ADMINISTRATIVE LAW

Second Edition

By

Alfred C. Aman, Jr.
Dean and Roscoe C. O'Byrne Professor of Law
Indiana University School of Law–Bloomington

William T. Mayton
Simmons Professor of Law
Emory University, School of Law

HORNBOOK SERIES®

WEST GROUP

A THOMSON COMPANY

ST. PAUL, MINN., 2001

610 Opperman Drive
P.O. Box 64526
St. Paul, MN 55164–0526
1–800–328–9352

ISBN 0–314–23875–1 (hard cover)
ISBN 0–314–23938–3 (soft cover)

TEXT IS PRINTED ON 10% POST CONSUMER RECYCLED PAPER

To the Students and Alumni of
Indiana University School of Law—Bloomington

A.C.A.

For Leigh Anne, Wesley, Elizabeth, and Luke

W.T.M.

*

Preface to Second Edition

In this treatise, we set forth a comprehensive analysis of administrative law in the United States. Administrative law continues to evolve in interesting ways in all of its various dimensions. The primary purpose of this new edition of the treatise is to update our coverage of the law and its on-going development since 1992, when the first edition appeared. Some of the changes that this book documents and discusses concern new issues of technology. Computers, for example, have changed the ways in which administrative agencies deal with Freedom of Information Act requests and they also affect the ways in which agencies collect, store, and share data concerning individuals. Technological change creates both opportunities for more transparent and efficient regulatory approaches but also new privacy concerns. This edition tracks these and related changes. More broadly, we address the new developments in the law of standing, congressional attempts to make agencies more accountable, the constitutionality (or lack thereof) of the Line Item Veto Act, among other issues. Both the domestic and international context of U.S. regulation and administrative law have also changed since the first edition and some of these developments also find their way into this book.

Though many of these new developments in administrative law are significant, the fundamental purposes of this book remain the same: to assess and explain fundamental doctrines of administrative law, placing some of the most important aspects of those doctrines in a historical context, and setting forth the current state of the law. The book also remains a work intended to serve practitioners, scholars, and students of administrative law. Our aim is also to provide a useful guide for practitioners and scholars in any discipline who may be coming to administrative law and its interesting issues for the first time. The respective responsibility of the authors for the updated chapters in this edition remains as it was in the first edition.

Acknowledgments — Professor Aman

As with the first edition, the second edition of this book has also required the help, patience, and inspiration of many people. I wish to thank, in particular, the students at Indiana University School of Law-Bloomington who, over the last several years, have helped me work on this update. These students are: Sean Carton '02, Ursula Doyle '97, Rene Garza '02, Marc Malooley '01, Jacob Pond '01, John Snethen '01, Lena Snethen '03, Andrew Straw '97, and Yu-Chi Wang '97. I want to offer my special thanks to John Snethen, who worked very closely with me on this book over the last two years and especially at the conclusion of this project. His dedication, hard work and careful research were invaluable to this enterprise.

Even in the computerized world in which we now live, the production of a book of this sort requires tremendous care, attention to detail, and a great deal of typing and revision. I want to thank, with deep appreciation, my secretary, Jeanine Wiese, who prepared virtually all of the updates and changes to my chapters in this treatise. Not only did she do this in a most professional and competent manner, but with a great deal of humor and good spirit throughout. In addition, I also wish to thank my administrative assistant, Jan Turner, who helped out in various ways in this book, including working on specific parts of some of the chapters. I also wish to thank all of my colleagues at Indiana University School of Law-Bloomington for their insights and encouragement throughout. In particular, I wish to thank Professors Paul Craig, Steve Johnson, Rob Fischman and John Applegate for their willingness to discuss a wide variety of stimulating administrative law issues with me and for their insights and help. Finally, I especially want to thank my wife, Carol Greenhouse, who deserves the largest thanks of all for her encouragement and help throughout.

My portion of this edition of the book is dedicated to the students at Indiana University School of Law-Bloomington. I have been Dean at this law school for the last 10 years and have come to know many of these students well over these years, either as law students or now, as alums. Their energy, imagination, and intellectual commitment to understanding and analyzing new approaches to new and old problems in administrative law have been on-going inspiration for me. Their sense of community at this law school has helped create a truly humane, total learning environment, which I have found enormously exciting and sustaining.

Acknowledgments — Professor Mayton

I thank Emory for its support, and Carol Grafman, J.D., Emory, 1999, and Benjamin Sawyer, 3L, Emory for their research assistance. I thank my colleague, Bill Buzbee, for being there to work through some of the issues. Otherwise, I have gained solace from the continual support of Joseph (Joey) Mayton.

Westlaw® Overview

Administrative Law, Second Edition, offers a detailed and comprehensive treatment of principles and issues in administrative law practice. To supplement the information contained in this book, you can access Westlaw, a computer-assisted legal research service of West Group. Westlaw contains a broad array of legal resources, including case law, statutes, expert commentary, current developments, and various other types of information.

Learning how to use these materials effectively will enhance your legal research abilities. To help you coordinate the information in the book with your Westlaw research, this volume contains an appendix listing Westlaw databases, search techniques, and sample problems.

*

Summary of Contents

Table of Contents

Page

PART THREE. CONSISTENCY IN AGENCY ACTION

*

Research References

Key Number System: Administrative Law and Procedure ⟸1 et seq, (to(15A)); Constitutional Law ⟸59 et seq. (to(92)); Constitutional Law ⟸318 (92k318)

Am Jur 2d, Administrative Law §§ 1 et seq.; Admiralty § 84; Alternative Dispute Resolution §§ 1 et seq.; Americans With Disabilities Act: Analysis and Implications §§ 149-178; Appellate Review §§ 28, 55; Bankruptcy § 157; Civil Rights § 474; Constitutional Law §§ 890-972; Consumer and Borrower Protection §§ 419-430; Courts §§ 48-53; Customs Duties and Import Regulations §§ 394-401; Declaratory Judgments § 92; Energy and Power Sources §§ 17, 143; Federal Courts §§ 1109, 2486-2488; Freedom of Information Acts §§ 1 et seq.; Indians § 88; Injunctions § 182; Job Discrimination §§ 1213, 1214, 1223, 1226, 1966-1986, 1992-2011; Labor and Labor Relations §§ 211, 220, 225, 232, 929, 931, 1182, 2614, 2755; Pollution Control §§ 685-687, 1163-1211, 1680-1737; Records and Recording Laws §§ 32-46; State and Local Taxation §§ 109, 110

Corpus Juris Secundum, Aeronautics and Aeronautics §§ 28-41; Agriculture §§ 8-24; Aliens §§ 220-224; Attorney and Client § 36; Carriers §§ 220, 222, 287, 352, 366; Civil Rights §§ 345-362; Colleges and Universities § 18; Constitutional Law §§ 1176-1180; Evidence § 37; Employer-Employee Relationship § 84; Health and Environment §§ 100, 103, 107, 111, 133-145; Insurance §§ 36, 38, 40; Intoxicating Liquors §§ 117-124; Labor Relations §§ 1210-1255; Licenses §§ 19, 61; Mandamus § 25; Monopolies §§ 184-188; Officers and Public Employees §§ 152-174; Public Administrative Law and Procedure §§ 1 et seq.; Records §§ 76-86; Social Security and Public Welfare §§ 265-270; Taxation §§ 1765-1769; Telecommunications §§ 8, 11, 79, 99, 102, 170; Workmen's Compensation §§ 700-729

ALR Index: Administrative Procedure Act; Alternative Dispute Resolution; Due Process; Federal Tort Claims Act; Freedom of Information Acts; Right to Know Law; Sunshine Laws

ALR Digest: Administrative Law §§ 1 et seq.; Appeal and Error § 277; Constitutional Law §§ 441-680; Labor §§ 57, 145, 148; License § 29; Records and Recording Laws § 6.5; Unemployment Compensation § 19

Am Jur Legal Forms 2d, Federal Tort Claims Act §§ 113:1 et seq.; Social Security and Medicare §§ 235:24-235:28; Veterans and Veterans' Laws §§ 255:11-255:13

Am Jur Pleading and Practice (Rev), Administrative Law §§ 1 et seq.; Certiorari § 80; Civil Rights § 86; Federal Criminal Procedure §§ 96, 97; Freedom of Information Act §§ 1 et seq.; Housing Laws and Urban Redevelopment §§ 14, 15; Initiative and Referendum §§ 61, 62;

Licenses and Permits §§ 23, 24; Patents §§ 11-24; Social Security and Medicare §§ 91-95; Telecommunications §§ 39-59; Veterans and Veteran's Laws §§ 22-49

77 Am Jur Trials 1, Representing Law Enforcement Officers in Personnel Disputes and Employment Litigation; 76 Am Jur Trials 1, Arbitration Evidence: Putting Your Best Case Forward; 50 Am Jur Trials 407, Litigation under the Freedom of Information Act; 48 Am Jur Trials 587, Public School Liability: Constitutional Tort Claims For Excessive Punishment and Failure To Supervise Students; 44 Am Jur Trials 507, Alternative Dispute Resolution: Commercial Arbitration; 32 Am Jur Trials 1, Due Process Considerations in Suspension of a Physician's Hospital Staff Privileges; 26 Am Jur Trials 327, Representation of An Alien In Exclusion, Rescission and Deportation Hearings

55 POF3d 313, Proof That School Board Improperly Expelled Student from School; 55 POF3d 155, Citizens' Suits Under the Comprehensive Environmental Response, Compensation and Liability Act (CERCLA) and the Emergency Planning and Community Right-to-Know Act (EPCRA); 54 POF3d 65, Proof That Firearm License Holder was Improperly Denied License to Carry Concealed Weapon; 53 POF3d 301, Proof That Food Stamp License Holder's License Was Improperly Revoked

10 POF2d 221, Adequate Notice to Governmental Entity of Claim

ADMINISTRATIVE LAW

Second Edition

*

INTRODUCTION

The complexity of administrative law can be avoided, if only for the moment, by speaking at a high level of generality. This is how we speak in this introduction.

Administrative law pertains to those agencies of government assigned the task of implementing various social, economic, and quality of life programs within our nation. These agencies include the Social Security Administration, the Environmental Protection Agency, the Federal Aviation Agency, the Securities and Exchange Commission, and many, many more. Agencies are generally created by, and draw their power from, the legislature. By the legislature, they are established by an organic act that both provides for their organization, and transmits, or delegates, electronic media, securities markets, and labor relations, you will of course recognize that Congress has established and delegated a regulatory power to the Commission, and the National Labor Relations Board.

The public sector that is comprised of agencies that is subject to administrative law is huge, which fact is denoted by the federal Administrative Procedure Act as it provides that federal administrative law basically covers the whole federal structure, excepting Congress and federal courts.[1] But some structures of government, albeit nominally within the scope of a general administrative law, have in practice stayed outside it. Notably, structures pertaining to international relations and to the operation of the military have been excluded from much of the body of law known as administrative law. So has the enforcement of criminal law, but for the different reason, that special constitutional safeguards, those of the fourth, fifth and sixth amendments to the Constitution, pertain to this process. But with the exclusions aside, still we are left with much of government, the part pertaining to the civil affairs of ordinary people, as the range of administrative law.

This public sector, the range of administrative law, is as important as it is large. For a time, courts and judges drew attention to this prominence. In 1952, Mr. Justice Jackson wrote that "The rise of administrative bodies probably has been the most significant legal trend of the last century and perhaps more values today are affected by their decisions than those of all the courts...."[2] Also, judges described how

1. Administrative law pertains to the operations of agencies, and the Administrative Procedure Act defines an agency as "each authority of the Government, ... but does not include (A) the Congress, (B) the courts of the United States...." 5 U.S.C.A. § 551(1).

2. Federal Trade Commission v. Ruberoid Co., 343 U.S. 470, 487, 72 S.Ct. 800, 810, 96 L.Ed. 1081 (1952).

much administrative law was part of their own work; for the Supreme Court, it was the "largest category of cases decided on the merits."[3] Today, the position of administrative law, its prominence and how it pertains to government action that affects us daily (by benefactory programs, quality of life programs, social insurance, commercial regulation, and licensing respecting services, trades, and professions) is simply a given.

In the rise of administrative law, the Thirties, the time of the New Deal, are taken to be watershed years. As they were. This is not to say that agencies had not previously been a part of American government. They had. The Interstate Commerce Commission had been established, primarily for rate regulation of railroads, in 1887. In the "Progressive era," the 1890's to about the start of the first World War, other regulatory laws, including the Federal Trade Commission Act, the Meat Inspection Act, and the Pure Food and Drugs Act, were passed.[4] The Federal Radio Commission, the predecessor of the Federal Communications Commission, was established during the Hoover Administration.

Also, certain ideas about government and knowledge—the justifications for administrative government—were already in place at the time of the New Deal. The scientific method had come to be seen as a superior means of solving social problems; it would " 'place men's relations where they never yet have been placed, under the control of trained human reason.' "[5] Expertise, that is, specialized and usually compartmentalized knowledge, was part of the method, and so was inductive reasoning and data. These ideas justified a reliance on organization and experts and investigation and data, the basic administrative system. Also, the hope was that placing social programs in bureaus responsive to scientific truth, as opposed to politics, would protect these programs from " 'the political winds that sweep Washington.' "[6]

An ideology in support of an administrative state was in place. The facts completed the New Deal commitment to this state of government were the urgency caused by the Great Depression and a strong President, disposed to use any means at hand to end the crisis. Therefore, in the New Deal, agencies were created at an accelerated pace. These new agencies were largely involved in market regulation, (e.g., the Securities

3. Clark, 13 Ad.L.Rev. 6 (1960). Mr. Justice Clark also described administrative law as " 'the most important body of law presently current and reasonably foreseeable.' " Id.

4. Rubin, 38 Stan.L.Rev. 1189, 1216 et seq. (1986). This article provides an excellent history of federal administrative law in this country.

5. W. Nelson, the Roots of American Bureaucracy, 1880–1900, 82 (1982) (quoting E.L. Godkin).

6. Commodity Futures Trading Com'n v. Schor, 478 U.S. 833, 835, 106 S.Ct. 3245, 3248, 92 L.Ed.2d 675 (1986). These aspirations of scientifically refined decisional process were described in relation to the Federal Trade Commission. This Commission, it was said, was delegated its broad power over commerce on a faith in a "commission composed of eminent lawyers, economists, businessmen, and publicists" that would develop "a body of precedent and tradition and a continuous policy." T. Henderson, The Federal Trade Commission 19 (1924). See also J. Landis, The Administrative Process (1928). An intellectual history respecting the justifications for an administrative state is provided by W. Nelson, supra, note 5. See also, Rubin, supra, note 4.

and Exchange Commission) and in providing a new measure of personal, economic security (e.g., the Social Security Administration). The more important fact of this period, however, was not the kind or necessarily the number of agencies. Indeed, in terms of quantity, the Nixon administration established as many new agencies as did that of FDR.[7] Rather, the important part of the New Deal was the nature of turn made in coming to agencies. This turn was toward a new commitment by government to act positively, to itself identify and solve economic and social problems as opposed to leaving these matters to a free market and private solutions. The usual form of these governmental solutions were programs roughed-in by Congress and then delegated to agencies.

There were reservations, grave ones, about this departure. Some reservations were purely social and economic, respecting the wisdom in creating a large public sector as the New Deal was doing. Other reservations were about the instrumentalities of this sector, the agencies themselves. The harsh assessment, of a 1937 presidential commission, was that agencies now comprised a "headless 'fourth branch' of government, a haphazard collection of irresponsible agencies and uncoordinated powers." [8] This matter of "irresponsible agencies and uncoordinated power" was seen as a structural and procedural problem, albeit procedure in very upper-case terms. These issues of structure and procedure are still with us; they are the body of administrative law. Among other things, this is to say that in the United States, administrative law is not about the substance of what agencies do. Instead, it is about the structures and processes by which they do what they do.

The reservations about structure and procedure can be separated into three categories. One of these categories is about "deranged" governmental structures.[9] The Constitution commits the basic powers of government to branches designed to receive and to exercise these powers. Article I defines legislative power and commits it to Congress; Article III does the same respecting judicial power and the courts. Article II assigns "the executive Power" to the President. With the rise of the administrative state, a considerable portion of these powers were allocated to agencies rather than the constitutionally prescribed branches. In some major constitutional cases, such as *Crowell v. Benson, Humphrey's Executor v. United States,* and *Schecter Poultry v. United*

7. This wave of new agencies came in the late Sixties and early Seventies. In their "quality of life" goals, these new agencies differed from those of the New Deal. The goals of these new agencies pertained to consumer protection and health, safety and the environment. Among these agencies were the Environmental Protection Agency, the Occupational Safety and Health Administration, and the Consumer Product Safety Commission. For a discussion of the significant Acts and agencies established in this period, see Rubin, note 4, at 1278, *et seq.*

8. President's Committee on Administrative Management, Report with Special Studies (1937) (the "Brownless Report").

9. "Deranged" is the term used by Justice Jackson. In describing the prominence of agencies, he pointed out that "They [had] become a veritable fourth branch of the Government, which has deranged our three-branch legal theories." Federal Trade Commission v. Ruberoid Co., 343 U.S. 470, 487, 72 S.Ct. 800, 810, 96 L.Ed. 1081 (1952).

States, the Supreme Court tried to say how and how much of these powers could be assigned to agencies.

The second reservation about agencies was that they might degrade the rule of law. Within agencies, power is combined: agencies typically held legislative, executive, and judicial power. This sort of combined power structure allows agencies to more expeditiously develop and enforce policies. But combined power also allows agencies to act more arbitrarily, to use ad hoc solutions and sanctions rather than solutions and sanctions formally prescribed by standing laws.

A third reservation was a lawyer's reservation, whether an agency of combined power and loose structure could fairly determine the rights of individuals.[10] How, for instance, could an organization, itself responsible for devising and enforcing certain standards, impartially judge a person whom it had charged with violating those standards?

These original reservations about agencies were the subject of some great court cases, some of which we have mentioned. But the main effort at quieting these concerns came from Congress, by means of the Administrative Procedure Act.[11] In 1939, President Roosevelt established a committee, consisting of distinguished judges, practitioners, and scholars, to study agency practices, and the study was directed by Professor Walter Gellhorn. The committee's report, the "Attorney General's Report," was issued in 1941.[12] This report remains one of the most authoritative and informative documents on agencies. Also, it was the basis for the federal Administrative Procedure Act, which (after the war years) was passed in 1946. This Act remains in force, as the charter for federal administrative law and, in the past at least, as a model for state administrative procedure acts.[13]

The feature that agencies share is combined power. Otherwise, agencies come in a bewildering variety of forms and structures. Independent regulatory commissions are established outside of, and independent of, executive departments. Other agencies, for instance the Internal Revenue Service in the Treasury Department, are established within one of these departments. In all instances, the internal organization of agencies varies greatly. The Administrative Procedure Act deals with

10. Report of the Special Committee on Administrative Law, 63 A.B.A.Rep. 331 (1938).

11. This Act is codified at 5 U.S.C.A. §§ 551–559, 701–706, 1305, 3105, 3344, 5372, 7521. The Act is also set out in the appendix to this book.

12. The Attorney General's Committee on Administrative Procedure, Administrative Procedure in Government Agencies, S.Doc. No. 8, 77th Cong., 1st Sess. (1941).

13. As described by the Supreme Court, the Administrative Procedures Act, "represents a long period of study and strife; it settles long-continued and hard-fought contentions, and enacts a formulation on which opposing social and political forces have come to rest." Wong Yang Sung v. McGrath, 339 U.S. 33, 41, 70 S.Ct. 445, 450, 94 L.Ed. 616 (1950).

In 1946, the same year the Administrative Procedure Act was enacted, the National Conference of Commissioners on Uniform State Laws adopted a "Model State Administrative Procedure Act." This Act was revised in 1961 and in 1981. Most states have an administrative procedure act and most of these acts are based on the Model Act. The Model Act is included in the appendix to this book.

this variety of structures by identifying agency functions, rather than forms, and then prescribing procedures accordingly.[14] Two of the Act's major divisions are for the legislative and judicial functions of agencies. By these provisions, for surrogate legislative and adjudicatory structures, the Act meets some concerns about allocations of legislative and judicial power to agencies. By another measure, a requirement that agencies act under codified and published rules, the Act responds to rule of law concerns.

Also, the Administrative Procedure Act assumes that the courts have a major role in assuring that agencies stay within their jurisdiction, act lawfully, and make reasonable decisions. Accordingly, in a third major part the Act provides for judicial review of agency actions, and defines the scope of that review.

As a final product, the Administrative Procedure Act has never been free of criticism. One criticism is of the Act's fundamental assumption, that the variety of agencies and social programs can be brought in under a unitary procedure. Another criticism is that in its attention to rulemaking, adjudication, and judicial review, the Act leaves some things out. For instance, the Act does little for agency action that is "informal." Informal action denotes agency action that is neither adjudication nor rulemaking, and includes common and commonly important agency actions, such as money grants.

Despite these criticisms, the terms of the Act have changed little. The idea that administrative practice is too varied to be bound by a single code has never taken hold. The greater splintering of practice, which a non-unified code might produce, is not appealing. Moreover, Congress retains control over the procedures of specific agencies, and for a specific agency Congress may (and often has) provide procedures that differ from the Administrative Procedure Act and that are tailored for that agency.[15] The courts themselves, out of a sense of what Professor Kenneth Culp Davis has identified as "administrative common law," have here and there filled in respecting some perceived deficiencies in the Act. For instance, to fill the perceived deficit respecting informal agency actions, the Supreme Court has created a procedure: that such agency action be supported by a record sufficient to show its rationality.[16]

14. A side-effect of this, the bewildering variety of agency forms and the Administrative Procedure Act's unitary and functional approach to these forms, is the demand it makes on students and practitioners. They must come to administrative law understanding some basics of jurisprudence. They must, for instance, understand that which is law making and that which is law applying. Often, neither function comes with a label, or the right label.

15. The Administrative Procedure Act recognizes this, that Congress may provide more specific procedures for specific agencies, as it states that "it does not limit or repeal additional requirement imposed by statute...." 5 U.S.C.A. § 559.

16. Citizens to Preserve Overton Park, Inc. v. Volpe, 401 U.S. 402, 91 S.Ct. 814, 28 L.Ed.2d 136 (1971).

The terms of the Administrative Procedure Act have not been substantially changed. However, the Act is interpreted and enforced by the courts. These interpretations have been cyclical, depending on how the administrative method is regarded as a solution to social problems. Presently, the courts do not have the same faith—in the primacy of experts presumably operating according to scientific principles—as they have had. Consequently, the courts have more rigorously enforced portions of the Administrative Procedure Act that might bolster the decisional processes of administrative agencies. These parts are rulemaking, which provides for public impute into the reasoning of agency, and judicial review as it submits agency action to the scrutiny of the courts.

Today, administrative law is still unfolding. Not all developments, of course, have involved the Administrative Procedure Act. The constitutional requirement of due process of law has been expanded by the courts, to place them in a supervisory position respecting state and federal adjudications. State practice, while following the same lines as federal practice, has developed some of its own wrinkles.[17] Also, apart from the initial emphasis, on rulemaking, adjudication, and judicial review, another dimension has been added to the Administrative Procedure Act.

This additional dimension is about information, the value in it and the harm. In 1966, the Freedom of Information Act was added to the Administrative Procedure Act, to provide for (subject to certain exemptions) public access to information held by agencies. In 1974, the Privacy Act was added, to limit the agencies respecting information harmful to individuals. To open agency processes to public inspection, the Administrative Procedure Act was amended by the Government in the Sunshine Act of 1976.

Our account of an unfolding administrative law is presented according to the customary distinction between the legislative and judicial functions of agencies. Otherwise, we cover "informal" agency actions. We also devote a major part of the book to judicial review, the timing and availability of review and the scope of review. We also cover a particular remedy offered by the courts, damages actions against public official. Another major part of the book relates to agency information, how to gain access to it and how to be protected from it.

17. See Bonfeld, The Federal APA and State Administrative Law, 72 Va.L.Rev. 297 (1986).

Part One

LEGISLATIVE POWER IN AGENCIES

Delegations of legislative power from representative assemblies to administrative agencies are a large part of modern American government. These delegations take lawmaking out of a region of representative government and into a zone of government by specialists presumed to act according to more disinterested and scientific judgments of good social policy. Otherwise, because administrative lawmaking is not subject to the same structural constraints—imposed by separated powers and by the consensus necessary in a bicameral legislature—as is Congress, a transfer of legislative power to agencies makes possible a greater range and volume of lawmaking than if such power were retained by Congress. In this way, delegations of legislative power are, as Professor Jaffe has said, the "dynamo of the modern social services state."[1]

The action itself, delegating legislative power to agencies, may in some cases be subject to question by means of a constitutional doctrine known as the delegation doctrine. Over the last several years, this doctrine has been diagnosed, alternatively, as dead and resurrected.[2]

1. Jaffe, An Essay on the Delegation of Legislative Power, 47 Colum.L.Rev. 561, 592 (1947).

2. Regarding the morbidity of the doctrine, see K. Davis, Administrative Law Text 27 (1972). In recent years, however, life signs have been apparent. For arguments favoring the delegation doctrine, see T. Lowi, The End of Liberalism: Ideology, Policy, and the Crisis of Public Authority (1969); Aranson, Gellhorn & Robinson, A Theory of Legislation Delegation, 68 Cornell L.Rev. 1 (1982); Lowi, Two Roads to Serfdom: Liberalism, Conservatism, and Administrative Power, 36 Amer.U.L.Rev. 295, 307 (1987); McGowan, Congress, Court, and Control of Delegated Power, 77 Colum.L.Rev. 1132 (1977); Schoenbrod, Separation of Powers and the Powers that Be: The Constitutional Purposes of the Delegation Doctrine, 36 Amer.U.L.Rev. 355 (1987); Wright, Beyond Discretionary Justice, 81 Yale L.J. 575 (1972). For modern Supreme Court cases that at least support the doctrine as a canon of statutory interpretation, see Industrial Union Dept. v. American Petroleum Institute, 448 U.S. 607, 100 S.Ct. 2844, 65 L.Ed.2d 1010 (1980); Hampton v. Mow Sun Wong, 426 U.S. 88, 96 S.Ct. 1895, 48 L.Ed.2d 495 (1976); National Cable Television Ass'n, Inc. v. United States, 415 U.S. 336, 94 S.Ct. 1146, 39 L.Ed.2d 370 (1974) These cases are discussed at Sec. 1.2, infra. In the states, the delegation has never been diagnosed as dead, and there it remains as a check on overly broad delegations. E.g., In re Initiative Petition No. 332, 776 P.2d 556 (Okl.1989); Boreali v. Axelrod, 71 N.Y.2d 1, 523 N.Y.S.2d 464, 517 N.E.2d 1350 (1987); Fitanides v. Crowley, 467 A.2d 168 (Me. 1983); Thygesen v. Callahan, 74 Ill.2d 404, 24 Ill.Dec. 558, 385 N.E.2d 699 (1979); Commissioner of Agriculture v. Plaquemines Parish Com'n Council, 439 So.2d 348 (La.1983). See A. Bonfeld & M. Asimow,

The present condition of the doctrine is discussed in Chapter 1. Within the agency, delegated legislative power is subject to procedural controls. These controls are largely the rulemaking requirements of federal and state administrative procedure acts. Rulemaking is the subject of Chapters 2 and 3.

State and Federal Administrative Law, 451–61 (1988).

For a view of delegation in other countries, see Currie, Distribution of Powers After Bowser, 1986 S.Ct.Rev. 19, 21 & n. 42 (1986); F. Bennion, Statutory Interpretation 133 et seq. (1984) (English practice). In Germany, an idea of a non-delegable legislative power, as Currie points out, is thought to be an implication of the rule of law and separated powers. In Germany, constitutional law "entrusts to the lawmaker in the first instance the decision which public interest are so important that the liberty of the individual must be subordinated. From this duty of decision the democratic lawmaker may not withdraw at pleasure." BVerGe 33, 125 (159) (1979), quoted in Currie, supra.

For a more favorable view of delegations, see Mashaw, Prodelegation: Why Administrators Should Make Political Decisions, 1 Jour.L.Econ. & Organ. 80 (1985). See also Pierce, Political Accountability and Delegated Power: A Response to Prof. Lowi, 36 Amer.U.L.Rev. 391 (1987); Stewart, The Reformation of American Administrative Law, 88 Harv.L.Rev. 1671, 1693–98 (1975). Professors Pierce and Stewart do not necessarily favor broad delegations, but they do doubt the viability of legal controls of legislative delegations.

Chapter 1

THE DELEGATION DOCTRINE

Table of Sections

The first sentence of the body of the Constitution provides that "All legislative Powers herein granted shall be vested in a Congress of the United States."[1] Certainly, this provision establishes that Congress has a supreme legislative power and that it is the main policy-making branch of government. This provision has not, however, never been taken to mean that Congress holds legislative power exclusively or that it cannot delegate some portion of legislative power.[2]

Some delegation is unavoidable. This part is ordained by limitations of knowledge and language. In relation to knowledge, the point, as H.L.A. Hart has said, is that "we are men, not gods." Legislators without perfect foresight do the best they can: they enact statutes providing for the general good.[3] A statute setting the speed limit at fifty-five miles per hour may be generally good, but certainly not always. What, for instance, about medical emergencies? Therefore, in the implementation of this statute, new and more specific rules about speeding, as for medical emergencies, are bound to emerge. In relation to the different matter of precision of language, the point is that even if Congress had perfect knowledge, it cannot usually draft an act in other than

1. U.S. Const. Art. I, § 1.

2. As said by John Marshall, "Congress may certainly delegate to others, powers which the legislature may rightfully exercise itself." Wayman v. Southard, 23 U.S. (10 Wheat.) 1, 15–16, 6 L.Ed. 253 (1825).

3. H. Hart, The Concept of Law 125 (1975). For a classic exposition of the legislator's lack of omniscience and the resultant necessity of some degree of delegation of discretion, so as to allow for the adjustment of statutes to unforeseeable circumstances, to those who apply the statute, see Plato, The Statesman, as excerpted in J. White, The Legal Imagination 627–28 (1973).

general terms. At a point, specification renders a statute awkward, unwieldy, and internally inconsistent.[4]

In another part, delegation is not inevitable, but it is, as the Supreme Court has said, "necessary that the exertion of legislative power does not become a futility."[5] One such necessity was explained by Thomas Jefferson. The resources of Congress, he said, may be usefully conserved by avoiding the diversion of that body "from great to small objects,"[6] and so power respecting these "small objects" is delegated. Indeed, agencies with decision costs lower than Congress are often better at working through "a labyrinth of detail" than is Congress. In *Mistretta v. United States,* the Court upheld Congress's delegation to the United States Sentencing Commission of the authority to establish mandatory sentencing guidelines. The Court explained that "Developing proportionate penalties for hundreds of different crimes by a virtually limitless array of offenders is precisely the sort of intricate, labor-intensive task for which delegation to an expert body is especially appropriate."[7]

The lower decision costs of agencies also makes possible an adaptability that explains another portion of delegation. By establishing primary standards and then delegating to an agency the task of adjusting these standards to current conditions, Congress can create a useful "flexibility in the face of changing circumstances." This flexibility is perhaps most useful where technology is rapidly developing, such as in environmental controls. Here, Congress can avoid freezing technology by setting general standards and committing their implementation to an agency.[8]

4. Hans Lieber demonstrated the futility and the illusion of statutes as itemized prescriptions. He showed how "Men have at length found out that little or nothing is gained by attempting to speak with absolute clearness and endless specifications, but that human speech is the clearer, the less we endeavor to supply by words and specifications that interpretation which common sense must give to human words." H. Lieber, Legal and Political Hermenuetics 18–20 (2d ed. 1880), quoted in W. Eskridge and P. Frickey, Cases and Materials on Legislation: Statutes and Public Policy 574–75 (1988).

5. Sunshine Anthracite Coal Co. v. Adkins, 310 U.S. 381, 398, 60 S.Ct. 907, 914, 84 L.Ed. 1263 (1940).

6. The Writings of Thomas Jefferson 424–25 (P. Ford ed. 1894).

7. 488 U.S. 361, 379, 109 S.Ct. 647, 658, 102 L.Ed.2d 714 (1989). See also United States v. Shreveport Grain & Elevator Co., 287 U.S. 77, 85, 53 S.Ct. 42, 44, 77 L.Ed. 175 (1932) ("That the legislative power of Congress cannot be delegated is clear," the Court said. "But Congress may declare its will, and after fixing a primary standard devolve upon administrative officers the power to fill in the details."). See generally J. Landis, The Administrative Process 70 (1938).

8. J. Wilson, The Politics of Regulation, 303 (1980); Ackerman & Hassler, The New Deal: Coal and the Clean Air Act, 89 Yale L.J. 1466 (1980).

Another area appropriated for delegation of a law-making authority may be identified by reference to the fact that Congress is not always in session, and when it is, its acts are, as we have said, subject to a level of decision costs that hinder quick action. Congress might, therefore, by statute identify certain events, establish standards of action with respect to these events, and then delegate (to a body that sits continuously and that is better suited to prompt reaction) a "contingent" authority to react to these events according to these standards. See The Aurora v. United States, 11 U.S. (7 Cranch) 382, 383, 3 L.Ed. 378 (1813). For a more extensive review of early delegations of a contingent legislative power, see Panama Refining Co. v. Ryan, 293 U.S. 388, 422, n. 9, 55 S.Ct. 241, 249, n. 9, 79 L.Ed. 446 (1935).

Finally, legislative power may be delegated not out of any sort of necessity but because Congress deems it to be the better solution to some problems. In particular, Congress may wish to gain the assistance of professionals in working out a particular program. These specialists, for instance scientists and technicians at the Environmental Protection Agency, may have expertise not usually shared by legislators.[9] Thus Congress may establish the rudiments of a program and delegate the elaboration of it to an agency. In constitutional text, support for this sort of pragmatic and evolutionary movement in government can be found in the "necessary and proper clause" of Article I. The flexibility asserted by that clause includes the "Powers vested by this Constitution in the Government of the United States, or in any Department or Officer thereof."[10]

* * *

By consensus, it is a proper thing for Congress to identify social problems and work through the rudiments of a solution, and then to turn the program thus established over to an agency and its professionals for implementation: knowing that within this frame of things the agency gains a portion of lawmaking power.[11] It is, however, quite

9. As explained by the Court, "in our increasingly complex society, replete with ever changing and more technical problems, Congress simply cannot do its job absent an ability to delegate power under broad general directives." Mistretta v. United States, 488 U.S. 361, 368, 109 S.Ct. 647, 652, 102 L.Ed.2d 714 (1989). ("Broad general directives" did not mean no directives, however. In *Mistretta,* the Court carefully examined the delegation to the United States Sentencing Commission so as to assure that it contained standards to guide the Commission.) In relation to policy implementation by experts, it has been said that the Federal Trade Commission was delegated its broad authority over commercial matters on a faith in "trained experts" and a "commission composed of eminent lawyers, economists, businessmen, and publicists" which would develop "a body of precedent and tradition, and a continuous policy." T. Henderson, The Federal Trade Commission 19 (1924). Delegation to agency professionals, on the hope that they might better develop social policy by means of disinterested social judgment and expeditious procedures, came to the front during the New Deal. J. Landis, The Administrative Process (1938). The hope that is sometimes expressed, but not necessarily realized, is that by delegation to professions who operate on the basis of disinterested judgments shaped by objective, scientific truths, social policy might be removed from a seemingly insecure region of politics. As the Supreme Court has said, "broad regulatory powers ... were most appropriately vested in an agency ... relatively immune from the 'political winds that sweep Washington.'" Commodity Futures Trading Com'n v. Schor, 478 U.S. 833, 106 S.Ct. 3245, 92 L.Ed.2d 675 (1986).

10. U.S. Const. Art. I, § 8. In apparent relation to the necessary and proper clause, delegations may be justified, as the Court has said, by "common sense and the inherent necessities of governmental coordination." J.W. Hampton Jr., & Co. v. United States, 276 U.S. 394, 406, 48 S.Ct. 348, 351, 72 L.Ed. 624 (1928). See A.L.A. Schechter Poultry Corp. v. United States, 295 U.S. 495, 524, 55 S.Ct. 837, 840, 79 L.Ed. 1570 (1935).

11. This justification, and delegation in prototype form, may be seen in the Securities Act of 1933 and the creation of the Securities Exchange Commission. Following the 1928 crash, Congress turned to various problems of the national stock market. The solutions that Congress arrived at were not generally prescriptive. Instead, they were enabling. By the Securities Act of 1933, Congress did not prohibit stock sales but instead tried to enhance the stock market by inculcating public confidence in it. Congress did so by disclosure requirements, requiring that persons and institutions offering new "securities" for sale disclose information relevant to the value of the security. 15 U.S.C.A. § 77. Congress enacted statutory guidelines pertinent to

another thing for Congress *not* to legislate in some primary manner, but to instead turn to an agency to say, "Here is the problem, deal with it." Today, this maneuver is likely to be seen as an unacceptable passing of the buck, the buck being Congress's responsibility under Article I for "important choices of social policy."[12] That important choices of social policy ought to be made in Congress—and not by unelected officials and a bureaucratic process—seems a requirement of Article I and an implication of the Constitution's profound regard for consensual government.[13]

Reserving important social choices to an elected Congress, as opposed to delegating them to agencies, is also consistent with other constitutional considerations, related to, but still somewhat apart from, the blunt fact of our norm of representative government. Within Article I, the Constitution tries to distill and to protect public values by a certain process of deliberation among politically responsible officials. When delegation takes lawmaking out from under Article I, the result is lawmaking by bureaucratic officials who, to use Justice Brennen's phrase, are not "responsive in the same degree to the people."[14] Such unresponsiveness may amount to something more than public values being assessed by other than democratic principles. It may also mean that these values are ignored. If Congress does not itself strike a balance as regards conflicting values, but instead only identifies a goal, then an option available to an agency is to pursue such a goal single-mindedly

disclosure and then established an expert agency, the Securities and Exchange Commission, to carry out the program so established. Id. As it has worked within the statutory guidelines, the Commission has made a considerable amount of legal rules itself. In relation to the key question of what is a security, for instance, the '33 Act left sufficient room for the Commission to over time and in its expertise develop standards for what is and is not a security.

12. Industrial Union Dept., AFL–CIO v. American Petroleum Institute, 448 U.S. 607, 685, 100 S.Ct. 2844, 2885, 65 L.Ed.2d 1010 (1980) (Rehnquist, J. concurring). See also Boreali v. Axelrod, 71 N.Y.2d 1, 523 N.Y.S.2d 464, 517 N.E.2d 1350 (1987) ("Manifestly, it is the province of the peoples' elected representatives, rather than appointed administrators, to resolve difficult social problems by making choices among competing ends"). The idea that the Congress should make primary social choices is also consistent with modern legislative theory. For instance, Prof. Rubin argues that we should understand modern legislatures for what they are: not bodies that promulgate standards of conduct (law in a classical sense), but bodies that "generate internal government instructions." These instructions are mostly directives to agencies. Still, Rubin does not suppose that these instructions are without substance. Rather, establishing these directives is a policy-making operation. Rubin, Law and Legislation in the Administrative State, 89 Colum.L.Rev. 369 (1989).

13. The direction of consensual government is that of assuring "that the fundamental issues in our society will be made not by appointed officials but by the body immediately responsible to the people." Arizona v. California, 373 U.S. 546, 626, 83 S.Ct. 1468, 1511, 10 L.Ed.2d 542 (1963) (Harlan, J., dissenting). See also Daughters of Miriam Center for the Aged v. Mathews, 590 F.2d 1250, 1257 (3d Cir.1978) ("The constitutional legitimacy that inheres in Congress by virtue of its accountability to the electorate is absent, however, from the administrative process, and consequently, serious questions are continually being raised—and with increased frequency—regarding the legitimacy of the administrative apparatus within the framework of American government. Near the center of the growing concern over legitimacy lies the apprehension that the critical choices of our society will more and more be made by administrative personnel who are not, as a practical matter, accountable to anyone.").

14. United States v. Robel, 389 U.S. 258, 276, 88 S.Ct. 419, 430, 19 L.Ed.2d 508 (1967) (concurring).

and without regard to other values and interests.[15] (For example, the old Atomic Energy Commission, established with the goal of promoting nuclear power, operated single-mindedly, advancing nuclear power without much regard to safety or environmental concerns.) Agency officials may be disinclined to consider conflicting values, because of their enthusiastic belief in the agency's goal or because they may be "grateful for the opportunity to escape responsibility for the intellectually difficult and politically touchy task of making such trade-off decisions."[16]

Article I also aspires to a lawmaking process that is "circumspect," that is, careful about how government uses its monopoly on power and in being careful, protective of non-coercive alternatives, as offered by consensual agreements and private markets, to government regulation. Accordingly, Article I was originally explained as working to instill a "circumspection in forming the laws" so as to avoid one of government's worst parts, an "undigested and inaccurate code of laws."[17] This pru-

15. *See* Hampton v. Mow Sun Wong, 426 U.S. 88, 96 S.Ct. 1895, 48 L.Ed.2d 495 (1976). In this case, which is discussed at Sec. 1.1, supra, the Supreme Court distinguished between the decisional processes of Congress, which are more likely to be responsive to a range of values, and those of an agency, which are more single-minded and relatively insensitive to values not associated with its mission. As regards how the "mission orientation" of agencies can blind them to the "tradeoffs any regulatory course entails," see generally "The Regulatory Reform Act," S.Rep. No. 97–284, 97th Cong., 1st Sess., at 60–61 (1981). A balanced description of this mission orientation is provided by this description of the decisional processes at the Consumer Products Safety Commission:

> In making their decisions, though, agency officials, including the commissioners, would seem to have a bias in favor of the agency's "doing something." The CPSC is not in charge of keeping down the cost of living, or saving people an ounce of inconvenience, or maximizing freedom of choice (even through officials do take such factors into consideration). The CPSC is in the business of reducing injury from consumer products, and it is hardly surprising that its bias is towards taking measures which promote that goal, even when they have attendant costs.

Kelman, Regulation by the Numbers—A Report on the Consumer Product Safety Commission, The Public Interest 83, 90–91 (1974). See also W. Lilley and J. Miller III, The New "Social Regulation," 47 The Public Interest 49–60 (1977), reprinted in part in G. Robinson, E. Gellhorn, H. Bruff, The Administrative Process, 422–26 (4th ed. 1993).

In the last several years, Congress has been concerned about the insularity of agency decisional processes and has put controls in place to broaden these processes. It has identified certain values, such as preservation of the environment, and then by legislation (such as the National Environmental Policy Act, 42 U.S.C.A. § 4321 *et seq.* required agencies to include these values in their decisional processes). The Regulatory Flexibility Act, 5 U.S.C.A. § 601, is another example of this sort of value-enhancing act. It directs agencies to consider regulatory alternatives such as might be less injurious to the interests of small businessmen. For a general discussion and description of congressional acts directing agencies to include certain values in their decisional processes, see Diver, Policymaking Paradigms in Administrative Law, 95 Harv.L.Rev. 393 (1981).

16. E. Bardach & R. Kagan, Going By the Book 48–49 (1982).

17. James Wilson, one of the three or four most influential delegates to the constitutional convention, thus explained Article I at the ratification convention in his home state of Pennsylvania. 2 The Debates in the Several State Conventions on the Adoption of the Federal Constitution 447 (J. Elliot ed. 1836) (hereinafter referred to as Elliot's Debates.) As explained by the Supreme Court, Article I consists of "enduring checks ... to protect the people from the improvident exercise of power." Immigration & Naturalization Service v. Chadha, 462 U.S. 919, 957, 103 S.Ct. 2764, 2787, 77 L.Ed.2d 317 (1983). See Mayton, The Possibilities of Collective Choice: Arrow's Theorem, Article I, and the Delega-

dence about lawmaking is in part mechanically induced in that Article I requires a high level of agreement, a consensus among the House, the Senate and the President. The decision costs implicit in this level of agreement impede a high volume of lawmaking, and from the standpoint of circumspection in lawmaking, this impediment is not a bad idea. In this respect, James Madison justified Article I by saying that "the facility and excess of lawmaking seem to be the diseases to which our governments are most liable."[18] Of course, today a facility and excess of lawmaking does not, to many, seem a disease at all. Rather, a high volume of regulation and social services seems desirable. From that point of view, a delegation of lawmaking out of the high decision costs of Article I and on to a zone of lower decision costs in an agency, where that greater volume is then possible, makes sense. In this respect, one of the more astute and more observations about modern American government is that of Professor Louis Jaffe as he noted that the delegation of legislative power to agencies is "the dynamo of the modern social services state."[19]

Also, reserving primary social choices for Congress is consistent with the aspiration, which following James Madison in Federalist No. 10 we have ever since identified with Article I, of breaking the force of special interests in politics by means of the political process established by Article I.[20] That agencies "unduly favor organized interest, especially the interests of regulative or client business firms and other organized groups at the expense of diffuse, comparatively unorganized interests" is not an uncommon observation.[21] Within the agency, there are "no regular political forces or processes in the national government [with] the capacity of regularly pushing interest groups back toward the more public and generalized legislative process."[22]

Finally, you should note that reserving important social choices to Congress has a significant relation to federalism. The representation that the states have in Congress and the decision costs and checks of Article I that slow the rush of national legislation together tend to

tion of Legislative Power to Administrative Agencies, 1986 Duke L.J. 948, 957–58.

18. The Federalist No. 62.

19. Louis L. Jaffe,

20. See Federalist No. 10 (Madison).

21. Stewart, The Reformation of American Administrative Law, 88 Harv.L.Rev. 1667, 1684–85 (1975).

22. Lowi, Two Roads to Serfdom: Liberalism, Conservatism, and Administrative Power, 36 Amer.U.L.Rev. 295, 297–98 (1987). For Congress acting under Article I, the decisional process is one of "bargaining on the rule." This description signifies a relatively permanent solution to a problem, in something of a one-shot process. In a one-shot process, various interests including the not so well-heeled interests (who are unlikely to have the resources for anything more than one good shot) can be expected to come forward to make their case and exert their influence.

But what if Congress does not resolve the problem but instead passes it on, saying to an agency "Here is the problem, you deal with it?" Then, according to Lowi, the process changes, to "bargaining on the order." In the agency, issues get strung-out over time, which benefits strong special interest groups comparatively more than weaker interests. On a day-in and day-out basis, the stronger special interests can be counted on to be at the agency pressing their interest, whereas weaker interests lack the resources to do so. T. Lowi, The End of Liberalism (1969).

decentralize government, moving some part of public matters to local government.[23] Justice Brandeis had this decentralizing feature in mind on the occasion of the Court's destruction, on delegation doctrine grounds, of probably the most extensive transfer of legislative power to a bureaucracy as has occurred in this nation's history. On the day that this decision, in *Schechter Poultry*, was announced, Brandeis sent this rather excited message to President Roosevelt: "This is the end of this business of centralization. As for your young men, you call them together and tell them to get out of Washington—tell them to go home, back to the states. That is where they must do their work."[24]

In view of these surpassing purposes—of consensual government, of an order of deliberation so as to identify and respect public values, of a "circumspection in forming the laws," of federalism—the delegation doctrine is something more than a quaint injunction against delegating legislative power to agencies. Rather, it is derived from legitimate inferences respecting constitutional structure and supported by empirical observations as to whether and when delegations of legislative power to agencies are consistent with the constitutional process. By these means, the delegation doctrine as we have it today wraps around a consensus, in the courts at least, which is that "important choices of social policy" are to be in Congress and not in the agencies.[25]

23. Under Article I, when national solutions are chosen, the states participate in the choice. The Senate is elected from and directly apportioned to the states and the House is elected from the states. The President may largely represent a national constituency, but still "the mode of his selection [the electoral college operating in the states] and the future of his party require that he also be responsive to local values that have large support within the states." H. Wechsler, The Political Safeguards of Federalism: The Role of the States in the Composition and Selection of the National Government, 54 Column.L.Rev. 543 (1954). The virtues of the Constitution's allocation of power between state and federal governments are well-known. In our large country local conditions vary, and local laws and local arrangements may better accommodate these variations, and, at the same time, provide various "laboratories of social experimentation," as Brandeis put it. New State Ice Co. v. Liebmann, 285 U.S. 262, 52 S.Ct. 371, 76 L.Ed. 747 (1932). The "prairie socialism" of North Dakota (state owned bank, state subsidized coal gasification plant, various cooperative arrangements) is, for instance, a useful adjustment to the particular social and economic conditions of that state. In the laboratories of social experimentation, better solutions to national as well as to local problems have often evolved, an example being how economic deregulation of airlines was inspired by the successes of unregulated intrastate airline operations in California and Texas. Empirical confirmation came from comparing fares in California and Texas—where new firms and price competition had been allowed—with flights elsewhere in the nation where competition had been restricted by the Civil Aeronautics Bureau. A traveler flying 476 miles from San Francisco to San Diego paid $27. On comparable routes elsewhere in the country the traveler paid at least sixty percent more. Civil Aeronautics Board Practice & Procedure, Subcomm. on Administrative Practice and Procedure, Senate Comm. on the Judiciary, 94th Cong., 1st Sess. 3 (1975).

24. Arthur Schlesinger, The Age of Roosevelt: The Politics of Upheaval 282, 280 (1960).

25. Various scholars dissent from this consensus. Professor Mashaw, arguing "prodelegation," believes that many of the qualities identified in the text above, for instance consensual government and the right sort of decisional process, do not attach just to Congress. Instead, they are suffused throughout government. Outside of Congress, the President represents a unitary national interest in counterbalance to agency single-mindedness in pursuit of its goals. By ordinary standards of judicial review, the courts stand to check agency usurpations of power, and by a contemporary requirement of reasoned decision-mak-

But it is also the case that given less than omniscient lawmakers and the imprecision of language, some lesser amount of delegation is inevitable. Moreover, pragmatic reasons, such as avoiding the diversion of Congress from "large objects to small" and making allowances for adjustments to rapidly changing circumstances, support a measure of delegation. Given these things, a substantial amount of delegation has, as we all know, been found to be good and tolerable under Article I.

A substantial amount of delegation being the case, the problem for the courts, and the main problem in the delegation doctrine, is this: how are judges to distinguish between the important choices of social policy that may not be delegated and the power that may be delegated. Given the difficulty of this distinction, it might be said that while the delegation doctrine is a "fundamental element of our constitutional system" it is not a part that is judicially enforceable because the courts cannot reliably distinguish between good and bad delegations.[26] But this is not what the courts have said. While the delegation may have in recent years may seen to have seen scant enforcement, the courts as we shall see have never "repudiated the principle" that primary choices of social policy must be made in Congress. They have maintained this principle by requiring that legislative power be delegated according to statutory standards, the presence of which are taken as showing that Congress has in some rudimentary way identified and thought through a social problem.

As often as not, this requirements of standards is referred to as a requirement that delegations of power be according to "intelligible principles". However it is stated, the courts have maintained this condition of delegated power in two ways. One way has been to nullify legislative acts that are bereft of standards. This mode is not uncommon in state courts. In the federal courts, it has not been much used to nullify statutes. (This is not, though, to say that is never so used.)[27] More frequently, this requirement of statutory standards is used as a canon of interpretation. Here, the courts review carefully a particular agency claim to power, in light of an assumption that Congress does not—not in the area of basic social choices—lightly give up legislative power by

ing the courts stand to reduce irrational exercises of legislative power. Mashaw, Prodelegation: Why Administrators Should Make Political Decisions, 1 Jour.L.Econ. & Organ. 80, 98 (1985) Given this suffusion, some portion of legislative power can be assigned to an agency without disrupting the constitutional scheme, so Prof. Mashaw's argument goes.

26. Mistretta v. United States, 488 U.S. 361, 415, 109 S.Ct. 647, 677, 102 L.Ed.2d 714 (1989)(Scalia, dissenting). In doubting the viability of the delegation doctrine, Justice Scalia asked whether delegation should not be a matter solely of "parliamentary concern" as in England. The practice in England is that "Although Parliament is often compelled to delegate legislative power, it prefers to retain some measure of control over the exercise of the power." F. Bennion, Statutory Interpretation 136 (1984). According to Bennion, the English courts, however, would not presume to overturn an act of Parliament on the grounds of an overly broad delegation. Instead, their role is to "superintend" the delegation, to assure that the agency acts "in good faith" and "within the four corners of the powers given by the legislature." Id., quoting Carltona Ltd. v. Commissioners of Works, [1943] 2 E.R. 560, 564.

27. See South Dakota v. U.S. Department of Interior, 69 F.3d 878 (8th Cir. 1995).

means of open-open delegations. In the "*Benzene Case,*" the Occupational Safety and Health Administration tried to reduce carcinogens in the workplace, and in doing so claimed the power freely to balance between death and productivity in American industry.[28] The Supreme Court, however, denied the agency all the power it claimed. The Court did so by interpreting the statutory allocation of power more narrowly than the agency did. As explained by the Court, "If the Act had not required that the risk from a toxic substance be quantified sufficiently to enable the Secretary to characterize it as significant in an understandable way, the statute would make such a 'sweeping delegation of legislative power' that it might be unconstitutional."

The delegation in the courts, their reasons for deploying it, and the methods by which they have deployed it are discussed in the next section.

§ 1.1 THE DELEGATION DOCTRINE IN THE COURTS

Before the New Deal, the delegation doctrine consisted of a series of decisions that spoke of a "non-delegable" legislative power in Congress. While these cases consistently approved the delegation in question, this approbation was contingent on Congress retaining a primary legislative power.[1] Moreover, the delegations approved by courts in these cases did not much involve private conduct within the domestic sphere. Instead, these delegations involved matters such as presidential authority in foreign affairs[2] or agency management of public property.[3] These delegations were, therefore, limited in subject matter; they did not generally pertain to broad-scale agency regulation of domestic conduct.

Accordingly, in 1928 Professor Ernst Fruend wrote that "the appropriate sphere of delegable authority is where there are no controverted issues of policy or of opinion" and that "a delegation so undefined [as to transcend this sphere] is too uncommon to call for much comment."[4] In

28. Industrial Union Dept., AFL–CIO v. American Petroleum Institute, 448 U.S. 607, 100 S.Ct. 2844, 65 L.Ed.2d 1010 (1980).

§ 1.1

1. E.g., Wichita R. & Light Co. v. Public Utilities Com'n, 260 U.S. 48, 58–59, 43 S.Ct. 51, 54–55, 67 L.Ed. 124 (1922) ("The maxim that a legislature may not delegate legislative power has some qualifications, as . . . in the creation of administrative boards to apply to the myriad details of rate schedules the regulatory policy power of the state"); Field v. Clark, 143 U.S. 649, 692, 12 S.Ct. 495, 504, 36 L.Ed. 294 (1892) ("[Tariff Act] does not in any real sense invest the President with the power of legislation"); United States v. Shreveport Grain & Elevator Co., 287 U.S. 77, 85, 53 S.Ct. 42, 44, 77 L.Ed. 175 (1932) ("that the legislative power cannot be delegated is clear, but Congress may declare its will, and after fixing a primary standard devolve upon administrative officers the power to fill in the details").

2. J.W. Hampton, Jr., & Co. v. United States, 276 U.S. 394, 48 S.Ct. 348, 72 L.Ed. 624 (1928). The reasons justifying broad delegations to the President in the realm of foreign affairs are discussed at § 1.3(a), infra.

3. U.S. v. Grimaud, 220 U.S. 506, 31 S.Ct. 480, 55 L.Ed. 563 (1911).

4. E. Fruend, Administrative Power Over Persons and Property 218 (1928). See Panama Refining Co. v. Ryan, 293 U.S. 388, 55 S.Ct. 241, 79 L.Ed. 446 (1935). In this pre-New Deal era, probably the most extensive delegation of power approved by the Court was to the President in J.W. Hampton, Jr., & Co. v. United States, 276 U.S. 394, 48 S.Ct. 348, 72 L.Ed. 624 (1928). This

two prominent cases in the next few years, *Panama Refining* and *Schechter Poultry,* the Supreme Court confirmed Fruend's description of the appropriate sphere of delegation, at least for the time. Both cases arose under the National Industrial Recovery Act of 1933, in Congress' initial and ill-considered attempt to cope with the Great Depression.

Understandably, in the crisis of the Depression a "clash of values and policies became particularly acute."[5] On the one hand, there was a demand for increased government regulation and market control. On the other hand, a solution was seen in a free market and in making good the competitive premises of capitalism. In the meantime, business and labor were at odds. Without resolving these various conflicts itself, Congress by means of the National Industrial Recovery Act, simply passed them on through the President and on to his sub-delegate, the National Recovery Administration ("NRA"). The NRA was generally supposed to devise codes of "fair competition" for the entire nation. But acting without direction from Congress, it soon became "a crisis-laden agency with little apparent policy direction and ad hoc procedures."[6]

In *Panama Refining,* the Court was concerned with only a part of the National Industrial Recovery Act, Sec. 9(c) that gave the President a discretionary power "to prohibit the transportation" of "hot oil" among the states.[7] Congress' authority to delegate this rather broad power was questioned. Respecting this question, Chief Justice Hughes defined the Court's role as that of "look[ing] to the statutes" to see whether Congress had "declared a policy" and "set up a standard for the President's action."

In the Court's view, Congress had not. Congress had, to be sure, provided an extensive statement of its "purposes" such as (a) to "remove obstructions" to commerce, (b) to "provide for the general welfare" by "promoting" cooperative action among industrial groups, (c) to "induce" labor-management unity, (d) to "eliminate unfair competitive practices," (e) to "promote the fullest utilization" of existing productive capacity, (f) to "reduce" unemployment, and so on. But in these "diverse objectives broadly stated," Congress' failure to itself establish national policy was

case is, however, distinguishable on the grounds that it involved the shared power of the President and Congress in foreign affairs. See § 1.3(a), infra. Otherwise, the Court found that Congress had provided standards, albeit broad, to guide the President.

The *Hampton* case involved the Tariff Act of 1922 in which Congress had established tariff duties but had delegated to the agency the considerable authority to vary these duties so as to equalize "cost of production" between the United States and other nations. At the same time, though, Congress provided statutory guidelines for ascertaining these "costs of production." The Court found this delegation to be justified by an "intelligible principle" standard: "If Congress shall lay down by legislative act an intelligible principle to which the person or body authorized to fix such rates is directed to conform, such legislative action is not a forbidden delegation of legislative power." 276 U.S. at 409, 48 S.Ct. at 352.

5. E. Gellhorn, G. Robinson, & H. Brueff, The Administrative Process 47 (2d ed. 1980). See also L. Jaffe, Judicial Control of Administrative Action 60–72 (1965).

6. E. Gellhorn, G. Robinson, & H. Bruff, supra at 48.

7. Panama Refining Co. v. Ryan, 293 U.S. 388, 55 S.Ct. 241, 79 L.Ed. 446 (1935).

apparent to the Court.[8] These statutory purposes were simply a recital, without resolution, of the values and interests that had confronted Congress.

Four months later in *Schechter Poultry,* a unanimous Court struck down the National Industrial Recovery Act in its entirety and put the NRA to rest.[9] Under the Act, Congress had, as we said, broadly delegated to the NRA the power to establish "codes of fair competition" for the various businesses and industries of the country. The NRA might itself write these codes or it might approve codes as submitted to it by various trade groups.

Unfortunately, Congress had provided no standards respecting the content of these codes. All Congress had done was to provide the above list of diverse and conflicting purposes and to otherwise state a few homilies such as the codes should be "truly representative" and impose "no inequitable restrictions or admission to membership" in a business or industry. Also, Congress had established virtually no procedural requirements for the NRA respecting the formulation and approval of these codes. As it was constituted, the NRA included and represented business interests in its decisional processes while affording labor and consumer groups little input.[10] Consequently, the NRA appeared to be, and was, rubber-stamping hastily prepared and anti-competitive codes in gross amounts. What all this amounted to, as described by Justice Cardozo, was "delegation running riot."[11]

"Circumspection in forming the law" was especially run down.[12] Because the NRA was relatively unconfined by procedures, and given the like-mindedness of the participants in the process (conflicting interests such as consumers or labor had, as we said, been excluded), decision costs at the NRA were minimal. And so it pumped out the Codes. The NRA "in the course of its short life from August 1933 to February 1935 . . . formulated and approved 546 codes and 185 supplemental codes filling 18 volumes and 13,000 pages; and 685 amendments and modifications."[13]

The complete sense of *Schechter* also requires an attention to federalism. In their Brooklyn market, the Schechter Brothers were selling kosher chickens at a price below that set by an NRA "Live Poultry Code," and they were prosecuted for that. As to them, the NRA

8. 293 U.S. at 416 & n.6 418, 55 S.Ct. at 246 & n.6 247.

9. A.L.A. Schechter Poultry Corp. v. United States, 295 U.S. 495, 55 S.Ct. 837, 79 L.Ed. 1570 (1935).

10. E.g., L. Lorwin, Economic Consequences of the Second World War 427–28 (1941). In Yakus v. United States, 321 U.S. 414, 426, 64 S.Ct. 660, 668, 88 L.Ed. 834 (1944), the Court explained that under the National Industrial Recovery Act the formulation of codes of fair competition was effectively "delegated . . . to private individuals engaged in the industries to be regulated."

11. 295 U.S. at 553, 55 S.Ct. at 853 (concurring).

12. Regarding "circumspection in forming the law," see § 1.1 and n.25, supra.

13. L. Jaffe, Judicial Control of Administrative Action 61 (1965). In this regard, it has been suggested that it was this large number of codes rather than the delegation of power that most bothered the justices in *Schechter Poultry.* A. Schlesinger, The Age of Roosevelt: The Politics of Upheaval 282 (1960).

seems to have been set loose, as a fox in the hen house, to disrupt their market without much attention to competition and customers. In upsetting local markets, the delegation to the NRA seems to have been an ill-favored substitute for the more carefully deliberated and calibrated use of power required by our federal-state system. Thus Justice Brandeis, as we have said, in excited, *ex cathedra* comments told Tom Corcoran that "This is the end of this business of centralization. As for your young men, you call them together and tell them to get out of Washington—tell them to go home, back to the states. That is where they must do their work."[14]

The Court, as it overturned the delegation of law-making power in *Schechter,* formally did so on the basis of Congress' failure to confine and condition this power by means of substantive and procedural controls. Respecting substance, the Court found that the NRA had been delegated a largely unfettered power over an enormously broad subject matter: "The vast array of commercial and industrial activities throughout the country." Respecting procedures, the Court noted that other broad delegations, to the Federal Trade Commission, the Interstate Commerce Commission, and the Federal Radio Commission, had been accompanied by at least a minimal set of procedural controls. "The National Industrial Recovery Act," the Court then said, "dispenses with this administrative procedure and, with any administrative procedure of an analogous character."

After *Schechter Poultry,* the delegation doctrine, according to reports, had something of a decline. Certainly it was on the wane in the Supreme Court's 1943 decision in the "*Networks Case*."[15] This decision established the broadest possible power in the Federal Communications Commission and is the single decision in which a majority of the Court approved a wholly open-ended and non-trivial grant of regulatory power to a federal agency. The Federal Communications Commission had promulgated regulations upsetting certain contractual arrangements between network companies and local broadcasting stations. It claimed the power to do so in that the Communications Act of 1934 had delegated to it, the Commission, the broadest of power, that of regulating the broadcast industry according to the Commission's view of the "public interest." Certain networks disagreed and brought suit. They contended that the Commission's charter, the Communications Act, more narrowly limited the Commission's power "to the engineering and technical aspects" of the electronic media and that that more limited power did not give the Commission the authority generally to regulate, as it now wished to, their business. The "public interest" claimed by the Commission would, the networks argued, render the Act "an unconstitutional delegation of legislative power."

14. A. Schlesinger, Jr., supra, at 280.

15. National Broadcasting Company v. United States, 319 U.S. 190, 63 S.Ct. 997, 87 L.Ed. 1344 (1943).

The Act's history and terms supported the network's narrow reading of it. History showed that the Act's origins lay in the inability of private enterprise to reach such agreements as would eliminate electronic interference among radio stations operating on adjacent frequencies.[16] The text of the Act sets out the Commission's power in detail, largely in relation to those matters of electronic interference. The Commission's "general powers" are largely established by Sec. 303 of the Act. In its preamble, Sec. 303 states that "the Commission from time to time, as public convenience, interest or necessity requires, shall . . .," and this "shall" is then followed by standards defining the scope of the Commission's power. These standards are fairly specific, and mostly pertain to technical matters of electronic interference.[17]

In the Communications Act, then, the "public convenience, interest or necessity" language does not stand alone, as a general and unlimited grant of power to regulate in the public interest. Instead, that power is defined and conditioned by the standards that immediately follow the public interest language, which was the networks substantial argument.[18] But Justice Frankfurter, writing for the majority in the *Networks*

16. 319 U.S. at 211–12, 63 S.Ct. at 1007–08. See also FCC v. Sanders Bros. R.S., 309 U.S. 470, 60 S.Ct. 693, 84 L.Ed. 869 (1940) ("The fundamental purpose of Congress in respect of broadcasting was the allocation and the use of radio frequencies by prohibiting [interfering uses]."). Because of this failure, the industry itself "called upon Congress to remedy the situation through legislation." In response, Congress established the Radio Act of 1927, which in its substantive provisions was then substantially reenacted in the Communications Act of 1934.

17. In this regard, § 303 in relevant part provides that:

Except as otherwise provided in this Act, the Commission from time to time, as public convenience, interest, or necessity requires, shall—

(a) Classify radio stations;

(b) Prescribe the nature of the service to be rendered by each class of licensed stations and each station within any class;

(c) Prescribe the nature of the service to be rendered by each class of licensed stations and each station within any class;

(d) Determine the location of classes of stations or individual stations;

(e) Regulate the kind of apparatus to be used with respect to its external effects and the purity and sharpness of the emissions from each station and from the apparatus therein;

(f) Make such regulations not inconsistent with law as it may deem necessary to prevent interference between stations and to carry out the provisions of this Act: Provided, however, That changes in the frequencies, authorized power, or in the times of operation of any station, shall not be made without the consent of the station licensee unless, after a public hearing, the Commission shall determine that such changes will promote public convenience or interest or will serve public necessity, or the provisions of this Act will be more fully complied with. . . .

48 Stat. 1082 (1934), codified at 47 U.S.C.A. § 303.

18. See Mayton, The Illegitimacy of the Public Interest Standard at the FCC, 38 Emory L.J. 715 (1989). Professor Louis Jaffe has also concluded that the Communications Act of 1934 was not intended to delegate a general power to act in the public interest to the Federal Communications Commission. "The use of 'public interest,' in the statute," he wrote, "did not manifest a congressional intent to give the Commission general powers to regulate the industry or to solve any problems other than the problem of interference which gave rise to the legislation." L. Jaffe, the Illusion of the Ideal Administration 1183, 1192 (1954).

In their argument in the *Networks Case*, plaintiffs relied not only on the history and terms of the 1934 Act, but from the Supreme Court's previous and first interpretation of this Act, in *FCC v. Sander Brothers R.S* 309 U.S. 470, 475, 60 S.Ct. 693, 697, 84 L.Ed. 869 (1940). In this 1939 decision, the Court had flatly stated that "the Act does not essay to regulate the business of the

Case, could not accept such a parsimonious view of agency power; otherwise, the "facilities of radio" might not, as he saw it, be put "to the best practicable service to the community."[19] Consequently, Frankfurter found the most expansive language of the 1934 Act, the "public interest, convenience and necessity" language in the prologue of Sec. 303, to be a general and unconditioned grant of power. Since then, the Federal Communications Commission has been considered to be the recipient of an open-ended "public interest" delegation.[20] Justice Murphy, in his dissent in the *Networks Case,* was, however, no doubt correct as he stated that "We gratuitously bestow upon an agency power which Congress has not granted."[21]

Outside of rate regulation or minor matters suited to administrative routine, the *Networks Case,* as we said, seems to be the only case where the Supreme Court has approved (or, more accurately, helped construct) an entirely open-ended delegation.[22] For about forty years following

licensee. The Commission is given no supervisory control of the programs, of business management or of policy." 309 U.S. at 475, 60 S.Ct. at 697. In *Sanders Bros.,* a unanimous Court had found that the general "public convenience, interest, or necessity" language of the Act was "given meaning and contour by the other provisions of the statute," 309 U.S. at 473, 60 S.Ct. at 696 (just as the plaintiffs in the *Networks Case* argued).

19. 319 U.S. at 216, 63 S.Ct. at 1009 (here Justice Frankfurter is quoting out of context the opinion of the Court in FCC v. Sanders Bros. R.S., 309 U.S. 470, 475, 60 S.Ct. 693, 697, 84 L.Ed. 869 (1940)).

20. At most, the "public convenience, interest, or necessity" language on which Justice Frankfurter relies supports the residual and discretionary authority of the FCC to choose among otherwise qualified applicants for a license according to this general formula. See Jaffe, The Illusion of the Ideal Administration, 86 Harv.L.Rev. 1183, 1191 et seq. (1973). But, in no sense, does this language appear to be a basis for a general regulatory authority as regards the manner in which a licensee does business, or, indeed, the unlicensed networks. A unanimous Court in FCC v. Sanders Bros. R.S., 309 U.S. 470, 60 S.Ct. 693, 84 L.Ed. 869 (1940), had previously stated this. See note 28 supra.

The textual obstacles that beset Frankfurter in the *Networks Case* are indicated by his admission that, "True enough, the Act does not explicitly state that the Commission shall have power to deal with network practices found inimical to the public interest." 319 U.S. at 218–19, 63 S.Ct. at 1010–11.

21. 319 U.S. at 227–28, 63 S.Ct. at 1014–15. In terms of securing the highest and best use of the broadcast media, various studies have shown that the "gratuity" conferred in the *Networks Case* has not worked so well. See H. Friendly, The Administrative Agencies 53 (1962) (citing Landis, Report on Regulatory Agencies to the President–Elect 53 (1960), for the proposition that "Despite considerable technical excellence on the part of its staff, the Commission has drifted, vacillated and stalled in almost every major area. It seems incapable of policy planning, of disposing within a reasonable period of time the business before it, of fashioning procedures that are effective to deal with its problems."). See also Coase, The Federal Communications Commission, 2 J.L. Econ. 1 (1959); Kalven Broadcasting, Public Policy and the First Amendment, 10 J.L. Econ. 15 (1967); In re Complaint of Syracuse Peace Council, 2 FCC Rec. 5043, 5055 (1987).

22. Public interest delegations respecting rate regulation are generally confined by market forces and by common-law practices. Outside of rate regulation, wholly open-ended delegations have been for relatively minor matters such as grading exported tea, Buttfield v. Stranahan, 192 U.S. 470, 24 S.Ct. 349, 48 L.Ed. 525 (1904), or for the proprietary concerns of government, U.S. v. Grimaud, 220 U.S. 506, 31 S.Ct. 480, 55 L.Ed. 563 (1911). Otherwise, the more open-ended delegations have been in foreign affairs, where Congress and the Executive share power. See Sec. 1.3, infra.

The large and broad delegation to the Federal Trade Commission, at least the original delegation respecting "unfair methods of competition," 15 U.S.C.A. § 45(a),

Schechter Poultry, however, the Court did approve a number of delegations while disapproving of none. Some of the larger delegations approved by the Court were for market controls such as World War II price controls or price supports in agriculture. In these cases, Congress had made the decision to impose price and market controls, established guidelines, and delegated to agencies. Had Congress tried to do much more, that effort would have violated Thomas Jefferson's injunction about legislatures about not being diverting from large objects to small. In *United States v. Rock Royal Co-op., Inc.*[23] and *Yakus v. United States*[24] delegations pertaining to price controls and to parity pricing in agriculture were approved on the grounds that Congress had conditioned the delegations with standards sufficient to control agency discretion and to provide a baseline for judicial review of agency action. The Court may, or may not (see the dissent in *Rock Royal*), have been overly generous in assessing the strength of the strings in place to bind the agencies. Still, it insisted on the strings. The Court did not, as Professor Currie has said, "repudiate[ ] the principle."[25]

The decision in *Yakus* further developed the principle in an important way. This development was about judicial review. In this regard, the Court explained that the delegation doctrine's requirement of statutory standards made judicial review of agency action feasible inasmuch as those standards provided courts a baseline for constraining agency action.[26] In *American Power & Light Co. v. SEC,* the Court further explained this "baseline for judicial review" requirement:

> [It is] constitutionally sufficient if Congress clearly delineates the general policy, the public agency which is to apply it, and the boundaries of this delegated authority. Private rights are protected

seems to have been done on the understanding that that language referred to common law standards of unfair competition, and that these standards would confine the agency. See Arthur, Farewell to the Sea of Doubt, Jettisoning the Constitutional Sherman Act, 74 Cal.L.Rev. 263 (1986).

23. 307 U.S. 533, 59 S.Ct. 993, 83 L.Ed. 1446 (1939), rehearing denied 308 U.S. 631, 60 S.Ct. 66, 84 L.Ed. 526 (1939).

24. 321 U.S. 414, 64 S.Ct. 660, 88 L.Ed. 834 (1944).

25. Currie, The Distribution of Powers After Bowsher, 1986 S.Ct. Rev. 19, 21. As Professor Currie explains, in cases commonly cited for the demise of the delegation doctrine, there was "no absence of standards to guide the exercise of delegated authority". In *Yakus,* the World War II price control statute in question had "essentially required preservation of preexisting price levels with adjustments for charging costs." Id. In *Fahey v. Mallonee,* 332 U.S. 245, 67 S.Ct. 1552, 91 L.Ed. 2030 (1947), another seemingly open-ended delegation, the statutory scheme incorporated such common law standards as would guide agency authority. See Sec. 1.2 at n. 22, supra.

Outside of the *Networks Case*, the decision that is probably the weakest in terms of the delegation doctrine is the elaborately reasoned lower court opinion in Amalgamated Meat Cutters v. Connally, 337 F.Supp. 737 (D.D.C.1971). The court in this case thought that good procedures and agency action in supplying standards might cure the ills of an open-ended delegation. As discussed at sec. 1.4, infra, that thought seems to have been wrong.

26. In *Yakus,* the Court explained that "Only if we could say that there is an absence of standards for the guidance of the Administrator's action, so that it would be impossible in a proper proceeding to ascertain whether the will of Congress has been obeyed, would we be justified in overriding its choice of means of effecting its declared purpose." 321 U.S. at 425–26, 64 S.Ct. at 667–68.

by access to the courts to test the application of the policy in the light of these legislative declarations.[27]

* * *

In 1974 the delegation doctrine turned up alive, in *National Cable Television Association, Inc. v. United States*[28] where the Court applied the principle that "Congress is not permitted to advocate or to transfer to others the essential legislative functions with which it is ... vested." By the Independent Offices Appropriation Act, Congress authorized agencies to become more "self-sustaining" by assessing "fees" against regulated industries. The amount of the fee was to be determined according to the "direct and indirect cost to the government, value to the recipient, public policy or other interests served, and other pertinent facts...."[29] Under this provision, the Federal Communications Commission imposed charges of about a million dollars a year on cable television firms. These firms sued, claiming that these charges were unlawfully imposed. The Supreme Court agreed, on the ground that Act in its most open-ended terms left the agency free to pick among competing values "in the manner of" a legislative body.[30] The Court, therefore, "narrowed" the Act by nullifying its indeterminate "public policy or other interests served" provision while leaving its more determinate "value to the recipient" provision in place.

The delegation doctrine was called upon again, not to nullify but to serve as a canon of interpretation, in the Supreme Court's 1980 decision in the *"Benzene"* case.[31] The Occupational Safety and Health Administration had been delegated the power to "assure, to the extent feasible, ... that no employee will suffer material impairment of health or functional capacity...."[32] Pursuant to this authority, the agency had published a rule requiring industry to limit benzene in the workplace to no more than one part benzene in one million parts of air. Industry

27. 329 U.S. 90, 105, 67 S.Ct. 133, 142, 91 L.Ed. 103 (1946). Federal Power Com'n v. New England Power Co., 415 U.S. 345, 94 S.Ct. 1151, 39 L.Ed.2d 383 (1974).

28. 415 U.S. 336, 342, 94 S.Ct. 1146, 1149, 39 L.Ed.2d 370 (1974). See also Federal Power Com'n v. New England Power Co., 415 U.S. 345, 94 S.Ct. 1151, 39 L.Ed.2d 383 (1974). 415 U.S. at 342, 94 S.Ct. at 1149. This case's endorsement and application of has been described as limited in that it represents only a special instance of a delegation doctrine relating to a special power of Congress, its power to tax. J. Freedman, Crisis and Legitimacy: The Administrative Process and American Government 80–86 (1978). However, the Court did not so limit its opinion. Also, how could a judge in any principled way say which legislative powers are special and which are not. Accordingly, in Skinner v. Mid–America Pipeline Co., 490 U.S. 212, 216, 109 S.Ct. 1726, 1729, 104 L.Ed.2d 250 (1989), the Court found "no support ... for Mid–Atlantic's contention that the text of the Constitution or the practices of Congress require the application of a different and stricter nondelegation doctrine in cases where Congress delegates discretionary authority to the executive under its taxing power."

29. 31 U.S.C.A. § 483a.

30. 415 U.S. at 416, 94 S.Ct. at 1142. In particular, the Court objected to the Act's "public policy or interest served" measure of charges, because that measure "if read literally, carries an agency far from its customary orbit and puts it in search of revenue in the manner of an Appropriations Committee of the House." *Id.* at 341.

31. Industrial Union Dept. v. American Petroleum Institute, 448 U.S. 607, 100 S.Ct. 2844, 65 L.Ed.2d 1010 (1980).

32. 29 U.S.C.A. § 655(b)(5).

argued that attaining such a low-level of benzene would be exceptionally costly and would not redress any significant health problems. Thus stated, the issue was whether the agency had been delegated the power to impose health regulations on industry without regard to the costs of these regulations or the risk involved. In a five to four decision, the Court overturned the rule.

One of the five, Chief Justice Rehnquist, was of the opinion that the delegation should be nullified because it violated the Article I norm of consensual government. "It is the hard choices and not the filling in of the blanks," Rehnquist wrote, "which must be made by the elected representatives of the people." The hard choice in question was "whether the statistical probability of future death should ever be disregarded in light of the economic costs of preventing those deaths." Congress, as Rehnquist determined from the legislative history, had been troubled by how far economic costs should be counted in establishing health standards, but had been unable to reach agreement in the matter. Instead, by the "legislative mirage" of the "to the extent feasible" condition of statute, Congress had "simply avoided a choice which was both fundamental ... and yet politically so divisive that the necessary decision or compromise was difficult, if not impossible, to hammer out on the legislative forge." Thus Congress, in Rehnquist's view, had passed the buck to the agency, and he considered that grounds for overturning the statute.[33]

The agency's benzene rule was overturned, but the statute saved, as Rehnquist joined a plurality of four. This plurality—while not opting for nullification as had Rehnquist—nonetheless interpreted the Act to avoid an open-ended delegation. This plurality found that the delegation to which Rehnquist had objected (the agency's power to "assure, to the extent feasible, ... that no employee will suffer material impairment of health or functional capacity") was limited by other parts of the Act. These other parts were read as requiring that the Occupational Safety and Health Administration find a "significant risk of harm" to workers, which finding the agency had not made in enacting the benzene rule. This statutory interpretation was shaped by the delegation doctrine, the doctrine operating as a canon of interpretation. The plurality explained that if the Act did not "requir[e] that the risk from a toxic substance be quantified sufficiently to enable the Secretary to characterize it as significant in an understandable way, the statute would make such a 'sweeping delegation of legislative power' that it might be unconstitutional...."[34]

33. Rehnquist would have overturned the benzene rule by voiding, on delegation doctrine grounds, that portion of the Occupational Safety and Health Act which empowered the agency to "assure, to the extent feasible, ... that no employee will suffer material impairment of health or functional capacity...." As this portion of the Act was eliminated, the benzene rule was then controlled by more stringent portions of the Act, which portions it failed to meet. 448 U.S. at 687–88, 100 S.Ct. at 2886–87.

34. 448 U.S. at 646, 100 S.Ct. at 2866. The plurality explained that "in the absence of a clear mandate in the Act" it was "unreasonable to assume" that Congress had given the Commission "unprecedented

In modern case law, another decision, *Hampton v. Mow Sun Wong,*[35] stands in a seemingly enigmatic relation to the delegation doctrine. This relation is not so obscure, however, from a point of view of the right sort of decisional processes. As previously said, Article I tries to assure an order of deliberation and debate that distills and protects public interests and values.[36] In *Hampton v. Mow Sun Wong,* the Court struck a Civil Service Commission rule barring aliens from federal jobs. The Court did so because the Commission's decisional process was too thin to support the rule.

The Commission had argued that barring aliens from federal employment served important public interests such as encouraging aliens to qualify for naturalization, assuring an undivided loyalty in sensitive positions, and providing a bargaining chip for securing reciprocal treatment for U.S. citizens in other nations. The Court was of the opinion that these interests might have justified the rule, *if the rule had been passed by Congress*.[37] The Court was not, however, "willing to presume that the Civil Service Commission was deliberately fostering [interests] so far removed from its normal responsibilities." These normal responsibilities were those attendant to its statutory goal of "promot[ing] the efficiency" of the federal work force. In short, in *Hampton v. Mow Sun Wong* the Court found that the process of delegation had resulted in a truncated decisional process (an agency in service of a limited set of interests) that would not support an infringement of important private rights.

In 1995 the Eight Circuit deployed the delegation doctrine in its strongest form, to annul a open-ended delegation on the grounds that in it Congress had avoided the lawmaking responsibility assigned it by Article I and in doing so had created an unfortunate "agency fiefdom." The federal "Indian Reorganization Act of 1934" (the "IRA") in Sec. 465 authorizes the Department of Interior to acquire land to be held "in trust" for "the purpose of providing land to Indians." Land so acquired is not subject to state taxes or regulation. In South Dakota v. Department of Interior,[38] the state claimed that the Department's acquisition of some ninety acres, partly within a municipality and ostensibly for an industrial park, was bad in that the authorizing statute, Sec. 465 of IRA, was so open-ended as to violate the delegation doctrine. The court of appeals was mindful that a delegation was proper so long as it was according to an intelligible principle, which here meant that "at a minimum Congress ... articulate and configure the underlying public use that justifies an acquisition." The court, however, could find no such articulation or configuration, that instead the agency had been autho-

power over American industry." 448 U.S. at 644, 100 S.Ct. at 2865.

35. 426 U.S. 88, 96 S.Ct. 1895, 48 L.Ed.2d 495 (1976).

36. See § 1 supra.

37. 426 U.S. at 100, 96 S.Ct. at 1903.

38. 69 F.3d 878 (8th Cir.1995), opinion vacated on other grounds,106 F.3d 247 (8th Cir.1996).

rized to acquire any sort of land for any sort of use and that over time the result had become that of the out-of-control "agency fiefdom".

* * *

The foregoing cases have been federal cases. In the states, the delegation doctrine is also used, and used more extensively, so that in the states there has never been a suspicion of its death.[39] For instance, New York's highest court held that a delegation to agencies of the power to make "trade-offs" between health and privacy in relation to control on smoking in public places was unconstitutional. "Manifestly," the court said, "it is the province of the peoples' elected representatives, rather than appointed administrators, to resolve difficult social problems by making choices among competing ends."[40]

§ 1.2 IS THE DELEGATION DOCTRINE A WORKABLE JURIDICAL PRINCIPLE?

The history of the delegation doctrine in the courts shows the courts' own reasons for enforcing it. Their main reason, that "important choices of social policy" should be made by democratic assemblies rather than in the agencies, has been discussed at some length. Another reason, one that we have not heretofore identified, is that the structure of American government tends toward a certain discipline, of regulation according to standing rules and regular procedures. We refer to this discipline as the rule of law, and broad delegations and unfettered agency processes, so that lawmaking becomes as casual and irresponsible as it was by the National Recovery Administration in *Schechter Poultry,* are contrary to it. A third reason sounds in the courts' special function of limiting agency power. In this respect, the statute that delegates power to agencies should be precise enough for courts to understand whether an agency is acting consistent with its allotted power.[1]

The history of the doctrine in the courts also shows that the courts have developed two different ways of implementing it. One way, used infrequently and reluctantly (at least in federal courts) has been to overturn statutes. More modestly and more often, the courts have used the doctrine as a canon of interpretation. As a canon of interpretation, the doctrine is consistent with a function of courts in a society careful about power. This function is to prevent power from growing, this time according to bureaucratic tendencies to expand their turf. Here, the delegation doctrine simply requires that the courts be especially mindful about exactly how much power Congress has delegated to an agency. In

39. See, e.g., In re Initiative Petition No. 332, 776 P.2d 556 (Okl.1989); Boreali v. Axelrod, 71 N.Y.2d 1, 523 N.Y.S.2d 464, 517 N.E.2d 1350 (1987); Fitanides v. Crowley, 467 A.2d 168 (Me.1983); Thygesen v. Callahan, 74 Ill.2d 404, 24 Ill.Dec. 558, 385 N.E.2d 699 (1979); Commissioner of Agriculture v. Plaquemines Parish Com'n Council, 439 So.2d 348 (La.1983). See A. Bonfeld & M. Asimow, State and Federal Administrative Law, 451–61 (1988).

40. Boreali v. Axelrod, 71 N.Y.2d 1, 8, 523 N.Y.S.2d 464, 471, 517 N.E.2d 1350, 1356 (1987).

§ 1.2

1. See *Yakus v. United States,* 321 U.S. 414, 64 S.Ct. 660, 88 L.Ed. 834 (1944).

this way, the courts may work with Congress, not against it. In this way, the Eleventh Circuit refused to find that the Interstate Commerce Commission had been broadly delegated the power to implement a "national transportation policy."[2]

The Commission, by means of its selective reading of its charter, had ignored the detail that defined and confined its power. Instead, the Commission tried to expand its power by fastening on such expansive and open-ended phrases as might be found in the Interstate Commerce Act. According to such phrases, the Commission claimed that it had been statutorily authorized to implement a "national transportation policy." This mode of interpretation—by which the agency emphasizes the broad terms of its charter while ignoring the detail—had been the method of the Federal Communications Commission in the *Networks Cases*. But in sharp contrast to the method of the Supreme Court in the *Networks Cases,* the Eleventh Circuit found that the Interstate Commerce Commission's power was not to be measured by such vague and general phrases as might be found in its charter. "Such a reading," the court said, "would make superfluous much of the rest of the Act, with its detailed guidelines and delegations of authority." Moreover, "construing the National Transportation Policy, which paraphrased, says little more than 'go forth and do good,' as a congressional grant of rule making authority might well amount to an unconstitutional delegation of legislative authority."[3]

* * *

The courts, then, have justified the delegation doctrine and developed ways of enforcing it. Nonetheless, a doubt remains about whether the doctrine is susceptible to judicial enforcement. The doctrine requires the courts to make judgments about the precision that Congress must bring to bear it drafting statutes, about whether the statutes define and confine agency power with sufficient precision. The doubt is whether this judgment can be consistently and reliably made. A prominent expression of this reservation is that of Justice Scalia, who said that the requisite precision comes down to a matter of degree and that therefore "it is small wonder that we have almost never felt qualified to second-guess Congress regarding the permissible degree of policy judgment that can be left to those executing or applying the law."[4] In assessing this

2. The Fifth Circuit refused to find that the Interstate Commerce Commission had been delegated this power in two related case, Global Van Lines, Inc. v. ICC, 714 F.2d 1290 (5th Cir.1983), and Central Forwarding, Inc. v. ICC, 698 F.2d 1266 (5th Cir.1983).

3. Central Forwarding, Inc. v. ICC, 698 F.2d 1266, 1283 (5th Cir.1983).

4. Mistretta v. United States, 488 U.S. 361, 416, 109 S.Ct. 647, 677, 102 L.Ed.2d 714 (1989) (dissenting). Scalia's full comment on the doctrine is as follows:

[W]hile the doctrine of unconstitutional delegation is unquestionably a fundamental element of our constitutional system, it is not an element readily enforceable by the courts. Once it is conceded, as it must be, that no statute can be entirely precise, and that some judgments, even those involving policy considerations, must be left to the officers executing the law and the judges applying it, the debate over unconstitutional delegation becomes a debate not over a point of principle but over a question of degree.... Since Congress is no less en-

reservation, we should first note that Scalia did not say never; rather, he said "almost never," as he had to considering that the doctrine has been enforced in the courts (and considering that he would himself have held the delegation then before the Court unconstitutional).

Another thing is that as the courts have constructed the doctrine it operates more as a matter of discernible principle than as a matter of immeasurable degree. The main principle, of course, is that Congress must make primary social choices and then express this choice in terms appreciable to agencies and to courts reviewing agency action. The requisite expression of legislative is variously referred to as a standard or as an "intelligible principle."[5] The requisite standard defines and confines agency power and provides the substantive baseline for court review of this action. The judgment as to whether Congress has laid down such a standard involves an assessment more of the quality of a statute than an estimate of degree. The courts application of this criterion of standards is marked by qualitative expressions, such as whether the agency has been left free to select among important social values "in the manner of" a legislative assembly. Other applications of the doctrine, which we have yet to consider, involve qualitative assessments such as whether the agency has been delegated the power to determine important personal rights. It is only atop a baseline of standards that Congress determines the "degree" of authority that it delegates. The Supreme Court has explained:

dowed with common sense than we are, and better equipped to inform itself of the necessities of government; . . . it is small wonder that we have almost never felt qualified to second-guess Congress regarding the permissible degree of policy judgment that can be left to those executing or applying the law.

5. Limiting delegations by a measure of standards is an obvious and natural requirement. According to James Madison, "If nothing more were required, in exercising a legislative trust, than a general conveyance of authority—without laying down any precise rules by which the authority conveyed should be carried into effect—it would follow that the whole power of delegation might be transferred by the legislature from itself. . . ." IV Elliot's Debates, at 560. See also Mistretta v. United States, 488 U.S. 361, 371, 109 S.Ct. 647, 654, 102 L.Ed.2d 714 (1989); Skinner v. Mid–America Pipeline Co., 490 U.S. 212, 109 S.Ct. 1726, 104 L.Ed.2d 250 (1989); National Cable Television Ass'n, Inc. v. United States, 415 U.S. 336, 94 S.Ct. 1146, 39 L.Ed.2d 370 (1974); A.L.A. Schechter Poultry Corp. v. United States, 295 U.S. 495, 55 S.Ct. 837, 79 L.Ed. 1570 (1935); Wayman v. Southard, 23 U.S. (10 Wheat.) 1, 42–43, 6 L.Ed. 253 (1825).

For a more general discussion of the requirement of standards, see Pound, The Administrative Application of Legal Standards, Report of the 42nd Meeting of the American Bar Association (1919), reprinted in Separation of Powers and Independent Agencies, Cases and Selective Readings, Sen.Doc. 49, 91st Cong., 1st Sess. 17 (1969); Merrill, Standards—A Safeguard for the Exercise of Delegated Powers, 47 Neb.L.J. 469 (1968); S.Rep. 97–284, 97th Cong., 1st Sess. 164 (1983) ("One primary mechanism for control of agency discretion is the requirement that when the legislature delegates power, it must establish an intelligible principle to govern the delegation").

In the states, a test more formulaic than an unadorned requirement of standards has at times been used as a measure of a good delegation. Under this test, a delegation is valid if it identifies:

(1) The *persons* and *activities* potentially subject to regulations;

(2) the *harm* sought to be prevented;

(3) the general *means* intended to be available to the administrator to prevent the identified harm.

Thygesen v. Callahan, 74 Ill.2d 404, 24 Ill.Dec. 558, 385 N.E.2d 699 (1979).

> [E]ach enactment must be considered to determine whether it states the purpose which the Congress seeks to accomplish and the standards by which that purpose is to be worked out with sufficient exactness to enable those affected to understand these limits. Within these tests the Congress needs specify only so far as is reasonably practicable.[6]

* * *

The material to which the delegation doctrine is applied is generally statutory. As said by the courts, their main task is that of "looking to the statutes" to see whether in them Congress has "set up a standard."[7] However, the courts do on occasion look outside the statute, to extrinsic material that may operate to define agency power consistent with the delegation doctrine. In this respect, the courts have approved otherwise open-ended statutory provisions where the blank check might be filled in by reference to common-law standards or to established administrative practices. In a leading case, *Fahey v. Mallonee*,[8] Congress had delegated to the federal Home Loan Bank a broad authority with respect to reorganizations and receiverships of failing banks and the argument was that this was a "delegation of legislative functions . . . without adequate standards." The Court in rejecting this claim of inadequate standards noted that "banking is one of the longest regulated" businesses and that "well-defined practices" provided a background of standards sufficient to control agency power.

§ 1.3 SOME SPECIAL CONDITIONS OF THE DELEGATION DOCTRINE

The general form of the delegation doctrine is that delegations with standards will not be questioned by the courts, while open-ended delegations about basic social choices will be. Within this general form, however, the courts may make some special assumptions about the delegation doctrine. These assumption are about the relative capabilities of Congress and its delegate as regards a delegated power. According to assumptions about capabilities, the courts may either favor or disfavor a delegation. Presently, the cases reveal three conditions—of foreign affairs, private organizations, and personal liberties—where these assumptions operate.

§ 1.3.1 Foreign Affairs

Under the Constitution, the conduct of foreign affairs does not belong exclusively to Congress. Instead, responsibility is shared with the executive. Moreover, the executive branch has special capacities in this

6. United States v. Rock Royal Co-op., Inc., 307 U.S. 533, 574, 59 S.Ct. 993, 1013, 83 L.Ed. 1446 (1939).

7. Panama Refining Co. v. Ryan, 293 U.S. 388, 415, 55 S.Ct. 241, 246, 79 L.Ed. 446 (1935).

8. 332 U.S. 245, 249, 67 S.Ct. 1552, 1553, 91 L.Ed. 2030 (1947).

area. Consequently, in foreign affairs broad delegations to the executive branch are more than usually tolerable. In *United States v. Curtiss–Wright Export Corp.,*[1] the Supreme Court spoke of the "unwisdom of requiring Congress in this field of governmental power to lay down narrowly defined standards by which the President is to be governed."

The *Curtiss–Wright* case involved a delegation to the President of a law-making authority with respect to international arms sale by American companies. The Court assessed this delegation in relation to its international affairs subject-matter, and stated that the constitutional question was "assuming (but not deciding) that the challenged delegation, if it were confined to internal affairs would be invalid, may it nevertheless be sustained on the ground that its exclusive aim is to afford a remedy for a hurtful condition within a foreign territory?" The Court's answer, an unequivocal yes, was based on its assessment of the special capabilities of the White House in foreign affairs and on the shared responsibilities, under the Constitution, of Congress and the President in foreign affairs. In this regard, the Court explained:

> It is quite apparent that if, in the maintenance of our international relations, embarrassment—perhaps serious embarrassment—is to be avoided and success for our aims achieved, congressional legislation which is to be made effective through negotiations and inquiry within the international field must often accord to the President a degree of discretion and freedom from statutory restriction which would not be admissible were domestic affairs alone involved. Moreover, he, not Congress, has the better opportunity of knowing the conditions which prevail in foreign countries.... He has his confidential sources of information. He has his agents in the form of diplomatic, consular and other officials.[2]

§ 1.3.2 Private Organizations and Occupational Licensing Boards

Delegations of law-making power to private organizations are especially suspect. In *Schechter Poultry,* for example, the Court disfavored the authority conveyed to private trade associations to formulate their own "codes of fair competition" because these associations might thereby protect themselves at the expense of competitors and consumers.[3] Private organizations may be inclined to act in their own interest and contrary to the Article I norm of laws made for the whole community. Consequently, delegation of governmental power to them is especially suspect. It is, as the Supreme Court has said, "delegation in its most obnoxious form; for it is not even delegation to an official or an official body, presumptively disinterested, but to private persons whose interests

§ 1.3

1. 299 U.S. 304, 321–22, 57 S.Ct. 216, 221–22, 81 L.Ed. 255 (1936).

2. 299 U.S. at 320, 57 S.Ct. at 221. See also Florsheim Shoe Co. v. United States, 570 F.Supp. 734, 742 (CIT 1983), order affirmed 744 F.2d 787 (Fed.Cir.1984).

3. A.L.A. Schechter Poultry Corp. v. United States, 295 U.S. 495, 537, 55 S.Ct. 837, 846, 79 L.Ed. 1570 (1935).

may be and often are adverse to the interests of others in the same business."[4]

This assumption about delegation to private associations ("delegation in its most obnoxious form") has been most often applied in the field of occupational licensing. As stated by the New Jersey Supreme Court, "We think such a power to determine who shall have the right to engage in an otherwise lawful enterprise may not validly be delegated by the Legislature to a private body ... at least where the exercise of such power is not accompanied by adequate legislative standards or safeguards...."[5] Trappings of sovereignty (a state-created licensing board whose public members are actually practitioners of the regulated occupation) may, however, be sufficient to remove private associations from an assumption of ineligibility to exercise law-making power. Still, the courts

4. Carter v. Carter Coal Co., 298 U.S. 238, 311, 56 S.Ct. 855, 872, 80 L.Ed. 1160 (1936). In this case, the Court held unconstitutional a delegation of "the power to fix maximum hours of labor to a part of the producers [of coal] and the miners—namely 'the producers of more than 2/3 of the annual national tonnage production for the preceding calendar year' and 'more than 1/2 of the miners employed.'" Id. at 310, 56 S.Ct. at 872. See also Grendel's Den, Inc. v. Goodwin, 662 F.2d 88, 92–93 (1st Cir.1981) (after synthesizing the case law, the court concluded that "legislative bodies may not abrogate their responsibility to formulate and impose policy regarding matters such as zoning or the issuance of government privileges, by delegating this responsibility to private parties 'uncontrolled by any standard or rule prescribed by legislative action ...' ").

Delegation to private organizations are more common in the states and probably as a result, much of the case law respecting such delegations has arisen in the states. E.g., Stewart v. Utah Public Serv. Comm'n, 885 P.2d 759 (Sup.Ct., Utah 1994) ("the Legislature cannot constitutionally delegate to the private parties governmental power that can be used to further private interests contrary to the public interest"); Corvallis Lodge No. 1411 v. Oregon Liquor Control Comm'n, 67 Or.App. 15, 677 P.2d 76 (Or. App.1984); Salt Lake City v. International Association of Firefighters, 563 P.2d 786 (Utah 1977) ("The legislature may not surrender its legislative authority to a body wherein the public interest is subjected to the interest of a group which may be antagonistic to the public interest."); Fink v. Cole, 302 N.Y. 216, 97 N.E.2d 873 (1951); Sante Fe Natural Tobacco Co. v. Judge, 963 F.Supp. 437 (D.Pa.1997). See generally 1 F. Cooper, State Administrative Law 84–85 (1965).

Where the actions of private organizations are subject to review by a public body, the chance for self-interested action by these organizations may be eliminated. Consequently, where such review is present, delegations to these organizations have been upheld. E.g., Todd & Co. v. SEC, 557 F.2d 1008, 1012–13 (3d Cir.1977); Corum v. Beth Israel Medical Center, 373 F.Supp. 550, 552–53 (S.D.N.Y.1974).

5. Group Health Ins. v. Howell, 40 N.J. 436, 445, 193 A.2d 103, 108 (1963). See also Rogers v. Medical Association, 244 Ga. 151, 259 S.E.2d 85 (1979); United Chiropractors of Washington, Inc. v. State, 90 Wash.2d 1, 578 P.2d 38 (1978) (en banc); Blumenthal v. Board of Medical Examiners, 57 Cal.2d 228, 18 Cal.Rptr. 501, 368 P.2d 101 (1962) (en banc); Garces v. Department of Registration & Ed., 118 Ill.App.2d 206, 254 N.E.2d 622, 628–29 (1969). The Supreme Court (under due process and not the delegation doctrine) has in the context of board adjudications especially limited the power of occupational licensing boards. In Gibson v. Berryhill, 411 U.S. 564, 93 S.Ct. 1689, 36 L.Ed.2d 488 (1973), the Court held that an optician licensing board whose members were drawn wholly from one wing (self-employed practitioners) of the occupation could not itself adjudicate unprofessional conduct charges brought against the other wing ("commercially," or non-self-employed practitioners). The Court based this holding on the fact that the monetary gain to the self-employed practitioners would unfairly infect their decisional processes. On the other hand, the Court has refused to extend this holding to the lawmaking functions of such licensing boards. Friedman v. Rogers, 440 U.S. 1, 17, 99 S.Ct. 887, 898, 59 L.Ed.2d 100 (1979), rehearing denied 441 U.S. 917, 99 S.Ct. 2018, 60 L.Ed.2d 389 (1979).

are suspicious, and at times they have specially insisted on standards specific enough to limit such a licensing board's opportunities to act out of self-interest. Where the state legislature had delegated "to an administrative licensing board made up of interested members of the industry" an unconfined power to establish minimum prices for dry cleaning, the California Supreme Court overturned the delegation because of the legislature's failure to "establish an ascertainable standard" to control the board.[6]

While delegations to private organization may be suspect, they are by no means inappropriate. Indeed, such delegations in limited and technical areas, for instance wiring and electrical codes, are quite useful.[7] Information is a most valuable commodity, and it is often expensive to duplicate it. Consequently, if the private sector does have knowledge that has been distilled to usable standards, the most efficient course may be for government to adopt these standards. The legitimacy of this course will, however, turn on whether these standards have been formulated by private groups that are so constituted as to dampen special interests and whether these standards involve limited and technical areas as opposed to broad matters of public interest.

§ 1.3.3 Personal Liberties

A third assumption about delegation of legislative power relates to personal liberties. Given the goal-oriented tendencies of agencies, constitutionally protected liberties may be slighted when agencies are delegated power respecting those liberties. In *Hampton v. Mow Sun Wong,* the Civil Service Commission had issued a rule denying federal jobs to aliens. The Supreme Court found that this rule restricted an important personal liberty, and then overturned it. The Court was unwilling "to presume" that the Commission, whose statutory goal was that of "promoting the efficiency" of the civil service, would include in its decisional processes the values pertinent to an infringement of this liberty by the rule in question.[8] In *Kent v. Dulles,* the Court narrowly construed the power delegated to immigration officials, and thereby denied them the authority to withhold passports because of the applicant's political

6. State Board of Dry Cleaners v. Thrift–D–Lux Cleaners, 40 Cal.2d 436, 441, 254 P.2d 29, 36 (1953) (*en banc*). See also Group Health Ins. v. Howell, 40 N.J. 436, 193 A.2d 103 (1963); Allen v. California Bd. of Barber Examiners, 25 Cal.App.3d 1014, 102 Cal.Rptr. 368 (1972) (overturning an open-ended delegation of power to a licensing board, and explaining that "None of the cited cases, however, involve the delegation of a power to fix prices to an administrative agency made up of interested members of the industry" and that "under such circumstances 'the courts . . . insist upon stringent standards to contain and guide the exercise of the delegated power' "); Cassidy v. Indiana State Bd. of Registration and Examination in Optometry, 244 Ind. 137, 191 N.E.2d 492, 498 (1963) (Where a state statute gave a licensing board the unbridled authority to determine what was "unprofessional conduct," the court stated that "this complete abrogation of legislative authority, if relied upon by the board, would be unconstitutional").

7. See generally, Hamilton, the Role of Nongovernmental Standards in the Development of Mandatory Federal Standards Affecting Safety or Health, 56 Tex.L.Rev. 1329 (1978).

8. 426 U.S. 88, 105, 113–14, 96 S.Ct. 1895, 1906, 1910–11, 48 L.Ed.2d 495 (1976). See Sec. 1.2 at n. 51, supra.

affiliations. In doing so, the Court indicated that sort of action was possible only if done, specifically and deliberately, by Congress. "If that 'liberty' is to be regulated," the Court said, "it must be pursuant to the law-making functions of Congress."[9]

§ 1.4 THE AGENCIES AS SURROGATES FOR LEGISLATURES, AND THE RULE OF LAW AND PROCEDURALISM

An attitude about delegation is not to worry about how broadly Congress delegates power to agencies, and to instead pay attention to how the agency uses the power. This attention to how an agency uses power has been directed to two things. One is whether an agency deploys its power consistent with the rule of law, whether an agency has made open-ended delegations more specific by itself developing rules and standards.[1] The second thing is whether an agency develops rules and standards by processes that simulate the democratic processes of Article I. In this respect, rulemaking under the Administrative Procedure Act is said to "serve as a Congressionally mandated proxy for the procedures which Congress itself employs in fashioning its 'rules,' as it were, thereby insuring that agency 'rules' are also carefully crafted (with democratic values served by public participation) and developed after consideration of relevant considerations."[2]

Both these matters, the rule of law and good rulemaking procedures, are important in administrative law. But in terms of establishing an administrative process that is a surrogate for Article I, these matters have not had much of a reception in the courts. As said by the U.S. Supreme Court, such measures "furnish protections against arbitrary use of properly delegated legislative authority," but they "cannot validate an unconstitutional delegation. . . ."[3]

9. 357 U.S. 116, 129, 78 S.Ct. 1113, 1120, 2 L.Ed.2d 1204 (1958). See also Greene v. McElroy, 360 U.S. 474, 506–07, 79 S.Ct. 1400, 1418–19, 3 L.Ed.2d 1377 (1959).

§ 1.4

1. As said by Prof. Davis, "the basic purpose" of the delegation doctrine "is unsatisfactory and should be changed. It should no longer be either to prevent delegation of legislative power or to require meaningful statutory standards." Instead, the doctrine should "gradually grow into a broad requirement . . . that offices with discretionary power should do about as much as possible to structure this discretion through standards, principles, and rules." I K. Davis, Administrative Law Treatise, 3.15, at 297–08 (2d ed. 1978).

2. Community Nutrition Institute v. Young, 818 F.2d 943, 951 (D.C.Cir.1987) (Starr, concurring). According to Prof. Davis, delegations are not problematic so long as administrative discretion is "guided by administrative rules adopted through procedure like that prescribed by the federal Administrative Procedure Act." K. Davis, Discretionary Justice: A Preliminary Inquiry 219 (1969).

3. United States v. Rock Royal Co-op., Inc., 307 U.S. 533, 574, 59 S.Ct. 993, 1013, 83 L.Ed. 1446 (1939).

If rule promulgation could cure open-ended delegations, the National Recovery Administration, because it compiled eighteen volumes and 13,000 pages of rules and regulations, should have been holding spades when the constitutionality of its delegated power was tested in *Schechter Poultry*. See L. Jaffe, Judicial Control of Administrative Action 61 (1965). This delegation to the National Recovery Administration was of course held unconstitutional, on the basis that it was a standardless delegation of power over the "vast array of commercial

That agency procedures cannot be counted on to save a bad delegation is supported by the elaborately reasoned but finally unsuccessful district court decision in *Amalgamated Meat Cutters v. Connally.*[4] The Economic Stabilization Act of 1970 gave the President broad wage and price controls respecting the American economy. The Act provided that the President might "issue such orders and regulations as he may deem appropriate to stabilize prices, rents, wages and salaries."[5] When President Nixon implemented this broad authority by setting wage and price controls, his authority to do so was challenged under the delegation doctrine, the claim being that the Economic Stabilization Act under which he acted was a grant of "unbridled legislative power." The court, however, found that the delegation was constitutional, in significant part because the procedures that the delegate was bound to follow sufficiently harnessed the power.

"The Rule of Law," the court said, had "been beleaguered but not breached." Any action taken by the executive under the freeze had "to be in accordance with further standards as developed by the Executive." This "requirement, inherent in the Rule of Law and implicit in the Act," meant "that however broad the discretion of the Executive at the outset, the standards once developed limit the latitude of subsequent executive action." However, "further standards as developed by the Executive" did not happen as the court anticipated. As subsequent studies showed, the President's sub-delegate, the Cost of Living Council, did not confine its power by a regime of standing rules. Instead, it tended to act ad hoc, by means of orders and exemptions issued for the situation at hand. Rather than binding legal standards, the product was more "a welter of regulations, circulars, orders, releases and question-and-answer statements whose legal status was often uncertain."[6] The court was also hopeful that an otherwise blank check could be reliably filled-in under the rulemaking procedures of the Administrative Procedure Act. But agency practice turned out to be inconsistent with that part of the opinion, too. The Cost of Living Council "employed highly secretive procedures that impeded both effective participation by affected parties and judicial review."[7]

* * *

In a well-known opinion issued as the twentieth century turned over, the court of appeals for the District of Columbia Circuit professed to use the delegation doctrine to overturn clean air rules issued by the

and industrial activities throughout the country," in A.L.A. Schechter Poultry Corp. v. United States, 295 U.S. 495, 539, 55 S.Ct. 837, 847, 79 L.Ed. 1570 (1935).

4. 337 F.Supp. 737 (D.D.C.1971).

5. 12 U.S.C.A. § 1904.

6. See generally J. Mashaw & R. Merrill, Administrative Law: The American Public Law System 16–19 (2d ed. 1985). As the courts were called upon to provide relief from inconsistent applications of the wage price freeze, they refused such relief because (paradoxically) the broad scope of delegated power was to them an indication of the "desire of Congress to give the executive broad discretion."

7. Id. at 19 (relying on Baldwin County Electric Membership Corp. v. Price Commission, 481 F.2d 920, 924–28 (Emer.Ct.App.1973)) (J. Hastie, dissenting); Note, The Administration of Economic Controls: the Economic Stabilization Act of 1970, 29 Case W.Res.L.Rev. 458 (1979).

Environmental Protection Agency. The Clean Air Act gives the EPA the power to establish clean air rules "requisite to protect the public health" with an "adequate margin of safety" based on the "latest scientific knowledge." Under this delegation, the agency issued rules for allowable levels of particulate matter (dust) and ozone. In *American Trucking Associations v. Environmental Protection Agency*,[8] the court of appeals overturned these rules, on the grounds that the "construction" of the Clean Air Act on "which the agency relied . . . effects an unconstitutional delegation of legislative power."

Both particulate matter and ozone are pollutants for which no safe level has been identified: Any level bears some risk. In this context, where any level above zero has some risk, the problem for the court was that the EPA had failed to explain how it had identified an acceptable risk. In this respect, the court said that the agency had not acted according to an "intelligible principle." But while the court used the language of the delegation doctrine, it admittedly deviated from the doctrine's main rational, which is to require that Congress make the primary policy choice and then make that choice evident through an intelligible principle that would guide the agency. The court deviated from this rational by requiring that the EPA, as opposed to Congress, supply the "intelligible principle." And in doing so the EPA would, as the court acknowledged, "make the fundamental policy choices."

On review, the Supreme Court entirely rejected the notion that an agency might cure a "standard delegation" by itself (rather than Congress) making the choice and supplying the standard. The Court explained, "We have never suggested that an agency rather can cure an unlawful delegation of legislative power by adopting in its discretion a limiting construction of the statute." The Court did, however, continue the ordinary requirement, that Congress must provide the Environmental Protection Agency with an "intelligible principle" respecting how it was to set national air quality standards. Congress, in the Court's view, had done so.[9]

8. 175 F.3d 1027 (D.C.Cir.1999), modified and rehearing denied, 195 F.3d 4 (D.C.Cir.1999); reversed, Whitman v. American Trucking Ass'ns, 531 U.S. 457, 121 S.Ct. 903, 149 L.Ed.2d 1 (2001).

9. In this respect, the sufficiently intelligible principle, as described by the Court was that "for a discrete set of pollutants and based on published air standards and based on published air quality criteria that reflect the latest scientific knowledge, [the] EPA must establish uniform national standards at a level that is requisite to protect public health from the adverse effects of the pollutant in the ambient air." Whitman v. American Trucking Ass'ns, 531 U.S. 457, 121 S.Ct. 903, 149 L.Ed.2d 1 (2001).

Chapter 2

RULEMAKING

Table of Sections

Inevitably, administrative agencies are recipients of some greater or lesser amount of legislative power. Some lesser amount is ordained by limitations of language and the fact that Congress is not omniscient; some greater amount is deliberate, as Congress may determine that some part of public policy is best filled in by agencies. And just so, "the power of an administrative agency to administer a congressionally created ... program *necessarily* requires the formulation of policy and the making of rules."[1]

1. Chevron U.S.A., Inc. v. Natural Resources Defense Council, Inc., 467 U.S. 837, 843, 104 S.Ct. 2778, 2781, 81 L.Ed.2d 694 (1984); Morton v. Ruiz, 415 U.S. 199, 231, 94 S.Ct. 1055, 1072, 39 L.Ed.2d 270 (1974). Generally speaking, agencies deploy the power they hold, legislative as well as judicial, according to a certain classification—of standards, rules, and orders. This classification and its generalizations are bound to be imperfect. But if this unruly area is to be talked about at all, some such terminology, some such ordering, seems essential.

Standards and rules both include agency action that is determinative of conduct across a class of people, and this class-like effect is of course the hallmark of legislation. Because standards and rules both pertain to the legislative work of agencies, we will frequently use these terms interchangeably.

However, these two terms do differ. A standard does not ordinarily describe or proscribe specific conduct. Instead, it describes the goal toward which conduct should be oriented. Such care as exercised by a reasonable person is an instance. Driving safe enough for conditions is another. Rules are more specific than standards. A legislative body, after determining that speed on public highways should be limited in the interest of safety, might establish the standard that "vehicles should not be driven faster than conditions allow." This standard, because of its generality (what is too fast for conditions?) may, however, be hard to apply. To avoid this difficulty in application, the legislative body might forego the standard and instead choose to achieve its goal of highway safety through rules. It might enact a rule setting a speed limit of 55 miles per hour in the country and anoth-

The manner—the procedural processes by which an agency implements this law-making power—is generally *not* subject to constitutional controls. This is the legacy of the Holmes-written opinion in *Bi–Metallic v. State Board of Equalization.*[2] There are, however, statutory controls. Congress has established a process of rulemaking for law-making by federal agencies. State administrative procedure acts have similar rulemaking procedures.

Rulemaking as thus established has two parts. One part is about decisional processes; the other part is about the rule of law. In relation to decisional processes, the Administrative Procedure Act provides that "the agency shall give interested persons an opportunity to participate in the rulemaking through submission of written data, view, or arguments."[3] By this provision, rulemaking is participatory (open to persons likely to be affected by a proposed rule) and comprehensive (assesses the range of interests at stake in a proposed rule). Also, as presently required by the courts rulemaking must be demonstrably rational: the agency should be able to show that it "has ... genuinely engaged in reasoned decision-making."[4]

The second part of rulemaking pertains, as we said, to the rule of law and to an aspiration of impartial and consistent regulation by means of standing rules. In this regard, the Administrative Procedure Act requires codification and publication of agency-made rules of conduct and further provides that "a person may not in any manner be required to resort to, or be adversely affected by, a matter required to be published ... and not so published."[5] This idea of rulemaking—of official action according to standing rules arrived at by open procedures—corresponds to what Lon Fuller described as the inner morality

er rule setting 45 miles per hour within cities.

Orders are contrasted to standards and rules in that they are associated *not* with the lawmaking but with the law applying functions of agencies. An "order" is addressed to individuals. It ordinarily represents an agency determination that an individual has acted inconsistent with some rule or standard administered by it. The Administrative Procedure Act provides that " 'adjudication' means agency processes for the formulation of an order." 5 U.S.C.A. § 551(7). The Act's rather broad and ambiguous definition of a rule is at 5 U.S.C.A. § 551(4). As an order is particular and personal, it is appropriately the product of the more intense and focused processes of the adjudicatory method. The distinctions between rules, standards, and orders are more fully discussed in Chap. 4, § 4.5.

2. 239 U.S. 441, 36 S.Ct. 141, 60 L.Ed. 372 (1915). In one respect, however, rulemaking has in a few cases been to a due process constraint. In relation to the rule of law, that agencies define and thus confine their discretion by means of published rules, due process has in some few situations been applied by the courts to require codified and published rules. See Chap. 3, Sec. 3.3, infra. In not being generally subject to constitutional constraint, rulemaking procedures differ greatly from adjudicatory procedure, which are. See Chap. 7, Sec. 7.1, infra.

3. 5 U.S.C. § 553(c).

4. Greater Boston Television Corp. v. FCC, 444 F.2d 841, 851 (D.C.Cir.1970), cert. denied 403 U.S. 923, 91 S.Ct. 2233, 29 L.Ed.2d 701 (1971). See Chap. 3, Sec. 3.3, infra.

5. 5 U.S.C. § 552(a) & 553. Regarding the need for codification and publication of rules, see G. Bentham, Of Promulgation of the Laws, in 1 Works 155 (Bowring ed. 1859). See also Griswold, Government in Ignorance of the Law, 48 Harv.L.Rev. 198 (1934).

of law, concerns of which, he said, reach their most "poignant intensity in administrative law."[6]

The tension that Fuller signaled is this. Within administrative law, the idea of regularity and order, of regulation according to rules, has a powerful competitor. The competition is a vision of substantive rationality, of judging agency action according to how instrumental it is in achieving agency goals. In this light, an agency, rather than acting within the confines of published rules, may prefer to have its hands free, to be able to act outside or without rules so that it may then most expeditiously reach the solution that at the time seems best to contribute to its goals.

The conflict between instrumentalism and the rule of law is illustrated by one of the most influential administrative law cases, *SEC v. Chenery Corp.*[7] The management of a holding company had acquired stock in the company. When this transaction came under its jurisdiction, the Securities Exchange Commission was of the view that management's stock-ownership created a conflict of interest contrary to the Commission's goals. That transaction, however, had been made in good faith, and no agency rules, or laws of any source—then, at the time management acted—had identified the transaction as improper. Still, by means of an order cut for the occasion, the Commission required management to give up its stock. The issue this action created—respecting the instrumentalism of the agency (it was determined to eliminate what it saw as a bad practice, whether or not it had a rule on point) and rule of law values as claimed by the stockholders—split the Supreme Court five to four.

* * *

In this chapter, the subject of rulemaking is divided into three sections. In two sections, we discuss rulemaking first in terms of its decisional process and then second in terms of codification and publication. In the last section we try to locate the zone where rulemaking is required. In this last section, the conflict that we identified, between agency instrumentalism and regulation according to standing rules arrived at by prescribed and open procedures, is a main issue.

§ 2.1 THE DECISIONAL PROCESSES OF RULEMAKING

The Administrative Procedure Act requires that rulemaking be participatory and comprehensive, and as the Act is presently interpreted, it also requires that rulemaking be "demonstrably rational." Rulemaking is made participatory by Section 553 of the Act, which requires that "the agency shall give interested persons an opportunity to participate in the rulemaking through submission of written data, views, or argu-

6. Fuller, Positivism and Fidelity to Law—A Reply to Professor Hart, 71 Harv. L.Rev. 630, 648 (1958).

7. 332 U.S. 194, 67 S.Ct. 1575, 91 L.Ed. 1995 (1947). The case is more extensively discussed in Chap. 3, Sec. 3.1, infra.

ments."[1] This participation by interested parties should also assure that rulemaking is comprehensive. The input of "interested persons" requires an agency assessment of the range of interests affected by a rule.[2] The third part of rulemaking, that it be demonstrably rational, seems largely a requirement of modern courts, imposed by them through their power to review and correct agency action. Today, reviewing courts insist that an agency show that it "has ... genuinely engaged in reasoned decision-making."[3] These courts have, therefore, required that agencies produce the data underlying a rule, show how they arrived at the rule from this data, and show how the rule relates to their statutory goals.[4]

While courts now favor and underwrite the decisional processes of rulemaking, this has not always been the case. For a time, when courts were willing to defer to agency expertise—(an expertise that courts then referred to as "an intuition of experience which outruns analysis"[5]) the courts did not enthusiastically enforce these processes. Although the Administrative Procedure Act provides for public participation in rulemaking, the agency was left free to ignore information and analysis as

§ 2.1

1. 5 U.S.C.A. § 553(c).

2. See generally Diver, Policymaking Paradigms in Administrative Law, 95 Harv. L.Rev. 393 (1981). The synoptic nature of rulemaking, that it should assess the range of private interests affected by a rule, was a basis of decision in Gas Appliance Manufacturers Ass'n, Inc. v. Secretary of Energy, 722 F.Supp. 792 (D.D.C.1989). There, the Secretary had relied almost exclusively on the input of one group in formulating standards, and the court held that this was improper rulemaking. The Secretary, the court held, had to hear comment and objections from all the interested public.

3. Greater Boston Television Corp. v. FCC, 444 F.2d 841, 851 (D.C.Cir.1970).

4. An illustration of rationality review is provided by Kennecott Copper Corp. v. EPA, 462 F.2d 846 (D.C.Cir.1972). The Environmental Protection Agency had enacted a national air-quality standard limiting concentrations of sulfuric oxides to no more than sixty micrograms per cubic meter of air. However, a report on which the agency had relied said that the less stringent level of eighty-five micrograms was acceptable. Therefore, industry attacked the rule on the grounds that it did not make sense considering that the report that the EPA had relied on identified eighty-five as being safe. The court agreed, at least to the extent that the agency had the burden of explaining how it rationally could arrive at the sixty-microgram standard. Consequently, the rule was remanded for the agency "to supply an implementing statement that will enlighten the court as to the basis on which he reached the 60–microgram standard...." 462 F.2d at 859.

An aspiration of rationality review is that a requirement that agencies be judged according to "a single, comprehensive, detailed justification" would "force the various sub-units within an agency to pursue their differences on questions of fact, interpretation or policy until they could be resolved" and "force the agency to choose between alternative data, theories and methodologies and create a coherent case upon which scrutiny by the courts can be focused." Pederson, Formal Records and Informal Rulemaking, 85 Yale L.J. 38, 73 (1975). See also A. Howard, G. Gunther, D. Horowitz, and R. Stewart, The Courts: Separation of Powers 80 (1983) ("a real and healthy impact on the decisional processes of agencies"). For a criticism of rationality review, at least as imposed by the courts, see Sax, The (Unhappy) Truth about NEPA, 26 Okla.L.Rev. 239 (1973). Also, rationality review, in its present form in the courts, requires a rulemaking record. Unfortunately, the viability of such a record is open to question. See Sec. 2.1.5, infra.

Rationality review by the courts is discussed in detail in Chap. 12 on judicial review.

5. Chicago, Burlington & Quincy R. Co. v. Babcock, 204 U.S. 585, 598, 27 S.Ct. 326, 329, 51 L.Ed. 636 (1907). See Greater Boston Television Corp. v. FCC, 444 F.2d 841, 852 (D.C.Cir.1970), cert. denied 403 U.S. 923, 91 S.Ct. 2233, 29 L.Ed.2d 701 (1971).

provided by this participation. The agency might receive such material, and then gently slide it into the handiest receptacle for waste products.[6] Also, no burden of rationalization, no burden of explanation and justification respecting the substance of a rule, was placed upon the agency. Not by the courts.

Presently, however, courts are of the view that rulemaking informed only by agency expertise is not as good as rulemaking that includes the participation of the private sector, and absent this participation courts are not so willing to defer to agency findings. There are several reasons for this change in attitude,[7] the strongest of which is that experience has shown that the substance of a rule is not, as New Dealers may have assumed, all that susceptible to a wholly abstract and objective determination by disinterested agency professionals. Experts are important, but the worth of a rule depends on how it accommodates the interests of the various individuals and entities, *as seen by them,* that the rule affects. This modern attitude about rulemaking is shown in statements from the bench such as the following:

> [M]ost important of all, high-handed agency rulemaking is more than just offensive to our basic notions of democratic government, a failure to seek at least the acquiescence of the governed eliminates a vital ingredient for effective administrative action.... Charting changes in policy direction with the aid of those who will be affected by the shift in course helps dispel suspicions of agency predisposition, unfairness, arrogance, improper influence, and ulterior motivation.[8]

6. E.g., Lansden v. Hart, 168 F.2d 409 (7th Cir.1948), cert. denied 335 U.S. 858, 69 S.Ct. 132, 93 L.Ed. 405 (1948). In terms of the Administrative Procedure Act, such denigration of the input of the private sector was justified on the grounds that all the Act provided was an "opportunity" to comment, with the agency left with the discretion to use this comment as it pleased, or not at all. 5 U.S.C.A. § 553(c). As we later discuss, see Sec. 2.1.4, infra, the better, and today the prevailing account view is that Congress intended that the agency include this input from the private sector in its decisional process.

7. A weaker reason is that public participation by means of rulemaking serves as a proxy for democratic processes. As expressed by the courts, this reason is one of "reintroduc[ing] public participation and fairness to affected parties after governmental authority has been delegated to unrepresentative agencies." Batterton v. Marshall, 648 F.2d 694, 703 (D.C.Cir.1980). The weakness in this reason is that agency officials are not responsible, at the polls, as are elected representatives. It remains the case that the "legitimacy that inheres in Congress by virtue of its accountability to the electorate is absent ... from the administrative process." More fully stated, this sense of the futility in supposing that administrative processes can substitute for democratic processes is as follows:

> The constitutional legitimacy that inheres in Congress by virtue of its accountability to the electorate is absent, however, from the administrative process, and consequently, serious questions are continually being raised—and with increased frequency—regarding the legitimacy of the administrative apparatus within the framework of American government. Near the center of the growing concern over legitimacy lies the apprehension that the critical choices of our society will more and more be made by administrative personnel who are not, as a practical matter, accountable to anyone....

Daughters of Miriam Center for the Aged v. Mathews, 590 F.2d 1250, 1257 (3d Cir. 1978).

8. Chamber of Commerce of U.S. v. OSHA, 636 F.2d 464, 470 (D.C.Cir.1980).

Another strong reason for enforcing rulemaking is simply the value of information. There is often a gap between what the private sector knows and what an agency can know, removed as it is from the hands-on, day-to-day work of the private sector that it would regulate. Rulemaking's right to comment, however, attaches to "interested" parties, those who are likely to be affected by agency action. These parties, interested and close to the action as they are, are good sources of information. Also, they have the incentive—being affected by the proposed rule—to come forward with their information. Interested parties can, therefore, usually be counted on to come forward out of the private sector, to identify gaps in agency information and to supply additional information so as to at least save the agency the costs of producing that information itself. Also, interested parties are often good sources of critical analysis of inferences and decisions made by the agency from the information that it does have. Therefore, courts now routinely assert that the purpose of rulemaking is to " 'assur[e] that the agency will have before it the facts and information relevant to a particular administrative problem, as well as suggestions for alternative solutions.' "[9]

Moreover, where an agency operates at the margins of scientific knowledge, scientists in the private sector provide a unique and useful check on the soundness of agency decisions. And at this leading edge, the value of other checks on agency error are diminished. In particular, the check of judicial review, because it depends on lay judges who are understandably not up to date on the science of a particular area, is diminished. Consequently, courts tend to insist on a rulemaking process that includes the "scrutiny of the scientific community and the public."[10]

* * *

Although rulemaking has evolved into a more rigorous process, the basic notice, comment and publication framework established in 1946 by the Administrative Procedure Act has remained intact. When Congress has changed rulemaking, the change usually has been in the direction of adding to this basic structure, by trying to better guarantee its inclusive, synoptic and public-regarding features. By means of the National Environmental Protection Act, Congress has required agencies to include environmental values in their decisional processes.[11] Similarly, by means of the Regulatory Flexibility Act Congress has specifically required that agencies involved in rulemaking take into account the interests of small businesses.[12] The most extensive requirement that agencies try to be

9. American Hosp. Ass'n v. Bowen, 834 F.2d 1037, 1044 (D.C.Cir.1987).

10. International Harvester Co. v. Ruckelshaus, 478 F.2d 615, 652 (D.C.Cir. 1973).

11. 42 U.S.C.A. § 4331 et seq.

12. 42 U.S.C.A. §§ 601–612. See P. Verkuil, A Critical Guide to the Regulatory Flexibility Act, 1982 Duke L.J. 213 (1982). Respecting the relation, in terms of their effect on agency decisional processes, of the National Environmental Act and the Regulatory Flexibility Act, see W. Gellhorn, C. Byse, P. Strauss, T. Rakoff, & R. Shotland, Administrative Law, Cases and Comments, 157–58 (8th ed. 1987). Also, the Paperwork Reduction Act of 1980, 44 U.S.C.A. § 3501 et seq., has the purpose of forcing federal agencies to keep in mind paperwork costs

synoptic, to consider and balance all things, has, however, been imposed not by Congress but by the President. By the executive order of the last six holders of that office, the President has imposed a regime of "cost benefit analysis" under which a major agency rule must be supported by an analysis and balance of the societal costs and benefits of the rule, an analysis that is subject to review by the Office of Management and Budget.[13]

Some statutory changes respecting rulemaking have been more particular, pertaining to specific agencies. The overall trend of these changes has been to reinforce the basic elements of rulemaking as provided by the Administrative Procedures Act. For example, for the Environmental Protection Agency, the Clean Air Amendments of 1977 reinforced the notice and comment provisions of rulemaking by requiring detailed notice about the methodology used in arriving at the substance of a proposed rule and by requiring that the agency respond to "significant comments" from that sector about the substance of the rule.[14] Some of these new "reinforcing" procedures may, however, have departed from the minimalist theory of rulemaking, by intensifying the process in the direction of adjudication. The Federal Trade Commission Improvement Act of 1974 seems the most radical departure.[15] This Act gives interested parties the right to make oral argument as well as written comment, and then further provides for cross-examination. The Act states that if "the Commission determines that there are disputed issues of fact it is necessary to resolve," then it must provide interested parties the opportunity to file "rebuttal submissions" and "such cross-examination of persons as the Commission determines to be appropriate, and (ii) to be required for a full and true disclosure with respect to such issues." The Act also requires that the Commission maintain a relatively elaborate record of the proceedings and that courts review this record according to a substantial evidence form of review.

These features—cross-examination, extensive record requirements, and a substantial evidence form of review—are ordinarily part of adjudication. Their infusion into rulemaking thus creates what is known as "hybrid rulemaking." Initially, the thought was that these more intensive procedures would provide for a more extensive, and therefore better, examination of issues in rulemaking. But there have been second thoughts, along the lines that hybrid procedures make rulemaking

imposed on persons, small businesses, and local government.

13. Cost best analysis is currently required by Ex. Order No. 12,866, reprinted at 5 U.S.C. § 601. This matter of executive control and cost-benefit analysis is discussed at Chap. 15, Sec. 15.1.3, infra.

14. 42 U.S.C. § 7607(d).

15. 15 U.S.C. § 57(a). For other "hybrid" rulemaking enactments, see the Consumer Product Safety Act, 15 U.S.C.A. § 2058(d); Occupational Safety and Health Act of 1970, 29 U.S.C.A. § 651 et seq., and also the 1977 Clean Air Amendments, 42 U.S.C.A. § 7607(d). These provisions generally provide for oral argument, require a rulemaking record, and perhaps provide for a substantial evidence form of review, all of which procedures are ordinarily associated with adjudication.

rather cumbersome, without commensurate gains in the accuracy or fairness of the process.[16]

In the remainder of this section we discuss the various parts of the basic framework for the decisional processes of rulemaking.

§ 2.1.1 The Pre-notice Part of Rulemaking

(a) Setting the Agenda

The Administrative Procedure Act requires that agencies publish notice of proposed rules in the Federal Register. But before this event occurs, and the process established by Sec. 553 of the Administrative Procedure Act begins, the agency exercises an important authority: it establishes the rulemaking agenda. Agency resources are limited; it cannot address every problem. In the pre-notice period, the agency decides which problems may, or may not, require a regulatory response in the form of a rule.[17]

Agency control of its rulemaking agenda is qualified, but only weakly, by the Administrative Procedure Act. Sec. 553(e) of the Act provides that "each agency shall give an interested person the right to petition for the issuance, amendment, or repeal of a rule." This provision, while it requires agencies to receive and to consider rulemaking initiatives from the private sector, does not require the agency to accept the substance of the petition.[18] Moreover, until the last several years,

16. See generally, Hamilton, Procedures for the Adoption of Rules of General Applicability: The Need For Procedural Innovation in Administrative Rulemaking, 60 Cal.L.Rev. 1276, 1283–1313 (1972). Hybrid rulemaking is discussed at Sec. 2.2, infra. As for the courts, the Supreme Court has rather archly held that they (the courts) have no power of their own (as some sort of administrative common law) to require procedures (in the manner of hybrid rulemaking) additional to the minimal notice and comment procedures of Sec. 553 of the Administrative Procedure Act. Vermont Yankee Nuclear Power Corp. v. N.R.D.C., 435 U.S. 519, 98 S.Ct. 1197, 55 L.Ed.2d 460 (1978).

17. In Natural Resources Defense Council, Inc. v. SEC, 606 F.2d 1031, 1053 (D.C.Cir.1979), the court explained why it is that the power to control its rulemaking agenda should lie primarily with the agency:

> An agency's discretionary decision not to regulate a given activity is inevitably based, in large measure, on factors not inherently susceptible to judicial resolution—e.g., internal management considerations as to budget and personnel; evaluations of its own competence; weighing of competing policies within a broad statutory framework. Further, even if an agency considers a particular problem worthy of regulation, it may determine for reasons lying within its special expertise that the time for action has not yet arrived. The area may be one of such rapid technological development that regulations would be outdated by the time they could become effective, or the scientific state of the art may be such that sufficient data are not yet available on which to premise adequate regulations. The circumstances in the regulated industry may be evolving in such a way that could vitiate the need for regulation, or the agency may still be developing the expertise necessary for effective regulation.

18. In a leading case, WWHT, Inc. v. FCC, 656 F.2d 807, 813 (D.C.Cir.1981) the court, after reviewing Sec. 553(e) and its legislative history, stated that while it was "plain that an agency must receive and respond to petitions for rulemaking, it is equally clear from the legislative history that Congress did not intend to compel an agency to undertake rulemaking merely because a petition has been filed." The court then explained that "When petitions for rulemaking are filed, [Sec. 553(e)] requires the agency to 'fully and promptly consider them, take such action as may be required,

agency discretion respecting these private petitions was considered to be so complete as not to be subject to judicial oversight.[19]

Presently, though, denials of rulemaking petitions are subject to review.[20] The scope of this review, however, is narrow, "limited to ensuring that the [agency] has adequately explained the facts and policy concerns it relied on [in rejecting a petition] and to satisfy ourselves that these facts have some basis in the record. . . ."[21] In the rare case where a court finds that an agency has not met its burden of explanation about why it denied a rulemaking petition, the remedy is not mandatory rulemaking. Instead, the court remands the matter to the agency. On remand, the agency's choice is either to "explain [its] decision or to institute rulemaking."[22]

The weak right to petition under Sec. 553(e) may, however, be strengthened in special cases. One such case is where an agency refuses

and . . . notify the petitioner in case the request is denied. The agency may either grant the petition, undertake public rule making proceedings or deny the petition.' "

19. See generally, Stewart and Sunstein, Public Programs and Private Rights, 95 Harv.L.Rev. 1193, 1267–89 (1982). Along with the tradition of unreviewable prosecutorial discretion, non-review of agency rulemaking petitions is supported by the fact that such review would entail a "supervisory and managerial role that courts traditionally eschew." Id. at 1283.

20. WWHT, Inc. v. FCC, 656 F.2d 807, 817 (D.C.Cir.1981). In this case the court rejected the view that an agency's discretion to reject a rule making petition was unreviewable according to 5 U.S.C.A. § 701(a)(1), which makes unreviewable "agency action committed to agency discretion by law." See also American Horse Protection Ass'n, Inc. v. Lyng, 812 F.2d 1 (D.C.Cir.1987); Professional Drivers Council v. Bureau of Motor Carrier Safety, 706 F.2d 1216 (D.C.Cir.1983). On the "committed to agency discretion by law" exception to judicial review, see Chap. 12, Sec. 12.6, infra.

21. National Ass'n of Regulatory Utility Com'rs v. U.S. Department of Energy, 851 F.2d 1424, 1430 (D.C.Cir.1988); WWHT, Inc. v. FCC, 656 F.2d 807, 817 (D.C.Cir.1981).

Also, agency denials of rulemaking petitions remain reviewable, notwithstanding the premise of Heckler v. Chaney, 470 U.S. 821, 105 S.Ct. 1649, 84 L.Ed.2d 714 (1985), which is that agency enforcement decisions are generally unreviewable. American Horse Protection Ass'n, Inc. v. Lyng, 812 F.2d 1 (D.C.Cir.1987), on remand 681 F.Supp. 949 (1988). *Heckler v. Chaney* and the "committed to agency discretion" exception to reviewability are discussed at Chap. 12, Sec. 12.6, infra. But while denial of rulemaking petitions remain reviewable even in the wake of *Heckler v. Chaney,* that decision has given the lower courts pause, and since *Chaney* they say that "an Agency's refusal to institute rulemaking procedures is at the high end of the range" that shades toward unreviewability and that "only in the rarest and most compelling of circumstances" will the refusal to institute rulemaking be overturned. National Ass'n of Regulatory Utility Com'rs v. U.S. Department of Energy, 851 F.2d 1424, 1430 (D.C.Cir.1988).

For some of the rare cases where the court actually found that an agency had abused its discretion in not instituting rulemaking, see American Horse Protection Ass'n, Inc. v. Lyng, 812 F.2d 1 (D.C.Cir. 1987), on remand 681 F.Supp. 949 (1988); Geller v. FCC, 610 F.2d 973 (D.C.Cir.1979). In these cases, the courts found that the agency had not provided a reasoned basis for its refusal to institute rulemaking. *In American Horse Protection Ass'n, Inc. v. Lyng,* the court noted that "an agency may be forced by a reviewing court to institute rulemaking proceedings if a significant factual predicate of a prior decision on the subject (either to promulgate or not to promulgate specific rules) has been removed." 812 F.2d 1, 5 (D.C.Cir.1987). The court also thought that the agency's failure to institute rulemaking was based on an erroneous interpretation of the Act, almost as if, in the circumstances of that case, the refusal to institute rulemaking amounted to an error of law. 812 F.2d at 6–7. Also, the court cared little for cruelty to animals, as was alleged in the case.

22. American Horse Protection Ass'n, Inc. v. Lyng, 812 F.2d 1, 7–8 (D.C.Cir.1987).

a rulemaking petition for purely legal reasons, as for instance when it declines the petition on the grounds that it would require the agency to act outside its statutory power.[23] This sort of statutory reason for declining a rulemaking petition reason more involves a pure question of law, a matter of statutory interpretation, that lies within the ordinary competence of a court. Also, this reason does not itself directly involve agency discretion respecting the deployment its regulatory resolves, a matter of discretion not within the ordinary competence of the courts.

The weak right to petition has some greater force where Congress has specially limited an agency's general discretion respecting its regulatory agenda. The usual such limit is that of an "action forcing statute." By such a statute, Congress requires that rules implementing delegated power be enacted either within a specified period[24] or upon the occurrence of certain triggering events such as the existence of a "grave danger" from toxic substances to employees.[25] Where Congress has so qualified agency discretion, the courts may require agencies to be more responsive to rulemaking petitions. The court may review denials of such petitions with an eye toward whether these denials are consistent with the conditions of the action forcing statute. In appropriate cases—as where petitioners established a "grave danger" from toxic substances as ought to trigger rulemaking—the courts have ordered the agency to commence rulemaking as requested by public petition.[26]

(b) Forming a Proposal: The Negotiated Rulemaking Act of 1990

Once the agency determines that a regulatory response in the form of a rule is in order, then a proposal is drafted, which is then subject to the notice and comment process of Sec. 553. Usually, the agency alone composes the substance of the proposed rule. But by an amendment—the Negotiated Rulemaking Act of 1990—to the Administrative Procedure Act, Congress has authorized agencies to use a process of negotiation to determine the substance of a proposed rule.[27] This process

23. See WWHT, Inc. v. FCC, 656 F.2d 807, 818–819 (D.C.Cir.1981). See generally John H. Reece, Administrative Law: Procedures and Practice, 229–231 (1995).

24. E.g., the Asbestos Hazard Emergency Response Act of 1986 requires that the Environmental Protection Agency publish proposed rules within sixty days of the Act's enactment and final rules within three hundred and sixty days. 15 U.S.C. § 2601 et seq. Generally, see Tomlinson, Report on the Experience of Various Agencies with Statutory Time Limits Applicable to Licensing or Clearance Functions and to Rulemaking, 1978 Administrative Conference Recommendations and Reports 119, 216–233.

25. E.g., the Occupational Safety Health Administration is required to provide "temporary emergency standards" if it determines that "employees are exposed to grave dangers from exposure to substances determined to be toxic or physically harmful or from new hazards." 29 U.S.C. § 655(c).

26. See Public Citizen Health Research Group v. Auchter, 702 F.2d 1150 (D.C.Cir. 1983).

27. The Negotiated Rulemaking Act of 1990, 5 U.S.C.A. § 561 et seq. As originally enacted, the Act contained a sunset provision by which it would have expired in 1996. In 1996 Congress repealed the sunset provision and established the Negotiated Rulemaking Act as a permanent part of the Administrative Procedure Act. Pub. L. 104–320, Sec. 11(a), 110 Stat. 3873. The seminal article about negotiated rulemaking is Har-

supplements the ordinary decisional processes of rulemaking; it does not replace them. Also, the process is not mandatory. Whether or not it is used is left to agency discretion.

If an agency decides to use negotiation, it must give notice of that choice in the Federal Register. This notice shall include "a description of the subject and scope of the rule to be developed," a list of "interest likely to be significantly affected by the rule," and the "persons proposed to represent such interests."[28] This notice should also inform the public that they may apply for, or nominate others, for inclusion on the negotiating committee.[29]

The agency is a member of the committee, and no more than that. Sessions are led not by the agency but by a "facilitator," a person skilled in negotiation who "impartially aids in the discussions and negotiations."[30] Negotiations can produce a proposed rule only on the basis of consensus, which the Act defines as "unanimous concurrence among the interests represented on a negotiated rulemaking committee."[31] That proposed rule—hopefully with the kinks worked out and the various interests mollified—is then submitted to notice and comment as required by the ordinary process of Sec. 553.

The purpose of negotiated rules is to supplement rulemaking by a process of collaboration between the regulated sector, interest groups, and the agency. In this respect, negotiated rulemaking has been described "as educational, as offering a forum for presenting arguments and evidence, and as a chance to generate new ideas and opinions with informed people holding diverse opinions." Be that as it may, negotiation will not likely suit every proposed rule. It rests on certain assumptions, "that affected interests in society could be represented in a committee of 15 to 20 people, that people would be willing to invest the time and resources to work through issues to a consensus, that the parties would be counted on to negotiate in good faith, that the Agency could commit to issuing a proposed rule based on the parties consensus."[32] These assumptions are often hard to met. The Act, though, anticipates this circumstance. It does so by more-or-less identifying these assumptions as factors to be considered by the agency in determining whether or not to use negotiated rulemaking in the first instance.[33]

* * *

ter, Negotiating Regulations: A Cure for the Malaise?, 71 Georgetown L.Rev. 1 (1982).

28. 5 U.S.C. § 584(a).

29. The act provides that "Persons who will be significantly affected by a proposed rule and who believe that their interest will not be adequately represented ... may apply for, or nominate another person for, membership on the negotiated rulemaking committee...." 5 U.S.C. § 584(b).

30. 5 U.S.C. § 582(4).

31. 5 U.S.C. § 582(2).

32. Fiorino, Regulatory Negotiation as a Policy Process, 48 Public Ad. Rev. 764, 768 (1988).

33. 5 U.S.C. § 563(a). One of the more troubling assumptions of negotiated rulemaking is that the agency can convene a group that truly represents the interests affected by a rule. Out of this concern, the Act doubles-up in its assurances of representation. Adequate representation is a matter to be taken into account in deciding whether to use negotiation. Id. If the agency decides to use negotiation, then it "may"

Negotiated rulemaking has had its critics, whose concern is that it diminishes the legitimacy of the administrative state. Agency input to social solutions is in significant part justified by the idea that agency scientists and experts impart a disinterested and objective measure of the common good. In contrast, negotiated rulemaking emphasizes deals and tradeoffs among special interests. This process of deals and tradeoffs has been described, and criticized, as one of substituting "privately bargained interests" for the pursuit of "the public interest through law and reasoned decision making."[34] In *USA Group Loan Services Inc. v. Riley*,[35] Judge Posner was similarly critical of the process. The issue before the court was whether an agency was bound by a commitment to regulated entities, respecting the substance of a proposed rule, that it may have made during negotiation under the Act. The court of appeals, per Judge Posner, held it was not. "We have no doubt," Posner wrote, "that the Negotiated Rulemaking Act did not make the [commitment] enforceable." "The practical effect of enforcing it would be to ... extinguish notice and comment rulemaking in all cases in which it was preceded by negotiated rulemaking." More generally, Judge Posner wrote against the policy of an agency bound by commitments made during the bargaining sessions of negotiated rulemaking. "It sounds like," he said, "an abdication of regulatory authority to the regulated, the full burgeoning of the interest-group state, and the final confirmation of the 'capture' theory of administrative regulation."

Concerns that the bargaining of negotiated rulemaking may too much displace the presumably disinterested judgments of agencies should, however, be hedged by the facts that the agency still controls the agenda. It identifies the problem and the need for a rule and whether circumstances (which include whether a rounded and full representation of the various interests at stake is possible) warrant negotiation. In negotiation, the agency can refuse to agree to the deal and in doing so destroy the necessary consensus. Finally, the proposal of the negotiating committee is subject to the rest of the rulemaking process and in theory the agency may amend or drop the proposed rule in response to the public comment generated by this process.[36] The final result, the rule, is still subject to judicial review, an additional safeguard on the side of the general public interest.

use "convenors" to "identify people who will be significantly affected by a proposed rule." 5 U.S.C.A. § 563 (b). Then, after notice, persons who feel that their interests are inadequately represented may apply for inclusion on the committee. 5 U.S.C. § 564(b).

34. W. Funk, Bargaining Toward the New Millennium: Regulatory Negotiation and the Subversion of the Public Interest, 46 Duke L.Rev. 1351, 1356 (1997).

35. 82 F.3d 708 (7th Cir.1996).

36. As a practical matter, you might doubt whether the agency will likely modify a rule that it has subscribed to in the negotiation process. In this respect, and as the courts have noted, agency open-mindedness is essential to effective notice and comment. E.g, Advocates for Highway and Auto Safety v. Federal Highway Administration, 28 F.3d 1288, 1292 (D.C.Cir.1994) (in evaluating the agency's responsiveness to public comment "The touchstone of our inquiry is thus the agency's open-mindedness").

§ 2.1.2 Notice of Rulemaking

Section 553(b) of the Administrative Procedure Act provides that "General notice of proposed rule making shall be published in the Federal Register."[37] This notice must include "(1) a statement of the time, place, and nature of public rule making proceedings; (2) reference to the legal authority under which the rule is proposed; and (3) either the terms or substance of the proposed rule or a description of the subjects and issues involved." While the courts may not invalidate rulemaking in each and every failure to meet this three-part prescription respecting notice,[38] they will certainly overturn the whole, large process in case of "prejudicial" failures of notice.[39] That which is prejudicial is determined in relation to the purpose of notice in rulemaking. This purpose is to establish an effective opportunity for interested parties to participate in rulemaking by means of "responsive data or argument" about a rule.[40] To be "responsive" interested parties must be informed of the "legal basis," the substance, and the data underlying the proposed rule. The rule of thumb is that the notice must "fairly appraise interested persons of the subjects and issues the agency was considering."[41]

That interested parties must be fairly appraised of the legal basis of a rule is made clear in *Global Van Lines, Inc. v. ICC.*[42] That case involved

37. 5 U.S.C. § 553(b).

38. The notice requirement may not, however, be transformed into what the courts have referred to as an "elaborate treasure hunt" by which parties dissatisfied with a rule may score the record for some dissonance between the result of rulemaking and the notice given. Small Refiner Lead Phase–Down Task Force v. EPA, 705 F.2d 506, 549–50 (D.C.Cir.1983). In *United Steelworkers of America v. Schuylkill Metals Corp.*, the Secretary of Labor had issued regulations establishing wage requirements for workers transferred out of a particular job because of their sensitivity to lead. 828 F.2d 314, 317 (5th Cir.1987) (1990). When these regulations were applied to require employers to continue to provide overtime pay and bonuses ("premium payments") to transferred lead-sensitive employees, the rule was challenged on the grounds of inadequate notice of rulemaking. In the notice, the Secretary had referred to "rate of pay." This was said not to give adequate notice that "premium payments" were also proposed. The court of appeals found otherwise. The notice had referred to benefits " 'that would maintain the rate of pay, seniority and other rights of an employee . . . [when] the employee is transferred or removed from his or her job as a result of an increased health risk from exposure to lead.' " That and other similar language in the notice, the court held, was sufficient "to appraise fairly interested parties."

39. E.g., McLouth Steel Products Corp. v. Thomas, 838 F.2d 1317, 1323–24 (D.C.Cir.1988). See generally Texas v. Lyng, 868 F.2d 795, 797–98 (5th Cir.1989). When an agency completely fails to provide procedures as required by Section 553, the harmless error defense is not available to it. United States Steel Corp. v. Environmental Protection Agency, 595 F.2d 207 (5th Cir. 1979).

40. Notice should be "sufficient to appraise interested parties of the issues involved, so they may present responsive data or argument relating thereto." Administrative Procedure Act Legis. Hist., S. Doc. 248 at 200, 258 (Report of the Senate Judiciary Committee.).

41. United Steelworkers of America v. Schuylkill Metals Corp., 828 F.2d 314, 317 (5th Cir.1987). See American Med'l Ass'n v. Reno, 57 F.3d 1129, 1132–33 (D.C.Cir.1995) In Small Refiner Lead Phase–Down Task Force v. EPA, 705 F.2d 506, 547 (D.C.Cir. 1983), the court broke the purposes of notice in rulemaking down as follows: to improve the accuracy of rulemaking through "exposure to diverse public comment," to be fair to interested parties by means of the chance to express their views, and to provide for more effective judicial review of the final rule by allowing the rule's critics to "develop evidence in the record to support their objections."

42. 714 F.2d 1290 (5th Cir.1983).

an important deregulation issue, the Interstate Commerce Commission's statutory authority to remove restrictions on transportation services provided by "freight forwarders." The Commission had eliminated these restrictions by a rule. When its power to do so was challenged in the Fifth Circuit, the Commission claimed that its authority to eliminate the restrictions came from a certain provision of the Interstate Commerce Act. The Commission, however, had not referred to this particular statutory authority in its notice of rulemaking. Consequently, the court of appeals overturned the rule, stating that "The Commission's failure to articulate the legal basis that its counsel now advances for the rule ... effectively deprived the petitions of any opportunity to present comment on what amounts to half the case."[43]

Notice must, of course, be given of the substance of a proposed rule. In this respect, Sec. 553(b) provides that the agency may publish "either the terms or substance of the proposed rule or a description of the subjects and issues involved." By which ever or by what combination of these means the agency choices, the notice must, as we have said, "fairly appraise interested persons of the subjects and issues the agency was considering." Whether interested parties have been fairly appraised is a fact-intensive inquiry, varying according to the context of each case.[44] Interested parties were not fairly appraised where the agency merely reprinted an existing set of regulations in forty pages of the federal register without clearly indicating the parts of these regulations that it wished to amend.[45] Nor were interested parties fairly appraised where only some "knowledgeable manufacturers" would grasp the relation between the subjects identified by the notice and the substance of the final rule.[46]

To assure that interested parties are fairly appraised of the substance of a proposed rule, courts today require that notice identify the data and methodology used by the agency in formulating a rule. A leading decision on this point is *United States v. Nova Scotia Food Products Corp.*[47] The Federal Drug Administration had adopted a rule that required certain protections against botulism in commercially marketed fish. This rule was objected to by firms that packed and sold whitefish. Instead of establishing separate standards for various species of fish, the agency had lumped all species together under one general

43. 714 F.2d at 1298. See also National Tour Brokers Ass'n v. United States, 591 F.2d 896, 899–901 (D.C.Cir.1978). On the other hand, where a failure to give adequate notice of the "legal authority" for a rule was not prejudicial, that is, interested parties had not been deprived of an effective right to comment, the courts have refused to vacate a rule. Trans–Pacific Freight v. FMC, 650 F.2d 1235, 1259 (D.C.Cir.1980).

44. "The adequacy of notice in any case must be determined by a close examination of the facts of the particular proceeding which produced a challenged rule." American Medical Ass'n v. United States, 887 F.2d 760, 768 (7th Cir.1989).

45. AFL–CIO v. Donovan, 757 F.2d 330, 339 (D.C.Cir.1985).

46. Wagner Elec. Corp. v. Volpe, 466 F.2d 1013, 1019–20 (3d Cir.1972). Nor where interested parties, even highly sophisticated parties, fairly appraised by a footnote out of kilter with the thrust of the notice of a proposed rule. MCI Telecommunications Corp. v. FCC, 57 F.3d 1136 (D.C.Cir.1995).

47. 568 F.2d 240 (2d Cir.1977).

botulism rule. The whitefish firms claimed that botulism in whitefish had already been eliminated by practices developed and applied in that industry. This objection, about the overinclusiveness of the agency rule, was made in procedural terms. The whitefish people argued that the agency had failed to give them notice of the scientific data upon which it had relied in establishing the rule and that they had therefore been denied the opportunity to show that a different and less burdensome rule was sufficient for whitefish.

This argument prevailed. The court of appeals found that the agency's notice was inadequate and that the rule in question was therefore invalid. In relation to notice of data and method, the court explained that "Scientific research is sometimes rejected for diverse inadequacies of methodology and statistical results are sometimes rebutted because of a lack of adequate gathering technique or of supportable extrapolation...." Therefore, "To suppress meaningful comment by failure to disclose the basic data relied upon is akin to rejecting comment altogether."[48]

While the direction in notice of rulemaking has been toward detailed notice,[49] the optimum detail remains a matter of balance. Often, the sophistication and expertise of interested parties in the private sector may be great or greater than that of the agency. For such parties, the best notice is detailed and specific, covering data and methodology. But other interested parties may not be similarly sophisticated and knowledgeable. For these parties, such detail might obscure the general points of a proposed rule. A balance of intelligibility may, however, be achieved by a form of notice often used by the agencies. This form includes a preamble that states the basic purposes and the general impact of a proposed rule, a reference to the legal authority under which the rule is promulgated, and the text of the proposed rule. This general description is, however, accompanied by an appendix containing more detailed information such as would be useful to more sophisticated parties.[50]

48. 568 F.2d at 252. See also Portland Cement Ass'n v. Ruckelshaus, 486 F.2d 375, 393–94 (D.C.Cir.1973).

49. This has been especially so in scientific and technical areas, where the knowledge and expertise of the private sector may equal or exceed that of the agency. Accordingly, many of the leading cases requiring fairly comprehensive notice about the data on which a rule is based have involved matters of science and technology in general and the environmental area in particular. See, e.g., Portland Cement Ass'n v. Ruckelshaus, 486 F.2d 375 (D.C.Cir. 1973); PPG Industries, Inc. v. Costle, 659 F.2d 1239, 1249–51 (D.C.Cir.1981). Congress, moreover, has with respect to the Environmental Protection Agency especially required that notice as provided by that agency include a summary of "the factual on which the proposed rule is based" and the "methodology" used in obtaining and analyzing the data. 42 U.S.C. § 7607(3).

50. See Administrative Conference of the United States, A Guide to Federal Agency Rulemaking 119 (1983). In the interest of intelligibility in notice, the courts have generally disapproved of forms of notice that attempt to incorporate by reference. In PPG Industries, Inc. v. Costle, 659 F.2d 1239, 1249–50 (D.C.Cir.1981) the court overturned an Environmental Protection Agency rule where the notice of rulemaking had referred to certain internal agency guidelines for measuring air quality without setting forth the substance of these measurements.

§ 2.1.3 Notice and Changes in a Proposed Rule: The Principle of "Logical Outgrowth"

The Environmental Protection Agency had identified three pollutants in its notice of a proposed rule, but then the final rule added a fourth pollutant. Because of this deviation, the District of Columbia Circuit, in *American Frozen Food Institute v. Train,* remanded the rule for an additional round of notice and comment respecting the fourth pollutant.[51] Here, the deficiency in notice involved a change in an agency's position during rulemaking. The rule about which notice was given was one thing, the final rule something else.

The result in *American Frozen Food Institute v. Train* is, however, the exception. Ordinarily, a change in position during rulemaking is *not* to be condemned or penalized. An agency change of position during rulemaking usually shows that the rulemaking process has been effective. Therefore, a second stage of notice and comment should not be required simply because a final rule differs from the proposed rule. Such a requirement would "lead to the absurdity that in rulemaking under the APA the agency can learn from its proposals only at the peril of starting a new procedural round of commentary."[52]

The courts have tried to avoid disincentives to "learning during rulemaking." They have done so according to whether a final rule is a "logical outgrowth" of the rule proposed in the original notice.[53] If the rule is a logical outgrowth, the courts assume adequate notice, and do *not* require new notice and a new round of comment. Whether the final rule is a "logical outgrowth" of the proposed rule is a fact-intensive question that is sometimes, as the court in *Chocolate Manufacturers*

51. American Frozen Food Institute v. Train, 539 F.2d 107, 135 (D.C.Cir.1976).

52. International Harvester Co. v. Ruckelshaus, 478 F.2d 615, 632 n. 51 (D.C.Cir.1973). (In this case the Environmental Protection Agency), in part on the basis of information received during public comment, had developed a new methodology for analyzing data concerning automobile emissions. The complainant asked for a new opportunity to comment on this new data. The court refused, saying that "the requirement of a submission of a proposed rule does not automatically generate a new opportunity to comment merely because a rule promulgated by the agency differs from the rule it proposed, at least in response to submissions." 478 F.2d at 632.

53. E.g., American Medical Ass'n v. United States, 887 F.2d 760 (7th Cir.1989). As said by the court in this case, a perspective of "logical outgrowth" is "whether parties affected by a final rule were put on notice that 'their interests [were] at stake.' "Here, the rule as proposed had not been opposed by the American Medical Association, and so it offered no comment. During the course of rulemaking, however, the substance of the rule changed, and in final form the rule was not agreeable to the American Medical Association, which then objected to the adopted rule on grounds of inadequate notice. The court, however, found that the rule was a logical outgrowth of the originally proposed rule. Further, the court explained that:

> The AMA's sole explanation for its failure to comment is that the rule as initially proposed looked fine to it, and therefore the association saw no need to intervene in the rulemaking. But ... an agency's proposed rule is merely that, a proposal. While an agency must explain and justify its departure from a proposed rule, it is not straitjacketed into the approach initially suggested on pain of triggering a further round of notice-and-comment.

887 F.2d at 769. See also American Water Works Ass'n v. EPA, 40 F.3d 1266 (D.C.Cir. 1994); Health Insurance Ass'n v. Shalala, 23 F.3d 412 (D.C.Cir.1994).

Association v. Block said, "not easy to answer."[54] In the *Chocolate Manufacturers* case, the Department of Agriculture had issued a rule that prohibited chocolate flavored milk in a federally funded food program for infants and young children. The Chocolate Manufacturers Association objected to the rule on grounds that the Department had not given adequate notice that the elimination of chocolate-flavored milk would be considered in the rulemaking process. The court of appeals, because it found that the final rule was *not* a "logical outgrowth" of the rule proposed in the original notice, agreed. The court explained:

> At the time the proposed rulemaking was published, neither the [Chocolate Manufacturers Association] nor the public in general had any indication from the history of the [federal program] or any other food distribution programs that flavored milk was not part of the acceptable diet for women and children without special dietary needs. The discussion in the preamble to the proposed rule was very detailed and identified specific foods which the agency was examining for excess sugar. This specificity, together with total silence concerning any suggestion of eliminating flavored milk, strongly indicated that flavored milk was not at issue.[55]

* * *

The agency, to help with notice of a rule in change during rulemaking, can keep an open file known and accessible to interested parties, which file contains new data and developments as they may come in after the original notice. The courts may require such a file. As they have said, "[I]nformation that is material to the subject at hand should be disclosed as it becomes available."[56]

§ 2.1.4 The Right to Comment

The right of public participation in rulemaking is bare-boned: The Administrative Procedure Act rather thinly provides that "An agency shall give interested persons an opportunity to participate in rule making through submission of written data, view, or arguments with or without opportunity for oral presentation."[57] This opportunity of some

54. 755 F.2d 1098, 1105 (4th Cir.1985).

55. 755 F.2d at 1106–07.

56. Portland Cement Association v. Ruckelshaus, 486 F.2d 375, 394 (D.C.Cir. 1973), cert. denied, 417 U.S. 921, 94 S.Ct. 2628, 41 L.Ed.2d 226 (1974). But if at all possible, pertinent information should be disclosed in the original notice at the commencement of rulemaking, "in order that rulemaking proceedings to determine standards be conducted in orderly fashion...." Id.

In the case of an inadequate opportunity to participate in rulemaking because of a late submission, it is "incumbent on the petitioner objecting to the agency's late submission of documents to indicate with 'reasonable specificity' what portions of the documents to object to and how it might have responded if given the opportunity." Small Refiner Lead Phase–Down Task Force v. Environmental Protection Agency, 705 F.2d 506, 540–41 (D.C.Cir.1983). See also Air Transport Ass'n v. Civil Aeronautics Board, 732 F.2d 219 (D.C.Cir.1984); Texas v. Lyng, 868 F.2d 795, 797–98 (5th Cir.1989).

57. 5 U.S.C. § 553(c). Ordinarily, agencies will limit interested parties to written comment.

input is unadorned by the more elaborate and intensive procedures that are characteristic of adjudication. In the multi-interest and multi-party context of rulemaking, the decision costs associated with adversarial processes may stunt the development of a rule without necessarily improving the data base. Also, adversarial processes tend to transfer control of rulemaking to those who are competent in such processes (lawyers) and away from those competent with respect to the substance of a rule (agency personnel and interested parties from the private sector).

The opportunity to comment is, therefore, in form minimal. But it is not meager. The right to comment better grounds agency action in the actual values and interests of the people subject to the action and it better "assur[e] that the agency will have before it the facts and information relevant to a particular administrative problem, as well as suggestions for alternative solutions."[58] The courts, therefore, will not credit rulemaking as "fully reasoned" unless the agency takes into account the data and critical analysis and identification of interests and priorities as offered by public comment. Accordingly, a demand reviewing courts has been that an agency must respond—either by modifying a rule or by explaining why not—to "significant comments" or "comments of cogent materiality" from the private sector.[59]

Textual support for requiring agencies to respond to significant comment is found in Sec. 553(c) of the Administrative Procedure Act. This section establishes the opportunity to comment and then immediately provides that "After consideration of the relevant matter presented, the agency shall incorporate in the rules adopted a concise general statement of their basis and purpose." Because it thus refers to an agency "consideration of the relevant matter presented," Sec. 553(c) is taken as directing that comment from the private sector in fact be a part of the agency's decisional process. The courts then enforce this directive by requiring the agency to respond to significant comments.[60]

58. American Hosp. Ass'n v. Bowen, 834 F.2d 1037, 1044 (D.C.Cir.1987).

59. United States v. Nova Scotia Food Products Corp., 568 F.2d 240 (2d Cir.1977); Portland Cement Ass'n v. Ruckelshaus, 486 F.2d 375, 393–94 (D.C.Cir.1973), cert. denied 417 U.S. 921, 94 S.Ct. 2628, 41 L.Ed.2d 226 (1974). In the *Portland Cement* case, the Environmental Protection Agency had issued clean air standards pertaining to cement dust. In the original notice for the proposed rule, the agency failed to provide all pertinent data as to its methodology. In particular it did not reveal the methodology used in evaluating information developed at two test sites. When detailed test data was later revealed to the industry, the Portland Cement Company submitted the data to an expert who in a new comment to the agency concluded that agency inferences from the data were seriously flawed. An issue before the court was whether the agency had to respond to this new comment; the court concluded that the agency was obliged to respond. In this respect, the court explained that "it was not consonant with the purpose of a rule-making proceeding to promulgate rules on the basis of . . . data that [to a] critical degree, is known only to the agency," and that "this agency, particularly when its decisions can literally mean survival of persons or property, has a continuing duty to take a 'hard look' at the problems involved in its regulatory task, and that includes an obligation to comment on matters identified as potentially significant by the court order remanding for further presentation."

60. This textual direction is reiterated in Sec. 553's legislative history as it reads that the "agency must consider the data argument so presented by interested par-

An agency need not, however, formally respond to all comment, but only to sufficiently material comment. As explained in *Portland Cement Ass'n v. Ruckelshaus,* "comments must be significant enough to step over a threshold requirement of materiality before any lack of agency response or consideration becomes of concern."[61] An illustration of comment sufficiently important to warrant an agency response is provided by the Second Circuit's previously discussed opinion in *United States v. Nova Scotia Food Products Corp.*[62] In relation to a Food and Drug Administration rule about packing whitefish, interested parties had offered comment to the effect that present practices protected the public health and that the new practice ordered by the agency made the commercial marketing of whitefish unfeasible. The agency, however, had not responded to these points in its "statement of basis and purpose" for the final rule. The court held that this lack of explanation was reversible error. "It is not in keeping with a rational process," the court said, "to leave vital questions, raised by comments which are of cogent materiality, completely unanswered."

Judicial review that requires agencies to respond to "comments of cogent materiality" may check agency tendencies to ignore input from the private sector. On the other hand, this form of review makes rulemaking more cumbersome for agencies: They must anticipate which comment a court may think significant and must then assume a burden of explanation in relation to that comment. Also, this form of review is a litigation tool for losers in rulemaking, who can cause a strung-out and sequential rulemaking process, consisting of a series of remands for agency responses to overlooked comments. In short, while Sec. 553 may direct agencies to include the information gained from comment by the private sector on the proposed rule, it is a larger and different step to suppose, as the courts now do, that they have the authority to force agencies to respond to what they (the courts) think are comments of "cogent materiality." Such a requirement may, among other things, increase the decision costs of rulemaking beyond the point contemplated by Sec. 553, a matter which we will shortly discuss more fully.[63] In any event, our review of case law in the 1990's shows little deployment of the "comment of cogent materiality" requirement.

§ 2.1.5 The Rulemaking Record

In adjudication, the record consists of all the evidence and argument adduced at a hearing and the grounds for decision must be taken from this record.[64] The rulemaking record is something less. Mainly, it is *not* a

ties" and that in its "required statement of the basis and purpose" the agency should "with reasonable fullness" show that it has done so. Administrative Procedure Act Legis. Hist., S.Doc. 248 at 201.

61. 486 F.2d 375, 394 (D.C.Cir.1973), cert. denied 417 U.S. 921, 94 S.Ct. 2628, 41 L.Ed.2d 226 (1974).

62. 568 F.2d 240 (2d Cir.1977).

63. See discussion at Sec. 2.2, infra.

64. The record requirements for adjudication are found in Sec. 556 and Sec. 557 of the Administrative Procedure Act. In accordance with the understanding that the grounds for decision in an adjudication are limited to evidence and arguments that are

requirement that rulemaking decision be wholly "on the record" as in the case of an adjudication.[65] Instead, because the rulemaking record is largely incidental to modern requirements of a rational process, this record consists of proofs of decisional processes, proofs sufficient to show such rationality to a reviewing court.[66]

Initially, the courts had little use of such a "record." Agency rules were treated about the same as statutes enacted by Congress: the courts would not overturn a rule unless the party challenging the rule could show that it was inconceivable that the rule might serve some legitimate purpose.[67] For such a weak form of review, no record was needed. Also, a record requirement was initially seen as inconsistent with the structure and nature of rulemaking. Rulemaking was understood as a broad process, which included information offered by sources other than the notice and comment hearing required by the Administrative Procedure Act and which processed all information by a policy-making apparatus spread throughout the various subunits of an agency.[68] Such a diffuse process is not easily reduced to a record.[69]

made part of the record, Sec. 556(e) provides that "[t]he transcript of testimony and exhibits, together with all papers and requests filed in the proceeding, constitutes the exclusive record for decision. . . ." 5 U.S.C.A. § 556(e). For rulemaking, the Administrative Procedure Act has no definition of what a record should be nor does it generally require that rulemaking should be "on the record".

65. As said by the Court of Appeals for the District of Columbia:

> We do not expect the agency to discuss every item of fact or opinion included in the submissions made to it in informal rulemaking. We do expect that, if the judicial review which Congress has thought it important to provide us be meaningful, the "concise general statement of . . . basis and purpose" mandated by [APA Sec. 553] will enable us to see what major issues of policy were ventilated by the informal proceedings and why the agency reacted to them as it did.

Automotive Parts & Accessories Ass'n v. Boyd, 407 F.2d 330, 338 (D.C.Cir.1968). On the relation of the rulemaking record to the statement of basis and purpose required by Sec. 553(c) of the Administrative Procedure Act, see text at note 79, infra.

66. An exception to this is where, for specific agencies, Congress has especially established a substantial evidence standard of review for rules and then provided for a rulemaking record. Here, then, the requirement of a rulemaking record is related to the substantial evidence form of review. For authorities criticizing this scheme, see note 79, infra.

67. Pacific States Box & Basket Co. v. White, 296 U.S. 176, 56 S.Ct. 159, 80 L.Ed. 138 (1935).

68. "The purpose of notice is to allow interested parties to make useful comment and not to allow them to assert their 'rights' to insist that a rule take a particular form. The agency, in rulemaking, can look beyond the particular hearing record since it otherwise would be unable to draw upon its expertise." Pacific Coast European Conference v. United States, 350 F.2d 197, 205 (9th Cir.1965) cert. denied, 382 U.S. 958, 86 S.Ct. 433, 15 L.Ed.2d 362 (1965). In this regard, the Administrative Procedure Act does not preclude ex parte contacts in rulemaking. For a description of how diffuse rulemaking is, see Pederson, Formal Records and Informal Rulemaking, 85 Yale L.J. 59 (1975).

69. Accordingly, the Administrative Procedure Act's requirement of a "concise general statement of a basis and purpose" of a rule was initially interpreted as being unrelated to judicial review. Instead, it was viewed as a general information provision that merely required the agency to explain briefly the rule for the public at large. This view of § 553(c), as creating something less than a record requirement, has indirect support in other terms of the Administrative Procedure Act. In the case of adjudication, the Act specifically requires a record, defines what should be in the record, and then provides that grounds for decision be limited to evidence and arguments contained in this record. 5 U.S.C. §§ 556–557. When Congress wanted to impose a record requirement, it did so by means of such

Today, courts still understand the difficulties of compiling a rulemaking record. What has changed, however, is their attitude about reviewing agency action. Presently, the courts insist that rulemaking be "fully reasoned," and so they incidentally require the agency to produce a record that shows its reasoning.[70] According to the Supreme Court, in *Citizens to Preserve Overton Park, Inc. v. Volpe,* whatever "presumption" of validity to which an agency action may be entitled, that presumption should not be sufficient to "shield [the] action from a thorough, probing, in-depth review" of the underlying decisional processes. Toward that end, the Court remanded the agency action for lower court review based on the "full administrative record" underlying the action in question.[71]

As soon as a rulemaking record was viewed as essential to a more rigorous and extensive judicial review of rules, the text of the Administrative Procedure Act was newly interpreted so as to require such a record. Initially, the courts had read the Sec. 553(c) requirement of a "concise general statement of a basis and purpose" as not pertaining to judicial review but as merely requiring public information about the rule. But as the courts' attitude about rulemaking changed so did their reading of this section. They commenced to read it as requiring a rulemaking record sufficient for judicial review. As explained by the District of Columbia Circuit, "the 'purpose of requiring a statement of the basis and purpose is to enable courts, which have the duty to exercise review, to be aware of the legal and factual framework underlying the agency action.' "[72]

* * *

detail, and not by a cursory reference to a concise general statement of basis and purpose as in § 553.

70. As explained by the District of Columbia circuit, "Whatever the law may have been in the past, there can now be no doubt that implicit in the decision to treat the promulgation of rules as a 'final event' in an ongoing process of administration is an assumption that an act of reasoned judgment has occurred, an assumption which further implicates the existence of a body of material—comments, transcripts, and statements in various forms declaring agency expertise or policy—with reference to which such judgment was exercised." Home Box Office, Inc. v. FCC, 567 F.2d 9, 54 (D.C.Cir. 1977), cert. denied 434 U.S. 829, 98 S.Ct. 111, 54 L.Ed.2d 89 (1977).

71. 401 U.S. 402, 415, 91 S.Ct. 814, 823, 28 L.Ed.2d 136 (1971). Perhaps the rise of pre-enforcement review of agency rules has been another reason for the courts' present requirement of a rulemaking record. Initially, the substance of a rule could be reviewed only in the context of an agency action enforcing the rule, and this enforcement action provided a factual context and a record against which the substance of a rule might be tested. But after the Supreme Court decision in *Abbott Laboratories v. Gardner,* the courts were opened to pre-enforcement review of rules. With such review, however, there was no agency adjudication, and no record such as there would be in the case of such adjudication, to aid the court. Consequently, courts engaged in pre-enforcement review tended to ask for a rulemaking record, as it might provide a context for review of a rule. See Verkuil, Review of Informal Rulemaking, 60 Va. L.Rev. 185, 205 (1974).

72. Action on Smoking and Health v. CAB, 699 F.2d 1209, 1216 (D.C.Cir.1983). See also UMW v. Dole, 870 F.2d 662, 666 (D.C.Cir.1989); Automotive Parts & Accessories Ass'n v. Boyd, 407 F.2d 330, 338 (D.C.Cir.1968) ("We do not expect the agency to discuss every item of fact or opinion included in the submissions made to it in informal rulemaking." We do expect that, if the judicial review which Congress has thought it important to provide us be meaningful, the "concise general statement of . . . basis and purpose mandated by [Sec. 553] will enable us to see what major issues

At this point, after trying to understand the source of the rulemaking-record requirement, the question is: what is that record anyway; what should it include? The Administrative Procedure Act does not specifically require such a record, and so the Act, unsurprisingly, does not define it.[73] Instead, the rulemaking record is defined by its origins in rationality review, in the needs of courts trying to assure that an agency "has considered all relevant factors . . . and that it has demonstrated 'a rational connection between the facts found and the choices made.' "[74]

A rulemaking record that meets this standard of rationality review—showing facts found and choices made—will have both historical and statutory underpinnings. The historical underpinning consists of the materials actually relied upon by an agency in reaching a decision, so that the courts can review these materials—as a contemporaneous picture of agency decisional processes—to see whether the rule was arrived at rationally. An implication of the record as a documentary history is this: because this record must consist of materials on which an agency decision was actually based, it cannot include materials produced after the decision. Specifically, the record cannot include materials produced *post hoc,* as by agency attorneys trying to justify a rule to a reviewing court.[75]

To supplement the historical approach to building the record, the courts also require that an agency produce a "procedural" record. This record consists of evidence and argument presented under an obligatory set of procedures and considerations.[76] Agencies must reveal to interested parties the data and methodology underlying proposed rules and to respond to material comments from these parties. Under a procedural approach, therefore, a rulemaking record should include such data and

of policy were ventilated by the informal proceedings and why the agency reacted to them as it did.").

A record requirement specific to some agencies may be implied where Congress has for these agencies required reviewing courts to determine that an agency rule is supported by "substantial evidence." This scope of review requirement may be seen as implying a rulemaking record, so that the courts can tell if a rule is indeed supported by such evidence. E.g., Industrial Union Department, AFL–CIO v. Hodgson, 499 F.2d 467 (D.C.Cir.1974). See also Verkuil, supra, at 222–26.

In the *Hodgson* case, though, Judge McGowan was skeptical about a substantial evidence form of review for proceedings not formally on the record. "[H]ere Congress," he said, "with no apparent awareness of the anomaly—has explicitly combined an informal agency procedure with a standard of review traditionally conceived of as suited to formal adjudication or rulemaking." For a sharper criticism, see Scalia and Goodman, Procedural Aspects of the Consumer Products Safety Act, 20 Calif.L.Rev. 899, 933–36 (1973).

73. The "concise general statement of basis and purpose" requirement of Sec. 553(c) hardly amounts to a definition of a record. In any event, it is not the definition that has evolved.

74. Independent U.S. Tanker Owners Committee v. Lewis, 690 F.2d 908, 922 (D.C.Cir.1982).

75. Citizens to Preserve Overton Park, Inc. v. Volpe, 401 U.S. 402, 91 S.Ct. 814, 28 L.Ed.2d 136 (1971); Camp v. Pitts, 411 U.S. 138, 142, 93 S.Ct. 1241, 1244, 36 L.Ed.2d 106 (1973) (The record must consist of material "already in existence, not some new record made initially in the reviewing courts.") Cf. SEC v. Chenery Corp., 318 U.S. 80, 88, 63 S.Ct. 454, 459, 87 L.Ed. 626 (1943).

76. The differences between an historical and a procedural approach to the rulemaking record are examined in Pederson, Formal Records and Informal Rulemaking, 85 Yale L.J. 38, 62 et seq. (1975).

methodology and responsive comments about it.[77] Statutes may also prescribe an obligatory set of considerations. For instance, in *Citizens to Preserve Overton Park, Inc. v. Volpe* the agency was statutorily required to determine whether there were "prudent alternatives" to road construction through public parks. The rulemaking record, therefore, should show that such considerations were in fact part of the agency's decisional process.[78]

In sum, the rulemaking record probably should contain the data and agency inferences therefrom that underlie a rule, public comment on the rule and agency responses thereto, a transcript of hearings held on the rule, if any, and a statement of the agency's authority to enact the rule. Residually, the historical approach of *Overton Park* requires that the record include all other materials, such as internal studies, relied upon by the agency in enacting the rule.[79]

A problem in the foregoing definition of the rulemaking record is the assumption: that there is such a documentary record, at least one that can coherently be produced. In rulemaking, information comes from a variety of sources, which include the comment generated by public participation in rulemaking and information produced by the agency or acquired by the agency outside the notice and comment process. In various sub-units, the agency digests all this information. This sort of decentralized and diffuse process is not easily captured within the four corners of the record, a difficulty of several unfortunate consequences. One such consequence is that the record can be incoherent, just a "sump in which the parties have deposited a sundry mass of materials."[80] Also, its looseness leaves the record easy to contrive, as "a collection of self-serving evidence" by the agency.[81] Finally, the rulemaking record may be

77. E.g., Gas Appliance Manufacturers Ass'n, Inc. v. Secretary of Energy, 722 F.Supp. 792, 796 (D.D.C.1989).

78. 401 U.S. 402, 404, 91 S.Ct. 814, 817, 28 L.Ed.2d 136 (1971). See also Gas Appliance Manufacturers Ass'n, Inc. v. Secretary of Energy, 722 F.Supp. 792 (D.D.C. 1989); UMW v. Dole, 870 F.2d 662 (D.C.Cir. 1989).

79. In enactments over the last several years, Congress has for some agencies more specifically outlined the contents of the rulemaking record. These requirements, as they bind the agencies to which they pertain, at the same time also provide some sense of what a rulemaking record should be. In this regard, the rulemaking record for the Environmental Protection Agency, as defined by the Clean Air Act amendments of 1977, includes comment on the rule, transcripts of public hearings if any, and a statement of basis and purpose containing a "summary of (a) the data on which the proposed rule is based; (b) the methodology used in obtaining the data and analyzing the data; and (c) the major legal interpretations and policy considerations underlying the rule." Also, the Clean Air Act amendments require the record to include agency "response to each of the significant comments, criticisms, and new data introduced by public participation in rulemaking under the Act." 42 U.S.C. § 7607(d)(7)(A).

Generally speaking, the rulemaking record has not been tightly defined, and such definition as there is has been subject to various exceptions. In fact, the looseness of the concept has caused some observers to doubt whether a rulemaking record, as a single, comprehensive justification for a rule, is possible. Stark and Wald, 33 Ad. L.Rev. 333 (1984).

80. Natural Resources Defense Council, Inc. v. SEC, 606 F.2d 1031, 1052 (D.C.Cir.1979).

81. Id.

so ambiguous that a judge, supposing to base her opinion on the record, may in fact do no more than indulge her policy preferences.[82]

§ 2.2 VERMONT YANKEE, HYBRID RULEMAKING, AND A NOTE ON DECISION COSTS

Hybrid rulemaking combines the rather thin procedural processes of rulemaking with some of the more intensive processes of adjudication, on the hope that the rule produced will be better and better supported by a record. The rise and fall of "hybrid rulemaking" under the Administrative Procedure Act is, however, a story of something else, the "iron rule of decision costs."

In the Seventies, the sparseness of rulemaking procedures was the cause of some dissatisfaction. The lower courts, especially in the District of Columbia Circuit, commenced to impose procedures more intensive than the bare notice and comment procedures of Sec. 553. For instance, in *Mobil Oil Corp. v. FPC,* the District of Columbia circuit overturned a Federal Power Commission rule setting minimum rates for piping natural gas.[1] Although the rule had been enacted on the basis of procedures fully in accordance with Sec. 553, the court found that these procedures did not fully "test, criticize and illuminate" the "evidentiary" basis of it. Accordingly, the court remanded the rule for more intensive procedures. (The court suggested cross-examination.) This more intensive process is what is known as hybrid rulemaking, because it tries to add more depth to rulemaking by adding adjudicatory procedures.

Hybrid rulemaking under the Administrative Procedure Act had a short life. It was terminated by the Supreme Court in *Vermont Yankee Nuclear Power Corp. v. Natural Resources Defense Council, Inc.*[2] The District of Columbia Circuit had upset an Atomic Energy Commission rule about nuclear waste disposal, largely because of the agency's failure to provide rulemaking procedures to the satisfaction of the court. In particular, the court of appeals thought that environmental interest groups should have been able to more thoroughly examine, by means of

82. Judge McGowan has explained this phenomenon as follows:

> [The rulemaking record] is indistinguishable ... from the proceedings before a legislative committee hearing on a proposed bill—letters, telegrams, and written statements from proponents and opponents, including occasional oral testimony not subjected to adversary cross-examination.... The resulting policy choices ... are virtually immune to judicial scrutiny....
>
> When ... policy choices are largely committed to agency rulemaking, the record before the reviewing court is essentially the same. No matter how the standard of review is articulated, there is wide latitude for judges to vote their policy views in the same manner as does the legislature. No matter how sensitive judges are of the necessity for restraint ..., the opportunities and the consequent temptations are great to come down on the side of the judge's personal conceptions of policy.

McGowan, Congress and the Courts, 62 Am.Bar.Ass'n J. 1588, 1589–90 (1976).

§ 2.2

1. 483 F.2d 1238 (D.C.Cir.1973).

2. 435 U.S. 519, 98 S.Ct. 1197, 55 L.Ed.2d 460 (1978), on remand 685 F.2d 459 (D.C.Cir.1982). While hybrid rulemaking, as we said, no longer exists as a "general" condition of rulemaking, it does remain, where—for a specific agency—Congress has required some form of it. E.g., Federal Trade Commission Improvement Act 15 U.S.C. 57a.

cross-examination, a study relied upon by the agency. In no uncertain terms and in an unanimous decision, the Supreme Court held that the lower court had erred. The Administrative Procedure Act "established the maximum procedural requirements," those of notice and comment, "which Congress was willing to have the courts impose upon agencies in conducting rulemaking procedures." Further, the Court explained that while "Agencies are free to grant additional procedural rights in the exercise of their discretion, . . . reviewing courts are generally not free to impose them if the agencies have not chosen to grant them."[3]

This interment of hybrid rulemaking was driven by the fear that procedures additional to those required by Sec. 553 would set the decision costs for rulemaking so high as to impede it. If courts claimed the power to require additional procedures whenever they thought bare-boned notice and comment procedures inadequate, then the safe course for an agency bent on protecting a rule from the courts would be to surround the rule with a full complement of adjudicatory procedures. This course would burden rulemaking with an unacceptable decision cost, the huge cost of adjudicatory procedures in the multi-party, multi-interest context of rulemaking.[4] Therefore, the Court in *Vermont Yankee* removed the power of courts to impose rulemaking procedures greater than those stipulated in Sec. 553.

But while it eliminated hybrid rulemaking under the Administrative Procedure Act, *Vermont Yankee* seems to have left unchanged the more rigorous decisional process for rules that we have described in this chapter. In this regard, the Court specifically approved one of these more exacting processes—the rulemaking record—as it said that courts must determine whether rules are "sustainable" based "on the administrative record made."[5] The reason for letting these processes stand appears to be this: these more rigorous processes for rules—that agencies fully reveal data and methodology, respond to material comments, and provide reviewing courts with a record of their decisional processes—are

3. 435 U.S. at 524, 98 S.Ct. at 1202. See C. Byse, Vermont Yankee and the Evolution of Administrative Procedure: A Somewhat Different View, 91 Harv.L.Rev. 1283, 1829 (1978) ("in enacting APA Sec. 553 in 1946, Congress established a new general model of rulemaking procedure. There is no suggestion that the legislative history of the section was declaratory of the common law or that it was a delegation of power to the courts to develop desirable procedural models. On the contrary, the legislative history indicates that the question whether additional procedures are to be employed is an *agency* question, not a judicial one: 'Considerations of practicality, necessity, and public interest . . . will naturally govern the *agency's* determination of the extent to which public proceedings should go' ") (emphasis in original). For a less favorable assessment of *Vermont Yankee,* see R. Stewart, Vermont Yankee and the Evolution of Administrative Procedure, 91 Harv.L.Rev. 1805 (1978).

4. See generally Hamilton, Procedures for the Adoption of Rules of General Applicability: The Need For Procedural Innovation in Administrative Rulemaking, 60 Calif.L.Rev. 1276, 1283–1313 (1972). The Food and Drug Administration is one of the few agencies which is specially required by statute to conduct rulemaking according to adjudicatory procedures, and in a classic case, given all the interested parties in the industry and all the lawyers and all the procedures, it took that agency nine years to determine how much of peanut butter should be comprised of peanuts. W. Gellhorn, C. Byse, and P. Strauss, Administrative Law, Case and Comments 733–34, 747–50 (6th ed.).

5. 435 U.S. at 549, 98 S.Ct. at 1214.

now considered as processes prescribed by the Administrative Procedure Act itself.

Moreover, while *Vermont Yankee* disestablished hybrid rulemaking under the Administrative Procedure Act, that decision did not, of course, preclude Congress from itself prescribing hybrid procedures for specific agencies, and Congress has done so, as noted in the introduction to this chapter.

Still, *Vermont Yankee* did disestablish hybrid rulemaking as it might be imposed by the courts of their own motion. And still that decision is a statement of concern about the high decision costs and about whether such costs might make rulemaking impracticable.[6] If the costs get too high, a likely result, as Justice Scalia has pointed out, is one of displacement: agencies will continue to produce rules, but they will try to do without rulemaking, and the law may afford them the opportunities.[7] These opportunities largely involve skirting the zone of rulemaking by using adjudication rather than rulemaking to make rules. We discuss these opportunities in the next two sections.

6. An example of the decision costs associated with the modern rulemaking process is provided by this account of rulemaking:

Under the Toxic Substances Control Act, EPA was required to write a Pre-Manufacturer Notification rule; in essence, this requires a company to notify us before moving from development to large-scale production of a chemical. The proposed rule brought forth 192 commentators at 29 public meetings, and 300 pages of comment raising 400 discrete issues, each requiring an EPA response. Our defense comprised 300 pages of response, 800 pages of economic analysis performed at a cost of $600,000, and 500 pages of related analysis on regulatory impact....

Costle, Brave New Chemical: The Future Regulatory History of Phlogiston, 33 Ad.L.Rev. 195, 199–200 (1981), quoted at W. Gellhorn, C. Byse, P. Strauss, T. Rakoff and R. Shotland, Administrative Law, Cases and Comments, 485 (8th ed. 1987).

In a leading decision on rulemaking, United States v. Florida East Coast Ry. Co., 410 U.S. 224, 93 S.Ct. 810, 35 L.Ed.2d 223 (1973), the Court again, with an eye toward freeing rulemaking of the burden of adjudicatory procedures, interpreted the Administrative Procedure Act in favor of the notice and comment procedures of Sec. 553. In this case the Court held that Sec. 553(c), which calls for adjudicatory procedures "When rules are required by statute to be made on the record after opportunity for an agency hearing", was so narrow as to virtually eradicate this exception to notice and comment procedures. The Court did this by holding that only where a statute literally tracks the hearing on the record language of Sec. 553(c) is the exception available. Thus, statutory formulations such as "a full hearing," or whatnot, do not qualify for the exception. Thus in most cases of agency rulemaking, the spare notice and comment procedures of Sec. 553, with their lower decisions costs, are the norm.

7. Scalia, Back to Basics: Making Law Without Making Rules, Regulation 25 (Jul./Aug. 1981). See also Mashaw and Harfst, Regulation and Legal Culture: The Case of Motor Vehicle Safety, 4 Yale J. on Reg. 258, 263 (1987); Scanlon and Towowsky, Back Door Rulemaking: A View From the CPSC Regulation 22 (Jul./Aug. 1984).

Chapter 3

RULEMAKING AND THE RULE OF LAW

Table of Sections

Aspirations of the rule of law—of government according to a regime of standing rules that provide notice of the demands of government and that at the same time better assure that these demands are evenly distributed—are, as the Supreme Court has said, part of "the nature and the theory" of American government.[1] The relevant "nature and theory" of government comes out of the separated powers structure of American government.

Federalist No. 47 asserts that "The accumulation of all powers, legislative, executive, and judiciary, in the same hands, whether of one, a few, or many, and whether hereditary, self-appointed, or elective, may justly be pronounced the very definition of tyranny." "Tyranny" here refers to the old, despised practice of prerogative power, power under which law is discretionary and unstable, where it is no more than the wishes at the time of a government official. The classically American disdain for this sort of power was expressed by the U.S. Supreme Court in Yick Wo v. Hopkins where the Court explained that "the very idea that one man may be compelled to hold his life, or the means of living, or any material right essential to the enjoyment of life, at the mere will of

1. As explained by the Supreme Court, "When we consider the nature and the theory of our institutions of government, the principles upon which they are supposed to rest, and review the history of their development, we are constrained to conclude that they do not mean to leave room for the play and action of purely personal and arbitrary power." Yick Wo v. Hopkins, 118 U.S. 356, 369–70, 6 S.Ct. 1064, 1070–71, 30 L.Ed. 220 (1886). In this case, the Court overturned the action of a state licensing board because the broad discretion exercised by a California licensing board had been applied partially, to the disadvantage of Chinese licensees. In rule of law terms, the Court objected to the discretion given the board because "It lays down no rules by which its impartial execution can be secured or partiality and oppression prevented."

another, seems to be intolerable in any country where freedom prevails. . . ."[2]

How a combination of power, whether in the hands of one or several, allows for prerogative power may be understood by reference to a distinction, current at the time of Federalist No. 47, between combined and separated powers. This distinction was as follows: "While they [legislative, executive, and judicial powers] are kept separate, general laws are made by one body of men . . . and when made they must be applied by the other, let them effect whom they will." But "When these offices are united in the same person or assembly, particular laws are made for particular cases, springing often times from partial motives [special interests] and directed to private ends."[3]

* * *

Today, a large & complex society is often taken as requiring a greater measure of rapidity and responsiveness than separated powers can admit. And so, government power has again been combined, combined within agencies for a more efficient development of various government programs.[4] Such was the great initiative of New Deal. This combination of power, though, again provides the opportunity for prerogative power and *ad hoc* action that separated powers was supposed to avoid. However, both Congress and the courts have kept in mind the original aspiration—of government according to standing rules rather than prerogative power—and both have established safeguards accordingly.

By means of the Administrative Procedure Act, Congress has established a requirement of regulation according to standing rules. The Act requires codification and publication in the Federal Register of rules of conduct and provides that "a person may not in any manner be required to resort to, or be adversely affected by a matter required to be published in the Federal Register and not so published."[5] This part of rulemaking, as the Court has noted, is responsive to rule of law values. It "provides notice of what conduct will be sanctioned and promotes equality of treatment among similarly situated [persons]."[6]

2. 118 U.S. 356, 370, 6 S.Ct. 1064, 1071, 30 L.Ed. 220 (1886).

3. W. Paley, Political and Moral Philosophy, Book VI, Ch. 8 (1785). See also 2 J. Story, Commentaries on the Constitution 1–7 (1833). John Marshall described legislation in a government of separated laws in the same ideal way, as productive of "laws made under no resentments, and without knowing on whom they were to operate." Ex parte Bollman, 8 U.S. (4 Cranch) 75, 127, 2 L.Ed. 554 (1807). For a modern discussion of how generality is an essential quality of law, see F.A. Hayek, The Constitution of Liberty 148–161 (1960).

4. As expressed by a main proponent, this New Deal ideology was "If in private life we were to organize a unit for the operation of an industry, it would scarcely follow Montesquieu's lines," yet "the direction of any large corporation presents difficulties comparable in character to those faced by an administrative commission." J. Landis, The Administrative Process 10 (1938).

5. 5 U.S.C. § 552(a). Regarding the advantages of codification and publication of rules, see G. Bentham, Of Promulgation of the Laws, in 1 Works 155 (Bowring ed. 1859).

6. Dixon v. Love, 431 U.S. 105, 97 S.Ct. 1723, 52 L.Ed.2d 172 (1977).

Outside of the Administrative Procedure Act, the courts, in a particular group of due process cases, have imposed their own rule of law requirements. We will consider both these cases and the Administrative Procedure Act's codification and publication requirements shortly. But first we will briefly address the arguments, pro and con, for agency regulation according to rules.

§ 3.1 REGULATION ACCORDING TO RULES

"Liberty under government," John Locke said, "consists of a standing rule to live by, common to everybody in that society."[1] Liberty under government is thus based on government according to standing rules. Standing rules underpin this liberty in two ways. The first way, as denoted by the phrase "common to everybody in that society," is an idea of government by general rules rather than by the will of an official.[2] The second way is to enhance the practical capacity of a person to plan, to order his or her life and work in some forehanded way.

The relation of "liberty under government" to a person's capacity to plan is implicit in Federalist No. 62, which states, "Law is defined to be a rule of action; but how can that be a rule, which is little known and less fixed."[3] In concrete circumstances, this relation was used by the second circuit in *E.I. Du Pont de Nemours & Co. v. FTC.*[4] Here, the court tried to confine, by a prescription of regulation according to standing rules, the Federal Trade Commission's broad authority respecting unfair methods of competition. "The Commission," the court said, "owes a duty to define the conditions under which conduct claimed to facilitate price uniformity would be unfair so that businesses will have an inkling as to what they can lawfully do rather than be left in a state of complete unpredictability."[5]

§ 3.1

1. J. Locke, Second Treatise on Government, Chap. IV, Para. 22 (Laslett ed. 1960).

2. "For, the very idea that one man may be compelled to hold his life, or the means of living, or any material right essential to the enjoyment of life, at the mere will of another, seems to be intolerable in any country where freedom prevails. . . ." Yick Wo v. Hopkins, 118 U.S. 356, 370, 6 S.Ct. 1064, 1071, 30 L.Ed. 220 (1886).

3. On one side, a rule tells an individual of the circumstances in which government will impose a burden or confer a benefit. On its other side, the rule directs agency officials to treat the private sector according to its terms and limits the power of the official to those terms. Thus, the agency same as the private sector is bound by rules. See Nader v. Bork, 366 F.Supp. 104 (D.D.C.1973) (holding that President Nixon was bound by the rules he had set regarding the tenure of the Watergate special prosecutor). See also Arizona Grocery Co. v. Atchison, Topeka, & Santa Fe Railway Co., 284 U.S. 370, 52 S.Ct. 183, 76 L.Ed. 348 (1932). Consequently, where regulatory authority is exercised according to rules, individuals are by these rules authoritatively informed as to what they can count on from agency officials. These rules, therefore, extend the range in which these individuals can predict the consequences of their action and in which they can act.

4. 729 F.2d 128 (2d Cir.1984).

5. 729 F.2d at 139. As individual liberty is diminished, so may be the productivity of a society. As explained by Madison in Federalist No. 62, no "prudent" merchant, manufacturer, or farmer "will hazard his fortune" when "he can have no assurances that his preparatory labor and advances will not render him a victim to an inconstant government." See Lawrence, Mass. v. CAB, 343 F.2d 583, 587 (1st Cir.1965). See also H. Friendly, The Administrative Agencies, The Need for Better Definition of

The other important part of a standing rule is, as we said, its generality. Locke spoke of rules "common to everyone in that society;" the modern Supreme Court has said that a law should be "general in its operation upon the subjects to which it relates."[6] Rules are general as they proscribe conduct abstractly, let the consequences fall on whom they may.[7] A rule will not say that Jones may not drive faster than sixty-five miles per hour. Rather, it will say that no one can. This generality is important as it enhances "distributive" justice, that is, an evenhanded distribution of the benefits and burdens of government. By this same measure, generality also serves the important goal of inculcating respect for a legal system. This measure helps assure, and helps a citizen to see, that the burdens and benefits of its government are evenly distributed and shared by the powerful as well as the weak.[8]

Outside the agency, then, private individuals may prefer regulation by means of rules as it enhances their forehanded action and as it better assures an impartial and even distribution of the burdens and benefits of government. Within the agency, regulation by rules may also be pre-

Standards 20 (1962) According to Friendly, a "reason for definite standards of administrative adjudication is the social value in encouraging the security of transactions." He explains that "An airline considering an investment of $100,000,000 in additional jet transports, which it thinks necessary to give adequate service on its routes over a decade, ought to have some notion whether it will be allowed to serve the existing and anticipated traffic, along with other airlines then certified, or whether its very success in traffic development will become the basis for additional authorizations. So ought the lenders who will be providing the money." Friendly concludes that therefore it is essential that agencies of broad discretionary power develop standards "to the point of affording a fair degree of predictability of decision in the great majority of cases, and an intelligibility in all."

6. O'Bannon v. Town Court Nursing Center, 447 U.S. 773, 799, 100 S.Ct. 2467, 2482, 65 L.Ed.2d 506 (1980) (Blackmun, J., concurring), quoting Dent v. West Virginia, 129 U.S. 114, 124, 9 S.Ct. 231, 234, 32 L.Ed. 623 (1889). In Fletcher v. Peck, 10 U.S. (6 Cranch) 87, 136, 3 L.Ed. 162 (1810), the Court explained that "it is the peculiar province of the legislature to prescribe general rules for the government of society; the application of those rules in society to be the duty of their departments."

7. F.A. Hayek has described this quality of generality thusly:

> The concept of freedom under law ... rests on the contention that when we obey laws, in the sense of general abstract rules laid down irrespective of their application to us, we are not subject to another man's will and are therefore free. It is because the lawgiver does not know the particular cases to which his rules will apply, and it is because the judge who applies them has no choice in drawing the conclusions that follow from the existing body of rules and the particular facts of the case, that it can be said that laws and not men rule. Because the rule is laid down in ignorance of the particular case and no man's will decides the coercion used to enforce, the law is not arbitrary. This, however, is true only if by "law" we mean the general rules that apply equally to everybody. This generality is probably the most important aspect of that attribute of law which we have called its "abstractness." As a true law should not name any particulars, so it should especially not single out any specific person.

F.A. Hayek, The Constitution of Liberty 153–54 (1960).

8. E.g., Baker–Chaput v. Cammett, 406 F.Supp. 1134, 1139 (D.N.H.1976). Apart from matters of fairness and integrity, the generality of rules acts as a check on the processes and quality of lawmaking. When all similarly situated individuals and enterprises—irrespective of their political clout—are subject to a rule, the rule maker must necessarily proceed with care and circumspection, with a due regard to all relevant interests, in formulating the rule. Railway Express Agency v. New York, 336 U.S. 106, 112–13, 69 S.Ct. 463, 466–67, 93 L.Ed. 533 (1949) (Jackson, J., concurring).

ferred, for additional reasons. One is that regulation according to rules enhances routine and neutrality. Agency officials, as their decisions turn on the application of pre-determined rules to the facts as presented to them, are able to act abstractly rather than personally. It is the rule, not them, that decides the case. Also, agency officials may prefer regulation by means of codified and published rules because it is efficient. The private sector tends to conform to the substance of agency regulations: once this substance is settled and then revealed. As the private sector by its own motion conforms to rules, regulation according to rules reduces agency enforcement costs.

But as there are advantages to regulation according to rules, there are disadvantages, certainly from the point of view of agencies and agency officials. In large part, the disadvantages are in terms of "substantive rationality," the idea that agency action should be measured according to how instrumental it is in achieving agency goals. Instead of having its hands bound by rules, an agency might prefer to be as free as possible to reach as expeditiously as possible the result that presently seems best to contribute to its goals. It would prefer to proceed *ad hoc* by orders cut for the occasion; it would prefer to treat each case according to its own merits rather than forcing it to a perhaps poorly fitting rule. On similar grounds, public officials may object to being "rule bound." This thorny professionalism is shown in a probation officer's remarks about sentencing guidelines and new bureaucratic methods in his profession, that he was now a "bean counter" and that "the probation officer's knowledge, experience, and judgment are no longer crucial in the sentencing process."[9]

Considering these disadvantages, the Supreme Court in *SEC v. Chenery* refused to hold administrative agencies to a strict discipline of regulation according to rules.[10] The Securities Exchange Commission, acting pursuant to a broad statutory authority to oversee reorganizations of public utility holding companies, had ordered the management of a company to give up its own stock in the company. The Commission believed that this inside-ownership created a conflict of interest potentially injurious to the company's public shareholders. Management, however, had bought the stock in good faith, and under any standard existing at the time of this purchase, this purchase was completely lawful. The Court's task, therefore, was to ascertain whether the agency's order, which relieved management of six million dollars in profit on the stock, was consistent with the rule of law.

9. Natali, The Probation Officer, Bean Counting and Truth in in Sentencing, 1 Federal Sentencing Reporter 102 (1991). See generally, E. Bardach and R. Kagan, Going by the Book (1982).

The solution to rule-bound behavior, however, is not necessarily to do away with rules. Rather, the problem is also that of the optimal precision of rules, with having standards in place that are not too narrow and that yet do not fail to channel the discretion of public officials. See e.g., Varnon, The Role of the Probation Officer in the Guideline System, 1 Federal Sentencing Reporter 63 (1991). See generally Diver, The Optimal Precision of Rules, 93 Yale L.J. 65 (1983).

10. SEC v. Chenery Corp., 332 U.S. 194, 67 S.Ct. 1575, 91 L.Ed. 1995 (1947).

The Court stated that "The function of filling in the interstices of the [Holding Company Act] should be performed as much as possible through the quasi-legislative promulgation of rules to be applied in the future." The Court, however, then tempered this presumption of regulation by rules. The Court reasoned "that problems may arise which the administrative agency could not reasonably foresee . . . [or] the problems might be so specialized and varying in nature as to be impossible of capture within the boundaries of a general rule." Consequently, the conclusion of a majority of the Court was that while an agency should ordinarily regulate by means of rules, it might instead act more instrumentally. An agency might in its "informed discretion" resort to *ad hoc* orders addressed to the situation at hand.[11]

The power that *Chenery* approves, to act "for the public good without the prescription of Law"[12]—may be used as the Court imagined, instrumentally to advance the general good. However, this power can also be used partially to indulge some bad tendencies, tendencies that

11. 332 U.S. at 202–03, 67 S.Ct. at 1580–81. The discretion so conferred on agencies is quite broad. This breadth may be shown in relation to the Court's justification respecting "problems . . . which the administrative agency could not reasonably foresee." In one part, this justification has to do with the fact that general rules are susceptible of bad applications. Rulemakers are not omniscient and language is not perfect, and so situations are bound to arise where an application of a rule makes no sense. In this situation, a solution is to seek out the equity in the statute. As explained in U.S. v. Kirby, 74 U.S. (7 Wall.) 482, 486, 19 L.Ed. 278 (1868), "All laws should receive a sensible construction, and it will always, therefore, be presumed that the legislature intended exceptions to its language which would avoid results of this character." Another part to the matter, of "problems ariz[ing] which the administrative agency could not reasonably foresee," is not of an exception to a rule but rather where there is no rule at all. No rule at all was the circumstance in *Chenery.* This circumstance is the most objectionable from a rule of law standpoint, because an individual who acted lawfully has to bear the brunt of a retrospective order.

To protect the individual in these circumstances, *Chenery* stated one limitation to an agency discretion to dispense with rules: such discretion should not give rise to impermissibly retroactive orders. The measure of such retroactivity was a balancing test. The private injury caused by an agency order making something illegal *ex post* was to be balanced against the public interest served by the order. In the words of the Court:

> [S]uch retroactivity must be measured against the mischief of producing a result which is contrary to a statutory design or to legal and equitable principles. If that mischief is greater than the ill effect of the retroactive application of a new standard, it is not the type of retroactivity which is condemned by law.

332 U.S. at 203, 67 S.Ct. at 1580. In *Chenery,* this public interest versus private interest balancing came down to whether denying management the profits of its stock transactions was "outweighed by the dangers inherent in such purchases from the statutory standpoint." As is so often the case where the public interest is pitted against private injury, the agency determination of public interest carried a momentum hardly to be denied by the courts. The majority explained that the Commission "derived its conclusions from the particular facts in the case, its general experience in reorganization matters and its informed view of statutory requirements." 332 U.S. at 204, 67 S.Ct. at 1581. Retroactivity is discussed at Chap. 10, Sec. 10.3, infra.

12. J. Locke, 2d Treatise on Government, Chap. 14, Para. 160 (Laslett ed.1960) (The justification for this discretion was that "because it is impossible to foresee, and so by laws to provide for, all Accidents and Necessities, that may concern the public; or to make such Laws, as will do no harm, if they are Executed with an inflexible rigor, on all occasions, and upon all Persons, that may come in their way, therefore there is a latitude left to the Executive power, to do many things of choice, which the Laws do not prescribe.")

regulation under general rules is meant to avoid. Freed of general rules, an agency has more opportunity to favor special interests, to act partially, out of "partisan zeal or animosity, from favoritism and other improper influences and motives easy of concealment and difficult to be detected...."[13] Another bad tendency is the inclination of bureaucracies to expand their authority. An agency may enhance its authority by dispensing with general rules and instead treating law as a divisible product, as orders which must be bargained for by those subject to the agency.[14]

§ 3.2 REGULATION ACCORDING TO RULES: THE ADMINISTRATIVE PROCEDURE ACT AND OTHER STATUTORY CONSIDERATIONS

While the Court in *Chenery* acted in view of constitutional considerations of due process, it nonetheless refused to preclude an agency from penalizing conduct that had not been proscribed by a standing rule. The Constitution, however, is not the only set of procedural constraints for agencies. The leading role in establishing such constraints has belonged to Congress, and as Congress has delegated legislative power to agencies it has enacted measures aimed at assuring that agencies use that power consistent with rule of law values.[1] Consistent with the idea of "standing rules promulgated and known to the people," Congress by Sec. 552 and Sec. 553 of the Administrative Procedure Act *requires* codification and

13. Yick Wo v. Hopkins, 118 U.S. 356, 373, 6 S.Ct. 1064, 1072, 30 L.Ed. 220 (1886). See also T. Lowi, The End of Liberalism: Ideology, Policy, and the Crisis of Public Authority 107 (1969).

14. As explained by an able player in the process:

Unless the administrator has effective bargaining power, little can be expected. He must have sanctions or desired favors which he can exchange for changes in practice.... He may be asked to exercise his discretion, for example, to accelerate the effective date of registration [of a new security]. Then, if the need of the registrant is sufficiently urgent, a trade may be consummated. In return for the favor of the administrator, the registration may amend his practice in the administrator's conception of justice and equity.

Wilson, The Dead Hand of Regulation, 25 Public Interest 39, 50 (1971) (quoting Abe Fortas).

§ 3.2

1. At least in part, this action in Congress was in response to a history of agency disregard of rule of law values. This history is summarized in L. Jaffe, Judicial Control of Administrative Agencies 61–62 (abridged ed. 1965). The particular instance recounted by Jaffe has to do with the major New Deal case of Panama Refining Co. v. Ryan, 293 U.S. 388, 55 S.Ct. 241, 79 L.Ed. 446 (1935). The various 546 codes of the National Recovery Administration were scattered about in various places so that there was a great deal of confusion as to exactly what was required of private industry. In *Panama Refining,* it turned out that the code provision in question had in fact been amended out of existence by a non-published action. Such was the chaos. A "valuable consequence of such Act," as Jaffe recounts it, "was the Federal Register Act [44 U.S.C.A. § 301] which provides for publication of Executive Orders and rules and regulations in the daily Federal Register." This act, as Jaffe further explained, provides "that no document required to be so published shall be valid against any person not having actual knowledge unless and until filed for publication." Id. See also Griswold, Government in Ignorance of the Law, 48 Har.L.Rev. 198 (1934).

The Administrative Procedure Act, as discussed above, specifically establishes a similar scheme for agency rules and standards. This Act was not, however, in force when the agency action in *SEC v. Chenery* occurred. Accordingly, the case was not decided under the Act and its rule of law provisions.

publication in the Federal Register of rules of conduct and provides that "a person may not in any manner be required to resort to, or be adversely affected by a matter required to be published in the Federal Register and not so published."[2] This codification and publication requirement was meant to bind agency to a regime of standing rules so as to better assure impartial agency action and to "require[] agencies to set out in advance the legal standards that will be applied so that 'actions can be guided and strategies planned.' "[3]

This statutory requirement of regulation according to rules would seem to be in no way abated by the *Chenery* decision, the reason being that the circumstances of that case arose prior to the Administrative Procedure Act and were not decided under the Act. *Chenery* should not, therefore, be controlling precedent respecting the Act. The decision that most closely addresses the codification and publication requirements of the Act, and affirms their rule of law basis, is *Morton v. Ruiz*.[4] In this case, the Supreme Court overturned a Bureau of Indian Affairs determination respecting eligibility for government benefits because that agency had failed to publish eligibility standards as required by the Act. Speaking against a bureaucratic tendency to regulate by "*ad hoc* determination" rather than by published rules, the Court asserted that "the agency must, at a minimum, let the standard be generally known so as to ensure that it is being applied consistently and so as to avoid both the reality and the appearance of arbitrary denial of benefits to potential beneficiaries."[5]

For reasons not altogether clear, the holding in *Morton v. Ruiz* in practice seems limited to circumstances where tangible economic goods are distributed by an agency. In these circumstances, a requirement of rules may be seen as especially necessary in order, as the Court said in *Morton v. Ruiz,* to "avoid both the reality and appearance of arbitrary denial of benefits to potential beneficiaries." In contrast, the "regulation according to published rules" holding of *Morton v. Ruiz* does not appear to have been extended to "command and control" orders (such as those of economic regulatory agencies like the Federal Trade Commission or Securities Exchange Commission) that are unadorned by such tangible benefits and that instead require or condemn certain conduct.[6] This limitation, though, of the codification and publication requirements of the Administrative Procedure Act to tangible economic benefits is a limitation of case law, and not of the Act. No such limitation is in the Act. Instead, Sec. 552(a)(1) requires publication and codification of all agency produced rules of conduct that may "adversely" affect a person.

2. 5 U.S.C.A. § 552(a).

3. Alliance for Cannabis Therapeutics v. Drug Enforcement Administration, 15 F.3d 1131, 1136 (D.C.Cir.1994). (1974) as it is discussed in the text above.

4. 415 U.S. 199, 94 S.Ct. 1055, 39 L.Ed.2d 270 (1974).

5. 415 U.S. at 231, 94 S.Ct. at 1072. See also Davidson v. Glickman, 169 F.3d 996 (5th Cir.1999).

6. See Gellhorn & Robinson, Perspectives on Administrative Law, 75 Colum.L.Rev. 771, 792–93 (1975).

§ 3.3 REGULATION ACCORDING TO RULES: DUE PROCESS

The courts have occasionally seen a connection between constitutional structure and the rule of law.[1] But when modern courts have sought to conform agency power to rule of law values, they have generally not referred to structure, and have instead referred to due process.[2] Why? Probably because of the easy open-endedness of the phrase and because of the historic relation of due process to fairness. In any event, due process has been the handle, as is shown in Justice Brennan's assertion that

> By demanding that government articulate its aims with a reasonable degree of clarity, the Due Process Clause ensures that state power will be exercised only on behalf of policies reflecting a conscious choice among competing social values; reduces the danger of caprice and discrimination in the administration of the laws; and permits meaningful judicial review of state actions.[3]

The larger part of the rule of law/due process cases has been in the context of agencies tending to treat law as a divisible product and of courts trying to block this tendency by prescribing general rules. In *Holmes v. New York Housing Authority,*[4] an agency had failed to promulgate rules to control the allocation of public housing among certain categories of applicants. The Second Circuit, on due process grounds, ordered the agency to promulgate such rules. The court stated:

> It hardly need be said that the existence of an absolute and uncontrolled discretion in an agency of government vested with the administration of a vast program, such as public housing, would be an intolerable invitation to abuse.... For this reason alone due process requires that selections among applicants be made in accordance with "ascertainable standards."

In *Hornsby v. Allen,*[5] the "intolerable invitation to abuse" was in the distribution of liquor licenses. To block this abuse, the court ordered the licensing agency to establish and publish general rules of eligibility for such licenses.

§ 3.3

1. *E.g.,* Yick Wo v. Hopkins, 118 U.S. 356, 369–70, 6 S.Ct. 1064, 1070–71, 30 L.Ed. 220 (1886).

2. In his thorough exposition on due process, Prof. Rubin concludes that in due process a "basic value is essentially the rule of law, that is, the treatment of individuals in accordance with legal standards." Rubin, Due Process in the Administrative State, 72 Cal.L.Rev. 1044, 1103 (1984).

3. Whisenhunt v. Spradlin, 464 U.S. 965, 969, 104 S.Ct. 404, 407, 78 L.Ed.2d 345 (1983) (dissenting).

4. Holmes v. New York City Housing Auth., 398 F.2d 262, 265 (2d Cir.1968).

5. 326 F.2d 605 (5th Cir.1964). See also White v. Roughton, 530 F.2d 750, 754 (7th Cir.1976) ("The requirements of due process include a determination of the issues according to articulated standards"); Mayer v. Wing, 922 F.Supp. 902, 910–12 (S.D.N.Y., 1996); Harnett v. Board of Zoning, 350 F.Supp. 1159, 1161 (D.Virgin Islands 1972). ("There is a tendency for regulatory systems which operate without clearly enunciated standards to be inherently irrational and arbitrary").

Using a due-process based prescription of standing rules, the courts, along with trying to assure evenhandedness, have also tried to assure a measure of stability in agency action. They have required agencies to develop, codify, and publish rules so that the private sector is informed of what it can expect from government and manage its affairs accordingly.[6] In this context, a requirement of rules has been described and applied as an aspect of a vagueness doctrine.

But unlike the usual vagueness doctrine case, the claim is not against the statute itself. Rather, the claim is against an agency, for its failure to render a vague statute more specific by implementing it through rules. In *Soglin v. Kauffman*,[7] the administration of the University of Wisconsin had expelled some students under a "misconduct" standard. Because "misconduct" was too vague to be a useful rule of conduct, the court overturned the University's action. As explained by the Court:

> No one disputes the power of the university to protect itself by means of disciplinary actions against disruptive students. Power to punish and the rules defining the power are not, however, identical. Power alone does not supply the standards needed to determine its application to types of behavior or specific instance of "misconduct."

* * *

Same as the codification and publication requirements of the Administrative Procedure Act, due process requirements of regulation according to standing rules have in practice been associated with distributions of tangible economic benefits, such as a license or welfare or a subsidy. These requirements do not appear to have been extended to "command and control" orders (such as those of economic regulatory agencies like the Federal Trade Commission or Securities Exchange Commission) that are unadorned by such tangible benefits and that instead require or condemn certain conduct.[8] Otherwise, due-process based rule of law requirements in practice relate to the level of government involved. The rule-of-law/due process cases generally involve state agencies. This may be happenstance. Or it may indicate that state agencies are looser in their regard for rule of law values. Or, more likely, these cases show that federal courts act against state agencies more confidently than they do against federal agencies.[9]

6. E.g., Clark v. Fremont, 377 F.Supp. 327, 335 (D.Neb.1974) (Due process violated absent "ascertainable standards" by which a licensee could assess "contemplated conduct").

7. 418 F.2d 163 (7th Cir.1969). See also White v. Roughton, 530 F.2d 750, 754 (7th Cir.1976) ("The requirements of due process include a determination of the issues according to articulated standards"); Mayer v. Wing, 922 F.Supp. 902, 910–12 (S.D.N.Y., 1996); Harnett v. Board of Zoning, 350 F.Supp. 1159, 1161 (D.Virgin Islands 1972). ("There is a tendency for regulatory systems which operate without clearly enunciated standards to be inherently irrational and arbitrary").

8. See Gellhorn & Robinson, Perspectives on Administrative Law, 75 Colum.L.Rev. 771, 792–93 (1975).

9. There are exceptions. In Mobil Oil Exploration and Producing v. FERC, 885 F.2d 209, 225–26 (5th Cir.1989), the Feder-

But in the range where the due process has been applied to require conformity to rule of law values, it has been strongly applied. Here, the courts have rejected arguments to the effect that a discretion to proceed by *ad hoc* orders rather than by rules is necessary to permit an agency to make decisions finely tuned to the facts and circumstances of an individual case. As stated by one court, this interest in fine tuning does not "outweigh the individual's interest in being protected from arbitrary and capricious decision making."[10]

Finally, the rule of law context of due process does not directly involve the usual use of due process, which is procedures and whether an individual has fairly been heard when the government acts against him personally. Still, there is a connection, between regulation according to rules and contemporary concerns about procedural protections and fair hearings. Procedures and hearings offer little protection without such rules and standards as might give content to the hearings. As the Fifth Circuit has so succinctly stated, "The idea of a hearing is fine. But what is to be heard?"[11]

al Energy Regulatory Commission had by adjudication established a certain requirement about time limits for selling natural gas. Because this requirement had been established by adjudication rather than rulemaking, the court ruled that the codification requirements of § 553 did not apply. Still, the court held that that the requirement should be published in the Federal Register. The legal basis that the court used was due process.

10. Baker–Chaput v. Cammett, 406 F.Supp. 1134, 1140 (D.N.H.1976). In this regard, the court explained that "to require the agency to formulate standards will neither force unrealistic rigidity in the content of these standards nor bring about administrative inefficiency." *Id.* See also Hill v. Federal Power Commission, 335 F.2d 355, 363 (5th Cir.1964).

11. Block v. Thompson, 472 F.2d 587, 588 (5th Cir.1973) *(per curiam)*. Somewhat more elaborately, the court in White v. Roughton, 530 F.2d 750, 754 (7th Cir.1976), in holding that a welfare program without standards violated due process explained that

> The requirements of due process include a determination of the issues according to articulated standards. The lack of such standards in this case deprives any hearing, whether before an agency or a court, of its meaning and value as an opportunity for the plaintiffs to prove their qualifications for assistance.

See also Raper v. Lucey, 488 F.2d 748 (1st Cir.1973).

Chapter 4

THE ZONE OF RULEMAKING

Table of Sections

Rulemaking is generally considered a superior process for agency-produced law in that it makes for better rules and, it is hoped, in some measure fills in for the loss of democratic representation entailed by delegation of legislative power to agency. In this latter respect, the courts commonly say that "The essential purpose of according § 553 notice and comment opportunities is to reintroduce public participation and fairness to affected parties after governmental authority has been delegated to unrepresentative agencies."[1] But however much the courts or anyone extols the virtue of rulemaking, the unfortunate fact is that in the decades since its inception the kinds of agency action subject to rulemaking have yet to be established with any confidence or security.

Indeed, this important area, the appropriate zone of rulemaking, has been described as "enshrouded in considerable smog," "tenuous,"

1. Dia Navigation Company v. Pomeroy, 34 F.3d 1255 (3d Cir., 1994).

"blurred," and "baffling."[2] The confusion that has been engendered is understandable when one considers that in this area as in few others, instrumentalism, in the form of the agency's wish to reach the result most consistent with its goals at the time, runs head on into the "inner moralities of law" (Lon Fuller's phrase). To the agency, the decisional processes of rulemaking may seem a waste of time and rule of law constraints—of no agency action except under codified and published rules—may seem to stymie its responsive action. Less commendably, the agency may not wish to have its policies exposed and questioned through the open and public processes of rulemaking.

Frequently, then, an agency may prefer to avoid rulemaking. Some courts read the Administrative Procedure Act to indulge this preference. These courts find that the Act gives agencies a sort of discretion respecting procedural modes that would allow them to avoid rulemaking. In contrast, other courts read the Act as establishing a zone in which rulemaking is mandatory. We will discuss these approaches in the next two sections, and this discussion will conform to the forms in which agency avoidance of rulemaking has presented itself. In one form, the problem is that of defining the kind of agency action that amounts to a rule so as to be subject to rulemaking. In its other form, the problem involves an alternative process to rulemaking: because an agency holds judicial as well as legislative powers, it has at hand adjudicatory processes as well as the legislative processes of rulemaking. Agencies have turned to these adjudicatory processes—and the incremental and *ad hoc* approach to regulation that they offer—as an alternative means of making rules.

§ 4.1 IDENTIFYING THE AGENCY ACTION SUBJECT TO RULEMAKING: WHAT IS A RULE?

The Supreme Court has recognized that as the agencies produce rules they are in the business of producing laws, of the same order as those made by Congress.[1] When an agency makes a rule, then, the applicability of a legislative process is naturally called into question, and under the Administrative Procedure Act that process is rulemaking as established by Sec. 553. A weakness, though, in this rather straightforward approach—that rulemaking is for making rules—is that in administrative law a consensus has not yet developed as to just when it is that an agency makes a rule.

In determining when an agency makes a rule, a good place to start is with some fairly secure propositions about laws (and a rule is a law). A law is a course of conduct prescribed by government for a class of

2. E.g., Community Nutrition Institute v. Young, 818 F.2d 943, 946 (D.C.Cir.1987).

§ 4.1

1. Immigration & Naturalization Service v. Chadha, 462 U.S. 919, 103 S.Ct. 2764, 77 L.Ed.2d 317 (1983).

people.[2] The rulemaking activity of an agency, therefore, is that agency action which *instills* such a course of conduct. Classically, government instills a course of conduct by means of a sanction. Drivers who exceed the speed limit are liable for the fine set out in the relevant statute or ordinance, and to avoid this sanction they generally stay under the limit. In administrative law, however, the sanction that can instill a course of conduct may be less formal and much more subtle.

A legislative body that operates within a separation of powers framework cannot implement the laws that it makes. Instead, it depends on the executive and judicial branches for that task. The legislature, therefore, must straightforwardly publish its laws in the canonical form of a statute. This formal publication is essential in order to tell the other branches of the conduct that they should prescribe. Agencies, however, as they may wish to implement a particular policy are not similarly encumbered by a dependence on other institutions. The whole power of government, its legislative, executive, and judicial power, is consolidated within the agency. Consequently, publication of rules formally designated as such is unnecessary in agency law making.

An agency that wishes to induce a certain course of conduct need not depend on prosecutorial or judicial bodies independent of it and thus need not formally communicate it wishes as by a formally designated law. The agency may only informally suggest a course of conduct, by a communiqué that it denotes as less than a rule of law and that has not been subjected to the prior public examination of the rulemaking process of Sec. 553, and then informally but effectively stand ready to enforce this suggestion by means of its own, self-contained, prosecutorial and adjudicatory power. The private sector knows this, and that the agency by its combined power can at least impose litigation costs should they act contrary to an agency-suggested course of conduct. Also, an agency often directly dispenses and controls things of value—licenses, subsidies, welfare, and so forth—and the recipients of these things simply cannot risk losing them by acting contrary to an agency recommendation.[3] So, like no other part of government an agency may if it wishes effectively make law in an informal and perhaps disguised manner.[4]

2. The Administrative Procedure Act follows this point, that a law is a course of conduct for a class, in that the Act distinguishes between rules (class-like agency action) and orders (agency action affecting) a person particularly. 5 U.S.C. Sec. 551(4), (6). See Sec. 4.5.3, infra.

3. American Trucking Ass'ns, Inc. v. Interstate Commerce Com'n, 659 F.2d 452, 471–72 (5th Cir.1981).

4. In this respect, Judge Mikva has described the possibilities of "agency gamesmanship" as follows:

> Policy or interpretive rules that are not "law" ... can nonetheless serve many of the same functions as substantive rules of law. If you are a regulated party, and the agency issues an interpretive rule or policy statement indicating its present view of the law, you will probably make serious efforts to comply with that rule even if it is not formally binding. At a minimum, the rule alerts you to the kind of conduct that the agency regards as worthy of prosecution; at a maximum, the rule may effectively dictate how the agency will conduct its adjudications.

JEM Broadcasting Co. v. FCC, 22 F.3d 320 (D.C.Cir.1994). Otherwise, the common observation is that an agency can regulate by means of "a raised eyebrow." E.g., E. Bannon, 2 A History of Broadcasting in the United States 29–35. For an instance of

An instance of this, and as well an instance of the ability of the courts to detect such *de facto* lawmaking, is provided by the Supreme Court in its 1941 decision in *Columbia Broadcasting System v. United States*.[5] The Federal Communications Commission, in what it characterized as an "expression of the general policy we will follow exercising our licensing power," had announced its disfavor of certain contractual relationships between local and network radio stations. When this action was challenged by the networks as being in effect an illegal rule, the Commission claimed that its action was merely a "policy statement" without the effect of law. The Commission claimed that it had simply stated its position with respect to future license renewal proceedings and that such a position had no present legal effect, and therefore was not a rule subject to review.

The Supreme Court, however, did not buy that argument, because it was about an artificial rather the real effect of the Commission's action. The reality was that broadcast stations, motivated by the risk of losing their licenses in renewal proceedings, would immediately conform to the Commission's "policy statement." Considering this "expected conformity," the Court found that the alleged policy statement in question was in its "practical operation" an agency-made rule of conduct. In this respect, the Court held that "the particular label placed upon it [the agency action] by the Commission is not necessarily conclusive, for it is the substance of what the Commission has purported to do and has done which is decisive."[6]

Because of the multitude of forms of agency action, this directive of the *Columbia Broadcasting System* case—to look not to labels but to the "practical operation" of an agency action—provides an excellent starting point for identifying the appropriate zone of rulemaking, and for defining the exceptions to rulemaking.

§ 4.2 THE STATUTORY EXCEPTIONS TO RULEMAKING

Persons who stand to be affected by an agency action are surely those "interested parties" to whom rights of participation in rulemaking, as provided by the Administrative Procedure Act, pertain. These persons, having the incentive to do so, can best be counted on to bring forward interests pertinent to the proposed rule and to provide useful data and

such regulation, where the FCC "suggested" that the major television networks institute a "family viewing" hour, see Writers Guild of America, West, Inc. v. Federal Communications Com'n, 423 F.Supp. 1064, 1072 (C.D.Cal.1976), reversed sub nom., Tandem Prods., Inc. v. Columbia Broadcasting Sys., Inc., 609 F.2d 355 (9th Cir.1979).

5. 316 U.S. 407, 62 S.Ct. 1194, 86 L.Ed. 1563 (1942).

6. Id. at 416, 62 S.Ct. at 1199. In *Immigration and Naturalization Service v. Chadha*, 462 U.S. 919, 952, 103 S.Ct. 2764, 2784, 77 L.Ed.2d 317 (1983).the Court reaffirmed that it is not form but the "character and effect" that counts in determining whether a governmental action amounts to a law. Referring to Congress, the Court approved the proposition that whether congressional acts are legislative depends not on form but upon "whether they contain matter which is properly to be regarded as legislative in its character and effect."

critical analysis of the rule. Also, basic concerns of fairness and acceptability require that those affected by an agency decision have some say in the formulation of it. Therefore, a policy of assuring that those persons affected by agency rules participate in their formulation guides the court as they try to identify the zone of rulemaking.[1]

Most often, this policy applies in relation to marking, and limiting, the exceptions to rulemaking. The Administrative Procedure Act excepts "interpretive rules, general statements of policy, or rules of agency organization, procedure, or practice" from rulemaking.[2] The latter two exceptions, for policy statements and procedural rules, are most often identified and isolated according the real-world effect of an agency action: if an agency action in effect instills a rule of conduct in the private sector, then the action is a rule of substance that *cannot* be excepted from rulemaking as a policy statement or procedural rule.[3]

The interpretive rule exception is, however, more complicated. An interpretive rule may reach primary behavior; that is, it may present a binding course of conduct. Nonetheless, the rule need not be set down for rulemaking, the reason being that the rule of conduct presented by the rule is not the product of the rule itself. Rather, the interpretive rule merely "reminds" the public of, or perhaps "clarifies" a conduct already prescribed by a previous statute or rule.[4]

§ 4.2.1 Procedural Rules

The "procedural rules" exception is established by Sec. 553(b) as it exempts "rules of agency organization, procedure, or practice" from the notice and comment requirements of rulemaking.[5] This exception, as its text denotes, generally involves matters relating to the conduct of agency proceedings and to the internal organization of agencies. As stated by the court of appeals for District of Columbia Circuit, a "useful articulation of the exemption's critical feature is that it covers agency actions that do not themselves alter the rights or interests of parties, although it may alter the manner in which the parties present themselves or their viewpoints to the agency."[6] Agency action that does not alter rights and

§ 4.2

1. The courts apply the Administrative Procedure Act's rulemaking requirement "in light of" the "policy goals of maximum participation and full information." American Hospital Ass'n v. Bowen, 834 F.2d 1037, 1044 (D.C.Cir.1987). To "advance these purposes, the Administrative Procedure Act broadly defines rules subject to Administrative Procedure Act § 553 procedures and carves out only limited exceptions." Batterton v. Marshall, 648 F.2d 694, 703–04 (D.C.Cir.1980).

2. 5 U.S.C. § 553(b).

3. As expressed by the District of Columbia Circuit, these exemptions to rulemaking for policy statements and procedural rule are "limited situations where substantive rights are not at stake." American Hospital Ass'n v. Bowen, 834 F.2d 1037, 1045 (D.C.Cir.1987).

4. Essentially, an interpretive rule is "hortatory and instructional." Gibson Wine Co. v. Snyder, 194 F.2d 329, 331 (D.C.Cir. 1952). In *Gibson,* the court distinguished between agency actions "which create law, usually implementary to an existing law;" & interpretive rules, which "are statements as to what an administrative officer thinks the statute or regulation means."

5. 5 U.S.C. § 553(b).

6. American Hosp. Ass'n v. Bowen, 834 F.2d 1037, 1047 (D.C.Cir.1987); JEM Broadcasting v. FCC, 22 F.3d 320 (D.C.Cir. 1994).

interests does not, not in the judgment of Congress, "merit the administrative burdens of public input proceedings." [7]

An illustration of the "cannot alter rights or interests" measure of procedural rules is provided by *Pharmaceutical Manufacturers Ass'n v. Finch.*[8] The Food, Drug, and Cosmetic Act had been amended to require that the "effectiveness" of new drugs be established by "substantial evidence." Under this amendment, the Food and Drug Administration, without prior public participation, issued regulations prescribing test procedures for determining the effectiveness of drugs. The agency contended that inasmuch as it had denoted the rules as "interpretive and procedural" it was exempt from rulemaking requirements. The court disagreed. Its starting point was that the agency characterization of its action—"a facile semantic distinction"—was not dispositive, and indeed did little to "clarify whether the regulations were subject to [rulemaking]." Instead, the "basic purpose" of rulemaking considered in light of the rule's "impact on the regulated industry" was the better approach.

Using this more pragmatic approach, the court found that the regulations were "pervasive in their scope and have an immediate and substantial impact" on the way that drug companies "conduct their everyday business." The standards, as the court noted, applied to more than 2,000 drug products and "place[d] all of them in jeopardy, subject to summary removal by order of the FDA." Otherwise, the court noted that there was "considerable confusion" as to the substantive validity of the regulation and that many questions that had arisen might have been avoided had the agency educated itself through rulemaking. Consequently, on the basis that the drug companies were "interested parties" who were assured rights of participation by Sec. 553, the court overturned the agency action because of its violation of those rights.

That a procedural rule may not alter primary conduct—the way people and firms go about their business—is also shown by *National Association of Home Health Agencies v. Schweiker.*[9] The Medicare Act provides for reimbursement to "home health agencies" (firms that provide at-home health care and that are referred to as "HHA's"). Typically, the amount of reimbursement to an HHA is determined by "intermediaries" selected by the HHA. The Secretary of Health and Human Services, however, issued a regulation in which it itself designated the intermediaries to be used by HHA's in determining reimbursement. Certain HHA's then claimed that the regulation was invalid in that it had been promulgated without affording them a right of prior participation in forming the rule as provided by Sec. 553. The Secretary, however, argued that they had no such right because the rule related to the manner in which reimbursements were paid. The rule, therefore, was procedural and thus exempt from rulemaking.

7. United States Dept. of Labor v. Kast Metals Corp., 744 F.2d 1145, 1153 (5th Cir. 1984).

8. 307 F.Supp. 858 (D.Del.1970).

9. 690 F.2d 932 (D.C.Cir.1982).

The court of appeals for the District of Columbia Circuit rejected this defense and ordered rulemaking, because the rule "substantially affected" the business interests of the HHA's. Among other things, these companies would have to scrap present electronic billing systems and to train new personnel, and compliance costs would be several million dollars for the industry. While those costs might not have been sufficient "to persuade the Secretary to rescind the [rule], the potential impact [was] such that the fairness element of Sec. 553 requires that HHA's involved be given a chance to present their case to the Secretary before he acts."

§ 4.2.2 General Statements of Policy

The range of the exemption for policy statements is not defined by the Administrative Procedure Act.[10] The courts, however, have roughly but usefully identified this exception in terms of what it may *not* be. A policy-statement "does not establish a 'binding norm' "and "is marked by the absence" of a practical alteration of "existing rights and obligations."[11] If the statement so alters existing rights and obligations, then persons so affected should have had the chance "as interested parties" to participate in the formulation of the alleged "policy."[12]

In *Lewis–Mota v. Secretary of Labor,* the Second Circuit reviewed certain changes—about job requirements for aliens seeking a "permanent resident" status—made by the Secretary of Labor without rulemaking.[13] Prior to these changes, the Secretary had published schedules listing occupations in which labor was in short supply, and an alien merely had to submit a general statement of his qualification for such an occupation. Importantly, the alien did not have to show that he had received a specific job offer. The Secretary, however, in what he characterized as a general statement of policy, eliminated this practice and required aliens to show proof of specific job offers in order to qualify as permanent residents. On review, the court noted that "the particular label ... is not, for our purposes, conclusive; rather, it is what the agency does in fact." The court then found that the agency action was outside the policy-statement exception and therefore subject to rulemaking. The court explained:

10. The Sec. 553 exception for general statements of policy, like the other exceptions, is not defined by the Administrative Procedure Act itself. The Attorney General's Report does contain some language describing a policy statement, but this description relates to publication requirements for administrative agencies, and is an argument for requiring publication of a policy statement. Administrative Procedure in Government Agencies, Report of the Committee on Administrative Procedure, Appointed by the Attorney General 26–27 (1941).

11. Iowa Power and Light Co. v. Burlington Northern, Inc., 647 F.2d 796, 811 (8th Cir.1981), cert. denied 455 U.S. 907, 102 S.Ct. 1253, 71 L.Ed.2d 445 (1982).

12. Pickus v. U.S. Board of Parole, 507 F.2d 1107, 1112 (D.C.Cir.1974) ("The outer boundary of the General Policy exemption derives from the Congressional purpose in enacting 553—that the interested public should have an opportunity to participate, and the agency should be fully informed, before rules having such substantial impact are promulgated").

13. 469 F.2d 478 (2d Cir.1972).

> We look then to what the [agency] in fact did. We find that it changed existing rights and obligations by requiring aliens of the class of appellants to submit proof of specific job offers as well as a statement of their qualification; it thereby made it more difficult for employers to fill vacancies in the occupations no longer pre-certified. By virtue of this substantial impact both upon the aliens and employers, notice and opportunity for comment by the public should first be provided.

Because it shows how the courts can examine the language and structure of a professed policy statement to determine its actual, real world effect, the District of Columbia Circuit opinion in *Pickus v. United States Board of Parole* is another instructive case.[14] The Parole Board had issued guidelines specifying many of the factors that it would use in deciding whether to parole prisoners and it had characterized these guidelines as "general statements of policy." But considering the language, the structure, and the effect of the guidelines, the court of appeals for the District of Columbia Circuit disagreed. The guidelines, the court said, "were of a kind calculated to have a substantial effect on ultimate parole decisions" and "cannot help but focus the decision maker's attention on the Board-approved criteria." The guidelines "narrow[ed] [the decision maker's] field of vision" and minimiz[ed] the influence of other factors whose significance might have been differently articulated had [Sec. 553] been followed.

The circumstances in which the policy statement exception may rightfully be claimed are illustrated by the Eighth Circuit decision in *Iowa Power & Light Co. v. Burlington Northern, Inc.*[15] The Interstate Commerce Commission by a "policy statement" had stated that it would determine on a case-by-case basis the reasonableness of contract rates between railroads and shippers. The railroads, however, claimed that the statement amounted to a rule that should have been set down for rulemaking. The court of appeals disagreed, because the statement "in no way established a binding norm for future rate cases, but instead left the Commission free to exercise considerable discretion" as to the propriety of a rate. The statement in question did not refer to the substance of agency rate determinations. Instead, it merely referred to the form—a case-by-case evaluation—in which the determinations would be made. Moreover, the railroads had made no showing as to how the action could in any significant way affect their primary behavior. Therefore, the court ruled the Administrative Procedure Act did not require rulemaking.

§ 4.2.3 Interpretive Rules

Unlike procedural and policy rules, an interpretive rule properly contains a course of conduct. Still, this rule is exempted from rulemak-

14. 507 F.2d 1107 (D.C.Cir.1974).

15. 647 F.2d 796 (8th Cir.1981), cert. denied 455 U.S. 907, 102 S.Ct. 1253, 71 L.Ed.2d 445 (1982).

ing, the reason being that the course of conduct contained in the rule is derivative. An interpretive rule is one that describes, clarifies, and reminds the public of a statutory standard or a pre-existing rule.[16] Often, the interpretive rule exception is applied when Congress has not delegated broadly but has itself prescribed the rule of conduct in question. The agency may present this rule, perhaps with some interpretation problems worked out, to the public; still, the rule is *not* the agency's own doing.[17] In this situation, where the agency is not itself making law, rulemaking would be superfluous, and so it is not required.[18]

For the courts, then, the question is not, (as with the policy statement or procedural rules exceptions), whether the agency action in question amounts to a rule of conduct. That interpretive rules contain rules of conduct is a given. The question is whether the agency has itself made that rule or whether it is merely presenting and perhaps clarifying a rule made by Congress.[19] In *Cabais v. Egger*,[20] Congress had by statute required that pension benefits be offset against a person's unemployment compensation. In a letter that it characterized as an interpretive ruling, the Department of Labor informed the states of some of their responsibilities under this amendment. Persons whose unemployment compensation would suffer by an offset for pensions claimed that this letter was invalid because its content should have been the product of rulemaking. For the most part, the court in *Cabais* rejected this claim, because "the letter simply construes the language and intent of the [relevant statutes] and 'reminds' the states of 'existing duties.' " For example, the letter dealt with "a prorating [against unemployment compensation] on a weekly basis of pensions received on a monthly basis." The court found that this was simply an interpretation of the

16. Chemical Waste Management, Inc. v. U.S. EPA, 873 F.2d 1477, 1482 (D.C.Cir. 1989) ("In general ... our cases ... have emphasized the distinction between rules which create new legal obligations and those which simply restate or clarify existing statutes or regulations"); British Caledonian Airways, Ltd. v. CAB, 584 F.2d 982, 989–90 (D.C.Cir.1978). See also Chamber of Commerce v. OSHA, 636 F.2d 464, 469 (D.C.Cir.1980) (interpretive rules "only provide a clarification of statutory language ... the interpreting agency only 'reminds affected parties of existing duties' "); Guardian Federal Savings and Loan Ass'n v. Federal Savings and Loan Insurance Corp., 589 F.2d 658, 664 (D.C.Cir.1978) ("an interpretive rule is merely a clarification or explanation of an existing statute or rule").

17. Syncor v. Shalala, 127 F.3d 90 (D.C.Cir.1997) ("The legal norm is one that Congress has devised; the agency does not purport to modify that norm, in other words, to engage in lawmaking"); Hoctor v. Department of Agriculture, 82 F.3d 165 (7th Cir. 1996); Gibson Wine Co. v. Snyder, 194 F.2d 329, 331 (D.C.Cir.1952).

18. "The function of Sec. 553's first exemption, that for interpretive rules, is to allow agencies to explain ambiguous terms in legislative enactments without having to undertake cumbersome proceedings." American Hospital Ass'n v. Bowen, 834 F.2d 1037, 1045 (D.C.Cir.1987).

19. As noted by the third circuit in Dia Navigation Co. v. Pomeroy, 34 F.3d 1255, 1264 (3d Cir.1994):

> What distinguishes interpretive from legislative rules is the legal base upon which the rule rests. If the rule is based on specific statutory provisions, and its validity stands or falls on the correctness of the agency's interpretation of those provisions, it is an interpretive rule. If, however, the rule is based on an agency's power to exercise its judgment as to how best to implement a general statutory mandate, the rule is likely a legislative one.

20. 690 F.2d 234 (D.C.Cir.1982).

statute's requirement of an offset of pensions "reasonably attributable to such week."[21]

The clearest instance in which an agency is itself prescribing new rules, so that the interpretive rule exception should *not* apply, is where Congress has established broad statutory standards. And perhaps (but not necessarily) specifically extended a rulemaking power to the agency: By such authorization of rulemaking, Congress may have acknowledged that as the agency implements a statute it will be making new law as opposed to interpreting and applying the statute. In *Chamber of Commerce v. OSHA,*[22] the head of the Occupational Safety and Health Administration announced in a speech that a failure of employers to pay their employees for time spent accompanying an agency inspector during a "walkaround" inspection of the work place would be prosecuted by the agency as a "discrimination" against these employees—respecting their exercise of rights created by Occupational Safety and Health Act—prohibited by the Act. One month later, this requirement was published in the Federal Register and made retroactive to the date of the speech.

The Occupational Safety and Health Administration had not, however, subjected this "walkaround pay" rule to rulemaking. Instead, the agency characterized its action as merely its "interpretation" of the statutory prohibition of discrimination, and therefore not an independent exercise of lawmaking power such as to be subject to rulemaking. On review, the court of appeals disagreed. It found that the agency was not merely interpreting a pre-existing standard created by Congress, but was instead using the broad discretionary power conveyed to it by Congress to create a new rule of conduct for the regulated sector. As explained by the court, the "walkaround-pay regulation does not merely explain the statute, the effect of an interpretive rule." Instead, the rule in question "effectively enunciates a new requirement heretofore nonexistent," and the Occupation Safety and Health Administration was "exercising the authority Congress delegated to it to 'fill up the details' by establishment of administrative rules and regulations...."[23]

21. 690 F.2d at 238. The court did, however, find that certain parts of the letter "impose[d] an obligation on the states not found in the statute itself" and was not, therefore, interpretive. The parts that established formulae for determining individual contributions to pension funds and that determined individual contributions to pension funds imposed obligations not found in the statute and thus were subject to rulemaking.

22. 636 F.2d 464 (D.C.Cir.1980).

23. 636 F.2d at 471–72. (J. Bazleon, concurring). See also Syncor v. Shalala, 127 F.3d 90 (D.C.Cir.1997); Southern California Aerial Advertisers' Ass'n v. FAA, 881 F.2d 672 (9th Cir.1989); Credit Union Nat. Ass'n v. National Credit Union Admin. Bd., 573 F.Supp. 586 (D.D.C.1983). In the *Credit Union National Ass'n* case, Congress had granted a federal agency broad authority to superintend the liquidation of insolvent federal credit unions. In carrying out this responsibility, the agency had established certain priorities for paying the creditors of an insolvent credit union. The agency characterized this schedule of priorities as consisting of "interpretive" rules, and did not follow rulemaking procedures. The court, however, rejected this characterization, stating that the rules' true nature could not be "disguised by the simple semantic maneuver of claiming it 'clarifies or explains,'" In this regard, the court noted that the rules: (1) had an undeniable "substantial impact" on a class consisting of creditors affected by the priorities; and (2) "implemented" a statute as opposed to merely clarifying a pre-existing statutory standard.

§ 4.3 LOCATING THE ZONE: PRAGMATICS VERSUS THE "FORCE OF LAW" APPROACH TO RULEMAKING

As shown in the previous section, courts tend to determine the exceptions to rulemaking pragmatically, in light of the context and effect of agency action. They look to this context and effect to determine whether or not the agency action has instilled or is likely to instill a course of conduct across a regulated sector. They consider that such a course of conduct is the hallmark of a rule that should been subjected to the open processes of Sec. 553. In this respect, the courts explain that "When an agency action has 'palpable effects' upon the regulated industry and the public in general, it is necessary to expose that action 'to the test of prior examination and comment by the affected parties.' "[1] Or, as explained by the District of Columbia Circuit in 1999, when an agency action in effect has a "substantial impact" upon private parties and "puts a stamp of [agency] approval upon on a given type of behavior," it is a rule subject to rulemaking.[2] The indices by which these rule-like effects are determined are various: by whether the private sector, to avoid litigation costs or the risk of losing a license or other benefit controlled by the agency, will conform to an agency-suggested course of action; by whether, as in *Pickus v. United States Board of Parole*,[3] the

For an excellent discussion of how and when statutory terms may, 0r may not, general legislative rules, see Hoctor v. Department of Agriculture, 82 F.3d 165 (7th Cir.1996).

An opinion by Judge Williams in American Mining Congress v. Mine Safety & Health Admin., 995 F.2d 1106 (D.C.Cir. 1993) presented a four-part test for determining whether an alleged interpretive rule was that or was instead an agency-made rule that should have subjected to rulemaking. This test is "(1) whether in the absence of the rule there would not be an adequate legislative basis of enforcement action or other agency action to confer benefits or ensure performance of duties, (2) whether the agency has published the rule in the Code of Federal Regulations, (3) whether the agency has explicitly invoked its general legislative authority, or (4) whether the rule effectively amends a prior legislative rule. If the answer to any of these questions is affirmative, we have a legislative, not an interpretive rule."

§ 4.3

1. National Helium Corp. v. FEA, 569 F.2d 1137, 1146 (Emer.Ct.App.1977). In the past, this pragmatic approach has been referred to as the "substantial impact" test. Today, though, courts tend to follow a pragmatic approach without referring to it as a "substantial impact" test, the reason probably being that of avoiding the academic criticism, which will shortly be discussed above that was heaped on the "substantial impact" test. Today, the courts avoid this name but follow the method.

2. Chamber of Commerce v. Department of Labor, 174 F.3d 206, 211 (D.C.Cir. 1999).

3. 507 F.2d 1107 (D.C.Cir.1974). This case is discussed at Sec. 4.2.3, supra. This same approach, that of a textual analysis of an agency statement to determine whether its officials might well understood the statement as establishing criteria that they were obliged to enforce, was followed in *Community Nutrition Institute v. Young*, 818 F.2d 943 (D.C.Cir.1987). The Food and Drug Administration had published certain "action levels" that notified food producers of allowable levels of contaminants. It claimed that inasmuch as these "action levels" had been denoted as policy statements they did "not bind courts, food producers, or the FDA." However, the court of appeals for the District of Columbia Circuit instead found that the announced contaminants levels were rules subject to rulemaking. The alleged "policy statement" had been stated in mandatory terms; the agency had said that food with contaminants in excess of the announced levels "will be deemed to be adulterated." In this light, "the agency's own words strongly suggest[ed] that action levels are not musings about what the FDA

agency by the terms of an alleged policy statement has so committed itself to enforcing the statement that it has made a rule; or by whether, as in *United States Telephone Ass'n v. FCC*,[4] an agency by its practice has shown that it will in fact enforce a purportedly non-binding policy position. True, the assessment of whether an agency action in fact instills a course of conduct is at time difficult. It turns on various contextual factors and is "extraordinarily case specific."[5] On the other hand, the underlying theory is straightforward.

A considerable level of theoretical complexity has, however, been sustained in that courts have struggled with a choice between this pragmatic approach and a competing measure of rulemaking. This other measure is most commonly known as the "force of law" test.[6] In this test, the word "force" is misleading, because it has little to do with the actual effect of an agency action and little to do with whether an action in fact causes people to act in a certain way.

Instead, the force of law approach is rather a formal method. It is said to require two separate conditions. First, Congress must formally denote a grant of rulemaking power to an agency.[7] Such a grant of power would be accomplished by statutory language stating that the agency may implement a statute by such rules and regulations as are consistent with it. An instance of such a statutory grant is Sec.14(b) of the Securities Exchange Act of 1934, which forbids certain persons "to give, or to refrain from giving a proxy" contrary "to such rules and regulations as the Commission may prescribe." This is a clear instance of formally denoted rulemaking power. The fact is, though, that such a formal delegation of rulemaking power is unnecessary, and not always

might do in the future but rather that they set a precise level of . . . contamination that FDA deems permissible."

4. United States Telephone Ass'n v. FCC, 28 F.3d 1232 (D.C.Cir.1994). The FCC labeled a certain schedule of fines as non-binding guidelines that constituted a policy statement. The court noted, though, that in "the schedule of fines has been employed in over 300 cases and only in 8 does the Commission even claim that it departed from the schedule." This being the case, the court held that the alleged policy statement was in fact a rule of conduct for which the rulemaking procedures of Sec. 553 were necessary. In this case, the court also looked to the text of the purported "guidelines" and found that it was so detailed and specific that it was "hard to imagine" that the agency would publish it "if it did not intend to use that framework to cabin its discretion."

5. American Hospital Ass'n v. Bowen, 834 F.2d 1037, 1045 (D.C.Cir.1987).

6. It is also known as the "legal effects" test.

7. 2 K. Davis, Administrative Law Treatise 7.8, at 36 (2d ed. 1979). See also American Postal Workers Union v. United States Postal Service, 707 F.2d 548, 558 (D.C.Cir.1983), cert. denied 465 U.S. 1100, 104 S.Ct. 1594, 80 L.Ed.2d 126 (1984). A moderate statement of this condition, and perhaps the origin of it, is found in Ernst Freund's work on administrative power:

> All these types of unquestionably valid rulemaking may be supposed to be covered by the ordinary delegation of power to make rules and regulations to carry a statute into effect; and the power probably exists without express delegation, a possible difference being that the express delegation makes the rule binding upon the administrative authority while it stands whereas a rule voluntarily made may perhaps be looked upon in the same manner as "administrative rules" are looked upon in courts of equity, namely as rules of guidance by which the authority is not rigorously bound.

E. Freund, Administrative Powers Over Persons and Property 215 (1928).

the case. *Whenever* Congress, as it usually does, broadly delegates substantive power to an agency, the agency as it implements that power necessarily gains the power to make rules. As the courts have noted, "The power of an administrative agency to administer a congressionally created ... program necessarily requires the formulation of policy and the making of rules to fill any gap left, implicitly or explicitly, by Congress."[8] The Federal Trade Commission is delegated the power to proscribe "unfair methods of competition" and "deceptive acts or practices" in commerce. In its well-known opinion in *National Petroleum Refiners Ass'n v. FTC*,[9] the District of Columbia Circuit held that the Commission had the power to make and to publish rules of substance notwithstanding that Congress had not specifically granted it a rulemaking power. The "denoted grant of legislative power" condition to the force of law approach is, then, wrong in its premises. This particular fault, though, seems insignificant. The reason is that the courts—probably in tacit recognition of the futility of the exercise—easily imply, or else overlook, such a grant.

The larger problem with the force of law approach lies in its second condition, that an agency must denote a rule as a "legislative" rule and not as something else such as a policy statement.[10] The logic of this condition seems to be this. The "legislative rule" characterization signifies that the agency considers the rule to be an "authoritative" subset of the statute that the agency implements. The rule is said to be authoritative in that in an enforcement action, the only matter open for question is whether the conduct in question violates the "legislative" rule. Whether the rule itself is legitimate, whether it is within the agency's delegated power, is not open for question. Lesser agency positions, such as interpretive rules or policy statements, are not similarly authoritative (the legitimacy of the rule is open to question), and are therefore said to be without the force of law. This being the case, these are not subject to rulemaking.[11] That it is how the force of law test goes. However, this

8. Morton v. Ruiz, 415 U.S. 199, 231, 94 S.Ct. 1055, 1072, 39 L.Ed.2d 270 (1974). Cf. Chevron, U.S.A., Inc. v. Natural Resources Defense Council, Inc., 467 U.S. 837, 104 S.Ct. 2778, 81 L.Ed.2d 694 (1984) (recognizing that Congress may implicitly, by virtue of broad delegations, delegate a rulemaking power to agencies). See also McGowan, Reflections on Rulemaking Review, 53 Tul.L.Rev 681, 683 (1979) ("administration [of broad statutes] inevitably involves lawmaking...."). The breadth of rulemaking power that is the inevitable result of delegation of substantive power to an agency varies, of course, with the breadth of the delegation.

9. 482 F.2d 672 (D.C.Cir.1973).

10. K. Davis, Administrative Law Sec. 6.18 (1st ed. Supp.1970) ("A rule which the agency designates as interpretive and as 'merely declarative of the commission's view' is surely an interpretive rule"). A more moderate statement of the weight given the agency's own characterization of its action is that "The crucial question is whether the agency intends to exercise delegated [lawmaking] power ... and the intent usually can best be found in what the agency says at the time of issuing the rules." Firestone Synthetic Rubber & Latex Co. v. Marshall, 507 F.Supp. 1330, 1334 (E.D.Tex. 1981).

11. As explained in the leading "force of law" case:

> In subsequent administrative proceedings involving a substantive rule, the issues are whether the adjudicated facts conform to the rule and whether the rule should be waived or applied in that particular instance.
>
> A general statement of policy on the other hand, does not establish a "binding norm." It is not finally determina-

central part of it, that a rule not formally designated a legislative rule is without an authoritative and substantive effect, is rather artificial. This artificiality, as we have said, was identified and disallowed in *Columbia Broadcasting System v. United States* where the Supreme Court held that "the particular label placed upon it [the agency action] by the Commission is not necessarily conclusive, for it is the substance of what the Commission has purported to do and has done which is decisive."[12]

When an agency publishes a rule of substantive content, the regulated sector understands that the agency is likely to enforce the stated position against them, whether or not the agency has characterized its position as a "legislative rule."[13] This private sector is, therefore, likely

tive of the issues or rights to which it is addressed. The agency cannot apply or rely upon a general statement of policy as law because a general statement of policy only announces what the agency seeks to establish as policy.... When the agency applies the policy in a particular situation, it must be prepared to support the policy just as if the policy statement had never been issued.

Pacific Gas & Electric Co. v. Federal Power Commission, 506 F.2d 33, 38–39 (D.C.Cir.1974). The force of law distinction between legislative or substantive rules and all other rules and policy statements is perhaps best explained by way of illustration. The Federal Trade Commission, which has the power to prohibit "unfair or deceptive acts or practices in commerce," may promulgate as a legislative rule a rule defining a gas station's failure to post octane ratings as an unfair or deceptive act or practice. In a Commission enforcement against a gas station for violation of this octane-posting rule, that station, because the rule has been designated as legislative (and thus authoritative), will not be allowed to argue against that rule's predicate, that the failure to post octane ratings is a deceptive act or practice. Rather, all the hearing can be about is whether the gas station has violated the standard of conduct contained in the rule: did it, or did it not, post octane ratings? In this sense, a legislative rule is said to have the force of law.

In contrast, interpretive rules, or general statements of policy, are not supposed to be authoritative, and to have the force of law. Consequently, if an agency designates a rule as interpretive, and a person acts contrary to the standard of conduct expressed in it, the agency in an enforcement action must this time prove that the defendant's act violated the statute under which the interpretive rule was issued. Thus, if our octane posting rule is designated as interpretive, the gas station in an enforcement action is free to argue that a failure to post octane ratings is not an unfair or deceptive act or practice under the Federal Trade Commission Act.

12. 316 U.S. 407, 62 S.Ct. 1194, 86 L.Ed. 1563 (1942).

13. Within an agency, its officials are likely to treat a policy statement as a binding rule. This tendency has been explained as follows:

> [the policy statement thus will come to be treated as binding in practical sense.... The ordinary dynamics of bureaucratic behavior make this a highly probable prospect for any given policy statement. Those who make adjudicatory decisions will tend to apply policy statements in the same routinely controlling way as they apply legislative rules.

Robert A. Anthony & David A. Codevilla, Pro. Ossification: A Harder Look at Agency Policy Statements, 31 Wake Forest L.Rev. 667, 678 (1996).

On review of agency adjudication, courts tend to disregard the labels and to treat legislative rules and policy statements alike and to apply about the same standard of review to each. Indeed, even at the time the Administrative Procedure Act was enacted, the distinction in terms of judicial review between legislative and non-legislative rules had become "blurred" and useless. According to the Attorney General Report on which the Act was based:

> This distinction between statutory [substantive] regulations and interpretive regulations is, however, blurred by the fact that the courts pay great deference to the interpretive regulations of administrative agencies, especially where these have been followed for a long time. In upholding certain regulations issued by the Commissioner of In-

to adjust its conduct accordingly. This point seems illustrated by what is probably the leading case for the force of law approach, the District of Columbia Circuit opinion in *Pacific Gas & Electric Co. v. Federal Power Commission*.[14]

This case involved the Federal Power Commission's choice between regulatory alternatives for curtailing the use of natural gas in times of shortages. Such curtailment could be based either on contract rights of customers or on the Commission's assessment of the utility of the "end use" of the gas. In a "statement of policy" issued without rulemaking, the Commission chose the latter route and announced that curtailment of natural gas usage was to be based on the Commission's view of the utility of its end use. Customers whose contract rights suffered under this approach sought to overturn it because of the Commission's failure to follow rulemaking procedures. The court, however, found that rulemaking was not required. Because the Commission had characterized its action as a policy statement, this action could not, as the court saw it, have the requisite "force of law." As explained by the court, the Commission had merely "announce[d] the general policy which the Commission hopes to establish in [these] subsequent proceedings."

More likely, the agency announcement had the immediate effect of causing members of the regulated sector to forgo valuable contract rights. They would give up these rights rather than suffer the litigation costs necessary to challenge the Commission's position, especially so given the probability—in light of the Commission's already announced position—of losing. Consequently, natural gas users "had to begin an immediate search for alternative energy sources, to negotiate long-range commitments for other fuels and to purchase equipment for burning them."[15] These parties were surely the "interested parties" whose needs and analysis should have been included in the Commission's decisional processes by means of rulemaking. Such participation was, however, denied by the route of characterization, by the agency denoting its action as a policy statement. In this respect, and as one court has explained, "all administrative agencies easily could circumvent the provisions of the Administrative Procedure Act by promulgating substantive rules or eligibility requirements in internal 'staff manuals' and designating them to be policy statements or interpretive rules."[16]

ternal Revenue, the Supreme Court has stated that "it is the settled rule that the practical interpretation of an ambiguous or doubtful statute that has been acted upon by officials charged with its administration will not be disturbed except for weighty reasons."

Attorney General's Comm. on Admin. Proced., Final Report, S.Doc. No. 8, 77th Cong., 1st Sess., 100 (1941) (emphasis added). This same point has more recently been made by Justice Scalia, as he explained that "In an era when our treatment of agency positions is governed by *Chevron*, the 'legislative rules vs. other actions' dichotomy ... is an anachronism." EEOC v. Arabian American Oil Co., 499 U.S. 244, 260, 111 S.Ct. 1227, 1236, 113 L.Ed.2d 274 (1991) (concurring)].

14. 506 F.2d 33 (D.C.Cir.1974).

15. Asimow, Public Participation in the Adoption of Interpretive Rules and Policy Statements, 75 Mich.L.Rev. 520, 536–37 (1977).

16. Herron v. Heckler, 576 F.Supp. 218, 231 (N.D.Cal.1983) For a discussion and criticism of such "de facto rulemak-

In the years succeeding years the *Pacific Gas & Electric*, judges acknowledged that that the force of law approach of that case indulged "agency gamesmanship" wherein:

> [P]olicy or interpretive rules that are not "law" . . . can nonetheless serve many of the same functions as substantive rules of law. If you are a regulated party, and the agency issues an interpretive rule or policy statement indicating its present view of the law, you will probably make serious efforts to comply with that rule even if it is not formally binding.[17]

The force of law test, though, does provide a "bright-line" measure of the applicability of rulemaking[18] whereas a more pragmatic, effects oriented test, is, as we said, hard to apply. Also, the force of law approach permits a more active government; it allows the agency to act where it might be unwilling to do so if the basis of its action was subject to the inconvenience and delay, and as well the examination and exposure, of rulemaking. No one, of course, thinks that avoidance of public examination is in and of itself a good reason for agencies to avoid rulemaking. However, the rest of it, the delay and decisions costs of rulemaking, have somewhat blunted the initial enthusiasm for the process, and perhaps this disappointment has contributed somewhat to such backing as the agency-friendly force of law test has gained.

For the most part, though, courts, out of considerations of fairness to affected parties and of what these parties might contribute to agency proceedings, have largely been unwilling to allow agencies to use the force of law approach to avoid rulemaking, not when for all practical purposes the agency has in fact induced a course of conduct in the private sector. In the 1970's the courts commenced to turn away from the force of law method and its "facile semantic distinctions."[19] Instead, they looked, as we have said, to the practical effect of an agency action and to whether in effect the action amounted to an agency prescribed rule of conduct.[20] In this regard, the Second Circuit announced that

ing," see "The Regulatory Reform Act," Sen. Judiciary Comm., Rep. No. 97–284, 97th Cong., 1st Sess. 111 (1981).

See also Anthony, Interpretive Rules, Policy Statements, Guidances, Manuals and the Like—Should Agencies Use Them to Bind the Public?, 1992 Duke L.J. 181.

17. JEM Broadcasting Co. v. FCC, 22 F.3d 320 (D.C.Cir.1994).

18. In Community Nutrition Institute v. Young, 818 F.2d 943 (D.C.Cir.1987), Judge Starr, dissenting, acknowledged that "the law has certainly evolved since *Pacific Gas*" but thought that the District of Columbia circuit should "reembrace the case," largely because the force of law approach provided a bright-line, the agency characterization, for locating agency action subject to rulemaking. While he advocated a return to the force of law approach, Judge Starr recognized the danger in it: "Agencies may yield to temptation and seek to shield their regulations from the scrutiny occasioned by notice-and-comment procedures, choosing instead to cast would-be regulations as interpretive rules." 818 F.2d at 950–53.

19. Pharmaceutical Manufacturers Association v. Finch, 307 F.Supp. 858, 863 (D.Del.1970).

20. The approach, which was initially known as the "substantial impact test," possibly originated in the Third Circuit decision in Texaco, Inc. v. Federal Power Commission, 412 F.2d 740, 744–45 (3d Cir. 1969). The Federal Power Commission, without the prior participation of interested parties, had imposed a new requirement of compound rather than simple interest rates on refunds paid by natural gas companies. To avoid rulemaking, the Commission had

"While the Secretary strenuously argues that he was merely announcing 'a general statement of agency procedure or practice,' . . . the label that the participating agency puts upon its given exercise of administrative power is not, for our purposes, conclusive; rather, it is what the agency does in fact."[21]

This turn to a pragmatic approach to rulemaking, though, had its critics, most notably Kenneth Culp Davis.[22] They argued that this approach was inconsistent with the Administrative Procedure Act in that the Act established the "force of law" method rather than a pragmatic method as the appropriate measure for rulemaking. This argument, as it was continued, was that inasmuch as the pragmatic approach is not authorized by the Administrative Procedure Act, it is simply a court made add-on, a piece of procedural activism by the courts that violates the injunction of *Vermont Yankee*[23] against that sort of initiative.

However, *Vermont Yankee* is violated only if the Administrative Procedure Act actually prescribes the force of law approach. But the Act does not; it does not prescribe or otherwise endorse the "force of law" approach. The method of this approach, which is that the rules subject to the prior examination by rulemaking are only those that the agency designates as "substantive" or "legislative" rules, is not in the terms of the Act. The Act, in Sec. 553, simply makes rulemaking procedures mandatory ("shall" is the operative language) for a "rule." It is, then, important to understand what constitutes a rule. Is it agency action that

simply characterized its action as a policy statement rather than a rule. The court, however, looking to the purposes of rulemaking, set aside the action because of the agency's failure to subject it to rulemaking. In doing so the court explained that

> [Section 553 of the Administrative Procedure Act] was enacted to give the public an opportunity to participate in the rulemaking process. It also enables the agency promulgating the rule to educate itself before establishing rules and procedures which have a substantial impact on those regulated.... These procedures must be followed when an agency is exercising its legislative function.
>
> The Federal Power Commission also made a combined powers argument in support of its no rulemaking position. The agency claimed that because it had judicial power, it could apply its compound interest rate through the medium of adjudication, without ever formulating a general rule. Its argument, then, was that since it could avoid stating a general rule, and thus avoid rulemaking, it really made no sense to require rulemaking of it when it stated a general rule.

The court rejected that argument. See also Guardian Federal Savings and Loan Ass'n v. Federal Savings and Loan Insurance Corp., 589 F.2d 658, 666 (D.C.Cir. 1978).

21. Lewis–Mota v. Secretary of Labor, 469 F.2d 478, 481–82 (2d Cir.1972). See also the Ninth Circuit decision in Mt. Diablo Hosp. Dist. v. Bowen, 860 F.2d 951, 956 (9th Cir.1988), in which the court stated that

> The label that an agency gives to a particular statement of policy is not dispositive. [authority omitted] "This court must into the substance and effect of the policy pronouncement...." Thus, it does not matter whether the Secretary calls his pronouncements in the 1982 Manual or the 1984 Memorandum policy statements, interpretative rulings, or substantive rulings. We must independently determine the effect of the Secretary's statements, and decide whether they were adopted according to the appropriate procedures.

22. 2 K. Davis, Administrative Law 7.15–7.16 (2d ed. 1978).

23. Vermont Yankee Nuclear Power Corp. v. Natural Resources Defense Council, Inc., 435 U.S. 519, 98 S.Ct. 1197, 55 L.Ed.2d 460 (1978). This part of *Vermont Yankee* is discussed in Chap. 2 at Sec. 2.2.

the agency denotes as a rule (the force of law method) or is it agency action that in fact instills a course of conduct (the pragmatic method)? The Act in its mostly unhelpful definition of a rule does not say. It loosely defines a rule as "a statement of general ... application and future effect designed to implement, interpret, or prescribe law or policy,"[24] a definition that lumps together both descriptive (interpretive) rules and prescriptive rules. This definition, as well as Sec. 553 itself, says nothing about the force of law approach nor does it imply it.[25] On the other hand, neither can the terms of the Act be read as embracing a pragmatic approach to rulemaking.[26] The Act is silent, or mostly so,[27] here as well.

As Judge Wald has said, perhaps the force of law approach to identifying agency-made rules of conduct was in the air at the time the Administrative Procedure Act was adopted, and thus it is silently a part of the Act. On the other hand, the artificiality of that approach had then been identified, by the U.S. Supreme Court and by the prestigious Attorney General's Report, done under the direction of Walter Gellhorn, that was the basis of the Act. The Report explained that rules that the agency had not designated as rules of conduct nonetheless might have a practical effect on how the private sector does business. Most significantly, the Report concluded that "Consequently the *procedures* by which these regulations are prescribed become important to private interests."[28] In the years in which the bill that became the Act was before

24. 5 U.S.C.A. Sec. 551(5).

25. The terminology of "legislative" or "substantive" rules that is associated with the force of law approach is not part of the notice and comment procedures of Sec. 553. This section prescribes notice and comment for "rules," without ever mentioning "legislative" or "substantive" rules. Where the term "substantive" is used in the Act, it is used with the codification and publication parts of rulemaking. Here, it is used to provide that "substantive" rules are subject to these requirements. 5 U.S.C.A. §§ 552(a) & 553(d). While the Administrative Procedure Act itself does not define a "substantive rule as it is used in connection with these codification and publication requirements," the Supreme Court, in Morton v. Ruiz, 415 U.S. 199, 94 S.Ct. 1055, 39 L.Ed.2d 270 (1974), did so, and did so in a manner consistent with the pragmatic approach to rulemaking. In determining the applicability of these publication requirements, the Court looked to the real-world effect of the agency action, to whether it "affect[ed] individual rights and/or obligations."

26. Some courts, however, looking to the general purposes of rulemaking under the Administrative Procedures, have found that the pragmatic approach is indeed required by the Act. Batterton v. Marshall, 648 F.2d 694, 708–710 (D.C.Cir.1980). See also Mobil Oil Corp. v. Department of Energy, 610 F.2d 796, 804 (Emer.App.1979); Associated Dry Goods Corp. v. EEOC, 543 F.Supp. 950, 964–65 (E.D.Va.1982), reversed 720 F.2d 804 (4th Cir.1983).

27. See Morton v. Ruiz, supra. In Chrysler Corp. v. Brown, 441 U.S. 281, 99 S.Ct. 1705, 60 L.Ed.2d 208 (1979), the Court explained, "in Morton v. Ruiz ... we noted a characteristic inherent in the concept of a 'substantive rule.' We described a substantive rule—or a 'legislative-type rule,' ... as one 'affecting individual rights and obligations.' "

28. Attorney General's Comm. on Admin. Proced., Final Report, S.Doc. No. 8, 77th Cong., 1st Sess, 100 (1941)(italics added). More fully stated, the Report noted the practical effect on the private sector of rules not denoted as "legislative rules" according to the force of law approach as follows.

> This distinction between statutory regulations rules [denoted by the agency as rules of substance] and interpretive regulations is, however, blurred by the fact that the courts pay great deference to the interpretive regulations of administrative agencies, especially where these have been followed for a long time. In upholding certain regulations issued by

Congress, the Supreme Court had, as we have said, held that "the particular label placed upon it [the agency action] by the Commission is not necessarily conclusive, for it is the substance of what the Commission has purported to do and has done which is decisive."[29]

It is, therefore, hard to say that the force of law approach, being in the air, was silently embraced by the Administrative Procedure Act. The pragmatic approach, respecting "the substance of what the Commission has purported to do and has done" had also had an airing. This, and the fact that the Administrative Procedure Act does not by its terms endorse the force of law method, would seem to rebut the argument that the Administrative Procedure Act established the force of law method. On the other hand, it cannot be said that the Act endorses a pragmatic method. This particular indeterminacy, though, would seem to leave the courts free, to interpret the Act, as they have, according to whether in effect an agency has established a course of conduct for the private sector and to then require that that action be subject to notice and comment procedures.

Still, certain curious events occurred in some of the courts, and in these events the confusion about the appropriate zone of rulemaking was compounded. In response to the rising academic criticism, some courts stated that they were dropping the pragmatic method in favor of the force of law approach. Or they said so.[30] The opinions that most conspicuously said so did so in the context of interpretive rules, a context where neither the force of law nor the pragmatic method is relevant.[31] In the case of interpretive rules, the fact that a rule contains a course of conduct—the point to which both methods are directed—is a given. The problem in these cases is whether the rule is of the agency's own making or whether the rule merely carrying forward and perhaps clarifying a rule made by Congress. In this context, there is simply no problem—

the Commissioner of Internal Revenue, the Supreme Court has stated that "it is the settled rule that the practical interpretation of an ambiguous or doubtful statute that has been acted upon by officials charged with its administration will not be disturbed except for weighty reasons." Although the courts at times avoid the effect of this doctrine by refusing to apply administrative interpretations which they consider inadmissible, the doctrine has sufficient weight to give much finality to the interpretive regulations of administrative agencies. Consequently, the procedures by which these regulations are prescribed become important to private interests and will be considered in the report.

29. Columbia Broadcasting System v. United States, 316 U.S. 407, 416, 62 S.Ct. 1194, 86 L.Ed. 1563 (1942).

30. See, e.g., Energy Reserves Group, Inc. v. Department of Energy, 589 F.2d 1082, 1094 (Emer.Ct.App.1978) (after citing Davis' Administrative Law Treatise, the court stated that "persuasive and controlling legal authorities" did not support the pragmatic method). Although some courts purported to abandon the substantial impact test, they did not do so. Rather, these courts still looked to the effect of an agency action on the private sector and determined the applicability of rulemaking according to that effect. See, e.g., Firestone Synthetic Rubber & Latex Co. v. Marshall, 507 F.Supp. 1330, 1335 (E.D.Tex.1981) (the practical effect of the agency's action used as a measure of whether the agency "intended" that its rule be "legislative.")

31. E.g., Cabais v. Egger, 690 F.2d 234 (D.C.Cir.1982) discussed at (Sec. 4.2.3, supra); American Postal Workers Union v. U.S. Postal Service, 707 F.2d 548 (D.C.Cir. 1983), cert. denied 465 U.S. 1100, 104 S.Ct. 1594, 80 L.Ed.2d 126 (1984).

about whether the agency action is in fact a rule of conduct—that might be resolved by resort to either the force of law or a pragmatic method.[32]

But when courts have been faced with the problem that is addressed by the pragmatic and force of law methods, that of identifying whether an agency action is in fact a rule of conduct, they have—the academic counterattack notwithstanding—generally continued to make that identification pragmatically. To be sure, the central feature of the force of law approach, which is how the agency labels its action, is not excluded from consideration. As the courts say, an agency's characterization of its action is a factor (significant for what it may say about how the agency will enforce the action) that they do consider. But, wholly unlike the force of law approach, the agency characterization is not dispositive. Instead, the label is but one of a number of factors, such as the entire text of the agency pronouncement, the industry context, and the agency's influence in this context, that the courts consider.[33] This perseverance of the pragmatic method has included the District of Columbia Circuit, whose opinion in *Pacific Gas & Electric Co. v. Federal Power Commission* had been the strongest endorsement of the force of law approach. In *Community Nutrition Institute v. Young*,[34] however, the District of Columbia Circuit abandoned the formalism of that approach.

The Food and Drug Administration had established "action levels" that notified food producers of allowable levels of contaminants. Various public interest groups and consumers claimed that these contaminant levels were in reality rules enacted without rulemaking procedures and were invalid as such. The Food and Drug Administration, however, claimed that the contaminant levels had been denoted as "policy statements," that as such these levels did "not bind courts, food producers, or the FDA," and that companies thus remained free to contest the substance of the levels in such enforcement actions as the agency might bring. Just so, the agency maintained that under *Pacific Gas*/force of law method, the food containment levels it had announced were not subject to rulemaking.

32. Metropolitan School District v. Davila, 969 F.2d 485, 493 (7th Cir.1992); Cabais v. Egger, 690 F.2d 234 (D.C.Cir.1982)("Interpretive rules and substantive rules may both vitally affect private interests, thus the substantial impact test has no utility in distinguishing between the two").

33. Accordingly, the Ninth Circuit has explained that "The label that an agency gives to a particular statement of policy is not dispositive" and that in determining the applicability of rulemaking "This court must inquire into the substance and effect of the policy pronouncement." Mt. Diablo Hosp. Dist. v. Bowen, 860 F.2d 951, 956 (9th Cir.1988). See Zhang v. Slattery, 55 F.3d 732, 745–46 (2d Cir.1995) (" 'the label that the particular agency puts upon its given exercise of administrative power is not ... conclusive; rather, it is what the agency does in fact' "); Dia Navigation Co. v. Pomeroy, 34 F.3d 1255, 1264 (3d Cir. 1994) ("Thus, courts have inquired into the agency's characterization of the rule.... The more basic determination, however, involves whether 'by its action the agency intends to create new law, rights or duties.' Courts have also looked more broadly to 'the impact that a given rule has on those to whom the rule applies' ").

34. 818 F.2d 943 (D.C.Cir.1987). See also Professionals and Patients for Customized Care v. Shalala, 56 F.3d 592 (5th Cir. 1995); Alaska v. Department of Transportation, 868 F.2d 441 (D.C.Cir.1989). See also Guardian Federal Savings and Loan Ass'n v. Federal Savings and Loan Insurance Corp., 589 F.2d 658, 666 (D.C.Cir.1978).

In *Community Nutrition v. Young*, however, the court instead found that the announced contaminant levels were rules of conduct subject to rulemaking. In doing so, it found that it would give "some, but not overwhelming deference" to the agency's characterization of its action as a policy statement. What was more important, though, was the overall text and context of the action. The text of the alleged policy statement, the court found, "suggests that both levels have a present effect and are binding."[35] A relevant context was that the Food and Drug Administration had required food producers to secure exemptions to the announced contaminant levels. If the contaminant levels were not binding, the court noted, "it would scarcely be necessary to require that 'exceptions' be obtained." Another contextual factor was that the agency, in various ancillary statements, had put the industry on notice that deviations from its "policy statement" would be subject to prosecution. (And the industry, to avoid these litigation costs, would of course tend to comply with the containment levels.) Taking these things together (a "consideration of various factors"), the court held that the Food and Drug Administration, its policy statement disclaimer notwithstanding, had in fact established a presently binding norm that was subject to rulemaking.[36]

In 1999, as the first century of administrative law closed, the District of Columbia continued this pragmatic approach. In *Chamber of Commerce v. Department of Labor* the court explained, "of course, whether a rule has the force of law will bear upon its classification," but that factor was not "controlling". More to the point was whether the agency action "has a 'substantial impact' upon private parties and 'puts a stamp of [agency approval] or disapproval on a given type of behavior.' " That stamp, as the case most amply illustrates, is best determined pragmatically.[37]

* * *

35. The operative text of the alleged policy statement was that

> [A]n action level for an added poisonous or deleterious substance . . . may be established to define the level of contamination at which food will be deemed to be adulterated. An action level may prohibit any detectable amount of substance in food.

"This language," the court said, "speaking in terms of 'defin[ing]' and 'prohibit[ing]' clearly reflects an interpretation of action levels as presently binding norms."

36. That the decision in *Community Nutrition Institute v. Young* disowned the force of law method was made clear by the dissent. Judge Starr acknowledged that "the law has certainly evolved since *Pacific Gas*" but still he thought that the circuit should "reembrace the case," largely because the force of law approach provided a bright-line measure, that of agency characterization, for locating agency action subject to rulemaking. While he advocated a return to the force of law approach, Judge Starr recognized the danger in it: "Agencies may yield to temptation and seek to shield their regulations from the scrutiny occasioned by notice-and-comment procedures, choosing instead to cast would-be regulations as interpretive rules." 818 F.2d at 950–53.

37. Chamber of Commerce v. Department of Labor, 174 F.3d 206, 211–13 (D.C.Cir.1999). OSHA argued that a new "directive," inasmuch as it gave employers an option of self-inspective versus an OSHA inspection was either procedural or a policy statement, or both, and therefore exempt from rulemaking. However, to qualify for self-inspection, an employer had to agree to some new substantive conditions respecting plant safety. The Court of Appeals held that this procedural choice would in fact have a "substantial impact" on the "safety practices of thousands of employees" and that the "value of ensuring that OSHA is well-

To summarize, on the whole the courts work pragmatically to locate the appropriate zone of rule making. This method is better attuned to how agencies of combined power actually make law. This method is, though, at times hard to apply. It requires various assessments, as in *Pickus v. United States Board of Parole*[38] that featured a careful reading of an alleged "policy statement" agency to determine whether the agency had so committed itself to a position that the statement in fact amounted to an agency-prescribed rule of conduct or as in *Columbia Broadcasting System v. United States* where the Court examined industry conditions and an agency's position and power in these conditions to determine whether the agency had in fact established a rule of conduct. While the pragmatic method is hard to apply, the force of law approach, in contrast, provides "bright line" rules. Otherwise, the force of law approach better allows the agency to avoid the decision costs of rulemaking and thus to produce more law more quickly. Which too many is not a bad thing. But on the whole this argument from efficiency has not been weighty enough to convince the courts.

We might add that much of the foregoing analysis, respecting the appropriate zone of rulemaking under the Administrative Procedure Act, rests on lower court, as opposed to U.S. Supreme Court, opinions. To be sure, the Supreme Court opinion in *Columbia Broadcasting System v. United States* is the archetype of the pragmatic method. That opinion, though, was issued five years before the Administrative Procedure Act was passed. Strictly speaking, then, the *Columbia Broadcasting System* case is not an interpretation of the Act. Under the Act, the Supreme Court has not yet to address definitively the matter of how to determine when an agency action amounts to a rule subject to rulemaking.[39]

informed and responsive to public comments before it adopts a policy is therefore considerable." Accordingly, the court held that the agency action was in fact a rule of substantive effect for which rulemaking was necessary.

38. 507 F.2d 1107 (D.C.Cir.1974).

39. Prof. Davis, in his critique of the pragmatic approach to rulemaking, found support for the competing force of law approach in the Supreme Court's opinions in Batterton v. Francis, 432 U.S. 416, 97 S.Ct. 2399, 53 L.Ed.2d 448 (1977), and General Electric Company v. Gilbert, 429 U.S. 125, 97 S.Ct. 401, 50 L.Ed.2d 343 (1976). Neither of these opinions, however, are about the appropriate zone of rulemaking procedures. In *Batterton v. Francis,* the agency had in fact provided rulemaking. 432 U.S. at 423 & n. 6, 97 S.Ct. at 2404 & n. 6. Instead of being about procedures and the appropriate zone of rulemaking, these cases are about the substance of agency action, whether the *content* of the rules in question was consistent with the standards set by relevant statutes. Some of the terminology of the force of law approach is found in those cases, but only in relation to the substantive question of how much the Court should defer to the *substance* of the rules in question. And in these substantive review cases, the Court in fact deferred no more to a "legislative rule" (which is what *Batterton v. Francis* had) than to a lesser agency action, which was the case in *General Electric Company v. Gilbert.* As much as anything, these cases support the later observation, by Justice Scalia, that "In an era when our treatment of agency positions is governed by *Chevron,* the 'legislative rules vs. other actions' dichotomy ... is an anachronism." EEOC v. Arabian American Oil Co., 499 U.S. 244, ___, 111 S.Ct. 1227, 1236, 113 L.Ed.2d 274 (1991) (concurring).

In Whirlpool Corp. v. Marshall, 445 U.S. 1, 100 S.Ct. 883, 63 L.Ed.2d 154 (1980), the Court recognized the distinction drawn above, between procedural review of rules (whether rulemaking is necessary) and substantive review (the content of rules). The Court stated that the issue before it was one of content, whether the rule in question

§ 4.4 THE GOOD CAUSE EXEMPTION

As the Administrative Procedure Act provides for rulemaking it does not at the same time prescribe a strait jacket. For the exceptional circumstances that require action more immediate than by rulemaking or for action inconsistent with the open processes of rulemaking, rulemaking may be waived for good cause. Sec. 553 provides that when the agency "for good cause finds ... that notice and public procedure thereon are impracticable, unnecessary, or contrary to the public interest," then the agency can for the time being forego public participation in establishing a rule.[1] Similarly, codification and publication requirements may be waived "for good cause found and published with the rule."[2]

The agency has an important obligation of explanation and justification when it uses these exceptions to rulemaking, which obligation checks overuse of the "good cause" exception. Under the Administrative Procedure Act, an agency claiming these exceptions must do so on the basis of published findings and reasons. The Act specifically requires that agencies claiming the exceptions "incorporate[] the finding and a brief statement of reasons therefor in the rules issued."[3] These findings and this statement are subject to judicial review.

As to justification, the "good cause" provision does not allow an agency to avoid rulemaking simply because it does not consider rulemaking to be the optimal decisional process. In this respect, the exemption is not, as the courts have said, an "escape hatch."[4] Rather, it applies in these limited circumstances: (1) where rulemaking might defeat legitimate agency goals, (2) where the rule is so "technical or minor" that it

was an "interpretive regulation constitutes a permissible gloss" on the relevant statute. The Court then carefully pointed out that it "accepted the Secretary's designation of the regulation as interpretive" for this purpose only, and that it was not considering the procedural issue of whether the regulation "qualifies as an 'interpretive rule' within the meaning of the Administrative Procedure Act, 5 U.S.C. § 553." 445 U.S. at 10 & n. 15.

§ 4.4

1. 5 U.S.C.§ 553(b).

2. 5 U.S.C. § 553(d)(3).

3. 5 U.S.C. § 553(b) (notice and comment). Similarly, the exception pertaining to publication is "for good cause found and published." 5 U.S.C.A. § 553(d)(3). Requiring an agency to provide findings and reasons for the good cause exemption should diminish such careless and evasive use of the exemption as might diminish the integrity of the rulemaking requirement. In this regard, the courts have generally required such findings and reasons and then reviewed them carefully. E.g., Southern California Aerial Advertisers' Ass'n v. FAA, 881 F.2d 672, 677 (9th Cir.1989). At times, however, the courts, at least where the reasons for the exemption were "obvious," have approved the good cause exemption even though the agency failed to provide such findings and reasons. E.g., DeRieux v. Five Smiths, Inc., 499 F.2d 1321, 1333 (Emer.Ct.App.1974), cert. denied 419 U.S. 896, 95 S.Ct. 176, 42 L.Ed.2d 141; California v. Simon, 504 F.2d 430 (Emer.App.1974). In these cases the findings and reasons requirement was characterized as "technical."

4. E.g., Zhang v. Slattery, 55 F.3d 732, 746–47 (2d Cir.1995), cert. denied 516 U.S. 1176, 116 S.Ct. 1271, 134 L.Ed.2d 217 (1996) ("a mere recitation that good cause exists, coupled with a desire to provide immediate guidance, does not amount to good cause"); National Fed. of Federal Employees v. Devine, 671 F.2d 607, 610 (D.C.Cir. 1982) (the exemption is not an "escape route" and "the courts will closely examine the agency's proffered rationale").

has no significant effect on the public, or (3) where an emergency does not allow time for rulemaking.[5]

The defeating-legitimate-agency-goals application of the good-cause exemption has been used in situations where rulemaking undercuts the purpose of the rule. In *DeRieux v. Five Smiths, Inc.,* the court, respecting a "cost-freeze" (of season tickets for professional football set by the Cost of Living Council) without rulemaking approved that omission. The publicity caused by the public processes of rulemaking participation would have caused a "massive rush to raise prices." In turn, this "rush to raise prices" would have contributed to the very inflationary spiral that the price freeze was supposed to defeat.[6]

Where Sec. 553 excuses rulemaking that is "unnecessary" or "impracticable," it seems to exempt rules pertaining to technical or minor matters. Professor Bonfield has illustrated these technical or minor matters in a couple of ways. He says that the "exemption seems to cover

5. E.g., Levesque v. Block, 723 F.2d 175, 184 (1st Cir.1983). The court stated, "Impracticability ... exist[s] when the agency could not both follow section 553 and execute its statutory duties.... Public procedures are 'unnecessary' ... when the regulation is technical or minor. Finally, '[p]ublic interest' supplements the terms 'impracticable' or unnecessary; it requires that public rulemaking procedures shall not prevent an agency from operating and that, on the other hand, lack of public interest in rule-making warrants an agency to dispense with public procedure." Generally, "Courts are more inclined to uphold [an agency's resort to the good cause exemption] if the agency responded to circumstances beyond its control, if the emergency rule is of limited scope or duration, and if the agency initiated prompt follow-up proceedings allowing for public participation." A Guide to Federal Agency Rulemaking 75 (Ad.Conf., 2d ed. 1991). See also Jordon, The Administrative Procedure Act Good Cause Exemption, 36 Admin.L.Rev. 113 (1976); Note, 68 Geo.L.J. 765 (1980).

"Action forcing statutes" that require rulemaking within a certain period or upon the occurrence of some triggering event do not seem to constitute good cause for avoiding rulemaking. A Guide to Federal Agency Rulemaking, supra, at 74–75.

6. 499 F.2d 1321, 1332 (Emer.Ct.App.1974), cert. denied 419 U.S. 896, 95 S.Ct. 176, 42 L.Ed.2d 141 (1974). See also National Fed. of Federal Employees v. Devine, 671 F.2d 607 (D.C.Cir.1982). In this case, the "open season" in which federal employees might transfer freely from one health benefit plan to another was postponed pursuant to a regulation promulgated without public participation. The agency's reliance on the good cause exemption was approved because:

> [T]he agency would have been compelled to take action which was not only impracticable but also potentially harmful. The purpose of an open season is to permit employees to make an informed choice among health benefit plans; yet no accurate information about 1982 contract terms was available, nor could it possibly have been made available.... If open season had been held as scheduled, the resulting actuarial disarray might have posed a serious threat to the financial stability of the benefit program.

671 F.2d at 610–11.

An issue that arises from time to time is whether time constraints that Congress may attach to regulatory measures (that rules must be promulgated within a certain period) may excuse, under the good cause exemption, rulemaking. Generally speaking, the answer seems to be that they do not, with the "presumption" being that "Congress expects agencies to comply with the Administrative Procedure Act, even at the expense of short statutory time constraints, unless the statute expressly dictates otherwise." Levesque v. Block, 723 F.2d 175, 184 (1st Cir.1983). As said by the Fifth Circuit, "the mere existence of deadlines for agency action, whether set by statute or court order, does not in itself constitute good cause...." United States Steel Corp. v. EPA, 595 F.2d 207, 213 (5th Cir.1979). See also New Jersey v. United States Environmental Protection Agency, 626 F.2d 1038, 1049–50 (D.C.Cir.1980). But see United States Steel Corp. v. EPA, 605 F.2d 283 (7th Cir.1979), cert. denied 445 U.S. 939,

situations where a rule involved is in fact of such a minor nature, like the rule requiring government loan instruments to be signed in ink, that public procedures would be a predictable and indisputable waste of time." At a different level, he explains that where agency actions are not especially creative, as in the Department of Agriculture's publication of penalty rates derived from mathematical computations ordained by statute, public participation in the formulation of those rates is "unnecessary."[7]

Emergencies, as we said, might also meet the good cause exemption. In *Nader v. Sawhill,* the Cost of Living Council, without public participation as ordinarily required by rulemaking, increased the price of crude oil by one-dollar per barrel.[8] In arguing that its action was exempt from rulemaking under the good-cause exception, the Cost of Living Council said that cost increase "had to be done promptly and without advance notice of the price change" to avoid adversely affecting the market during a period of national shortage. The district court agreed, finding that "An emergency matter was presented which required immediate action and hearings are not possible." The court of appeals approved this finding, but not without some misgivings. The court added, "Assuming less calamitous circumstances, we fully expect that any future decisions will take the utmost advantage of full and open public procedures."[9] "Less calamitous circumstances" were evident in *Asbestos Information Association v. OSHA.*[10] The Occupational Safety and Health Administration had promulgated an emergency ruling respecting asbestos, and the court vacated the rule because it had not been subject to notice and comment. The court explained that the "risk analysis" in the ruling was "precisely the type of data that may be more uncritically accepted after public scrutiny through notice-and-comment rulemaking, especially when the conclusions it suggests are controversial or subject to different interpretations."

100 S.Ct. 1332, 63 L.Ed.2d 773 (1980). Generally, see Note, 68 Geo.L.J. 765 (1980).

7. Bonfield, Public Participation in Federal Rulemaking Relating to Public Property, Loans, Grants, Benefits, or Contracts, 118 U.Pa.L.Rev. 540, 592 (1970). In the illustration above, dealing with penalty rates as ordained by statute, the agency also may not be said to be making a rule, but simply applying a rule already made by Congress. If this is the case, then the agency action would also qualify for the "interpretive" rule exception to rulemaking. See Sec. 4.2.3, supra.

8. 514 F.2d 1064 (Emer.Ct.App.1975).

9. 514 F.2d at 1069. Compare Consumers Union v. Zarb, 523 F.2d 1404 (Emer.Ct.App.1975) (per curiam) (where the Federal Energy Administration had six months to act, the emergency gasoline shortage ... [did] not ... rise to the level of "good cause.")

Where the Department of Labor summarily extended the filing deadline for miners claiming disability benefits caused by black lung, the Tenth Circuit approved that action under the good cause exemption to rulemaking. North American Coal Corp. v. Director, O.W.C.P., 854 F.2d 386 (10th Cir. 1988). The court explained that the " 'good cause' exemption is essentially an emergency procedure; and this exemption is an important safety valve to be used *where delay would do real harm.*" The court concluded that "the loss or delay of medical benefits to many eligible coal miners was a real harm and the extension of the filing deadline operated as a safety valve to prevent this harm." (emphasis added).

10. 727 F.2d 415 (5th Cir.1984).

§ 4.5 THE CHOICE BETWEEN ADJUDICATION AND RULEMAKING

Agencies usually hold both legislative power and judicial power. Accordingly, the Administrative Procedure Act provides two different processes—rulemaking and adjudication—for these two different powers. Respecting these two processes, the courts have said, "Trial-like procedures are particularly appropriate for retrospective determination of specific facts about individual parties.... Notice and comment procedures, on the other hand, are especially suited to determining legislative facts and policy of general, prospective applicability."[1]

Apart from "retrospective determination of specific facts about individual parties," agency adjudication is sometimes called on to carry another weight, that of making rules. For various reasons, an agency may wish to avoid regulation by means of rulemaking and a codified set of rules, and to instead regulate in a more *ad hoc* manner by means of adjudication. Considering decisional processes alone, the case can be made for allowing agencies to develop rules by adjudication as well as by rulemaking. But other considerations, rule of law values really, generate a different answer. Also, by means of the Administrative Procedure Act Congress has taken a position in this matter, and it is against the use of adjudication to make rules.

§ 4.5.1 The Choice Between Rulemaking and Adjudication: Considerations Respecting Decisional Processes

Somewhat inaptly, the choice between rulemaking and adjudication is sometimes referred to as a choice between legislative and common-law methods.[2] More accurately, this choice may be expressed and explained, as Professor Colin Diver did in an influential article in the early 1980's,

§ 4.5

1. National Small Shipments Traffic Conference, Inc. v. ICC, 725 F.2d 1442, 1447–48 (D.C.Cir.1984). See also Bowen v. Georgetown University Hosp., 488 U.S. 204, 215–20, 109 S.Ct. 468, 475–78, 102 L.Ed.2d 493 (1988) (Scalia, J., concurring). This basic distinction was stated by Justice Holmes as follows:

> A judicial inquiry investigates, declares and enforces liabilities as they stand on present or past facts and under laws supposed already to exist. Legislation on the other hand looks to the future and changes existing conditions by making a new rule to be applied thereafter to all or some part of those subject to its power.

Prentis v. Atlantic Coast Line Co., 211 U.S. 210, 226, 29 S.Ct. 67, 69, 53 L.Ed. 150 (1908).

2. This analogy is inapt because the contexts of administrative and common law are not sufficiently similar. Common law adjudication typically happens on top of customary standards, those of contracts, torts, and property law. These established standards are over time adjusted by case law, but only at the margins. The system, therefore, is one of stability and marginal adjustments. The same stability and marginal adjustments cannot be expected of agency adjudication. An agency may often be delegated a lawmaking responsibility for which there are no time honored and established standards as in contracts or property. Instead, the agency, for instance the NLRB as it set out to define "unfair labor practices" or the FCC as it was charged with regulating the new broadcast media, is often starting from scratch. These areas of agency regulation, then, are simply not the areas of marginal adjustments to established standards wherein the common law method works so well.

as one between the comprehensive processes of rulemaking and the incremental and sequential processes of adjudication.[3] Otherwise, and perhaps more importantly, the choice may be viewed as between power-limiting processes (rulemaking) and power-enhancing processes (adjudication).

In terms of decisional processes, rulemaking tries to "canvass all the competing considerations."[4] Any number of social problems may warrant such a comprehensive assessment. For instance, the matter of an acceptable level of carcinogens in an industrial environment simultaneously affects differing interests such as health, wages, and productivity and a number of parties, such as workers, management and public health people, who hold these interests differently. The open and participatory processes of rulemaking (and various add-on requirements such as cost-benefit analysis) are meant to accommodate and to assess such a range of parties and interests.

Whereas rulemaking accommodates a comprehensive decisional process, adjudication does not.[5] Because of its different set of procedures—designed for an intensive and retrospective examination of the conduct of accused individuals—adjudication is generally too cumbersome to do a good job of rulemaking. As was explained by Judge Skelly Wright, "Especially in the rapidly expanding realms of economic, environmental and energy regulation, the policy disputes are too sharp, the technological considerations too complex, the interests affected too numerous, and the missions too urgent for agencies to rely on the ponderous workings of adjudication."[6] Also, adjudication is characteristically bilateral, the agency versus a particular party. This particular party against whom an agency proceeds cannot be counted on to have the resources or the incentive to bear the cost of representing interests and values other than his own.[7] Indeed, the agency may pick him as a party for this very reason.

3. See Diver, Policymaking Paradigms in Administrative Law, 95 Harv.L.Rev. 393 (1981).

4. NLRB v. Wyman–Gordon Co., 394 U.S. 759, 783, 89 S.Ct. 1426, 1439, 22 L.Ed.2d 709 (1969) (Harlan, J., dissenting).

5. In 1946, the Senate Committee on the Judiciary, in its report on the Administrative Procedure Act, expressed a similar conclusion:

Proceedings are classed as rule making under this act not merely because, like the legislative process, they result in regulations of general applicability but also because they involve subjects demanding judgments based on technical knowledge and experience.... In many instances of adjudication, on the other hand, the accusatory element is strong, and individual compliance or behavior is challenged; in such cases, special procedural safeguards should be provided to insure fair judgments on the facts as they may properly appear of record. The statute carefully differentiates between these two basically different classes of proceedings so as to avoid, on the one hand, too cumbersome a procedure, and to require, on the other hand, an adequate procedure.

S.Rep. No. 752, app. at 39. Since 1946, this assessment has been reaffirmed by another congressional study that found that rulemaking is a more efficient process for developing new rules and standards than adjudication. 4 Sen.Comm. on Governmental Affairs, 95th Cong., 1st Sess., Study on Federal Regulation 26–35 (1977).

6. Wright, The Courts and the Rule Making Process: The Limits of Judicial Review, 59 Cornell L.Rev. 375, 376 (1974).

7. Because these problems with adjudication arise from the narrow scope of the process, a solution may be seen in broaden-

But while rulemaking may be a generally superior process for establishing agency standards, it may be that it is not in all circumstances the better *decisional* process.[8] A rulemaking process, synoptic and comprehensively rational as it tries to be, is best suited to static conditions, where the problem remains still as it is studied. Where conditions are dynamic and evolving, the already prodigious task of assessing and weighing interests that a comprehensive process requires is increased considerably.[9] In rapidly changing circumstances, predictions and broad prescriptions may be futile. In these circumstances, adjudication is appealing, because it does not require a global judgment and because it reduces the agency's task to manageable assessments of the more limited interests of the limited number of parties to an adjudication.[10] The usual statement of this advantage to adjudication is from *SEC v. Chenery Corp.*:

> [T]he agency may not have had sufficient experience with a particular problem to warrant rigidifying its tentative judgment into a hard and fast rule. Or the problem may be so specialized and varying in nature as to be impossible of capture within the boundaries of a general rule.[11]

ing the scope of adjudication, by allowing parties representing a wider range of interests to intervene. This solution, however, immediately creates other problems. An appropriate level of intervention may render an adjudicatory process too cumbersome. Adjudication is necessarily attended by procedural rights, such as confrontation and cross-examination, that create decision-costs. As the number of parties and interests starts to expand, the costs assessed by these procedures can become intolerably high.

The greater damage, though, is that intervention to protect public values may destroy the integrity of the adjudicatory process itself. The main purpose of adjudication is to determine whether individuals have conformed to commonly understood standards of conduct. As Lon Fuller has so persuasively argued, a just system of law requires "institutionally designed and assured" means for a litigant to present "proofs and recent arguments for a decision in his favor," and "whatever destroys the meaning of that participation destroys the integrity of adjudication itself." Fuller, The Forms and Limits of Adjudication, 92 Harv.L.Rev. 351, 364 (1978). An individual's "meaningful participation" in an adjudication of his rights can, however, be subvented and smothered by intervenors trying to vindicate other, broader interests. Consider, for instance, a supposedly "adjudicatory" opinion of the National Labor Relation Board that devoted "seven pages to a hypothetical discussion of how it would decide cases involving other parties and other fines, and only four pages . . . to the case at hand." Peck, A Critique of the NLRB's Performance in Policy Formulation: Adjudication and Rulemaking, 117 U.Pa.L.Rev. 254, 273 (1968).

8. Lindbloom, The Science of Muddling Through, 19 Pub.Adm.Rev. 79 (1959). See also Diver, Policymaking Paradigms in Administrative Law, 95 Harv.L.Rev. 393 (1982).

9. Greater Los Angeles Council on Deafness, Inc. v. Community Television of Southern California, 719 F.2d 1017 (9th Cir.1983); First National Monetary Corp. v. Commodity Futures Trading Commission, 677 F.2d 522 (6th Cir.1982).

10. An agency goal may involve a range of interests such as (a), (b), (c), (d), and (e), all of varying intensities. The multi-party, multi-interest processes of rulemaking require an assessment of all these interests. In the bipolar context of adjudication, however, only a limited number of interests, perhaps only one interest at a time, need be assessed. In a National Labor Relations Board adjudication, for example, an employer may want more of (e), the union less.

11. 332 U.S. 194, 202–03, 67 S.Ct. 1575, 1580–81, 91 L.Ed. 1995 (1947).

The idea of rulemaking by adjudication is that over time and out of a sequence of adjudications aimed at discrete problems as they present themselves, agency standards of broad application should emerge. This notion, of solving just a piece of the problem at a time, is the general justification of rulemaking by adjudication.[12] It has been sufficiently strong to make the case that an agency should have the discretion to determine whether a particular problem is better solved by rulemaking by making rules through adjudication.

§ 4.5.2 The Choice Between Rulemaking and Adjudication: Considerations of Agency Accountability and the Rule of Law

So far as decisional processes are concerned, the comprehensive processes of rulemaking seem generally preferred to adjudication. But only generally so. As discussed above, as a decisional process the incrementalism of the adjudicatory method may occasionally have its place. The choice between rulemaking and adjudication, however, involves more than simply picking the better decisional process.

Rulemaking imposes a discipline of agency action according to the rule of law. This discipline, as we have discussed it, is one of agency action according to codified and published rules. Such rules better assures predictable, consistent, and impartial agency action. By them, the private sector is thereby authoritatively informed of what it can count on from government. Planning, economic and personal, is therefore enhanced, and so is the range of choices of individuals. Consequently, the Second Circuit, respecting how the Federal Trade Commission should deploy its open-ended power to proscribe "unfair methods of competition," has said that "the Commission owes a duty to define the

12. There are various other considerations respecting this choice between rulemaking and adjudication. For a sketch of these various considerations, see A Guide to Federal Agency Rulemaking, 100–106 (Admin.Conf.2d ed. (1991)). See also National Petroleum Refiners Ass'n v. FTC, 482 F.2d 672 (D.C.Cir.1973).

An additional consideration worthy of note is that the incremental and sequential process of adjudication assure no self-correcting mechanism, no effective mode of self-study. Adjudication guarantees no analysis, such as a comprehensive assessment of the interests involved in a policy, to determine whether an agency is appropriately on course. This problem has been succinctly described by Professor Lowi with respect to Interstate Commerce Commission regulation of the transportation industry: "Since 1920 . . . Congress benefited not from fifty years' experience, but from one year's experience fifty times over." T. Lowi, The End of Liberalism: Ideology, Policy, & the Crisis of Public Administration 111 (1969). In a study of the National Labor Relation Board's practice of regulation by means of adjudication, Professor Bernstein reached the same sort of conclusion:

> [A]n enormous number of Board doctrines are based upon untested suppositions. For example, we have had more than twenty-five years of litigation about organizing activities on and off company property but little data on how employees actually react to various organizing devices. We simply do not know what makes an employee feel fear in election situations. We do not even know whether substantial groups of employees regard Board elections as truly secret. If many do not, the whole Board election process is askew.

Bernstein, The NLRB's Adjudication–Rule Making Dilemma Under the Administrative Procedure Act, 79 Yale L.J. 571, 582 (1970). See also Gifford, Discretionary Decisionmaking in the Regulatory Agencies: A Conceptual Framework, 57 S.Cal.L.Rev. 101, 117–21 (1983).

conditions under which the conduct claimed to facilitate price uniformity would be unfair so that business would not be left in a state of complete unpredictability.''[13]

But to an agency sure of itself and anxious to get on with its program, this discipline of the rule of law is likely to be seen as an unwarranted constraint. The conflict here, between rule of law values and an agency's preference for unfettered power, is basic. Prof. Unger has described this conflict as involving ''two different ways of ordering human relations'':

> One way is to establish rules to govern general categories of acts and persons, and then to decide particular disputes among persons on the basis of the established rule. This is legal justice. The other way is to determine goals and then, quite independently of rules, to decide particular cases by a judgment of what decision is most likely to contribute to the predetermined goals, a judgment of instrumental rationality.[14]

An agency, then, may seek to escape the constraints of regulation according to standing rules, so that it may freely, by adjudication and orders, bring its best judgment at the time to bear on the problem at hand. As expressed in a famous article by a past chairman of the Civil Aeronautics Bureau, ''it is a good working hypothesis that the agencies have uniformly failed to promulgate specific and clear policies and standards as by rules and rulemaking, not from an inability, or ignorance, or ineptitude, but from an *unwillingness* to limit themselves in the exercise of power.''[15]

The ''rules'' produced by adjudications are not canonical statements of an agency position; they are instead that which the agency may glean from the various opinions that were issued to justify the result in particular cases. The agency may choose among its backlog of opinions and by ''file drawer law'' produce the rule it wants in a given case. In this respect, Judge Henry Friendly described how a change in Federal Communications Commission policy was ''slipped into an opinion in such a way that only careful readers would even know what had happened, without articulation of reason, and the prior authorities not overruled, so that the opinion writer remained free to pull them out of the drawer whenever the agency wishes to reach a result supported by the old rule but not the new.''[16]

13. E.I. du Pont De Nemours & Co. v. FTC, 729 F.2d 128, 139 (2d Cir.1984). For these same reasons, James Madison, in Federalist No. 62, asserted that the freedom and productivity of a society were enhanced by government action made predictable by virtue of standing rules. These matters and the rule of law are discussed in Chapter 3.

14. R. Unger, Knowledge and Politics 89–90 (1975).

15. Hector, Problems of the CAB and the Independent Regulatory Commissions, 69 Yale L.J. 931 (1960). See also H. Friendly, The Federal Administrative Agencies: The Need for Better Definition of Standards (1962).

16. H. Friendly, supra, at 62. How rulemaking can preclude such arbitrariness is shown in a more responsible FCC action, where the Commission refused to subject certain members of the broadcast industry to the vagaries of an uncertain case law. In this action it had been contended that ''Commission precedent'' established a rule

As agency flexibility and power is thus enhanced by *ad hoc* lawmaking, so may accountability be diminished. An agency may hide the ball among its various opinions and diffuse responsibility among the various agency officials that produce adjudications. Legislative oversight and presidential initiatives, such as cost-benefit analysis, may be avoided when the agency's position has not been openly and definitely published as a rule.[17] Also, accountability of a different sort, to interested parties in the private sector, may be avoided by resort to adjudication. For instance, the Securities Exchange Commission developed its standard restricting the use of inside information by stockbrokers by adjudication rather than by rulemaking. As described by Professor William Cary, a past Chairman of the Commission, that body chose adjudication because it not wish to deal with inputs and objections from the stock exchanges and brokerage firms as would have been the case with rulemaking.[18] Justice Douglas further explained that "the survival of a questionable rule seems somewhat more likely when it is submerged in the facts of a government case than when rule making is used" and that while "rule making is no cure-all ... it does force important issues into full public display and in that sense makes for more responsible administrative action."[19]

§ 4.5.3 Administrative Procedure Act Constraints on the Choice Between Adjudication and Rulemaking

Simply in terms of the best decisional process, an agency may at times usefully rely on adjudication rather than rulemaking for developing rules and standards. But because an agency may also use the adjudicatory mode of regulation to avoid accountability and to diminish rule of law values, then perhaps its discretion to use adjudication as an alternative to rules and rulemaking should be curtailed. And it has been. One such curtailment, a weak one, has been due process. The courts have been particularly concerned with a fair and even distribution of the burdens and benefits of agency-made laws. Under the heading of due process they have tried to maintain such a fair and even distribution by requiring agencies to define and to confine their power by means of codified and published rules. These due process constraints, though,

allowing only attorneys to represent corporations in Commission proceedings, and the Commission Review Board recognized both that such a rule was within the Commission's power and that there were sound policy reasons for such a rule. Nonetheless, the Review Board found the "rule" invalid on procedural grounds because it had not been codified and published as required by the Administrative Procedure Act. The Review Board noted that an uncertain case law could not substitute for published rules and that "[w]hether a corporation must be represented by counsel is a matter too fundamental, too general in applicability ... to be made the subject of an ad hoc rule applicable when remembered." Advanced Electronics, 21 F.C.C.2d 239 (1970).

17. A. Scalia, Back to Basics: Making Law Without Making Rules, Regulation 25 (July/August 1981).

18. W. Cary, Politics and the Regulatory Agencies 82–85 (1967).

19. NLRB v. Wyman–Gordon Co., 394 U.S. 759, 779, 89 S.Ct. 1426, 1436, 22 L.Ed.2d 709 (1969) (Douglas, J., dissenting).

have been limited, to those situations where an agency is distributing tangible benefits or where "personal" liberties are involved.[20]

The broader constraint, respecting the choice between rulemaking and adjudication, comes at the hands of Congress and by the means of the Administrative Procedure Act. While it is often said that the Administrative Procedure Act as it provides for both rulemaking and adjudication thereby gives agencies the discretion to choose between the two, this interpretation is not faithful to the terms of the Act. Rather, the Act, closely read, differentiates between rulemaking and adjudication so as to establish rulemaking as the process for making rules.

The precise manner by which the Administrative Procedure Act separates rulemaking and adjudication is as follows. Under Sec. 553 of the Act, an agency "shall" give notice of proposed rulemaking and the agency "shall give interested parties an opportunity to participate in rule making."[21] In similarly mandatory terms, the Act requires that rules be codified and published and further provides that "a person may not ... be adversely affected" by an unpublished rule.[22] The event for which these notice, comment, and codification publication requirements are mandatory is "rule making."

Rulemaking is a defined term. It is defined by the Act as the agency process for "formulating, amending, or repealing a rule."[23] In turn, a "rule" is defined as a "statement of general ... applicability and future effect designed to implement, interpret, or prescribe law or policy."[24]

"Adjudication" is also defined. It is defined as the process for formulating an "order," and an order is then defined as "the final disposition ... of an agency in a matter *other than rule making*."[25] Whatever the vagaries of this definition are otherwise, Congress was specific on the point that "the term 'order' is essentially and necessarily defined to exclude rules."[26]

By this separation of rulemaking and adjudication, the Act precludes the use of adjudication to develop rules. Because an "order"—an outcome of adjudication—may not include rules, adjudication may not be used for the production of rules. Instead, rulemaking is for rules, just as the Act's definition of a rule says it is. This is, as Justice Harlan has said, the "natural interpretation" of the Act.[27]

Moreover, the legislative history of the Act clearly shows that the text that produced this "natural reading" was not some sort of mishap

20. See Chap. 3, § 3.3.

21. 5 U.S.C. § 553(b) & (c).

22. 5 U.S.C. § 552(a). See also 5 U.S.C.A. § 553(d).

23. 5 U.S.C. § 551(5).

24. 5 U.S.C. § 551(4).

25. 5 U.S.C. §§ 551(6), (7).

26. H.Rep. No. 1980 79th Cong., 2d Sess. 20 (1946). See NLRB v. Wyman–Gordon Co., 394 U.S. 759, 780, 89 S.Ct. 1426, 1437, 22 L.Ed.2d 709 (1969) (Harlan, J., dissenting).

27. NLRB v. Wyman–Gordon Co., 394 U.S. 759, 780, 89 S.Ct. 1426, 1437, 22 L.Ed.2d 709 (1969) (dissenting). See also Bowen v. Georgetown University Hosp., 488 U.S. 204, 215–20, 109 S.Ct. 468, 475–78, 102 L.Ed.2d 493 (1988) (Scalia, J., concurring).

of draftsmanship. The Senate report on the Act explains that the "definition of 'rule' . . . prescribes the kind of operation that is subject to Sec. 4 [rulemaking] rather than Sec. 5 [adjudication]."[28] The House Report states that the Act's "definition [of a rule] is important because it determines whether section 4 [rulemaking] rather than section 5 [adjudication] applies to a regulatory operation."[29]

It is the case, then, that the Administrative Procedure Act distinguishes between rulemaking and adjudication so as to preclude the use of adjudication for developing rules.[30] But as we shall shortly discuss, this interpretation of the Act has not altogether been embraced in the courts.

§ 4.5.4 Control of the Choice Between Adjudication and Rulemaking: The Case Law

Congress acted conservatively, to harness agency discretion by establishing rulemaking an exclusive process for agency-made rules of conduct. Accordingly, a number of courts have looked to the Administrative Procedure Act and have found that it establishes rulemaking as an exclusive and mandatory process. Other times courts have acted otherwise. With little or no regard to the Administrative Procedure Act, these courts have found that agencies may in their discretion choose between rulemaking and adjudication, with the choice of adjudication subject to reversal by the courts according to an abuse of discretion form of review. This form of review, as you may note, transfers control of agency processes to courts and away from Congress and the Administrative Procedure Act.

28. S. Rep. No. 752, 79th Cong., 1st Sess. 11 (1946).

29. H.Rep. No. 1980, supra, at 20. This point of distinction between rulemaking and adjudication was underscored by Justice Douglas, as he explained "The Committee reports make plain that the Act 'provides quite different procedures for the legislative and judicial functions of administrative agencies'." NLRB v. Wyman–Gordon Co., 394 U.S. 759, 776, 89 S.Ct. 1426, 1435, 22 L.Ed.2d 709 (1969) (dissenting).

The committee reports also show some part of the policy basis for this distinction:

> Proceedings are classed as rule making under this act not merely because, like the legislative process, they result in regulations of general applicability but also because they involve subjects demanding judgments based on technical knowledge and experience.... In many instances of adjudication, on the other hand, the accusatory element is strong, and individual compliance or behavior is challenged; in such cases, special procedural safeguards should be provided to insure fair judgments on the facts as they may properly appear of record. The statute carefully differentiates between these two basically different classes of proceedings so as to avoid, on the one hand, too cumbersome a procedure, and to require, on the other hand, an adequate procedure.

S. Rep. No. 752, app. at 39. Since 1946, this assessment has been reaffirmed by another congressional study. Study on Federal Regulation 26–35, 4 Sen. Comm. on Governmental Affairs, 95th Cong., 1st Sess. (1977).

30. See Mayton, The Legislative Resolution of the Rulemaking Versus Adjudication Problem in Agency Lawmaking, 1980 Duke L.Jour. 103 (1980). However, on the Supreme Court, only Harlan and Douglas, in their dissents in Wyman–Gordon, have taken seriously the task of explicating and applying the Administrative Procedure Act. NLRB v. Wyman–Gordon Co., 394 U.S. 759, 780–83, 89 S.Ct. 1426, 1437–39, 22 L.Ed.2d 709 (1969). As they did so they concluded the process was mandatory.

§ 4.5.5 The Supreme Court Decisions

SEC v. Chenery is the foundation on which the presumed discretion of agencies to develop rules by adjudication as well as by rulemaking is said to rest. But in truth, *Chenery* cannot bear that weight. The circumstances of *Chenery* arose prior to the Administrative Procedure Act, and the case was decided without any reference to the Act.[31] More importantly, *Chenery* did not fully assess the issues involved in the choice between rulemaking and adjudication. The opinion is wholly unconcerned with the decisional processes appropriate to the formulation of a rule. Instead, it involved a different issue, that of a prerogative "to act for the public good" in the absence of a standing rule.[32]

Eventually, the Supreme Court did address the issue of whether under the Administrative Procedure Act an agency might use adjudication rather than rulemaking to create a rule. The Court did so in an unusual opinion, *NLRB v. Wyman–Gordon Co.*[33] Here, six justices found that the Act established rulemaking as an exclusive process for rules of general application. A plurality of four, however, opted for a result that confused the issue.

The circumstances of *Wyman–Gordon* were that the National Labor Relations Board by adjudication attempted to develop a rule of general application. Two employers had mailed anti-union material to their employees during the course of an election of union representation. The unions then asked the employers to furnish them with the names and addresses of those employees so that they could distribute rebuttal information. The employers refused. In the course of its adjudication respecting the propriety of the employers' inaction, the Board invited "certain interested parties to file briefs and to participate in oral arguments." At the end of the adjudicatory proceedings against the two employers, the Board announced a new standard, the so-called *Excelsior* Rule, which was to apply prospectively "in all election cases."[34] Under this rule, employers were required to provide a list of employee names and addresses to the National Labor Relations Board, which would then make the list available to all parties to an election.

When the Board later tried to apply this rule to the Wyman–Gordon Company, that firm objected on the grounds that this "rule" had been arrived at by adjudication rather than rulemaking. The First Circuit Court of Appeals agreed with this objection, and, accordingly, overturned

31. The assumption that *Chenery* is an Administrative Procedure Act case is an error too frequently made. Bowen v. Georgetown University Hosp., 488 U.S. 204, 210, 109 S.Ct. 468, 472, 102 L.Ed.2d 493 (1988) (Scalia, J., concurring).

32. See discussion at Chap. 3, Sec. 3.1, supra.

33. 394 U.S. 759, 89 S.Ct. 1426, 22 L.Ed.2d 709 (1969). One way in which this opinion is unusual is that the Court actually worked through the text of the Act as this text relates to rulemaking. Most of the time, the courts, as Justice Scalia has recently explained, shirk this particular task of statutory interpretation. Bowen v. Georgetown University Hosp., 488 U.S. 204, 210, 109 S.Ct. 468, 472, 102 L.Ed.2d 493 (1988) (concurring).

34. 156 N.L.R.B. 1236, 1239 (1966).

the rule.[35] On review, the Supreme Court agreed with that court in principle. The Court found (1) that the Board action, as it was meant to establish a general standard of conduct for union representation elections, amounted to a rule and (2) that this rule was enacted without complying with the rulemaking requirements of Sec. 553 of the Administrative Procedure Act. In particular, the Board's invitation to selected parties to intervene in the underlying adjudication did not satisfy the requirement of notice to, and opportunity to comment by, all interested parties. Consequently, a majority of the justices felt that the process was an inadequate decisional process, for the reason that:

> The rule-making provisions of [the Administrative Procedures Act], which the Board would avoid, were designed to assure fairness and a mature consideration of rules of general application.... They may not be avoided by the process of making rules in the course of adjudicatory proceedings.[36]

After subscribing to this position, a plurality of four then opted for a confusing result. Apparently, this plurality was of the view that the *Excelsior* rule was sound in substance, that a remand for new proceedings would surely lead to its reenactment, and that therefore a remand for rulemaking would be "meaningless."[37] But as Justice Harlan argued in dissent, how could the Court presume to assess the merits of the rule when it had not been informed by a "recanvass[ing]" of "all of the competing considerations" in a rulemaking proceeding?[38] Harlan understood the Administrative Procedure Act as making rulemaking mandatory and as precluding the use of adjudication as a substitute. He stated the consequences of softening this position as follows: "Either the rulemaking provisions are to be enforced or they are not."

Five years later, the Supreme Court in the same term decided two cases dealing with an agency's power to dispense with rulemaking. In one of these cases, *NLRB v. Bell Aerospace Co.,* the Court seemed to focus on the decisional processes appropriate to developing a rule.[39] In the second, *Morton v. Ruiz,*[40] the Court looked to rule of law values.

35. 397 F.2d 394 (1st Cir.1968).

36. 394 U.S. at 764, 89 S.Ct. at 1429.

37. 394 U.S. at 766–67, n. 6, 89 S.Ct. at 1430 n. 6.

38. 394 at 783, 89 at 1439. In another case Justice Harlan explained that federal courts should not pass on the substance of agency standards "until [the agency] has first illumined the regulatory problems involved through an appropriate exercise of its rule-making powers." California v. Lo–Vaca Gathering Co., 379 U.S. 366, 372, 85 S.Ct. 486, 490, 13 L.Ed.2d 357 (1965) (dissenting).

In *Wyman–Gordon,* the Justices divided as follows. The plurality of four, who thought the rule to be valid even though it was based on bad procedures, was joined by three other justices who concurred on the basis that an agency could, in its discretion, use adjudicatory processes as an alternative means for developing rules. They relied on *Chenery* for that proposition.

Justices Harlan and Douglas, dissenting, thought the rule to be procedurally invalid because the agency had not followed the rule making procedures of Sec. 553. And unlike the plurality, they were unwilling to uphold a procedurally bad rule.

39. 416 U.S. 267, 94 S.Ct. 1757, 40 L.Ed.2d 134 (1974). The case was argued in 1973.

40. 415 U.S. 199, 94 S.Ct. 1055, 39 L.Ed.2d 270 (1974).

The circumstances of *NLRB v. Bell Aerospace Co.* were these. Prior to 1970, the National Labor Relations Board had interpreted the National Labor Relations Act as inapplicable to "managerial employees." These employees, therefore, had no right to union representation under the Act. But in 1970 the Board, in the context of an adjudication, changed its position. Twenty-five "buyers" at a Bell Aerospace plant had sought union representation. The company opposed this action on the grounds that these buyers were managerial employees who were not subject to the labor laws under which they sought to organize.

For its refusal to bargain with the buyers, an unfair labor practice complaint was filed against the company. In its adjudication of this complaint, the Board changed its position about managerial employees and held that such employees—except those who might be placed in "a conflict of interest" situation because of competing management and union interests—were covered by the labor laws and entitled to union representation. On review, the Second Circuit held against the Board on both substantive and procedural grounds.[41] The substantive grounds were that the Board's previous position, that all managerial employees were excluded from the labor laws, was the correct interpretation of the National Labor Relations Act.

On procedural grounds, the court of appeals held that the Board proceeding was invalid as an improper attempt at rulemaking. The Board decision was meant "to fit all cases at all times," and this kind of global ruling was appropriately made only by the rulemaking processes of the Administrative Procedures Act, and not through adjudication as attempted by the Board. Judge Friendly, writing for the court, explained this position as follows:

> [I]f the opinions of six Justices in Wyman–Gordon mean anything, they must be read as demanding rule-making here.... The Board was prescribing a new policy, not just with respect to 25 buyers in Wheatfield, N.Y., but in substance ... "to fit all cases at all times." There must be tens of thousands of manufacturing, wholesale and retail units which employ buyers, and hundreds of thousands of the latter. Yet the Board did not even attempt to inform industry and labor organization ... of its proposed new policy and to invite comment thereon....

On review, the Supreme Court agreed with the Second Circuit on the substantive issue.[42] It agreed that the Board's previous view, that all managerial employees were outside the labor laws, had been correct. The Court, however, did not view rulemaking, the procedural issue, the same as the Second Circuit. Rather, the Court stated, "Consideration of that issue was unnecessary." The Court's view was that it had corrected the Board's misinterpretation of the labor laws by reinstating the Board's previous interpretation. The Board's task on remand, therefore, was

41. 475 F.2d 485 (2d Cir.1973), affirmed in part, reversed in part, 416 U.S. 267, 94 S.Ct. 1757, 40 L.Ed.2d 134 (1974).

42. NLRB v. Bell Aerospace Co., 416 U.S. 267, 291, 94 S.Ct. 1757, 1770, 40 L.Ed.2d 134 (1974).

simply to apply the old standard of exclusion of managerial employees to the twenty-five buyers in question. Apparently, the Court considered this Board action as adjudication pure and simple—respecting only the Bell Aerospace buyers—and not, as Judge Friendly had said, a proceeding designed to generate a rule "to fit all cases at all times."

At this point, the *Bell Aerospace* opinion, as at least one court would later explain, seemed to have "reserved the question whether the board would have to use rulemaking to adopt a new standard of general applicability."[43] The opinion, however, did not stop at this point. It continued in a more expansive vein. Referring to *SEC v. Chenery,* the Court stated that as a general proposition "the Board is not precluded from announcing new principles in an adjudicative proceeding, and . . . the choice between rule making and adjudication lies in the first instance within the Board's discretion." Whatever its status, holding or dictum, this sentence has become the quotable part of the case, and has been widely taken as affirmation of the proposition that an agency can, at its discretion, make rules by adjudication as well as rulemaking.

After *Bell Aerospace,* the Court handed down its last decision to date that much involves the rulemaking versus adjudication issue. This decision was in *Morton v. Ruiz,* which involved eligibility standards for certain government benefits.[44] Here, the Court, as we have previously discussed, was concerned with the relation of rulemaking and the rule of law, with assuring that agency authority be implemented through codified and published rules so as to insure a fair and even-handed distribution of law and its benefits and burdens. The Court held that under the Administrative Procedure Act, eligibility standards had to be established by published rules to assure that these standards were "being applied consistently and so as to avoid both the reality and the appearance of arbitrary denial of benefits." The Court objected to what it characterized as "ad hoc determinations" by the agency, and in this relation the Court explained:

> The Administrative Procedure Act was adopted to provide, *inter alia,* that administrative policies affecting individual rights and obligations be promulgated pursuant to certain stated procedures so as to avoid the inherently arbitrary nature of unpublished ad hoc determinations.

When used as a means of developing new standards, adjudication necessarily involves the "*ad hoc*" determinations disapproved in *Morton v. Ruiz.*[45] Therefore, to read *Bell Aerospace* as approving the *ad hoc*

43. According to Judge Wright, "in *Bell Aerospace* the Court held merely that in deciding whether the buyers who worked for a particular employer were managerial employees the NLRB was free to proceed by adjudication. The Court expressly reserved the question whether the Board would have to use rule making to adopt a new general standard for determining when an employee is a managerial employee." Chisholm v. FCC, 538 F.2d 349, 390 (D.C.Cir.1976).

44. 415 U.S. 199, 94 S.Ct. 1055, 39 L.Ed.2d 270 (1974).

45. Both the Tenth and Eleventh Circuits have read *Morton v. Ruiz* in this way. Curry v. Block, 738 F.2d 1556 (11th Cir. 1984); Matzke v. Block, 732 F.2d 799 (10th Cir.1984).

development of rules by adjudication is to have the Court going in two different directions in the same term.

§ 4.5.6 Lower Court Practice

Since *Bell Aerospace* and *Morton v. Ruiz,* the Supreme Court has not again directly addressed the issue of whether rulemaking is a mandatory process for the development of rules. In the lower courts, however, the issue has continued and has generated a considerable amount of litigation. In this litigation, two different approaches to legal controls respecting an agency's choice of rulemaking modes have surfaced. Under one approach, the courts subscribe to the *Bell Aerospace* dictum that the "choice between rule making and adjudication lies in the first instance within the Board's discretion."[46] Under this approach, the Courts themselves have an ultimate (albeit infirm) control over procedures, by means of an abuse of discretion form of review.

The other approach adheres to the principles in *Wyman–Gordon,* that the Administrative Procedure Act is controlling and that under it rulemaking "may not be avoided by the process of making rules in the course of adjudicatory proceedings."[47] Both these approaches are discussed below.[48]

a. The Abuse of Discretion Standard

The courts that hold that an agency choice of adjudication over rulemaking is subject only to an abuse of discretion form of review have had one primary concern: whether a new rule of conduct, as developed in

46. See, e.g., E.g., Miranda v. National Transp. Safety Board, 866 F.2d 805, 808 (5th Cir.1989). A number of lower courts, however, only purport to follow *Bell Aerospace.* On examination, this rhetoric about agency discretion to establish new rules of conduct by adjudication rather than rulemaking is mitigated by the fact that the agency was not actually promulgating a new rule of conduct. For instance, in Sheet Metal Workers v. NLRB, 716 F.2d 1249, 1257 (9th Cir.1983), the court eventually concluded that the agency had not been involved in developing a rule of conduct. In this regard, the court concluded "the rule at issue in the instant case involves not an alteration of pre-existing lawful relationships (rendering lawful that which had been previously unlawful) but rather the imposition of a different remedy for conduct that had long been considered improper." The case cited above, Miranda v. National Transp. Safety Board, 866 F.2d 805, 806–807 (5th Cir.1989) involved an agency interpretation of an existing (albeit open-ended) aviation safety rule. See also British Caledonian Airways, Ltd. v. CAB, 584 F.2d 982, 992–93 (D.C.Cir.1978). Where no rule of conduct is being created, there is simply no occasion for rule making. See Sec. 4.2.3, supra.

47. NLRB v. Wyman–Gordon Co., 394 U.S. 759, 764, 89 S.Ct. 1426, 1429, 22 L.Ed.2d 709 (1969).

48. However, first we might illustrate the division among the courts. In 1978, Congress provided mortgage relief to farmers. The Eighth Circuit then held that under that enactment, the Secretary of Agriculture was required to establish substantive standards defining the scope of mortgage relief. Allison v. Block, 723 F.2d 631 (8th Cir.1983). In doing so, the court explained that while "rulemaking would better insure a uniform set of substantive standards ..., we recognize that the Secretary may decide to develop the criteria through adjudicative processes which give some precedential effect...." 732 F.2d at 637–38. However, two other circuits, the Tenth and the Eleventh, held that rulemaking was mandatory for developing standards under the mortgage relief act. Curry v. Block, 738 F.2d 1556 (11th Cir.1984); Matzke v. Block, 732 F.2d 799 (10th Cir.1984).

an adjudication, may fairly be applied to a party to that adjudication—to penalize the party for conduct done when the rule was not in force.

A statement of this concern is that "agencies may not impose undue hardship by suddenly changing direction, to the detriment of those who have relied on past policy."[49] In *Ruangswang v. Immigration and Naturalization Service,* a native of Thailand had sought to avoid deportation by qualifying as an "investor" (in a domestic enterprise) under Immigration and Naturalization Service regulations.[50] But in an adjudication, which occurred at the time she was making investments that would have qualified for the exemption, the Service changed the rules. Under these new standards, the Service found that Mrs. Ruangswang failed to qualify for the investor exemption. The Ninth Circuit, however, overturned this agency action, on the basis that as Mrs. Ruangswang could not have known of the new standards when she acted, they were unfairly applied to her. The court stated that "applying the standards of Bell Aerospace, we hold there was an abuse of discretion in attempting to establish a new standard . . . and applying it to Mrs. Ruangswang in an adjudicatory process."[51]

Apart from their concern with retrospective lawmaking, the lower courts have also been concerned about the wisdom of establishing an original policy determination of broad effect by means of a single adjudication. In this regard, the Ninth Circuit's position is that "a promulgation or an announcement of a broad policy determination in a single adjudicative proceeding" amounts to an abuse of discretion.[52]

From another direction, where rulemaking has been avoided so as to diffuse agency accountability for a rule, that avoidance has been counted as an abuse of discretion. In *National Wildlife Federation v. Clark,* the court explained that agency discretion to choose between rulemaking and adjudication did not "give an agency or department the option between judicially reviewable rulemaking and ad hoc decisions which it could protect from effective judicial review."[53]

b. Rulemaking as Mandatory

Rather than an abuse of discretion standard, lower court decisions have, as we said, alternatively subscribed to the *Wyman–Gordon* proposition that rulemaking "may not be avoided by the process of making rules

49. Anaheim v. FERC, 723 F.2d 656, 659 (9th Cir.1984).

50. 591 F.2d 39 (9th Cir.1978).

51. 591 F.2d at 46. See also Patel v. INS, 638 F.2d 1199 (9th Cir.1980) (discussed infra); Curry v. Block, 738 F.2d 1556 (11th Cir.1984). Contra, see Mehta v. INS, 574 F.2d 701 (2d Cir.1978).

52. Matzke v. Block, 732 F.2d 799, 802 (10th Cir.1984).

53. 577 F.Supp. 825, 829 (D.D.C.1984). See also Curry v. Block, 738 F.2d 1556 (11th Cir.1984), where the court ordered that the Farmer's Home Administration implement loan-servicing and foreclosure-avoidance measures through rulemaking rather than adjudication. The court found that "under the circumstances of this case, in which many farmers are in dire need of the relief Congress intended to be made available to them, the Secretary's implementation of this program through adjudication would be an abuse of discretion."

in the course of adjudicatory proceedings."[54] The Ninth Circuit in *Ford Motor Co. v. FTC*[55] is a well-known decision of this sort. The Federal Trade Commission in an adjudicatory proceeding had found that the Francis Ford Motor Company's repossession of automobiles amounted to an "unfair trade practice" under the Federal Trade Commission Act. The Act had been violated by Francis Ford's "failure to give defaulting customers more than wholesale value for their repossessed cars, ... [and by] improperly charging them indirect expenses such as overhead and lost profits."

On review, the Ninth Circuit overturned the Commission's action. The court first identified the nature of the action, which was that of "establish[ing] a *rule*," (The rule thus established was that a secured creditor had "to credit the debtor with the 'best possible' value of the repossessed vehicle," and "forb[ade] the creditor from charging the debtor with overhead and lost profits.") Because the agency had produced this rule through an adjudication, "the narrow issue presented [was] whether the F.T.C. should have proceeded by rulemaking in this case rather than by adjudication." Regarding this issue, the court found that the controlling principle was that "agencies can proceed by adjudication to enforce discrete violations of *existing* laws where the effective scope of the rule's impact will be relatively small; but an agency must proceed by rulemaking if it seeks to change the law and establish rules of widespread application."[56] The Commission had violated this principle, as the court explained:

> Credit practices similar to those of Francis Ford are widespread in the car dealership industry; and the [Uniform Commercial Code] section the F.T.C. wishes us to interpret exists in 49 states. The F.T.C. is aware of this. It has already appended a "Synopsis of Determination" to the order, apparently for the purpose of advising other automobile dealerships of the results of this adjudication. To allow the order to stand ... would do far more than remedy a discrete violation of a singular Oregon

54. Also, the lower courts have read Morton v. Ruiz, 415 U.S. 199, 94 S.Ct. 1055, 39 L.Ed.2d 270 (1974) as requiring rulemaking. Curry v. Block, 738 F.2d 1556 (11th Cir.1984); Matzke v. Block, 732 F.2d 799 (10th Cir.1984).

55. 673 F.2d 1008 (9th Cir.1981).

56. In arriving at this principle the court relied on the Ninth Circuit's decision in Patel v. INS, 638 F.2d 1199 (9th Cir. 1980). In this case, the Immigration and Naturalization Service ("INS") had by a rule provided that an alien might avoid deportation if he engaged in "a commercial or agricultural enterprise in which he had invested a substantial amount of capital." Then, by means of an adjudication, the INS amended this rule to add that the investment "must tend to expand job opportunities" in the United States. When the INS tried to apply this new standard to an alien who had invested according to the requirements of the original rule, the court of appeals held that it could not. In this regard, it concluded that the adjudication adding the "job opportunities requirement" announced a broad, generally applicable requirement. Thus the adjudication functionally amended the original rule about alien investments. As such, the adjudication "was an improper circumvention of the rulemaking requirement." (Also, the court noted that the job opportunity amendment had been considered and rejected in the rule making process for the original rule.)

law as the F.T.C. contends; it would create a national interpretation of U.C.C. sec. 9–504.

One year later, in *Montgomery Ward & Co. v. F.T.C.,* the Ninth Circuit again set aside an agency adjudication.[57] The case involved whether an adjudication was merely an application of an existing rule or an amendment to the rule. The court found that the adjudication amounted to an amendment to the existing rule, and set the adjudication aside. If the agency wished to amend the rule, the court said, "it may do so in a formal rule-making proceeding." In this relation, the court explained:

> Adjudication allows an agency to apply a rule to particular factual circumstances and to provide an interpretation of the required conduct in light of those circumstances. An adjudicatory restatement of the rule becomes an amendment [subject to rulemaking], however, if the restatement so alters the requirements of the rule that the regulated party had inadequate notice of the required conduct.[58]

* * *

The thrust of these lower court opinions seems to be that where the agency is not just clarifying or filling-in with respect to an existing standard of conduct, but flat-out establishing a new rule, then that action is subject to being overturned by the courts. It will be overturned under either an abuse of discretion or a mandatory rulemaking form of review.

Or both approaches simultaneously, as in the Ninth Circuit decision in *Anaheim v. FERC.*[59] On an application for a rate increase, the Federal Energy Regulatory Commission has the statutory authority to suspend the rate increase for up to five months pending a hearing. In an adjudication, the Commission announced that it would exercise its statutory authority to "suspend for only one day where our preliminary analysis indicates that no more than ten percent of the increase appears

57. 691 F.2d 1322, 1329 (9th Cir.1982).

58. For cases holding that the rule-making process of the Administrative Procedure Act is an exclusive process for either making or amending rules, see First Bancorporation v. Board of Governors, 728 F.2d 434 (10th Cir.1984); Patel v. INS, 638 F.2d 1199 (9th Cir.1980).

The *First Bancorporation* case involved a Federal Reserve Board order to the effect that negotiated withdrawal accounts (NOW accounts) amounted to demand deposits that should be subject to reserve and interest limitations for banks. The court held this order, arrived at in an adjudication, improper inasmuch as it was an "attempting to propose legislative policy by an adjudicative order." In so holding, the court explained that the fact that "the Board's order is an attempt to construct policy by adjudication" was "evident" in that it "examined no specific facts as to the potential adverse effects of unregulated Foothill NOW accounts" and instead made only "broad conclusions" respecting "public policy objectives." 728 F.2d at 438.

See also Matzke v. Block, 732 F.2d 799 (10th Cir.1984). For a state case that extensively reviews the issue, and determines that rulemaking is mandatory for agency-made rules of conduct, see Metromedia, Inc. v. Director, Div. of Taxation, 97 N.J. 313, 478 A.2d 742 (1984). See also Megdal v. Oregon State Bd. of Dental Examiners, 288 Or. 293, 605 P.2d 273 (1980) (J. Linde). See generally, A. Bonfield, State Administrative Rule Making, 119–23 (1986).

59. 723 F.2d 656 (9th Cir.1984).

to be excessive." The use of adjudication to establish this rate-suspension decision was questioned in court, and the court announced two constraints. First was the abuse of discretion constraint, which the court expressed as "agencies may not impose undue hardship by suddenly changing direction, to the detriment of those who have relied on past policy." This limit, the court found, had not been exceeded inasmuch as the Commission had merely "strengthened and clarified a previously recognized exception to the general rule of five-month suspension." The second constraint was the Administrative Procedure Act requirement of rulemaking: the court stated that the "agencies may not use adjudication to circumvent the Administrative Procedure Act's rule making procedures." However, this limitation was not transgressed either, because "FERC's clarification of its suspension policy ... was a minor adjustment, a fine tuning of doctrine that does not require rulemaking unless it imposes a severe hardship or circumvents existing rules." This result, the court noted, was altogether consistent with the circuit's previous decision in *Ford Motor Co. v. FTC.* This case, the court said, stood for the proposition that "agencies can proceed by adjudication to enforce discrete violations of *existing* law" but that "an agency must proceed by rulemaking if it seeks to change the law and establish rules of widespread application." In *Anaheim v. FERC,* the agency had not established such a general rule.

§ 4.6 CONCLUSION

As it authorizes Congress to make all laws "necessary and proper" for the "execution" of the various powers of government, the Constitution acknowledges an important fact about deployment of government power. Because Congress is best situated to make comprehensive, system-wide judgments, it is the institution better suited to establish processes respecting how such power is deployed.

With respect to agency lawmaking, Congress has made some choices and established a process. This statutory process of rulemaking harnesses agency power by requiring that it be exercised according to codified and published rules arrived at by a prescribed decisional process. In some instances, this process will surely diminish an agency's ability to exercise its power over private individuals in the manner that the agency then deems most consistent with its substantive goals. In these instances, the agency will want the flexibility to act in an *ad hoc* manner, to act against the individual outside the confinement of rulemaking and standing rules. A careful reading of the Administrative Procedures Act, however, shows the judgment of Congress that outside the "good cause exemption" of Sec. 553, the overall cost of giving agencies this sort of flexibility precludes it. But among the courts, there is no present consensus favoring this reading.

Part Two

AGENCY ADJUDICATION

Agencies routinely determine whether a person's conduct conforms to the laws they implement and impose sanctions when a person has acted wrongfully. This application of law constitutes adjudication, and this fact of agency adjudication raises various issues. One set of issues involves how an agency can be assigned judicial power under a constitutional structure that at least nominally places that power in courts especially constituted to receive it. Under the federal Constitution, Article III defines the judicial power of the United States and then provides for federal courts to receive that power.

Another set of issues arises inside the agency. Here, the assumption is that agencies constitutionally hold judicial power and the concern is how, within the agency, this power is exercised. There are two main sources of control respecting how an agency exercises adjudicatory power. One source of control is the due process clauses of the fifth and fourteenth amendments. Presently, the institution that exercises this control is the courts. Apart from the courts and due process, the other main source of control is the body that creates agencies, the legislature. For federal agencies, Congress has, by means of the Administrative Procedure Act, established a basic set of procedures for agency adjudication.[1] State legislatures have acted similarly.

Another issue associated with adjudication is that agencies frequently assess money remedies such as civil fines, reparations, or back-pay. Agencies do so, of course, without juries; juries being incompatible with the structure and function of agencies. This omission, however, ought to be squared with the right to a jury trial as guaranteed by the seventh amendment.

This part addresses these various matters—Article III, the seventh amendment, due process, and the Administrative Procedure Act—as each of them pertain to agency adjudication.

1. 5 U.S.C. § 551 et seq.

Chapter 5

ALLOCATION OF JUDICIAL POWER

Table of Sections

Although the Constitution says that the "judicial Power of the United States, shall be vested in one supreme Court and in such inferior Courts as the Congress may from time to time ordain and establish,"[1] much of that power is instead exercised by administrative agencies. These agencies typically determine whether the conduct of individuals conforms to the laws that the agencies implement. As agencies make these determinations, they find facts and interpret statutes and other sources of federal law. In this capacity they perform a judicial function equivalent to the "federal question jurisdiction" of federal courts under Article III.

The reasons for allocating judicial power to administrative agencies, as Congress has done, are several. Advantages of specialization are gained by assigning a single function, *e.g.*, deciding Social Security disability claims, to a single body staffed by experts. With such an assignment, procedures streamlined for that function can then be better developed and applied.[2] Such expertise and streamlined procedures contribute to the "inexpensive and expeditious" processes that Congress has favored for so many public programs and that the courts have so often approved.[3] In the words of Justice Brennan, "when Congress creates a

1. U.S. Constitution Art. III, § 1.

2. See J. Mashaw, Bureaucratic Justice (1983). Professor Mashaw argues that in the context of Social Security disability programs, expedition of adjudication by professionalism and streamlined procedures has not sacrificed equity and accuracy in adjudication.

3. Among other things, this sort of process offers the individual a cheaper, and therefore a viable, means of a fair resolu-

statutory right, it clearly has the discretion, in defining that right, to create presumptions, or assign burdens of proof, or prescribe remedies; it may also provide that persons seeking to vindicate that right must do so before particularized tribunals created to perform the specialized adjudicative tasks related to that right."[4]

Apart from these reasons of expertise and efficiency, Congress has sometimes assigned judicial functions to administrative agencies in order to secure a forum more hospitable to legislative goals. To avoid the hostility to labor that the courts had then shown, Congress, as it established a right of labor to bargain collectively with management, assigned the primary responsibility of protecting that right to the National Labor Relations Board.[5] More commonly, Congress may not be troubled by a specific hostility of the courts; rather, Congress may simply wish to avoid a certain psychological perspective of courts. A judge, it is said, "has a breadth of vision and relative disinterestedness qualified by potential prejudice for the status quo." In contrast, the agency typically "has the special knowledge, sympathy, and potential intolerance of an expert."[6] To promote a public program, Congress might substitute the knowledge, sympathy, and intolerance of the agency for the more comprehensive and conservative perspective of a court.

There is, then, a utility in assigning judicial power to agencies. Still, when Congress assigns that power the question is: how can it do so consistent with the Constitution's allocation of that power to courts constituted under Article III? The care in this allocation was described by Justice Frankfurter:

> No provisions of the Constitution, barring only those that draw on arithmetic, ... are more explicit and specific than those pertaining to courts established under Article III. "The judicial power" which is "vested" in these tribunals and the safeguards under which their judges function are enumerated with particularity. Their tenure and compensation, the controversies which may be brought before them, and the distribution of original and appellate jurisdiction among these tribunals are defined and circumscribed, not left at large by vague and elastic

tion of claims involving the government. See, e.g., Myron v. Hauser, 673 F.2d 994, 1001 (8th Cir.1982) ("Congress ... sought to encourage inexpensive and expeditious adjudication of customer claims against commodity professionals by requiring the CFTC to establish a reparation procedure for the resolution of claims arising under the Act"). Generally, see L. Jaffe & N. Nathanson, Administrative Law, Cases and Materials, 122–25 (4th ed. 1976). As Professors Jaffe and Nathanson wrote, the need that was often seen was that of "an agency which was sympathetic, which cost the worker little or nothing and had no other business." Id. at 123. On Congress's perception that administrative procedures more expeditious than judicial procedures would benefit labor, see NLRB v. United Food and Commercial Workers Union, 484 U.S. 112, 108 S.Ct. 413, 98 L.Ed.2d 429 (1987).

4. Northern Pipeline Construction Co. v. Marathon Pipe Line Co., 458 U.S. 50, 83, 102 S.Ct. 2858, 2877, 73 L.Ed.2d 598 (1982).

5. L. Jaffe & N. Nathanson, Administrative Law, Cases and Materials 136–38 (4th ed. 1976).

6. Id. at 123.

phrasing.[7]

Because Article III so carefully vests the "judicial Power of the United States" in courts constituted under it, this Article plausibly implies that *if* the United States chooses to exercise this power, it must do so *only* through the medium of these courts.[8] This implication might be taken as precluding an allocation of any part of the judicial power of the federal government to administrative agencies.[9]

Such an absolutist reading of Article III is, however, attenuated by the Constitution's "necessary and proper clause." This clause pertains not only to the substantive powers of Congress, but also to "all other powers vested ... in the Government of the United States, or in any Department or Officer thereof." As it thus includes the powers of *all* the departments of the federal government, the clause would seem to give Congress some room in which to allocate—according to expediencies such as we have identified—some amount of judicial power to agencies. Indeed, that Congress may do so, may distribute some amount of judicial power "pursuant to its powers under Article 1," has been "long recognized" in the courts.[10]

Nonetheless, in a distribution of judicial power to agencies the overall constitutional plan cannot be disregarded.[11] And so, if we under-

7. National Mut. Ins. Co. v. Tidewater Transfer Co., 337 U.S. 582, 646, 69 S.Ct. 1173, 1196, 93 L.Ed. 1556 (1949) (dissenting).

8. In Federalist No. 78, Alexander Hamilton may have been the first one to argue for such an implication. The judicial power of the United States, he said, should be exercised "through one supreme tribunal, and a certain number of inferior ones" as provided in Article III. This pronouncement cuts against the common argument that Article III is not mandatory because it contemplates that the judicial power it defines may be exercised by the states in their courts rather than in federal courts. While it is true that the states may hold this judicial power, the point remains that if the United States itself chooses to exercise judicial power, the forum for that is an Article III court. Moreover, allocating judicial power to state courts is not, in the context of separated powers, functionally the same as allocating judicial power to agencies. "Because they are relatively insulated from federal political pressure, state courts are capable of exercising a check on the departure from separation-of-powers principles by Congress, the national executive, or their agents." Fallon, Our Legislative Courts, Administrative Agencies, and Article III, 101 Harv.L.Rev. 916, 939 (1988). Agencies cannot claim to be so inclined.

9. For instance, in Senate debate about the creation of a Federal Trade Commission with the power to by adjudication develop a body of federal law respecting unfair commercial practices, Sen. Sutherland persistently argued that "We have no right to confer this power upon the administrative body, ... it is a judicial power, and belongs to the courts." 51 Cong.Rec. 12652 (1914).

10. See Thomas v. Union Carbide Agr. Products Co., 473 U.S. 568, 583, 105 S.Ct. 3325, 3334, 87 L.Ed.2d 409 (1985) ("the Court has long recognized that Congress is not barred from acting pursuant to its powers under Article 1 to vest decision making authority in tribunals that lack the attributes of Article III courts"). As put most bluntly by Justice White, it is "too late to return to the simplicity of the principle pronounced in Article III and defended so vigorously and persuasively by Hamilton.... " Northern Pipeline Const. Co. v. Marathon Pipe Line Co., 458 U.S. 50, 113, 102 S.Ct. 2858, 2893, 73 L.Ed.2d 598 (1982) (dissenting).

11. Northern Pipeline Const. Co. v. Marathon Pipe Line Co., 458 U.S. 50, 71, 74, 102 S.Ct. 2858, 2871, 2873, 73 L.Ed.2d 598 (1982) (Rejecting the contention "that pursuant to any of its Art. I powers Congress may create courts free of Art. III's requirements whenever it finds that course expedient" and rejecting "a rule of broad legislative grace that could effectively eviscerate the constitutional guarantee of an independent Judicial Branch of the Federal Government").

stand that Congress may allocate some portion of the judicial power to agencies, but at the same time understand that Congress cannot wholly disassemble constitutionally prescribed structure, the logical inquiry that follows is along these lines. First, what are the purposes underlying the Constitution's assignment of the judicial power to "Article III" courts? Second, how consistent with these purposes is a reallocation of that power to an agency? A third inquiry is whether courts should defer to a legislative choice about allocating judicial power to agencies. Unfortunately, case law has not generally followed this sort of analysis, not until recently. Until recently, case law has developed along a line that, in a distinction it makes between "public" and "private" rights, is irrelevant respecting the purposes of Article III. We will try to trace this fault line, but as we do so we must keep in mind that it crosses what has been "one of the most confusing and controversial areas of constitutional law."[12]

12. Northern Pipeline Construction Co. v. Marathon Pipe Line Co., 458 U.S. 50, 93, 102 S.Ct. 2858, 2883, 73 L.Ed.2d 598 (1982); Thomas v. Union Carbide Agr. Products Co., 473 U.S. 568, 583, 105 S.Ct. 3325, 3334, 87 L.Ed.2d 409 (1985) (an " 'area of frequently arcane distinctions and confusing precedents' ").

In these areas, some clarity can be gained by distinguishing between two separate institutions, legislative courts and administrative agencies. E.g., Crowell v. Benson, 285 U.S. 22, 52 S.Ct. 285, 76 L.Ed. 598 (1932); Glidden Co. v. Zdanok, 370 U.S. 530, 549, 82 S.Ct. 1459, 1472, 8 L.Ed.2d 671 (1962), rehearing denied 371 U.S. 854, 83 S.Ct. 14, 9 L.Ed.2d 93 (1962). The case law also pertains to another kind of court, a territorial court. This court is one established by Congress pursuant to its power to establish governing bodies in United States territory outside the states. As such, this power does not implicate separation of powers problems and federalism problems as might judicial power in the hands of administrative agencies. As said by John Marshall, "the same limitation [Article III] does not extend to the territories. In legislating for them, Congress exercises the combined powers of the general and of a state government." American Ins. Co. v. 356 Bales of Cotton, 26 U.S. (1 Pet.) 511, 546, 7 L.Ed. 242 (1828). See also Palmore v. United States, 411 U.S. 389, 93 S.Ct. 1670, 36 L.Ed.2d 342 (1973).

Legislative courts and administrative agencies are often lumped together, as in:

Legislative courts

Are but agencies in drag;

Glidden is but paint.

Federal Jurisdiction Haiku, 32 Stan. L.Rev. 229 (1979). But this has to be poetic (or haikuic, whatever) license. "Legislative courts" appropriately refers to institutions such as the old court of customs and patent appeals. Such an institution and agencies are alike in that they both exercise judicial power without being constituted according to Article III. Otherwise, however, they differ markedly.

Legislative courts do not combine the whole power of government—legislative, executive, and judicial—as agencies typically do. Instead, legislative courts typically hold only a judicial power, and they hold it only in a discrete and specialized area, such as patents. In the case of the United States Customs Court, jurisdiction includes classifications of imports, applicable rates of duty, and anti-dumping cases. 28 U.S.C.A. § 1582. Obviously, this jurisdiction, while limited and specialized, is, nonetheless, quite significant. See Re, Litigation Before the United States Custom Court, 19 U.S.C.A. xvii. See also Katz, Federal Legislative Courts, 43 Harv.L.Rev. 894, 908–12 (1930).

In comparison to legislative courts, modern administrative agencies exercise a judicial power of a much greater breadth, and these agencies also hold legislative and executive power. The Federal Trade Commission, for instance, has judicial power of an incredible breadth, respecting "unfair methods of competition" and "deceptive acts or practices in commerce." Moreover, it combines this power with legislative and executive power. 15 U.S.C.A. § 45. The Commission makes the rules, decides when to prosecute, and then sits in judgment. The point is, agencies stand to undermine the Article III idea of a separate and inde-

§ 5.1 CROWELL v. BENSON: A REASONABLE DECISION WITH SOME UNFORTUNATE TALK ABOUT PUBLIC AND PRIVATE RIGHTS

The grand assault on assigning judicial power to agencies rather than courts constituted under Article III came in *Crowell v. Benson*.[1] This New Deal case involved a major social initiative, a workman's compensation scheme established by Congress and implemented by an agency, the United States Employees Compensation Commission. By statute, Congress had made maritime employers liable to their employees for their on-the-job injuries "irrespective of fault" and according to a fixed schedule of damages. The responsibility for administering this scheme was placed in the Employees Compensation Commission. Clearly, the Commission performed a judicial function as it determined "the circumstances, nature, extent and consequences of the injuries sustained by the employee" and awarded compensation according to a table of damages for those injuries.[2]

This allocation of power was challenged by an employer, on the grounds that in it Congress had assigned the Commission a judicial function that the Constitution reserved to federal courts. In its analysis of this argument, the Court noted that all compensation orders of the Commission were appealable to an appropriate federal district court, and that in significant respect, this right of appeal reserved judicial power to an Article III court. Commission orders was subject to review according to a division between issues of law and fact. The form of review was *de novo* as to matters of law and, in effect, "substantial evidence" for factual matters.[3] Respecting issues of law, the Commission's judicial power was clearly valid. A reviewing court had full power, under the *de novo* standard of review prescribed by Congress, to itself determine matters of law and to reverse contrary agency decisions. "Interpretation of the laws," the Court explained, is "the proper and peculiar responsibility of the courts." Under the facts of *Crowell*, this responsibility had been fully reserved for Article III courts.

The Commission's power to make factual determinations was, however, considerably insulated from judicial review. These important determinations, so long as they were not "without evidence or 'contrary to the indisputable character of the evidence,' "bound the courts. Consequently, in factual matters the agency had been allocated a significant judicial power, and the question was whether this allocation of power was consistent with Article III.

pendent judiciary as legislative courts do not. See Currie, Bankruptcy Judges and the Independent Judiciary, 16 Creighton L.Rev. 441 (1983).

§ 5.1

1. 285 U.S. 22, 52 S.Ct. 285, 76 L.Ed. 598 (1932).

2. 285 U.S. at 54, 52 S.Ct. at 294.

3. Reviewing courts might overturn factual findings that were "without evidence or 'contrary to the indisputable character of the evidence.' " 285 U.S. at 50, 52 S.Ct. at 292.

An answer was arrived at by way of analogy. The Commission's "findings of fact" the Court explained, "were closely analogous to the findings of the amount of damages that are made, according to familiar practice, by commissioners or assessors; and the reservation of full authority to the court to deal with matters of law provides for the appropriate exercise of the judicial function in this class of cases." Considering this "familiar practice" of delegating fact-finding to referees, the Court concluded, "there is no requirement that in order to maintain the essential attributes of judicial power, all determinations of fact in constitutional courts shall be made by judges." This "agencies as adjuncts to courts" explanation is not, however, altogether persuasive. The adjuncts the Court spoke of, referees and trustees and so forth, work for the courts for specific purposes. Agencies have much more power and their own purposes.

But overall, the result in *Crowell*—that the essential attributes of judicial power are retained in Article III courts so long as those courts may fully correct agency determinations on matters of law and overturn unreasonable findings as to matters of fact—seems reasonable, certainly in the circumstances of that case. The Commission's authority had been limited to a narrow area (on-the-job injuries in the maritime industry) where agency expertise and routine might usefully supplant the general processes of federal courts. In this context, the Court was "unable to find any constitutional obstacle to the action of the Congress in availing itself of a method shown by experience to be essential in order to apply its standards to the thousands of cases involved, thus relieving the court of a most serious burden while preserving their complete authority to insure the proper application of the law."

§ 5.1.1 Public and Private Rights

While the result in *Crowell* is reasonable, a rationale used by the Supreme Court en route to that result is not. This rationale turned on a distinction, between public rights and private rights, a distinction apparently offered as a means of determining when judicial power is appropriately allocated to agencies. While this public and private distinction might have been taken as a best-forgotten dictum,[4] it has not at all been disremembered. It is how the courts, today, often speak of Article III and agencies.

4. In *Crowell,* the Court found that the adjudications of the United States Employees Commission were subject to Article III, and that the constraints of that Article were met inasmuch as the Commission's findings were subject to review in an Article III court. Thus, the case, as regards the general issue of allocations of judicial power to agencies, could be read for no more than that. Also, in a sense the public right/private right distinction is dictum confounded in that the actual holding in *Crowell* was to set aside the agency action on the grounds that a trial de novo was appropriately held in federal district court on what a "jurisdictional fact," the existence of a master-servant relationship, that the case involved. Regarding the (dormant) jurisdictional fact doctrine, W. Gellhorn, C. Byse, & P. Strauss, Administrative Law, Cases and Comments, 287ff (7th ed. 1979). Enroute to the jurisdictional fact issue, the Court interjected the public right/private discussion.

According to this talk, "private rights" relate to suits between private individuals over rights or duties arising under the common law.[5] Article III, it is said, pertains to these kinds of rights and actions, and any allocation of these private rights to agencies must first be squared with Article III. But not a public right; instead, this matter is free of the constraints of Article III.

A public right, according to *Crowell v. Benson,* is one "which arises between the government and persons subject to its authority in connection with the performance of the constitutional functions of the executive or legislative departments."[6] It refers to government acting "in its sovereign capacity to enforce rights created by statutes."[7] Unlike a private right, adjudication respecting this sort of right is not at all subject to Article III: "There need be no Art. 111 court involvement in any adjudication of a 'public right.'"[8] Therefore, the reasoning goes, Congress in its discretion can outright assign such matters to an agency. As said in *Crowell v. Benson,* "there are matters, involving public rights . . . which Congress may or may not bring within the cognizance of the courts of the United States, as it may deem proper."[9]

Given the broad definition of public rights, of government acting "in its sovereign capacity to enforce rights created by statutes," virtually all the judicial work of agencies can be said to be exempt from Article III. For instance, because "an agency like the FTC enforces 'public rights,'" Congress should be "wholly free to commit determinations of cases involving such rights to agencies."[10] And apparently, almost any private, common-law sort of action may be converted by Congress to a matter of public right and thereby moved outside the zone of Article III courts.[11]

5. Atlas Roofing Co., Inc. v. Occupational Safety and Health Review Com'n, 430 U.S. 442, 97 S.Ct. 1261, 51 L.Ed.2d 464 (1977). See also Myron v. Hauser, 673 F.2d 994 (8th Cir.1982).

6. 285 U.S. 22, 52 S.Ct. 285, 76 L.Ed. 598 (1932), quoting Murray's Lessee v. Hoboken Land & Improvement Co., 59 U.S. (18 How.) 272, 15 L.Ed. 372 (1855).

7. Atlas Roofing Co. v. Occupational Safety and Health Review Com'n, 430 U.S. 442, 458, 97 S.Ct. 1261, 1271, 51 L.Ed.2d 464 (1977); Northern Pipeline Const. Co. v. Marathon Pipe Line Co., 458 U.S. 50, 108, 102 S.Ct. 2858, 2890, 73 L.Ed.2d 598 (1982).

8. Northern Pipeline Construction Co. v. Marathon Pipe Line Co., 458 U.S. 50, 108, 102 S.Ct. 2858, 2890, 73 L.Ed.2d 598 (1982).

9. 285 U.S. at 50, 102 S.Ct. at 2860.

10. B. Schwartz, Administrative Law 64–65 (2d ed. 1984).

11. Atlas Roofing Co. v. Occupational Safety and Health Review Com'n, 430 U.S. 442, 458, 97 S.Ct. 1261, 1270, 51 L.Ed.2d 464 (1977). Also, a lower court opinion, Myron v. Hauser, 673 F.2d 994 (8th Cir. 1982), shows how Congress can change private rights to public rights. This case involved a reparation hearing by a federal agency, the Commodities Future Trading Commission. In that hearing a private individual—on the basis that the defendant, a commodities broker, had in violation of the Commodity Futures Trading Commission Act of 1974, 7 U.S.C. § 18(g), committed fraud in the sale of sugar options to him—recovered $24,592 from the defendant. The defendant then challenged the reparation proceeding, claiming that as was an action between private individuals, it was a judicial proceeding with respect to a private right and therefore subject to the constraints of Article III. The Eighth Circuit, however, found that the agency action was with respect to a public right, stating that:

> Congress, acting under the commerce clause, has regulated commodity options transactions.... The customer does receive a benefit in the form of a reparations award. However, the fact that the statute and regulations are enforceable

But this elasticity is not the main problem with the public and private rights distinction. The problem lies in the fact that the distinction itself is unresponsive to the reasons for separating the judicial power from executive and legislative power and assigning that power to courts constituted to receive it.[12] The most important part of the judicial

in favor of a private party does not preclude administrative adjudication.

673 F.2d at 1005.

12. The Court in *Crowell v. Benson* lifted the public right/private right distinction out of an antebellum case of no particular relevance to modern administrative government. This case was Murray's Lessee v. Hoboken Land & Improvement Co., 59 U.S. (18 How.) 272, 15 L.Ed. 372 (1855).

In 1833, Samual Swartwout, the customs collector for the port of New York, was one million dollars in arrears to the federal government for accounts received in his job. Pursuant to statute, the Treasury Department issued a distress warrant, and under this warrant Swartwout's property was sold to satisfy the debt. The validity of the distress warrant was then challenged on various grounds, one of which was that the determination of debt was a judicial matter that belonged to Article III judges rather than Treasury Department officials.

The Supreme Court agreed that the Treasury Department's action was a judicial matter that *could* have been assigned to Article III courts. The Court, however, disagreed that it *had* to be assigned to an Article III court. Indeed, there was a tradition to the contrary respecting this particular kind of debt. The Court explained that while "the auditing of the accounts of a receiver of public moneys may be, in an enlarged sense, a judicial act," Anglo–American tradition established that it need not be, that government could by its own audit determine the debt due it from its revenue officials. 59 U.S. (18 How.) at 274.

In arriving at this holding, about the revenue-collecting activities of the executive branch, the Court, as Justice Scalia has said, "uttered the words". Granfinanciera, S.A. v. Nordberg, 492 U.S. 33, 57, 109 S.Ct. 2782, 2798, 106 L.Ed.2d 26 (1989) (concurring). The Court in *Murray's Lessee* made the statement, picked-up and repeated out of context in *Crowell v. Benson,* that "there are matters, involving public rights ... which Congress may or may not bring within the cognizance of the courts of the United States, as it may deem proper." 59 U.S. (18 How.) at 283.

Justice Scalia has made a determined effort to put the public and private rights distinction in correct historical perspective. Granfinanciera, S.A. v. Nordberg, 492 U.S. 33, 109 S.Ct. 2782, 106 L.Ed.2d 26 (1989). As explained by him, the distinction made in *Murray's Lessee v. Hoboken Land & Improvement Co.* was in the context of a waiver of sovereign immunity. There, the federal government had by an act of Congress consented to be sued over the attachment of property of a revenue official, and it was in relation to this consent to be sued that the Court explained that matters of "public right" could by Congress be committed to a non-Article III body. The Court in *Murray's Lessee* had stated that the "United States may consent to be sued, and may yield this consent upon such terms and under such restrictions as it may think just." (59 U.S. (18 How.) at 283.) In this context, the power of Congress to assign matters as public rights to non-Article III courts is derivative of sovereign immunity and limited to the historic context of sovereign immunity and waivers of it. Accordingly, Justice Scalia states that "what we meant by public rights were not rights important to the public, or rights created by the public, but rights of the public, that is, rights pertaining to claims brought by or against the United States." 492 U.S. at 58, 109 S.Ct. at 2799.

Behind *Murray's Lessee,* in the English origins of judicial review of agency action, there appears to be little if any support for legislative power to withdraw public law matters from judicial review simply because these matters had instead been committed to agency adjudication. In fact, these origins seem to go the other way, toward a power in the courts to superintend agency determinations in matters committed to them. The tenor of these antecedents is indicated by the pronouncement of Lord Coke that "to this Court of King's Bench belongs authority, not only to correct errors in judicial proceedings, but other errors and misdemeanors extra-judicial ...; so that no wrong or injury, neither private nor public, can be done, but that it shall be here reformed or punished by due course of law." Baggs Case, 77 Eng.Rep. 1271 (1615). For a discussion of these antecedents see Chap. 12, Sec. 12.2.

For a more generous view of the breadth of the public rights doctrine, see Fallon, Our Legislative Courts, Administrative Agencies, and Article III, 101 Harv.L.Rev. 916, 951 et seq. (1988).

power created by Article III consists of federal question jurisdiction, cases arising under the Constitution and laws of the United States.[13] A public right, as it involves government acting "in its sovereign capacity to enforce rights created by statutes" would be a crucial part of this jurisdiction. But as a "public right," these cases arising under the Constitution and laws of the United States may be committed to agency adjudication without reference to Article III.

Only for common law claims—the area of private rights—does Article III, under the public rights/private rights dichotomy, apply to agency adjudication. This area is not insignificant. In our political system, where the background social and economic ordering is by private arrangements protected by the common law, a judicial power authoritatively to mediate disputes arising out of this ordering is important. Except, that is, in terms of Article III, where these private rights are not that important, not really. As was made abundantly clear in *Erie R. Co. v. Tompkins,* this area of private rights is by the Constitution largely reserved to the states and state courts.[14] And it is an area of a federal concern only derivatively, as part of the diversity jurisdiction established by Article III. The relatively limited purpose of this jurisdiction is to provide an alternative federal forum for out-of-state litigants, to protect them from a possible in-state bias of state courts. This purpose is clearly not that of establishing federal courts as a font of "private rights".

Because the public and private rights distinction protects only diversity jurisdiction and allows the courts' important federal question jurisdiction to be allocated to agencies without reference to Article III or its purposes, the distinction is surely deficient. Worse than that, it is beside the point.

§ 5.2 JUDICIAL POWER UNDER ARTICLE III

In recent years the Supreme Court has come back to the problem, of allocation of judicial power to agencies, that it first addressed in *Crowell v. Benson.*[1] As it has returned, the Court has perhaps maintained the

13. U.S. Const. Art. III, § 2.

14. 304 U.S. 64, 58 S.Ct. 817, 82 L.Ed. 1188 (1938).

§ 5.2

1. The relevant cases are Northern Pipeline Const. Co. v. Marathon Pipe Line Co., 458 U.S. 50, 102 S.Ct. 2858, 73 L.Ed.2d 598 (1982); Thomas v. Union Carbide Agr. Products Co., 473 U.S. 568, 105 S.Ct. 3325, 87 L.Ed.2d 409 (1985), and Commodity Futures Trading Com'n v. Schor, 478 U.S. 833, 106 S.Ct. 3245, 92 L.Ed.2d 675 (1986). The decision in *Schor,* which is the main administrative law case in this area, is discussed in the text above.

Thomas v. Union Carbide Agriculture Products Co. was also an important initial step toward a functional, purpose-oriented view of Article III. As a condition to registering a pesticide, the Federal Insecticide, Fungicide, and Rodenticide Act requires pesticide manufacturers to submit research data concerning the pesticide's effect on health, safety, and the environment to the Environmental Protection Agency. 7 U.S.C.A. § 136 et seq. To "spread the costs of generating adequate information regarding the safety, health, and environmental impact of a potentially dangerous product," the Act includes "data sharing" provisions, which allow a manufacturer seeking registration to use data previously submitted by other registrants. If such data are used, the user must compensate the previous registrant for the data. Compensation, if it cannot be agreed upon is subject to arbitration, with the arbitrator's decision subject to ju-

public rights/private form of discourse started in *Crowell.* The Court has, however, more-or-less emptied this form of any substance. In *Commodity Futures Trading Commission v. Schor,* the Court renounced a "doctrinaire reliance on formal categories," and in doing so dispensed with the method of the public rights/private rights distinction.[2] Instead, the "constitutionality of a given delegation of adjudicative functions to a non-Article III body should be assessed by reference to the purposes underlying the requirements of Article III."

The Commodities Exchange Act provides for a reparations hearing by the Commodities Futures Exchange Commission, wherein customers of commodities brokers may seek redress for broker violations of the Act. In *Schor,* customers had filed a complaint with the Commission, alleging that certain debits charged to them by their brokers were void under the Act. In that agency proceeding, the brokers counterclaimed for the debit balance.

An administrative law judge ruled for the brokers on all counts, including their counterclaim. At that point, the customers turned around and brought an action in federal court, asking that the agency ruling on the brokers' counterclaim be set aside, on the grounds that the agency could not constitutionally adjudicate that claim as it involved ordinary contract matters squarely within the category of a private right under *Crowell v. Benson.* But as we said, the Court declined a "doctrinaire reliance on formal categories" and instead "look[ed] to the purposes" of Article III.

The Court described these purposes in terms of (1) a "personal right" to "an impartial and independent federal adjudication" and (2) certain "public functions" pertaining to "the role of the independent judiciary within the constitutional scheme of tripartite government." The extent to which Article III stands as a "personal guarantee of an impartial and independent federal adjudication" was not, however, at issue in *Schor.* Whatever claim the petitioners may have had to this guarantee, they had waived by choosing the agency forum and its reparations process.

dicial review for "fraud, misrepresentation or other misconduct."

Certain chemical firms claimed that this scheme violated Article III. They claimed that the arbitration involved "private rights" subject to Article III and that the standard of review, for "fraud, misrepresentation or other misconduct," was not a sufficient reservation of judicial power in these courts. The Supreme Court rejected these claims, largely with a purpose-oriented view of Article III.

The arbitration system was limited to specialized factual assessments (determining compensation for the use of scientific data pertaining to the registration of pesticides). Moreover, the Act's provision for federal court review reserved an " 'appropriate exercise of the judicial function' " in those courts. 473 U.S. at 592, 105 S.Ct. at 3338. Also, as explained by Justice Brennan in his concurrence, such review "encompasses the authority to invalidate an arbitrator's decision when that decision exceeds the arbitrator's authority or exhibits a manifest disregard for the governing law," thereby "preserving the judicial authority over questions of law.... " 473 U.S. at 601, 105 S.Ct. at 3343. Given this limited scope of agency-held judicial power, the delegation of this power did not seriously undercut "the independent role of the judiciary in our constitutional scheme." 473 U.S. at 590, 105 S.Ct. at 3337.

2. 478 U.S. 833, 847–48, 106 S.Ct. 3245, 3254–55, 92 L.Ed.2d 675 (1986).

The public functions part of Article III could not, however, be waived. "When these Article III limitations are at issue," the Court explained, "notions of consent and waiver cannot be dispositive because the limitations serve institutional interests that the parties cannot be expected to protect." The Court, therefore, asked whether the allocation of judicial power to the Commodities Exchange Commission undercut Article III in its public function respecting "the role of the independent judiciary within the constitutional scheme of tripartite government," and found that the allocation did not.

In the next sections we will more generally discuss agencies and these Article III matters, of an impartial and independent federal forum and the role of an independent judiciary in our form of government.

§ 5.2.1 Public Functions: The Role of an Independent Judiciary

In *Schor,* the allocation of judicial power to the agency was only for a specialized area—commodities trading—that seemed especially fit for resolution by an expert and streamlined process. Moreover, Commission orders were subject to judicial review, according to a "weight of the evidence" form of review for matters of fact and *de novo* review for matters of law. Considering these various factors—the limited subject matter of agency jurisdiction, agency expertise respecting this subject matter, and the availability of judicial review—the Court determined that any infringement of Article III and its standard of an independent federal judiciary was "*de minimis.*"[3]

A more general examination of the functions and purposes of an independent judiciary in our form of government now seems in order, so as better to understand when (as in *Schor*) an allocation of judicial power to agencies does not undercut these functions. Foremost among these functions is maintaining the limitations and dispersals of power that are so much a part of our constitutional structure. In this function, the courts act as an "intermediary for the people," set in place to keep the other parts of government "within the limits assigned to their authority."[4] In relation to agencies, the courts continue their role as an intermediary for the people, by checking tendencies of agencies to enlarge on the authority that Congress has delegated to them.[5]

Keeping power within prescribed limits stands in the tradition of *Marbury v. Madison.* This function of courts does not, however, exhaust the range of public functions assigned to federal courts by Article III. As

3. 478 U.S. at 856, 106 S.Ct. at 3259.

4. Federalist No. 78 (Hamilton). Using a metaphor of containment, Hamilton described the courts as "the bulwarks of a limited Constitution.... "

5. In the words of Justice Brennan, the courts "function as a check on any aggrandizing tendencies in the other branches." Thomas v. Union Carbide Agr. Products Co., 473 U.S. 568, 594, 105 S.Ct. 3325, 3339, 87 L.Ed.2d 409 (1985). The courts also mediate government power in another sense. Respecting the power that government legitimately holds, the courts try to assure that this power is not used to violate individual rights that the Constitution shields, as by the Bill of Rights.

explained by Alexander Hamilton in Federalist No. 78, "it is not with a view to infractions of [constitutional limits] only that an independent judiciary was established." Rather, an independent judiciary was also established *to interpret and apply laws passed by Congress.* In this function, Hamilton said, "the firmness of the judicial magistracy is of vast importance in mitigating the severity and confining the operation of such laws."

According to the deepest traditions of Anglo–American jurisprudence, courts work in the context of whole law and "the permanent interests of the community."[6] As explained by Professor Harry Wellington, the generalist perspective of courts "enable judges to discern, better than others with ... limited vision, the enduring principles and longer range concerns that tend to be forgotten where either the interests of factions collide or the perspective of bureaucrats prevail."[7]

Bureaucratic adjudication is by officials with a perspective perhaps distorted by whatever policy or program the agency is about and who

6. This tradition, that the courts may "mitigate" legislation in light of the permanent interests of the community, is seen in canons of interpretation variously described as the "equity in the statutes." See J. Gough, Fundamental Law in English History 19–47 (1955). Or as the "constructive intent" of the "reasonable legislator." See Mayton, Law Among the Pleonasms: The Futility and Aconstitutionality of Legislative History in Statutory Interpretation, 41 Emory L.J. 113 (1992).

That courts may "mitigate" legislation in light of the permanent interests of the community, may have been the theory of Lord Coke in Dr. Bonham's case, as he held that courts may review acts of Parliament according to "common right and reason". See id. at 30–47; Jaffe, The Right to Judicial Review, 71 Harv.L.R. 401, 416–17 (1958). As explained by Jaffe "Coke's philosophy, his statements in Dr. Bonham's Case and the Institutes were a mighty source of ... oracular authority." It was not necessary to their thinking that the courts be independent of parliament in any absolute sense. It was enough that legislation would be interpreted in the light of "reason" and the "common law".

In American jurisprudence, how the courts apply statutes to preserve the permanent values of the community is shown starkly in the celebrated New York Court of Appeals decision in Riggs v. Palmer, 115 N.Y. 506, 22 N.E. 188 (1889). There, to prevent his grandfather from changing his will and to gain "a speedy enjoyment" of the grandfather's property, the grandson poisoned the grandfather. The daughters of the deceased brought suit to prevent the grandson from taking possession. According to the terms of the applicable statutes, however, the grandson inherited the property. Nonetheless, the court found against the grandson, stating:

> [A]ll laws, as well as all contracts, may be controlled in their operation and effect by general, fundamental maxims of the common law. No one shall be permitted to profit by his own wrong, or to found any claim upon his own iniquity, or to acquire property by his own crime. These maxims are dictated by public policy, have their foundation in universal law administered in all civilized countries, and have nowhere been superseded by statutes.

115 N.Y. at 51, 22 N.E. at 190. This power of the courts to modify statutes in light of ingrained community interests enjoys a broad support, in one form or another, among a range of scholars. See, e.g., B. Cardozo, The Nature of the Judicial Process 42 (1921) ("in the end, the principle that was thought to be most fundamental, to represent the larger and deeper social interests, put its competitors to flight"); Dworkin, The Model of Rules, 35 U.Chi.L.Rev. 14, 29 (1977) ("the Court cited the principle that no man may profit from his own wrong as a background standard against which to read the statute of wills and in this way justified a new interpretation of the statute").

7. Wellington, The Nature of Judicial Review, 91 Yale L.J. 486, 493 (1982). These qualities, as we associate them with courts, create an essential, a necessary "public and private confidence" in courts. Federalist No. 78 (Hamilton).

may not be as inclined, by training, experience or position, to as balanced a view as Article III courts.[8] How this works, this difference in perspective, is illustrated by *Textile Workers Union v. Darlington Manufacturing Co.*[9] The National Labor Relations Act makes it an unfair labor practice for a business to discharge employees because they join a union. When a company went out of business to avoid unions, the Union argued "that an employer may not go completely out of business without running afoul of the Act if such action is prompted by a desire to avoid unionization." The National Labor Relations Board agreed, finding that the employer had indeed committed an unfair labor practice by choosing to go out of business. The Supreme Court, however, disagreed. In the context of our ingrained interest in economic freedom, the Union's claim would "represent such a startling innovation that it should not be entertained without the clearest manifestation of legislative intent.... " Consequently, the Court in the *Textile Workers Union* case held that "so far as the Labor Relations Act is concerned, an employer has the absolute right to terminate his entire business for any reason he pleases."

From a public choice point of view, Article III courts may "mitigat[e] the severity" of laws passed by Congress in quite another way, by impeding special interests working through government to gain private benefits at a collective cost.[10] As Professor Macey has explained, legislators may pass a statute with high-sounding but vague "public interest" language, and with a special-interest beneficiary hidden behind this language.[11] By this form of statute they may avoid the political costs they would incur if the special-interest purpose were explicit. This promotion of special interests may, however, be diminished by the operation of an independent judiciary in a government of separated powers.

A separate and independent judiciary, given its inclination toward the permanent interests of the community, should tend to ignore the implicit special interest, and to enforce the statute only according to its "public interest" tenor.

The ultimate effect of this interaction between courts and Congress should be to force legislators to bear the political costs of special-interest legislation, which in turn should diminish the amount of such legislation. Legislators, to insure court enforcement of special legislation, must specifically identify the interest that this legislation serves. And this

8. The Supreme Court has acknowledged this bad possibility. "A danger in allocating judicial power to agencies," the Court has said, is that of "sapp[ing] the judicial power as it exists under the Federal Constitution" by "establish[ing] a government of bureaucratic character alien to our system." Northern Pipeline Const. Co. v. Marathon Pipe Line Co., 458 U.S. 50, 86, 102 S.Ct. 2858, 2879, 73 L.Ed.2d 598 (1982). See Wellington, supra, 91 Yale L.J. at 502.

9. 380 U.S. 263, 85 S.Ct. 994, 13 L.Ed.2d 827 (1965).

10. In Federalist No. 10, Madison described this harm of special interests as "the injury of the private rights of particular classes of citizens by unjust and partial laws."

11. Macey, Promoting Public–Regarding Legislation Through Statutory Interpretation: An Interest Group Model, 86 Colum.L.Rev. 223–268 (1986).

identification informs their constituency, so that the legislators are forced to bear the political costs of special interest legislation. Thus, it is that as envisioned in Federalist No. 78, judicial review "not only serves to moderate the immediate mischiefs of those [laws] which may have been passed, but it operates as a check upon the legislative body in passing them."[12]

§ 5.2.2 The "Personal Right" to "An Impartial and Independent Federal Adjudication"

The "personal right" recognized in *Commodity Futures Trading Commission v. Schor,* that of "an impartial and independent federal adjudication,"[13] is secured by Article III by its provision for tenured judges sitting in courts separated from the political branches. But as judicial power is allocated to agencies, this insulation and independence of judges is threatened by the combination of power within agencies: the agency that adjudicates quite likely also legislates and prosecutes. Whether an independent and impartial adjudication is possible in such an environment of combined power has been a long-standing concern of administrative law.[14]

Congress and the President have wrestled with the problem. In 1937, the President's Committee on Administrative Management recommended that the judicial function of agencies be completely separated from the "administrative function," and lodged in a tribunal that would "sit as an impartial, independent body to make decisions affecting the public interest and private rights upon the basis of the records and findings presented to it by the administrative section."[15] Since this report, various presidential commissions have similarly recommended that agencies be divested of judicial functions.[16] But in only one case, that of the National Labor Relations Board, has such a complete divestiture been made.[17]

12. The full quote is that judicial review:

> not only serves to moderate the immediate mischiefs of those [laws] which may have been passed, but it operates as a check upon the legislative body in passing them; who, perceiving that obstacles to the success of iniquitous intention are to be expected from the scruple of the courts, are in a manner compelled by the very motives of the injustice they meditate to qualify their attempts.

Federalist No. 78 (Hamilton).

13. 478 U.S. 833, 848, 106 S.Ct. 3245, 3255, 92 L.Ed.2d 675 (1986).

14. See, e.g., Wong Yang Sung v. McGrath, 339 U.S. 33, 70 S.Ct. 445, 94 L.Ed. 616 (1950).

15. Report of the President's Committee on Administrative Management 41–42 (1937).

16. For instance, the second Hoover Commission proposed that the adjudicatory functions of the Federal Trade Commission and the National Labor Relations Board be taken out of those agencies and placed in an "Administrative Court of the United States." Commission on organization of the Executive Branch, Legal Services and Procedure 61–62 (1955). In 1971, the "Ash Commission" recommended an administrative court. The President's Council on Executive Organization, a New Regulatory Framework: Report on Selected Independent Regulatory Agencies 20, 54 (1971).

17. In 1947 in the Labor Management Relations Act, 61 Stat. 136 (1947), Congress separated the Office of General Counsel from the National Labor Relations Board. For a review from the bench of this separation of functions, see NLRB v. United Food and Commercial Workers Union, 484 U.S. 112, 108 S.Ct. 413, 98 L.Ed.2d 429 (1987).

Congress has, however, provided for an internal separation of functions so as to establish a measure of independence for agency personnel engaged in judging. By means of the Administrative Procedure Act, Congress has provided that agency adjudicatory hearings are to be presided over by "administrative law judges" whose appointment, salary, and tenure are controlled not by the agencies but by the Civil Service Commission.[18] Within the agency, administrative law judges are further insulated from the prosecutorial side of the agency as the Administrative Procedure Act provides that these judges "may not . . . be responsible to or subject to the supervision or directions of an employee or agent in the performance of investigative or prosecuting functions for an agency."[19] These Administrative Procedure Act provisions, which establish something of an internal separation of functions, are discussed more fully in Chapter 8.

Apart from Congress, the courts have addressed the agency combination of functions problem. In doing so, they have not, however, generally relied on Article III, *Commodity Futures Trading Commission v. Schor* notwithstanding. Instead of Article III, the courts have usually acted in relation to due process of law as guaranteed by the fifth and fourteenth amendments.[20] In the case of large, compartmentalized agencies, the courts have thought that functions are separated enough, inside the agency, for an impartial adjudication as required by due process. Even where such internal separation is lacking, for instance in a smaller agency such as a state licensing board, the Supreme Court, presuming an "intellectual discipline" on the part of officials, has ruled that a combination of functions does not in and of itself violate due process.[21]

18. 5 U.S.C. §§ 3105, 5372 & 7521.

19. 5 U.S.C. § 554(d)(2). The success of these Administrative Procedure Act provisions in assuring that administrative law judges are insulated against agency pressures, is a matter of debate. A harsh assessment is that " 'Rather than having the independence of a district court judge, they are essentially on the payroll and subjected to the pressures of agencies.' "Moss, Judges Under Fire: ALJ Independence at Issue, 77 ABA Journ. 56 (Nov., 1991).

20. Analyzing allocations of judicial power to agencies by reference only to due process may truncate analysis. Due process focuses on whether an agency provides a "fair" hearing, by which we mean such things as whether it reaches accurate results while respecting the autonomy and dignity of the person. See Chapter 7, Sec. 7.6.1, infra. While this sort of focus on fair procedures is of course important, it may be too limited. This focus does not reach the structural functions assigned to Article III courts (such as an inclination to keep the other parts of government within their constitutional spheres and an aptitude in "mitigating the severity" of laws passed by Congress) and whether a rerouting of judicial power to agencies might diminish these functions. Of course, due process might be broadly construed to include these matters—open-ended constructions of due process are not unheard of. But such overloading has to weaken due process in its core function of assuring fair procedures to the individual facing the collective might of the state. So, perhaps it is best to judge allocations of judicial power to agencies according to the constraints of Article III.

21. Withrow v. Larkin, 421 U.S. 35, 95 S.Ct. 1456, 43 L.Ed.2d 712 (1975). The precise holding was that "the mere exposure to evidence presented in nonadversary investigative procedures is insufficient in itself to impugn the fairness of the Board members at a later adversary hearing." The Court qualified this holding by saying that it did not "preclude a court from determining that in the special facts and circumstances present in the case before it that the risk of unfairness is intolerably high."

§ 5.3 KEEPING DELEGATIONS OF JUDICIAL POWER CONSISTENT WITH ARTICLE III

In the last several years, the Supreme Court has measured the constitutionality of allocations of judicial power to agencies by whether that allocation diminishes the "essential attributes" of judicial power.[1] These attributes, we suppose, are synonymous with the purposes of Article III and qualities of judicial power as discussed in the preceding sections. These essential attributes would, therefore, include an impartial and balanced point of view, an inclination to keep the other parts of government within their constitutional spheres, and an aptitude at "mitigating the severity" of laws passed by Congress.

A way of assuring that these essential attributes of judicial power are kept in courts is to assure that agency action is subject to judicial review. Federal court review of agency adjudications, as a means of preserving judicial power, was the method that was actually and originally approved in *Crowell v. Benson.* There, the court could fully correct the agency in matters of law and overturn unreasonable findings as to matters of fact. For most allocations of judicial power to agencies, this form of review should preserve "the proper and peculiar responsibility of the courts" in the "interpretation of the laws" and should check unreasonable factual findings by agencies.[2] At the same time, it accommodates the economies incident to original agency adjudication. Consequently, given the narrowly circumscribed power committed to the agency in *Crowell v. Benson* (on-the-job injuries in the maritime area—where agency expertise and routine might usefully supplant the more ponderous processes of federal courts) the Court in that seminal case was "unable to find any constitutional obstacle to the action of the Congress in availing itself of a method shown by experience to be essential in order to apply its standards to the thousands of cases involved, thus relieving the courts of a most serious burden *while preserving their complete authority to insure the proper application of the law.*"[3]

Too much, however, can be made of judicial review of agency action as a means of assuring that the "essential attributes" of Article III power remains in the courts. While "the presence of appellate review by

§ 5.3

1. Commodity Futures Trading Commission v. Schor, 478 U.S. 833, 850, 106 S.Ct. 3245, 3256, 92 L.Ed.2d 675 (1986); Northern Pipeline Construction Co. v. Marathon Pipe Line Co., 458 U.S. 50, 81, 102 S.Ct. 2858, 2876, 73 L.Ed.2d 598 (1982). See Kalaris v. Donovan, 697 F.2d 376, 388 (D.C.Cir.1983), cert. denied 462 U.S. 1119, 103 S.Ct. 3088, 77 L.Ed.2d 1349 (1983), rehearing denied 463 U.S. 1236, 104 S.Ct. 30, 77 L.Ed.2d 1451 (1983) (Article III requires only that the ultimate "judicial power" be reserved in the Article III courts; it does not require that all adjudicative bodies . . . be constituted as Article III courts).

2. Federalist No. 78 (Hamilton).

3. 285 U.S. 22, 54, 52 S.Ct. 285, 293, 76 L.Ed. 598 (1932). See also United States v. Raddatz, 447 U.S. 667, 681–83, 100 S.Ct. 2406, 2415–16, 65 L.Ed.2d 424 (1980), rehearing denied 448 U.S. 916, 101 S.Ct. 36, 65 L.Ed.2d 1179 (1980) (holding that the Federal Magistrates Act, 28 U.S.C.A. § 636(b)(1) (1982), which allows federal district court to accept magistrates' assessment of the credibility of testimony received in a pre-trial motion to suppress evidence, did not by that allowance violate Article III).

an Article 111 court will go a long way toward insuring a proper separation of powers,"[4] a long way is not all the way, which was a point made in *Northern Pipeline Constr. Co. v. Marathon Pipe Line*. In this case, Justice Brennan wrote that "the constitutional requirements for the exercise of the judicial power must be met at all stages of adjudication, and not only on appeal, where the court is restricted to considerations of law, as well as the nature of the case as it has been shaped at the trial level."[5]

The point underscored by Brennan is that appellate review cannot fully be counted on to redress all the errors in initial agency adjudication. Moreover, judicial review is expensive and perhaps untimely: given its length it may come too late. As a practical matter, then, the agency tribunal is for many individuals the only tribunal. What are we to make of this? Probably, that the judicial power thus held by an agency should not approach "the range of jurisdiction and powers normally vested only in Article 111 courts."[6] In *Marathon Pipe Line,* federal court review of non-Article 111 bankruptcy courts was not enough to save the constitutionality of those courts, and *Crowell v. Benson* was distinguished because there "the agency ... made only specialized, narrowly confined factual determinations regarding a particularized area of law." "In contrast," the power of bankruptcy judges "encompasse[d] not only traditional matters of bankruptcy but drew in a broad range of other civil actions as well."[7]

4. Northern Pipeline Construction Co. v. Marathon Pipe Line Co., 458 U.S. 50, 115, 102 S.Ct. 2858, 2894, 73 L.Ed.2d 598 (1982). For an "appellate review theory," which at a minimum would provide "a right of access to a constitutional court to police the separation of powers and provide guarantees against administrative arbitrariness," see Fallon, Our Legislative Courts, Administrative Agencies, and Article III, 101 Harv.L.Rev. 915, 969 (1988). In practice, Congress subscribes to an appellate review theory in that it ordinarily provides for judicial review (de novo as to questions of law and substantial evidence as to questions of fact) of agency action. If Congress doesn't explicitly provide for judicial review, the courts presume that Congress intended some such form of it. See Abbott Laboratories v. Gardner, 387 U.S. 136, 141, 87 S.Ct. 1507, 1511, 18 L.Ed.2d 681 (1967) ("only upon a showing of 'clear and convincing evidence' of a contrary legislative intent should the courts restrict access to judicial review").

5. 458 U.S. 50, 86 & n. 39, 102 S.Ct. 2858, 2879 & n. 39, 73 L.Ed.2d 598 (1982). In the *Marathon Pipe Line* case, the Northern Pipeline Construction Co. had filed a petition for reorganization in bankruptcy court organized under the Bankruptcy Reform Act of 1978. Northern then sued Marathon Pipe Line in that court asserting various common law claims including breach of contract and misrepresentation. Marathon moved to dismiss this suit, claiming that the 1978 act unconstitutionally conferred judicial power on a non-Article II court. On review, a divided Supreme Court upheld this claim. While the members of the Court were unable to agree on any common rationale for its holding, this holding, as later described in Thomas v. Union Carbide Agr. Products Co., 473 U.S. 568, 594, 105 S.Ct. 3325, 3339, 87 L.Ed.2d 409 (1985), was "that Congress may not vest in a non-Article III court the power to adjudicate, render final judgment, and issue binding orders in a traditional contract action arising under state law, without consent of the litigants, and subject only to ordinary appellate review [in federal court]."

6. Commodity Futures Trading Com'n v. Schor, 478 U.S. 833, 835, 106 S.Ct. 3245, 3248, 92 L.Ed.2d 675 (1986).

7. Northern Pipeline Construction Co. v. Marathon Pipe Line Co., 458 U.S. 50, 84–85, 102 S.Ct. 2858, 2878–79, 73 L.Ed.2d 598 (1982). See also Commodity Futures Trading Com'n v. Schor, 478 U.S. 833, 106 S.Ct. 3245, 92 L.Ed.2d 675 (1986); Thomas v. Union Carbide Agr. Products Co., 473 U.S. 568, 594, 105 S.Ct. 3325, 3339, 87 L.Ed.2d 409 (1985).

A regard for "the range of jurisdiction and powers" conferred on agencies requires care by Congress respecting the subject matter that it commits to agency adjudicatory power, even if that adjudication is subject to judicial review. In this light, *Crowell v. Benson,* where agency expertise and routine was usefully brought to bear with respect to a limited subject matter, was an exemplar of an appropriately delegated judicial power.

Chapter 6

THE SEVENTH AMENDMENT AND THE AGENCIES

Table of Sections

Sec.

Adjudicatory power has been a power essential to agencies, and apparently just as essentially, agencies supplement this power by money remedies such as civil fines, reparations, or an award for back pay. When agencies adjudicate and issue these orders, they do so without juries. The lay wisdom of juries is incompatible with institutions whose *raison d' etre* is efficiency and expertise. Same as the Supreme Court has said, "jury trials would be incompatible with the whole concept of administrative adjudication." [1] Given this incompatibility, Prof. Hart long ago noted that the seventh amendment "with a little different interpretation" might have been "a major safeguard against bureaucracy."[2]

A safeguard, or, from a different view, an impediment to an efficient as well as fair and accurate mode of adjudication as by agencies. The Supreme Court has favored this latter view. To date, it has found that agencies are not subject to the seventh amendment.[3]

§ 6.1 NLRB v. JONES & LAUGHLIN STEEL CORPORATION

In the late Thirties, the newly created National Labor Relations Board found the Jones & Laughlin Steel Corporation guilty of an unfair

1. Curtis v. Loether, 415 U.S. 189, 194, 94 S.Ct. 1005, 1008, 39 L.Ed.2d 260 (1974).

2. Hart, The Power of Congress to Limit the Jurisdiction of Federal Courts: Exercise in Dialectic, 66 Har.L.Rev. 1362 (1953).

3. Atlas Roofing Co. v. Occupational Safety and Health Review Com'n, 430 U.S. 442, 450, 97 S.Ct. 1261, 1266, 51 L.Ed.2d 464 (1977). More recently, the Court has said that "In certain situations, of course, Congress may fashion causes of action that are *closely analogous* to common-law claims and place them beyond the ambit of the Seventh Amendment by assigning their resolution to a forum in which jury trials are unavailable." Granfinanciera, S.A. v. Nordberg, 492 U.S. 33, 52, 109 S.Ct. 2782, 2796, 106 L.Ed.2d 26 (1989) (emphasis added).

labor practice in firing employees active in union affairs. The Board then ordered the company to reinstate the employees with back-pay. In its major-league New Deal decision in *NLRB v. Jones & Laughlin Steel Corporation*,[1] the Supreme Court held that Congress had acted within the commerce clause in enacting the National Labor Relations Act and establishing the National Labor Relations Board. In a couple of terse paragraphs added at the end, the opinion also addressed whether the back-pay remedy prescribed by the Board amounted to a "money judgment" in violation of the seventh amendment.

The Court resolved the jury trial issue by interpreting the seventh amendment according to a certain historical method. The amendment provides that the "right of trial by jury shall be preserved." The Court emphasized the word "preserved," and explained that what the amendment preserved was the "right which existed under the common law when the Amendment was adopted." Because the National Labor Relations Act established a "statutory proceeding" that was "unknown to the common law" in 1791, the Court found that a civil jury was not required.[2]

In 1974, however, the historical approach of *Jones & Laughlin* was undercut, by the Supreme Court's unanimous decision in *Curtis v. Loether*.[3] In that case, the plaintiff claimed that a landlord had violated the fair housing provisions of the Civil Rights Act of 1968, because he had refused to rent her an apartment because of her race. She asked for compensatory and punitive damages as provided by the Act.[4] The case was tried by a district court judge without a jury; this judge found for the plaintiff. The defendant-landlord appealed, and the question before the Supreme Court was whether the bench trial had violated her rights, if any, to a jury trial as provided by the seventh amendment.

The plaintiff argued against the application of the amendment on grounds of policy and precedent, and was unsuccessful in both arguments. On policy grounds, she claimed that a jury trial might expose her, a black woman, to the racial prejudice of the jury and that the delay of a jury trial might impede a timely enforcement of the Act. But these policy reasons, the Court found, were in and of themselves "insufficient to overcome" a constitutional command.

In terms of precedent, the plaintiff relied on *NLRB v. Jones & Laughlin* and argued that "the Amendment is inapplicable to new causes of action created by congressional enactment." But *Jones & Laughlin* and its historical method notwithstanding, the Court rejected plaintiff's argument. The Court stated:

§ 6.1

1. NLRB v. Jones & Laughlin Steel Corp., 301 U.S. 1, 57 S.Ct. 615, 81 L.Ed. 893 (1937).

2. 301 U.S. at 48, 57 S.Ct. at 629. For a thorough, and critical, discussion of the historical approach to interpreting the seventh amendment, see Wolfram, The Constitutional History of the Seventh Amendment, 57 Minn.L.Rev. 639 (1973).

3. 415 U.S. 189, 94 S.Ct. 1005, 39 L.Ed.2d 260 (1974).

4. 42 U.S.C. § 3612 ("The court may . . . award to the plaintiff actual damages and not more than $1000 punitive damages").

> Whatever doubt may have existed should now be dispelled. The Seventh Amendment does apply to actions enforcing statutory rights, and requires a jury trial upon demand, if the statute creates legal rights and remedies, enforceable in an action for damages in the ordinary court of law.

Under this reasoning, whether an action existed in 1791 would not seem to be the key to the seventh amendment. Rather, the key seems to be the quality of the action, whether the action for which a civil jury is requested shares qualities of the common-law sort of action for which the jury trial is preserved. The Court explained that "a jury trial must be available if the action involves right and remedies of the sort *typically* enforced in an action at law." In relation to the case before it, the Court reasoned that "A damage action under the statute sounds basically in tort—the statute merely defines a new legal duty, and authorizes the courts to compensate a plaintiff for the injury caused by the defendant's wrongful breach."[5] Because the action "involve[d] right and remedies of the sort *typically* enforced in an action at law," it was subject to the seventh amendment.

But what about *Jones & Laughlin?* Was that case, decided as it was according to a more formalistic method, therefore wrongly decided? No, the Court explained because in that case the statutory rules were enforced in an *agency* rather than in a *court. Jones & Laughlin,* the Court said, "merely stands for the proposition that the seventh amendment is generally inapplicable in administrative proceedings, where jury trials would be incompatible with the whole concept of administrative adjudication."

In contrast, the enforcement of statutory rights had, in *Curtis v. Loether*, been committed to a court rather than an agency, and this, the Court said, made all the difference. In the Court's view, "when Congress provides for enforcement of statutory rights in an ordinary civil action in the district courts, where there is obviously no *functional justification* for denying the jury trial right, a jury trial must be available.... "[6]

If "functional justification" is the measure, then a full job of it would seem to require an identification of the functions of the civil jury

5. 415 U.S. at 195, 94 S.Ct. at 1009 (emphasis added). The Court also quoted Justice Story, in Parsons v. Bedford, 28 U.S. (3 Pet.) 433, 446–47, 7 L.Ed. 732 (1830), for the proposition that "[b]y *common law,* [framers of the Amendment] meant ... not merely suits, which the *common* law recognized among its old and settled proceedings, but suits in which *legal* rights were to be ascertained.... " 415 U.S. at 193, 94 S.Ct. at 1007. This approach, of how the action in question shares qualities of the common law action for which the jury trial is preserved, has been continued by the Court in its more recent decision in this area in Granfinanciera, S.A. v. Nordberg, 492 U.S. 33, 109 S.Ct. 2782, 106 L.Ed.2d 26 (1989). In relation to whether, as in *Curtis v. Loether,* a statutory action involving a money sanction had to be committed to a jury, the Court in *Granfinanciera v. Nordberg* said that "First, we compare the statutory action to 18th-century actions brought in the courts of England prior to the merger of the courts of law and equity." The Court held that the matter in question, allegedly fraudulent transfers involving bankruptcy, could not be decided without the aid of a seventh amendment jury.

6. 415 U.S. at 195, 94 S.Ct. at 1009 (emphasis added).

and how it might be useful, and then to compare the functions of agencies. This sort of functionalism is not an easy task, certainly it is one that the Court has not undertaken.[7] Still, some jury functions are obvious.[8] The grand function of the civil jury has to be that of rectifying and decentralizing government power according to community interests.[9] By reference to reasons identified in the ratification debates on the Constitution, the jury may as well be considered as "a security against the corruption" of magistrates and more generally as a guard against abuse of power by government officials.[10]

From this jury trial side of things, it would appear that the Court in *Curtis v. Loether* had it backwards as it distinguished between bench trials (subject to the amendment) and agencies (not subject). Agencies would seem to be *more* subject to political pressures, and *less* likely to interpose community values between the defendant and government, than are judges. On the administrative side, however, there are countervailing interests of efficiency and of accuracy in adjudication as made possible by agency experts. So far these interests have been a controlling justification. As said by the Court:

> Congress is not required by the Seventh Amendment to choke the already crowded federal courts with new types of litigation or prevented from committing some new types of litigation to administrative agencies with special competence in the relevant field.... This is the case even if the Seventh Amendment would have required a jury where the adjudication of these rights is

7. Justice White, dissenting in Granfinanciera, S.A. v. Nordberg, 492 U.S. 33, 109 S.Ct. 2782, 106 L.Ed.2d 26 (1989), which involved the application of the seventh amendment to proceedings in bankruptcy, does survey some of the functions of the civil jury, and he does so consistent with the discussion, of "jury equity" and "of juries serving as popular checks on life-tenured judges," in the text above.

8. For an examination of the functions that the seventh amendment may perform, see Wolfram, The Constitutional History of the Seventh Amendment, 57 Minn.L.Rev. 639 (1973).

9. As well as being indicated by the result in *Curtis v. Loether,* such a view of the first amendment may be seen in that opinion's quotation of, and reliance on, Justice Story's description of the seventh amendment. Justice Story wrote that "[b]y *common law,* [framers of the amendment] meant ... not merely suits, which the *common* law recognized among its old and settled proceedings, but suits in which *legal* rights were to be ascertained.... " Parsons v. Bedford, 28 U.S. (3 Pet.) 433, 446–47, 7 L.Ed. 732 (1830), quoted in Curtis v. Loether, 415 U.S. at 193, 94 S.Ct. at 1008.

10. Fed. No. 83 (Hamilton). See also II Records of the Federal Convention 587 (M. Farrand ed. 1937) (Gerry, arguing that civil juries guard against corrupt judges). See generally Note, Article III Implications for the Applicability of the Seventh Amendment to Federal Statutory Actions, 95 Yale L.J. 1459, 1465–66 (1986).

Luther Martin, addressing the Constitution's failure to guarantee trial by jury, stated that:

> Thus, Sir, jury trials, ... are taken away not only in a great variety of questions between individual and individual, but in every case, whether civil or criminal, arising under the laws of the United States, or the execution of those laws. It is taken away in those very cases, where, of all others, it is most essential for our liberty to have sacredly guarded and preserved, in every case, whether civil or criminal, between government and its officers on the one part, and the subject or citizen on the other.

III Records of the Federal Convention 80–81 (M. Farrand ed. 1937). See also Kirst, Administrative Penalties and the Civil Jury: The Supreme Court's Assault on the Seventh Amendment, 126 U.Pa.L.Rev. 1281, 1313–28 (1978).

assigned to a federal court of law instead of an administrative agency.[11]

§ 6.2 ATLAS ROOFING CO. v. OCCUPATIONAL SAFETY & HEALTH REVIEW COMMISSION: THE CLOSELY ANALOGOUS AND THE PURELY TAXONOMIC

Apparently because it considered common-law remedies for unsafe working conditions to be inadequate, Congress enacted the Occupational Safety and Health Act. The Act establishes a statutory duty on the part of industry to avoid unsafe or unhealthy working conditions and authorizes the Secretary of Labor to promulgate safety and health rules toward these goals. Under the Act, civil penalties of up to $10,000 may be assessed against employers who violate these rules. The employer may challenge such an assessment in an evidentiary hearing before an administrative law judge. This hearing is reviewable by the Commission, and then a final order as rendered by the Commission is subject to review by a federal court of appeals. On review, the Commission's factual findings are conclusive if supported by substantial evidence.[1]

In this process (which occurs in an area previously occupied by only the common law) there is no jury. In *Atlas Roofing Co. v. Occupational Safety & Health Review Commission,* the argument was that absent a jury, the process was constitutionally deficient.[2] This argument was brought by an employer, which after exhausting the administrative process offered by the Commission found itself assessed with a six hundred dollar civil fine.

As the employer saw it, *Curtis v. Loether* stood for the proposition that general rules of law backed by money fines required a jury trial. The employer argued that "a suit in a federal court by the government for violation of a statute . . . is classically a suit at common law." The Supreme Court did not deny that a court action in damages for violation of a statute was "classically a suit at common law." Instead, the Court found that this proposition was inapposite, because here the civil action was in an *agency* and not a *court* as had been the case in *Curtis v. Loether.* The Supreme Court justified this distinction between courts and agencies by resort to the historical method and by a new angle under this method.

As reiterated in *Atlas Roofing,* the historical approach is that the seventh amendment is "declaratory" of the law in 1791. The twist of *Atlas Roofing* was that under the law at that time, the availability of a jury trial depended on the *identity* of the forum. When the amendment

11. Atlas Roofing Co. v. Occupational Safety and Health Review Com'n, 430 U.S. 442, 455, 97 S.Ct. 1261, 1269, 51 L.Ed.2d 464 (1977).

§ 6.2

1. Occupational Safety and Health Act of 1970, 29 U.S.C. § 651 et seq.

2. 430 U.S. 442, 97 S.Ct. 1261, 51 L.Ed.2d 464 (1977).

was added to the Constitution, equity, admiralty, and military courts operated without juries and the jurisdiction of these forums at times overlapped with law courts. Consequently, the same or similar issues might or might not have been decided by juries, depending on the forum. The Court thus concluded that under a historical approach the "right to a jury trial turns not solely on the nature of the issue to be resolved but also on the forum in which it is to be resolved." This being so, the function of the seventh amendment, the Court said, was to "prevent Congress from depriving a litigant of a jury trial in a 'legal action' before a tribunal *customarily* utilizing a jury as its fact-finding arm. . . ."

Under this identity-of-the-forum key to the seventh amendment, Congress does not violate the amendment as it assigns civil actions to an agency, because the agency is not "a tribunal customarily utilizing a jury as its fact-finding arm." No jury is required "even if the Seventh Amendment would have required a jury where the adjudication of those rights is assigned to a federal court of law instead of an administrative agency." The Court also explained that the identity-of-the-forum approach had its agreeable policy implications. "Congress," the Court said, "is not required by the Seventh Amendment to choke the already crowded federal courts with new types of litigation or prevented from committing some new types of litigation to administrative agencies with special competence in the relevant field."

The reasoning behind the identity-of-the-forum approach to the seventh amendment is not airtight. In this respect, the history used by the Court is incomplete. While availability of the jury trial may have turned on the identity of the tribunal, it is also true that this fact was a major complaint of the colonists against England. By shifting civil cases to admiralty courts, the British had deprived them of the right to trial by jury. The British did this for violations of the Stamp and Sugar Acts. Moreover, a vice-admiralty court sitting in Nova Scotia was given jurisdiction respecting a wider range of matters in the colonies.[3] The colonists, therefore, formally complained that Parliament had extended "the Courts of Admiralty beyond their ancient limits, giving them a concurrent jurisdiction, in causes heretofore cognizable only in courts of Common Law."[4] So, in terms of the practices that caused Americans to worry

3. See generally J. Reid, The Constitutional History of the American Revolution, (1986). See also Grey, Origins of the Unwritten Constitution: Fundamental Law in American Revolutionary Thought, 30 Stan. L.Rev. 843, 870 (1978).

4. From the "last petition of grievances" submitted by New York to England, and quoted at J. Reid, supra, 191. See also J. Reid at 205, quoting a protest by London merchants against Parliament's "fisheries and trade bill" on the grounds that it would "aggravate" legitimate colonial grievances:

> [A]mong the other grievances of which our fellow-subjects in *America* so generally complain, is of their being deprived of Trial by Jury in particular cases, and the extension of the jurisdiction of Admiralty Courts; which grievances your Petitioners, with much concern find are not only continued, but extended by the present Bill.

Also, in the British Parliament, it had been moved that "the powers of Admiralty and vice-Admiralty courts in America shall be restrained within their ancient limits, and the trial by jury, in all civil cases, where the same may be abolished, restored. . . . " Id. at 224.

about losing the civil jury and to add the seventh amendment, the *Atlas Roofing* identity-of-the-forum argument is off the mark.

In *Atlas Roofing,* the petitioner also argued that if the seventh amendment may be avoided simply by assigning a civil action to an agency rather than a court, then Congress could "utterly destroy the right to a jury trial by always providing for administrative rather than judicial resolution of a vast range of cases." This argument the Court said, was "well put." But it was, the Court added, ultimately "unpersuasive." It was unpersuasive in light of a certain limitation to Congress' power to avoid the amendment by the assigning civil actions to agencies route. This limitation, or supposed limitation, was a new use of the public rights and private rights distinction of *Crowell v. Benson.*[5]

Congress, the Court explained, could not assign just any case to an agency free of the seventh amendment. Instead, the amendment was inapplicable only when Congress assigned "public rights" to an agency.[6] Consequently, "Wholly private tort, contract, and property cases, as well as a vast range of other cases [were] not at all implicated." In short, because Congress might assign only public rights to an agency free of the seventh amendment, there was no chance that Congress might eliminate seventh amendments rights simply by transferring civil actions en mass to agencies.

This reasoning, of course, is circular: When Congress commits a matter that otherwise subject to the seventh amendment to an agency, by that very act, as the Court would have it, the matter becomes a public right free of the seventh amendment. The point is illustrated by *Myron v. Hauser.*[7] By statute, the Commodities Futures Trading Commission can hear claims, sounding in deceptive sales practices and fraudulent transactions, for reparations (damages) brought by customers against brokers selling options in commodities. In the instant case, the Commission had found that a broker had "committed fraud" by not disclosing relevant information and by making misleading statements to a customer. The Commission awarded the customer some $24,000 for his "out-of-pocket losses."

The broker claimed that the agency action was essentially a private action for money damages in violation of the seventh amendment. The court of appeals, though, did not accept this "interesting argument." On the authority of *Atlas Roofing,* the court found that the Commission reparations process amounted to a public right exempted from the jury

5. 285 U.S. 22, 52 S.Ct. 285, 76 L.Ed. 598 (1932). See Chap. 5, Sec. 5.1, supra.

6. More fully stated, the Court's response to the argument that Congress could destroy the right to a jury trial by assigning civil actions to agencies was that

> The argument is well put but it overstates the holdings of our previous cases and is in any event unpersuasive. Our prior cases support administrative fact-finding in only those situations involving "public rights," e.g., where the Government is involved in its sovereign capacity under an otherwise valid statute creating enforceable rights. Wholly private tort, contract, and property cases, as well as a vast range of other cases, are not at all implicated.

430 U.S. at 458, 97 S.Ct. at 1271.

7. 673 F.2d 994, 997 (8th Cir.1982).

trial requirement. But the "public right" had been created by Congress out of these circumstances:

> At least seventy-five per cent of all claims [heard by the Commission] involved fraud, a cause of action known to the common law since at least 1789—two years before the adoption of the seventh amendment. The remedy in CFTC reparations—damages—is the same remedy available at common law. Thus, CFTC reparations are simply an old remedy in a new forum.[8]

* * *

The Supreme Court has said that "purely taxonomic" changes in a cause of action are insufficient to avoid the seventh amendment. But at the same time, though, the Court has also endorsed the proposition that "Congress may fashion causes of action that are closely *analogous* to common-law actions and place them beyond the ambit of the Seventh Amendment by assigning their resolution to a forum in which jury trials are unavailable."[9]

§ 6.3 CONCLUSION: THE SEVENTH AMENDMENT AS AN INSTITUTIONAL ARRANGEMENT

Probably, the substance of the Supreme Court opinions about agencies and the seventh amendment is simply that trial by jury is "incompatible" with an "administrative forum," and that to save this forum, the Court has held agencies free of a jury requirement. Undoubtedly, when all was said and done by the Court in *Atlas Roofing,* the bottom-line was:

> We cannot conclude that the [seventh amendment] rendered Congress powerless—when it concluded that remedies available in a court of law were inadequate to cope with a problem within Congress' power to regulate—to create new public rights and remedies by statute and commit their enforcement, if it chooses, to a tribunal other than a court of law—such as an administrative agency—in which facts are not found by juries.[1]

The case law, then, is perhaps best understood as interpreting the seventh amendment not as conveying a personal right but as instead establishing an institutional arrangement, using a jury to rectify civil actions according to community interests. As an institutional arrange-

8. Markham, The Seventh Amendment and CFTC Reparations Proceedings, 68 Iowa L.Rev. 87, 120–21 (1982).

9. Granfinanciera, S.A. v. Nordberg, 492 U.S. 33, 52, 61, 109 S.Ct. 2782, 2796, 2800, 106 L.Ed.2d 26 (1989).

§ 6.3

1. Atlas Roofing Co. v. Occupational Safety and Health Review Com'n, 430 U.S. 442, 460, 97 S.Ct. 1261, 1272, 51 L.Ed.2d 464 (1977). See also Shelter Framing Corp. v. Carpenters Pension Trust, 543 F.Supp. 1234, 1246 (C.D.Cal.1982) ("Several leading cases ... indicate clearly that when Congress legislates in the economic field and sets up an administrative scheme for determining a financial liability, there is no right to trial by jury under the Seventh Amendment in the common law sense"). Contra, see Federalist No. 83 (the jury is "an excellent method of determining questions of property").

ment, the amendment, same as with other institutional arrangements, is subject to congressional power under the necessary and proper clause of Article I of the Constitution. Consequently, the amendment would not, as the Court said in *Atlas Roofing,* bar Congress from "creat[ing] new public rights and remedies by statute and commit[ing] their enforcement, if it choose[s], to a tribunal other than a court of law."[2]

Of course, the amendment does look like a right. And even if the amendment is considered as just an institutional arrangement, still, Congress's power of rearrangement ought not to be without bounds. This power ought to be exercised with some regard to the functions that the seventh amendment should perform in our government.

2. Atlas Roofing Co. v. Occupational Safety and Health Review Com'n, 430 U.S. 442, 460, 97 S.Ct. 1261, 1272, 51 L.Ed.2d 464 (1977). The Court reaffirmed this view, of the seventh amendment as an institutional arrangement subject to control by Congress, in Granfinanciera, S.A. v. Nordberg, 492 U.S. 33, 42, 109 S.Ct. 2782, 2790, 106 L.Ed.2d 26 (1989). Here, the Court said that "if these factors [whether traditionally this was a matter subject to a jury trial] indicate that a party is entitled to a jury trial under the Seventh Amendment, we must decide whether Congress may assign and has assigned resolution of the relevant claim to a non-Article III body that does not use a factfinder."

Chapter 7

DUE PROCESS

Table of Sections

The due process clauses of the fifth and fourteenth amendments promise that neither the federal nor state governments shall deprive a person of "life, liberty, or property, without due process of law." "Life, liberty, or property" might plausibly be read as a unit and given the "open-ended, functional interpretation" that government cannot "seriously hurt you without due process of law."[1] The modern Supreme Court, however, does *not* read due process in this open-ended way. Instead, it requires that a person claiming due process must establish an interest definable as either "life" or "liberty" or "property."[2]

§ 7.1 WHEN DUE PROCESS APPLIES: THE ADJUDICATORY MODE OF AGENCY ACTION

Before the definitional exercise, about what constitutes liberty or property in the administrative state is relevant, an even more rudimentary inquiry is necessary. This inquiry is about whether or not the agency is acting in an "adjudicatory" mode as it may take liberty or property. If the agency action is *not* adjudicatory, due process does not apply.

Whether an agency action is adjudicatory depends not on how an agency labels its action but on the *effect* of the action.[1] This "effects" datum, and some of its qualities, was identified by the Supreme Court in *Londoner v. Denver* and *Bi–Metallic Investment Co. v. State Board of Equalization*.[2] The key quality identified in these cases is whether a person is "exceptionally affected, in each case on individual grounds."[3]

Both cases, *Londoner* and *Bi–Metallic,* involved assessments against property owners in Denver, Colorado. In *Londoner,* the city had decided to improve a certain street. The costs of this improvement were to be borne by the owners of property that fronted the street, in an amount proportionate to the benefit to their property from the improvement. These property owners sued, contending that "the assessment on their lands had been made without notice and opportunity for hearing." The Supreme Court agreed, and ruled that the property owners could not be assessed for the street improvement without a hearing consistent with due process of law.

The second decision, *Bi–Metallic Investment Co. v. State Board of Equalization,* involved an across-the-board increase of forty per cent in the valuation of taxable property in Denver. The plaintiff, which had property subject to the new valuation, contended that in that valuation "it was given no opportunity to be heard and that therefore its property will be taken without due process of law." This time, however, the Court rejected the claim to due process.

1. J. Ely, Democracy and Distrust, A Theory of Judicial Review 19 (1980).

2. Board of Regents of State Colleges v. Roth, 408 U.S. 564, 92 S.Ct. 2701, 33 L.Ed.2d 548 (1972). See sec. 7.4.1, infra.

§ 7.1

1. This effect-of-the-agency-action datum also counts under the Administrative Procedure Act in determining whether rulemaking or adjudicatory procedures, as provided by the Act, apply. United States v. Florida East Coast Railway Co., 410 U.S. 224, 93 S.Ct. 810, 35 L.Ed.2d 223 (1973), on remand 368 F.Supp. 1009 (M.D.Fla.1973).

2. 210 U.S. 373, 28 S.Ct. 708, 52 L.Ed. 1103 (1908); 239 U.S. 441, 36 S.Ct. 141, 60 L.Ed. 372 (1915).

3. Bi–Metallic Investment Co. v. State Board of Equalization, 239 U.S. 441, 446, 36 S.Ct. 141, 142, 60 L.Ed. 372 (1915).

The difference in *Londoner* (subject to due process) and *Bi–Metallic* (not subject) is as follows. In *Londoner* the persons claiming due process had been particularly affected: The assessment against each individual varied according to how each person's property was separately benefited.[4] In *Bi–Metallic,* however, the agency action applied alike—"common to all and peculiar to none"—to a class of people. All the property owners in Denver had had their property valuation increased by the same amount, thus they all were "equally concerned."

Practicality was one reason that agency action of class-like effect was not subject to due process. When "a rule of conduct applies to more than a few people," Holmes wrote, "it is impracticable that every one should have a direct voice in its adoption." Thus "there must be a limit to individual argument in such matters if government is to go on."[5] Another reason was about fair chances of participation in governmental processes. The action in *Bi–Metallic* was of city-wide effect, and Holmes wrote that as "the sweep of government power broadens so too does the power of the affected group to protect its interests outside rigid constitutionally imposed procedures."[6] One part of this sweep is that groups generally have resources and political potencies greater than that of an individual. Another part is that an action of broad effect, as in *Bi–Metallic,* usually affects a community of interests. When such a variety of interests are consulted, as even by a bare right to comment as in rulemaking, that variety in itself is likely to illume the various sides of the issues relevant to an agency action.

But when an action affects a person specially, according to her circumstances, there is a new set of dynamics. The power of the group to protect its interests, or a variety of interests, is no longer a factor. Also, who has better knowledge of the circumstances of an individual specially affected than that individual? Simply in the interest of an accurate assessment of those circumstances a person who is especially affected ought to be heard. Accordingly, Holmes distinguished *Londoner* and its requirement of due process from *Bi–Metallic* by explaining that in the former case the property owners had "been exceptionally affected [by varying rates of assessment against their property] in each case upon individual grounds."[7]

As the Court has said, "The pragmatic considerations identified by Justice Holmes in *Bi–Metallic* . . . are as weighty today as they were in 1915."[8] Commentators and individual justices have, however, advanced

4. The general plan approved by the municipality was to charge the cost of street improvement to owners of property adjacent to the street. In relation to this plan, the Court in *Londoner* held that there was no right to a hearing under due process. In its implementation, however, the plan required an assessment against individual property owners according to how each piece of property benefitted by the improvement, and this assessment was subject to due process.

5. 239 U.S. at 445, 36 S.Ct. at 142.

6. 210 U.S. at 383, 28 S.Ct. at 712. See O'Bannon v. Town Court Nursing Center, 447 U.S. 773, 800, 100 S.Ct. 2467, 2483, 65 L.Ed.2d 506 (1980).

7. 239 U.S. at 446, 36 S.Ct. at 142.

8. Minnesota State Bd. for Community Colleges v. Knight, 465 U.S. 271, 286, 104

an additional reason for a right to be heard by individuals "exceptionally affected." As explained by Justice Blackmun, "when government acts in a way that singles out identifiable individuals—in a way that is likely to be premised on suppositions about specific persons—it activates the special concern about being personally *talked to* about the decision rather than simply being *dealt with*." This reason to be heard is commonly referred to as a "dignitary interest".[9]

* * *

As it is used to distinguish between either individual or class-like actions, the effects datum of *Londoner* and *Bi–Metallic* seems a workable criterion for due process.[10] At the margins, however, there are some difficult cases, for instance when the agency action by its terms applies to a class, but that class has only a single member. In *Anaconda Company v. Ruckelshaus* the Environmental Protection Agency had issued a "rule," as it said, controlling emissions of sulfur oxide.[11] However, only one plant was subject to the rule and the owners of that one plant claimed the right to a due process hearing. From the fact that the alleged "rule" applied to only plant, the court might have found that the agency action was sufficiently focused to be subject to due process. The court, however, was more flexible, and considered factors such as whether the class was closed or subject to be opened to new members and whether there was such a community of interests involved so as to make rulemaking a fair and effective process. As said by the Court, the "fact that Anaconda alone is involved is not conclusive on the question as to whether the hearing should be adjudicatory, for there are many other interested parties and groups who are affected and are entitled to be heard."[12] Looking to these other factors, the court found that indeed the agency action was not adjudicatory and not subject to due process.

S.Ct. 1058, 79 L.Ed.2d 299 (1984). See also Logan v. Zimmerman Brush Co., 455 U.S. 422, 433, 102 S.Ct. 1148, 71 L.Ed.2d 265 (1982).

9. O'Bannon v. Town Court Nursing Center, 447 U.S. 773, 801, 100 S.Ct. 2467, 65 L.Ed.2d 506 (1980). See also Minnesota State Bd. for Community Colleges v. Knight, 465 U.S. 271, 285, 104 S.Ct. 1058, 79 L.Ed.2d 299 (1984)' Logan v. Zimmerman Brush Co., 455 U.S. 422, 433, 102 S.Ct. 1148, 71 L.Ed.2d 265 (1982). So far, however, this dignitary interest has not gained the approval of a majority of the Court. In Dixon v. Love, 431 U.S. 105, 114, 97 S.Ct. 1723, 52 L.Ed.2d 172 (1977), the Court specifically refused to take a "dignitary interest" into account when calculating the procedures due a person. See Sec. 7.6.1, infra.

10. A modern illustration of the operation of the distinction is provided in Air Line Pilots Association, Intern. v. Quesada, 276 F.2d 892 (2d Cir.1960). The Federal Aviation Agency had promulgated a regulation barring airline pilots from flying after they reached age sixty. It had done so on the basis of a rulemaking process that, comprehensively, included comment from the industry and the Airline Pilots Association, medical studies, and experts in aviation safety and medicine. Thirty-five airline pilots, each over sixty, claimed that the rulemaking process was inadequate, that as the agency's action "deprive[d] them of property in their pilots' license," they were each entitled to an adjudicatory hearing. *Id.* at 894. While acknowledging that the thirty-five pilots had indeed been deprived of a property interest, the court, because of the class-like effect of the agency action (an age limit for all commercial pilots), held that they had no constitutional claim to a hearing.

11. 482 F.2d 1301 (10th Cir.1973).

12. 482 F.2d at 1306. See Law Motor Freight, Inc. v. CAB, 364 F.2d 139, 142–43 (1st Cir.1966), cert. denied 387 U.S. 905, 87 S.Ct. 1683, 18 L.Ed.2d 622 (1967) (in finding that the operating territory of a single

§ 7.1.1 The Necessity of a Fact in Dispute

For due process to apply, there must be some fact in dispute. Consider an eighteen year-old who applies for a taxi-driver license, but is turned down because of a rule requiring that licensees be age twenty-one. This person is specially affected and his liberty is taken. But he probably has no claim to a due process hearing. Why? Because there seems to be no fact in dispute: the rule says twenty-one and he is eighteen.[13] In *Weinberger v. Hynson Westcott & Dunning,* the Supreme Court sustained a Food and Drug Administration regulation that denied a hearing where the petitioner failed to show that a substantial factual issue was in issue. The Court explained that "When it clearly appears from . . . the reasons and factual analysis in the request for the hearing that there is no genuine and substantial issue of fact" there is no due process claim to a hearing.[14]

The criterion of a substantial issue of fact was the basis of decision in *New Motor Vehicle Board v. Orrin W. Fox Co.*[15] Under a state statute, new car dealerships in California had to be approved by a state board. Specifically, such approval was required when an existing dealership in the vicinity of the proposed dealership protested the establishment of the new dealership. Upon such a protest and within sixty days, a hearing was held to determine whether the new competition would be unduly injurious to existing dealerships and to the "public interest."[16] Within thirty days of this hearing, the board had to hand down its decision. During the pendency of this process, the proposed dealership was enjoined. So, simply by entering a protest an existing dealership could delay (for ninety days) the opening of a competing business. Two prospective dealerships claimed that such a delay amounted to a "taking" without a hearing of an interest protected by due process. A three-judge district court agreed.

The Supreme Court, however, overturned that court, because the ninety-day delay was not contingent upon any factual dispute. Instead, under state law the delay was imposed automatically, on the protest of an existing dealership. That dealership did not have to show cause, nor did the state board have any discretion to refuse to impose the delay.

air freight forwarder could be defined by a rule, the court predicated its holding on the generality of the rule, stating that the Civil Aeronautics Bureau "has declared new ground rules available to the air carrying industry" even "though the occasion was the application of one company for pickup and delivery tariffs"). See generally Rabin, Due Process and the Administrative State, 42 Cal.L.Rev. 1044, 1126 (1984).

13. Only if the applicant was able to establish a factual issue about the application of the twenty-one years of age rule to him—for instance that he is twenty-two and not eighteen—would he have a claim to a hearing.

14. Weinberger v. Hynson, Westcott & Dunning, Inc., 412 U.S. 609, 620, 93 S.Ct. 2469, 2478, 37 L.Ed.2d 207 (1973). See also United States v. Florida East Coast Ry. Co., 410 U.S. 224, 254, 93 S.Ct. 810, 825, 35 L.Ed.2d 223 (1973).

15. 439 U.S. 96, 99 S.Ct. 403, 58 L.Ed.2d 361 (1978).

16. 439 U.S. at 102. In *Fox,* the adjudicatory fact condition showed that the problem complained of was not procedural but substantive. It was substantive in that the action complained of was the decision of the state legislature to impose an unqualified advantage of delay on existing dealerships.

There was, in short, nothing about the taking (the ninety-day delay) that could be questioned at a hearing. In ordering the delay, the board had "neither found nor assumed the existence of any adjudicative facts."

§ 7.1.2 Inspections, Examinations, and Testing

The element of a fact in dispute pertains to both ends of a certain continuum of administrative discretion. This continuum is one that runs from no discretion to full discretion. At either end of this continuum, no hearing is required. The reasons for this are pragmatic. At the "no discretion" end of the continuum there is no fact in dispute and agency action is compelled by law. Because there are no factual issues to be resolved at a hearing no hearing is required by due process. (See *Weinberger v. Hynson Westcott & Dunning* and *New Motor Vehicle Board v. Orrin W. Fox Co.* as discussed in the preceding section.)

At the other end of the continuum, where there is full discretion, there may also be no need for a hearing, for the reason that that discretion cannot be beneficially examined in a hearing. In the context of full discretion, consider the circumstances of a person that fails the road test necessary to a driver's license and fails because his examiner found that he was not, as the test required, proficient in parallel parking. The person tested, however, disagrees about his proficiency. This is a dispute about conduct peculiar to an individual, yet it will not be examined at a hearing. It will not be examined because a decision about that conduct is best made by the examiner applying her expertise to circumstances especially observed by her. That sort of expert judgment cannot be usefully questioned at a hearing. As explained by the Connecticut Supreme Court, if "administrative fact-finding requires technical or professional expertise," then that fact-finding may "appropriately depend upon inspection, examination, or testing, rather than upon an adversary hearing."[17]

Fact-finding that cannot be usefully questioned at a hearing often involves matters of "pure administrative routine," such as Department of Agriculture inspections regarding the quality of meat or a building inspector's judgment about compliance with safety standards. In *Board of Curators v. Horowitz,* this rational, about action that cannot be usefully tested at a hearing, was extended to academia. The Supreme Court found that a student's dismissal from medical school had not violated due process, and in doing so noted the disutility of a hearing in an academic context. "The determination whether to dismiss a student for academic reasons," the Court explained, "requires an expert evaluation of cumulative information and is not readily adapted to the procedural tools of judicial or administrative decision-making."[18]

17. Connecticut Light and Power Co. v. Norwalk, 179 Conn. 111, 425 A.2d 576, 581 (1979). Coterminous with due process, the Administrative Procedure Act does not require an adjudicatory process in the case of "proceedings in which decisions rest solely on inspections, tests, or elections." 5 U.S.C. § 554(a)(3).

18. The underlying principle in *Horowitz,* that an adjudicatory hearing may serve no useful purpose in a decision turn-

§ 7.2 DUE PROCESS: HISTORY AND DEVELOPMENT

Past the threshold criteria, of an agency action particular to an individual, a person may have a call on the courts, courtesy of due process, to correct agency processes. In response to such a call, modern courts have assumed a large power of superintending agency procedures. Examination of this power inevitably involves what the courts now describe as a "familiar two-part inquiry." The first question is whether an individual has asserted an interest—in life, liberty or property—to which due process applies. The second question is: considering that due process applies, what process is due?

Before commencing this two-part inquiry, we will briefly examine the origins of due process. History has a particular relevance to due process, as Justice Frankfurter has explained:

> "[D]ue process" unlike some legal rules is not a technical conception with a fixed content unrelated to time, place and circumstances.... Representing a profound attitude of fairness ... "due process" is compounded of history, reason, the past course of decisions, and stout confidence in the strength of the democratic faith which we profess.[1]

* * *

In 1215, the Magna Carta provided that "No free man shall be taken or imprisoned or disseised or outlawed or exiled or in any way ruined, nor will we go or send against him, except by the lawful judgment of his peers or by the law of the land." The phrase "by the law of the land" (*per legem terrae)* is in sound and meaning the precursor of the modern phrase, due process of law.[2]

ing upon expert discretion, has been applied in various contexts. In *Greenholtz v. Nebraska Penal Inmates,* the Court found that the decision of a parole board not to grant a parole need not be tested by an adjudicatory hearing. Noting that such a hearing was "designed to elicit specific facts," they found that in the action in question, "there is no set of facts which if shown mandate a decision favorable to the individual." Instead, the decision turned on a " 'discretionary assessment of a multiplicity of imponderables' " involving predictive assessments of what a man "may become rather than what he has done." 442 U.S. 1, 10, 14, 99 S.Ct. 2100, 60 L.Ed.2d 668 (1979). See also Parham v. J.R., 442 U.S. 584, 609, 99 S.Ct. 2493, 61 L.Ed.2d 101 (1979) ("Common human experience and scholarly opinion suggest that the supposed protections of an adversary proceeding to determine the appropriateness of medical decisions for the commitment and treatment of emotional illness may well be more illusory than real").

§ 7.2

1. Joint Anti–Fascist Refugee Committee v. McGrath, 341 U.S. 123, 162, 71 S.Ct. 624, 95 L.Ed. 817 (1951) (concurring opinion).

2. See, e.g., Murray's Lessee v. Hoboken Land & Improvement Company, 59 U.S. (18 How.) 272, 276, 15 L.Ed. 372 (1855) ("The words 'due process of law' were undoubtedly intended to convey the same meaning as the words 'by the law of the land' in Magna Carta."). The phrase "process of law" first appeared as a phrase of law-French, *process de ley,* in an English legal document of the early fourteenth century. Not long afterward, in its 1354 reissue under Edward III, Magna Carta was written in official English for the first time. "In place of *per legem terrae,* are the words 'by due process of law.' " C. Miller, the Forest of Due Process, Nomos XVIII 4 (1977). See also Easterbrook, Substance and Due Process, 1982 Sup.Ct.Rev. 85 (1982).

"By the law of the land," was not, however, in meaning co-extensive with modern due process. Under it, the courts did not, as they now do, claim the power to themselves devise and develop procedures. Instead, "by the law of the land" was a guarantee pertaining to positive law. The standing laws, the laws of the land, were to be applied equally to all. In this context, the phrase was a guarantee against such "arbitrary action of the crown," in disregard of the sanctuary of the general laws, as might jeopardize the liberty or property of a person.[3]

In its original context, as just as a surety of positive law, the due process clause has had important modern applications. In the McCarthy era, government sometimes felt that those associated with communism were not entitled to the same legal process as everybody else. In *Vitarelli v. Seaton,* an employee at the Department of Interior, had been suspended without pay for reasons that included "sympathetic association" with members of the communist party.[4] In overturning this action, the Court found that the procedures afforded the employee were not consistent with those generally afforded by applicable departmental regulations. For the Court, Justice Harlan wrote that because "the proceedings attendant upon petitioner's dismissal from government service . . . fell substantially short of the applicable departmental regulations, we hold that such dismissal was illegal and of no effect."[5]

The larger, modern application of due process, however, lies outside of this positive law context. Modern due process involves quite a different thing, a power of the courts to correct procedures as provided by positive law, so as to make those procedures consistent with the courts' own ideas of good process. The origins of this form of due process seem to lie in Lord Coke's opinion in *Dr. Bonham's Case.*[6] Henry VIII had established a medical licensing board, a "college perpetual of doctors and grave men to restrain the boldness of wicked men, who professed physic more for avarice than out of confidence of a good conscience." By act of Parliament, the board was authorized to assess fines in the amount of one hundred pounds, half to go to the crown, the other half to board members. When Dr. Bonham was summoned by the board to answer a charge of practicing medicine without a license, he refused to comply with the summons. Consequently, he was fined a hundred pounds and jailed seven days for contempt. Thereafter, Bonham brought a tort action for false imprisonment, and in that action Lord Coke ruled in Bonham's favor.

Lord Coke considered this split fine to be a pecuniary bias that spoiled Bonham's chance of a fair hearing. Because the board kept half

3. Dent v. West Virginia, 129 U.S. 114, 123–24, 9 S.Ct. 231, 233–34, 32 L.Ed. 623 (1889).

4. 359 U.S. 535, 536–37, 79 S.Ct. 968, 971, 3 L.Ed.2d 1012 (1959).

5. Id. at 545, 79 S.Ct. at 975. See also Service v. Dulles, 354 U.S. 363, 77 S.Ct. 1152, 1 L.Ed.2d 1403 (1957); United States ex rel. Accardi v. Shaughnessy, 347 U.S. 260, 74 S.Ct. 499, 98 L.Ed. 681 (1954). See generally Rubin, Due Process in the Administrative State, 72 U.Cal.L.Rev. 1056–57 (1984).

6. 8 Co.Rep. 107, 77 Eng.Rep. 638 (1610).

of Bonham's fine, its members were both "judges" and "parties" in the proceeding against Bonham. But because this arrangement had been established by Parliament, it was consistent with the law of the land/positive law form of due process. At this point, Lord Coke departed from this form. He made his famous statement that "the common law will controul Acts of Parliament, and sometimes adjudge them to be utterly void: for when an Act of Parliament is against common right and reason, or repugnant, or impossible to be performed, the common law will controul it, and judge such Act to be void.... "

In the United States, the Supreme Court in its first notable exposition on due process expressed a view of it compatible with *Dr. Bonham's Case.* In *Murray's Lessee v. Hoboken Land & Improvement Co.,* the Court assumed the power to correct procedures as established by Congress. The Court, *per* Justice Curtis, stated:

> It is manifest that it was not left to the legislature to enact any process that might be devised. The article is a restraint on the legislature as well as on the executive and judicial powers of government....[7]

However, this special judicial power, not merely to enforce processes as provided by positive law but to correct these processes, was circumscribed in an important way. Judges were not to superintend agency procedures according to their own subjective notions of good or bad processes. Instead, as said in *Murray's Lessee v. Hoboken* judges were to look outside themselves to "settled usages and modes of proceeding."[8] They might correct agency processes, but only according to established principles such as fair notice, the opportunity to rebut and present evidence, and a disinterested judge.[9]

The power of the courts to correct process was contained in another respect; it was contained by means of the subject-matter of the process. Due process was based on conservative notions of liberty and property. Liberty was taken to mean an absence of state-imposed constraints on personal mobility.[10] An even more limiting construction, at least in relation to the modern public sector, was that of property. Property referred to things *owned* by an individual, to those things that an individual, under the security of general laws of the state might himself acquire, use, and dispose of as he wished.[11] If Jones acquired a carriage by a contract of sale, it was his to put to any non-injurious use and to

7. 59 U.S. (18 How.) 272, 277, 15 L.Ed. 372 (1855).

8. 59 U.S. (18 How.) at 277. In this statement, the Court followed the lead of Lord Coke in *Dr. Bonham's Case.* Coke had stated acts against "common right and reason, or repugnant, or impossible to be performed" as the measure of a judge's power. This implies that a judge is to rely on custom, rather than his conscience, in determining what process is due. 8 Co.Rep. at 118a, 77 Eng.Rep. at 652.

9. Measuring due process according to established principle differs from the modern test of due process, which is an open-ended balancing test. See sec. 7.8.3, infra.

10. Board of Regents v. Roth, 408 U.S. 564, 571, 92 S.Ct. 2701, 2705, 33 L.Ed.2d 548 (1972).

11. A. Honore', Ownership 107 in Oxford Essays in Jurisprudence (A. Guest ed. 1961).

dispose of as he wished. As ownership was an essential element of property, it was an element essential to claiming the protection of due process.

This concept of due process rested easily in a privately ordered society, where conservative notions of liberty and property were largely sufficient to cover the personal interests that might be jeopardized by the limited government of that society. But today government acts more often and more positively—by redistribution of wealth programs and more intensive regulatory schemes—to correct what it sees as defects in free-market ordering of social and economic relations. As the state has assumed this greater role, the portion of wealth generated by it rather than by the private sector has increased. This new wealth includes welfare to individuals or subsidies to business. It also includes public jobs, expanded in number and importance as government has grown. Also, in an active regulatory role the state controls a larger number of otherwise private activities by means of occupational and business licenses.

Unlike wealth privately gained, this new wealth—that generated by the newly expansive public sector—was *not* protected by due process,[12] at least not initially. There were two reasons for this. One was that wealth generated by the public sector, such as welfare, was not "owned."[13] Absent ownership, it was not property and was not subject to due process.

Another reason that government-generated resources were not subject to due process was the "privilege doctrine". This doctrine and its demise, at least in relation to due process, is the subject of the next section.

§ 7.3 THE FALL OF THE PRIVILEGE DOCTRINE

Justice Holmes baldly stated the privilege doctrine as he said "The petitioner may have a constitutional right to talk politics, but he has no constitutional right to be a policeman."[1] Because one could not claim a government job as a matter of right, one could not claim rights, including constitutional rights, associated with the job.

These rights, being appurtenant to other benefits, were lesser-included claims. The judgment, of whether, how much, and on what

12. This distinction was noted in Lynch v. United States, 292 U.S. 571, 577, 54 S.Ct. 840, 78 L.Ed. 1434 (1934), the Court held that insurance policies purchased from the government by individuals "create vested rights" subject to due process. In contrast:

> Pensions, compensation allowances, and privileges are gratuities. They involve no agreement of parties; and the grant of them involves no vested rights. The benefits conferred by gratuities may be redistributed or withdrawn at any time in the discretion of Congress.

13. Today, such wealth is still not owned. What is changed is that the Supreme Court has held that ownership is not essential to due process-protected property. See sec. 7.4.1, infra.

§ 7.3

1. McAuliffe v. Mayor of New Bedford, 155 Mass. 216, 220, 29 N.E. 517, 517–18 (1892).

terms a portion of the public fisc should be distributed as welfare, is a judgment that lies with Congress. Consequently, as welfare is created and distributed by government, it is defeasible according to the will of Congress. Under the privilege doctrine, this condition of defeasibility simply overrode what in context were seen as lesser conditions, such as that of a welfare claimant to due process. As stated by one court, "When the licensee takes this privilege he does so subject to the provisions of the statutes under which it is granted; and if these statutes say or fairly imply that he is entitled to no notice or hearing before revocation, he cannot be heard to complain if he is given none."[2]

Today, the privilege doctrine has generally collapsed. One reason has been a solicitude for personal rights.[3] Another reason is that a loss of a government benefit has come to be seen as a penalty imposed by government, in much the same way as such as a fine would be seen as a penalty: a penalty imposed to coercive a person into adhering to a prescribed form of conduct. As explained by the Supreme Court, the "denial of a public benefit may not be used by the government for the purpose of creating an incentive enabling it to achieve [indirectly] what it may not command directly."[4]

As the privilege doctrine fell, it did so generally but not quite completely. One vestige of it remains in immigration. In *Landon v. Plasencia* the Court reaffirmed that an "alien seeking admission to the United States requests a privilege, and has no constitutional rights regarding his application, for the power to admit or exclude aliens is a sovereign prerogative."[5] Other remnants of the doctrine arise out of the fact that the typically blunt statements of it obscured some important and credible interests that the doctrine sometimes served. As an employer, for instance, government has a proprietary interest in a happy and productive work force. Therefore government does not necessarily have

2. Smith v. Iowa Liquor Control Com'n, 169 N.W.2d 803 (Iowa 1969). See generally Van Alstyne, Cracks in the "The New Property": Adjudicative Due Process in the Administrative State, 62 Cornell 445 (1977). Historically, there were exceptions to the privilege doctrine, for instance the "learned profession" exception in occupational licensing. Ex parte Robinson, 86 U.S. (19 Wall.) 505, 512, 22 L.Ed. 205 (1874).

3. E.g. United Public Workers v. Mitchell, 330 U.S. 75, 100, 67 S.Ct. 556, 569, 91 L.Ed. 754 (1947) ("Congress may not enact a regulation providing that no Republican, Jew or Negro shall be appointed to federal office, or that no federal employee shall attend Mass or take any active part in missionary work.")

4. Elrod v. Burns, 427 U.S. 347, 361, 96 S.Ct. 2673, 2683, 49 L.Ed.2d 547 (1976). See also Perry v. Sindermann, 408 U.S. 593, 597, 92 S.Ct. 2694, 2697, 33 L.Ed.2d 570 (1972) ("If the government could deny a benefit to a person because of his constitutionally protected speech or associations, his exercise of those freedoms would in effect be penalized and inhibited. This would allow the government to 'produce a result which [it] could not command directly.' ") Regarding the fall of the privilege doctrine, see Van Alstyne, The Demise of the Right–Privilege Distinction in Constitutional Law, 81 Harv.L.Rev. 1439 (1968).

5. 459 U.S. 21, 103 S.Ct. 321, 74 L.Ed.2d 21 (1982). However, once an alien "gains admission to the country and begins to develop the ties that go with permanent residence his constitutional status changes accordingly." Id. Consequently, a deportation hearing is outside the privilege doctrine, and comes under the protection of due process.

to tolerate speech, such as that of an employee accusing his superintendent of bribery, that is inimical to this interest.[6]

But these are the exceptions. Across the board, the privilege doctrine fell. This fall was essential to expanding due process to include forms of wealth created and distributed by government, as in *Bell v. Burson* where the Court held that a driver's license was "not to be taken away without . . . due process." This holding, the Court explained, was "an application of the general proposition that relevant constitutional restraints limit state power to terminate an entitlement whether the entitlement is denominated a 'right' or a 'privilege.' "[7]

§ 7.4 STATUTORY ENTITLEMENTS AND THE NEW PROPERTY

The demise of the privilege doctrine meant that government could no longer ignore due process for benefits distributed by government. But while this was a *necessary* step to extending due process to such circumstances, it was not in itself a step *sufficient* to bring about this end. Another step remained. The protections offered by due process are not free floating: they pertain only to "life, liberty, or property." After the fall of the privilege doctrine, benefits created or distributed by government still did not generally qualify as either of the three. Consequently, it could not be said that there was a taking of life, liberty, or property in relation to most government benefits.

Property was the best means for extending due process to such wealth. Government benefits are ordinarily financial; this economic angle immediately brings the idea of property to mind. Nonetheless, in 1971 when in *Bell v. Burson* the Court held that the privilege doctrine could not exclude government benefits from due process, a necessary step of inclusion—of defining these benefits as property—had not been done.[1] The Court passed over this problem in *Bell,* but only for the moment.

In the mid-Sixties, Professor Charles Reich published his famous article on "The New Property."[2] Reich reviewed the modern breadth of the public sector and how various forms of wealth—cash benefits, licenses, jobs, and so forth—were now created, distributed, and controlled by the state. His particular concern, however, was not with positive government and a large public sector *per se*. Rather, it was that the beneficiaries of wealth generated by the public sector held that wealth only conditionally. Benefits stood to be diminished or eliminated at any time by government, usually because the recipient had not

6. Arnett v. Kennedy, 416 U.S. 134, 94 S.Ct. 1633, 40 L.Ed.2d 15 (1974).

7. 402 U.S. 535, 539, 91 S.Ct. 1586, 1589, 29 L.Ed.2d 90 (1971).

§ 7.4

1. 402 U.S. 535, 91 S.Ct. 1586, 29 L.Ed.2d 90 (1971).

2. Reich, The New Property, 73 Yale L.J. 733 (1965). In a particular historical context, Reich was complaining of a prerogative power in agencies, a power unconfined by law, such as the Stuarts had claimed for the Crown in England, but which was not ever thought to be suited to America.

maintained a certain behavior or status. As agency officials made these discretionary determinations, they were invested with a large and unconfined power over the lives of beneficiaries.

The discretionary bureaucratic power that Reich wrote against might be diminished by a delegation doctrine that requires Congress to limit agency discretion by means of tight standards. Courts might also more vigorously enforce rule of law concepts to require that agencies themselves limit that discretion by means of agency promulgated rules. However, the approach that Reich himself advocated for securing a measure of autonomy and privacy for beneficiaries of government wealth was to treat this government-generated wealth as the property of its beneficiaries. "Property," Reich wrote, "draws a circle around the activities of each private individual or organization. Within that circle, the owner has a greater degree of freedom than without.... Within, he is master and the state must explain and justify any interference."

* * *

Under the ordinary terms of property, the circumference of Reich's protected circle is marked by ownership. As has been said by A.M. Honore, the "concentration in the same person of the right ... of using as one wishes, the right to exclude others, the power of alienating and an immunity from expropriations is a cardinal feature of the institution."[3] Unfortunately, there are difficulties if not impossibilities in establishing ownership, and the security and autonomy that it entails, in relation to government benefits. These difficulties were examined by the Supreme Court in *Flemming v. Nestor*,[4] where the issue was whether by amending the Social Security Act Congress could terminate the old age benefits then received by one Epram Nestor. Mr. Nestor claimed he owned those benefits, and that therefore Congress could not eliminate them. The lower court agreed, finding that Nestor had an "accrued property right" protected against such defeasance by due process of law.

The Supreme Court, however, held that Nestor did not enjoy the security of ownership. Justice Harlan, in his opinion for the court, explained why. Social Security benefits were subject to the "judgment and preferences [of Congress] as to the proper allocation of the Nation's resources which evolving economic and social conditions will of necessity in some degree modify." Consequently, "To engraft upon the Social Security system a concept of 'accrued property rights' would deprive it of the flexibility and boldness in adjustment to ever-changing conditions which it demands."[5]

3. Honore, Oxford Essays on Jurisprudence 107, 113 (A. Guest ed. 1961). The relation of ownership to due process in the modern administrative state is discussed in Terrell, "Property," "Due Process," and the Distinctions Between Definition and Theory in Legal Analysis, 70 Geo.L.J. 861 (1982). It is, as Prof. Terrell says, "one thing to say that a welfare claimant has some sort of amorphous property interest in benefits prior to their receipt, but it is quite another to argue the more precise proposition that the claimant *owns* these future benefits."

4. 363 U.S. 603, 80 S.Ct. 1367, 4 L.Ed.2d 1435 (1960).

5. Id. at 610, 80 S.Ct. at 1372. See also O'Bannon v. Town Court Nursing Center, 447 U.S. 773, 795–96, 100 S.Ct. 2467, 2480–

Inasmuch as *Flemming v. Nestor* recognized the residual power of the legislative branch to reduce or terminate benefits such as welfare, a recipient cannot claim to own them. In the context of due process, this means that that "a welfare recipient is not deprived of due process when the legislature adjusts benefit levels."[6]

§ 7.4.1 The New Property Recognized and Identified: *Board of Regents v. Roth* and the Theory of Statutory Entitlements

Today, the Supreme Court has not in any way presumed to alter the *substantive* power of the state to reduce or terminate the benefits that form the "new property." In short, the Court has not acted to provide the security of "ownership" of public benefits, an inaction displeasing to the author of the "New Property." In the 1990's Professor Reich wrote, "I continue to insist that it makes a vital difference whether or not the individual owns and has sovereignty over the economic means of survival."[7] But then, same as Justice Harlan explained, ownership is impossible in the context of public benefits, considering that the stream of benefits necessarily involve Congress's "judgment and preferences as to the proper allocation of the Nation's resources, which evolving economic and social conditions will of necessity in some degree modify."[8]

While the Court cannot decree ownership, it might, however, search for some other measure of security for the holders of public benefits. It did so search and what it found was due process: The Court extended the protection of due process to the "new property" that consisted of government-generated wealth. An acclaimed but incomplete move in so extending due process came in *Goldberg v. Kelly.* The question in *Goldberg* was "whether a State that terminates public assistance payments [welfare] to a particular recipient without affording him the opportunity for an evidentiary hearing prior to termination denies the recipient procedural due process. . . . "[9] A majority of the Supreme Court answered in the affirmative, saying that due process required such a hearing.

The premise essential to that requirement of a hearing, however, was that an interest in receiving welfare benefits was property, and the common understanding of *Goldberg* is that it established that premise. But that is not precisely so. In *Goldberg,* the state chose to concede that due process applied and to instead argue that the summary pretermina-

81, 65 L.Ed.2d 506 (1980) ("public benefits are not held in fee simple"). See generally B. Barry, Political Argument 149–151 (1965).

6. E.g., Logan v. Zimmerman Brush Co., 455 U.S. 422, 432, 102 S.Ct. 1148, 1155, 71 L.Ed.2d 265 (1982).

7. Reich, Beyond the New Property: An Ecological View of Due Process, 56 Brooklyn L.Rev. 731, 736 (1990).

8. Flemming v. Nestor, 363 U.S. 603, 610, 80 S.Ct. 1367, 1372, 4 L.Ed.2d 1435 (1960), rehearing denied 364 U.S. 854, 81 S.Ct. 29, 5 L.Ed.2d 77 (1960).

9. Goldberg v. Kelly, 397 U.S. 254, 255, 90 S.Ct. 1011, 1013, 25 L.Ed.2d 287 (1970).

tion procedures it afforded the plaintiffs were consistent with due process.[10] Because of this concession, the point of whether welfare benefits constituted property was not an issue in the case.[11]

But while the Court in *Goldberg v. Kelly* neither justified nor defined welfare as property, a justification and definition was forthcoming—in the Court's exceedingly important opinion in *Board of Regents v. Roth*.[12] In its facts, *Roth* was a public employment case. David Roth, a non-tenured assistant professor, had been employed at a state university under a one-year contract. Under state law, the renewal of such contracts was by "the unfettered discretion of university officials" and "no reason for non-retention need be given." By the terms of his contract, Roth's sole right relating to retention was timely notice of the contract's renewal or non-renewal.

Roth was given timely notice that his contract would not be renewed. Otherwise, he was given "no reason for the decision and no opportunity to challenge it in any sort of hearing." Roth sued, on the grounds that "the failure of the University officials to give him notice of any reason for non-retention and opportunity for a hearing violated his right to procedural due process of law." In deciding this claim, the Court established much of the modern framework of due process.

The Court first of all demolished the notion, then of some moment, that due process is a free-floating right, applicable whenever the government has harmed an individual in some "important" way. The lower court in *Roth* had found that due process applied to Roth's interest in keeping his job simply because of the worth of the job to him. The Court, however, disagreed. It explained that in determining whether there is a right to due process, a court should "look not to the 'weight' [importance] but to the *nature* of the interest at stake." By the "nature of the interest at stake" the Court referred to the fact that by their terms, the due process clauses of the fifth and fourteenth amendments apply only with respect to the "life, liberty, or property" of an individual. Accordingly, the importance of an interest is insufficient to trigger due process; instead, a court must determine whether that interest may be classified as either life or liberty or property.[13] Under *Roth,* therefore, the Court identified another initial task in applying due process, one of definition.

10. "Appellant does not contend that procedural due process is not applicable to the termination of welfare benefits." 397 U.S. at 261, 90 S.Ct. at 1017.

11. Instead, in a footnote, Justice Brennan for the majority simply stated that "it may be realistic today to regard welfare entitlements as more like 'property' than a 'gratuity,'" and relied on Prof. Reich's "new property" thesis in support of this observation. 397 U.S. at 262 & n. 8, 90 S.Ct. at 1017 & n. 8.

12. 408 U.S. 564, 92 S.Ct. 2701, 33 L.Ed.2d 548 (1972).

13. 408 U.S. at 556–57. See also Meachum v. Fano, 427 U.S. 215, 224, 96 S.Ct. 2532, 49 L.Ed.2d 451 (1976) ("We reject at the outset the notion that any grievous loss visited upon a person by the state is sufficient to involve the procedural protections of the Due Process Clause.") Inasmuch as the "importance" of plaintiff's interest in itself be insufficient to trigger due process, neither will the unimportance be enough to defect a claim to due process. In Goss v. Lopez, 419 U.S. 565, 95 S.Ct. 729, 42 L.Ed.2d 725 (1975), some students at a public school had been suspended, not expelled, and for only a ten-day period. While

This done, the Court then made one of the greater changes ever in public law. In *Roth,* the Court expanded the definition of property to include the "new property," which consisted of a certain interest in benefits generated by government. This new property was justified by considerations of reliance and security. "It is a purpose of the ancient institution of property," the Court said, "to protect those claims upon which people rely in their daily lives, reliance that must not be arbitrarily undermined." Today, people rely on welfare, business subsidies, public jobs, and so forth in the same way that they had relied on traditional forms of wealth that constituted traditional property. This reliance, the Court said, ought not to be "arbitrarily undermined" by the action of public officials. So, to provide more security to the beneficiaries of this government-distributed wealth the Court defined "entitlements" to this wealth as a property interest subject to the protections of due process.

To illustrate such an entitlement, the Court explained that "the welfare recipients in *Goldberg v. Kelly* ... had a claim of entitlement to welfare payments that was grounded in the statute defining eligibility for them." An entitlement might be created by a statute or other authoritative "rules or understandings" about government benefits. As stated in *Roth,* "Just as the welfare recipient's 'property' interests in welfare payments was created and defined by statutory terms, so [Roth's] 'property' interest [if any] in employment ... was created and defined by the terms of his appointment."

While the Court defined the interests newly subject to the procedural protections of due process, it carefully explained that neither the courts nor the Constitution controlled the substance of those interests. Instead, these interests were "created and their dimensions ... defined by existing rules or understandings that stem from an independent source such as state law." These independent sources include statutes, regulations, or contracts such as might form the basis for a claim of entitlement to some benefit created and distributed by the state. The relation between this power to create property interests, a substantive power itself not subject to constitutional control, and the procedural, and constitutional, control of due process has been explained by the Court as follows: "Although the underlying substantive interest is created by 'an independent source such as state law,' federal constitutional law deter-

the this was a mild infringement of the student's "entitlement" property rights in a public education, this infringement, the Court found, was not so insubstantial as to fail to qualify for due process. In this regard the controlling principle as stated in *Ross* was that "as long as a property deprivation is not *de minimis,*" then its "gravity" is simply "irrelevant" to the question of the applicability of due process. An instance of "*de minimis*" is provided in Bell v. Wolfish, 441 U.S. 520, 542–43, 99 S.Ct. 1861, 60 L.Ed.2d 447 (1979), where the Court found that detaining two prisoners in a room constructed for one did not create a level of discomfort sufficient to give rise to a taking of liberty within the meaning of due process.

While the gravity of a deprivation is not seen as generally relevant to the applicability of due process, it is generally relevant to the separate question of how much process is due, a matter discussed at sec. 7.6.5, supra.

mines whether that interest rises to the level of a 'legitimate claim of entitlement' protected by the Due Process Clause."[14]

§ 7.4.2 The Scope of the *Roth* Entitlements System

The range of interests subject to due process under *Roth* is not unlimited. But it is quite impressive. In its public employment context, *Roth* brought within due process those employees with the status of permanent employment (employees who may be fired only upon a showing of cause). Otherwise, the entitlement theory of *Roth,* subject to certain qualifications, pertains " 'to the whole domain of social and economic fact.' "[15]

A student's interest in avoiding a ten-day suspension from a public school may not immediately strike you as property. Nonetheless, in *Goss v. Lopez* the Court used entitlement theory to define it is a "property interest" subject to due process.[16] The entitlement that constituted property was located in the state statutes that established the public school system, particularly the statute that "direct[ed] local authorities to provide a free education to all residents between five and twenty-one years of age." Besides public education, the entitlement theory of *Roth* has established property interests in such areas as occupational and professional licensing,[17] government disability insurance,[18] services provided by public utilities,[19] and public housing.[20] (Moreover, *Roth's* entitlement theory has extended beyond property, and used—rather questionably—to define liberty.[21])

But while it is expansive, the range of interests subject to due process under the entitlements theory of *Roth* is not, as we said, open-ended. It has been qualified and limited in some important respects, and it is to these qualifications and limitations that we now turn.

(a) "Mutual Understanding" of Entitlement

One of the first qualifications of *Roth* (a qualification implied by the requirement that an entitlement be grounded in some positive act of the state) is that a sufficient claim of entitlement is more than "an abstract need or desire" or "unilateral expectation" of some benefit. Rather, the claim of entitlement must be grounded in a "mutual understanding"

14. Memphis Light, Gas and Water Div. v. Craft, 436 U.S. 1, 9, 98 S.Ct. 1554, 56 L.Ed.2d 30 (1978).

15. Logan v. Zimmerman Brush Co., 455 U.S. 422, 430, 102 S.Ct. 1148, 1154, 71 L.Ed.2d 265 (1982).

16. 419 U.S. 565, 95 S.Ct. 729, 42 L.Ed.2d 725 (1975).

17. Barry v. Barchi, 443 U.S. 55, 99 S.Ct. 2642, 61 L.Ed.2d 365 (1979) (horse trainer's license).

18. Mathews v. Eldridge, 424 U.S. 319, 96 S.Ct. 893, 47 L.Ed.2d 18 (1976).

19. Memphis Light, Gas and Water Div. v. Craft, 436 U.S. 1, 11–12, 98 S.Ct. 1554, 56 L.Ed.2d 30,(1978) ("Because petitioners may terminate service only 'for cause,' respondents assert a legitimate claim of 'entitlement' within the protection of the Due Process Clause.").

20. Holbrook v. Pitt, 643 F.2d 1261 (7th Cir.1981) (Section 8 housing assistance).

21. Discussed at Sec. 7.5.2, infra.

between the individual and the state, an understanding created by independent and objective sources such as statutes, agency rules, or employment contracts.[22]

In *Roth* itself, the plaintiff, David Roth, failed to establish the requisite mutual understanding of permanent employment. While he may have had some expectation of being retained past the term of his one-year teaching contract, that expectation was, as the Court explained, unilateral. The state had agreed to employ Roth for only a year. Roth may have wanted a new contract, but there was no "state statute or University rule or policy that secured his interest in re-employment." What would qualify as "mutual understanding" was marked by *Roth's* companion case, *Perry v. Sindermann*.[23]

Similar to *Roth,* the plaintiff in *Perry v. Sindermann* had been employed as a teacher at a state institution under a one-year contract. As in *Roth,* the state without a hearing chose not to renew his contract. Unlike *Roth,* however, "independent and objective sources" in state law might establish a mutual understanding of permanent employment sufficient to create, for the teacher, the requisite property interest in his job. These sources included a "faculty guide" that while saying that the college "has no tenure system" at the same time explained that the "administration of the College wishes the faculty member to feel that he has permanent tenure as long as his teaching services are satisfactory." Another source was a state-wide regulation that provided that a teacher, like the plaintiff, who had been employed in the state's system of colleges and universities for more than seven years had "some form of tenure."

Since *Roth* and *Perry v. Sindermann,* the Court has further identified the zone of "mutual understanding" necessary to establish an expectancy or entitlement that qualifies for due process. In particular, the Court has defined what is not within the zone. Most prominently and most ironically, what is not within the zone includes an agency power that is wholly discretionary. The irony is that the intellectual force behind the "new property" was, as we said, that of protecting the denizens of the administrative state against discretionary bureaucratic power. But as it turns out, wholly discretionary power is by the definition of new property outside the protection of due process. In *Connecticut Board of Pardons v. Dumschat,*[24] a prisoner claimed that the Board's rejection of his petition for a commutation of his sentence was subject to due process. A state statute granted the Board of Pardons the power to commute sentences but the power so conveyed was wholly discretionary. There were no statutes or standards or rules, no "mandated shalls," to bind the Board of Pardons and to confine its power. As the Board's

22. As explained in Perry v. Sindermann, 408 U.S. 593, 601, 92 S.Ct. 2694, 33 L.Ed.2d 570 (1972), a "person's interest in a benefit is a 'property' interest for due process purposes if there are such rules or mutually explicit understandings that support his claim of entitlement to the benefit and that he might invoke at a hearing."

23. 408 U.S. 593, 92 S.Ct. 2694, 33 L.Ed.2d 570 (1972).

24. 452 U.S. 458, 101 S.Ct. 2460, 69 L.Ed.2d 158 (1981).

power was in no way confined, there was perforce no basis for the "mutual understanding" between the individual and the state that might qualify as a property interest. Accordingly, the Court found that in respect to his commutation, the prisoner had no property interest subject due process.[25]

Nor may historical practice in and of itself give rise to a mutual understanding sufficient to establish a property interest, at least not according to *Leis v. Flynt*.[26] Under state law, a state court had a wholly discretionary power to allow, or not allow, an out-of-state lawyer from practicing before him. This discretion notwithstanding, in *Leis v. Flynt*, the claim was that of a mutual understanding between out-of-state lawyers and judges sufficient to establish an "expectancy" protected due process. The history in these state courts of routinely allowing out-of-state lawyers to practice before them was said to have the requisite mutual understanding. The U.S. Supreme Court, however, held no, that the simple fact of a formally discretionary power to bar out-of-state lawyers in and of itself defeated the claim to due process.[27]

(b) Already Acquired Benefits

Under *Roth*, property interests are limited to persons who are already receiving a benefit. The Court summarily, but deliberately, stated that due process is a "safeguard of the security of interests that a person *has already acquired* in specific benefits."[28] *Applicants* for a benefit, therefore, have no such property interest. Accordingly, where a person claimed a right to a hearing in connection with the denial of his application for public housing, the court denied that claim, on the grounds that "It has long been settled that a party aggrieved by loss of a pre-existing right or privilege may enjoy procedural rights not available to one denied the right or privilege in the first instance."[29]

25. In *Dumschat v. Connecticut,* the Court distinguished its previous holding, in *Greenholtz v. Nebraska,* 442 U.S. 1, 99 S.Ct. 2100, 60 L.Ed.2d 668 (1979), that a state statute respecting pardons established a liberty interest protected by due process. Unlike the circumstances of *Dumschat,* the power of government officials to grant pardons had in *Greenholtz* been defined and limited by standards.

26. 439 U.S. 438, 443, 99 S.Ct. 698, 58 L.Ed.2d 717 (1979).

27. *Connecticut Board of Pardons v. Dumschat* is entirely in accord. There, the state statute that granted the Board of Pardons the power to commute sentences had made that power completely discretionary. The prisoner, however, tried to derived a claim of entitlement from the Board's past practices. These past practices were that "some 75 percent of all lifers received some favorable action from the pardon board prior to completing their minimum sentences." But this past practice was not enough. As explained by the Court, "no matter how frequently a particular form of clemency has been granted, the statistical probabilities standing alone generate no constitutional protections." 452 U.S. 458, 465, 101 S.Ct. 2460, 69 L.Ed.2d 158 (1981).

28. In dissent, Justice Marshall would have included at least applicants for public jobs within the zone of due process. "In my view," he wrote, "every citizen who applies for a government job is entitled to it unless the government can establish some reason for denying the employment. This is the 'property' right that I believe is protected by the Fourteenth Amendment and that cannot be denied 'without due process of law.' " 408 U.S. at 588–89.

29. Sumpter v. White Plains Housing Authority, 29 N.Y.2d 420, 425, 328 N.Y.S.2d 649, 652, 278 N.E.2d 892 (1972).

While the Court in *Roth* gave no reason for its assertion that only those already in receipt of benefits could have a property interest, a couple of reasons are evident. One reason is vested interests, that is, the greater value of wealth presently held. Generally speaking, only on the basis of resources in hand do people "embark their capital, bestow their labour, or shape the course of their lives."[30]

A second reason for the "already acquired" limit has to be the impracticability of providing a hearing to anyone who has no greater interest in a benefit other than that he wants it. For instance, in the public employment context of *Roth,* the cost of a due process hearing for the many applicants for government jobs would obviously be quite large.

(c) Indirect Beneficiaries

"Indirect beneficiaries" of a government program may not gain a property interest in benefits distributed pursuant to that program. Consequently, while a person may have a property interest in, say, a continued electrical service to his own home by a public utility, that person would not likely be able to claim a property interest in continued electricity to a public school attended by his children. This latter interest would probably be too indirect, which point is made in *O'Bannon v. Town Court Nursing Center.*[31]

The Department of Health, Education, and Welfare had certified a nursing home, the Town Court Nursing Center, Inc., as a "skilled nursing facility." With this certification, the home was eligible to receive state and federal funds for providing nursing care to the aged. About a year after this certification was granted, the Department proceeded to withdraw this certification and Town Court's eligibility for government funds. A group of elderly residents at the Town Court home, who stood to be transferred against their wishes to another home, objected. They claimed that they had a statutory entitlement to a continued residence in the nursing home and that this entitlement was protected by due process. The issue thus presented was "whether approximately 180 elderly residents of a nursing home ... have a constitutional right to a hearing before a state or federal agency may revoke the home's authority to provide them with nursing care at government expense."

In resolving this issue, the Court distinguished between "direct" and "indirect" beneficiaries of a government program. In this respect, the Court explained that "Although decertification will inevitably necessitate the transfer of all those patients who remain dependent on Medicaid benefits, it is not the same for purposes of due process analysis as a decision to transfer a particular patient or to deny financial benefits, based on his individual needs or financial situation." While this general transfer of patients would likely impose hardships on the residents, that "impact," the Court said, "which is an indirect and incidental result of

30. J. Bentham, A Fragment on Government and an Introduction to the Principles of Morals and Legislation (Harrison ed. 1948).

31. 447 U.S. 773, 100 S.Ct. 2467, 65 L.Ed.2d 506 (1980).

the Government's enforcement action, does not amount to a deprivation of any interest in life, liberty, or property."

The justifications offered in *O'Bannon* for its distinction between direct and indirect effects of an agency action involve considerations of (1) practicality and (2) derivative representation. Practicality is implicated by the unpredictable (and more randomly generated) number of hearings that would be required if incidental effects of agency action give rise to a hearing.[32] Also, given the attenuated interests and knowledge of those indirectly affected, such hearings would not be uniformly useful, either to the state or to the individual.

The consideration respecting derivative representation is that "as the sweep of government action broadens, so too does the power of the affected to protect its interests outside rigid constitutionally imposed procedures."[33] As government action broadens to include a community of interests, those interests may effectively be heard by means other than a due process hearing.

§ 7.5 LIBERTY

Perhaps especially in administrative law, the idea of liberty has acquired two sides. The usual and stronger side is the "natural liberty" to act, to do, to be: free of constraints of government. The other, weaker side is that of liberty as a species of positive law, like the entitlements recognized in *Board of Regents v. Roth*.[1] In the following sections we will discuss these two aspects of liberty within the meaning of due process, and we do so by starting with natural liberty.

32. Hearings would tend to be more randomly generated because of the attenuated causation associated with indirect effects of agency actions. 447 U.S. at 780.

Also, we might point out that the Court's concern with the practicality is similar to the reasoning of Holmes in Bi–Metallic Investment Co. v. State Board of Equalization, 239 U.S. 441, 445, 36 S.Ct. 141, 142, 60 L.Ed. 372 (1915). When "a rule of conduct applies to more than a few people," Holmes wrote, "it is impracticable that every one should have a direct voice in its adoption" and thus "there must be a limit to individual argument in such matters if government is to go on."

33. 447 U.S. at 800–01. This distinction between direct and indirect beneficiaries sounded in the *Bi–Metallic* and *Londoner* cases discussed in sec. 7.1, above. In this respect, and as explained by Justice Blackmun:

> "[T]he case for due process protection grows stronger as the identity of the persons affected by a government choice becomes clearer; and the case becomes stronger still as the precise nature of the effect on each individual comes more determinately within the decisionmaker's purview."

447 U.S. at 800–01.

§ 7.5

1. We are here considering liberty as a source of procedural protections, and in this sense positive forms of liberty are those "statutory entitlements" that qualify for procedural protections. Another sense of positive liberty, one that we are not concerned with, involves a duty of the state to provide for the welfare of its citizens, so as to effectively increase their freedom of choice, by such measures as are designed to lift them above a level of subsistence living. Examples of such positive rights are provided in the Universal Declaration of Human Rights, which includes such interests as social security, special care and assistance to mothers, education, and so forth. See B. Barry, Political Argument 149 (1965). In the United States, the courts have refused to recognize these interests as a source of constitutional obligations. See, e.g., Richardson v. Perales, 402 U.S. 389, 91 S.Ct. 1420, 28 L.Ed.2d 842 (1971) (education); Roe v. Wade, 410 U.S. 113, 93 S.Ct. 705, 35 L.Ed.2d 147 (1973) (abortions); Flemming

§ 7.5.1 Natural Liberty

Liberty might be liberally construed, to mean doing whatever one wants free of the constraints of government, as in driving one hundred miles-per-hour if you like.[2] But when considering "liberty" as a source of constitutional rules, such an expansive interpretation of it has been impracticable. Instead, liberty is confined to a loosely defined set of personal interests.[3] Of these interests, the one that forms the historically validated core of liberty is a freedom from state-imposed physical constraints. Blackstone, for instance, defined liberty as "the power of locomotion . . . without imprisonment or restraint, unless by due course of law."[4]

Physical constraints are, of course, most commonly the product of the criminal law. However, they are not foreign to administrative law. Immigration officials constrain the movement of an alien by deportation, thereby taking his liberty. Prison officials take a person's liberty when they return him to confinement by revoking his parole.[5] In a smaller way, an administrative apparatus can restrict "locomotion," as when a state agency suspends a driver's license.[6] Also, in *Ingraham v. Wright* the Supreme Court found that the containment and "intrusion on personal security" of a school paddling constituted a taking of liberty.[7]

Natural liberty, though, is today taken as more that a freedom from constraints on movement. *In Board of Regents v. Roth,* the Court confirmed that liberty "denotes not merely freedom from bodily restraint" but includes the capacity "to acquire useful knowledge, to marry, establish a home and bring up children." Also, liberty included the capacity "to engage in any of the common occupations of life."[8] That occupational choices warrant constitutional protection is to the Court a

v. Nestor, 363 U.S. 603, 80 S.Ct. 1367, 4 L.Ed.2d 1435 (1960) (social security).

2. In this assumption of liberty as a freedom from governmental constraint, we speak of liberty in the sense that is sometimes referred to (most notably by Isaiah Berlin) as negative liberty. Negative liberty—a freedom from government restraint—is usually contrasted with positive liberty, which is the in-fact range of choices open to an individual. Because the due process clause speaks of a government "taking" liberty, liberty in the negative sense seems a reasonable assumption in the due process context.

3. In the context of constitutional rules, the broader construction of liberty has been in the case of "substantive due process," that is, a court's appraisal of the substance of a law according to whether it bears a "reasonable relation to some purpose within the competency of the state." Meyer v. Nebraska, 262 U.S. 390, 399–400, 43 S.Ct. 625, 67 L.Ed. 1042 (1923). As regards economic matters, that broader construction has been considerably shrunken, as an unwarranted judicial meddling with the work of the legislature. Still, in the context of "personal" liberties, the doctrine of substantive due process remains vital.

4. 1 W. Blackstone, Commentaries on the Law of England: Of the Rights of Persons 134. See Monaghan, Of "Liberty" and "Property," 62 Cor.L.Rev. 405, 411–14 (1977).

5. But as we shall discuss, the definition of liberty in this prison administration context is not so simple. See sec. 7.5.2, supra.

6. See Bell v. Burson, 402 U.S. 535, 91 S.Ct. 1586, 29 L.Ed.2d 90 (1971).

7. 430 U.S. 651, 97 S.Ct. 1401, 51 L.Ed.2d 711 (1977).

8. 408 U.S. 564, 572, 92 S.Ct. 2701, 2706, 33 L.Ed.2d 548 (1972). In *Roth,* the Court, quoted a substantive due process

self-evident proposition. "It requires no argument," the Court has said, "to show that the right to work for a living in the common occupations of the community is of the very essence of the freedom and opportunity that it was the purpose of the [fourteenth] Amendment to protect."[9] Consequently, the Court has found that due process conditions the procedures by which the state may restrict "a range of such choices."[10]

Most often, the "range of occupational choices" is restricted by administrative licensing boards. These boards—which may control entry into, as well as the practice of, a trade or profession—usually consist of full-time practitioners of the regulated trade or profession. The opportunity that these board members gain is to use their state-endowed power to create and to enhance an occupational monopoly to their own advantage and to the disadvantage of individuals seeking entry into that occupation.[11] Accordingly, in *Gibson v. Berryhill* the Court found that the chance of an occupational licensing board to act in its own self-interest so tainted the Board's decisional processes as to violate due process.[12]

§ 7.5.2 Liberty as a Product of Positive Law: The Strange Idea of "State–Created Liberty"

As it has preferred to anchor interests protected by due process in positive law, the Supreme Court has not fully exploited—in fact it has on

case, Meyer v. Nebraska, 262 U.S. 390, 399, 43 S.Ct. 625, 626, 67 L.Ed. 1042 (1923), for the proposition that:

> Without doubt [liberty] denotes not merely freedom from bodily restraint but also the right of the individual to contract, to engage in any of the common occupations of life, to acquire useful knowledge, to marry, establish a home and bring up children, to worship God according to the dictates of his own conscience, and generally to enjoy those privileges long recognized as essential to the orderly pursuit of happiness by free men.

Id.

9. Truax v. Raich, 239 U.S. 33, 41, 36 S.Ct. 7, 10, 60 L.Ed. 131 (1915). See also Schware v. Board of Bar Examiners, 353 U.S. 232, 238–39, 77 S.Ct. 752, 755–56, 1 L.Ed.2d 796 (1957) ("A state cannot exclude a person from the practice of law or from any other occupation in a manner . . . that contravene[s] Due Process. . . . ").

10. The taking of a single job, however, is not a restriction of a range of occupational choices and a taking of liberty. If, however, the employee is a permanent employee, then under the entitlement theory of *Roth,* she would have a property interest in that job. See sec. 7.4.1, infra.

11. In these licensing boards, as Professor Walter Gellhorn has explained, history has turned around, and the guilds of the middle-ages replicated: "The thrust of occupational licensing, like that of the guilds, is toward decreasing competition by restricting access to the occupation; toward a definition of occupational prerogatives that will debar others from sharing in them; toward attaching legal consequences to essentially private determinations of what are ethically or economically permissible practices." W. Gellhorn, Individual Freedom and Government Restraints, 114 (1956).

12. 411 U.S. 564, 93 S.Ct. 1689, 36 L.Ed.2d 488 (1973). In this case, a state licensing board had proposed to determine whether certain optometrists—by practicing in the employ of a corporation providing optometric services—should forfeit their license for unprofessional conduct. Supposedly, by such corporate employment professionals might lose independence of judgment. The licensing board, however, was comprised wholly of independently employed optometrists, who stood to gain personally by eliminating corporate competitors. So, on grounds of bias, on the idea that those with "substantial pecuniary interest in legal proceeding should not adjudicate these disputes," the Court sustained the lower court finding that the board action violated the due process protected occupational choices of the optometrists before it. Id. at 579.

occasion shrunk—the broad platform of rights embraced by natural liberty. In *Leis v. Flynt,* out-of-state lawyers claimed that their interest in being allowed to represent their client, Larry Flynt (of *Hustler* magazine) within Ohio was, under entitlement theory, an interest subject to due process.[13] The Court, however, found that state law committed the attorneys' capacity to represent their client to the unconfined discretion of the trial-court judge. The attorneys could not, therefore, show the "requisite mutual understanding" between them and the state, and so, according to entitlement theory, they had no interest protected by due process. But did not the lawyers have an interest in liberty in their own right as persons, a liberty that existed apart from the grace of the state? Justice Stevens thought so. In dissent, he sharply criticized the implication of the majority opinion, that "liberty does not exist apart from specific state authorization."[14]

The origin of "state-created" liberty seems to lie in modern prisoners' rights cases. In these cases, the due process problem, as the Court saw it, was this: how could a convict claim that his liberty was taken by some action of prison officials when he had already lost all his liberty pursuant to a full criminal trial? The Court's solution to this problem was in *Morrissey v. Brewer.*[15] Two prisoners who had been on parole claimed that revocation of their paroles was a taking of liberty, and therefore subject to a due process hearing. The problem with this claim to due process, as least in the Court's view, was that these prisoners did not have any liberty to lose. They had lost it, by due process of law, when they were tried and sentenced to prison.

The decision in *Morrissey,* however, was handed down on the same day as *Roth v. Board of Regents* and in *Roth's* statutory entitlement theory the Court saw a solution to the no-liberty-to-lose problem. In *Morrissey* as in *Roth,* the plaintiffs were trying to maintain a particular status: the status in Roth being that of college professor, the status in *Morrissey* being that of a parolee. The conditions necessary for the parolee status had been created by state statutes. These statutes, the Court found, might create an entitlement on the part of parolees that amounted to a liberty interest in the same way that a statutory scheme of, say, welfare benefits might create an entitlement that yielded a property interest.[16]

In subsequent cases, this concept of liberty as a form of entitlement was continued and phrases such as "state-created liberty" or liberty as a

13. 439 U.S. 438, 99 S.Ct. 698, 58 L.Ed.2d 717 (1979), rehearing denied 441 U.S. 956, 99 S.Ct. 2185, 60 L.Ed.2d 1060 (1979).

14. 439 U.S. at 456, 99 S.Ct. at 708. Liberty is rightfully thought of as something that a person naturally has—a "cardinal inalienable right"—rather than a privilege extended by the state. Meachum v. Fano, 427 U.S. 215, 230, 96 S.Ct. 2532, 2541, 49 L.Ed.2d 451 (1976) (Stevens, J., dissenting), rehearing denied 429 U.S. 873, 97 S.Ct. 191, 50 L.Ed.2d 155 (1976).

15. 408 U.S. 471, 92 S.Ct. 2593, 33 L.Ed.2d 484 (1972).

16. 408 U.S. at 493–94, 92 S.Ct. at 2606–07. For a more complete explication of liberty as a statutory expectancy, see, e.g., Connecticut Bd. of Pardons v. Dumschat, 452 U.S. 458, 101 S.Ct. 2460, 69 L.Ed.2d 158 (1981); Wolff v. McDonnell, 418 U.S. 539, 94 S.Ct. 2963, 41 L.Ed.2d 935 (1974).

"statutory creation of the state" were used to describe this concept.[17] In these cases however, the reasoning of *Morrissey* became subject to doubt. From the bench, Justice Stevens, as we have noted, criticized *Morrissey* as it stood for a strictly positivist view of liberty. Such a view of liberty might make sense, Stevens said, if man were "a creature of the state." But he is not. Instead, it is "self-evident that all men were endowed by their creator with liberty as one of the cardinal unalienable rights." And it is "that basic freedom which the Due Process Clause protects, rather than the particular rights or privileges conferred by specific laws or regulations."[18]

A particular problem with the positive law/entitlement theory of *Morrissey* is that it is defeasible by the state, by the simple option of making all bureaucratic decisions wholly discretionary. In *Connecticut Board of Pardons v. Dumschat,* the Court held that a state statute that provided for commutation of prison sentences, but that had "no definition" and "no criteria" to "guide and control the agency" in such commutations, could not give rise to a liberty interest that triggered due process.[19] In short, there is no liberty if there are no standards controlling bureaucratic discretion. Therefore, Justice Stevens has charged that under a positive law concept of liberty, the "process of sentencing, parole release, parole revocation, and ultimate discharge could all be totally arbitrary."[20]

The concept of state-created liberty may have been useful in the context in which it was created, that of convicted criminals in *Morrissey.* But the concept was not necessary, not even for the result in *Morrissey.* The convicts could have been considered as retaining their status as human beings with some residuum of natural liberty that would support their claim to due process.[21] In the construct of positive liberty that the Court did create, there is a danger of diminishing liberty in its natural

17. E.g., Vitek v. Jones, 445 U.S. 480, 488–89, 100 S.Ct. 1254, 1261–62, 63 L.Ed.2d 552 (1980); Wolff v. McDonnell, 418 U.S. 539, 558, 94 S.Ct. 2963, 2975, 41 L.Ed.2d 935 (1974).

18. Meachum v. Fano, 427 U.S. 215, 230, 96 S.Ct. 2532, 49 L.Ed.2d 451 (1976).

19. 452 U.S. 458, 466, 101 S.Ct. 2460, 69 L.Ed.2d 158 (1981). Further, the Court has said that unless the decision-maker is required to base his decisions on "objective and defined criteria" . . . then the state has not created a constitutionally protected liberty interest. Olim v. Wakinekona, 461 U.S. 238, 249, 103 S.Ct. 1741, 75 L.Ed.2d 813 (1983).

In *Dumschat,* the Court distinguished its previous holding, in *Greenholtz v. Nebraska,* 442 U.S. 1, 99 S.Ct. 2100, 60 L.Ed.2d 668 (1979), that a state statute respecting pardons established a liberty interest protected by due process. Unlike the circumstances of *Dumschat,* the power of government officials to grant pardons had in *Greenholtz* been defined and limited by standards.

20. Connecticut Bd. of Pardons v. Dumschat, 452 U.S. 458, 470, 101 S.Ct. 2460, 69 L.Ed.2d 158 (1981) (dissenting).

21. 408 U.S. at 482. The Court in *Morrissey,* concerned with parole revocations, had noted the hardship of a parolee who "may have been living on parole for a number of years and . . . living a relatively normal life at the time of the revocation." In such circumstances, it seems reasonable to suppose (1) a residuum of natural liberty even with convicts and (2) that this residuum is disturbed by a parole revocation. The same residual natural liberty would seem to be at work in other prisoner's rights cases, involving such matters as solitary confinement or transfer to a mental institution.

sense, where it is a universal and more reliable measure of the rights of the individual against the state.

§ 7.6 THE PROCESS THAT IS DUE

The full due process question involves a "familiar two-part inquiry." To this point, we have addressed the first part, about when due process applies. The second part of this inquiry, to which we now turn, is what process is due?[1] Logically, the process due a person involves identification of the goals that a good process should serve. Historically, the process due a person is anchored in the Anglo–American of an adversarial hearing.

The process that is due also involves a consideration of institutions, whether the legislative or the judicial branches should have the plenary power of selecting and balancing among legitimate societal goals, and then determining the process due. In one part, agency processes involve programmatic choices, such as trying to design a unitary process for a massive program such as Social Security. In another part, the question is more personal, whether a particular individual has been treated right. A system that is generally fair still may fail in specific cases.

Presently, the Supreme Court has up and down the line, for programmatic choices as well as individual cases, claimed a plenary power for the courts to say what process is due. The courts exercise this power by a balance, their own balance, among public goals and individual interests.[2]

§ 7.6.1 Fairness, Accuracy, Security, Autonomy: The Goals of Due Process

Fairness refers to agency action according to known standards that are impartially applied though revealed procedures. *Known* standards allow a person to better understand what government expects of her, so that she can plan her life in some forehanded way.[3] Known standards

§ 7.6

1. Brock v. Roadway Express, Inc., 481 U.S. 252, 262–63, 107 S.Ct. 1740, 1747–48, 95 L.Ed.2d 239 (1987); Morrissey v. Brewer, 408 U.S. 471, 481, 92 S.Ct. 2593, 2600, 33 L.Ed.2d 484 (1972) ("Once it is determined that due process applies, the question remains what process is due.")

2. Mathews v. Eldridge, 424 U.S. 319, 348–49, 96 S.Ct. 893, 909–10, 47 L.Ed.2d 18 (1976) (discussed, infra, at sec. 7.6.5). See also Goldberg v. Kelly, 397 U.S. 254, 262–63, 90 S.Ct. 1011, 1017–18, 25 L.Ed.2d 287 (1970) ("The extent to which procedural due process must be afforded the [welfare] recipient is influenced by the extent to which he may be 'condemned to suffer grievous loss,' and depends upon whether the recipient's interest in avoiding that loss outweighs the governmental interest in summary adjudication"); Cafeteria & Restaurant Workers Union v. McElroy, 367 U.S. 886, 895, 81 S.Ct. 1743, 1748, 6 L.Ed.2d 1230 (1961), rehearing denied 368 U.S. 869, 82 S.Ct. 22, 7 L.Ed.2d 70 (1961).

3. For instance, in Dixon v. Love, 431 U.S. 105, 97 S.Ct. 1723, 52 L.Ed.2d 172 (1977), involving the application of a well-defined criteria for the suspension of driver's licenses, the Court noted that "the decision to use objective rules in this case provides drivers with more precise notice of what conduct will be sanctioned and promotes equality of treatment among similarly situated drivers. The approach taken by the District Court would have the contrary result of reducing the fairness of the system, by requiring a necessarily subjective inquiry in each case as to a driver's 'disrespect' or 'lack of ability to exercise ordinary

also limit the allocation choices of agency officials. They require that choices be made according to principle rather than the preference of the official. *Revealed* procedures—procedures seen and comprehended—are essential to an individual's effective and comfortable participation in the agency's application of its standards to her.[4]

Fairness relates to accuracy, to whether the outcome of a process advances the right goal. A welfare agency might distribute cash benefits by drawing lots. Such a process is revealed and impartial.[5] Yet it hardly seems fair, because it is not an accurate response to the goal of distribution of benefits to indigent persons. Therefore, a process should be responsive to substantive goals by implementing them as *accurately* as is possible.[6] This interest in accuracy is held both collectively and individually. There is obviously a general societal interest in a public program being applied to individuals according to its goals. At the same time, an individual is more likely to feel fairly treated when an agency action affecting him is consistent with societal goals.[7]

Security in relation to the state is another goal of due process. In *Board of Regents v. Roth,* the Court emphasized that due process was "a safeguard of the *security* of interests that a person has . . . in specific benefits."[8] In the courts, however, this goal of security, at least in relation to what process is due,[9] has been treated as the composite of the aforementioned goals of fairness and accuracy. If the law applying processes of agencies are accurate and fair, then the interest in security as described in *Roth* has been served.[10]

and reasonable care.' " Id. at 115, 97 S.Ct. at 1729. See also Joint Anti–Fascist Refugee Committee v. McGrath, 341 U.S. 123, 170, 71 S.Ct. 624, 647, 95 L.Ed. 817 (1951) (Frankfurter, concurring) ("a democratic government must therefore practice fairness, and fairness can rarely be obtained by secret one-sided determination of facts decisive of rights."). On the need for known standards, see Chap. 3, supra.

4. That processes be appropriately revealed was required in Memphis Light, Gas and Water Div. v. Craft, 436 U.S. 1, 13–15, 98 S.Ct. 1554, 1562–64, 56 L.Ed.2d 30 (1978), as the Court there found that notice was inadequate as it failed to inform utility customers of procedures for protesting termination of utility services. Regarding that deficiency, the Court noted "Mrs. Craft's repeated efforts to obtain information about what appeared to be unjustified double billing" and "good faith [but misinformed] efforts to pay [her] utilities as well as straighten out the problem." Id. at 14, 98 S.Ct. at 1562.

5. It was just because drawing lots was deemed as an impartial method that this was finally used as the means for selecting draftees during the Vietnam war.

6. 436 U.S. at 14, 98 S.Ct. at 1562 ("[t]he function of legal process, as that concept is embodied in the Constitution, and in the realm of factfinding, is to minimize the risk of erroneous decisions"); Goss v. Lopez, 419 U.S. 565, 579, 95 S.Ct. 729, 738, 42 L.Ed.2d 725 (1975) ("The Student's interest is to avoid unfair or mistaken exclusion from the educational process"); Morrissey v. Brewer, 408 U.S. 471, 484, 92 S.Ct. 2593, 2601, 33 L.Ed.2d 484 (1972) ("[s]ociety thus has an interest in not having parole revoked because of erroneous information").

7. Morrissey v. Brewer, 408 U.S. 471, 484, 92 S.Ct. 2593, 2601, 33 L.Ed.2d 484 (1972); Goss v. Lopez, 419 U.S. 565, 579, 95 S.Ct. 729, 738, 42 L.Ed.2d 725 (1975).

8. 419 U.S. at 576, 95 S.Ct. at 737.

9. An individual's interest in security is, however, considerably important otherwise. It underlies the entitlement theory of when process is due. See sec. 7.4.1, supra.

10. That the interest in security is comprised of interests in fairness and accuracy seems substantiated by the number of cases following *Roth* (where this security interest was acknowledged) in which the

A remaining goal of due process, at least in terms of scholarly support, is an individual's sense of her own worth and dignity.[11] In massive public programs with thousands of proceedings (the usual workload of welfare programs) the individual may be seen as a number rather than as a person. In this light, the courts' general insistence on special constitutional rules when agencies act against a particular person may be seen as recognition of that individual's interest in being treated as a person, as recognition of her autonomy and worth. As explained by Justice Blackmun, "when government acts in a way that singles out identifiable individuals—in a way that is likely to be premised on suppositions about specific persons—it activates the special concern about being personally talked to about the decision rather than simply being dealt with."[12]

In *Dixon v. Love,* however, the Court refused to include a dignitary interest in its due process calculus, at least not in the context of that case. A truck driver's license had been summarily suspended after he exceeded a certain number of points assessed for accumulated traffic offenses. He was entitled to an evidentiary hearing after the suspension, but the truck driver argued that he was also entitled to oral argument prior to suspension. The Court, because it found little chance of an "erroneous deprivation" of his license under the point system, was not sympathetic. "Such an appearance might make the licensee feel that he has received more personal attention," the Court said, "but it would not serve to protect any substantive rights."[13]

§ 7.6.2 Adversarial Hearings: The Trial Type Model

While the process due a person might be calculated freshly and wholly rationally, by identifying goals and by then devising procedures that best serve these goals, it has not been wholly the product of such a method. Due process is also a product of history. Here, the starting point has been a certain tradition, of "a trial according to some settled course of judicial proceedings."[14] According to this model, a due process hearing consists of procedures designed for adversarial processes. A reasonably

Court's main concern was the fairness and accuracy of agency procedures. See Dixon v. Love, 431 U.S. 105, 114, 97 S.Ct. 1723, 1728, 52 L.Ed.2d 172 (1977); Goss v. Lopez, 419 U.S. 565, 95 S.Ct. 729, 42 L.Ed.2d 725 (1975); Morrissey v. Brewer, 408 U.S. 471, 92 S.Ct. 2593, 33 L.Ed.2d 484 (1972).

11. See Mashaw, Administrative Due Process: The Quest for a Dignitary Value, 61 Bos.L.Rev. 885 (1981). Among other things, Professor Mashaw surveys the relevant literature and concludes that "The unifying thread in this literature is the perception that the effects of process on participants, not just the rationality of substantive results, must be considered in judging the legitimacy of public decisionmaking." Id. at 886. For a criticism of "dignity" as a due process value, see Easterbrook, Substance and Due Process, 1982 Sup.Ct.Rev. 85, 115–18.

12. O'Bannon v. Town Court Nursing Center, 447 U.S. 773, 801, 100 S.Ct. 2467, 2483, 65 L.Ed.2d 506 (1980), on remand 626 F.2d 1114 (3d Cir.1980) (*quoting* L. Tribe, Amer. Const. Law 503–04 (1978)). See generally M. Buber, I and Thou (R. Smith Trans., 1958).

13. Dixon v. Love, 431 U.S. 105, 114, 97 S.Ct. 1723, 1728, 52 L.Ed.2d 172 (1977).

14. Murray's Lessee v. Hoboken Land & Imp. Co., 59 U.S. (18 How.) 272, 280, 15 L.Ed. 372 (1855), supra, at 280. In that opinion, though, Justice Curtis carefully added that this implication of an adjudicatory model was "not universally true." Id.

full list, as verified by the Supreme Court, of these procedures is as follows:

1. notice of a proposed action;

2. disclosure of the grounds of the agency action and the evidence the agency is relying upon;

3. an opportunity to present one's own evidence, witnesses, and reasons;

4. confrontation and cross-examination of adverse witnesses;

5. an impartial tribunal;

6. a written statement by the tribunal of the evidence relied upon and the reasons for its decision;

7. right to counsel.[15]

The courts need not impose all of these procedures in a given case.[16] Rather, some combination of them may be imposed, depending on the circumstances. Some procedures may be omitted because at times they are counter-productive. For instance, in prison disciplinary proceedings, a right to counsel has been rejected because "it would inevitably give the proceedings a more adversarial cast and tend to reduce their utility as a means to further correctional goals."[17] At other times, parts of the adjudicatory model may be omitted simply because their contribution to a hearing is slight in relation to their costs. In the context of professional judgments and reports, for example, cross-examination may contribute only slightly to the reliability of evidence while being quite costly: the expert has to appear and be paid for his time.[18]

As a matter of consensus among the courts, however, an adjudicatory model (and no doubt any procedural model) would in all circumstances require certain elements of the above list. These elements

15. Morrissey v. Brewer, 408 U.S. 471, 489, 92 S.Ct. 2593, 2604, 33 L.Ed.2d 484 (1972). See also Goldberg v. Kelly, 397 U.S. 254, 90 S.Ct. 1011, 25 L.Ed.2d 287 (1970). For a discussion of these various elements, see Friendly, Some Kind of Hearing, 123 U.Pa.L.Rev. 1267 (1975).

16. "A procedural rule that may satisfy due process in one context may not necessarily satisfy procedural due process in every case." Bell v. Burson, 402 U.S. 535, 540, 91 S.Ct. 1586, 1589, 29 L.Ed.2d 90 (1971).

17. This disutility of counsel, as more fully explained by the Court, is that "The role of the hearing body itself, . . . being 'predictive and discretionary' as well as factfinding, may become more akin to that of a judge at a trial, and less attuned to the rehabilitative needs of the individual probationer or parolee." Wolff v. McDonnell, 418 U.S. 539, 570, 94 S.Ct. 2963, 2981, 41 L.Ed.2d 935 (1974).

18. In such cases, while there may be "professional disagreement" with the conclusions of the expert, there are not usually involved questions of "credibility or veracity," where confrontation and cross-examination are useful. Richardson v. Perales, 402 U.S. 389, 406–07, 91 S.Ct. 1420, 1429–30, 28 L.Ed.2d 842 (1971) (involving medical evidence). See also Wolff v. McDonnell, 418 U.S. 539, 567, 94 S.Ct. 2963, 2980, 41 L.Ed.2d 935 (1974); Mathews v. Eldridge, 424 U.S. 319, 343–44, 96 S.Ct. 893, 907, 47 L.Ed.2d 18 (1976). In Brock v. Roadway Express, Inc., 481 U.S. 252, 266, 107 S.Ct. 1740, 1750, 95 L.Ed.2d 239 (1987), the Court, in the context of a pretermination hearing in the employment area, found that "[t]o allow the employer and employee an opportunity to test the credibility of opposing witnesses during the investigation would not increase the reliability of the preliminary decision sufficiently to justify the additional delay."

include notice,[19] disclosure of the agency's reasons for its proposed action,[20] an opportunity for an individual to present his reasons and to refute those of the agency,[21] and an unbiased decision-maker.[22] In this short list, history and logic combine: the goals of accuracy and fairness and autonomy identified in the previous section could hardly be met except on the basis of notice and an opportunity to present and refute evidence before an impartial person.

§ 7.6.3 *Goldberg v. Kelly* and the Trial–Type Model

The trial-type form of process, of a hearing "according to some settled course of judicial proceedings," arose when a private ordering of social and economic relations was the norm, and government regulation the exception.[23] Then, when government acted it did so in isolated episodes, such as whether an item had been properly taxed or whether certain behavior violated some general rule such as a criminal law. An adversarial hearing, adapted as it was to reproducing and examining the limited range of circumstances associated with a singular event, was suited to this episodic context.

In modern times, this form of due process was reinforced when it was a useful antidote to the poisons of McCarthyism. Main features of the adversarial method, such as confrontation and cross-examination, usefully counteracted some bad government practices, for instance false charges and faceless informers.[24] In *Goldberg v. Kelly,* however, the Court may have gone overboard in embracing the juridical model.

Goldberg v. Kelly involved the constitutionality of procedures for terminating welfare payments (under the Aid to Families with Dependent Children program) in New York City.[25] The general form of these procedures was notice to recipients and consultation with them prior to termination of payments. These pre-termination procedures were backed

19. Notice should be "reasonably calculated" to inform a person both of the grounds of an agency action with respect to him and of whatever procedures the agency offers that person in connection with hearing his objections. Memphis Light, Gas and Water Div. v. Craft, 436 U.S. 1, 13–16, 98 S.Ct. 1554, 1562–64, 56 L.Ed.2d 30 (1978). See also Mullane v. Central Hanover Bank & Trust Co., 339 U.S. 306, 314, 70 S.Ct. 652, 657, 94 L.Ed. 865 (1950) ("An elementary and fundamental requirement of due process in any proceeding which is to be accorded finality is notice reasonably calculated, under all the circumstances, to apprise interested parties of the pendency of the action and afford them an opportunity to present their objections.")

20. Brock v. Roadway Express, Inc., 481 U.S. 252, 259–60, 107 S.Ct. 1740, 1746–47, 95 L.Ed.2d 239 (1987).

21. This minimum element of due process is recognized as such in Cleveland Bd. of Educ. v. Loudermill, 470 U.S. 532, 546, 105 S.Ct. 1487, 1495, 84 L.Ed.2d 494 (1985) ("The tenured public employee is entitled to oral or written notice of the charges against him, an explanation of the employer's evidence, and an opportunity to present his side of the story."). See also Memphis Light, Gas and Water Div. v. Craft, 436 U.S. 1, 17–19, 98 S.Ct. 1554, 1564–66, 56 L.Ed.2d 30 (1978); Goss v. Lopez, 419 U.S. 565, 581, 95 S.Ct. 729, 740, 42 L.Ed.2d 725 (1975).

22. Dr. Bonham's Case, 8 Co.Rep. 107, 77 Eng.Rep. 638 (1610).

23. E.g., Horwitz, The History of the Public Private Distinction, 130 U.Pa.L.Rev. 1423 (1982).

24. Davis, The Requirement of a Trial Type Hearing, 70 Harv.L.Rev. 193 (1956).

25. 397 U.S. 254, 90 S.Ct. 1011, 25 L.Ed.2d 287 (1970).

by a full, post-termination hearing. If the post-termination hearing showed that payments to a recipient had been erroneously terminated, then payments were resumed and back payments paid. In *Goldberg*, the plaintiffs, whose payments had been terminated, claimed that the pre-termination procedures afforded them were inadequate and that the process due them required an evidentiary hearing prior to termination of payments.

The pre-termination procedures at issue in *Goldberg* were caseworker intensive. These procedures were as follows:

> A caseworker who has doubts about the recipient's continued eligibility must first discuss them with the recipient. If the caseworker concludes that the recipient is no longer eligible, he recommends termination of aid to a unit supervisor. If the latter concurs, he sends the recipient a letter stating the reasons for proposing to terminate aid and notifying him that within seven days he may request that a higher official review the record, and may support the request with a written statement prepared personally or with the aid of an attorney or other person. If the reviewing official affirms the determination ineligibility, aid is stopped immediately and the recipient is informed by letter of the reasons for the action.

In assessing these procedures, the Court was struck by the dire straits of welfare recipients whose payments were erroneously terminated, individuals who might be "deprived of the very means by which to live" pending the full evidentiary hearing. With this concern in mind, the Court determined that the pre-termination procedures were deficient.

The Court ordered that the caseworker-intensive mode of process used by the agencies be replaced by an adversarial and evidentiary process. Rather in the form of a code, the Court prescribed nearly the full bag of adjudicatory procedures. These procedures included notice, right to counsel, confrontation and cross examination of adverse witnesses, an impartial hearing examiner, a decision on the record supported by a transcript, and a statement of findings and evidence.

Two years later in *Morrissey v. Brewer,* the Court, in the context of parole revocation hearings, again required an adjudicatory form of process and imposed a procedural code similar to that of *Goldberg*.[26] However, these cases, *Goldberg* and *Morrissey*, represented the high-water mark of the adjudicatory model.

§ 7.6.4 Post–*Goldberg*: The Emergence of Alternatives to Trial–Type Procedures

Since *Goldberg v. Kelly,* the courts have not at all backed away from that case's main proposition of the applicability of due process to public programs. Because of doubts about the adversarial processes adopted in

26. 408 U.S. 471, 92 S.Ct. 2593, 33 L.Ed.2d 484 (1972).

that case, the courts have, however, turned away from that model of due process and toward some alternatives.

In the first place, the doubts about *Goldberg* were whether the adversarial processes it ordered in fact offered a good measure of compassion and comfort to individuals caught in the bureaucratic system. For whatever reason—the fact that adversarial processes tend to displace civility or because of the huge case load in welfare—the trial-type hearing ordered in *Goldberg* seems to have offered only cold comfort to welfare claimants. These hearings, it is said, have tended toward a "police court environment," where "claimants certainly are not made to feel that an informal process has been designed to provide for a full, relaxed opportunity to present their case."[27] Nor does it seem that the adjudicatory model gives claimants an effective opportunity to present their claims: they frequently lack the resources and the knowledge essential to vindicating claims by the contentious methods of the adversarial system.[28]

In programmatic terms, the expense and delay of the adversarial model has taxed administrative systems.[29] Also, because judicial supervision of agency procedures is *ex post* and because the measure of this supervision is presently an unpredictable balancing test, the incentive to an agency hoping to achieve a secure result, one with some insulation against judicial review, is to pile on the procedures. As the Supreme Court has said in another context, "The agencies, operating under [a] vague injunction to employ the 'best' procedures and facing the threat of reversal if they did not, would undoubtedly adopt full adjudicatory procedures in every instance."[30] The weight of this "proceduralization" may fall on the individual as a dead weight. A cost is also assessed against public programs, where the expense of an adversarial model of process inevitably consumes some portions of the appropriation for such programs.[31]

27. D. Blum, The Welfare Family and Mass Administrative Justice, 36–40, 50–51 (1974), quoted in W. Gellhorn, et al., Administrative Law, Cases and Comments 572–73 (8th ed. 1987).

28. The adversarial hearing presumes contestants who are evenly matched, which may not be the case, especially in social welfare programs where a claimant cannot be expected to have the resources to participate effectively in an adversarial process. Wedemeyer & Moore, The American Welfare System, 59 Cal.L.Rev. 326, 342 (1966). See also Wolff v. McDonnell, 418 U.S. 539, 567, 94 S.Ct. 2963, 41 L.Ed.2d 935 (1974).

29. Delays are generally detrimental to the agency's goals. Also, they may hurt the individual asking for due process. That delay in providing a hearing can itself constitute a violation of due process, see Brock v. Roadway Express, Inc., 481 U.S. 252, 267, 107 S.Ct. 1740, 95 L.Ed.2d 239 (1987); Cleveland Bd. of Educ. v. Loudermill, 470 U.S. 532, 546–47, 105 S.Ct. 1487, 84 L.Ed.2d 494 (1985). Delay does not, of course, always harm an individual. For instance, if a person is presently receiving a benefit of some sort, and the hearing is about the termination of that benefit, that person might prefer that the hearing be delayed.

30. Vermont Yankee v. Natural Resources Defense Council, Inc., 435 U.S. 519, 546–47, 98 S.Ct. 1197, 1213, 55 L.Ed.2d 460 (1978).

31. The expense of adversarial hearings may diminish resources, such as the Social Security Trust Fund, otherwise available to the beneficiaries of a governmental program. Richardson v. Perales, 402 U.S. 389, 406, 91 S.Ct. 1420, 28 L.Ed.2d 842 (1971) ("With over 20,000 disability claim hearings annually, the cost of providing live

Finally, a problem with the adjudicatory model is that at times it is beside the point: it is simply inapposite to the work of agencies. In social welfare programs, the individual and the agency are involved in a dynamic relation in which the agency must continually assess the status of that individual so as to make predictive judgments about her future abilities or needs. Here cooperation, civility, constancy, and forward-thinking are in order,[32] and the hostile, adversarial and backward-looking characteristics of adjudicatory hearings seem manifestly inappropriate.[33] Also, in this sort of agency work the adjudicatory model may operate perversely, as it deflects decisional responsibilities away from the best qualified people. When due process converts agency processes into trial-type processes, decisional responsibility tends to shift toward those competent in those processes (lawyers) and to move away from those competent with respect to substance (the caseworker).

Because of these drawbacks to trial-type procedures, various agencies have tried various alternatives. One alternative is the "inquisitorial" hearing. In administrative law, this sinister-sounding process is simply a variation of the trial-type model in which the administrative law judge assumes responsibilities ordinarily performed by the separate legal counsel of the two sides to a hearing. Also, the administrative law judge may assist an underrepresented party in preparing his case.[34] Another alternative process, one that seems especially appropriate in the context of the dynamic agency/client relationships of welfare programs, is that of a "managerial" system of process. Instead of trying to correct agency decisions by a separate and after-the-fact evidentiary hearing, a managerial system concentrates on improving the agency decisional process. Such a system consists of quality controls internal to the agency and involving "the development of standards, the evaluation of performance against those standards, and action to upgrade substandard performance."[35]

medical testimony at those hearings ... would be a substantial drain on the trust fund...."); Goldberg v. Kelly, 397 U.S. 254, 90 S.Ct. 1011, 25 L.Ed.2d 287 (1970) (Berger, C.J., dissenting) ("The history of the complexity of the administrative process followed by judicial review as we have seen it for the past 30 years should suggest the possibility that new layers of procedure may become an intolerable drain on the very funds earmarked for food, clothing, and other living essentials.")

32. The element of civility, which is perhaps too often ignored in due process calculations, is however seen in Board of Curators v. Horowitz, 435 U.S. 78, 90, 98 S.Ct. 948, 955, 55 L.Ed.2d 124 (1978), as the Court found that an adversarial process was inappropriate to questions of academic performance inasmuch as it was detrimental to the "educator, adviser, friend, and, at times, parent-substitute roles" of a teacher.

33. See generally Mashaw, The Management Side of Due Process: Some Theoretical and Litigation Notes on the Assurance of Accuracy, Fairness, and Timeliness in the Adjudication of Social Welfare Claims, 59 Cornell L.Rev. 772 (1972). Regarding adjudicatory processes, Mashaw says that the "information which is available on the [Aid to Families with Dependent Children] program should substantially decrease our confidence that the procedural rights afforded recipients in *Goldberg v. Kelly* provided substantial assurance of fairness and accuracy."

34. E.g., Richardson v. Perales, 402 U.S. 389, 91 S.Ct. 1420, 28 L.Ed.2d 842 (1971).

35. Mashaw, supra note 33, at 791.

In view of these concerns, the courts, as we said, turned away from the trial-type mode of due process prescribed in that case and toward the alternatives. We will follow this progression, on up to *Mathews v. Eldridge* where the Court stated:

> The judicial model of an evidentiary hearing is neither a required, nor even the most effective, method of decision-making in all circumstances.... In assessing what process is due ... substantial weight must be given to the good faith judgments of the individuals charged by Congress with the administration of social welfare programs.[36]

An early expression of this newer attitude came in *Richardson v. Wright*.[37] A three-judge district court had found that the Social Security Administration's termination procedures for disability payments violated due process, and that decision was appealed to the Supreme Court. During the pendency of this appeal, the Department of Health, Education, and Welfare promulgated new regulations that substantially met the district court's objections to the procedures in question. Consequently, the Supreme Court vacated the district court order and directed the Social Security Administration to reprocess the disability claim under the new regulations. As it gave the agency's initiative a chance, the Court explained that in "the context of a comprehensively complex administrative program, the administrative process must have a reasonable opportunity to evolve procedures to meet needs as they arise."

As the Court became willing to give other branches of government more room to develop processes, it also began to say that the adjudicatory structure was not an exclusive structure for these processes. In *Richardson v. Perales,* the Court held that in a Social Security disability hearing due process did not include a right of confrontation and cross-examination of adverse medical witnesses (doctors) and that written submissions from those witnesses would do.[38]

More dramatically, *Richardson v. Perales* departed from the adjudicatory model of *Goldberg* as in *Richardson* the Court held that an inquisitorial process was consistent with due process. In the disability hearing, the administrative law judge had assumed responsibilities ordinarily performed by separate legal counsel for both claimant and govern-

36. Mathews v. Eldridge, 424 U.S. 319, 348–49, 96 S.Ct. 893, 47 L.Ed.2d 18 (1976).

37. 405 U.S. 208, 92 S.Ct. 788, 31 L.Ed.2d 151 (1972).

38. 402 U.S. 389, 91 S.Ct. 1420, 28 L.Ed.2d 842 (1971). In *Richardson, Goldberg v. Kelly* and that decision's confident emphasis on confrontation and cross-examination was distinguished in that while the credibility and veracity of witnesses were a factor in *Goldberg*, these things were not similarly implicated by the medical opinions involved in the "Social Security disability claim" context of *Richardson*. Here, the professional nature of opinions and the "routine of the medical examination" as well as the routine of the agency was, the Court said, a sufficient guarantee of impartial and unbiased reports. Also, the "sheer magnitude of the administrative burden" was a factor in the Court's decision not to require confrontation and cross examination with respect to medical evidence. In this regard the Court stated that "[w]ith over 20,000 disability claim hearings annually, the cost of providing live medical testimony at those hearings, where need has not been demonstrated by a request for a subpoena, ... would be a substantial drain on the trust fund."

ment. He prepared evidence for both sides, generally aided an unrepresented claimant in preparing his case, and then at the hearing decided the case. This "three-hat role" of the administrative law judge, the Court found, was fair to the individual and provided for a more efficient resolution of his claim. This being the case, the arguments against the system "assume[d] too much and would bring down too many procedures designed, and working well, for a governmental structure of great and growing complexity."

This disaffection with the adjudicatory model continued in other contexts, for instance public education. In *Goss v. Lopez,*[39] the Court agreed that a high-school suspension was subject to due process. The Court, however, did not agree that the process should be adversarial. One reason was the costs in money and time. "To impose ... even truncated trial-type procedures," the Court explained, "might well overwhelm administrative facilities in many places and, by diverting resources, cost more than it would save in educational effectiveness." Another reason was doubts about effectiveness, that "further formalizing the suspension process and escalating its formality and adversary nature may ... destroy its effectiveness as part of the teaching process."[40]

Perhaps the most thorough reexamination of the adjudicatory model occurred in prison administration cases. In *Morrissey v. Brewer,*[41] the Court's initial reaction—same as in *Goldberg v. Kelly*—had been to establish adversarial and evidentiary procedures as the due process norm. In prison administration, however, the decisions subject to due process are not often simple assessments of past behavior. Instead, they are predictive and evaluative, involving assessments of the future behavior of inmates and the welfare of the individual and society in general.[42] Such a decision, as Professor Kadish said, involves a "discretionary assessment of a multiplicity of imponderables, entailing primarily what a man is and what he may become rather than simply what he has done."[43] For these kinds of decisions, the Court, in the years following *Morrissey,* came to see adversarial processes as not especially helpful,[44]

39. 419 U.S. 565, 95 S.Ct. 729, 42 L.Ed.2d 725 (1975).

40. Rather than a hearing along the lines of an adjudicatory model, the Court prescribed an informal process consisting of "oral or written notice of the charges against him [the student] and, if he denies them, an explanation of the evidence the authorities have and an opportunity to present his side of the story." 419 U.S. at 581.

41. 408 U.S. 471, 92 S.Ct. 2593, 33 L.Ed.2d 484 (1972).

42. Hewitt v. Helms, 459 U.S. 460, 474, 103 S.Ct. 864, 74 L.Ed.2d 675 (1983).

43. Kadish, The Advocate and the Expert—Counsel in the Peno–Correctional Process, 45 Minn.L.Rev. 803, 813 (1961), quoted in Greenholtz v. Nebraska Penal Inmates, 442 U.S. 1, 10, 99 S.Ct. 2100, 60 L.Ed.2d 668 (1979).

44. For instance in Wolff v. McDonnell, 418 U.S. 539, 563, 94 S.Ct. 2963, 41 L.Ed.2d 935 (1974), the Court noted the "unwisdom in encasing ... disciplinary procedures in an inflexible constitutional straitjacket that would necessarily call for adversary proceedings typical of the criminal trial [and that would] very likely raise the level of confrontation between staff and inmate, and make more difficult the utilization of the disciplinary process as a tool to advance the rehabilitative goals of the institution."

and instead came to rely on "informal non-adversarial evidentiary review."[45]

§ 7.6.5 *Mathews v. Eldridge*

The present method for determining the process due a person is set out in *Mathews v. Eldridge.*[46] The plaintiff, Eldridge, had been receiving disability payments for chronic anxiety and back sprain and diabetes, for about four years. In 1972, he filed a routine, periodic report on his disability. Upon receiving this report, the agency monitoring his condition obtained additional reports from his physician and from a psychiatric consultant. Considering these various reports, and other information in his file, that agency informed Eldridge that his disability benefits would end that month.

Eldridge was, however, entitled to a full post-termination hearing, with reinstatement of back benefits should this hearing show that his termination had been erroneous. Rather than pursuing such a hearing, Eldridge brought a federal court action, claiming that the agency's pre-termination procedures violated due process. He relied, of course, on *Goldberg v. Kelly.* The same as the plaintiffs in that case, he stood to be in bad circumstances (disabled) if the initial termination decision was erroneous, and as in *Goldberg* this crucial decision had not been the product of evidentiary hearing. Therefore, on the authority of *Goldberg v. Kelly* the lower court found for Eldridge. The Supreme Court, however, disagreed, and held that the system was constitutional.

In *Mathews v. Eldridge,* the Court first of all established a three-part test for assessing the process due a person, the parts of which it described as follows:

45. Hewitt v. Helms, 459 U.S. 460, 476, 103 S.Ct. 864, 74 L.Ed.2d 675 (1983). See also Gagnon v. Scarpelli, 411 U.S. 778, 788, 93 S.Ct. 1756, 36 L.Ed.2d 656 (1973) ("due process is not so rigid as to require that the significant interests in informality, flexibility, and economy must always be satisfied"). An instance of the Court's reliance upon "informal, non-adversarial review" is provided by Greenholtz v. Nebraska Penal Inmates, 442 U.S. 1, 99 S.Ct. 2100, 60 L.Ed.2d 668 (1978). In that case the Court overturned a lower court's requirements (1) of a "formal hearing" before the parole board for an inmate eligible for parole and (2) that adverse decisions be accompanied by a statement of the evidence relied upon by the Board.

Regarding the formal hearing requirement, the Court found that the informal hearing already provided by the state was sufficient. At that hearing an inmate eligible for review might appear before the Board and introduce such statements or letters as he wished. This appearance, as the court saw it, "provided the inmate with an effective opportunity first, to insure that the records before the board are in fact the records relating to his case; and, second, to present any special considerations demonstrating why he is an appropriate candidate for parole." 442 U.S. at 15, 99 S.Ct. at 2108. Because the parole decision was one "that must be made largely on the basis of the inmate's files," the Court found that this informal hearing "adequately safeguards against serious risks of error and thus satisfies due process." 442 U.S. at 15.

Regarding the second requirement imposed by the trial judge, that of a statement of the evidence that the parole board relied upon, the Court found that as the parole decision was "essentially an experienced prediction based on a host of variables," such a requirement was of little value in explaining the Board's decision. At the same time such a statement of evidence, the Court said, had a bad effect, it "would tend to convert the process into an adversary proceeding. . . . " 442 U.S. at 16.

46. 424 U.S. 319, 96 S.Ct. 893, 47 L.Ed.2d 18 (1976).

> First, the private interest that will be affected by the official action; second, the risk of an erroneous deprivation of such interest through the procedures used, and the probable value, if any, of additional or substitute procedural safeguards; and finally, the government's interest, including the function involved and the fiscal and administrative burdens that the additional or substitute procedural requirement would entail.

This test included the private interest versus governmental interest parts of *Goldberg*. But consistent with the case law after *Goldberg,* the test added (1) an assessment of the marginal contribution to the accuracy of an agency action of a claimed procedural requirement, and (2) a calculation of the "fiscal and administrative burden that [an] additional or substitute procedural requirement would entail." In a matter that we will return to, the Court emphasized that in applying this three-part test the courts should not address the circumstances of the individual claiming due process, but the courts should instead consider the "generality" of cases.[47] The balancing process prescribed by the Court is, therefore, overtly utilitarian and legislative-like.

After establishing this general, balancing test, the Court applied it to the Social Security disability procedures in question. Out of the "private interest" part of the test, the argument was that an erroneous agency action removed benefits from a person unable to work and that this was as serious a deprivation as in *Goldberg v. Kelly.* The Court, however, found the private interest in disability cases not so pressing as in *Goldberg,* considering "the possibility of access to private resources" and the "availability to government welfare programs" for disabled persons.[48]

The Court then moved to the new second part of its test—the probable value, from the standpoint of accuracy, of "additional procedural safeguards." Eldridge had claimed a right to a personal appearance and oral argument prior to termination of benefits. (The agency's pretermination procedures allowed only written submissions.) By classifying disability as a strictly medical question, the Court was able to find that little could be gained by a personal appearance. This medical question turned on " 'routine, standard, and unbiased medical reports by physician specialists,' "and this routine, standardization and impartiality seemed an assurance of probative value sufficient to eliminate the need for an oral evidentiary hearing.

Additionally, the recipient had full access to the evidence upon which the agency relied, and the opportunity to submit comment and additional medical evidence, in written form, to the agency. These procedures, the Court found, "enable[d] the recipient to 'mold' his

47. 424 U.S. at 344, ("procedural due process rules are shaped by the risk of error inherent in the truth-finding process as applied to the generality of the cases").

48. Justice Brennan, dissenting, characterized this distinction of *Goldberg* as "speculation." Indeed, the majority itself was not enthusiastic about its distinction, as it said that "the degree of difference [between the plights of the disability claimant and the welfare claimant] can be overstated." 424 U.S. at 341.

argument to respond to the precise issues which the decisionmaker regards as crucial."

The Court then considered the third part, the governmental interest part, of its due process balance. This interest now included the "fiscal or administrative burden" of substitute or additional procedures. In the massive Social Security program, the additional cost of a more formal pre-termination hearing "would not be insubstantial,"[49] and so that cost was a significant factor.

Finally, the Court in *Matthews v. Eldridge* formally endorsed the movement away from adjudicatory procedures as an exclusive form of procedure for administrative law. "The judicial model of an evidentiary hearing," the Court explained, "is neither a required, nor even the most effective method of decisionmaking in all circumstances." The Court also acknowledged that it had no exclusive competence in these matters and that "substantial weight must be give to the good-faith judgments of the individuals charged by Congress with the administration of social welfare programs that the procedures they have provided assure fair consideration of the entitlement claims of individuals."

§ 7.7 THE TIMING OF A HEARING

The process due a person involves an inquiry into the kind of hearing and procedures he should have. But that inquiry does not always complete the problem. Sometimes another question, one of timing, remains: when is the process that is due, due?

A person would expect to be heard *before* he is deprived of liberty or property. And, indeed, a prior hearing is the norm.[1] Occasionally, however, an agency may wish to deviate from this norm. It may wish to avoid the delay associated with a prior hearing; it may, for instance, wish to immediately seize food or drugs that it believes to be unsafe.[2] Other times, an agency may choose to not dispense *entirely* with a prior hearing but to instead provide a summary form of prior hearing. Then, after it has acted, then provide a full hearing.[3] The point is: there are enough of these exceptions to make the timing of a hearing sometimes complicated.

§ 7.7.1 The Property Rights Exception

The Supreme Court once said that "where only property rights are involved" no prior hearing is required, and that instead a post-depriva-

49. The Court added that: "Significantly, the cost of protecting those whom the preliminary administrative process has identified as likely to be found undeserving may in the end come out of the pockets of the deserving, since resources available for any particular program of social welfare are not unlimited."

§ 7.7

1. Memphis Light, Gas and Water Div. v. Craft, 436 U.S. 1, 19, 98 S.Ct. 1554, 56 L.Ed.2d 30 (1978).

2. Ewing v. Mytinger & Casselberry, Inc., 339 U.S. 594, 70 S.Ct. 870, 94 L.Ed. 1088 (1950) (misbranded drugs); North American Cold Storage Co. v. Chicago, 211 U.S. 306, 29 S.Ct. 101, 53 L.Ed. 195 (1908) (putrid chicken).

3. See, e.g., Barry v. Barchi, 443 U.S. 55, 99 S.Ct. 2642, 61 L.Ed.2d 365 (1979) (suspension of a horse trainer's license where a race horse in his care had been drugged).

tion hearing will do.[4] When "only property" is taken, post-deprivation remedies are often effective to redress the injury. Usually, the injury can be measured in dollars and that amount paid as damages.[5] But given the expanded definition of property "interests" in *Roth v. Board of Regents,* the "only property" exception would operate to give the state an unexpectedly large opportunity to postpone a hearing. Possibly for this reason, and also because of the Court's estimate of the severity of a deprivation in new property cases, the property-rights exception to the norm of a prior hearing is today more moderately stated and applied.

This more tempered measure is that "where the potential length or severity of the deprivation [of property] does not indicate a likelihood of serious loss and where the procedures underlying the decision to act are sufficiently reliable to minimize the risk of erroneous determination, government may act without providing additional advance procedural safeguards."[6] The Court is, then, concerned with the likelihood of serious loss, even in the case of "mere" property and will temper the notion, that with property a post-deprivation hearing will do, accordingly. Thus, in such otherwise different cases *as Goldberg v. Kelly* and *Matthews v. Eldridge*, the Court required some sort of a hearing prior to the deprivation of important social benefits.[7]

In the public employment context, the interests of the employee and the state with respect to a pre-termination hearing were assessed in *Arnett v. Kennedy*,[8] where a federal civil servant had been dismissed after

4. Ewing v. Mytinger & Casselberry, Inc., 339 U.S. 594, 599–600, 70 S.Ct. 870, 94 L.Ed. 1088 (1950); Bowles v. Willingham, 321 U.S. 503, 520, 64 S.Ct. 641, 88 L.Ed. 892 (1944).

5. In contrast, when a person's liberty is taken, an injury not generally susceptible of redress in terms of dollars, a person may not similarly be made whole by post-deprivation remedies. As Justice Stevens has explained:

> When only an invasion of a property interest is involved, there is a greater likelihood that a damages award will make a person completely whole than when an invasion of the individual's interest in freedom from bodily restraint and punishment has occurred. In the property context, therefore, frequently a post-deprivation state remedy may be all the process that the Fourteenth Amendment requires.

Ingraham v. Wright, 430 U.S. 651, 701, 97 S.Ct. 1401, 51 L.Ed.2d 711 (1977) (dissenting).

In Dixon v. Love, 431 U.S. 105, 113, 97 S.Ct. 1723, 52 L.Ed.2d 172 (1977), the Court compared a state action depriving a person of his liberty (by suspending his license to drive a truck) with deprivation of a property interest (cash payments under social security disability insurance): "Unlike the social security recipients in Eldridge, who at least could obtain retroactive payments if their claims were subsequently sustained, a licensee is not made entirely whole if his suspension or revocation is later vacated."

6. Memphis Light, Gas and Water Div. v. Craft, 436 U.S. 1, 98 S.Ct. 1554, 56 L.Ed.2d 30 (1978).

7. Respecting social welfare programs, in both *Goldberg v. Kelly,* and Mathews v. Eldridge, 424 U.S. 319, 96 S.Ct. 893, 47 L.Ed.2d 18 (1976), the Court found that due process required some sort of process before termination of payments. The difference between the two cases, of course, was that in *Goldberg v. Kelly* the Court required trial-type pre-termination processes, while in the latter case, the Court backed away from formal, evidentiary-type processes, stating that "the ordinary principle established by our decisions [is] that something less than an evidentiary hearing is sufficient prior to adverse administrative determinations." Mathews v. Eldridge, 424 U.S. at 343. See also Dixon v. Love, 431 U.S. 105, 113, 97 S.Ct. 1723, 52 L.Ed.2d 172 (1977).

8. This assessment appears in the opinions of the six justices who found that a property interest was implicated in that

a summary pre-termination hearing but was entitled to a full post-termination hearing and back pay if reinstated. The government's substantial interest in a summary and expeditious means of removing an employee from its work force was described as follow:

> Prolonged retention of a disruptive or otherwise unsatisfactory employee can adversely affect discipline and morale in the work place, foster disharmony, and ultimately impair the efficiency of an office or agency. Moreover, a requirement of a prior evidentiary hearing would impose additional administrative costs, create delay, and deter warranted discharges.[9]

The countervailing interest, that of the employee, was assessed as "the continuation of his public employment pending an evidentiary hearing" and the avoidance of a "temporary disruption of income" prior to that hearing, and, possibly, in avoiding the "stigma" that might be associated with an erroneous initial determination. On balancing these interests, the important concurrence in *Arnett* found that the "procedures minimize the risk of error in the initial removal decision and provided for compensation for the affected employee should that decision eventually prove wrongful" and that due process did *not*, therefore, require "a prior evidentiary hearing."[10]

Subsequently, the holding in *Arnett*, that due process did not in that case require a prior evidentiary hearing, was followed by the lower courts in a strict and mechanistic way. This way was that in public employment due process did not require a hearing prior to termination where a post-termination hearing with reinstatement and back pay was available. This perception of *Arnett* was, however, corrected in *Cleveland Board of Education v. Loudermill*.[11] A school board had dismissed a school security guard when it found out that he was a convicted felon. And it did so immediately, with no prior hearing. The dismissed employee was, however, entitled to a full hearing and reinstatement with back pay if his summary dismissal was found to be erroneous. This post-

case. Arnett v. Kennedy, 416 U.S. 134, 94 S.Ct. 1633, 40 L.Ed.2d 15 (1974).

9. 416 U.S. at 168 (Powell, concurring). In *Cleveland Board of Education v. Loudermill,* 470 U.S. 532, 544–45, 105 S.Ct. 1487, 84 L.Ed.2d 494 (1985), Justice Brennan stated an additional and quite different governmental interest with respect to firing its employees:

> [A] governmental employer also has an interest in keeping citizens usefully employed rather than taking the possibly erroneous and counter-productive step of forcing its employees onto the welfare rolls. [In] those situations where the employer perceives a significant hazard in keeping the employee on the job, it can avoid the problem by suspending with pay.

10. 416 U.S. at 170–71, 94 S.Ct. at 1652. Later, in Cleveland Board of Education v. Loudermill, 470 U.S. 532, 105 S.Ct. 1487, 84 L.Ed.2d 494 (1985), the Court described the appropriate test as "balancing the private interest in retaining employment, the governmental interest in the expeditious removal of unsatisfactory employees and the avoidance of administrative burdens, and the risk of of an erroneous termination." 470 U.S. at 542–43. Regarding the possibility of stigma, which involved the employee's claim that by the initial decision to fire him he was "in effect accused of dishonesty," Justice Rehnquist, in his plurality opinion, found that the post-termination evidentiary hearing afforded the employee an adequate " 'opportunity to clear his name.' " 416 U.S. at 157.

11. 470 U.S. 532, 105 S.Ct. 1487, 84 L.Ed.2d 494 (1985).

deprivation hearing backed by reinstatement and back pay being the case, a lower federal court found that process consistent with due process.

A majority of the Supreme Court disagreed. It noted the "severity of depriving a person of the means of his livelihood," and that finding employment elsewhere "will take some time and is likely to be burdened by the questionable circumstances under which he left his previous job." Consequently, the majority held that the lower court had erred in reading *Arnett* as wholly eliminating the need for a prior hearing.[12]

§ 7.7.2 Emergency Action

To avoid imminent public injury, government may act against a person without a hearing prior to that action. Some of the clearest instances of this "emergency action exception" to the norm of a prior hearing involve substances, usually food or drugs, that an agency has provisionally determined to be detrimental to the public health.[13] The courts have approved seizures of such substances without a previous hearing even where an erroneous seizure might result in irreparable injury to the owner, such as the damage to the good will of a drug company generated by a seizure of drugs characterized as dangerous.

Outside the food and drug area, the Court upheld the federal strip mining act as it provided for a summary order against surface mining that posed an immediate danger to public health and safety. The Court relied on an "exception to the normal rule that due process requires a hearing prior to deprivation of a property right," this exception being that "summary administrative action may be justified in emergency situations."[14]

§ 7.7.3 Common Law Remedies

The Court seems to have established something of a new exception—relating to common law remedies against government officials—to the norm of a prior hearing.

A suggestion of this exception appeared in *Paul v. Davis*.[15] Here the Court, in finding that due process was not violated in relation to an

12. 470 U.S. at 543–45. Consistent with *Mathews v. Eldridge,* however, the majority in *Loudermill* did not require a full evidentiary hearing prior to termination. Instead, it held that the prior hearing should simply provide "oral or written notice of the charges against him, an explanation of the employer's evidence, and an opportunity to present his side of the story." 470 U.S. at 546.

13. E.g., Ewing v. Mytinger & Casselberry, Inc., 339 U.S. 594, 70 S.Ct. 870, 94 L.Ed. 1088 (1950) (misbranded drugs); North American Cold Storage Co. v. Chicago, 211 U.S. 306, 29 S.Ct. 101, 53 L.Ed. 195 (1908) (putrid chicken).

14. Hodel v. Virginia Surface Mining and Reclamation Ass'n, Inc., 452 U.S. 264, 300, 101 S.Ct. 2352, 69 L.Ed.2d 1 (1981). See also Federal Deposit Ins. Corp. v. Mallen, 486 U.S. 230, 108 S.Ct. 1780, 100 L.Ed.2d 265 (1988) (upholding the Federal Deposit Insurance Corporation's authority summarily to suspend bank officers indicted for a felony involving dishonesty or breach of trust.)

15. 424 U.S. 693, 96 S.Ct. 1155, 47 L.Ed.2d 405 (1976). A police flier distributed to merchants in Louisville, Kentucky

injury to reputation inflicted by state officials, noted that relief might instead be gained by common-law actions against those officials. The plaintiff's "interest in reputation," the Court said, was simply one of a "number [of private interests] which the State may protect against injury by virtue of its tort law, providing a forum for vindication of those interests by means of damages actions."[16]

Civil remedies might alleviate the need for a prior hearing in a couple of ways. Damages may make the plaintiff whole, thus redressing the "taking." Another way is by diminishing the chances of a wrongful taking in the first place, because damages assessed against state officials after the fact should tend to reduce error by inducing care before the fact. The incentive is to avoid tort liability by acting carefully in the first place.[17]

The suggestion of *Paul v. Davis,* about a common law remedy diminishing the need for a prior administrative hearing, became a basis of decision in *Ingraham v. Wright.*[18] In this case, the Court found that a school paddling was a "bodily restraint and punishment" that amounted to a taking of liberty. The Court, however, held that this taking did not require a hearing prior to the paddling. State law provided civil actions for a wrongful paddling, and the threat of damages inculcated a prudence that should diminish the risk of erroneous corporal punishment.[19] *Ingraham* was followed on this point in *Parratt v. Taylor,* where the claim was that due process was violated inasmuch as the state negligently and without a prior hearing took plaintiff's personal property.[20] In denying that claim, the Court noted the availability of a state tort action for damages and emphasized that the plaintiff could be made whole for his loss of property in that action. "The [tort] remedies provided could have fully compensated the respondent for the property loss he suffered,

had identified persons "arrested" or "active" in shoplifting. Plaintiff's name appeared on that flyer. But while he had been arrested for shoplifting, those charges had subsequently been dismissed. Consequently he filed an action seeking damages and declaratory and injunctive relief respecting injury to his reputation as might have been caused by the flyer.

16. See also Ingraham v. Wright, 430 U.S. 651, 701, 97 S.Ct. 1401, 51 L.Ed.2d 711 (1977) (Stevens, J., concurring) ("It may also be true—although I do not express an opinion on the point—that an adequate state remedy for defamation may satisfy the due process requirement when a state has impaired an individual's interest in his reputation. On that hypothesis, ... *Paul v. Davis* may have been correctly decided on an incorrect hypothesis.")

17. There is, of course, a balance here, involving the fact that an exposure to civil sanctions may cause government officials to become overly cautious and to refrain from action that benefits the public. On damages actions against public officials, see Chap. 14.

18. 430 U.S. 651, 674, 97 S.Ct. 1401, 51 L.Ed.2d 711 (1977).

19. 430 U.S. at 678 ("teachers and school authorities are unlikely to inflict corporal punishment unnecessarily or excessively when a possible consequence of doing so is the institution of civil or criminal proceedings against them.") Also, the Court was of the opinion that the fact that paddlings were administered on the spot, "in response to conduct directly observed by teachers" reduced the risk of erroneous paddlings. 430 U.S. at 677–78.

20. 451 U.S. 527, 101 S.Ct. 1908, 68 L.Ed.2d 420 (1981). Insofar as this case held that the negligent loss of property by a state official amounted to a "taking of an interest protected by due process," it has been overruled. Daniels v. Williams, 474 U.S. 327, 106 S.Ct. 662, 88 L.Ed.2d 662 (1986); Davidson v. Cannon, 474 U.S. 344, 106 S.Ct. 668, 88 L.Ed.2d 677 (1986).

and we hold that they are sufficient to satisfy the requirements of due process."[21]

Post-deprivation common law remedies do not, however, in all instances remove the need for a prior hearing. In *Memphis Light, Gas and Water Division v. Craft,* the Court found that due process required a hearing before a public utility terminated a customer's service because of non-payment of bills.[22] The Court rejected the utility's argument that "the available common-law remedies of a pre-termination injunction, a post-termination suit for damages, and post-termination action for a refund" were "sufficient to cure any perceived inadequacy" in the utility's procedures. As regards injunctive relief, the Court explained that this remedy was "likely to be bounded by procedural constraints and too susceptible to delay to provide an effective safeguard against an erroneous deprivation."[23]

§ 7.8 A CRITIQUE OF THE DUE PROCESS EXPLOSION

Tangible costs of the "due process explosion" include paperwork and the litigation costs—time and money—of a judicialized process. These costs are collectively borne. But as well, they may be assessed more pointedly, against the very beneficiaries of a public program. The reason is that "new layers of procedural protections may become an intolerable drain on the very funds earmarked for food, clothing, and other living essentials."[1] Not so tangible costs of the due process explosion include a diminished spontaneity and responsiveness, on the part, for instance, of a public school teacher in the classroom who foregoes on-the-spot disciplining of an errant student so as to avoid the red tape of modern due process.

These various costs are not unknown nor are various players in the field without power to ease them. The Supreme Court has said that "conserving scarce fiscal and administrative resources" should be taken

21. 451 U.S. at 544. Another factor in the Court's finding that due process did not require a prior hearing was the unfeasibility of such a hearing where the property was taken negligently. In this regard the Court noted that "the loss is not a result of some established state procedure and the State cannot predict precisely when the loss will occur. It is difficult to conceive of how the State could provided a meaningful hearing before the deprivation takes place." 451 U.S. at 541. In *Parratt,* the court also noted a federalism element common to state cases such as *Parratt* and *Paul v. Davis*. This element was that the fourteenth amendment was not meant to be a "font of tort law to be superimposed upon whatever systems may already by administered by the States." 451 U.S. at 544.

22. 436 U.S. 1, 98 S.Ct. 1554, 56 L.Ed.2d 30 (1978). The hearing required by the Court in this case was quite informal and limited, just a conversation between the utility and the customer.

23. Moreover, in the context of utility bills, the sums of money were typically "too small to justify engaging counsel" for such post-termination relief as might be available. 436 U.S. at 20–21.

§ 7.8

1. Wheeler v. Montgomery, 397 U.S. 280, 284, 90 S.Ct. 1026, 25 L.Ed.2d 307 (1970) (Berger, J., dissenting). Because the gross national product is not infinite, the amount of money left to be distributed to welfare recipients will go down as administrative expenses go up.

into account in determining the process due.[2] There are some problems, however, that a strict attention to "conserving scarce fiscal and administrative resources" cannot correct. Two problems of this sort are identified below.

§ 7.8.1 A Perverse Incentive of Entitlement Theory

There is, at least in the abstract, a certain perverse incentive in entitlement theory. This incentive has largely remained in the abstract because of the apparent good sense of public officials.

The justification for extending due process to "entitlements" to public benefits is to "protect those claims upon which people rely in their daily lives, reliance that must not be arbitrarily undermined."[3] Entitlement theory can, however, cut against this security and autonomy. Where agency power is wholly discretionary, where it is unconfined by standards, a person interested in a benefit distributed by that agency can have no expectations, no "entitlement" that amounts to a property interest.

In *Connecticut Board of Pardons v. Dumschat,* the Court held that a state statute that provided for commutation of prison sentences, but that had "no definition, no criteria, no mandated 'shalls' " to guide the agency with respect to such commutations, could not give rise to an entitlement subject to due process.[4] In public employment, the Court has similarly held that a property interest in such employment can be defeated by providing no job security whatsoever, by simply making employment wholly dependent on the "will and pleasure" of administrative officials.[5] The theory of these cases is that "If the decisionmaker is not required to base its decisions on objective and defined criteria, then the person disadvantaged by that decision has no claim to due process."[6]

Under entitlement theory, then, government may avoid the costs to it of a due process hearing simply by making agency action entirely

2. Mathews v. Eldridge, 424 U.S. 319, 349, 96 S.Ct. 893, 47 L.Ed.2d 18 (1976).

3. Board of Regents v. Roth, 408 U.S. 564, 577, 92 S.Ct. 2701, 33 L.Ed.2d 548 (1972).

4. 452 U.S. 458, 466, 101 S.Ct. 2460, 69 L.Ed.2d 158 (1981). In *Dumschat,* the Court distinguished its previous holding, in Greenholtz v. Inmates of Nebraska Penal & Correctional Complex, 442 U.S. 1, 99 S.Ct. 2100, 60 L.Ed.2d 668 (1979), that pardons were subject to due process. It distinguished *Greenholtz* on the grounds that in that case the power of the board had been defined and limited by standards, while the board was not so limited in *Dumschat.*

5. Bishop v. Wood, 426 U.S. 341, 345, 96 S.Ct. 2074, 2077, 48 L.Ed.2d 684 (1976).

6. Olim v. Wakinekona, 461 U.S. 238, 249, 103 S.Ct. 1741, 1747, 75 L.Ed.2d 813 (1983), on remand 716 F.2d 1279 (9th Cir. 1983). Another instance of how the *Roth* entitlements system can diminish standards is provided in Bishop v. Wood, 426 U.S. 341, 96 S.Ct. 2074, 48 L.Ed.2d 684 (1976). In that case a city ordinance had, on its face, rather clearly established a status of permanent employment sufficient to constitute a property interest. Id. at 345, 96 S.Ct. at 2077. Accordingly, a policeman fired without a hearing claimed that his due process rights had been violated. This claim was avoided, though, as the state courts were said to have interpreted this ordinance as creating a security no greater than a job held at the "will and pleasure of the city." Id. at 345, 96 S.Ct. at 2077. So the due process right to a hearing, and probably more importantly the assurances of permanent employment under the ordinance, were defeated.

discretionary. Assuring objective and defined criteria and eliminating purely discretionary power was a driving force behind entitlement theory. Therefore, inasmuch as entitlement theory provides an incentive for action according to the "will and pleasure" of administrative officials, the theory is intrinsically contradictory.[7] But while the incentive to avoid due process and its costs simply by making agency action wholly discretionary is real enough, legislatures and agencies do not seem to have responded to it. Instead, they appear to have ignored the incentive and to have with good faith and common sense stayed true to the goals—personal security and autonomy—of due process.

§ 7.8.2 Allocation of Institutional Resources

Under the modern system of due process, the judiciary has assumed a plenary role in supervising the law-applying processes of agencies. Courts, however, are not so well positioned or well constituted for this role, at least not to perform in the legislative-like manner they have adopted.

Courts are poorly positioned in that they operate *ex post.* They do not and cannot participate in the original and hopefully systemic creation of procedures. Instead, they operate only after this event, to upset arrangements already made.

Courts are not so well constituted inasmuch as due process as they have made it requires comprehensive and system-wide judgments for which they are ill-suited.[8] The Supreme Court has established a wide-ranging balancing test, consisting of the private interest, the governmental interest, and the costs to the system. Also, rather than applying this test according to the circumstances of the individual before him, a judge, the Court has said, should apply it in light of "the generality of cases."[9]

Attending the "generality of cases" is a utilitarian method characteristic of legislatures. The methods of courts are more atomic. With their attention necessarily drawn to bipolar disputes and limited to issues relevant to that dispute, judges tend to adjust procedures to meet the interests of particular parties and cases. Such a process is not given to the broad, system-wide determinations, to programmatic choices in complex systems such as social security or welfare.

7. As stated by Professor (now judge) Stephen Williams, "at the margin the entitlements approach set up incentives against the evolution of clear substantive criteria for government allocation (or termination) of benefits—an odd way of protecting people from government." Williams, Liberty and Property: The Problem of Government Benefits, 12 J. of Legal Studies 3, 14 (1983).

8. As the courts' programmatic choices are logically more suspect than the more comprehensive work of Congress, these court decisions are, perversely, more permanent. Because they are due process-based constitutional pronouncements, they are writ in stone, or at least supposed to be. This factor was the bottom line in Justice Black's dissent in *Goldberg v. Kelly,* as he stated that "I feel that new experiments in carrying out a welfare program should not be frozen into our constitutional structure. It should be left, as are other legislative determinations, to the Congress.... " 397 U.S. 254, 279, 90 S.Ct. 1011, 1026, 25 L.Ed.2d 287 (1970).

9. Mathews v. Eldridge, 424 U.S. 319, 344, 96 S.Ct. 893, 907, 47 L.Ed.2d 18 (1976).

In this context, the Supreme Court has encouraged the courts to give some deference to the programmatic choices of Congress and agencies. The exhortation, however, may not be sufficiently bright-line to have much effect at the working, trial-court level. Otherwise, the Supreme Court has simply denied that it has intruded into legislative matters. It has done so by saying that due process attends to merely procedural matters (an appropriate task) for the courts, while matters of substance in public programs are left to Congress and agencies. But as Judge Easterbrook (among others) has shown, this particular substantive-procedural dichotomy is more supposed than real, and the procedural responsibilities that the courts have assumed in fact intrude on legislative choices.[10]

The procedural aspects of a public program, such as welfare, are ineluctably connected to that program's substantive parts, such as the amount and the conditions of cash payments to the program beneficiaries. In part, this relation is caused by fiscal constraints. In a world of limited resources, the expenses associated with administering a program are important to a legislature as it determines how much cash can be delivered to the program's beneficiaries. But besides such fiscal considerations, procedures also implicate such things as whether fairness and civility are best served by reliance on, say, a managerial and case worker intensive mode of administration as opposed to adversarial systems. These considerations, all relating to the public acceptance of and satisfaction with a program such as welfare, are intrinsic features of a whole program, and these considerations and the trade-offs they require are part of the legislative calculus in establishing that program.

The courts, therefore, cannot realistically suppose that matters of process are divorced from substantive legislative work, and they "cannot logically be reticent about revising the substantive rules but unabashed about rewriting the procedures to be followed in administering those rules."[11]

* * *

Shortly after the entitlements theory of due process was established in *Roth,* the matter of whether its new arrangements responded to optimal allocations of institutional responsibilities—specifically, whether Congress might not be better suited than the courts to establish procedures for the civil service system—came before the Court. In *Arnett v. Kennedy,*[12] a plurality opinion, by exploiting a certain logical flaw in this entitlements system of *Roth,* attempted to shift a primary responsibility for these procedures back to Congress.

Mr. Arnett, an employee of the Office of Economic Opportunity, had been removed from his job, on the grounds that "in reckless disregard of the actual facts" he had publicly accused his supervisor of taking a bribe.

10. Easterbrook, Substance and Due Process, 1986 Supreme Court Rev. 85.

11. Id. at 113.

12. 416 U.S. 134, 94 S.Ct. 1633, 40 L.Ed.2d 15 (1974).

The procedures to which Arnett was entitled included a summary pre-termination hearing consisting of notice of the charges against him, a chance to review the evidence supporting these charges, and a chance to reply orally and in writing to these charges. These more summary procedures were followed by a full post-termination evidentiary hearing, with reinstatement and back pay should Arnett prevail at that hearing. Arnett objected to these procedures, on the grounds that the *pre*-termination hearing was not up to the process due him.[13]

All members of the Court agreed that because he could be removed only "for cause," Arnett had an expectancy that under *Roth* amounted to a property interest. But Justice Rehnquist, writing for a plurality, used *Roth*'s statutory-expectancy theory to stand Arnett's due process claim on its head. The Lloyd–La Follete Act created Arnett's property interest in his job, and that same Act also provided for the procedure that Arnett objected to. This being so, the procedures Arnett got were in fact his statutory expectancy. As explained by Rehnquist, "Here the property interest which appellee had in his employment was itself conditioned by the procedural limitations which had accompanied the grant of that interest." Because a *Rothian* property interest is based in positive law, Arnett simply could not claim more property than that law provided.

This logic was not divorced from policy. As Rehnquist further explained, "Congress was obviously intent on according a measure of statutory job security to government employees which they have not previously enjoyed, but was likewise intent on excluding more elaborate procedural requirements which it felt would make the operation of the new scheme unnecessarily burdensome in practice."[14] Rehnquist thought that the courts should defer to these procedural choices, because, manifestly, these procedures were part of substance. The substance being the overall level of job security that Congress thought appropriate for the civil service.

However sound Rehnquist's opinion might be in relation to comparative legislative and judicial competence, the Court has thoroughly repudiated it and the *Arnett* plurality behind it. In *Cleveland Board of Education v. Loudermill*,[15] a local board of education, on learning that a school security guard had a prior felony conviction, promptly, without a

13. Id. at 138–39 (emphasis added). Arnett's problem, though, was that the supervisor to whom these procedures were addressed and who made the initial decision to remove him from his job was the very person whom Arnett had accused of bribery. Consequently Arnett, when he was notified of the charges against him, refused to exhaust the administrative processes afforded him. Instead, claiming that due process required a "trial-type hearing before an impartial officer," and that such a hearing must be provided "before he could be removed from his employment," Arnett filed suit in federal court. 416 U.S. at 139. Also Roth claimed that he could not be fired because his statements about his supervisor were protected by the first amendment. This claim was denied.

14. Consequently, Rehnquist wrote that "The employee's statutorily defined right is not a guarantee against removal without cause in the abstract, but such a guarantee as enforced by procedures which Congress has designated for the determination of cause." 416 at 152.

15. 470 U.S. 532, 105 S.Ct. 1487, 84 L.Ed.2d 494 (1985).

prior hearing, fired him. Under state law, the employee could be removed from his job only for cause. But as state law established this entitlement, it also established that it could be vindicated only by means of a *post*-termination hearing. This being the case, the district court rejected the employee's claim that he was entitled to a *pre*-termination hearing. On the basis of *Arnett,* that court held that "because the very statute that created the property right in continued employment also specified the procedures for discharge, and because those procedures were followed, Loudermill was, by definition, afforded all the process that was due him."[16]

On review, the Supreme Court summarily denied the proposition that the substance and procedure dichotomy of *Roth* did not make sense. For the Court, Justice Brennan summarily asserted that "the categories of substance and procedure are distinct," and that " 'while the legislature may elect not to confer a property interest in [public] employment, it may not constitutionally authorize the deprivation of such an interest, once conferred, without appropriate procedural safeguards.' "

§ 7.8.3 Another Direction: Away From Balancing and Back to Principles

The opinion in *Cleveland Board of Education v. Loudermill* no doubt ended the *Arnett v. Kennedy* attempt to deflect programmatic responsibility for administrative procedures away from the courts and back towards Congress and the agencies. Consequently, so far as Supreme Court case law is concerned social programs involve a bifurcation of substance and process, with the legislature responsible for the substance of these programs and the courts holding a special plenary power respecting process.

Accepting that the Court will not give up what it sees as its primary power to supervise procedures, we still may ask whether it might not exercise this power in a manner more deferential to the programmatic choices of Congress and the agencies. One possibility is that of discarding the utilitarian measure of the process that is due a person and instead returning to the original plan of due process. This plan, as stated in cases such as *Dr. Bonham's Case* and *Murray's Lessee v. Hoboken Land & Improvement Co,* was that the courts should determine the procedures owed a person not by a balancing test but by a set of principles made according to "settled usages and modes of proceedings."

In *Mathews v. Eldridge,* as we said, the Court firmed up the modern plan, an expansive three-part balancing test to be applied, not from the standpoint of the individual, but from the standpoint of the "generality of cases." This utilitarian calculus seems a matter of legislative rather than judicial competence. Moreover, it is contrary to what has long been understood as the "touchstone" of due process, which is the protection of an *individual* (as opposed to collectivities) "against arbitrary action of

16. 470 U.S. at 541.

government."[17] Also, constitutional text guarantees a "person" (as opposed to a class) due process. So, rather than looking to the "generality of cases," perhaps a court should follow its natural inclination of looking to the party before it to see whether that individual has been fairly treated.

Once this proper context of due process, a concern for the individual as opposed to the public at large, is in view, then some new steps (one of them back in time) seem in order. The step back is to the one referred to above, that of discard the legislative-like balancing test of *Mathews v. Eldridge* and returning to the more principled method of cases such as *Dr. Bonham's Case* and *Murray's Lessee v. Hoboken Land & Improvement Co.*[18] In these cases, the courts, as we said, assessed procedures not by a balancing test but by a set of principles established according to "settled usages and modes of proceedings."

When they act out of understood principles—such as no man should be a judge in his own case as in *Dr. Bonham's Case*—courts avoid the structural engineering for which they are not so well suited. Courts may and should leave the programmatic choices to Congress for systems such as the civil service or Social Security. At the same time, though, the courts should not relinquish their task of protecting the individual caught up in these systems, and in this respect they can rescue an individual from the warps of a generally fair procedural scheme. For instance, in *Arnett v. Kennedy* the Court need not have been concerned, as it was, with the whole civil service system. Instead, it could have attended to Arnett's specific problem, which was that of a distortion in the system. This distortion was that the person who presided over Arnett's *pre*-termination hearing was probably biased because Arnett had accused of taking a bribe. Instead of generally addressing the civil service system the Court could have acted more specifically, by applying the principle (as established by "settled usages and modes of proceedings") that a judge cannot be a party in his own case.

This idea, that the process due a person comes out of principles as opposed to an ad hoc balancing of social and personal goals, is not necessarily a static idea. New principles or variations on principles may evolve. In *Mathews v. Eldridge,* the Court applied its utilitarian (balancing of interests in the context of the "generality of cases") approach to due process, and in doing so upheld a summary pre-termination procedure for Social Security disability benefits. But had the Court proceeded differently, had it assessed the disability program not from a utilitarian standpoint but from the standpoint of whether that program was consistent with a set of principles owed an individual, it might have reached a different result. Here's how: A relevant, albeit evolutionary, principle pertains to the "dignitary interest" that a number of people have

17. Wolff v. McDonnell, 418 U.S. 539, 558, 94 S.Ct. 2963, 41 L.Ed.2d 935 (1974).

18. 8 Co.Rep. 107, 77 Eng.Rep. 638 (1610); 59 U.S. (18 How.) 272, 15 L.Ed. 372 (1855).

identified as appropriate to due process.[19] The principle is that in the administrative state, a person should not be shifted around as a number: as an agency exercises a power over an individual that individual should be heard from, personally. In *Mathews v. Eldridge,* the plaintiff's complaint was that he had not been so heard. His disability benefits had been terminated on the basis of papers and reports, without a personal appearance by him. He had no chance to see and talk to those officials, faceless to him, who were stopping his disability benefits. Indeed, his anonymity before the state seems to have been the cause of his complaint.

Finally, arriving at the process due a person on the basis of an understood set of principles ought to provide for a greater certainty about, and stability in, agency action. Under the balancing test now used, "the results ... have been quite unpredictable," and "the lack of any principled standards in this area means that these procedural due process cases will recur time and again."[20] With an understood set of principles, the Congress and the agencies ought to be able, in a forehanded way, to conform public programs to due process.

19. See sec. 7.6.1, supra.

20. Mashaw, The Management Side of Due Process: Some Theoretical and Litigation Notes on the Assurance of Accuracy, Fairness, and Timeliness in the Adjudication of Social Welfare Claims, 59 Cornell L.Rev. 772 (1972).

Chapter 8

FORMAL AGENCY ADJUDICATION

Table of Sections

---

§ 8.1 OVERVIEW

The procedural requirements for formal agency adjudication are set forth in sections 554, 556 and 557 of the APA. These provisions provide for an initial decision to be rendered, in most cases,[1] by an impartial Administrative Law Judge (ALJ) based on a record compiled before her. The decision includes both findings of fact, supported by substantial

§ 8.1

1. The APA also provides that the Commission itself could, if it chose to, hear the case in the first instance. See 5 U.S.C.A. § 557(b).

evidence in the record, and conclusions of law.[2] It usually is appealable to the Commission or agency head which "has all the powers which it would have in making the initial decision except as it may limit the issues on notice or by rule."[3] The factfinding processes of formal agency adjudication do not differ significantly from traditional courtroom proceedings. Agency adjudicators, however, are in a different position. Unlike generalist judges, agency adjudicators are expected to be steeped in the complexities of their regulatory fields. They are expected to have acquired substantial experience with both the law in their area and the range of factual situations to which it applies.

Most agencies combine rulemaking, investigatory and adjudicatory functions at the top of the Commission or agency. The combination of these functions aids policymaking considerably, and enables an agency more effectively and efficiently to carry out its statutory mission; however, the combination of adjudicatory policymaking, and investigatory power within the same agency, and particularly within the same decisionmakers, can give rise to problems of bias and conflicts of interest. This combination of functions, coupled with specific agency statutory missions, can sometimes undercut the perception, and at times the reality, of the adjudicatory independence necessary to ensure fairness. The APA speaks directly to this possibility. The Act mandates a strict separation of an agency's investigative and adjudicatory staffs below the top of the Commission or agency.[4] It also prohibits ex parte contacts and undue influence on the decision making processes.[5] Other statutes seek to insulate ALJ's from direct control of agency heads and commissioners concerning salary and tenure decisions.[6]

The APA provisions for formal agency adjudication have long served as the framework for most adjudicatory disputes, particularly those arising in the context of economic regulation. The APA was passed in 1946, and it was initially applicable to the New Deal agencies established earlier. There has, however, been a major shift in both the volume and the nature of the adjudication to which these APA provisions now apply. Today, the primary focus of federal agency adjudication involves benefits litigation involving social security claims.[7] This shift reflects a change in

2. 5 U.S.C.A. § 557(c).

3. 5 U.S.C.A. § 557(b).

4. 5 U.S.C.A. § 554(d).

5. 5 U.S.C.A. § 557(d)(1)(A), (B), (C), (D) and (E).

6. See infra sec. 8.5.2.

7. As Jeffrey Lubbers of the United States Administrative Conference has pointed out, this shift is dramatically illustrated by comparing the numbers of ALJ's now engaged in economic regulatory adjudication with those involved in what are essentially benefits programs. Shortly after the APA was passed, there were 196 ALJ's—64% of whom (125) were assigned to economic regulatory agencies and 6.6% (or 13) to the Social Security Administration. By 1984, there were 1121 ALJ's. Three agencies employed 85% (951) of them and 24 of the 29 agencies employed 12 or fewer. Only 6.5% or 73 ALJ's were in the 12 economic regulatory agencies, while 67.8% or 760 ALJ's were in Social Security. This trend has continued. The bulk of the increase in ALJs occurred between 1947 and October 1982, by which time they numbered 1,183. Jeffery S. Lubbers, *APA-Adjudication: Is The Quest For Uniformity Faltering?*, 10 Admin. L.J. Am. U. 65 (1996).

From the end of the 1982 to 1998, the number of ALJs increased only 12%, to 1,426, see United States Office of Personnel management, Demographic Profile of the

the nature of formal adjudication at the federal level: "the administrative law judge in today's Federal Government has become less an organizer and initial decider of regulatory policy issues and more the (often final) dispenser of disability benefits or arbiter of civil money penalties—cases where fact finding, demeanor evidence, fairness and speed are hallmarks, and policy issues absent or submerged."[8]

The increased focus on individual fact patterns and the individual benefits at stake in such cases underscore the importance of ensuring uniformity and consistency in the agency decisions rendered, along with regard for the speed with which they are provided. The legal issues that arise are often technical, centering on fact-finding, substantial evidence, and the role of medical testimony.[9] Moreover, the trade-off between the cost of additional procedure and the use of these funds for substantive benefits is increasingly apparent.[10] Along with the change in the volume and nature of agency adjudication at the federal level, however, there have been changes in the administrative structures within which adjudication occurs. Congress has established a number of independent commissions whose sole responsibility is adjudication.[11] The Department of Labor, for example, enforces its mine safety and occupational health and safety programs before two independent adjudicatory agencies—the Occupational Safety and Health Review Commission[12] and the Federal Mine Safety and Health Review Commission.[13] Another purely adjudicatory agency, the National Transportation Safety Board, entertains claims involving the denial, revocation or suspension of pilot licenses,[14] and the Merit Systems Protection Board is an independent adjudicatory board that hears employee appeals.[15] In addition to the creation of independent commissions, a number of proposed reforms would increase ALJ independence. Perhaps the most prominent reform would create a nationwide corps of federal ALJ's not tied to any one agency. The basic theory underlying this proposal is that an ALJ corps would "maximize decision-

Federal Workforce, OMSOE–OWI–7, 95 tbl.3 (1999) (hereinafter OPM Demographic), available at United States Office of Personnel management (visited June 24, 2000) <http://www.opm.gov/index.htm>, with 1,257 men, 6.9% of whom were minorities, and 169 women, 1.7% of whom were minorities. Id. At 131, 167.

Of the ALJs employed by 31 Federal agencies in 1997, H.R. Rep. No. 104–879, at 65 (1997), the majority of the ALJs (1,150 of 1,387, or 82.9%) was at the Social Security Administration. United States Office of Personnel Management, Occupations of Federal White Collar and blue Collar Workers, OMSOE–OWI–56–25, 98 tbl. W–E (1998) (hereinafter OPM Occupations), available at United States Office of Personnel Management (visited June 24, 2000) <http://www.opm.gov/index.htm>.

8. Lubbers, supra note 7, at 385. See also Lubbers, A Unified Corps of ALJ's: A Proposal to Test the Idea at the Federal Level, 65 Judicature 266, 268–272 (1982) [hereinafter Lubbers, A Unified Corps].

9. They also, on occasion, involve some larger issues such as agency nonacquiescence to arguably inconsistent judicial determinations involving challenges to their procedures. See generally, Estreicher and Revesz, Nonacquiescence by Federal Administrative Agencies, 98 Yale L.J. 679, 692–718 (1989).

10. See generally, J. Mashaw, Bureaucratic Justice (Yale Univ. Press, 1983).

11. Lubbers, supra note 7 at 385.

12. 29 U.S.C.A. § 661 (1982).

13. 30 U.S.C.A. § 823 (1982).

14. National Transportation Safety Board, 49 U.S.C.A. §§ 1442, 1429 (1982).

15. 5 U.S.C.A. § 1201 (1982).

al independence of ALJ's by shifting their status from agency employees, subject to formal controls over personal behavior and to the agency's powers over reductions in force, to employees of the central panel, with no subservience whatever to any agency for which they hold hearings."[16]

A number of proposed reforms seek to increase the efficiency of the administrative adjudicatory process by providing, for example, for the retraining, transfer, and reassignment of judges as needed.[17] Perhaps the most prominent reform would create a nationwide corps of federal ILJs not tied to any one agency. The basic theory underlying this proposal is that an ALJ corps would ensure "adherence to constitutional and statutory standards of fairness in the ALJ process and to convey to the public that this is indeed the case. Since ALJs are currently employees of the agencies in which they serve, the appearance of impartiality has sometimes been questioned."[18]

There are many variations on the adjudicatory themes we shall now set forth. As we shall see, the formal adjudicatory provisions of the APA are not always triggered by the relevant agency enabling act. Adjudicatory provisions, thus, can and do differ from agency to agency. The Administrative Procedure Act, however, sets forth an important structural and procedural framework for agency adjudication. It is a basic touchstone that remains relevant today, even with the shift away from economic regulatory litigation to benefits litigation. We shall begin by first examining how the formal adjudicatory provisions of the APA come into play. Section three will then examine just what these procedures entail. The remaining sections of this chapter will then examine the administrative structure within which these procedures are applied.

§ 8.2 TRIGGERING THE FORMAL ADJUDICATORY PROVISIONS OF THE APA

Sections 554, 556 and 557 of the APA set forth the procedural requirements for formal adjudication. These provisions of the Act deal with the combination of functions that are common in most agencies by attempting to establish at least a modicum of judicial independence on the part of the ALJs who hear cases at the trial level of the agency proceedings. They thus deal with such issues as bias, ex parte contacts and who may or may not seek to exercise influence over these initial decisionmakers. In addition, they mandate procedures, that ensure a decision on the record, made by an impartial judge and supported by

16. Rosenblum, The Central Panel System: Enhancing Administrative Justice, 65 Judicature 235 (1981). See generally, Lubbers, supra note 8.

17. See, e.g., Reorganization of the Federal Administrative Judiciary Act, H.R. 1802, 104th Cong. (1995); H.R. Rep. No. 104–879, at 65–66 (1997); Administrative Law Judge Conference of the united States Act. H.R. 3961, 105th Cong. (1998). See Daniel J. Gifford, Federal Administrative Law Judges: The Relevance of Past Choices to Future Directions, 49 Admin. L.Rev. 1 (1997).

18. Reorganization of the Federal Administrative Judiciary Act, H.R. 1802, 104th Cong. (1995); H.R. Rep. No. 104–879, at 66 (1997). See also Victor Rosenblum, The Central Panel System: Enhancing Administrative Justice, 65 Judicature 235 (1981).

substantial evidence in the record. The APA entitles a party "to present his case or defense by oral or documentary evidence, to submit rebuttal evidence, and to conduct such cross-examination as may be required for a full and true disclosure of the details."[1]

These general provisions do not necessarily apply to all federal agency adjudications. Since the APA is a generic statute, its formal adjudicatory provisions must be triggered by the statutes that govern a particular agency's regulatory responsibilities. Section 554 of the APA states that sections 554, 556 and 557 of the Act apply "in every case of adjudication required by statute to be determined on the record after opportunity for an agency hearing."[2]

Determining whether an Act of Congress triggers the formal adjudicatory hearing procedures of the APA is not always easy.[3] Statutes seldom use the precise language "on the record after opportunity for a hearing." It has, therefore, been necessary for courts to determine when congressional statutes trigger the APA's adjudicatory provisions. Several judicial approaches have been taken.

§ 8.2.1 Judicial Approaches to Triggering Formal Adjudicatory Hearings Under the APA

The Supreme Court first dealt with the issue of when the APA's formal adjudicatory provisions were triggered in *Wong Yang Sung v. McGrath*,[4] a case involving a deportation hearing. The Court took what ultimately turned out to be a misguided constitutional approach to this question. Wong Yang Sung was a Chinese merchant marine who had overstayed his shore leave. He was arrested by Immigration and Naturalization Service (INS) officials. After a hearing before an Immigration Inspector, the inspector recommended that he be deported. The Acting Commissioner approved and the Board of Immigration Appeals affirmed. Wong Yang Sung then sought a writ of habeas corpus arguing that the administrative hearing he was given was not in conformity with all of the procedural protections required by sections 554, 556 and 557 of the APA. In particular, Wong Yang Sung did not have the kind of hearing examiner provided for by the APA. The government admitted noncompliance with the APA, but argued that the Immigration Act of 1917 did not trigger the formal adjudicatory procedures of the APA and that the procedures the agency provided fully satisfied the constitutional demands of the Due Process Clause.

§ 8.2

1. 5 U.S.C.A. § 556(d).

2. 5 U.S.C.A. § 554(a) (1986). Sections 556 and 557 also may apply if formal rulemaking proceedings are required. Section 553(c) provides for formal rulemaking procedures "[w]hen rules are required by statute to be made on the record after opportunity for an agency hearing."

3. Some commentators believe formal proceedings should be initiated only in sanction cases. See, Verkuil, The Emerging Concept of Administrative Procedure, 78 Colum. L. Rev. 258, 296 and n. 189, 321–22 (1978); Pedersen, The Decline of Separation of Functions in Regulatory Agencies, 64 Va. L. Rev. 991 (1978).

4. 339 U.S. 33, 70 S.Ct. 445, 94 L.Ed. 616 (1950), superseded by statute as stated in Ardestani v. I.N.S., 502 U.S. 129, 112 S.Ct. 515, 116 L.Ed.2d 496 (1991).

The majority of the Court, with Justice Jackson writing the opinion, disagreed. The Court reasoned that the Due Process Clause of the Fourteenth Amendment clearly required a hearing in a case of this sort. It then ruled, in effect, that the constitutional requirement of a hearing necessarily triggered the adjudicatory provisions of the APA. In so doing, the Court thus rejected the argument that "the limiting words render the Administrative Procedure Act inapplicable to hearings, the requirement for which has been read into a statute by the Court in order to save the statute from invalidity."[5] In the majority's view, the constitutional requirement of procedural due process of law derived from the same source as Congress' power to legislate and, where applicable, "permeates every valid enactment of that body."[6] The Court thus read the APA's language "in every case required by statute to be determined on the record" in § 554(a) to include the Constitution as well.[7] It, in effect, erroneously equated the procedural requirements of the Due Process Clause with those set forth in the APA.

Given this interpretation of section 554(a), INS could not possibly prevail. When comparing the procedures used by INS with those mandated by the APA, the Court noted that Wong Yang Sung had not received a proper APA hearing. In particular, the APA's requirement that the hearing examiner be separate from the prosecutorial and policy-making functions of the agency was violated in this case. The Court thus concluded that "[w]hen the Constitution requires a hearing, it requires a fair one, one before a tribunal which meets at least currently prevailing standards of impartiality."[8]

This expansive reading of section 554 did not last long when it came to dealing with immigration issues. Soon after this decision, Congress statutorily exempted the application of the APA in immigration contexts.[9] The implication of *Wong Yang Sung* that there was a constitutional basis for a formal APA adjudicatory hearing in immigration proceedings was rejected by the Supreme Court in *Marcello v. Bonds*[10]. *In Marcello,* an alien had been convicted of a felony. He was ordered deported pursuant to the terms of Immigration and Nationality Act of 1952.[11] The terms of the Act provided for an evidentiary hearing "specially adapted to meet the needs of the deportation process." The Act provided that this procedure was to be the "sole and exclusive procedure

5. Id. at 50, 70 S.Ct. at 454.

6. Id. at 49, 70 S.Ct. at 453.

7. Id. at 50, 70 S.Ct. at 454. ("We would hardly attribute to Congress a purpose to be less scrupulous about the fairness of a hearing necessitated by the Constitution than one granted by it as a matter of expediency.")

8. Id.

9. Because aliens were involved, Congress did not consider itself bound by the court's constitutional reasoning. Six months after *Wong Yang Sung* was decided, Congress specifically provided, in the Supplemental Appropriations Act of 1951, 64 Stat. 1048, that deportation proceedings under the Immigration Act of 1917 were not to be governed by the APA.

10. 349 U.S. 302, 75 S.Ct. 757, 99 L.Ed. 1107 (1955), rehearing denied 350 U.S. 856, 76 S.Ct. 38, 100 L.Ed. 761 (1955).

11. Section 241(a)(11) of the 1952 Act provides that a felony conviction at any time is grounds for an alien's deportation.

for determining the deportability of an alien under this section."[12] After a hearing administered under these provisions, Marcello was ordered deported. He challenged the procedure as violative of the APA on grounds similar to those invoked in *Wong Yang Sung*. Justice Clark, speaking for the majority, rejected Marcello's arguments, relying both on the legislative history of the 1952 Act and the Due Process Clause. Justice Clark found that the history of the Act clearly indicated a desire on the part of Congress to exempt such cases from the formal adjudicatory procedures of the APA. Moreover, he held that the relationship between the hearing officer and his supervisors did not "strip the hearing of fairness and impartiality as to make the procedure violative of due process."[13] In so doing, Justice Clark treated the procedural requirements of the due process clause as separate and distinct from the statutory procedural requirements of the APA.[14]

This approach is in accord with the relatively flexible approach the Supreme Court has taken to due process issues in cases such as *Mathews v. Eldridge*.[15] Simply because the Constitution may require a hearing does not mean that this hearing must be an APA adjudicatory hearing.

The same is not true, however, when a statute clearly requires a "hearing on the record." But since statutes often are not that clear, other judicial approaches have developed to determine when formal adjudicatory hearings ought, in fact, to be triggered. The most straight-

12. 349 U.S. at 309, 75 S.Ct. at 761.

13. Id. at 311, 75 S.Ct. at 762.

14. After *Wong Yang Sung* came down, most lower courts simply ignored its essential holding. Indeed, the decisionmaking costs of requiring formal adjudication whenever the due process clause applied would have been excessively high. See, Note, The Requirement of Formal Adjudication under Section 5 of the Administrative Procedure Act, 12 Harv. J. Legis. 194, 218–41 (1975). See, e.g., Clardy v. Levi, 545 F.2d 1241 (9th Cir.1976). See generally, Bonfield, The Definition of Formal Agency Adjudication under the Iowa Administrative Procedure Act, 63 Iowa L.Rev. 285, 357 (1977).

15. See chapter 7, supra. The Supreme Court, however, has held that *Mathews* is not appropriate in the military context. Weiss v. U.S., 510 U.S. 163, 164, 114 S.Ct. 752, 127 L.Ed.2d 1 (1994). Nor is *Mathews* appropriate in the criminal context when determining the constitutionality of state procedural rules. Medina v. California, 505 U.S. 437, 112 S.Ct. 2572, 120 L.Ed.2d 353 (1992). Also, the 7th Circuit has held that application of the *Mathews* balancing test "may be appropriate in the context of a judicial determination of a motion for summary judgment when there are no genuine issues of material fact. A court may not, however, apply a balancing test when deciding a motion to dismiss." Smith v. McDonald, 1998 WL 259536 (1998). "(The growth of the disability programs at issues in *Mathews* eventually prompted the SSA to announce a 'Disability Reengineering Project Plan' that it claimed would revamp the process and have 'the right decision ... made the first time.)' " See 59 Fed. Reg. 47887 (Sept. 19 (1994)). See also Walters v. National Ass'n of Radiation Survivors, 473 U.S. 305, 105 S.Ct. 3180, 87 L.Ed.2d 220 (1985), on remand 111 F.R.D. 595 (N.D.Cal. 1986). The 9th Circuit reviewed the district court's conclusions on remand regarding the due process and First Amendment claims *de novo*, and reversed the decision. It applied the *Mathews* test in finding that the government had a significant interest in the fee limit, that non-need based benefits do not create as strong an interest as need-based benefits (but that applicants do not have weaker interests than recipients), and that, *inter alia*, the district court's "abstract discussion of the complexities involved in IR claims" did not "provide a sufficient basis for determining that the probability of error under the present system for adjudicating IR claims is truly 'extraordinarily strong.' " 994 F.2d 583, 591 (9th Cir.1992), cert. denied, 510 U.S. 1023, 114 S.Ct. 634, 126 L.Ed.2d 592 (1993).

forward is what might be called a "magic words" approach. If the statute in question does not state precisely that a "hearing on the record" is required, the APA is not triggered.[16] All doubts are thus resolved in favor of a non-APA hearing.

Even if courts reject a simple "magic words" approach, they often find ways of avoiding "the imposition of costly, formal proceedings they deem unnecessary.[17]" Increasingly, courts' reluctance to interpret ambiguous legislative histories has resulted in greater procedural discretion for the agencies involved, in lieu of greater congressional clarity. This is in contrast to the more expansive, functional approaches courts have taken to such issues in the past. In *Seacoast Anti–Pollution League v. Costle*,[18] for example, the First Circuit took a functional approach to determine the appropriate adjudicatory procedures for an environmental licensing case. The dispute in that case arose when the Public Service Company of New Hampshire (PSCO) sought a license to discharge heated water into the Hampton–Seabrook Estuary. The controlling statute, the Federal Water Pollution Control Act of 1972[19], generally prohibited the discharge of any pollutant, including heated water, but permitted exceptions where it could be shown that the EPA standards were "more stringent than necessary" to protect indigenous fish and wildlife.[20] The Act provided that this exception should be allowed "after opportunity for public hearing."[21] In *Seacoast,* application for an exception was heard by an ALJ at a public hearing, whose procedures were less formal than an APA adjudicatory proceeding under sections 554, 556 and 557. The permit was eventually granted and challenged by a group of environmentalists. They claimed that the public hearing process was inconsistent with the requirements of formal adjudication under the APA and they argued that the Water Pollution Control Act, in effect, triggered these procedures.

From the outset, Judge Coffin rejected the notion that only the precise words "on the record" could trigger APA procedures.[22] Instead,

16. This was, essentially, the approach the Court used when dealing with formal rulemaking under the APA, in United States v. Florida East Coast Ry. Co., 410 U.S. 224, 93 S.Ct. 810, 35 L.Ed.2d 223 (1973), on remand 368 F.Supp. 1009 (M.D.Fla.1973), affirmed 417 U.S. 901, 94 S.Ct. 2595, 41 L.Ed.2d 207 (1974). See sec. 8.2.2, infra.

17. See, e.g., City of West Chicago, Ill. v. United States Nuclear Regulatory Com'n, 701 F.2d 632, 646 (7th Cir.1983) ("Taking into account the technical, scientific nature of the issues, the absence of credibility questions, and the apparent lack of controverted issues of material fact, the additional value of an oral hearing in this case is minimal.")

18. 572 F.2d 872 (1st Cir.1978), cert. denied sub nom. Public Serv. Co. v. Seacoast Anti Pollution League, 439 U.S. 824, 99 S.Ct. 94, 58 L.Ed.2d 117 (1978).

19. 33 U.S.C.A. § 1251 et seq. (1982).

20. Id. at § 1326(a).

21. Id.

22. Prior to *Seacoast* two other circuits rejected the "magic words" approach. See Marathon Oil Co. v. E.P.A., 564 F.2d 1253 (9th Cir.1977) (Nature of proceeding is determinative factor as to whether APA is applicable); United States Steel Corp. v. Train, 556 F.2d 822 (7th Cir.1977) (Absence of words "on the record" is not conclusive bar to APA hearing). In Union of Concerned Scientists v. U.S. NRC, 735 F.2d 1437, 1444 n. 12 (D.C.Cir.1984), cert. denied 469 U.S. 1132, 105 S.Ct. 815, 83 L.Ed.2d 808 (1985), the D.C. Circuit stated that "when a statute calls for a hearing for

the APA's applicability turned on "the substantive nature of the hearing Congress intended to provide."[23] With respect to the instant case, the Court reasoned that the granting of a discharge exception to a specific applicant was not a policy decision, but was clearly an adjudicatory decision in which only the rights of a specific applicant would be affected. This kind of proceeding clearly required adjudicatory procedures.[24] The statutory protections of the APA were, therefore, necessary to protect the public from an arbitrary lessening of strict environmental standards. The Court thus equated the statutory language of "public hearing with" hearing on the record.[25]

The fact that an adjudicative decision is called for, however, does not and should not automatically mean that formal APA adjudication procedures are required. Despite the initial acceptance of the *Seacoast* approach,[26] later cases have not so easily invoked formal evidentiary hearings simply because the issues involved were adjudicatory in nature. In *Chemical Waste Management, Inc. v. U.S. E.P.A.*,[27] the D.C. Circuit explicitly rejected the presumption that when a statute calls for a hearing in an adjudicative context, the hearing is governed by "on the record" procedures.[28] In that case, the Court was asked to construe the Hazardous and Solid Waste Amendments of 1984. That Act authorized corrective orders for violations of its provisions after a "public hearing." The Court noted, however, that the Act "does not, by its terms, indicate whether Congress intended that formal or informal hearing procedures be used."[29] The Court invoked the doctrine in *Chevron U.S.A., Inc. v. NRDC*.[30] It concluded that this lack of specificity on the part of Congress authorized the agency to choose its own adjudicatory procedures. As long as these procedures were reasonable, they need not be the same as the formal adjudicatory proceedings specified by the APA. The fact that the EPA had, at one time, interpreted its statute so as to require formal APA proceedings did not mean it could not change that interpretation, "pro-

an adjudication the hearing is presumptively governed by 'on the record procedures,' notwithstanding omission of the phrase 'on the record' in the statute." But see, Chemical Waste Management, Inc. v. U.S. E.P.A., 873 F.2d 1477 (D.C.Cir.1989) (rejecting this presumption).

23. 572 F.2d at 876.

24. Id. (citing Marathon Oil Co. v. EPA, 564 F.2d 1253, 1262 (9th Cir.1977) ("In summary, the proceedings below were conducted in order 'to adjudicate disputed facts in particular cases,' not 'for the purposes of promulgating policy-type rules or standards' ")).

25. An exceptions proceeding can also be seen as a form of informal adjudication or administrative equity necessitating more flexible agency procedures. See chapter 9, sec. 9.4, infra.

26. See, e.g., United States Lines, Inc. v. Federal Maritime Com'n, 584 F.2d 519, 536 (D.C.Cir.1978) (Exact phrase "on the record" is not an absolute prerequisite for application of the formal APA hearing requirements); Steadman v. SEC, 450 U.S. 91, 96–97 n. 13, 101 S.Ct. 999, 1005–06, n. 13, 67 L.Ed.2d 69 (1981), rehearing denied 451 U.S. 933, 101 S.Ct. 2008, 68 L.Ed.2d 318 (1981) (absence of "on the record" language does not preclude application of '554).

27. 873 F.2d 1477 (D.C.Cir.1989).

28. Id. at 1481. This presumption was first stated in the D.C. Circuit in Union of Concerned Scientists v. U.S. N.R.C., supra note 37.

29. Id. at 1480.

30. 467 U.S. 837, 104 S.Ct. 2778, 81 L.Ed.2d 694 (1984), rehearing denied 468 U.S. 1227, 105 S.Ct. 28, 82 L.Ed.2d 921 (1984). This case is discussed in full in chapter 13, sec. 13.7.2, infra.

vided that its new interpretation is otherwise legally permissible and is adequately explained."[31]

The D.C. Circuit Court of Appeals reached a similar result in *Railroad Commission of Texas v. United States*.[32] The Staggers Rail Act of 1980,[33] requires Interstate Commerce Commission certification before state authorities can regulate intrastate rail traffic. For certification, the Act simply provides that the "Commission may take action under this section only after a full hearing."[34] The Court held that this provision did not trigger APA formal proceedings, stating that a "fundamental and well-recognized distinction exists between a requirement that an agency provide a 'hearing' and a requirement that an agency provide a 'hearing on the record.' "[35] Formal APA hearing proceedings attach only when a "hearing on the record" is required. The fact that the statute in the instant case required a "full hearing" did not alter the Court's conclusion. Not only did the Court insist on the statutory words "on the record" to trigger APA proceedings, it also reduced the "nature of the hearing" analysis adopted in *Seacoast* to simply one of many factors involving the exercise of agency discretion. "The [agency] has substantial flexibility," the Court emphasized, "to structure the hearings it must provide."[36]

Reliance solely on the magic words "on the record" can be too wooden an approach for determining when formal APA procedures are appropriate in an adjudicatory context. Congress' use of a phrase other than "hearing on the record" does not always indicate rejection of the procedural protections of the APA. On the other hand, simply because an adjudicatory issue is present does not mean that the full range of APA procedures is required. A more complex contextual approach is appropriate for resolving such issues. Taking the nature of the agency action into account, along with the significance of the decision involved, the need for agency expedition and, in particular, any clear indications from the legislative history as to what Congress may have intended, is the most appropriate approach to such issues. Just as courts have increasingly interpreted the hearing requirement of the due process clause more flexibly, so too are they increasingly likely to treat the APA's formal adjudicatory provisions with flexibility, giving increasing deference to the efficiency concerns of the agency involved and its choice of adjudicatory procedures.

31. 873 F.2d at 1481.

32. 765 F.2d 221 (D.C.Cir.1985).

33. 49 U.S.C.A. § 10101 et seq. (1982).

34. Id. at § 11501(f).

35. 765 F.2d at 227.

36. Id. at 228 (citing Sea–Land Service, Inc. v. United States, 683 F.2d 491, 495 (D.C.Cir.1982) citing United States Lines, Inc. v. FMC, 584 F.2d 519, 537 (D.C.Cir. 1978)). According to *Sea–Land Service, Inc.*, the Interstate Commerce Commission was required to conduct an evidentiary hearing if "disputed issues of material fact" existed. 683 F.2d at 496 (citations omitted). The court here concluded that the denial was justified on non-factual grounds, precluding the possibility that the Railroad Commission of Texas could obtain formalized adjudicatory proceedings on another theory. 765 F.2d at 228–29. See also, Buttrey v. United States, 690 F.2d 1170 (5th Cir.1982), cert. denied 461 U.S. 927, 103 S.Ct. 2087, 77 L.Ed.2d 298 (1983).

§ 8.2.2 Triggering Formal Rulemaking Proceedings

Section 553(c), like section 554(a), provides that "when rules are required by statute to be made on the record after opportunity for an agency hearing, sections 556 and 557 ... apply.... "[37] Formal rulemaking proceedings usually are triggered only by the presence of the words "on the record." This is as it should be. Given the fact that rules involve policy determinations, adjudicatory provisions usually are neither appropriate nor particularly helpful in such proceedings.

The leading case on this issue is *United States v. Florida East Coast Railway*.[38] The issue before the Court was whether the Interstate Commerce Commission (ICC) had to conform to sections 553, 556 and 557 of the APA when setting rail rates pursuant to section 1(14)(a) of the Interstate Commerce Act.[39] A 1966 Amendment to section 1(14)(a) enlarged the ICC's authority to prescribe per diem charges for the use by one railroad of freight cars owned by another.[40] After subsequent investigation and numerous hearings, the ICC initiated the rulemaking procedures that ultimately gave rise to the challenged order. It directed certain line-haul railroads to compile and report detailed information concerning the supply and demand of freight cars. In response, twenty railroads voiced questions about this procedure, and the ICC held an informal conference to allay these fears. The ICC adopted an interim report in 1969. That report announced its tentative decision to adopt incentive per diem charges on standard boxcars based upon information it had compiled. The railroads were given 60 days' notice to file written statements on this report and to request an oral hearing. When these procedures were challenged, the District Court ultimately found them inadequate. In that court's view, section 1(14)(a) of the Interstate Commerce Act triggered the formal rulemaking procedures of the APA.

Relying almost exclusively on the Supreme Court's opinion in *United States v. Allegheny–Ludlum Steel Corp.*,[41] Justice Rehnquist reversed the District Court's decision. He ruled that the *Allegheny–Ludlum* Court's holding that the "after hearing" language of section 1(14)(a) "was not the equivalent of a requirement that a rule be made 'on the record after opportunity for an agency hearing' as the latter term is used in '553(c) of the Administrative Procedure Act.' "[42] Furthermore, section 1(14)(a) was not contravened by the adoption of the 1966 Amendment[43]

37. 5 U.S.C.A. § 553(c).

38. 410 U.S. 224, 93 S.Ct. 810, 35 L.Ed.2d 223 (1973), on remand 368 F.Supp. 1009 (M.D.Fla.1973), affirmed 417 U.S. 901, 94 S.Ct. 2595, 41 L.Ed.2d 207 (1974).

39. The pertinent language of section 1(14)(a) provides: "The Commission may, *after hearing,* on a complaint or upon its own initiative without complaint, establish reasonable rules, regulations and practices with respect to car service by common carriers.... " 49 U.S.C.A. § 1(14)(a) (1970) (emphasis added).

40. The amendment was a direct result of chronic freight-car shortages on the nation's railways. For a fuller sense of the factual background, see United States v. Allegheny–Ludlum Steel Corp., 406 U.S. 742, 92 S.Ct. 1941, 32 L.Ed.2d 453 (1972).

41. 406 U.S. 742, 92 S.Ct. 1941, 32 L.Ed.2d 453 (1972).

42. 410 U.S. at 234, 93 S.Ct. at 815.

43. Justice Rehnquist pointed out that the amended section "does not by its terms add to the hearing requirement contained

Noting that an agency can function despite the presence of formalized rulemaking procedures, Justice Rehnquist declined to explicitly adopt a "magic words" approach. "[T]he actual words 'on the record' and 'after . . . hearing' used in § 553 [are] not words of art, and . . . other statutory language having the same meaning could trigger the provisions of '§ 556 and 557 in rulemaking proceedings.' "[44]

The Court was, however, unwilling to mandate trial-type proceedings.[45] Implicitly the Court understood that, while it may be hard to trigger adjudicatory proceedings in an adjudication,[46] it ought to be even more difficult to trigger such proceedings in a rulemaking context. As the Court indicated, policy decisions generally are best made in accordance with the less formal, legislative provisions of section 553.[47]

§ 8.2.3 Avoiding APA Adjudicatory Hearings—Administrative Summary Judgment

Agencies need not always grant a full blown adjudicatory hearing even when the statute clearly seems to require it. An agency may, for example, conclude that an issue raised in an adjudicatory proceeding has such broad significance for other cases that it is best decided in the context of a rulemaking rather than an adjudicatory proceeding.[48] A litigant may also have failed to request an adjudicatory hearing in a timely fashion.[49] More important, there often are cases in which an adjudicatory hearing is unnecessary because there are no material facts in dispute.[50] Administrative summary judgment is, thus, in order. The Supreme Court has long recognized that an agency need not order a

in the earlier language." 410 U.S. at 235, 93 S.Ct. at 816.

44. 410 U.S. at 238, 93 S.Ct. at 817.

45. Noting that "a recognized distinction [exists] in administrative law between proceedings for the purpose of promulgating policy-type rules or standards, on the one hand, and proceedings designed to adjudicate disputed facts in particular cases on the other," Justice Rehnquist found that the ICC procedures conformed to the requirements of section 1(14)(a). Id. at 245–46, 93 S.Ct. at 821.

46. Trial-like procedures are not always required in adjudication, however. Laird v. ICC, 691 F.2d 147, 154 (3d Cir. 1982), cert. denied 461 U.S. 927, 103 S.Ct. 2086, 77 L.Ed.2d 297 (1983); see Cerro Wire & Cable Co. v. Federal Energy Regulatory Com'n, 677 F.2d 124, 128–29 (D.C.Cir. 1982).

47. See generally, Hamilton, Procedures for the Adoption of Rules of General Applicability: The Need for Procedural Innovation in Administrative Rulemaking, 60 Cal.L.Rev. 1276 (1972); ACUS, Procedures for the Adoption of Rules of General Applicability (Recommendation No. 72–5), 1 C.F.R. § 305.72–5; but see, Dixon, Rulemaking and the Myth of Cross-Examination, 34 Admin.L.Rev. 389 (1982).

48. See, e.g., American Airlines, Inc. v. Civil Aeronautics Bd., 359 F.2d 624 (D.C.Cir.1966) (en banc), cert. denied 385 U.S. 843, 87 S.Ct. 73, 17 L.Ed.2d 75 (1966). See also Vermont Yankee Nuclear Power Corp. v. NRDC, 435 U.S. 519, 98 S.Ct. 1197, 55 L.Ed.2d 460 (1978), on remand 685 F.2d 459 (D.C.Cir.1982).

49. See, e.g., Shoreline Associates v. Marsh, 555 F.Supp. 169, 177 (D.Md.1983), affirmed 725 F.2d 677 (4th Cir.1984); Gables by the Sea, Inc. v. Lee, 365 F.Supp. 826, 829 (S.D.Fla.1973), affirmed 498 F.2d 1340 (5th Cir.1974), cert. denied 419 U.S. 1105, 95 S.Ct. 775, 42 L.Ed.2d 801 (1975).

50. For a discussion of the use of agency summary judgment proceedings when no factual dispute exists, see Ames & McCracken, Framing Regulatory Standards to Avoid Formal Adjudication: The FDA as a Case Study, 64 Calif.L.Rev. 14 (1976).

hearing if it would be useless:[51] "We cannot impute to Congress the design of requiring, nor does due process demand, a hearing when it appears conclusively from the applicant's 'pleadings' that the application cannot succeed."[52]

Courts generally defer to an agency's determination that a controversy raises no disputed issues of material fact;[53] however, there sometimes is confusion concerning the type of information that a protestant must initially proffer in order to establish that there truly is a disputed issue of fact in contention.

Two cases involving the Federal Reserve Board exemplify slightly different judicial approaches to these issues. In *Independent Ins. Agents of America, Inc. v. Board of Governors*,[54] the Eighth Circuit remanded for an evidentiary hearing, originally denied by the Board of Governors, to allow the protestants (IIAA) to substantiate their claim that the possible adverse effects of granting Mercantile Bancorporation's (Mercantile) application to sell credit-related property and casualty insurance through a nonbank acquisition outweighed the proposed benefits of this transaction. Despite the Board's review of written submissions and responses, the Court rejected Mercantile's contention that IIAA's objections were merely speculation, stating that "[t]he Board cannot deny a request for an evidentiary hearing when, as here, it is presented with legitimate contentions which place materials [sic] facts in dispute."[55]

The District of Columbia Circuit, in comparison, took a more restrictive view of the right to an evidentiary hearing. In *Connecticut Bankers Ass'n v. Board of Governors*[56] it required evidence—"as contrasted with

51. Weinberger v. Hynson, Westcott & Dunning, Inc., 412 U.S. 609, 93 S.Ct. 2469, 37 L.Ed.2d 207 (1973). See also State of Cal., Dept. of Education v. Bennett, 843 F.2d 333, 340 (9th Cir.1988); Vermont Dept. of Public Service v. F.E.R.C., 817 F.2d 127, 140 (D.C.Cir.1987); Ohio Power Co. v. F.E.R.C., 744 F.2d 162, 170 (D.C.Cir.1984) (citing Public Serv. Co. of N.H. v. F.E.R.C., 600 F.2d 944, 955 (D.C.Cir.1979), cert. denied 444 U.S. 990, 100 S.Ct. 520, 62 L.Ed.2d 419 (1979) and Citizens for Allegan County, Inc. v. F.P.C., 414 F.2d 1125, 1128 (D.C.Cir.1969)); City of Ukiah v. F.E.R.C., 729 F.2d 793, 799–800 (D.C.Cir.1984); Cerro Wire & Cable Co. v. F.E.R.C., 677 F.2d 124, 128–29 (D.C.Cir.1982); Cities of Batavia v. F.E.R.C., 672 F.2d 64, 91 (D.C.Cir. 1982); RKO General, Inc. v. F.C.C., 670 F.2d 215, 226 (D.C.Cir.1981), cert. denied 456 U.S. 927, 102 S.Ct. 1974, 72 L.Ed.2d 442 (1982); Independent Ins. Agents of America, Inc. v. Board of Governors, 646 F.2d 868, 869 (4th Cir.1981); Robinson v. Cheney, 876 F.2d 152 (D.C.Cir.1989).

52. *Weinberger,* 412 U.S. at 621, 93 S.Ct. at 2479. See also Veg–Mix, Inc. v. U.S. Dept. of Agriculture), 832 F.2d 601, 607 (D.C.Cir.1987) (citing Citizens for Allegan County, Inc. v. F.P.C., 414 F.2d 1125, 1128 (D.C.Cir.1969) ("the right of opportunity for hearing does not require a procedure that will be empty sound and show, signifying nothing"); Louisiana Land and Exploration Co. v. F.E.R.C., 788 F.2d 1132, 1137 (5th Cir.1986) (agency not required to hold hearing when proffered evidence is of no relevance); Huston v. Board of Governors, 758 F.2d 275, 284 (8th Cir.1985); Connecticut Bankers Ass'n v. Board of Governors, 627 F.2d 245, 250–51 (D.C.Cir.1980); Independent Bankers Ass'n of Ga. v. Board of Governors, 516 F.2d 1206, 1220 (D.C.Cir. 1975); American Bancorporation, Inc. v. Board of Governors, 509 F.2d 29, 39 (8th Cir.1974).

53. *Vermont Dept. of Public Service,* 817 F.2d at 140; see *Ohio Power Co.,* 744 F.2d at 170.

54. 658 F.2d 571 (8th Cir.1981), rehearing denied 664 F.2d 177 (8th Cir.1981).

55. Id.

56. 627 F.2d 245 (D.C.Cir.1980).

mere possibility or speculation''[57]—to dispute facts asserted or denied by the applicant, and substantially upheld the Board's denial of Connecticut Bankers Association's (CBA) request for a hearing. "[A] protestant does not become entitled to an evidentiary hearing merely on request, or on a bald or conclusory allegation that such a dispute exists. The protestant must make a minimal showing that material facts are in dispute, thereby demonstrating that an 'inquiry in depth' is appropriate.''[58] Before the Board had denied the request, it had required Citicorp, whose application to sell credit-related insurance and second-mortgage loans CBA opposed, to provide detailed answers to CBA's questions, and it allowed CBA to make an informal oral presentation to the Board's staff. In addition, the Board reviewed written arguments supporting the request for a hearing. The denial was issued after the Board satisfied itself that "there [were] no facts in dispute that bear upon the determination the Board must make.''[59]

The D.C. Circuit's approach for determining when a protestant has a right to an oral hearing is applicable in other regulatory contexts as well. The Department of Agriculture, the Federal Maritime Commission and the Federal Energy Regulatory Commission all subscribe to the view that mere allegations are insufficient to place material issues of fact in contention.[60] Both the Fourth and Tenth Circuits also appear to subscribe to the D.C. Circuit's view of a protestant's right to a hearing.[61] Agencies should exercise a significant amount of discretion over the kind of adjudicatory hearings they will require to resolve disputes. Not every case requires the full panoply of APA procedures. Not every litigant seeks to invoke additional procedural protections solely to further the public interest. Procedure should not be allowed to be used as a means of delay, but should function as a means of ensuring a fair and accurate decision. Summary judgment is an important procedural tool that enables agencies to avoid unnecessary hearings without compromising the fairness or accuracy of the decision making process.

§ 8.3 COMPARATIVE HEARINGS

As we have seen above, there are some contexts in which formal adjudicatory hearings are not necessary. Conversely, there also are some situations where to grant one entity a hearing is, in effect, to deny

57. Id. at 252.

58. Id. at 251 (citing Independent Bankers Ass'n of Ga. v. Board of Governors of the Federal Reserve System, 516 F.2d at 1220 n. 57).

59. Id. at 248.

60. See Veg–Mix, Inc. v. U.S. Dept. of Agriculture, 832 F.2d 601, 608 (D.C.Cir. 1987); Sea–Land Service, Inc. v. United States, 683 F.2d 491, 501 (D.C.Cir.1982); Cerro Wire & Cable Co. v. F.E.R.C., 677 F.2d 124, 129 (D.C.Cir.1982). In *Veg–Mix,* the D.C. Circuit compared the type of information a protestant must proffer to establish a disputed issue of fact with the burden placed on a party seeking summary judgment in a civil court action. 832 F.2d at 608.

61. See Independent Insurance Agents of America, Inc. v. Board of Governors, 646 F.2d 868, 869–70 (4th Cir.1981); Oklahoma Bankers Ass'n v. F.R.B., 766 F.2d 1446, 1451–52 (10th Cir.1985). Even the Eighth Circuit may be opting for more restrictive standards in light of a decision which relied heavily on the *Connecticut Bankers* opinion. See Huston v. Board of Governors, 758 F.2d 275, 284 (8th Cir.1985).

another of its right to a hearing. When an agency must choose between two or more applicants competing for a license, for example, or when granting one application will of necessity deny others, the agency may be compelled, under the *Ashbacker* doctrine, to hold a comparative hearing.

The Supreme Court created this doctrine in *Ashbacker Radio Corp. v. FCC*,[1] a case which arose under the Federal Communications Act.[2] Fetzer Broadcasting Co. and Ashbacker Radio Co. applied separately for licenses to operate a radio station on the same frequency in nearby communities. The Commission declared that the two applications were "mutually exclusive" because simultaneous operation on the same wavelength would cause electrical interference to both stations. After examining the Fetzer application, the Commission granted it without a hearing, and scheduled Ashbacker's application for a later hearing. Ashbacker appealed.

Section 309(a) of the Federal Communications Act provides that where the FCC is faced with mutually exclusive applications, it may grant one of them if the "public interest, convenience, or necessity would be served."[3] The Act also states that if the Commission does not grant an application, it must fix a hearing date and afford the applicant an opportunity to be heard. In *Ashbacker,* the Court concluded that because the grant of one application effectively denies another, any subsequent hearing would be a mere formality. By granting one application, the agency effectively deprives the other applicant of its statutory right to a hearing. In order to preserve all of the applicants' procedural rights, the *Ashbacker* court required the Commission to consolidate all mutually exclusive applications into one comparative hearing, providing all applicants an equal opportunity to compete for the license in the same proceeding.[4]

The FCC has promulgated rules to deal with comparative hearings.[5] Agencies may be excepted from applying the *Ashbacker* doctrine in

§ 8.3

1. 326 U.S. 327, 66 S.Ct. 148, 90 L.Ed. 108 (1945).

2. 47 U.S.C.A. § 151 et seq. (1982).

3. 326 U.S. at 330 n. 4, 66 S.Ct. at 150 n. 4.

4. Several courts have explained, however, that *Ashbacker* did not confer upon the applicants a constitutional right to a hearing. The doctrine merely provides that a commission must use the same set of procedures to process the applications of all similarly-situated persons who come before it seeking the same license. Maxcell Telecom Plus, Inc. v. FCC, 815 F.2d 1551 (D.C.Cir.1987) (Bork, J.). See also Multi–State Communications, Inc. v. FCC, 728 F.2d 1519 (D.C.Cir.1984), cert. denied 469 U.S. 1017, 105 S.Ct. 431, 83 L.Ed.2d 358 (1984) (Tamm, J.) (congressionally-mandated objective of bringing an operational VHF commercial television station to unserved states overrode statutory requirement to grant consolidated hearing to mutually exclusive applications).

5. When parties apply for mutually exclusive broadcast licenses, the FCC will conduct a comparative hearing on the applications' merits to determine which will best serve the public interest. The Commission examines various factors before choosing what it considers to be the most appropriate applicant for the license. See Albert, Constitutional Regulation of Televised Violence, 64 Va.L.Rev. 1299, 1322 (1978). See also, Robinson, The FCC and the First Amendment: Observations on 40 Years of Radio & Television Regulation, 52 Minn. L.Rev. 67, 116 (1967). It has also provided guidelines indicating what a "full hearing" entails, and how it will choose among the applicants. See Policy Statement on Com-

certain circumstances. For example, the *Ashbacker* Court explicitly stated that it found no suggestion that "the demands of the public interest were so urgent as to preclude the delay which would be occasioned by a hearing."[6] Agencies may also follow different procedures in cases involving temporary authorizations and interim permits.[7] Finally, the agency need not permit a late applicant to disrupt a hearing already in process. The *Ashbacker* holding only applies to parties whose applications have already been declared mutually exclusive, not to prospective applicants.[8]

Courts, however, often have discouraged FCC efforts to limit the applicability of *Ashbacker*. In *Citizens Communications Center v. FCC*,[9] for example, the D.C. Circuit held that a Commission policy statement on comparative hearings violated the Communications Act hearing requirement and the *Ashbacker* doctrine. The policy statement provided that in a hearing between an incumbent applying for renewal of its broadcasting license and a mutually exclusive applicant, a comparison of the two parties was required only if the incumbent could not demonstrate "substantial past performance without serious deficiencies."[10] Thus the "comparative" hearing was limited to a single issue: that of substantial past performance. This, the Court ruled, effectively stripped the challenger of its right to a hearing.[11]

FCC deregulatory policies and more market-oriented approaches towards the award of certain licenses have, to a large extent, rendered *Ashbacker* irrelevant in some regulatory contexts. For example, the FCC now awards licenses for cellular phones on the basis of a lottery. All applicants must meet a minimum standard of acceptability, but in place of a comparative hearing, there is only a lottery.[12] It is possible to challenge the winner of the lottery as unfit, but if such a challenge is successful the FCC either holds another drawing for the license or awards the license to the runner up in the first lottery. Such an approach, of course, undercuts any need for an *Ashbacker* hearing.

Although the physical nature of the broadcasting spectrum provided the original motivation for the *Ashbacker* doctrine, the doctrine has been

parative Broadcast Hearings, 1 F.C.C.2d 393 (1965). See also Johnston Broadcasting Co. v. F.C.C., 175 F.2d 351, 356–357 (D.C.Cir.1949).

6. 326 U.S. at 333, 66 S.Ct. at 151.

7. In Beloit Broadcasters, Inc. v. F.C.C., 365 F.2d 962 (D.C.Cir.1966), the court held that the FCC may award interim authority without a hearing if the public interest would be served and the regular licensing proceeding would not be prejudiced. See also Newark Radio Broadcasting Ass'n v. F.C.C., 763 F.2d 450, 454 (D.C.Cir. 1985) (permitting reduction in procedural panoply in interim applications where the Commission selected on interim operator because of public interest); Consolidated Nine, Inc. v. F.C.C., 403 F.2d 585 (D.C.Cir. 1968).

8. Reuters Ltd. v. FCC, 781 F.2d 946, 951 (D.C.Cir.1986). See also Great Western Packers Express, Inc. v. United States, 263 F.Supp. 347, 351 (D.Colo.1966).

9. 447 F.2d 1201 (D.C.Cir.1971). Although *Ashbacker* involved two original applications, the doctrine applies to renewal proceedings as well. Id. at 1211.

10. Id. at 1203.

11. For a criticism of the opinion, and a discussion of its aftermath, see, Geller, The Comparative Renewal Process In Television: Problems and Suggested Solutions, 61 Va.L.Rev. 471, 486–489 (1975).

12. Cellular Lottery Rulemaking, 90 F.C.C.2d 175 (1984).

applied in other areas in which multiple applicants compete for a single license.[13]

§ 8.4 THE ADMINISTRATIVE ADJUDICATIVE PROCESS

Assuming that formal adjudicatory proceedings are in order, the following sections examine the decisionmaking process the APA provides. We shall first consider aspects of the prehearing phase of the process, and then focus on certain procedural aspects of the hearing itself.

§ 8.4.1 Parties Under the APA

The APA defines a "party" to include "a person or agency named or admitted as a party, or properly seeking and entitled as of right to be admitted as a party in an agency proceeding, and a person or agency admitted by an agency as a party for limited purposes."[1] The individual who is the "obvious party" is the one subject to or the object of the agency's action such as an applicant for a license, a regulated utility seeking a rate increase or an entity or individual against whom the agency's rules are being enforced. Such persons, whose rights and duties are directly affected by the agency action involved, have a clear right to participate in the hearing.

The question that arises, however, is what persons or entities who are not the direct focus of any agency proceeding may participate. There are many categories of interested individuals or entities and they may have a variety of motives for participating in an adjudicatory proceeding. Competitors of an applicant for a license may, for example, have economic interests at stake. Consumers of electricity have a clear interest in the electricity rates set by the Federal Energy Regulatory Commission when an interstate electric utility that supplies the local companies that serve them applies for a rate increase. Similarly situated regulated entities may also have an interest in a proceeding that involves issues that ultimately affect their interests. Parties with varying degrees of interest in the case, from a direct interest in the legal principles that may be formulated to an unspoken desire to raise the costs of entry of a potential competitor all may wish to intervene in an agency proceeding.[2]

13. See, e.g., Delta Air Lines, Inc. v. CAB, 497 F.2d 608, 613 (D.C.Cir.1973), cert. denied 417 U.S. 930, 94 S.Ct. 2640, 41 L.Ed.2d 233 (1974); see also, Public Utilities Com'n v. FERC, 900 F.2d 269 (D.C.Cir. 1990).

§ 8.4

1. 5 U.S.C.A. § 551(3) (1982).

2. There has been much discussion of the intervention right and the need to allow for more effective public representation. See, e.g., Stewart, The Reformation of American Administrative Law, 88 Harv. L.Rev. 1669 (1975); Robinson, The Federal Communications Comm'n: An Essay on Regulatory Watchdogs, 64 Va.L.Rev. 169 (1978); Murphy, Hoffman, Current Models For Improving Public Representation in the Administrative Process, 28 Admin.L.Rev. 391 (1976); Butzel, Intervention and Class Actions Before the Agencies and the Courts, 25 Admin.L.Rev. 135, 136 (1973); Gellhorn, Public Participation in Administrative Proceedings, 81 Yale L.J. 359, 361 (1972); Cramton, The Why, Where and How of Broadening Public Participation in the Administrative Process, 27 Am.U.L.Rev. 981

While most of these potential parties to the proceeding may have a contribution to make to the record that will be compiled, the number of participants involved creates the possibility that the proceeding may become unwieldy. The APA allows some parties to be admitted "for limited purposes."[3]

The Administrative Law Judge, or presiding officer, may thus limit certain parties' right to cross-examination and try to prevent unnecessary duplication of efforts. Most parties, however, will seek to intervene and participate as a full party, with the right to submit evidence, cross-examine witnesses and appeal adverse decisions. The ALJ involved can still seek to limit duplication of efforts among these parties through skillful use of her discretionary powers.

§ 8.4.2 Intervention

Agency actions by their nature affect a broad range of public and private interests. Administrative law has witnessed a steady and continued expansion of public participation in most agency proceedings.[4] This expansion of participation rights sometimes has reflected the courts' concern with the inability of agencies adequately to represent the public interest.[5] It also reflects a pluralistic conception of the administrative process that sees the public interest as consisting of a tapestry of many strands. The public interest as well as the legitimacy of the agency's decisionmaking process thus demands that all important interests and viewpoints be represented.[6]

There are reasons, however, for imposing some limitations on those who wish to participate. Some interveners may not have a significant interest in the proceeding and may wish only to delay the agency's processes. Others may have a significant interest, but one that is already ably represented. Balanced against the need an agency has to be sure that the many facets of the public interest are represented is the agency's equally important need to proceed in an orderly and efficient manner.[7]

(1978); Note, Federal Agency Assistance to Impecunious Intervenors, 88 Harv.L.Rev. 1815 (1975); Comment, Public Participation in Federal Administrative Proceedings, 120 U.Pa.L.Rev. 702 (1972).

3. 5 U.S.C.A. § 551(4).

4. "The opportunity of citizen groups to intervene as parties in trial-type proceedings where their views are unrepresented . . . has been greatly broadened by statutes, administrative actions, and judicial decisions." ACUS, Public Participation in Administrative Hearing (Rec. No. 71–6), 1 C.F.R. § 305.71–6 (1988). The study also discusses agency concerns:

In order that agencies may effectively exercise their powers and duties in the public interest, public participation in agency proceedings should neither frustrate an agency's control of the allocation of its resources nor unduly complicate and delay its proceedings. Consequently, each agency has a prime responsibility to reexamine its rules and practices to make public participation meaningful and effective without impairing the agency's performance of its statutory obligations.

5. See, e.g., National Welfare Rights Organization v. Finch, 429 F.2d 725 (D.C.Cir.1970).

6. See Stewart, supra note 91.

7. See, e.g., Comment, Licensing of Nuclear Power Plants: Abuse of the Intervention Right, 21 U.S.F.L.Rev. 121 (1986).

The APA does not explicitly address the question of which interested persons are entitled to intervene in agency proceedings.[8] The opportunity to intervene usually depends on interpretation of agency rules or enabling acts.[9] These sources of law, however, frequently employ ambiguous language and amorphous "good cause" standards, leaving resolution of these issues largely to agency discretion.[10] The vagueness of the statutes and rules governing intervention has led many courts to look to other areas of the law to resolve these issues, particularly the law of standing. This is true even though the Article III constraints of a "case or controversy" do not bind an Article I administrative court. A party that lacks standing in federal court because there is no Article III "case or controversy" present need not be denied the right to intervene in an agency's adjudicative proceedings. By the same token, the right to intervene in an agency proceeding does not automatically entitle an intervener to judicial review in federal court.[11] Courts have, nevertheless, often relied on standing doctrines when deciding intervention questions arising at the agency level.

Initially, at least, the fact that the law of standing was expanding to grant increased access to the courts provided the doctrinal basis for a liberal approach to participation at the agency level. This was, in large part, promised on a pluralistic conception of administrative law that sought legitimacy for its decisions by ensuring the representation of various points of view.[12] In *Office of Communication of United Church of Christ v. FCC*,[13] for example, the Court took a liberal approach to standing in deciding to grant plaintiff's petition to intervene. The United Church of Christ had filed a petition on behalf of black citizens who lived in Jackson, Mississippi, and watched the television station at issue. The petition alleged that the present license holder engaged in racist programming and violated the FCC's fairness doctrine. Previously, the FCC had allowed intervention in licensing cases only to parties alleging electrical interference[14] or specific economic injury, and the Commission

8. Various provisions of the APA, however, touch on this issue. See, e.g., 5 U.S.C.A. §§ 554(c), 555(b), 555(e), 557(d)(1)(A) (regarding ex parte proceedings and interested persons in general), and 558(c) (1982).

9. "Administrative standing analysis must always begin with the language of the statute and regulations that provide for an administrative hearing." Ecee, Inc. v. FERC, 645 F.2d 339, 350 (5th Cir.1981), Koniag, Inc., Village of Uyak v. Andrus, 188 U.S.App.D.C. 338, 580 F.2d 601, 614 (1978), cert. denied 439 U.S. 1052, 99 S.Ct. 733, 58 L.Ed.2d 712 (1978) (Bazelon, J., concurring).

10. See, e.g., Federal Trade Commission Act, 15 U.S.C.A. § 45(b) (allowing intervention "upon good cause shown").

11. See Koniag, Inc., Village of Uyak v. Andrus, 580 F.2d 601 (D.C.Cir.1978), cert. denied 439 U.S. 1052, 99 S.Ct. 733, 58 L.Ed.2d 712 (1978).

12. The equation of a growing, liberal standing doctrine with intervention rights at the agency level was particularly prevalent in the 1960's and 1970's. See Stewart, supra note . Standing doctrine is not necessarily as liberally construed today. See chapter 12, sec. 12.7.4, infra.

13. 359 F.2d 994 (D.C.Cir.1966), appeal after remand 425 F.2d 543 (D.C.Cir. 1969).

14. See National Broadcasting Co. v. F.C.C., 132 F.2d 545 (D.C.Cir.1942), affirmed, 319 U.S. 239, 63 S.Ct. 1035, 87 L.Ed. 1374 (1943). In this case an individual sought a license to operate a new radio station. The station, if operated, would have electrically interfered with an already-existing station. The court permitted the opera-

so ruled in this case.[15] The Court, however, reversed the Commission on the basis of a liberal conception of the doctrine of standing:

> Since the concept of standing is a practical and functional one designed to insure that only those with a genuine and legitimate interest can participate in a proceeding, we can see no reason to exclude those with such an obvious and acute concern as the listening audience.[16]

The Court also set forth reasons independent of the doctrine of standing for requiring intervention in this case. The interveners in this case represented "all other television viewers in the State of Mississippi." The Court advanced a theory of agency representation that went beyond the requirements of Article III:

> The theory that the Commission can always effectively represent the listener interests in a renewal proceeding without the aid and participation of legitimate listener representatives fulfilling the role of private attorneys general is one of those assumptions we collectively try to work with so long as they are reasonably adequate. When it becomes clear, as it does to us now, that it is no longer a valid assumption which stands up under the realities of actual experience, neither we nor the Commission can continue to rely on it.[17]

The Court thus rejected the Commission's fear of clogged and unwieldy dockets, and held that "[i]n order to safeguard the public interest in broadcasting ... some 'audience participation' must be allowed in license renewal proceedings."[18]

A second landmark opinion in this area is *Scenic Hudson Preservation Conference v. Federal Power Commission*,[19] which provided judicial guidelines concerning the interested groups eligible to intervene in agency proceedings. The Court interpreted the Federal Power Act, which permits any party "aggrieved by an order issued by the Commission"[20] to

tor of the existing station to intervene as a party. For a similar case, see Interstate Broadcasting Co. v. F.C.C., 285 F.2d 270 (D.C.Cir.1960).

15. F.C.C. v. Sanders Bros. Radio Station, 309 U.S. 470, 60 S.Ct. 693, 84 L.Ed. 869 (1940). The party seeking to intervene need not be a competing broadcaster. In Philco Corp. v. F.C.C., 257 F.2d 656 (D.C.Cir.1958), cert. denied 358 U.S. 946, 79 S.Ct. 350, 3 L.Ed.2d 352 (1959) the party seeking to intervene was a manufacturer of radio and electronic equipment, who competed with Radio Corporation of America, the sole shareholder of NBC, a station operator. The stations gave RCA a competitive advertising advantage. The court held that where the operation of the stations strengthened the competitor's competitive position to such a degree as to have a direct economic effect on manufacturer, the manufacturer was a party in interest.

16. 359 F.2d at 1002.

17. Id. at 1003–04.

18. Id. at 1005. See also National Welfare Rights Organization v. Finch, 429 F.2d 725 (D.C.Cir.1970) where the court, in effect, reasoned backwards from the right to intervene in a judicial proceeding to the right to intervene at the agency level: "[t]he right of judicial review cannot be taken as fully realized, however, if appellants are excluded from participating in the proceeding to be reviewed." Id.

19. 354 F.2d 608 (2d Cir.1965), cert. denied 384 U.S. 941, 86 S.Ct. 1462, 16 L.Ed.2d 540 (1966).

20. § 313(b) (codified at 16 U.S.C.A. § 8251(b)).

obtain review in Circuit Court. The interveners were an unincorporated association consisting of a number of non-profit, conservationist organizations, and several towns. The Court explained that allowing this intervention was the only way to represent the public's aesthetic, conservationist, and recreational interests. Indeed, intervention was an efficient way of making these views known. The association represented several groups that would otherwise have had to intervene separately and thereby delay the administrative process.[21] The Commission could not, by itself alone, adequately protect the public and therefore "those who by their activities and conduct have exhibited a special interest in such areas, must be held to be included in the class of 'aggrieved' parties under § 313(b)."[22]

In short, the policy justifications that support an agency's decision to grant an intervention petition do not always coincide with the more stringent requirements of Article III standing. The need for an agency to inform itself as fully as possible on the issues before it, as well as the need, for legitimacy purposes, of including all relevant points of view in the decisionmaking process, militate in favor of granting intervention petitions more liberally than Article III standing.[23] "[A]gencies are free to hear actions brought by parties who might be without party standing if the same issues happened to be before a federal court."[24] This is true because "[t]he agencies' responsibility for implementation of statutory purposes justified a wider discretion, in determining what actions to entertain, than is allowed to the courts by either the constitution or the common law."[25]

Given the relatively liberal approach courts generally have taken to intervention issues, few credible parties are denied the opportunity to intervene.[26] Of greater relevance are such practical problems as finding

21. The D.C. Circuit cited this reasoning with approval in National Welfare Rights Organization v. Finch, 429 F.2d 725, 739 (D.C.Cir.1970) (holding welfare recipients and their state and national organizations may intervene in conformity hearings; the court stated that the National Organization could serve the common good of all participants since the class shared a unity of interest. This, in turn, would save agency resources).

22. 354 F.2d at 616 (emphasis added).

23. See Koniag, Inc., Village of Uyak v. Andrus, 188 U.S.App.D.C. 338, 343, 580 F.2d 601, 606 (1978), cert. denied 439 U.S. 1052, 99 S.Ct. 733, 58 L.Ed.2d 712 (1978); Nichols v. Board of Trustees of Asbestos Workers Local 24 Pension Plan, 835 F.2d 881 (D.C.Cir.1987). See also American Trucking Ass'ns, Inc. v. Interstate Commerce Comm'n, 673 F.2d 82, 85 n. 4 (5th Cir.1982), cert. denied 469 U.S. 930, 105 S.Ct. 324, 83 L.Ed.2d 261 (1984) (carriers and carrier associations sought to reopen ICC cases to determine whether agency disregarded or improperly applied a Court of Appeals' interpretation of the Motor Carrier Act of 1980); but see Erie–Niagara Rail Steering Comm. v. Surface Transp. Bd., 167 F.3d 111 (2d Cir.1999). (*American Trucking* unpersuasive dictum that rests upon pre–1975 cases ; hence, there is "no compelling support for the proposition that, despite the plain statutory language to the contrary, non-party petitions remain valid today.")

24. Gardner v. F.C.C., 530 F.2d 1086, 1090 (D.C.Cir.1976).

25. Id.

26. Butzel, supra note 91; Gellhorn, Public Participation in Administrative Proceedings, 81 Yale L.J. 359, 361 (1972). See also, Shapiro, Some Thoughts on Intervention Before Courts, Agencies and Arbiters, 81 Harv.L.Rev. 721 (1968).

the funds necessary for some interests realistically to have a chance to intervene in agency proceedings.[27]

§ 8.4.3 Notice and Pleadings

Failure to provide notice of an administrative proceeding is a jurisdictional defect that invalidates the administrative action until the defect is cured.[28] Administrative pleadings, however, are liberally construed, and easily amended.[29] As a result, problems concerning pleadings arise almost entirely in reference to the adequacy of the notice they provide.[30]

Due process guidelines inform courts in claims seeking to enforce a right to notice. This right includes advance notice of the time and place of a hearing and the issues likely to be raised in that hearing. *Memphis Light, Gas and Water Div. v. Craft*[31] dealt with the notice of the existence of a hearing. The Court held that when a utility seeks to terminate its service, due process is not satisfied if the notice of termination does not inform the customer of the availability of a procedure for protesting the proposed termination. The opinion stressed that the notice in this case affected "customers of various levels of education, experience, and resources," all of whom should have been informed of their right to contest the utility's termination order. Appropriate notice should, therefore, have included the designation of a place, specific hours, and a particular person before whom complaints could be submitted.[32]

On the other hand, in *Walthall v. United States*[33] the 9th Circuit has held that the Tax Equity and Fiscal responsibility Act of 1982 provides constitutionally adequate notice to indirect partners of multi-tiered partnerships who receive no written notice of administrative hearings under 26 U.S.C. § 6223, *et seq*. That statute requires that notice of an administrative hearing be sent to all partners whose name and address have been furnished to the IRS. Indirect partners are entitled to notice if they are identified on the partnership return or are identified by the tax

27. See generally, "Public Participation in Regulatory Agency Proceedings," Study on Federal Regulation pursuant to 5 Res. 71, Senate Committee on Governmental Affairs, 95th Cong., 1st Sess. (1977); "Federal Regulation and Regulatory Reform," Subcomm. on Oversight and Investigations of the House Comm. on Interstate and Foreign Commerce, 44th Cong. 2d Sess. 539 (1976). See also, Robinson, The Federal Communications Commission: An Essay on The Regulatory Watchdog, 64 Va.L.Rev. 169 (1978).

28. North Alabama Express, Inc. v. United States, 585 F.2d 783 (5th Cir.1978).

29. See Usery v. Marquette Cement Mfg. Co., 568 F.2d 902, 906 (2d Cir.1977) (holding Occupational Safety and Health Review Commission abused its discretion in refusing to allow amending complaint to charge violating general duty clause).

30. Kenneth Culp Davis, Administrative Law Treatise § 14.11 (2d ed. 1980).

31. 436 U.S. 1, 98 S.Ct. 1554, 56 L.Ed.2d 30 (1978).

32. 436 U.S. at 15 n. 15, 98 S.Ct. at 1563 n. 15. If, however, the party responding is aware of the procedural route it must follow in order to present a complaint, special notification of such options is not required. See Morgan v. United States Postal Serv., 798 F.2d 1162 (8th Cir.1986), cert. denied 480 U.S. 948, 107 S.Ct. 1608, 94 L.Ed.2d 793 (1987) (where plaintiff had actual knowledge of the procedures available for handicap determination action, agency was not required to publish the procedures in the Federal Register, and plaintiff should have exhausted administrative remedies before going to court).

33. 131 F.3d 1289 (9th Cir.1997).

matters partner in accordance with prescribed regulations. Furthermore, tax matters partners are required to keep all other partners informed of administrative proceedings. The Court reasoned that the Act was constitutional "because the government could conclude that it is 'reasonably certain' that tax matters partners would carry out their statutory duty to pass on notices to the other partners."[34]

Another central purpose of the notice requirement is to inform the parties of the substantive issues that will be involved. The APA states that notice must inform the party of "the matters of fact and law asserted."[35] Courts have equated this requirement with the Constitution: "The purpose of notice under the Due Process Clause is to apprise the affected individual of, and permit adequate preparation for, an impending 'hearing.' "[36] Adequacy of notice should be evaluated "with due regard for the practicalities and peculiarities of the case."[37] In a license revocation proceeding, for example, notice which merely informed the party of a hearing was not sufficient. It had to advise the person of the particular acts and omissions with which he was charged, to enable him to prepare his defense.[38]

Courts apply a reasonableness test to determine the adequacy of notice. Proper notice must reasonably apprise parties of the issues involved, and provide a reasonable amount of time to prepare their defense.[39] The focus generally is on whether the notice reasonably informs the individual of the matters the hearing will address.

Under certain circumstances, however, agency hearings may extend to issues not mentioned in the notice. This often happens when the parties, though lacking formal notice, have actual notice of the issues to

34. Id. at 1295. see also Kaplan v. United States, 133 F.3d 469 (7th Cir.1998).

35. 5 U.S.C.A. § 554(b)(3) (1982).

36. 436 U.S. at 14, 98 S.Ct. at 1562. See also Mullane v. Central Hanover Bank & Trust Co., 339 U.S. 306, 314, 70 S.Ct. 652, 657, 94 L.Ed. 865 (1950) ("An elementary and fundamental requirement of due process in any proceeding which is to be accorded finality is notice reasonably calculated, under all the circumstances, to apprise interested parties of the pendency of the action and afford them an opportunity to present their objections").

37. Mullane v. Central Hanover Bank & Trust Co., 339 U.S. 306, 314, 70 S.Ct. 652, 657, 94 L.Ed. 865 (1950); See also Intercontinental Indus., Inc. v. American Stock Exchange, 452 F.2d 935, 941 (5th Cir.1971), cert. denied 409 U.S. 842, 93 S.Ct. 41, 34 L.Ed.2d 81 (1972).

38. Wolfenbarger v. Hennessee, 520 P.2d 809 (Okl.1974).

39. Soule Glass and Glazing Co. v. NLRB, 652 F.2d 1055, 1074 (1st Cir.1981) ("Thus, the test is one of fairness under the circumstances of each case—whether the [individual] knew what conduct was in issue and had a fair opportunity to present his defense."); see also Southwest Sunsites, Inc. v. FTC, 785 F.2d 1431, 1435 (9th Cir. 1986), cert. denied 479 U.S. 828, 107 S.Ct. 109, 93 L.Ed.2d 58 (1986) (purpose of the APA notice requirement is satisfied, and there is no due process violation, if the party proceeded against "understood the issue" and "was afforded full opportunity" to justify its conduct citing Golden Grain Macaroni Co. v. FTC, 472 F.2d 882, 885 (9th Cir.1972), cert. denied 412 U.S. 918, 93 S.Ct. 2730, 37 L.Ed.2d 144 (1973)); North Alabama Express, Inc. v. United States, 585 F.2d 783, 787 (5th Cir.1978); Buckner Trucking, Inc. v. United States, 354 F.Supp. 1210, 1219 (S.D.Tex.1973) (reasonable notice is generally adequate absent a showing that an interested party was misled); Perry v. Planning Com'n, 62 Hawaii 666, 619 P.2d 95 (1980); F.T.C. v. Gratz, 253 U.S. 421, 430, 40 S.Ct. 572, 576, 64 L.Ed. 993 (1920) (Brandeis, J., dissenting) ("The function ... is solely to advise the respondent of the charges made").

be considered.[40] When a hearing is broader in scope than the notice provided, the doctrine set forth in *Kuhn v. CAB*[41] usually applies: "It is now generally accepted that there may be no subsequent challenge of issues which are actually litigated, if there has been actual notice and adequate opportunity to cure surprise."[42] If the parties understood the issues when the proceedings took place, "they cannot thereafter claim surprise or lack of due process because of alleged deficiencies in the language of particular pleadings. Actuality of notice there must be, but the actuality, not the technicality, must govern."[43]

In addition to actuality of notice, courts also examine whether expanding the scope of a hearing may have caused the parties any prejudice. Generally, "absent prejudice agencies can deviate slightly from theories initially alleged" in pleadings.[44] An example of a change in theory prejudicing a party is where the new theory would require new methods of proof.[45] Agencies may not change theories in midstream without giving the respondent reasonable notice of the change.[46] The important consideration in permitting an agency to rely on a new theory is the respondent's opportunity to present an argument, not that the result reached would most likely have been the same.[47] Courts may also consider whether new issues arising during a hearing are sufficiently

40. On the validity of actual notice see, e.g., Northern Colo. Water Conservancy Dist. v. FERC, 730 F.2d 1509, 1522 (D.C.Cir.1984) (no actual notice of proposed hydroelectric power project where newspaper notice failed to mention precise project location); National Steel & Shipbuilding Co. v. Director, Office of Workers' Compensation Programs, 616 F.2d 420, 421 (9th Cir. 1980); Common Carrier Conference Irregular Route v. United States, 534 F.2d 981, 983 (D.C.Cir.1976), cert. denied 429 U.S. 921, 97 S.Ct. 317, 50 L.Ed.2d 288 (1976).

41. 183 F.2d 839 (D.C.Cir.1950).

42. Id. at 841–42.

43. Id. at 842. For cases applying *Kuhn,* see Citizens State Bank of Marshfield, Mo. v. FDIC, 751 F.2d 209 (8th Cir. 1984) (holding agency did not err in considering loans not specifically enumerated in more definite statement where FDIC found Citizens Bank violated Truth In Lending Act); Conair Corp. v. NLRB, 721 F.2d 1355 (D.C.Cir.1983), cert. denied 467 U.S. 1241, 104 S.Ct. 3511, 82 L.Ed.2d 819 (1984) (holding employer did not receive fair notice and opportunity to respond to claim that in addition to threatening to discharge unfair practice strikers it actually did discharge striking employees on a specific date).

44. ITT Continental Baking Co., Inc. v. FTC, 532 F.2d 207, 218 (2d Cir.1976) ("[T]here is no real unfairness in the Commissioner's reference to the capacity of Wonder Bread advertisements to deceive adults in support of its finding that the advertisements were deceptive to children"); NLRB v. United Aircraft Corp., 490 F.2d 1105, 1111, 1112 (2d Cir.1973).

45. See, e.g., Southwest Sunsites, Inc. v. FTC, 785 F.2d 1431 (9th Cir.1986), cert. denied 479 U.S. 828, 107 S.Ct. 109, 93 L.Ed.2d 58 (1986) (fact that FTC applied new deception standard in reversing ALJ decision and finding land sale company engaged in unfair and deceptive practice did not violate due process where the new standard placed a heavier burden of proof on the FTC, and no new defenses or proof were required).

46. Rodale Press, Inc. v. FTC, 407 F.2d 1252, 1256 (D.C.Cir.1968) (persons charged with making representations in advertisements were improperly deprived of notice and hearing where the complaint was sustained on different theory from theory in complaint); see also NLRB v. Johnson, 322 F.2d 216, 219–20 (6th Cir.1963), cert. denied 376 U.S. 951, 84 S.Ct. 968, 11 L.Ed.2d 971 (1964); NLRB v. H.E. Fletcher Co., 298 F.2d 594 (1st Cir.1962). But see Advance Bronze, Inc. v. Dole, 917 F.2d 944 (6th Cir.1990); Faries v. Director, Office of Workers' Comp. Programs, 909 F.2d 170 (6th Cir.1990)—Change in *legal standard* during hearing *not* a violation of due process.

47. 407 F.2d at 1257.

related to the one relied on in the complaint.[48]

In addition to the general notice and pleading guidelines established by the due process clause, the APA specifically requires notice of: (1) the time, place, and nature of the hearing; (2) the legal authority and jurisdiction under which the hearing is to be held; and, (3) the matters of fact and law asserted.[49] Section 554(b)(3) provides that the agency must schedule hearings at a time and place convenient for the parties and their representatives. The APA does not, however, dictate what constitutes "timely" notice. Agency enabling acts often provide a minimum time period, as do some state administrative procedure acts.[50] In general, notice must allow the parties sufficient time to prepare their case.[51] There is no mechanical rule defining adequacy of time, and courts must make fact-specific determinations.

Unless an agency's own enabling statute or regulations specify otherwise, the APA does not require personal notice. Agencies may serve through the mails, and agency rules generally provide for service by registered mail. Courts have permitted service by ordinary mail where the individual could not show prejudice resulting from the agency's failure to use registered mail.[52]

§ 8.4.4 Discovery and Prehearing Conferences

Prehearing discovery in agency adjudicatory proceedings seeks to ensure that the parties to the proceeding have access to all relevant information before the proceeding begins. The goals of discovery are to expedite the proceedings, encourage settlement, and increase the fairness of the proceedings by eliminating, to a large extent, the element of surprise to the litigants involved. There is, however, no general federal requirement that agencies provide for pre-trial discovery.[53] Rather, the extent of pre-hearing discovery in agency adjudicatory proceedings is a

48. See, e.g. Kuhn v. CAB, 183 F.2d at 841 n. 2. See also, 14 C.F.R. § 61.51, and Cruz v. Lavine, 45 A.D.2d 720, 356 N.Y.S.2d 334 (2d Dept.1974) (In *Cruz,* the Court held that switching issues deprived petitioner of notice. 356 N.Y.S.2d at 335–36).

49. 5 U.S.C.A. § 554(b) (1982).

50. See, e.g., West's Ann.Cal.Govt.Code § 11509 (1988), providing that parties receive at least 10 days' notice of hearing.

51. Landon v. Plasencia, 459 U.S. 21, 35–36, 103 S.Ct. 321, 330–31, 74 L.Ed.2d 21 (1982), on remand 719 F.2d 1425 (9th Cir. 1983) (case remanded to determine whether 11 hours' notice of exclusion hearing before Immigration Law Judge allowed sufficient time for petitioner to prepare her case). See also Lawrence v. Department of Corrections, 81 Mich.App. 234, 265 N.W.2d 104 (1978) (notice must allow party enough time to prepare an answer); Randolph v. First Baptist Church of Lockland, 120 N.E.2d 485 (Ohio Com.Pl.1954) (notice must allow party sufficient time to prepare a defense or summon witnesses). But see Alexander v. Shiloh Baptist Church, 62 Ohio Misc.2d 79, 592 N.E.2d 918, 923 (Ohio C.P. 1991) (*Randolph* only means "that a church cannot change its constitution and, on the same day as the amendment, summarily expel a member without notice").

52. See Olin Industries v. NLRB, 192 F.2d 799 (5th Cir.1952), cert. denied 343 U.S. 919, 72 S.Ct. 676, 96 L.Ed. 1332 (1952), rehearing denied 343 U.S. 970, 72 S.Ct. 1055, 96 L.Ed. 1365 (1952).

53. The Administrative Conference, however, has recommended that agencies should adopt comprehensive discovery procedures. See Admin.Conf.Rec. 70–4, 1 C.F.R. § 305.70–4 (1988). See generally, Tomlinson, Discovery In Agency Adjudication, 1971 Duke L.J. 89 (1971).

matter of agency discretion and the amount and type of discovery available to parties, other than the agency, varies considerably from agency to agency.[54] Though courts have generally held that there is no constitutional right to discovery,[55] there are some situations where the denial of discovery could so undermine a hearing as possibly to violate due process.[56]

A potentially effective device for exchanging information among the parties to a proceeding—a means of practical discovery—is the prehearing conference. The APA explicitly provides for such "conferences for the settlement or simplification of the issues by consent of the parties."[57] An effective Administrative Law Judge may utilize such conferences to encourage the kind of exchange of information among litigants that may discourage unnecessary litigation and eliminate the element of surprise in the case. Unlike most civil proceedings in federal or state court, however, administrative adjudication usually involves direct testimony filed well before the case actually begins. The parties not only have a very detailed idea of the case to be presented, but sufficient time to prepare their questions for cross-examination.

§ 8.4.5 Cross-Examination

Once sections 556 and 557 have been triggered, the parties are entitled to a formal hearing.[58] This does not always mean that this hearing will be oral or that there will necessarily be opportunity for cross-examination.[59] Section 556 itself makes cross-examination contingent on the need "for a full and true disclosure of the facts."[60] The

54. Some agencies follow the Federal Rules of Civil Procedure; others follow a modified version and some have no discovery rules at all. See, e.g., 16 C.F.R. § 3.31–3.37 (1989) (Federal Trade Commission provides discovery rights pursuant to regulations similar to the Federal Rules of Civil Procedure); 29 C.F.R. §§ 102.117, 102.30(a) (1988) (NLRB reserves discovery matters to its own discretion and decides issues on a case-by-case basis).

The agencies themselves, however, usually have broad investigatory powers that include the power to subpoena information. For a discussion of these agency investigatory powers, see chapter 20, infra.

55. Silverman v. Commodity Futures Trading Com'n, 549 F.2d 28, 33 (7th Cir. 1977); NLRB v. Interboro Contractors, Inc., 432 F.2d 854, 857–58 (2d Cir.1970), cert. denied 402 U.S. 915, 91 S.Ct. 1375, 28 L.Ed.2d 661 (1971); Starr v. Commissioner of Internal Revenue, 226 F.2d 721, 722 (7th Cir.1955), cert. denied 350 U.S. 993, 76 S.Ct. 542, 100 L.Ed. 859 (1956).

56. See McClelland v. Andrus, 606 F.2d 1278, 1285–86 (D.C.Cir.1979); see also NLRB v. Valley Mold Co., 530 F.2d 693 (6th Cir.1976), cert. denied 429 U.S. 824, 97 S.Ct. 77, 50 L.Ed.2d 86 (1976); J.H. Rutter Rex Mfg. Co. v. NLRB, 473 F.2d 223 (5th Cir.1973), cert. denied 414 U.S. 822, 94 S.Ct. 120, 38 L.Ed.2d 55 (1973).

57. 5 U.S.C.A. § 556(c).

58. 5 U.S.C.A. §§ 553(c), 554(c)(2) (1982).

59. For a discussion of the flexibility § 556(d) affords in granting or denying cross-examination, see Auerbach, "Informal Rulemaking: A Proposed Relationship Between Administrative Procedures and Judicial Review," 72 NW.U.L.Rev. 15, 19 (1977); Nathanson, "Probing the Mind of the Administrator: Hearing Variations and Standards of Judicial Review Under the Administrative Procedure Act and Other Federal Statutes," 75 Colum.L.Rev. 721, 727–28, 730 (1975).

60. 5 U.S.C.A. § 556(d) (1982); for a discussion of cross-examination in general, see, Boyer, "Alternatives to Administrative Trial–Type Hearings for Resolving Complex Scientific, Economic, and Social Issues", 71 Mich.L.Rev. 111, 127–130 (1972). For a discussion of cross-examination and scientific

agency can exercise its discretion regarding the kind of formal hearing that takes place.[61] Cross-examination is not an absolute right conferred by the APA.[62] Rather, "its necessity must be established under specific circumstances by the party seeking it."[63] In most cases, agencies can and do limit cross-examination, particularly if the net effect of the cross-examination is to minimize repetition, delay and, thus unnecessary administrative costs.[64]

§ 8.4.6 Administrative Agency Evidentiary Rules

Section 556(d) of the APA provides that "[a] party is entitled to present his case or defense by oral or documentary evidence."[65] While an agency decision may be reversed if the agency refuses to receive competent, relevant and material evidence,[66] a decision to admit irrelevant, incompetent evidence will not result in reversal, as long as there is

decisionmaking, see Verkuil, "The Emerging Concept of Administrative Procedure," 78 Colum.L.Rev. 258, 306–9 (1978); see also McGarity, "Substantive and Procedural Discretion in Administrative Resolution of Science Policy Questions: Regulating Carcinogens in EPA and OSHA," 67 Geo.L.J. 729, 766–80 (1979).

61. Reilly v. Pinkus, 338 U.S. 269, 276, 70 S.Ct. 110, 114, 94 L.Ed. 63 (1949); Loesch v. F.T.C., 257 F.2d 882, 885 (4th Cir.1958), cert. denied 358 U.S. 883, 79 S.Ct. 125, 3 L.Ed.2d 112 (1958).

62. See Cellular Mobile Systems of Pa., Inc. v. F.C.C., 782 F.2d 182, 198 (D.C.Cir. 1985); Solis v. Schweiker, 719 F.2d 301, 302 (9th Cir.1983); Seacoast Anti–Pollution League v. Costle, 572 F.2d 872, 880 (1st Cir.1978), cert. denied 439 U.S. 824, 99 S.Ct. 94, 58 L.Ed.2d 117 (1978); American Public Gas Ass'n v. FPC, 498 F.2d 718, 723 (D.C.Cir.1974); Bryant v. Bowen, 683 F.Supp. 95, 100 (D.N.J.1988); National Trailer Convoy, Inc. v. United States, 293 F.Supp. 634, 636 (N.D.Okl.1968). But see Giant Food Inc. v. F.T.C., 322 F.2d 977, 984 (D.C.Cir.1963), cert. denied 376 U.S. 967, 84 S.Ct. 1121, 12 L.Ed.2d 82 (1964) (agencies cannot refuse to permit cross-examination or unduly limit it); State of Texas v. United States, 866 F.2d 1546 (5th Cir. 1989), rehearing denied 874 F.2d 812 (5th Cir.1989).

63. *Cellular Mobile Systems,* 782 F.2d at 198. The court went on to note that "the party fails to 'point to any specific weaknesses in the proof which might have been explored or developed more fully by that technique than by the procedures adopted by the Commission,' or fails specifically to 'suggest what questions were necessary' to explore the general issues to be examined, or fails to explain why written submissions, including rebuttal material, were ineffectual." Id. In a Social Security context, cross-examination is allowed if its denial will result in a prejudice to the claimant. See, e.g., Solis v. Schweiker, 719 F.2d at 302; Bryant v. Bowen, 683 F.Supp. at 100. See generally, Verkuil, supra note , at 313. But see, NLRB v. Doral Bldg. Services, where the Ninth Circuit was very critical of the NLRB for unduly limiting cross-examination. 666 F.2d 432 (9th Cir.1982).

64. See, e.g., Central Freight Lines, Inc. v. United States, 669 F.2d 1063, 1068 (5th Cir.1982) ("the burden of cross-examining the remaining 1,600 witnesses [following cross-examination of 127 witnesses] would have been tremendous"); American Public Gas Ass'n v. FPC, 498 F.2d 718, 723 (D.C.Cir.1974) ("petitioners have failed to demonstrate that cross examination was required for a full and true disclosure of the facts"). But see People of State of Ill. v. United States, 666 F.2d 1066, 1082–83 (7th Cir.1981), appeal after remand 698 F.2d 888 (7th Cir.1983) ("[o]nly by knowing that the parties here had the opportunity for cross-examination, can a reviewing court be assured that the ICC was relying on permissible evidence"); Bunker Hill Co. v. EPA, 572 F.2d 1286, 1305, n. 41 (9th Cir.1977) ("the limited number of parties involved . . . insures that cross-examination will not be administratively burdensome").

65. APA § 7(c) (codified at 5 U.S.C.A. § 556(d)).

66. See, e.g., Atlas Copco, Inc. v. EPA, 642 F.2d 458, 467 (D.C.Cir.1979); Russell–Newman Mfg. Co. v. N.L.R.B., 370 F.2d 980, 984 (5th Cir.1966), appeal after remand 407 F.2d 247 (5th Cir.1969). See also Pittsburgh Plate Glass Co. v. NLRB, 313 U.S. 146, 177, 61 S.Ct. 908, 923, 85 L.Ed. 1251 (1941) (Stone, J., dissenting).

substantial evidence in the record to support the agency's final decision.[67] In some cases, hearsay alone can constitute substantial evidence.[68]

For a variety of reasons, strict rules of evidence do not apply to administrative hearings.[69] Congress may explicitly provide for the admission of certain kinds of evidence in an agency setting, even though that evidence would be inadmissible in court proceedings.[70] Some courts have reasoned that the agency's chief function is investigation, and therefore it should not be hampered in its inquiry by narrow rules "where a strict correspondence is required between allegation and proof."[71] Implicit in these and other decisions is the belief that agencies, as "triers of fact" in administrative proceedings, are more sophisticated and expert in the subject matter before them. Therefore they do not require the same protective shield of evidentiary rules intended for jury trials.[72]

Absent express Congressional limitations, the administrative law judge has the power to make reasonable determinations as to the admissibility of materials in proceedings before her. This broad power is derived from the Administrative Procedure Act, which provides for "the exclusion of irrelevant, immaterial or unduly repetitious evidence."[73] Agencies usually apply this provision in such a way that favors inclusion rather than exclusion of evidence[74] and courts usually defer to the agency's decision either to include or exclude the evidence in question.[75]

67. See, e.g., Calhoun v. Bailar, 626 F.2d 145, 148 (9th Cir.1980), cert. denied 452 U.S. 906, 101 S.Ct. 3033, 69 L.Ed.2d 407 (1981).

68. See, Richardson v. Perales, sec. 8.4.7, infra.

69. Federal Trade Commission v. Cement Institute, 333 U.S. 683, 705–06, 68 S.Ct. 793, 805–06, 92 L.Ed. 1010 (1948), rehearing denied 334 U.S. 839, 68 S.Ct. 1492, 92 L.Ed. 1764 (1948); Calhoun v. Bailar, 626 F.2d 145 (9th Cir.1980), cert. denied 452 U.S. 906, 101 S.Ct. 3033, 69 L.Ed.2d 407 (1981).

70. See, e.g., the Social Security Act, 42 U.S.C.A. § 405(b) ("[e]vidence may be received at any hearing before the Secretary even though inadmissible under rules of evidence applicable to court procedure"). See also Richardson v. Perales, 402 U.S. 389, 400, 91 S.Ct. 1420, 1427, 28 L.Ed.2d 842 (1971).

71. I.C.C. v. Baird, 194 U.S. 25, 44, 24 S.Ct. 563, 568, 48 L.Ed. 860 (1904); I.C.C. v. Chicago, Rock Island & Pac. Ry. Co., 218 U.S. 88, 102, 30 S.Ct. 651, 656, 54 L.Ed. 946 (1909); Opp Cotton Mills v. Administrator, 312 U.S. 126, 155, 61 S.Ct. 524, 537, 85 L.Ed. 624 (1941); Federal Trade Com'n v. Cement Institute, 333 U.S. 683, 705–06, 68 S.Ct. 793, 805–06, 92 L.Ed. 1010 (1948).

72. See, e.g., Ohio Bell Tel. Co. v. Public Utilities Com'n of Ohio, 301 U.S. 292, 304, 57 S.Ct. 724, 730, 81 L.Ed. 1093 (1937) ("Regulatory commissions have been invested with broad powers within the sphere of duty assigned to them by law. Even in quasi-judicial proceedings their informed and expert judgment exacts and receives a proper deference from courts when it has been reached with due submission to constitutional restraints"). (See also K. Davis, Administrative Law, § 16.5 (1980)).

73. 5 U.S.C.A. § 556(d) (1982).

74. See, e.g., Meehan v. United States Postal Serv., 718 F.2d 1069 (Fed.Cir.1983); but see Second Taxing Dist. of City of Norwalk v. FERC, 683 F.2d 477 (D.C.Cir.1982).

75. For cases in which the court treats an agency's decision in this regard with deference, see, e.g., Yaffe Iron and Metal Co. v. EPA, 774 F.2d 1008, 1016–17 (10th Cir.1985) (excluding evidence as irrelevant); Alabama Ass'n of Ins. Agents v. Board of Governors of Fed. Reserve System, 533 F.2d 224 (5th Cir.1976), vacated 558 F.2d 729 (5th Cir.1977) (excluding evidence as irrelevant). But see, National Ass'n of Recycling Industries v. Federal Maritime Com'n, 658 F.2d 816, 824–25 (D.C.Cir.1980) (overruling FMC decision not to rely on ALJ's use of hearsay testimony); Garcia v. Califano, 463 F.Supp. 1098 (N.D.Ill.1979) (an ALJ can admit and weigh conflicting evidence, but cannot ignore any inadequacies in such evidence). See also Landess v. Weinberger, 490

Generally, the Federal Rules of Evidence do not bind an administrative law judge's decisions. Congress, however, sometimes limits by statute an agency's discretion to admit evidence that would be inadmissible in court. For example, Congress has provided that NLRB proceedings "shall, so far as practicable, be conducted in accordance with the rules of evidence applicable in the district courts of the United States under the rules of civil procedure for the district courts of the United States, adopted by the Supreme Court of the United States pursuant to section 2072 of title 28."[76] In *NLRB v. McClure Associates, Inc.*,[77] a general contractor discharged twelve employees, citing economic justifications. In support of its contention, the contractor offered an affidavit by the project builder to show that the builder had directed the contractor to reduce its work force on efficiency grounds. The ALJ refused to admit the affidavit on hearsay grounds: the affidavit was unreliable because the affiant was unavailable for cross-examination. The ALJ ruled that eight of the twelve discharged employees were fired for union activities, and the NLRB affirmed, ordering the eight reinstated with back pay. Regarding the evidentiary arguments, the NLRB ruled that the Federal Rules of Evidence applied. Because the affidavit was inadmissible under the Federal Rules, it was inadmissible in the hearing. The Fourth Circuit, deferring to agency discretion, affirmed.[78]

At times, Congress expressly directs an agency to consider only certain substantive factors in reaching its decisions. In such instances, the agency's discretion to exclude evidence about other kinds of factors is considerable. In *Lead Industries Association, Inc. v. EPA*,[79] for example, the petitioner sought review of an EPA administrator's promulgation of air quality standards for lead. The congressional mandate neither re-

F.2d 1187, 1189 (8th Cir.1974) (because the right to disability payments is a significant one to the applicant, the Secretary must closely scrutinize evidence to avoid miscarriages of justice).

76. 29 U.S.C.A. § 160(b). See, e.g., Carpenter Sprinkler Corp. v. NLRB, 605 F.2d 60, 66 (2d Cir.1979); see also Donovan v. Sarasota Concrete Co., 693 F.2d 1061 (11th Cir.1982) (although OSHA investigation was based on disputed probable cause, violative of the Fourth Amendment, no reason why OSHA should be restricted from evaluating whether evidence obtained from investigation meets the standards of admissibility for an OSHA proceeding).

The U.S. Department of Labor Standard provides, in part:

> (a) Applicability of Federal Rules of Evidence. Unless otherwise provided by statute or these rules, and where appropriate, the Federal Rules of Evidence may be applied to all proceedings held pursuant to these rules.

29 C.F.R. § 18.44 (1988).

77. 556 F.2d 725 (4th Cir.1977).

78. Id. One commentator has argued that the DOL standard should be uniformly adopted, and that the APA standard of "so far as practicable" should be discarded. Pierce, Use of the Federal Rules of Evidence in Federal Agency Adjudications, 39 Admin.Law Rev. 1 (Winter 1987). His argument, based on a survey of ALJ's, was that the APA standard was largely inefficient and confusing. Id. at 16–25. The DOL standard was favored because it permitted the ALJ to balance the probative value of evidence against the risk of delay, waste of agency time, or presentation of cumulative evidence. Id. at 25. The balancing test is provided in Fed.R.Evid. 403: "Although relevant, evidence may be excluded if its probative value is substantially outweighed by the danger of unfair prejudice, confusion of the issues, or misleading the jury, or by considerations of undue delay, waste of time, or needless presentation of cumulative evidence."

79. 647 F.2d 1130 (D.C.Cir.1980), cert. denied 449 U.S. 1042, 101 S.Ct. 621, 66 L.Ed.2d 503 (1980).

quired nor allowed the administrator to consider economic or technological feasibility in establishing air quality standards. The administrator refused to admit economic and technological evidence, and the petitioner appealed. The D.C. Circuit affirmed, noting "when Congress directs an agency to consider only certain factors in reaching an administrative decision, the agency is not free to trespass beyond the bounds of its statutory authority by taking other factors into account.... A policy choice such as this is one which only Congress, not the courts and not EPA, can make."[80]

The absence of explicit congressional direction favors admission, rather than exclusion, of all relevant evidence. In *Atlas Copco, Inc. v. EPA*,[81] EPA administrators promulgated noise emission standards and established testing and enforcement procedures for new portable air compressors. Eleven manufacturers sought review of the entire regulatory scheme. They argued that they were arbitrarily limited in presenting relevant evidence on an important issue, namely, the scope of the testing order. The D.C. Circuit vacated the EPA standards and remanded, noting that:

> [H]aving afforded a hearing procedure, the important inquiry is whether the Administrator may arbitrarily limit its scope, and we think the answer must be in the negative.... "One of the most important safeguards of the rights of litigants ... in proceedings before an administrative agency vested with discretion, is that it cannot rightly exclude from consideration facts and circumstances relevant to its inquiry which upon due consideration may be persuasive weight in the exercise of its discretion."[82]

Similarly, in *Catholic Medical Center of Brooklyn and Queens, Inc. v. NLRB*,[83] an employer petitioned for review and the NLRB cross-petitioned for enforcement of an NLRB order to the employer to cease and desist refusals to bargain with a certified union. At the hearing, the NLRB had refused to admit evidence offered by the employer which tended to show no such refusals. Judge Friendly vacated the order and remanded, stating:

> The Administrative Procedure Act, 5 U.S.C. § 556(d), provides that an "agency as a matter of policy shall provide for the exclusion of irrelevant, immaterial or unduly repetitious evidence." By negative implication an agency may thus not provide for the exclusion of relevant evidence not protected by a privilege or countervailing policy, defined in Federal Rules of Evidence 401, as "evidence having any tendency to mask the existence of any fact that is of

80. Id. at 1150.

81. 642 F.2d 458 (D.C.Cir.1979).

82. Id. at 467 (quoting the dissenting opinion of Justice Stone in Pittsburgh Plate Glass Co. v. NLRB, 313 U.S. 146, 177, 61 S.Ct. 908, 923, 85 L.Ed. 1251 (1941), rehearing denied 313 U.S. 599, 61 S.Ct. 1093, 85 L.Ed. 1551 (1941) (dissenting opinion) (citations omitted)).

83. 589 F.2d 1166 (2d Cir.1978).

consequence to the determination of the action more probable or less probable than it would be without the evidence."[84]

§ 8.4.7 Hearsay Evidence

Administrative tribunals freely admit hearsay evidence. An important issue that arises is whether such evidence can constitute substantial evidence and support an agency finding of fact. This issue was at the heart of the dispute in *Richardson v. Perales*.[85] There, a claimant sought review of the Social Security Administration's denial of disability benefits. Prior to the hearing, several government-paid physicians had examined Perales, but at the hearing only Perales's personal physician and one government specialist testified. The government specialist had not personally examined Perales; instead, he relied on reports which the other doctors had prepared following their examinations. Perales appealed, arguing that the specialist's testimony was hearsay and that the only evidence which should have been admitted was that of Perales's own physician. Alternatively, Perales argued that even if the specialist's testimony was admissible, it could not be the basis for a denial in the absence of corroborating evidence. These arguments articulated what had been known as "the residuum rule," that "[m]ere uncorroborated hearsay or rumor does not constitute substantial evidence."[86]

The *Perales* Court rejected these arguments and, in effect, the residuum rule itself. The Court determined that reliable hearsay could form the sole basis for an agency decision even when the record also contained adverse direct testimony:

> We conclude that a written report by a licensed physician who has examined the claimant and who sets forth in his report his medical findings in his area of competence may be received as evidence in a disability hearing and, despite its hearsay character and an absence of cross-examination, and despite the presence of opposing direct medical testimony and testimony by the claimant himself, may constitute substantial evidence supportive of a finding by the hearing examiner adverse to the claimant, when the claimant has not exercised his right to subpoena the reporting physician and thereby provide himself with the opportunity for cross-examination of the physician.[87]

84. Id. at 1170.

85. 402 U.S. 389, 91 S.Ct. 1420, 28 L.Ed.2d 842 (1971).

86. Id. at 407, 91 S.Ct. at 1430 (quoting Consolidated Edison Co. v. NLRB, 305 U.S. 197, 230, 59 S.Ct. 206, 217, 83 L.Ed. 126 (1938)). See also Watker v. Vermont Parole Board, 157 Vt. 72, 596 A.2d 1277, 1279 (Vt. 1991) criticizing the residuum rule.

87. 402 U.S. at 402, 91 S.Ct. at 1428. But see, Bethlehem Steel Corp. v. Clayton, 578 F.2d 113 (5th Cir.1978), rehearing denied 584 F.2d 389 (5th Cir.1978). In this unusual case, an employer filed a petition for review of an order awarding disability benefits under the Longshoremen's and Harbor Workers' Compensation Act, 33 U.S.C.A. § 901 et seq. The employer argued that the ALJ erred in admitting an *ex parte* report from the claimant's personal physician who examined the claimant following the disability-causing accident. The ALJ awarded the benefits, and the Benefits Review Board affirmed. On appeal, the employer asserted that the doctor's report was excludable hearsay and, if excluded, there

In short, hearsay evidence, once admitted, is subject to the substantial evidence test upon judicial review.[88] Courts have found that hearsay evidence alone is enough to satisfy the substantial evidence standard of review.[89]

Agencies have broad discretion when deciding whether or not to admit hearsay evidence. An objection to hearsay evidence at the time it is admitted usually is of little consequence when it comes to keeping the information out. The Court in *Calhoun v. Bailar*,[90] for example, suggest-

was insufficient evidence to support the ALJ's findings. The Fifth Circuit agreed with the employer, and vacated the order and remanded the case. 578 F.2d at 114. The appellate court ruled, in effect, that the hearsay was inadmissible because the right of cross-examination was denied on a crucial issue. The Fifth Circuit paid lip service to *Richardson v. Perales* by distinguishing between the Longshoremen's Act and the Social Security Act, which was the battleground in *Perales*. In fact, the court relied on a decision which was reversed by the Supreme Court in *Perales*. See Cohen v. Perales, 412 F.2d 44 (5th Cir.1969). The court also discounted as *dicta* its ruling in Young & Co. v. Shea, 397 F.2d 185, 188 (5th Cir.1968), cert. denied 395 U.S. 920, 89 S.Ct. 1771, 23 L.Ed.2d 237 (1969). That case had held that hearsay, if reliable, was admissible in proceedings under the Longshoremen's Act.

88. See Ordnance Research, Inc. v. United States, 609 F.2d 462, 475 n. 31 (Ct.Cl.1979) (substantial evidence is evidence which would "sufficiently convince a reasonable mind"). For a detailed discussion of this standard of review, see chapter 13, sec. 13.4.1, infra.

89. See, e.g., School Board of Broward County, Fla. v. Department of HEW, 525 F.2d 900 (5th Cir.1976) (hearsay evidence was only evidence available and court found it trustworthy).

See also, Mobile Consortium of CETA, Ala. v. U.S. Department of Labor, 745 F.2d 1416 (11th Cir.1984). In that case, the ALJ ordered the petitioner to repay misused CETA grant funds. The ALJ relied, in part, on some CETA participants' questionnaires and interview sheet responses, which contradicted the petitioner's fund application responses. The petitioner offered no evidence to explain the discrepancies which the ALJ found in its application, or to verify the information stated therein. The ALJ chose to believe the questionnaires. Mobile Consortium appealed, arguing that the evidence was inadmissible hearsay, but the Eleventh Circuit affirmed: "In ... cases where the participants' applications were contradicted by responses listed on signed questionnaires or interview sheets, the ALJ could properly choose to believe the latter, particularly since the Consortium offered nothing to indicate eligibility apart from the applications themselves.... [A]lterations and discrepancies ... appearing ... in responses directly keyed to an applicant's eligibility, provided a substantial basis upon which the ALJ could reasonably conclude that the eligibility of the participants had not been established." 745 F.2d at 1419. See also, National Association of Recycling Industries, Inc. v. Federal Maritime Com'n, 658 F.2d 816 (D.C.Cir.1980). In *Perales* the Court held that hearsay evidence from an examining physician in a disability hearing, without cross-examination and despite the fact that there was opposing medical testimony, may constitute substantial evidence "when the claimant has not exercised his right to subpoena the reporting physician and thereby provide himself with the opportunity for cross-examination of the physician." 402 U.S. at 402. In Lopez v. Chater, 8 F.Supp.2d 152, 156 n. 2 (D.P.R.1998) the court went a step further when it noticed that "due process does not require that a disability benefit claimant be permitted to subpoena consulting physicians," though it is questionable whether the court in *Chater* correctly interpreted the law. The U.S. Court for the Federal Circuit has held that substantial evidence failed to support the discharge of a U.S. Air Force major where the accused were effectively precluded form countering hearsay evidence when he was denied the opportunity to confront and cross-examine the witnesses who produced the evidence. But see Doe v. United States, 132 F.3d 1430, 1434 (Fed.Cir.1997). Furthermore, the Montana Supreme Court has also held that where a claimant does not bear the burden of proof, it is a denial of due process to admit hearsay evidence without allowing the claimant the opportunity to confront and cross-examine the witnesses. Bean v. Montana Bd. of Labor Appeals, 290 Mont. 496, 965 P.2d 256 (1998).

90. 626 F.2d 145, 150 (9th Cir.1980), cert. denied 452 U.S. 906, 101 S.Ct. 3033, 69 L.Ed.2d 407 (1981).

ed that a motion to strike at the conclusion of the hearing would be more appropriate than objection at the time of introduction because the administrator would then have the entire record from which to evaluate the hearsay's reliability, trustworthiness and probative value. Failure to object, however, may be seen by a reviewing court as corroboration of the hearsay, thereby "curing" any defects.[91]

Because the substantial evidence test measures the weight accorded hearsay evidence, a court is more easily able to find that hearsay evidence is substantial if it has been corroborated.[92] Some courts have also sustained agency decisions based on hearsay evidence because the opponent of the hearsay failed to cross-examine the declarants.[93]

Not all hearsay evidence, of course, constitutes substantial evidence. This is especially true when there is trustworthy direct testimony to contradict it. In *Hoska v. U.S. Dept. of the Army*,[94] for example, the Army revoked a civilian employee's security clearance, resulting in his dismissal. The Army alleged security violations, an unfavorable psychiatric evaluation, and incidents of sexual misconduct which reflected poor judgment and emotional instability. The Army built its case almost entirely on hearsay.[95] The D.C. Circuit reversed, finding that uncorroborated hearsay lacked sufficient assurance of truthfulness and was not enough to overcome the sworn testimony of the employee.[96] The Court's opinion also impliedly suggested that the Army's evidence was inconsistent, the declarants were not disinterested, and the employee did not have access to the hearsay statements prior to the hearing.[97]

Some courts have held that multiple hearsay is insufficient to constitute substantial evidence. In *Cooper v. United States*,[98] for example, a Navy civilian employee was discharged for "disgraceful conduct." The Civil Service Commission, relying on hearsay evidence, upheld the dismissal, but the Court of Claims reversed, holding that the decision was unsupported by substantial evidence. The police report relied upon by the Commission constituted multiple hearsay in that the police were actually reporting interviews between witnesses and other investigators.

91. See, e.g., Sears v. Department of Navy, 680 F.2d 863 (1st Cir.1982); Hayes v. Department of the Navy, 727 F.2d 1535 (Fed.Cir.1984).

92. See, e.g., Diggin v. United States, 661 F.2d 174, 178 (Ct.Cl.1981) (hearsay evidence corroborated and thus "reveals sufficient assurance of its truthfulness"). See also, Fairfield Scientific Corp. v. United States, 611 F.2d 854 (Ct.Cl.1979), appeal after remand 655 F.2d 1062 (Ct.Cl.1981); Martin–Mendoza v. INS, 499 F.2d 918 (9th Cir.1974), cert. denied 419 U.S. 1113, 95 S.Ct. 789, 42 L.Ed.2d 810 (1975), rehearing denied 420 U.S. 984, 95 S.Ct. 1417, 43 L.Ed.2d 667 (1975); Coates v. Califano, 474 F.Supp. 812, 818–19 (D.Colo.1979).

93. See Williams v. U.S. Department of Transportation, 781 F.2d 1573 (11th Cir. 1986), rehearing denied 794 F.2d 687 (11th Cir.1986); Klinestiver v. Drug Enforcement Admin., 606 F.2d 1128, 1130 (D.C.Cir. 1979).

94. 677 F.2d 131 (D.C.Cir.1982).

95. Id. at 138.

96. Id. at 139–40. See also, Reil v. United States, 456 F.2d 777 (Ct.Cl.1972); McKee v. United States, 500 F.2d 525 (Ct. Cl.1974).

97. Cf. Johnson v. United States, 628 F.2d 187, 190–91 (D.C.Cir.1980).

98. 639 F.2d 727 (Ct.Cl.1980).

The Court felt the report "should not have been given any probative force without *some* assurance of its credibility and reliability."[99]

Some courts have also reversed agency decisions because the agency failed to indicate clearly why it did not find certain testimony credible. In *Tieniber v. Heckler*,[100] for example, the petitioner appealed from a denial of social security benefits. The ALJ found that the petitioner was not disabled because she failed to provide objective medical evidence of her disability. The petitioner presented her own direct testimony, corroborated by her daughter's direct testimony, but the ALJ rejected their evidence as subjective. The Eleventh Circuit remanded the case back to the agency because it had failed to "articulate its credibility finding of no disability is supported by substantial evidence."[101] The Court noted that where credibility of witnesses is a crucial factor, the ALJ is justified in rejecting both direct testimony and hearsay if he does not believe it. But he must state as much in order to withstand a challenge of arbitrary and capricious conduct.[102]

A case that helps synthesize courts' approaches to hearsay evidence in administrative proceedings is *Calhoun v. Bailar*.[103] There, a postal superintendent challenged his discharge from employment, for falsifying mail volume records, on the ground that the administrator's findings were not supported by substantial evidence. His dismissal was based on affidavits of four of his subordinates, stating that the superintendent had directed them or others to falsify the records. On direct testimony, each affiant disavowed his respective affidavit. The hearing examiner found the affidavits more credible than the disavowals; the District Court for the Northern District of California upheld the dismissal, and the Ninth Circuit affirmed. After reviewing the guiding principles of admissibility and weight accorded hearsay under *Richardson v. Perales*,[104] the Court identified eight factors bearing on the reliability, probative value and fair use of hearsay evidence:

(1) the independence or possible bias of the declarant;

(2) the type of hearsay material submitted, e.g., independent reports, routine reports;

(3) whether written statements are signed and sworn, as opposed to unsigned, unsworn, oral or anonymous statements;

(4) whether or not the statements are contradicted by direct testimony;

99. Id. at 730 (emphasis in original). See also, TRW–United Greenfield Div. v. NLRB, 716 F.2d 1391 (11th Cir.1983).

100. 720 F.2d 1251 (11th Cir.1983).

101. Id. at 1255.

102. See also, Duvall v. United States, 647 F.2d 131 (Ct.Cl.1981); Faulkner Radio, Inc. v. FCC, 557 F.2d 866 (D.C.Cir.1977).

103. 626 F.2d 145 (9th Cir.1980), cert. denied 452 U.S. 906, 101 S.Ct. 3033, 69 L.Ed.2d 407 (1981).

104. 402 U.S. 389, 91 S.Ct. 1420, 28 L.Ed.2d 842 (1971).

(5) whether or not the declarant is available to testify and, if so, whether or not the party objecting to the hearsay statements subpoenas the declarant;

(6) whether the declarant is unavailable and no other evidence is available;

(7) the credibility of the declarant if she is a witness, or of the witness testifying to the hearsay;

(8) whether or not the hearsay is corroborated.

As the *Calhoun* Court noted, such an analysis "encourages the full development of the record and allows the administrative examiner to determine questions of reliability and probative value in the first instance. If the hearing examiner overrules an objection or a motion to strike, the reviewing court is nonetheless presented with a developed record."[105]

§ 8.4.8 Official Notice

In adjudicatory cases at the agency level, factual issues inevitably arise about which the agency knows a great deal. Such issues may be related directly to the agency's expertise or relate to certain aspects of the parties' situation of which the commission has a good deal of prior knowledge. The question thus presented is to what extent can the agency rely on its expertise and prior knowledge in making findings of fact? Moreover, to what extent should the parties involved in the litigation be allowed to refute these factual findings?

In an adjudicatory proceeding, a fundamental principle of administrative law is that the decisionmaker must rely only on evidence that was produced at the administrative hearing and is thus a part of the administrative record.[106] The APA thus requires that "[t]he transcript of testimony and exhibits, together with all papers and requests filed in the proceeding, constitutes the exclusive record for decision."[107] One major exception to this rule is the official notice doctrine.

The APA recognizes the official notice doctrine. Section 556(e) of the APA states that "[w]hen an agency decision rests on official notice of a material fact not appearing in the evidence in the record, a party is entitled, on timely request, to an opportunity to show the contrary."[108] The range of facts capable of being judicially noticed by trial courts is narrower than the range of facts eligible for official notice by an agency. As in other areas of administrative procedure, comparison with federal court procedure is, nevertheless, instructive. Rule 201 of the Federal Rules of Evidence limits judicial notice to facts that are beyond dispute

105. 626 F.2d at 150.

106. See, e.g., Mazza v. Cavicchia, 15 N.J. 498, 105 A.2d 545, 554 (1954) (Chief Justice Vanderbilt noted that "nothing must be taken into account by the administrative tribunal in arriving at its determination that has not been introduced in some manner into the record of the hearing") (quoting Benjamin, Administrative Adjudication in New York).

107. Section 7(d), 5 U.S.C.A. § 556(e) (1982).

108. 5 U.S.C.A. § 556(e) (1982).

and are "generally known within the territorial jurisdiction of the trial court" or "capable of accurate and ready determination by resort to sources whose accuracy cannot reasonably be questioned."[109] Due to the specialized expertise that agencies bring to the problems before them, the breadth of noticeable facts is broader in agency litigation. The issues over which litigation often ensues under this provision are the extent to which the agency makes clear that these facts are the basis of its decision and the extent to which an opportunity to contest them has been provided.[110] The more that courts require such opportunities to contest such facts, the more limited the doctrine of official notice becomes in actual practice.

Deficiencies involving the official notice doctrine appear to have been at the heart of Justice Cardozo's rejection of its use in *Ohio Bell Tel. Co. v. PUC of Ohio*.[111] In that case, the Ohio Public Utilities Commission took official notice of certain economic trends prevailing in 1934 to aid it in property valuation for rate-making purposes for the years 1926–1933. Specifically, the Commission took "official notice" of certain price, labor and land value trends to update the record before it. Not only did the Commission thereby appear to rely on just one year's data to fix rates relating to the preceding nine years, but this data itself was neither of a general nature nor the product of the Commission's own expertise. As Judge Cardozo noted: "The Commission, withholding from the record the evidential facts that it has gathered here and there, contents itself with saying that . . . it went to journals and tax lists, as if a judge were to tell us, 'I looked at the statistics in the Library of Congress, and they teach me thus and so.' This will never do if hearings and appeals are to be more than empty forms."[112] Indeed, the information upon which the Commission relied was in no record to which the Court could refer, thus hampering any meaningful challenge of that decision in court.

More recently, some courts have taken a more lenient approach. In *Puerto Rico Maritime Shipping Authority v. Federal Maritime Com'n*,[113] oil prices were crucial in determining the coming year's shipping rates, and the forecast of rising oil prices submitted by one of the carriers was rejected by the Commission. The Commission took official notice of newspaper articles and other sources that indicated that oil prices were stagnant. The PRMSA objected to the use of official notice of information not submitted by any of the parties, suggesting that it controverted *Ohio Bell*.[114]

109. Rule 201(e) of the Federal Rules of Evidence states: A party is entitled upon timely request to an opportunity to be heard as to the propriety of taking judicial notice and the tenor of the matter noticed. In the absence of prior notification, the request may be made after judicial notice has been taken. Fed.R.Evid. 201(e) (1988).

110. See, e.g., Banks v. Schweiker, 654 F.2d 637, 641–42 (9th Cir.1981).

111. 301 U.S. 292, 57 S.Ct. 724, 81 L.Ed. 1093 (1937).

112. Id. at 303, 57 S.Ct. at 730.

113. 678 F.2d 327 (D.C.Cir.1982), cert. denied 459 U.S. 906, 103 S.Ct. 210, 74 L.Ed.2d 167 (1982).

114. Id. at 339.

The Court held otherwise, commenting that "both the nature of the information noticed and the use made of it by the Commission"[115] distinguished the instant case. The information that the Commission used *was* documented in the record, and any information gleaned from outside the record was characterized as "general and gross economic and financial information:"[116] it was "common knowledge" of the sort that would have been allowed by the Court in *Ohio Bell.* The Commission was thus justified, and indeed expected, on the grounds of fairness to both the carriers and the shippers, to consider any estimate of future fuel prices to achieve a just rate. In this situation, the rates could be adjusted in the future to reflect rises in oil prices if the carrier found the rates too low. The shippers, however, had no comparable method to reduce rates if the initial rate over-estimated the rise in oil prices, and would be required to pay the inflated rates for the full year.

In *Banks v. Schweiker,*[117] however, the Court refused to allow the Social Security Administration (SSA) to give effect to facts which, though common knowledge, should have been capable of refutation. Banks was a recipient of supplemental security income disability benefits (SSID). He had also become eligible for social security disability insurance benefits (SSDB). Aware that the receipt of the two benefits might occasion an overpayment in the first quarter he was to receive SSDB, he claimed that he had called the Social Security District Office and had been told that he was entitled to cash both SSDB and SSID checks. The administrative law judge doubted Banks's story, and made passing reference during an exchange with Banks, to its unlikelihood in light of the training and capacities of SSA personnel.[118] Only later, in his written report, did the ALJ take official notice of the "practices and customs of SSA district offices",[119] and conclude that no one at an SSA district office would have advised Banks to cash all of the checks he had received.

After the SSA's Appeals Council affirmed the ALJ's decision, which was in turn affirmed by the district court, the U.S. Court of Appeals for the Ninth Circuit reversed the decision and remanded it to the Secretary. The Court considered two issues. The first was a contention by Banks that official notice is prohibited in SSA cases. Banks cited the Social Security Act[120] and the agency's regulations,[121] which seem to prohibit the use of official notice in disability cases "because the Secretary's decision [must] be based on evidence adduced at the hearing."[122] The Court held otherwise, stating that neither Congress nor the SSA intended such a result, for it would unduly restrict the agency. The Court distinguished between two theories of official notice. A "rule of caution" is typified by Rule 201 of the Federal Rules of Evidence[123] and a "belief that the taking of evidence, subject to established safeguards, is

115. Id. at 340.

116. Id.

117. 654 F.2d 637 (9th Cir.1981).

118. Id. at 641–42.

119. Id. at 640–42.

120. 42 U.S.C.A. § 1383(c)(1) (1982).

121. 20 C.F.R. § 416.1457(a).

122. 654 F.2d at 640.

123. Fed.R.Evid. 201 (1988).

the best way to resolve controversies involving disputes of adjudicative facts."[124] The Court noted, however, that the standard under which this hearing was held was the "rule of convenience," a standard that, according to SSA regulations, allows evidence at a hearing not otherwise acceptable in court under Rule 201.[125] The "rule of convenience" was justified by the huge number of cases the agency must handle. The Court concluded that the ALJ's official notice of office custom was acceptable. In a footnote, however, the Court commented that "we do not share his belief that such practices are invariably followed or that district offices give infallible advice."[126]

The second issue that the Court addressed also stemmed from its distinction between doctrines of caution and convenience. As a result of the less strict standard of the rule of convenience, the Court argued that it is even more vital that the party to the hearing be given "on timely request, ... an opportunity to show the contrary."[127] Noting that Banks had not had the opportunity to rebut the fact noticed, the Court next considered whether he had made a timely request. The Court concluded that if, as was true in this case, an ALJ takes official notice of a fact after the hearing and does not allow the claimant the chance to refute it, the appellant's request for *review* of the case, on the grounds that the ALJ took improper notice, will qualify as a timely request. In short, "the ALJ must adequately inform the claimant that he is, in fact, taking official notice and must indicate the facts noticed and their source with a degree of precision and specificity."[128] The ALJ must, in effect, give notice of official notice; failure to do so may be grounds for reversal and remand, as the Court so held in *Banks v. Schweiker*.

Generally, an administrative agency may not take notice of data from annual reports required by law to be filed with the agency, even if the party is given notice of the agency's intent to do so. In *United States v. Abilene & So. Ry. Co.*,[129] the Court held that the effect of noticing large blocks of information is that the party to the adversarial relationship is not aware of specific references in the decision. "The requirement that in an adversary proceeding specific references be made, is essential to the preservation of the substantial rights of the parties."[130]

124. 654 F.2d at 640.

125. Id.

126. 654 F.2d at 641 n. 8.

127. 5 U.S.C.A. § 556(e) (1982).

128. 654 F.2d at 642.

129. 265 U.S. 274, 44 S.Ct. 565, 68 L.Ed. 1016 (1924).

130. Id. at 289, 44 S.Ct. at 570. *Abilene* involved an appeal by the Interstate Commerce Commission from a federal court injunction prohibiting enforcement of a Commission order concerning the division of joint freight fees for traffic on connecting railway lines to shore up an ailing line at the expense of others. The Commission gave notice that they would probably consider the annual reports of the various carriers. The court held that this warning did "not mean that the Commission will take judicial notice of all the facts contained in such documents. Nor does it purport to relieve the Commission from introducing, by specific reference, such parts of the reports as it wishes to treat as evidence. It means that as to these items there is no occasion for the parties to serve copies." Id. The Court adds that the Commission's notice that it would rely upon "voluminous annual reports is tantamount to giving no notice whatsoever." Id. at 290, 44 S.Ct. at 570. As a result, the Commission's decision was based on inadmissible evidence and was therefore void.

Agency abuse of official notice, however, is not *per se* cause for reversal of agency decisions. In *Market St. Ry. Co. v. Railroad Com'n of Cal.*,[131] the Supreme Court refused to invalidate an agency order that was based, in part, upon monthly reports that were not introduced into the record. The Commission had directed that the railway, a private San Francisco cable car company, reduce its fees from seven cents to six cents. The railway contended that "the order is invalid under the due process clause because it is based on matters outside the record."[132] The Commission admitted taking information from the railway's monthly reports that were filed after the hearing was closed.

Justice Jackson noted that the Commission erred in using these reports, but that the Commission would have reached the same result without them, the information was correct, and there was no contention on the part of the railway that they could have controverted it. The railway was not prejudiced by it, nor would it gain by "cross-examination, rebuttal or impeachment of its own auditors."[133] Justice Jackson added that: "due process deals with matters of substance and is not to be trivialized by formal objections that have no substantial bearing on the ultimate rights of parties."[134]

More recently, *Air Products & Chem., Inc. v. FERC*[135] considered a number of issues brought out in the above cases, and though it recognized the validity of Justice Jackson's *Market St. Ry.* analysis, the Court concluded that prejudice to the parties did result from the agency's faulty use of the official notice doctrine. *Air Products* concerned various natural gas producers and interstate pipeline companies that were denied certificates of public convenience and necessity authorizing transportation of natural gas produced in an offshore federal domain. In 1978, the Commission reversed the bulk of an ALJ opinion issued in 1975, without further hearing or introduction of new evidence, because it perceived the need for a general curtailment of natural gas supplies. It relied upon evidence outside the record in doing so.

FERC took official notice of then existing natural gas supplies in a manner reminiscent of *Ohio Bell:* "The FERC has in no way, either in its decisions below or in its briefs on appeal, identified the 'various reports on curtailments and supplies' it relied upon in finding a serious curtailment situation in the interstate market or in finding the probability of a worsening curtailment situation. Thus, at this time, neither this Court nor any petitioner knows what information the FERC looked to in reaching this decision."[136] Since it is essential that the opposing party have the opportunity to rebut the evidence, "an agency should either disclose the contents of what it relied upon or, in the case of publicly-available information, specify what is involved in sufficient detail to

131. 324 U.S. 548, 65 S.Ct. 770, 89 L.Ed. 1171 (1945), rehearing denied 324 U.S. 890, 65 S.Ct. 1020, 89 L.Ed. 1438 (1945). See also McLeod v. INS, 802 F.2d 89 (3d Cir.1986).

132. Id. at 561, 65 S.Ct. at 777.

133. Id. at 562, 65 S.Ct. at 777.

134. Id.

135. 650 F.2d 687 (5th Cir.1981).

136. Id. at 696–97.

allow for meaningful adversarial comment and judicial review.[137] Significantly, the Court did note that '[a] caveat placed upon this rule is that the mere fact that an agency has looked beyond the record without opportunity to a party for rebuttal does not invalidate its action unless substantial prejudice is shown to result.' "[138] The Court, however, determined that there was substantial prejudice in this case because evidence outside the record was used between the decisions in 1975 and 1978 without giving notice of what the Commission considered.[139]

The Court identified two bases for its decision. First, both Section 556(e) of the APA and fair play demand that the petitioner be given a chance to respond to evidence relied upon by FERC. Second, official notice of unspecified information in agency files precludes effective judicial review. The Court thus rejected FERC's argument that use of the evidence in question was permissible because it involved a legislative judgment within the agency's expertise. The Court viewed the data FERC relied upon as factual, as opposed to being in the nature of a forecast of the future.[140] It concluded that where the agency relies "on the existence of certain determinable facts, the [agency] must, in form as well as substance, find those facts from evidence in the record."[141]

§ 8.4.9 Scope of Review versus Burden and Standard of Proof

The substantial evidence standard of judicial review applies when a court assesses the validity of an agency's findings of fact.[142] This standard and the scope of judicial review that it implies should not be confused with the burden of going forward that a party in an administrative case may carry or the applicable burden of proof or persuasion that that party's evidence must meet in that hearing. As a threshold matter, § 7(c) of the APA places the burden of proof on the proponent of a rule or of an order.[143] The APA, however, does not define "burden of proof." In *Director, Office of Workers' Compensation Programs v. Greenwich Collieries*,[144] the Court had to decide whether "burden of proof" included the "burden of persuasion,"[145] or whether "burden of proof" imposed only the "burden of production"[146] or, in effect, the burden of going

137. Id. at 697.

138. Id.

139. For cases raising similar issues, see United States v. Pierce Auto Freight Lines, 327 U.S. 515, 66 S.Ct. 687, 90 L.Ed. 821 (1946); Marathon Oil Co. v. E.P.A., 564 F.2d 1253 (9th Cir.1977), Association of Mass. Consumers, Inc. v. United States SEC, 516 F.2d 711 (D.C.Cir.1975), cert. denied 423 U.S. 1052, 96 S.Ct. 781, 46 L.Ed.2d 641 (1976).

140. 650 F.2d at 699. See FPC v. Transcontinental Gas Pipe Line Corp., 365 U.S. 1, 81 S.Ct. 435, 5 L.Ed.2d 377 (1961).

141. Id. at 696.

142. See infra chapter 13, sec. 13.4.1.

143. 5 U.S.C.A. § 556(d) (1996). See also Director, Office of Workers' Compensation Programs v. Greenwich Collieries, 512 U.S. 267, 270, 114 S.Ct. 2251, 129 L.Ed.2d 221 (1994).

144. 512 U.S. 267, 114 S.Ct. 2251, 129 L.Ed.2d 221 (1994).

145. The doctrine that "if the evidence is evenly balanced, the party that bears the burden of persuasion must lose." Id. at 272.

146. "[A] party's obligation to come forward with evidence to support its claim." Id.

forward on the proponent of a rule or order. If the latter were true, the APA would not conflict with the approach taken by the Department of Labor to various claims disputes. This, however was not the case.

The issue arose when the Department of Labor (DOL), in adjudicating claims under the Black Lung Benefits Act (BLBA) and under the Longshore and Harbor Workers Compensation Act (LHWCA), applied its so-called "true doubt" rule. The true doubt rule shifted the burden of persuasion to a party who opposed a benefits claim under the BLBA, or to a party who opposed a benefits claim under the BLBA, or to a party who opposed a benefits claim under the LHWCA. The Court, however, reasoned that Congress intended "burden of proof" to have the meaning accepted by the legal community in 1946, when the APA was enacted.[147] At that time, the definition of "burden of proof" included the burden of persuasion. That being the case, under the true doubt rule of the DOL, a claimant would win if the evidence was evenly balanced because the burden of persuasion would have been shifted. Under § 7(c) of the APA, however, a claimant would lose if the evidence was evenly balanced because the claimant, or proponent of the order, would not have carried their burden of proof. The Court concluded that the DOL could not allocate the burden of persuasion in a way that conflicted with the APA and, thus, held that the true doubt rule violated § 7(c) of the APA.[148]

The APA usually has been interpreted to require that a preponderance of the evidence test apply in administrative proceedings.[149] In *Steadman v. SEC*,[150] for example, the Court upheld the SEC's use of a preponderance-of-the-evidence standard of proof in a case involving allegations of fraud and the imposition of a sanction that would, in effect, bar an individual from continued association with certain investment companies. Petitioner argued that the evidence in the proceeding had to meet a clear-and-convincing standard of proof. The Court, however, agreed with the SEC and upheld the imposition of the sanction.[151]

Determining who has the burden of proof in an administrative proceeding can be crucial to the outcome of the case. This is particularly

147. Id. at 275.

148. For a criticism of the time-bound, textualist approach to interpreting the APA taken by the Court in Greenwich Collieries, see Peter L. Strauss, Changing Times: The APA at Fifty, 63 U. Chi. L.R. 1389, 1392–93, 1420 (1996). But see Stephen F. Williams, The Era of "Risk–Risk" and the Problem of Keeping the APA Up to Date, 63 U. Chi. L.R. 1375, 1385–87 (1996) (arguing that a more elastic interpretation of "burden of proof" than the one in Greenwich Collieries would lead to different standards of proof among agencies).

149. 5 U.S.C.A. § 556(d) (1982).

150. 450 U.S. 91, 101 S.Ct. 999, 67 L.Ed.2d 69 (1981) rehearing denied 451 U.S. 933, 101 S.Ct. 2008, 68 L.Ed.2d 318 (1981).

151. Cf. Woodby v. INS, 385 U.S. 276, 282, 284, 87 S.Ct. 483, 486, 487, 17 L.Ed.2d 362 (1966) (held that the standard of proof was "clear, unequivocal and convincing evidence" for a deportation case, and stated that "an appellate court in a criminal case ordinarily does not ask itself whether it believes that the evidence at the trial established guilt beyond a reasonable doubt, but whether the judgment is supported by substantial evidence.)" But see, Vance v. Terrazas, 444 U.S. 252, 100 S.Ct. 540, 62 L.Ed.2d 461 (1980), rehearing 445 U.S. 920, 100 S.Ct. 1285, 63 L.Ed.2d 606 (1980) (upheld Congress' lowering of the *Woodby* standard in denaturalization cases to a preponderance of the evidence standard since the *Woodby* standard was based on administrative common law).

true in environmental, health and safety cases where it can be difficult, if not impossible, to prove that something is, in fact, safe or unsafe. Section 556(d) of the APA states that "except as otherwise provided by statute, the proponent of a rule or order has the burden of proof."[152] Some environmental statutes often are interpreted as altering this burden of proof requirement. In *Environmental Defense Fund v. EPA*,[153] for example, the court held that the enabling act under which the EPA could order the suspension of certain pesticides took precedence over the APA.[154] On the other hand, the Court in *Industrial Union Dep't v. American Petroleum Inst.*,[155] in effect, ruled that the burden of proof on the Occupational Health and Safety Administration (OSHA) when setting standards "reasonably necessary" to ensure safe employment.[156]

§ 8.5 THE STRUCTURE OF ADMINISTRATIVE ADJUDICATION

Thus far, we have examined the nature of an administrative hearing. We shall now examine the administrative structure within which this hearing occurs. Because most administrative agencies combine rulemaking, adjudicatory and enforcement functions at the top of the agency's decisionmaking hierarchy, there is a need to insulate those involved

152. 5 U.S.C.A. § 556(d). But see, NLRB v. Transportation Management Corp., 462 U.S. 393, 403–04 n. 7, 103 S.Ct. 2469, 2475–76 n. 7, 76 L.Ed.2d 667 (1983) (court interprets § 556(d) to mean a burden of going forward).

153. 548 F.2d 998, 1015 (D.C.Cir. 1976), supplemental opinion (1977) cert. denied sub nom. Velsicol Chem. Corp. v. EPA, 431 U.S. 925, 97 S.Ct. 2199, 53 L.Ed.2d 239 (1977).

154. The court noted:

> Section 7(c) of the APA provides that the proponent of a rule or order shall have the burden of proof "[e]xcept as otherwise provided by statute." Because we held in our panel opinion that § 7(c) was not intended to govern the allocation of the burden of persuasion, we found it unnecessary to decide whether suspension hearings held under FIFRA might not qualify as a situation where the location of the burden of proof was "otherwise provided by statute." Velsicol's challenge has led us to focus again on the problem. We have examined the relationship between FIFRA and the APA and conclude that suspension hearings do indeed fall within the exceptions to § 7(c).

Id. at 1015. The court went on to note that it "has repeatedly held that the 1964 amendments to FIFRA were specifically intended to shift the burden of proof from the Secretary (now the Administrator) to the registrant." Id. at 1015 (citing) EDF, Inc. v. Ruckelshaus, 142 U.S.App.D.C. 74, 93, 439 F.2d 584, 593 (1971); see also EDF, Inc. v. EPA [Aldrin and Dieldrin], 167 U.S.App. D.C. 71, 76, 510 F.2d 1292, 1297 (1975).

155. 448 U.S. 607, 100 S.Ct. 2844, 65 L.Ed.2d 1010 (1980).

156. Id. at 639. OSHA argued that it needed only to set rational standards with no findings, but the Court said that to ensure "safe" employment implied that OSHA must first find that the workplace was "unsafe." The law did not imply that the workplace must be "risk free," which would have left OSHA at liberty to promulgate the strictest standards with no need to show that the workplace was unsafe to start with. Moreover, the fact that the law required OSHA to set "the" standard and not "a" standard implied that OSHA must choose one from among several possible standards that would satisfy the law—which again implied that OSHA had to first show that a workplace was unsafe. Finally, the Court noted that the law required OSHA to make policy tradeoffs by using a cost-benefit analysis of the standards—again which implied that OSHA first had to find a workplace unsafe. Id. at 639–46. It is clear that the *Benzene* case now sets "the applicable legal standard" for OSHA. American Dental Association v. Martin, 984 F.2d 823, 825 (7th Cir.1993) (opinion by Judges Posner, Coffey, and Easterbrook.)

in adjudication from those involved in enforcement. It is thus important to examine the role played by the Administrative Law Judge (ALJ) and the various means used by the APA to ensure the fairness and neutrality of that person's decisions. We being, first, with some of the background issues that helped shape the adjudicatory structure established by the APA.

§ 8.5.1 Background: The Institutional Decision and the *Morgan* Cases

Adjudication of disputes by an agency rather than by a state or federal Court was a major development accompanying the vastly increased role of administrative decisionmaking in the Twentieth Century. Prior to passage of the APA, the Supreme Court addressed a number of concerns raised by administrative adjudication in four cases, commonly referred to today as the *Morgan*[1] cases.

The Morgan cases involved rate-making proceedings begun by the Department of Agriculture in 1930. The Secretary of Agriculture fixed the rate structure of market agencies engaged in livestock trade at the Kansas City Stock Yards. The Packers and Stockyards Act provided that if these rates were challenged, the Secretary would, after a full hearing, determine what constituted a "just, reasonable, and non-discriminatory" rate.[2]

Morgan I[3] reached the Supreme Court after the district court struck from the complaint allegations that the Secretary issued his rate order without having personally heard or read any of the evidence presented at the hearing.[4] The Court, through Chief Justice Hughes, concluded that the district court erred in dismissing this allegation. The Court objected to the fact that the Assistant Secretary, who had heard the evidence in this case, had no final responsibility for the order ultimately issued. The Secretary had that responsibility, but he did not actually hear the evidence. In one of the most-oft quoted statements on this issue, Justice Hughes stated that: "The one who decides must hear."[5] Under the Court's reasoning in *Morgan I,* the agency could continue to employ assistants to pursue inquiries and sift through and analyze the evidence. But an agency would be presumed to offer a substantial hearing only if the officer who issued the order was, in fact, the one who considered and appraised the evidence.[6]

Strict compliance with *Morgan I* was difficult. The Secretary of Agriculture could not possibly hear all of the cases under his jurisdiction.

§ 8.5

1. Morgan v. United States, 298 U.S. 468, 56 S.Ct. 906, 80 L.Ed. 1288 (1936), Morgan v. United States, 304 U.S. 1, 58 S.Ct. 773, 82 L.Ed. 1129 (1938); United States v. Morgan, 307 U.S. 183, 59 S.Ct. 795, 83 L.Ed. 1211 (1939); United States v. Morgan, 313 U.S. 409, 61 S.Ct. 999, 85 L.Ed. 1429 (1941).

2. 7 U.S.C.A. § 211(a) 1021.

3. Morgan v. United States, 298 U.S. 468, 56 S.Ct. 906, 80 L.Ed. 1288 (1936).

4. Id. at 475 n. 1, 56 S.Ct. at 909 n. 1.

5. Id. at 481, 56 S.Ct. at 911.

6. Id. at 481–82, 56 S.Ct. at 911–12.

The Court's opinion, however, did allow for the delegation of this decision-making authority. The person to whom the matter was delegated then had responsibility for the decision in the case; however, the realities of administrative decisionmaking often meant that that one individual relied heavily on others.[7]

The second *Morgan* case[8] involved an allegation that the Secretary had based his decision on information received from ex parte contacts.[9] There had been a lengthy hearing before a hearing examiner, but no preliminary decision had been issued. The record that was compiled was then submitted to the Secretary. Briefs were filed by industry, but the Secretary accepted the agency's findings of fact, having first discussed those findings with the agency's lawyers. Industry advocates, however, never saw these findings until they appeared in the Secretary's order.[10] Stating that it is not the function of the Court to probe the Secretary's mental processes in reaching his conclusion,[11] the Court nevertheless held that the appellants did not receive a full hearing. They did not have an opportunity to know and address the opposing party's claims.[12] The Court stressed the adversarial nature of this proceeding and objected to the fact that the prosecutor in the case had prepared all of the findings, presented them to the fact-finder without showing them to the opposing party, and then allowed the fact-finder (who was part of the prosecuting unit) to make his decision solely or mostly on the basis of those findings.[13]

In 1941, the Supreme Court, speaking through Justice Frankfurter, again considered these issues. In the fourth *Morgan* case to reach the Court,[14] the district court had authorized the market agencies to depose

7. Most cases have not taken *Morgan I's* requirement that the decisionmaker actually "hear" the case too literally. See F. Cooper, State Administrative Law 447–51 (1965); Guerrero v. N.J., 643 F.2d 148, 149 (3d Cir.1981) ("administrative officers charged with a decision need not personally hear testimony but may instead rely on a written record"); Estate of Varian v. Commissioner of Internal Revenue, 396 F.2d 753, 755 (9th Cir.1968), cert. denied 393 U.S. 962, 89 S.Ct. 402, 21 L.Ed.2d 376 (1968) (Supreme Court statement in *Morgan I* that "[t]he one who decides must hear" "means simply that the officer who makes the findings must have considered the evidence or argument"); Southern Garment Mfrs. Ass'n v. Fleming, 122 F.2d 622, 626 (D.C.Cir.1941) (" 'hear' is used in the artistic sense of requiring certain procedural minima to insure an informed judgment by the one who has the responsibility of making the final decision and order"). But see Matter of Univ. of Kan. Faculty, 2 Kan. App.2d 416, 581 P.2d 817 (1978).

8. Morgan v. United States, 304 U.S. 1, 58 S.Ct. 773, 82 L.Ed. 1129 (1938) (*Morgan II*).

9. Id. at 17–18, 58 S.Ct. at 776.

10. Id. The Secretary relied heavily on the agency's findings (the Court notes the approximately 10,000 pages of transcript of oral evidence and over 1,000 pages of statistical exhibits), dipping into the "bulky record ... from time to time to get its drift."

11. Id. at 18, 58 S.Ct. at 776.

12. Id. at 18–19, 58 S.Ct. at 776–77.

13. Id. at 19–20, 58 S.Ct. at 776–77. The opinion analogized the administrative hearing to court proceedings, stating that the Secretary's reliance on the Bureau's findings was akin to a judge basing his or her holding on ex parte communications, having used findings of fact prepared by the plaintiff's attorney and without having provided the defendant an opportunity to know their contents in advance.

14. United States v. Morgan, 313 U.S. 409, 61 S.Ct. 999, 85 L.Ed. 1429 (1941). As a condition of the interlocutory injunction in the first *Morgan* case, Morgan had to pay a fund into the lower court constituting the difference between the scheduled rates and

the Secretary and inquire into the process by which he reached his conclusions. This inquiry included his subjective state of mind, the degree of understanding of the record he had, and the extent of the consultation he engaged in with his subordinates.[15] Justice Frankfurter objected.[16] Claiming that an analogous examination of a judge would be "destructive to judicial responsibility,"[17] Justice Frankfurter concluded that it is not a function of the Court to probe the mental processes of the Secretary.[18]

Subsequent developments in the law have rendered many of the *Morgan* issues irrelevant. This is because courts have authorized broad delegations of power to initial decisionmakers.[19] Moreover, as we shall

those prescribed by the order. *Morgan II* set aside the Secretary's order, and the district court ordered return of the impounded funds to Morgan. In United States v. Morgan, 307 U.S. 183, 59 S.Ct. 795, 83 L.Ed. 1211 (1939) (*Morgan III*), the Court held that the district court erred in holding Morgan entitled to the money since there was a proceeding pending before the Secretary concerning the reasonableness of the rates. The district court should therefore have waited for that determination and for the Secretary's final order, and then made its distribution order with a full record before it.

The Court noted that "in construing a statute setting up an administrative agency and providing for judicial review of its action, court and agency are not to be regarded as wholly independent and unrelated instrumentalities of justice, each acting in the performance of its prescribed statutory duty without regard to the appropriate function of the other in securing the plainly indicated objects of the statute." 307 U.S. at 191, 59 S.Ct. at 799. The statute should be construed so as to allow the agency and the court to attain those ends through coordinated action. Id.

15. 313 U.S. at 422, 61 S.Ct. at 1004.

16. Id. Of course, the only person who really knows whether *Morgan I* was followed is the agency head, and if he or she cannot be questioned, there is little for the litigant to do. As Professor Schwartz stated: "[a]s a practical matter ... what the Supreme Court said in *Morgan IV* all but eliminates the *Morgan I* rule as an enforceable principle of our administrative law." Schwartz, Institutional Administrative Decisions and the Morgan Cases: A Re–Examination, 4 J. Public Law 49, 65 (1955).

17. 313 U.S. at 422, 61 S.Ct. at 1004.

18. Id. ("although the administrative process has had a different development and pursues somewhat different ways from those of courts, they are to be deemed collaborative instrumentalities of justice and the appropriate independence of each should be respected by the other"). But see Citizens to Preserve Overton Park, Inc. v. Volpe, 401 U.S. 402, 91 S.Ct. 814, 28 L.Ed.2d 136 (1971) (authorizing the probing of mental processes where the administrator made no contemporaneous findings or gave no explanation for his decision).

19. See, e.g., National Nutritional Foods Ass'n v. FDA, 491 F.2d 1141 (2d Cir.1974), cert. denied 419 U.S. 874, 95 S.Ct. 135, 42 L.Ed.2d 113 (1974) (concerning a claim that the agency head must "personally familiarize himself with 1,000 pages of formal exceptions, 20,000 letters, and the staff's views about them, and read the relevant portions of the record)," Id. at 1146, Judge Friendly explained that "[w]ith the enormous increase in delegation of lawmaking power which Congress has been obliged to make to agencies, both independent and in the executive branch, and in the complexity of life, government would become impossible if courts were to insist on anything of the sort. It would suffice under the circumstances that Commissioner Schmidt considered the summaries of the objections and of the answers contained in the elaborate preambles and conferred with his staff about them." Id. KFC National Management Corp. v. NLRB, 497 F.2d 298 (2d Cir.1974), cert. denied 423 U.S. 1087, 96 S.Ct. 879, 47 L.Ed.2d 98 (1976) (the Court quoted *Morgan I's* "one who decides must hear" and qualified: "However, the Court was quick to add—in a passage often forgotten by its critics—that this principle did not preclude every delegation of adjudicative responsibility") 497 F.2d at 304; Braniff Airways, Inc. v. CAB, 379 F.2d 453, 461 (D.C.Cir.1967) ("We agree ... that 'despite its immediately appealing quality, the broad ideal that agency heads should do personally what they purport to do is for many functions impractical and unworkable' "); NLRB v. Cherry Cotton Mills, 98

now see, the Administrative Procedures Act provides for the separation of agency investigatory and agency adjudicatory functions.[20]

§ 8.5.2 The Administrative Law Judge

The Administrative Procedures Act created the position of Administrative Law Judge (ALJ). Prior to this Act, hearing examiners, as they were then called, usually were "subordinate employees chosen by the agencies, and the power of the agencies to control and influence such personnel made questionable the contention of any agency that its proceedings assured fundamental fairness."[21] They were perceived as "mere tools of the agency concerned"[22] and thus as substantially undermining the faith of the administrative process.

The APA sought to allay these fears by vesting ALJs with an independence from their respective agencies.[23] Tenure[24] and compensation[25] decisions were removed from agency control and vested largely in the Civil Service Commission, now the Office of Personnel Management. In addition, ALJs were exempted from performance ratings required for other civil service employees.[26] They could be removed by the agency, which employed them only for cause and after a hearing before the Merit Systems Protection Board.

The APA also followed essentially a judicial model when it came to ensuring that an ALJ was insulated from certain officials within an agency that is otherwise pursuing a variety of non-judicial tasks. Section

F.2d 444, 447 (5th Cir.1938), rehearing denied 98 F.2d 1021 (5th Cir.1938); NLRB v. Baldwin Locomotive Works, 128 F.2d 39, 47 (3d Cir.1942) ("we may not dogmatically tell the Board that it must 'hear' in some one particular manner so long as it does 'hear', i.e. consider the evidence and argument").

20. See sec. 8.5.4, infra. Yet, some persistent issues remain. In Citizens to Preserve Overton Park, Inc. v. Volpe, 401 U.S. 402, 91 S.Ct. 814, 28 L.Ed.2d 136 (1971), for example, plaintiffs challenged the Secretary of Transportation's decision to use federal funds to build a highway through a park as arbitrary and capricious. The Court asked the district court to examine, on remand, whether the Secretary considered all relevant statutory factors in making his decision. In conducting this inquiry, the Supreme Court made clear that the district court had the authority to require administrative officials who participated in the decision to explain their action. Id. at 420. Recognizing that there was a possible conflict with *Morgan IV,* Justice Marshall distinguished the two cases. In *Morgan,* said Marshall, the administrative findings and the decision were made simultaneously. Here there were no contemporaneous findings and the Court remanded for the development of an administrative record that might include testimony by the administrators involved. This case is discussed in detail in chapter 9, sec. 9.2, infra.

21. Lubbers, Federal Administrative Law Judges: A Focus On Our Invisible Judiciary, 33 Admin.L.Rev. 109 (1981). See also Nash v. Califano, 613 F.2d 10, 14 (2d Cir.1980) (hearing examiners had "limited independence from the agencies they served"); Administrative Procedure Act–Legislative History, S.Doc. No. 248, 79th Cong., 2d Sess. (1946); Thomas, The Selection of Federal Hearing Examiners: Pressure Groups and the Administrative Process, 59 Yale L.J. 431 (1950).

22. Ramspeck v. Federal Trial Examiners Conference, 345 U.S. 128, 131, 73 S.Ct. 570, 572, 97 L.Ed. 872 (1953), rehearing denied 345 U.S. 931, 73 S.Ct. 778, 97 L.Ed. 1360 (1953).

23. Lubbers, supra note 266, at 111.

24. 5 U.S.C.A. § 5362 (1976).

25. Id.

26. 5 U.S.C.A. § 4301 (1976).

554(d) of the Act sets forth the basic guidelines respecting internal separation of functions. In particular, "an employee or agent engaged in the performance of investigative or prosecuting functions" may not consult with an ALJ on any fact in issue before him. In 1941 the Attorney General, acting at the direction of President Roosevelt, examined this issue in a well-known report.[27] As noted by the Ninth Circuit:

> In responding to the much criticized union of the investigative, prosecutive, and adjudicative functions within agencies, the committee report [of the Attorney General's Committee] suggested the creation of hearing commissioners, now administrative law judges, as a "separate unit in each agency's organization".... Two reasons ... were given for this recommended separation: "the investigators, if allowed to participate [in adjudication], would be likely to interpolate facts and information discovered by them ex parte and not adduced at the hearing ... " and "[a] man who has buried himself in one side of an issue is disabled from bringing to its decision that dispassionate judgment which Anglo–American tradition demands of officials who decide questions."[28]

The provisions in the APA thus seek to promote the neutrality of the agency decisionmaker.[29] This neutrality, in turn, "serves as the ultimate guarantee of a fair and meaningful proceeding."[30] It has long been argued that the independence and neutrality of ALJ's could be significantly enhanced by their removal from particular agencies and the creation of a unified corps of ALJ's and a central panel system. Reforms to this effect often have been proposed in Congress.[31]

Providing for ALJ decisional independence does not, of course, give the ALJ completely free reign over the cases he hears. He has a basic obligation "to develop a full and fair record."[32] APA provisions concern-

27. Report of the Attorney General's Committee on Administrative Procedure 50 (1941), S.Doc. No. 8, 77th Cong., 1st Sess. 50 (1941).

28. Grolier Inc. v. F.T.C., 615 F.2d 1215, 1219 (9th Cir.1980), cert. denied 464 U.S. 891, 104 S.Ct. 235, 78 L.Ed.2d 227 (1983).

29. In the words of Justice White, "the process of agency adjudication is currently structured so as to assure that the hearing examiner exercises his independent judgment on the evidence before him, free from pressures by the parties or other officials within the agency." Butz v. Economou, 438 U.S. 478, 513, 98 S.Ct. 2894, 2914, 57 L.Ed.2d 895 (1978).

30. Marshall v. Jerrico, Inc., 446 U.S. 238, 250, 100 S.Ct. 1610, 1617, 64 L.Ed.2d 182 (1980). ("This requirement of neutrality in adjudicative proceedings safeguards the two central concerns of procedural due process, the prevention of unjustified or mistaken deprivations and the promotion of participation and dialogue by affected individuals in the decisionmaking process." Id. at 242). See also Nash v. Califano, 613 F.2d 10 (2d Cir.1980). Courts have also recognized ALJs' functional comparability to judges. See Butz v. Economou, supra note (ALJs, like judges, enjoy absolute immunity from liability in damages for actions taken in their quasi-judicial capacity).

31. See Symposium, The Central Panel System: A New Framework for the Use of Administrative Law Judges, 65 Judicature 233–277 (1981); see also, Lubbers, Federal Agency Adjudication: Trying to See the Forest and the Trees, 31 Fed.Bar News & Journal 383 (1984). See S. 594, 101st Cong. 1st Sess. (1989).

32. Clark v. Schweiker, 652 F.2d 399, 404 (5th Cir.1981) (citing Barker v. Harris, 486 F.Supp. 846, 849 (N.D.Ga.1980)); see also Benson v. Schweiker, 652 F.2d 406 (5th Cir.1981).

ing ex parte contacts,[33] separation of functions[34] and bias[35] also significantly confine the manner in which ALJs exercise their discretion.

§ 8.5.3 Ex Parte Contacts

Formal agency adjudication, like a trial in federal court, should be based solely on the record compiled before the ALJ. This principle is embodied in § 556(e) of the APA, which provides that "[t]he transcript of testimony and exhibits, together with all papers and requests filed in the proceeding, constitutes the exclusive record for decision."[36] The primary reason for this requirement, similar to the theory behind the decisional independence of the ALJ, is fairness to litigants.[37] This requirement that decisions be based solely on the record can, however, easily be undercut by ex parte contacts.

The APA did not originally deal with the issue of ex parte contacts. Claims of improper influence were initially analyzed only under the Due Process Clause of the Constitution.[38] A 1976 Amendment to the APA, however, provided explicit provisions for dealing with ex parte contacts in the context of formal agency adjudications. Section 557(d)(1) now prohibits any "interested person outside the agency" from making "an ex parte communication relevant to the merits of the proceeding" to any decisionmaker.[39] By statute, a decisionmaker encompasses more than just an ALJ; it also includes "a member of the body comprising the agency" or "other employee who is or may reasonably be expected to be involved in the decisional process."[40] Similarly, decisionmakers are prohibited from making ex parte contacts with any "interested person."[41]

When an improper ex parte contact occurs, the APA requires that it be placed on the public record.[42] If the contact was oral, a memorandum stating the substance of the communication must be submitted.[43] Sanctions for parties who try improperly to influence a decisionmaker are potentially severe; the offending party may be required to show cause "why his claim or interest in the proceeding should not be dismissed, denied, disregarded or otherwise adversely affected."[44] The provisions for prohibition come into effect when a proceeding is noticed for hearing or when the agency so designates.[45]

Whether the ex parte contact is self-serving is an important factor in a court's decision to sanction the offending individual or agency. In *Doe*

33. 5 U.S.C.A. § 557(d)(1) (1982).

34. Id. at § 554(d).

35. Id. at § 556(b).

36. Id. at § 556(e) (1982).

37. See Sierra Club v. Costle, 657 F.2d 298, 400 (D.C.Cir.1981).

38. See, e.g., WKAT, Inc. v. F.C.C., 296 F.2d 375, 383 (D.C.Cir.1961), cert. denied 368 U.S. 841, 82 S.Ct. 63, 7 L.Ed.2d 40 (1961); see also Massachusetts Bay Telecasters, Inc. v. F.C.C., 261 F.2d 55, 65–67 (D.C.Cir.1958), cert. denied sub nom. WHDH, Inc. v. F.C.C., 366 U.S. 918, 81 S.Ct. 1094, 6 L.Ed.2d 241 (1961).

39. 5 U.S.C.A. § 557(d)(1)(A) (1982).

40. Id. at § 557(d)(1)(C).

41. Id. at § 557(d)(1)(B).

42. Id. at § 557(d)(1)(C).

43. Id. at § 557(d)(1)(C)(ii).

44. Id. at § 557(d)(1)(D).

45. Id. at § 557(d)(1)(E).

v. Hampton,[46] for example, the Court of Appeals for the D.C. Circuit reviewed the propriety of a request, made during an appeal by the Civil Service Commission's Appeals Examining Office (AEO), for an additional medical opinion. The question arose in the context of the dismissal of a civil servant[47] on grounds of mental disability. The civil servant appealed the dismissal. Rather than confine its review to the existing record, the AEO solicited the opinion of an additional medical expert, Dr. Eck. The AEO eventually sustained the dismissal, relying on the undisclosed medical statement of Dr. Eck. The civil servant brought suit alleging the communication between the AEO and Dr. Eck was an improper ex parte communication.

Speaking for the majority, Judge Tamm concluded that, though the communication was an ex parte contact, it was merely cumulative of the medical evidence already admitted into evidence. The ex parte contact constituted a non-prejudicial procedural error. The Court characterized the communication as improper, but it emphasized that Dr. Eck had no vested interest in the outcome of this case. The solicitation was not "a self-serving contact initiated by an interested party to add to its factual evidence or to proffer further justification for its actions after the record should have been closed."[48] In short, the contact was improper but harmless. The Court thus upheld the trial court's grant of summary judgment to the Civil Service Commission.[49]

Ex parte contacts can, in some cases, result in a dismissal of the proceedings. In *Professional Air Traffic Controllers Organization (PATCO) v. FLRA*,[50] the D.C. Circuit noted that ex parte communications, which "irrevocably taint" administrative decisions are sufficient grounds to vacate the proceedings.[51] Cases which merely fall short of being "paragons of administrative procedure," however, do not necessarily warrant such a sanction.[52] The PATCO case was an example of the latter. It developed out of the 1981 strike by the Professional Air Traffic Controllers Organization. The strike was endorsed by PATCO and significantly affected private and commercial air transportation in the United States.[53]

The union's endorsement of the strike led to charges of unfair labor practices. An administrative hearing held before an ALJ confirmed their validity. As a result, PATCO's status as the exclusive bargaining representative for the controllers was revoked. The Federal Labor Relations Authority (FLRA) subsequently rejected PATCO's claim that FLRA members[54] had engaged in improper ex parte contacts. Specifically, the

46. 566 F.2d 265 (D.C.Cir.1977).

47. The anonymous civil servant was formerly employed as a clerk-typist for the Department of the Treasury. 566 F.2d at 267.

48. Id. at 276.

49. Id. at 277–78.

50. 685 F.2d 547 (D.C.Cir.1982).

51. Id. at 574.

52. Id.

53. Over 70% of the nation's federally employed air traffic controllers walked off the job. 685 F.2d at 551.

54. "Members" here refer to the judicial decisionmakers who heard the *PATCO* case on appeal. By statute, they are held to the same standards as ALJs. 5 U.S.C.A. § 557(d)(1)(A) (1982).

challenged contacts included: (1) a conversation between FLRA General Counsel and a staff attorney concerning the attorney's memorandum on the revocation of the unions' exclusive recognition status while a FLRA decisionmaker was present;[55] (2) a phone call from the Secretary of Transportation to one member of FLRA detailing the status of the strike negotiations;[56] and (3) a dinner between Albert Shanker, President of the American Federation of Teachers, and a FLRA decisionmaker which included comments by Shanker on the PATCO case.[57]

The Court of Appeals for the D.C. Circuit, recognizing that "one (or possibly two)" statutory infringements may have occurred, concluded that no parties were prejudiced by the proceedings and imposed no sanctions.[58] In addressing the first of the three ex parte contacts, Judge Edwards noted that "occasional and inadvertent contacts between the prosecuting and adjudicating arms of a small agency like the FLRA may be inevitable,"[59] but "accidental or passing references to a pending case do not *per se* deprive a party of a fair proceeding."[60] Though the conversation between the General Counsel and a staff attorney should have waited until the decisionmaker had left the office, the innocuous nature of the discussion did not "unfairly advantage the General Counsel in the prosecution of the case."[61]

With respect to the second set of ex parte contacts, the Court stated that the Secretary's telephone conversation was potentially an improper contact.[62] It declined, however, to decide the issue. The Court recognized the good faith belief by the decisionmaker that no wrongdoing had occurred and went on to chastise the decisionmaker for not reporting "close cases" such as this one.[63] It concluded that sanctions were unnecessary and it ultimately justified its conclusion upon the lack of prejudice created by the contact.[64]

The final ex parte contact, the dinner, was the "most troublesome" of the communications for the Court.[65] It found that Mr. Shanker clearly was an "interested person" under section 557(d) of the APA. He was president of a major public sector labor union and he had a special interest in the union movement and the law that applied to labor disputes in the public sector.[66] The fact that Mr. Shanker freely admitted that his motive in inviting the decisionmaker to dinner was specifically to discuss the PATCO situation made the contact all the more deplorable.[67] Nevertheless, the Court held that the *decisionmaker* had not

55. 685 F.2d at 566–67.

56. Id. at 558–59.

57. Id. at 559–60.

58. Id. at 575.

59. Id. at 567.

60. Id.

61. Id. Specifically, neither the General Counsel nor the decisionmaker expressed any view on the correct statutory interpretation of the issue of exclusive recognition of the union. Moreover, the General Counsel did not argue the facts before the decisionmaker. Id.

62. Id. at 568.

63. Id.

64. Id.

65. Id. at 569.

66. Id. at 569.

67. *"It is simply unacceptable behavior for any person to attempt to influence the decision of a judicial officer in a pending*

committed an "impropriety" by accepting the dinner invitation. A judge "must have neighbors, friends and acquaintances,[68] business and social relations, and be a part of his day and generation."[69]

The Court's primary difficulty with the decisionmaker's actions stemmed from the final fifteen minutes of the dinner conversation in which Mr. Shanker explicitly aired his views on the PATCO case. Noting that the decisionmaker should have terminated the evening then and there, the Court did not find that the contact warranted any sanction. "Though plainly inappropriate, the ex parte communication was limited to a ten or fifteen minute discussion, often couched in general terms.... This behavior falls short of the 'corrupt tampering with the adjudicatory process' found by this court in WKAT, Inc. v. FCC.... "[70]

§ 8.5.4 Separation of Functions

The hallmark of the administrative process is its ability to combine legislative, prosecutorial, investigative and adjudicatory functions. By combining these functions under one roof, an agency, in theory at least, can pursue its congressionally mandated duties with efficiency and effectiveness. Courts have long upheld the constitutionality of the combination of these functions within a single agency,[71] but legal difficulties may result when some functions are combined within the same decisionmaker or that decisionmaker has access to or can be influenced by superiors that perform conflicting functions within the agency.[72]

The most alarming combination of functions is that of adjudication and prosecution in the same decisionmaker. Closely related to this is the

case outside of the formal, public proceedings." Id. at 570 (emphasis in original).

68. Albert Shanker and the decisionmaker in question were former business and social acquaintances. Id. at 559.

69. Id. at 570, quoting Pennsylvania v. Local Union 542, International Union of Operating Engineers, 388 F.Supp. 155, 159 (E.D.Pa.1974) (quoting Ex parte N.K. Fairbank Co., 194 Fed. 978, 989 (M.D.Ala. 1912)).

70. Id. at 571, citing WKAT, Inc. v. FCC, 296 F.2d 375, 383 (D.C.Cir.1961), cert. denied 368 U.S. 841, 82 S.Ct. 63, 7 L.Ed.2d 40 (1961) (attempts made by several applicants for a television station to influence the outcome by factors unrelated to the merits justified their disqualification by the Commission).

71. See Withrow v. Larkin, 421 U.S. 35, 95 S.Ct. 1456, 43 L.Ed.2d 712 (1975); Marshall v. Jerrico, Inc., 446 U.S. 238, 100 S.Ct. 1610, 64 L.Ed.2d 182 (1980); Friedman v. Rogers, 440 U.S. 1, 99 S.Ct. 887, 59 L.Ed.2d 100 (1979); Hortonville Joint School Dist. No. 1 v. Hortonville Education Ass'n, 426 U.S. 482, 96 S.Ct. 2308, 49 L.Ed.2d 1 (1976), on remand 87 Wis.2d 347, 274 N.W.2d 697 (1979); FTC v. Cement Institute, 333 U.S. 683, 700–03, 68 S.Ct. 793, 92 L.Ed. 1010 (1948), rehearing denied 334 U.S. 839, 68 S.Ct. 1492, 92 L.Ed. 1764 (1948); Gibson v. FTC, 682 F.2d 554, 560 (5th Cir.1982), rehearing denied 688 F.2d 840 (5th Cir.1982); United States v. Litton Industries Inc., 462 F.2d 14, 16–17 (9th Cir.1972); Pangburn v. CAB, 311 F.2d 349, 356 (1st Cir.1962). But see, Gibson v. Berryhill, 411 U.S. 564, 93 S.Ct. 1689, 36 L.Ed.2d 488 (1973); Tumey v. Ohio, 273 U.S. 510, 47 S.Ct. 437, 71 L.Ed. 749 (1927); Ward v. Village of Monroeville, 409 U.S. 57, 93 S.Ct. 80, 34 L.Ed.2d 267 (1972). See also, Commodity Futures Trading Commission v. Schor, 478 U.S. 833, 106 S.Ct. 3245, 92 L.Ed.2d 675 (1986) (dealing with Article III implications of certain combination of functions).

72. See generally Asimow, When the Curtain Falls: Separation of Functions in the Federal Administrative Agencies, 81 Colum.L.Rev. 759 (1981). Pedersen, The Decline of Separation of Functions in Regulatory Agencies, 104 Va.L.Rev. 991 (1978), advocates a return to separation-of-functions practice under certain circumstances.

communication of information, off-the-record, from one involved with prosecution to an adjudicatory decisionmaker. Similarly, decisionmakers who have (or appear to have) prejudged the case before them also evince a kind of bias which can undermine the fairness and legitimacy of the decisionmaking process. The APA explicitly confronts these kinds of issues.

Section 554(d) of the APA mandates a "separation of functions" within the agency itself.[73] It requires that "[a]n employee or agent engaged in the performance of investigative or prosecuting functions for an agency in a case may not, in that or a factually related case, participate or advise in the decision."[74] The APA thus recognizes that while agencies may perform a variety of functions, individual employees may not. This separation-of-function requirement does not cover all agency proceedings;[75] licensing and ratemaking proceedings are specifically exempt from § 554(d).[76] Moreover, courts have generally held § 554(d) inapplicable to informal rulemaking proceedings[77] and to worker certification proceedings.[78]

§ 8.5.5 Structural Bias: Constitutional and APA Requirements

Withrow v. Larkin[79] explored the due process constitutional dimensions of the separation-of-functions requirement and authorizes a much broader combination of functions than does the APA. In *Withrow,* Dr. Larkin alleged that the authority of the Examining Board to investigate physicians, present charges, and rule on those charges and impose punishment violated his due process rights under the Constitution.[80] Justice White wrote the opinion for a unanimous court. The Court recognized that administrative agencies must conduct "fair trials",[81] but noted that "[t]he contention that the combination of investigative and adjudicative functions necessarily creates an unconstitutional risk of

73. See Utica Packing Co. v. Block, 781 F.2d 71, 76 (6th Cir.1986) (clear purpose of § 554(d) is to separate the investigative and prosecutorial functions from the adjudicative function).

74. 5 U.S.C.A. § 554(d).

75. Nor all agency functions. See Shultz v. S.E.C., 614 F.2d 561, 569 (7th Cir.1980) (prosecutor's drafting of SEC response letter dismissing employee was not violation of § 554(d); once decision to dismiss had been taken, drafting of letter was merely "ministerial").

76. 5 U.S.C.A. § 554(d) provides: "This subsection does not apply in determining applications for initial licenses ... [or] to proceedings involving the validity or application of rates."

77. See RSR Corp. v. F.T.C., 656 F.2d 718, 722 (D.C.Cir.1981); United Steelworkers of America, etc. v. Marshall, 647 F.2d 1189, 1213 (D.C.Cir.1980), cert. denied sub nom. Lead Industries Ass'n, Inc. v. Donovan, 453 U.S. 913, 101 S.Ct. 3148, 69 L.Ed.2d 997 (1981); F.T.C. v. Brigadier Industries Corp., 613 F.2d 1110, 1116 (D.C.Cir.1979); Lead Industries Ass'n, Inc. v. OSHA, 610 F.2d 70, 84 (2d Cir.1979).

78. N.L.R.B. v. Eskimo Radiator Mfg. Co., 688 F.2d 1315, 1320 (9th Cir.1982); In re Bel Air Chateau Hospital, Inc., 611 F.2d 1248, 1253 (9th Cir.1979).

79. 421 U.S. 35, 95 S.Ct. 1456, 43 L.Ed.2d 712 (1975), on remand 408 F.Supp. 969 (E.D.Wis.1975).

80. 421 U.S. at 41, 95 S.Ct. at 1461.

81. Id. at 46, 95 S.Ct. at 1464; see also *Utica Packing,* 781 F.2d at 77.

bias''[82] must overcome two important presumptions: (1) that of the honesty and integrity of an adjudicator; and (2) that the mere combination of prosecuting and adjudicating functions in a single agency usually is not enough to trigger a constitutional violation. Due process violations must turn on "a risk of *actual* bias or prejudgment."[83]

Justice White compared administrative processes to criminal processes. He pointed out that judges make a variety of preliminary determinations that are similar to an agency's decision to issue a complaint. For example, they issue arrest and search warrants and they may later preside at trial. The decision whether there is sufficient evidence to hold a defendant for trial may also be made by the trial judge.[84] Moreover, judges who preside over temporary restraining orders and preliminary injunction proceedings are not disqualified from later hearing the merits of the case.[85] Thus, the practice of agencies "to receive the results of investigations, to approve the filing of charges, . . . and then to participate in the ensuing hearings,"[86] does not by itself violate due process of law.[87] The Court was less tolerant, however, if individual bias, rather than structural bias, is evident. For constitutional purposes, courts have held that individual bias is clearly present if the decisionmaker has any monetary interest in the outcome of the case.[88]

Individual bias resulting from combined functions is more closely controlled by the APA. In *Grolier, Inc. v. F.T.C.*,[89] an encyclopedia seller named Grolier challenged the decision of ALJ von Brand as violative of

82. 421 U.S. at 47, 95 S.Ct. at 1464.

83. Id. (emphasis added).

84. Id. at 56, 95 S.Ct. at 1469.

85. Id.

86. Id.

87. See Marshall v. Jerrico, Inc., 446 U.S. 238, 100 S.Ct. 1610, 64 L.Ed.2d 182 (1980) (strict due process requirements do not apply to civil penalties assessed by Department of Labor Employment Standards Administrator, because his determination is akin to that of a prosecutor seeking a penalty, and because the risk of bias due to potential pecuniary benefit to agency is insignificant); Friedman v. Rogers, 440 U.S. 1, 18, 99 S.Ct. 887, 898, 59 L.Ed.2d 100 (1979), rehearing denied 441 U.S. 917, 99 S.Ct. 2018, 60 L.Ed.2d 389 (1979) ("reasonable for legislature to require that a majority of a [regulatory] Board be drawn from a professional organization that had demonstrated consistent support for the rules that the Board would be responsible for enforcing"); Hortonville Joint School Dist. No. 1 v. Hortonville Education Ass'n, 426 U.S. 482, 96 S.Ct. 2308, 49 L.Ed.2d 1 (1976), on remand 87 Wis.2d 347, 274 N.W.2d 697 (1979) (school board could both negotiate with teachers and fire them, after an illegal strike that took place when negotiations broke down); FTC v. Cement Institute, 333 U.S. 683, 68 S.Ct. 793, 92 L.Ed. 1010 (1948) (FTC Commissioners could testify before Congress on a matter they would later adjudicate). See also Air Products & Chemicals, Inc. v. F.E.R.C., 650 F.2d 687, 709–10 (5th Cir.1981); Kennecott Copper Corp. v. F.T.C., 467 F.2d 67 (10th Cir.1972), cert. denied 416 U.S. 909, 94 S.Ct. 1617, 40 L.Ed.2d 114 (1974), rehearing denied 416 U.S. 963, 94 S.Ct. 1983, 40 L.Ed.2d 314 (1974); F.T.C. v. Cinderella Career & Finishing Schools, Inc., 404 F.2d 1308, 1315 (D.C.Cir.1968).

88. See sec. 8.5.6, infra. See Tumey v. Ohio, 273 U.S. 510, 47 S.Ct. 437, 71 L.Ed. 749 (1927) (mayor could not rule on speeding violations where those fines paid his salary); Ward v. Village of Monroeville, 409 U.S. 57, 93 S.Ct. 80, 34 L.Ed.2d 267 (1972) (fines formed a substantial part of municipality's revenues). See also, Gibson v. Berryhill, 411 U.S. 564, 93 S.Ct. 1689, 36 L.Ed.2d 488 (1973) (Court would not allow a licensing board drawn from one-half of a state's optometrists to adjudicate whether other half engaged in unprofessional conduct).

89. 615 F.2d 1215 (9th Cir.1980) (*Grolier I*), appeal after remand 699 F.2d 983 (9th Cir.1983), cert. denied 464 U.S. 891, 104 S.Ct. 235, 78 L.Ed.2d 227 (1983).

§ 554(d).[90] Specifically, Grolier alleged that von Brand, the third ALJ[91] to preside over its unfair competition hearing, was unduly biased as a result of his previous position as attorney-advisor to the F.T.C. Commissioner during the period Grolier was intermittently investigated and charged.[92] The issue presented before the court was whether von Brand's employment as an "attorney-advisor" was an "investigative or prosecutorial function" under the terms of § 556(d).[93]

The Court adopted a broad view of § 554(d). Instead of limiting the provisions of § 554(d) to those individuals with the title of "investigator" or "prosecutor," the Ninth Circuit extended the prohibitions to "all persons who had, in that or a factually related case, been involved with ex parte information, or who had developed, by prior involvement with the case, a 'will to win.' "[94] The Court, however, refused to see von Brand's knowledge of all investigative and prosecutorial activities undertaken during his tenure as attorney-advisor as rendering him unqualified per se to preside at the hearing.[95] Instead, it focused upon actual involvement[96] and held that attorney-advisors are "precluded only from participating in cases in which they have actually performed such ['investigative and prosecuting'] functions, and in factually related cases."[97] The Ninth Circuit then remanded the case for further determination of von Brand's involvement with the *Grolier* case when he was an attorney-advisor.[98]

Another aspect of the *Grolier* case arose in *Gibson v. F.T.C.*[99] In that case, the F.T.C. instituted proceedings against discount merchandisers for alleged unfair trade practices. The ten month agency trial was, ironically, presided over by ALJ von Brand. Relying on the strength of *Grolier I,* Gibson asserted that von Brand's earlier position as attorney-

90. 5 U.S.C.A. § 554(d).

91. The original ALJ to preside over the *Grolier* case retired from federal service before rendering a decision. A second ALJ recused himself. Von Brand took the helm in 1975, two years after the start of the original hearing.

92. This period extended from 1963 to early 1971.

93. 615 F.2d at 1218.

94. Id. at 1220 (emphasis in original); see also *Utica Packing,* 781 F.2d at 76–77.

95. 615 F.2d at 1221.

96. Courts which have considered the question have focused "not upon the former position of the challenged adjudicator but upon his actual involvement, while in that former position, with the case he is now deciding." Id.; see also Au Yi Lau v. I.N.S., 555 F.2d 1036, 1043 (D.C.Cir.1977); Cisternas–Estay v. I.N.S., 531 F.2d 155, 158 (3d Cir.1976) cert. denied 429 U.S. 853, 97 S.Ct. 145, 50 L.Ed.2d 127 (1976); Twigger v. Schultz, 484 F.2d 856, 861 (3d Cir.1973); R.A. Holman & Co. v. S.E.C., 366 F.2d 446, 451–54 (2d Cir.1966), modified 377 F.2d 665 (2d Cir.1967) cert. denied 389 U.S. 991, 88 S.Ct. 473, 19 L.Ed.2d 482 (1967), rehearing denied 389 U.S. 1060, 88 S.Ct. 767, 19 L.Ed.2d 867 (1968); Amos Treat & Co. v. S.E.C., 306 F.2d 260, 265–67 (D.C.Cir. 1962).

97. 615 F.2d at 1221 (quoting *Au Yi Lau,* 555 F.2d at 1043).

98. The Ninth Circuit later concluded that Grolier did not adequately show that von Brand was involved in the *Grolier* investigation in his capacity as attorney-advisor. Grolier, Inc. v. F.T.C., 699 F.2d 983 (9th Cir.1983), cert. denied 464 U.S. 891, 104 S.Ct. 235, 78 L.Ed.2d 227 (1983) (*Grolier II*).

99. 682 F.2d 554 (5th Cir.1982) rehearing denied 688 F.2d 840 (5th Cir.1982), cert. denied 460 U.S. 1068, 103 S.Ct. 1521, 75 L.Ed.2d 945 (1983).

advisor for the F.T.C. violated § 554(d) and necessitated his disqualification.

The Fifth Circuit panel adopted the view of *Grolier I;* however, the Court went on to point out that the Ninth Circuit opinion in no way "foreclose[d] the possibility of waiver, a concept wholly compatible with placing the burden of establishing prior knowledge on the proponent."[100] The same policies which support timely objections and motions to disqualify judges are thus equally applicable to ALJ's.[101]

Turning to the specific facts of the case, the Court found that Gibson expressly waived any objection it might have had with respect to ALJ von Brand.[102] Not only had Gibson indicated it had no objection to von Brand continuing to preside over the case, but it also failed to raise the issue subsequent to the ALJ's decision, whether at oral argument, on appeal, or once *Grolier I* was handed down. In fact, Gibson raised the disqualification issue only after the F.T.C. issued its decision, which had been less favorable to Gibson than had been ALJ von Brand's.[103] Section 554(d) is thus subject to the complimentary concepts of timely objection and waiver.

§ 8.5.6 Personal Bias and Prejudgment

Structural bias can result from a combination of functions within a single agency. While such bias is rarely grounds for the disqualification of an ALJ,[104] the APA recognizes the need for ensuring that personal bias is also not present. It thus requires a high degree of neutrality on the part of the specific decisionmaker involved.[105] Section 556(b) requires that the "functions of presiding or participating" employees be conducted "in an impartial manner."[106] If they are not conducted in such a manner, the decisionmaker may be disqualified. Disqualification can occur either by self-disqualification by the decisionmaker or upon motion of the parties.[107] In the later case, courts adhere to the traditional rules of disqualification. They require that the claim be raised "as soon as practicable after a party has reasonable cause to believe grounds for disqualification exist."[108]

Proving specific allegations of personal bias is seldom an easy task. Over the years, most agencies and their administrators develop certain views of the world as they go about their tasks of formulating and

100. Id. at 563.

101. Id. at 566.

102. Id. at 563.

103. Id.

104. See sec. 8.5.5, supra.

105. 5 U.S.C.A. § 556(b).

106. Id.

107. Id.

108. Duffield v. Charleston Area Medical Center Inc., 503 F.2d 512, 515 (4th Cir.1974); see also Pfister v. Director, 675 F.2d 1314, 1318 (D.C.Cir.1982); Capitol Transportation, Inc. v. United States, 612 F.2d 1312, 1325 (1st Cir.1979); Marcus v. Director, 548 F.2d 1044, 1051–52 (D.C.Cir. 1976); Lloyd A. Fry Roofing Co. v. F.T.C., 371 F.2d 277, 286 (7th Cir.1966); Stieberger v. Heckler, 615 F.Supp. 1315, 1383 (S.D.N.Y.1985). Some decisions recognize that failure to object may be explained by reasonable fear of antagonizing the decisionmaker. E.g., N.L.R.B. v. Washington Dehydrated Food Co., 118 F.2d 980 (9th Cir.1941); Cupples Co. Mfrs. v. N.L.R.B., 106 F.2d 100 (8th Cir.1939).

implementing policies. These views often involve issues of law, policy, or legislative fact and represent the kinds of expertise that support the creation of administrative agencies in the first place.[109] They should not, however, be confused with bias or prejudgment. Indeed, "a complete tabula rasa" with respect to the agency "would be evidence of lack of qualification, not lack of bias."[110] This need for specialization must be weighed against the due process requirement of fairness to the parties, but reviewing courts often have a very difficult time determining when impermissible bias, as opposed to the exercise of expertise, has in fact occurred.

Courts have refused to find bias when decisionmakers have expressed public views of general matters of law and policy.[111] In *F.T.C. v. Cement Institute*,[112] for example, the bias claim centered upon the Federal Trade Commission's release of reports and Congressional testimony condemning the use of a particular pricing system in the cement industry. The Supreme Court held that such actions did not prevent the Commission from issuing complaints against companies using that pricing system. "The fact that the Commission had entertained such views as the result of its prior ex parte investigations did not necessarily mean that the minds of its members were irrevocably closed on the subject."[113] Moreover, had the commissioners been disqualified, no other tribunal would have been empowered to hold hearings on unfair trade practices.[114] An inability to prosecute these practices would clearly defeat the Congressional purposes behind the passage of the Trade Commission Act. As a result, a rule of necessity has been established allowing flexibility

109. Mattes v. United States, 721 F.2d 1125, 1132 (7th Cir.1983) (one of the main reasons for specialized agencies is to provide expert administrators for the enforcement of statutes). See generally, United Steelworkers v. Marshall, 647 F.2d 1189 n. 21, 1213 (D.C.Cir.1980), cert. denied 453 U.S. 913, 101 S.Ct. 3148, 69 L.Ed.2d 997 (1981); Association of National Advertisers, Inc. v. FTC, 627 F.2d 1151 (D.C.Cir.1979), cert. denied 447 U.S. 921, 100 S.Ct. 3011, 65 L.Ed.2d 1113 (1980).

110. Laird v. Tatum, 409 U.S. 824, 835, 93 S.Ct. 7, 14, 34 L.Ed.2d 50 (1972) (memorandum of Justice Rehnquist on motion that he disqualify himself from participation in a case).

111. See generally *Laird v. Tatum*, supra note 355; F.T.C. v. Cement Institute, 333 U.S. 683, 68 S.Ct. 793, 92 L.Ed. 1010 (1948), rehearing denied 334 U.S. 839, 68 S.Ct. 1492, 92 L.Ed. 1764 (1948); Parchman v. U.S. Dept. of Agriculture, 852 F.2d 858, 866 (6th Cir.1988), rehearing denied Sept. 27, 1988. Related is Sierra Club v. Costle, 657 F.2d 298 (D.C.Cir.1981) (off-the-record contacts between the EPA, the President and White House staff not a violation because EPA rulemaking is not a "rarified technocratic process, unaffected by political considerations or the presence of Presidential power." 657 F.2d at 408).

112. 333 U.S. 683, 68 S.Ct. 793, 92 L.Ed. 1010 (1948), rehearing denied 334 U.S. 839, 68 S.Ct. 1492, 92 L.Ed. 1764 (1948).

113. Id. at 701, 68 S.Ct. at 803.

114. Id. See also, United States v. Will, 449 U.S. 200, 212, 101 S.Ct. 471, 479, 66 L.Ed.2d 392 (1980) ("the ancient Rule of Necessity prevails over the disqualification standards"); NLRB v. Baldwin Locomotive Works, 128 F.2d 39, 58 (3d Cir.1942); Brinkley v. Hassig, 83 F.2d 351, 357 (10th Cir.1936).

within the contours of the rule of disqualification.[115] Where disqualification for bias would make an administrative decision impossible, the doctrine of necessity mandates a decision, despite the fact that the decisionmakers may not be wholly impartial.[116]

While ideological commitments are usually insufficient to trigger disqualification, financial or personal commitments produce the opposite result.[117] A decisionmaker must recuse herself "in any case in which she has a substantial interest, has been of counsel, is or has been, a material witness, or is so related to or connected with any party or his attorney as to render it improper"[118] to participate in the case.

Some of the most common and most difficult disqualification questions arise when a litigant claims a decisionmaker has prejudged the issues as a result of prior exposure to the evidence. In *Cinderella Career & Finishing Schools, Inc. v. F.T.C.*,[119] for example, the prejudgment issue centered on a public speech made by the Chairman of the F.T.C., Paul Rand Dixon. The speech included derogatory statements about advertisements that "offer college education in five weeks" and ads that entice people to become an "airline's hostess by attending a charm school."[120] At the time the statements were made, a proceeding by the F.T.C. against Cinderella Career & Finishing Schools (Cinderella) for charges of deceptive trade practices[121] was pending before the Chairman. Despite Cinderella's request that the Chairman recuse himself, Dixon participated in the decision in the case.

115. At least one exception exists to this general rule. In Pillsbury Co. v. F.T.C., 354 F.2d 952 (5th Cir.1966) the court, in principle, disqualified an entire agency on the basis of Congressional interference with its decision process. But the passage of time and changes in personnel diluted the effect of prejudgment and, by the time the case came before the Court, it could remand it to a new Commission for further proceedings. Id. at 965.

116. The doctrine or rule of necessity has been discussed in the context of federal judges sitting on a case involving the reduction of their pay. In United States v. Will, 449 U.S. 200, 101 S.Ct. 471, 66 L.Ed.2d 392 (1980), the Supreme Court concluded that even though each of its members had a financial outcome in the proceedings they must hear the case. The Court quoted approvingly from the Supreme Court of Pennsylvania: "The true rule unquestionably is that wherever it becomes necessary for a judge to sit even where he has an interest—where no provision is made for calling another in, or where no one else can take his place—it is his duty to hear and decide, however disagreeable it may be." 449 U.S. at 213–14, 101 S.Ct. at 480 (quoting Philadelphia v. Fox, 64 Pa. 169, 185 (1870)).

117. See supra sec. 8.5.5. See Tumey v. Ohio, 273 U.S. 510, 47 S.Ct. 437, 71 L.Ed. 749 (1927) (mayor could not rule on speeding violations where those fines paid his salary); Ward v. Village of Monroeville, 409 U.S. 57, 93 S.Ct. 80, 34 L.Ed.2d 267 (1972) (fines formed a substantial part of municipality's revenues). See also, Gibson v. Berryhill, 411 U.S. 564, 93 S.Ct. 1689, 36 L.Ed.2d 488 (1973) (court would not allow a licensing board drawn from one-half of a state's optometrists to adjudicate whether other half engaged in unprofessional conduct).

118. 28 U.S.C.A. § 455.

119. 425 F.2d 583 (D.C.Cir.1970).

120. Id. at 590.

121. F.T.C. alleged that Cinderella advertised "courses of instruction which qualify students to become airline stewardesses" and that its graduates "were qualified to assume executive positions." Id. at 584.

The Court found Dixon's actions to be of "questionable discretion and very poor judgment."[122] It remanded the case to the F.T.C. for reconsideration without the participation of Chairman Dixon and set out a test for disqualification: "whether a disinterested observer may conclude that [the decisionmaker] has in some measure adjudged the facts as well as the law of a particular case in advance of hearing it."[123] This standard takes both actual fairness as well as the appearance of propriety into account. The Court was concerned that a decisionmaker's ability to adjudicate impartially would be impaired by making statements before the public concerning matters presented in litigation.

Rulemaking proceedings, however, involve different considerations. The *Cinderella* test is not applicable. The D.C. Circuit has made it very clear that "[t]he *Cinderella* view of a neutral and detached adjudicator is simply an inapposite role model for administrators who must translate broad statutory commands into concrete social policies."[124] Because of the inherent differences between adjudication and rulemaking,[125] the D.C. Circuit has developed a second standard for disqualification in the rulemaking context. An agency official can be disqualified "only when there has been a clear and convincing showing that he has an unalterably closed mind on matters critical to the disposition of the proceeding."[126]

This higher standard was applied in *United Steelworkers of America, etc. v. Marshall*[127] where a standard for occupational exposure to lead came under attack. The official who set the standard, Assistant Secretary of Labor Eula Bingham, was charged with prejudgment bias on the issue. The Secretary had addressed a United Steelworkers of America conference about the dangers of exposure to lead just five days before the Secretary of Labor signed the final standard but thirty days after Bingham had effectively made her own decision.

The Court of Appeals for the D.C. Circuit held that the health standard should not be vacated. While recognizing the possibility of disqualification of agency officials for prejudgment of issues, Chief Judge Wright found that Bingham's comments did not meet a "clear and convincing" standard of proof. Rather, they merely showed a general predisposition on a matter of policy, "the sort held legally harmless in

122. 425 F.2d at 591.

123. Id. at 590 (quoting Gilligan, Will & Co. v. SEC, 267 F.2d 461, 469 (2d Cir. 1959), cert. denied 361 U.S. 896, 80 S.Ct. 200, 4 L.Ed.2d 152 (1959)).

124. Association of National Advertisers, Inc. v. FTC, 627 F.2d 1151, 1168–1169 (D.C.Cir.1979), cert. denied 447 U.S. 921, 100 S.Ct. 3011, 65 L.Ed.2d 1113 (1980).

125. See chapter 4, supra.

126. *Association of Nat. Advertisers*, 627 F.2d at 1195; see also United Steelworkers of America, etc. v. Marshall, 647 F.2d 1189, 1209 (D.C.Cir.1980), cert. denied sub nom. Lead Industries Ass'n v. Donovan, 453 U.S. 913, 101 S.Ct. 3148, 69 L.Ed.2d 997 (1981).

127. 647 F.2d 1189 (D.C.Cir.1980), cert. denied sub nom. Lead Industries Ass'n v. Donovan, 453 U.S. 913, 101 S.Ct. 3148, 69 L.Ed.2d 997 (1981).

F.T.C. v. Cement Institute."[128] The statements were made *after* Bingham had decided the lead standard and *after* the record had been closed. The Court was unwilling to engage in what it called "judicial mindreading" and construe Bingham's remarks retroactively.[129] It upheld both the validity of the rulemaking proceedings and the standard formulated therein.[130]

128. Id. at 1210.

129. 647 F.2d at 1210.

130. See also, Association of National Advertisers v. FTC, 627 F.2d 1151 (D.C.Cir. 1979), cert. denied 447 U.S. 921, 100 S.Ct. 3011, 65 L.Ed.2d 1113 (1980). See generally, Strauss, Disqualification of Decisional Officials in Rulemaking, 80 Colum.L.Rev. 990 (1980); Gellhorn and Robinson, Rulemaking "Due Process": An Inconclusive Dialogue, 484 U.Chi.L.Rev. 213 (1981). For a discussion of the role of OMB in the rulemaking process, see chapter 15, sec. 15.2, infra.

Chapter 9

INFORMAL AGENCY PROCESSES AND ACTIONS

Table of Sections

§ 9.1 OVERVIEW

Informal agency actions are "the lifeblood of the administrative process."[1] The agency procedures that may accompany them run the gamut from no procedure at all, to little more than notice of a decision and a reason for the agency's action, to procedures that begin to approximate, but not quite duplicate, those set forth in sections 554, 556 and 557 of the APA.

§ 9.1

1. Final Report of the Attorney General's Committee on Administrative Procedure, S.Doc. No. 8, 77th Cong., 1st Sess. 35 (1941). See Gardner, "The Procedures By Which Informal Action is Taken," 24 Admin.L.Rev. 155, 156 (1972). See also, Freedman, Summary Action By Administrative Agencies, 40 U.Chi.L.Rev. 1 (1972) ("More than 90 percent of the work of the federal administrative agencies is done informally, without an adjudicatory hearing.").

By definition, informal agency actions are those that fall outside the rulemaking and adjudicatory provisions of the APA. But even in the context of rulemaking and adjudication, there are a number of informal preliminary decisions, ranging from briefing schedules and hearing dates to settlement negotiations and consent decrees that also constitute informal agency action. In short, informal agency actions comprise the everyday business of an administrative agency's substantive agenda.[2]

The APA speaks directly to a certain kind of informal decisionmaking in Section 555(e), a kind which addresses agency denials "in whole or in part of a written application, petition, or other request of an interested person made in connection with any agency proceedings."[3] With some exceptions,[4] Section 555(e) requires prompt notice "of the denial" and "a brief statement of the grounds for denial."[5] Most informal agency actions, however, are taken without "a written application, petition or other request from an interested person" and thus lie completely outside the specific procedures provided by the APA. This does not mean that all such actions escape judicial review or do not require certain minimal procedures before they are valid. As we shall see, *Citizens to Preserve Overton Park, Inc. v. Volpe*[6] provides for judicial review of agency actions that fall outside of the APA's procedural requirements for rules and orders. Moreover, the due process clause of the fifth and fourteenth amendments may in certain contexts, also require certain minimum procedures.[7] In most cases, an agency's own regulations will govern the procedures used to make certain informal determinations.

This chapter will not repeat the due process analysis of Chapter 7,[8] nor will it examine the scope of judicial review of informal agency actions, discussed in Chapter 13.[9] It will, however, set forth the basic procedural requirements some courts have demanded when agencies take certain informal actions. In so doing, it will examine some reoccurring informal agency decisionmaking contexts that require agency adjudicatory action. These contexts include an agency's grant or denial of individual requests for exceptions to its rules, or declaratory orders

2. Informal agency processes have occasionally come under scholarly scrutiny. Some of these studies look at the process in a general way. See, e.g., K. Davis, Discretionary Justice, A Preliminary Inquiry (1969); Ernest Gellhorn & Ron Levin, Administrative Law And Process In A Nutshell 160–193 (3d ed.1990); Gardner, supra note 1; Freedman, supra note 1; Lockhart, The Origin and Use of Guidelines for the Study of Informal Action in Federal Agencies, 24 Admin.L.Rev. 167 (1972); Sofaer, The Change-of-Status Adjudication: A Case Study of the Informal Agency Process, 1 J. Legal Stud. 349 (1972). Other studies focus on certain aspects of the informal process, such as granting exceptions to rules. See Aman, Administrative Equity: An Analysis of Exceptions to Administrative Rules, 1982 Duke L.J. 277 (1982). Still other approaches look at the informal procedures of a single agency. See, e.g., J. Mashaw, Bureaucratic Justice (1982) (social security cases); Aman, Bargaining For Justice: An Analysis of the Use and Limits of Conditions By The Federal Reserve Board, 74 Iowa L.Rev. 837 (1989).

3. 5 U.S.C.A. § 555(e).

4. 5 U.S.C.A. § 555(e) states: "Except in affirming a prior denial or when the denial is self-explanatory, ... " Id.

5. Id.

6. 401 U.S. 402, 91 S.Ct. 814, 28 L.Ed.2d 136 (1971).

7. See supra chapter 7.

8. Id.

9. See chapter 13, sec. 13.10.3, infra.

regarding the meaning of those rules, when applied to a particular, regulated entity. These requests may also include rulings, no-action letters and other procedural devices by which the regulated seek to shape agency policy to their own circumstances. This treatise refers to these various types of individualized agency actions, particularly exceptions processes, as "Administrative Equity."

Closely related to Administrative Equity is an agency's use of conditions in an attempt to fine tune its regulatory powers to the specific circumstances of the regulated entity before it. This chapter thus examines the use and the limits of an agency's conditioning powers as another informal adjudicatory context. This chapter also examines a third decisionmaking context, one that involves emergencies and an agency's duty to act quickly and, usually, informally.

The second half of this chapter will examine various dispute resolution approaches that provide other, usually less formal alternatives to APA adjudicatory and rulemaking procedures. These include the use of settlement, mediation, minitrials, arbitration and negotiated rulemaking at the agency level.

§ 9.2 INFORMAL AGENCY ACTION

Section 554 of the APA requires formal trial-type procedures "in every case of adjudication required by statute to be determined on the record after opportunity for a hearing. . . . "[1] Though this provision's applicability is limited by the statutory "on the record" requirement, the APA's definition of adjudication is, in fact, extremely broad.[2] It includes all agency actions that are not rulemaking, including, for example, government grants, licensing decisions, contract determinations, and the various kinds of high volume cases associated with programs such as social security or workmen's compensation, welfare or veterans benefits. As discussed in Chapter 7,[3] the due process clause requires that certain minimal procedures be used in many of these contexts. But quite apart from the constitution, courts have also imposed certain procedural requirements for agency decisions that do not easily fit within APA adjudicatory or rulemaking frameworks. The leading cases are *Citizens to Preserve Overton Park, Inc. v. Volpe*[4] and *Camp v. Pitts.*[5]

In *Overton Park,* the agency action at issue was the Secretary of Transportation's decision to release federal highway funds to help finance a state highway in Memphis, Tennessee. This kind of decision was

§ 9.2

1. 5 U.S.C.A. § 554 (1986).

2. 5 U.S.C.A. § 551. This section defines rules and orders. Any action that is not a rule is, by APA definition, an order. Order is thus a residual category in the APA and, because orders usually result from adjudication, informal agency actions often are called informal agency adjudications.

3. See chapter 7, supra. See also, Verkuil, A Study of Informal Adjudication Procedures, 43 U.Chi.L.Rev. 739 (1976).

4. 401 U.S. 402, 91 S.Ct. 814, 28 L.Ed.2d 136 (1971).

5. 411 U.S. 138, 93 S.Ct. 1241, 36 L.Ed.2d 106 (1973).

essentially a desk decision thought at the time to have been fully within the executive's discretion. It was not the kind of agency action normally associated with adjudicatory proceedings, findings of fact and conclusions of law. Yet, the decision was clearly an important one and one that was likely to have an enormous impact on the community involved. The proposed highway would cut through an urban park in Memphis. Petitioners alleged that the Secretary of Transportation had failed to consider seriously alternative highway routes which were more likely to satisfy the environmental requirements of the relevant statutes that applied. In this regard, section 4(f) of the 1966 Department of Transportation Act barred the use of federal funds in environmentally harmful highway projects unless there was no "feasible and prudent alternative."[6] Despite the fact that the highway in question raised significant environmental concerns, the Secretary approved its federal funding without any explanation whatsoever. The statute involved did not require a hearing at this stage of the decisionmaking process and the Secretary's decision was made without the formalities of a record, findings of fact, or conclusions of law. Petitioners nevertheless alleged that the Secretary's action was irreconcilable with the specific requirements and criteria of section 4(f) of the Department of Transportation Act. Because the Secretary provided no reasons for his actions that were contemporaneous with his decision, there was no way to determine how or whether he had concluded that there was no "feasible and prudent alternative" to the route in question.

On review, the Supreme Court first sought to determine precisely what kind of administrative action it was reviewing. It recognized that the action "was plainly not an exercise of a rulemaking function."[7] The APA categorizes administrative actions as either rules or orders, and provides for adjudicatory and rulemaking processes. The action in question must, therefore, have been a kind of adjudication,[8] though not the kind that triggers sections 556 and 557 of the APA. The Court was thus dealing with an informal order or informal adjudication.

The Court rejected arguments that this kind of decision was committed to agency discretion and concluded that there was substantive law to apply.[9] It then determined the applicable standard of judicial review.[10] In so doing, the Court first sought to determine whether the Secretary had acted within the scope of his authority. Because the relevant statute involved required a comparison of alternative highway routes, the Court had to determine not only what the Secretary decided, but how he had come to this decision. Did he consider the relevant statutory factors in making this judgment or, by implication, was he improperly influenced by irrelevant factors such as political pressure?

6. 401 U.S. at 405, 91 S.Ct. at 818 (citing 49 U.S.C.A. § 1653(f)).

7. Id. at 414, 91 S.Ct. at 822.

8. 5 U.S.C.A. § 551(6) defines orders very broadly: "order means the whole or a part of a final disposition ... of an agency in a matter other than rulemaking but including licensing," § 551(7) defines adjudication as "agency process for the formulation of an order[.]"

9. 401 U.S. at 413, 91 S.Ct. at 822.

10. Id. at 415, 91 S.Ct. at 823.

The absence of reasons issued contemporaneous with the Secretary's decision left such questions unanswerable.

The Supreme Court remanded the case to district court, but in so doing it resisted explicitly requiring the Secretary to file contemporaneous findings of fact and conclusions of law.[11] Had the court held that the production of written findings of fact and legal conclusions were required for all informal decisions of this sort, an enormous "bureaucratic delay could have been imposed on the agencies."[12] Instead, the Court assumed that there already existed "an administrative record that allows the full, prompt review of the Secretary's action.... "[13] It thus remanded the case to the District Court for plenary review of the Secretary's decision "on the full administrative record that was before the Secretary at the time he made his decision."[14]

On remand, however, it became clear that no such administrative record actually existed; it had to be assembled by reconstructing the decisionmaking process. This proved to be a long and arduous process. The district court rejected attempts by lawyers to substitute sworn statements and *post hoc* rationalizations for the Secretary's decision and it sought to determine what actually occurred at the time the decision was made. After a 25–day trial that included taking affidavits of the Secretary and testimony of his subordinates, the district court reversed the Secretary's decision and remanded the case to the agency for another determination in accordance with applicable law. The Secretary ultimately concluded that the highway as planned violated the law. He was unable to show that use of the park land was the only prudent and feasible course, especially in light of the broad environmental protection objectives of statutes then in effect. Quite apart from the fact that Court did not actually require findings and reasons "[w]hat starts out by definition to be neither a decision on the administrative record nor an administrative hearing on the record becomes in substance both."[15]

Camp v. Pitts[16] is an important follow-up case to *Overton Park.* It demonstrates that an agency engaged in informal decisionmaking need not overly "judicialize" its processes to survive judicial review, provided it can point to a reason for its action issued contemporaneously with its decision. In *Camp,* the Supreme Court accepted as adequate a very brief statement by the Comptroller of Currency setting forth his reasons for denying a branch bank application. The Comptroller denied the application because there was no need for additional banking services in the particular community. The Court noted that "[u]nlike *Overton Park,* in the present case there was contemporaneous explanation of the agency

11. Id. at 420, 91 S.Ct. at 825.

12. See, e.g., California Legislative Council for Older Americans v. Weinberger, 375 F.Supp. 216 (E.D.Cal.1974).

13. 401 U.S. at 419, 91 S.Ct. at 825.

14. Id. at 420, 91 S.Ct. at 825.

15. Nathanson, Probing the Mind of the Administrator: Hearing Variations and Standards of Judicial Review Under the Administrative Procedure Act and Other Federal Statutes, 75 Colum.L.Rev. 721, 768 (1975).

16. 411 U.S. 138, 93 S.Ct. 1241, 36 L.Ed.2d 106 (1973).

decision. The explanation may have been curt, but it surely indicated the determinative reason for the final action taken: the finding that a new bank was an uneconomic venture. . . . ''[17]

Despite the simplicity of the procedural requirements for judicial review in *Camp,* the Supreme Court's decision in *Overton Park* raised, without conclusively resolving, a number of issues. Foremost among these was precisely what constitutes a record in an administrative proceeding. While sections 556(e) and 557 of the APA define a record for purposes of formal, ''on the record'', APA proceedings,[18] record requirements for informal agency action are less precise and less demanding.[19] At a minimum, Judge (now Justice) Scalia indicated that in informal cases like *Camp,* ''whether the administrator was arbitrary must be determined on the basis of what he had before him when he acted, and not on the basis of 'some new record made initially in the reviewing court'. That 'administrative record' might well include crucial material that was neither shown to nor known by the private parties in the proceeding—as indeed appears to have been the situation in *Camp* itself.''[20]

When the contemporaneous findings available to the Administrator are not as readily apparent as they were in *Camp,* the Court must try to recreate the record actually before the agency. This, of necessity, rules out the use of *post hoc* litigation affidavits. Such a record can be recreated either by (1) requiring agency officials to testify personally as to the underlying basis of their opinion at the time they made the decision, or (2) remanding the case for a reconstruction of the administrative record based on actual memoranda and other documents actually before the administrator at the time of decision; or (3) a combination of these two techniques. To avoid the lengthy litigation such cases can engender, the *Camp v. Pitts* approach is the model to follow. If administrative findings issued contemporaneously with the decision exist, the usual deference accorded most agency decisions will apply.[21]

17. Id. at 143, 93 S.Ct. at 1244.

18. These provisions require the exclusive record be comprised of transcripts, exhibits, papers filed in the proceeding, formal rulings and decisions that follow a stated format and records of any forbidden ex parte communications. See 5 U.S.C.A. §§ 556(e) and 557.

19. For a discussion of what constitutes a record in informal rulemaking proceedings, see Pedersen, Formal Records and Informal Rulemaking, 85 Yale L.J. 38 (1975).

20. Association of Data Processing Service Organizations, Inc. v. Board of Governors, 745 F.2d 677, 684 (D.C.Cir.1984).

Though this approach to the exclusivity of the record was, in effect, affirmed in Vermont Yankee Nuclear Power Corp. v. Natural Resources Defense Council, Inc., 435 U.S. 519, 98 S.Ct. 1197, 55 L.Ed.2d 460 (1978), there are many exceptions made in an informal rulemaking context. See Stark and Wald, Setting No Records: The Failed Attempts to Limit the Record in Review of Administrative Action, 36 Admin.L.Rev. 373, 373–74 (1984) (authors list 8 exceptions to exclusivity of record rule and note that ''[A]n examination of these exceptions reveals that they are now so far-reaching that they can be applied in almost any case.'').

21. See Butz v. Glover Livestock Commission Co., 411 U.S. 182, 185–86, 93 S.Ct. 1455, 1458–59, 36 L.Ed.2d 142 (1973), rehearing denied 412 U.S. 933, 93 S.Ct. 2746, 37 L.Ed.2d 162 (1973). This, of course, does not mean that all such findings or reasons will satisfy a reviewing court. See, e.g., Independent U.S. Tanker Owners Committee

§ 9.3 INFORMAL AGENCY ACTION AND THE APA—SECTION 555(E)

The APA is not completely silent when it comes to procedures applicable to some forms of informal agency action. Section 555(e) states that "[p]rompt notice shall be given of the denial in whole or in part of a written application, petition, or other request of an interested person made in connection with any agency proceedings. Except in affirming a prior denial or when the denial is self-explanatory, the notice shall be accompanied by a brief statement of the grounds for denial." The underlying purposes of this section are to ensure the overall fairness of agency proceedings[1] and to provide a basis for judicial review.[2] Closely related to the promotion of fairness is the belief that a statement of reasons promotes better decisionmaking.[3] Other purposes behind the section are to "keep the administrative agency within proper authority and discretion, avoid or prevent arbitrary, discriminatory, and irrational action by the agency, and inform the aggrieved person of the grounds of the administrative action so he can plan his course of action (including the seeking of judicial review)."[4]

But as Professor Davis has noted: "Opinions requiring findings and reasons . . . almost never mention 555(e) even when it is clearly applicable . . . [T]he decisions are the same whether or not the APA applies. No significant difference is discernible among the circuits."[5] The Attorney General's Manual itself states that section 555(e) "has no application to matters which do not relate to rule making, adjudication or licensing. Generally it is not applicable to the mass of administrative routine unrelated to those proceedings."[6] Thus, courts have avoided extensive

v. Lewis, 690 F.2d 908 (D.C.Cir.1982) (court overturned agency decision, noting *inter alia* that "where an agency's analytic task *begins* rather than ends with a set of forecasts, sound practice would seem to dictate disclosure of those forecasts so that interested parties can comment upon the conclusions properly to be drawn from them." Id. at 926) (emphasis in original).

§ 9.3

1. See, e.g., Roelofs v. Secretary of Air Force, 628 F.2d 594 (D.C.Cir.1980); Mower v. Britton, 504 F.2d 396 (10th Cir.1974); Childs v. U.S. Board of Parole, 511 F.2d 1270 (D.C.Cir.1974).

2. See, e.g., City of Gillette, Wyo. v. FERC, 737 F.2d 883 (10th Cir.1984); Fraga By and Through Fraga v. Smith, 607 F.Supp. 517 (D.Or.1985); George Transfer & Rigging Co. v. United States, 380 F.Supp. 179 (D.Md.1974), affirmed 419 U.S. 1042, 95 S.Ct. 613, 42 L.Ed.2d 636 (1974).

3. Dunlop v. Bachowski, 421 U.S. 560, 95 S.Ct. 1851, 44 L.Ed.2d 377 (1975) ("compels [the Secretary] to cover the relevant point and eschew irrelevancies, and . . . the need to assure careful administrative consideration 'would be relevant even if the Secretary's decision were unreviewable.' "Id. at 572, 95 S.Ct. at 1860) (citation omitted).

4. Matlovich v. Secretary of Air Force, 591 F.2d 852, 857 (D.C.Cir.1978). See also Dunlop v. Bachowski, 421 U.S. 560, 95 S.Ct. 1851, 44 L.Ed.2d 377 (1975), for a broad discussion of why reasons are necessary under the Labor–Management Reporting and Disclosure Act for failure to pursue irregularities in a union election.

5. 3 Kenneth Culp Davis, Administrative Law Treatise § 14.24, at 114 (2d ed. 1980). See also Walter Gellhorn & Clark Byse et al., Administrative Law 474 (8th ed. 1987). (5 U.S.C.A. § 555(e) has had little actual impact).

6. Attorney General's Manual On the Administrative Procedure Act at 70 (1947).

use of this provision, though they often employ the basic reasoning behind it.[7]

On occasion, though, courts do explicitly rely on section 555(e). In *Roelofs v. Secretary of the Air Force,*[8] a serviceman challenged the validity of an Air Force regulation authorizing the Air Force to discharge servicemen convicted by civilian authorities of certain kinds of offenses. These offenses included crimes resulting in prison terms greater than one year. The regulation in contention required that servicemen convicted of such crimes receive a less than honorable discharge.

Thomas Roelofs pleaded guilty to a charge of heroin possession and was sentenced to eighteen months in prison. The trial judge stayed execution of this sentence until Roelofs completed his remaining months of his military service. The Air Force, however, initiated a discharge proceeding against him and issued an undesirable discharge. Roelofs applied to the Air Force Discharge Review Board to upgrade his discharge to honorable. The review board responded by upgrading him to a general but not an honorable discharge. It gave no reasons for its decision, and Roelofs' appeal to the Air Force Board for Corrections was denied, again without any stated reasons. He then sought judicial review.

The Court held that § 555(e) required a statement of reasons to accompany the denial of a serviceman's request for an Honorable Discharge.[9] Section 555(e)'s exception for "self-explanatory" denials was inapplicable to this case.[10] No explanation whatsoever had been provided and, in the Court's view, the decision to upgrade from a dishonorable to a general, but not to an honorable discharge was not at all "self-explanatory."[11] The Court noted that the relevance of § 555 is not limited to cases where a specific statutory prescription exists, and "[t]he requirement of 'a brief statement of the grounds for denial' obtains even though the request pertains to a matter of discretion or grace, not one of entitlement."[12] The court described section 555(e) as a modest require-

7. See, e.g., French's Estate v. FERC, 603 F.2d 1158 (5th Cir.1979).

8. 628 F.2d 594 (D.C.Cir.1980).

9. Id. at 595.

10. There also are two statutory exceptions to 555(e)'s requirement of a statement of grounds: if the denial is an affirmation of a prior denial, or the denial is self-explanatory. George Transfer & Rigging Co. v. United States, 380 F.Supp. 179 (D.Md. 1974), affirmed 419 U.S. 1042, 95 S.Ct. 613, 42 L.Ed.2d 636 (1974); Northeast Broadcasting, Inc. v. FCC, 400 F.2d 749 (D.C.Cir. 1968). But note that "prior denial would satisfy this requirement only where the grounds previously stated remain the actual grounds and sufficiently notify the party." See Sen. Committee Report, S.Doc.No. 248, 79th Cong., 2d Sess. 265–68 (1946) cited in *Roelofs,* 628 F.2d at 600 n. 33; Memphis Light, Gas & Water Div. v. FPC, 243 F.2d 628 (D.C.Cir.1957); Plumbers Local Union No. 519 v. Construction Industry Stabilization Committee, 479 F.2d 1052 (1973).

But cf. *Roelofs,* 628 F.2d at 600–01; NRDC v. SEC, 389 F.Supp. 689 (D.D.C. 1974), later appealed 432 F.Supp. 1190 (1977), reversed 606 F.2d 1031 (D.C.Cir. 1979).

11. 628 F.2d at 601.

12. Id. at 600 (footnote omitted). Prior to a 1976 statutory requirement that denials of parolee parole include reasons. Applications for parole were subject to the requirements of 555(e). See King v. United States, 492 F.2d 1337 (7th Cir.1974). But cf. Beltone Electronics Corp. v. FTC, 402 F.Supp. 590 (N.D.Ill.1975) (implies that certain degree of formality in proceeding required to apply 555(e)); Reed v. United States, 388 F.Supp. 725 (D.Kan.1975) (written reasons for denial of parole required only upon written request).

ment that probably does not add to, and may even diminish, the burden on the agency imposed by the APA's provision for judicial review. As the court noted, section 706 of the APA authorizes any aggrieved person to bring a lawsuit if the denial of the relief was arbitrary and capricious agency action.[13]

It would be a rare case indeed in which the plaintiff could not make a plausible enough contention to require the government to state the reasons for its action. When the reasons have not been asserted by the agency at the time the action is taken, there is a prospect of further proceedings to develop those reasons. The burden is lessened if the agency provides at least some statement of reasons at the time it takes its action.[14]

As the above quote implies, even though Section 555(e) does not require a statement of reasons for every agency denial of a request within its power to grant, practicality and efficiency suggest that it is very much in the agency's best interest to provide reasons.

Courts have held that the statement of grounds for denial of a petition must be specific[15] and that it must contain both conclusions that respond to the evidence presented and reasons for those conclusions.[16] Courts have also held, however, that the statement need not be exhaustive and that general reasons for denial often are sufficient.[17] Courts that find the statement of reasons insufficient will require the agency to provide an adequate statement, or, especially if it appears that the agency's decision was an arbitrary and capricious one, courts may also require a new hearing.[18]

§ 9.4 OTHER INFORMAL AGENCY ACTIONS AND PROCESSES

It is impossible to categorize all informal agency actions and the various contexts in which they occur, but some types of informal agency actions occur in many, if not most, agencies and some generalizations may be in order. Many agencies, for example, have processes for considering requests for exceptions, waivers, and exemptions to, or interpretations, clarifications or modifications of existing agency rules. These requests represent attempts by individual applicants to have an agency review their own, peculiar, individual circumstances. They are, therefore, adjudicatory proceedings and they seek either relief from the application

13. 628 F.2d at 601.

14. Id.

15. Trailways of New England, Inc. v. CAB, 412 F.2d 926 (1st Cir.1969).

16. Meadville Master Antenna, Inc. v. FCC, 443 F.2d 282 (3d Cir.1971), petition for review denied 535 F.2d 214 (1976).

17. Gardner v. FCC, 530 F.2d 1086 (D.C.Cir.1976); French's Estate v. FERC, 603 F.2d 1158 (5th Cir.1979).

18. See Bowman v. U.S. Bd. of Parole, 411 F.Supp. 329 (W.D.Wis.1976) (denial of parole requires statement sufficient to show decision not arbitrary); Natural Resources Defense Council v. SEC, 389 F.Supp. 689 (D.D.C.1974), appeal after remand 432 F.Supp. 1190 (1977), reversed 606 F.2d 1031 (D.C.Cir.1979) (reversing District Court's determination that SEC was "arbitrary and capricious" in refusing to order corporate disclosure of factors claimed to be of importance to the "ethical investor").

of a general rule to their own peculiar factual situations or in the alternative, a declaration of just what their rights and duties under the law may be. These kinds of requests, especially those dealing with exceptions and waivers, generate case law that constitutes what might be called "Administrative Equity", complete with its own set of general, but substantive, maxims and procedural requirements.[1]

Closely related to the issues of how the regulated seek to shape the law to their own peculiar circumstances, are attempts by agencies to tailor their regulatory powers to the specific applicant before them. To do this, agencies often issue conditional orders or seek voluntary consent from the party before it to assure that certain of its specific regulatory goals are carried out. Conditions and voluntary commitments can, therefore, be important regulatory tools for many agencies, particularly those engaged in the administration of regulatory programs whose success depends on an agency's ability informally to tailor its regulatory demands to fit the peculiar facts of the party before it.[2] These conditions and commitments are usually imposed or agreed upon after an informal process that occurs before any of the more formal adversarial processes apply.

In addition, there are also a number of agencies that must act quickly to, for example, seize or recall dangerous goods or suspend temporarily the licenses of entities at risk of significantly harming individuals or environment.[3] Informal action is often synonymous with summary actions or emergency procedures. This chapter will now examine these various informal decisionmaking contexts.

§ 9.4.1 Administrative Equity

Administrative equity serves as a bridge between general, collectively determined rules and the reality of the particular case.[4] It refers to a body of substantive principles and norms that, on occasion, may justify the granting of individual exceptions, exemptions or waivers to rules that generally apply to others. Administrative equity is most often

§ 9.4

1. See Aman, Administrative Equity: An Analysis of Exceptions To Administrative Rules, 1982 Duke L.J. 277 (1982) [hereinafter Aman, Administrative Equity].

2. See Aman, Bargaining For Justice: An Examination of The Use and Limits of Conditions By The Federal Reserve Board, 74 Iowa L.Rev. 837 (1989) [hereinafter Aman, Bargaining For Justice].

3. See, e.g., Freedman, Summary Action By Administrative Agencies, 40 U.Chi. L.Rev. 1 (1972).

4. This section draws heavily on Aman, Administrative Equity, supra note 49. For other articles dealing with these issues see also Schuck, When The Exception Becomes The Rule: Regulatory Equity And The Formulation Of Energy Policy Through An Exceptions Process, 1984 Duke L.J. 163 (1984); Note, Regulatory Values and the Exceptions Process, 93 Yale L.J. 938 (1984); Leventhal, Principled Fairness and Regulatory Urgency, 25 Case W.Res. L.Rev. 66 (1974); Comment, The Exceptions Process: The Administrative Counterpart To A Court Of Equity And The Dangers It Presents to the Rulemaking Process, 30 Emory L.J. 1135 (1981). For a recent article that applies the principles of administrative equity to certain programs at EPA, see Dennis D. Hirsch, Bill and Al's Xl–Ent Adventure: An Analysis of the EPA's Legal Authority to Implement the Clinton Administration's Project Xl, 1998 U. Ill. L. Rev. 129.

concerned with the impact of a regulatory scheme on those who must bear the brunt of its costs. It is usually the regulated, not the beneficiaries of the regulation, who seek exceptions or modifications to agency rules.[5] The principles used by regulators to grant or deny these requests constitute the substance of administrative equity. They allow the administrator "to rectify the shortcoming ... of the lawgiver due to the generality of his statement."[6]

Administrative equity takes many forms. For example, the Department of Energy Act confers on the Secretary specific power to make adjustments to rules of general applicability.[7] Adjustments include exceptions, exemptions, modifications, rescissions, and interpretations. Similarly, other agencies provide opportunities for modifications[8] and waivers,[9] no-action letters,[10] variances[11] or rulings.[12] All of these various adjustments provide a mechanism for relief from general rules for individual applicants. They fall into two broad categories: those that resemble declaratory orders and those that resemble injunctions.

Some adjustments are closely akin to declaratory orders or advisory opinions.[13] Rulings or interpretations, for example, usually involve requests to determine whether a particular regulation actually applies to certain facts and, if so, with what result. Such determinations, made before any agency action has been taken, apply only to the petitioner. They generally predate any actual dispute between the agency and a party, are rendered by agency staff and are not subject to judicial review.[14] Similarly, rescissions and modifications usually apply only to particular orders and particular petitioners. Exceptions to rules, as well as waivers, variances, and the like are more like injunctions. The petitioner does not seek a clarification of the application of a rule; he seeks an order indicating that the rule does not, in fact, apply to him at all. This kind of adjustment enjoins the application of the rule to the petitioner.[15]

5. This need not always be the case. See Aman, Administrative Equity, supra note 49 at 280.

6. Id. at 281, citing Aristotle, Nicomachean Ethics, Book 5, at 142 (M. Ostwald trans. 1962).

7. 42 U.S.C.A. § 7174(a) (Supp. III 1979).

8. See, e.g., 47 U.S.C.A. §§ 203(b)(2), 316(a) (1976) (modification).

9. 47 C.F.R. § 1.3 (1989) (waiver procedure) (FCC).

10. See, e.g., Fed.Sec.L.Rep. (CCH) § 76,001.

11. See, e.g., 29 U.S.C.A. § 665 (1976).

12. Fed.Taxes (P–11) § 26,708.

13. The APA specifically authorizes the issuance of declaratory orders in the context of formal adjudicatory cases in 5 U.S.C.A. § 554(e). See generally, Powell, Sinners, Supplicants and Samaritans: Agency Advice Giving in Relation to Section 554(e) of the Administrative Procedure Act, 63 N.C.L.Rev. 339, 366 (1985).

14. See Kixmiller v. SEC, 492 F.2d 641, 643–44 (D.C.Cir.1974) ("[W]e think members of the Commission's staff ... have no authority to make orders.... "). For an analysis of the advice-giving role of administrative agencies, see Powell, supra note 61.

15. There are, in fact, three broad categories of exceptions: hardship exceptions, fairness exceptions and policy exceptions. See Aman, Administrative Equity, supra note 49 at 293–323.

These kinds of agency actions usually are authorized by statute. Some statutes authorize the agency to grant only exceptions to rules.[16] Others authorize a wide variety of modifications.[17] Apart from statutory authorization, an agency's own rules or policy statements often provide authority for similar exceptions.[18]

These statutes or agency rules usually set forth criteria for granting or denying relief. Some statutes contain broad criteria, giving the administrator enormous discretion in applying the standards. For example, the Department of Energy Organization Act authorizes the Secretary to grant adjustments if there is "special hardship, inequity or unfair distribution of burdens."[19] Other acts are more specific in their criteria. The Occupational Safety and Health Act, for example, provides that the Secretary of Labor may grant adjustments to allow "reasonable variances, tolerances, and exemptions ... as he may find necessary and proper to avoid serious impairment of the national defense."[20]

Quite apart from an agency's own enabling act or rules, some courts have suggested that the authority to grant exceptions to rules may be implied as well.[21] Courts have failed, however, to explain explicitly the basis of this authority and whether it is statutory or constitutional.

16. See, e.g., Natural Gas Policy Act of 1978, 15 U.S.C.A. § 3412(c) (1988). See generally, R. Noland & W. Penniman, The FERC Adjustments Process Under Section 502(c) of the Natural Gas Policy Act of 1978, 1 Energy L.J. 79 (1980).

17. See, e.g., National Traffic and Motor Vehicle Safety Act of 1966, as amended, 15 U.S.C.A. §§ 1410, 1417 (1988); Federal Mine Safety and Health Act of 1977, 30 U.S.C.A. §§ 811(c), 811(e), 814(g) (1988); Water Pollution Control Act Amendments of 1972, 33 U.S.C.A. § 1342 (1988); Safe Drinking Water Act, 42 U.S.C.A. § 300g–4 (1982); Nuclear Non–Proliferation Act of 1978, 42 U.S.C.A. § 2155a (1982); Clean Air Act, 42 U.S.C.A. § 7410 (1982); Shipping Act of 1916, 46 U.S.C.A. §§ 814, 833a (1982); Communications Act of 1934, 47 U.S.C.A. §§ 203(b)(2), 214(a) (1982) (common carriers), 47 U.S.C.A. §§ 316, 359 (1982) (radio); Federal Aviation Act of 1958, 49 U.S.C.A. §§ 1386(b)(1), 1432(c) (1976).

18. See, e.g., F.P.C. Order No. 467, discussed in Pacific Gas & Elec. Co. v. FPC, 506 F.2d 33 (D.C.Cir.1974).

19. 42 U.S.C.A. § 7194(a) (1982).

20. 29 U.S.C.A. § 665 (1988).

21. See, e.g., Chemical Manufacturers Association v. Natural Resources Defense Council, Inc., 470 U.S. 116, 105 S.Ct. 1102, 84 L.Ed.2d 90 (1985) (upholding the EPA's creation of fundamentally different factor (FDF) variances with respect to toxic pollutants in the face of statutory language prohibiting the modification of standards for toxic pollutants); WAIT Radio v. FCC, 418 F.2d 1153, 1157 (D.C.Cir.1969), later appealed 459 F.2d 1203 (1972), cert. denied 409 U.S. 1027, 93 S.Ct. 461, 34 L.Ed.2d 321 (1972) (ordering the FCC to entertain requests for waivers from its "clear channel" rules, noting that "a system where regulations are maintained inflexibly without any procedure for waiver poses legal difficulties"). See also, Heckler v. Campbell, 461 U.S. 458, 103 S.Ct. 1952, 76 L.Ed.2d 66 (1983) (upholding Social Security Administration regulations establishing a "grid" of categories for considering disability appeals, but noting that an administrative law-judge will not apply the rules contained is the guidelines when they fail to describe a claimant's particular limitations. Id. at 462 n. 5 and 468 n. 11, 103 S.Ct. at 1955 n. 5 and 1958 n. 11).

But see, Air Line Pilots Ass'n Intern. v. Quesada, 276 F.2d 892, 896 (2d Cir.1960) (upholding FAA's refusal to grant any exceptions to its rule that all pilots reaching the age of 60 must retire); see also, Starr v. FAA, 589 F.2d 307 (7th Cir.1978); Rombough v. FAA, 594 F.2d 893 (2d Cir.1979) Gray v. FAA, 594 F.2d 793 (10th Cir.1979) See generally, Comment, Mandatory Retirement of Airline Pilots: An Analysis of the FAA's Age 60 Retirement Rule, 33 Hastings L.J. 241 (1981).

§ 9.4.2 Administrative Equity, Declaratory Procedures and Judicial Review

Agencies provide for equitable adjustments and rulings with varying degrees of informality. At one end of the spectrum, an agency may interpret its rules and orders over the telephone. A private party may simply speak with agency staff and receive an interpretation of agency law. Questions arise, however, when parties rely on this advice to their detriment. Can the agency change an interpretation once it has given this advice? What if the advice relied upon was wrong? Can a party seek judicial review of such interpretation? Usually an agency is not bound by the advice of its staff[22] and such advice is not judicially reviewable.[23] The application of estoppel principles to agency advice depends to a large degree on the extent of the reliance by and the potential harm to the public.[24] Many agencies, however, agree to be bound by the informal advice,[25] and, as a practical matter, informal staff rulings are illustrative of what the agency itself is likely to do.

The APA provides that an agency "may issue a declaratory order to terminate a controversy or remove uncertainty" and that such orders are to have binding effect on the agency and the party involved.[25] Such declaratory orders qualify as final agency action and are reviewable in federal court. Because such declaratory orders are produced only in the context of formal adjudicatory hearings, they are rare.[26]

The usual situation is somewhat analogous to that of a federal litigant who seeks to challenge a law that has not, as yet, been applied to him. Article III requires that there be a real "case or controversy."[27] Because most agency declaratory advice is informal, such litigants usually lack the requisite standing, and the case is not ripe for judicial review. A litigant that disagrees with an agency's advice or interpretation can most clearly obtain review by ignoring the advice and defending its own interpretation of the law in an enforcement proceeding. In other contexts, the courts may be willing to step in without requiring the party to risk civil or criminal penalties: for example, courts have concluded in some cases that certain no-action letters issued by the SEC were sufficiently final to justify judicial review.[28]

22. See Wilmington Chemical Corp. v. Celebrezze, 229 F.Supp. 168 (N.D.Ill.1964).

23. See authorities cited in note 61, supra.

24. See, e.g., Federal Crop Ins. Corp. v. Merrill, 332 U.S. 380, 68 S.Ct. 1, 92 L.Ed. 10 (1947); but see, Moser v. United States, 341 U.S. 41, 71 S.Ct. 553, 95 L.Ed. 729 (1951). See generally Ernest Gellhorn & Ron Levin, Administrative Law and Process in a Nutshell 183–190 (3d ed. 1990).

25. See, e.g., 16 C.F.R. §§ 1.1, 1.3 (1990) (Federal Trade Commission); 26 C.F.R. §§ 602.201(a), 601.201(d) (1990) (Internal Revenue Service).

25. 5 U.S.C.A. § 554(e) (1988). See Gellhorn & Levin, supra note 72, at 184.

26. For a detailed treatment of this section of the APA, see Powell, supra note 61.

27. See, e.g., Younger v. Harris, 401 U.S. 37, 91 S.Ct. 746, 27 L.Ed.2d 669 (1971); Samuels v. Mackell, 401 U.S. 66, 91 S.Ct. 764, 27 L.Ed.2d 688 (1971); Perez v. Ledesma, 401 U.S. 82, 91 S.Ct. 674, 27 L.Ed.2d 701 (1971). For agency declaratory orders, see Helco Prods. Co. v. McNutt, 137 F.2d 681 (D.C.Cir.1943).

28. See Medical Committee for Human Rights v. SEC, 432 F.2d 659 (D.C.Cir.1970) vacated 404 U.S. 403, 92 S.Ct. 577, 30 L.Ed.2d 560 (1972); but see, Kixmiller v. SEC, 492 F.2d 641 (D.C.Cir.1974).

Since petitioners formally request the agency to waive the application of an otherwise applicable rule, exceptions or waivers usually result in more elaborate procedures. Usually the petitioner files an application, and interested competitors often intervene. The denial or grant of relief is usually treated as a final order. Exceptions requests usually focus on the particular needs of the applicants and the peculiar, distinct, and adverse manner in which it is claimed a rule affects those needs. Such exceptions requests are necessarily adjudicatory in nature. Informal adjudicatory procedures are appropriate for such matters, but agency processes vary in this regard.[29] Some statutes authorizing equitable relief may themselves trigger the APA's formal adjudicatory procedure.[30]

§ 9.4.3 Other Informal Agency Actions—Conditions and Commitments

Requests for exceptions, waivers and other adjustments are initiated by the regulated. Such requests may result in clarification of existing law or, in the case of exceptions and waivers, exemption from certain rules altogether. They usually turn on the peculiar circumstances of the petitioner involved. Agencies also can take the peculiar facts of an applicant into account by tailoring their regulatory powers to that entity. Indeed, somewhat akin to exceptions are conditional orders or an applicant's advance voluntary consent to certain agency requirements. While exceptions and waivers often result in less regulation for the regulated entities who seek them, conditions and commitments usually represent a form of more specific, individual regulatory requirements. In both instances, regulation is shaped largely by the individual needs of the particular regulated entity with which the agency deals.

Agencies usually exercise power to condition their orders on certain actions in response to an application for a license, merger authorization, or some other kind of regulatory permission. In this sense, the agency has something the applicant wants and a regulatory bargaining context potentially may be established.[31] The procedural and substantive issues in these various application contexts vary, but individualized petitions that seek permission to engage in certain activity, such as building and operating a nuclear power plant or merging with or acquiring a bank as part of a bank holding company enable the agency involved to condition its grant of authority. It can, in effect, say "yes, but" and then provide certain regulatory requirements, often quite specific to the factual cir-

29. For a detailed examination of the Department of Energy Exceptions Process, see Schuck, supra note 52.

30. See, e.g., Seacoast Anti–Pollution League v. Costle, 572 F.2d 872 (1st Cir. 1978), cert. denied 439 U.S. 824, 99 S.Ct. 94, 58 L.Ed.2d 117 (1978). This case is discussed in chapter 8, sec. 8.2.2, supra.

31. For an analysis of agency conditions, see Aman, Bargaining For Justice, supra note 50. This section draws heavily on this article. See also, Tomlinson & Mashaw, "The Enforcement Of Federal Standards In Grant–In–Aid Programs: Suggestions For Beneficiary Involvement," 58 Va. L.Rev. 600 (1972). Most application processes are initially informal, though an ultimate denial of the benefits sought in some programs may later result in more formal adjudication. See, e.g., Mathews v. Eldridge, 424 U.S. 319, 96 S.Ct. 893, 47 L.Ed.2d 18 (1976).

cumstances of the applicant involved. Conditional orders can thus be important regulatory tools in certain kinds of programs.

Conditions are particularly common in application proceedings, such as those carried out pursuant to the Bank Holding Company Act.[32] Because the nature of the application process is informal, a great deal of negotiation occurs between the staff of the Federal Reserve Board (Board) and the applicants seeking Bank Holding Company status or the acquisition of a bank or nonbank. Orders are not so much decreed as they are negotiated and, in that process, conditions are often attached by the Board before an applicant's request is granted.[33]

The various substantive contexts in which an agency issues a conditional order or agrees to grant certain authority in light of an applicant's voluntary commitment to carry out or abstain from carrying out certain activities raise a number of issues. In general, these include questions of law, policy and fact. Working at this level of generality, at least five types of agency conditions or commitments are possible.[34] A perfect condition is one that is based on clear law, clear agency policy and is narrowly tailored to the facts of a particular applicant before the agency. This kind of condition allows the agency to tailor its regulatory demands to fit the precise situation of the applicant before it. Such a condition, being so narrow and fact-specific, is unlikely to have any precedential value. It allows the applicant to obtain approval of its proposed action in a manner that ensures the agency's regulatory duties and goals are fully carried out. The informal give and take between agency staff and private counsel constitute the only procedure available in most cases involving this kind of informal agency action.

A second kind of condition can be called a policy condition. Such a condition is fact-specific and within the agency's legal authority, but it may implicate policies not yet fully articulated by the agency. Such a condition can raise procedural issues similar to those involved in determining whether an agency should use adjudication or rulemaking when formulating policy.[35] But policy making at so early a stage in the agency's proceedings, however, raises its own difficulties. The bargaining process usually consists of a discussion between a staff member of the agency and private counsel. By voluntarily agreeing to a condition, the applicant knows that it can expedite its petition, but such a condition or voluntary commitment often is treated as essentially a *fait accompli* by the agency that reviews the order. Policy made in this manner, especially significant policy, does not begin to receive the kind of public scrutiny applied to the results of rulemaking proceedings. When the case proceeds to consider-

32. 12 U.S.C.A. § 1842 (1988). See Aman, Bargaining For Justice, supra note 50.

33. For the most part, conditions are authorized by the Bank Holding Company Act. See, e.g., Pauline B. Heller, Federal Bank Holding Company Law § 7.08, at 7–63 n. 10 (1992).

34. For examples of these five types of conditions and an analysis of their substantive and procedural significance, see Aman, Bargaining For Justice, supra note 50, at 891–892.

35. See chapter 4, sec. 4, supra.

ation by the full commission or board, there may not have been a full policy review. Given the voluntary nature of the commitment it is not likely that courts will review this aspect of the order. Thus, the policy involved receives even less outside scrutiny than if it had been developed in an adjudication. This kind of ad hoc approach to policymaking is thus relatively invisible and not necessarily consistent or well thought out. Conditions with significant policy implications are, thus, not appropriate for the very informal processes of negotiation that occur in such contexts.

An even more controversial third kind of condition is one in which the parties agree to take or forego certain actions over which the agency's actual regulatory authority is uncertain. An applicant eager to close a deal or avoid protracted litigation may be willing to agree to such a condition, thus allowing the agency to extend its regulatory jurisdiction informally and in a manner that also is effectively immune from judicial review. A fourth type of agency condition is one that does not relate to the specific facts in the petition of the applicant. Such a condition is wholly prospective in nature and designed to prevent future action that may or may not be contemplated by the applicant. This kind of regulation may avoid future litigation, but it can be particularly coercive when demanded of an applicant whose own factual situation does not necessarily raise or justify the restriction. Finally, a fifth type of condition or commitment is the null condition, one that is clearly beyond the authority of the Commission to impose, and thus not grounded in any known or articulated policy, and that is not even fact-specific to the applicant involved.

These types of conditions have both legal and policy effects. Since most of them are negotiated informally, they create law in an entirely informal manner. They usually come out of the bargaining phase of the administrative process and, as such, are not subject to the kinds of procedural checks found in more adversarial phases of the process. Given the often voluntary nature of the agreement between applicants and agency staff, neither the policy implications nor the respective merits of these conditions are likely to be reviewed either by the full commission granting the applications or a court reviewing the process.

Nevertheless, attaching conditions to orders is an effective regulatory device. Conditions not only allow an application to proceed, but do so in a manner that is legally sound. Overuse of conditions, however, particularly those that are not fact-specific and grounded on reasonably clear agency authority and policy, can raise fairness concerns. Applicants seeking governmental benefits are seldom in a strong bargaining position. Applicants in the Bank Holding Act context, for example, are usually putting together financial deals that require quick action and approval. Their ability to bargain with the agency or pursue litigation to prove their point is likely to be limited by the realities of the transactions they wish to undertake. In such contexts, the voluntary nature of the commitments they enter into may be exaggerated.

Unwise use of conditions can also have adverse policy effects. If the condition agreed to raises important policy issues, it is not likely the full Board will consider it thoroughly. Conditions that have already been agreed upon are likely to be seen as a *fait accompli*. This is particularly true when the policies involved are not readily apparent, controversial or both. Indeed, the manner in which such conditions are publicized may also have adverse rule of law effects. For example, to the extent that conditions appear only in letters of transmittal between the parties and the agency, they may constitute a form of secret law. This is particularly true if they contain policy implications of significance beyond the particular applicant in the case, and they are not publicized or made easily accessible to the public.

Conditions are even more common in Congressional grant-in-aid programs, where they clearly have significant policy-making effects. Federal grants have strings attached and some of these "strings" or conditions attempt to "encourage the grantee to engage in or expand programs benefiting third parties, such as welfare recipients, highway users, school children, and the poor who need medical attention."[36] Such grants, conditioned or otherwise, are excluded from coverage under the rulemaking provisions of the APA. Section 553(a)(2) specifically exempts rules relating to government "loans, grants, benefits, or contracts." This, of course, makes it even more difficult for petitioners to resist conditions. By and large, courts have upheld the use of such Congressional conditions.[37]

§ 9.4.4 Summary Action

Another important agency use of informal procedure is summary action. These actions are often taken like temporary restraining orders, during a perceived emergency and are effective only for a temporary period. Usually the government justifies such action on the ground that a serious and, most often, an irreparable harm is likely to ensue from a failure to act. The assumption is that if the agency were to provide an extensive hearing before acting, the harm it sought to avoid would very likely occur. In such cases, the government acts first and asks questions later.

36. Tomlinson & Mashaw, supra note 80, at 602.

37. See generally, South Dakota v. Dole, 483 U.S. 203, 107 S.Ct. 2793, 97 L.Ed.2d 171 (1987). For a general discussion of conditions imposed by Congress, see Sullivan, Unconstitutional Conditions, 102 Harv.L.Rev. 1415 (1989); Rosenthal, Conditional Federal Spending and the Constitution, 39 Stan.L.Rev. 1103 (1987); Kriemer, Allocational Sanctions: The Problem of Negative Rights In a Positive State, 132 U.Pa.L.Rev. 1293 (1984).

As far as agency conditions are concerned, the statutory authority to grant or deny individual applicant requests usually implies the power to condition the grant. See Heller, supra note 82, at § 7.04 at 7–25 (1986). For cases where courts have found agency conditions beyond this statutory authority, see, e.g., Securities Industry Ass'n v. Board of Governors, 839 F.2d 47, 67–68 (2d Cir.1988); First Bancorporation v. Board of Governors, 728 F.2d 434 (10th Cir.1984).

Historically, common law authority to act against nuisances gave the states the power to deal summarily with a wide variety of potential harms.[38] Exercising their broad police powers, states passed a variety of statutes dealing, for example, with unwholesome food,[39] diseased animals[40] and trees,[41] potentially insolvent banks,[42] the temporary suspension of utility rates,[43] the destruction of fire hazards,[44] and the licensing of businesses located on unsafe premises.[45] As Professor Freedman has concluded, "the authority of the states to act summarily has thus been as extensive as the substantive reach of nuisance and of the police power."[46]

Like the states, the federal government has also recognized the need for summary action. For example, Congress has given agencies authority to "seize adulterated or misbranded foods, drugs, cosmetics and hazardous substances; to appoint conservators to take possession of banks whose financial situations are thought to be precarious; to halt trading in certain securities; and to suspend many of the various licenses that the federal government requires to engage in particular activities."[47] In addition, various health and environmental statutes similarly provide an agency with authority to take prompt action.[48]

Courts have usually upheld the statutory authority under which agencies engage in informal, summary proceedings. Statutory authority alone, however, is not dispositive of the question. Constitutional issues also are involved. As in most cases, the constitutionality of the statutory authorizations depends on the context in which summary action occurs.

One context in which summary agency action is generally upheld is war. In *Bowles v. Willingham,*[49] for example, the Supreme Court upheld the constitutionality of the Emergency Price Control Act of 1942. That

38. See generally, Freedman, supra note 51. This section draws heavily on this excellent article.

39. See, e.g., North American Cold Storage Co. v. Chicago, 211 U.S. 306, 29 S.Ct. 101, 53 L.Ed. 195 (1908); see, generally, Freedman, supra note 51 at 3–4.

40. See, e.g., Miller v. Horton, 152 Mass. 540, 26 N.E. 100 (1891).

41. See, e.g., Miller v. Schoene, 276 U.S. 272, 48 S.Ct. 246, 72 L.Ed. 568 (1928), Balch v. Glenn, 85 Kan. 735, 119 P. 67 (1911).

42. See, e.g., State Savings & Commercial Bank v. Anderson, 165 Cal. 437, 132 P. 755 (1913).

43. See, e.g., Driscoll v. Edison Light & Power Co., 307 U.S. 104, 59 S.Ct. 715, 83 L.Ed. 1134 (1939), rehearing denied 307 U.S. 650, 59 S.Ct. 831, 83 L.Ed. 1529 (1939).

44. See, e.g., Jackson v. Bell, 143 Tenn. 452, 226 S.W. 207 (1920).

45. See, e.g., Genesee Recreation Co. v. Edgerton, 172 App.Div. 464, 158 N.Y.S. 421 (1916).

46. Freedman, supra note 51 at 40.

47. Id. at 3–4.

48. See, e.g., Consumer Product Safety Act, 15 U.S.C.A. § 2061 (1988) (condemnation and seizure of products constituting imminent hazards); Federal Food, Drug, and Cosmetic Act, 21 U.S.C.A. §§ 334 (seizure of adulterated or misbranded food, drugs, or cosmetics), 455(c) (condemnation and destruction of adulterated poultry), 606(b)(2) (adulterated meat), 1034(c) (bad eggs) (1988); Federal Insecticide, Fungicide, and Rodenticide Act, 7 U.S.C.A. § 136k(a)–(c) (1988) ("Stop sale, use, or removal" orders against pesticides or devices in violation of Act, and seizure and destruction of same).

49. 321 U.S. 503, 64 S.Ct. 641, 88 L.Ed. 892 (1944). For a case involving World War I legislation, see Stoehr v. Wallace, 255 U.S. 239, 41 S.Ct. 293, 65 L.Ed. 604 (1921).

Act allowed the Price Administration to establish maximum rents by order and without a full hearing. Those wishing to challenge the order could do so only after the order had taken effect.

In addition to wartime measures, courts have also looked with favor on summary governmental action aimed at protecting federal revenue[50] and protecting the public from economic injury,[51] as well as from injuries to health due to impure food, drugs,[52] unsafe chemicals, or carcinogens. Automobile recall cases are a recent and important example not only of informal agency processes at work, but of how informal processes develop to avoid the costs, rigidity and the inevitable delay that result from formal legal processes, particularly those that lead to protracted agency and court battles.[53]

Not all of legislative authorization of summary or less than full adjudicatory procedures has been upheld. The Supreme Court in *Goldberg v. Kelly*[54] held that the "brutal need" of those on welfare required that there be a full adjudicatory hearing before termination of benefits could occur. Similarly, in *Sniadach v. Family Finance Corp.*,[55] the Court held a state's summary garnishment statute unconstitutional because it failed to provide for a hearing prior to seizure in rem of an individual's wages. In both of these cases, the Court held that the litigants' economic vulnerability outweighed the fiscal needs of the opposing parties.[56] As has been noted in our chapter dealing with the Due Process Clause, however, the trend seems now very much in the other direction. Courts are now more willing to engage in a form of cost-benefit analysis when it comes to pre-termination procedures involving, for example, social security disability benefits.[57] Courts are, in effect, increasingly inclined to defer to the legislature in such matters, and consequently give much greater discretion to the agency in determining when summary procedures are appropriate.[58]

50. Phillips v. Commissioner, 283 U.S. 589, 51 S.Ct. 608, 75 L.Ed. 1289 (1931). But see Kahn v. United States 753 F.2d 1208 (3d Cir.1985). An excellent discussion of this and the other contexts described in this section can be found in Freedman, supra note 51, at 9–20.

51. See, e.g., Fahey v. Mallonee, 332 U.S. 245, 67 S.Ct. 1552, 91 L.Ed. 2030 (1947) (need to protect depositors from failing bank).

52. North American Cold Storage Co. v. Chicago, 211 U.S. 306, 29 S.Ct. 101, 53 L.Ed. 195 (1908); Ewing v. Mytinger & Casselberry, Inc., 339 U.S. 594, 70 S.Ct. 870, 94 L.Ed. 1088 (1950), rehearing denied 340 U.S. 857, 71 S.Ct. 69, 95 L.Ed. 627 (1950).

53. See Mashaw and Harfst, Regulation and Legal Culture: The Case of Motor Vehicle Safety, 4 Yale J. On Reg. 257 (1987). For a discussion of how overly complex rulemaking procedures can encourage attempts to bypass this aspect of the administrative process, see generally, chapter 4, supra.

54. 397 U.S. 254, 90 S.Ct. 1011, 25 L.Ed.2d 287 (1970). This case is discussed in detail in chapter 7, sec. 7.6.3, supra.

55. 395 U.S. 337, 89 S.Ct. 1820, 23 L.Ed.2d 349 (1969).

56. See also, Wisconsin v. Constantineau, 400 U.S. 433, 437, 91 S.Ct. 507, 510, 27 L.Ed.2d 515 (1971); Bell v. Burson, 402 U.S. 535, 91 S.Ct. 1586, 29 L.Ed.2d 90 (1971).

57. See, e.g., Mathews v. Eldridge, 424 U.S. 319, 96 S.Ct. 893, 47 L.Ed.2d 18 (1976).

58. Id. See also, Walters v. National Association of Radiation Survivors, 473 U.S. 305, 105 S.Ct. 3180, 87 L.Ed.2d 220 (1985), on remand 111 F.R.D. 595 (N.D.Cal.1986).

§ 9.4.5 Agency Press Releases

Agencies usually enforce the laws Congress has asked them to administer. While most enforcement proceedings involve formal adjudicatory procedures, there also are informal and often indirect methods for achieving the same result. One approach is the use of publicity. If an agency announces that it fears a certain product may be harmful and, as a result, it may at some future date need to recall or ban that product, the mere announcement of its concern can have a profound effect on the market for the product in question.[59] Similarly, choosing very famous and, thus, highly visible persons as targets for enforcement can highlight the allegedly wrongful behavior involved and discourage similar behavior on the part of others.

The use of media, however, can also be a source of considerable concern. Bad publicity is instantaneous and it can have a very damaging effect prior to any kind of hearing, formal or informal. Some agencies have rules or policies aimed at controlling the publicizing of matters that may harm those they regulate.[60] But barring such internal restraints, administrators can impose the sanction without the usual constraints of notice, a hearing, reasons or judicial review. In most cases, the use of publicity is an informal sanction and is limited only by the discretion and good sense of the agency involved.

§ 9.5 ALTERNATIVE DISPUTE RESOLUTION TECHNIQUES

Administrative agencies and the procedures they employ arose, in part, as an alternative dispute resolution mechanism. They were in reaction to the formality, cost and delay experienced by parties who had to litigate their regulatory disputes in federal and state courts.[1] Some critics now contend that the administrative process itself has become unduly formal, costly and time-consuming.[2] Moreover, many administrative agencies must deal with an enormous caseload.[3] Some of these cases involve disputes that are inherently more amenable to alternative dispute resolution (ADR) methods. Arbitration, for example, may be more efficient than administrative adjudication for resolving monetary disputes between private parties, especially if these disputes do not involve

59. See Gellhorn, Adverse Publicity By Administrative Agencies, 86 Harv.L.Rev. 1380 (1973).

60. See, e.g., 28 C.F.R. § 50.2. (Justice Dept.).

§ 9.5

1. See Gellhorn, Alternative Means of Dispute Resolution In Government: A Sense of Perspective, 1 Admin.L.J. 459, 460 (1987).

2. Id. *See also*, 141 Cong. Rec. S10105 (daily ed. July 17, 1995) (statement of Sen. Roth).

3. *See, e.g.*, Simler v. Harrison County Hospital, 110 F.Supp.2d 886, 890 (S.D.Ind. 2000) (noting that the Equal Employment Opportunity Commission is "an agency with an admittedly heavy caseload"); Stockman v. Federal Election Comm'n, 944 F.Supp. 518, 521 (E.D.Tex.1996) (noting that the FEC manages "a burgeoning caseload involving thousands of respondents and complex financial transactions"); United States v. Gorman Towers Apartments, 857 F.Supp. 1335, 1338 (W.D.Ark.1994) (suggesting that the Department of Housing and Urban Development faces a heavy caseload).

significant policy or legal issues.[4] Proponents of ADR also argue that the primary value of these techniques is that they increase the satisfaction of the participants involved.[5] For the most part, participants are more directly involved in the decisionmaking process itself and that process is usually cheaper and faster. For reasons such as these, alternative dispute resolution techniques are now consistently proposed as an important reform of the administrative decisionmaking process.[6] They include processes that have long been a part of the administrative process, such as settlement and negotiation. But they also include less commonly used techniques such as arbitration, mediation and mini-trials.

Since 1996, every Federal agency has established some sort of ADR infrastructure and many agencies have taken advantage of these procedures.[7] By the mid–1990's, for example, the Environmental Protection Agency had used mediation and arbitration to resolve at least thirty cases[8] that involved Superfund, Clean Water Act, and Resource Conservation and recovery Act disputes.[9] In the early 1990s, the Federal Deposit Insurance Corporation estimated a savings of $13 million in legal costs in settling disputes that arose out of the Savings and Loans Scandals, and the Resolution Trust Corporation estimated it saved $114 million during the same period.[10] The Air Force and the Army Corps of

4. In 1998, Congress passed the Alternative Dispute Resolution Act of 1998, Pub. L. No. 105–315, 112 Stat. 2993 (codified at 28 U.S.C. §§ 651–58 (1999)), which authorizes U.S. District Courts to implement ADR programs. A brief survey of proposed legislation from the 106th Congress shows that lawmakers regularly incorporate arbitration into legislation and resolutions. See, e.g., H.R. 495, 106th Cong. (1999) (providing for arbitration in taking cases pursuant to the 1973 Endangered Species Act); H.R. 1283, 106th Cong., §§ 301–07 (1999) (providing for alternative dispute resolution in the settlement of asbestos injury claims); H.R. 1412, 106th Cong. (1999) (amending the National Labor Relations Act to require the arbitration of initial contract negotiation disputes); H.R. 2550, 106th Cong. (1999) (providing the right to arbitration to owners of private property affected by regulatory restrictions); S.747, 106th Cong. (1999) (directing the Surface Transportation Board to adopt expedited arbitration as a dispute resolution mechanism); S.2703, 106th Cong. (1999) (making arbitration available to postmasters in employment disputes); H.R. 4593, 106th Cong. (2000) (requiring the EEOC to mediate employee claims arising under civil rights laws); H.Res. 479, 106th Cong. (2000) (expressing the sense of the House, inter alia, that international arbitration panels should be created as a bankruptcy mechanism for heavily indebted nations).

5. See Willard, "Uses for Alternative Dispute Resolution: Better Ways to Resolve Some Public Sector Controversies," 1 Admin.L.J. 479, 493 1987. See also Fleming, "Institutionalizing Alternative Dispute Resolution: Where Does the Government Go from Here?," 1 Admin.L.J. 509, 519 (1987). See also, Tom R. Tyler, Citizen Discontent with Legal Procedures: A Social Science Perspective on Civil Procedure Reform, 45 Am.J.Com.L. 871, 882 (1997); Jody Freeman & Laura I. Langbein, Regulatory Negotiation and the Legitimacy Benefit, 9 N.Y.U. Envtl.L.J. 60, 121 (2000).

6. Supra note 113.

7. Supra note 113. See also Peter R. Steenland, Jr. & Peter A. Appel, The Ongoing Role of Alternative Dispute Resolution in Federal Government Litigation, 27 U. Tol. L. Rev. 805 (1996).

8. S. Rep. No. 104–245, 104th Cong., at 2 (1996).

9. See 141 Cong. Rec. S12959 (daily ed. September 8, 1995) (statement of Sen. Grassley).

10. Id. The FDIC prefers mediation and mini-trials to arbitration. See FDIC, Guide for Outside Legal Counsel (updated April 30, 1996) http://www.fdic.gov/buying/legal/guide/case.html#alterdispuresol. For the FDIC policy on ADR, see 62 Fed. Reg. 66370, Dec. 18, 1997. The FDIC success suggests that ADR may be particularly appropriate for claims that involve astronomically high sums of money, such as the

Engineers also have a long history of using ADR.[11] The Administrative Conference of the United States (ACUS) reported that "partnering" was responsible for a "dramatic decline in the volume of contract claims and appeals experienced by the Army Corps of Engineers (from 1,079 claims in 1988 to 314 in 1994, and from 742 appeals in 1991 to 365 in 1994)."[12] The Army Corps of Engineers also used dispute resolution in fifty-five contract disputes between 1989 and 1994, fifty-three of which were successful; one claim for $55 million was settled for $17 million in four days.[13] Furthermore, the Air Force successfully settle more than 100 Equal Employment Opportunity disputes through mediation in 1992 and 1993, which saved more than 44 million in complaint processing costs.[14] Perceived problems with ADR has resulted in only nominal use of ADR by some Federal agencies.[15] When ADR is used, it is usually invoked in government contracts, workplace disputes, and enforcement and program disputes.[16]

much-hyped anticipated fallout from the Y2K computer glitch. See Y2K in the Courts: Will We be Capsized by a Wave of Litigation?, Hearing on the Specific Liability Bills Circulating in the Senate and Potential for Court Overload, and the Effects that Y2K Litigation May Have on the Operation of Businesses Either Faced With Lawsuits or Forced to Seek legal Recourse Through the Court System of the Senate Special Comm. on the Year 2000 Technology Problem, 106th Cong. (1999) (statement of Hon. William Steele Sessions on appropriateness of ADR in resolving anticipated Y2K disputes).

11. H.R. Rep. No. 104–597, 104th Cong., at 2 (1996).

12. Id.

13. 142 Cong. Rec. H11451 (daily ed. Sept. 27, 1996) (statement of Rep. Gekkas). Air Force personnel also testified that the Air Force had used ADR to resolve more than 1,000 civilian personnel disputes, with a settlement rate close to eighty percent. 142 Cong. Rec. H5788 (daily ed. June 4, 1996) (statement of Rep. Reed). Also, fifty-three Air Force contracting cases had gone through ADR by the mid–1990s, and all had been resolved. Id. The Air Force then began adding ADR clauses to contracts to ensure that disputes did not drive up acquisition costs. Id.

14. H.R. Rep. No. 104–597, 104th Cong., at 2 (1996).

15. See Jonathan D. Mester, Note & Comment, The Administrative Dispute Resolution Act of 1996: Will the New Era of ADR in Federal Administrative Agencies Occur at the Expense of Public Accountability?, 13 Ohio St.J. on Disp. Resol. 167, 172–73 (1997); 141 Cong. Rec. S12959 (daily ed. September 8, 1995) (statement of Sen. Grassley). For example, it was not until 1996 that the Department of Defense issued a directive that established an ADR coordinating committee chaired by the DOD General Counsel with specialists representing each of the services to resolve civil claims involving DOD. See Major Kathryn R. Sommerkamp et. al., Developments of 1996—The Year in Review, 1997 Army Law 3, 53 (1997). On the other hand, arbitration has captured the imagination of international governing bodies, such as the World Trade Organization. The World Intellectual property Organization (WIPO) is in the process of drafting arbitration protocols to resolve disputes that arise out of "cybersquatting," or the bad faith registration of multiple Internet domain names with the intention of selling them to a business that failed to register them first, which gain the attention of Congress in the late 1990s. See, e.g., Cybersquatting and Consumer Protection: Ensuring Domain Name Integrity, Hearing on S. 1255 Before the Senate Comm. on the Judiciary, 106th Cong. (1999). Experts have advised legislators that congressional action had been or soon would be mooted by the proposed WIPO rules on mandatory arbitration, which were expected to become the global standard for Internet registries. Id. at 77 (testimony of A. Michael Froomkin, University of Miami School of Law). See also WIPO Arbitration and Mediation Center, at <http://arbiter.wipo.int/center/index.html>.

16. See H.R. Rep. No. 104–597, 104th Cong., at 2 (1996).

No one can deny the importance of flexibility, informality and an appropriate fit of procedure to substance. Nor can efficiency values be ignored, particularly in programs with enormous caseloads. But critics of ADR maintain that the application of these techniques to the administrative process do not always result in more expeditious dispute resolution.[17] More fundamentally, ADR skeptics maintain that ADR can "replace the rule of law with nonlegal values"[18] and that ADR "falls too far on the private law side of the public/private quandary, threatening rights-based jurisprudence and the rule of law, public accountability, and even the judiciary itself."[19] In one sense, ADR can be viewed as a procedural analogue to substantive decontrol. Carried too far, some techniques can, in effect, privatize administrative procedures raising not only philosophical and policy issues,[20] but important constitutional and statutory questions as well.[21]

Settlements reached through ADR are subject to limited judicial review prior to final approval and entry. The standard of permissible review is whether the agreement is "fair and adequate and [is] not unlawful, unreasonable, or against public policy."[22] The settlement becomes a final agency action upon entry by the court,[23] or by an ALJ at the agency level.[24] Despite this legal status, however, a plaintiff may be

17. See Patricia M. Wald, ADR and the Courts: An Update, 46 Duke L.J. 1445, 1447 (1997) (stating that ADR "has not made a huge impact, on cost or delay in the federal trial courts"). But see Rosemary O'Leary, Tracy Yandle, & Tamilyn Mooreb, 14 Ohio St.J. on Disp. Resol., 515, 515 (1999) (finding that a national survey of environmental dispute resolution (EDR) programs in every state and the District of Columbia shows "no state that has a fully operating EDR program has been disappointed"); Marshall J. Breger, Should An Attorney Be Required To Advise A Client Of ADR Options?, 13 Geo.J.Legal Ethics 427, 428–29 nn.1–2 (2000) (noting the proliferation of government and corporate ADR programs). See also The Alternative Dispute Resolution Act of 1998, P.L. 105–315, 112 Stat. 2993, amending 28 U.S.C. § 651 et seq. (authorizing the courts to use ADR in federal civil actions). In passing the 1998 Act, Congress found that ADR "has potential to provide ... greater satisfaction of the parties ... greater efficiency in achieving settlements ... [and the] potential to reduce the large backlog of [federal] cases. P.L. 105–315 § 2."

18. Edwards, Alternative Dispute Resolution: Panacea or Anathema?, 99 Harv. L.Rev. 668, 677 (1986).

19. ADR, the Judiciary, and Justice: Coming to Terms with the Alternatives, 113 Harv. L. Rev. 1851, 1854 (2000).

20. See, e.g., Fiss, Against Settlement, 93 Yale L.J. 1073, 1085 (1984). See also, Jack B. Weinstein, Some Benefits and Risks of Privatization of Justice Through ADR, 11 Ohio St.J.Disp. Resol. 241, 256–63 (1996). Judge Weinstein argues that ADR creates power imbalances between parties depending on their skill at manipulating ADR; that ADR can only be afforded by the wealthy, which leaves the poor to use traditional dispute mechanisms and so reduces the effectiveness of those traditional mechanisms; and that ADR removes the burden to monitor the public's interest in disputes.

21. See generally, Bruff, Public Programs, Private Deciders: The Constitutionality of Arbitration In Federal Programs in Studies, in Administrative Law and Procedure 88–1, Agency Arbitration 7 (Admin.Conf. of the U.S., Office of the Chairman, 1988); Note, Rethinking Regulation: Negotiation As An Alternative To Traditional Rulemaking, 94 Harv.L.Rev. 1871 (1981); Harter, Negotiating Regulations: A Cure For Malaise, 71 Geo.L.J. 1, 102–112 (1982) [hereafter Harter, Negotiating Regulations].

22. United States v. Georgia–Pacific Corp., 960 F.Supp. 298, 298 (N.D.Ga.1996).

23. United States v. Int'l Bhd. of Teamsters, 120 F.3d 341 (2d Cir.1997).

24. See, e.g., 29 CFR § 2570.65 (1999). Cf. Chem. Manufacturers Ass'n v. EPA, 26 F. Supp. 2d 180, 187 (D.D.C.1998) (finding that as a matter of law, a settlement policy is not final agency action).

unable to obtain judicial review if the governing statute lacks a provision for granting it.[25] Even if the statute does provide for review, two potential problems remain. First, a decision to settle is sometimes analogous to a decision not to prosecute, and the prosecutorial discretion of an agency is not reviewable.[26] Second, settlements that propose new policies or new interpretations of existing statutes may not be ripe for review. Until an agency action takes place, the interests of the parties to the settlement have not been affected, and no case or controversy exists for judicial review.[27] If an agency formally promulgates or withdraws a rule, however, such action is ripe for review.

§ 9.5.1 Administrative Dispute Resolution Act

The Administrative Dispute Resolution Act was designed to "authorize and encourage federal agencies to use mediation, conciliation, arbitration, and other techniques for the prompt and informal resolution of disputes.... "[28] The Act amends the APA to authorize parties involved in disputes arising under federal administrative programs to agree to use alternative dispute resolution methods to resolve these disputes; agency use of ADR remains completely discretionary. The Act sets forth guidelines to help determine the cases to which ADR techniques are most appropriate. It also requires that each agency adopt a formal ADR policy, appoint personnel and provide for their training in ADR methods.[29] Seven of the new code sections establish procedures for arbitration and include provision for enforcement and judicial review of arbitration awards.[30] Voluntary arbitration is authorized when all parties consent, subject to a thirty-day waiting period before awards become final[31] and until any judicial review[32] of awards has been completed. Sections 5

25. See NLRB v. United Food and Commercial Workers Union, 484 U.S. 112, 133, 108 S.Ct. 413, 98 L.Ed.2d 429 (1987) (stating that the attempted use of the APA judicial review provisions without statutory authority was "absurd" and contrary to Congressional intent).

26. See Heckler v. Chaney, 470 U.S. 821, 105 S.Ct. 1649, 84 L.Ed.2d 714 (1985).

27. See J.V. Peters & Co. v. Administrator, EPA, 767 F.2d 263, 264 (6th Cir. 1985) (stating that to allow a cause of action "prior to a response action would debilitate the central function" of the legislation that empowers the agency).

28. Pub.L. 101–552, 104 Stat. 2736 (1990) (codified as amended at 5 U.S.C.A. §§ 571–584) (quoting the preamble), permanently reauthorized by P.L. 104–320, § 9, 110 Stat. 3872 (1996). The amendments to the ADRA also removed the prohibition against federal employees using ADR in employment disputes, removed the oversight authority of the Administrative Conference of the United States, permanently authorized the use of negotiated rulemaking by Federal agencies, and exempted communication between a party and a neutral in an ADR proceeding from disclosure under the Freedom of Information Act (FOIA). See also 142 Cong. Rec. S11849 (daily ed. Sept. 30, 1999).

29. Id., at § 3(a) ("Each agency shall adopt a policy that addresses the use of alternative means of dispute resolution and case management."); at § 3(b) ("The head of each agency shall designate a senior official to be the dispute resolution specialist of the agency."); and, § 3(c) ("Each agency shall provide for training on a regular basis for the dispute resolution specialist of the agency and other employees involved in implementing the policy of the agency developed under subsection (a).").

30. 5 U.S.C.A. §§ 575–581.

31. Id. § 580(b) ("The award in an arbitration proceeding shall become final 30 days after it is served on all parties.") Subsection (c)makes a final award binding on all parties.

32. Id. at § 581. Subsection (a) stipulates that any party "adversely affected or aggrieved by an award made in an arbitra-

through 8 of the Act amend various other sections of U.S. Code titles to facilitate agency implementation of ADR, and Section 9 provides guidelines for representation and assistance by nonattorneys. All records and information produced during settlement are confidential and, unless otherwise discoverable, cannot be used in litigation or disclosed without permission.[33]

The Act acknowledges that ADR is not appropriate in all circumstances. The private gains in efficiency and reduced expense may, in some cases, exact too high a price in terms of reduced public oversight and general accountability for legal pronouncements, in effect, placing lawmaking in private hands. The Act thus attempts to address such concerns by proscribing ADR in certain cases, typically those involving a need to take into account the interests of those not party to the specific dispute. The interests of other private parties or the public at large are particularly relevant when there is a need for a definitive administrative resolution of a dispute that can provide precedential authority, or when private ADR proceedings significantly would prevent full public disclosure.[34]

The remaining sections of this chapter will now examine some of the more common ADR techniques used on a regular or experimental basis by various federal agencies. They will describe these ADR techniques generally as well as their implementation at certain, specific agencies. They shall also examine some of the key legal issues that can arise when these techniques are applied to disputes in the administrative process.

§ 9.5.2 Settlement—An Overview

The essence of a settlement is that the parties to a dispute themselves render a decision in the case by means of a negotiated agreement.[35] All records and information produced during settlement are

tion proceeding conducted under this subchapter may bring an action for review of such award only pursuant to the provisions of sections 9 through 13 of Title 9." Under subsection (b), a decision by an agency whether to use a dispute resolution proceeding is not subject to judicial review.

33. For a discussion of the advantages and drawbacks of secrecy and out-of-court settlements, see David Luban, Settlements and the Erosion of the Public Realm, 83 Geo. L.J. 2619 (1995). See also Laurie Kratky Dore, Secrecy by Consent: The Use and Limits of Confidentiality in the Pursuit of Settlement, 74 Notre Dame L.Rev. 283 (1999).

34. Id. § 572(b)(1–6).

35. By settlement, we mean to include the various methods parties use to reach a consensus-based solution. For instance, if the parties are unable to reach an agreement between themselves, they may rely on the services of a mediator. A mediator is a third-party who "at a minimum, ... arranges meetings, assists in the exchange of information, tenders proposals at the request of one party or another, and assists the parties in developing clearer statements of their interests." Suskind & Ozawa, Mediated Negotiation in the Public Sector, 27 Am.Behavioral Scientist 255, 256 (1983), reprinted in Chairman of the Admin. Conf. of the United States, Sourcebook: Federal Agency Use of Alternative Means of Dispute Resolution 189–90 (1987). A mediator facilitates negotiation. The result is binding only if the parties agree to it in writing.

A minitrial is a voluntary, expedited, nonjudicial procedure through which management officials for each party meet to resolve disputes. Discovery is kept to a minimum. In a proceeding free from such constraints as the Federal Rules of Evidence and Civil Procedure, representatives of the parties present abbreviated versions of their cases before high-level officials of the

confidential and, unless otherwise discoverable, cannot be used in litigation or disclosed without permission.[36] While some administrative proceedings involve only two parties—a regulated entity and the agency—administrative litigation more typically involves more parties, representing a variety of interests and viewpoints. Rate cases before the Federal Energy Regulatory Commission, for example, regularly involve many more parties than just the interstate utility seeking a rate increase; these additional participants usually include the various customers of the utility, such as local intrastate utility companies, other interstate utilities with an interest in the proceeding, as well as some of the many industrial, residential and commercial users of the electricity or gas to be sold. The more parties involved, the more difficult it is to settle the issues in dispute. This is especially true when "the distance between those on the line and those with decisional authority" is great.[37] Parties are thus usually unwilling to negotiate unless it is clear that they are dealing with an agency official who possesses the power to settle the matter.[38]

Settlement is a dispute resolution technique that has long been a part of the administrative process. The APA explicitly speaks to settlement in section 554(c), requiring agencies to give "all interested parties opportunity for . . . offers of settlement . . . when time, the nature of the proceeding, and the public interest permits[.]"[39] A participant in a proceeding may have a right to request the appointment of a settlement judge,[40] which is an administrative law judge (ALJ) who is not permanently assigned to the case, but is able to "preside over conferences and settlement negotiations and assess the practicalities of the potential

parties to the dispute. Following the presentations, the officials enter into settlement discussions. See sec. 9.5.7, infra.

36. For a discussion of the advantages and drawbacks of secrecy and out-of-court settlements, see David Luban, Settlements and the Erosion of the Public Realm, 83 Geo. L.J. 2619 (1995). See also Laurie Kratky Dore, Secrecy by Consent: The Use and Limits of Confidentiality in the Pursuit of Settlement, 74 Notre Dame L.Rev. 283 (1999).

37. Harter, Points On A Continuum: Dispute Resolution Procedures and the Administrative Process, 1 Admin.L.J. 141, 206 (1987) [hereinafter Harter, Points On A Continuum].

38. See Smith, Alternative Means of Dispute Resolution: Practices and Possibilities in the Federal Government, 1984 Mo.J. of Dispute Resolution 9, 21. Similarly, there is a disincentive to bargain if a settlement is subject to multiple layers of review within the agency and can be undone at each of these levels. Harter, Points on a Continuum, supra note 146, at 206. In addition to the numbers of parties and the ability of the agency official involved to act authoritatively, there are a variety of other factors that may affect settlement, including the nature of the issues involved. Are they sufficiently crystallized to allow for settlement§ The issues need genuinely to be in doubt so that the parties are unsure of the outcome, should the case be litigated. Moreover, the parties must be willing to negotiate in good faith. See ACUS Recommendation 82–4, 1 C.F.R. § 305.82–4 (1984).

39. 5 U.S.C.A. § 554(c) (1988). See also 5 U.S.C.A. § 558(c) (1988). See Michigan Consol. Gas Co. v. FPC, 283 F.2d 204, 224 (D.C.Cir.1960), cert. denied sub nom. Panhandle E. Pipe Line Co. v. Michigan Consol. Gas Co., 364 U.S. 913, 81 S.Ct. 276, 5 L.Ed.2d 227 (1960). For a discussion of how settlement at the agency level differs from settlement in civil court actions, see Pennsylvania Gas & Water Co. v. FPC, 463 F.2d 1242, 1246 (D.C.Cir.1972).

40. See, e.g., Federal Regulatory Energy Commission (FERC) rules, 18 C.F.R. § 385.603(c)(1) (2000).

settlement."[41] The settlement judge does not preside over the case should negotiations fail, but "acts a bit like a mediator ... by giving his reaction to the case."[42] Because the settlement judge plays no role in any formal adjudication, parties may be more willing to settle. The APA does not require an agency to accept a settlement,[43] nor does the APA require that parties unanimously accept a settlement.[44] The most important factor in identification of cases amenable to settlement judge participation is fact-specificity; broad policy or legal questions generally render cases unsuitable for settlement.[45]

The APA does not mandate any particular agency procedures, and different agencies have developed different settlement strategies. For example, the Federal Energy Regulatory Commission (FERC) sometimes will sever contesting parties from a settlement to facilitate resolution of the dispute.[46] The severed party, however, may lack the resources to pursue the litigation on its own, or it may find itself excluded from recurring agency litigation that creates "regulars" who work easily with one another and who have agendas that differ from the agenda of the excluded party. Another example of agency settlement strategies can be found at the Environmental Protection Agency (EPA), which uses ADR to manage its enormous backlog of Superfund cases.[47] After the EPA lists a hazardous waste site as a priority pursuant to the 1986 Superfund Amendments Reauthorization Act (SARA),[48] it may decided to negotiate with the potentially responsible parties (PRPS).[49] If the EPA decides to negotiate, the PRPs are required to submit a cleanup proposal to the Agency, subject to approval by the EPA and the appropriate federal court[50] after a thirty-day public notice-and-comment period on the pro-

41. Id. at § 385.603(g) (2000). Walker, supra note 148, at 343–347.

42. Harter, Points on a Continuum, supra note 146, at 208.

43. See Pennsylvania Gas & Water Co. v. FPC, 463 F.2d 1242, 1246 (D.C.Cir.1972) (a regulatory agency "may responsibly exercise its initiative by terminating the proceedings at virtually any stage" if the agency finds that the evidence before it justifies such action). Walker, supra note 148, at 344–345.

44. Cities of Lexington, etc., Ky. v. FPC, 295 F.2d 109, 121 (4th Cir.1961) ("[t]here is nothing in the Administrative Procedure Act which expressly requires unanimous consent of all the participating parties to an agreement of settlement"). For a discussion of how public utility commissions have abandoned the principle of unanimity in settling rate cases, and the use of ADR in such cases, see Stefan H. Krieger, Problems for Captive Ratepayers in Nonunanimous Settlements of Public Utility Rate Cases, 12 Yale J. on Reg. 257 (1995). Cf. Alan P. Buchmann & Robert S. Tongren, Nonunanimous Settlements of Public Utility Rate Cases: A Response, 13 Yale J. on Reg. 337 (1996) (disputing Krieger's claim that unanimous settlements are necessary to protect certain consumer groups).

45. D. Joseph & M. Gilbert, Breaking the Settlement Ice: The Use of Settlement Judges in Administrative Proceedings in Recommendations and Reports 19–20 (Admin. Cong. of the U.S. Office of the Chairman, 1998).

46. This tactic received judicial approval in United Mun. Distributors Group v. FERC, 732 F.2d 202 (D.C.Cir.1984), and was reaffirmed by Arctic Slope Reg'l Corp. v. FERC, 832 F.2d 158 (D.C.Cir.1987), cert. denied 488 U.S. 868, 109 S.Ct. 175, 102 L.Ed.2d 145 (1988).

47. See generally, Shana A. Samson, Note & Comment, Using Alternative Dispute Resolution to Streamline Superfund, 15 Ohio St. J. on Disp. Resol. 519 (2000).

48. Pub. L. No. 99–499, 100 Stat. 1678 (codified at 42 U.S.C. § 9622 (1999)).

49. 42 U.S.C. § 9622(a) (1999).

50. United States v. Shaffer Equip. Co., 158 F.R.D. 80, 82 (D.C.W.Va.1994)

posal.[51] There are, in effect, a range of ADR mechanisms that provide agencies with opportunities to craft efficient, effective dispute settlement strategies.

§ 9.5.3 Settlement at FERC

The Federal Energy Regulatory Commission (FERC) routinely uses settlement techniques to reduce its caseload. In describing its intention to follow the practices of its predecessor, the Federal Power Commission (FPC), FERC has stated that:

> . . . the agency has a strong policy favoring the disposition of cases through settlements. The FPC and the courts recognized that the Commission could not possibly cope with the flood of business engendered by its jurisdictional statutes if the outcome of a substantial proportion of that business were not the result of voluntary settlements entered into by the parties . . . We adhere to that view.[52]

Any party or participant to a proceeding may request, by formal motion or otherwise, a settlement conference, which the Commission staff or decisional authority may grant.[53] The presiding judge can entertain settlement offers or a separate settlement judge may be appointed.[54] Any participant may file a motion for the appointment of a settlement judge with the presiding judge or the Commission.[55] The presiding judge may also request the Chief Administrative Judge to appoint a settlement judge.[56] Settlement conferences may be formal or informal. An informal settlement can be convened by any party, participant or Commission staff. Unlike formal settlement conferences,[57] informal conferences are not subject to Commission rules regarding notice and participation requirements.

FERC regulations authorize the use of a settlement judge.[58] A settlement judge is an Administrative Law Judge (ALJ) who, though not assigned to the case to render a decision, will "preside over conferences and settlement negotiations and assess the practicalities of a potential settlement."[59] A settlement judge is in a unique position to facilitate the settlement process because the parties may be more willing to reveal their bottom line to a judge who is not involved in the actual decision should settlement negotiations break down. The settlement judge thus "acts a bit like a mediator and a bit like the neutral adviser in a minitrial by giving his reaction to the case."[60]

("[T]he Court must be convinced that [the Superfund settlement] is fair, adequate, and reasonable, and consistent with the Constitution and the mandate of Congress.") (citation omitted).

51. 42 U.S.C. § 9622 (1999).

52. 44 Fed.Reg. 34,936 (1979).

53. 18 C.F.R. § 385.601(a) (1990).

54. Id. at § 385.603.

55. Id. at § 385.603(c)(1).

56. Id. at § 385.603(c)(2).

57. Id. at § 385.601(b)(1)–(2).

58. 18 C.F.R. § 385.603. The Occupational Safety and Health Review Commission also has rules permitting the use of settlement judges. 29 C.F.R. § 220.101.

59. 18 C.F.R. § 385.603(g). See generally, Walker, supra note 148, at 343–347.

60. Harter, Points on a Continuum, supra note 146, at 208.

Settlement offers may be unanimous or contested. The Commission usually approves all uncontested offers of settlement, as long as the proposal "appears to be fair and reasonable and in the public interest."[61]

Unanimity among the negotiating parties, however, will not automatically validate the settlement. Settlement orders must be certified by the presiding officer, and the Commission has acknowledged that because such unanimous offers of settlement do not always comport with the public interest, they cannot be automatically accepted.[62]

When an offer of settlement is contested, the Commission may approve the offer if "(1) the record contains substantial evidence upon which a reasoned decision can be based, or (2) the Commission finds that no general issue of material fact exists.[63] Courts have upheld this approach. In *Cities of Lexington v. FPC,*[64] for example, the court found that '[t]here is nothing in the Administrative Procedure Act which expressly requires unanimous consent of all the participating parties to an agreement of settlement;' indeed, to demand such unanimity 'would effectually destroy the settlement provision.' "[65] FERC may also sever contested issues from a negotiated agreement.[66] This option, however, is rarely exercised because many settlement offers contain "non-severability" clauses prohibiting such excision.[67]

More common is the severing of contesting parties from a settlement in order to expedite resolution of the dispute. If the Commission decides to sever a party, it then proceeds with the agreement as if it were uncontested, while allowing the contesting party a hearing on the merits of the contested issues.[68] The Court of Appeals for the District of Columbia upheld this technique in *United Municipal Distributors Group v. FERC.*[69] In that case, the petitioner challenged two Commission orders approving a negotiated settlement of rate increases as to all consenting parties, but remanding the case for a full administrative hearing on behalf of the contesting petitioner. The Court of Appeals approved the arrangement as a fair exercise of FERC procedures because it provided the settlers' the benefit of their negotiations while protecting non-settlers due process rights.[70] The ratepayer that objected could independently challenge the rates it was being charged on its own, if it so chose.

61. 18 C.F.R. § 385.602(g)(3).

62. Id. See also, Walker, supra note 148, at 350. Such orders have no precedential value or effect in future litigation.

63. 18 C.F.R. § 385.602(h) (1990). Walker, supra note 148, at 350–51 ("The Commission has held that the objections of a party with no present and immediate interest in a settlement will not render a settlement contested." Id. at 351). Similarly, the rules provide that the objection of Commission staff alone will not render an otherwise uncontested offer of settlement contested. 18 C.F.R. § 385.601 (1990).

64. 295 F.2d 109 (4th Cir.1961).

65. Id. at 121.

66. 18 C.F.R. § 385.602(h)(1)(iii).

67. Walker, supra note 148, at 353.

68. Id.

69. 732 F.2d 202 (D.C.Cir.1984). But see Northern Natural Gas Co., 35 FERC § 61,105 (1986), discussed in Walker, supra note 148, at 355.

70. The court noted: "In this case, in contrast, UMDG, as sole objector to the settlement, is in no wise being required to accept the settlement against its will. To the contrary, FERC's action permits UMDG to preserve its objection, while allowing the noncontesting parties to have the benefit of

The D.C. Circuit reaffirmed the legality of this approach in *Arctic Slope Regional Corp. v. FERC.*[71] In that case, FERC approved a multiparty settlement of an oil pipeline rate case involving the TransAlaska Pipeline System. The proceedings that were settled had gone on for some time without getting near a final conclusion. Petitioner Arctic challenged the settlement on the grounds that the agreed upon rate-setting methodology did not assure "just and reasonable" rates. In response, the Commission severed this petitioner from the case and allowed settlement to proceed as if it were uncontested. In so doing, the Commission made clear that this settlement was not being imposed on Arctic, in as much as Arctic retained the right independently to contest the rates so determined.[72] Moreover, the Commission emphasized that 1) agreement on the rate-setting method would not be taken to guarantee that the rates determined thereby would be just and reasonable, and 2) the settlement would have no precedential value in subsequent proceedings before the Commission. The Circuit Court affirmed, noting that there were "a number of public-interest advantages flowing from the arrangement" including "the fact that rates have come down substantially ... [and] that the State of Alaska has received substantial refunds redounding to the benefit of its citizens; and that ... competition will be increased in the settlement's wake."[73] The Court also noted that "it is of no little moment that the entities charged with protecting the public interest, including the State of Alaska and the Department of Justice, have heartily approved of the settlement."[74]

Despite the Court's approval of this aspect of FERC's regulations, it is important to note the practical difficulties it may pose for the severed party or parties to the case. Independent pursuit of a large, complicated piece of litigation can be a formidable, if not impossible, task. The resources necessary to contest the issues in a case like *Arctic Slope,* for example, are beyond most parties.[75] Moreover, there is always a risk in this kind of litigation that certain parties take on the status of "regulars." Any kind of recurring agency litigation tends to produce a similar cast of characters who interact with one another so much that they may be able to settle matters among themselves far more easily than they may be able to when more ideologically driven, or less frequent participants in the administrative process are involved. This does not, in and of itself, always lead to a bad result. When, however, some of the nonsettling parties are public interest groups who believe that the public discourse would benefit from a judicial resolution of the dispute, there is a risk that parties that are not "regulars," or parties that seek a principled resolution of issues, will be precluded from trying the case on

a settlement determined by the Commission to be fair and reasonable and in the public interest." 732 F.2d at 209. (footnote omitted). See also, 18 C.F.R. § 385.602(h)(1)(ii)(B) (1981).

71. 832 F.2d 158 (D.C.Cir.1987), cert. denied 488 U.S. 868, 109 S.Ct. 175, 102 L.Ed.2d 145 (1988).

72. Id. at 166–67.

73. Id. at 167.

74. Id.

75. Id. at 161 ("The administrative proceedings in the *Arctic Slope* case involved over 15,000 exhibits and more than 65,000 pages of transcript.").

their own. It is, of course, for the agency to strike an appropriate balance, in such cases. Yet a procedure that allows for the severability of contesting parties can make it relatively easy to avoid confronting the principled conflicts often underlying factual disagreements and the philosophical issues that render settlement difficult or, in some cases, unwise. This is not to argue that a settlement conference is necessarily the place to raise such broad issues. Ideally, cases in which some parties affirmatively seek to change an agency's policy or an agency's legal interpretation of its own powers are, perhaps, best reserved for petitions for rulemaking proceedings.

§ 9.5.4 Settlement at EPA—Superfund Negotiations

Despite, or perhaps because of, the complexity of environmental disputes,[76] such cases have proven especially amenable to ADR techniques.[77] From an efficiency perspective, EPA's overwhelming and exponentially increasing case backlog,[78] coupled with budgetary constraints and Congressional legislation requiring enforcement, leave the agency few options in attempting to manage its workload.[79] For private parties, incentives to settle include the relatively high cost, risk and delay[80] of litigation, combined with the opportunity to reduce their actual liabili-

76. See Anderson, Negotiation and Informal Agency Action: The Case of Superfund, 1985 Duke L.J. 261, 328 (1985) (environmental ADR successful despite tenet that such disputes are "too hotly contested, value-laden, redistributive, and multi-faceted to permit consensual solutions." Anderson's study became the basis of ACUS Recommendation 84–4, Negotiated Cleanup of Hazardous Waste Sites Under CERCLA, 1 C.F.R. § 305.84–4). See also Susskind & Weinstein, Towards A Theory of Environmental Dispute Resolution, 9 Envtl.Aff. 311, 324 (1980) (environmental disputes unique due to irreversibility of ecological effects, indeterminacy of the nature, boundaries, and costs of damage, uncertainty of identification of all responsible parties, and inclusion of participants representing the "public interest" (including unborn generations)).

77. "Approximately ninety percent of EPA's judicial cases are settled." Mays, Applying Alternative Dispute Resolution to Government Litigation and Enforcement Cases, 1 Admin.L.J. 527, 544, 545 (1987). See generally G. Bingham, Resolving Environmental Disputes: A Decade of Experience (1985) (78% success record in ten-year study of mediated environmental disputes.)

78. At present, nearly 30,000 hazardous-waste sites have been inventoried and 1,175 of these are on EPA's National Priority list; a total of 43 sites have been cleaned up. Clean Sites, Inc., Making Superfund Work 1–2 (1989), cited in Gilbert, Alternative Dispute Resolution and Superfund: A Research Guide, 16 Ecology L.Q. 803, 804 (1989).

79. Chief Judge Wald of the D.C. Circuit has noted that: "[I]t is obvious to almost everyone that voluntary settlements are the best and perhaps the only hope for Superfund's success". Wald, supra note 126, at 8. In addition to straightforward practical reasons, "rapid risk reduction lies at the heart of the EPA's statutory mission." Anderson, supra note 185, at 324. Congressional deadlines provide further incentive for the agency to resolve disputes as rapidly as possible. See Leue, Private Party Settlements in the Superfund Amendment and Reauthorization Act of 1986 (SARA), 8 Stanford Envtl.L.J. 131, 147 (1989). Settlement also brings with it the benefit of cooperation by a private sector with superior technical and financial resources, and assists in motivating PRPs' technological progress in cleanup and minimization to avoid further litigation. Id. at 144.

80. Due to CERCLA's scheme of joint and several strict liability, Potentially Responsible Parties (PRPs) are liable for delay-related transaction costs and incremental costs created by site deterioration, as well as being vulnerable to potential civil litigation. Anderson, supra note 185, at 321–322.

ty.[81]

Critics contend, however, that these practical advantages are offset by acute policy concerns about the effects of application of ADR to environmental disputes. Among these are the circumvention of the judiciary as guardian of the public interest,[82] the danger of privatization as well as compromise or disregard of legal standards and public values,[83] and the potential exclusion of interested participants.[84]

These concerns were apparently borne out in the early Superfund settlements that were widely regarded as overgenerous to responsible parties.[85] In an attempt to strike a balance between settlements that imposed few, if any, of the clean-up costs on offending parties and those that imposed all such costs on alleged violators, Congress enacted hazardous waste settlement procedures in the Superfund Amendments and Reauthorization Act (SARA) of 1986.[86] SARA's goals specifically included the need "to expedite effective remedial actions and minimize litigation" between EPA and potentially responsible parties (PRPs).[87] SARA expressly authorized EPA to use negotiations and settlement procedures to secure cleanup agreements with PRPs.[88] It provides EPA

81. The fact that federal cleanup expenses may exceed the cost of equivalent private cleanups by thirty percent or more, potential Justice Department recovery of reimbursement actions, evidentiary problems created by joint and several strict liability, and public-image damage all provide additional incentive for PRPs to settle. Anderson, supra note 185, at 301–302, 321–322. Benefits more intrinsic to settlement itself include the fact that a consensually based agreement created by the principals incorporates a far better understanding of the underlying technical and factual basis than would a judicial order, and may consequently be more sensitive to implementation concerns.

82. Fiss, supra note 129.

83. Edwards, supra note 127.

84. L. Bacow & M. Wheeler, Environmental Dispute Resolution 19 (1984).

85. See Anderson, supra note 185, at 283–84. The following are examples of CERCLA settlements that "drew severe criticism for their generosity to the responsible parties":

(a) In its first CERCLA settlement, an assistant to the EPA administrator allegedly leaked the Agency's lowest bargaining figure to the principal generator at the General Disposal Site in Santa Fe Springs, California. The generator then offered the amount ($700,000) to the EPA when negotiations were verging on failure. The EPA accepted the offer and released the generator from all federal claims under all statutes. No consent decree was entered.

(b) In United States v. Seymour Recycling Corp., 554 F.Supp. 1334 (S.D.Ind. 1982), a district court upheld as reasonable an agreement in which the EPA settled with a group of parties who generated about half of the hazardous waste at a site. It was considered a "sweetheart deal" because the group was allowed to pay for part of the surface cleanup, which cost approximately half of what the rest of the generators had to pay. In addition, the EPA released the group from liability for any of the groundwater cleanup.

(c) In 1982, the EPA reached a settlement with generators to the Chem–Dyne site near Hamilton, Ohio. The generators agreed to pay 70% of the estimated costs of surface cleanup and groundwater studies (this was 30% below its negotiating goal and 10% below the amount the EPA then required to enter negotiations). The EPA released the generators from further surface cleanup liability. It also agreed that should the nonsettling generators who were then being sued implead the settling generators, and the court enter judgment against the settlers, the United States would pay the contribution. Again, no consent decree was entered and thus the settlement was not subject to public comment.

86. 100 Stat. 1678 (codified at 42 U.S.C.A. § 9622).

87. 42 U.S.C.A. § 9622(a).

88. 42 U.S.C.A. § 9622(a). For a perspective on resolution "mechanisms", as opposed to resolution "procedures", and

with subpoena powers[89] as well as authorization for limited judicial review of its decisions.[90] In addition, SARA addresses several previously recurrent disincentives to PRP settlement participation,[91] dealing to some extent with de minimis settlements,[92] covenants not to sue,[93] cost recovery settlement,[94] consent decrees,[95] and mixed funding (combining Superfund and PRP funds to finance site cleanups).[96] These factors, combined with the heavy burden of proof borne by PRPs, provide strong motivation for PRPs to resolve disputes and minimize their liability through settlement procedures.

Under the provisions of SARA, once a hazardous waste site is listed as a priority and the agency makes its discretionary determination to negotiate with PRPs, it is required to furnish them with specified information and notification of its intent to proceed. A 120–day moratorium on EPA–PRP negotiations follows notification, during which EPA may, at its option, prepare nonbinding allocations of costs among the PRPs.

their potential impact on environmental dispute resolution, see Painter, The Future of Environmental Dispute Resolution, 28 Nat.Resources J. 145, 166 (1988). This was a key departure from legislative precedent under the Comprehensive Environmental Response, Compensation and Liability Act of 1980 (CERCLA), also known as "Superfund", 42 U.S.C.A. §§ 9601–9675 which SARA amended.

Enacted in December 1980, CERCLA provided EPA with two procedural approaches for enforcement of hazardous-waste cleanup: the agency was authorized either to pay for governmental treatment of the site and then pursue collection against the responsible parties, or to compel actual private-party cleanup. Three categories of liable parties were established: facility or site owners or operators (both at the time of hazardous waste disposal and at the time of EPA action), those arranging for treatment or disposal or transportation for that purpose of hazardous waste to the site (generators), and parties transporting waste to the site. Habicht, Encouraging Settlements Under Superfund, Nat. Resources & Env't Fall 1985, at 3, 4.

For a concise guide to CERCLA research material, see generally Alexander, CERCLA 1980–1985: A Research Guide, 13 Ecology L.Q. 311 (1986).

89. 42 U.S.C.A. § 9622(e)(3)(B).

90. SARA prohibits judicial review of EPA remedial action under CERCLA § 104 or of administrative orders under § 106, with certain exceptions. 42 U.S.C.A. § 9613(h) (1992 Supp.). For these exceptions, judicial review is limited to the administrative record, and agency action must be upheld unless the court finds the action was arbitrary and capricious or otherwise not in accordance with the law. 42 U.S.C.A. § 9613(j)(1), (2) (1992 Supp.). Such judicial review is allowed if the action involves (a) diversity jurisdiction or common-law state grounds such as nuisance, (b) recovery for costs or contribution under § 107, (c) enforcement, or recovery for violation of, an administrative order issued under § 106(a), (d) reimbursement for § 106 costs if a compliant PRP can establish non-liability for those costs, (e) private citizens alleging under § 310 that the response action violates a provision of SARA, (f) the U.S., brought to compel remedial action under § 106. 42 U.S.C.A. § 9613(h) (1992 Supp.). See Mays, Settlements with SARA: A Comprehensive Review of Settlement Procedures Under the Superfund Amendments and Reauthorization Act, 17 Envtl.L.Rep. (Envtl.L.Inst.) 10101, 10110–10111 (1987) [hereinafter Mays, Settlements with SARA].

91. 42 U.S.C.A. § 9622(b) (1992 Supp.). De minimis parties as defined by the EPA are "low volume, low toxicity disposers who would not normally make a significant contribution to the costs of clean up in any case." 50 Fed.Reg. 5036 (1985), as quoted by Kowalski, Why Can't We Just Settle These Superfund Cases Once and For All?, 5 Va.J. of Nat.Resources L. 179, 189 (1985).

92. 42 U.S.C.A. § 9622(g), 179 (1992 Supp.).

93. 42 U.S.C.A. § 9622(f).

94. 42 U.S.C.A. § 9622(h).

95. 42 U.S.C.A. § 9622(d).

96. 42 U.S.C.A. § 9622(b).

Within 60 days of notification the PRPs must tender a good-faith proposal either for gathering information (including a reliable estimate of potential clean-up costs) or for cleanup. If the PRPs fail to meet the 60–day deadline, the agency may then commence action against them, and the PRPs forfeit their opportunity to take the lead in initial informational development.[97] EPA, however, has customarily offered PRPs the chance to conduct remedial action despite prior uncooperative behavior.[98]

The resulting agreement between the government and PRPs for remedial action is then entered as a consent decree in the appropriate federal court,[99] for a 30–day public-comment period; commentary received during this period indicating that the decree is "inappropriate, improper or inadequate"[100] may result in withdrawal of the decree by the agency. The court may sign and accept the decree, rendering it a final agency order. Before approving a settlement under CERCLA, however, the court may review the settlement to determine that it is "fair, adequate, and reasonable, and consistent with the Constitution and the mandate of Congress."[101]

While SARA may have succeeded in encouraging PRPs to settle with EPA, its safeguard provisions may also have slowed down the actual settlement process. In addition, some tension exists between Federal authority under SARA and state authority under both the Resource Conservation and Recovery Act[102] and state law.[103] Commentators agree that ample room remains for improvement in EPA's settlement facilitation process.[104]

97. 42 U.S.C.A. § 9622(e).

98. Mays, Settlements with SARA, supra note 199, at 10104 (1987). The statutory moratorium periods may be lengthened at the agency's discretion. See also Environmental Protection Agency, Guidance on the Use of Alternative Dispute Resolution Techniques in Enforcement Actions, 18 Envtl. L.Rep. (Envtl.L.Inst.) 35,123 (1988) [hereinafter Guidance].

99. De minimis parties, defined by EPA as "low volume, low toxicity disposers who would not normally make a significant contribution to the costs of clean up in any case," (50 Fed.Reg. 5036 (1985)) are excepted from this requirement. 42 U.S.C.A. § 9622(g).

100. 42 U.S.C.A. § 9622(i)(3).

101. City of New York v. Exxon Corp., 697 F.Supp. 677, 692 (S.D.N.Y.1988) (citation omitted).

102. 42 U.S.C.A. §§ 6901–6987 (1982).

103. See generally Hoard & Lyons, Negotiating with Environmental Regularity Agencies: Working Towards Harmony, 31 Air Force L.R. 201, 205.

104. See generally Note, Superfund Settlements: The Failed Promise of the 1986 Amendments, 74 Va.L.Rev. 123 (1988); Leue, supra note 188; Strock, Settlement Policy Under the Superfund Amendments and Reauthorization Act of 1986, 58 U.Colo.L.Rev. 599, 629 (1988). EPA has also been criticized for its lack of a uniform national hazardous waste policy. See Hoard & Lyons, supra note 212, at 210. For criticism of EPA's policy of encouraging a large PRP (or group thereof) to control the clean-up process on a site, charging that CERCLA's threat of joint and several liability of each PRP leads to the large PRP coercing an unjustly large contribution to cleanup costs from de minimis PRP's, see Sperling, Foxes, Hens, and Ostriches: EPA's Oversight of Private Party Superfund Agreements, Admin.Law News, Summer 1990, at 6.

EPA settlements also occur in a variety of other statutory and litigation contexts. In addition to SARA, number of other environmental statutes allow for settlement of enforcement actions; See Rosin, EPA Settlements of Administrative Litigation, 12 Ecol. L.Q. 363, 364 n. 11–12. Settlement can also

§ 9.5.5 EPA and the Use of ADR Generally

EPA also employs a variety of other ADR techniques. It considers mediation and nonbinding arbitration to be the primary forms of ADR useful in the environmental context. Minitrials and fact-finding, however, are also, on occasion, employed by EPA.[105]

In determining whether to use ADR generally and what kind of ADR process, in particular, EPA considers several factors, including actual or potential impasse, agency familiarity with the legal issues involved, and the existence of relatively well-settled law and precedent in the area under review. Additionally, the agency determines whether the case involves a large number of parties or issues and whether non-parties whose ADR input is considered valuable have expressed interest in participating.[106] In order to proceed with ADR, the agency and all defendants must agree on the necessity of using a neutral third party (e.g., a mediator or arbitrator); beyond this, less than unanimous agreement is necessary to proceed.[107] PRPs and defendants "buy in" to the ADR process by paying an amount equal to that paid by EPA for fees required by the neutral third party; the exact financial terms are generally reduced to a written agreement before ADR is initiated.[108] The method of selecting the neutral third party is determined by all the parties.[109]

The agency recommends that third party neutrals have the following qualifications: demonstrated experience, subject-matter expertise, and lack of involvement with another phase of the enforcement process for that particular case. Neutrals must disclose any relationship or interest that might give rise to bias. In addition, a corporate entity serving as third-party neutral must submit a list of all persons who will or may be significantly involved on its behalf in the ADR process.[110]

Subsequent proceedings will vary according to the parties' choice of terms and type of ADR. All records and information generated in the course of ADR are confidential and, unless otherwise discoverable, cannot be used in litigation or disclosed without permission.[111]

Settlements reached through ADR are subject to limited judicial review prior to final approval and entry. The standard of permissible review is whether the agreement is "fair and adequate and [is] not unlawful, unreasonable, or against public policy."[112]

Upon entry by the court or, on occasion, by an ALJ at the agency

occur in the context of legal and policy proceedings. 50 Fed.Reg. 47212 (1985).

105. Guidance, supra note 207, at 35,-124.

106. Id. at 35,125.

107. Id. at 35,126.

108. Exceptions may be made in unusual circumstances. Id. at 35,127.

109. CERCLA settlement actions are excepted from this requirement by CERCLA § 107. Id. at 35,126.

110. Id. at 35,126–35,127.

111. Id. at 35,127.

112. United States v. Hooker Chemicals and Plastics Corp., 540 F.Supp. 1067, 1072 (W.D.N.Y.1982).

level, the settlement becomes a final agency action.[113] Despite this legal status, however, a plaintiff may be unable to obtain judicial review if the governing statute lacks a provision for granting it. In *NLRB v. United Food and Commercial Workers Union,*[114] the Supreme Court characterized the attempted use of APA judicial review provisions in such a context as "absurd", and commented that, given the governing statute, "this hazard to the functioning of the 'lifeblood' of the administrative process could certainly not have been the congressional intention."[115] Prior to the enactment of CERCLA and SARA, a 1976 decision found that, in reviewing EPA settlement agreements, "the court will not review substantive judgments made by the Administrator of the EPA ... but will merely ensure good faith compliance with the provisions of the agreement."[116]

Even if the statute does provide for review, two potential problems remain. First, in some enforcement contexts, a decision to settle is closely analogous to a decision not to prosecute. Such prosecutorial decisions are committed to agency discretion and are thus unreviewable.[117] Even if the court finds that there is law to apply, however, obtaining review of settlements that propose to make policy or provide new interpretations of existing statutes is problematic and may not be ripe for review. Until agency action takes place, none of the parties' interests have been affected and no concrete controversy exists for judicial purposes at the time of settlement.[118] Once formal agency enforcement action relating to the promulgation or withdrawal of a rule actually takes place, however, such action becomes ripe for review.[119]

113. Natural Resources Defense Council v. Costle, 561 F.2d 904 (D.C.Cir.1977) (motion to intervene by impacted third parties timely upon implementation proceedings); City of New York v. Exxon Corp., 697 F.Supp. 677 (S.D.N.Y.1988) (though the contribution and apportionment issues in question might never ripen, ruling on settlement would affect nonsettling defendants' litigation strategy, such ruling therefore held appropriate); United States v. Hooker Chemicals and Plastics Corp., 540 F.Supp. 1067 (W.D.N.Y.1982) (right to intervene granted by Clean Water Act supported granting of a motion to intervene prior to approval of settlement agreement by the court). But see B.R. MacKay & Sons, Inc. v. United States, 633 F.Supp. 1290 (D.Utah 1986) (no judicial review of final agency action prior to government cost recovery action).

114. 484 U.S. 112, 108 S.Ct. 413, 98 L.Ed.2d 429 (1987), on remand 840 F.2d 171 (3d Cir.1988).

115. 484 U.S. at 133, 108 S.Ct. at 426.

116. Natural Resources Defense Council, Inc. v. Train, 6 Envtl. L.Rep. 20,588, 8 Env't Rep.Cas. (BNA) 2120 (D.D.C.1976).

117. See NLRB v. United Food and Commercial Workers Union, 484 U.S. 112, 108 S.Ct. 413, 98 L.Ed.2d 429 (1987), on remand 840 F.2d 171 (3d Cir.1988); see also, Heckler v. Chaney, 470 U.S. 821, 105 S.Ct. 1649, 84 L.Ed.2d 714 (1985).

118. "[U]ntil regulations are promulgated, there is not a concrete controversy.... [A]pproval of the agreement creates no precedent on the legality of the specific regulations which may emerge." Natural Resources Defense Council, Inc. v. Train, 8 Env't Rep.Cas. (BNA) 2120, 2121 (D.D.C. 1976); see also S.E.C. v. Canadian Javelin Ltd., 64 F.R.D. 648, 650–51 (S.D.N.Y.1974); United States v. Carter Products, Inc., 211 F.Supp. 144, 148 (S.D.N.Y.1962). See also J.V. Peters & Co. v. Administrator, EPA, 767 F.2d 263, 264 (6th Cir.1985) ("allowance of a cause of action prior to a response action would debilitate the central function" of the legislation empowering the agency).

119. Rosin, EPA Settlements of Administrative Litigation, 12 Ecology L.Q. 363, 376–78 (1985).

§ 9.5.6 Mediation

Mediation is closely related to traditional settlement techniques. Like settlement judges or presiding officers, mediators are neutral third parties who assist the litigants in negotiating an agreement; however, unlike a judge or an arbitrator, the mediator has no power to impose a decision on the parties.[120] Mediation is a common dispute resolution device in labor matters; it has also been used in family disputes[121] and, increasingly, in environmental matters.[122] A judge sympathetic to mediation may play a key role in encouraging the parties to employ this technique.

The mediator's many and varied functions often require a considerable personal reservoir of perception, diplomatic talent, and ability to accommodate the often complex issues involved. If involved from the beginning of a dispute, the mediator may sound out the parties' grievances, propose negotiation as a viable technique (thereby allowing each party to avoid compromising its posture in the dispute), identify parties that should be included, and assist in structuring the negotiations.[123] The mediator, in confidential meetings with individual parties, can help them assess the potential costs of litigating the dispute, establish the degree to which, and areas in which they are willing to make concessions, and separate their actual needs and interests from their negotiation postures.[124]

Once negotiations have begun, the mediator may submit to the participants sensitive concerns and potential solutions proposed anonymously by one party, thus "taking the heat off" the proposer. In individual meetings, he or she can help the parties assess proposals realistically and present the other side's perspective as data to be considered in positional analyses. Finally, the mediator may act as manager of the parties' commitment to the negotiation process, maintaining lines of communication and recognizing and assisting the parties in dealing with volatile issues. Should negotiations encounter difficulty or threaten to break down, the mediator will seek commonalities between the parties and endeavor to pull the parties back on track.[125]

120. See John D. Feerick, Toward Uniform Standards of Conduct for Mediators, 38 S. Tex. L. Rev., 455, 458 (1997). In this sense, a mediator is also a facilitator. Since a facilitator rarely gets involved in the substance of the issues under negotiation, a facilitator is not also a mediator.

121. See Jean R. Sternlight, Lawyers' Representation of Clients in Mediation: Using Economics and Psychology to Structure Advocacy in a Nonadversarial Setting, 14 Ohio St.J. on Disp. Resol. 269, 283 (1999) (discussing the advantages and drawbacks of family dispute mediation).

122. Diane R. Smith, "Rough Justice," "Fairness," and the Process of Environmental Mediation, 34 Val. U.L. Rev. 367 (2000); Elaine Smith, Danger–Inequality of Resources Present: Can the Environmental Mediation Process Provide an Effective Answer?, 1996 J. Disp. Resol. 379 (1996).

123. See Stephen B. Goldberg et al., Dispute Resolution 107 (1985).

124. See Harter, Points On A Continuum, supra note 146, at 148–149.

125. Id.

§ 9.5.7 Minitrials

The minitrial has been described as "a carefully structured, private settlement negotiation where counsel for opposing parties present condensed versions of their cases in the presence of senior executives from each side who possess the ultimate authority to settle the dispute."[126] The idea behind the minitrial is that the parties can resolve a dispute on their own more efficiently if litigant representatives with settling authority are educated about the strengths and weaknesses of each side, giving summary presentations of their best cases under the eye of a jointly selected neutral advisor. After each case is presented, the parties meet privately to negotiate an agreement. The minitrial is confidential and nonbinding. Usually, no transcript is made of the proceeding.[127] Minitrials have had some success in saving both time and money.[128]

Many scholars assume that minitrial work best in disputes over mixed questions of law and fact.[129] Some scholars, however, argue that if the question at issue is one of pure law, or if precedent is being established, then the minitrial is not appropriate. Others counter that the minitrial is too new to discount completely its effectiveness in controversies over questions of law.[130] Still others note that a dispute over facts may require lengthy discovery, whereas the minitrial is valued for its speedy disposition of the case. There is evidence suggesting minitrial work best in factual, technical cases.[131] Some practicing attorneys, however, have expressed skepticism with regard to minitrials. Results from a 1990–91 American Bar Association Forum on a Construction Industry survey[132] and a 1994 Multidisciplinary Survey on Dispute Avoidance and Resolution in the Construction Industry[133] revealed that these attorneys strongly favor other dispute resolution mechanisms over minitrials,[134] and that, in fact, minitrials are frequently used in ways not thought sound by dispute resolution theorists.[135]

When minitrials are used, the parties involved usually draft a minitrial agreement specifying the names of the principals, the issues involved, whether or not a neutral advisor will facilitate negotiations, and the allocation of expenses.[136] Additionally, the parties should be careful to limit the duration and scope of discovery so as to ensure the benefit of the expedited mechanism. Finally, the parties should agree to suspend traditional litigation for the duration of the minitrial.

126. Douglas A. Henderson, Avoiding Litigation With the Mini–Trial: The Corporate Bottom Line as Dispute Resolution Technique, 46 S.C. L. Rev. 237, 238 (1995).

127. Id. at 239–41.

128. The average time for a minitrial is five days, and the average direct cost is $25,000. Id. at 250.

129. See Henderson, supra note 235, at 245.

130. Id.

131. Id.

132. Id. at 247–65.

133. See Thomas J. Stipanowich, Beyond Arbitration: Innovation and Evolution in the United States Construction Industry, 31 Wake Forest L. Rev., 65, 124–79 (1996).

134. Id. at 90–123.

135. See Henderson, supra note 235, at 261.

136. Edelman & Carr, supra note 108, at 12.

§ 9.5.8 Arbitration

Arbitration is adjudication performed by private adjudicators. It is a common alternative means of private dispute resolution. Public arbitration is performed by courts and administrative agencies. Using private arbitrators to adjudicate disputes arising in public programs can raise a variety of constitutional, legal and practical problems. Nevertheless, arbitration does offer some promise in some administrative contexts.

Arbitration is a flexible procedure ranging in appearance from the formality of a trial to completely informal discussion and negotiation.[137] Parties face a plethora of options. They may engage in full discovery, use sworn witnesses, present elaborate briefs, and fully argue their cases, or they may opt for a simple, fast hearing facilitating expeditious resolution of their dispute. One of the great benefits of arbitration is the ability to select an arbitrator with special expertise in the subject matter of a particular dispute.

Arbitration may be binding or advisory, voluntary or mandatory. In voluntary arbitration, the parties agree either before or after a conflict has arisen to submit their dispute to arbitration. The parties also agree on the arbitration procedures to be used. In mandatory arbitration, arbitration procedure as well as the result is imposed on the parties.

Though arbitration is generally a private ADR technique, a number of statutes authorize administrative agencies to use it.[138] For example, the Agricultural Adjustment Act[139] grants the Secretary of Agriculture the authority to arbitrate disputes arising out of the sale and distribution of milk;[140] the South Pacific Tuna Act of 1988[141] gives the Secretary of State and Secretary of Commerce the authority to appoint an arbitrator "[i]n the event of a dispute requiring the establishment of an arbitral tribunal" in disputes that arise under the Treaty on Fisheries Between the Governments of Certain Pacific Island States and the Government of the United States of America;[142] and under the Comprehensive Environ-

137. See Harter, supra note 146, at 154.

138. See, e.g., 7 U.S.C. § 136a(c)(1)(F)(iii) (2000) (arbitration provided under the Federal Insecticide, Fungicide, and Rodenticide Act (FIFRA)); 7 U.S.C. § 671 (1999) (authorizing Secretary of Agriculture to use arbitration to settle milk disputes); 16 U.S.C. § 973n (2000) (empowering Secretary of State and Secretary of Commerce to name an arbitrator to settle South Pacific Island tuna fishing disputes); 17 U.S.C. § 801 (2000) (authorizing Librarian of Congress to convene copyright royalty arbitration panels); 39 U.S.C. § 1207 (providing for arbitration in U.S. Postal Service employee labor disputes); 42 U.S.C. 4083 (1999) (authorizing the Director of the Federal Emergency Management System to arbitrate Federal flood insurance claims); 42 U.S.C. § 9622(h)(2) (1999) (authorizing arbitration in settlements under the Comprehensive Environmental response, Compensation and Liability Act ("Superfund")).

139. Ch. 25, 48 Stat. 31, as amended by Ch. 296, § 3, 50 Stat. 248.

140. 7 U.S.C. 671(a) (1999). See also United States v. Borden Co., 308 U.S. 188, 201–2, 60 S.Ct. 182, 84 L.Ed. 181 (1939) (finding that an arbitration award approved by the Secretary would be a defense to antitrust litigation).

141. Pub. Law No. 100–330, § 2, 102 Stat. 591.

142. April 2, 1987, T.I.A.S. No. 11100. See also Republic of Kazakhstan v. Biedermann Int'l, 168 F.3d 880, 881 (5th Cir. 1999) ("References in the United States Code to 'arbitral tribunals' almost uniformly concern an adjunct of a foreign government or international agency").

mental response, Compensation and Liability Act ("Superfund"),[143] the Environmental Protection Agency is authorized to arbitrate settlements where the cost of cleanup does not exceed $500,000.[144]

Although Administrative arbitration is based on agency precedent,[145] it cannot be used as precedent.[146] In fact, an agency should not consider using arbitration, or ADR in general, if "a definitive or authoritative resolution of the matter required for precedential value, and such a proceeding is not likely to be accepted generally as an authoritative precedent."[147] Final arbitration awards are binding on all parties, including the federal government, and may be enforced pursuant to the Federal Arbitration Act (FAA) (codified at 9 U.S.C. §§ 9–13).[148]

The standard of judicial review for binding agency arbitration is not settled,[149] but at least four approaches now exist. First, parties can waive all judicial review.[150] If that does not occur, some courts will only reverse the agency if it is shown that the agency award has no basis in evidence and contravenes the law.[151] Others determine whether the law incorporates the standard of review found in the Alternative Dispute Resolution Act[152] and the Federal Arbitration Act. Under this standard, a federal district court must determine whether a contested agency arbitration award is the result of bias, fraud, corruption, or arbitrator misconduct,[153] or if the award is "clearly inconsistent with the factors" in 5 U.S.C. § 572 (1999).[154] Finally, still another approach would review an award in the usual manner, pursuant to the APA.[155] If the law provides for

143. Pub. L. No. 96–510, Title I, § 101, 94 Stat. 2767.

144. 42 U.S.C. § 9622(h)(2) (1999). Cf. Disston Co. v. Sandvik, Inc., 750 F.Supp. 745, 746 (W.D.Va.1990) (noting that "[n]o reported cases consider whether or not CERCLA claims may be subject to binding arbitration clauses"); United States v. Acton Corp., 733 F.Supp. 869, 871 (D.N.J. 1990) (approving a CERCLA settlement between private parties that relied on ADR).

145. 732 F.2d 213 (D.C.Cir.1984).

146. 5 U.S.C. § 580(d) (1999). See also H.R. Rep. No. 104–597, at 3 (1996).

147. 5 U.S.C. 572(b)(1) (1999).

148. 5 U.S.C.A. § 580 (c) (Supp. 2000).

149. See 1995 OLC LEXIS 17, at *2–4. See generally Patricia M. Wald, ADR and the Courts: An Update, 46 Duke L.J. 1445, 1451–56 (1997) (discussing the standard of judicial review of agency-annexed ADR).

150. See Commodity Futures Trading Comm'n v. Schor, 478 U.S. 833, 849, 106 S.Ct. 3245, 92 L.Ed.2d 675 (1986) (finding that a decision to seek relief in an agency proceeding waived any right to a full trial).

151. See National Ass'n of Broadcasters v. Librarian of Congress, 146 F.3d 907, 924 (D.C.Cir.1998) (applying an "arbitrary manner" standard of review, which is more deferential than the APA standard of review).

152. Pub. L. No. 101–552, 104 Stat. 2736 (1990), permanently reauthorized by Pub.L. No. 104–320, § 9, 110 Stat. 3872 (1996).

153. 9 U.S.C. § 10(a) (1999). See also United States v. Georgia–Pacific Corp., 960 F.Supp. 298, 299 (N.D.Ga.1996) ("[T]he Court should approve of the settlement if it determines that the settlement is fair and reasonable, and resolves the controversy in a manner consistent with the public interest.").

154. Id. Cf. Harter, supra note 146, at 83 (arguing that arbitration award should be reviewed "only for gross deviation from policy or procedure, which is the administrative analog of the award's being outside the proper scope of the arbitrator's authority"); Tenaska Washington Partners II, L.P. v. United States, 34 Fed. Cl. 434, 443 (Fed. Cl.1995) (finding that review of an agency arbitration award is limited to "a claim of corruption, fraud, or undue means").

155. See National Ass'n of Broadcasters v. Librarian of Congress, 146 F.3d at 920 9cataloguing the "list of administrative transgressions set forth in the APA".

administrative adjudication and an appeal of the agency decision to be determined by arbitration, a party may be required to exhaust all administrative and arbitral remedies before seek judicial review.[156]

Administrative arbitration raises several possible constitutional problems. Article III problems are the most significant. The specific issue raised by agency arbitration is the extent to which adjudicative authority assigned to federal courts may be granted not to administrators, as in *Crowell v. Benson,* but to private decisionmakers. This was at issue in *Thomas v. Union Carbide Agr. Products Co.*[157] There, petitioners challenged the use of arbitration to resolve disputes over EPA's requirement that manufacturers seeking to register a pesticide must give EPA research data on the product's likely effects on health, safety, and the environment. EPA considers this data not only in connection with the original registration of the pesticide, but also when later applicants seek to register similar products. The later registrants must compensate earlier registrants for the use of the earlier data, and if there is a disagreement over the amount of compensation, the dispute is resolved by arbitration, not agency adjudication. The Supreme Court rejected arguments that only private rights were involved, noting that:

> Congress, acting for a valid legislative purpose pursuant to its constitutional powers under Article I, may create a seemingly "private" right that is so closely integrated into a regulatory scheme as to be a matter appropriate for agency resolution with limited involvement by the Article III judiciary. To hold otherwise would be to erect a rigid and formalistic restraint on the ability of Congress to adopt innovative measures such as negotiation and arbitration with respect to rights created by a regulatory scheme.[158]

The Court recognized Congress' desire to streamline procedures in this area through binding arbitration.[159] Arbitration was important for the effective administration of a public program. Moreover, there was little danger of undermining Article III judicial power since the firms involved consented to arbitration and thus "no unwilling defendant is subjected to judicial enforcement power.... "[160] Finally, the Court found that FIFRA's limited scope of judicial review provided the necessary and legitimizing Article III link to these arbitration procedures.[161]

The Court's analysis in *Thomas* and its impact on agency arbitration is consistent with the relatively flexible approach to Article III issues the Supreme Court took in *Schor v. Commodity Futures Trading Commis-*

156. See, e.g., Fillinger v. Cleveland Soc'y for the Blind, 587 F.2d 336, 338 (6th Cir.1978).

157. 473 U.S. 568, 105 S.Ct. 3325, 87 L.Ed.2d 409 (1985).

158. Id. at 593–94, 105 S.Ct. at 3339–40.

159. Id. at 573–75, 105 S.Ct. at 3329–30.

160. Id. at 591, 105 S.Ct. at 3338.

161. Id. at 592–93, 105 S.Ct. at 3339. The standard for judicial review "protects against arbitrators who abuse or exceed their powers or willfully misconstrue their mandate under the governing law." See generally, Fletcher, Privatizing Securities Disputes Through the Enforcement of Arbitration Agreements, 71 Minn.L.Rev. 393 (1987).

sion.[162] In that case, the Supreme Court held that the CFTC could render a decision on a state law counterclaim arising out of the same transaction as did the original dispute before the agency, because "the courts would still be called upon to enforce the order; the legal rulings would be subject to *de novo* review; the range of issues presented was narrow; and, the scheme did not oust the courts of jurisdiction because the parties could still proceed there instead of before the agency."[163] The Court compared the CFTC option to arbitration and argued that only the choice of alternative procedure minimized separation of powers concerns.[164]

Arbitration can also raise Article II concerns. Arbitrators must be appointed and this can raise separation of powers issues. While much has been written about the separation of powers doctrine, little has been written about the relevance of it to agency ADR.[165] The doctrine of separation of powers developed by the Supreme Court rests on four assumptions:[166] (1) that "[w]hen any branch acts, it is presumptively exercising the power the Constitution has delegated to it,"[167] (2) that each branch should not "exceed that outer limits of its power, even to accomplish desirable objectives,"[168] (3) that no branch may "impair another in the performance of its Constitutional duties,"[169] and (4) that "Congress cannot delegate to the Courts, or to any tribunals, powers which are strictly and exclusively legislative."[170] Article II separation of powers issues could be implicated were Congress to aggrandize power to itself by appointing or retaining removal or continuing authority over an arbitrator[171] who had authority that was constitutionally vested in the Executive Branch,[172] or if a decision of the President were subject to arbitration.[173] Nevertheless, the functional approach to separation of

162. 740 F.2d 1262 (D.C.Cir.1984), vacated 473 U.S. 922, 105 S.Ct. 3551, 87 L.Ed.2d 674, reinstated 770 F.2d 211 (D.C.Cir.1985), reversed, 478 U.S. 833, 106 S.Ct. 3245, 92 L.Ed.2d 675 (1986).

163. Harter, Points On a Continuum, supra note 146, at 167 (footnotes omitted).

164. Professor Bruff has argued that:

In both *Thomas* and *Schor* the Court associated coercion with inherent judicial power. That casts some doubt on strictly nonconsensual arbitration, for example in regulatory enforcement. Nevertheless, the Court's characterization of FIFRA registrations as "voluntary" may signal its intention to employ a narrow definition of coercion.

Bruff, supra note 130, at 34.

Professor Bruff also has noted that there are statutory limits to arbitration as well.

Courts will not defer in all cases. See Wilko v. Swan, 346 U.S. 427, 74 S.Ct. 182, 98 L.Ed. 168 (1953), and Alexander v. Gardner–Denver Co., 415 U.S. 36, 94 S.Ct. 1011, 39 L.Ed.2d 147 (1974).

165. See Neil Kinkopf, Of Devolution, Privatization, and Globalization: Separation of Powers Limits on Congressional Authority to Assign Federal Powers to Non–Federal Actors, 50 Rutgers L. Rev. 331, 333 (1998).

166. Id. at 338–39

167. INS v. Chadha, 462 U.S. 919, 951, 103 S.Ct. 2764, 77 L.Ed.2d 317 (1983).

168. Id.

169. Clinton v. Jones, 520 U.S. 681, 701, 117 S.Ct. 1636, 137 L.Ed.2d 945 (1997).

170. Wayman v. Southard, 23 U.S. (10 Wheat) 1, 42, 6 L.Ed. 253 (1825).

171. 1995 OLC LEXIS 17, at *56.

172. Id. at *59. Cf. Morrison v. Olson, 487 U.S. 654, 108 S.Ct. 2597, 101 L.Ed.2d 569 (1988) (holding that the President must retain some control over federal prosecutorial power).

173. 1995 OLC LEXIS 17, at *60. Agency ADR still calls for sensitivity to Article II separation of powers issues, par-

powers adopted by the Court in *Morrison v. Olson*[174] suggests that there is a good deal of room for private arbitration, even in an enforcement setting. Arbitration seems particularly suited to cases where the arbitrator's primary role is limited to factfinding and the application of well-settled principles of law and policy to the facts.

Arbitration can also raise Appointments Clause[175] issues under Article II. Justice Scalia, in *Printz v. United States*,[176] suggested that the power over inferior officers[177] conferred to the Executive by the Appointments Clause is what enables the President to "take Care that the law be faithfully executed" (U.S. Const. art. II § 3).[178] It could be argues that to appoint a neutral third party who is not an Executive Branch official to arbitrate agency disputes unconstitutionally places Executive authority outside the sphere of Executive control.[179] In the late 1980s, U.S. Department of Justice attorneys argued that the assignment of an arbitrator to a dispute by an agency violated the Appointments Clause.[180] In 1995, the DOJ reversed its position,[181] and argued in memorandum from the Office of Legal Council[182] that, with certain exceptions, the United States could enter binding arbitration.[183] The Appointments Clause, according to the DOJ, was implicated "only if there is created or an individual is appointed to (1) a position of employment[184] (2) within

ticularly since Congress spent the last decade of the twentieth century "shearing" Federal power from the Federal government by assigning State power to non-State actors. See Kinkopf, supra note 274, at 332. See also Jonathan D. Mester, Note & Comment, The Administrative Dispute Resolution Act of 1996: Will the New Era of ADR in Federal Administrative Agencies Occur at the Expense of Public Accountability?, 13 Ohio St. J. on Disp. Resol. 167 (1997).

174. 487 U.S. 654, 108 S.Ct. 2597, 101 L.Ed.2d 569 (1988). For a detailed discussion of Morrison v. Olson, see chapter 15, sec. 15.4.5, infra.

175. U.S. Const. Art. II, § 2, cl. 2.

176. 521 U.S. 898, 117 S.Ct. 2365, 138 L.Ed.2d 914 (1997).

177. For the meaning of "officer" within the Appointments Clause, see United States v. Hartwell, 73 U.S. (6 Wall.) 385, 393, 18 L.Ed. 830 (1900); United States v. Smith, 124 U.S. 525, 8 S.Ct. 595, 31 L.Ed. 534 (1888).

178. Id. at 922. Cf. Buckley v. Valeo, 424 U.S. 1, 131, 96 S.Ct. 612, 46 L.Ed.2d 659 (1976) (finding that the Appointments Clause encompasses "all appointed officials exercising responsibility under the public laws of the Nation").

179. But see Kinkopf, supra note 274, at 336 (arguing that "[u]nder the established separation of powers doctrine . . . the Printz dictum and the argument from the Appointments Clause are untenable"). Cf. Harold H. bruff, Public Programs, Private Deciders: The Constitutionality of Arbitration in Federal Programs, 67 Tex. L. rev. 441, 487 (1989) ("Comparison of a private delegation with the government function it displaces must include consideration of the legal constraints on that function, to see how much discretion the executive actually loses and to what extent the executive retains control over arbitration.").

180. See 1995 OLC LEXIS 17, at *2–4.

181. Id. at *1. Approximately one year after the DOJ submitted its opinion, president Clinton revoked Executive Order 12,-778, 56 Fed. reg. 55,195 (1991), which had forbidden litigation counsel for federal agencies from seeking or agreeing to binding arbitration. See Exec. Order No. 12,988, 61 Fed. Reg. 4,729 (1996).

182. OLC memoranda are binding on the DOJ and other Executive Branch agencies. See Tenaska Washington Partners II, L.P. v. United States, 34 Fed. Cl. 434, 439 (Fed. Cl. 1995).

183. The phrase "binding arbitration" does not have a settled meaning. Id. at *6. The DOJ takes it to mean that judicial review of an arbitral decision is narrowly limited, or is reviewable only for arbitrator fraud or for arbitrary and capricious decision making. Id. at *7.

184. See generally United States v. Maurice, 26 F. Cas. 1211, 1214 (C.C.D.Va. 1823) (No. 15,747), opinion by Marshall,

the federal government[185] (3) that is vested with significant authority pursuant to the laws of the United States."[186] Following the analysis of the DOJ, the firing of a private contractor to act as an arbitrator in a single case would not violate the Appointments Clause. One the other hand, if an agency employed a full-time arbitrator, that arbitrator would have to be appointed pursuant to the Appointments Clause.[187] Justice Scalia's *Printz* dictum also implies that the final judgment of an arbitrator would violate the Take Care Clause[188] by subordinating the President's judgment to the arbitrator's judgment and thereby co-opt the President's duty to "faithfully" execute the law.[189] In the opinion of the DOJ, however, the "Take Care" clause only requires the President to follow whatever valid legal requirement resulted from the arbitrator's decision.[190]

In *Tenaska Washington Partners II, L.P. v. United States*,[216] the issue before the U.S. Court of Federal Claims was whether the United States could enter binding arbitration. The Bonneville Power Administration (BPA), an agency of the Department of Energy, entered an agreement with a private energy supplier, Tenaska. BPA executed a contract to buy energy from Tenaska for twenty years, but later refused to perform on the contract. Tenaska sued BOA in the U.S. Court of federal claims. BPA, relying on an arbitration provision contained in its contract with Tenaska, moved to stay discovery in anticipation of filing a motion to compel arbitration. Tenaska argued that BPA lacked both constitutional and statutory authority to enter binding arbitration. The court, relying on a 1995 DOJ memorandum on binding arbitration,[217] found no constitutional prohibitions against BPA entering binding arbitration and further found that Congress had empowered the BPA officer to settle any claim, which implied that the officer could settle any claim by arbitration.[218] Although *Tenaska* is a rare case of agency arbitration that has been litigated, the court noted that "[a] new era of federal arbitration may be dawning, the extent of which remains to be seen."[219]

Article I and due process issues can also arise. Delegation of administrative power to private decisionmakers recalls the teaching of *Carter v.*

Circuit Justice (finding that a person may be employed under contract by the government without becoming an officer); United States v. Germaine, 99 U.S. (9 Otto) 508, 25 L.Ed. 482 (1878) (finding that a federal officer's duties are continuing and permanent, not intermittent and occasional).

185. See Germaine, supra note 293, at 510 (finding that Appointments Clause pertains only to those persons who hold a federal government office).

186. See Buckley v. Valeo, 424 U.S. at 126; 1995 OLC LEXIS 17, at *11. Cf. Confederated Tribes of Siletz Indians of Oregon v. U.S. Dep't of Interior, 841 F.Supp. 1479, 1486 (D.C.Or.1994).

187. 1995 OLC LEXIS 17, at *30–38.

188. U.S. Const. art. II, § 1, cl. 1; id. art. II, § 3.

189. 1995 OLC LEXIS 17, at *50.

190. Id. at *53. See also Kendall v. United States ex rel. Stokes, 37 U.S. (12 Pet.) 524, 609–13, 9 L.Ed. 1181 (1838) (holding that the executive branch had to comply when Congress ordered the Solicitor of the Dep't of Treasury to resolve a dispute between the Postmaster General and several contractors).

216. 34 Fed. Cl. 434 (Fed. Cl. 1995).

217. 1995 OLC LEXIS 17.

218. 34 Fed. Cl. at 442–43.

219. Id. at 440.

Carter Coal Co.,[220] where the Court invalidated a statute delegating power to set maximum hours and minimum wages for the coal industry, holding, in effect, that a delegation to private decision makers violated the Due Process Clause.[221] Delegations can also raise Article I issues as well, particularly if the delegation is vague or without standards. These issues, however, rarely become serious unless there is a wholesale delegation to private parties, without guidance or supervision from either public officials or Congress. Most arbitration provisions could easily be structured to avoid these difficulties.[222]

Due process concerns have arisen in the context of arbitration and medicare reimbursements. In *Schweiker v. McClure,*[223] the Supreme Court unanimously upheld the adjudication of disputed medicare claims by private insurance carriers without a right of appeal. The Court rejected a variety of fairness arguments, and relied heavily on the fact that the private carriers who made these decisions had no monetary conflict of interest.[224] Their salaries and any resulting claims were paid by the government, not their employers. Moreover, the nature of the decision was determined by statute and regulation; they had to operate under procedures specified by the agency.[225] Most arbitration, it would seem, easily could fall within the guidelines set forth in this case.

§ 9.5.9 Negotiated Rulemaking

ADR is not limited to adjudicatory contexts. Faced with the increasingly adversarial atmosphere of agency rulemaking, the lengthy proceedings that hybrid rulemaking often involve, and the almost inevitable judicial appeals that result, both the agencies and parties involved have increasingly expressed interest in a negotiated approach to policymaking.[226] The Negotiated Rulemaking Act of 1990[227] is designed to encourage negotiations between agencies and affected parties prior to the notice and comment period of the APA.[228] If the head of an agency determines that negotiated rulemaking is in the public interest, she may appoint a convener who identifies affected parties and establishes the topics of concern to those parties.[229] The affected parties form a negotiated rule-

220. 298 U.S. 238, 56 S.Ct. 855, 80 L.Ed. 1160 (1936). See generally, Liebmann, Delegation to Private Parties in American Constitutional Law, 50 Ind.L.J. 650 (1975).

221. Id. at 311, 56 S.Ct. at 872.

222. FIFRA's delegation to arbitrators may, however, be in violation of even these most basic principles. See, e.g., the district court opinion in Union Carbide Agricultural Products Co. v. Ruckleshaus, 571 F.Supp. 117, 124 (S.D.N.Y.1983) rev'd sub nom. Thomas v. Union Carbide Agr. Prods. Co., 473 U.S. 568, 105 S.Ct. 3325, 87 L.Ed.2d 409 (1985). But see PPG Industries, Inc. v. Stauffer Chemical Co., 637 F.Supp. 85, 87 (D.D.C.1986).

223. 456 U.S. 188, 102 S.Ct. 1665, 72 L.Ed.2d 1 (1982).

224. Id. at 195–97, 102 S.Ct. at 1669–71.

225. Id. at 197, 102 S.Ct. at 1671.

226. See Harter, supra note 146.

227. Pub.L. 101–648, § 3(a), 104 Stat. 4969 (codified as amended at 5 U.S.C.A. §§ 561–70 (1996 & supp. 2000)), permanently reauthorized by the Administrative Dispute Resolution Act of 1996, Pub.L. No. 104–320, § 11(a), 110 Stat. 3870, 3873.

228. 5 U.S.C.A. § 551 (1996).

229. 5 U.S.C.A. § 563 (1996).

making committee[230] of not more than twenty-five members[231] that tries to reach a consensus as to what the agency rule should be.[232] If the negotiated rulemaking committee reaches a consensus about the proposed rule, it reports the proposed rule to the agency,[233] which may adopt the proposed rule of the committee as the basis of its proposed regulation, which is then published for comment pursuant to the APA.

The Act received its first judicial interpretation in *USA Group Loan Services, Inc. v. Riley*.[234] The issue was whether an agency official's promise to abide by the consensus of a negotiated rulemaking committee was enforceable. The Court held that such a promise was not enforceable. The controversy in *USA Group Loan Services* involved the Department of Education (DOE) and a student loan "servicer," which is a third party that contracts to perform student loan record-keeping for schools and to collect student loans for banks. Subsequent to an APA negotiated rulemaking procedure in which the services had rejected a DOE limited-liability proposal, the DOE prescribed regulations that made the servicers liable for the total of any uncollectable student loan overpayment that was caused by servicer misfeasance. The servicers argued that during the negotiated rulemaking, a DOE official had promised that a cap would be placed on servicer liability. The final DOE regulations provided no such cap. The court found that not only did the Negotiated Rulemaking Act not make the DOE official's promise enforceable,[235] but that to enforce the official's promise would "extinguish notice and comment rulemaking in all cases in which it was preceded by negotiated rulemaking,"[236] because "the comments would be irrelevant if the agency were already bound by promises that it had made to the industry."[237]

Administrative law scholars continue to debate the merits of negotiated rulemaking. The debate falls within two broad categories: statistical and normative. Under the statistical category, Professor Cary Coglianese argues that negotiated rulemaking has failed to achieve proponents' instrumental goals of reducing the time spent developing regulations and reducing subsequent judicial challenges to regulations.[238] According to

230. 5 U.S.C.A. § 564 (1996).

231. 5 U.S.C.A. § 565 (1996).

232. 5 U.S.C.A. § 566(a) (1996).

233. 5 U.S.C.A. § 566(f) (1996).

234. 82 F.3d 708 (7th Cir.1996), opinion by Posner, Chief J.

235. But see William Funk, Bargaining Toward the New Millennium: Regulatory Negotiation and the Subversion of the Public Interest, 46 Duke L.J. 1351, 1363–65 (1997) (arguing that a bad faith promise might be enforceable).

236. 82 F.3d at 714.

237. Id. at 714–15. The Court also said that the official's promise was analogous to a settlement offer, which is not admissible as evidence if the settlement fails. Id. at 715. Chief Judge Posner came under criticism from some administrative law scholars when he referred to negotiated rulemaking as "a novelty in the administrative process," and when he added that "[i]t sounds like an abdication of regulatory authority to the regulated, the full burgeoning of the interest-group state, and the final confirmation of the 'capture' theory of administrative regulation." Id. at 714. For criticism of Chief Judge Posner's statements, see Philip J. Harter, First Judicial Review of Reg Neg a Disappointment, Admin. & Reg. L. News, Fall 1996, at 1; Funk supra note 293, 319, 329, at 1363–65 (arguing that the Court misunderstood the negotiated rulemaking process).

238. See Cary Coglianese, Assessing Consensus: The Promise and Performance

Coglianese, less than one-tenth of one percent of agency regulations are adopted through the use of negotiated rulemaking.[239] Moreover, Coglianese states that the average time for negotiated rulemaking proceedings is 2.8 years, compared to 3.1 years when negotiated rulemaking is not used.[240] Finally, Coglianese also notes that the litigation rate for negotiated rulemaking is no lower than the litigation rate for rules overall.[241] Professors Langbein and Kerwin have countered Coglianese's conclusions with their own data, which purportedly show that participants in negotiated rulemaking experience greater satisfaction with the substance of the final rule than they would have absent negotiated rulemaking.[242] Implicit in this debate are certain legal norms. In the case of Coglianese, the concern is that negotiated rulemaking places special-interest consensus building over autonomous agency rulemaking.[243] In the case of Langbein and Kerwin, it is argued that greater satisfaction with the rule translates into great legitimacy for the rule.[244]

§ 9.5.10 The Legality of ADR in Agency Rulemaking Proceedings

Some commentators have suggested several legal impediments to the effective use of alternative dispute resolution by federal agencies, particularly negotiated rulemaking. Specifically, the delegation doctrine,[245] the Federal Advisory Committee Act[246] (FACA), and the general ban on ex parte communications all pose potential problems for negotiated rulemaking.[247] Even if these legal problems are surmounted, others such as the standard of judicial review[248] best suited to the procedure, and the question of who has standing to challenge a negotiated rule, also remain.[249]

Using private individuals to draft a proposed regulation may contravene the delegation doctrine. Although Congress may constitutionally authorize nonelected agency officials to issue rules, an agency cannot subsequently transfer that decisionmaking power to unaccountable private citizens.[250] Negotiated rulemaking, however, need not necessarily

of Negotiated Rulemaking, 46 Duke L.J. 1255 (1997).

239. Id. at 1276.

240. Id. at 1283–84.

241. Id. at 1309. Harter has called Coglianese's research "significantly flawed." See Philip J. Harter, Assessing the Assessors: The Actual Performance of Negotiated Rulemaking, 9 N.Y.U. Envtl. L.J. 32, 32 (2000).

242. Laura I. Langbein & Cornelius M. Kerwin, Regulatory Negotiation Versus Conventional Rule Making: Claims, Counterclaims, and Empirical Evidence, 10 J. Pub. Administration Research & Theory 599, 599 (2000).

243. See Funk, supra note 293, 319, 329, at 1374–79.

244. See Jody Freeman & Laura I. Langbein, Regulatory Negotiation and the Legitimacy Benefit, 9 N.Y.U. Envtl. L.J. 60, 121 (2000).

245. See William Funk, Bargaining Toward the New Millennium: Regulatory Negotiation and the Subversion of the Public Interest, 46 duke L.J. 1351, 1373–74 (1997).

246. Pub. L. No. 92–463, 86 Stat. 770 (1972) (codified as amended at 5 U.S.C.A. App. 2 §§ 1–15 (West 1996)).

247. Note, supra note 175, at 1871.

248. Id. at 1356–65.

249. Id.

250. In Carter v. Carter Coal Co., 298 U.S. 238, 56 S.Ct. 855, 80 L.Ed. 1160 (1936), the Supreme Court invalidated a

run afoul of the delegation doctrine. Courts have differentiated between private groups rendering ultimate decisions and private groups acting in a strictly advisory capacity.[251] Clearly, negotiating committees would appear to fall into the latter, permissible category. Under the Negotiated Rulemaking Act, the agency is not bound to accept the committee's suggestions for the proposed rule. Furthermore, the negotiated rulemaking committee must include a representative of the agency, as distinguished from committees consisting entirely of representatives of private groups.[252] As one commentator has stated, "[B]lessed by Congress and structured to conform to the requirements of the Constitution, the APA, and FACA, negotiated rulemaking does not raise serious legal questions."[253]

Compliance with the Federal Advisory Committee Act (FACA), however, potentially is a more difficult legal problem. Although a negotiating group serves an advisory function, it must be chartered under the FACA only if it is "established" and "utilized" by the government.[258] Thus, a

statute granting representatives of coal producers and coal miners the authority to set industry-wide wage and hour standards. The Court found that the plan was "legislative delegation in its most obnoxious form[,] . . . to private persons whose interests may be and often are adverse to the interests of others in the same business." Id. at 311, 56 S.Ct. at 872. Similarly, the Supreme Court in A.L.A. Schechter Poultry Corp. v. United States, 295 U.S. 495, 55 S.Ct. 837, 79 L.Ed. 1570 (1935) struck down a law permitting representative trade associations to draft codes regulating hours, wages, and other conditions of the poultry industry. Private delegation continues to be subjected to rigorous scrutiny.

See also, Gibson v. Berryhill, 411 U.S. 564, 93 S.Ct. 1689, 36 L.Ed.2d 488 (1973) (invalidating on due process grounds a decision by a state board, composed solely of independent optometrists, revoking the licenses of competitor corporate optometrists); Aqua Slide 'N' Dive Corp. v. Consumer Product Safety Com'n., 569 F.2d 831, 843–44 (5th Cir.1978) (courts should defer more to the opinions of agency officials than to those of private consultants). See cases cited in Note, supra note 175, at 1882 n. 63.

251. See, e.g., Sunshine Anthracite Coal Co. v. Adkins, 310 U.S. 381, 399, 60 S.Ct. 907, 915, 84 L.Ed. 1263 (1940) (denying a delegation challenge because the statute provided for a public commission's approval, disapproval, or modification of the private group's proposal); First Jersey Securities, Inc. v. Bergen, 605 F.2d 690, 697–700 (3d Cir.1979), cert. denied 444 U.S. 1074, 100 S.Ct. 1020, 62 L.Ed.2d 756 (1980) (permitting self-regulation in a securities market where the Securities and Exchange Commission retained a significant oversight function). See also Jody Freeman, The Private Role in Public Governance, 75 N.Y.U. L. Rev. 543 (2000); Mark Seidenfeld, Empowering Stakeholders: Limits on collaboration as the Basis for Flexible Regulation, 41 Wm and Mary L. Rev. 411 (2000); Hans A. Linde, Structures and Terms of Consent: Delegation, Discretion, Separation of Powers, Representation, Participation, Accountability?, 20 Cardozo L. Rev. 823 (1999).

252. 5 U.S.C.A. §§ 565(b) and 566(b). On a more practical level, even if the agency were to relinquish its authority to private individuals, a fully balanced representation of interests might guard against the very harm the delegation doctrine seeks to prevent. In negotiated rulemaking, interested parties take responsibility for the substance of the rule and thus are accountable to themselves, thereby "replicating the process of pluralistic decision at the agency level," at least in a strictly procedural sense. See Harter, Negotiating Regulations, supra note 130, at 109. See also Perritt, Negotiated Rulemaking Before Federal Agencies, supra note 173, at 1695 (suggesting that the delegation doctrine is met not only in the above two ways, but that the doctrine actually overlaps existing requirements of the APA and need not be addressed separately).

253. See Funk, supra note 329, at 1374.

258. See Public Citizen v. United States Dep't of Justice, 491 U.S. 440, 109 S.Ct. 2558, 105 L.Ed.2d 377 (1989). For a criticism of how the court used statutory

peer review group established by a private environmental organization to advise the EPA on certain environmental rules would not be an advisory committee under the FACA if the EPA did not strictly manage the group.[259] This Act requires that all advisory committee meetings be open to the public and that notice of such meetings be published in the Federal Register.[260] The prevailing view, however, is that negotiations work best when conducted in private.[261] Consequently, some commentators have proposed that the FACA be amended to exempt negotiating groups from public meeting requirements.[262] The Negotiated Rulemaking Act states that agencies have the authority under FACA to establish negotiated rulemaking committees,[263] and assigns to the facilitator responsibility for keeping minutes and records of committee meetings in compliance with FACA.[264] This information is then transmitted to the agency along with the committee's report on the proposed rule.[265]

Another potential difficulty with negotiated rulemaking is the general ban on ex parte communications. Courts generally have looked askance at private contacts between the agency and affected parties even during informal rulemaking proceedings so as to ensure that the public record accurately reflects the basis for the agency's decisions.[266] This ban on private contacts responds to a fear that the record will be a sham, concealing the true rationale for the rule, and that those affected by the rule will be unable to challenge the record both at the time it occurs and in later adjudication.[267] The informality of recordkeeping[268] and the likelihood of private deliberations in the negotiating process could bring charges of improper influence or agency "capture", thus giving cause for application of the ban to negotiated rulemaking.

The D.C. Circuit has carved out exceptions to the total restriction enunciated in *Home Box Office*. In *Sierra Club v. Costle*,[269] the Court allowed private contacts where the informal rulemaking clearly was of a

construction to reach its holding in Public citizen, see Animal Legal Defense Fund v. Shalala, 104 F.3d 424, 427–30 (D.C.Cir. 1997) (noting that the term "utilized" is construed very narrowly).

259. Cf. Byrd v. United States Environmental Protection Agency, 174 F.3d 239, 245–48 (D.C.Cir.1999).

260. 5 U.S.C.A. App. 2 § 10 (West 1996).

261. See Funk, supra note 329, at 1372.

262. Id. at 1373.

263. Negotiated Rulemaking Act of 1990, Pub.L. No. 101–648, § 2(6), 104 Stat. 4969 (1990) ("Agencies have the authority to establish negotiated rulemaking committees ... under the Federal Advisory Committee Act ..... The process has not been widely used ... [because agencies are] uncertain as to the authority for such rulemaking.").

264. 5 U.S.C.A. § 566(d)(3) (specifically referring to the recordkeeping requirements of §§ 10(b) and 10(c) of FACA).

265. Id. at § 566(g). The Act also provides for agency reimbursement of certain expenses of committee members in accordance with § 7(d) of FACA. Id. at § 588(c).

266. See Home Box Office, Inc. v. FCC, 567 F.2d 9 (D.C.Cir.1977) (per curiam), cert. denied 434 U.S. 829, 98 S.Ct. 111, 54 L.Ed.2d 89 (1977). supra.

267. See Perritt, Negotiated Rulemaking Before Federal Agencies, supra note 173, at 1698.

268. See Harter, The Role of Courts in Regulatory Negotiation—A Response to Judge Wald, 11 Colum. J. Envtl.L., 51, 71 (1986) [hereinafter Role of Courts] (EPA organizational protocols for negotiated rulemaking prohibit the use of electronic recording devices).

269. 657 F.2d 298, 402 (D.C.Cir.1981).

policymaking nature. In another case, the Court found that the ban applied only to rules in which parties were vying for "a specific valuable privilege."[270] In *United Steelworkers of America v. Marshall,*[271] the Court permitted ex parte contacts where OSHA used consultants to draw conclusions from the public record and to help the agency draft the preamble to the rule.

These cases suggest that negotiated rulemaking could survive a challenge based on the ban on ex parte contacts. First, if the agency provides a full factual record, the public, through participation in the negotiations or notice and comment stages, will still be afforded an opportunity to challenge the actual basis of the rule, even if the specific analysis and evaluation in the negotiations are not recorded.[272] Second, courts might accept deliberations between the agency and the participants focusing solely on policy if they occur after the record is closed.[273]

The standard of judicial review in negotiated rulemaking has proved to be the most controversial issue raised by negotiated rulemaking procedures. Prior to passage of the Negotiated Rulemaking Act, Philip Harter, a leading proponent of negotiated rulemaking, suggested that courts use a "less stringent" standard of review towards negotiated rules.[274] Rather than making a "searching and careful"[275] review of the agency decision in light of the entire record, courts should examine whether the rulemaking was conducted "in a manner calculated to negate dangers of arbitrariness and irrationality."[276] This purely procedural approach would eliminate the need for a thorough review of the factual basis of the decision and, as long as the rule falls within the agency's jurisdiction,[277] adequate interest-group representation and consensus would in theory at least, have been achieved.

This approach drew considerable fire from Chief Judge Patricia M. Wald,[278] who argues that negotiated rulemaking "represents the latest outgrowth of a pluralist approach to administrative law",[279] and that in changing the standard of review, it may actually increase judicial involvement. By attempting to replicate the political process, agencies

270. Action for Children's Television v. FCC, 564 F.2d 458 (D.C.Cir.1977). Negotiated rulemaking should not be attempted where parties would have to compromise basic values to reach agreement. See Perritt, Negotiated Rulemaking Before Federal Agencies, supra note 173, at 1653 (observing another factor in the OSHA failure: participants, namely those at risk of developing a serious disease, would be compromising a basic value).

271. 647 F.2d 1189, 1217 (D.C.Cir. 1980), cert. denied 453 U.S. 913, 101 S.Ct. 3148, 69 L.Ed.2d 997 (1981).

272. See Perritt, Negotiated Rulemaking Before Federal Agencies, supra note 173, at 1700.

273. Id.

274. Harter, Negotiating Regulations, supra note 130, at 103 (footnote omitted).

275. Citizens to Preserve Overton Park, Inc. v. Volpe, 401 U.S. 402, 416, 91 S.Ct. 814, 824, 28 L.Ed.2d 136 (1971).

276. Harter, Negotiating Regulations, supra note 130, at 107.

277. See Harter, Role of Courts, supra note 348, at 63 (asserting that the process will keep the proposal within the agency's authority because "presumably some party would be better off if it did [remain within bounds] and that party would likely insist on compliance").

278. Chief Judge, United States Court of Appeals for the District of Columbia Circuit.

279. Wald, supra note 126, at 24.

leave to the courts the difficult problems of how to develop legal standards "for identifying relevant interest groups, and for assessing the extent of their participation and the 'negotiation' process."[280]

These difficulties are made plain at the preliminary stage of granting standing to plaintiffs. Judge Wald would grant standing to anyone who was adversely affected by the rule and who submitted comment concerning the rule to the agency.[281] Harter feels this would give too great an incentive to parties to sit out the negotiations and then individually challenge the final rule.[282] Although he earlier argued that a party should be precluded from challenging the rule if its interest had been represented in the negotiations,[283] he has since revised his opinion, stating that the party need not be precluded but "should be put to a relatively higher burden of knocking down the agreement others forged."[284]

Part of this higher standard involves determining if the party was adequately represented in the negotiations. Judge Wald finds it unwise for courts to engage in a determination of this fact.[285] Proponents of negotiated rulemaking, however, argue that making this determination is valid, in large measure due to balanced representation.[286]

To Judge Wald, the most troubling aspect of Harter's proposed standard is the emphasis on consensus as a quantifier of a negotiated rule's legality. She resists the notion of equating consensus with "reasonableness".[287] Because political logrolling can undermine the negotiation process, a collection of signatures on a draft should not be the basis for a cursory review of the decisionmaking. Furthermore, increasing the use of subgroups or caucuses will create an additional risk of inappropriate bargaining. The Negotiated Rulemaking Act would appear to resolve this debate in favor of Judge Wald.[288] It provides that an agency's negotiated rulemaking activity be subjected to judicial review "otherwise provided by law," and specifically eschews any heightened level of deference for rules resulting from such negotiation.[289]

280. Id. at 7.

281. Id. at 22.

282. This problem is presumably avoided by the convener's rejection of issues in which specific parties see a better alternative to negotiation. In addition, before participating parties are to agree to make a good faith effort to reach an agreement; the agency may allow them "to withdraw from the negotiations at any time without prejudice." Harter, Role of Courts supra 348 at 71 (from EPA organizational protocols).

283. Harter, Negotiating Regulations, supra note , at 102–107.

284. Harter, Role of Courts supra note 348, at 67.

285. Wald, supra note 126.

286. See Perritt, Negotiated Rulemaking Before Federal Agencies, supra note 173, at 1702 (observing that "the same action taken by negotiators and sponsoring agencies to avoid delegation and ex parte communication problems will also reduce the likelihood that a court would find a negotiated rule to be arbitrary and capricious.").

287. Wald, supra note 126, at 22. And, indeed, the two have been functionally equated. Prior to passage of the Negotiated Rulemaking Act, the EPA, for instance, has committed itself "to use any consensus reached—if within its statutory authority—as the basis of its proposed rulemaking." 53 Fed.Reg. 51,003 (1988).

288. See Funk, supra note 329, at 1357–58.

289. 5 U.S.C.A. § 570.

As we have seen, negotiated rulemaking is a procedure that engages affected parties in the early stages of regulatory agency deliberations. The process is designed to encourage the ranking and communication of interests by each involved party and by the agency. If it is effective, it can facilitate the creation of equitable and enforceable regulations, and reduce the incidence of court challenges. Unfortunately, the procedure also shows the potential for rules based on inappropriate bargaining. Despite this danger, proponents of negotiated rulemaking are nevertheless inclined towards the "amputation of meaningful judicial review."[299] It remains to be seen just how significant and useful negotiated rulemaking will be in the future, though its use will likely increase as agencies implement the Negotiated Rulemaking Act.

§ 9.5.11 Case Management

Another approach to encouraging the efficient resolution of agency adjudication involves case management techniques. The Administrative Conference of the United States (ACUS) adopted Recommendation 86–7, *Case Management as a Tool for Improving Agency Adjudication,* to further the "prompt, efficient and inexpensive processing of adjudicative proceedings."[300] It suggested that agencies set time goals for agency adjudication, focus on training agency personnel in ADR, and actively clarify and develop the record to resolve ambiguities early in the proceedings. In addition, ACUS recommended telephone conferences "to hear motions, to hold prehearing conferences, and even to hear the merits of administrative proceedings where appropriate."[301] A decade after the ACUS made its recommendations, however, many agencies have not implemented case management strategies.[302] For example, a disability claim before the Social Security Administration, the caseload of which accounts for more than eighty percent of all agency adjudications, can take about 900 days to adjudicate. many applicants die before their case is resolved.[303] This state of affairs has led the Social Security Administration to begin to experiment with some case management strategies.[304]

299. Wald, supra note 126, at 33.

300. 1 C.F.R. § 305.86–7 (1990).

301. Id.

302. See The Hon. Jeffrey S. Wolfe & Lisa B. Proszek, Interaction Dynamics in Federal Administrative Decision making: The Role of the Inquisitorial Judge and the Adversarial lawyer, 33 Tulsa L.J. 293, 349 (1997) (arguing that ALJs should be given case management authority).

303. See Management of Disability Cases: Hearing Before the House Subcommittees on Social Security and Human Resources of the Committee on Ways and Means, 106th Cong. 5 (1999) (statement of Rep. Shaw).

304. Id. at 13–17 (testimony of Social Security Commissioner Kenneth Apfel).

Part Three

CONSISTENCY IN AGENCY ACTION

Consistency is a prime value in a legal system. Consistency pertains to distributive justice, treating like cases alike. It also pertains to foreseeability, where it has a temporal dimension: standards of conduct should be stable over time, as security for those who have relied on them.

In administrative law, consistency is, or should be, assured and erratic agency action avoided, by confirming agency action to published rules and standards. The principle of consistency also has a rather specific application, for persons whom an agency has dealt with on a particular basis. In this context, consistency is maintained according to doctrines borrowed from the courts and the common law, these doctrines being res judicata and promissory estoppel.

Chapter 10

CONSISTENCY ACCORDING TO FORMAL RULES AND STANDARDS

Table of Sections

By a published regulation, the Interstate Commerce Commission had set "reasonable" rates for the carriage of goods by rail. The Commission, however, proceeded to find that a rate within the regulation was nonetheless unreasonable. In *Arizona Grocery Co. v. Atchison, Topeka & Santa Fe Ry.*,[1] the railroads objected to this action on rule of law grounds. "They should not," they argued, "be required to pay reparations on shipments which moved under rates approved or prescribed by the Commission as reasonable." The Commission responded on grounds of instrumental rationality, that it was obliged to depart from a rule when "it clearly appeared that our previous findings" the rule would not serve the goals entrusted to it by Congress. On review, the private sector's interest in a consistent agency position prevailed. The Supreme Court announced: "The carrier is entitled to rely upon the [Commission's] declaration as to what will be a lawful ... rate." Therefore, the "Commission ... may not in a subsequent proceeding ignore its own pronouncement.... "

Holding an agency to its rules does not mean that an agency cannot change its position. But it does mean that that change should be consistent with the rule of law. Accordingly, when an agency wishes to change a rule, it should do so prospectively, by a new rule for future conduct. In *Arizona Grocery,* the Court explained that the Commission "was bound to recognize the validity of the rule of conduct prescribed by it and not to repeal its own enactment with retroactive effect." The Commission could, however, "repeal the order as it affected future

1. 284 U.S. 370, 52 S.Ct. 183, 76 L.Ed. 348 (1932).

action, and substitute a new rule of conduct as often as occasion might require, but this was obviously the limit of its power. . . ."

Today, *Arizona Grocery* stands for the proposition that agency rules, unless and until they are amended or repealed, bind the agency as well as the private sector.[1] The decision is also bedrock for the publication and codification requirements of the Administrative Procedure Act. Under the Act, the agency is required to codify and publish its rules in the Federal Register.[2] Further, the Act provides that "a person may not in any manner be required to resort to, or be adversely affected by, a matter required to be published in the Federal Register, and not so published."[3]

Generally, the principle that an agency is bound by its own rules is limited to rules that have some significant effect on a person. If a rule does not affect the conduct of a private individual or the outcome of an agency decision with respect to that individual, it is usually not subject to this principle. Thus, agency procedural or housekeeping rules that do not "confer important procedural benefits upon individuals" fall outside the principle of *Arizona Grocery*.[4]

* * *

1. E.g., Nader v. Bork, 366 F.Supp. 104 (D.D.C.1973). In this case, the court held that the United States Attorney General's dismissal of Archibald Cox, the Watergate Special Prosecutor, was illegal because it violated regulations previously issued by the Attorney General. Without the regulations, the Attorney General "would have had the authority to fire Mr. Cox at any time and for any reason" However, "he had chose to limit his own authority in this regard by promulgating the Watergate Special Prosecutor regulation" and "it is settled beyond dispute that under such circumstances an agency regulation has the force and effect of law and is binding upon the body that issues it."

That an agency is bound by its own rules is also supported by Supreme Court decisions—made in the politically charged atmosphere of McCarthyism—where the Court held agencies to their regulations so as to better assure even and equal treatment of those charged with disloyalty. United States v. Shaughnessy, 347 U.S. 260, 74 S.Ct. 499, 98 L.Ed. 681 (1954); Service v. Dulles, 354 U.S. 363, 77 S.Ct. 1152, 1 L.Ed.2d 1403 (1957); Vitarelli v. Seaton, 359 U.S. 535, 79 S.Ct. 968, 3 L.Ed.2d 1012 (1959).

2. 5 U.S.C. § 553(c).

3. 5 U.S.C. § 552(a). See chap. 3, sec. 3.2, supra. In Morton v. Ruiz, 415 U.S. 199, 94 S.Ct. 1055, 39 L.Ed.2d 270 (1974), the Supreme Court overturned an action of the Bureau of Indian Affairs because of its failure to act under a rule published according to the requirements of the Administrative Procedure Act. The Court asserted that "the agency must, at a minimum, let the standard be generally known so as to assure that it is being applied consistently and to avoid both the reality and the appearance of arbitrary denial of benefits to potential beneficiaries."

4. American Farm Lines v. Black Ball Freight Service, 397 U.S. 532, 538, 90 S.Ct. 1288, 1292, 25 L.Ed.2d 547 (1970).

In United States v. Caceres, 440 U.S. 741, 99 S.Ct. 1465, 59 L.Ed.2d 733 (1979), the Court held admissable certain evidence that the Internal Revenue Service had acquired in violation of its own regulation. This regulation required the Service to obtain prior Justice Department approval of electronic surveillance. In finding that evidence gained in violation of this rule need not be excluded, the majority explained that this was not "a case in which the Due Process Clause is implicated because an individual has reasonably relied on agency regulations promulgated for his guidance or benefit and has suffered substantially because of their violation by the agency." *United States v. Caceres,* therefore, would seem to mean that where defendant has not based his primary out-of-court conduct on an agency rule, the need for an agency to follow its own rule is diminished.

The principle of *Arizona Grocery,* that an agency is "bound to recognize the validity of the rule of conduct prescribed by it and not to repeal its own enactment with retroactive effect," pertains to *formally* designated rules of conduct. This principle of consistency is not, however, understood to apply to standards developed by adjudication.[5] Prior agency decisions may, of course, be taken as precedent, and by this means a degree of consistency may be maintained. The agencies, however, do not have quite the same tradition, as do the courts, in deciding like cases alike. Nor do agencies operate in the context of a subject matter, such as contract, torts, or property rules, where stable standards of conduct have evolved over time. Nor do they have the same stability of personnel as do courts.

An agency setting and applying standards through adjudication may, therefore, vacillate, and in doing so deny expectations of predictable and even-handed regulation.[6] The courts, however, have stepped-in, in support of these expectations, by establishing such additional safeguards—for adjudication—as a requirement of "reasoned decision-making," a retroactivity doctrine, and the "*Ashbacker* doctrine."

5. In *Arizona Grocery,* the agency had claimed that the only measure of consistency applicable to its rate structure was res judicata and that res judicata should not be so rigorously applied as to bind the agency to its "previous findings" when it later appeared that they were wrong. The Court rejected this argument on the grounds of a distinction between the rulemaking and the adjudicatory activities of agencies. Whatever the measure of res judicata, it was inapplicable to the requirement of consistency in rules. The Court explained that the "Commission's error arose from a failure to recognize that when it prescribed a maximum reasonable rate for the future it was performing a legislative function, and that when it was sitting to award reparation it was sitting for a purpose judicial in its nature. That in this capacity, it was bound to recognize the validity of the rule of conduct prescribed by it and not to repeal its own enactment with retroactive effect." 284 U.S. 370, 389, 52 S.Ct. 183, 186, 76 L.Ed. 348 (1932).

Perhaps abetted by this distinction between adjudication and rulemaking *Arizona Grocery's* principle of consistency has generally been limited to agency action under published and codified rules. But not completely. In National Conservative Political Action Committee v. Federal Election Commission, 626 F.2d 953 (D.C.Cir.1980), the court invalidated an advisory opinion, issued by the Commission and for and favorable to the Democratic National Committee (DNC), where the Commission had failed to provide public notice of the Committee's request for the opinion. The Federal Election Campaign Act as well as the Commission gave interested parties the right to comment on such request for advisory opinions, and while the Commission failed to publish notice of the receipt of the DNC request, its practice had been to publish such requests in the Federal Register and in its own newsletter. Even though this practice had not been encapsulated by means of a formally published rule, the court nonetheless invalidated the DNC opinion. The court explained that "prior notice is required where a private party justifiably relies upon an agency's past practice and is substantially affected by a change in that practice.... Thus, Congress' mandate, the Commission's regulations, and considerations of fundamental fairness lead us to conclude that [the advisory opinion] was unlawfully issued and is without force and effect."

Regarding agency discretion to develop rules and standards by adjudication rather than rulemaking, see chap. 4, sec. 4.5, supra.

6. As observed by Judge Friendly, there is a tendency among the agencies to treat precedent as "file-drawer law," to be pulled from among the welter of reported cases when it suits the agency's purposes and otherwise to be disregarded. H. Friendly, The Federal Administrative Agencies 63 (1962).

§ 10.1 CONSISTENCY BY "REASONED DECISION-MAKING" IN ADJUDICATION

When agency adjudication defeats expectations of foreseeability and even-handed action, the courts may in certain circumstances overturn that action on the grounds that it is "arbitrary and capricious." The circumstances are that the agency has acted without a "reasoned explanation." As explained by Judge Levanthal:

> An agency's view of what is in the public interest may change, either with or without a change in circumstances. But an agency changing its course must supply a reasoned analysis indicating that prior policies and standards are being deliberately changed, not casually ignored.... [1]

In relation to *even-handed* action, "reasoned decision-making" was required by the Fourth Circuit in *Contractors Transport Corp. v. United States*.[2] The Interstate Commerce Commission had denied a trucking company's request to transport iron and steel products in a certain area, on the grounds that the trucking service in this area was adequate. For another company, the Commission granted a similar application for the same area, without reference to the adequacy of existing service. On the petition of the carrier whose request had been denied, the court of appeals reversed the Commission's action as to that carrier. Because of its "disparate treatment of similarly situated applicants," the Commission was required to provide "a rational basis" for its decision.[3]

Another Interstate Commerce Commission case, *Greyhound Corp. v. ICC,* provides an example of the reasoned-decision requirement as it is used to assure *predictable* agency action.[4] In past orders, the Commission had established that it would not require prior approval of stock transactions by companies subject to its jurisdiction. Therefore, when the Greyhound Corporation reorganized, its expectation was that it would

§ 10.1

1. Greater Boston Television Corp. v. FCC, 444 F.2d 841, 852 (D.C.Cir.1970). See also Atchison, Topeka & Santa Fe Ry. Co. v. Wichita Bd. of Trade, 412 U.S. 800, 806–09, 93 S.Ct. 2367, 2374–75, 37 L.Ed.2d 350 (1973); McHenry v. Bond, 668 F.2d 1185, 1192 (11th Cir.1982) Because "An agency must either conform to its prior norms and decisions or explain the reason for its departure from such precedent," the court in *McHenry v. Bond* found that where the National Transportation Safety Board had in previous adjudications established that a certain medical problem was not a sufficient basis to revoke the license of an airline pilot, it was reversible error, at least without a reasoned decision, to take the license of a pilot because of that ailment.

2. 537 F.2d 1160 (4th Cir.1976).

3. 537 F.2d at 1162. See also IBM Corp. v. United States, 343 F.2d 914, 923 (Cl.Ct.1965) (where the Internal Revenue Service by a private ruling found that Remington Rand Company did not have to pay an excise tax and then in similar circumstances found that IBM had to pay the tax, the court found that IBM was entitled to "like treatment."). In Doubleday Broadcasting Co. v. FCC, 655 F.2d 417, 423 (D.C.Cir. 1981), the Federal Communications Commission had denied a company's request to use the same call sign at one station that it used in another. The Commission's practice, though, as established by other adjudicated cases, had been to grant such a request. In this context, the court overturned the Commission action, stating that "[t]he Commission may not decide a case one way today and a substantially similar case another way tomorrow, without a more reasonable explanation than is offered here."

4. 551 F.2d 414 (D.C.Cir.1977), *appeal after remand*, 668 F.2d 1354 (D.C.Cir.1981).

not be required to gain the Commission's approval of associated stock transactions. The Commission, however, required that Greyhound submit all such stock transactions to it for its approval.

The court of appeals for the District of Columbia, in view of the Commission's "indifferen[ce] to the rule of law," overturned the Commission's action respecting Greyhound. The Commission's "duty" was to abide by "established precedents" or to make out a case why not. "We do not remand," the court said, "for the Commission merely to reiterate its decision with some new words of explanation added."[5]

§ 10.2 RETROACTIVITY

With respect to foreseeability—keeping standards stable over time as security for those who rely on them—the courts have added another degree of protection by means of a "retroactivity doctrine." The substance of this doctrine is that when a person has acted according to prevailing standards of conduct and an agency changes the standards (usually by means of adjudication[1]) to deny this person the fruits of her action, the courts may overturn the agency order.

This doctrine is grounded in *SEC v. Chenery,* where the Court held that while an agency should ordinarily regulate by means of rules, it might in its "informed discretion" resort to *ad hoc* orders addressed to the situation at hand. Legal control over this discretion was to be maintained by the retroactivity doctrine. The measure of an impermissible retroactivity was the balance of the private injury caused by a retroactive agency order versus the public interest served by the agency order.[2]

5. 551 F.2d at 418. In this context of consistency, the requirement that a change of direction be demonstrably reasoned is a product of expectations of predictable and even-handed agency action. But as well, a reviewing court's abhorrence to an agency's sudden departure from a previous position may be something of a matter of statutory construction. The courts have the ultimate authority respecting what a statute means. Inasmuch as a court has acceded to a settled agency position as the appropriate interpretation of the statute, the agency is, as it were, bound by the statute not to disregard its previous position. This may be what Justice Marshall had in mind as he explained that "a settled course of behavior embodies the agency's informed judgment that, by pursuing that course, it will carry out the policies committed to it by Congress." Atchison, Topeka & Santa Fe Ry. v. Wichita Bd. of Trade, 412 U.S. 800, 807, 93 S.Ct. 2367, 2375, 37 L.Ed.2d 350 (1973).

§ 10.2

1. Where an agency does act retroactively by a rule, so as to penalize a person for conduct that was lawful when done, the Administrative Procedure Act has been interpreted as itself proscribing that retroactivity. The Act defines a rule as an action of "future effect." 5 U.S.C. § 551(4). In his concurrence in Bowen v. Georgetown University Hospital, 488 U.S. 204, 109 S.Ct. 468, 102 L.Ed.2d 493 (1988), Justice Scalia interpreted this "future effect" provision as precluding retroactive rules.

2. In the words of the Court:

> [S]uch retroactivity must be measured against the mischief of producing a result which is contrary to a statutory design or to legal and equitable principles. If that mischief is greater than the ill effect of the retroactive application of a new standard, it is not the type of retroactivity which is condemned by law.

332 U.S. 194, 203, 67 S.Ct. 1575, 1581, 91 L.Ed. 1995 (1947). In *Chenery,* the balance in issue was whether denying management the profits of certain stock transactions was "outweighed by the dangers inherent in such purchases from the statutory standpoint." In *Chenery,* as is so often the case where the public interest is pitted against

The balancing test of *Chenery* was more fully developed in *NLRB v. Majestic Weaving Co.,* where Judge Friendly described certain degrees of retroactivity.[3] The least "obnoxious" degree of retroactivity is when the agency had previously taken no position one way or the other on the substantive issue in question. More obnoxious is the case where "an agency alters an established rule defining permissible conduct which has generally been recognized and relied on throughout the industries that it regulates." The "judicial hackles still raise more," Friendly added, when a "financial penalty is assessed for action that might well have avoided if the agencies changed disposition had been made earlier made known."

The retroactivity doctrine is most often based on due process and fundamental fairness. Additionally, as in *NLRB v. Majestic Weaving Co.,* the doctrine has been grounded in judicial review as provided by the Administrative Procedure Act. Under the Administrative Procedure Act, retroactive agency action may be reversible as "arbitrary" or "capricious" agency action.[4] Whether based on due process or the Administrative Procedure Act, the doctrine is usually, but not exclusively, applied in the context of adjudication. Adjudication, as we said, presents greater possibilities for inconsistent agency action, and thus it presents more occasions for the application of the doctrine of retroactivity.

Finally, the retroactivity doctrine has emerged in something of a more specialized context. A long-standing problem in administrative law is whether agencies may make rules by adjudication as well as by rulemaking procedures. In this context, the courts sometimes find that where a new agency position upsets expectations of consistent agency action, the agency can establish this position only by prospective rules developed through rulemaking.[5]

§ 10.3 COMPARATIVE HEARINGS

Agencies sometimes have the power to distribute scarce resources, scarce because an agency decision to allocate the resource to one person deprives all other persons of it. For instance, a license to operate a broadcasting station on a frequency within an area necessarily deprives all others of that opportunity. In these circumstances of agency-induced scarcity, a degree of consistency and equality is arrived at by means of "comparative hearings" among the applicants for a broadcast license.[1]

This prescription of comparative hearings is known as the *Ashbacker* doctrine after the Supreme Court opinion in *Ashbacker Radio Corp. v.*

private injury, the agency determination of public interest carried a momentum hardly to be denied by the courts.

3. 355 F.2d 854 (2d Cir.1966).

4. 5 U.S.C. § 706(2)(A).

5. See chap. 4, sec. 4.5.6, supra.

§ 10.3

1. Greater Boston Television Corp. v. FCC, 444 F.2d 841 (D.C.Cir.1970). As for the particular subject of comparative hearings, the findings must cover all the substantial differences between the applicants, and the ultimate conclusion must be based on a composite consideration of the findings as to each applicant.

FCC.[2] Under the Communications Act of 1934, persons or firms wishing to build new broadcasting stations must gain the approval of the Federal Communications Commission. The Act also provides that applicants are entitled to a hearing on their request. In *Ashbacker,* the Federal Communications Commission had received two different applications to build and operate a commercial radio station. Because both these applications were for stations on the same frequency in the same area, they were mutually exclusive. The Commission granted one application and scheduled a hearing on the other. However, this other hearing, after the license had already been granted, was pointless. The Court explained:

> We do not think it is enough to say that the power of the Commission to issue a license on a finding of public interest, convenience or necessity supports its grant of one of two mutually exclusive applications without a hearing of the other. For if the grant of one effectively precludes the other, the statutory right to a hearing which Congress has accorded applicants before denial of their applications becomes an empty thing.

This right to a comparative hearing has been extended beyond *Ashbacker* and physical exclusivity (where two radio stations could not operate on the same frequency) to economic exclusivity. When two airlines could not profitably operate on the same route, the *Ashbacker* doctrine was applied to require comparative hearings among applicants for the route. As said by the court, "If the grant of one of several applications for a new route does, as a matter of economic necessity, preclude the grant of any other application, the doctrine of *Ashbacker* clearly applies."[3]

In practice, the *Ashbacker* doctrine has been difficult in application. A comparative hearing "must cover all the substantial differences between the applicants and the ultimate conclusion must be based on a composite consideration of the findings as to each applicant."[4] It is, therefore, hard to judge just how extensive the comparative hearing that *Ashbacker* requires should be.

2. 326 U.S. 327, 66 S.Ct. 148, 90 L.Ed. 108 (1945).

3. Delta Air Lines, Inc. v. Civil Aeronautics Board, 275 F.2d 632, 638 (D.C.Cir. 1959).

4. Greater Boston Television Corp. v. FCC, 444 F.2d 841, 851 (D.C.Cir.1970).

Chapter 11

CONSISTENCY, AND THE DOCTRINES OF RES JUDICATA AND ESTOPPEL

Table of Sections

The norm of consistency in agency action also has a quite specific application, to persons with whom an agency has dealt with on a particular basis. This application is according to two different doctrines, res judicata and promissory estoppel. Res judicata pertains to adjudication, to whether an agency that has acted against a person by means of adjudication is, respecting that person, thereafter bound by that adjudication. Estoppel involves the extent to which an agency is bound by promises made by its officials to a person.

§ 11.1 RES JUDICATA

The doctrine of res judicata, or "claim preclusion" as it is also called, is that a judgment in an action precludes the parties to a lawsuit, or those in privity with them, from relitigating issues that were, or could have been, raised in the action.[1] The subsumed doctrine of collateral

§ 11.1

1. Montana v. United States, 440 U.S. 147, 153, 99 S.Ct. 970, 973, 59 L.Ed.2d 210

estoppel, or "issue preclusion" as it is sometimes called, is that once a court has "decided an issue of fact or law" that is "necessary" to a judgment, that decision is conclusive with respect to that issue should arise in a future adjudication.[2] Res judicata (claim preclusion) prevents the *case* from being relitigated; collateral estoppel (issue preclusion) pertains to an issue and not to the case, and prevents the relitigation of particular issues resolved in a case. For convenience, we will usually refer to these matters of claim and issue preclusion together, under the heading of res judicata.

The doctrine of res judicata is a product of civil actions in courts. The Supreme Court has, however, established that in principle it applies as well to administrative adjudication: "When an administrative agency is acting in a judicial capacity and resolves disputed issues of fact properly before it which the parties have had an adequate opportunity to litigate, the courts have not hesitated to apply res judicata to enforce repose."[3] In practice, however, this endorsement is probably too sweeping.

In civil actions tried before courts, res judicata protects expectations of "repose" among private litigants. It saves them the costs, of money and time, of redundant litigation. Also, this doctrine offers something to the courts: it conserves judicial resources from the depredations of repetitious litigation.[4] As an individual's interest in respite from litigation and the public interest in the most efficient use of the courts thus coincide, res judicata can be expected to be, and is, a doctrine of

2. Id. See also Continental Can Company v. Marshall, 603 F.2d 590, 594–96 (7th Cir.1979).

3. United States v. Utah Construction & Mining Co., 384 U.S. 394, 422, 86 S.Ct. 1545, 1560, 16 L.Ed.2d 642 (1966) (holding that factual findings by the Board of Contract Appeals bound the Court of Claims, according to collateral estoppel, in a subsequent suit for damages). As the Court endorsed the application of the doctrines of res judicata and collateral estoppel to administrative agencies, it did so against a background of hostility to such an application of the doctrines. This hostility, however, was in large part an aspect of an era in which the quality of an administrative adjudication was not as good as it is today.

"In an earlier era, decisions of administrative agencies usually were arrived at by so-called 'executive procedures,' that is, unilateral decision by an official on the basis of whatever information he deemed it appropriate to take into account. Parties did not have a right to present evidence or argument and sometimes had no rights of participation at all.... It followed that an administrative determination could not have res judicata effects on legal rights or on disputed issues upon which such rights might depend." Restatement (Second) of Judgments sec. 83 & commentary at 269 (1982). See also Pearson v. Williams, 202 U.S. 281, 284–85, 26 S.Ct. 608, 609–10, 50 L.Ed. 1029 (1906) (Holding that res judicata did not apply to a hearing before an immigration board inasmuch as the "board is an instrument of the executive power, not a court," and that such decisions "have long been recognized as decisions of the executive department, and cannot constitute res judicata in a technical sense").

Today, agency adjudication, as it has been improved by the Administrative Procedure Act and due process, is better thought of. Consequently, the "well settled doctrine that that res judicata and equitable estoppel does not ordinarily apply to decisions of administrative tribunals," Churchill Tabernacle v. FCC, 160 F.2d 244 (D.C. Cir. 1947), has abated. Restatement (Second) of Judgments, supra. See also Continental Can Co. v. Marshall, 603 F.2d 590, 593–94 (7th Cir. 1979).

4. Montana v. United States, 440 U.S. 147, 153–54, 99 S.Ct. 970, 973–74, 59 L.Ed.2d 210 (1979).

considerable force. But in the agencies, the doctrine, because of some different public concerns, "is applied with less rigidity than its judicial counterpart."[5] One of these differing concerns is an agency's interest in instrumental action. By design, agencies serve special goals, and in pursuit of these goals their ideas of good policy change. In effecting these changes, the agency would rather avoid having it hands tied by res judicata. For instance, in the Sixties the Federal Trade Commission determined that a particular company's advertising did not amount to a "deceptive act or practice." Then, in the more consumer-conscious Seventies, the Commission reversed itself, and found that that same advertising by that same company was deceptive.[6]

Respecting an avoidance of res judicata—so as to free up agencies to change position when their view of the public interest changes—the cases show a distinction between an agency acting to serve proprietary interests and an agency acting in the public interest. In a proprietary action, for instance an adjudication respecting contract rights between the government and a private company, the courts readily have found that res judicata applies to agencies. Accordingly, in *United States v. Utah Construction & Mining Co.,* a government contracts case, the Court asserted that as against agencies, "the courts have not hesitated to apply res judicata to enforce repose."

But where an agency action is not proprietary, and is instead more obviously tinged with the public interest, the courts have at times hesitated in limiting that action according to res judicata. In *Churchill Tabernacle v. Federal Communications Commission,* the Commission had initially approved certain arrangements respecting the ownership and control of a radio station.[7] Several years later, however, the Commission set the matter down for a new hearing, and in that hearing determined that those arrangements "rendered [the licensee] incapable of discharging in the public interest the responsibilities imposed upon it by the [Communications] Act of 1934." On appeal, the licensee claimed that the Commission was estopped by its previous approval of the arrangements in question. The court of appeals for the District of Columbia Circuit, however, refused to hold the Commission to its previous decision. It refused to do so because of the Commission's obligation to a greater public interest:

5. Parker v. Califano, 644 F.2d 1199, 1202 (6th Cir.1981).

6. Cf. FTC v. Raladam Co., 316 U.S. 149, 62 S.Ct. 966, 86 L.Ed. 1336 (1942) (The courts had earlier overturned, because the evidence did not establish injury to competitors, a Federal Trade Commission determination that a company had engaged in an unfair method of competition by misrepresenting the fat-reducing quality of a certain product. Thereafter, the Commission brought the case again, this time finding injury to competitors, and issued a cease and desist order against the company; in this second action, the Supreme Court ruled against the company respecting its defense of res judicata.); Commissioner of Internal Revenue v. Sunnen, 333 U.S. 591, 599, 68 S.Ct. 715, 720, 92 L.Ed. 898 (1948) ("change or development in the controlling legal principle may make [the first] determination obsolete or erroneous.") See Churchill Tabernacle v. FCC, 160 F.2d 244, 246 (D.C.Cir.1947) (discussed in text, infra).

7. 160 F.2d 244 (D.C.Cir.1947).

> [T]he Commission is empowered to establish a new policy, and apply it to the renewal of an old license, despite the fact it is inconsistent with a previous decision. This follows from the statutory duty of the Commission to examine each application for renewal of license as an original proceeding and grant or refuse it in the public interest.[8]

In speaking to the "statutory duty of the Commission to examine *each application* for renewal of license as an *original* proceeding" the court in *Churchill Tabernacle* identified another factor pertinent to res judicata in administrative law. Agencies may be under statutory directives that specially limit the application of res judicata. In this relation, the *Restatement 2d of Judgments* provides that res judicata may be inapplicable if "incompatible with a legislative policy that ... [t]he tribunal in which the issue subsequently arises be free to make an independent determination of the issue in question."[9]

* * *

The *Restatement 2d of Judgments* generally provides that "final determinations by an administrative tribunal has the same effects under res judicata ... as a judgment of a court." This approbation, however, is conditioned on whether the proceeding in that tribunal "entail the essential elements of adjudication."[10] The Supreme Court has set the same condition, that res judicata depends on whether acts in "a *judicial capacity* and resolves disputed issues of fact properly before it which the parties have had *an adequate opportunity to litigate*."[11] Given the various forms of agency action, it cannot be presumed that all actions characterized as adjudicatory actually conform to the essential elements of adjudication. Consequently, this "essential elements" condition has considerable importance in administrative law, so that the applicability of res judicata cannot be "viewed in isolation from the administrative process."[12]

The essential elements of administrative adjudication are basically those of a fair hearing. The *Restatement* identifies these elements as notice, the opportunity "to present evidence and legal argument in support of the party's contentions and fair opportunity to rebut evidence and argument by opposing parties," and a decision, according to identified rules of law. This decision must be in reference to "specified parties

8. 160 F.2d at 246. See also Porter & Dietsch, Inc. v. FTC, 605 F.2d 294, 299–300 (7th Cir.1979), cert. denied 445 U.S. 950, 100 S.Ct. 1597, 63 L.Ed.2d 784 (1980); Louis Stores, Inc. v. Department of Alcoholic Beverage Control, 57 Cal.2d 749, 758, 22 Cal.Rptr. 14, 371 P.2d 758, 762 (1962) (when, in a new hearing to revoke a wholesale liquor license, the licensing authority decided against the licensee on issues decided in his favor at a previous hearing, the courts on review refused to hold the authority bound by collateral estoppel inasmuch as the "public interest and effect on third parties" required that it be able to reexamine and reinterpret the applicable statutes as it applied to the license.)

9. Restatement (Second) of Judgments sec. 83.

10. Id.

11. United States v. Utah Const. & Min. Co., 384 U.S. 394, 422, 86 S.Ct. 1545, 1560, 16 L.Ed.2d 642 (1966).

12. Purter v. Heckler, 771 F.2d 682, 691 (3d Cir.1985).

concerning a specific transaction, situation, or status." Moreover, the *Restatement* requires a "rule of finality" which would "specify[ ] a point in the proceeding when presentations are terminated and a final decision is terminated."[13]

§ 11.1.1 Res Judicata Across Forums

A question that frequently arises is whether an agency adjudication is binding in subsequent actions in forums other than the agency. Should, for example, an administrative determination that a school teacher's dismissal was not racially motivated be conclusive in a subsequent federal court action involving the same issue? In the past, the practice was that an administrative determination would *not* be given such a preclusive effect. Today, however, the practice has changed. The initial impression, of agency adjudication as "executive action" unentitled to preclusive effect, has faded.[14] An agency determination about a matter within its jurisdiction will not, simply because it was rendered by an agency, be denied a preclusive effect in another forum. Instead, the courts now look to the quality of the agency determination in question. If it is possessed of the "essential elements of adjudication," then that determination may be given a conclusive effect across forums.[15]

The question posed above, whether an administrative determination that a job termination was not racially motivated should be conclusive in a subsequent federal court action, was at issue in *Yancy v. McDevitt*.[16] A school board had determined that racial prejudice was not a motive in the job termination of a public school teacher. The teacher then brought a federal court action, under 42 U.S.C. § 1983, in which he claimed that his dismissal was racially motivated. The district court, however, entered a summary judgment against him on the grounds that the school board's finding of no racial motivation was conclusive. On appeal, the Eighth Circuit Court of Appeals affirmed the lower court decision and held that "the fact that [the teacher's] termination was litigated before what amounts to an administrative tribunal rather than a court [does not] prevent the application of issue preclusion." Instead, the relevant question was whether the agency adjudication conformed to the essential elements of adjudication. The court held that the adjudication did so conform and that relitigation of the board's allegedly discriminatory motive was thus precluded.[17] (We should quickly add that where an

13. Restatement (Second) of Judgments Sec. 83. Additionally, the Restatement provides that the "essential elements of an adjudication" may include "Such other procedural elements as may be necessary to constitute the proceeding a sufficient means of conclusively determining the matter in question. . . ."

14. E.g. Bowen v. United States, 570 F.2d 1311, 1322 (7th Cir.1978).

15. Restatement (Second) of Judgments Sec. 83. The "essential elements of adjudication," as required by this provision, are discussed in the preceding section.

16. 802 F.2d 1025 (8th Cir.1986).

17. 802 F.2d at 1029–30. The court relied on the Restatement (Second) of Judgments Sec. 83 as it provides that an administrative determination may be conclusive "insofar as the proceeding resulting in the judgment entailed the essential elements of adjudication."

Another instructive case respecting the modern application of res judicata to agency

administrative proceeding does not conform the "essential attributes" of adjudication, the courts have adamantly refused to give that proceeding preclusive effect in subsequent adjudications.)[18]

Apart from the "essential elements of adjudication," the availability of res judicata across forums may depend upon such additional factors as compatibility of evidentiary standards or burdens of persuasion. Or differing legal standards. In *Harary v. Blumenthal,* an accountant, previously acquitted in a criminal trial on bribery charges, was brought before the Internal Revenue Service for a disbarment proceeding.[19] The grounds for disbarment were the same bribery charges involved in the previous criminal trial, and so the accountant argued that the agency was estopped by the not-guilty determination in that trial. But because of the lower standard of proof in administrative proceedings and because the issue in the Internal Revenue Service proceeding was somewhat different (fitness to practice rather than criminality) the court of appeals refused to find that the agency was bound by the previous criminal action.

Across agency forums, res judicata again depends on whether the initial decision was arrived at according to the essential elements of adjudication. Also, decisions by an agency of "primary responsibility" for the matter in question will generally be given conclusive effect by other agencies (assuming that that decision was arrived at according to the essential elements of adjudication). The National Bituminous Coal Commission had determined that the Sunshine Coal Company was a produc-

actions is Bowen v. United States, 570 F.2d 1311 (7th Cir.1978), where the court found that that a prior National Transportation Safety Board determination of pilot error was preclusive in a court action brought by the pilot under the Federal Tort Claims Acts. In the court action, the pilot claimed that air traffic controllers had negligently failed to warn him of the icing conditions that had caused him to crash. At a previous hearing (pertaining to suspension of the pilot's license), the National Transportation Safety Board had found that air traffic controllers had in fact properly advised the pilot of the icing conditions and that the pilot had operated his aircraft contrary to this advice and had in " 'a careless or reckless manner' ... enter[ed] into the cloud cover." In finding that this prior administrative determination was conclusive respecting the pilot's contributory negligence, the court stated:

> [H]ere the underlying policy, *viz.,* that one fair opportunity to litigate an issue is enough, is best served by the rule that issue preclusion applies to a final administrative determination of an issue properly before an agency acting in a judicial capacity when both parties were aware of the possible significance of the issue in later proceedings and were afforded a fair opportunity to litigate the issue and to obtain judicial review.

18. In Nasem v. Brown, 595 F.2d 801 (D.C.Cir.1979), Mr. Nasem claimed that he was fired in reprisal for a claim of racial discrimination that he had filed against the Army; the Army claimed Nasem's work was unsatisfactory. When Nasem brought a Title VII action in federal court, the court of appeals for the District of Columbia held that the Army was *not* barred from relitigating in that action issues decided in an earlier proceeding by the Civil Service Commission's Office of Federal Equal Employment Opportunity. The court, looking to the "adequacy" of the administrative determination, found it deficient. In this regard, the court referred to "the inability of the parties to present live witness testimony in a proceeding that necessarily turns on retaliatory motivation" and "thus demands that the decision maker weigh witness credibility." See also Montana v. United States, 440 U.S. 147, 99 S.Ct. 970, 59 L.Ed.2d 210 (1979) (claim preclusion denied where "there is reason to doubt the quality, extensiveness, or fairness of the procedures followed in the prior litigation.").

19. 555 F.2d 1113 (2d Cir.1977).

er of bituminous coal subject to the Bituminous Coal Act. In *Sunshine Anthracite Coal Co. v. Adkins,*[20] the Supreme Court held that that Coal Commission determination was binding in an Internal Revenue Service proceeding where the coal company's tax liability was predicated on whether it was subject to the Bituminous Coal Act. The Commission, and not the IRS, had been primarily assigned the responsibility of making that decision. The "Commissioner of Internal Revenue [was] merely the agency to collect taxes." It was *not*, the Court found, the administrative agent whom Congress has designated to determine what coal is exempt from the . . . tax.[21]

§ 11.1.2 Collateral Estoppel

Collateral estoppel, as we said, precludes the relitigation of such issues as may have been decided in a case. Once a court has "decided an issue of fact or law" that is "necessary" to a judgment, that decision is conclusive with respect to that issue if it arises in a future adjudication.[22] Today, collateral estoppel applies to agency adjudication in much the same way as it does to courts. But with this significant exception. Traditionally, collateral estoppel has required "mutuality of estoppel". In recent years, though, their requirement of "mutuality" has been eased in civil litigation in courts. For agencies, though, the mutuality requirements remains firm.

In shorthand, mutuality of estoppel may be described as limiting collateral estoppel to future disputes *between the parties* to the case in which an issue was originally resolved. A feature of modern civil procedure, however, is that collateral estoppel has been extended, so that it may be had without "mutuality of estoppel." This is to say that collateral estoppel may prevent the relitigation of an issue even as against a person who was not a party to the case in which the issue was resolved. Assume that issue x is decided in a civil action between Acme and Bates. With mutuality of estoppel eliminated, Acme may then rely on that judgment respecting that issue in a subsequent civil action, not against Bates but against Cox who was not a party to the original action.

In *U.S. v. Mendoza*, the Supreme Court explained that the reason for having dropped mutuality of estoppel in ordinary civil actions was to "relieve parties of the costs and vexation of multiple lawsuits" and to "conserve judicial resources." At the same time, though, the Court

20. 310 U.S. 381, 60 S.Ct. 907, 84 L.Ed. 1263 (1940).

21. 310 U.S. at 401, 60 S.Ct. at 916. See also FTC v. Texaco, Inc., 517 F.2d 137, 147 (D.C.Cir.1975) (preclusive effect given to prior determination of Federal Power Commission regarding gas reserves where, among other things, the Commission had "particular expertise on the factual issues involved"); National Ass'n of Women's and Children's Apparel Salesmen, Inc. v. FTC, 479 F.2d 139, 144 (5th Cir.1973), cert. denied 414 U.S. 1004, 94 S.Ct. 360, 38 L.Ed.2d 240 (1973) (given the National Labor Relations Board's "particular expertise" regarding the matter at hand—whether certain organizations constituted "labor organizations"—it was "proper for the FTC to accord dispositive weight to the Board's holding").

22. Montana v. United States, 440 U.S. 147, 153, 99 S.Ct. 970, 59 L.Ed.2d 210 (1979).

explained that agency litigation was "different" and then laid down the rule that the requirement of mutuality of estoppel *remained in place* in actions where an agency was a party.

The Court's explanation of how agency litigation is different was along these lines. A dispute about agency policy may break out in several different forums. To be sure, adjudication between the agency and a particular person, respecting that policy, ought to settle the issues between that person and the agency, and collateral estoppel would assure that. However, if mutuality of estoppel is dropped, then all other parties in all other forums in which the developing policy is at issue could similarly claim that the agency was estopped. If, for instance, the agency in developing its policy has some issues decided against it an action against Smith. Without mutuality of estoppel, that decision on those issues would from then on be preclusive everywhere and with anybody. For this reason, the Court in *Mendoza* stated that a "rule allowing nonmutual collateral estoppel against the Government in such cases would substantially thwart the development of policy by freezing it to the first decision first final rendered in a matter." Additionally, the Supreme Court noted that "allowing only one final determination would deprive this Court of the benefit it would receive from permitting several courts of appeals to explore a difficult question before this Court grants certiorari."

For these and other reasons, the Court in *Mendoza* retained the mutuality of estoppel requirement in agency litigation. At the same time, though, the Court in a companion case made clear that collateral estoppel—so long as the mutuality requirement was met—continued to apply to agency adjudication.[23]

§ 11.2 PROMISSORY ESTOPPEL: THE RELIABILITY OF GOVERNMENT ADVICE

When government makes assurances to us individually, we should expect it to stand by its word.[1] In private law, this sort of expectation is subject to legal protection, by principles of estoppel that hold private citizens to promises that they have made and others have relied upon.[2]

23. United States v. Stauffer Chemical Co., 464 U.S. 165, 104 S.Ct. 575, 78 L.Ed.2d 388 (1984). So long as collateral estoppel was subject to the mutuality of estoppel, it would, the Court said, serve private and public interests in economy in litigation without "freez[ing] the development of the law." As well, the Court rejected the government's argument that to preserve an agency's flexibility in developing a congressionally mandated program, the agency should not be collaterally estopped respecting pure question of respecting questions of law.

§ 11.2

1. There is a legitimate interest of "citizens in some minimum standard of decency, honor and reliability in their dealing with Government." Heckler v. Community Health Services, Inc., 467 U.S. 51, 60–61, 104 S.Ct. 2218, 2224–25, 81 L.Ed.2d 42 (1984). See also Brandt v. Hickel, 427 F.2d 53, 56 (9th Cir.1970) ("some forms of erroneous advice are so closely connected to the basic fairness of the administrative decision making process that the government may be estopped from disavowing the misstatement.")

2. The dissertation about estoppel most relied upon in the courts is J. Pomer-

Similar protection might be expected where government is the promisor. In many ways, however, the doctrine of promissory estoppel does not apply to government as it applies in private transactions. Here, there are additional considerations, such as the rule of law, separation of powers, sovereign immunity, and the fiscal and managerial integrity of public programs.

In *Federal Crop Insurance Corporation v. Merrill,* farmers who had bought crop insurance from a federal agency had done so on the representation, by a local agency official, that the crop was insurable. Unfortunately, their crop was destroyed. When they tried to make good on their insurance, payment was denied. The reason given was that according to published regulations, their crop was uninsurable. In private law, the principal is bound by the representations of agents acting within the scope of their actual or apparent authority.[3] Accordingly, the Utah Supreme Court held that the agency was estopped, the same as a private insurance company, to deny the representations of its agent. Therefore, the agency should pay the claim.[4] This state court decision was appealed to the United States Supreme Court, which Court, while willing to "assume that recovery could be had against a private insurance corporation," was unwilling to assume that the Government was "just another private litigant." The Supreme Court, therefore, refused to hold the agency estopped.[5]

Since *Federal Crop Insurance Corporation v. Merrill,* the Supreme Court has never *held* that government can be estopped by the representations of its officials. At the same time, though, the court has declined to rule that an agency can never be estopped. Instead, the Court has refused to say "that there are no cases in which the public interest in ensuring that the Government can enforce the law free from estoppel might be outweighed by the countervailing interest of citizens in some minimum standard of decency, honor and reliability in their dealing with Government."[6] Consistent with this dictum, there is a somewhat unruly

oy, 3 Equity Jurisprudence Sec. 801 et seq. (5th ed. 1941). Pomeroy describes the "doctrine of equitable estoppel" as "pre-eminently the creature of equity," and that its "object is to prevent the unconscientious and inequitable assertion or enforcement of claims or [rights] which might have existed or been enforceable by other rules of law." Id. at sec. 802.

3. Restatement (Second) of Agency sec. 265; W. Seavey, Agency sec. 8E, at 14 (1964).

4. Merrill v. Federal Crop Insurance Corp., 67 Idaho 196, 174 P.2d 834 (1946).

5. Federal Crop Insurance Corp. v. Merrill, 332 U.S. 380, 383, 68 S.Ct. 1, 3, 92 L.Ed. 10 (1947).

6. Heckler v. Community Health Services, Inc., 467 U.S. 51, 60, 104 S.Ct. 2218, 2224, 81 L.Ed.2d 42 (1984). In this case, the Court found that there was no estoppel against the agency because of the claimants failure to meet the ordinary, private law elements of the doctrine. These elements, and *Heckler v. Community Health Services, Inc.*, are discussed in the next section infra.

Besides the leading case of *Federal Crop Insurance v. Merrill,* an important Supreme Court decision denying estoppel is Utah Power & Light Co. v. United States, 243 U.S. 389, 37 S.Ct. 387, 61 L.Ed. 791 (1917), where the Court found that estoppel could not be applied to mistakes of law by government officials. In that case, electrical power companies, when the federal government tried to enjoin them from the use of forest "reservation" land, claimed that it was estopped from doing so. The companies claimed that they had been assured by government officials that "the reservations

body of lower court decisions holding that in appropriate circumstances the government may be estopped. This case law has no doubt been driven by the expansion of modern government into what was previously the unshared turf of economic arrangements by the private sector. As the Seventh Circuit has explained, "with the growth of the federal government and the broadening of government interaction with private parties, many courts have reconsidered their reluctance to apply the doctrine of equitable estoppel against the government."[7]

This "reconsideration" of promissory estoppel is discussed in the rest of this section. But whatever the extent of the newer case law, the case remains that because government is sufficiently different from other parties it "may not be estopped on the same terms as any other litigant."[8] In at least this respect, *Federal Crop Insurance Corporation v. Merrill* still rules.

§ 11.2.1 The Elements of the Private Law of Estoppel

To estop government at all, one must first meet the private law elements of the doctrine, and only then go on to meet additional factors peculiar to government. As the Supreme Court has said, "When an estoppel is asserted against the government, the private party surely cannot prevail without at least demonstrating that the traditional elements of estoppel are present."[9] Thus, before discussing the public law of estoppel it seems useful to pause for a moment to look at the private law.

When Jones makes representation to Smith, who reasonably relies to his detriment on that representation, Jones is then estopped to deny the truth of that representation.[10] In this general form, estoppel includes

would not be an obstacle to the Construction or operation" of hydroelectric plants on the lands, and in reliance the companies built the plants. The Supreme Court, however, ruled "the United States is neither bound nor estopped by acts of its officers or agents in entering into an arrangement or arrangements to do or cause to be done what the law does not sanction or permit." 243 U.S. at 408–09, 37 S.Ct. at 391. On estoppels pertaining to mistakes of law, see also Automobile Club v. Commissioner, 353 U.S. 180, 77 S.Ct. 707, 1 L.Ed.2d 746 (1957).

7. Portmann v. United States, 674 F.2d 1155 (7th Cir.1982).

8. Heckler v. Community Health Services, Inc., 467 U.S. 51, 60, 104 S.Ct. 2218, 2224, 81 L.Ed.2d 42 (1984). See also U.S. Immigration and Naturalization Serv. v. Hibi, 414 U.S. 5, 8, 94 S.Ct. 19, 21, 38 L.Ed.2d 7 (1973) ("It is well settled that the Government is not in a position identical to that of a private litigant with respect to the enforcement of laws enacted by Congress.").

9. Heckler v. Community Health Services, Inc., 467 U.S. 51, 61, 104 S.Ct. 2218, 2224, 81 L.Ed.2d 42 (1984); Lyng v. Payne, 476 U.S. 926, 935–36, 106 S.Ct. 2333, 2339–40, 90 L.Ed.2d 921 (1986), rehearing denied 478 U.S. 1031, 107 S.Ct. 11, 92 L.Ed.2d 766 (1986). For lower court cases holding that the agencies might not be estopped where the private law elements of estoppel were not met, see Santoni v. FDIC, 677 F.2d 174, 178–79 (1st Cir.1982); Radioptics, Inc. v. United States, 621 F.2d 1113, 1129–30 (Ct. Cl.1980); Robbins v. Reagan, 780 F.2d 37, 53 (D.C.Cir.1985).

10. A more specific description of the elements of the doctrine, as provided by Pomeroy, is as follows:

1. There must be conduct—acts, language, or silence—amounting to a representation or a concealment of material facts.

2. These facts must be known to the party estopped at the time of his said conduct, or at least the circumstances must be such that knowledge of them is necessarily imputed to him.

elements of reasonable reliance on a representation and detrimental change in position caused by this reliance. Respecting these elements, the Supreme Court decision in *Heckler v. Community Health Services, Inc.*, involving a claim of estoppel in Medicare payments, is instructive.[11]

The government reimburses health care providers for services to Medicare patients. Providers may elect to receive these payments through a "fiscal intermediary" that does the accounting. Community Health Services was a provider in the Medicare program and received payments through the intermediation of the Travelers Insurance Companies.

Community Health Services asked Travelers whether it might be reimbursed for wages paid CETA employees, even though it otherwise received grants respecting the wages and fringe benefits of such employees under "CETA" (the Comprehensive Employment and Training Act). Travelers "orally advised" Community Health Services that the CETA funds were "seed money" that the Health and Human Services "Provider Reimbursement Manual" had said was reimbursable. In fact, Travelers was wrong. Health and Human Services operating procedures instead required Travelers to refer such a question to it. When Travelers finally did that, Health and Human Services ruled that the CETA funds were not covered and that Community Health Services had been overpaid some $70,000. When Health and Human Services tried to recoup this amount, Community Health Services claimed that the agency was estopped to do so by the representations of Travelers, the fiscal intermediary.

In these circumstances, the Court held that private law requirements of estoppel—those of detrimental and reasonable reliance—had not been met. To start with, the Court could not see how Community Health Services could claim detrimental injury it that in had no right to the compensation. The government had essentially given Community Health Services an interest free loan over a three-year period. Instead of injury, Community Health Services had, in the Court's view, bettered itself, by "expand[ing] its operations" by the interim use of funds to which it was not entitled.

The Court also found that Community Health Services could not "reasonably rely" on the representations in question. Community Health Services knew that Traveler's appropriate role was that of a mere "conduit" between Health and Human Services and the claimant. Know-

3. The truth concerning these facts must be unknown to the other party claiming the benefit of the estoppel, . . .

4. The conduct must be done with the intention, or at least with the *expectation,* that it will be acted upon by the other party, or under such circumstances that it is both natural and probable that it will be so acted upon.

5. The conduct must be relied upon by the other party, and, thus relying, he must be led to act upon it.

6. He must in fact act upon it in such a manner as to change his position for the worse; . . .

J. Pomeroy, 3 Equity Jurisprudence sec. 805 (5th ed. 1941).

11. 467 U.S. 51, 61, 104 S.Ct. 2218, 2224, 81 L.Ed.2d 42 (1984).

ing this, Community Health Services did not seek a more dispositive answer. Moreover, the reasonableness of Community Health Services' reliance was "further undermined because the advice it received from Travelers was oral." An estoppel based on oral representations, as the Court noted, increased the possibility of fraud in staking a claim to government benefits. Also, written advice would have better represented a deliberate and reflective agency opinion in the matter. Consequently, the Court concluded that Community Health Services accepted "an oral policy judgment by an official who, it should have known, was not in the business of making policy." This was not "reasonable reliance."[12]

§ 11.2.2 Public Law of Promissory Estoppel: The Elements

While the private law elements of promissory estoppel are necessary to establishing a case against the government, they are not in themselves sufficient, because "government may *not* be estopped on the same terms as any other litigant."[13] Considerations such as rule of law, separation of powers, sovereign immunity, and an appropriate regard for the fiscal and administrative integrity of public programs are the reasons for this difference.

(a) Rule of Law

Because of expectations of predictability and even-handedness in agency action, the idea of government according to standing rules is a powerful force in administrative law. Close to a century ago, Judge Sanborn, in reversing an agency because of its deviation from a rule about use of government land, said:

> [R]ights [were not] left to the arbitrary and whimsical discretion of the officers before whom their cases happened to arise, without law or rule to guide them. Such a deplorable condition of affairs would have been in conflict with the fundamental principles of civilized government, which attempts by a uniform administration of law, to secure equal rights to all, free from the arbitrary and whimsical will of any.[14]

In accord is the modern Supreme Court: "When the Government is unable to enforce the law because the conduct of its agents has given rise to an estoppel, the interest of the citizenry as a whole in obedience to the rule of law is undermined."[15]

12. 467 U.S. at 65–66, 104 S.Ct. at 2226–27. Although the court's consideration of reasonable reliance was in terms of the private law, some of the factors it included were nonetheless peculiar to the public sector, as it spoke to the "necessity for ensuring that governmental agents stay within the lawful scope of their authority, and that those who seek public funds act with scrupulous exactitude." Id.

13. Heckler v. Community Health Services, 467 U.S. at 60, 104 S.Ct. at 2224.

14. Germania Iron Co. v. James, 89 Fed. 811, 814 (8th Cir.1898).

15. Heckler v. Community Health Services, 467 U.S. 51, 60 (1984). See also Berger, Do Regulations Really Bind Regulators?, 62 NW.U.L.Rev. 137, 149–50 (1967) ("Compliance with a regulation which has 'the force of law' ... is required by due

This relation, between the rule of law and estoppel, was justification for the leading decision against estopping the government, the previously mentioned Supreme Court decision in *Federal Crop Insurance Corp. v. Merrill.*[16] In more detail, the circumstances of that case were that private insurers considered crop insurance "too great a commercial risk." Congress, therefore, enacted the Federal Crop Insurance Act and created the Federal Crop Insurance Corporation "to insure, upon such terms and conditions not inconsistent with the provision of this title, as it may determine, producers of wheat ... against loss in yields due to unavoidable causes, including drought." Pursuant to this delegation, the Federal Crop Insurance Corporation promulgated and published regulations in the Federal Register, and among these regulations was one that precluded insurance for "reseeded wheat." Two brothers applied for crop insurance and in doing so informed the Corporation's county agent that it was seeking insurance for four hundred acres of spring wheat reseeded on winter wheat, and the agent advised the farmers that the crop was insurable. This representation was contrary to the published regulation about reseeded wheat, but the farmers had no knowledge of that.

When the crop was destroyed by drought, the Federal Crop Insurance Corporation refused to pay and did so because of the regulation denying insurance for reseeded wheat. The farmers then sued. The U.S. Supreme Court, in an opinion by Justice Frankfurter, "assumed that recovery could be had against a private insurance corporation." The Court, however, was unwilling to say that the Government was "just another private litigant." One main difference was the duty imposed by the rule of law: "Just as everyone is charged with knowledge of the United States Statutes at Large, ... the appearance of rules and regulations in the Federal Register gives legal notice of their contents."[17] Because the farmers, the same as the agency officials, were charged with notice of, and compliance with, standing rules, they could not base a claim on representations contrary to those rules.

If administrative officials were able to change agency rules by their own representations, these officials would perforce gain the power to distribute agency benefits unequally at their discretion, which discretion is contrary to the rule of law. Perhaps this is the sense of the bald assertion, in *Federal Crop Insurance Corp. v. Merrill,* that "Men must turn square corners when they deal with the government."[18]

process in its primal sense; i.e., a regulation, like a statute, is a part of 'the law of the land' which must be observed by an official for the protection of the citizen.").

16. 332 U.S. 380, 68 S.Ct. 1, 92 L.Ed. 10 (1947).

17. 332 U.S. at 384–85, 68 S.Ct. at 3.

18. Public laws would include statutes of Congress and agency regulations published in the federal register. Whether it would include agency directives that are not so published would seem an open question. The Supreme Court has, however, indicated that non-published, internal agency directives, such as operational or instructional manuals, do not amount to rules binding the public sector. See Morton v. Ruiz, 415 U.S. 199, 94 S.Ct. 1055, 39 L.Ed.2d 270 (1974).

(b) Separation of Powers

Assume that Congress by statute establishes that to receive a certain benefit a person must meet conditions X, Y, and Z. Further assume that an agency official, mistakenly or otherwise, tells a person that Z is not necessary. If the courts should hold that government is bound by this representation that is contrary to the statute, that holding, as one court has said, "would infringe upon Congress' exclusive constitutional authority to make law."[19] This alleged infringement is another reason that for promissory estoppel, government is "not just another private litigant."

This separation of powers element to estoppel can be overstated. Congress may set X, Y, and Z as essential conditions of some program. But as Justice Stevens has explained, these conditions are just that, *programmatic* elements. And the program, and Congress' will, is not defeated by the occasional use of promissory estoppel to prevent injustice to a particular person.[20] Against estoppel, though, the response is that in the context of one of its programs, Congress itself can provide for the individualized justice of promissory estoppel, and where it wishes to do so has done so. Leaving the decision about promissory estoppel to Congress, then, makes the doctrine consistent with separation of powers. Otherwise, the separation of powers argument against estoppel can be stated somewhat more functionally. The bureaucracy that implements a federal program is large and imperfect. Mistakes will be made, mismanagement will happen. Also, in this vast bureaucracy there are ample opportunities for collusion and fraud, where some official makes unauthorized promises deliberately. If binding, these mistakes, mismanagements, and collusions might be so extensive as to do overall (indeed, "programmatic") damage to the project. Thus, the better regard for Congress if for the courts not to elevate these mistakes and collusions by means of promissory estoppel.[21]

19. Portmann v. United States, 674 F.2d 1155, 1159 (7th Cir.1982). See also Montilla v. United States, 457 F.2d 978, 986–87 (Ct.Cl.1972) ("[W]e know of no case where an officer or agent of the government . . . has estopped the government from enforcing a law passed by Congress. Unless a law has been repealed or declared unconstitutional by the courts, it is a part of the supreme law of the land and no officer or agent can by his action or conduct waive its provisions or nullify its enforcement.").

In Automobile Club v. Commissioner, 353 U.S. 180, 183, 77 S.Ct. 707, 709, 1 L.Ed.2d 746 (1957), the Court held that promissory estoppel could not bar an agency from correcting its wrong interpretation of the controlling public law. In that case, the Internal Revenue Service had in a letter ruling advised the Automobile Club that it was exempted from federal income taxes. Some time later, the Service determined that its earlier ruling was "grounded upon an erroneous interpretation of the term 'club'" in the Code and retroactively reversed that ruling. Id. When the Automobile Club claimed that the Service was estopped by its previous ruling, the court held that the Service could not be estopped from correcting a mistake of law.

20. *Office of Personnel Management v. Richmond,* 496 U.S. 414, 435–36, 110 S.Ct. 2465, 110 L.Ed.2d 387 (1990).

21. Heckler v. Community Health Services, Inc., 467 U.S. 51, 65, 104 S.Ct. 2218, 2226, 81 L.Ed.2d 42 (1984); Schweiker v. Hansen, 450 U.S. 785, 789–90, 101 S.Ct. 1468, 1471–72, 67 L.Ed.2d 685, rehearing denied 451 U.S. 1032, 101 S.Ct. 3023, 69 L.Ed.2d 401 (1981). See Raven–Hansen, Regulatory Estoppel: When Agencies Break Their Own Laws, 64 Tex.L.Rev. 1, 33–42 (1985). Where the courts do not see an estoppel as contrary to congressional purpose, they are more likely to uphold it.

In view of these considerations, the Supreme Court, in *Office of Personnel Management v. Richmond*,[22] handed down one of its stronger decisions against estoppel. In this case, Mr. Richmond, a former federal employee (a shipyard welder) had applied for and received federal funded disability payments. Thereafter, he took on part-time work and in doing so asked a federal employee-relations specialist whether that part-time employment might disqualify him for disability benefits. That government official orally and in writing advised Richmond that he would not be disqualified. On the basis of this advice, Richmond took the part time work. This advise was wrong inasmuch as Congress had recently amended the relevant law in terms that would disqualify Richmond and both the oral and written advice that Richmond had received was out of date. Richmond therefore stood to lose six months of disability payments (about $4000). To avoid this loss, Richmond argued promissory estoppel, that that the government was bound by the representation of its agents. The Court held no, that promissory estoppel could not be used to defeat Congress' precise statutory directive about disability payments. In this holding, the Court, as we said, relied on separation of powers considerations such as we have presented.

But as well the Court endorsed a particular sort of textual argument against estoppel. The "Appropriations Clause" of Article I of the Constitution provides that "No Money shall be drawn from the Treasury, but in consequence of Appropriations made by Law." Richmond was asking that money (the disability benefit) be withdrawn from the treasury contrary to what Congress had appropriated. He was, therefore, asking the Court to order an (unauthorized) appropriation, and that the Court, out of formal, separation of power considerations, could not do. In this respect, the majority stated: "We hold that that payments of money from the Federal Treasury are limited to those authorized by statute." Three concurring and two dissenting justices had reservations about such a broad pronouncement. In particular, Justice Stevens, concurring, thought that promissory estoppel would not in all instances be so contrary to the intent of Congress as to amount to an unauthorized appropriation. In this respect, he made the point, as previously stated, that appropriations for projects such as disability insurance are programmatic in nature and that in some instances promissory estoppel might well serve the program and the appropriation.[23]

Brandt v. Hickel, 427 F.2d 53 (9th Cir. 1970).

Where an agency-made rule rather than a statute is involved, it might seem that the separated powers basis of estoppel ("Congress' exclusive constitutional authority to make law") has no application. The rules that are misrepresented are the products of the agency, not Congress. E.g., Portmann v. United States, 674 F.2d 1155, 1159 (7th Cir.1982) (the "separation of powers" principle is of less appeal "where only an agency's own regulations are at stake."). However, Congress has delegated this authority to the agency, to be exercised according to processes prescribed by law, such as rulemaking, and rulemaking and published rules inform Congress as to the substance of delegated authority. Cf. Federal Crop Insurance Corp. v. Merrill, 332 U.S. 380, 381–82, 68 S.Ct. 1, 2, 92 L.Ed. 10 (1947). As this substance is varied by means of estoppels, the plenary powers of Congress may be diminished, albeit more indirectly.

22. 496 U.S. 414, 110 S.Ct. 2465, 110 L.Ed.2d 387 (1990).

23. As explained by Professor Asimov, "the application of estoppel hardly means

(c) Sovereign Immunity

Sovereign immunity, which holds that government may not be sued without its consent,[24] has had a particular application to estoppels against government. Where an estoppel is used offensively—to establish a cause of action in damages against the state—sovereign immunity precludes the estoppel (unless of course Congress has otherwise waived that immunity). How this works is illustrated by the Ninth Circuit opinion in *Jablon v. United States*.[25]

A physician had signed-up for the Air Force on the understanding that he would receive a bonus of $37,000 for enlisting. But before reporting for active duty, he was arrested for an alleged violation of a state law regulating prescription drugs. Because of this arrest, the Air Force revoked the physician's orders to active duty. He then sued the United States in damages for breach of contract, contending that an Air Force recruiting officer had promised him he would be paid his $37,000 bonus for taking the oath of office, which he had done.

The Ninth Circuit Court of Appeals assumed that the physician had satisfied the traditional elements of a claim of estoppel. Nonetheless, the court dismissed his claim. Where an estoppel is used offensively—to create an action in damages for breach of contract—then according to settled rules of sovereignty government has to consent to the action. The Tucker Act, by which the federal government consents to contract actions against it, did not include claims based on estoppel. Therefore, the court concluded that "the government has not waived its sovereign immunity with regard to a promissory estoppel cause of action."

While sovereign immunity may bar promissory estoppels asserted offensively, as part of a contract action in damages, such immunity does *not* include estoppels offered defensively, to deny government a claim or defense that it otherwise might have.[26] For instance, in *FDIC v. Harri-*

the repeal of a statute; it would simply preclude the retroactive correction as to particular individuals of a particular mistake." M. Asimow, Advice to the Public From Federal Administrative Agencies 60 (1973).

24. Sovereign immunity is discussed at chap. 12, sec. 12.1.

25. 657 F.2d 1064 (9th Cir.1981).

26. In *Jablon v. United States,* the court distinguished between promissory estoppel and equitable estoppel. Equitable estoppel, the court explained, was used defensively, as a shield to prevent the government from asserting a claim or a defense which it otherwise would have had. In contrast, promissory estoppel was used offensively, as a sword to create a cause of action in contract. "[P]romissory estoppel is used to create a cause of action, whereas equitable estoppel is used to bar a party from ... instituting an action it otherwise would have." As further explained by the court:

> Dr. Jablon's "estoppel theory" is not an equitable estoppel theory. He is not attempting to bar the government from raising a defense to an independent cause of action which he is asserting. Instead, he is relying on a promissory estoppel to create his right of recovery. Thus, the "estoppel" of which he speaks is promissory estoppel. The equitable "estoppel" cases he cites are inapposite.

The court added that while the courts had applied equitable estoppel theories to government, it could find no cases "that actually awarded the plaintiff money damages on a promissory estoppel theory." 657 F.2d at 1069 & n. 9. See Schuhl v. United States, 3 Cl.Ct. 207 (1983); Biagioli v. United States, 2 Cl.Ct. 304, 307–08 (1983).

son, the court defined the estoppel in question as equitable and permitted private parties to assert it as a defense to a debt collection action brought against them by the FDIC.[27]

(d) Fiscal and Administrative Integrity

Agencies often implement vast and complex programs. Within this large apparatus, control is maintained by rules and regulations that bind various sub-units. As estoppel denies the authority of rules, it shunts authority to the lower levels of an agency. Thus, the agency's capacity centrally to manage and control field operations is diminished. In *Schweiker v. Hansen,* Ms. Hansen met for fifteen minutes with a field representative of the Social Security Administration to ask him whether she was eligible for "mother's insurance benefits."[28] The official made certain representations to her. However, this official, the field representative, lacked the authority to make those representations. Instead, the agency's written requirements and field manual provided that the eligibility determinations in question had to be made more deliberately, on written application. When Ms. Hansen later claimed that the Social Security Administration was bound by the assurances made to her by the field representative, the Supreme Court held that estoppel was inappropriate. The Court explained that "if [the field representative's] minor breach of such a manual suffices to estop petitioner, then the government is put 'at risk that every alleged failure by an agent to follow instructions to the last detail in one of a thousand cases will deprive it of the benefit of the written application requirement which experience has taught to be essential to the honest and effective administration of the Social Security Laws.' "[29]

27. 735 F.2d 408 (11th Cir.1984), rehearing denied 768 F.2d 1353 (11th Cir. 1985) (discussed, infra). See also United States v. Fox Lake State Bank, 366 F.2d 962 (7th Cir.1966), where the government was estopped from bringing an action under the Civil False Claims Act against a bank that had heavily relied on the advice of federal agents in preparing the claims application in question.

Regarding sovereign immunity and equitable actions that may include the transfer of money from government to the private sector, see chap. 12, sec. 12.5, infra.

28. 450 U.S. 785, 101 S.Ct. 1468, 67 L.Ed.2d 685 (1981), rehearing denied 451 U.S. 1032, 101 S.Ct. 3023, 69 L.Ed.2d 401 (1981).

29. 450 U.S. at 789–90, 101 S.Ct. at 1471–72. More fully described, the circumstances of *Schweiker v. Hansen* were as follows. When the Social Security Administration field representative told the claimant that she was ineligible for benefits, he at the same time failed to tell her such benefits were available only to those who file written applications. Also, the internal Social Security Administration handbook instructed field representatives to advise applicants of the advantages of filing written applications and to recommend to applicants uncertain about their eligibility that they file written applications. Some time later the individual filed a written application, which was approved, and she then began receiving benefits. She then claimed benefits retroactive to the time the field representative erroneously told her she was not eligible and failed to advise her to submit a written application. The Second Circuit Court of Appeals found for her, holding that "misinformation provided by a Government official combined with a showing of misconduct (even if it does not rise to the level of a violation of a legally binding rule) should be sufficient to require estoppel." 450 U.S. at 787, 101 S.Ct. at 1470.

On review, the Supreme Court disagreed. The Court explained that while it had "never decided what type of conduct by a government employee will estop the Government from insisting upon compliance

Moreover, estoppel opens agencies to bogus claims, based on contrived representations of government officials. These claims, even as they are defeated, consume scarce agency resources.[30] Professor Raven–Hansen has argued that the possibility of fraud and collusion need not be a general objection to estoppel, and "because fraud is ultimately a problem of proof in the estoppel context, it should be treated as such."[31] Still, agency resources must be diverted to disproving these claims and in vast public programs, the amount of these resources and the overall managerial problems may be significant. Accordingly, the Supreme Court appears to have established a presumption against estoppel based solely on oral representations.[32]

(e) Evolution of Public Policy

A claim of a private interest by means of an estoppel might preclude an agency from acting according to its view of the greater public interest. In *Deltona Corp. v. Alexander,* a developer of ocean-front property had undertaken some extensive projects.[33] At some early stage of the project, the practice of the Army Corps of Engineers had been to grant dredge and fill permits for such projects so long as they did not impede navigable water ways. The developer claimed that consistent with this practice, the Corps of Engineers had promised such permits to it.

with valid regulations governing the distribution of welfare benefits," it had recognized "the duty of all courts to observe the conditions defined by Congress for charging the public Treasury.... " 450 U.S. at 788, 101 S.Ct. at 1470. From this standpoint, the Court made the point discussed in the text above, that the administrative integrity of a public program should not be put at risk by the field representative's disregard of standard operating procedures. Otherwise, the Court seemed to be of the opinion that the ordinary private law elements of estoppel had not been fully met. In this regard the Court stated that the field representative's actions "did not cause [the claimant] to take action, ... or fail to take action, ... that [she] could not correct at any time." 450 U.S. at 789, 101 S.Ct. at 1471.

While maintaining the integrity of public programs is a matter of considerable importance in estoppel cases, it is not a dispositive consideration. In Brandt v. Hickel, 427 F.2d 53 (9th Cir.1970), an individual, Brandt, had submitted a non-competitive oil and gas lease bid to a regional office of the Bureau of Land Management, and that office advised her that she had thirty days to cure deficiencies in it and resubmit it. Subsequently, the Secretary of Interior ruled that the local office's action in giving the applicant thirty days in which to resubmit the lease was invalid. On review, however, the Ninth Circuit held that the Secretary was estopped to deny the representation of the local office, even though action "was unauthorized by statute, regulation, or decision." 427 F.2d at 56. To the "Secretary's understandabl[e] concern[ ] that the estoppel doctrine can have a deleterious effect on administrative regularity," the court's response was that "administrative regularity must sometimes yield to basic notions of fairness." 427 F.2d at 57.

30. E.g., Lovell Mfg. v. Export–Import Bank, 777 F.2d 894, 898 (3d Cir.1985), on remand 654 F.Supp. 63 (W.D.Pa.1987). Othertimes, a concern about fraud seems to be in the background of opinions denying estoppel. In Heckler v. Community Health Services, Inc., 467 U.S. 51, 65, 104 S.Ct. 2218, 2226, 81 L.Ed.2d 42 (1984) the Court stated the "necessity for ensuring that governmental agents stay within the lawful scope of their authority, and that those who seek public funds act with scrupulous exactitude." See generally, Raven–Hansen, Regulatory Estoppel: When Agencies Break Their Own Laws, 64 U.Tex.L.Rev. 1 54–56 (1985).

31. Raven–Hansen, supra, at 55.

32. Heckler v. Community Health Services, Inc., 467 U.S. 51, 63–66, 104 S.Ct. 2218, 2225–27, 81 L.Ed.2d 42 (1984).

33. 682 F.2d 888 (11th Cir.1982).

The Corps' policies, however, changed to include other public interests, especially environmental concerns. Because of these new concerns, the Corps finally denied the developer the permits. The developer, on the basis of the alleged representations that the permits were forthcoming, sought to have the denial of them estopped. The Eleventh Circuit, however, was of the opinion that such an estoppel would tie the hands of the Corps in carrying out public policy. Therefore, the court found that an estoppel was inappropriate as a matter of law. The court explained that the "act of granting a sec. 404 permit is unquestionably an exercise of the government's sovereign power to protect the public interest" and that "in fact, the entire rational behind the sec. 404 permit is to insure that the public interest in environmental safety and quality is preserved."[34]

In accommodating public policy, by preserving agency flexibility to pursue its statutory goals, one should, however, not forget that the public interest is comprised of aggregated private interests, and that the private interest of being able to rely on government representations is considerable.

§ 11.2.3 Public Law of Estoppel: Summary

While various factors, the rule of law, sovereign immunity, and so forth, mitigate against estopping government, they have not, in terms of what the lower courts do, resulted in a flat rule against such estoppels. Instead, because of the "countervailing interest of citizens in some minimum standard of decency, honor and reliability in their dealing with Government" the courts from time to time hold government to its representations according to the standards of estoppel. But it is hard to say when the courts will do this, which should not be surprising. Estoppel, after all, is an equitable doctrine applied according to the circumstances of the case, and such application does not lend itself to a set of predictive rules.

Still, some guidelines can be offered. First of all, in dealing with government the burden is always on the claimant to know the rules: "Anyone entering into an arrangement with the government takes the risk of having accurately ascertained that he who purports to act for the government stays within the bounds of his authority."[35] Secondly, sovereign immunity operates to bar *damage* claims based on estoppel. Thirdly, and as we will shortly discuss, in the context of the proprietary functions

34. 682 F.2d at 892. See also Organized Fishermen of Florida v. Hodel, 775 F.2d 1544, 1549 (11th Cir.1985), cert. denied 476 U.S. 1169, 106 S.Ct. 2890, 90 L.Ed.2d 978 (1986) ("Although commercial fishing was deemed consistent with [the National Park Service's] conservation function for forty years, it is not surprising nor inequitable that the NPS, in exercising its conservation function, might prohibit commercial fishing today." Representations to the contrary could not "reasonably" be relied on).

35. Federal Crop Insurance Corporation v. Merrill, 332 U.S. 380, 384, 68 S.Ct. 1, 3, 92 L.Ed. 10 (1947).

of government, promissory estoppel may be especially available as a defense against government claims.[36]

Apart from these guidelines, the decisions of the courts are in themselves instructive, for instance the opinion of the Seventh Circuit in *Portmann v. United States*.[37] A postal clerk had told a graphic arts designer, who had mailed some films of considerable commercial value via the United States Post Office, that her films were insured up to $50,000. But after the films were lost in the mail, she was told that her insurance was limited by postal regulations to five hundred dollars. She then sued for the full value of the films, claiming that the Post Office was bound by the representations of its clerk.

That claim of estoppel seemed to run counter to *Federal Crop Insurance v. Merrill,* where the Supreme Court had held that in selling insurance the government could not be estopped by the representations of its agents. The court of appeals, however, found the Post Office bound by the representations of its employee and distinguished *Federal Crop Insurance v. Merrill* on the following grounds. First, in *Merrill,* the government was the only source of insurance, so that "even if [the claimant] had been given accurate information, he would not have been able to procure the insurance he desired from an alternate private source." In contrast, the postal customer could "have elected instead to do business with a private carrier." Second, the regulation misrepresented in *Federal Crop Insurance v. Merrill* had been clear and explicit. In *Portmann* the regulation was "any thing but explicit." Consequently, the court felt that the claimant could more reasonably rely on the postal clerk's advice. Third, the claim in *Portmann* was not against the public as was the case in *Federal Crop Insurance v. Merrill.* The court explained that "because the operations of the Postal Service are financed almost entirely from a self-sustaining fund generated out of the business revenue received by the Service, the *Merrill* Court's reasoning, that only Congress has the power to charge the public treasure, is ... inapplicable to the instant situation."[38]

Finally, the court in *Portmann* reasoned that the " 'proprietary' or commercial character of the government activity at issue in the instant case militates in favor of allowing an estoppel claim...." We discuss this topic, the relation of estoppel to proprietary functions, below.

§ 11.3 ESTOPPEL AND PROPRIETARY FUNCTIONS

The distinction drawn in *Portmann v. United States,* whether an agency is acting in a proprietary rather than a sovereign capacity, has

36. On occasion the courts have eschewed reliance on guidelines or principles, and instead posited an open-ended balancing test as the measure of estoppels against government. As described by one court, such a test involves whether "the government's wrongful conduct threatens to work a serious injustice and if the public's interest would not be unduly damaged by the imposition of estoppel." United States v. Lazy FC Ranch, 481 F.2d 985, 989 (9th Cir.1973).

37. 674 F.2d 1155 (7th Cir.1982).

38. 674 F.2d at 1163–64.

been an important factor in estoppel cases.[1] Where government has acted in a proprietary capacity, "courts have tended to find no significant obstacles to the use of estoppel based on the conduct of government agents acting within the scope of their actual or apparent authority."[2] The substance of the proprietary and sovereign function distinction has been described as follows:

> Proprietary governmental functions include essentially commercial transactions involving the purchase or sale of goods and services and other activities for the commercial benefit of a particular government agency. Whereas in its sovereign role, the government carries out unique governmental functions for the benefit of the whole public, in its proprietary capacity the government's activities are analogous to those of a private concern.[3]

This distinction may not, however, be easy to see, because "even routine operational contracts of federal agencies may be conditioned on a variety of special requirements imposed by Congress or the Executive for the promotion of national policy goals, thus adding a 'sovereign' element to other purely commercial transactions."[4]

The difficulty in the distinction notwithstanding, the courts have identified a number of proprietary actions of government, and held the government subject to estoppel in them. In *FDIC v. Harrison,* the Federal Deposit Insurance Corporation ("FDIC") had been appointed receiver for the insolvent Southern National Bank.[5] The FDIC then purchased the assets of the bank, which included three notes. Three individuals had borrowed thirty thousand dollars from the bank. For tax reasons, these three persons divided the promissory note for this loan into three parts. Each person was primarily liable for one part and assumed a limited guarantee for the other two parts.

When FDIC officials first made demand on the three persons responsible for the thirty-thousand dollar loan, these officials told them that each person need pay only the amount of his own note, and that he would not be held to the guarantees respecting the other notes. The FDIC thereafter changed its position, and tried to collect from all three persons in their capacity as guarantors of the other notes. At that point, these individuals asserted that the agency was estopped by its officials

§ 11.3

1. 674 F.2d 1155 (7th Cir.1982).

2. 674 F.2d at 1160–61.

3. FDIC v. Harrison, 735 F.2d 408, 411 (11th Cir.1984), rehearing denied 768 F.2d 1353 (11th Cir.1985).

4. Portmann v. United States, 674 F.2d 1155, 1161 (7th Cir.1982). An instance of where an element sovereignty is added to otherwise commercial dealings, so as to prevent a claim of estoppel is provided by Cox v. Kurt's Marine Diesel, 785 F.2d 935 (11th Cir.1986). A sheriff, in an agreement whereby his office recovered its expenses of keeping an arrested ship, misestimated these expenses. The court held that he could not by the agreement be estopped from bringing an action to recover the additional expense inasmuch as in arresting the ship he "was acting for the public at large by assisting the federal judicial system in the resolution of a dispute, a governmental function." The fact that the expense in question, an insurance expense, was commercial in nature, did not change this.

5. 735 F.2d 408, 411 (11th Cir.1984), rehearing denied 768 F.2d 1353 (11th Cir. 1985).

previous representations to the contrary. The First Circuit agreed, and held that the "FDIC was equitably estopped."

The FDIC had argued against estoppel on public policy grounds. It argued that it was acting to serve a public purpose, "the stability of the banking system," and that in this capacity the FDIC was trying to collect the notes in question. While mindful of the agency's public responsibilities, the court still did not see this as a reason for not holding the agency to its promises, not when it had assumed a proprietary role, of commercial enterprise as done by a commercial bank. The court explained that "although the debt collecting activities of the Corporation ... might be viewed in a broad sense as contributing to the accomplishment of the Corporation's purpose of maintaining a stable banking environment, the FDIC was primarily serving as an instrument of the banking industry when it became receiver for the failed Southern National Bank." Consequently, the court saw "no reason not to apply the traditional rules of equitable estoppel to the conduct of the FDIC in this case."[6]

§ 11.4 ESTOPPEL: SUMMARY

In administrative law, the doctrine of estoppel is about government standing behind the assurances of its officials. In private law, doctrines of estoppel often hold a person to a promise made to another, when the other person has relied on that promise to his detriment. This private law doctrine can be considered as establishing a norm in administrative law, but it is a norm that is modified considerably. In administrative law, considerations such as rule of law, separation of powers, sovereign immunity, and an appropriate regard for the fiscal and administrative integrity of public programs sometimes produce different results.

Some guidelines, as we have said, can be offered, the first one being that in dealing with government, the person himself has to know agency rules and cannot rely on representations about these rules by officials.[1] The second is that sovereign immunity operates to bar claims for damages based on promissory estoppel and the third is that the proprietary functions of government make a difference. For proprietary functions, estoppel may be especially available as a defense against government claims.[2]

6. See, also, United States v. Georgia–Pacific Co., 421 F.2d 92 (9th Cir.1970) (government estopped from claiming that land was part of a national forest after advising the Georgia–Pacific Company that was outside the forest and the company then invested $350,000 in managing it). Contra, see FDIC v. Roldan Fonseca, 795 F.2d 1102 (1st Cir.1986) (Where efforts of the FDIC to foreclose on a mortgage and to collect on a note were claimed to be foreclosed by alleged FDIC representations on which the property owners claimed they relied to their detriment, the court denied the defense of promissory estoppel as a matter of law.).

§ 11.4

1. To reiterate, "any one entering into an arrangement with the government takes the risk of having accurately ascertained that he who purports to act for the government stays within the bounds of his authority." Federal Crop Insurance Corporation v. Merrill, 332 U.S. 380, 384, 68 S.Ct. 1, 3, 92 L.Ed. 10 (1947).

2. On occasion the courts have eschewed reliance on guidelines or principles, and instead posited an open-ended balancing test as the measure of estoppels against government. As described by one court, such a test involves whether "the govern-

Finally we should add that as we have discussed estoppels, we have naturally focused on the pathological, on the bad promises of government officials. But bad promises do not by any means represent agency practice. As explained by Prof. Asimow:

> It seems fair to say that there is a well established custom: Advice in writing from staff officials who are highly placed, and who routinely give written advice, can be relied upon. Thus, the highly confused law on estoppel of the government gives a distorted impression of what happens; disappointment of genuine reliance interest is the rare exception.[3]

ment's wrongful conduct threatens to work a serious injustice and if the public's interest would not be unduly damaged by the imposition of estoppel." United States v. Lazy FC Ranch, 481 F.2d 985, 989 (9th Cir.1973).

3. M. Asimow, Advice to the Public from Federal Administrative Agencies 7–8 (1973).

Chapter 12

THE AVAILABILITY AND TIMING OF JUDICIAL REVIEW

Table of Sections

Whether and when the courts will review an agency action, or failure to act, are reasonably complicated matters. These matters, the availability and timing of judicial review, are about divisions of labor between courts and agencies. These divisions turn on the comparative abilities of agencies and courts and on such practical matters as allocating work between agencies and court so as to avoid redundant work. Also, the availability and timing of review implicates constitutional concerns about the role of the courts in a government of separated powers. According to the Supreme Court:

> Judicial adherence to the doctrine of the separation of powers preserves the courts for the decision of issues, between litigants, capable of effective determination.... When the courts act continually within these constitutionally-imposed boundaries ... their ability to perform their function as a balance for the peoples' protection against abuse of power by other branches of government remains unimpaired.[1]

While both are similarly grounded in separated powers and a sensible division of work between courts and agencies, the availability and the timing of review are, nonetheless, separately identified. Questions about the *availability* of judicial review are expressed as matters of jurisdiction, standing, and sovereign immunity. Availability of review also includes questions highlighted by the Administrative Procedure Act, of the extent to which Congress has "precluded" review or has so "committed" a matter to agency discretion that it is beyond review. *Timing* of review is identified by reference to the pendency and maturity of agency actions. In this relation, timing involves doctrines of ripeness and exhaustion of administrative remedies. It also involves the doctrine of primary jurisdiction, whether an action is best initiated in an agency or a court.[2]

We will discuss the timing and the availability of judicial review according to the foregoing categories, or doctrines, of ripeness, exhaustion, *et al.* But as you consider these doctrines, you should do so with a

1. United Public Workers v. Mitchell, 330 U.S. 75, 90–91, 67 S.Ct. 556, 564–65, 91 L.Ed. 754 (1947).

2. These questions of availability and timing of review generally relate to court actions initiated by a private individual. At times, these questions and the impediments they present can be substantially avoided should a person act more passively and defensively, to await an "enforcement action." By an enforcement action, the agency proceeds against the individual in court, to gain the assistance of the court in forcing the individual to do whatever it is that the agency wants of him. See sec. 12.3, infra.

particular caution in mind. This is that in practice these doctrines are not all that neat and separate; often, they converge and overlap,[3] as we will from time to time point out. Generally speaking, though, the confusion that may be entailed by the occasional convergences of ripeness, exhaustion, *et al*. can be dissipated by remembering that these doctrines, while emphasizing somewhat different factors, share the common goal of managing a sensible allocation of work between courts and agencies. Before considering these matters of availability & tuning of review, we will briefly discuss, and then set aside for awhile, the matter of sovereign immunity.

§ 12.1 SOVEREIGN IMMUNITY

In government litigation, sovereign immunity is a serious matter. Potentially, it is an absolute barrier to suits against the government.

Sovereign immunity refers to the immunity of government to suits against it. In England, this immunity came to be seen as an aspect of royalty and was based on the maxim that "the King can do no wrong."[1] Given this basis in royalty, the strong argument against sovereign immunity in the United States is its general incompatibility with the republican government that the Constitution establishes. A more specific argument is that the text of Article III of the Constitution eliminated the doctrine. Article III extends judicial power to "controversies to which the United States shall be a Party" without excluding cases in which the United States is a party defendant. Article III, then, may be read as thus endorsing suits against the United States. This endorsement, of course, would signify the general incompatibility of sovereign immunity with the republican government established by the Constitution.[2]

3. The illustration of these convergences that has gained some fame is the D.C. Circuit's opinion in Ticor Title Ins. Co. v. FTC, 814 F.2d 731 (1987), where each of the three judges determined the reviewability of an agency action according to the three separate doctrines of ripeness, exhaustion, and finality.

§ 12.1

1. In its origins, governmental immunity may not be so firmly anchored in abstract notions of sovereignty, such as "the King can do no wrong," as we may today believe. In feudal England the highest court was the King's court, and the King was not subject to suit in his own court. Still, it was not presumed that the King could not do wrong under the law, as was seen in the "petitions of right" developed in the thirteenth century. If these petitions were approved in council, the King could not refuse them. Engdahl, Immunity and Accountability for Positive Government Wrongs, 44 U.Colo.L.Rev. 1,3 (1972). Later, Blackstone provided the somewhat different basis for the doctrine as he said that "the King can do no wrong." The King, Blackstone said, might be poorly advised and poorly served by "wicked" counselors and ministers, but the King himself could not do wrong. W. Blackstone, 1 Commentaries on the Law of England 237–39 (1765). Generally see Engdahl, supra; P. Schuck, Suing Government: Citizen Remedies for Official Wrongs 33–35 (1983).

2. See the opinions of Justices Wilson and Jay in Chisholm v. Georgia, 2 U.S. (2 Dall.) 419, 1 L.Ed. 440 (1793). See also P. Schuck, supra, at 35–36 ("Read literally, [Article III] seemed to abrogate governmental immunity altogether, for the text did not expressly distinguish between cases in which governmental entities were plaintiffs and cases in which they were defendants. On the other hand, Article III might plausibly be understood to have incorporated *sub silentio* the English common law tradition of governmental immunity waivable only with government's express consent.").

But any sort of departure—on general principles of republican government or the text of Article III or both—was the route not taken. By the time of the Civil War, sovereign immunity was firmly established in this country. For the federal government this immunity was achieved by case law, by a process of accretion in which the reasons for or against immunity were never squarely faced. As said by Justice Miller in 1882, "while the exemption of the United States ... from being subjected as defendants to ordinary actions in the courts ... has been repeatedly asserted here, the principle has never been discussed or the reasons for it given, but it has always been treated as an established doctrine."[3] In the states, sovereign immunity was established not just by case law but also by formal constitutional amendment. The eleventh amendment provides that no state can be sued "by Citizens of another State, or by Citizens or Subjects of any Foreign State." By its terms, the amendment bars only those suits brought by "citizens of another state." Be that as it may, the courts themselves have extended the amendment to include immunity against suits brought by a state's own citizens.[4]

But while it is today entrenched doctrine, sovereign immunity is *not* the wholesale barrier to judicial review that it might be. A reason is that state and federal governments can, by a legislative enactment, waive it.[5] Such a waiver has at times been done specially and specifically, as when a legislature, federal or state, in establishing an agency provides for judicial review of actions of that agency. That provision is deemed a waiver as to the actions of that agency.

More importantly, at least in the case of the federal agencies, immunity has been more generally and broadly waived. In 1976, Congress—looking to the "patchwork" and "not altogether logical body of law" that in many views the doctrine of sovereign immunity had become[6]—waived federal immunity for much of the usual forms of judicial review of agencies. The Administrative Procedure Act was amended to provide that "An action in a court of the United States seeking relief other than money damages ... shall not be dismissed nor relief therein be denied on the ground that it is against the United

3. United States v. Lee, 106 U.S. 196, 207, 1 S.Ct. 240, 249, 27 L.Ed. 171 (1882).

4. Hans v. Louisiana, 134 U.S. 1, 10 S.Ct. 504, 33 L.Ed. 842 (1890). Today, the U.S. Supreme Court tends to endorse state sovereign immunity not just as a product of the Eleventh Amendment but as an inherent part of state sovereignty. Alden v. Maine, 527 U.S. 706, 119 S. Ct. 2240, 144 L.Ed.2d 636 (1999). Schapiro, Balancing, Justice, & the Eleventh Amendment: Justice Stevens Theory of State Immunity, 27 Rutgers L.J. 563 (1996).

5. E.g., United States v. Mitchell, 463 U.S. 206, 212, 103 S.Ct. 2961, 2965, 77 L.Ed.2d 580 (1983) ("It is axiomatic that the United States may not be sued without its consent and that the existence of consent is a prerequisite for jurisdiction.") Such consent can be had only by formal legislative action. E.g., United States v. Shaw, 309 U.S. 495, 60 S.Ct. 659, 84 L.Ed. 888 (1940).

6. Cramton, Non–Statutory Review of Federal Administrative Action: The Need for Statutory Reform of Sovereign Immunity, Subject Matter Jurisdiction, and Parties Defendant, 68 Mich.L.Rev. 389, 432 (1970), quoted at Senate Comm. on the Judiciary, Judicial Review of Agency Action, Sen. Rep.No. 94–996, 94th Cong., 2d Sess. 3 (1976).

States. . . ."[7] This waiver of immunity covers much of the substance of this chapter. It includes actions to set aside agency orders or rules or, more generally, actions for declaratory and injunctive relief respecting agency action or inaction.

But by its terms, the Administrative Procedure Act's waiver of immunity stops short of "money damages." By construction of the Supreme Court, however, this exception for "money damages" has been narrowed, so that the fact that money is asked for does not necessarily imply damages. In this respect, actions arising at law for injuries to person and property have been contrasted to equitable remedies requiring the transfer of money. The Administrative Procedure Act's exclusion of money damages includes the former but not the latter. In this respect, the courts have emphasized that civil actions for damages have historically been compensatory (i.e, in a tort action money recoveries are to compensate for injuries received). Thus, where the compensatory-for-injury-suffered element is lacking, a recovery of money from an agency is not necessarily "damages." In view, then of the equity versus actions-at-law distinction and of the compensatory element essential to damages, the Court in *Bowen v. Massachusetts* announced that "the fact that a 'judicial remedy may require one party to pay money to another is not a sufficient reason to characterize the action as money damages.' "[8]

Under Medicaid, if the Secretary of Health and Human Services determines that a state is not in compliance with applicable regulations, the Secretary may disallow federal reimbursements to the state for its expenditures under the program. Massachusetts brought a federal court action contesting a disallowance of some six million dollars. It requested declaratory and injunctive relief, in the form of a court order requiring reimbursement for the six million dollars. The agency claimed that this relief was barred by sovereign immunity. The state, however, claimed that sovereign immunity had been waived by Sec. 702 of the Administrative Procedure Act. The agency in turn disputed that waiver, saying that the suit was for damages. The Supreme Court, in *Bowen v. Massachusetts*, found that contrary to the agency's contention, the action was *not* for damages and that this being the case, sovereign immunity had been

7. Pub.L. 94–574, 90 Stat. 2721 (1976), codified at 5 U.S.C.A. § 702. According to the report of the Senate Judiciary Committee, this amendment was based in part on the importance that Congress attached to the use of judicial review to control agency action. In this regard, the report stated that "It is now generally accepted that courts can make a useful contribution to the administration of Government by reviewing the legality of official conduct which adversely affects private persons." Sen.Comm. on the Judiciary, Judicial Review of Agency Action, Sen.Rep. No. 94–996, 94th Cong., 2d Sess. 3 (1976). In this context of the availability of review, the report recognized that while special statutory review provisions waived immunity in a number of situations, these waivers were incomplete, especially as regards "many of the functions performed by the older executive departments." Id.

The general waiver of immunity as provided by 5 U.S.C.A. § 702 nullified the Supreme Court decision in Larson v. Domestic & Foreign Commerce Corp., 337 U.S. 682, 69 S.Ct. 1457, 93 L.Ed. 1628 (1949), insofar as that decision held that sovereign immunity barred actions for injunctive relief against the government.

8. 487 U.S. 879, 893, 108 S.Ct. 2722, 2731, 101 L.Ed.2d 749 (1988).

waived by the Administrative Procedure Act. In this respect, the Court explained:

> Our cases have long recognized the distinction between an action at law for damages—which are intended to provide a victim with monetary compensation for an injury to his person, property, or reputation—and an equitable action for specific relief—which may include an order providing for the reinstatement of an employee with back pay, or for "the recovery of specific property or moneys. . . ."

* * *

For damages proper, that is compensatory relief for injury to person or property, the federal government has waived immunity in two important areas. For tort actions, the immunity has partially been waived by the Federal Tort Claims Act. For contract actions, immunity has more extensively been waived by the Tucker Act.[9] We will describe these waivers in Chapter 14 on "Money Damages."

§ 12.2 ORIGINS OF JUDICIAL REVIEW

The origins of judicial review of agency action establish a tradition that is somewhat peculiar to Anglo–American jurisprudence and that is too quickly taken for granted. This tradition is that ordinary, generalist judges—acting on the petition of ordinary citizens—stand ready to assure that administrative power is exercised according to law and in light of permanent community interests.[1]

§ 12.2.1 Common Law Actions

The power of courts to correct and contain the power of administrative officials seems to be anchored in *Dr. Bonham's Case,* which was decided in 1610.[2] A medical licensing board, a "college perpetual of physicians and grave men," had been established by Act of Parliament during the reign of King Henry VIII. Bonham had persisted in a medical practice unlicensed by the board. For this unlicensed practice, he was imprisoned for seven days for contempt of the board. Consequently, Bonham brought an action for false imprisonment against the board

9. Additionally, immunity has been waived in actions "to quiet title to an estate or interest in real property in which an interest is claimed by the United States." 28 U.S.C. §§ 1346(f) 1402(d), 2409(a).

§ 12.2

1. As interpreted by Dicey, these origins of judicial review exclude "the idea of any exemption of officials or others from the duty of obedience to the law which governs other citizens or from the jurisdiction of the ordinary tribunals." Dicey, Law of the Constitution 202 (9th ed. 1945). See generally, Henderson & Jaffe, Judicial Review and the Rule of Law, 72 Law Quarterly 345 (1956).

2. 8 Co.Rep. 107, 77 Eng.Rep. 638 (K.B. 1610). See Jaffe, The Right to Judicial Review, 71 Harv.L.Rev. 401, 412–13 (1958). Much of the material in this section is taken from Jaffe's work, id. and from Henderson & Jaffe, Judicial Review and the Rule of Law, 72 Law Quarterly 345 (1956). See also E. Henderson, Foundations of English Administrative Law (1963).

members. By that tort action, he sought to gain judicial review of the propriety of the board's action against him.

The Court of Common Pleas took the case. In his opinion for the court, Lord Coke found that the board's action was procedurally deficient inasmuch as its members were biased. They kept for themselves a portion of the fines they imposed for unlicensed practice, and Coke held that this fee-splitting violated due process. Also, Coke found that the board's determination that Bonham was "insufficient and inexpert in the art of medicine" was reviewable. Explaining that "they [the board] are not made judges nor a court given them," Coke wrote that review by a court was essential if Dr. Bonham was to have an "adequate remedy."[3]

The form of review in *Dr. Bonham's Case,* a common-law action against agency officials, remains alive and reasonably healthy. But perhaps more important than this form of review is the tradition that *Dr. Bonham's Case* heads up. This tradition is that ordinary courts and generalist judges stand ready to assure—on the petition of private citizens—that administrative power is exercised lawfully.[4]

From a strictly logical perspective, review of agency action by generalist courts is by no means ordained. To many people, it makes more sense to establish specialist courts, expert in the subject matter and manner of agency regulation, to review agency work. Indeed, this is the European practice, where review is by specialized tribunals, such as

3. 8 Co.Rep. at 121, 77 Eng.Rep. at 657. In support of his finding that administrative decisions were traversable in an action for false imprisonment, Coke distinguished between the office of a judge, which was recognized by statute, and the offices of administrative officials, which were not similarly recognized. In this regard, Coke stated that "the record of force made by a justice of peace is not traversable, because he doth it as Judge, by the statutes of 14 Ric. 2. and 8 Hen. 6. and so there is a difference when one makes a record as a Judge and when he doth a thing by special authority (as they did in this case at bar) and not as a Judge." 8 Co.Rep. at 121, 77 Eng.Rep. at 658.

4. The tradition of review of agency action by ordinary, generalist courts is punctuated by this interesting event in English history. As recounted by Professors Henderson and Jaffe, in 1616, the Attorney General (Roger Bacon) with the Privy Council issued an order barring the common law courts from interfering with the work of the Sewer Commission. (The Sewer Commission, one of the first of the administrative agencies, is discussed at sec. 12.2.2, infra.) Speaking to the need for speed and efficiency and of avoiding a frustration of the work of the Sewer Commission, the order stated that "it can neither stand with law, nor with Common Sense or Reason . . . to restrain the Commissions from making new Works to withstand the Fury of the Waters." Rather than in common law courts, complaints should be brought to "the Court of Sewers or this Table if they receive not justice at the Commissioners' hands. . . ." Henderson & Jaffe, supra note 14, at 353–54.

So, from 1616 until 1643, when the prerogative courts were abolished, common law courts were "effectively excluded control of the Sewer Commissions." In this period, a system of control of administrative action resembling continental administrative courts was perhaps in the making. Not only did the council order require the common law courts to relinquish jurisdiction, but it "la[id] down that if there is a question of the legality of the Sewer Commission's action, it is to be decided by 'this Table'. Thus, as in the Continental droit administratif, the legality of administrative action is to be tested exclusively within the administrative hierarchy itself." But as the prerogative courts were abolished in the time of Cromwell, the common law courts again reasserted their power. Thus, the possibility, that "the Council and its brood of prerogative courts together would fulfill the functions of the French Conseil d'Etat and Tribunal des Conflits" passed. Henderson & Jaffe, supra note 14, at 353–55.

the French *Conseil d'Etat* and subordinate *Tribunaux Administratifs.* In the United States, proposals have from time to time been made to depart from the tradition of generalist courts, and to instead establish special administrative courts according to the European model. The system, has however, resisted the change, a resistance that Professors Currie and Goodman have described as grounded in a preference for generalist judges:

> The more time one devotes to a particular subject, the less time one has to learn about others. Analogy has been one of the geniuses of the common law; it surely has its place in administrative review. To put blinders on judges and confine them to narrow compartments not only creates the risk of disuniformities but also enhances the danger that issues may be resolved on the basis of ignorance as to past experience in related fields.[5]

§ 12.2.2 Prerogative Writs

As judicial review of agency action continued after *Dr. Bonham's Case,* it expanded to include review by the prerogative writs, certiorari and mandamus, as well as by common-law actions. By these writs, judicial review moved from official action in violation of the common law to a greater scope, official action outside of delegated authority.[6]

Review by these writs came out of a first great sphere of administrative power, the jurisdiction of England's Sewer Commissions. The Commissions consisted of members appointed by the Crown for terms of three years. From about the thirteenth century, their work was maintaining the bridges and dikes of England's marshes and fens. Later, they undertook extensive drainage projects to gain arable land.[7] These projects, involving condemnation of private property and assessments against property owners to pay the costs of public works, caused conflicts presently familiar. Special interests, the developers, were influential in the work of the Commissions. Now and then, the soulful voice of the environmentalist could be heard in opposition.[8]

In short, the Sewer Commissions exercised considerable discretionary power over important matters. Trying to contain this power, English courts in the seventeenth century came to rely upon certiorari. Previously, this writ had not been a mode of substantive review, but merely a

5. Currie & Goodman, Judicial Review of Administrative action: Quest for the Optimum Forum, 75 Colum.L.Rev. 1, 62–88 (1975) (presenting the pros and cons of generalist versus specialist courts).

6. One view is that "It may reasonably be said that these two new remedies, certiorari 'to quash' and mandamus, made possible the whole complex structure of modern administrative law". E. Henderson, supra note 14, at 1.

7. See generally W. Holdsworth, 10 A History of English Law 199–206 (1938).

8. In perhaps the first environmental poem, the lamprey was said to protest the draining of the great fens around Cambridge and Ely as follows:

> Behold the great design, which they do now determine,
>
> Will make our bodies pine, a prey to crows and vermin:
>
> For they do mean all Fens to drain, and waters overmaster,
>
> All will be dry, and we must die, lest Essex calves want pasture.

means of removing a record from one court to another. In 1643, however, the King's Bench in *Commins v. Massam* cautiously asserted a power of review over the Sewer Commission by means of certiorari.[9] The court reasoned that as the Commission was subject to review by means of common-law actions, it should be subject to review by means of certiorari. According to Justice Heath "Without question in trespass or replevin, their [the Commission's] proceedings are examinable here, and I see no reason but upon the same ground in a certiorare [they could not similarly be examined]."[10]

After *Commins v. Massam,* there was a "small but steady stream" of certiorari issued by the King's Bench to review Sewer Commission actions, and a variety of other official acts.[11] A fundamental reason for this steady use of the writ seems to have been a felt need for an independent judiciary to contain official action within limits established by law. In holding that municipal orders taxing the lands of foreign merchants were reviewable by means of certiorari, Chief Justice Hale explained that there ought to be "some jurisdiction to which the party might appeal if he were injured, otherwise the corporation will be party and judges and all, and they will tax the lands of the foreign to what value they please. . . ."[12]

Mandamus, the other writ to which we have referred, is generally used to compel an official to perform a duty required by law. As a mode of review of administrative action, the writ seems to have arrived fully formed, in 1615 in *James Bagg's Case*.[13] Baggs, who had been removed

9. 82 Eng.Rep. 473 (K.B.1643) (certiorari used to question Sewer Commission's authority to assess payments for improvements to land).

10. 82 Eng.Rep. 473 (K.B.1643). Previous to *Commins v. Massam,* an order of the Sewer Commission had been reviewed by means of a common law action. In *Rooke's Case,* 77 Eng.Rep. 209, 5 Co.Rep. 99a (C.P. 1599), the plaintiff's property had been taken to satisfy a Sewer assessment to pay for improvements to the banks of the Thames. The plaintiff, claiming that the assessment was improper because the Commission erred in limiting assessments to property on the Thames, rather than more generally assessing all benefited property, brought an action in replevin against the Commission. The Commission, however, argued that the action involved an unreviewable discretionary act. The Commission argued that in keeping with its statutory authority it was bound to act according "to their discretions," and that this discretion was not reviewable by the courts. Lord Coke disagreed, saying "yet these proceedings ought to be limited and bound within the rule of reason and law. For discretion is a science or understanding to discern between shadows and substance, between equity and colourable glosses and pretenses, and not to do according to their wills and private affections. . . ." 77 Eng.Rep. at 210, 5 Co.Rep. at 100.

11. Henderson & Jaffe, supra note 14, at 356.

12. The King v. The Corporation of Winchelsea, 2 Lev. 86; 3 Keb. 154 (1673), Freeman 99. This particular case might be seen as arguing for a judicial check in a special circumstance, where property was taxed without the representation of property owners (foreign owners) in the decision. However, the idea of the need of some independent jurisdiction (i.e., the courts) to check against abuse of power runs throughout the cases that we have mentioned in this section. See also The Case of Cardiff Bridge, 91 Eng.Rep. 135 (1700) (in issuing a writ of certiorari in connection with a levy to repair Cardiffe bridge, Chief Justice Hale declared that "wherever any new jurisdiction [public authority] is rested, be it by private or public Act of Parliament, they are subject to the inspections of this Court, by writ of error, or by certiorari or by mandamus.")

13. 77 Eng.Rep. 1271, 11 Co.Rep. 94 (K.B. 1615). On the origins of mandamus, as recounted by Professors Henderson and Jaffe:

from his position as a chief burgess of Plymouth by his fellow officers, applied to the King's Bench for reinstatement in his office, his "freehold" as he said. The court ordered the burgesses to show cause for Bagg's removal, and in reply they told of Bagg's persistent and obscene efforts to impugn the authority of a succession of Lord Mayors. The court, however, judged this return insufficient and by mandamus ordered Bagg reinstated. Lord Coke's sweeping assertion of judicial authority was that:

> [T]o this Court of King's Bench belongs authority, not only to correct errors in judicial proceedings, but other errors and misdemeanors extra-judicial . . .; so that no wrong or injury, neither private nor public, can be done, but that it shall be here reformed or punished by due course of law.[14]

A century and a half later, Lord Mansfield described mandamus just as generously, stating that "it ought to be used upon all occasions where the law has established no specific remedy, and where in justice and good government there ought to be one."[15]

Mandamus was, however, more constrained than Coke or Mansfield said. A principal limitation was that it applied only to the ministerial, and not to the discretionary, acts of government officials. The United States Supreme Court, in its 1840 decision in *Decatur v. Paulding,* adopted this ministerial/discretionary duty distinction, and applied it in a stingy fashion.[16]

Congress had authorized pensions for the widows of navy officers. By a writ of mandamus, the widow of Stephen Decatur claimed that the Secretary of Navy, because of his improper interpretation of the pertinent statute, had not paid her rightful amount. The Court, however, held that the writ could not be used to review the act in question, as it involved the judgment and discretion of a department head. Chief Justice Taney, writing for the Court, and perhaps calling on his own experience as the Secretary of Treasury, explained that:

> The interference of the courts with the performance of the ordinary duties of the executive departments of the government, would be productive of nothing but mischief; and we are quite satisfied that such a power was never intended to be given to them. Upon the very subject before us, the interposition of the courts might throw the pension fund and the whole subject of pensions, into the greatest confusion and disorder.

Mandamus is something of a mystery. For about ten years before James Bagg's Case, the Court of King's Bench had been granting judgments by which plaintiffs who had been unjustly removed from municipal office were restored to it, but the origin of this rather surprising activity is not at all clear. From this meager beginning Coke conceived the notion of a sweeping jurisdiction over all errors judicial and extra-judicial, as stated in Bagg's Case. Henderson & Jaffe, supra note 2, at 359.

14. 77 Eng.Rep. at 1277–78, 11 Co. Rep. at 98.

15. 97 Eng.Rep. 823, 824–25, R. v. Barker, 3 Burr. 1265, 1267 (K.B. 1762).

16. 39 U.S. (14 Pet.) 497, 10 L.Ed. 559 (1840).

However, Taney was not of the view that the courts should *never* review acts such as those of the Secretary. He simply thought that review by mandamus was extraordinary, and thus unwarranted in light of a general policy against judicial disruption of administrative work. But if Congress had by statute authorized the courts to decide this kind of case, then certainly the courts would do so. They would, Taney said, then interpret the pertinent statutes and correct executive action inconsistent with them.[17]

§ 12.3 FORMS OF REVIEW

Excepting tort action against agency officials, the forms used in these origins of judicial review of agency action have withered. Especially in federal courts, little remains of the writs of certiorari and mandamus.[1] One reason is that today, just as Justice Taney called for in 1840 in *Decatur v. Paulding*,[2] the legislature often prescribes a special form of judicial review for a particular agency, and where such special statutory review is available, it is usually a convenient, if not a required, form of review.[3] Another reason is that when special statutory review is unavailable or inadequate, declaratory and injunctive relief under a general jurisdiction statute (most often federal question jurisdiction) suffices as back-up form of review. Same as special statutory review, this alternative, of declaratory and injunctive relief, is generally superior to the prerogative writs.

In federal practice, certiorari as a form of review of agency action was written off—in favor of the injunction—by the Supreme Court in Degge v. Hitchcock.[4] The Postmaster General had barred complainants from use of the mails after finding that they had engaged in fraudulent representations. By a writ of certiorari, the complainants sought judicial review that action, alleging that the Postmaster General acted in excess of his authority and that the evidence did not show fraud. The Supreme Court held that as it was brought, the case could not be heard. Certiorari was an extraordinary remedy appropriate only where "there was no other method of preventing injustice." The Court, though, further found an action in equity would provide injunctive relief from "an arbitrary exercise of statutory power, or a ruling in excess of the jurisdiction

17. Respecting "special statutory review," which Taney was essentially calling for, see sec. 12.4.1, infra.

§ 12.3

1. While the use of these writs have diminished, the power to use them is still there. Federal court authority is generally provided by the All Writs Statute of the Judiciary Act of 1789, which is codified at 28 U.S.C. § 1651(a). Mandamus is especially provided by 28 U.S.C. § 1361. This latter statute was enacted to provide to all federal courts the jurisdiction that had previously existed only in federal courts in the District of Columbia. Those courts have subject matter jurisdiction in mandamus inasmuch as they have such jurisdiction under the common law as the District of Columbia carried with it when it was taken from the territory of Maryland. Kendall v. United States, 37 U.S. (12 Pet.) 524, 9 L.Ed. 1181 (1838).

2. 39 U.S. (14 Pet.) 497, 10 L.Ed. 559 (1840).

3. See discussion at sec. 12.4.1, infra.

4. 229 U.S. 162, 33 S.Ct. 639, 57 L.Ed. 1135 (1913).

conferred." This being the case, there was no need of certiorari as a form of review of administrative action.[5]

While mandamus has not been so formally interred as has certiorari, it has been a troublesome form of review, and its use has diminished. Review under mandamus requires a determination whether an agency action is ministerial or discretionary, with review available only where the action is ministerial. But administrative action usually involves some discretion, and courts are commonly called on to review either the appropriate scope of that discretion or whether it was abused. In this broad context of discretion, the ministerial/discretionary duty distinction has been "unsound and unworkable, more apt to label the result than explain it."[6]

In any event, federal question jurisdiction, under 28 U.S.C. § 1331, largely eliminates the need to resort to prerogative writs at all. Section 1331 provides a general jurisdictional basis for declaratory and injunctive relief, and these forms come without the baggage, such as the ministerial/discretionary distinction of mandamus, of the prerogative writs. Indeed, a mandatory injunction, that is, one that imposes some sort of affirmative duty (as opposed to prohibiting an action), is the functional equivalent of mandamus.

To this point, we have discussed forms of review when an individual initiates a legal action against an agency. At times, however, a person opposing an agency position need not initiate a legal action. Instead, he may act contrary to the agency's position, and await an agency action against him. The National Labor Relations Act, for instance, provides that National Labor Relations Board orders have to be enforced by means of a Board application to a federal court of appeals. In this enforcement action, a person subject to the order may present whatever claims they have about agency improprieties. A person seems assured of this opportunity by an inherent quality of an independent judiciary: if the courts are called on by the other branches to act against an individual, the courts must by their lights insure that justice is done that individual.[7] Moreover, this mode of review is assured by the Administrative Procedure Act as it provides that "agency action is subject to judicial review in civil or criminal proceedings for judicial enforcement."[8]

Using an agency enforcement action as a form of review avoids the litigation expenses of other forms of review, which require a person to

5. In state courts, certiorari has been said to be available on a limited basis, for agency action that is judicial in nature, in excess of jurisdiction and not a mere "error in judgment," and where "no other plain, speedy, and adequate remedy" presents itself. Timonds v. Hunter, 169 Iowa 598, 151 N.W. 961 (1915) (Deemer C.J., dissenting); Davidson v. Whitehill, 87 Vt. 499, 89 A. 1081 (1914).

6. Jaffe, Judicial Control of Administrative Action 181 (1965).

7. Cf. United States v. Mendoza–Lopez, 481 U.S. 828, 837, 107 S.Ct. 2148, 2154, 95 L.Ed.2d 772 (1987) ("where a determination made in an administrative proceeding is to play a critical role in the subsequent imposition of a criminal sanction, there must be some meaningful review of the administrative proceeding"); McKart v. United States, 395 U.S. 185, 89 S.Ct. 1657, 23 L.Ed.2d 194 (1969).

8. 5 U.S.C. § 703.

initiate a court action. Also, in privately initiated action hurdles of standing, ripeness, or exhaustion of remedies will have to be cleared. For the private litigant, however, these hurdles are generally absent in an agency-initiated enforcement action.

§ 12.4 JURISDICTION AND VENUE

Availability of review depends upon a court with jurisdiction and venue. In the past, jurisdiction and venue respecting agency actions have been restricted by certain spurious conditions to jurisdictional statutes and by venue statutes that centralized litigation in the District of Columbia. Today, however, Congress has removed these impediments and limitations, so that a lack of jurisdiction or venue is no longer much of a problem. Instead, the problem is more likely to be that of picking the best forum from among the courts where jurisdiction and venue may be had.

§ 12.4.1 Special Statutory Review and General Jurisdictional Statutes

Federal courts are courts of limited jurisdiction, and so, jurisdiction may not be presumed. Instead, in each case the plaintiff must show that Congress has by statute authorized the court to hear that case.[1] In administrative law, statutes conferring jurisdiction are of two kinds. One kind is a general jurisdictional statute, the most important of which is federal-question jurisdiction under 28 U.S.C. § 1331. The other kind is commonly referred to as "special statutory review." Special statutory review is simply the jurisdiction conferred when Congress, as it often does, specially provides a particular form of review for a particular agency. In prototype form, the Federal Trade Commission Act provides that Commission orders are reviewable in the "court of appeals of the United States, ... by filing in the court, within sixty days from the date of service of such order, a written petition praying that the order of the Commission be set aside."[2] As this provision provides a form of review, it also provides for subject-matter jurisdiction in the court of appeals.

Special statutory review is the favored form of review when it is available. In this respect, the Administrative Procedure Act provides that, "The form of proceeding for judicial review is the special statutory review proceeding relevant to the subject matter" and that only in the "absence or inadequacy" of statutory review may an action be brought

§ 12.4

1. E.g., Telecommunications Research and Action Center v. FCC, 750 F.2d 70, 74 (D.C.Cir.1984) (" 'Jurisdiction is, of necessity, the first issue of an Article III court. The federal courts are courts of limited jurisdiction, and they lack the power to presume the existence of jurisdiction in order to dispose of a case on any other grounds.' ").

2. 15 U.S.C.A. § 45(c). In full, § 45(c) provides that "Any person, partnership, or corporation required by an order of the Commission to cease and desist from using any method of competition or act or practice may obtain a review of such order in the court of appeals of the United States, ... by filing in the court, within sixty days from the date of service of such order, a written petition praying that the order of the Commission be set aside."

under a general jurisdiction statute.[3] Special statutory review, and the concomitant jurisdiction, is generally favored because it represents Congress's particular estimate of an optimal allocation of business between a specific agency and the courts. This form of review often provides a space in which agencies for a time may act unimpeded by the courts. For instance, special statutory review of Social Security Claims is conditioned on a claimant first obtaining a final decision by the agency with respect to the claim in question.[4]

Also, special statutory review is usually in a court of appeals, out of Congress's judgment that review of agency action is best done by appellate courts rather than by trial courts. Agency action is often on the basis of a record compiled by the agency, and searching a record for errors, or the appropriate evidentiary support, is the usual function of an appellate court.[5] Moreover, courts of appeals are collegial bodies suited to maintaining a coherent body of law over a large geographic area, and thus they are generally more adept at resolving the broad issues of national regulatory policy involved in many agency actions.[6]

Congress has established statutory review provisions for a number of agencies; thus, special statutory jurisdiction is widely available. But not completely: Situations remain where a person would like to gain judicial review of an agency action but jurisdiction by means of special statutory review is either "absent or inadequate." In these circumstances of the absence or inadequacy of a special jurisdictional statute, the Administrative Procedure Act and the courts have recognized that a

3. 5 U.S.C.A. § 702. In the courts, the preference for special statutory review goes back to *Decatur v. Paulding,* where Justice Taney wrote that while the Court would not review a Department of Treasury decision in a general jurisdiction situation, it would be inclined to review the decision if Congress had specially authorized such review. 39 U.S. (14 Pet.) 497, 10 L.Ed. 559 (1840). See discussion at sec. 12.2.2 note 20, infra.

4. 42 U.S.C. § 405(g). To protect against stale claims, this section also provides that review must be applied for within sixty days after a claimant has by mail received notice of the decision. See generally Weinberger v. Salfi, 422 U.S. 749, 95 S.Ct. 2457, 45 L.Ed.2d 522 (1975). For a thorough explication of the factors relevant to such an optimum allocation of judicial resources, see Currie and Goodman, Judicial Review of Federal Administrative Action: Quest for the Optimum Forum, 75 Colum.L.Rev. 1 (1975).

5. However, in United Gas Pipe Line Co. v. Federal Power Commission, 181 F.2d 796 (D.C.Cir.1950), cert. denied 340 U.S. 827, 71 S.Ct. 63, 95 L.Ed. 607 (1950), the court on direct appeal went so far as to engage in factual review of an agency regulation where a record had not been developed by a "quasi-judicial" hearing at the agency. The authority of that case, though, has been considerably weakened, even in the District of Columbia. As explained in Deutsche Lufthansa Aktiengesellschaft v. CAB, 479 F.2d 912, 916 (D.C.Cir.1973), "it is the availability of a record for review and not the holding of a quasi judicial hearing which is now the jurisdictional touchstone."

6. Congress will, however, occasionally provide for statutory review in federal district court. For instance, Social Security Administration dispositions of applications for old age, survivors', or disability benefits under Social Security are channeled to federal district court. 42 U.S.C.A. § 405(g), 421(d). Advantages offered by district court review include the convenience to private litigants of the greater dispersion of those courts, the district court's superiority when evidence must be taken, and the economy in a single judge deciding a case rather than three judges of a panel of the court of appeals. Of course, appeals may be taken to the court of appeals, and thus the economy gained by review by a single district judge may be lost. However, only a portion of litigants are likely to appeal. See generally, Currie and Goodman, supra.

court may review an agency action under a general jurisdiction statute,[7] most likely federal-question jurisdiction under 28 U.S.C. § 1331.

Since the amount in controversy was removed from it, § 1331 has been a comprehensive basis of jurisdiction. It broadly provides subject-matter jurisdiction for cases arising under the Constitution and laws of the United States.[8] Because federal agency actions involve questions about the construction and application of federal law (be it an agency rule, a federal statutes, or the Constitution), they are generally subject to federal-question jurisdiction. Apart from § 1331, other general jurisdictional statutes, such as mandamus, remain on the books.[9] But given the

7. The Administrative Procedure Act provides that in the "absence or inadequacy" of special statutory review, then a party may seek review by "any form of legal action, including actions for declaratory judgments or writs of prohibitory or mandatory injunction or habeas corpus, in a court of competent jurisdiction." 5 U.S.C. § 703. As to the courts receptivity to general jurisdictional statutes, see Califano v. Sanders, 430 U.S. 99, 97 S.Ct. 980, 51 L.Ed.2d 192 (1977)

8. 28 U.S.C.A. § 1331. See Califano v. Sanders, 430 U.S. 99, 97 S.Ct. 980, 51 L.Ed.2d 192 (1977) (the "obvious effect" of amending Sec. 1331 to remove the amount in controversy requirement "is to confer jurisdiction on federal courts to review agency action"). See also Abbott Laboratories v. Gardner, 387 U.S. 136, 139–48, 87 S.Ct. 1507, 18 L.Ed.2d 681 (1967); Association of National Advertisers, Inc. v. FTC, 627 F.2d 1151 (D.C.Cir.1979), cert. denied 447 U.S. 921, 100 S.Ct. 3011, 65 L.Ed.2d 1113 (1980).

9. Federal district courts have original jurisdiction in actions "in the nature of mandamus." 28 U.S.C. § 1361. Another general jurisdiction statute is 28 U.S.C.A. § 1137, which provides that "The district courts shall have original jurisdiction of any civil action or proceeding arising under any Act of Congress regulating commerce or protecting trade and commerce against restraints and monopolies." When Federal question jurisdiction was encumbered by an amount in controversy requirement, these statutes, unencumbered by that requirement, were useful. But with § 1331 now amended to remove the amount in controversy requirement, the use of these statutes has diminished.

An action for declaratory and injunctive relief under Sec. 1331 should be as effective as mandamus, and it is simpler as it is not encrusted with the barnacles—most notably the ministerial act condition—that mandamus has gathered. In an exceptional circumstance, however, mandamus may still be useful in gaining jurisdiction where federal question jurisdiction is unavailable. Such a circumstance is found in the District of Columbia federal court of appeals opinion in Ganem v. Heckler, 746 F.2d 844 (D.C.Cir.1984). The Social Security Act provides for statutory review of benefit determinations, and then, on the face it, makes this form of review exclusive by precluding review under federal question jurisdiction. The Act provides that:

> No findings of fact or decision of the Secretary shall be reviewed by any person except as herein provided. No action against the United States, the Secretary, or any officer or employee thereof shall be brought under sections 1331 or 1346 of Title 28 to recover on any claim arising under this subchapter.

42 U.S.C. § 405(h).

Whether this preclusion of jurisdiction applied as well to mandamus under Sec. 1361 was at issue in *Ganem v. Heckler*. An alien then residing in Iran claimed Social Security benefits that had accrued during her residency in the United States. Such benefits, however, were available to foreign residents only upon a finding by the Secretary of Health and Human Services that the country in which the claimant resided had a social security system that treated claims of American citizens similarly. With respect to Iran, the Secretary had not made that determination, on the grounds that it was unable to do under the regime of the Aytollah Khomeini. The Secretary's position, apparently, was that verification could be made only by means of direct contact with responsible government officials in Iran and that such contact was impossible. Nonetheless, the nonresident alien, by means of an action in mandamus with jurisdiction under Sec. 1361, asked the District of Columbia Circuit to compel the Secretary to make the determination.

The threshold question was whether the Social Security Act's preclusion of review

broad applicability of federal-question jurisdiction, there is usually no need to resort to these other statutes.

* * *

To summarize, jurisdiction to review agency actions may be gained by a general jurisdiction statute or by special statutory review, with special statutory being favored except where it is absent or inadequate.[10] Special statutory review is absent where Congress has not provided a particular form of review for a particular agency. It is inadequate when Congress has provided for a particular form of review, but that review cannot redress the agency action in question. In this respect, inadequacy of review has been described as involving a "manifest infringement of substantial rights irremediable by the statutorily-prescribed method of review."[11] In Leedom v. Kyne,[12] the National Labor Relations Board had certified a bargaining unit, but such unit had not been approved by an election among employees as specified by the National Labor Relations Act. Congress had provided for review of Board actions, but it had done so only for "Board orders." The Board certification in question did not constitute an order, and so the complaint against the Board was filed in federal district court under a general jurisdictional statute. The Board then argued that the special review provisions of the National Labor Relations Act "foreclosed review of its action by an original suit in a District Court." The Supreme Court, however, did not agree, stating that:

> This case ... involves "unlawful action of the Board [which] has inflicted an injury on the [respondent]." Does the law "apart from the review provisions of the ... Act" afford a remedy? We think the answer surely must be yes.

under federal question jurisdiction applied as well to mandamus. The sense of the Act, as it provided for statutory review, and then otherwise precluded review under federal question jurisdiction, might have well been taken as specially providing a form of review and then precluding review overall under other general jurisdictional statutes. The court of appeals, however, read the Act literally and found that as it denoted only federal question jurisdiction, the Act did not preclude jurisdiction under mandamus. In doing so, the court noted that mandamus, unlike federal question jurisdiction, is available only where the plaintiff establishes a "clear right" to the relief sought. As discussed in sec. 12.5, infra, on "preclusions of review," courts are especially reluctant to forego judicial review when clearly an agency has acted unlawfully. Because mandamus focuses on "a complete abnegation" by the agency of its statutory responsibilities, then perhaps the court in *Ganem v. Heckler* was correct as it insisted on a literal preclusion of review according to mandamus.

In one respect, the court's holding in *Ganem v. Heckler* is not clear. While the court throughout its opinion refers to jurisdiction in mandamus as provided by statute, that is, 28 U.S.C.A. § 1361, the court also described its holding as pertaining to the common-law jurisdiction in mandamus enjoyed by the District of Columbia Circuit but not federal courts generally. In this regard, the court stated, "we conclude that, whatever Congress' intent with respect to other federal courts, there is nothing to indicate that Congress intended to abolish the historic common law power of federal courts in the District to issue writs of mandamus to federal officials." 746 F.2d at 850. Regarding the common-law mandamus jurisdiction of the District of Columbia Circuit, see sec. 12.3 and note 1, supra.

10. 5 U.S.C. § 702.

11. Nader v. Volpe, 466 F.2d 261, 266 (D.C.Cir.1972).

12. 358 U.S. 184, 79 S.Ct. 180, 3 L.Ed.2d 210 (1958).

The reason the plaintiff could "surely" rely on general subject-matter jurisdiction was that the complaint involved a "patently" wrongful agency action, and an " 'absence of jurisdiction of the federal courts' would mean 'a sacrifice or obliteration of a right which Congress' has given professional employees, for there is no other means within their control . . . to protect and enforce that right."

Today, the courts may permit review, outside of special statutory review and under a general jurisdiction statute, where something less than a "patently" unlawful agency action is at stake.[13] This seems a direction of *Abbott Laboratories v. Gardner*, where the Supreme Court allowed direct review, under a general jurisdiction statute, of a Food and Drug Administration rule, even though Congress had provided only for judicial review of agency orders (as opposed to rules) and even though something less than a patent illegality was involved.[14]

§ 12.4.2 Jurisdiction: Agency Inaction

At times, an agency charged with implementing some program may not do so at a pace consistent with its statutory responsibility, and a person may ask the courts to prompt agency action. For instance, the courts may be asked to get a regulatory program underway by compelling rulemaking. These suits, to redress agency inaction or delay, are no small part of public law, particularly when deregulation is part of an agency's agenda. Suits to compel agency action raise a number of issues, such as whether an agency's regulatory agenda is so committed to an agency's discretion as to be unreviewable and whether such suits are ripe.[15] Our present concern, however, is that of an appropriate form of review and subject-matter jurisdiction for it.

Without agency action, special statutory review, keyed as it is to reviewing some form of completed agency action, at first glance seems an

13. For instance, in ITT World Communications, Inc. v. Federal Communications Commission, 699 F.2d 1219 (D.C.Cir. 1983), the court focused more on the differing capacities of trial and appellate courts and on the injury to the private party. ITT was of the opinion that the Federal Communications Commission had unlawfully held closed meetings with European administrators. The company, therefore, sued the Commission in federal district court under general federal question jurisdiction. The district court, however, refused to hear the case. In that court's opinion, the appropriate form of review was special statutory review of Commission orders in the court of appeals as provided by the Communications Act.

On review, the court of appeals held that the district court had erred in dismissing the case, and in doing so it focused on the injury in denying review under a general jurisdictional statute and that the suit involved factual inquiries better suited to a trial court than an appellate court. In relation to injury, the court found that ITT was faced with injury " 'beyond the capabilities of the statutorily-prescribed form of review to repair.' " The Commission's closed meetings were not calculated to result in a reviewable final order, "but rather to lead to unreviewable action by foreign administrations." 699 F.2d at 1232.

Since the *World Communications v. ITT* case, the Federal Trade Commission Act has been amended to establish an "exclusive jurisdiction for the review of rules in the federal court of appeals." 15 U.S.C.A. § 57a(e).

14. 387 U.S. 136, 87 S.Ct. 1507, 18 L.Ed.2d 681 (1967) (discussed at sec. 12.10.1, infra).

15. See discussion at Sec. 12.6 ("committed to agency discretion") and Sec. 12.9 ("ripeness"), infra.

unlikely basis of jurisdiction. Instead, an action in federal district court for declaratory and injunctive relief, pursuant to that court's federal-question jurisdiction, would seem to be in order. In a given case, perhaps it is. Still, among the lower courts there has been considerable uncertainty as to the proper court (district court by means of federal question jurisdiction or the court of appeals by means of special statutory review) and proper basis of jurisdiction in cases of agency inaction or delay. In the District of Columbia, however, this uncertainty seems to have been settled in favor of the jurisdiction in the court of appeals when special statutory review lies in that court.

The Federal Communications Act provides that "The court of appeals has exclusive jurisdiction to enjoin, set aside, suspend ... or to determine the validity of ... final orders [of the Federal Communications Commission]."[16] In *Telecommunications Research and Action Center v. FCC,* however, the Commission had issued no order.[17] Rather, the complaint was that the Federal Communications Commission had unreasonably delayed determining whether American Telephone and Telegraph should reimburse rate payers for alleged overcharges. The question was "whether a petition to compel unreasonably delayed agency action properly lies in this court or in the district court, or whether the two courts have concurrent jurisdiction."

The court of appeals held that according to the special statutory form of review, it had an exclusive jurisdiction. It held that "where a statute commits final agency action to review by the court of appeals, the appellate court has exclusive jurisdiction to the suits seeking relief that might affect its future statutory power of review."[18] To perfect this jurisdiction, the court relied on the jurisdiction vested by the All Writs Statute, to issue "all writs necessary or appropriate in aid of jurisdiction."[19] And in relation to good management of judicial resources, the court explained that:

> Appellate courts develop an expertise concerning the agencies assigned them for review. Exclusive jurisdiction promotes judicial economy and fairness to the litigants by taking advantage of that expertise. In addition, exclusive jurisdiction eliminates duplicative and potentially conflicting review, ... and the delay and expense incidental thereto.[20]

16. 28 U.S.C. § 2342(1).

17. As the court noted, there was "no final order—indeed, the lack of a final order is the very gravamen of the petitioners' complaint." 750 F.2d 70, 75 (D.C.Cir.1984).

18. 750 F.2d at 74. The court added that "Because the statutory obligations of a court of appeals to review on the merits may be defeated by an agency that fails to resolve disputes, a circuit may resolve claims of unreasonable delay in order to protect its future jurisdiction." 750 F.2d at 75. See also Oil, Chemical and Atomic Workers International Union v. Zegeer, 768 F.2d 1480 (D.C.Cir.1985).

19. 28 U.S.C. § 1651(a). The All Writs Statute, of course, is not itself a basis of jurisdiction.

20. 750 F.2d at 78. To its holding of appellate court review of claims of agency inaction, the court noted an exception where the claim against the agency was not subject to the jurisdiction of the appellate court. "In such cases", the court explained, "district court review might be predicated on general federal question jurisdiction statute, 28 U.S.C. Sec. 1331."

§ 12.4.3 Jurisdiction: State Agencies

Claims that state administrative agencies have violated federal law may generally be brought in federal district court under federal-question jurisdiction. The cases that may be brought under § 1331 include claims established by § 1983 of the Civil Rights Acts, which establishes a cause of action against state officials who deprive a person of rights secured by federal law (statutory as well as constitutional law). A § 1983 action has the considerable advantage of a broad range of remedies: the statute provides for damages as well as injunctive relief, and also for attorney fees.[21]

For claims under § 1983, jurisdiction is also provided by 28 U.S.C. § 1343(3), the jurisdictional component of the Civil Rights Acts.[22] The jurisdiction that § 1343(3) provides is not, however, as complete as that of federal question jurisdiction under § 1331. Federal question jurisdiction includes claims based on violations of federal statutory law, but Sec. 1343(3) of the Civil Rights Acts, which by its terms is limited to constitutional claims, does not. For instance, a person may bring an action under § 1983 (which establishes a cause of action for statutory as well as constitutional claims) against a state agency for violations of the federal Social Security Act. But jurisdiction to hear that action cannot be established under § 1343(3).[23] However, this § 1983 action may instead be brought in federal district court under federal question jurisdiction.[24]

§ 12.4.4 Venue

Apart from subject-matter jurisdiction, a plaintiff's choice of forum is conditioned by rules of venue. These rules pertain to location, to where a suit may be brought. At one time, they centralized litigation against federal agencies in the District of Columbia. But today, to accommodate the convenience of private litigants and to enhance the responsiveness of a central bureaucratic apparatus to local concerns and conditions, venue rules have been extended so as to allow suits to be

21. 42 U.S.C. § 1983. Attorney fees are available, for statutory as well as constitutional violations, by means of the Civil Rights Attorney's Fees Awards Act of 1976, codified at 42 U.S.C.A. § 1888. See Maine v. Thiboutot, 448 U.S. 1, 100 S.Ct. 2502, 65 L.Ed.2d 555 (1980); Maher v. Gagne, 448 U.S. 122, 100 S.Ct. 2570, 65 L.Ed.2d 653 (1980). Also, actions brought against state agencies under Sec. 1983 are excepted from the general requirement of exhaustion of administrative remedies. Patsy v. Board of Regents of State of Florida, 457 U.S. 496, 102 S.Ct. 2557, 73 L.Ed.2d 172 (1982), on remand 693 F.2d 558 (5th Cir.1982). An older view of the statute, that its application was limited to personal rights, e.g., speech, and that property rights were excluded from its coverage, has been rejected, and the statute held applicable to both personal and property rights, Lynch v. Household Finance Corp., 405 U.S. 538, 92 S.Ct. 1113, 31 L.Ed.2d 424 (1972).

22. Section 1343(3) provides that:

> The district courts shall have original jurisdiction of any civil action authorized by law to be commenced by any person . . . (3) To redress the deprivation, under color of state law, statute, ordinance, regulation, custom or usage, of any right, privilege or immunity secured by the Constitution of the United States or by any Act of Congress providing for equal rights of citizens. . . .

23. Maine v. Thiboutot, 448 U.S. 1, 100 S.Ct. 2502, 65 L.Ed.2d 555 (1980).

24. Chapman v. Houston Welfare Rights Organization, 441 U.S. 600, 99 S.Ct. 1905, 60 L.Ed.2d 508 (1979).

brought nation-wide.[25] The general venue statute, 28 U.S.C. and § 1391(e), allows the person suing an agency or agency official to sue where he resides, where the cause of action arose, or where the defendant resides.[26]

Sec. 1391 is, as we said, a general venue statute, to which particular statutes may create exceptions for particular agencies.[27] Where these special venue statutes apply, they, and not 28 U.S.C. § 1391, control the location of a suit.[28] These statutes, however, are similar to § 1391 in that they are generally concerned with the convenience of parties aggrieved by agency action. In this regard, special venue statutes often provide that the person suing the agency may sue where the cause of action arose or where that person resides or does business.[29] Otherwise, these special rules are at times concerned with directing litigation to where the impact of agency regulation is felt. For example, certain Department of Energy actions are reviewable "only" in "the circuit which contains the area or greater part of the area within which the rule, regulation, or order is to have effect."[30]

* * *

25. See District Courts—Jurisdiction—Venue, U.S. Code Congressional & Admin.News, S.Rep. Nos. 1992, 2784 (1962). Localizing litigation may not, however, always be viewed as a particularly strong interest in actions against federal agencies. Those agencies are typically concerned with implementing national standards, and the reviewing courts role is to say how that standard should be applied, and not to concentrate on local interests. Sunstein, Participation, Public Law, and Venue Reform, 49 U.Chi.L.Rev. 976, 983 (1982).

26. Sec. 1391(e) provides that:

> A civil action in which a defendant is an officer or employee of the United States or any agency thereof acting in his official capacity or under color of legal authority, or an agency of the United States, or the United States, may, except as otherwise provided by law, be brought in any judicial district in which (1) a defendant in the action resides, or (2) a substantial part of the events or omissions giving rise to the claim occurred, or a substantial part of property that is the subject of the action is situated, or (3) the plaintiff resides if no real property is involved in the action.
>
> 28 U.S.C. § 1391(e).

For a discussion of the various interests relevant to venue in agency litigation, see Sunstein, Participation, Public Law, and Venue Reform, 49 U.Chi.L.Rev. 976 (1982). See also Stafford v. Briggs, 444 U.S. 527, 533–45, 100 S.Ct. 774, 779–85, 63 L.Ed.2d 1 (1980).

27. These special venue provisions are usually created when Congress, as it provides for a certain form of judicial review for a given agency, at the same time specifies where that review may be located. For example, as the Federal Trade Commission Act provides that a party subject to a Commission order may gain review of that order in a federal court of appeals, it also provides that such review may be had "within any circuit where the method of competition or act or practice in question was used or where [the party] resides or carries on business." 15 U.S.C. § 45(c).

28. That special venue statutes are exclusive where they apply, see Save Our Cumberland Mountains, Inc. v. Clark, 725 F.2d 1422, 1429–31 (D.C.Cir.1984), vacated on other grounds 857 F.2d 1516 (D.C.Cir. 1988) (*en banc*).

29. For example, the Federal Trade Commission Act provides for venue "where the method of competition or act or practice in question was used or where [the party] resides or carries on business." 15 U.S.C.A. § 45(c). See also 7 U.S.C.A. § 608(c)(15) (Sec'y of Agriculture); 8 U.S.C. § 1105(a)(2) (INS deportation and exclusion orders); 42 U.S.C.A. § 405(g) (social security).

30. However, contrary to the modern practice of decentralizing review of agency action and accommodating the convenience of those suing the government, a few special venue rules limit judicial review for a few agency actions to the District of Columbia. Some of these are older pieces of legis-

Modern venue rules provide various locations where a plaintiff may bring an action. At the same time, an agency action often has a nationwide effect that generates various and numerous plaintiffs in numerous places. These various plaintiffs will choose among the various venues for their own convenience and tactical advantage. Therefore, an outcome of modern, and liberal venue provisions has been that of multiple filings in various courts with respect to the same agency action.

For federal courts of appeals, an initial response to this multiple-filing problem was a statutory "first-filing rule." Under this rule, the court of appeals where a petition for review was first filed took the case, and the other courts where the same action had also been filed transferred those cases to that first court.[31] This first-filing rule was meant to provide an easy, mechanical means of determining venue in cases of multiple filings. However, the rule was not altogether successful in that respect. It resulted in elaborate races to the courthouse (involving state of the art electronics and communications equipment). In the frequent photo finishes, resolving arguments over who won the race was not the highest use of a judge's time.[32] Also, the first-filing rule was disadvantageous to those who lacked the technological resources to run the race, to monitor agency action and to then race electronically to the forum of their choice.[33]

Consequently, in 1988 Congress provided a simpler process: "random selection" among the various courts of appeals in which parties seeking judicial review might file. If more than two parties file at different courts within ten days of issuance of an agency order, then the judicial panel on multidistrict litigation chooses among the courts by "means of random selection." The court so selected has the case, and the various appeals are consolidated in it.[34] Arbitrary choices of forums as

lation, such as the Federal Communications Commissions Act, 15 U.S.C.A. § 402(b) (restricting review of the Commission's licensing "decisions and orders" to the court of appeals for the District of Columbia). Some are not so old, e.g., 15 U.S.C.A. § 766(c) (establishing venue in Washington for Department of Energy rules and orders other than under the Emergency Petroleum Allocation Act).

31. 28 U.S.C. § 2112(3).

If proceedings have been instituted in two or more courts of appeals ... the agency ... or officer concerned shall file the record in that one of such courts in which a proceeding ... was first instituted. The other courts in which such proceedings are pending shall then transfer them to the court of appeals in which the record has been filed.

32. E.g., City of Gallup v. FERC, 702 F.2d 1116, 1125 (D.C.Cir.1983) ("This case demonstrates the difficulties of administering [the first filing system] when faced with the zealous representatives employing modern technology [in the race to the court house]. Yet until Congress changes the present scheme, courts must deal with it as best they can."); United Steelworkers v. Marshall, 592 F.2d 693, 695 (3d Cir.1979) ("Unlike race tracks ... courts are not equipped with photoelectric timers, and we decline the invitation to speculate which nose would show as first in a photo finish" and "courts of appeals lack means of holding hearings on disputed factual matters, and such a course would inevitably cause delays in the reviewing process.") See generally Court for Multiple Appeals, Pub. L.No. 100–236, 5 U.S.C. Cong. & Adm. News 3198 (1987).

33. For an illustration of the resources that attorneys have devoted to these races, see Associated Gas Distributors v. Federal Energy Regulatory Com'n, 738 F.2d 1388 (D.C.Cir.1984). See also 5 U.S.C. Cong. & Adm. News at 3199.

34. 28 U.S.C. § 2112 (3), as amended by Pub.L.No. 100–236, 101 Stat. 1731 (1988). To qualify for the lottery, parties

result from this new rule of random selection may be mitigated by the condition of *forum non conveniens*. Sec. 2112(5) of Title 28 provides that "for the convenience of the parties in the interests of justice" the court that gets the case by lottery may transfer it to "any other court of appeals."[35]

§ 12.5 LIMITATIONS TO JUDICIAL REVIEW: LEGISLATIVE PRECLUSION OF REVIEW

By its general jurisdiction and venue statutes, Congress has provided a broad avenue to the courts to persons aggrieved by agency action. At times, however, this route may be restricted, by limitations, or "preclusions of review" as they are commonly called, imposed by Congress with respect to a particular agency. An instance of preclusion of review is in *Weinberger v. Salfi*.[1] Mrs. Salfi claimed that a Social Security Administration rule, which limited the benefits of widows and stepchildren of deceased wage earners, was unconstitutional. For that claim, she filed a class action in federal district court under its general federal-question jurisdiction.

That court heard the case and decided it for her. On review, however, the Supreme Court overturned the lower-court decision, on the grounds that federal-question jurisdiction for Salfi's claim had been specially precluded. It had been by precluded by Sec. 405(h) of the Social Security Act as it provided that "No action against the United States, the Secretary, or any officer or employee thereof shall be brought under section 1331."[2]

appealing an agency action must file copies of their petition for review with the agency within ten days of the agency action.

35. See generally United Steelworkers v. Marshall, 592 F.2d 693, 695 (3d Cir. 1979); American Public Gas Ass'n v. FPC, 555 F.2d 852 (D.C.Cir.1976). Outside of statutory authority, the courts have claimed an inherent authority to transfer case "in the interest of justice and sound judicial administration." AT&T v. FCC, 519 F.2d 322, 325 (2d Cir.1975).

In administrative law, the doctrine of *forum non conveniens* applies not just to problems in multiple filings but more generally to all matters of forum selection. In this larger form, the doctrine may exist as an inherent power of the courts. However, it also has a statutory basis, both for district courts (28 U.S.C. § 1404(a)) and courts of appeals (the above-mentioned 28 U.S.C. § 2112(a)). These statutes authorize transfer to other courts according to broad standards of the convenience of the parties and the interests of justice, and the application of these standards is largely factual and discretionary. District court transfers under § 1404(a) are, however, limited to courts where the action "might have been brought." This "might have been brought" condition is taken as meaning that the transferee court must have subject-matter jurisdiction, personal jurisdiction, and venue in the action being transferred. For courts of appeals, however, this jurisdictional limit seems lacking, inasmuch as Sec. 2112(5) simply provides that transfer according to *forum non conveniens* may be to "any other court of appeals."

§ 12.5

1. Weinberger v. Salfi, 422 U.S. 749, 95 S.Ct. 2457, 45 L.Ed.2d 522 (1975).

2. See also Shalala v. Illinois Council on Long Term Care, 529 U.S. 1, 120 S.Ct. 1084, 146 L.Ed.2d 1 (2000). In Weinberger v. Salfi, the Court found that review by means of general federal question jurisdiction had been precluded. The Court explained, however, that review of the issue in question—whether the Social Security's Administration's "duration of relationship test" for survivors benefits for widows and stepchildren was unconstitutional—was not absolutely precluded. Instead, review was conditioned on the plaintiff claiming juris-

This matter of a legislative preclusion of judicial review has been a source of theoretical difficulties and seemingly clashing principles. The justification for preclusion is generally that of efficiency and fairness. In terms of efficiency, a preclusion of review provides the agency a space in which it has the "opportunity to correct its own errors, to afford the parties and the courts the benefit of its experience and expertise, and to compile a record which is adequate for judicial review."[3] The fairness, it is said, is that for some public programs preclusion of review may "provid[e] for the administration of the benefits ... with maximum efficiency and convenience for individuals entitled to benefits."[4] For smaller claims, the adversarial processes and costs of judicial review may make the program unfeasible. Consequently, some public programs might best function without the disruption by the courts and litigation expenses associated with judicial review.[5]

But from another and more structural sort of standpoint, preclusion of review does not look so good. Understandably, the courts respect the judicial power assigned them by Article III and the role they play in a government of separated powers. Under this power and in this role, the courts stand as a check "against the absolutely uncontrolled and arbitrary action of a public and administrative officer."[6] From this standpoint, courts are reluctant to forego review of agency actions.

diction under, and exhausting remedies as required by, the Social Security Act. The Act provides that "Any individual, after any final determination of the Secretary made after a hearing to which he was a party, may obtain review of such decision by a civil action commenced within sixty days after the mailing to him of notice of such decision...." 42 U.S.C.A. § 405(g). In *Salfi,* the Court found that the Social Security Administration had waived its claims that the named plaintiff, Mrs. Salfi, had not secured a final decision as required by § 405(g), and held that the district court therefore had jurisdiction to hear her claim under that section. Because the rest of her class could not be said to have secured a hearing and final decision by the Secretary as required by § 405(g), for them review was precluded.

3. 422 U.S. at 765, 95 S.Ct. at 2466.

4. 422 U.S. at 765, 95 S.Ct. at 2466. Justice (then Judge) Scalia also addressed this point when he said that preclusion may avoid the "judicialization, and even the lawyerization" of a social welfare program. Gott v. Walters, 756 F.2d 902 (D.C.Cir. 1985).

5. In relation to the Veterans' Administration, the Court has explained that preclusion of review (1) "prevent[ed] the courts from becoming involved in the day-to-day determinations and interpretation of Veterans' Administration policy" and (2) assured "that the technical and complex determinations and applications of Veterans' Administration policy connected with veterans' benefits will be adequately and uniformly made." Johnson v. Robison, 415 U.S. 361, 370, 372, 94 S.Ct. 1160, 1167, 1168, 39 L.Ed.2d 389 (1974). The avoidance of "judicialization of agency processes" has, by a number of courts, been seen as a prime justification for preclusion of review. See St. Louis University v. Blue Cross Hosp. Service, 537 F.2d 283, 289 (8th Cir.1976), cert. denied 429 U.S. 977, 97 S.Ct. 484, 50 L.Ed.2d 584 (1976) ("Judicial review of the amounts of all Medicare payments would bring the courts into the complex interplay between physician and hospital in determining the appropriate charges for technical services.... Determining the amount of these charges is a matter peculiarly suited to determination by a specialized agency.")

6. American School of Magnetic Healing v. McAnnulty, 187 U.S. 94, 23 S.Ct. 33, 47 L.Ed. 90 (1902). This stand is made by judicial review of agency action, and in this relation it is understood that "the presence of appellate review by an Art. III court will go a long way toward insuring a proper separation of powers." Northern Pipeline Construction Co. v. Marathon Pipe Line Co., 458 U.S. 50, 115, 102 S.Ct. 2858, 2894, 73 L.Ed.2d 598 (1982). For an "appellate review theory," which at a minimum would

It may seem, therefore, that the matter of legislative preclusion of review stands in opposition to the courts' role of checking the "uncontrolled and arbitrary action of a public and administrative officer." But that does not appear to be much the case. For the most part, Congress has not on any sustained basis tried to take away, nor have the courts in principle relinquished, their power ultimately to assure that agency officials act lawfully. Certainly Congress may wish to shape and defer review, so as to give an agency room to work. But this deferral does not and has not entailed the further proposition that review is not at some point available. Rather, careful examination of a preclusion of review usually shows that it merely postpones review until such time as the agency has had first crack at resolving the problem in question.[7] This sort of deferral (as opposed to a complete denial of review) was fact the case in *Weinberger v. Salfi,* with which decision we introduced this subject.

In *Weinberger v. Salfi*, the Court held that while the Social Security Act prevented the plaintiffs from commencing an action in federal district court prior to exhausting administrative remedies, the Court at the same time noted and emphasized that judicial review was yet available. It was available after a plaintiff first filed for relief from the agency itself and then, as provided by the Act, filed for review of an agency denial of that relief. In this respect, the Act provided that "Any individual, after any final determination of the Secretary made after a hearing to which he was a party, may obtain review of such decision by a civil action commenced within sixty days after the mailing to him of notice of such decision."[8]

* * *

The major exception to the general practice, of merely shaping and deferring agency action as opposed to barring it, had been the Veterans' Administration. For much of that agency's history, review of its actions was absolutely precluded. Its organic act provided that decisions of "law or fact under any law administered by the Veterans' Administration providing benefits for veterans ... shall be final and conclusive and no ... court of the United States shall have power or jurisdiction to review any such decision...."[9] This absolute preclusion of review was a major source of historical support favoring Congress' general power to preclude

provide "a right of access to a constitutional court to police the separation of powers and provide guarantees against administrative arbitrariness," see Fallon, Our Legislative Courts, Administrative Agencies, and Article III, 101 Harv.L.Rev. 915, 969 (1988). And see chap. 5, supra.

7. Cf. Shalala v. Illinois Council on Long Term Care, 529 U.S. 1, 120 S.Ct. 1084, 146 L.Ed.2d 1 (2000).

The principles of preclusion of review sometimes merge with the doctrine of exhaustion of administrative remedies that is discussed in Sec. 12.9. This doctrine often calls on the courts to postpone review until such remedies as the agency might itself offer are "exhausted."

8. 42 U.S.C. § 405(g).

9. 38 U.S.C. § 211(a). As will be shortly discussed in text above, this provision was amended in 1988, by Pub.L. 100–687, 102 Stat. 4105, 4122 (1988), to remove the restriction against review of legal questions and agency rules.

review of agency action.[10] But viewed in its whole, this Veterans' Administration preclusion of review is better seen as an aberration of history rather than a calculated practice.

The first Congress provided for disability benefits for Revolutionary War veterans and tried to give the federal courts the responsibility of administering the scheme. The courts refused to take that job, on the grounds that it was an administrative task, and not a matter of judicial power under Article III. Congress then enacted new legislation placing the administration of veterans' benefits with the Secretary of War.[11] Thus began a nearly two-hundred year tradition of administering veterans' benefits wholly outside the courts. In the first half of this century, when constitutional doubts about this system began to surface, they were quickly buried under the privilege doctrine. According to that doctrine, recipients of government benefits could not complain that unconstitutional conditions attached to the benefits. Several years ago, however, the privilege doctrine fell, so that it did insulate constitutional matters, such as the availability of judicial review, from being questioned.[12]

Consequently, in modern times the Veterans' Administration absolute preclusion of review came to be questioned on grounds that it unwisely and unconstitutionally kept the courts from checking unlawful action in that agency. Congress responded to these concerns about reviewability by amending the Veterans' Administration Act to eliminate the absolute preclusion.[13]

* * *

Under Article III and in a government of separated powers, the general and undiminished function of the courts is to assure that agencies conform to the Constitution and to the power delegated them by Congress.[14] Congress has respected this function. What then, is the topic of statutory preclusion of judicial review about?

10. Also, this preclusion has been taken as illustrative of the policy grounds—a "beneficial non-adversarial system"—supporting preclusions. Id. at 5795.

11. See Veterans' Judicial Review and Benefit Improvement Act, 7 U.S. Code Cong. & Admin. News, 5782, 5790 (1988). Also, a suit for veterans' benefits is a suit against the treasury, and was therefore considered particularly within the range of sovereign immunity. Id. at 5791.

12. See chap. 7, sec. 7.3, supra.

13. 38 U.S.C. § 211(a), amended, Pub.L. 100–687, 102 Stat. 4105, 4122 (1988).

14. As explained by the Supreme Court:

> It has never been the policy of Congress to prevent the administration of its own statutes from being judicially confined to the scope of authority granted or to the objectives specified. Its policy could not be otherwise, for in such a case statutes would in effect be blank checks drawn to the credit of some administrative officer or board.

Bowen v. Michigan Academy of Family Physicians, 476 U.S. 667, 106 S.Ct. 2133, 90 L.Ed.2d 623 (1986), quoting S.Rep. No. 752, 79th Cong., 1st Sess. 26 (1945).

The unconstitutionality of absolute preclusions of judicial review may be deduced from the courts' function, under *Marbury v. Madison,* of assuring that government in all its parts operates within constitutionally prescribed limits. 5 U.S. (1 Cranch) 137, 176, 2 L.Ed. 60 (1803). In relation to *Marbury,* the court of appeals for the District of Columbia Circuit has explained that "Not

The topic is that of statutory interpretation and locating the space in which Congress may have shaped and deferred review so as to give the agency first crack at implementing its program. The Administrative Procedure Act identifies this topic of as one of interpretation as it provides that agency actions are reviewable "except *to the extent* that ... statutes preclude judicial review."[15] Below, we examine various issues pertaining this matter of determining "the extent" which Congress may have precluded judicial review.

§ 12.5.1 Implied Preclusion of Review

Claims of legislative preclusion of judicial review are examined in light of a "strong presumption" against them, and only upon "clear and convincing evidence" are the courts to understand that Congress has precluded review.[16] Ordinarily, only clear statutory language constitutes clear and convincing evidence. This being the case, a sustainable implied preclusion is uncommon.

How claims of implied preclusion might be made, and how the courts usually deny them, is illustrated by the Supreme Court decision in *Stark v. Wickard*.[17] In various provisions, the Agriculture Marketing Agreement Act of 1937 created special statutory forms of review for actions of the Secretary of Agriculture. These provisions for judicial review did not, however, provide for review of the particular action in question, which involved an alleged error of law in an agency milk-marketing order. For this error, the plaintiffs sought injunctive relief in federal district court under a general jurisdiction statute. Because this kind of suit was not one of the forms of actions established by the Agriculture Marketing Agreement Act, the Secretary argued that Congress had meant to preclude it, albeit it had not expressly done so.

The Supreme Court refused to find that federal court review had been "impliedly" precluded as the Secretary argued. The Court emphasized the nature of the agency action in question, an alleged error of law about the agency's statutory authority. Respecting this alleged error, the Court explained that "The responsibility of determining the limits of statutory grants of authority ... is a judicial function entrusted to the court by Congress by the statutes establishing courts and marking their jurisdiction." Further, "If the absence of jurisdiction meant a sacrifice or obliteration of a right which Congress had created, the inference would

only is it daring to suggest that Congress, though subject to the checks and balances of the Constitution, may create a subordinate body free from those constraints; it also beggars the imagination to suggest that judicial review might be less crucial to assuring the integrity of administrative action than it is to make certain that Congress will operate within its proper sphere." Ralpho v. Bell, 569 F.2d 607, 620 (D.C.Cir.1977), rehearing denied 569 F.2d 636 (D.C.Cir.1977). See also Federal Legislative Courts, 43 Harv.L.Rev. 894, 908–12 (1930).

15. 5 U.S.C. § 701(a)(1) (emphasis added).

16. Abbott Laboratories v. Gardner, 387 U.S. 136, 140–41, 87 S.Ct. 1507, 1511–12, 18 L.Ed.2d 681 (1967); accord, Bowen v. Michigan Academy of Family Physicians, 476 U.S. 667, 106 S.Ct. 2133, 90 L.Ed.2d 623 (1986); McNary v. Haitian Refugee Center, 498 U.S. 479, 111 S.Ct. 888, 112 L.Ed.2d 1005 (1991).

17. 321 U.S. 288, 64 S.Ct. 559, 88 L.Ed. 733 (1944).

be strong that Congress intended that the statutory provisions governing the general jurisdiction of those courts to control."

An exception to the rule—that claims of implied preclusion are presumptively denied—is the Supreme Court's 1984 decision in *Block v. Community Nutrition Institute.*[18] In a case brought by a consumer, the Court held that the Agriculture Marketing Agreement Act had precluded review of consumer complaints respecting milk-marketing orders. The Court so held notwithstanding the fact that the Act did not *expressly* preclude such review. Whether a "particular statute" precludes review, the Court said, "is determined not only from its express language, but also from the structure of the statutory scheme, its objectives, its legislative history, and the nature of the administrative action involved." From this viewpoint, the Court found that "Suits of this type [consumer suits] would effectively nullify congress' intent to establish an equitable and expeditious procedure for testing the validity of orders...."

Also, consumer suits "would severely disrupt [a] complex and delicate administrative scheme" and would work to provide "[milk] handlers with a convenient device for evading the statutory requirement that they first exhaust their administrative remedies." In this respect, a lesson of *Block v. Community Nutrition Institute* would seem to be that if Congress has specifically provided for certain forms of review of agency action and if an alternative form of review can diminish the efficacy of the specially provided forms, then the courts may find that this alternative form has been precluded. Because this sort of implied preclusion turns on the availability of review in some form, it does not eliminate the courts as a check on agency lawlessness.

§ 12.5.2 Limited and Absolute Preclusion of Review

A "limited" preclusion of review is not necessarily disfavored. On the other hand, an absolute preclusion is. When Congress limits review it does so in a bounded way, so as merely to provide the agency with a space in which its expertise and specialized processes can operate uninterrupted by the courts.[19] Judicial review may be shaped or postponed, to allow the agencies to filter a myriad of fact-based claims, such as Social Security claims, that are suited to resolution by specialist agencies and special procedures.[20] Also, filtering claims through a single agency—in

18. 467 U.S. 340, 104 S.Ct. 2450, 81 L.Ed.2d 270 (1984). For a more recent Supreme Court decision, which in applying a "clear and convincing evidence" form of review to a claim of statutory preclusions nonetheless implied such a preclusion from the structure and purposes of the relevant Act, see NLRB v. United Food and Commercial Workers Union, 484 U.S. 112, 108 S.Ct. 413, 98 L.Ed.2d 429 (1987).

19. E.g., St. Louis University v. Blue Cross Hosp. Service, 537 F.2d 283, 289 (8th Cir.1976), cert. denied 429 U.S. 977, 97 S.Ct. 484, 50 L.Ed.2d 584 (1976) ("Judicial review of the amounts of all Medicare payments would bring the courts into the complex interplay between physician and hospital in determining the appropriate charges for technical services.... Determining the amount of these charges is a matter peculiarly suited to determination by a specialized agency.")

20. A winnowing of claims within an agency can "provid[e] for the administration of the benefits ... with maximum efficiency and convenience for individuals entitled to benefits." United States v. Erika,

contrast to a decentralization through the courts—enhances a uniformity in determining these claims.

When judicial review is so shaped and deferred, but still ultimately available to assure that the agency is acting lawfully, the courts' stand against the "uncontrolled and arbitrary action of a public and administrative officer" is not undercut.[21] Consequently, if there is room for interpretation the courts tend to find that Congress has limited rather than barred review.[22]

In *Bowen v. Michigan Academy of Family Physicians,* certain physicians challenged the validity, on statutory and constitutional grounds, of a Medicare regulation that provided for higher reimbursements to "board certified" physicians than to uncertified "family physicians."[23]

Inc., 456 U.S. 201, 203, 102 S.Ct. 1650, 1652, 72 L.Ed.2d 12 (1982). As explained by the Ninth Circuit, "Several courts have explicitly noted that, owing to economies of scale, reviewing the validity of statutory and regulatory provisions applicable to large classes of program beneficiaries is an inefficient use of judicial resources." Devine v. Cleland, 616 F.2d 1080, 1085 (9th Cir. 1980). See Plato v. Roudebush, 397 F.Supp. 1295, 1303 (D.Md.1975).

21. American School of Magnetic Healing v. McAnnulty, 187 U.S. 94, 23 S.Ct. 33, 47 L.Ed. 90 (1902). See also Ralpho v. Bell, 569 F.2d 607, 622–23 (D.C.Cir.1977), rehearing denied 569 F.2d 636 (D.C.Cir.1977). A court's commitment to checking unlawful agency action is of course a natural function of judiciary operating independently within our system of separated powers. To some extent, though, this commitment—as it often involves questions of law pertaining to the statutory authority essential to an agency's action—also turns on "a nice appreciation, presumably shared by Congress, that courts of law possess a particular expertise in statutory interpretation." Barlow v. Collins, 397 U.S. 159, 166, 90 S.Ct. 832, 837, 25 L.Ed.2d 192 (1970).

22. "Indeed, it has become something of a time-honored tradition for the Supreme Court and lower federal courts to find that Congress did not intend to preclude altogether judicial review. . . ." Bartlett v. Bowen, 816 F.2d 695 (D.C.Cir.1987). See Oestereich v. Selective Service System Local Bd. No. 11, 393 U.S. 233, 239, 89 S.Ct. 414, 417, 21 L.Ed.2d 402 (1968) (Harlan, J., concurring). For a case decision showing the considerable reluctance of courts to read statutes as creating absolute preclusions of review, see Johnson v. Robison, 415 U.S. 361, 367, 94 S.Ct. 1160, 1165, 39 L.Ed.2d 389 (1974) (discussed at note 27, infra).

23. 476 U.S. 667, 106 S.Ct. 2133, 90 L.Ed.2d 623 (1986). The claim of preclusion was based on § 405(h) of the Social Security Act which is incorporated into the Medicare Act. 42 U.S.C.A. § 1395(ii).

An exception to the rule against absolute preclusions of review is provided by Briscoe v. Bell, 432 U.S. 404, 97 S.Ct. 2428, 53 L.Ed.2d 439 (1977). In this case, the governor of Texas, claiming that the Attorney General of the United States had wrongfully determined that Texas was, with respect to "language minorities, subject to the Voting Rights Act, brought an action for declaratory and injunctive relief in federal district court in the District of Columbia." While the Voting Rights Act provided that a "determination or certification by the Attorney General . . . shall not be reviewable in any court. . . ," 42 U.S.C.A. § 1973(b), the district court ruled that this "apparent preclusion of judicial review was not absolute" and that it retained "jurisdiction to consider the 'pure legal question' of whether the Executive officials had correctly interpreted an Act of Congress." 432 U.S. at 408, 97 S.Ct. at 2430. The Supreme Court overruled the district, and found that judicial review had been precluded. The Supreme Court found that in this case the "heavy burden of overcoming the strong presumption that Congress did not mean to prohibit all judicial review" had been met.

But *Briscoe v. Bell* may, in comparison with the usual run of administrative law cases, be exceptional inasmuch as it involved the power especially bestowed on Congress, by the fourteenth and fifteenth amendments, to end voting discrimination. In this regard, the Court explained that the preclusion before it "may well be 'an uncommon exercise of congressional power,'" that "in attacking the pervasive evils and tenacious defenders of voting discrimination, Congress acted within its 'power to enforce' the Fourteenth and Fifteenth

The Secretary of Health and Human Services claimed that the Medicare Act had precluded judicial review of the regulation, both impliedly and expressly. The Supreme Court disagreed. While noting that the Act did preclude review of certain discretionary "amount determinations," the Court at the same time found that it was an "extreme position," and one that it would not take, to say that "Congress ... intended no review at all of substantial statutory and constitutional challenges to the Secretary's administration of ... the Medicare program."

As the Court in *Bowen* indicated, the courts consider an absolute preclusion of review as an "extreme position." An absolute preclusion is one that is extensive enough to prevent the courts from holding agencies to lawful limits, limits set by the Constitution, by Congress, and by an agency's own rules. This sort of preclusion is to be contrasted with a limited preclusion that, while allowing agencies a space for their expertise and methods, still reserve to the courts the power to check unlawful agency action. When they have appeared, absolute preclusions have presented "serious questions" of constitutionality.[25] Article III of the Constitution places the judicial power of the United States in federal courts. When matters within this power are committed to agencies and denied to courts, then the question that arises is whether this preclusion of respecting judicial power is an unconstitutional departure from Article III's allocation of that power to courts. This question is, we believe, best resolved by the analysis (which emphasizes the role of the courts in checking unlawful government action) required by the Supreme Court in *Commodity Futures Trading Comm'n v. Schor*.[26] For that analysis we refer you to Chapter 5 on the judicial power, at Sec. 5.2.

But more often than they undertake to say whether or not an absolute preclusion of review is constitutional, the courts will avoid that analysis by construing the preclusion in question as less than absolute, a practice that is amply illustrated by the Supreme Court's opinion in *Johnson v. Robison*.[27] The Veterans' Administration had, as provided by statute, denied educational benefits to a conscientious objector named Robison. Robison then sued the agency in federal court, claiming that this denial of benefits violated his constitutional rights to the free exercise of religion and the equal protection of the laws. In defense, the Veterans' Administration moved that the suit be dropped under the Act's provision at the time that "decisions of the Administrator on any questions of law or fact under any law administered by the Veterans' Administration providing benefits for veterans and their dependents or survivor shall be final and conclusive and no other official or any court of the United States shall have power or jurisdiction to review any such decision. . . ."

Amendments by appropriate legislation." 432 U.S. at 414, 97 S.Ct. at 2434.

25. Johnson v. Robison, 415 U.S. 361, 367, 94 S.Ct. 1160, 1165, 39 L.Ed.2d 389 (1974). See also Bartlett v. Bowen, 816 F.2d 695, 699 (D.C.Cir.1987).

26. 478 U.S. 833, 106 S.Ct. 3245, 92 L.Ed.2d 675 (1986).

27. 415 U.S. 361, 94 S.Ct. 1160, 39 L.Ed.2d 389 (1974).

The stringency of these terms did not faze the Court. The presumption against an absolute preclusion of review, the Court explained, was strong. The Court, therefore, closely examined the purposes and the language of the seemingly absolute preclusion, and found that its jurisdiction to hear Robison's claim was denied by neither. The purposes, the Court found, were (1) "to insure that benefits claims will not burden the courts with expensive and time consuming litigation and (2) to insure that the technical and complex determinations and applications of Veterans' Administration policy will be adequately and uniformly made." Review of claims about the unconstitutionality of legislation implemented by the Veterans' Administration would not contravene these purposes. These sorts of claims, the Court stated, "cannot be expected to burden the courts by their volume, nor do they involve technical considerations of Veterans' Administration policy." Nor did the text of preclusion, as it might seem, necessarily include plaintiff's claim. This text pertained to questions arising "under" a statute administered by the Veterans' Administration. The plaintiff Robison, the Court reasoned, was not attacking a decision made by the Veterans' Administration *under* the conscience objector statute it administered. Instead, his attack was against the statute itself; it was against Congress and its decision not to extend, by means of the statute, benefits to conscientious objectors.

§ 12.5.3 Constitutional and Statutory Review

Robison is sometimes taken as showing that a presumption against preclusion of judicial review operates most strongly in the context of constitutional challenges to agency action. An unfortunate flipside to this view is the implication that a preclusion of review respecting merely statutory rights is not so suspect.[28] This implication seems unfortunate. While arguments against preclusion of review of statutory claims may lack the rhetorical appeal of arguments about precluding constitutional claims, review of statutory claims is nonetheless as serious a matter. Practically speaking, statutory review is as important to individuals, for instance welfare recipients or social security claimants whose livelihood is tied to statutory enactment, as is constitutional review.[29]

Review of statutory rights is, however, also important in more *public* ways. The assumption of delegating government power to agencies is that these agencies stay within their statutory authority. Statutory

28. This distinction between constitutional and statutory review was suggested by Justice Brandeis concurring in St. Joseph Stock Yards Co. v. United States, 298 U.S. 38, 77, 56 S.Ct. 720, 737, 80 L.Ed. 1033 (1936) where he wrote that "When dealing with constitutional rights (as distinguished from privileges offered by the Government) there must be the opportunity of presenting in an appropriate proceeding at some time, to some court, every question of law raised."

29. Webster v. Doe, 486 U.S. 592, 618, 108 S.Ct. 2047, 2061, 100 L.Ed.2d 632 (1988) (Scalia, J., dissenting). Scalia also makes the important point, that "the only respect in which a constitutional claim is necessarily more significant than any other kind of claim is that, regardless of how trivial its real-life importance may be in the case at hand, it cannot be asserted against the action of the legislature itself, whereas a constitutional claim can."

review by the courts is the best means of enforcing this assumption. Also, as we discussed in Chapter 5, an aspiration of separated powers is that judicial review of statutes will improve the statute. Judges can also be expected to have a balance of views and of values, a sense of the interest of the moving party in relation to the permanent interests of the whole community. Judges can also be expected to interpret congressional enactments toward these ends, as an administrative agency, whose perspective may be distorted by its program and which may not be as inclined by training, experience or position to comprehensive views, cannot.[30] For these reasons, there is little reason to treating preclusion of review respecting statutory rights any different than preclusion of review respecting constitutional rights.

§ 12.6 LIMITATIONS TO JUDICIAL REVIEW: COMMITTED TO AGENCY DISCRETION

Should a court defer to an agency decision within the scope of its lawful authority? Should a court treat that decision deferentially, as, for example, an appellate court might defer to the discretionary judgments of a lower court? This question is not new. In *Dr. Bonham's Case,* Lord Coke found that a medical board's finding that Dr. Bonham was "insufficient and inexpert in the art of medicine" was reviewable.[1] But this part

30. These qualities "enable judges to discern, better than others with . . . limited vision, the enduring principles and longer range that tend to be forgotten where either the interests of factions collide or the perspective of bureaucrats prevail." Wellington, The Nature of Judicial Review, 91 Yale L.Rev. 486, 493, 502 (1982). That the courts may mitigate legislation so as to favor the permanent interests of the community may have been the theory of Lord Coke in *Dr. Bonham's case,* where he asserted review of acts of Parliament according to "common right and reason." As explained by Prof. Jaffe, "Coke's philosophy, his statements in Dr. Bonham's Case and the Institutes were a mighty source of . . . oracular authority." It was not necessary to their thinking that the courts be independent of parliament in any absolute sense. It was enough that legislation would be interpreted in the light of "reason" and the "common law." Jaffe, The Right to Judicial Review, 71 Harv.L.Rev. 401, 416–17 (1958).

§ 12.6

1. 8 Co.Rep. at 121, 77 Eng.Rep. at 658. Coke distinguished between the office of a judge, which was recognized by statute, and the office of administrative officials, which were not so recognized. In this regard, Coke stated that "the record of force made by a justice of peace is not traversable, because he doth it as Judge, by the statutes of 14 Ric. 2. and 8 Hen. 6. and so there is a difference when one makes a record as a Judge and when he doth a thing by special authority (as they did in this case at bar) and not as a Judge." Id. While Coke apparently meant that medical board factual findings were reviewable, still, the error that the board was charged with was one of law, whether Dr. Bonham was statutorily exempted from the board's jurisdiction, rather than a factual matter that would be more particularly a matter of administrative discretion.

In Rooke's Case, 77 Eng.Rep. 209, 5 Co.Rep. 99a (C.P., 1599), property had been taken to satisfy a Sewer Commission assessment to pay for improvements to the Thames. The property owner, arguing that the assessment was improper in that the Commission erred in limiting assessments to the property on the banks of the Thames rather than assessing all benefited property, brought an action in replevin against it. In defense, the Commission argued that under the appropriate statute it was to act according "to their discretions", and that this discretion was not reviewable by the courts. Lord Coke, finding against the Commission, disagreed, saying that:

> [Y]et these proceedings ought to be limited and bound within the rule of reason and law. For discretion is a science or understanding to discern between shadows and substance, between equity and

of the case, an assumption that courts might fully review agency discretion as to a matter within its expertise, did not thrive. Rather, the practice that soon developed was that English courts deferred to administrative discretion so long as the officials operated within limits set by law. The court's practice was stated thusly: "they are enabled by statute to proceed according to their discretions" and "if they proceed secundum, aequum & bonum, we cannot correct them; but if they proceed where they have no jurisdiction . . . then they are to be corrected here."[2] As we shall see, modern courts are somewhat more prone to review a matter that might be cast as properly within an agency's expertise. Nonetheless, that sort of discretionary act enjoys a degree of protection, according to the "committed to agency discretion" exception to review of the Administrative Procedure Act.

* * *

As we have seen, the Administrative Procedure Act provides that judicial review may be limited "to the extent that statutes preclude review." In the same section, the Act also provides that review may be barred when "an agency action is committed to agency discretion by law."[3] As this proximity indicates, these two limitations—preclusions of review and committed to agency discretion—to judicial review are related.[4] Still, they differ in significant respects.

The matter of a preclusion of review emphasizes statutory interpretation and how far Congress meant to go in clearing a zone in which the agencies may act unimpeded by the courts. In contrast, the "committed to agency discretion" exception to review more narrowly focuses on the agency act in question. With respect to that act the inquiry is, at bottom, largely functional. It is whether the act involves a discretion that the courts may usefully review.[5] Suppose that the Veterans' Administration, acting within delegated authority, purchases x-ray plates and the claim is that those plates are inferior to other similarly priced plates. Should a court review that claim? Probably not, because courts are not likely to be shoppers any smarter than the agency.

colourable glosses and pretenses, and not to do according to their wills and private affections. . . .

77 Eng.Rep. at 210, 5. Co.Rep. at 100.

2. Commins v. Massam, 82 Eng.Rep. 473 (K.B. 1643). See also Groenvelt v. Burwell, 1 Ld.Raym. 454, 1 Salk 144 (1700) (in denying that a board finding of malpractice was traversable, Lord Holt stated that "The judges do not understand medicine sufficiently to make a judgment").

3. 5 U.S.C. § 701(a)(2).

4. When a statute says that "the Commission may, upon the complaint of an interested party or upon its own initiative, order a hearing concerning the lawfulness or a rate" we certainly may say that the statute commits the matter to agency discretion, and that therefore the matter is "committed to agency discretion by law" within the meaning of § 701(a)(2) of the Administrative Procedure Act. See Southern Railway Co. v. Seaboard Allied Milling Corp., 444 U.S. 890, 100 S.Ct. 194, 62 L.Ed.2d 126 (1979). At the same time, we might also say that the statute by that same measure precludes review within the meaning of § 701(a)(1) as it refers to "statutes that preclude review."

5. Heckler v. Chaney, 470 U.S. at 826, 405 S.Ct. at 1653. S. Breyer & R. Stewart, Administrative Law and Regulatory Policy 1073–74 (2d ed.1985) ("The cases suggest that [committed to agency discretion] may have a somewhat broader scope, focusing on the 'practical and policy implications of unreviewability' ").

In the following discussion, we will first examine committed-to-agency-discretion the limitation to judicial review from the standpoint of the courts' ability sensibly to review agency action. Today, this is largely an inquiry about whether there are "meaningful standards" that a court might use to judge an agency action. Then, we will examine committed-to-agency-discretion in terms of optimizing decisional resources as between agencies and courts. Finally, we will address the extent to which agency *in* action is an unreviewable portion of discretion.

§ 12.6.1 The "Meaningful Standards" Criteria

Administrative decisions generally involve discretion, and those actions are ordinarily reviewable.[6] The Administrative Procedure Act follows this convention of reviewability inasmuch as the Act generally provides judicial review of "abuse of discretion."[7] However, the Act's "committed to agency discretion" exception to judicial review also establishes a "narrow" zone of discretion that is unreviewable.[8] The problem is finding that zone.

Courts ordinarily judge the propriety of agency action according to whether it is consistent with some legal standard.[9] Where no such standards are available, review would mostly be futile. The absence of standards may, therefore, be considered an indicia of the committed to agency discretion limitation to judicial review. Accordingly, in *Heckler v. Chaney* the Supreme Court explained that this limitation applies where there is "no meaningful standard against which to judge the agency's exercise of discretion."[10] No such standard would likely be available in

6. For a review of the various forms of agency discretion, see Kock, Judicial Review of Administrative Discretion, 54 Geo. Wash.L.Rev. 469 (1986).

7. 5 U.S.C.A. § 706.

8. 5 U.S.C.A. § 701. See Heckler v. Chaney, 470 U.S. 821, 838, 105 S.Ct. 1649, 1659, 84 L.Ed.2d 714 (1985). See also Davis, Administrative Arbitrariness Is Not Always Reviewable, 51 Minn.L.Rev. 643 (1967). Contra see Berger, Administrative Arbitrariness, A Reply to Prof. Davis, 114 U.Pa. L.Rev. 763 (1966).

9. Standards may be drawn from a variety of sources, such as applicable statutes, the agency's own rules, and constitutional requirements. In this relation of standards, "Judicial review is available when the plaintiff alleges a violation of 'constitutional, statutory, regulatory, or other legal mandates or restrictions.'" Merrill Ditch–Liners, Inc. v. Pablo, 670 F.2d 139 (9th Cir.1982).

10. Heckler v. Chaney, 470 U.S. at 830, 105 S.Ct. at 1655. See also City of Santa Clara v. Andrus, 572 F.2d 660, 666 (9th Cir.1978), cert. denied 439 U.S. 859, 99 S.Ct. 176, 58 L.Ed.2d 167 (1978) ("If, however, no law fetters the exercise of administrative discretion the courts have no standard against which to measure the lawlessness of agency action. In such cases no issues susceptible of judicial review are prescribed. . . ."). Florida v. United States, 768 F.2d 1248 (11th Cir.1985) ("If there are judicially manageable standards available for judging how and when an agency should exercise its discretion, then it is impossible to determine even whether the agency abused its discretions"). This latter case, *Florida v. United States,* involved a land acquisition decision for the benefit of the Seminole Indians. In finding that this decision was unreviewable, the court noted that the relevant statute stated that the land acquisition was within the discretion of the Department of Interior and that the statute at the same time "does not delineate the circumstances under which exercise of this discretion is appropriate." 768 F.2d at 1256. From a functional point of view, the court added that decision to buy the land included factors such as budgetary considerations, the particular needs of the Indians, governmental resources for overseeing the land, and securing the cooperation of state and local officials, and that for these

our previous illustration, about the courts being in no position to say that one kind of x-ray plates is better than the other.

Nor was such a "meaningful standard" available in *Heckler v. Chaney*. The peculiar circumstances of that case were that inmates sentenced to death by an injection of lethal drugs claimed that the drugs were not in compliance with laws administered by the Food and Drug Administration and that the agency should therefore take various investigatory and enforcement actions.[11] The Food and Drug Administration refused to do so. The Court saw that refusal as an instance of prosecutorial discretion unbounded by standards, and thus not susceptible to meaningful judicial review.[12]

The meaningful standards criteria of *Heckler v. Chaney* was drawn from the "no law to apply" formula of the Court's earlier opinion in *Citizen's to Preserve Overton Park v. Volpe*.[13] A citizen's group had challenged the Secretary of Transportation's decision to allocate federal funds for the construction of an interstate highway through a public park in Memphis. The Secretary, however, claimed that the decision was unreviewable as it had been committed to agency discretion. The Supreme Court disagreed. The committed to agency discretion exception, the Court explained, is "very narrow," and only "applicable in those rare instances where 'statutes are drawn in such broad terms that in a given case there is no law to apply.' "[14] By statute, the Secretary's approval of funds was subject was conditioned on there being no "prudent and

reasons the agency decision to buy the land should not be reviewed. (This functional approach to the reviewability of agency discretion is discussed in the next preceding section.).

See generally, Koch, Judicial Review of Administrative Discretion, 54 Geo. Wash.L.Rev. 469, 494ff (1986).

11. The injury possibly caused by noncompliance with federal drug laws was a tortured rather than a quick and painless death. Chaney v. Heckler, 718 F.2d 1174, 1177 (D.C.Cir.1983), rehearing denied 724 F.2d 1030 (D.C.Cir.1984).

12. As stated by the Court, the reasons for "this general unsuitability for review" were that:

> First, an agency decision not to enforce often involves a complicated balancing of a number of factors which are peculiarly within its expertise. Thus, an agency must not only assess whether a violation has occurred, but whether agency resources are best spent on this violation or another, whether the agency is likely to succeed if it acts, whether the particular enforcement action best fits the agency's overall policies, and indeed, whether the agency has enough resources to undertake the action at all.

470 U.S. at 831, 105 S.Ct. at 1655. See generally Wayte v. United States, 470 U.S. 598, 105 S.Ct. 1524, 84 L.Ed.2d 547 (1985). See also Investment Co. Institute v. FDIC, 728 F.2d 518 (D.C.Cir.1984) (A "simple exercise of 'prosecutorial discretion' " is unreviewable because "there are no general standards to govern the agency exercise of discretion.").

In *Heckler v. Chaney*, the Court distinguished its previous decision in Dunlop v. Bachowski, 421 U.S. 560, 95 S.Ct. 1851, 44 L.Ed.2d 377 (1975) where it held that an act of prosecutorial discretion was reviewable. In that case, the Court explained, there was "statutory language which supplied sufficient standards to rebut the presumption of unreviewability...." 470 U.S. at 833, 105 S.Ct. at 1656.

The matter of prosecutorial discretion is also considered in sec. 12.6.4, infra, dealing with the reviewability of agency inaction or delay.

13. Citizens to Preserve Overton Park, Inc. v. Volpe, 401 U.S. 402, 91 S.Ct. 814, 28 L.Ed.2d 136 (1971).

14. Citizens to Preserve Overton Park, Inc. v. Volpe, 401 U.S. 402, 410, 91 S.Ct. 814, 820, 28 L.Ed.2d 136 (1971) quoting S.Rep. 752, 79th Cong., 1st Sess. 26 (1945).

reasonable" alternatives to the route selected. Considering this "prudent alternative route" standard, the Court held that the agency action was reviewable, according to whether the Secretary's decision was based on the factors that Congress had made relevant to determining alternative routes. "Plainly" there was "law to apply," and thus the funding decision had not been "committed to agency discretion so as to be unreviewable."

Overton Park referred to " 'statutes ... drawn in such broad terms that in a given case there is no law to apply.' " This statement may suggest that in the case of standardless delegations of legislative power, for instance the public-interest delegation to the Federal Communications Commission, there would be no law to apply and thus on a broad scale, agency action would be unreviewable. But this seems too expansive a reading of the "no law to apply" principle. Even in open-ended statutes, agency discretion is not necessarily unlimited. Today, courts review agency action under those statutes so as to assure a degree of rationality by the agency.[15] Accordingly, even under wholly open-ended statutes the agency must operate according to "traditional standards of rationality and fair process,"[16] and in these standards there would, it would seem, be law to apply.

§ 12.6.2 Optimizing Decisional Resources: Functional Considerations

In practice, the committed to agency discretion exception to judicial review has not turned solely on the presence or absence of standards against which the agency action might be judged. Application of the exception has also included purely functional considerations respecting optimal allocations of decisional responsibility between agencies and courts.[17]

Langevin v. Chenango Court, Inc. involved the reviewability of an FHA approval of a rent increase by a federally subsidized landlord.[18] Because standards were available against which the increase might be judged, the court felt that review of a rent increase was not "beyond judicial competence."[19] Nonetheless, the court held that the decision had

15. This rationality has been described as "Whether the decisionmaking process incorporated reasonably discoverable facts and, weighed all relevant factors", and generally, that the conclusions reached by the agencies were consistent with the evidence before it. Koch, supra note 12 at 475. See FCC v. WNCN Listeners Guild, 450 U.S. 582, 101 S.Ct. 1266, 67 L.Ed.2d 521 (1981).

16. Heckler v. Chaney, 470 U.S. 821, 853, 105 S.Ct. 1649, 1667, 84 L.Ed.2d 714 (1985) (Marshall, J., concurring).

17. As one court has put it "In practice the determination whether there is law to apply necessarily turned on pragmatic considerations as to whether the agency determination is the proper subject of review." Natural Resources Defense Council, Inc. v. SEC, 606 F.2d 1031, 1034 (D.C.Cir.1979).

18. 447 F.2d 296 (2d Cir.1971). By regulatory agreement, rent increases were limited to those "necessary to compensate for any net increase ... in taxes ... and operating and maintenance expenses over which owners have no effective control." 447 F.2d at 303.

19. Rent increases were limited to those "necessary to compensate for any net increase ... in taxes ... and operating and maintenance expenses over which owners have no effective control." 447 F.2d at 303.

been committed to agency discretion and was therefore unreviewable. Writing for the court, Judge Friendly emphasized "the managerial nature" of the decision and the "need for expedition to achieve the congressional objective."

Judges inevitably look to practical considerations respecting the relative responsibilities and abilities of the courts and agencies. Respecting the "managerial nature" of an agency action, the courts understand that Congress may entrust agencies with developing a program, such as public housing, where a particular decision may be part of "coordinated management in all its phases."[20] Other considerations include the relative expertise of the courts and the agency as it comes to understanding the subject matter of a dispute, how judicial review would interfere with informal agency processes, the need for expedition, the obviousness of a law violation, and so forth.[21]

§ 12.6.3 Optimizing Decisional Resources: Separation of Powers Considerations

Agency discretion may also implicate matters, usually foreign or military affairs, that are "confided by our Constitution to the political departments of the government."[22]

In *Curran v. Laird,* the National Maritime Union sued the Secretary of Defense and other officials on the grounds that foreign vessels were being used to ship cargo to Vietnam when federal law required that domestic vessels be used.[23] The Court of Appeals for the District of Columbia, however, refused to hear the case, and it did so on the basis that the availability of domestic shipping was a matter committed to agency discretion within the meaning of the Administrative Procedure Act. The court relied on the Administrative Procedure Act, but as well its reasoning was grounded in a constitutional allocation of power in these matters to the executive branch. The court explained that the "case before us involves decisions relating to the conduct of national defense; the President has a key role; the national interest contemplates and requires flexibility in management of defense resources; and the particular issues call for determinations that lie outside sound judicial domain in terms of aptitude, facilities, and responsibility."

The Supreme Court has on similar grounds, in *Chicago & Southern Air Lines v. Waterman Steamship Corp.,* refused to review a presidential decision pertaining to commercial international air routes.[24] In doing so,

20. Board of Governors v. Agnew, 329 U.S. 441, 450, 67 S.Ct. 411, 416, 91 L.Ed. 408 (1947). (Rutledge, J., concurring).

21. These factors as they pertain to the committed to agency discretion exception to judicial review are carefully reviewed in Saferstein, A Functional Analysis of "Committed to Agency Discretion," 62 Harv. L.Rev. 367 (1968).

22. Chicago & Southern Air Lines v. Waterman Steamship Corp., 333 U.S. 103, 68 S.Ct. 431, 92 L.Ed. 568 (1948). This basis for declining judicial review is akin to and sometimes the same as the political question doctrine in constitutional law.

23. 420 F.2d 122 (D.C.Cir.1969) (*en banc*).

24. 333 U.S. 103, 68 S.Ct. 431, 92 L.Ed. 568 (1948).

the Court referred to the superior information and capacities of the executive branch in these international matters, and to a constitutional allocation of the these matters to the political branches:

> Such decisions are wholly confided by our Constitution to the political departments of the government.... They are delicate, complex, and involve large elements of prophecy. They are and should be undertaken only by those directly responsible to the people whose welfare they advance or imperil. They are decisions of a kind for which the judiciary has neither aptitude, facilities nor responsibility....[25]

Deference in international matters notwithstanding, the courts sometimes review an agency action in this area, particularly when the action is subject to ordinary legal standards. In *Japan Whaling Association v. American Cetacean Society,* wildlife conservation groups contended that the Secretary of Commerce had not, as required by federal statute, certified that Japan was harvesting whales in contravention of the International Convention for Regulation of Whaling.[26] The Secretary's defense was that his failure to certify was justified by a new executive agreement between the United States and Japan. The argument was that the "present actions are unsuitable for judicial review because they involve foreign relations and that a federal court, therefore, lacks the judicial power to command the Secretary of Commerce, an Executive Branch official, to dishonor and repudiate an international agreement."

The Supreme Court disagreed, and heard the case on the merits. The Court emphasized that respecting the merits, its task involved ordinary judicial skills, the application of legal standards to a particular set of facts. The Court explained, "the Secretary's decision not to certify Japan for harvesting whales in excess of the [treaty] presents a purely legal question of statutory interpretation." This question called for "no more than the traditional rules of statutory constructions, and then applying this analysis to the particular set of facts." The court could "not shirk this responsibility" merely because our decision may have significant political overtones.

§ 12.6.4 Committed to Agency Discretion: Inaction or Delay

Dissatisfaction with an agency may result from its inaction as well as its action. The public may, for instance, feel that agencies are not moving swiftly enough in assuring that hazardous waste is safely disposed. Is such inaction or delay subject to judicial review? Possibly. The

25. 333 U.S. at 111, 68 S.Ct. at 436. The Court here noted that "The President, both as Commander-in-Chief and as the Nation's organ for foreign affairs, has available intelligence services whose reports are not and ought not to be published to the world."

26. 478 U.S. 221, 106 S.Ct. 2860, 92 L.Ed.2d 166 (1986). Certification requirements were imposed by the Fisherman's Protective Act of 1967, as amended. 22 U.S.C. § 1978.

Administrative Procedure Act declares that courts may "compel agency action unreasonably delayed."[27] For various reasons, however, courts will act only sparingly to compel agency action.

Often, questions of agency inaction or delay are considered unreviewable because they are "committed to agency discretion" within the meaning of the Administrative Procedure Act. Generally, these questions involve agency enforcement matters—either wholesale enforcement by rulemaking or more discrete enforcement by adjudication—of whatever program the agency is supposed to implement. Agency resources are not unlimited, and an enforcement decision involves an assessment of resources and priorities that the agency itself is ordinarily better suited to make. As explained by the Supreme Court:

> [A]n agency decision not to enforce often involves a complicated balancing of a number of factors which are peculiarly within its expertise. Thus, an agency must not only assess whether a violation has occurred, but whether agency resources are best spent on this violation or another, whether the agency is likely to succeed if it acts, whether the particular enforcement action best fits the agency's overall policies, and indeed, whether the agency has enough resources to undertake the action at all.[28]

Agency inaction may also be because of uncertainty. A problem may not be sufficiently close to a solution for the agency to act. (This uncertainty principle is particularly acute in agencies working on the edge of science and technology. But it is not, however, absent in sociology and economics.) In the face of uncertainty, agency action carries a risk of error, a chance of waste and unnecessary hardship.[29] And if agency expertise means anything, it means that the agency has the better sense of when its grip is too infirm to warrant action.[30]

27. 5 U.S.C. § 706(2). The reviewability of inaction or delay is also recognized by the Administrative Procedure Act as it defines "agency action" to include "failure to act". 5 U.S.C.A. § 501(13).

28. Curran v. Laird, 420 U.S. 122 (D.C.Cir.1969). See also Natural Resources Defense Council, Inc. v. SEC, 606 F.2d 1031, 1046–47 (D.C.Cir.1979).

29. For an argument, from a constitutional perspective, against regulation in the context of uncertainty, see Mayton, The Possibilities of Collective Choice: Arrow's Theorem, Article 1, and the Delegation of Legislative Power to Administrative Agencies, 1986 Duke L.J. 948, 957–63 (1986).

30. Cf. Oil, Chemical and Atomic Workers International Union v. Zegeer, 768 F.2d 1480, 1488 (D.C.Cir.1985) (in declining to find that the Mine, Safety, and Health Administration had unreasonably delayed rulemaking on mine radiation standards, the court stated that it was "cognizant ... of the complex scientific and technical issues involved in deciding whether to revise the current standards and in formulating a revision" and that the "difficulty and uncertainty inherent in the venture caution us against second-guessing...."); Natural Resources Defense Council, Inc. v. SEC, 606 F.2d 1031, 1046 (D.C.Cir.1979) ("Further, even if an agency considers a particular problem worthy of regulation, it may determine for reasons lying within its special expertise that the time for action has not yet arrived. The Area may be one of such rapid technological development that regulations would be outdated by the time they could become effective, or the scientific state of the art may be such that sufficient data are not yet available on which to premise adequate regulations. The circumstance in the regulated industry may be evolving in a way that could vitiate the need for regulation, or the agency may still be developing the expertise necessary for effective regulation.").

Accordingly, the courts usually defer to agency discretion not to regulate. But there are exceptions. Where uncertainty exists with respect to human health and safety, the courts have sometimes thought that the agencies should act, and chance error on the side of health and safety.[31]

The courts have also been reluctant to review claims of inaction for reasons quite apart from an agency managing its own regulatory resources. One reason is that agency inaction does not implicate a traditional concern of the courts, which is protecting individuals *against* government. As said by the Supreme Court, "when an agency refuses to act it does not exercise its coercive power over an individual's liberty or property rights, and thus does not infringe upon areas that courts often are called upon to protect."[32] Another reason is that claims of inaction may not be reviewable because they are unripe. The concrete context and factual record associated with agency action are often lacking in inaction. Consequently, issues presented by claims of delay or inaction may be too abstract for sound adjudication.[33] In *Natural Resources Defense Council, Inc. v. SEC,* where the court *did* review a charge of inaction in rulemaking, it was prompted to do because these problems of justiciability had been alleviated.[34] The agency had "in fact held a rulemaking proceeding and compiled a record narrowly focused on the particular rules suggested but not adopted." These matters of justiciability are more fully considered in Sec. 12.9, below, which deals with ripeness.

* * *

Because of the considerations stated above, the Court speaks of agency inaction as "presumptively unreviewable." But a presumption is not necessarily a bar.[35] At times, an agency's discretion to proceed at its own pace may have been curbed by Congress. Wisely or no, Congress

31. E.g., Telecommunications Research and Action Center v. FCC, 750 F.2d 70, 80 (D.C.Cir.1984) ("delays that might be unreasonable in the sphere of economic regulation are less tolerable when human health and welfare are at stake"); Environmental Defense Fund, Inc. v. Ruckelshaus, 439 F.2d 584, 598 (D.C.Cir.1971) (that courts are "increasingly asked to review administrative action that touches on fundamental personal interests in life, health, and liberty" and these "interests have always had a special claim to judicial protection, in comparison with the economic interests at stake in a rulemaking or licensing proceeding").

32. Heckler v. Chaney, 470 U.S. 821, 834, 105 S.Ct. 1649, 1657, 84 L.Ed.2d 714 (1985).

33. See Heckler v. Chaney, 470 U.S. at 834, 105 S.Ct. at 1657. ("when an agency does act to enforce, that action itself provides a focus for judicial review, inasmuch as the agency must have exercised its power in some manner. That action can at least be reviewed to determine whether the agency exceeded its statutory powers").

34. 606 F.2d 1031, 1042–43 (D.C.Cir. 1979).

35. As surveyed by Prof. Sunstein, the qualification to a presumption of non-reviewablity include "(1) review of a refusal to undertake rulemaking"; (2) inaction based on a conclusion that statutory jurisdiction is lacking; (3) cases in which an "agency has 'consciously and expressly adopted a general policy' that is so extreme as to amount to an abdication of its statutory responsibilities"; (4) refusal to enforce properly adopted agency rules; (5) nonenforcement that violates constitutional rights; and—the catch-all category—(6) cases in which the governing substantive statute sets priorities or circumscribes "an agency's power to discriminate among issues or cases it will pursue." Sunstein, Reviewing Agency Inaction After Heckler v. Chaney, 52 U.Chi.L.Rev. 653, 675 (1985).

may seek to force solutions to a problem, to force agency action by setting time limits or identifying triggering events for agency action.[36] These time limits or triggering events may be seen as standards against which the courts can measure the lawfulness of inaction.

There are as well various other circumstances in which inaction may be reviewed. In *Dunlop v. Bachowski,* the Court found that a National Labor Relations Board refusal to investigate and to file suit to set aside a union election was reviewable.[37] The Board was "required to file suit if certain 'clearly defined' factors were present." Therefore, the Board's decision not to prosecute "was not 'beyond the judicial capacity to supervise.' " Where an agency's refusal to regulate is based on an allegedly wrong assessment of its statutory authority, the courts have also reviewed that inaction. In *American Textile Manufacturers Institute, Inc. v. Donovan,* the Court found that the Occupation Safety and Health Administration's refusal, based on cost-benefit analysis, to regulate with respect to certain toxic materials was reviewable.[38] In *Heckler v. Chaney,* the Supreme Court also noted as reviewable circumstance in which an agency has " 'consciously and expressly adopted a general policy' that is so extreme as to amount to an abdication of its statutory responsibilities."[39]

This "extreme" was present where agency inaction was deemed so massive that it amounted to dereliction in implementing to a whole public program. In *Adams v. Richardson,* the claim was that the Department of Health, Education, and Welfare had failed to take steps against school segregation as required by Title VI of the Civil Rights Act of 1964.[40] Title VI, however, provided that such action need not be undertaken until the Department had "determined that compliance cannot be secured by voluntary means," and the department's defense was that the pace at which it enforced Title VI was a matter committed to its discretion and non-reviewable as such. The court of appeals disagreed, stating that:

> Although the Act does not provide a specific limit to the time period within which voluntary compliance may be sought, it is clear that a request for voluntary compliance, if not followed by responsive action on the part of the institution within a reasonable time, does not relieve the agency the responsibility to enforce Title VI. . . . A consistent failure to do so is a dereliction of duty reviewable in the courts.[41]

36. E.g. the Asbestos Hazard Emergency Response Act of 1986 requires that the Environmental Protection Agency publish proposed rules within sixty days of the Act's passage, and final rules within three hundred and sixty days. 15 U.S.C.A. § 2001 et seq., 33 U.S.C.A. § 1317(a).

37. 421 U.S. 560, 95 S.Ct. 1851, 44 L.Ed.2d 377 (1975).

38. American Textile Manufacturers Institute, Inc. v. Donovan, 452 U.S. 490, 509, 101 S.Ct. 2478, 2490, 69 L.Ed.2d 185 (1981).

39. 470 U.S. at 833 & n. 4, 105 S.Ct. at 1656 & n. 4.

40. 480 F.2d 1159, 1162 (D.C.Cir.1973) (en banc).

41. 480 F.2d at 1163. In this regard, the trial court had held that the Dept. of Health, Education and Welfare, "having found that a school district is in presump-

In *Heckler v. Chaney,* the Court also noted that its opinion of non-reviewability of agency enforcement proceedings did not necessarily extend to agency inaction or delay in rulemaking.[42] A reason for thus distinguishing inaction in rulemaking is that a rule is likely to have a greater regulatory impact than a single enforcement action. Also, the Administrative Procedure Act provides for some private participation in an agency's rulemaking agenda. It provides that "each agency shall given an interested person the right to petition for the issuance, amendment, or repeal of a rule."[43] Still, the various reasons (limited agency enforcement resources or uncertainty about the existence or the solution to a problem) that support agency discretion about initiating action also apply to rulemaking.[44] Consequently, claims that an agency should have adopted such and such a rule or initiated rulemaking proceedings are in fact generally not reviewed, unless they fall within an exception to the norm of non-reviewability (such as action forcing statutes) as we have considered.[45]

* * *

tive violation of Title VI, and having failed during a substantial period of time to achieve voluntary compliance, then unless the presumption has been overcome by further information defendants [HEW] have a duty to commence enforcement proceedings." Adams v. Richardson, 356 F.Supp. 92, 97 (D.D.C.1973), modified 480 F.2d 1159 (D.C.Cir.1973).

42. 470 U.S. at 825 & n. 2, 105 S.Ct. at 1652 & n. 2.

43. 5 U.S.C.A. § 553(e). In American Horse Protection Ass'n, Inc. v. Lyng, 812 F.2d 1 (D.C.Cir.1987), on remand 681 F.Supp. 949 (D.D.C.1988) the court explained that the District of Columbia Circuit maintained that inaction in rulemaking was reviewable. The court particularly relied on the Administrative Procedure Act, noting that the Act "requires agencies to allow interested persons to 'petition for the issuance, amendment, or repeal of a rule,'" and that "when such petitions are denied, to give a brief statement of the reasons for denial [5 U.S.C.A. § 555(e) (1982)]." The court explained that these "two provisions suggest that Congress expected that agencies denying rulemaking must explain their action." 812 F.2d at 4.

44. See, e.g., Natural Resources Defense Council, Inc. v. SEC, 606 F.2d 1031 (D.C.Cir.1979).

45. In something of a departure from the above described zone of non-reviewability, the court of appeals for the District of Columbia, in its careful opinion in Natural Resources Defense Council, Inc. v. SEC, 606 F.2d 1031 (D.C.Cir.1979), stated a somewhat broader conception of reviewability of agency inaction in rulemaking. That broader conception of reviewability focused on the justiciability of claims of inaction. The court stated that "discretionary decisions not to adopt rules are reviewable where . . . the agency has in fact held a rulemaking proceeding and compiled a record narrowly focused on the particular rules suggested but not adopted."

Public interest groups had petitioned the SEC for rules requiring corporate disclosure about their environmental policies. While the SEC, after rulemaking, did adopt rules requiring disclosure of the financial effects of corporate compliance with environmental laws, these rules were too limited to suit the petitioners, and so they brought suit. In this action, the court of appeals divided petitioners' complaint into two parts. One part was that the SEC had failed to consider alternatives and factors as required by the National Environmental Protection Act ("NEPA"). The other part was that the agency's decision not to adopt the rules proposed by petitioners was "arbitrary and capricious."

The court held that the SEC's inaction was reviewable in relation to the allegation that it had failed to comply with NEPA. As this review focused on a specific part—compliance with NEPA—of the SEC's regulatory agenda, it would not, the court thought, seriously interfere with that agenda. Also, there would be "law to apply," whether the agency's decisional process included factors make relevant by NEPA. Accordingly, the

Even if agency inaction is reviewable, getting judicial review is not the same as getting results. The usual form of relief is that of a remand, for the agency to consider its inaction in light of whatever deficiency, such as an agency failure to include some relevant factor in its decisional process, that the court has identified. This sort of remand ordains no particular result: the agency may clean-up its decisional processes and then reach the same decision.

§ 12.7 STANDING

Standing pertains to the plaintiff, as a threshold condition that all persons who would dispute an agency action in court must satisfy. At its core, standing is of a constitutional order. It is inferred from Article III of the Constitution as that Article provides for courts invested with "the judicial power of the United States."[1] As determined by the courts, this "judicial power" inheres in them only when a plaintiff has "standing,"

court said that it "would exercise relatively careful scrutiny to ensure that the SEC has scrupulously followed NEPA procedures. . . ."

But as to the charge that the agency's failure to adopt the proposed rules was arbitrary and capricious, judicial review could not be so precisely focused. Also, because such review goes directly to the kind of regulatory action an agency should undertake, it more directly undercuts agency discretion with respect to its regulatory agenda. With these things in mind the court related the question of reviewability to the question of the scope of review, stating that "In cases where courts have evidenced serious doubts about the reviewability of agency action, they have tended to couple their decision to review with a particularly narrow scope of review." Accordingly, the court limited the scope of its review—of petitioner's claim that the agency erred in not adopting the rules they proposed—to the less intrusive standards of "rationality review." In this regard, the court stated that "our review of the Commission's factual, and particularly its policy, determinations will perforce be an narrow one, limited to ensuring that the Commission has adequately explained the facts and policy concerns it relied on and to satisfying ourselves that those facts have some basis in the record." 606 F.2d at 1052–53.

Following Natural Resources Defense Council, Inc. v. SEC, the court of appeals for the District of Columbia Circuit has reviewed charges of inaction or delay in rulemaking in American Horse Protection Ass'n, Inc. v. Lyng, 812 F.2d 1 (D.C.Cir. 1987) (see note 57, supra); Oil, Chemical and Atomic Workers International Union v. Zegeer, 768 F.2d 1480 (D.C.Cir.1985) (reviewing a charge of undue delay in rulemaking); WWHT, Inc. v. FCC, 656 F.2d 807 (D.C.Cir.1981). In American Horse Protection Ass'n, Inc. v. Lyng, 812 F.2d 1, 4 (D.C.Cir.1987), the court summarized its position on the reviewability of inaction in rulemaking thusly:

> [R]efusals to institute rulemaking proceedings are distinguishable from other sorts of nonenforcement decisions insofar as they are less frequent, more apt to involve legal as opposed to factual analysis, and subject to special formalities, including a public explanation. *[Heckler v.] Chaney* therefore does not appear to overrule our prior decisions allowing review of agency refusals to institute rulemakings.

§ 12.7

1. *Steel Co. v. Citizens for a Better Environment*, 523 U.S. 83, 118 S.Ct. 1003, 1016, 140 L.Ed.2d 210 (1998). Because standing is of a constitutional order, whenever a lack of standing appears, at the trial court or on appeal and either by the motion of a party or on the court's own motion, the case is then immediately dismissed and any and all previous decisions respecting the merits in that case are null and void. From the outset of the proceedings, the court was not possessed of the judicial power essential to decisions on the merits. 118 S.Ct. at 1012–17.

A further note: The fact that we address standing in federal courts is not to suggest that standing is an exclusively federal. It is not; standing is required in state courts under state constitutions, in the same general form as it is required in federal courts.

with the qualifications that count as standing being derived from certain assumptions respecting that power. These assumptions are, first of all, about the competency of courts, whether the dispute a plaintiff brings to them may be capably resolved by judicial methods. Secondly, these assumptions are about the appropriate function of courts in a democracy that features separated power. Out of these assumptions the elements of standing have, by the courts, been presented somewhat axiomatically, by maxims conveniently stated but not always easily applied.

A plaintiff, it is said, must have a certain "personal stake" in the case that he or she brings to a court.[2] The personal stake must be such that the plaintiff will be (a) affected by and thus grounded in the circumstances of the agency action in question and (b) *adversely* affected so that she will resolutely argue the facts and law pertinent to the action. As the courts see it, a plaintiff so sited in and affected by the facts of a case better assures their informed resolution of the case.

Also, the requisite "personal stake" must be such as to distinguish those agency actions that are suitable for judicial review from those actions better suited to correction and control by the other branches.[3] This means that standing must work to separate the business of the courts from the more political work best done by the legislative branch. Similarly, a purpose of standing as emphasized in the 1990's is that of avoiding judicial usurpation of executive functions. In the federal system, Article II assigns to the President the task of assuring that the laws are "faithfully executed." Accordingly, the federal courts may measure and deny standing according to whether a plaintiff calls upon them to assume a supervisory role over administrative agencies that might usurp this executive function.[4]

In service of these matters of a sound adjudication and an appropriate separation of judicial, legislative, and executive powers, the courts have identified the "personal stake" essential to standing according to

Except that in state courts standing does not seem to be stringent and to have acquired the complexities as in federal courts.

2. The question that standing presents is whether the plaintiff has "alleged such a personal stake in the outcome of the controversy as to warrant *his* invocation of federal court jurisdiction and to justify exercise of the court's remedial powers on his behalf." Warth v. Seldin, 422 U.S. 490, 498–99, 95 S.Ct. 2197, 2204–05, 45 L.Ed.2d 343 (1975).

3. One of the first persons to understand this, how the requirement of a personal stake in litigation helps keep the courts out of the "daily aggressions" of special interests and politics, was Alexis de Tocqueville. His observation was that in American courts "The errors of the legislator are exposed only to meet a real want; and it is always a positive and appreciable fact that must serve as the basis of a prosecution." 1 Democracy in America 102, 280 (1945), *quoted in* Sierra Club v. Morton, 405 U.S. 727, 92 S.Ct. 1361, 31 L.Ed.2d 636 (1972).

4. Lujan v. Defenders of Wildlife, 504 U.S. 555, 560–61, 112 S.Ct. 2130, 2136–37, 119 L.Ed.2d 351 (1992). (to transfer from the President to the courts "the undifferentiated public interest in executive officers compliance with the law" is to "transfer from the President to the courts the Chief Executive's most important constitutional duty," to "take Care that the Laws be faithfully executed. Art. II, Sec. 3."); Allen v. Wright, 468 U.S. 737, 761, 104 S.Ct. 3315, ___, 82 L.Ed.2d 556 (1984) (The Constitution, assigns to the Executive Branch the duty, after all, to "take Care that the Laws be faithfully executed" and this assignment "counsels against recognizing standing in a case brought . . . to seek restructuring of the apparatus established by

this universal measure. The essential personal stake is that a person must "be injured in fact" by the agency action that he or she challenges.[5] Injury-in-fact underwrites sound adjudication by assuring as a rule of thumb that the plaintiff's interest in the case at hand is sufficiently great, sufficiently sited in the facts, and sufficiently opposed to the agency's position as to provide "the concrete adverseness which sharpens the presentation of issues."[6]

"Injury-in-fact" serves a separation of powers as it limits courts to the judicial function as it has been understood since *Marbury v. Madison*. In and since *Marbury*, courts have understood that at times they might decide matters of great moment to the nation. But at the same time courts have understood that they might do so only in the context of cases brought by individuals seeking to avoid real and appreciable injury to them.[7] The pronouncement of *Marbury* was that it was an appropriate function, and indeed duty, of the courts to be open to "every individual to claim the protection of the laws, whenever he receives an injury."[8] The courts must thus be open and must decide, but as they do so their decisions are, under the terms of *Marbury,* grounded in the concrete circumstances of the injury that a person claims. In this way, the courts avoid the more general, more abstract, and more comprehensive disputes that are typically the domain of the political branches and in this way standing is "founded on a concern about the proper—and properly limited—role of the courts in a democratic society."[9]

the Executive Branch to fulfill its legal duties").

5. Association of Data Processing Service Organizations, Inc. v. Camp, 397 U.S. 150, 152, 90 S.Ct. 827, 829, 25 L.Ed.2d 184 (1970).

6. "We may reasonably expect that a person so harmed will, as best he can, frame the relevant questions with specificity, contest the issues with the necessary adverseness, and pursue the litigation vigorously." Association of Data Processing Service Organizations, Inc. v. Camp, supra, at 172, 90 S.Ct. at 841 (Brennan, concurring).

7. Accordingly, in Warth v. Seldin, 422 U.S. 490, 499, 95 S.Ct. 2197, 45 L.Ed.2d 343 (1975), the Court noted that "The Art. III judicial power exists only to redress or otherwise to protect against injury to the complaining party, even though the court's judgment may benefit others collaterally." *See also* Massachusetts v. Mellon, 262 U.S. 447, 448, 43 S.Ct. 597, 601, 67 L.Ed. 1078 (1923) ("We have no power per se to review and annul acts of Congress.... That question may be considered only when the justification of some direct injury suffered or threatened, presenting a justiciable issue, is made to rest upon such an act").

8. Marbury v. Madison, 5 U.S. (1 Cranch) 137, 163, 2 L.Ed. 60 (1803).

9. Warth v. Seldin, supra note 7, 422 U.S. at 498. The Supreme Court's disinclination to attribute standing to a person that claims only a "generalized grievance," one where an injury is to the public, may be laid to these separation of powers concerns. As said by the Supreme Court, "the Court has sometimes determined that where a large numbers of Americans suffer alike, the political process rather than the judicial process, may provide the more appropriate remedy for a widely shared grievance." Federal Election Commission v. Akins, 524 U.S. 11, 23, 118 S.Ct. 1777, 1785, 141 L.Ed.2d 10 (1998). This case, *Federal Election v. Akins*, does, however, does seem to relax, if only for the circumstances at hand, the Court's aversion to hearing "generalized grievances." In *Atkins* the Court held that a plaintiff that complained of the Federal Election Commission's wrongfully refused to require a political group to divulge information about election related activities, had standing, notwithstanding the government contention that the information was owed not to the plaintiff specifically but to the public at large. In this holding, the Court emphasized that this information was useful to the plaintiff's important interest in voting, and on this basis distinguished the case from other decisions denying standing where the duty was to the public generally.

The cases carry out this fundamental regard for separated powers. In *Allen v. Wright,* plaintiffs, who were parents of children attending public schools, brought a nation-wide class action alleging that the Internal Revenue Service had inadequately implemented federal law that denied tax exempt status to racially discriminatory private schools and that some number of such private schools had therefore not been identified by the Service and thus had wrongly received a tax break. A claim of injury was that the chances of plaintiffs' children at receiving a racially integrated education in their public schools were diminished inasmuch as white students were drawn from these schools by segregated private schools. This claim of injury, the Court held, was for several reasons too attenuated and uncertain to count as injury-in-fact. As plaintiffs failed to state an injury to them, their stake in the action was reduced to that of an undifferentiated interest in how an agency, the IRS, performed its public law responsibilities. That, the Court explained, would not do for standing:

> Carried to its logical end, [plaintiffs] approach would have the federal courts as virtually continuing monitors of the wisdom and soundness of Executive action; such a role is appropriate for the Congress acting through its committees and the "power of the purse;" it is not the role of the judiciary, absent actual present or immediately threatened injury resulting from unlawful governmental action.[10]

So, in parts pertaining to assuring a sound adjudication and in other parts to maintaining an appropriate separation between that which suits judicial resolution and that which is more appropriate for political determination, standing remains a "complicated specialty of federal jurisdiction."[11]

And complicated all the more so today: The basic "injury-in-fact requirement has been elaborated so that it includes considerations of 'causation' ('a causal connection between the injury and the conduct complained of')" and "redressability" (that the injury will "likely . . . be redressed by a favorable decision").[12] Also, wholly apart from injury-in-fact, the Supreme Court has for administrative law especially established a second measure that it speaks of as standing. This measure is that the plaintiff be within a statutory "zone of interests." And apart from injury-in-fact, causation, redressability, and the "zone-of-interests" test, standing also entails a concept of "associational standing" and further entails the curiously inter-related concepts of "prudential standing" and "standing statutes."

In the succeeding sections, we discuss these various parts, trying to understand the difficult question of standing. The question may be

10. Allen v. Wright, 468 U.S. 737, 758, 104 S.Ct. 3315, 3328, 82 L.Ed.2d 556 (1984).

11. U.S. ex rel. Chapman v. FPC, 345 U.S. 153, 156, 73 S.Ct. 609, 612, 97 L.Ed. 918 (1953).

12. Bennett v. Spear, 520 U.S. 154, 167, 117 S.Ct. 1154, 1163, 137 L.Ed.2d 281 (1997); Lujan v. Defenders of Wildlife, 504 U.S. 555, 560–61, 112 S.Ct. 2130, 2136–37, 119 L.Ed.2d 351 (1992).

difficult but it is necessary. For some time, the courts have understood that "the judicial power" is not an altogether malleable power, that it must, as we said, conform to the competency of courts and to the "the proper—and properly limited—role of the courts in a democratic society."[13] Commencing with *Marbury v. Madison*, the courts have also understood that the plaintiff's injury and interest in a case, *i.e.*, standing, is key to a properly defined judicial power. There may or may not be better terms by which to deploy the judicial power, but the fact is that these terms of standing are those that the courts have settled on and are those that the courts will likely keep.

Still, the particular adjustment of these terms to the various social policies implemented by administrative agencies has been and will be a matter of debate. One constant part of this debate is this: those who have standing influence agency implementation of social policy. People with the power to sue can expose the agency to judicial review and possible correction, and certainly to the expenses and delays of that review. Standing thus creates special "stakeholders" who may skew agency policy simply because they hold the power to take the agency to court.[14] Accordingly, a concern is that in its complexity, standing may be too easily manipulated by courts so as to create their own preferred body of stakeholders and thus their own preferred social policy. This seems more a possibility than a practice. However, the possibility in and of itself places a burden on the courts of keeping standing neutral and agnostic in terms of social policy and to do so by as much as possible not allowing standing to establish special classes of stakeholders.

§ 12.7.1 The Administrative Law Origins of Standing

Standing is ubiquitous. It is required in all cases, be they common law, constitutional, or statutory in origin. But while standing is universal in its application, the origins of it as it is today are largely in the public law context that is administrative law. It is here—in the circumstances of private parties with partial interests trying to curtail agencies presumably bent on the larger, collective good—that the problems that standing entails were first encountered and first answered.

In this context of reconciling private interests and agency visions of the public good, the courts developed what was known as either the "legal wrong" or "legal interest" measure of standing. In 1970, though, standing underwent a tidal change. In *Association of Data Processing v. Camp*, the legal-wrong/legal-interest was supplanted by the present injury-in-fact and zone-of-interest requirements. The legal-wrong/legal interest measure (which we will for convenience refer to as the "legal-

13. Warth v. Seldin, 422 U.S. 490, 498, 95 S.Ct. 2197, 45 L.Ed.2d 343 (1975). *See also* Hayburn's Case, 2 U.S. (2 Dall.) 409, 1 L.Ed. 436 (1792); Massachusetts v. Mellon, 262 U.S. 447, 448, 43 S.Ct. 597, 601, 67 L.Ed. 1078 (1923).

14. Buzbee, Expanding the Zone, Tilting the Field: Zone of Interests and Article III Standing Analysis, Bennett v. Spear, 49 Ad. L.Rev. 763, 768–73 (1997).

wrong test") is now usually thought of as hopelessly wrong-headed and thus appropriately dumped, which may be generally correct.

The legal-wrong test was restrictive and in being so left a number of agency actions outside the range of judicial review. Nor was the test a model of clarity, at least not in the way we today approach the problem of availability of review. Today we try to separate questions of standing from those of jurisdiction (or "reviewability") as might be conferred by statutory provisions for judicial review of agency actions. As we have discussed, by jurisdictional statutes Congress often establishes a division of labor between courts and agencies, by shaping and limiting judicial review so as to give agencies a primary space in which to resolve the matters delegated to them. Under the legal-wrong, questions of standing and jurisdiction were often lumped together. But while the legal-wrong test was subject to these criticisms of being unduly restrictive and of conflating jurisdiction and standing, a important and enduring theme runs through the cases that applied this test, the theme being that of identifying an appropriate connection between the plaintiff, the agency action in question, and the public law program at stake. The necessity of an appropriate connection reemerges, as we shall see, in such facets of modern standing as "causation" and the "zone of interest" tests.

* * *

The 1938 Supreme Court decision in *Alabama Power Company v. Ickes* is a prime example of the legal-wrong/legal-interest measure of standing.[15] A New Deal agency, the Federal Emergency Administrator, intended to grant subsidies (a package of loans and grants) to municipal power companies. A private utility company, Alabama Power, sued to enjoin those federal subsidies on the constitutional ground that they violated the reserve power of the states and on the statutory ground that the subsidies were not authorized by the relevant acts of Congress. The plaintiff claimed it had standing inasmuch as it would suffer financial loss by the competition of the utility companies that the federal grants and loans would revive.

But to have standing, the Court explained, the plaintiff must allege a "wrong which results in the violation of a legal right." Suppose, said the Court, that Grocer A seeks to borrow from a company whose corporate charter might not allow the loan. Suppose that a rival, Grocer B, seeks to enjoin the loan on the grounds that it exceeded the lender's power. Could B bring the suit? Certainly not, said the Court, because the loan to Grocer A, however unlawful it might otherwise be, violated no legal duty that the lender owed the plaintiff, Grocer B. This same reasoning, the Court then explained, applied to Alabama Power. That firm complained of the competitive injury to it cause by the allegedly unlawful subsidies to rival utilities. But this competition was itself lawful and in it these utilities violated no duty owed Alabama Power. Hence,

15. 302 U.S. 464, 58 S.Ct. 300, 82 L.Ed. 374 (1938).

the allegedly improper subsidies cause no "legal wrong" to Alabama Power.

* * *

The wrongful acts of the New Deal agencies might indeed cause collateral damage, as the subsidies in *Alabama Power v. Ickes* may have caused incidental competitive injury. (Given the economic focus of the New Deal agencies, this sort of economic injury was frequently incurred and frequently challenged.) But for standing it was not enough that an agency act be wrong and injurious. Rather, the allegation had to be that the agency had erred by violating a duty that it owed directly and specifically to the plaintiff. These sorts of duties were typically established by the common law. Thus, should an agency trespass on a person's property, that person would have standing to sue on the trespass. Or should an agency break a contract with a person that person had standing to sue on the contract. Infrequently, a statute might be particular and direct enough to establish a duty that ran from an agency to a person. In that case, the person had standing to sue the agency if it violated that duty.[16] But the instances where statutes created such a bilateral relation were infrequent.

As the legal wrong test limited standing to instances of bilateral relation (A owes a duty to B), it generally precluded standing where a plaintiff sought to correct the agency where it had erred in its public responsibilities (even though the plaintiff might suffer collateral injury). In the usual multi-lateral, public-interest context of public law, no special duties ran to an individual, no bilateral relations are implicated, and standing to correct agency error in the law was, under the legal-interest/legal wrong test, hard to come by. With the New Deal and a new faith in agencies as prime repositories of the public welfare, this result was not unwelcome. In its public responsibilities an agency might resolve various interests, balancing, say, productivity against safety against consumer costs, and so forth. In terms of standing the idea was that in their efforts to serve the greater public interest, agencies should not be burdened, impeded, or harassed by individuals suing to maintain only

16. See The Chicago Junction Case, 264 U.S. 258, 44 S.Ct. 317, 68 L.Ed. 667 (1924). In this case, the Interstate Commerce Commission had approved the New York Central's acquisition of a rail terminal in Chicago. Prior to this purchase, the terminal had been open to the various railroads coming into Chicago. New York Central, though, planned to reserve the terminal for its own exclusive use. Railroads who thus stood to lose the use of the terminal, and to lose it to their competitor the New York Central, then sued. The Commission, however, argued that the "plaintiffs' have not the legal interest necessary to entitle them to challenge the order." 264 U.S. at 262, 44 S.Ct. at 318. The Court held that the plaintiffs' did have a sufficient "legal interest." It found that the injury complained of was not simply the general injury "incident to more effective competition." Instead, the issue at stake was whether plaintiffs had been denied equal access to the terminal when such access, it was alleged, had been specially guaranteed the plaintiffs by the relevant statutes. In the Court's view, "by reason of this legislation, the plaintiffs ... have a special interest in the proposal to transfer the control to that company." 264 U.S. at 267, 44 S.Ct. at 320. At issue, then, was a statutory duty running to plaintiffs.

their own particular and hence smaller interest. Justice Frankfurter stated these terms as follows:

> In these agencies are lodged the resources for compounding the manifold ingredients of "the public interest." To entrust the vindication of this public interest to a private litigant professing a special stake in the public interest is to impinge on the responsibility of the public authorities designated by Congress.[17]

But faiths change, and agencies came to be viewed not simply as general repositories of the public interest. To be sure, agencies were typically delegated large public responsibilities, but as attitudes changed it was more clearly seen that these responsibilities were defined and contained by law. In this light, agency decisions were not disembodied determinations of the public interest and courts were not out of their element as they might correct these decisions. Rather, courts were acting squarely within their competence as they interpreted the law to which agencies were subject. Consequently, individuals complaining about agency actions were not seen as just "private litigant professing a special stake" who might "impinge" on the greater responsibility of agencies to serve the greater collective good. Rather, these individual were seen more as litigants who might usefully get the courts plugged into an administrative system at a good place to correct error.[18] Qualification to sue might now be measured *not* by the bilateral arrangements of the legal-wrong/legal-interest test but instead by whether a party had a sufficient stake in the action to be a good plaintiff. As much as any case, the Supreme Court decision in *FCC v. Sanders Brothers Radio Station* was seen as marking this change in attitude and its relation to standing.[19]

17. L. Singer & Sons v. Union Pacific R. Co., 311 U.S. 295, 61 S.Ct. 254, 85 L.Ed. 198 (1940) (concurring). Frankfurter added that "to allow any private interest to thrash out the complicated questions ... is to invite dislocation of the scheme which Congress has devised for the expert conduct of the litigation of such issues. It would also put upon the district courts the task of drawing fine lines in determining when a private claim is so special that it may be set apart from the general public interest and give the claimant power to litigate a public controversy." 311 U.S. at 307, 61 S.Ct. at 259. See also Johnson v. Chesapeake & Ohio Ry. Co., 188 F.2d 458, 458–59 (4th Cir.1951), cert. denied 342 U.S. 833, 72 S.Ct. 43, 96 L.Ed. 630 (1951) (*per curiam*).

18. Office of Communication of United Church of Christ v. FCC, 359 F.2d 994, 1003–04 (D.C.Cir.1966), appeal after remand 425 F.2d 543 (D.C.Cir.1969).

The court here found that the agency is "directed by Congress to protect the public interest" and the theory that the agency does so is "one of those assumptions that we collectively work with so long as they are reasonably adequate". But "When it becomes clear, as it does to us now, that it is no longer a valid assumption ... neither we nor the Commission can continue to rely upon it." See also Scenic Hudson Preservation Conference v. FPC, 354 F.2d 608 (2d Cir.1965), cert. denied 384 U.S. 941, 86 S.Ct. 1462, 16 L.Ed.2d 540 (1966) ("In order to insure that the Federal Power Commission will adequately protect the public interest in the aesthetic, conservational, and recreational aspects of power development, those who by their activities and conduct have exhibited special interest in such areas, must be held to be included in the class of 'aggrieved' parties' ").

19. *FCC v. Sanders Brothers Radio Station*, 309 U.S. 470, 477 60 S.Ct. 693, 698, 84 L.Ed. 869 (1940). The Court referred to Sanders Brothers "standing" to appeal the Commission's decision. More accurately, though, the case was about subject-matter jurisdiction, whether the judicial review provisions of the Communications Act provided the courts with jurisdic-

The Sanders Brothers and another company, a newspaper, had both applied for permits for a radio station in East Dubuque, Illinois. In a consolidated hearing, the Federal Communications Commission considered both applications and then granted both permits. Pursuant to the judicial review provisions of the Federal Communications Act, Sanders Brothers appealed this action. It claimed that the Commission had erred in granting the other permit because advertising revenues would not adequately support two stations in that locale. Sanders Brothers cast this argument in terms of a competitive injury to it and claimed that the Communications Act required that the Commission take such injury into account as it granted broadcast permits.

The Commission opposed the appeal on the basis that the Communications Act, as it provided for judicial review of Commission actions, did so only for persons "aggrieved or whose interests are adversely affected by" the action. The Commission reasoned the Communications Act did not make competitive injury a factor that it should take into account in granting licenses. This meant that the Commission was under no duty to assure that Sanders Brothers or anyone else was free of competitive injury. In turn, because Sanders Brothers, in that it alleged only competitive injury, could not have suffered a "legal wrong" and could not, therefore, be an aggrieved or adversely affected party as required by the Act.

On the merits, the Supreme Court found that same as the Commission argued, it was not required to take competitive injury into account in granting broadcast permits. But that did not mean that Sanders Brothers lacked "standing" to appeal the Commission's action in granting a license. The idea behind the statutory "aggrieved or adversely affected" condition of judicial review, the Court reasoned, was that "one likely to be financially injured ... would be the only person having a sufficient interest to bring to the attention of the appellate court errors of law in the action of the Commission." Thus, "standing" to seek judicial review was tied not to the merits of the Commission's action but to the allegation of an injury sufficient to cause a party reliably to bring to the court possible agency errors. In this way, standing commenced to be aligned with what are today considered as the Article III grounds of simply securing a good plaintiff.

§ 12.7.2 The New Measure of Standing: *Association of Data Processing Service Organization v. Camp*

In 1970, the Supreme Court disowned the legal-wrong test of standing and rather abruptly established the modern framework of standing. In *Association of Data Processing Service Organizations, Inc. v. Camp,*[20]

tion to hear Sanders Brothers appeal. Be that as it may, the *Sanders Brothers* case was and is widely considered as a standing case and the part of it that focused on whether the plaintiff is so injured as to be a good plaintiff is relevant to standing.

20. 397 U.S. 150, 90 S.Ct. 827, 25 L.Ed.2d 184 (1970).

plaintiffs who sold data processing services challenged a Comptroller of Currency decision that permitted national banks to provide similar services. The plaintiffs' interest in bringing the suit was simply that of avoiding the competitive injury caused by banks entering their line of work. Because plaintiffs had no legally protected right to be free of competition, the lower court dismissed their case for lack of standing. On review, the Supreme Court, in an opinion by Justice Douglas, reversed that decision and dismissed, for all time, the legal-wrong/legal-interest test.

That test was defective in that it went "to the merits." "The question of standing", Douglas then said, "is different." Evidently, Douglas considered that standing ought to be a singular inquiry, apart from and antecedent to the questions of law and fact that constitute the merits of a case, and that this more detached inquiry could be generated by grounding standing in Article III. For the Court, Justice Douglas wrote that standing "is to be considered in the framework of Article III." In this framework, the question was "whether the dispute will be presented in an adversary context and in a form historically viewed as capable of judicial resolution." This context and form was assured by requiring that the plaintiff be "injured in fact, economic or otherwise." In the instant case, the financial injury that plaintiffs faced because of bank competition met this "injury in fact" requirement.

A majority of the Court went further. For this majority, Douglas was not content to leave standing to a constitutional minimum of "injury in fact," at least not in the administrative law context. In this context, Douglas asserted that standing involved the additional question of "whether the interest sought to be protected by the complainant was arguably within the zone of interests to be protected or regulated by the statute ... in question." In the instant case, the "statute in question" was a provision of the Bank Service Corporation Act that stated that "No bank service corporation may engage in any activity other than the performance of bank services." The majority concluded that as the Act thus limited "banks to banking" it included a non-banking competitor within "the zone of interests protected by it."

This second, "zone-of-interests" requirement was derived from the Administrative Procedure Act. As said by Justice Douglas, "[T]he Administrative Procedure Act grants standing to a person aggrieved by agency action within the meaning of a relevant statute." In this respect, Justice Douglas referred to and paraphrased Sec. 702 of the Act, which section provides that a person "adversely affected or aggrieved by agency action within the meaning of a relevant statute is entitled to judicial review thereof."[21]

* * *

The opinion in *Association of Data Processing* is, as we shall see, in certain respects a somewhat cobbled effort. Nonetheless, the opinion was

21. 5 U.S.C. Sec. 702.

sufficiently well-timed to be the new foundation for standing in the administrative state. This foundation is of two parts: (1) whether the plaintiff was injured-in-fact by the action and (2) whether plaintiff's injury was "arguable within the zone of interests to be protected or regulated by the statute ... in question." In creating this foundation, Justice Douglas said, the Court was but following "the trend toward enlarging the class of people who may protest administrative actions."

However, Justice Brennan, who concurred and dissented, thought the Court had in one respect needlessly restricted standing and had thus violated its goal of "enlarging the class of people who may protest administrative actions." The "injury-in-fact" requirement, he agreed, was constitutionally required and therefore essential to standing. But the second requirement, that a plaintiff's interest be within the zone of interests of a relevant statute was an extra and unnecessary hurdle that needlessly restricted access to the courts. Unlike Douglas, Brennan found no purchase for the zone-of-interest restriction in the Administrative Procedure Act. Sec. 702 of that Act, he wrote, was not meant to limit review above and in addition to the constitutional minimum of injury-in-fact. According to the prevailing view, which Douglas had ignored, Sec. 702 established a presumption in favor of judicial review for persons harmed by agency implementation of statutory law.[22] For this and other reasons, Brennan was of the opinion that injury-in-fact should be the sole test of standing and that the additional "within the zone of interests" requirement was a misplaced limitation to standing.

But whatever its weaknesses, *Association of Data Processing* did detach standing from prior requirements of a bilateral, duty-invested relation between plaintiff and agency, a relation hard to satisfy in many cases. Also, the Article III-based goal that *Association of Data Processing* freshly embraced, that of securing a plaintiff who will thoroughly and vigorously prosecute a case, is a worthy if not an essential goal. But laudable as the new basis and aspiration of standing might be, the path that standing has taken after *Association of Data Processing* has not been altogether straight and clear. In the next sections we will pick up this path, and we will do so in the context of the two-part test of *Association of Data Processing:* Its injury-in-fact requirement, which has become more elaborate by addition of requirements of causation and "redressability", and its "zone of interests" requirement, which as Justice Brennan anticipated, has been something of a problem.

§ 12.7.3 Injury–In–Fact

As a common measure of standing, the injured-in-fact measure of standing has much to recommend it. It is a generally reliable means of

22. 397 U.S. at 168, 90 S.Ct. at 838. The prevailing, and judicial-review favoring view of Sec. 702, was that "the Administrative Procedure Act ... embodies the basic presumption of judicial review to one 'suffering legal wrong because of agency action, or adversely affected or aggrieved by agency action within the meaning of a relevant statute,' 5 U.S.C. Sec. 702." Abbott Laboratories v. Gardner, 387 U.S. 136, 87 S.Ct. 1507, 18 L.Ed.2d 681 (1967).

securing a plaintiff grounded in the facts and with a stake in the action that assures a vigorous presentation of the case. As the injury must be personal, it is responsive to the felt notion—and the premise of *Marbury v. Madison*—that a person who is in some singular way the victim of a public action ought especially to have access to the courts.

Certain characteristics of injury-in-fact are established. To prevent waste, the injury need not be completed; instead, it may be prospective. If too far in the future, though, the injury may be so speculative as to implicate the courts in advisory opinions. The courts, therefore, require that injury if not "eminent" be at least close at hand.[23] The injury—present or prospective—that suffices for standing includes a wide range of impairments. It includes a plaintiff's economic well-being and health. It includes her aesthetic concerns such as those that might be associated with environmental damage.[24] It includes infringement of common-law and constitutional rights. The injury can be, and often is, of a statutory source; that is, "the actual or threatened injury required by Art. III" may exist solely by virtue of "statutes creating legal rights, the invasion of which creates standing."[25] The injury may be "procedural," which injury commonly consists of an agency *not* adhering to a decisional requirement, such as cross-examination, that is owed an individual. But it is also the case that a failure to observe procedural requirements that are not specifically owed to individuals (*e.g.*, the form of environmental analysis required by the National Environmental Policy Act) can count for "procedural" injury that confers standing.[26]

But however broadly the impairments—economic, aesthetic, procedural, or otherwise—that constitute "injury" are defined, it remains the case that injury-in-fact must be particular to the plaintiff. The injury must be "personal" and "distinct," which among other things means that the general objection that an agency is incorrectly enforcing the law does not, not by itself, count as standing.

In *Lujan v. Wildlife Defenders,* plaintiffs alleged that the Department of Interior had wrongfully determined that Endangered Species Act did not apply to U.S.-supported projects in foreign nations. But because plaintiffs failed to allege a sufficiently imminent injury to themselves, they were—in the Court's view—left in the position of asserting a general grievance respecting the agency's alleged failure properly to implement the Endangered Species Act. That general grievance did not constitute standing. As said by Justice Scalia, "a plaintiff

23. Lujan v. Defenders of Wildlife, 504 U.S. 555, 112 S.Ct. 2130, 119 L.Ed.2d 351 (1992).

24. For example, the allegation that plaintiff lived near the Tyger River, and "that it looked and smelled polluted; and that he would like to fish, camp, swim, and picnic in and near the river ... as he did when he was a teenager" established injury in fact. Friends of the Earth v. Laidlaw Environmental Services, 528 U.S. 167, 120 S.Ct. 693, 145 L.Ed.2d 610 (2000).

25. Havens Realty Corp. v. Coleman, 455 U.S. 363, 374, 102 S.Ct. 1114, 1121, 71 L.Ed.2d 214 (1982).

26. Bennett v. Spear, 520 U.S. 154, 117 S.Ct. 1154, 137 L.Ed.2d 281 (1997). See also Lujan v. Defenders of Wildlife, 504 U.S. 555, ___, nn.7–8, 112 S.Ct. 2130, 119 L.Ed.2d 351 (1992).

raising only a generally available grievance about government—claiming only harm to his and every citizen's interest in proper application of the Constitution and laws, and seeking relief that no more directly and tangibly benefits him than it does the public at large—does not state an Article III case or controversy."[27] This sort of generalized grievance is taken as an indication that the conflict at hand is more about the collective good than individual injury and in being so better suited to resolution by the political branches than by the courts.[28]

While there is much to be said for the injury-in-fact requirement, it has not, in one respect, fully met the aspirations of *Association of Data Processing.* As the Court in that case established the modern framework of standing, it did so with the aim of disconnecting standing from the merits, so that standing would not entail a preliminary inquiry into the merits. That disconnect has not always been accomplished, particularly in the context of injury-in-fact as it might be based on an invasion of rights created by statute.

Under the Fair Housing Act, housing firms must not lie to people—because of their race—about the availability of housing. Section 804(d)of the Act makes it unlawful for a firm "To represent to any person because of race, color, religion, sex, or national origin that any dwelling is not avoidable for inspection, sale, or rental when such dwelling is in fact so available."[29] In *Havens Realty v. Coleman,*[30] a housing firm allegedly gave false information, for reasons of race, about the availability of rental apartments. For that alleged misrepresentation, a suit was filed claiming that Sec. 804(d) of the Act had been violated.

The plaintiffs included "testers," people hired (by a public interest firm) to pretend to seek housing so that the truthfulness of housing information might be checked. Injury-in-fact as claimed by these testers was based on Sec. 804(d) of the Fair Housing Act. Clearly, the rights and duties established by that provision ran to persons who sought housing and then were lied to because of their race. However, the testers had not sought housing, just information. In this context, the Court—for purposes of determining standing—went ahead and made a determination of the scope, that is, of the merits, of Sec. 804(d). That statute, the Court found, broadly "conferred on all 'persons' a legal right to truthful information about 'available housing.' " Therefore, "That the tester may have approached the real estate agent fully expecting that he would

27. Lujan v. Defenders of Wildlife, 504 U.S. 555, 560–61, 112 S.Ct. 2130, 2136–37, 119 L.Ed.2d 351 (1992). The Supreme Court has, however, distinguished an injury that is "widely shared" from the untenable "generalized grievance." For instance, the injury of a "mass tort," albeit widely shared, would nonetheless confer standing. *See* Federal Election Commission v. Akins, 524 U.S. 11, 118 S.Ct. 1777, 141 L.Ed.2d 10 (1998). In the same way, a widely shared injury based on statutory right, if that injury is specific and concrete and non-abstract in relation to the plaintiff, may also confer standing. *Id.*

28. Richardson and also Lujan v. Defenders of Wildlife, 504 U.S. 555, 560–61, 112 S.Ct. 2130, 2136–37, 119 L.Ed.2d 351 (1992).

29. 42 U.S.C. Sec. 3604(d).

30. Havens Realty Corp. v. Coleman, 455 U.S. 363, 374, 102 S.Ct. 1114, 1121, 71 L.Ed.2d 214 (1982).

receive false information, and without any intention of buying or renting a home, does not negate the simple fact of injury within the meaning of Sec. 804(d)."

In relation to standing and injury-in-fact, the lesson of *Havens Realty* is that in cases of statutory injury, courts in determining standings have not and probably cannot wholly abjure from preliminary findings respecting the merits, notwithstanding that those sort of findings were disapproved in *Association of Data Processing*.[31]

§ 12.7.4 Ideological Plaintiffs an "Associational" Standing

However extensive the interests covered by the injury-in-fact requirement may be, purely ideological interests are not among them. In *Sierra Club v. Morton*,[32] the Sierra Club claimed that the United States Forest Service's approval of a Walt Disney project on lands adjacent to the Sequoia National Forest violated several statutory provisions and sought judicial review of that approval. While the Supreme Court recognized that the "attendant changes to the ecology in the area" was an injury that would support standing, it nonetheless held that the Sierra Club had no standing because it was not itself injured. The rule laid down by the Court was that "the injury in fact test requires more than injury to a cognizable interest. It requires that the party seeking review be himself among the injured." The Sierra Club was not "among the injured" in that "Nowhere in the pleadings or the affidavits did the Club state that its members use Mineral King for any purpose, much less that they use it in anyway that would be significantly affected by the proposed actions. . . ."

As explained by the Court, "a mere 'interest in a problem,' no matter how long-standing the interest and no matter how qualified the organization is in evaluating the problem" is not enough for standing. The reasons for this bar to merely ideological plaintiffs are several. A reliable and "objective basis" by which to separate a sufficiently resourceful and committed ideological plaintiff from the "small and short-lived" litigants seems to be lacking. Also, ideological plaintiffs might create an element of paternalism, and inaccuracy. Not standing precisely in the injured party's shoes, these plaintiffs might not, on the average, understand the pinch.[33] Moreover, opening the courts' doors to parties who are not directly injured might politicize judicial processes. In *Sierra*

31. See generally William A. Fletcher, The Structure of Standing, 98 Yale L.J. 221 (1988).

32. Sierra Club v. Morton, 405 U.S. 727, 92 S.Ct. 1361, 31 L.Ed.2d 636 (1972).

33. As the Supreme Court has explained:

> The Art. III aspect of standing also reflects a due regard for the autonomy of those persons likely to be most directly affected by a judicial order. The federal courts have abjured appeals to their authority which would convert the judicial process into no more than a vehicle for the vindication of the value interests of concerned bystanders.

Valley Forge Christian College v. Americans United for Separation of Church and State, Inc., 454 U.S. 464, 473, 102 S.Ct. 752, 70 L.Ed.2d 700 (1982).

Club v. Morton, the Court referred to Alexis de Tocqueville's "famous observation" that "Scarcely any political question arises in the United States that is not resolved, sooner or later, into a judicial question." But as the Court also noted, less familiar was his "further observation that judicial review is effective largely because it is not available simply at the behest of a partisan faction, but is exercised only to remedy a particular, concrete injury."[34]

But while the Supreme Court held that an ideological interest was insufficient for standing, the Court did not at the same time deny the capacity of the Sierra Club, or any similar ideological organization, to bring a suit, once one or some number of its members are injured in some conventional, non-ideological way.[35] An association's capacity to sue on behalf of injured members is known as "associational standing." The justification for such standing is that of bringing the often significant resources of an association into play, once one of its members is injured. "Besides financial resources," the Court has said, "organizations often have specialized expertise and research resources relating to the subject matter of the lawsuit that individual plaintiffs lack" and "these resources can assist both courts and plaintiffs."[36]

Injury to members, though, does not automatically confer standing on an association. The association's injured members may be so few, or their injury so unrelated to the association's ordinary interests, as to render the association a stranger to the cause of action.[37] Or, associational standing may be inappropriate because the case at hand "requires the participation of individual members."[38] In *Warth v. Seldin,* the Court denied associational standing because "whatever injury might have been suffered is peculiar to the individual member concerned, and both the fact and extent of injury would require individualized proof."[39]

34. 405 U.S. at 740–41, 92 S.Ct. at 1368–69, quoting Alex de Tocqueville, 1 Democracy in America 102, 280 (1945).

35. In *Sierra Club v. Morton*, the association lacked standing because it failed to allege a non-ideological injury to it or to its members. But where such injury has been alleged, the Court has found standing. This basis of associational standing has been explained by the Court thusly: "The association must allege that its members, or any one of them, are suffering immediate or threatened injury as a result of the challenged action of the sort that would make out a justiciable case had the members themselves brought suit." Warth v. Seldin, 422 U.S. 490, 511, 95 S.Ct. 2197, 2211, 45 L.Ed.2d 343 (1975).

36. International Union, United Automobile, Aerospace and Agricultural Implement Workers of America v. Brock, 477 U.S. 274, ___, 106 S.Ct. 2523, 91 L.Ed.2d 228 (1986). The case-law development of associational standing is summarize in United Food & Commercial Workers Union v. Brown Group, Inc., 517 U.S. 544, 116 S.Ct. 1529, 134 L.Ed.2d 758 (1996).

37. See International Union, United Automobile, Aerospace and Agricultural Implement Workers of America v. Brock, supra.

38. Hunt v. Washington State Apple Advertising Com'n, 432 U.S. 333, 343, 97 S.Ct. 2434, 2441, 53 L.Ed.2d 383 (1977).

39. 422 U.S. 490, 515–16, 95 S.Ct. 2197, 2213–14, 45 L.Ed.2d 343 (1975) (associational standing is subject to the condition that "the nature of the claim and of the relief sought does not make the individual participation of each injured party indispensable to proper resolution of the cause."). But even in the event of peculiar and individualized injury, associational standing may be appropriate where the substantive questions of a case may be decided apart from the question of injury. International Union, United Automobile, Aerospace & Agricultural Implement Workers of America v. Brock, 477 U.S. 274, 106 S.Ct. 2523, 91 L.Ed.2d 228 (1986).

Given this possibility of a divergence of interests among an association and its members, the Supreme Court has established a three-part test of associational standing that is aimed at avoiding this divergence. This test, as described by the Court, is as follows:

> [W]e have recognized that an association has standing to bring suit on behalf of its members when: (a) its members would otherwise have standing to sue in their own right; (b) the interests it seeks to protect are germane to the organization's purpose; and (c) neither the claim asserted nor the relief requested requires the participation of individual members in the lawsuit.[40]

An application of this test of associational standing, in the Supreme Court's 1996 decision in *United Food and Commercial Workers Union v. Brown Group, Inc.*, is discussed below in Sec. 12.7.6 on "Prudential Rules and Standing Statutes."

§ 12.7.5 Causation and Redressability

For plaintiff's injury to count as standing, it must be appropriately connected to the agency action in question. If the injury is not so connected, the plaintiff may be so distant from the agency action as to be a stranger to it. This sort of distance does not tend to produce plaintiffs so grounded in and affected by an agency action that they can reliably be counted on to knowledgeably and vigorously present the facts and law pertinent to the action. Also, if a plaintiff is too far removed from the agency action, a decision against the agency may not reach him, may not affect him much if at all. In this case, the decision of the court would resemble a forbidden advisory opinion.

A certain link between plaintiff's injury and the agency action in question is, therefore, required by the courts. This link is established by the requirements of causation ("a causal connection between the injury and the conduct complained of") and "redressability" (that the injury will "likely ... be redressed by a favorable decision").[41] Indeed, these matters of causation and redressability are now so strongly in place that the courts speak of standing as a "triad" consisting of injury-in-fact, causation, and redressability.

§ 12.7.5(a) Causation.

Causation, or rather the lack of it, is illustrated by *Allen v. Wright.* As previously discussed, plaintiffs in this case had alleged that the Internal Revenue Service had inadequately implemented federal law that denied tax exempt status to racially discriminatory private schools, that some unspecified number of such private schools had therefore not been identified by the IRS, and that these schools had thus wrongly received a

40. Hunt v. Washington State Apple Advertising Com'n, 432 U.S. 333, 343, 97 S.Ct. 2434, 2441, 53 L.Ed.2d 383 (1977).

41. Bennett v. Spear, 520 U.S. 154, 167, 117 S.Ct. 1154, 1163, 137 L.Ed.2d 281 (1997).

tax break. The plaintiffs were parents of children attending public schools. A claim of injury was that their children's chances of receiving a racially integrated education in their public schools were diminished inasmuch as white students were drawn from these schools by segregated private schools. This alleged injury, though, did not confer standing, because the link of causation between it and the agency action in issue was entirely too conjectural. As explained by the Court:

> It is, first, uncertain how many racially discriminatory private schools are in fact receiving tax exemptions. Moreover, it is entirely speculative ... whether a tax exemption from any particular school would lead the school to change its policies.... It is just as speculative whether any given parent of a child attending such a private school would decide to transfer the child to public school as a result of any changes in educational or financial policy made by the private school once it was threatened with loss of tax-exempt status. It is also pure speculation whether, in a particular community, a large enough number of the relevant school officials and parents would reach decisions that collectively would have a significant impact on the racial composition of the public schools.[42]

Certainly, the connection between a plaintiff's injury and the agency action in question should not be merely speculative. However, certain applications of this requirement stand to impair the ability of the courts to hear and correct a most important sector of agency action. Increasingly, Congress has favored and established agency programs that *facilitate* social goals by a set of incentives such as subsidies, tax breaks, or newly established property rights. Congress may choose these methods of assisting desirable conduct over conventional methods of compelling such conduct by command and control regulation. Facilitating as opposed to compelling private activity is less restrictive; it leaves room for private choice and adaptation to local circumstances. Thus, it may be a more accurate and efficient means of attaining the behavior best suited to a given social policy. In terms of standing, the problem is that a crudely calibrated measure of causation may defeat judicial review of agency implementation of program that depends on facilitation rather than compulsion. This problem emerged in *Simon v. Eastern Kentucky Welfare Rights Organization*[43] and was then repaired in subsequent cases.

To promote more generous medical services, Congress, by means of the Internal Revenue Code, provides a tax exempt status for corporations "organized and operated exclusively for ... charitable ... purposes."[44] The Internal Revenue Service had allowed such status only when a hospital provided full services to indigents. But then the Service changed that rule to so that hospitals might qualify for the tax exemp-

42. Allen v. Wright, 468 U.S. 737, 758, 104 S.Ct. 3315, 3328, 82 L.Ed.2d 556 (1984).

43. 426 U.S. 26, 96 S.Ct. 1917, 48 L.Ed.2d 450 (1976).

44. 26 U.S.C.A. § 501(c)(3).

tion by providing only emergency assistance to indigents. In *Simon v. Eastern Kentucky Welfare Rights Organization,* this new rule was challenged on grounds both substantive (that it violated the Code) and procedural (that appropriate rulemaking procedures had not been followed).

The plaintiffs were indigents who had been refused medical services by hospitals qualifying as charitable organizations under the new rule. This refusal of services, the Court found, amounted to "actual injury."[45] However, the court also found that this injury did not confer standing because it was not causally connected to the IRS ruling that plaintiffs challenged. Plaintiffs had alleged that the ruling had "encouraged" hospitals not to provide full services to indigents. In this context of facilitating rather than compelling charitable services, the hospital of course remained free to refuse indigent services and to forego the tax benefit and in given circumstances that choice might make better sense, in terms of economic or any number of factors, to a hospital. This being so, the Court found that the necessary causation was lacking. As stated by the Court, it was "purely speculative whether the denials of service specified in the complaint fairly can be traced to petitioners' 'encouragement' or instead result from decisions made by the hospitals without regard to the tax implications."

That statement is open to question. Surely a hospital decision regarding indigent services would not, as the Court said, be made "without regard to the tax implications." Businesses do not operate without regard to tax implications, Congress had not expected that hospitals would act without regard to tax implications, and so it had provided a tax incentive to influence the decision. Thus, it seems that the Court did not link the plaintiffs' injury to the appropriate wrong. The wrong plaintiffs complained of was not simply that of being denied services by a private hospital (which denial was not, by the way, a wrong); instead, the wrong was that the Internal Revenue Service had misconstrued the set of incentives that Congress had established for such services. Was that misconstruction connected to plaintiffs? Yes, they were indigents turned out by hospitals operating under the allegedly wrong set of incentives and their interest was in medical services according to the incentives Congress had established.[46]

45. Respecting the plaintiffs' injury, the Court stated: "The obvious interest of all respondents, to which they claim actual injury, is that of access to hospital services. In one sense, of course, they have suffered injury to that interest. The complaint alleges specific occasions on which each of the individual respondents sought but was denied hospital services solely due to his indigency. . . ." 426 U.S. at 40–41, 96 S.Ct. at 1925–26.

46. In *Association of Date Processing,* the plaintiff's claim, as Justice Brennan explained, was not "and by its very nature could not be, that they have been and will be illegally denied the provision of indigent medical services by the hospitals. Rather, if respondents have a claim cognizable under the law, it is that the Internal Revenue Code requires the Government to offer economic inducements to the relevant hospitals only under conditions which are likely to benefit respondents." 426 U.S. at 48, 56 (concurring and dissenting). See also Chayes, Public Law Litigation and the Burger Court, 96 Harv.L.Rev. 4, 18–19 (1982), where Chayes explains that what was at stake in *Eastern Kentucky Welfare*

To not regard that as a interest sufficient for standing is, as we said, to limit judicial review where Congress has chosen to facilitate rather than to compel a selected social policy.[47] Where the method is to facilitate, the purpose of judicial review, as Justice Brennan explained, ought to remain the same, that of "ensur[ing] that the attainment of congressionally mandated goals is not frustrated by illegal action."[48] Fortunately, since *Simon v. Eastern Kentucky Welfare Workers* the Court has changed the restrictive "but for" causation of that case to better to allow for such review.

One change has been linguistic, substituting a formula of "a substantial likelihood" of inducement of injury for the "but for" causation of *Eastern Kentucky Welfare Workers*. To facilitate development of nuclear power, the Price Anderson Act limited the liability of private industry to 560 million dollars per catastrophe. In *Duke Power Co. v. Carolina Environmental Study Group, Inc.,*[49] the Duke Power Company proposed to build nuclear power plants. Environmental plaintiffs wished to avoid that construction and toward that end they asked the courts to find the Price Anderson Act unconstitutional. The injury they asserted was largely environmental ("the thermal pollution of . . . lakes in the vicinity"). For this injury, though, causation as required by *Eastern Kentucky Welfare Workers* could not be satisfied. Even if the Court overturned the Price Anderson Act's incentive of limited liability, Duke Power might yet build the plants. Be that as it may, in *Duke Power* the Court found causation. The trial court had found a "substantial likelihood" that the plants would not be built and that the environmental injury would thus be averted if the Price Anderson Act was overturned. That "substantial likelihood," the Supreme Court ruled, was a connection sufficient for standing.

A case that more directly correlates causation to programs that seek to facilitate rather than to coerce socially beneficial programs is the Supreme Court decision on the "line-item veto." The Line Item Veto Act of 1996 authorized the President to veto portions of a bill without vetoing the entire bill. In *Clinton v. New York*, the bill was challenged as unconstitutional in that the "Presentment Clause" of the Constitution allowed the President to veto a bill only in its entirety. Using the line-

Rights Organization was "not the interest in obtaining free medical services at a particular hospital but in having hospitals' decisions reflect accurately the incentive structure that Congress established." 426 U.S. at 56, 96 S.Ct. at 1932.

47. *Eastern Kentucky Welfare Rights Organization* seems to have no application to command and control regulation. For instance, in *Association of Data Processing*, the agency, acting according to command and control regulation, had rescinded its previous rule prohibiting banks from providing data processing services to customers. That action, as the Court held, injured bank competitors. That injury certainly was traceable to the agency action, because "but for" the rule rescission, the banks would not have been in the data processing business. The relief that plaintiffs requested was reinstatement of the rule, and certainly that relief would remove plaintiffs injury. In just this way, the *Eastern Kentucky Welfare Rights Organization* factors of causation and redress are automatically satisfied in the context of command and control regulation.

48. 426 U.S. at 65, 96 S.Ct. at 1937.

49. 438 U.S. 59, 98 S.Ct. 2620, 57 L.Ed.2d 595 (1978).

item veto, President Clinton had vetoed a item of the Tax Payers Relief Act of 1997 that permitted "owners of curtain food refiners and processors to defer the recognition of gain if they sell their stock to eligible farmers cooperatives." The purpose of this item was " 'to facilitate the transfer of refiners and processors to farmers' cooperatives.' " A plaintiff, the Snake River Cooperative, was such a cooperative; it had been formed for the purpose of acquiring processing facilities and it now planned to use the tax benefit that Congress had provided to sellers of these facilities as a "bargaining chip" in its acquisitions.

Of course, Congress had provided only an incentive—the "bargaining chip"—to sellers. In no way were sellers compelled to sell to plaintiffs and so it could not be assured that they would. That lack of assurance was said to defeat Snake River's standing on grounds of insufficient causation. The Supreme Court held otherwise, saying that "a denial of a benefit in the bargaining process can itself create an Article III injury" and that "by depriving [the Snake River Cooperative] of their statutory bargaining chip, the [veto] inflicted a sufficient likelihood of economic injury to establish standing under our precedents."[50] *Clinton v. New York* thus recognizes that when Congress chooses to facilitate certain private action by means of incentives that change the economic environment in which such actions occur, an actor in that environment has standing to claim that an agency has misconstrued the incentives required by Congress.[51]

§ 12.7.5(b) Redressability

"Redressability" is whether the injury complained of will "likely . . . be redressed by a favorable decision." In relation to causation, redressability is, a sense, redundant. If the agency action in question has caused

50. 524 U.S. 417, 118 S.Ct. 2091, 2101 & 2101 at n. 21, 141 L.Ed.2d 393 (1998).

51. For related cases, in which the Court held that plaintiff's interest and injury was caused by a decisional process that failed to conform to the law, see Regents of University of California v. Bakke, 438 U.S. 265, 98 S.Ct. 2733, 57 L.Ed.2d 750 (1978), Northeastern Florida Chapter of Associated Gen. Contractors v. Jacksonville, 508 U.S. 656, 113 S.Ct. 2297, 124 L.Ed.2d 586 (1993), In *Bakke*, the plaintiff, claimed that an admissions process at a state medical school that established a quoto system of racial preferences was unconstitutional. If the admissions process was expunged of this allegedly illegal factor, however, that action would not have guaranteed plaintiff admission. There may have been candidates more qualified than he available. But this possibility, the Court held, did not deny standing. The plaintiff's interest, the Court found, was in an appropriate decisional process with respect to admissions. In this regard, the Court stated:

> The constitutional element of standing is plaintiff's demonstration of any injury to himself that is likely to be redressed by favorable decision of his claim. The trial court found such an injury, apart from his failure to be admitted, in the University's decision not to permit Bakke to compete for all 100 places in the class, simply because of his race. Hence the constitutional requirements of Art. III were met.

438 U.S. at 280–81 & n. 14, 98 S.Ct. at 2742–44 & n. 14. In *Northeastern Florida Chapter of Associated Gen. Contractors v. Jacksonville*, an association of contractors challenged the city of Jacksonville's affirmative action program. Even though there was no assurance that a contractor would receive a contract absent the program, the Court found standing, on the basis that the injury was in the negotiation process to which plaintiffs were subject and not in an "ultimate inability" to receive a contract. 508 U.S. at 666, 113 S.Ct. at 2203.

plaintiff's injury, then a court's correction of that action will likely redress it; if not so caused, then correction will not likely redress it. In just this sense, causation and redressability are in a number of cases conflated and these two legs to the "triad" of standing are in fact only one. Otherwise, redressability is open to the criticism that it transmutes what had been a more moderate element of equity into a harder requirement of standing.[52]

In any event, there are few cases in which redressability has been a dispositive element of standing. The Supreme Court's decision in *Steel Co. v. Citizens for a Better Environment*[53] is, however, such a case. The "Community Planning and Right to Know Act" requires firms using toxic substances to file annual reports identifying such substances and the firm's methods for disposing of them.[54] The Environmental Protection Agency may bring actions to enforce the Act, but if it declines to do so the Act provides that "any person may commence a civil action in his own behalf against . . . [a]n owner or operator of a facility" for failure to file required reports. In 1995, Citizens for a Better Environment, a public interest group, notified the Environmental Protection Agency that a small manufacturer, the steel company, had failed to file reports as required by the Act. Upon that notice, the company filed all the overdue reports and the Environmental Protection Agency declined to bring an against the company.

The public interest group then brought it own court action against the steel company under the "citizens suit" provision of the Community Planning and Right to Know Act. As plaintiffs, the public interest group asked for declaratory relief, asked for access to defendant's facilities and future compliance reports, asked that the defendant be assessed a civil penalty of $25,000 per violation, and asked that it (plaintiff) be reimbursed its litigation costs. None of these remedies, the Court found, would redress any injury that plaintiffs had suffered under Act. Thus, plaintiff had no standing inasmuch as it failed the requirement of redressability.

Declaratory relief would be pointless inasmuch as defendant had already admitted that it had wrongly failed to report. Access to defendant's facilities and future compliance reports, as further requested by the plaintiff, might avoid future failures to comply with the Act. However, plaintiff "had not alleged a continuing violation or the imminence of a future violation" of the Act nor did the facts of the case provide a basis for such allegation. The civil penalty that plaintiff requested would be paid to the United States Treasury rather than the plaintiff. This penalty, therefore, was not compensation to plaintiff for such damage as

52. The Supreme Court has recognized that "redressability" works to transmute to constitutional law what previously been more flexible matter of equity. Considerations of redressability, the Court has explained, " 'obviously shade into those determining whether the complaint states a sound basis for equitable relief.' " Allen v. Wright, 468 U.S. 737, 760, 104 S.Ct. 3315, 82 L.Ed.2d 556 (1984).

53. 523 U.S. 83, 118 S.Ct. 1003, 140 L.Ed.2d 210 (1998).

54. 42 U.S.C. Sec. 11046(a)1.

it may have suffered.[55] The litigation costs that plaintiff had incurred would amount to compensation for actual costs to plaintiffs. But these costs are a constant byproduct of litigation and recognition of them would allow each plaintiff to establish standing to bring a case simply by bringing the case. That sort of bootstrapped standing the Court would not allow. It did so by citing and following the established rule that " 'an interest in attorney's fees is . . . insufficient to create an Article III case or controversy.' "

§ 12.7.6 Procedural Injury

Often, a plaintiff will challenge an action on grounds that the agency has failed to follow procedures required by law. The alleged procedural error may be an ordinary one of, say, a failure to provide a proper hearing as required by due process or to provide rulemaking procedures as required by the Administrative Procedure Act. In these sorts of cases, a plaintiff alleges that an agency has failed to provide a procedure—such as a right to cross examination or a right as an interested party to comment on a proposed rule—that is owed directly to him. This is a standard model of procedural error. To it, in modern times, has been added a different sort of procedure & error.

Today, Congress often requires that agencies conform to certain decisional processes that require them to take into account specially identified public interests or values. These "procedural" requirements do not ordain a particular result. Instead, they simply require that the agency identify certain hazards or costs and take them into account before taking some action or the other. The National Environmental Policy Act, which requires agencies to identify and then include in their decisional processes the environmental costs of a proposed agency action, but does not mandate any particular decision, is an instance of such a process. In *Lujan v. Defenders of Wildlife*, Justice Scalia described these sort of "procedural rights" as having a "special" weight in the context of standing. Be that as it may, standing to challenge procedural error does give rise to some problems. In particular, alleged procedural errors present these two problems of standing. One problem is that of an appropriate *connection* (or "nexus") between the plaintiff's interest and the procedural scheme in question. The other problem is one of causation as we spoke of in the previous section.

When a person complains of an agency's failure to provide her with, say, a hearing consistent with due process, the courts as we know do not question that person's standing to contest that sort of procedural injury: The procedures in question are directly that individual, and this is

55. But where the defendant has not ceased its bad acts, then a civil penalty, because of their ordinary "deterrent" effect, may meet the redressability requirement as it may deter those continuing acts. Friends of the Earth v. Laidlaw, 528 U.S. 167, 120 S.Ct. 693, 145 L.Ed.2d 610 (2000)("the civil penalties sought by [plaintiff] carried with them a deterrent effect that made it likely ... that the penalties would redress [plaintiff's] injuries by abating current [environmental] violations and preventing future ones").

clearly a "connection" sufficient for standing. On the other hand, where procedures are owed more to the public at large than to a specific person, this matter of an appropriate connection is more difficult. Where a plaintiff complains of the public injury caused by a failure to file, say, an environmental impact statement, that plaintiff may well be out of court because she has not alleged a sufficiently particular injury and has in fact alleged no more than a "generalized grievance." As explained by the District of Columbia Circuit:

> In this type of case, which includes suits demanding preparation of an EIS [environmental impact statement] ... the plaintiff must show that the government act performed without the procedure in question will cause a distinct risk to a particularized interest of the plaintiff. The mere violation of a procedural requirement does not permit any and all persons to sue to enforce the requirement.

This basic requirement, that for procedural injury a plaintiff must assert more than a generalized (and thus public) interest in an agency's conforming to a prescribed decisional process, was set in *Lujan v. Defenders of Wildlife*. The dictum of that case, though, was that this relation need not be especially difficult to obtain. In this respect, Justice Scalia used the example of a "geographic nexus," and said that a person who lived next to a proposed damn would because have standing to challenge an agency failure to follow environmental impact procedures respecting the dam.[56] Accordingly, the ninth circuit, in *Douglas County v. Babbitt*,[57] held that the plaintiff's "proprietary interest" in lands adjacent to a federal land management project, for which project plaintiff alleged that an environmental impact statement was owing, was a "concrete interest" sufficient for standing.

A second problem respecting procedural standing is, as we said, one of causation. A person injured by an agency rule may challenge the rule on the ground that the agency failed to follow rulemaking procedures in adopting it. But even with appropriate procedures, the agency may still enact the very same rule. So then, one cannot say with certainty that the procedural error caused the injury. Under the rule of causation, as discussed above, this might be an issue in gaining standing. But as we all know it is not such an issue, not in an ordinary procedural case such as rulemaking. In these cases, the courts routinely grant standing, even though the agency might in a new and procedurally correct action reach the same substantive result. The fact is, the courts are simply unwilling to allow a procedural incorrect action to stand. The question is: In the newer procedural injury type cases, where Congress requires that an agency take into account certain costs and hazards of some proposed action (as in the environmental accounting required by National Environmental Policy Act or by the Endangered Species Act) will the requirement of causation be similarly bypassed or presumed?

56. Florida Audubon Society v. Bentsen, 94 F.3d 658, 664 (D.C.Cir.1996).

57. 48 F.3d 1495, 1501 (9th Cir.1995).

The indications are that causation will indeed be similarly bypassed or presumed. In *Douglas County v. Babbitt*, the plaintiff had alleged that in the agency—in designating an area as a "critical habitat"—was required to first complete the environmental audit required by the National Environmental Policy Act. The court found standing, even though causation was "uncertain". It was "uncertain whether the findings of an EIS [environmental impact statement] would affect the Secretary's critical habitat designation." But as the court explained, "under *Lujan*, these concerns are not important."

The prescription of *Lujan v. Defenders of Wildlife* is that "procedural rights" are "special." The way that they are special, according to Justice Scalia'a famous illustration, is that a claim of procedural error (as under the Endangered Species Act at issue in *Lujan* or as under the National Environmental Policy Act) is exempt from a requirement of causation in much the same way that claims of procedural error in, say, rulemaking are exempt from such a requirement. In this respect, Scalia's illustration was that a person opposed to "the proposed construction of federally licensed dam . . . has standing to challenge the licensing agency's failure to file an impact statement even though he cannot establish with any certainty the statement will cause the license to be withheld or altered."[58]

* * *

A point of clarification, and reiteration, may be in order. While procedural errors are not subject to a causation requirement, it remains the case that with broad-scale, public-regarding processes such as those

58. 505 U.S. at __ & n.22. As regards the process at issue in Lujan (that the agencies were required, by the Endangered Species Act, to consult with the Secretary of Interior, Scalia added that the inapplicability of causation to this sort of process was why "we do not rely on the government's argument that, even if the other agencies were required to consult with the Secretary, they may not have followed his advice.)"

In its 1997 decision in *Bennett v. Spear*, 520 U.S. 154, 117 S.Ct. 1154, 137 L.Ed.2d 281 (1997), the Court did find causation in relation to the decisional processes itself, as opposed to causation in relation to the agency action to which the decisional process pertained. In this case, though, the Court, did not find that causation had to be linked to the decisional process. The facts of *Bennett v. Spear* were that under Endangered Species Act a federal agency must consult with the Fish and Wildlife Service whenever an action by that federal agency threatens the habitat of an endangered species. Technically, such an opinion is advisory in that the agency requesting does not necessarily have to comply with it.

The Fish and Wildlife Service had issued a "biological opinion" to the Bureau of Reclamation of the Dept. of Interior respecting its "Klamath Water Project." This opinion advised the Bureau to maintain certain water levels in certain lakes, this to protect the habitat of two endangered species of fish. Ranchers who stood to lose irrigation water if such new water levels were imposed sued. They alleged that in the biological opinion in question, the Fish and Wildlife service had misapplied certain provisions of the Endangered Species Act. The government contended that the ranchers lacked standing in that " 'the proximate cause of their injury is an (as yet unidentified) decision by the Bureau regarding the volume of water allocated to [plaintiffs], not the opinion itself.' " The Court rejected this argument. While the biological opinion "theoretically serv[ed] an 'advisory function,' " the Court noted that "in reality it has a powerful coercive effect." This "virtually determinative effect" for the most part was that officials in compliance with such an opinion could not be held liable for any violations of the Endangered Species Act.

of the National Environmental Policy, the plaintiff must show a particularized injury that is caused by the agency action for which an environmental impact statement was needed. As said by the D.C. Circuit in *Florida Audubon Society v. Bentsen*,[59] "To prove causation, a plaintiff seeking the preparation of an EIS [environmental impact statement] must demonstrate that the particularized injury that the plaintiff is suffering or likely to suffer is fairly traceable to the agency action that implicated the need for an EIS."

In *Audubon Society* case, plaintiffs had alleged that the Internal Revenue Service was required to make an environmental impact study before it provided a tax credit for a certain fuel additive, ethyl tertiary butyl. The tax credit was the agency action that "implicated the need for an EIS." The injury attributed to this tax credit was that it would stimulate production of crops from which the fuel additive was to be manufactured, and that this crop production would cause agricultural pollution to lands in the vicinity of plaintiffs. The court found that this allegation of particularized injury failed at the point of causation. The injury laid to the tax-credit injury was too attenuated and speculative and causation failed because of "the uncertainty of several individual links and because of the number of speculative links that must hold to connect the challenged acts to the asserted particularized injury."

§ 12.7.7 Standing Statutes and Prudential Rules

The question presented by "standing statutes" is whether Congress, independent of Article III-based standing as established by the courts, can by statute itself provide for standing. An instance of such a statute is provided by the Endangered Species Act as it provides that "any person may commence a civil suit on his own behalf" to enjoin violations of the Act. In *Lujan v. Defenders of Wildlife*, plaintiffs argued that this provision specially gave them standing, irrespective of their standing, or lack of it, under Article III, to dispute an alleged violation of the Endangered Species Act. Justice Scalia, writing for a plurality, rejected that contention, saying that persons suing under the provision still had to meet Article III requirements for standing as the courts had established. Because plaintiffs had failed to meet these requirements, their suit was dismissed. Under this view, "standing statutes" do not modify or eliminate the necessity of standing as defined by the courts according to Article III.

This reduction of standing statutes has had its critics, on and off the Court, the gist of which is that a generous part of the enforcement of public policy ought to lie with interested citizens, as least when Congress has provided for such enforcement by a standing statute (or, as these statutes are often referred to, by a "citizen's suit" provision).[60] Be that as it may, from the outset, from *Hayburn's Case* and *Marbury v.*

59. 94 F.3d 658 (D.C.Cir.1996) (en banc).

60. E.g., Sunstein, What's Standing After Lujan? Of Citizen Suits, "Injuries", and Article III, 91 Mich.L.Rev. 163 (1992).

Madison,[61] the courts have considered themselves best suited to define the judicial power and at least since *Massachusetts v. Mellon*[62] have obviously defined standing as an incident of that power. Moreover, the case can and has been made that the Article III based rules that the courts employ are significantly related to the laudable goals of assuring good plaintiffs and separating the courts work from that of the political branches.[63] Accordingly, in *Raines v. Byrd* a majority of the Supreme Court found that Congress could not by statute create standing to review its Line–Item Veto Act. For that majority, Chief Justice Rehnquist stated that "It is settled that Congress cannot erase Article III's standing requirements by statutorily granting the right to sue to a plaintiff who would not otherwise have standing."[64]

If standing statutes do not eliminate or amend the Article III requirements for standing, are these statutes of no effect? Rehnquist answered that as well, pointing out that standing statutes are effective, in that they "eliminate[] any prudential standing limitations." The "prudential limitations" that standing statutes do eliminate differ from Article III standing in this way. Prudential standing, it is said, is not based on Article III but is instead based on the courts' independent and non-derived power of "self-governance." In this respect, prudential standing rules are said to go beyond Article III, to assure an even more circumspect deployment of judicial power than Article III of its own force requires. This circumspection is significantly, but not exclusively, directed at avoided separation of powers problems.[65] If, however, Congress has

61. Hayburn's Case, 2 U.S. (2 Dall.) 409, 1 L.Ed. 436 (1792); Marbury v. Madison, 5 U.S. (1 Cranch) 137, 2 L.Ed. 60 (1803).

62. 262 U.S. 447, 448, 43 S.Ct. 597, 601, 67 L.Ed. 1078 (1923). Commentators critical of court-made rules of standing in general and injury-in-fact in particular have claimed that the requirement of injury-in-fact is relatively recent, commencing with Association of Data Processing v. Camp in 1970, and that therefore this rule cannot claim a good pedigree. But in 1923 in *Massachusetts v. Mellon*, well before the modern administrative state, the Court had taken as established that it could not hear a case unless the plaintiff complained of a distinct injury. In that case, Mrs. Mellon had sought to overturn an act of Congress on the grounds that it exceeded the limited-powers structure of Article I. The Court refused to hear her claim because she presented only a generalized grievance as opposed to a particular injury to her. In this respect, the Court stated:

> We have no power *per se* to review acts of Congress on the ground that they are unconstitutional. That question may be considered only when the justification for some direct injury suffered or threatened, presenting a justiciable issue, is made to rest upon such an act. Then the power exercised is that of ascertaining and declaring the law applicable to the controversy.... The party who invokes the power must be able to show, not only that the statute is invalid, but that he has sustained or is immediately in danger of sustaining some direct injury as a result of its enforcement.

63. Brillmayer, The Jurisprudence of Art. III: Perspectives on the "Case or Controversy" Requirement, 93 Harv.L.Rev. 297 (1979).

64. 521 U.S. 811, 820 & n. 3, 117 S.Ct. 2312, 2317 & n. 3, 138 L.Ed.2d 849 (1997). Similarly, in Steel Co. v. Citizens for a Better Environment, 523 U.S. 83, 118 S.Ct. 1003, 140 L.Ed.2d 210 (1998) the Court held that the standing statute in that case did not eliminate the need for Article III standing as determined by courts. See also Gladstone Realtors v. Village of Bellwood, 441 U.S. 91, 100, 99 S.Ct. 1601, 1608, 60 L.Ed.2d 66 (1979).

65. But as discussed at page ___, the neither rational for nor the definition of prudential rules is all that clear. Also, as discussed at page ___ the notion that prudential rules are somehow qualitatively dif-

by statute specially provided a plaintiff with "standing," the separation of powers problems that are the main concern of prudential rules are diminished. By this "standing statute", Congress has presumably acquiesced respecting such infringement of its turf that judicial review might otherwise be. Accordingly, standing statutes are thought to "significantly lessen[] the risk of unwanted conflict with the Legislative Branch."[66]

Therefore, it is the position of the courts that standing statutes "eliminate[] any prudential standing limitations." This complex relation of standing statutes and prudential rules is probably best understood by an example, which is provided by the Supreme Court decision in *United Food & Commercial Workers Union v. Brown Group*.[67]

The Worker Adjustment and Retraining Notification Act ("WARN Act") requires certain employers to give employees or their union sixty days notice of a plant closing or layoff. An employer who fails to do so is liable to "each aggrieved employee" in damages consisting of back pay. The WARN Act further provides that this suit for damages may be brought by the employee or by a union acting as the "representative of employees ... aggrieved" under the Act. In the *United Food* case, a union sued the Brown Shoe Company for damages owed to employees who were allegedly laid off in violation of the Act.

The union claimed "associational standing." But as previously discussed, to qualify for such standing a plaintiff must among other things establish that "neither the claim asserted nor the relief requested requires the participation of individual members in the lawsuit."[68] Inasmuch as damages owed to an individual are ordinarily determined according to the circumstances of that individual, such a claim for damages is a classic instance of a claim that "requires the participation of individual members."[69] Because the Union brought a claim for damages to its members, the court of appeals held that it did not qualify for associational standing.

The Supreme Court, though, held otherwise. Clearly, the union failed the part of associational standing that denies such standing when the plaintiff asserts damages claims on the part of its members. Still, the union had sued under a statute, that of the WARN Act, that provided for standing in this very circumstance. And the rule, as we have said, is that standing statutes trump prudential rules. The question, then, was whether the test of associational standing that the union failed was a prudential or an Article III gauge of standing.

That distinction was hard to make, because as the Court noted, the definition of prudential rules has been altogether clear. But however

ferent from "Article III rules" is a notion about which we may properly be skeptical.

66. 521 U.S. at 820, 117 S.Ct. at 2317.

67. 517 U.S. 544, 116 S.Ct. 1529, 134 L.Ed.2d 758 (1996).

68. See Sec. 12.____.

69. In relation to association standing, the Court noted that "our cases have not ... clearly disentangled the constitutional from the prudential stands of associational standing." 517 U.S. at 555.

difficult it might be to separate prudential from Article III requirements, that distinction was necessary in *United Food.* To make the distinction, the Court looked to the purposes of associational standing's bar to damages action. These purposes, the Court found, were to "guard against . . . litigating the a case to the damages stage only to find the plaintiff lacking . . . the evidence necessary to show the harm with sufficient specificity" and to "hedge against any risk that the damages recovered by the association will fail to find their way into the pockets of the members on whose behalf injury is claimed." These purposes were for "administrative convenience and efficiency" in the courts. As such they were "matters of judicial self government" rather than elements of Article III standing. The part of associational standing that precluded damages actions was, therefore, a prudential rule that Congress, as it had, might eliminate by means of a standing statute.

* * *

As a postscript, we might reiterate the skepticism, as expressed in *United Food & Commercial Union Workers Union v. Brown Group* above, about the courts' ability to "disentangle" prudential and Article III rules. That skepticism seems well-founded. These rules presumably flow from different well-heads, Article III on the part of "constitutional standing rules" and the courts' "self-governance" on the part of standing rules, but surely this assumption is incorrect. Both rules in fact have the same origin. This origin is in the "judicial power" invested in courts by the Constitution and the courts long-standing assumption that the character of this power is such that courts may take only those cases that they can—consistent with their methods and resources—competently resolve and that courts can resolve consistent with their place in a democratic government.[70] Being similarly derived, prudential rules and "Article III" rules are qualitatively the same. They are on the same continuum and differ only in that prudential rules are generally further out on that continuum. It is thus entirely unexceptional that "it has not always been clear in the opinions of this Court whether particular features of the 'standing' requirement have been required by Art. III ex proprio vigore, or whether they are requirements that the Court itself has erected and which were not compelled by the language of the

70. The Supreme Court has long maintained Article III and prudential rules of standing are alike "founded in concern about the proper—and properly limited—role of the courts in a democratic society." Warth v. Seldin, 422 U.S. 490, 500, 95 S.Ct. 2197, 2205, 45 L.Ed.2d 343 (1975). The Court also noted the symmetry of prudential and Article III rules by explaining that "without [prudential rules]—closely limited to Art. III concerns but essentially matter of judicial self-governance—the courts would be called upon to decide abstract questions of wide public significance even though other governmental institutions may be more competent to address the questions and even though judicial intervention may be unnecessary to protect individual rights." 422 U.S. at 500. 95 S.Ct. at 2206. In *Gladstone, Realtors v. Village of Bellwood,* 441 U.S. 91, 100–01, 99 S.Ct. 1601, 1608, 60 L.Ed.2d 66 (1979), prudential standing was explained by reference to the Article III standard that courts do not litigate generalized grievances. As said by the Court: "a plaintiff may still lack standing under the prudential principles by which the judiciary seeks to avoid deciding questions of broad social import where no individual rights would be vindicated."

Constitution."[71] In this light, it might also be expected that courts would, as they have, defer to standing statutes by allowing Congress by those statutes to eliminate the extension of standing that prudential rules represent and to not allow Congress to eliminate the closer in (*i.e.*, "irreducible") elements of standing.

§ 12.7.8 The Zone-of-Interests Test

As established by *Association of Data Processing v. Camp*, standing to challenge agency action in court consists of two requirements: the Article III "injury-in-fact" requirement and the additional requirement that the injury be "within the zone of interests to be protected or regulated by the statute . . . in question."[72] As we have said, the second, "zone-of-interests" test was somewhat abruptly derived from Sec. 702 of the Administrative Procedure Act. Sec. 702 provides that "A person suffering legal wrong because of agency action, or adversely affected or aggrieved by agency action within the meaning of a relevant statute is entitled to judicial review thereof."[73]

As established in *Association of Data Processing,* the zone-of-interests test was a limitation, an extra and additional hurdle that an injured plaintiff must meet. However, Sec. 702, the Administrative Procedure Act provision on which the zone-of-interests restriction was based, had been generally interpreted *not* as a *limit* to, but as a *presumption in favor of*, judicial review.[74] Accordingly, Justice Brennan, as we have said, dissented. He thought that the Article III's injury-in-fact basis of standing was sufficient, and that the addition of the zone-of-interests test was an unnecessary and unwise restriction of judicial review. Over time, Brennan's reservations about the zone-of-interests test were borne out.

As previously discussed, persons and organizations with the power to sue can and will tax the agency with the costs of judicial review, these costs being the possibility that the courts will overturn an agency and the certainty of the expenses and delays of judicial review. If by operation of standing that power is limited to only a segment of those interested in a statute, then standing creates special "stakeholders" who may skew agency implementation of the statute simply because they hold an exclusive power to impose costs on an agency by taking it to court. The zone-of-interests test may create such a body of stakeholders. As the test was formulated in *Association of Data Processing*, the majority spoke of interests "protected" by the relevant statute. Thus, the zone-of-interests test was initially viewed as providing judicial review

71. Valley Forge Christian College v. Americans United for Separation of Church and State, 454 U.S., 464, 471, 102 S.Ct. 752, 758, 70 L.Ed.2d 700 (1982).

72. 397 U.S. 150, 153, 90 S.Ct. 827, 829, 25 L.Ed.2d 184 (1970).

73. 5 U.S.C.A. Sec. 702. See Sec. 12.6.1, supra.

74. This generous, judicial review favoring view of Sec. 706. was that "the Administrative Procedure Act . . . embodies the basic presumption of judicial review to one 'suffering legal wrong because of agency action, or adversely affected or aggrieved by agency action within the meaning of a relevant statute,' 5 U.S.C. Sec. 702." Abbott Laboratories v. Gardner, 387 U.S. 136, 87 S.Ct. 1507, 18 L.Ed.2d 681 (1967).

only for the "beneficiaries" of a statute and as blocking review by anyone else.[75]

Limiting standing to beneficiaries may skew the courts' enforcement of a statute. When Congress makes social policy, that policy is usually a compromise of competing interests. For instance, in the context of banking regulation, banks, bank clients, and bank competitors often will have opposing interests in a proposed bill and often the resulting statute will be defined, at least at the margins, by a compromise of these interests. When these margins are moved—either shrunk or expanded—this compromise is upset and the will of Congress is undone. Insofar as the zone-of-interests test is read as allowing only the beneficiaries of a statute to sue under the statute, then, by virtue of their exclusive power to call on the courts respecting the statute, the boundaries of the statute stand to move in the direction favored by beneficiaries.

Avoidance of such a distortion produced some otherwise odd decisions. In *Investment Company Institute v. Camp,* investment companies sought to overturn a ruling by the Comptroller of Currency that permitted national banks to enter the mutual fund business.[76] These plaintiffs contended that the federal Glass–Stegall Act precluded banks from providing investment services such as selling mutual funds. These plaintiffs, being investment companies who stood to lose money because of bank competition, were thus injured and thus met the injury-in-fact requirement of standing.

These plaintiffs, however, might be denied standing inasmuch as they were not "beneficiaries" of the relevant statute and thus they might fail the zone-of-interests test. The obvious reason that the Glass–Stegall Act precluded banks from providing investment services was that such services would be "destructive of prudent and disinterested commercial banking and of public confidence in the commercial banking system."[77] As the Act thus protected bank customers by limiting banks to banking, it probably was not meant to protect the bank competitors who had brought the instant case. As Justice Harlan explained, "neither the language of the ... Act nor the legislative history evinces any congressional concern for the interest of [plaintiffs] and others like them in freedom from competition. Indeed it is reasonably plain that, if anything, the Act was adopted in spite of its anti-competitive effect rather than because of it."[78]

75. Accordingly, in *Association of Data Processing,* the Court found that the regulatory statutes in question, as they limited the business of banks, were meant to benefit the plaintiffs. 397 U.S. at 155, 90 S.Ct. at 830. In *Barlow v. Collins,* the companion case to *Association of Data Processing,* the Court found that plaintiffs, who were tenant farmers challenging a Department of Agriculture regulation with respect to payments due them under the "Uplands Cotton Program" established by Congress, were within the zone of interests inasmuch as "implicit in the statutory provisions and their legislative history is a congressional intent that the Secretary protect the interests of tenant farmers." 397 U.S. 159, 164–65, 90 S.Ct. 832, 836–37, 25 L.Ed.2d 192 (1970).

76. 401 U.S. 617, 91 S.Ct. 1091, 28 L.Ed.2d 367 (1971).

77. 401 U.S. at 634, 91 S.Ct. at 1100.

78. 401 U.S. at 640, 91 S.Ct. at 1103. And in *Association of Data Processing v. Camp*, 397 U.S. 150, 90 S.Ct. 827, 25

Thus, the investment companies might have been denied standing because they were not the statutory beneficiaries who met the zone-of-interests test. But had the Court had refused to hear this complaint, that of injured competitors, that refusal would have tended to foreclose judicial review of extensions of banking authority beyond that intended by the Glass–Steagal Act. The acknowledged beneficiary group, bank clients, might bring such a suit, but it is hard to see how they would have the incentive to do so. In this context, the majority simply relaxed the zone-of-interests test, by glossing over any requirement (as imposed by the zone-of-interests test) that plaintiffs be beneficiaries of the statute in question.

Decisions such as *Investment Company Institute v. Camp* have made for at least an erratic application of the zone-of-interests test.[79] To avoid these irregularities and to avoid a one-sided measure of standing such as results from a zone-of-interests test that limits standing to statutory beneficiaries, the Court has realigned and redefined the zone-of-interests test. It commenced to do in *Clarke v. Securities Industry Association.*[80]

In *Clarke v. Securities Industry Association,* the Court first of all recognized that Sec. 702 of the Administrative Procedure Act, from which provision the zone-of-interests test was derived, is indeed directed to "reviewability" and to a presumption favoring judicial review.[81] The Court explained that "The zone of interests test is a guide for deciding whether, in view of Congress's evident intent to make agency action presumptively reviewable, a particular plaintiff should be heard to complain of a particular agency decision." Secondly, the Court found that the zone-of-interests test did not limit the class of qualified plaintiffs to statutory beneficiaries. In this respect, the Court explained that "there need be no indication of a congressional purpose to benefit the would-be plaintiff."

The facts of *Clarke v. Securities Industries* were that two national banks had obtained the Comptroller of Currency's permission to offer discount brokerage services at branch offices outside their home states. The McFadden Act prohibits bank branches outside a bank's home state,[82] but the Comptroller had ruled that discount brokerage services were sufficiently different from ordinary banking for the branch banking limitation to be inapplicable. Securities dealers who stood to lose busi-

L.Ed.2d 184 (1970), the Court was just as disingenuous as it found bank competitors were beneficiaries of a statute that obviously benefited bank clients, and not them. See Stewart, The Reformation of Administrative Law, 88 Harv.L.Rev. 1669, 1733 (1975).

79. Control Data Corp. v. Baldrige, 655 F.2d 283, 294 (D.C.Cir.1981), cert. denied 454 U.S. 881, 102 S.Ct. 363, 70 L.Ed.2d 190 (1981). As this case documents and explains, the zone of interests condition, while in theory a necessary part of standing, was only variously applied and then with a considerable lack of uniformity. A court's application of the zone-of-interests test may skew its decision on the merits of the case.

80. 479 U.S. 388, 107 S.Ct. 750, 93 L.Ed.2d 757 (1987).

81. As said by the Court, "The zone of interests test is a guide for deciding whether, in view of Congress's evident intent to make agency action presumptively reviewable, a particular plaintiff should be heard to complain of a particular agency decision." 479 U.S. at 399, 107 S.Ct. at 757.

82. 12 U.S.C.A. §§ 36 & 81.

ness to banks that provided discount brokerage service sought to overturn this ruling in the courts. In doing so, these plaintiffs contended that the Comptroller of Currency had misinterpreted the McFadden Act.

The Comptroller of Currency, though, argued that these securities dealers lacked standing to press this claim because they failed the zone-of-interests test. They failed, the Comptroller argued, because "Congress passed the McFadden Act not to protect securities dealers but to establish competitive equality between state and national banks." The Court rejected this argument, because "in particular there need be no indication of a congressional purpose to benefit the would-be plaintiff." Otherwise, the Court explained that the zone-of-interests test should not be "especially demanding" and should be generously applied in favor of standing. As said by the Court:

> The zone of interests test is a guide for deciding whether, in view of Congress's evident intent to make agency action presumptively reviewable, a particular plaintiff should be heard to complain of a particular agency decision. In cases where the plaintiff is not itself the subject of the contested regulatory action, the test denies a right of review if the plaintiff's interests are so marginally related to or inconsistent with the purposes implicit in the statute that it cannot reasonably be assumed that Congress intended to permit the suit.

Those few cases, where the "plaintiff's interests are so marginally related to or inconsistent with" the relevant statute that review should be denied, were later illustrated, by Justice Scalia, according to the following hypothetical: "[T]he failure by an agency to comply with a statutory provision requiring 'on the record hearings' would assuredly have an adverse effect upon the company that has the contract to record and transcribe the agency's proceedings; but since the provision was obviously enacted to protect the interests of the parties to the proceedings and not those of the reporters, that company would not be 'adversely affected with meaning of the statute.' "[83] As thus reduced to a requirement of connection, to a requirement that a plaintiff's interest not be unrelated to or inconsistent with the purposes of the public law in question, the zone-of-interest test may after all be useful.

* * *

Four years after the Supreme Court offered this refreshed definition of the zone-of-interests test it declined to follow it, in *Air Couriers v. American Postal Workers Union*. More recently, though, the Court has returned to and applied the zone-of-interests test in the liberal manner of *Clarke v. Securities Industries*.

Air Courier v. American Postal Workers Union[84] involved the U.S. Postal Service's statutory monopoly for the carriage of mail and the postal unions' long standing effort to protect that monopoly. Congress

83. Lujan v. Defenders of Wildlife, 497 U.S. at 883, 110 S.Ct. at 3186.

84. 498 U.S. 517, 111 S.Ct. 913, 112 L.Ed.2d 1125 (1991).

had provided some relief from that monopoly by authorizing the Postal Service to suspend it "upon any mail route where the public service requires the suspension." Under this provision, the Postal Service enacted a rule that allowed for expedited delivery in the international sector by private companies such as Fed–Ex or UPS. Because their job security was threatened by this relaxation of the postal monopoly, postal employees, through their unions, brought a court action to overturn it. The question considered by the Supreme Court was whether postal employees were within the zone of interests of the statutes that established the postal monopoly.

The Court held that postal employees were not. On review of the text and the history of the statutes that created the postal monopoly, the Court found no "indication that the [statutes] were intended for the benefit of postal workers." Because they were not beneficiaries, a majority of the Court held that they failed the zone-of-interests test and thus had no standing. This holding, obviously, is contrary to the direction, as stated in *Clarke v. Security Industries,* that "there need be no indication of a congressional purpose to benefit the would-be plaintiff."

In 1998, though, the Court returned to the generous view of the zone of interests test it had stated in *Clarke v. Security Industries.* The Court did so in *National Credit Union Administration v. First National Bank & Trust Co.*[85] The agency, the National Credit Union Administration, had interpreted its enabling act, the Federal Credit Union Act, as providing for federally chartered credit unions for "multiple unrelated employee groups." Thus, AT & T Family Credit Union (a party to the case) had as its clients and members the employees of such diverse companies as Duke Power, Coca–Cola Bottling Company, Ciba–Geigy, Lee Apparel, and American Tobacco. The plaintiffs (commercial banks) contended that these unrelated employee groups were unlawful in that the Federal Credit Union Act, as it limited credit unions to "groups having a common bond of occupation" did not permit the inclusion of such diverse occupations in a single credit union.

The agency contended that the plaintiffs bank lacked standing because they were not within the requisite zone of interests. The banks' interest was that of avoiding the competition of credit unions and the Federal Credit Union Act, the agency contended, was not meant to benefit banks by shielding them from competition. The Court's (relatively) straight forward response to this argument was to reassert the holding of *Clarke Securities* that there "does not have to an 'indication of congressional purpose to benefit the would-be plaintiff.' " Instead, the Court determined whether the plaintiff's interest was "arguably" related to the statute in question. In this respect, the banks' interest was in the "markets" that credit unions could serve (and in, of course, limiting these markets). The Federal Credit Union Act provision in question was directed to appropriate markets. This common ground of markets was, the Court held, a relation sufficient to meet the zone of interests test. It

85. 522 U.S. 479, 118 S.Ct. 927, 140 L.Ed.2d 1 (1998).

was "irrelevant," the Court reiterated, that "Congress did not intend to benefit commercial banks."

§ 12.8 TIMING OF REVIEW

Judicial review of agency action includes matters of timing. Review may not be presently available, but deferred, until such time as the agency has fully completed its work and the impact of this work is evident. The doctrines most concerned with timing of review are exhaustion of administrative remedies and ripeness.

Ripeness requires that an issue be sufficiently developed, final, and then felt, so as to be "justiciable". Exhaustion of administrative entails a primacy to the relief and remedies offered by agencies; the doctrine, as stated by the courts, is that "no one is entitled to judicial relief ... until the prescribed administrative remedy has been exhausted."[1] On the whole, ripeness and exhaustion of remedies are more alike than different; they both involve an appropriate maturation of a person's dispute with an agency.[2]

These doctrines differ, however, in their emphasis. Exhaustion of remedies stresses a primary resort to administrative processes so as to assure that agency decision-making is not unduly disrupted and taxed by judicial review. In this respect, the doctrine has been described, most notably by Prof. Jaffe, as an expression of "administrative autonomy."[3] This "autonomy" is vested in agencies by Congress. The doctrine of exhaustion, therefore, is conditioned by the will of Congress. As said by the Supreme Court, "appropriate deference to Congress' power ... requires fashioning of exhaustion principles in a manner consistent with congressional intent and any applicable statutory scheme."[4]

As exhaustion is largely for the agencies, to reserve for them a space in which for a time they may work undisturbed, ripeness, in contrast, is for the courts. It is for them a self-examination of their ability and place in a government of separated powers. This examination is generally considered by the courts to be required of them by Article III of the Constitution. They view that Article as limiting their power to "concrete" cases, which in the context of administrative law means developed, final, and felt agency actions. As courts thus insist on completed agency action, that insistence better assures the courts of the knowledge gained from applied agency expertise, and provides them with a record already developed by the agency. In these ways, ripeness conserves the

§ 12.8

1. McKart v. United States, 395 U.S. 185, 193, 89 S.Ct. 1657, 1662, 23 L.Ed.2d 194 (1969).

2. For a comparison of the ripeness and exhaustion doctrines, see Ticor Title Insurance Co. v. Federal Trade Com'n, 814 F.2d 731 (D.C.Cir.1987).

3. L. Jaffe, Judicial Control of Administrative Action 425 (1965). See McKart v. United States, 395 U.S. 185, 195, 89 S.Ct. 1657, 1663, 23 L.Ed.2d 194 (1969) (the exhaustion doctrine is meant to prevent the "frequent and deliberate flouting of administrative processes" that "weaken the effectiveness of an agency by encouraging people to ignore its procedures").

4. McCarthy v. Madigan, 503 U.S. 140, 112 S.Ct. 1081, 117 L.Ed.2d 291 (1992).

resources of courts "for the decision of issues, between litigants, capable of effective determination" and assures that "their function as a balance for the peoples' protection against abuse of power by other branches remains unimpaired."[5]

Insofar as ripeness is grounded in Article III, it would seem—in comparison to the exhaustion requirement—to be the more basic condition, one that must be met before the case that is brought against an agency is within the zone of the "judicial power" that Article vests in agencies. Exhaustion, in contrast, is not constitutionally grounded and is not a similarly essential predicate of judicial power. Logically, then, we should consider ripeness ahead of exhaustion and this we shall do. Still, we should again remember that exhaustion and ripeness are more alike than different and remember that the courts do not always rigorously differentiate between the two. We should also know that the courts do not necessarily and always treat ripeness as a constitutional doctrine. In *Abbott Laboratories v. Gardner*, for instance, the Court more-or-less presented ripeness as a manifestation of an equitable-like discretion in the courts.[6]

§ 12.9 RIPENESS

Each summer, aliens domiciled in the continental United States traveled to Alaska, not then a state, to work in salmon and herring canneries. As the canning season approached in 1953, the Immigration and Naturalization Service announced that when those aliens returned from Alaska, the Service would treat them as aliens entering the United States for the first time. This agency action would create greater entry barriers for these aliens, and the possibility that some of them might be denied reentry to the country. For them, a suit for declaratory relief was then brought, on statutory and constitutional grounds, in federal court. On review, the Supreme Court held that such relief could not be granted.

Because the agency had yet to apply its newly-announced policy, the Court held that the case was unripe. The Court explained that "Appellants in effect asked the District Court to rule that a statute the sanctions of which had not been set in motion . . . because an occasion for doing so had not arisen, would not be applied to them if in the future such a contingency should arise." This contingency and lack of context raised Article III problems that Justice Frankfurter, writing for the Court, found insufferable. "Determinations of the scope and constitutionality of legislation in advance of its immediate adverse effect in the

5. United Public Workers v. Mitchell, 330 U.S. 75, 90–91, 67 S.Ct. 556, 564–65, 91 L.Ed. 754 (1947).

6. Ripeness often involves a claim for declaratory and injunctive relief, and in this context, Justice Harlan, speaking for the Court in *Abbott Laboratories v. Gardner*, explained that "The injunctive and declaratory remedies are discretionary, and courts traditionally have been reluctant to apply them to administrative determinations unless these arise in the context of a controversy 'ripe' for judicial resolution." 387 U.S. 136, 87 S.Ct. 1507, 18 L.Ed.2d 681 (1967).

context of a concrete case," he wrote, "involves too remote and abstract an inquiry for the proper exercise of the judicial function."[1]

As it insists on completed agency action, ripeness is similar to the exhaustion doctrine. But the direction from which it comes is different. While exhaustion springs from a concern, a regard for agency autonomy, that is external to the courts, ripeness comes from within the courts: It is their self-concern "for the proper exercise of the judicial function." Ripeness is, therefore, for the courts an exercise in self-governance, an exercise that the federal courts generally take as a necessary condition of the "judicial power" invested in them by Article III of the Constitution.

Ripeness is a matter of general principle. How this generality works out can best be seen contextually, by reference to the circumstances in which problems of ripeness commonly arise. Accordingly, we will discuss ripeness by reference to the circumstances of preenforcement review, informal agency action, and agency advisory opinions.

§ 12.9.1 Ripeness and Preenforcement Review

When an agency acts against an individual formally, by means of an order issued after a hearing, that action will, perforce, be ripe for review. The individual is demonstrably affected by the agency, there are few if any contingencies (the agency action has been reduced to a final order), and there is an evidentiary record to assist the court in its review.

But for various reasons, individuals may wish *not* to await such an enforcement action. They may instead prefer to take the offensive, to sue the agency and to gain the advantages, such as choice of forum, of that initiative. Moreover, more than litigation tactics are often involved in preenforcement review of an agency action. An agency position may present a Hobson's choice to those who are subject to it and who believe it to be wrong. If a person chooses not to conform to the agency's position, he faces the cost of an agency enforcement action (litigation expenses plus the chance of losing and whatever sanction that entails). Also, that person stands to lose his investment in whatever venture the agency disallows. On the other hand, if he conforms, he foregoes advantageous conduct to him and to society.

A means of avoiding this predicament and the costs of it is immediately to test the agency position by a court action for declaratory relief. This was, for instance, the route taken in *International Longshoremen's and Warehousemen's Union v. Boyd* in relation to new restrictions on resident aliens. In that case this route was, as we previously discussed, denied on grounds of ripeness. But today, largely on the basis of *Abbott Laboratories v. Gardner*,[2] preenforcement relief is not necessarily barred. Instead, in administrative law (and unlike other areas of the law such as

§ 12.9

1. International Longshoremen's and Warehousemen's Union v. Boyd, 347 U.S. 222, 223–24, 74 S.Ct. 447, 448–49, 98 L.Ed. 650 (1954).

2. Abbott Laboratories v. Gardner, 387 U.S. 136, 87 S.Ct. 1507, 18 L.Ed.2d 681 (1967).

preenforcement review of criminal statutes[3]) there is a "judicial willingness" to save "a regulated entity [from] the dilemma of enduring costly compliance measures or risking civil and criminal penalties."[4] (This "judicial willingness," though, is somewhat restrained outside the "dilemma" of compliance costs versus civil or criminal penalties.)

The circumstance of *Abbott Laboratories* were that Congress had required that a drug's generic name, along with its proprietary name, be placed "prominently" on labels and advertising. After a rulemaking proceeding, the Food and Drug Administration published regulations requiring that the generic name "accompany each appearance" of a drug's proprietary name on everything, on labels, enclosures, and advertising and other promotional literature. The drug industry thought that the Food and Drug Administration had gone overboard with its "everytime" requirement and asked for declaratory and injunctive relief in federal district court. That court refused this relief because in its preenforcement context, the case was unripe.

The Supreme Court, in an opinion by Justice Harlan, held otherwise. Harlan explained that ripeness is about the "avoidance of abstract disagreements over administrative policies," and then established a framework for avoiding such "abstract disagreements." The framework included a two-part test for ripeness, which was stated as follows: "the *fitness* of the issues for judicial decision and the *hardship* to the parties of withholding court consideration." Today, this two-part test is routinely applied in determining ripeness.

Fitness for Review. For ripeness, fitness pertains to the *nature* of the issue at hand and to the *finality* of the agency's position respecting the issue. The "nature" of the issue largely pertains to whether the issue is factual or legal. With legal issues, involving as they do interpretations of text such as statutes, the courts are doing what they are familiar with and best at, and they are unlikely to benefit from further agency proceedings. In a case of factual issues, on the other hand, the courts especially benefit both from a concrete context in which to view the facts and from a record developed according to an agency's own expert assessment of the issues. In *Abbott Laboratories,* the issue at hand was legal, "whether the statute was properly constructed . . . to require the established [generic] name of the drug to be used every time the proprietary name is employed."

The finality part of the ripeness has as its purpose avoiding review of intermediate agency positions. Controversies with respect to such positions are likely to be more "remote and abstract" than a court would like and courts might well think that "further administrative action is needed to clarify the agency's position."[5] Also, judicial intervention at

3. See Younger v. Harris, 401 U.S. 37, 91 S.Ct. 746, 27 L.Ed.2d 669 (1971).

4. Ciba–Geigy Corp. v. U.S. Environmental Protection Agency, 801 F.2d 430, 438 n. 10 (D.C.Cir.1986).

5. Action Alliance of Senior Citizens v. Heckler, 789 F.2d 931, 940 (D.C.Cir.1986). As well, judicial intervention short of a final agency position raises the concern that is a particular focus of the doctrine of exhaus-

this intermediate point places a court in the position of spinning its wheels: the agency may later change its position and thereby nullify the court's action.

In *Abbott Laboratories,* the agency position in question was clearly and formally final: it had been arrived at by means of rulemaking and stated in a published rule. But as Justice Harlan indicated, such formality is not a necessary index of finality; instead, finality is to be measured in a "flexible" and "pragmatic" way. This pragmatic view of finality, and the importance of identifying precisely the action that may be "final," is shown in the District of Columbia Circuit opinion in *Ciba–Geigy v. United States Environmental Protection Agency.*[6] The Ciba–Geigy Company had been informed by the Environmental Protection Agency that it faced an enforcement action backed by civil and criminal penalties unless it changed the labeling of a certain pesticide. Ciba–Geigy wrote back, stating that prior to an enforcement action for "misbranded" substances it was, under the applicable statutory scheme, entitled to a "preenforcement hearing." By return letter, the agency replied that the company had no statutory right to such a hearing. Ciba–Geigy then brought a federal court action for declaratory and injunctive relief. The district court, however, dismissed the action because it was unripe in that the agency had yet to issue a misbranding order or take any final action of any sort.

The court of appeals, however, was of the opinion that the lower court had been misdirected respecting finality. The appellate court noted that the precise issue raised by the company was the legal one of whether it was statutorily entitled to a certain preenforcement hearing. Respecting this issue, the agency letter to Ciba–Geigy "unequivocally stated EPA's position on the question whether registrants were entitled to a ... hearing before labeling changes could be required." The court added that "we have no reason to believe that the EPA Director of Pesticide Programs [the author of the letter] lacks authority to speak for EPA on this issue or that his statement of the agency's position was 'only the ruling of a subordinate official' that could be appealed to a higher level of EPA's hierarchy." Consequently, the letter showed that the agency had "come to rest" in its position so that the court of appeals saw "not the slightest danger that judicial review will interrupt the orderly processes of administrative decision-making."

* * *

Finally, we should emphasize that a factor important to the courts in determining fitness for review has been a felt need for "context": Even if an issue is simply one of statutory interpretation, the courts may yet wish to see it applied in a real-world circumstances. In *Diamond Shamrock Corp. v. Costle* some chemical companies challenged Environ-

tion of administrative remedies, that of a too early, perhaps unnecessary, and therefore improper intrusion into the agency's decisional processes. Ohio Forestry Ass'n v. Sierra Club, 523 U.S. 726, 118 S.Ct. 1665, 140 L.Ed.2d 921 (1998).

6. 801 F.2d 430 (D.C.Cir.1986).

mental Protection Agency regulations pertaining to the discharge of pollutants into navigable waters.[7] Before pollutants might be discharged, a permit had to be secured. Under existing regulations, the receipt of that permit was conditioned on effluent limitations set in absolute terms: that is, company seeking a permit was given no set-off for effluents already in the water.

The chemical companies claimed that effluent limitations should be set in "net terms," so that a company was not responsible for pollutants not its own, and they brought a court action so alleging. Had the companies applied for and been denied a permit, judicial review as to that denial was available. The chemical companies were not, however, willing to abide by this ordinary, post action, means of judicial review. They sought immediate, preenforcement review in which they alleged that the agency's action in setting effluent limitations in gross terms was in excess of statutory authority.

This time, though, the court found that the case was unripe and that review should be sought later, when and if a permit was denied. The court thought that both it and the agency would gain from agency experience in applying the effluent limitations. The agency was not "barred from changing its policy as further experience was gained" and the "impact of the regulations [would] in part depend in part upon their interpretation by the EPA's regional administrators." Judicial review would generally be "facilitated by waiting until the administrative policy is implemented for then a court can be freed, at least in part, from theorizing about how a rule will be applied and what its effect will be."[8]

Hardship to the Parties. In *Diamond Shamrock Corp. v. Costle,* the court's professed need for context was conditioned by another factor, the fact that the chemical companies had made a less than compelling case of hardship if review were presently denied. This being the case, the court was "unwilling to disrupt this administrative process when 'no irremediable adverse consequences flow from requiring a later challenge to this regulation.' "[9]

7. 580 F.2d 670 (D.C.Cir.1978).

8. 580 F.2d at 674. The principle about not "theorizing" about how a rule will be applied was, the court said "particularly apt in the instant case" where the limitations up for review were not absolute but relative, depending on the existing pollution in a given stream.

9. In *Diamond Shamrock*, the plaintiffs had claimed, but failed to substantiate, any irremediable effects of the agency action. In their challenge to permits for the discharge of pollutants into streams, the plaintiffs had asserted that the permit system would presently cause them to modify their waste-water treatment systems. But they did not show how "presently—before such permits are issued—they must begin to make such modifications." In their briefs the companies made allegations but did back them up. In this regard, the court noted that

> Appellants contend in their brief that the regulations "now operate to control [their] business affairs" and to place them in an "acute dilemma" because of the stringent deadlines the Act imposes for achieving compliance with permits and the lead times needed to design and construct conforming treatment facilities.... Yet, appellants have failed to substantiate this bare assertion either in their briefs or at oral argument. They have not, for example, alleged that design or construction must commence before a permit issues or that they could not meet the deadlines. Indeed, at oral

This factor of "irremediable injury" is an aspect of the second part, the "hardship to the parties part," of *Abbott Laboratories'* "two-fold" test of ripeness. This element of hardship, we might add, seems not altogether an implication of the Article III norm that courts hear only "justiciable" cases, that is, cases sufficiently developed and concrete so that the courts can better decide them. Logically, a case might be so developed and concrete without regard to the "hardship" suffered by plaintiff. This being so, this factor of hardship is perhaps best derived, as Harlan said it should be, from the courts' ordinary discretionary and equitable power respecting the declaratory and injunctive relief that is the usual form of preenforcement relief.[10] Be this as it may, "hardship" is a factor in ripeness and it usually consists of costs that cannot be redressed by judicial review at some later time.

In *Abbott Laboratories,* the drug companies faced considerable marketing costs if they complied with the Food and Drug Administration's labeling requirements. If they chose not to comply, they faced not just a cease and desist order, but "serious" criminal and civil penalties for the distribution of "misbranded drugs." Moreover, given public sensitivities respecting drug products, just having to defend in a criminal and civil action stood to deplete a valuable stock of goodwill. These costs were hardship enough, the Court found.

* * *

The "judicial willingness" to provide preenforcement review seems of late to have been somewhat restrained, restrained not in the case of an agency-imposed duty backed by penalties as was the context of *Abbott Laboratories* but in the case of agency-distributed benefits. In *Reno v. Catholic Social Services,*[11] public interest groups brought class actions respecting the Immigration and Naturalization Service's interpretation—expressed in certain regulations—of a statutory requirement that aliens seeking a certain residency status first establish a "continuous physical presence" in the United States. The Court identified the residency status that aliens might hope to achieve as a benefit, and then held that judicial review ahead of an agency refusal to award that benefit was unripe. In doing so, the Court distinguished agency-conferred benefits from agency-imposed duties. In this respect, the Court noted that in the case of a duty allegedly owed by a plaintiff, a finding for the plaintiff would be sufficient to relieve the plaintiff of that duty.

> argument this court repeatedly pressed counsel for appellants to state what effect the regulations now have on their clients, but counsel's only response was that they "know it's going to come."

580 F.2d 670, 673 (D.C.Cir.1978). A lesson here is that while the courts may have expressed a "judicial willingness" to save "a regulated entity [from] the dilemma of enduring costly compliance measures or risking civil and criminal penalties," that willingness is predicated on that entity establishing this hardship to the satisfaction of the court. Unsubstantiated assertions of costs and hardships will not do.

10. "The injunctive and declaratory remedies are discretionary, and courts traditionally have been reluctant to apply them to administrative determinations unless these arise in the context of a controversy 'ripe' for judicial resolution." Abbott Laboratories, 387 U.S. 136 (1967).

11. 509 U.S. 43, 113 S.Ct. 2485, 125 L.Ed.2d 38 (1993).

But in the case of a benefit, a finding for plaintiff would not, not usually, by itself be similarly sufficient to gain the benefit. In *Reno v. Catholic Social Services,* the finding respecting a "continuous presence" that plaintiffs hoped to establish in the courts was necessary to receiving the benefit, but it was not sufficient. This was because an alien had to satisfy statutory requirements apart from a continuous presence in order to claim the benefit. This being the case, the agency action was not final in relation to the plaintiffs. In her concurrence, Justice O'Connor emphasized that this distinction, that plaintiffs had challenged a necessary but not a sufficient basis for the conferral of benefit, was the basis for the majority's holding of unripeness and that she "would not go so far as to state that a suit challenging a benefit-conferring rule is necessarily unripe."

§ 12.9.2 Ripeness and Informal Actions

Abbott Laboratories dealt with formal agency action consisting of rulemaking and an officially promulgated rule. Many times, however, the form and effect of an agency action may not be so clear. The agency may seek to regulate by means less straightforward than by formally established rules.

In *Columbia Broadcasting System v. United States,* the Federal Communications Commission issued "an expression of the general policy we will follow in exercising our licensing power."[12] This policy statement expressed the Commission's disfavor of certain contractual arrangements between local stations and the networks. The Columbia Broadcasting System, contending that this action was outside the Commission's statutory authority, sought review of it.

The Commission, however, argued that there was nothing for a court to review; that its "policy statement" bound nothing and nobody, that any effect, if it should occur, would be in the context of a license revocation and that relief could then be had on review of that revocation. The agency position, in short, was that their action was unreviewable because it had no present legal effect.

Chief Justice Stone, writing for the Court, took a more practical view of things. He looked not to the "label" but instead to "the substance of what the Commission has purported to do and has done." The substance was that the broadcast stations, rather than risking their licenses in renewal proceedings, would immediately give up the network contracts that the Federal Communications Commission had said it disfavored. The Commission action was, therefore, calculated to instill conformity, and it was, in its "practical operations, an order promulgating regulations which operate to control . . . contractual relationships." Thus, the Commission's action was presently reviewable. By this practical view of agency operation—disregarding the agency's characterizations of its action in favor of the effect of the action on the private

12. 316 U.S. 407, 62 S.Ct. 1194, 86 L.Ed. 1563 (1942).

sector—the courts have in hand a means of determining the ripeness of agency action according to real-world consequences.

§ 12.9.3 Ripeness and Agency Advisory Opinions

The agencies themselves may try to avoid the waste associated with a person or firm either refraining from some venture or going ahead with it but risking a sanction and the loss of invested resources should an agency decide that the venture was illegal. The agencies may try to avoid this waste by an advisory opinion as to whether they consider the venture permissible. These opinions come in various forms. For instance, the Securities and Exchange Commission, after considering a venture as described to it, will provide a letter (a "no-action letter") from the Commission's staff, saying whether or not the staff will recommend prosecution if that venture is undertaken.[13]

If a person or company does not like the advice it gets from an agency, may it seek judicial review of that agency's advisory opinion? Ordinarily, the answer is no, usually on the grounds that such opinions are not "fit" for review within the meaning of *Abbott Laboratories.* Often, the advisory opinion will not amount to a final agency decision, as fitness requires. For instance, Security Exchange Commission no-action letters are opinions issued by the staff, not the Commission itself.[14] An advisory opinion might also be unfit in that the matter it presents—as in the case of some planned but not yet executed venture—involves inchoate factual issues.[15] Also, aside from considerations of ripeness, the courts are aware that advisory opinions are a valuable service that the agencies provide and that if agencies are taken to court on the basis of advisory opinions, then that service might dry up.[16] All things considered, judicial review of advisory opinions is not usually forthcoming.

But sometimes the courts may consider advisory opinions ripe for review, and in this regard the opinion in *National Automatic Laundry and Cleaning Council v. Shultz* is instructive.[17] A trade association of laundromat operators, had presented a fact situation typical of the industry to the Administrator of the Wage and Hour Division of the Department of Labor and had asked for his opinion whether laundromats were subject to wage and hour requirements of the Fair Labor

13. See Lemke, The SEC No–Action Letter Process, 42 Bus. Lawyer 1019, 1023 (1987) ("Individuals benefit by obtaining expert advice" as to "appropriate conduct under the law").

14. Kixmiller v. SEC, 492 F.2d 641 (D.C.Cir.1974). But see Medical Committee for Human Rights v. SEC, 432 F.2d 659 (D.C.Cir.1970), vacated as moot 404 U.S. 403, 92 S.Ct. 577, 30 L.Ed.2d 560 (1972), where the court held that an SEC no-action letter about its proxy rules was reviewable. Unlike *Kixmiller,* though, the Commission had in the *Medical Committee for Human Rights* case reviewed and approved the no-action letter, a distinction that the court in *Kixmiller* found significant. 492 F.2d at 644.

15. E.g., New York Stock Exchange v. Bloom, 562 F.2d 736 (D.C.Cir.1977).

16. "Advisory opinions should, to the greatest extent possible, be available to the public as a matter of routine; it would be unfortunate if the prospect of judicial review were to make an agency reluctant to give them." National Automatic Laundry and Cleaning Council v. Shultz, 443 F.2d 689, 699–700 (D.C.Cir.1971).

17. 443 F.2d 689 (D.C.Cir.1971).

Standards Act. The Administrator wrote back and said that they were. The trade association then sought judicial review of the agency position stated in that letter.

The court, in an opinion written by Judge Leventhal, addressed the ripeness of this letter-opinion according to the *Abbott Laboratories* framework of fitness for review and hardship to the parties. Because the underlying issue was legal, a matter of statutory interpretation as to the scope of the Fair Labor Standards Act, the Administrator's advisory opinion was by this measure presently fit for review.

The problem was whether the agency letter amounted to a final agency action. *Abbott Laboratories* had involved a formally complete agency action (a rule enacted on the basis of a rulemaking process and then published in the federal register). While there were no such formal indices of finality in the instant case, the court nonetheless found that the agency action was sufficiently complete to be fit for review. The opinion addressed a matter of broad importance in the relevant industry group, this matter had been the subject of deliberation and study by the agency staff, and the opinion as rendered had come from the agency head. In these circumstances, it was unlikely that the opinion transmitted to the industry was tentative or up for reconsideration. As said by the court, "The opinion in this case was signed by the administrator; it was rendered on a broad legal question affecting an entire industry group; we take it as satisfying the aspect of finality which requires an authoritative agency ruling."

The agency also contended that the laundromat operators did not meet the second part of the *Abbott Laboratories* framework—hardship to the parties—in that the laundromats faced no penalties for non-compliance with the opinion. The agency contended that "if it later develops that the Administrator was correct, and they should have raised their wages to meet the statutory minimum, they have only to pay back the additional wages they should have been paying all along." The laundromat operators, however, were subject to actions for double-damages brought by employees for underpayment. In these actions, the agency interpretation of the statute might be deferred to by the court. Also, the Administrator's interpretation, when disseminated in the industry, might "stimulat[e] double-damage suits by employees who need not fear that they would be at odds with the Government officials involved." This risk, the court found, met the *Abbott Laboratories* standard of a hardship sufficient to qualify for present judicial review.

§ 12.10 EXHAUSTION OF ADMINISTRATIVE REMEDIES

There are several reasons for requiring a person to exhaust whatever remedies an agency may offer. Giving the agency first crack should help the agency, by giving it the chance to resolve matters committed to it by Congress in light of the agency's own policies and priorities.[1] Litigation costs and judicial intervention may so stifle a new and unfolding agency program that its fruition (the time when the program's merits and demerits can probably be most usefully assessed) is defeated. Also, a first resort to agencies is usually efficient. Specialized agencies offer processes streamlined to fit the matter at hand.[2] In light of these matters, the courts usually justify exhaustion of administrative remedies in terms of enhancing agency processes. They say that the doctrine allows "an administrative agency to perform functions within its special competence—to make a factual record, to apply its expertise."[3] Also, the courts are not unaware of how the doctrine serves them, the courts, as well. A record as first developed by the agency should be useful to the courts. At times, application of the doctrine may remove the need for judicial review, in those cases when the agency gives a complainant the relief she seeks.

We will discuss exhaustion of administrative remedies in three different contexts. First, we discuss the usual context, whether the courts should presently review an agency action or defer review pending further administrative action. Secondly, we address a more unusual application of the doctrine, where it may result not just in a deferral but also in a forfeiture of judicial review. Thirdly, we will discuss the doctrine in a context that especially and separately emphasizes "final agency action" as a condition of judicial review.

§ 12.10.1 The General Doctrine

For the exhaustion doctrine, bedrock in case law is found in Justice Brandeis's opinion in *Myers v. Bethlehem Shipbuilding Corporation*.[4] The National Labor Board had filed a complaint charging Bethlehem Shipbuilding with unfair labor practices at one of its plants and the Board had set a hearing on that complaint. If the Board found against Bethlehem Shipbuilding, judicial review was available. Under the National Labor Relations Act, the Board had to apply to a federal court of appeals for enforcement of whatever order it entered against a person or company.

Rather than abiding an agency hearing, Bethlehem Shipbuilding immediately filed suit in federal district court (under a general jurisdictional statute) and asked that the hearing be enjoined. Bethlehem contended that the Board lacked jurisdiction over it because the compa-

§ 12.10

1. "The exhaustion doctrine also acknowledges the commonsense notion of dispute resolution that an agency ought to have an opportunity to correct its own mistakes with respect to the programs it administers before it is haled into federal court." McCarthy v. Madigan, 503 U.S. 140, 112 S.Ct. 1081, 117 L.Ed.2d 291 (1992).

2. These agency processes may be compared to those of the court, which to accommodate the variety of cases that generalist courts must hear, are necessarily fuller and more cumbersome. Consequently it would often be more efficient for the agency to use its more streamlined processes to develop the record in a case.

3. Securities and Exchange Com'n v. G.C. George Securities, Inc., 637 F.2d 685 (9th Cir.1981).

4. 303 U.S. 41, 58 S.Ct. 459, 82 L.Ed. 638 (1938).

ny was not involved in interstate commerce as required by the National Labor Relations Act. In this respect, Bethlehem made the further argument, appealing at first glance, that without jurisdiction the Board hearing "would be futile" and that such a futile proceeding would cost the company considerably in terms of litigation expenses and "harmonious relations" with its employees.

The Supreme Court agreed that the Board had no jurisdiction over Bethlehem unless it was involved in interstate commerce. But because Congress had given the Board the power to determine whether a company was involved in interstate commerce, that question, the Court held, should first be decided by the agency. To do otherwise would "in effect substitute the District Court for the Board as the tribunal to hear and determine in the first instance" and would therefore violate "the long-standing rule of judicial administration that no one is entitled to judicial relief for a supposed or threatened injury until the prescribed administrative remedy has been exhausted."

In *Myers v. Bethlehem Shipbuilding,* the Court identified the doctrine as a "rule of judicial administration," a part of the inherent powers of courts. Thereafter, in 1946, the doctrine received a new support: it was "codified", as the Supreme Court has said, in Sec. 704 of the Administrative Procedures Act.[5] Sec. 704 identifies the agency actions that are "subject to review." These actions are those "made reviewable by statute and final agency action for which there is no adequate remedy in a court."[6] An agency action "made reviewable by statute" is, perforce, one where administrative remedies have been exhausted. As explained by the Court, "Perhaps the most common application of the exhaustion doctrine is in cases where the relevant statute provides that certain administrative procedures shall be exclusive."[7] Otherwise, Sec. 704 makes "final agency action" subject to review, and today such finality is itself a condition of exhaustion.

But neither as a rule of judicial administration nor as a statutory requirement of "final agency action" has the doctrine been absolute. While the doctrine was strongly stated in *Myers v. Bethlehem Shipbuilding Corp.,* that approbation was in circumstances that approximated the core case for exhausting administrative remedies: a factual issue within the agency's jurisdiction and with special statutory review respecting that issue available after the agency had acted.[8]

5. Bowen v. Massachusetts, 487 U.S. 879, 903, 108 S.Ct. 2722, 101 L.Ed.2d 749 (1988) ("the primary thrust of [Sec. 704] was to codify the exhaustion requirement"); Darby v. Cisneros, 509 U.S. 137, 113 S.Ct. 2539, 125 L.Ed.2d 113 (1993).

6. In this respect, Sec. 704 provides that "Action made reviewable by statute and final agency action for which there is no adequate remedy in a court are subject to judicial review." 5 U.S.C. § 704.

7. McKart v. United States, 395 U.S. 185, 193, 89 S.Ct. 1657, 1662, 23 L.Ed.2d 194 (1969).

8. The party seeking immediate judicial review may claim that the court presently has jurisdiction by means of a general jurisdiction statute such as federal question jurisdiction under 28 U.S.C. § 1331. A jurisdictional issue, then, is whether Congress, by providing a form of special statutory review meant to oust the courts of jurisdiction under a general jurisdiction statute.

Outside this core case, exhaustion of administrative remedies is not necessarily required and the courts will at times hear cases ahead of the processes that agencies may offer. When courts will hear cases ahead of the agencies is determined by various factors.[9] One factor concerns the nature of the issue that the court is asked to decide, whether the issue is factual or legal. For factual issues, the specialized agency is ordinarily considered the better forum, at least in terms of initially ironing out the issue and developing a record.[10] A court would, for instance, likely benefit from an agency record and opinion on the merits of a sophisticated pollution-control scheme. On the other hand, where the issue is legal, perhaps a matter of construing statutory language, the courts are more confident of their skills and not as likely to require exhaustion.[11] Certainly they are not as likely where an agency is operating under an apparent error of law and in doing so threatens the very "obliteration of a right which Congress has given."[12]

This last statement is from *Leedom v. Kyne.* In that case, the National Labor Relations Board had certified for collective bargaining a unit which included both professional and non-professional employees. This certification was an apparent violation of the National Labor Relations Act's proscription of this sort of combination of employees. Accordingly, the professional employees challenged the certification in a federal court action brought under a general jurisdiction statute. The National Labor Relations Act provided for judicial review of bargaining-unit certifications, but only after a Board hearing and final order. The Board strenuously argued that that process, being the command of Congress, had to be used.

The Supreme Court disagreed. The Board's certification decision constituted a legal error that was "clear," and "contrary to a specific prohibition in the Act." In this context, withholding immediate review in favor of the complainant's exhausting the statutory form of review would

The general answer to this question is no. Regarding subject-matter jurisdiction, see Sec. 12.4.1, supra.

9. This discretionary authority to take a case ahead of agency processes is usefully described in McCarthy v. Madigan, 503 U.S. 140, 112 S.Ct. 1081, 117 L.Ed.2d 291 (1992).

10. In the courts, the practice is that "exhaustion should be required ... when the nature of the case suggests that a factual record be developed prior to judicial review and that the issues would be more susceptible of judicial determination after being framed by the agency." Energy Co-op, Inc. v. U.S. Dept. of Energy, 659 F.2d 146, 148–49 (Temp.Em.Ct.1981). See also McKart v. United States, 395 U.S. 185, 193–94, 89 S.Ct. 1657, 1662–63, 23 L.Ed.2d 194 (1969) ("The agency, like a trial court, is created for the purpose of applying a statute in the first instance. Accordingly, it is normally desirable to let the agency develop the necessary factual background upon which decisions should be based").

11. Compare McKart v. United States, 395 U.S. 185, 89 S.Ct. 1657, 23 L.Ed.2d 194 (1969), with McGee v. United States, 402 U.S. 479, 91 S.Ct. 1565, 29 L.Ed.2d 47 (1971). In the former case, involving a *legal* issue about draft exemption, the Court had not required exhaustion. But in *McGee,* where the issue was factual, the court required exhaustion. The court explained that "Unlike the dispute about statutory interpretation involved in *McKart,* McGhee's claim to exempt status—as a ministerial student or a conscientious objector—depended on the application of expertise by administrative bodies in resolving underlying issues of fact." 402 U.S. at 486, 91 S.Ct. at 1569.

12. 358 U.S. 184, 79 S.Ct. 180, 3 L.Ed.2d 210 (1958).

likely have resulted in a " 'sacrifice or obliteration of a right which Congress' has given to professional employees." The Court, therefore, did not require exhaustion.

Still, we should remember that especially where a party seeks to avoid a statutorily prescribed administrative process, resort to that process is much the norm and Leedom v. Kyne much the exception. In *Ticor Title Ins. Co. v. Federal Trade Commission,*[13] the Commission had issued a complaint, alleging price fixing, against six title insurance companies. The companies claimed that in issuing the complaint, the Commission had assumed a prosecutorial function that Article II of the Constitution assigns to the executive branch. Rather than abiding the statutory form of review (a Commission hearing and then if necessary taking an appeal from the hearing), these companies sought immediate judicial review. Immediate review, they argued, was warranted because they challenged the very constitutionality of the process to be exhausted. In this respect, the companies claimed that the Commission, as a mere agent of Congress, was not competent to decide that its principle, Congress, had acted unconstitutionally. The court, however, required them to exhaust their remedies, constitutional claims or no, because they had not met the *Leedom v. Kyne* exception for a "clear" violation of law.[14]

Along with assessing the issue to be decided, exhaustion of remedies has involved an assessment of the injury a person may suffer if he is forced to exhaust administrative processes. In *Meyers v. Bethlehem Shipbuilding*, the company's claim of injury, its litigation costs for hearings that might turn out to be groundless, was not enough to escape the doctrine. These costs, the Court was later to say, are those that we can expect to bear "as part of the social burden of living under government."[15] Outside of litigation costs, however, the courts have found that injury to a plaintiff is relevant to the exhaustion question. Usually, this is injury of the sort that cannot be repaired should the plaintiff be forced to exhaust administrative remedies.[16]

* * *

13. 814 F.2d 731 (D.C.Cir.1987),

14. 814 F.2d at 740. The court further explained that " 'Halting or delaying an administrative proceeding whenever a party is able to allege a constitutional question that is not frivolous' would produce the very interference with agency processes that exhaustion doctrine is designed to prevent." Also, agency processes might render the constitutional issues moot, and in doing so serve the principle of avoiding gratuitous constitutional decisions by courts. See also Rosenthal & Co. v. Bagley, 581 F.2d 1258, 1261 (7th Cir.1978).

15. Allen v. Grand Central Aircraft Co., 347 U.S. 535, 74 S.Ct. 745, 98 L.Ed. 933 (1954). In Meyers v. Bethlehem Shipbuilding, Justice Brennen explained that "Lawsuits ... often prove to be have been groundless", Brandeis wrote, "but no way has been discovered of relieving a defendant of the necessity of a trial to establish that fact." 303 U.S. at 50–52.

But only usually will the courts *not* look at litigation costs. Especially if the alleged agency error is clear, a sensible judge may consider these costs as a factor weighing against exhaustion. *See* PepsiCo, Inc. v. Federal Trade Commission, 472 F.2d 179 (2d Cir.1972) (Friendly, J.).

16. Utah Fuel Co. v. National Bituminous Coal Commission, 306 U.S. 56, 59 S.Ct. 409, 83 L.Ed. 483 (1939). See also Boise Cascade Corp. v. F.T.C., 498 F.Supp.

Sec. 704 of the Administrative Procedure Act, as it provides that "Action made reviewable by statute and final agency action for which there is no adequate remedy in a court are subject to judicial review," is Congress's own presumption of exhaustion of administrative remedies.

In *Darby v. Cisneros*,[17] the Court addressed a longstanding problem in administrative law. This problem was whether discretionary appeals, to a higher agency authority, from a decision by an administrative law judge had to be "exhausted" before that ALJ decision could be reviewed by a court. In the instant case, a lower court had refused to review an ALJ decision that was subject to such a discretionary appeal to the head of the agency. The court reasoned that this possibility of an intra-agency appeal had to be "exhausted" prior to judicial review.

That lower court decision was reversed by the Supreme Court. In his opinion for the Court, Justice Blackmun, after expressing his astonishment that Sec. 704 had been so long overlooked as a solution to these exhaustion issues, turned to it and therein found the solution to the problem at hand. In its last sentence, Sec. 704 provides "Except as otherwise expressly required by statute, agency action otherwise final is final ... whether or not there has been presented ... an application ... for any form of reconsideration...." Within the meaning of this sentence, the Court found a useful rule certain: An ALJ decision subject to a discretionary appeal is final for purposes of judicial review. The lower court, therefore, had improperly required exhaustion.

While the Court quite aptly found a rule certain in Sec. 704 for the exhaustion problem before it, Justice Blackmun's opinion described the provenance of this rule in terms that have given rise to an expansive and probably unfortunate reading of the Court's decision. This description was as follows:

> Appropriate deference in this case requires the recognition that, with respect to actions brought under the APA, Congress effectively codified the doctrine of exhaustion of administrative remedies in [Sec. 704]. Of course, the exhaustion doctrine continues to apply as a matter of judicial discretion in cases not governed by the APA. But where the APA applies ... [c]ourts are not free to impose an exhaustion requirement as a rule of judicial administration where the agency action has become final under [Sec. 704].

The now common reading of this language is that for Administrative Procedure Act cases, *Darby* altogether eliminated the "common law" of exhaustion and instead left the doctrine to be determined solely according to Sec. 704.[18]

772, 777 (D.Del.1980), rehearing denied 498 F.Supp. 782 (1980); West v. Bergland, 611 F.2d 710, 718 (8th Cir.1979), cert. denied 449 U.S. 821, 101 S.Ct. 79, 66 L.Ed.2d 23 (1980); Ogletree v. McNamara, 449 F.2d 93, 99 (6th Cir.1971); Wolff v. Selective Service Local Board No. 16, 372 F.2d 817, 825 (2d Cir.1967).

17. 509 U.S. 137, 113 S.Ct. 2539, 125 L.Ed.2d 113 (1993).

18. Under this view, the common law of exhaustion, as it had been adumbrated just the year before *Darby* in McCarthy v. Madigan, 503 U.S. 140, 112 S.Ct. 1081, 117 L.Ed.2d 291 (1992), remains in place for

The "common law" of exhaustion refers to the exhaustion doctrine as the courts have developed it over the years, presumably according to the inherent power claimed in *Meyers v. Bethlehem Shipbuilding*. Discarding this alleged common law, as *Darby v. Cisneros* is said to do, has its problems. To start with, a complete disposal of the case law on exhaustion will likely cause more confusion than it cures. At the same time, this disposal stands to obliterate some sensible principles, as the courts have developed, respecting an appropriate allocation of labor between courts and agencies. Indeed, these very principles had been reviewed, restated, and approved by the Supreme Court, in *McCarthy v. Madigan*,[19] just one year prior to *Darby v. Cisneros*.

Moreover, even as Sec. 704 is the primary source of the exhaustion doctrine, in being so it does not wipe out the common law. On the whole Sec. 704 and the common-law it presumably displaces are much the same thing. Sec. 704 offers no precisely delineated measure of exhaustion; instead, its terms rather endorse the alleged "common law" doctrine. As it was enacted, Sec. 704 "codified" the doctrine previously developed in the courts.[20] Subsequently, the doctrine has evolved consistent with both *Myers* (the common-law bottom of exhaustion) and Sec. 704.

Sec. 704 is written in terms that accommodate this evolution. Sec. 704 defines the agency actions that are "subject to judicial review" as (1) those "made reviewable by statute" and (2) "final agency action for which there is no adequate remedy in a court." The "made reviewable by statute" provision gives a primacy to congressionally created agency processes and requires the exhaustion of them. That which has been characterized as the "common law" does the same: under it "the most common application of the exhaustion doctrine is in cases where the relevant statute provides that certain administrative procedures shall be exclusive."[21] Sec. 704's second provision, for "final agency action for which there is no adequate remedy in a court" is coterminous with the courts' practice of at times going ahead and reviewing final agency action where deferred review would not offer an "adequate" remedy.[22] Where deferred judicial review would be less than adequate has been delineated and identified by the courts in various ways, some of which we have

non-Administrative Procedure Act cases. See, e.g., Volvo v. Department of Labor, 118 F.3d 205 (4th Cir.1997). A constitutional tort would be one such non-APA case.

19. 503 U.S. 140, 112 S.Ct. 1081, 117 L.Ed.2d 291 (1992).

20. Bowen v. Massachusetts, 487 U.S. 879, 903, 108 S.Ct. 2722, 101 L.Ed.2d 749 (1988) ("the primary thrust of [Sec. 704] was to codify the exhaustion requirement").

21. McKart v. United States, 395 U.S. 185, 193, 89 S.Ct. 1657, 23 L.Ed.2d 194 (1969).

22. As the Administrative Procedure was presented to the Senate for its consideration, "final agency action" within the meaning of Sec. 704 was described as "any effective or operative agency for which there is no other adequate remedy in any court." The relation of the "made reviewable by statute" and "final agency action for which there is no adequate remedy in a court" provisions of Sec. 704 was explained as follow: Agency actions subject to review were "specific acts made reviewable by legislation and final agency action for there is no other adequate are subject to review under [Sec. 704]." Administrative Procedure Act, Legislative History, S. Doc. No. 248, 79th Cong., 2d Sess. at 368 (1946).

discussed and more of which the Supreme Court identified in its review of the exhaustion doctrine in *McCarthy v. Madigan.*[23]

So, while *Darby v. Cisneros* quite rightly acknowledges that by means of Sec. 704 the Administrative Procedure Act addresses exhaustion, it would seem quite wrong to think that either *Darby* or Sec. 704 generally displaces the alleged "common law" that has been in the works these many years. Rather, it makes more sense to say that Sec. 704 underwrites this common law.

§ 12.10.2 The Exhaustion Doctrine and Forfeiture of Judicial Review

The usual question addressed by the exhaustion doctrine is, as we have said, simply one of timing: whether a party has prematurely resorted to the courts. In *Myers v. Bethlehem Shipbuilding,* while the courts withheld immediate judicial review that review was ultimately available, by means of special statutory review if the Board found against Bethlehem.[24] At times, however, the exhaustion doctrine may involve consequences harsher than a postponement of review. By failing "to contest its rights in an available administrative forum," a party may "forfeit[] its right to judicial review."[25] An instance of the courts' reluctance to the deploy the exhaustion doctrine so as to eliminate the "right to judicial review" was provided by the Supreme Court decision in *McKart v. United States.*[26]

A draftee, McKart, was on trial for the crime of "willfully and knowingly failing to report for and submit to induction into the Armed Forces." His defense was that as the "sole surviving son" in his family, he was statutorily exempted from the draft. The district court, however, held that McKart could no longer raise that defense in court because "he had failed to exhaust the administrative remedies provided by the Selective Service System." McKart had failed to protest the classification to the local board and to then appeal that board's decision to a state board. Instead, when the local board had classified him "1A," McKart had simply failed to report for military duty.

The district court found McKart guilty of draft evasion and sentenced him to three years in prison. On review of that conviction, the Supreme Court noted that as applied to McKart the exhaustion doctrine amounted to a forfeiture of review. It "stripped" him of a defense in a criminal prosecution. In this forfeiture of review context, the Court found that exhaustion of administrative remedies could be applied only

23. 503 U.S. 140, 112 S.Ct. 1081, 117 L.Ed.2d 291 (1992). The one and only place where Sec. 704 states a specific rule (as opposed to general rules) is that (as covered above) the last sentence of Sec. 704 provides a specific rule respecting the exhaustion doctrine as applied to ALJ decisions.

24. Special statutory review of final Board orders was available because under the National Labor Relations Act the Board could enforce its orders only through a petition to a federal court of appeals. 29 U.S.C.A. § 160(e).

25. Energy Co-op, Inc. v. U.S. Dept. of Energy, 659 F.2d 146, 149 (Em.App.1981).

26. 395 U.S. 185, 89 S.Ct. 1657, 23 L.Ed.2d 194 (1969).

on a showing of a compelling state interest: "whether there is in this case a governmental interest compelling enough to outweigh the severe burden placed on petitioner."

The interest asserted by the government was grounded in efficiency. If McKart avoided Selective Service processes, other registrants would do the same and this would degrade orderly and efficient action in a highly important effort. The Court, however, found that efficiency was not a compelling interest: The Court thought that the "very presence of criminal sanctions is sufficient to ensure that the great majority of registrants will exhaust all administrative remedies before deciding whether or not to continue the challenge to their classifications." Otherwise, McKart's "sole surviving son" defense was solely a matter of statutory construction and resolution of this issue did "not require any particular expertise on the part of the appeal board" nor did it involve any exercise of board "discretion." Moreover, the statute seemed clearly in McKart's favor with respect to the exemption he claimed.

In *McKart v. United States,* a strict requirement of exhaustion of administrative remedies would have forfeited a defense based on a clear error of law. The courts have not rushed to extend the ruling of that case past these circumstances.[27]

§ 12.10.3 Final Agency Action

Judicial review is ordinarily available only at the point of "final agency action." This is the point at which the agency has considered, and has in some way taken a position, as to a particular matter.[28] Before that point, a person is generally required to resort to, and exhaust, administrative processes and remedies. "Final agency action" could thus be considered as a subset of exhaustion, and often it is. But as well, it has come to characterized by the courts as something of a separate prerequisite to judicial review. And here we will discuss it as such.

In *Federal Trade Commission v. Standard Oil Co.,*[29] the Court explained that the purpose of the "final agency action" principle was to gave "the agency an opportunity to correct its own mistakes and to apply its expertise." Letting the agency correct its own mistakes should in turn

27. In McGee v. United States, 402 U.S. 479, 91 S.Ct. 1565, 29 L.Ed.2d 47 (1971), a draftee was convicted of a willful failure to report for induction into military service. As in *McKart,* the draftee claimed a draft exemption which he had been unable to assert in his criminal trial because of his failure to assert it to the Selective Service Board. This time, however, the Supreme Court upheld the conviction. Unlike *McKart,* the draftee's objection was to a factual rather than a legal error in classification. Consequently, his failure to utilize Selective Services processes "implicate[d] decisively the policies served by the exhaustion requirement, especially the purpose of ensuring that the Selective Service system have full opportunity to 'make a factual record' and 'apply its expertise' in relation to a registrant's claim." See also Energy Co-op, Inc. v. U.S. Dept. of Energy, 659 F.2d 146, 149 (Em.App.1981).

28. "[T]he action must mark the 'consummation' of the agency's decision-making processes, ... it must not be of a merely tentative or interlocutory nature." Bennett v. Spear, 520 U.S. 154, 117 S.Ct. 1154, 137 L.Ed.2d 281 (1997). See also Dalton v. Specter, 511 U.S. 462, 114 S.Ct. 1719, 128 L.Ed.2d 497 (1994).

29. 449 U.S. 232, 101 S.Ct. 488, 66 L.Ed.2d 416 (1980).

avoid inefficient "piecemeal review." In the *Standard Oil* case, the Commission had issued a complaint alleging that eight major oil companies had contrived a national petroleum shortage. The Standard Oil Company of California ("Socal") contended that the complaint was groundless, simply the result of political pressures. The company turned this general contention into a particular legal argument by arguing that in the case of the Commission, ordinary prosecutorial discretion respecting when and where to file a complaint was qualified by the Federal Trade Commission Act. The Act required that "the Commission shall have reason to believe" that a violation has occurred.[30] Socal, therefore, asked the Commission to withdraw its complaint because it was based on politics and not such facts as would lead it to believe Socal had violated the law. When the Commission refused to do so, Socal sought to overturn that refusal in court.

The Supreme Court held that the agency determination was *not* final agency action and was therefore unreviewable. The Court explained that the Administrative Procedures Act established final agency action as the baseline for review, and noted the policies (giving an agency the chance to do its own work and avoiding delay and piecemeal review) underlying this finality requirement.[31] In relation to these policies, Socal had argued that it exhausted its administrative remedies inasmuch as it had asked the Commission to dismiss of the complaint and the Commission after due consideration had declined to do so. "By thus affording the Commission the opportunity to decide upon the matter," Socal argued, it had "satisfied the interest underlying the doctrine of exhaustion of remedies." Perhaps. But Socal, the Court explained, had "mistaken finality for exhaustion." The policies especially peculiar to finality, agency "efficiency and enforcement" remained relevant.

Also, Socal claimed that review of agency action at the point it became final—when the Commission entered an order against Socal—was not an "adequate remedy" within the meaning of the Administrative Procedure Act. In this regard, Sec. 704 of the Act provides that "final agency action for which there is no adequate remedy in a court" is subject to judicial review.[32] Socal argued that after a hearing on the merits, the Commission's failure to have "reason to believe" that a violation had occurred would be "insulated from review," because the court would lack an adequate record on that issue and would tend to look at "whether substantial evidence supported" the final agency order—as opposed to the initial "reason to believe" issue. In response to this argument, the Court noted that the Administrative Procedure Act directs a court to consider interlocutory matters on final review, that a

30. 15 U.S.C. § 45(b).

31. The Court also looked to the burden imposed upon Socal. In this regard, the Court noted that the complaint itself had no legal effect, that the burden facing Socal was that of the "expense and disruption of defending itself in protracted adjudicatory proceedings," and that this was not enough.

For the umpteenth time, the Court asserted that "the expense and annoyance of litigation is 'part and parcel of the social burden of living under government.'" 449 U.S. at 243.

32. 5 U.S.C. § 704.

court in reviewing these matters can take additional evidence, and that therefore it could not presume that review in the context of a final agency order would be inadequate.

Although *Federal Trade Commission v. Standard Oil Co.* staunchly applied the condition of final agency action to preclude judicial review of interlocutory orders, the case should not be taken as establishing an absolute bar against review of such orders. That such orders may sometimes be reviewed is recognized by the Administrative Procedure Act. Section 704 provides that a "preliminary, procedural or intermediate agency action or ruling not directly reviewable is subject to review on the review of the final agency action." The phrase "not directly reviewable" implies that some interlocutory actions are directly reviewable.[33]

In *PepsiCo, Inc. v. Federal Trade Commission,* the Federal Trade Commission had issued a complaint alleging that PepsiCo had "hindered ... competition ... by restricting its bottlers from selling outside of a designated geographical area."[34] Before the Commission, PepsiCo moved that the complaint be dismissed because the Commission had failed to join the soft drink bottlers whose business relations with PepsiCo were affected by the complaint. When the Commission denied that motion, PepsiCo filed suit in federal district court, asking that the agency proceedings against it be enjoined unless the bottlers were joined as parties. The district court dismissed this suit as "premature." The second circuit court of appeals, however, reversed the district court and held that the Commission's refusal to join the bottlers was presently reviewable.

The Federal Trade Commission Act provided a special statutory form of review, but only when the Commission had issued a cease and desist order. Because no such order had been issued, review under the Federal Trade Commission Act was not an option. However, Judge Friendly, writing for the court, found that judicial review had been more generally authorized by Sec. 704 of the Administrative Procedure Act. Somewhat provisionally, Judge Friendly accepted the "principle that one can find 'final agency action for which there is no other adequate remedy in a court' if an agency refuses to dismiss a proceeding that is plainly beyond its jurisdiction as a matter of law or is being conducted in a manner that cannot result in a valid order." Also, while noting that ordinary litigation expenses were not generally a reason sufficient to gain immediate judicial review, Judge Friendly explained that the instant case involved a possible "enormous waste of government resources and the continuing threat of a complete restructuring of an industry" and that "PepsiCo and the bottlers ... should not be placed under that threat in a proceeding that must prove to be a nullity."[35]

33. PepsiCo, Inc. v. Federal Trade Commission, 472 F.2d 179 (2d Cir.1972). See also Coca–Cola Co. v. Federal Trade Commission, 475 F.2d 299 (5th Cir.1973) cert. denied 414 U.S. 877, 94 S.Ct. 121, 38 L.Ed.2d 122 (1973); Seven–Up Co. v. Federal Trade Commission, 478 F.2d 755 (8th Cir.1973) cert. denied 414 U.S. 1013, 94 S.Ct. 379, 38 L.Ed.2d 251 (1973).

34. 472 F.2d 179 (2d Cir.1972).

35. 472 F.2d at 187. See also Coca-Cola v. Federal Trade Comm'n, 475 F.2d 299 (5th Cir. 1973); Seven-Up Co. v. Federal

§ 12.11 PRIMARY JURISDICTION

At times, both an agency and a court will have original jurisdiction over the same case or issue. In this context of concurrent jurisdiction, the question addressed by the doctrine of primary jurisdiction is whether, when a party chooses to initiate an action in the court, that court may decline to hear it in favor of an initial decision by the agency.[1] Generally speaking, the answer is that the court can do so. To achieve a "workable allocation of business between [the courts] and agencies"[2] the court may decline to hear the action so that a party is forced to turn to the agency of concurrent jurisdiction for its resolution of the matter in question. This judicial discretion to decline jurisdiction was established by the Supreme Court in its decision in 1907 in *Texas & Pacific Railway v. Abilene Cotton Oil Co.*[3]

Under the common law, a shipper might bring a court action against a carrier to recover charges in excess of a reasonable rate. This court remedy had been expressly preserved by the Interstate Commerce Act.[4] But the Act itself also prohibited unreasonable charges and gave the Interstate Commerce Commission the power to provide reparations to shippers for the amount of an overcharge. A carrier could, therefore, either file charges with the Interstate Commerce Commission or sue in federal court. In *Abilene Cotton* a shipper chose to sue in federal court, to recover the overcharge of an allegedly excessive rate. The Supreme Court, however, dismissed the court action in favor of primary agency jurisdiction. Notwithstanding the concurrent jurisdiction and choice of forums, court or agency, provided by the Interstate Commerce Act, the Court held that "a shipper seeking reparation predicated upon the unreasonableness of the established rate must ... primarily invoke redress through the Interstate Commerce Commission." If rate struc-

Trade Comm'n, 478 F.2d 755 (8th Cir. 1973).

§ 12.11

1. Primary jurisdiction differs from exhaustion of remedies in that primary jurisdiction involves the situation where Congress has specifically (and not just generally as by federal question jurisdiction) provided for court jurisdiction respecting the agency action in question. A somewhat fuller description of the difference is as follows: " '[e]xhaustion' applies where a claim is cognizable in the first instance by an administrative agency alone; judicial interference is withheld until the administrative process has run its course. 'Primary jurisdiction', on the other hand, comes into play whenever enforcement of the claim requires the resolution of issues which, under a regulatory scheme, have been placed within the special competence of an administrative body; in such a case the judicial process is suspended pending referral of such issues to the administrative body for its views." United States v. Western Pacific Railroad Co., 352 U.S. 59, 63–64, 77 S.Ct. 161, 1 L.Ed.2d 126 (1956).

2. CAB v. Modern Air Transport, 179 F.2d 622, 625 (2d Cir.1950). As described by the Supreme Court, the division of labor, between the courts and agencies, that primary jurisdiction is based upon is that "practical considerations dictate a division of functions between court and agency under which the latter makes a preliminary, comprehensive investigation of all the facts, analyses them, and applies to them the statutory scheme as it is construed". Federal Maritime Board v. Isbrandtsen Co., 356 U.S. 481, 498, 78 S.Ct. 851, 2 L.Ed.2d 926 (1958).

3. 204 U.S. 426, 27 S.Ct. 350, 51 L.Ed. 553 (1907).

4. The Act provided that "nothing in this Act ... shall in any way abridge or alter the remedies now existing at common law or by statute." 24 Stat. 379, § 2 (1887).

tures were determined in federal courts, these structures might vary from court to court. Such a result, the Court reasoned, was contrary to the uniform rate structure that the Act sought to achieve through the operation of a single agency, the Interstate Commerce Commission.[5]

Thus, the doctrine of primary jurisdiction, that courts with jurisdiction concurrent to that of an agency have the discretion to decline to in favor of an initial agency decision, was established. This discretion, as we said, is generally exercised toward the end of a "workable allocation of business between [the courts] and agencies." Such an allocation of business would, as in *Texas & Pacific Railway v. Abilene Cotton Oil Co.,* ordinarily incline toward a uniform regulatory scheme, by primarily channeling a class of cases to a single agency. But as well, a workable allocation of business between the courts and agencies includes the benefits achieved by a primary application of the specialized knowledge of an agency to matters within its field. Where the issues are factual, the courts—because of an agency's possibly superior fact-finding ability (superior by virtue of specialization, "insight gained through experience, and by more flexible procedure"[6])—may prefer that the agency render the initial decision. But where issues are legal, and therefore closer to their own abilities, the courts are more likely to take the case without remitting it to an agency for an initial decision.

This law-fact distinction was established in *Great Northern Railway v. Merchants' Elevator Co.*[7] The dispute here turned on an interpretation of the Interstate Commerce Act. Inasmuch as the case came down to this "legal" issue of statutory interpretation, the Court held that the lower court need not relinquish its jurisdiction in favor of an initial decision by the Commission. But Justice Brandeis, writing for the Court, explained that had the case involved more than statutory construction, if the issues had been "essentially of fact, and discretion in technical matters," an initial decision by the Commission would have been appropriate. In rate regulation, such factual issues involved "voluminous and conflicting evidence, for the adequate appreciation of which acquaintance with many intricate facts of transportation is indispensable and such acquaintance is commonly to be found only in a body of experts."[8]

Maintaining a uniform regulatory scheme and utilizing administrative expertise are considerations important to the doctrine of primary jurisdiction. Another consideration is whether the matter before the court involves an industry subject to heavy regulation. Here, "a system-

5. The Act, the Court explained, "cannot be construed as continuing in shippers a common law right, the continued existence of which would be absolutely inconsistent with the provisions of the act." "In other words, the Court added, 'the act cannot be held to destroy itself. 204 U.S. at 496, 27 S.Ct. at 336.' "

6. Far East Conference v. United States, 342 U.S. 570, 575, 72 S.Ct. 492, 96 L.Ed. 576 (1952).

7. 259 U.S. 285, 42 S.Ct. 477, 66 L.Ed. 943 (1922).

8. 259 U.S. at 291. See also Far East Conference v. United States, 342 U.S. 570, 574, 72 S.Ct. 492, 96 L.Ed. 576 (1952) ("in cases raising issues of fact not within the conventional experience of judges or cases requiring the exercise of administrative discretion, agencies created by Congress for regulating the subject matter should not be passed over").

atic and interrelated body of [agency] fact-finding and policy-making may be important enough to reduce the original jurisdiction of the courts to a secondary or supplementary role."[9] Also, subjecting the regulated industry to both courts and heavy agency regulation might create too much of a risk of conflicting commands. As the Supreme Court has explained, "In *Abilene,* the carrier, if subject to both agency and court sanctions, would be put in an untenable position when agency and court disagreed on the reasonableness of a rate."[10]

* * *

As there are reasons for a court to prefer an initial agency decision, there are also reasons for the court not to relinquish the jurisdiction Congress has assigned it. Often a plaintiff chooses a court because it is a forum by design and tradition hospitable to private rights. For the court to then refuse to hear the plaintiff in favor of an agency decision may be to sacrifice the individual plaintiff's rights in favor of a more general, public-law oriented remedy as provided by the agency. For instance, a cease and desist order as issued by an agency pursuant to a public law may not be a surrogate for an individual's claim for damages for injuries to her under the common law implemented by the courts.[11]

Where an agency does *not* have the power to provide the same relief as the court, the court may not simply dismiss the action. Instead, it may retain jurisdiction but stay its action pending an agency decision on an issue particularly within its competence.[12] In *General American Tank*

9. L. Jaffe, Judicial Control of Administrative Action, 133 (abridged ed., 1965). Cf. United States v. Radio Corporation of America, 358 U.S. 334, 350, 79 S.Ct. 457, 3 L.Ed.2d 354 (1959) (Finding no primary jurisdiction considering that there was "no pervasive regulatory scheme and no rate structures to throw out of balance" and therefore "sporadic action by federal courts can work no mischief").

10. Nader v. Allegheny Airlines, Inc., 426 U.S. 290, 96 S.Ct. 1978, 48 L.Ed.2d 643 (1976).

11. Nader v. Allegheny Airlines, Inc., 426 U.S. 290, 96 S.Ct. 1978, 48 L.Ed.2d 643 (1976). Also, remitting a matter to an agency, on primary jurisdiction grounds makes for a costly and lengthy piece of litigation. The plaintiff, after filing his action in court must then refile in an agency, prosecute the action there, and then come back to the courts if he wishes to gain judicial review of the agency's decision. In view of these costs, Justice Marshall has said that "wise use of the doctrine necessitates a careful balance of the benefits to be derived from utilization of agency processes as against the costs in complication and delay." Ricci v. Chicago Mercantile Exchange, 409 U.S. 289, 93 S.Ct. 573, 34 L.Ed.2d 525 (1973) (dissenting).

12. However, a preference for dismissal, at least where the whole case is within "the general scope" of an agency's jurisdiction, was described by Justice Frankfurter in Far East Conference v. United States, 342 U.S. 570, 72 S.Ct. 492, 96 L.Ed. 576 (1952). In that case (where the government was the plaintiff), Frankfurter explained:

> Having concluded that initial submission to the Federal Maritime Commission is required, we may either order the case retained on the District Court docket pending the Board's action, . . . or order dismissal of the proceeding. . . . As distinguished by the situation presented by the first *El Dorado* case, [308 U.S. 422, 60 S.Ct. 325, 84 L.Ed. 361 (1940)], which was a contract action raising only incidentally a question proper for initial administrative decision, the present case involves questions within the general scope of the Maritime board's jurisdiction. . . . An order of the Board will be subject to review by a United States Court of Appeals. . . . We believe that no purpose will here be served to hold the present action in abeyance in the District Court while the proceeding before the board and subsequent judicial review or enforcement of its order is being

Car Corp. v. El Dorado Terminal Co., a shipper, to recover amounts due it under a lease agreement for railroad cars, sued the leasing company.[13] The leasing company defended on the grounds that the payments that the shipper sought to recover amounted to an illegal transportation rebate. At the request of the Interstate Commerce Commission, the Supreme Court held that that agency had a primary jurisdiction over the rebate issue. However, the Court noted that apart from the rebate issue, the "action was an ordinary one ... on a written contract" where the district court was conventionally competent once the rebate issue was resolved. Consequently, the Court held that the court action should be stayed rather than dismissed. As explained by the Court,

> When it appeared in the course of litigation that an administrative problem, committed to the Commission, was involved, the court should have stayed its hand pending the Commission's determination of the unlawfulness and reasonableness of the practices under the terms of the [Interstate Commerce] Act. There should not be a dismissal, ... the cause should be held pending the conclusion of an appropriate administrative proceeding.[14]

Although stays may better preserve the court-forum chosen by the plaintiff, they are costly. The parties must bear the costs, the delay and litigation expense of the additional agency hearing that the stay requires. An alternative that may sometimes avoid this cost, while still gaining the expertise of the agency for the benefit of the court, is for the court to request an *amicus* brief from the agency. In a suit between gas companies for amounts claimed under tariffs filed with the Federal Energy Regulatory Commission, the court found that because interpretation of the tariffs turned on the Commission's order approving them, a decision in the case would be added by agency input. But rather than resorting to "the conventional practice in primary jurisdiction cases," of staying the case pending an agency hearing in the matter, the court instead asked the Commission to file an *amicus* brief explaining the order in question. Considering the limited nature of this question, surely the *amicus* route

> pursued. A similar suit is easily initiated later, if appropriate. Business-like procedure counsels that the Government's complaint should now be dismissed....

Where the Court dismisses an action, primary jurisdiction in an agency may for all practical purposes be the same as an exclusive jurisdiction. In *Abilene Cotton,* as the Court dismissed the rate case before it in favor of the Interstate Commerce Commission's jurisdiction in the matter, it explained that

> [W]e think that it inevitably follows from the context of the act that the independent right of an individual originally to maintain actions in courts to obtain pecuniary redress for violations of the act ... must be confined to redress of such wrongs as can, consistently with the context of the act, be redressed by courts without previous action by the Commission, and, therefore, does not imply the power in a court to primarily hear complaints concerning wrongs of the character of the one here complained of.

204 U.S. at 442, 27 S.Ct. at 356.

13. 308 U.S. 422, 60 S.Ct. 325, 84 L.Ed. 361 (1940), rehearing denied 309 U.S. 694, 60 S.Ct. 465, 84 L.Ed. 1035 (1940).

14. 308 U.S. at 433, 60 S.Ct. at 331. See also Israel v. Baxter Laboratories, Inc., 466 F.2d 272 (D.C.Cir.1972).

was, as the court said, here "a more efficient and expeditious alternative."[15]

While stays and agency amicus briefs may be useful means of preserving the rights of parties, the usual practice seems to be outright dismissal by the court. This is done, of course, on the assumption that the private party will have another crack at the courts, by means of review of the final agency action in the matter, and that this will sufficiently protect the private party's rights.[16]

§ 12.11.1 Additional Factors Pertaining to Division of Jurisdiction Between Courts and Agencies

As the doctrine of primary jurisdiction tries to allocate business between courts and agencies in some sensible way, the doctrine has not managed to do so in an uncomplicated way. The doctrine is discretionary, turning on a number of factors. "No fixed formula exists for applying the doctrine of primary jurisdiction" and in "every case the question is whether the reasons for existence of the doctrine are present and whether the purposes it serves will be aided by its application in the particular litigation."[17] This section more fully examines cases showing how this discretion is exercised.

Abilene Cotton was a core case for application of the doctrine of primary jurisdiction. The subject matter, reasonableness of rates in the transportation industry, involved factual matters of economics and tech-

15. Distrigas of Massachusetts Corp. v. Boston Gas Co., 693 F.2d 1113, 1119 (1st Cir.1982). The Supreme Court may have approved of using the *amicus* brief as a means of gaining agency expertise. In Rosado v. Wyman, 397 U.S. 397, 407, 90 S.Ct. 1207, 1215, 25 L.Ed.2d 442 (1970), the Court, in finding that the trial court had not erred in refusing to submit a matter (pertaining to the compatibility of state welfare law with federal law) to the Department of Health, Education, and Welfare according to the doctrine of primary jurisdiction, explained:

> The District Court ... made a considerable effort to learn the views of HEW. The possibility of HEW's participation, whether as a party or an amicus, was explored in the District Court and the Department at that stage determined to remain aloof. We cannot in these circumstances fault the District Court for proceeding to try the case.

16. The fact that a matter referred to an agency on primary jurisdiction grounds will eventually come before the courts again, as an incident of judicial review of completed agency action, seems to be a factor in finding primary jurisdiction in the agency in the first place. As said by the Supreme Court, "When there is a basis for judicial action, independent of agency proceedings, courts may route the threshold decision as to certain issues to the agency charged with primary responsibility for governmental supervision or control of the particular industry or activity involved". Port of Boston Marine Terminal Ass'n v. Rederiaktiebolaget Transatlantic, 400 U.S. 62, 68, 91 S.Ct. 203, 27 L.Ed.2d 203 (1970). What the allocation of functions between the courts and agencies according to the doctrine of primary jurisdiction can come down to, then, is that the agency makes "a *preliminary,* comprehensive investigation of all the facts, analyzes them, and applies to them the statutory scheme as it is construed." Federal Maritime Board v. Isbrandtsen Co., 356 U.S. 481, 498, 78 S.Ct. 851, 2 L.Ed.2d 926 (1958). See also Aircraft & Diesel Equipment Corp. v. Hirsch, 331 U.S. 752, 767, 67 S.Ct. 1493, 91 L.Ed. 1796 (1947) (initial agency decision "serve[s] as a foundation for or perchance to make unnecessary later judicial proceedings"). But as discussed in the text above, a final judicial review of an agency decision on a matter is not in all respects a surrogate for an initial court decision on that matter.

17. United States v. Western Pacific Railroad Co., 352 U.S. 59, 77 S.Ct. 161, 1 L.Ed.2d 126 (1956).

nology suited to administrative expertise. Also, because Congress had for better or worse committed the railroads to a pervasive and centralized scheme of agency regulation, the picture in *Abilene Cotton* was that of "a systematic and interrelated body of [agency] fact-finding and policy making . . . important enough to reduce the original jurisdiction of the courts to a secondary or supplementary role."[18] Moreover, in *Abilene Cotton* the agencies jurisdiction was truly concurrent: the agency could hear the very same claim (reparations for unreasonable rates) that had been presented in federal court and provide the same relief as was requested in that court.

Where these core features are not present, deferral to an agency is certainly not automatic. Identification of these features, for instance "what is a question of law best suited for judicial as opposed to agency determination?" is not automatic either, as is shown by a leading decision, *United States v. Western Pacific Railroad Co.*[19]

Without fuses, napalm bombs are an incendiary jelly-like substance. In the *Western Pacific* case, the government had shipped fuse-less napalm bombs by rail, and the issue was whether the government should pay the rate applicable to "incendiary bombs" or the lower rate for gasoline. Claiming the higher rate, the railroad sued the government in the court of claims. The court of claims refused to remit the case to the Interstate Commerce Commission under the primary jurisdiction doctrine. That court's reason was that the issues to be decided were not factual but legal, because they called for interpretation of the statutory tariffs for bombs and gasoline.

The Supreme Court, in an opinion by Justice Harlan, reversed, and held that the case was within the primary jurisdiction of the Commission. Harlan agreed that when a question was purely one of statutory construction, the courts might decide it without reference to an agency. But in Harlan's view, the tariffs in issue did not present such a pure matter of statutory construction. Whether the statute assigned tariff rates for bombs or for gasoline could not be considered abstractly. Instead, the reasons underlying the different tariffs had to be taken into consideration. For incendiary bombs, cost factors relating to the greater work in handling such a dangerous cargo must have been a reason for its higher rate. Therefore, in determining the right tariffs for the case at hand, a question was whether "the factors which make for high costs and therefore high rates on incendiary bombs also call for a high rate on steel casings filled with napalm gel." To answer that question, Harlan said, "there must be a close familiarity with these factors." That familiarity was "possessed not by the courts but by the agency. . . ." Thus, the simple fact that an issue involves a construction of language of legal significance, such as statutes or rules, does not necessarily mean that an initial agency decision is inappropriate. Rather, where the

18. L. Jaffe, Judicial Control of Administrative Action, 133 (abridged ed., 1965).

19. 352 U.S. 59, 65, 77 S.Ct. 161, 1 L.Ed.2d 126 (1956).

construction is in the context of complex and technical matters, it may sometime best be done initially by an agency expert in these matters.

Another core feature of *Abilene Cotton* was that the agency could hear the same claim and provide the same relief as could the court. Where the jurisdiction between court and agency is not so concurrent, the case for primary jurisdiction becomes weaker. Agency may not be altogether concurrent if it lacks the power to hear all the issues that a court can or it cannot as fully provide relief. (In antitrust cases, for instance, an agency might provide a degree of relief such as a cease and desist order but be unable to provide treble damages as can a court under the Sherman Act.) Because an agency might offer remedies that might aid the public at large, but not compensatory relief such as would suit the individual, the Court in *Nader v. Allegheny Airlines* refused to remit that individual to the agency's jurisdiction.[20]

In the *Allegheny Airlines* case, Ralph Nader had brought a court action, grounded in misrepresentation under the common law, against the Allegheny Airlines for "overbooking."[21] Somewhat parallel to the court's common-law jurisdiction, the Civil Aeronautics Board was empowered to "determine whether any air carrier . . . is engaged in unfair or deceptive practices" and to issue a "cease and desist" order. This being the case, the agency argued the courts should defer to the agency's jurisdiction. The Court was of a different opinion, which was that it should not sacrifice the plaintiff's rights in favor of the more general, public law oriented relief offered by CAB. In this regard, The Court explained that a "wrong may be of the sort that calls for compensation to an injured individual without requiring the extreme remedy of a cease-and-desist order."

§ 12.11.2 Primary Jurisdiction and the Antitrust Laws

Federal antitrust laws establish a standard of competitiveness in American business. These laws also create a privately held cause of action, which includes treble damages, enforceable in federal courts. Against this antitrust background, however, Congress has committed several industries to extensive agency regulation. In these industries, regulation not competition is usually the watchword, to the extent that sometimes these industries are exempted from the antitrust laws.

Whether a regulated industry has been "immunized" against the antitrust laws by such a regulatory scheme is often a difficult question for which there is no single method of finding the answer. Occasionally, the statutes pertaining to the regulated industry will specifically exempt certain activities from antitrust liability. For instance, farmers are by statute exempted from liability for joint marketing, even when it elimi-

20. 426 U.S. 290, 96 S.Ct. 1978, 48 L.Ed.2d 643 (1976).

21. "Overbooking" is the common practice by which the airlines deliberately book more passengers than seats for a given flight, on the understanding that ordinarily not all passengers who make reservations keep them. Nader had been bumped from an Allegheny Airlines flight when more passengers showed up than seats available.

nates competition and results in higher prices.[22] Other times, an agency may require or authorize business practices which otherwise would be illegal under the antitrust laws, and such an allowance operates as an exemption. In *Gordon v. New York Stock Exchange, Inc.,* the Supreme Court held that the fixed commission rates used by the stock exchanges, ordinarily per se violations of the Sherman Act, were exempted from the antitrust laws because the rates had been approved by the Securities Exchange Commission.[23] Taking matters a step further, in *United States v. National Association of Securities Dealers, Inc.* the Court held that certain price maintenance practices in the sale of mutual funds were exempted from the antitrust laws even though these practices had yet to be considered by the Securities Exchange Commission. The existence of a pervasive regulatory authority, not necessarily the exercise of it, was key.[24] As said by the Court, the "authority" of the Commission, the "federal agency responsible for regulating the mutual-fund industry ... will be seriously compromised if these agreements are deemed actionable under the Sherman Act." And so, the antitrust laws had "been displaced by the pervasive regulatory scheme."[25]

In these antitrust immunity cases, the primary jurisdiction question is often whether the court ought to defer to the responsible agency, for that agency to determine whether the conduct in issue had been immunized. Because the "scope of immunity may differ depending on the regulatory system and conduct at issue," the usual answer here, one arrived at somewhat reflexively, is simply to send the case to the agency for an initial decision.[26] But in *Ricci v. Chicago Mercantile Exchange,* the

22. 49 U.S.C. § 1384. Another instance is the Reed–Bulwinkle Act, 49 U.S.C.A. § 5b, which provides that an agreement between carriers that has been approved by the Interstate Commerce Commission is exempted from the antitrust laws.

23. 422 U.S. 659, 95 S.Ct. 2598, 45 L.Ed.2d 463 (1975). In finding the fixed rates exempt from the antitrust laws, the Court explained that

> The Securities Exchange Act was intended by the Congress to leave the fixing of reasonable rates of commission to the SEC. Interposition of the antitrust laws, which would bar fixed commission rates as per se violations of the Sherman Act, in the face of positive SEC action would preclude and prevent the operation of the Exchange Act, as intended by Congress and as effectuated through SEC regulatory activity.

24. 422 U.S. 694, 95 S.Ct. 2427, 45 L.Ed.2d 486 (1975).

25. 422 U.S. at 729, 735, 95 S.Ct. at 2447, 2480. For other industries and regulatory schemes, the courts, however, have not been as quick to find an immunity. In *United States v. RCA,* an exchange of television stations between the National Broadcasting Co. and the Westinghouse Broadcasting Co. was said to violate the Sherman Act, 358 U.S. 334, 79 S.Ct. 457, 3 L.Ed.2d 354 (1959). The defenses were that the transaction had been approved by the Federal Communications Commission and that the action was in any event within the primary jurisdiction of the Commission. The Court disagreed, saying that the "scope of immunity may differ depending on the regulatory system and conduct at issue," and that here "there was no pervasive regulatory scheme" as would justify deferral to the agency. 358 U.S. at 350, 79 S.Ct. at 466–67. See S. Breyer & R. Stewart, Administrative Law and Regulatory Policy 1180 (2d ed. 1985).

26. In Far East Conference v. United States, 342 U.S. 570, 72 S.Ct. 492, 96 L.Ed. 576 (1952), the Justice Department had brought an action against the conference (an association of shipping companies) alleging that its "dual rate" system (lower rates to companies who used only conference ships) was price fixing in violation of the antitrust laws. The conference was subject to regulation by the Federal Maritime Commission, and by statute that agency's approval of any agreement among shipping

Court presented a more analytic method for answering the primary jurisdiction question.[27]

Ricci, a dealer in commodities futures had sued on the grounds that the Chicago Mercantile Exchange and one of its members had conspired to deprive him of a seat on the exchange in violation of the antitrust laws. The Chicago Exchange was regulated by the Commodities Exchange Commission, and the question of whether Ricci's complaint was primarily within the jurisdiction of this Commission turned, as the Court said, on "three related premises." These premises were: (1) whether the Commodity Exchange Act established an antitrust immunity (2) whether "some facets of the dispute between Ricci and the Exchange are within the statutory jurisdiction of the Commodity Exchange Commission," and (3) whether "adjudication of that dispute by the Commission promised to be of material aid in resolving the immunity question."

As to the first premise: The Commodity Exchange Act provided that exchanges such as Chicago Mercantile Exchange were to operate under rules filed with the Department of Agriculture and enforced by the Commodity Exchange Commission. If the conduct in question had indeed been authorized by such a rule, there was a "plainly substantial issue" of antitrust immunity. The second premise, respecting agency jurisdiction, was satisfied in that the Exchange rules involved in the immunity question were within the Commission's power to enforce. Finally, the third premise, respecting the usefulness of remitting the case to the Commission, was also met. In this regard, the issue of immunity arose only if the denial of Exchange membership to Ricci "was in violation of the [Commodity Exchange] Act for failure to follow Commission rules."

lines exempted the agreement from the antitrust laws. A majority of the Court found, therefore, that the Commission had primary jurisdiction in the case. In doing so, the majority deferred to the Commission's broad responsibility and experience in these matters of shipping laws and practices. The dual rate agreement in question, however, had not been filed with, nor approved by, the Commission. Moreover, to the dissent the dual rate system was so patently contrary to the shipping laws that a referral to the agency was unnecessary. So, on this face of things, the antitrust immunity issue was one of law conventionally within the competence of the courts.

The dissent, as it turned out, seemed to have had the better view. The Federal Maritime Commission, when it considered the dual rate system, approved it. Subsequently, the system was again challenged in another antitrust action, Federal Maritime Board v. Isbrandtsen Co., 356 U.S. 481, 78 S.Ct. 851, 2 L.Ed.2d 926 (1958). Here the issue was the one raised by the dissent in the *Far East Conference* case, whether the dual rate system was illegal under the shipping laws themselves. The Court, disagreeing with the opinion that it had sought from the Commission, found the system in violation of these laws and thus outside any exemption to antitrust that they provided.

In a sense, the *Far Eastern/Isbrandtsen* cases merely illustrate a conventional operation of primary jurisdiction, where the "facts after they have been appraised by specialized competence serve as a premise for legal consequences to be judicially defined." 352 U.S. at 64–5, 77 S.Ct. at 165. On the other hand, given the costs in terms of litigation expense and delay of deferring the matter to the agencies, the referral to the agency may not have been worth it. As said by Justice Frankfurter in his dissent in *Isbrandtsen,* "it is a form of playfulness to make resort to the Board a prerequisite when the judicial determination of law could have been made precisely as though there had been no proceeding before the Board. This is to make a mockery of the doctrine of primary jurisdiction". 356 U.S. at 519, 78 S.Ct. at 872.

27. 409 U.S. 289, 93 S.Ct. 573, 34 L.Ed.2d 525 (1973).

Such a violation, the Court said, appeared to "pose issues of fact and questions about the scope, meaning, and significance of Exchange membership rules." These were "matters typically lying at the heart of an administrative agency's task," and " 'the courts, while retaining the final authority to expound the statute, should avail themselves of the aid implicit in the agency's superiority in gathering the relevant facts and in marshaling them into a relevant pattern.' "[28] In view of this resolution of its "three premises", the Court remitted Ricci to the primary jurisdiction of Commodities Future Exchange Commission.[29]

28. But while the Commission might determine whether Exchange rules applied and had been violated, the ultimate issue of antitrust immunity as might be provided by these rules was a legal one for the courts to decide. As explained by the Court the Commission was not "to decide either the question of immunity as such or that any rule of the Exchange takes precedence over antitrust policies. Rather, we simply recognize that Congress has established a specialized agency that would determine either that a membership rule of the Exchange has been violated or that it has been followed." 409 U.S. at 307.

29. The Court split five to four. A point made by the dissent was the Commission *might* undertake an investigation at Ricci's request, but Ricci could not count on the Commission doing anything at all. Whether or not it should institute an investigation and hearing into the practices that Ricci questioned lay wholly within the Commission's discretion. Consequently, Justice Marshall in dissent wrote that "The Court . . . remands petitioner to a procedure which he has no power to invoke, in which he has no right to participate if it is invoked, and which cannot provide the remedy he seeks [treble damages] even if he is allowed to participate."

Part 4

CONTROL OF AGENCY DISCRETION

Chapter 13

JUDICIAL REVIEW OF AGENCY DISCRETION

Table of Sections

§ 13.1 THE PURPOSES OF JUDICIAL REVIEW—AN OVERVIEW

Administrative agencies are created by Congress to carry out certain statutorily defined duties, goals and functions. A primary purpose of judicial review is to ensure that agencies do not go beyond their statutory powers in carrying out their tasks. If an agency could freely take actions that were *ultra vires,* that is, beyond its statutory authority, its decisions would completely undermine the separation of powers principles upon which the Constitution is based. Article I, § 1, for example, vests all legislative power in the elected representatives of a bicameral legislature. Agencies are to implement these statutes and neither amend nor ignore them.

Judicial review thus serves as an important check on the legality of the action that agencies may undertake. It also serves as an important check on Congress, as well. An agency must act within the statutory authority provided by Congress, but that authority must be in accord with the Constitution. Congress cannot, for example, authorize an administrative program that violates the First Amendment rights of individuals. Nor may it delegate its legislative powers in so diffuse a manner as to provide agencies with no legislative guidance at all. Similarly, Congress cannot provide agencies with authority that significantly undermines the executive or judicial branches of government. In short, separation of powers principles as well as specific clauses of the Constitution limit the power Congress can delegate to agencies. Courts play an important role as guardians of these constitutional principles and values.

Judicial review of such statutory and constitutional issues is fully in accord with the institutional expertise of the judiciary and the role that courts are expected to play in our constitutional system. Ever since *Marbury v. Madison,*[1] it is "emphatically the province and duty of the judicial department to say what the law is."[2] By training and experience judges are particularly adept at interpreting legal texts and resolving constitutional and statutory issues. As generalist judges they bring an important added dimension to their interpretive task. They are not part of any administrative agency and have no particular regulatory mission to fulfill. As federal judges in particular, they also have a position with life tenure and a salary that cannot be lowered. Such institutional characteristics enhance the ability of courts to apply their legal, interpretive skills in a relatively objective and independent manner. Courts can, when necessary, temper what may sometimes be the more narrow

§ 13.1

1. 5 U.S. (1 Cranch) 137, 2 L.Ed. 60 (1803).

2. Id.

interpretive perspective of a single, mission-oriented administrative agency.

Closely related to the role that courts may play in examining the constitutional and statutory validity of *what* administrative agencies can actually do, is judicial review of *why* agencies decide to exercise their power. It may, for example, constitutionally be fully within an agency's statutory powers to issue sanctions against employers who maintain unsafe working conditions in violation of the relevant statute involved. Before these sanctions can be imposed, however, the violations that trigger them must be based on facts that support the agency's conclusion that they actually occurred. An agency free to make whatever findings of fact it chooses to make can be capable of as much abuse as an agency free to disregard the limits of its statutory authority.

Judicial review of agency fact finding, however, is seldom as independent as judicial review of the statutory scope or constitutional validity of an agency's power. When courts review questions of law involving constitutional issues or claims of *ultra vires* agency action, one judicial decision usually can clear up any statutory confusion that may exist and provide the agency and its litigants with legal guidance in all the cases that are brought. Because of the particularized nature of questions of fact, however, different questions arise in virtually every case. For a court to retry every case that an agency has already tried at the administrative level would be economically and practically unworkable. Courts, thus, generally defer to agency findings of fact, provided they are supported in formal adjudicative proceedings by substantial evidence in the record.[3] If there is such support, courts will accept an agency's findings of fact, even though they might have not made those exact factual findings were they sitting at the trial level.

In addition to reasons of economy and practicality, there are other important reasons for this difference in judicial approach between questions of law and fact. Most administrative agencies are created to deal with certain specialized problems. They are expected to bring to their work as well as continually to develop an expertise with the problems with which they are concerned. Moreover, there is also an expectation that administrators in agencies will be exposed to various kinds of problems over and over again. There is usually a substantial caseload involved and thus, many opportunities for the agency to refine its approach to certain issues as well as to develop increasing knowledge and experience with regard to them. This specialized knowledge gives agency decisionmakers a comparative advantage in making the kinds of particularized judgments required in finding facts.

Similarly, the application of agreed upon law to these facts also usually is treated as a discretionary agency decision. This kind of expertise also provides the agency with the knowledge and legitimacy necessary to make the policy judgments required to address the general regulatory problems it was created to solve. Another purpose of judicial

3. See chapter 4, sec. 4.1, supra.

review is to ensure that such agency judgments are, in fact, reasonable. In playing such a role, courts generally give agencies broad leeway. In most cases, courts do not substitute their judgment for that of the agencies, but rather presume substantive agency results to be reasonable.

This presumption, however, does not prevent a court from looking closely at *how* an agency exercises its judgment and, specifically, the procedures an agency uses to exercise its power. The purpose of this kind of judicial review is not substantive quality control. It is, rather, to ensure that the agency has not abused its power in the process of making its decisions. It assumes that, in most cases, proper procedures will yield reasonable results. Thus, courts rarely substitute their judgment for that of the agency, provided the agency has used the proper procedures in making those judgments.

§ 13.2 THE STANDARDS AND SCOPE OF JUDICIAL REVIEW—THE APA

The basic purposes of judicial review set forth above are embodied in the APA.[1] This section will examine, in particular, the various legal standards set forth in section 706 of the APA and applied by federal courts when reviewing the substance of agency decisions and the procedures used in reaching them. These standards imply a particular scope of review. The ultimate scope of that review determines how far a court can go in overturning or remanding an agency decision.

Section 706(2)(C) gives courts the power to focus on *what* agencies actually do and to set aside agency action found to be "in excess of statutory jurisdiction, authority, or limitations, or short of statutory right."[2] In addition, to provide protection against those rare occasions when an agency's failure to act may be unlawful, section 706 allows the court to "compel action unlawfully withheld or unreasonably delayed."[3] In yet other contexts, an agency might act within its statutory authority, but its actions may nevertheless violate a constitutional provision. The APA authorizes the Court to hold unlawful or set aside agency action found to be "contrary to constitutional right, power, privilege, or immunity."[4]

Section 706 also provides for judicial review of *how* agencies exercise their power—that is, the processes that agencies use. The APA and agency enabling acts provide for certain procedural requirements when agencies make rules,[5] formally adjudicate[6] a dispute or take more informal action.[7] Pursuant to the APA, courts can set aside agency action that

§ 13.2

1. 5 U.S.C.A. §§ 701–706.

2. 5 U.S.C.A. § 706(2)(C). See, e.g., Maislin Industries, U.S., Inc. v. Primary Steel, Inc., 497 U.S. 116, 110 S.Ct. 2759, 111 L.Ed.2d 94 (1990), on remand 911 F.2d 1312 (8th Cir.1990) (agency cannot enact policy which conflicts with statute).

3. 5 U.S.C.A. § 706(1).

4. 5 U.S.C.A. § 706(2)(B).

5. See chapter 4, supra.

6. See chapter 8, supra.

7. See chapter 9, supra.

is "without observance of procedure required by law."[8]

Agencies often make a variety of other discretionary judgments such as deciding the policies they will pursue in order to carry out their statutory goals. Such policies are usually reviewable in court to determine why the agency exercised its powers the way it did. Such policy decisions may be set aside only if they are found to be "arbitrary, capricious, an abuse of discretion or otherwise not in accordance with law."[9] In engaging in this kind of review, courts also review the component parts of the discretionary decisions that agencies make. For example, in carrying out their adjudicatory duties, agencies make findings of fact. The APA provides that courts can set aside agency action in an adjudicatory case if it is premised on facts "unsupported by substantial evidence."[10] In a narrow band of cases, section 706 also allows for *de novo* judicial review of facts.[11]

To determine when these various standards of review apply, as well as the scope or intensity of judicial review that they trigger, it is important to note that the APA takes essentially a bi-polar approach to agency action, differentiating between rules and orders.[12] This approach requires that we ask a number of basic questions. First, it is necessary to understand the nature of the agency action under review. Is it a rule, an order or a form of informal agency action? If we are dealing with a statute that requires a hearing "on the record," the APA requires a formal adjudicatory hearing pursuant to sections 554, 556 and 557 before an order can be issued.[13] Judicial review of questions of fact in such on the record proceedings is pursuant to the "substantial evidence" standard set forth in section 706(2)(E). Similarly, rules made "on the record," require formal rulemaking proceedings which are also governed

8. 5 U.S.C.A. § 706(2)(D).

9. 5 U.S.C.A. § 706(2)(A).

10. 5 U.S.C.A. § 706(2)(E).

11. 5 U.S.C.A. § 706(2)(F).

12. A rule is "the whole or a part of an agency statement of general or particular applicability and future effect designed to implement, interject, or prescribe law or policy or describing the organization, procedure, or practice requirements of an agency...." 5 U.S.C.A. § 551(4) (1982). An order is "the whole or a part of a final disposition, whether affirmative, negative, injunctive, or declaratory in form, of an agency in a matter other than rule making but including licensing." 5 U.S.C.A. § 551(6). Compare § 553 (rule making) with § 554 (adjudication). There are, of course, many exceptions. See generally, Cass, Models of Administrative Action, 72 Va.L.Rev. 363 (1986). See also supra chapters 4 (Rulemaking) and 8 (Formal Adjudication).

13. 5 U.S.C.A. §§ 554, 556 and 557. See chapter 8, sec. 8.2.1, supra. Sections 556 and 557 set forth the procedures for formal hearings that are triggered by Sections 553 and 554 of the Act. Section 553(c) triggers formal rulemaking proceedings when an agency's enabling act requires that rules be made after a hearing "on the record." Similarly, section 554 likewise triggers the procedures set forth in sections 556 and 557 when an agency's enabling act requires that agency adjudications be made after a "hearing on the record."

The APA thus draws a bright line between formal and informal processes, both in the rulemaking and adjudicatory settings. The record which is mandated in formal settings consists of oral and written testimony and the findings of either the examiner (ALJ) or the Commission, if it sits at the trial level. Section 706(2)(E), through its reference to sections 556 and 557, provides for review of agency fact finding made in these processes, and thus applies to facts found pursuant to these formal procedures.

by sections 556 and 557.[14] Proceedings not subject to sections 556 and 557 usually result in the application of the arbitrary and capricious standard of judicial review in section 706(2)(A). Such proceedings include informal rulemaking proceedings under section 553 of the APA as well as various other informal agency actions that may be subject to judicial review.

The standard of review to be applied in any given case often will turn on how courts define and characterize the issues before them.[15] A court may, for example, characterize an issue as a question of fact, a question of law, a question of policy, a question of mixed fact and law, or a question of mixed policy and law. These issues, in turn, will trigger the application of a certain standard of review whose scope or intensity span the complete spectrum of judicial involvement in agency decisions—from no judicial review, for actions committed to agency discretion,[16] to *de novo* judicial review of certain other agency actions.[17] Between these two judicial approaches to agency decisions lie varying degrees of judicial deference to agency judgments.

The remaining sections in this chapter will examine the application of APA standards of judicial review in the variety of procedural and substantive contexts outlined above. The chapter will focus first on judicial review of questions of fact in formal and informal proceedings. The chapter next turns to judicial review of questions of law. It then analyzes judicial review of agency policy decisions. The chapter concludes by analyzing judicial review of a wide variety of discretionary agency decisions, including issues of law application to fact and policy. In so doing, it examines various contexts in which courts do or should defer to various agency judgments, including agency decisions not to act.

§ 13.3 THE LAW–FACT DISTINCTION

The law-fact distinction has long been part of American administrative law.[1] Its primary function is to allocate decisionmaking authority to make findings of fact and to interpret law between agencies and courts. For reasons set out above,[2] agencies are to have primary responsibility to make findings of fact. Courts are to have primary, if not sole, responsibility for certain kinds of questions of law.

14. 5 U.S.C.A. §§ 556, 557.

15. The APA, for example, explicitly distinguishes between questions of fact and questions of law. As to questions of law, the preamble of 5 U.S.C.A. § 706 states that "the reviewing court shall decide all relevant questions of law...." Section 706(E) provides for substantial evidence review of fact questions in formal agency proceedings.

16. 5 U.S.C.A. § 701(a)(2); see, e.g., Heckler v. Chaney, 470 U.S. 821, 832, 105 S.Ct. 1649, 1656, 84 L.Ed.2d 714 (1985) (enforcement discretion is presumptively "committed to agency discretion").

17. 5 U.S.C.A. § 706(2)(F); see, e.g., Porter v. Califano, 592 F.2d 770 (5th Cir. 1979), appeal after remand 648 F.2d 310 (1981) (free speech issues in administrative context receive *de novo* review). See also, infra sec. 13.7.2 (discussing review of questions of law).

§ 13.3

1. See Lee, The Origins of Judicial Control of Federal Executive Action, 36 Geo.L.Rev. 287, 302–306 (1948).

2. See sec. 13.1, supra.

Courts have, however, often found it difficult to separate law from fact, particularly when reviewing an agency's application of law to fact.[3] When agencies apply the appropriate legal standards to a set of agreed upon facts, their decisions should and usually are accorded deference by reviewing courts. The same reasons that justify deference to agency fact finding apply here as well. It is a particularized decision that relies heavily on the agency's expertise and experience in a multitude of such cases. Yet, commentators and courts have historically disagreed over whether such issues involved the review of questions of fact or questions of law.[4] Because the law-fact distinction failed to account adequately for a significant body of case law involving the application of law to facts,[5] it was often a source of confusion when applied by some courts.

In *O'Leary v. Brown–Pacific–Maxon,*[6] for example, the Supreme Court reviewed a compensation award made pursuant to the Longshoremen's and Harbor Workers' Compensation Act. The Court had to decide whether an employee's drowning occurred in the course of his employment. If so, his survivors were entitled to compensation under the Act. The decedent was at a company recreation center which was located near a body of water clearly marked as off-limits and dangerous to swimmers. He drowned while attempting to rescue two other men who apparently had ventured beyond the zone of safety. The Deputy Commissioner found as "fact" that the drowning required compensation because the death "arose out of and in the course of employment." The Court of Appeals reversed, but the Supreme Court affirmed the agency, holding that whether the injury was received "in the course of employment" was a question of "fact." The agency's determination in this regard was supported by substantial evidence and thus was reasonable.[7]

3. The standard and scope of judicial review applicable to such questions is discussed in detail, infra sec. 13.7.1. See NLRB v. Hearst Publications, 322 U.S. 111, 64 S.Ct. 851, 88 L.Ed. 1170 (1944), rehearing denied 322 U.S. 769, 64 S.Ct. 1148, 88 L.Ed. 1595 (1944), superseded by statute as stated in NLRB v. Town & Country Elec., Inc., 516 U.S. 85, 116 S.Ct. 450, 133 L.Ed.2d 371 (1995).

4. Compare Louis L. Jaffee, Judicial Control of Administrative Action 570–580 (1965) with Davis, Judicial Control of Administrative Action, 66 Colum.L.Rev. 635, 669 (1966). For an excellent modern discussion of these issues, see Levin, Identifying Questions of Law In Administrative Law, 74 Geo.L.Rev. 1 (1985).

5. Professor Jaffe was an early critic of such crude attempts to employ the law-fact distinction. He recognized that attempting to distinguish a fact from law was an exercise in "unanchored abstractness." He therefore argued that we should concentrate on distinguishing a "finding of fact from a conclusion of law." " 'A finding of fact' is the assertion that a phenomenon has happened or will be happening, independent of or anterior to any assertion as to its legal effect." Jaffe, supra note 24. It is, thus, "a description of a phenomenon independent of law making or law applying." Id. at 550. Jaffe contended that a finding of fact is distinguishable from a conclusion of law because a person untrained in the law should be able to make it. On the other hand, the process of attaching legal consequence to the fact pattern observed requires legal analysis and represents what he called a conclusion of law. Though analytically helpful, this approach failed to account for the tendency of many courts to describe the application of law to facts as a question of fact, particularly when they agreed with the outcome reached by the agency. On a theoretical level, Jaffe's approach also failed to distinguish sufficiently between questions of law that courts should review independently and those they should review in a posture deference to the agency. Id. at 548.

6. 340 U.S. 504, 71 S.Ct. 470, 95 L.Ed. 483 (1951).

As Professor Jaffe has pointed out, however, "the device of characterizing a question as one of fact or as 'mixed' permits a court to pretend that it *must* affirm the administrative action if it is 'supported by evidence' or is 'reasonable.' "[8] The inquiry in this case should, in fact, have been divided into two distinct parts. At the factfinding level, the court should first have determined whether the agency properly resolved the factual questions before it.[9] In the *O'Leary* case, such questions might have included what the decedent was doing at the time he attempted the rescue. Where were the other men? Did the decedent die by drowning? These are the types of inquiries that are appropriate for substantial evidence review. Such findings would establish the basic or raw facts of the case and would not necessarily be colored by any legal standard. They would, in effect, be independent of "any assertion as to their legal effect."[10]

The second level of analysis involves the law application stage. It requires that the court determine whether, based on the *O'Leary* facts, the decedent was acting in the course of his employment. This second level of analysis may result in the court deciding to defer to the agency's judgment, but this is true only if the Court concludes that the agency applied the appropriate legal standard to the facts of the case.[11] If so, we are not dealing with either a question of fact or law, but a mixed question of fact and law.[12] To treat this decision as a question of law is misleading if that implies that independent judicial review is in order. A question involving the application of law to facts on the other hand, is not an issue suitable for substantial evidence review either, nor is it the kind of a question of law that merits *de novo* judicial review. The substantial evidence test as envisioned by the APA is most properly applied only to the first stage of the inquiry—the determination of the raw or basic facts in the case. For an agency to exercise its statutory powers in such a case it is necessary that it make findings of fact that are supported by evidence in the record. The *de novo* scope of review is

7. Justice Frankfurter, writing for the majority, argued that this case did not involve a determination of the existence or nonexistence of a "simple external, physical event" but "a combination of happenings and inferences.... Yet the standards are not so severable from the experience of industry nor of such a nature as to be peculiarly appropriate for independent judicial ascertainment as' " "questions of law." 340 U.S. at 507–08, 71 S.Ct. at 472.

Three justices dissented, arguing that the employee had voluntarily initiated the rescue attempt and that it, thus, did not arise in the course of his employment. There was, they argued, no causal connection between his employment and his death. 340 U.S. at 509. For a case with similar issues and results, see O'Keeffe v. Smith, Hinchman and Grylls Associates, Inc., 380 U.S. 359, 85 S.Ct. 1012, 13 L.Ed.2d 895 (1965).

8. Jaffe, supra note 24, at 547.

9. Id. at 546.

10. Id. at 548.

11. See, e.g. NLRB v. Hearst Publications, 322 U.S. 111, 64 S.Ct. 851, 88 L.Ed. 1170 (1944), rehearing denied 322 U.S. 769, 64 S.Ct. 1148, 88 L.Ed. 1595 (1944), superceded by statute in NLRB v. Town & Country Elec., Inc., 516 U.S. 85, 116 S.Ct. 450, 133 L.Ed.2d 371 (1995) discussed infra in sec. 13.7.1.

12. See, Levin, supra note 24, at 12 (1985) (arguing that law application is best considered a question of discretion). See note 18, infra.

most appropriately applied to the initial determination of whether the agency's legal interpretation of "scope of employment" is in accord with the relevant statute involved.[13] Application of a properly conceived legal standard to a set of agreed upon facts supported by evidence in the record should evoke a form of reasonableness review by the courts that usually results in deference to the agency's judgment. From a functional point of view, this is precisely the kind of judgment that an agency is particularly well suited to make. It is most likely to have the expertise and experience necessary to apply the law to the facts in a manner that achieves uniformity in the large number of similar cases that are likely to come before it and, more importantly, in a manner that best advances the policy goals of the agency.

Another way in which courts historically have analyzed the law-fact distinction is set forth in *Saginaw Broadcasting v. F.C.C.*[14] The Saginaw case distinguished between "basic facts" and "ultimate facts" in this way: "The process [by which an agency reaches a decision] necessarily includes at least four parts: (1) evidence must be taken and weighed, both as to its accuracy and credibility; (2) from attentive consideration of this evidence a determination of facts of a basic or underlying nature must be reached; (3) from these basic facts the ultimate facts, usually in the language of the statute are to be inferred, or not, as the case may be; (4) from the finding the decision will follow by the application of the statutory criterion."[15] The *Saginaw* Court suggested that in an FCC permit proceeding the finding of ultimate fact is that the project will serve the "public interest, convenience, or necessity." "This ultimate fact, however, will be reached by inference from basic facts, such as, for example, the probable existence or nonexistence of electrical interference, in view of the number of other stations operating in the area, their power, wave length [sic], and the like."[16] The finding of ultimate facts involves the drawing of inferences in light of statutory requirements and thus, the process of law application for the resolution of what are, in reality, mixed questions of law and fact. These kinds of decisions resulted in the application of essentially a reasonableness test to the agency's decision.[17]

Courts have, nevertheless, sometimes merged the analytical stages of factfinding and law application, giving the erroneous impression that a substantial evidence standard is being applied to an issue of law application. Since the law-fact distinction alone cannot account for all issues involving law application, a residual category is necessary. That

13. See *NLRB v. Hearst,* supra note 31.

14. Saginaw Broadcasting Co. v. F.C.C., 96 F.2d 554 (D.C.Cir.1938), cert. denied 305 U.S. 613, 59 S.Ct. 72, 83 L.Ed. 391 (1938). This distinction has been elaborated upon by Professor Byse. See Byse, Requirements of Findings and Reasons in Formal Proceedings in Administrative Law, 26 Am.J.Comp.L. 393 (1978).

15. 96 F.2d at 559.

16. Id.

17. See, e.g., INS v. Jong Ha Wang, 450 U.S. 139, 144–45, 101 S.Ct. 1027, 1031–32, 67 L.Ed.2d 123 (1981).

category recognizes that there are a variety of mixed questions of law and fact that appropriately involve the exercise of agency discretion.[18]

The limitations of the law-fact distinction thus highlight *three* separate and distinct issues present in every instance of judicial review of agency action (or inaction). First, what were the facts that gave rise to the request for agency action in the first place? Second, given these facts, what legal authority governed the agency's response to these facts? What did the test of the relevant statutes actually say and what legal tests and standards did they set forth? Given agreement on the facts involved and on the meaning of the statutes to be applied, did the agency then properly apply these legal standards to the facts of the case? Judicial review of these three decisions takes place pursuant to different standards of judicial review that imply different degrees of judicial scrutiny. We shall now examine the application of these standards in various procedural contexts. We begin with questions of fact.

§ 13.4 JUDICIAL REVIEW OF QUESTIONS OF FACT

In *Crowell v. Benson,*[1] the Supreme Court rejected the constitutional argument that Congress could not vest fact-finding authority in an administrative agency without violating Article III of the Constitution. It impliedly upheld such fact-finding authority subject to judicial review of the reasonableness of the findings.[2] Except for so-called jurisdictional facts, the Court rejected any Article III requirement of *de novo* review.[3]

The APA provides three different standards of judicial review applicable to agency findings of fact. In a few cases, Section 706(2)(F) allows a court to review the facts *de novo,* as if it were the finder of fact in the first instance.[4] In on the record adjudicatory and formal rulemaking proceedings, section 706(2)(E) provides for "substantial evidence" review of agency fact finding.[5] If there is substantial evidence in the record, a court will affirm an agency's findings of fact, even if it might not have made those same findings were it the initial decision maker. By statute, the substantial evidence test sometimes applies to findings of fact made in the context of hybrid rulemaking proceedings. In informal rulemaking proceedings conducted under section 553 of the APA, however, as well as other informal agency actions subject to judicial review but falling outside of the specific procedural provisions of the APA, the arbitrary and capricious standard of review applies.[6] This standard thus applies to

18. As Professor Levin notes, questions of discretion would be "those normative issues which call for an inquiry into the 'rationality' of an agency's determination—a less intrusive inquiry than one in which the court independently decides whether the agency's determination was 'correct.'" Levin, supra note 24, at 12.

§ 13.4

1. 285 U.S. 22, 52 S.Ct. 285, 76 L.Ed. 598 (1932). See also United States ex rel. Vajtauer v. Commissioner of Immigration, 273 U.S. 103, 47 S.Ct. 302, 71 L.Ed. 560 (1927).

2. 285 U.S. at 46, 52 S.Ct. at 290.

3. 285 U.S. at 46, 52 S.Ct. at 290.

4. 5 U.S.C.A. § 706(2)(F). See sec. 13.6, infra.

5. 5 U.S.C.A. § 706(2)(E).

6. 5 U.S.C.A. § 706(2)(A).

proceedings that are not on the record proceedings in the same sense as those to which the substantial evidence standard applies. As we shall see, however, the very possibility of judicial review of agency actions of this sort has, over the years, required the compilation of at least some kind of record upon which to judge the agency's decision.

We shall examine the application of each of these standards, beginning with the most common—the substantial evidence standard.

§ 13.4.1 Judicial Review of Questions of Fact in the Record Proceedings—The Substantial Evidence Standard of Review

The leading case applying the substantial evidence standard to facts found in a formal adjudicatory agency proceeding is *Universal Camera Corp. v. NLRB.*[7] That case involved an employee re-instatement determination made by the NLRB. The Board reversed the decision of its own examiner who had found that the employee's dismissal did not violate the Act. Since the substantial evidence test had been in existence many years before passage of the APA, three general questions arose: (1) Did the substantial evidence standard apply to the whole record before the court, or could it be satisfied by looking only at those portions of the record that supported the agency's conclusion?[8] (2) Had the APA's codification of this standard altered the substantial evidence test as it had developed in other regulatory contexts?[9] and (3) what exactly was the scope of this newly codified standard as applied? In addition to these three questions, *Universal Camera* also considered the extent to which a court should defer to a hearing examiner's findings of fact when those

7. 340 U.S. 474, 71 S.Ct. 456, 95 L.Ed. 456 (1951). For a more recent case applying this standard to the NLRB, see *ABF Freight System, Inc. v. NLRB*, 510 U.S. 317, 114 S.Ct. 835, 127 L.Ed.2d 152 (1994) (the Supreme Court affirmed a Board decision regarding dismissal of an employee who had lied about his tardiness. The Board found that there was substantial evidence to support the claim that the employer's motivation to fire the employee was not based on tardiness, but on his earlier union activities).

8. This case dealt specifically with defining what substantial evidence meant for purposes of reviewing decisions of the National Labor Relations Board (NLRB) under the Taft–Hartley Act. At the time this case arose, there was some question as to whether the APA substantial evidence standard meant something different in the context of the Taft–Hartley Act. It had appeared that the Supreme Court was applying a very deferential standard to NLRB findings of fact, upholding them if there was any favorable or supporting evidence in the record. See, e.g., NLRB v. Nevada Consolidated Copper Corp., 316 U.S. 105, 62 S.Ct. 960, 86 L.Ed. 1305 (1942).

9. Justice Frankfurter's opinion, however, clearly equated the substantial evidence standard under the APA with that of the National Labor Relations Act. Id. In so doing, it was clear that the APA's standard was intended to tighten up the use of this standard by the Courts, but not substitute a new test. In fact, the APA's standard and that used in the NLRA were the same. See Florida v. United States, 292 U.S. 1, 54 S.Ct. 603, 78 L.Ed. 1077 (1934); Del Vecchio v. Bowers, 296 U.S. 280, 56 S.Ct. 190, 80 L.Ed. 229 (1935); NLRB v. Columbian Enameling & Stamping Co., 306 U.S. 292, 59 S.Ct. 501, 83 L.Ed. 660 (1939). For an early use of the term "substantial evidence," see ICC v. Union Pacific R.R., 222 U.S. 541, 548, 32 S.Ct. 108, 111, 56 L.Ed. 308 (1912) (courts will not examine facts further than to determine whether there is substantial evidence to sustain an agency order).

findings contradicted those of the Commission or Board involved. We shall discuss each of these issues in turn.

The Court in *Universal Camera* first determined that substantial evidence should be based on the whole record. Prior to *Universal Camera* a number of cases had at least hinted that reviewing courts need only look at portions of the record in isolation to find "substantial" evidence in support of an agency order.[10] This issue was addressed statutorily in both the APA[11] and the Taft–Hartley Amendments to the National Labor Relations Act.[12] Both these provisions mandated a look at "the whole record," and Justice Frankfurter's opinion clearly put this controversy to rest: "Whether or not it was ever permissible for courts to determine the substantiality of evidence supporting a Labor Board decision merely on the basis of evidence which in and of itself justified it, without taking into account contradictory evidence or evidence from which conflicting inferences could be drawn, the new legislation definitively precludes such a theory of review and bars its practice."[13]

The *Universal Camera* Court also concluded that the APA substantial evidence standard was not, therefore, a new standard.[14] In so doing, however, the Court made clear that this standard, which was also found in the Taft Hartley Act, demonstrated "a purpose to impose on courts a responsibility which has not always been recognized," and it viewed the adoption of the substantial evidence standard in the APA as "a response to pressures for stricter and more uniform practice, not a reflection of approval of all existing practices."[15] The Court also defined the relative roles of the Supreme Court and lower courts in cases of this sort, seeking to allocate primary responsibility for such decisions to the courts of appeals. The Supreme Court would intervene only in what ought to be rare instances when the standard appears to have been misapprehended or grossly misapplied.[16]

10. See, e.g., NLRB v. Waterman Steamship Corp., 309 U.S. 206, 226, 60 S.Ct. 493, 503, 84 L.Ed. 704 (1940) (Justice Black's language ambiguously suggests that the Court may look only to the evidence favorable to the agency position). Compare Stason, "Substantial Evidence" in Administrative Law, 89 U.Pa.Rev. 1026 (1941) with Jaffe, Judicial Review: Substantial Evidence on the Whole Record, 64 Harv.L.Rev. 1233 (1951).

11. 5 U.S.C.A. § 706.

12. 29 U.S.C.A. § 160(e) (1982).

13. 340 U.S. at 487–88, 71 S.Ct. at 464–65. See also Consolo v. FMC, 383 U.S. 607, 620, 86 S.Ct. 1018, 1026, 16 L.Ed.2d 131 (1966), on remand 373 F.2d 674 (D.C.Cir.1967) ("Congress was very deliberate in adopting [the substantial evidence] standard of review"); Spurlock v. Department of Justice, 894 F.2d 1328 (Fed.Cir. 1990).

14. "Retention of the familiar 'substantial evidence' terminology indicates that no drastic reversal of attitude was intended." 340 U.S. at 489, 71 S.Ct. at 465.

15. Id. at 489.

16. Id. at 491, 71 S.Ct. at 466; see also NLRB v. Pittsburgh S.S. Co., 340 U.S. 498, 502–03, 71 S.Ct. 453, 456, 95 L.Ed. 479 (1951) (lower courts have primary duty to apply the substantial evidence standard).

As far as the lower courts are concerned, some commentators have argued that review by Article III courts is often unnecessary. With regard to the NLRB, in particular, Judge Posner, for example, has noted that the administrative review process of ALJ decisions is usually perfunctory and, therefore, federal judicial review of the ALJ's decision is usually sought. "It would be easier and cheaper for Congress to establish within the Board a tier of credible appellate judges who would write opinions

These preliminary holdings by the Court did little to clarify any further the precise scope of the substantial evidence standard itself. The Court cites such prior formulations of the standard as: "Substantial evidence is more than a mere scintilla. It means such relevant evidence as a reasonable mind might accept as adequate to support a conclusion."[17] And substantial evidence "must do more than create a suspicion of the existence of the fact to be established.... It must be enough to justify, if the trial were to a jury, a refusal to direct a verdict when the conclusion sought to be drawn from it is one of fact for the jury."[18] Writing for the Court, Justice Frankfurter also attempted his own formulation: "Reviewing courts must be influenced by a feeling that they are not to abdicate the conventional judicial function. Congress has imposed on them responsibility for assuring that the Board keeps within reasonable bounds. That responsibility is not less real because it is limited to enforcing the requirement that evidence appear substantial when viewed, on the record as a whole, by courts invested with the authority and enjoying the prestige of the Court of Appeals. The Board's findings are entitled to respect; but they must nonetheless be set aside when the record before a Court of Appeals clearly precludes the Board's decision from being justified by a fair estimate of the worth of the testimony of witnesses or its informed judgment on matters within its special competence or both."[19] Applying these various formulations is, to say the least, more of an art than a science.[20]

Various commentators have attempted to define exactly what "substantial evidence" means. Professor Jaffe, for example, proposed that Courts examine the overall fairness of the entire fact-finding process.[21] Other approaches analogize agency fact finding to that of a trial court or

in all but frivolous cases than to continue expanding the federal courts so that they can keep up with a rising workload of administrative review cases." R. Posner, The Federal Courts: Crisis & Reform 161 (1985).

17. Consolidated Edison Co. v. NLRB, 305 U.S. 197, 229, 59 S.Ct. 206, 216, 83 L.Ed. 126 (1938). This has become the typical formulation of the standard. See Consolo v. FMC, 383 U.S. 607, 86 S.Ct. 1018, 16 L.Ed.2d 131 (1966), on remand 373 F.2d 674 (D.C.Cir.1967); NLRB v. Enterprise Ass'n of Steam Pipefitters, 429 U.S. 507, 97 S.Ct. 891, 51 L.Ed.2d 1 (1977); Newsweek, Inc. v. U.S. Postal Service, 663 F.2d 1186 (2d Cir.1981) remand affirmed 462 U.S. 810, 103 S.Ct. 2717, 77 L.Ed.2d 195 (1983); Beth Israel Hosp. v. NLRB, 437 U.S. 483, 98 S.Ct. 2463, 57 L.Ed.2d 370 (1978). Another formulation is that of Judge Hand in NLRB v. Remington Rand, 94 F.2d 862, 873 (2d Cir.1938) (substantial evidence is "the kind of evidence on which responsible persons are accustomed to rely in serious affairs").

18. NLRB v. Columbian Enameling & Stamping Co., Inc., 306 U.S. 292, 300, 59 S.Ct. 501, 505, 83 L.Ed. 660 (1939).

19. *Universal Camera,* 340 U.S. at 490, 71 S.Ct. at 466.

20. See Stork Restaurant v. Boland, 282 N.Y. 256, 274, 26 N.E.2d 247, 255 (1940) ("[t]here is often greater difficulty in applying the [substantial evidence] test than in formulating it").

21. In 1951 he wrote: "The word 'substantial,' coming as it does from a spectrum of words such as 'scintilla,' 'preponderance' and 'weight,' connotes the mechanics of judging. The concept of fairness relates to the attitude of judging. I would say, then, that the judge may—indeed must—reverse if as he conscientiously sees it the finding is not fairly supported by the record; or . . . he cannot conscientiously escape the conclusion that the finding is unfair." Jaffe, supra note 19, at 1239.

a jury.[22] In the trial court setting there are two standards for reviewing findings of fact: The jury-trial directed verdict test, which is essentially a reasonableness determination,[23] and the trial court-appellate court "clearly erroneous" standard.[24] Greater deference to jury fact finding is normally justified out of respect for decisions made by "persons embodying the underlying sense of fairness of the community."[25] Such deference need not be accorded to a trial judge by an appellate court; in some cases, however, the trial judge's very presence at the development of the record is an added factor favoring deference, particularly when issues of witness credibility are involved.

Deference to agencies, as noted above, is justified in part out of respect for agency expertise.[26] The deference accorded an agency is similar in result to the deference accorded to a jury in the context of a

22. These approaches view the relationship of an agency to a court as being similar to that of a trial court to a jury, or a trial court to an appellate court. See NLRB v. Columbian Enameling & Stamping Co., Inc., 306 U.S. 292, 300, 59 S.Ct. 501, 505, 83 L.Ed. 660 (1939). See also Stern, Review of Findings of Administrators, Judges, and Juries: A Comparative Analysis, 58 Harv. L.Rev. 70 (1944); Jaffe, supra note 19, at 1246–47. See Lamoille Valley R. Co. v. ICC, 711 F.2d 295 (D.C.Cir.1983) (while the "substantial evidence" standard requires facts supported by enough evidence to justify refusal to direct a verdict to the contrary in a jury case, the agency is expected to identify uncertain facts and state the considerations it found persuasive); Erickson Transport Corp. v. ICC, 728 F.2d 1057 (8th Cir.1984); Illinois Cent. R. Co. v. Norfolk & W. Ry. Co., 385 U.S. 57, 87 S.Ct. 255, 17 L.Ed.2d 162 (1966).

23. See Reconstruction Finance Corp. v. Bankers Trust Co., 318 U.S. 163, 170, 63 S.Ct. 515, 519, 87 L.Ed. 680 (1943). See also International Brotherhood of Electrical Workers v. NLRB, 448 F.2d 1127, 1142 (D.C.Cir.1971) (Judge Leventhal compares "clearly erroneous" rule and "substantial evidence" standard).

24. See Anderson v. Bessemer City, 470 U.S. 564, 575, 105 S.Ct. 1504, 1512, 84 L.Ed.2d 518 (1985) (application of clearly erroneous standard); United States v. U.S. Gypsum Co., 333 U.S. 364, 394–95, 68 S.Ct. 525, 541–42, 92 L.Ed. 746 (1948). Some statutes substitute a different test for the "substantial evidence" standard. See, e.g., Commodity Exchange Act, 7 U.S.C.A. § 8 (A "weight of the evidence" test applied). See infra sec. 13.7.

25. Stern, supra note 60, at 81. Substantial evidence is theoretically more restrictive than the "clearly erroneous" standard. Id. at 88–89.

26. Id. at 81–82. Consolo v. Federal Maritime Commission, 383 U.S. 607, 620, 86 S.Ct. 1018, 1026, 16 L.Ed.2d 131 (1966) ("substantial evidence" rule frees the courts from the burden of weighing the evidence, respects administrative expertise, and promotes the uniform application of statutes); 5 Jacob A. Stein et al., Administrative Law, at Ch. 51 (1992) (the purpose of the "substantial evidence" rule is to protect the integrity and autonomy of the administrative process plus deference to agency expertise and experience); FPC v. Florida Power & Light Co., 404 U.S. 453, 92 S.Ct. 637, 30 L.Ed.2d 600 (1972), rehearing denied 405 U.S. 948, 92 S.Ct. 929, 30 L.Ed.2d 819 (1972); but see, United States v. United States and Interstate Commerce Commission, 417 F.Supp. 851 (D.D.C.1976), affirmed 430 U.S. 961, 97 S.Ct. 1638, 52 L.Ed.2d 352 (1977) (judicial deference to agency expertise is not boundless and expertise is not sufficient by itself to sustain a decision); Darin & Armstrong, Inc. v. EPA, 431 F.Supp. 456 (N.D.Ohio 1976) (deference to agency does not lessen court's duty to thoroughly examine factual basis for agency conclusion to insure decisions are rational, reasonable and just in light of the evidence); Baltimore & O. R. Co. v. Aberdeen & Rockfish R. Co., 393 U.S. 87, 89 S.Ct. 280, 21 L.Ed.2d 219 (1968) (agency expertise is not a substitute for evidence in the record); Udall v. FPC, 387 U.S. 428, 87 S.Ct. 1712, 18 L.Ed.2d 869 (1967).

Applying the "substantial evidence" test is difficult because the reviewing court must consider the discretion to which the agency's expertise is entitled. See, Bowman Transp., Inc. v. Arkansas–Best Freight System, Inc., 419 U.S. 281, 95 S.Ct. 438, 42 L.Ed.2d 447 (1974); SEC v. New England Elec. System, 390 U.S. 207, 88 S.Ct. 916, 19 L.Ed.2d 1042 (1968).

motion for a directed verdict. As one judge ironically noted: "A wag might say that a verdict is entitled to high respect because the jurors are inexperienced in finding facts, an administrative finding is given high respect because the administrative officers are specialists (guided by experts) in finding a particular class of facts, but, paradoxically, a trial judge's finding has far less respect because he is blessed neither with jurors' inexperience nor administrative officers' expertness."[27] On balance, the application of the substantial evidence test is more akin to the judicial standard used in reviewing a directed verdict in a jury trial.[28]

Regardless of how one phrases the standard, the test is usually applied with considerable deference. Courts recognize that a decision may be reasonable even if it is one that a judge would not make herself. "[T]he possibility of drawing two inconsistent conclusions from the evidence does not prevent an administrative agency's finding from being supported by substantial evidence."[29] Courts have upheld agency findings even though substantial evidence also supports a different conclu-

27. Orvis v. Higgins, 180 F.2d 537, 540 n. 7 (2d Cir.1950), cert. denied 340 U.S. 810, 71 S.Ct. 37, 95 L.Ed. 595 (1950). See also Jaffe, supra note 19, at 1246.

28. For cases stating that the test for reviewing juries and agencies is the same, see Consolo v. FMC, 383 U.S. 607, 86 S.Ct. 1018, 16 L.Ed.2d 131 (1966), on remand 373 F.2d 674 (D.C.Cir.1967); Watson v. Gulf Stevedore Corp., 400 F.2d 649 (5th Cir. 1968), cert. denied 394 U.S. 976, 89 S.Ct. 1471, 22 L.Ed.2d 755 (1969); Continental Casualty Co. v. Holmes, 266 F.2d 269, 276 (5th Cir.1959), cert. denied 361 U.S. 877, 80 S.Ct. 140, 4 L.Ed.2d 114 (1959). For cases using a "clearly erroneous" standard for reviewing trial judges broader in scope than the "substantial evidence" standard for agency review, see Orvis v. Higgins, 180 F.2d at 540; United States v. U.S. Gypsum Co., 333 U.S. 364, 395, 68 S.Ct. 525, 542, 92 L.Ed. 746 (1948), rehearing denied 333 U.S. 869, 68 S.Ct. 788, 92 L.Ed. 1147 (1948); see also NLRB v. Southland Mfg. Co., 201 F.2d 244, 246–48 (4th Cir.1952); but see Vanderbilt, 30 N.Y.U.L.Rev. 1267, 1268 (1955); NLRB v. Southland Mfg. Co., 201 F.2d at 250 (Soper, J., concurring).

29. Consolo v. FMC, 383 U.S. at 620, 86 S.Ct. at 1026 (court ruling on sufficiency of evidence supporting damage award assessed by agency for non-competitive shipping practice); see also York v. Benefits Review Bd., 819 F.2d 134 (6th Cir.1987) (application of "substantial evidence" test to review of ALJ ruling upon Black Lung benefits); Turner v. Brock, 813 F.2d 1494 (9th Cir.1987) (Secretary of Labor's determination of eligibility for employee benefits is based on substantial evidence); NLRB v. Certified Grocers of Ill., Inc., 806 F.2d 744 (7th Cir.1986) (agency decision supported by substantial evidence even though contrary line of argument could also have been upheld on appeal); Consolidated Gas Transmission Corp. v. FERC, 771 F.2d 1536, 1548 (D.C.Cir.1985); Yaffe Iron and Metal Co. v. EPA, 774 F.2d 1008, 1014 (10th Cir.1985); American Fin. Services Ass'n v. FTC, 767 F.2d 957, 988 (D.C.Cir.1985), cert. denied 475 U.S. 1011, 106 S.Ct. 1185, 89 L.Ed.2d 301 (1986) (application of "substantial evidence" rule to FTC rulemaking); Pennzoil Co. v. FERC, 789 F.2d 1128, 1135 n. 20 (5th Cir.1986), appeal after remand 853 F.2d 1226 (1988), rehearing denied 861 F.2d 1279 (1988); National Ass'n of Broadcasters v. Copyright Royalty Tribunal, 675 F.2d 367, 375 (D.C.Cir.1982); Air Products & Chemicals, Inc. v. FERC, 650 F.2d 687, 695 (5th Cir.1981); United States v. FMC, 655 F.2d 247, 252 (D.C.Cir.1980); St. James Hospital v. Harris, 535 F.Supp. 751, 762 (N.D.Ill.1981), reversed 698 F.2d 1337 (7th Cir.1983) (opinions of competent persons may constitute substantial evidence); FPC v. Florida Power & Light Co., 404 U.S. 453, 464–65, 92 S.Ct. 637, 644–45, 30 L.Ed.2d 600 (1972), rehearing denied 405 U.S. 948, 92 S.Ct. 929, 30 L.Ed.2d 819 (1972) (well reasoned expert testimony, even if largely opinion, may in itself be substantial evidence when first-hand evidence is unavailable); Industrial Union Dept., AFL–CIO v. American Petroleum Institute, 448 U.S. 607, 100 S.Ct. 2844, 65 L.Ed.2d 1010 (1980) (whether the reviewing court would have reached a different conclusion is immaterial).

sion.[30]

Because the standard ordinarily provides for considerable deference, a person challenging an agency ruling is most likely to succeed if she can argue that essentially no evidence supports a given decision. A court will have little trouble reversing a decision which is totally unsupported by any evidence.[31] If some evidence supports a particular factual determination, convincing a court to reverse is difficult. Hearsay evidence alone can often be enough to constitute substantial evidence.[32] In other cases, however, the court may react to the existence of some, relatively weak, substantial evidence in the record by shifting the rhetoric to the soundness of an agency's reasoning or its failure to address certain issues adequately.[33] "Reasoned consideration" or "failure to consider" or "explain" are threads that can often be woven into substantial evidence analysis.[34]

In other contexts, however, courts may be affected by what is at stake in the proceeding they are reviewing. In *NLRB v. Walton Mfg. Co.*,[35] the Supreme Court flatly rejected what was then the Fifth Circuit's requirement that the evidence necessary to support Board orders imposing back pay awards on employers be greater than that necessary to justify prospective relief. Yet, there may be some contexts in which a court is likely to look closely at the amount of evidence an agency can muster. Issues with which the court arguably has as much experience or familiarity as does the agency may similarly receive stricter review.[36] As

30. *Consolo,* 383 U.S. at 620, 86 S.Ct. at 1026. See also Illinois Central R. Co. v. Norfolk & W. Ry. Co., 385 U.S. 57, 87 S.Ct. 255, 17 L.Ed.2d 162 (1966); NLRB v. United Ins. Co., 390 U.S. 254, 88 S.Ct. 988, 19 L.Ed.2d 1083 (1968) (Court of Appeals should not have displaced agency choice between conflicting views, each supported by substantial evidence, even though the agency didn't employ its expertise in making the decision). But see American Tunaboat Ass'n v. Baldrige, 738 F.2d 1013 (9th Cir.1984) (though the agency decision may have been supported by substantial evidence, where other evidence in the record detracts from that relied on by the agency, the court may find the agency rule to be arbitrary and capricious).

31. Department of Transportation Federal Highway Administration v. ICC, 733 F.2d 105 (D.C.Cir.1984) (court finds no substantial evidence to support fitness of carrier); Graham Hospital Ass'n v. Heckler, 739 F.2d 285 (7th Cir.1984) (court finds there is insufficient evidence to reasonably support agency's conclusion that hospital is not the sole community hospital); Port Norris Express Co. v. ICC, 687 F.2d 803 (3d Cir.1982) (decision unsupported by any evidence not only fails "substantial evidence" test, but also can be regarded as arbitrary and capricious); Abbotts Dairies Div. of Fairmont Foods, Inc. v. Butz, 389 F.Supp. 1 (E.D.Pa. 1975), rehearing denied 421 F.Supp. 415 (E.D.Pa.1976) (reversal of Secretary of Agriculture's new milk pricing system, as no evidence adduced from the hearing to show the desirability of the new system).

32. See, e.g., Richardson v. Perales, 402 U.S. 389, 91 S.Ct. 1420, 28 L.Ed.2d 842 (1971). But see Consolidated Edison Co. v. NLRB, 305 U.S. 197, 230, 59 S.Ct. 206, 217, 83 L.Ed. 126 (1938) ("[m]ere uncorroborated hearsay or rumor does not constitute substantial evidence"); Willapoint Oysters, Inc. v. Ewing, 174 F.2d 676, 691 (9th Cir. 1949), cert. denied 338 U.S. 860, 70 S.Ct. 101, 94 L.Ed. 527 (1949), rehearing denied 339 U.S. 945, 70 S.Ct. 793, 94 L.Ed. 1360 (1950). See Chapter 8, sec. 8.4.7, supra.

33. See, e.g., Maryland People's Counsel v. FERC, 761 F.2d 768, 774 (D.C.Cir. 1985); see also Office of Consumers' Counsel v. FERC, 655 F.2d 1132 (D.C.Cir.1980).

34. Id.

35. 369 U.S. 404, 82 S.Ct. 853, 7 L.Ed.2d 829 (1962), on remand 322 F.2d 187 (5th Cir.1963). See also *NLRB v. Pittsburgh S.S. Co.,* supra note 54.

36. See, e.g., Office of Consumers' Counsel, State of Ohio v. FERC, 783 F.2d 206, 223, 227–28 (D.C.Cir.1986) (deference

a practical matter, courts also may or may not give an agency much leeway depending upon such factors as the agency's general reputation, its thoroughness in the particular case under review and the size of the record, and the court's own sense of the merits of the case. Such factors are difficult to define explicitly in a court's opinion, but they can surely affect the "mood" of the case.[37]

§ 13.4.2 Conflict Between Agency Factfinders

Universal Camera also dealt with another aspect of the relationship of courts to agencies: how should a court review an agency decision when the agency disagrees with its own examiner's findings of fact? The agency has the power to reject an ALJ's findings of fact and reach its own independent conclusion on the record before it,[38] but how should a court treat an agency's findings when they are at odds with the factual determinations of the ALJ?

The Court in *Universal Camera* held that, pursuant to section 557(c) of the APA, the findings of an administrative law judge must be taken into account as part of the whole record when a court considers whether substantial evidence supports the agency's findings.[39] The Court essentially took a functional approach in determining whose findings of fact a court should look to:

> We do not require that the examiner's findings be given more weight than in reason and in the light of judicial experience they deserve. The "substantial evidence" standard is not modified in any way when the Board and its examiner disagree. We intend only to recognize that evidence supporting a conclusion may be less substantial when an impartial, experienced examiner who has observed the witnesses and lived with the case has drawn conclusions different from the Board's than when he has reached the same conclusion.[40]

is less when agency is outside its expertise). NLRB v. Universal Camera Corp., 190 F.2d 429, 430 (2d Cir.1951) (where agency's specialized experience is not relevant, judges are "as competent as the [agency] to pass upon issues of fact").

37. See SEC v. New England Electric System, 390 U.S. 207, 88 S.Ct. 916, 19 L.Ed.2d 1042 (1968) (deference shown to SEC findings); but see Baltimore & Ohio R.R. v. Aberdeen & Rockfish R. Co., 393 U.S. 87, 89 S.Ct. 280, 21 L.Ed.2d 219 (1968) rehearing denied 393 U.S. 1124, 89 S.Ct. 987, 22 L.Ed.2d 131 (1969) (ICC findings overturned). See generally, S. Breyer and R. Stewart, Administrative Law and Regulatory Policy 208 (2d Ed.1985). See also, Sidney Shapiro and Richard E. Levy, Judicial Incentives and Indeterminancy in Substantive Review of Administrative Decision, 44 Duke L. Rev. 1051 (1995) (federal courts less deferential in social security benefit cases in the 1980s).

38. See 5 U.S.C.A. § 557(b).

39. *Universal Camera,* 340 U.S. at 492–97, 71 S.Ct. at 467–69. See also FCC v. Allentown Broadcasting Corp., 349 U.S. 358, 75 S.Ct. 855, 99 L.Ed. 1147 (1955), reversing 222 F.2d 781 (D.C.Cir.1954) (question is not whether the agency erred in overruling the examiner's findings of fact but whether the agency's findings satisfy the substantial evidence standard based on the record as a whole, including the examiner's findings).

40. 340 U.S. at 496, 71 S.Ct. at 469. See also NLRB v. Marcus Trucking Co., 286 F.2d 583, 589 (2d Cir.1961) (court would not overturn agency's belief in witness' oral testimony unless "it is hopelessly incredible.")

The Ninth Circuit has developed more fully the functional approach suggested in *Universal Camera*. In *Penasquitos Village, Inc. v. NLRB*[41] the Board and the ALJ disagreed on findings of fact having to do with an employer's motive in discharging two employees. The ALJ accepted the employer's story, while the Board sided with the discharged employees. In reversing the ALJ, the Board's finding of improper motive was based primarily on inferences drawn from testimony specifically discredited at trial by the ALJ. The Court reversed the Board, noting that:

> in this case, credibility played a dominant role. The administrative law judge's testimonial inferences reduce significantly the substantiality of the Board's contrary derivative inferences. Particularly, removing the Board's finding of anti-union animus based upon alleged unlawful threats and interrogations ... leaves poorly substantiated the Board's other conclusion that the discharges were improperly motivated. Considering the record as a whole ... the Board's conclusion that Penasquitos committed unlawful labor practices is not supported by substantial evidence and must, therefore, be set aside.[43]

The dissent took issue with the majority's "dichotomy between 'credibility determinations based on demeanor ... *testimonial inferences*' and those based on 'inferences drawn from the evidence itself? ... derivative inferences ... ' "[44] It maintained that the traditional belief in the trier of fact as a kind of lie detector is but the product of myth and folklore. "Every trial lawyer knows, and most trial judges will admit, that it is not unusual for an accomplished liar to fool a jury (or, even, heaven forbid, a trial judge) into believing him because his demeanor is so convincing."[45] On the other hand, "many trial lawyers, and some trial judges, will admit that the demeanor of a perfectly honest but unsophisticated or timid witness may be—or can be made by an astute cross-

41. 565 F.2d 1074 (9th Cir.1977).

43. 565 F.2d at 1083–84. See also Garrison v. Heckler, 765 F.2d 710, 712 (7th Cir.1985) (Secretary's decision upheld where "supported by substantial evidence even if the ALJ's contrary decision was supported by substantial evidence"); American Tunaboat Ass'n v. Baldrige, 738 F.2d 1013 (9th Cir.1984) (derivative inferences drawn by ALJ are not entitled to special weight by the reviewing court but testimonial inferences are; the standard of review does not change simply because the agency disagreed with the ALJ; the significance of the ALJ's report depends largely upon the importance of credibility in the particular case); United States ex rel. Exarchou v. Murff, 265 F.2d 504, 507 (2d Cir.1959) (rejecting the hearing examiner's inability to believe that a divorced man and a divorced woman could live together without any sexual involvement); Gooding v. Willard, 209 F.2d 913 (2d Cir.1954) (defer to the determination of the fact finder unless the testimony is so inherently improbable that it is unworthy of belief as a matter of law); but see Edward J. Mawod & Co. v. SEC, 591 F.2d 588 (10th Cir.1979) (agency decision based on credibility should not be reversed unless contradicted by uncontrovertible documentary evidence or physical facts). See also, Sahn, Demeanor Evidence: Elusive and Intangible Imponderable, 47 A.B.A.J. 580 (1961).

44. 565 F.2d at 1084. Judge Duriway, in dissent, argued that, carried too far, this kind of distinction could easily result in a fact finder that resembles Shakespeare's Othello:

> The Moor is of a free and open nature,
>
> That thinks men honest that but seem to be so;
>
> And will as tenderly be led by the nose as asses are.

Id. at 1085.

45. 565 F.2d at 1084 (Duriway, J., dissenting).

examiner to be—such that he will be thought by the jury or the judge to be a liar."[46]

A related, unresolved issue is whether an agency decision that rejects uncontradicted testimony may nevertheless satisfy the substantial evidence standard. The courts of appeals favor the view that uncontradicted testimony may be disbelieved solely on the basis of the factfinder's determination of credibility.[47] The Ninth Circuit has specifically recognized this problem and held that the reasons for rejecting uncontradicted testimony on the grounds of credibility must be stated in the record.[48]

§ 13.5 JUDICIAL REVIEW OF QUESTIONS OF FACT IN INFORMAL AND HYBRID RULEMAKING PROCEEDINGS

Section 4 has examined judicial review of agency factfinding in the context of formal, on the record proceedings. The substantial evidence standard applies to facts in such proceedings that are based on a record compiled before an unbiased judge after an evidentiary hearing. The facts involved tend to be retrospective in nature and are best resolved by adducing the kind of evidence designed to prove who did what, when, where and how.

The specific, retrospective nature of the facts involved in such cases contrasts strongly with the broad, prospective nature of the facts involved in a rulemaking proceeding. Such proceedings are designed to establish broad based policies for the future. How much Benzene in the workplace will, over time, cause cancer in some individuals? Of necessity, resolution of such an issue elicits evidence that deals more in probabilities rather than certainties, and group averages rather than specific individual reactions.

The record in such proceedings is different than that involved in the formal proceedings examined above. At a minimum, it is likely to consist of the agency's notice of rulemaking, the comments that notice prompted, the final rule and a concise statement of the agency's basis for and purpose of this rule.[1] There is no requirement that agencies explicitly make findings of fact in such proceedings. Usually those facts are subsumed by the policy the agency ultimately chooses to adopt. The

46. Id. at 1085. Some of the social science literature suggests that the dissent's view may be the more accurate of the two. See e.g., R. Wodak–Engel, Determination of Guilt Discourse in the Courtroom in Language and Power 89 (C. Kramarae et al. eds., 1984).

47. NLRB v. Walton Mfg. Co., 369 U.S. 404, 82 S.Ct. 853, 7 L.Ed.2d 829 (1962), on remand, 322 F.2d 187 (5th Cir.1963); see also NLRB v. Cutting, Inc., 701 F.2d 659 (7th Cir.1983); Greyhound Lines–West v. Marshall, 575 F.2d 759 (9th Cir.1978); Buchman v. SEC, 553 F.2d 816 (2d Cir. 1977). But see Dickinson v. United States, 346 U.S. 389, 74 S.Ct. 152, 98 L.Ed. 132 (1953) (evidence presented must be accepted as true unless contradicted).

48. White Glove Building Maintenance, Inc. v. Brennan, 518 F.2d 1271, 1276 (9th Cir.1975).

§ 13.5

1. For a discussion of rules and rulemaking records, see chapter 4, supra.

arbitrary and capricious standard of review, therefore, usually applies to the overall reasonableness of that policy. As we shall see when we discuss judicial review of agency rules,[2] the arbitrary and capricious standard of review usually results in the judicial application of a relatively deferential rational basis test to the agency action under review.

Between these poles of adjudicative facts on the one hand and legislative or policy facts on the other, there is a good deal of middle ground that certain hybrid rulemaking statutes try to accommodate. Many of the environmental, health and safety statutes passed during the 1970's and early 1980's contain procedural provisions that combine aspects of informal rulemaking with judicial review provisions normally employed in formal adjudication.[3] Specifically, many such statutes require the use of a substantial evidence test for factfinding in the context of a rulemaking proceeding.[4] Statutes such as these raise a general question as to the meaning of substantial evidence in a policy-making context. They also raise questions concerning the kinds of facts to which the substantial evidence standard applies and how those facts should be developed in such proceedings. Finally, they raise the question of what, if any, difference exists between the substantial evidence standard and the arbitrary and capricious standard when applied in a rulemaking context.

One of the first cases to deal with these issues was *Industrial Union Dept., AFL–CIO v. Hodgson.*[5] In that case, the Secretary of Labor set standards regulating the levels of asbestos dust in industrial work places, pursuant to the Occupational Safety and Health Act. The union was not satisfied with these safety standards and it sought review. The D.C. Circuit had to confront what it termed an "anomal[ous]" statute—one that required a substantial evidence standard for a policy making proceeding.[6] As the Court noted, one problem with this combination is that of how to develop a "record [adequate] to permit meaningful performance of the required review."[7] In response to this problem, the Secretary voluntarily developed more formal procedures for certain kinds of factfinding. These procedures provided that a qualified hearing examiner should preside over an oral hearing, that witnesses should be cross-examined, and that a verbatim record be established for certain kinds of factual issues upon which agency policy would be based.[8] For other policy

2. See sec. 13.10, infra.

3. Such provisions are collected in Note, Convergence of the Substantial Evidence and Arbitrary and Capricious Standards of Review During Informal Rulemaking, 54 Geo.Wash.L.Rev. 541 (1986); see, e.g., Federal Trade Commission Improvement Act of 1975 § 202(e)(3)(A), codified at 15 U.S.C.A. § 57a(e)(3)(A); Securities Exchange Act of 1934 (1975 Amendments) § 25(b)(4), codified at 15 U.S.C.A. § 78y(b)(4); Interstate Land Sales Full Disclosure Act § 1411(a), 15 U.S.C.A. § 1710(a); Consumer Products Safety Act § 11(c), 15 U.S.C.A. § 2060(c); Toxic Substances Control Act § 19(c)(1)(B)(i), 15 U.S.C.A. § 2618(c)(1)(B)(i); Occupational Safety and Health Act § 6(f), 29 U.S.C.A. § 655(f); Federal Coal Mine Health and Safety Act § 106(a), 30 U.S.C.A. § 816(a).

4. Id.

5. 499 F.2d 467 (D.C.Cir.1974).

6. Id. at 469. The dispute arose under the judicial review provision of the Occupational Safety and Health Act, 29 U.S.C.A. § 665(f).

7. 499 F.2d at 474.

8. Id.

issues the record resembled that compiled in an informal rulemaking case. It included a "melange of written statements, letters, reports, and similar materials received outside the bounds of the oral hearing."[9] The court found that the procedure devised by the agency suited this type of statute very well:

> On a record of this mixed nature, when the facts underlying the Secretary's determinations are susceptible of being found in the usual sense, that must be done, and the reviewing court will weigh them by the substantial evidence standard. But, in a statute like OSHA where the decision making vested in the Secretary is legislative in character, there are areas where explicit factual findings are not possible, and the act of decision is essentially a prediction based upon pure legislative judgment, as when a Congressman decides to vote for or against a particular bill.[10]

In short, the court assumed that at least two categories of facts could exist in such a case: specific or adjudicative facts and policy or legislative facts. The former were amenable to more formal procedures and to substantial evidence review. Legislative facts, however, need not be subject to such additional procedures nor, arguably, to a substantial evidence standard of review.[11]

Hybrid statutes thus raise an additional issue: Does review of policy-making facts under the substantial evidence test differ from review under the arbitrary and capricious test of the APA?[12] Given the emer-

9. Id.

10. Id.

11. For other cases, see, Superior Oil Co. v. FERC, 563 F.2d 191, 199 (5th Cir. 1977); Citizens to Preserve Overton Park, Inc. v. Volpe, 401 U.S. 402, 91 S.Ct. 814, 28 L.Ed.2d 136 (1971). But see City of Chicago, Ill. v. FPC, 458 F.2d 731, 744–45 (D.C.Cir. 1971), cert. denied 405 U.S. 1074, 92 S.Ct. 1495, 31 L.Ed.2d 808 (1972) (judicial review of informal rulemaking must be "searching and careful," notwithstanding the "quasi-legislative" nature of such rulemaking). See also In re Permian Basin Area Rate Cases, 390 U.S. 747, 88 S.Ct. 1344, 20 L.Ed.2d 312 (1968). These cases set out an approach to judicial review of rulemaking based on a substantial evidence standard. While that case involved a formal rulemaking, the FPC (and FERC) has proceeded informally since then in a number of cases. See, e.g., Wisconsin Gas Co. v. FERC, 770 F.2d 1144, 1156 (D.C.Cir.1985), cert. denied 476 U.S. 1114, 106 S.Ct. 1968, 90 L.Ed.2d 653 (1986); Public Systems v. FERC, 606 F.2d 973, 979 (D.C.Cir.1979); American Public Gas Ass'n v. FPC, 567 F.2d 1016, 1029 (D.C.Cir.1977), cert. denied 435 U.S. 907, 98 S.Ct. 1456, 55 L.Ed.2d 499 (1978).

12. See authorities cited in Note, supra note 96, at 541, 542 n. 6. (citing legislative history to support the view that the standards are different). Specifically, it is noted that "such intent is reflected in the legislative history of the Consumer Products Safety Act, 15 U.S.C. §§ 2052–2083 (1982), where Congress indicated that it wanted courts to scrutinize the Commission's acts more closely than the arbitrary and capricious test would allow." See H.R.Rep. No. 1153, 92nd Cong., 2d Sess. 38 (1972); S.Rep. No. 749, 92nd Cong., 2d Sess. 35 (1972); 118 Cong.Rec. 31,378 (1972) (statement of Rep. Moss). In the debate over the standard of review for section 307 of the Clean Air Act, 42 U.S.C.A. § 7607(b)–(d) (1982), Senator Edmund Muskie opposed the House proposal for substantial evidence review, saying that "nothing in the bill or its legislative history was meant to single out EPA for special scrutiny." 123 Cong. Rec. 26,851 (1977) (statement of Sen. Muskie). See also Industrial Union Dept. v. American Petroleum Institute, 448 U.S. 607, 705, [100 S.Ct. 2844, 2896, 65 L.Ed.2d 1010] (1980) (Marshall, J. dissenting) (stating that the legislative choice of the substantial evidence standard in the Occupational Safety and Health Act of 1970, 29 U.S.C.A. § 655(f) (1982), represents a legislative judgment that regulatory action should be subject to review more stringent

gence of the hard look doctrine and the increasing demands by courts for reasoned decisionmaking on the part of the agency in rulemaking contexts,[13] "some courts and scholars have theorized that the two standards have actually converged and now operate in the same fashion."[14]

One of the leading cases in support of the convergence theory is Judge Friendly's opinion in *Associated Industries v. U.S. Dept. of Labor.*[15] In that case, the court reviewed an order by the Department of Labor, issued pursuant to the Occupational Safety and Health Act (OSHA), setting the minimum number of bathrooms required in industrial plants.

than the traditional arbitrary and capricious standard for informal rulemaking); Association of Data Processing Serv. Orgs. v. Board of Governors of the Fed. Reserve Sys., 745 F.2d 677, 685 (D.C.Cir.1984) (finding it conceivable that the inclusion of the substantial evidence standard in recent review provisions reflects legislative intent to scrutinize agency action more closely than the arbitrary and capricious standard); Union Oil Co. v. Federal Power Com'n, 542 F.2d 1036, 1041 (9th Cir.1976) (stating that Congress expects greater scrutiny when the enabling statute contains a substantial evidence test) [rejected by Superior Oil Co. v. FERC, 563 F.2d 191 (5th Cir.1977)]; Mobil Oil Corp. v. Federal Power Com'n, 483 F.2d 1238, 1257–60 (D.C.Cir. 1973) (stating that the inclusion of the substantial evidence test in the Natural Gas Act, 15 U.S.C.A. § 717r(b) (1982), suggested an intent to provide stricter review than that afforded under the arbitrary and capricious standard).

Statutes such as these may, however, authorize closer judicial review of an agency's reasons for its actions, if not the legislative facts on which its judgments are based. See sec. 13.10.6, infra.

13. For a detailed discussion of the hardlook doctrine and reasoned decisionmaking, see sections 13.10.4 and 13.10.5, infra.

14. Note, supra note 88, at 541, 543 (1982) (citing Pacific Legal Foundation v. Department of Transp., 593 F.2d 1338, 1343 n. 35 (D.C.Cir.1979), cert. denied, 444 U.S. 830, 100 S.Ct. 57, 62 L.Ed.2d 38 (1979) and noting its agreement with the emerging consensus of the courts of appeals that the difference between the arbitrary and capricious and substantial evidence tests is largely semantic and that the criteria used in both tests tend to converge); Friendly, "Some Kind of Hearing," 123 U.Pa.L.Rev. 1267, 1313 (1975) (stating that "the ... difference between the substantial evidence test and the arbitrary and capricious test can readily be exaggerated"); Garland, Deregulation and the Judicial Review, 98 Harv.L.Rev. 507, 533–34 (1985) (stating that after the emergence of the "hard look" doctrine, the difference between the substantial evidence and arbitrary and capricious standards was "fading"); Levanthal, Environmental Decisionmaking and the Role of the Courts, 122 U.Pa.L.Rev. 509, 540 (1974) (commenting that "[it] is not likely to be of great consequence whether the [court's] formula is put in terms like the need for 'substantial evidence' or ... whether the order was so lacking in a reasoned basis as to be 'arbitrary' "); Pedersen, Formal Records and Informal Rulemaking, 85 Yale L.J. 38, 48–49 (1975) (stating that the arbitrary and capricious test has been "transformed into something very close to substantial evidence review"); Scalia & Goodman, Procedural Aspects of the Consumer Product Safety Act, 20 UCLA L.Rev. 899, 935 n. 138 (1973) (noting that "in an evidentiary context the level of required support seems about the same whether the 'substantial evidence' or the 'arbitrary' test is used"); Verkuil, Judicial Review of Informal Rulemaking, 60 Va.L.Rev. 185, 222 (1974) (stating that "the substantial evidence test may be merely another way of expressing the rational basis test"). See also National Small Shipments Traffic Conference, Inc. v. CAB, 618 F.2d 819 (D.C.Cir.1980) (court said that it was following the emerging consensus of courts in rejecting the distinction); National Nutritional Foods Ass'n v. Weinberger, 512 F.2d 688, 705 (2d Cir. 1975), cert. denied 423 U.S. 827, 96 S.Ct. 44, 46 L.Ed.2d 44 (1975); ITT World Communications, Inc. v. FCC, 595 F.2d 897 (2d Cir.1979); American Public Gas Ass'n v. FPC, 567 F.2d 1016 (D.C.Cir.1977), cert. denied 435 U.S. 907, 98 S.Ct. 1456, 55 L.Ed.2d 499 (1978).

15. 487 F.2d 342 (2d Cir.1973).

The OSHA provision for judicial review stated:[16]

> The determinations of the Secretary shall be conclusive if supported by substantial evidence in the record considered as a whole.

The court noted the difficulty of reviewing informal rulemaking proceedings when there was no "statutory harmony" regarding the standard and scope of judicial review to be used.[17] The Labor Department argued that the substantial evidence test was inappropriate for this kind of legislative decision. They claimed that the APA's substantial evidence test[18] applies only to adjudicatory action under 5 U.S.C. § 554 or rules required to be made on the record.[19] The OSHA review provision, in their view, meant that the substantial evidence test applied only to "determinations" resulting from adjudication or rules required by statute to be determined on the record. The substantial evidence standard, they contended, should not be applied to the overall policy decision embodied in the rule.[20]

The Court held that the substantial evidence test applies generally to policy decisions, not just "determinations" made on the record. The Court noted that the plain meaning of the statute and its legislative history fully supported the proposition that the substantial evidence test was to apply the outcome of the rulemaking proceeding. Indeed the substantial evidence language appears in the very section of the statute "relating expressly to the determination of standards after notice and comment rulemaking."[21] Thus, the Court felt constrained to "determine and sustain the applicability of the substantial evidence test . . . at least in the context of informal rulemaking."[22]

The Court found that the application of either a substantial evidence or an arbitrary and capricious standard, however, would most likely produce the same result:

> "While we still have a feeling that there may be cases where an adjudicative determination not supported by substantial evidence within the test of [*Universal Camera*] would not be regarded as arbitrary and capricious . . . in the review of rules of general applicability made after notice and comment rulemaking, the two criteria do tend to converge."[23]

Applying this standard in this case, the court found that the agency had not met the burden of providing substantial evidence in support of the promulgation of its rule. The record revealed no witnesses in favor of the agency's position. In addition, the agency failed to respond to the various objections to its position.[24]

16. 29 U.S.C.A. § 655(f).

17. 487 F.2d at 345.

18. 5 U.S.C.A. § 706(2)(E).

19. 487 F.2d at 347.

20. Id. at 347–48.

21. Id.

22. Id. at 349.

23. Id. at 350.

24. Id. at 351–53.

In *Association of Data Processing Service Organizations, Inc. v. Board of Governors of the Fed. Reserve System,*[25] the court explicitly adopted the convergence theory in an opinion by Judge, now Justice Scalia. The court reviewed an order of the Federal Reserve Board approving Citicorp's application to establish a data processing subsidiary. A trade association sought review of the Board's order entered after notice and comment rulemaking, amending portions of the regulation[26] dealing with the performance of data processing by bank holding companies. As a result of consolidating appeals, the court was required to review both on-the-record adjudication and informal notice and comment rulemaking. Petitioners contended that what they viewed as the relatively more demanding substantial evidence test applied to both orders. An intervenor, Citicorp, argued for applying the substantial evidence test to the adjudication portion of the case, but the arbitrary and capricious test to the informal rulemaking portion of the case. The Court stated that this difference would not matter:

> "[I]n their application to the requirement of factual support the substantial evidence test and the arbitrary or capricious test are one and the same. The former is only a specific application of the latter, separately recited in the APA not to establish a more rigorous standard of factual support but to emphasize that in the case of formal proceedings the factual support must be found in the closed record as opposed to elsewhere."[27]

The Court further noted that the arbitrary and capricious test is a catch-all provision, "picking-up administrative misconduct not covered by the other more specific paragraphs."[28] In cases not governed by §§ 556 and 557 of the APA, the arbitrary and capricious test covers the need for factual support:

> When the arbitrary or capricious standard is performing that function of assuring factual support, there is no substantive difference between what it requires and what would be required by the substantial evidence test, since it is impossible to conceive of a "nonarbitrary factual" judgement supported only by evidence that is not substantial in the APA sense.[29]

Despite the convergence theory, the substantial evidence language incorporated into a policymaking proceeding sometimes triggers close judicial review of the reasons for an agency rule. Many of the hard look cases involve hybrid statutes, and the more demanding role that courts

25. 745 F.2d 677 (D.C.Cir.1984).

26. Id. at 680. See Bank Holding Company Act, 12 U.S.C.A. § 1848.

27. 745 F.2d at 683. In conclusion, the Court held that the distinction is largely semantic. "The distinctive function of paragraph (E) substantial evidence—what it achieves that paragraph (A) [arbitrary and capricious] does not—is to require substantial evidence to be found *within the record of closed-record proceedings* to which it exclusively applies." Id. at 684 (emphasis in original).

28. Id. at 683.

29. Id. The court also held that it could not apply a more rigorous review of the individual adjudicatory determination than it applied to the informal rulemaking decision which was a general determination with nationwide impact. Id. at 685.

occasionally play is arguably based on a judicial perception that by use of such statutes, Congress intended closer judicial scrutiny of the rationales of agency policy decisions.[30]

§ 13.6 DE NOVO REVIEW OF FACTFINDING

In addition to the judicial application of the arbitrary and capricious and the substantial evidence standards of review to agency factfinding, the drafters of § 706 of the APA also contemplated *de novo* judicial trial of facts in an unspecified, but potentially broad, range of circumstances. Section 706(2)(F) provides that courts may invalidate agency action that is "unwarranted by the facts to the extent that the facts are subject to trial *de novo* by the reviewing court."[1] When engaging in *de novo* review, a court can make its own independent findings of fact in addition to examining the record developed by the agency.[2]

De novo judicial review of agency factfinding was a common practice at the time the APA was passed.[3] Prior to the APA, the facts needed for meaningful judicial review in informal proceedings often were developed through a judicial trial.[4] The trend away from such judicial trials was reaffirmed by the Court's opinion in *Citizens to Preserve Overton Park, Inc. v. Volpe*.[5] In that case the Court agreed to review the Secretary of Transportation's decision to authorize federal funding for a highway whose route was chosen arguably in a manner that violated the relevant environmental statutes involved. The Court struggled with the question of what standard of judicial review to apply to the case. It concluded that the agency's action was, in effect, a form of informal adjudication. The Court then assumed that an administrative record was in existence. It, thus, rejected the application of *de novo* judicial review of the facts involved in favor of application of the arbitrary and capricious standard of review to the record that existed at the time the Secretary made his decision. In so doing, the Court narrowly construed § 706(2)(F), holding

30. See sections 13.10.5 and 13.10.6, infra. See also legislative histories recounted in note 88 supra.

§ 13.6

1. 5 U.S.C.A. § 706(2)(F). When this standard has been applied, there has been some question as to what "unwarranted by the facts" actually means. See, e.g., District of Columbia v. Pace, 320 U.S. 698, 701–02, 64 S.Ct. 406, 408, 88 L.Ed. 408 (1944) (usual standard for *de novo* review is to allow the court to overrule clearly erroneous findings, which allows the reviewing court to weigh the facts and reach conclusions based on its own judgment); Watson v. Gulf Stevedore Corp., 400 F.2d 649 (5th Cir.1968), cert. denied 394 U.S. 976, 89 S.Ct. 1471, 22 L.Ed.2d 755 (1969) (*de novo* review analogous to appellate review of an equity judgment decided without a jury). But see Modica v. United States, 518 F.2d 374, 376 (5th Cir.1975) (*de novo* review pursuant to the Food Stamp Act goes beyond the APA *de novo* standard and permits the court to decide the issue by a preponderance of the evidence).

2. See, e.g., Chandler v. Roudebush, 425 U.S. 840, 96 S.Ct. 1949, 48 L.Ed.2d 416 (1976); Williams v. Bell, 587 F.2d 1240 (D.C.Cir.1978).

3. See Levin, Scope of Review Doctrine Restated: An Administrative Law Section Report, 38 Admin.L.Rev. 239, 273–277 (1986). See also, Nathanson, Probing the Mind of the Administrator, 75 Colum.L.Rev. 721, 755 (1975).

4. Id.

5. Citizens to Preserve Overton Park, Inc. v. Volpe, 401 U.S. 402, 91 S.Ct. 814, 28 L.Ed.2d 136 (1971). This case is also discussed in chapter 9, sec. 9.2, supra.

that it applied in only two circumstances: (1) when "the action is adjudicatory in nature and the agency factfinding procedures are inadequate," or (2) when "issues that were not before the agency are raised in a proceeding to enforce nonadjudicatory agency action."[6]

De novo judicial review under § 706(2)(F) is, therefore, reserved for extraordinary cases.[7] *De novo* review of facts by courts has been largely confined to collateral matters such as the agency's rationale,[8] or the materials the agency relied on[9] in reaching its decision.

Quite apart from the APA, however, *de novo* review may be guaranteed by the Constitution or by statute.[10] A statute, however, must explicitly specify that *de novo* review is authorized. Such specification usually will not be presumed,[11] but it has, on occasion, been inferred from legislative history clearly indicating that this was Congress' intent.[12]

6. *Overton Park,* 401 U.S. at 415, 91 S.Ct. at 823; Camp v. Pitts, 411 U.S. 138, 142, 93 S.Ct. 1241, 1244, 36 L.Ed.2d 106 (1973); see also Environmental Defense Fund, Inc. v. Costle, 657 F.2d 275 (D.C.Cir. 1981); Baker v. Bell, 630 F.2d 1046 (5th Cir.1980); Parker v. Director, Office of Workers' Compensation Programs, 590 F.2d 748 (8th Cir.1979); Briggs v. Dalton, 939 F.Supp. 753 (D.Hawai'i 1996); Stauber v. Shalala, 895 F.Supp. 1178 (W.D.Wis. 1995); Montgomery Improvement Ass'n, Inc. v. Department of HUD, 543 F.Supp. 603 (M.D.Ala.1982); NAACP v. Wilmington Medical Center, Inc., 453 F.Supp. 280 (D.Del.1978). See also, Gordon G. Young, Judicial Review of Informal Agency Action on the Fiftieth Anniversary of the APA: The Alleged Demise and Actual Status of Overton Park's Requirement of Judicial Review "One the Record", 10 Admin. L.J. Am. U. 179, 221 (1996) (discussing the evidence for and existence of exceptions to the Overton Park rule, above and beyond the two actually enumerated in the Overton Park opinion).

7. See, e.g., National Organization for Women, Washington, D.C. Chapter v. SSA, 736 F.2d 727, 744–46 (D.C.Cir.1984) (Mikva, J. concurring); Porter v. Califano, 592 F.2d 770, 782–84 (5th Cir.1979), appeal after remand 648 F.2d 310 (1981) (involving an obviously biased agency adjudication). See also Levin, supra note 118, at 273–74 (noting that *Porter v. Califano* has been the only case since *Overton Park* to explicitly find one of the two stated circumstances in *Overton Park* for applying *de novo* review).

8. See Levin, supra note 118. See also *Overton Park,* 401 U.S. at 420–21, 91 S.Ct. at 825–26; Sierra Club v. United States Army Corps of Engineers, 772 F.2d 1043, 1051–52 (2d Cir.1985); United States v. Garner, 767 F.2d 104, 118 n. 20 (5th Cir. 1985); First Bank & Trust Co. v. Smith, 509 F.2d 663 (1st Cir.1975), appeal after remand 545 F.2d 752 (1976), cert. denied 430 U.S. 931, 97 S.Ct. 1551, 51 L.Ed.2d 775 (1977).

9. Levin, supra note 118, at 277.

10. See, e.g., Agosto v. INS, 436 U.S. 748, 98 S.Ct. 2081, 56 L.Ed.2d 677 (1978) (*de novo* trial of citizenship issue in deportation cases guaranteed by statute and by the Constitution); Chandler v. Roudebush, 425 U.S. 840, 96 S.Ct. 1949, 48 L.Ed.2d 416 (1976) (statutory guarantee of trial *de novo* of federal employee's Title VII claims); Porter v. Califano, 592 F.2d 770, 780 (5th Cir.1979), appeal after remand 648 F.2d 310 (1981) (*de novo* review allowed if constitutional rights are at issue); Williams v. Bell, 587 F.2d 1240 (D.C.Cir.1978) (*de novo* review authorized by Civil Rights Act of 1964); Izaak Walton League of America v. Marsh, 655 F.2d 346, 369 n. 56 (D.C.Cir. 1981), cert. denied 454 U.S. 1092, 102 S.Ct. 657, 70 L.Ed.2d 630 (1981) (judicial review under NEPA is not limited to the original administrative record because "[s]uits challenging environmental impact statements seek to ensure compliance with a statute other than the APA").

11. United States v. Carlo Bianchi & Co., 373 U.S. 709, 83 S.Ct. 1409, 10 L.Ed.2d 652 (1963). See also Consolo v. FMC, 383 U.S. 607, 86 S.Ct. 1018, 16 L.Ed.2d 131 (1966); Williams v. Califano, 593 F.2d 282 (7th Cir.1979).

12. See Perri v. BATF, 637 F.2d 1332 (9th Cir.1981); Stein's, Inc. v. Blumenthal, 649 F.2d 463 (7th Cir.1980).

De novo review is also possible when, quite apart from the statute involved, courts conclude that either jurisdictional or constitutional facts are in issue. Jurisdictional facts are those facts whose existence are essential if an agency's power is lawfully to be invoked.[13] Constitutional facts are those facts necessary for a court to determine the constitutionality of an agency's action.[14] Though modern courts seldom invoke the cases that gave rise to the jurisdictional and constitutional fact doctrines,[15] they have not been explicitly overruled.[16] The constitutional fact doctrine remains relevant[17] in cases involving personal as opposed to

13. The jurisdictional fact doctrine arises when a statute grants an administrative agency the power to make a specific decision, conditional on the presence of a certain fact, situation, or act. Since the question whether this condition existed in fact is the basis of the administrative agency's jurisdiction, a court must make such an independent determination, even though the agency already made the same determination as an initial step in reaching its decision. The determination whether a fact is "jurisdictional" depends strictly on the specific provisions of the statute which grants the agency its power to act. Dickinson, *Crowell v. Benson:* Judicial Review of Administrative Determinations of Questions of "Constitutional Fact," 80 Colum.L.Rev. 1055, 1059 (1931). Dickinson goes on to provide examples: suppose a statute confers an official power to kill diseased animals or confiscate "green" hides, and officials have taken such steps. The owners are entitled, under the jurisdictional fact doctrine, to introduce evidence in court on the issue of whether the animals were, "in fact," diseased, or the hides, "in fact" "green." A court will conduct this inquiry even though the agency officials had to make the same factual determination as a basis for their authority to act.

The jurisdictional fact doctrine is essentially dead today. Courts were never able to clearly distinguish between such facts and other facts in the case. See, e.g., Estep v. United States, 327 U.S. 114, 142, 66 S.Ct. 423, 436, 90 L.Ed. 567 (1946).

14. Ohio Valley Water Co. v. Ben Avon Borough, 253 U.S. 287, 40 S.Ct. 527, 64 L.Ed. 908 (1920), laid out the constitutional fact doctrine, and St. Joseph Stock Yards Co. v. United States, 298 U.S. 38, 56 S.Ct. 720, 80 L.Ed. 1033 (1936), developed it. This doctrine is analogous to the jurisdictional fact doctrine: "Just as a statute may confine jurisdiction to cases where a certain fact exists, so the constitution may be construed to limit jurisdiction to the presence or absence of a fact-situation." Dickinson, supra note 128, at 1067. That is, a constitutional fact is one which determines whether the agency act exceeds a constitutional limitation on its power.

15. See *Ohio Valley Water Co. v. Ben Avon Borough*; Crowell v. Benson, 285 U.S. 22, 52 S.Ct. 285, 76 L.Ed. 598 (1932); Ng Fung Ho v. White, 259 U.S. 276, 42 S.Ct. 492, 66 L.Ed. 938 (1922); St. Joseph Stock Yards Co. v. United States, 298 U.S. 38, 56 S.Ct. 720, 80 L.Ed. 1033 (1936).

16. See, e.g., M. Redish, Federal Courts: Cases, Comments and Questions 193 (1983); Schwartz, Does the Ghost of *Crowell v. Benson* Still Walk?, 98 U.Pa. L.Rev. 163 (1949); United States v. Raddatz, 447 U.S. 667, 710, 100 S.Ct. 2406, 2430, 65 L.Ed.2d 424 (1980), rehearing denied 448 U.S. 916, 101 S.Ct. 36, 65 L.Ed.2d 1179 (1980) (Marshall, J., dissenting) ("It may fairly be said that in certain respects at least, Mr. Justice Brandeis' views in *Crowell* and *St. Joseph Stock Yards* have become the law. . . .Yet neither *Crowell* nor *Ng Fung Ho* has been overruled, and the Court has cited both with approval in recent years."); Estep v. United States, 327 U.S. 114, 142, 66 S.Ct. 423, 436, 90 L.Ed. 567 (1946) (Justice Frankfurter regarding the doctrine of jurisdictional fact as stated in *Crowell:* "one had supposed that the doctrine had earned a deserved repose"); Associated Indemnity Corp. v. Shea, 455 F.2d 913, 914 n. 2 (5th Cir.1972) ("[s]uffice it to say, that although the Supreme Court has not expressly overruled *Crowell,* it simply does not follow it").

17. See Monaghan, Constitutional Fact Review, 85 Colum.L.Rev. 229, 260 (1985), arguing that despite *Crowell* 's decline in use in judicial review of agency decisions, the constitutional fact doctrine remains a part of the Supreme Court's general appellate jurisdiction. See e.g., Pittsburgh S.S. Co. v. Brown, 171 F.2d 175, 177 (7th Cir. 1948), reversing 81 F.Supp. 284 (N.D.Ill. 1947), modified 81 F.Supp. 285 (1947), supplemented by 81 F.Supp. 287 (1947) (confirming plaintiff's right to a *de novo* factual review of a compensation order under the

property rights.[18] In *Porter v. Califano,*[19] for example, the Southeastern Program Center of the Social Security Administration suspended the appellant without a hearing. She had written and distributed a letter which, among other things, criticized two of her superiors. When Porter exhausted her administrative appeals, she sued in district court, seeking review of the agency's decision, alleging, *inter alia,* violation of her First Amendment rights.

In setting aside the lower court's cursory rejection of Porter's constitutional claim, the Circuit Court explained that in § 706(2)(B) of the APA, Congress intended that courts make an independent assessment of a citizen's claim of constitutional right when reviewing agency decisionmaking.[20] The Court explained that "section 706(2)(B) explicitly authorizes the court to set aside any agency action 'contrary to constitutional right.' "[21] In a footnote the Court added that:

> Independent judicial judgment is especially appropriate in the First Amendment area. Judicial deference to agency fact-finding and decision-making is generally premised on the existence of agency expertise in a particular specialized or technical area. But in general, courts, not agencies, are expert on the First Amendment.[22]

The Court concluded that the District Court erred, and remanded the case "for a full hearing and independent judgment on Porter's constitutional claim."[23]

§ 13.7 JUDICIAL REVIEW OF QUESTIONS OF LAW

Previous sections in this chapter have examined the law-fact distinction and judicial review of questions of fact in various procedural contexts, pursuant to three standards of review. We shall now examine judicial review of questions of law. Section 706 of the APA provides a reviewing court with the authority to "decide all relevant questions of law, interpret constitutional and statutory provisions, and determine the meaning or applicability of the terms of an agency action."[1] A court is thus authorized to "hold unlawful and set aside agency action"[2] that it

Longshoremen's and Harbor Workers' Compensation Act as to whether the injury occurred on navigable waters, the court stated: "[n]one of the cases relied upon by the defendants ... furnish any substantial basis for the contention that the *Crowell* case is no longer binding upon inferior federal courts").

18. See, e.g., Ng Fung Ho v. White, 259 U.S. 276, 42 S.Ct. 492, 66 L.Ed. 938 (1922) (the court draws a distinction "between the right to liberty of a person and other constitutional rights"); Agosto v. INS, 436 U.S. 748, 753, 98 S.Ct. 2081, 2085, 56 L.Ed.2d 677 (1978) ("the Constitution requires that there be some provision for de novo judicial determination of claims to American citizenship in deportation proceedings").

19. 592 F.2d 770 (5th Cir.1979), appeal after remand 648 F.2d 310 (1981).

20. Id. at 780.

21. Id.

22. Id. at 780 n. 15. The Court also cites Quaker Action Group v. Hickel, 421 F.2d 1111, 1118 (D.C.Cir.1969).

23. Id. at 781–82. See also United States v. Means, 627 F.Supp. 247 (D.S.D. 1985), reversed on other grounds 858 F.2d 404 (8th Cir.1988), cert. denied 492 U.S. 910, 109 S.Ct. 3227, 106 L.Ed.2d 575 (1989).

§ 13.7

1. 5 U.S.C.A. § 706.

2. 5 U.S.C.A. § 706(2).

finds to be unconstitutional,[3] in excess of the agency's statutory powers,[4] made contrary to required procedures,[5] an abuse of discretion, "or otherwise not in accordance with law."[6]

Nowhere does the Act mention judicial deference to agency determinations of law, yet elaborate doctrines of judicial deference have developed over the years. In examining these doctrines of judicial deference to agency law making, it is necessary to distinguish among the types of questions of law involved, the procedural contexts or formats in which agencies interpret the law as well as the substantive, factual contexts which give rise to these issues.

Some questions of law go to the jurisdiction of an agency to act.[7] Others involve the application of a statutory term to a set of facts.[8] Other questions may involve consideration of the constitutional effects of certain agency action,[9] or an agency's interpretation of ambiguous statutory terms. We shall now examine these various types of questions of law, beginning with perhaps the most important distinction a court can make when engaging in judicial review—that between a question of law and a question of law application.[10] Still other questions of law may arise in the context of an agency interpretation of its own regulations.[11] Some of those regulations may have been promulgated as legislative rules pursuant to section 553 of the APA and others may be interpretative rules issued without notice and comment.[12]

3. 5 U.S.C.A. § 706(2)(B).

4. 5 U.S.C.A. § 706(2)(C).

5. 5 U.S.C.A. § 706(2)(D).

6. 5 U.S.C.A. § 706(2)(A).

7. See, e.g., Phillips Petroleum Co. v. Wisconsin, 347 U.S. 672, 74 S.Ct. 794, 98 L.Ed. 1035 (1954), rehearing denied 348 U.S. 851, 75 S.Ct. 17, 99 L.Ed. 670 (1954) (court extends Federal Power Commission's jurisdiction to include the price of natural gas at the wellhead).

8. See, e.g., NLRB v. Hearst Publications, 322 U.S. 111, 64 S.Ct. 851, 88 L.Ed. 1170 (1944), rehearing denied 322 U.S. 769, 64 S.Ct. 1148, 88 L.Ed. 1595 (1944), superceded by statute as stated in NLRB v. Town & Country Elec., Inc., 516 U.S. 85, 116 S.Ct. 450, 133 L.Ed.2d 371 (1995) (applying the statutory term "employee," after judicially determining its definition).

9. See, e.g., Porter v. Califano, 592 F.2d 770 (5th Cir.1979), appeal after remand 648 F.2d 310 (1981) (free speech issues); Bill Johnson's Restaurants, Inc. v. NLRB, 461 U.S. 731, 743–44, 103 S.Ct. 2161, 2170–71, 76 L.Ed.2d 277 (1983) (baseless lawsuit filed by an employer against an employee for exercising his rights under § 7 of the NLRA is not immunized by the First Amendment right to petition and may be enjoined by the NLRB); Florida Gulf Coast Bldg. and Const. Trades Council v. NLRB, 796 F.2d 1328, 1346 (11th Cir.1986), rehearing denied 806 F.2d 1070 (1986), affirmed 485 U.S. 568, 108 S.Ct. 1392, 99 L.Ed.2d 645 (1988) (peaceful and orderly distribution of handbills is a form of speech protected by the First Amendment and may not be enjoined by the NLRB as a violation of § 8(b)(4)(ii)(B) of the NLRA). See also, United States v. Nixon, 418 U.S. 683, 703–05, 94 S.Ct. 3090, 3105–06, 41 L.Ed.2d 1039 (1974).

10. See, e.g., Chevron, U.S.A., Inc. v. NRDC, 467 U.S. 837, 104 S.Ct. 2778, 81 L.Ed.2d 694 (1984), rehearing denied 468 U.S. 1227, 105 S.Ct. 28, 82 L.Ed.2d 921 (1984).

11. See, e.g., Ford Motor Credit Co. v. Milhollin, 444 U.S. 555, 100 S.Ct. 790, 63 L.Ed.2d 22 (1980) (involving, in part, application by the Federal Reserve Board of its own Regulation Z).

12. Traditionally courts have been more deferential to agency interpretations embodied in legislative rules as opposed to interpretative rules. See sec. 13.8.5, infra. Compare Chrysler Corp. v. Brown, 441 U.S. 281, 295, 99 S.Ct. 1705, 1714, 60 L.Ed.2d 208 (1979) (legislative or substantive rules) with Skidmore v. Swift & Co., 323 U.S. 134,

§ 13.7.1 Questions of Law and Questions of Law Application

As we have previously noted, judicial review of agency action usually involves at least three distinct questions—questions of fact, questions of law and questions of law application.[13] The application of law to facts results in what are commonly referred to as questions of mixed fact and law. Given agreement on the basic facts involved as well as the interpretation of the relevant law to be applied, courts generally defer to the result reached by the agency when it applies this law to the facts before it. The penchant of some courts, however, to collapse the law application stage of their analysis with the law formulation part of the process, particularly when they agree with the result reached by the agency, can make the judicial use of deferential language confusing and often misleading.

NLRB v. Hearst Publications, Inc.[14] demonstrates this potential for confusion. *Hearst* is often cited to support a limited judicial role in dealing with certain kinds of questions of law, particularly law application. Justice Rutledge, writing for the majority, stated:

> ... where the question is one of specific application of a broad statutory term in a proceeding in which the agency administering the statute must determine it initially, the reviewing court's function is limited. Like the commissioner's determination under the Longshoremen's & Harbor Workers' Act, that a man is not a "member of a crew" ... or that he was injured "in the course of his employment" ... and the Federal Communications Commission's determination that one company is under the "control" of another ..., *the Board's determination that specified persons are "employees" under this Act is to be accepted if it has "warrant in the record" and a reasonable basis in law.*[15]

On closer examination, however, the Court engages in a much more thorough and independent analysis of the law than this quote might indicate.

Hearst arose from the refusal of four Los Angeles newspapers to bargain collectively with a union representing newsboys who distributed their papers from newsstands on the streets. The newspapers argued

65 S.Ct. 161, 89 L.Ed. 124 (1944) (interpretative rules); but see Chevron, U.S.A., Inc. v. NRDC, 467 U.S. 837, 104 S.Ct. 2778, 81 L.Ed.2d 694 (1984), rehearing denied 468 U.S. 1227, 105 S.Ct. 28, 82 L.Ed.2d 921 (1984) (the Court's deferential approach fails to distinguish explicitly between the kinds of rules involved).

13. See sec. 13.3, supra.

14. 322 U.S. 111, 64 S.Ct. 851, 88 L.Ed. 1170 (1944), rehearing denied 322 U.S. 769, 64 S.Ct. 1148, 88 L.Ed. 1595 (1944), superceded by statute as stated in NLRB v. Town & Country Elec., Inc., 516 U.S. 85, 116 S.Ct. 450, 133 L.Ed.2d 371 (1995).

15. Id. at 131, 64 S.Ct. at 861 (emphasis added) (citations and footnotes omitted). *See also* Nationwide Mutual Ins. Co. v. Darden, 503 U.S. 318, 319, 112 S.Ct. 1344, 1346, 117 L.Ed.2d 581 (1992) (holding that when faced with a definition of "employee" which is completely circular and explains nothing all of the factors surrounding the employment relationship "must be assessed and weighed with no one factor being decisive" in determining the relevant definition to be applied to the situation).

that "newsboys" were not employees within the meaning of the National Labor Relations Act. Though the union was properly certified, the newspapers refused to bargain with it. The Board found that newsboys were employees and that the newspapers had, therefore, violated the National Labor Relations Act. It ordered them to cease and desist in these violations and to bargain collectively with the union upon request. The newspapers appealed. Though they were successful at the Circuit Court, the Supreme Court ultimately upheld the NLRB decision.

The principal question in the Supreme Court was whether the newsboys were "employees." Before concluding that the Board's legal conclusion was correct, the majority carefully examined whether the Board had, in fact, used the appropriate legal test in making its determination. The Court first discussed, but rejected, the argument that employees should be defined by resort to "common law standards."[16] The Court then discussed whether state law should govern an issue such as this and rejected that possibility. Instead, the issue was one that had to be "answered primarily from the history, terms and purposes"[17] of the National Labor Relations Act itself. In the case at hand, "it cannot be irrelevant that the particular workers in these cases are subject, as a matter of economic fact, to the evil the statute was designed to eradicate and that the remedies it affords are appropriate for preventing them or curing their harmful effects in the special situation."[18] Having independently determined that the Board's approach was consistent with that view, the Court then deferred to the result reached by the Board's application of the statute to the facts of this case.

With regard to the questions of law in this case, the *Hearst* Court engaged in a two-step analysis: (1) Did the agency devise the proper test to be applied to the facts of the case? (2) Assuming the Board used the proper factors in deciding what an employee was for purposes of the NLR Act, was its application of that term reasonable?[19] In the first step of its analysis, the court engaged in substantially *de novo* review. The Court deferred only when it was satisfied that the agency was applying the correct legal test to the facts at bar.[20]

16. Id. at 122, 64 S.Ct. at 856.

17. Id. at 124, 64 S.Ct. at 857.

18. Id. at 127, 64 S.Ct. at 858.

19. As we shall see infra, an important question today is how far can a court go in examining legislative history, once it is convinced that the statutory provision in question is ambiguous. Courts often disagree on just what constitutes ambiguity or when Congressional intent is clear or unclear. See sec. 13.7.3, infra.

20. This analysis is clearly implied in Walter Gellhorn et al., Administrative Law 379–92 (8th ed. 1987). Various commentators have developed this line of analysis more fully. See, e.g., Levin, Identifying Questions of Law in Administrative Law, 74 Geo.L.J., 23–26 (1985); Monaghan, Marbury and the Administrative State, 83 Colum.L.Rev. 1, 28–30 (1983); Note, The Chevron Legacy: Young v. Community Nutrition Institute Compounds the Confusion, 73 Corn.L.Rev., 113, 115–118 (1987).

Another case usually cited as a deference case is Gray v. Powell, 314 U.S. 402, 62 S.Ct. 326, 86 L.Ed. 301 (1941). In *Gray,* the Seaboard Airline Railway leased coal bearing lands and hired a contractor to extract the coal. They applied for an exemption from the provisions of the Bituminous Coal Code that was available for coal that was both produced and consumed by the same party. The National Bituminous Coal Commission denied the exemption, finding that Seaboard was not a "producer." Seaboard appealed to a United States Circuit

Packard Motor Car Company v. NLRB,[21] is traditionally considered at odds with *Hearst* and often is cited for the proposition that courts will take an independent approach to questions of law. Though the facts of that case were somewhat similar to those in *Hearst,* the Court did not agree with the NLRB's legal approach to this case. Both the majority and the dissenters explicitly engaged in their own independent legal analysis and none cited *Hearst* on the scope of review question.[22]

In *Packard,* like *Hearst,* the Board had to construe the statutory term "employee". It concluded that foremen were "employees" according to the National Labor Relations Act and thus they were "a unit appropriate for the purposes of collective bargaining."[23] The Supreme Court affirmed the Board's decision in a manner consistent with the analysis of *Hearst.* Though the *Hearst* court implicitly engaged in independent review, the *Packard* court did so explicitly. The majority concluded that the Board had determined Congress' intent correctly, stating that "[t]here is ... no ambiguity in this Act to be clarified by resort to legislative history ..."[24]

After the Court in *Packard* looked at the statute and found a clear answer, it went on to address the rationality of the Board's decision: "While we do not say that a determination of a unit of representation cannot be so unreasonable and arbitrary as to exceed the Board's power, we are clear that the decision in question does not do so."[25] While this language is not as deferential as the Court's formulation in *Hearst,* the Court, at this point, nevertheless defers to the agency's decision.

This synthesis of both the deference and independent review cases is consistent with the Report of the Attorney General's Committee on Administrative Procedure issued in 1941:

> To state the matter very broadly judicial review is generally limited to the inquiry whether the administrative agency acted within the scope of its authority. The wisdom, reasonableness, or expediency of the action in the circumstances are said to be matters of administra-

Court of Appeals for review, in accordance with the statute, and that court reversed the Commission's decision.

The Supreme Court affirmed the Commission's denial of exemption with very deferential language, but as Professor Nathanson pointed out:

> " ... the real issue in the *Gray* case could scarcely be appreciated if attention were centered exclusively on the exemptions clause ... Whether there was a rational basis for the administrative application of the term 'producer' itself depended upon a broader issue of statutory interpretation; namely, whether the regulatory provisions of the statute authorizing maximum and minimum prices could be applied to deliveries of coal which involved no change in ownership."

Nathanson, Administrative Discretion In The Interpretation of Statutes, 3 Vand.L.Rev. 470, 473–75 (1950). As to this question, the Court's review and decision was independent.

21. 330 U.S. 485, 67 S.Ct. 789, 91 L.Ed. 1040 (1947), superceded by statute as stated in NLRB v. Winnebago Television Corp., 75 F.3d 1208 (7th Cir. 1996). See Breyer, Questions of Law and Policy, 38 Admin.L.Rev. 363 (1986).

22. Justice Douglas cited *Hearst* once in his dissent but in support of an unrelated proposition. 330 U.S. at 495, 67 S.Ct. at 795 (Douglas, J. dissenting).

23. 330 U.S. at 488, 67 S.Ct. at 791.

24. 330 U.S. at 492, 67 S.Ct. at 794.

25. 330 U.S. at 491–92, 67 S.Ct. at 793.

tive judgment to be determined exclusively by the agency. But the narrow inquiry into the agency's authority to act as it did covers a wide field. The question whether Congress had the constitutional authority to authorize the administrative action is, of course, always in the background. Short of the constitutional issues are the questions of interpretation of the statutes conferring the authority....

Whether the factors upon which the administrative decision was based are such as the agency is permitted to consider and whether the factors which it rejected are such as it is permitted to reject, and what weight is required to be attached to various factors are all questions which the courts can review as questions of law.[26]

As we have just seen, cases such as *Hearst* and *Packard* involve both law formulation and law application issues. We shall now focus solely on law formulation. Our primary purpose is to determine when a court may engage in a relatively independent review of an agency interpretation of law and when it must defer to that interpretation.

§ 13.7.2 Independent Judicial Review of Questions of Law—*Chevron U.S.A. v. NRDC*

As the Attorney General's Report above suggests, there are a number of situations in which a Court will be asked to review agency actions that involve questions of law. In interpreting the law, an agency will, along with constitutional issues, have to take into account relevant statutory factors, weigh them appropriately and avoid relying on factors the law sought to exclude from consideration.[27] The interpretation of a statute whose text clearly sets forth those factors presents the kind of question of law that courts will usually always examine independently. If the text of the statute is, in the court's view, clear, and the agency's interpretation is at odds with the court's, the court will then freely disregard what it considers to be an erroneous agency view. Such an approach is fully in accord with one of the most fundamental purposes of judicial review discussed earlier,[28] namely to assure that the agency is carrying out its duties in accordance with the will of Congress.

Not all statutes, however, are clear. The provisions of a statute may be ambiguously drafted and capable of various interpretations. Congress

26. Final Report of the Attorney General's Committee on Administrative Procedure, 87–88 (1941).

27. For a case involving substantially *de novo* judicial review of constitutional issues, see, e.g., United States v. Nixon, 418 U.S. 683, 703–05, 94 S.Ct. 3090, 3105–06, 41 L.Ed.2d 1039 (1974).

For cases involving *de novo* judicial review of the statutory factors an agency did or did not consider, see, e.g., Dirks v. SEC, 463 U.S. 646, 103 S.Ct. 3255, 77 L.Ed.2d 911 (1983); Woodby v. INS, 385 U.S. 276, 87 S.Ct. 483, 17 L.Ed.2d 362 (1966). Compare Industrial Union Dept., AFL–CIO v. American Petroleum Institute, 448 U.S. 607, 100 S.Ct. 2844, 65 L.Ed.2d 1010 (1980) (plurality opinion) (Court reversed OSHA because its failure to consider, under the statute, whether its benzene rule would ameliorate a "significant risk") with American Textile Mfgrs. Institute, Inc. v. Donovan, 452 U.S. 490, 101 S.Ct. 2478, 69 L.Ed.2d 185 (1981) (OSHA affirmed, having considered the "feasibility" of its cotton dust rule).

28. See sec. 13.1, supra. See also, Boston v. Department of HUD, 898 F.2d 828 (1st Cir.1990).

may not have foreseen the circumstances that give rise to a particular application of the statute and, in those unforeseen circumstances, the statute may be capable of two or more reasonable interpretations.[29] Similarly, Congress may not have considered certain circumstances and the statute itself may be entirely silent on those issues.[30] The farther removed one becomes from the text of a statute in determining the legality of agency action, the more likely a court will defer to an agency's interpretation. This is because the interpretive expertise of the court usually should give way to the policy expertise of the agency involved.[31] Just as it is difficult to separate law from fact in certain contexts, it can also be difficult to separate law from policy.

In cases involving ambiguous or non-existent statutory guidance for certain agency actions, the legality of those actions tends to be assessed more in terms of the reasonableness of the policy undertaken than the correctness of the statutory interpretation involved. Courts are increasingly reluctant to go beyond the text of the statute involved in making their own independent judgments of what the law is. Not only do agencies tend to be more familiar with statutory issues presented in such contexts, they are much more likely to be aware of the policy implications of choosing one interpretation rather than another. When an agency makes this choice, not only does it use its expertise to do so, but its decision will lead to uniformity within the agency. When different statutory interpretations are possible, different judicial interpretations in different circuits can present an agency with conflicting obligations.

Chevron, U.S.A. Inc. v. NRDC[32] sets forth a deferential judicial approach to agency interpretations of law, one which we shall examine in detail. *Chevron* began as a challenge to EPA rules defining the phrase "stationary source" in the "new source review" program established by the 1977 amendments to the Clean Air Act.[33] The 1977 amendments imposed more stringent air quality requirements on states that had not yet reduced pollution to levels below certain ambient standards in what the statute called nonattainment areas. These provisions required permits "for the construction and operation of new or modified stationary sources" of air pollution.[34] A state could issue a permit for the construction of a new or modified major source in a nonattainment area only if

29. See, e.g., SEC v. Sloan, 436 U.S. 103, 112, 98 S.Ct. 1702, 1709, 56 L.Ed.2d 148 (1978) (pre-*Chevron* ruling in which the court overturned an agency interpretation of its statute, noting while the agency's interpretation of the statute was a permissible one, it was not the best one).

30. Chevron, U.S.A., Inc. v. NRDC, 467 U.S. 837, 104 S.Ct. 2778, 81 L.Ed.2d 694 (1984).

31. See, e.g., NLRB v. Curtin Matheson Scientific, Inc., 494 U.S. 775, 110 S.Ct. 1542, 108 L.Ed.2d 801 (1990) (In upholding NLRB policy against presuming that permanent strike replacement workers automatically oppose the strikers' union, the Court expressed its confidence that "the Board, with its vast reservoir of experience in resolving labor disputes, is better situated than members of this Court to determine the frequency with which unions demand displacement of striker replacements." Id. at 791, n. 9, 110 S.Ct. at 1551, n. 9).

32. 467 U.S. 837, 104 S.Ct. 2778, 81 L.Ed.2d 694 (1984), rehearing denied 468 U.S. 1227, 105 S.Ct. 28, 82 L.Ed.2d 921 (1984).

33. 42 U.S.C.A. § 7409.

34. 42 U.S.C.A. § 7502(b)(6).

the proposed source met these stringent requirements.[35] The EPA initially interpreted "stationary source" to include all individual pieces of pollution-emitting equipment within a plant.[36] The EPA, however, conducted a subsequent rulemaking proceeding, the end result of which was to repeal these earlier rules and to replace them with the so-called "bubble" approach. Under the "bubble" approach, EPA defined a major stationary source as the entire plant rather than the individual facilities within the plant.[37]

On appeal, the D.C. Circuit overturned the EPA's new interpretation of "stationary source." The court found that Congress had no specific intent concerning the term "stationary source," particularly as it applied to the bubble concept.[38] Nevertheless, the court reversed the agency based on its own interpretation of that term in light of the overall purposes of the amended Clean Air Act.

The Supreme Court reversed the Court of Appeals, and in so doing, appears to have narrowed the range of legal issues in which courts are expected to have the final say.[39] The Court disagreed with the D.C. Circuit's willingness to substitute its legal interpretation for that of the agency when the statute in question was ambiguous and was being

35. Id. See H.R.Rep. No. 95–564, 95th Cong., 1st Sess. 157 (1977). Indeed, some commentators have noted that statutory approach "applies to smokestacks, vents, and loading and transfer operations, notwithstanding the differing costs of controlling emissions from each." Stukane, EPA's Bubble Concept After *Chevron v. NRDC:* Who Is to Guard the Guards Themselves?, 12 Nat.Res. Lawyer, 647, 649 (1985); see also Note, An Overview of the Bubble Concept, 8 Colum.J. of Env'l Law, 137, 137 n. 1 (1982); Landau, Economic Dream or Environmental Nightmare? The Legality of the "Bubble Concept" in Air and Water Pollution Control, 8 Env'l Affairs, 741, 742 (1980).

36. As Stukane has argued, supra note 173, at 677, the D.C. Circuit has been inconsistent in its interpretation of these provisions. "In ASARCO, Inc. v. EPA, [578 F.2d 319 (1978)] the D.C. Circuit rejected the bubble concept as applied to NSPS. In Alabama Power Co. v. Costle, [636 F.2d 323 (1979)] the same court permitted the Agency to use the bubble concept in the regulations for the prevention of significant deterioration. Finally, in NDRC v. Gorsuch, [685 F.2d 718 (1982)] the decision reversed by the Court in *Chevron,* the D.C. Circuit held that the bubble concept could not be applied to the nonattainment areas."

37. It was thus possible to replace individual pieces of equipment within a plant without any pollution controls whatsoever if the owner could show that the net increase in *total* pollution would not exceed one hundred tons per year. The entire plant was, in effect, encased in an imaginary bubble for purposes of determining whether the requirements of the 1977 Act should apply. The net effect of the bubble concept was to lessen considerably the stringency and cost of the Carter rules that were repealed. It allows plants in non-attainment areas essentially to maintain the status quo when they replace individual pieces of equipment rather than having actually to lower their overall level of pollution. The bubble concept thus replaced the more absolutist approach to pollution control heretofore espoused by the EPA and affirmed by the courts with a regulatory approach designed to have much less of an impact on the costs borne by those creating the pollution, but also less impact on the curtailment of pollution in non-attainment areas. See generally, Stukane, supra note 173 at 666–668.

38. NRDC, Inc. v. Gorsuch, 685 F.2d 718 (D.C.Cir.1982).

39. Judge Starr called *Chevron* a watershed opinion, one that ushers in a new, more deferential, era in judicial review of questions of law. Starr, Judicial Review in the Post–*Chevron* Era, 3 Yale J.Reg. 283 (1986). Other commentators suggest that *Chevron* does not necessarily represent such a significant departure from past scope of review doctrine. See, e.g., Byse, Judicial Review of Administrative Interpretation of Statutes, 2 Ad.L.J. 255 (1988); Breyer, Judicial Review of Questions of Law and Policy, 38 Ad.L.Rev. 363, 380 (1986).

applied to a policy approach to pollution on which Congress provided no express direction. The Supreme Court set forth a revised two step approach to the review of questions of law:

If Congress has not directly addressed *the precise question at issue,* the court does not simply impose its own construction on the statute as would be necessary in the absence of an administrative interpretation. Rather, if the statute is silent or ambiguous with respect to the specific issue, the question for the court is whether the agency's answer is based on a permissible construction of the statute.[40]

To uphold the agency's interpretation, the court need not conclude "that the agency construction was the only one it permissibly could have adopted, or even the reading the court would have reached if the question had arisen in a judicial proceeding."[41] It need only conclude that the agency's interpretation was a "permissible" one.[42] Buttressing the

40. 467 U.S. at 843, 104 S.Ct. at 2782 (emphasis added) (footnotes deleted). See also INS v. Aguirre–Aguirre, 526 U.S. 415, 424, 119 S.Ct. 1439, 143 L.Ed.2d 590 (1999); Auer v. Robbins, 519 U.S. 452, 457, 117 S.Ct. 905, 137 L.Ed.2d 79 (1997); United States v. Haggar Apparel Co., 526 U.S. 380, 392, 119 S.Ct. 1392, 143 L.Ed.2d 480 (1999); Holly Farms Corp. v. NLRB, 517 U.S. 392, 398, 116 S.Ct. 1396, 134 L.Ed.2d 593 (1996); National Wildlife Federation v. Browner, 127 F.3d 1126 (D.C.Cir.1997).

41. Id. at 843 n. 11, 104 S.Ct. at 2782 n. 11. This approach contradicted an earlier Supreme Court opinion where the Court overturned an agency interpretation because it was not the "most natural or logical." See SEC v. Sloan, 436 U.S. 103, 113, 98 S.Ct. 1702, 1709, 56 L.Ed.2d 148 (1978).

42. Inherent in this approach to judicial review of agency interpretations of ambiguous statutory terms is an assumption that Congress has either explicitly or implicitly delegated this interpretive power to the agency. 467 U.S. at 843, 104 S.Ct. at 2782 ("If Congress has explicitly left a gap of authority to fill, there is an express delegation of authority to the agency to elucidate a specific provision of the statute by regulation. Such legislative regulations are given controlling weight unless they are arbitrary, capricious, or manifestly contrary to the statute. Sometimes the legislative delegation to an agency on a particular question is implicit rather than explicit. In such a case, a court may not substitute its own construction of a statutory provision for a reasonable interpretation made by the administrator of an agency."). Id. at 843–44, 1045 S.Ct. at 2782.

When Congress explicitly delegates legal interpretive power to an agency, a Court is clearly bound by a reasonable agency interpretation of a statutory term. See, e.g., Pauley v. BethEnergy Mines, Inc., 501 U.S. 680, 111 S.Ct. 2524, 115 L.Ed.2d 604 (1991) ("When Congress, through express delegation or the introduction of an interpretive gap in the statutory structure, has delegated policy-making authority to an administrative agency, the extent of judicial review of the agency's policy determinations is limited." 111 S.Ct. at 2534. The case involved an interpretation by the Secretary of Labor of the Black Lung Benefits Act, which the Court characterized as having produced "a complex and highly technical regulatory program. The identification and classification of medical eligibility criteria necessarily require significant expertise, and entail the exercise of judgment grounded in policy concerns. In those circumstances, courts appropriately defer to the agency entrusted by Congress to make such policy determinations.") See also, Montana v. Clark, 749 F.2d 740, 743 (D.C.Cir.1984), cert. denied 474 U.S. 919, 106 S.Ct. 246, 88 L.Ed.2d 255 (1985). See generally Monaghan, Marbury and the Administrative State, 83 Colum.L.Rev. 1, 25–28 (1983). For an excellent analysis of this facet and other aspects of the *Chevron* decision, see Anthony, Which Agency Interpretations Should Bind the Courts And The Public?, 7 Yale J. on Reg. 1, 33 (1990).

Where the delegation of legislative power is implicit, courts have sometimes presumed a delegation of legislative power in the face of a statutory gap. See Anthony, supra at 33, n. 140 (citing National Wildlife Federation v. Hodel, 839 F.2d 694, 741 (D.C.Cir.1988)), appeal after remand 733 F.Supp. 419 (D.D.C.1990) (clear evidence of congressional intent to preclude agency's interpretation is "a necessary prerequisite

Chevron court's deferential approach to agency legal interpretations[43] was the fact that certain agencies are connected to an electorally accountable branch of government—the executive. Justice Stevens thus spoke in terms of presidential deference:

> Judges are not experts in the field, and are not part of either political branch of the Government. Courts must, in some cases, reconcile competing political interests, but not on the basis of the judges' personal policy preferences. In contrast, an agency to which Congress has delegated policy-making responsibilities may, within the limits of that delegation, properly rely upon the incumbent administration's views of wise policy to inform its judgments. While agencies are not directly accountable to the people, the Chief Executive is, and it is entirely appropriate for this political branch of the Government to make such policy choices—resolving the competing interest which Congress itself either inadvertently did not resolve, or intentionally left to be resolved by the agency charged with the administration of the statute in light of everyday realities.[44]

Chevron's two step approach to judicial review has clearly changed the "mood" of reviewing courts when dealing with questions of statutory interpretation[45] and to some extent it has changed the law of judicial

here to rebut the inference that Congress meant to delegate to the Secretary the authority to interpret the general and ambiguous terms") (Wald, C.J.); National Fuel Gas Supply Corp. v. FERC, 811 F.2d 1563, 1569 (D.C.Cir.1987), cert. denied 484 U.S. 869, 108 S.Ct. 200, 98 L.Ed.2d 151 (1987) ("When Congress leaves gaps ... implicitly by enacting an ambiguously worded provision that the agency must interpret, it has ... implicitly delegated to the agency the power to fill those gaps. That delegation requires the courts to defer to an agency's decision.") (Bork, J.); Drummond Coal Co. v. Hodel, 796 F.2d 503, 507 (D.C.Cir.1986), cert. denied 480 U.S. 941, 107 S.Ct. 1593, 94 L.Ed.2d 782 (1987) ("Since Congress did not explicitly address the proper meaning of the words ... Congress has left a gap in the regulatory regime for the agency to fill....") (Silberman, J.). See also, National Credit Union Admin. v. First Nat. Bank, 522 U.S. 479, 118 S.Ct. 927, 140 L.Ed.2d 1 (1998); Investment Company Institute v. Conover, 790 F.2d 925, 935 (D.C.Cir.1986), cert. denied 479 U.S. 939, 107 S.Ct. 421, 93 L.Ed.2d 372 (1986); Lukhard v. Reed, 481 U.S. 368, 377 n. 3, 107 S.Ct. 1807, 1813 n. 3, 95 L.Ed.2d 328 (1987) (Scalia, J.); Dresser Industries, Inc. v. Commissioner of Internal Revenue, 911 F.2d 1128 (5th Cir.1990).

43. Several commentators have been very critical of the deference the court showed in *Chevron*. See, e.g., Farina, Statutory Interpretation and the Balance of Power in the Administrative State, 89 Colum.L.Rev. 452 (1989); Aman, Administrative Law In a Global Era: Progress Deregulatory Charge and the Rise of the Administrative Presidency, 73 Cornell L.Rev. 1101, 1223–1236 (1988); Sunstein, Constitutionalism After the New Deal, 101 Harv.L.Rev. 421 (1988); Mikva, How Should Courts Treat Administrative Agencies?, 36 Am.U.L.Rev. 1, 8 (1986); Shapiro & Glicksman, Congress, the Supreme Court, and the Quiet Revolution in Administrative Law, 1988 Duke L.J. 819, 871 (1988); but see, Scalia, Judicial Deference to Administrative Interpretations of Law, 1989 Duke L.J. 511 (1989); Pierce, *Chevron* and Its Aftermath: Judicial Review of Agency Interpretation of Statutory Provisions, 41 Vand.L.Rev. 301 (1988); Starr, supra note 177; but see National Rifle Association v. Reno, 216 F.3d 122, 132 (D.C.Cir.2000) ("Such deference, the Supreme Court recently explained, is justified because the responsibilities for assessing the wisdom of ... policy choices and resolving the struggle between competing views of the public interest are not judicial ones, ... and because of the agency's great familiarity with the ever-changing facts and circumstances surrounding the subjects regulated." (citations omitted)).

44. 467 U.S. at 865–66, 104 S.Ct. at 2793.

45. See, e.g., P. Shuck and D. Elliot, To the Chevron Station: An Empirical Study of Federal Administrative Law, 87

review of agency interpretations as well.[46] By asking first whether Congress spoke "precisely" to the statutory issue in question, and secondly, whether or not Congress' intent was "unambiguously clear" on that issue, the Supreme Court has narrowed the category of issues involving the kinds of questions of law that a Court is willing to examine closely, and has expanded the number of agency decisions to which it will defer.[47] Cases subsequent to *Chevron,* however, suggest that judicial implementation of *Chevron* leads to some very unpredictable results.

§ 13.7.3 Post–*Chevron*

As we have seen, implementation of the *Chevron* doctrine requires that a reviewing court determine whether there is clear and unambiguous congressional intent concerning the precise question in issue. Just what constitutes statutory clarity or ambiguity, the "precise issue" in question and how a reviewing court is to make such determinations leaves a great deal of room for judicial disagreement.

In *Young v. Community Nutrition Institute,*[48] for example, the majority found statutory ambiguity where the author of *Chevron,* Justice Stevens, found clarity. *Young* involved a dispute over the proper interpretation of section 346 of the Federal Food, Drug and Cosmetic Act. This section states that "the Secretary shall promulgate regulations limiting the quantity [of any harmful, but unavoidable, added substance] therein or thereon to such extent as he finds necessary for the protection of public health. . . ."[49] Respondents argued that this section mandated the promulgation of tolerance levels for unavoidable, unsafe substances in food. They contended that "shall promulgate" categorically required the creation of tolerance levels for any food that met the threshold requirements of the statute. The FDA, however, argued that the word "shall" is modified by the phrase "to such extent as he finds necessary

(1989) (Preliminary Report to the U.S. Admin. Conf.) (study shows greater deference by courts after *Chevron* was decided). See also, MCI Telecommunications Corp. v. American Telephone & Telegraph Co., 512 U.S. 218, 231, 114 S.Ct. 2223, 129 L.Ed.2d 182 (1994) (stating that "we must be guided to a degree by common sense as to the manner in which Congress is likely to delegate a policy decision of such economic and political magnitude to an administrative agency"); United States v. Estate of Romani, 523 U.S. 517, 530–31, 118 S.Ct. 1478, 140 L.Ed.2d 710 (1998) (stating that "the meaning of one statute may be affected by other acts, particularly where Congress has spoken subsequently and more specifically to the topic at hand").

46. See Starr, supra note 177. For a more recent and excellent analysis of *Chevron,* see Anthony, supra note 180; Anthony, Which Agency Interpretations Should Get Judicial Deference—A Preliminary Inquiry, 40 Admin.L.Rev. 121 (1988); see also, Cass R. Sunstein, Law and Administration After *Chevron*, 90 Colum. L.Rev. 2071, 2075 (1990) (noting that "[*Chevron*] has established itself as one of the very few defining cases in the last twenty years of American public law.").

47. See, e.g., Homemakers North Shore, Inc. v. Bowen, 832 F.2d 408, 411 (7th Cir.1987) ("An ambiguous legal rule does not have a single "right" meaning; there is a range of possible meanings; the selection from the range is an act of policymaking. The person who fleshes out the meaning of the rule is the true law-giver in the circumstances.") (Easterbrook, J.).

48. 476 U.S. 974, 106 S.Ct. 2360, 90 L.Ed.2d 959 (1986), appeal after remand 818 F.2d 943 (D.C.Cir.1987).

49. 476 U.S. at 977, 106 S.Ct. at 2363.

for the protection of public health." This makes the statute ambiguous, thereby requiring judicial deference to the agency's decision in this case.

Speaking for the majority, Justice O'Connor agreed, citing *Chevron* and deferring to the agency's interpretation of the statute. The majority found the statutory phrase "to the extent ... necessary" to be "ambiguous," noting that:

> "As enemies of the dangling participle well know, the English language does not always force a writer to specify which of two possible objects is the one to which a modifying phrase relates. A Congress more precise or more prescient than the one that enacted § 346 might, if it wished petitioner's position to prevail, have placed 'to such extent as he finds necessary for the protection of public health' as an appositive phrase immediately after 'shall' rather than as a free-floating phrase after 'the quantity therein or thereon.' A Congress equally fastidious and foresighted, but intending respondents' position to prevail, might have substituted the phrase 'to the quantity' for the phrase 'to such extent as.' But the Congress that actually enacted § 346 took neither tack."[49]

In the absence of such legislative improvements, the Court found that the wording of § 346 must remain ambiguous, and that FDA's interpretation was not an unreasonable one.

In dissent, Justice Stevens looked at the same statute and found it unambiguous. In his view, "the antecedent of the qualifying language is quite clearly the phrase 'limiting the quantity therein or thereon,' which immediately precedes it, rather than the word 'shall' which appears eight words before it. Thus, the Commissioner is to 'limit the quantity [of an added, unavoidable poisonous or deleterious substance] therein or thereon to such extent as he finds necessary for the protection of public health.' "[50] In Justice Stevens' view, "the task of interpreting a statute requires more than merely inventing an ambiguity and involving administrative deference."[51]

49. 476 U.S. at 980–81, 106 S.Ct. at 2365. See also, Smiley v. Citibank (South Dakota), N.A., 517 U.S. 735, 739, 116 S.Ct. 1730, 135 L.Ed.2d 25 (1996) (where Justice Scalia observed that "We accord deference to agencies under *Chevron*, not because of a presumption that they drafted the provisions in question, or were present at the hearings, or spoke to the principal sponsors; but rather because of a presumption that Congress, when it left ambiguity in a statute meant for implementation by an agency, understood that the ambiguity would be resolved, first and foremost, by the agency, and desired the agency (rather than the courts to possess whatever degree of discretion the ambiguity allows.)); Williams v. Babbitt, 115 F.3d 657 (9th Cir.1997), cert. denied, 523 U.S. 1117, 118 S.Ct. 1795, 140 L.Ed.2d 936 (1998) (interpreting the Reindeer Act of 1937 as not preculding non-native Alaskans from importing and owning reindeer)."

50. 476 U.S. at 985, 106 S.Ct. at 2367. In making this argument, Justice Stevens was also willing to buttress his interpretation with legislative history. See 476 U.S. at 985 n. 1, 106 S.Ct. at 2367 n. 1.

51. Id. at 988, 106 S.Ct. at 2368. For an example of a case in which the Court agreed on what was the clear and unambiguous interpretation of the statute involved and thus, reversed the agency's decision, see, e.g., Board of Governors v. Dimension Financial Corp., 474 U.S. 361, 106 S.Ct. 681, 88 L.Ed.2d 691 (1986); see also Maislin Industries, U.S., Inc. v. Primary Steel, Inc., 497 U.S. 116, 110 S.Ct. 2759, 111 L.Ed.2d 94 (1990), on remand 911 F.2d 1312 (8th Cir.1990) (Court reversed an agency interpretation of the Interstate Commerce Act in

In *Chemical Manufacturers Ass'n v. Natural Resources Defense Council,*[52] the Court took a broader approach than it did in *Young* in determining whether statutory ambiguity in fact existed.[53] This case involved a dispute over the proper interpretation of section 301(1) of the Clean Water Act, added by the 1977 amendments to that act. This provision states that "the administrator may not modify any requirement of this section as it applies to any specific pollutant which is on the toxic pollutant list under section 1317(a)(1) of this title."

Before enactment of this section, the EPA allowed variances from effluent limitations based on proof of "factors fundamentally different from those considered by EPA" in promulgating its effluent guidelines. The Natural Resources Defense Council argued that these variances were modifications within the meaning of the statute. The EPA contended that "modify" referred only to specific modifications allowed under other parts of the statute and that it did not, therefore, invalidate adjustments in effluent limitations made through the variance mechanism.

The majority opinion upheld the agency's interpretation, but in so doing, it engaged in what it considered to be a searching inquiry into legislative history and the purpose and structure of the statute.[54] Before deferring, the Court looked for guidance to the statute's legislative history and supporting policies and concluded that "neither the language nor the legislative history of the Act demonstrates a clear Congressional intent to forbid EPA's sensible variance mechanism."[55] By engaging in

part because previous judicial interpretations rendered that statute clear and unambiguous, thereby limiting the agency's flexibility).

52. 470 U.S. 116, 105 S.Ct. 1102, 84 L.Ed.2d 90 (1985).

53. For another example of the Court's inability to decide where a statute was clear or not, see, NLRB v. United Food and Commercial Workers Union, Local 23, 484 U.S. 112, 108 S.Ct. 413, 98 L.Ed.2d 429 (1987), on remand 840 F.2d 171 (3d Cir.1988) (Court split 4 to 4 on the question whether *Chevron* applied).

54. Chemical Mfrs. Ass'n v. Natural Resources Defense Council, Inc., 470 U.S. at 126, 105 S.Ct. at 1108.

55. Id. at 134, 105 S.Ct. at 1112. See Farina, supra note 181, at 460 n. 41: Professor Farina notes the many approaches to legislative history that the Court has taken in the wake of *Chevron:* "Justice Stevens' opinion treats legislative history as one of the 'traditional tools of statutory construction' to be used in determining congressional intent, y(3)27 although post-*Chevron* cases have seen increasing debate over whether and to what extent it ought to be consulted. Compare INS v. Cardoza–Fonseca, 480 U.S. 421, 452–53, [107 S.Ct. 1207, 1223–24, 94 L.Ed.2d 434] (1987) (Scalia, J., concurring in judgment) (vigorously criticizing use of legislative history) and K Mart Corp. v. Cartier, Inc., [486 U.S. 281, 290–96,] 108 S.Ct. 1811, 1817–19[, 100 L.Ed.2d 313] (1988) (Kennedy, J., writing in part for the court) (conducting purely textual analysis and avoiding reference to legislative history) with [Justice Brennan's approach in] *K Mart,* [486 U.S. at 300–09,] 108 S.Ct. at 1822–26 (Brennan, J., concurring in part and dissenting in part) (using legislative history and even statutory purpose to discover ambiguity in what majority found unequivocal statutory text); see also Regents of University of California v. Public Employment Relations Board, [485 U.S. 589, 603,] 108 S.Ct. 1404, 1413, [99 L.Ed.2d 664] (1988) (White, J., concurring in the judgment) (insisting that, if text is unambiguous, deference must be granted unless legislative history is 'quite clear' in foreclosing agency interpretation)."

See also Fort Stewart Schools v. Federal Labor Relations Authority, 495 U.S. 641, 110 S.Ct. 2043, 109 L.Ed.2d 659 (1990) ("There is no conceivable persuasive effect in legislative history that may reflect nothing more than the speakers' incomplete un-

this broad a search to determine Congressional intent, the Court approximates the approach taken in *NLRB v. Hearst.*[56]

Quite apart from how one determines whether the text of a statute is clear or not, the Court often disagrees even when it looks at the same congressional materials. In *Chemical Manufacturers,* Justice Marshall, in dissent, looked at the same congressional sources but found clear congressional intent to support the opposite result.[57] Justice Marshall, thus, also invoked *Chevron* as providing the proper framework for review, concluding that "[t]he plain meaning of § 301(1), the changes made prior to enactment of the bill containing this provision, and the clearly expressed congressional objectives in enacting § 301(1)—to deal vigorously and comprehensively with the extremely serious environmental problem caused by toxic pollutants—establish that this provision's scope was meant to be considerably broader than that attributed to it by EPA."[58]

In short, even when there is agreement on the application of *Chevron* principles to the case at hand, there may be disagreement over what the text of the statute actually says and the extent to which the court can go beyond the text to determine whether it is or is not ambiguous. The Supreme Court's opinion in *INS v. Cardoza—Fonseca*[59] suggests even more directly that in making such determinations, the Court may on occasion engage in the kind of independent judicial review that traditionally characterized its approach before *Chevron.* That is to say, the Court may be willing to go beyond the four corners of the statutory text to determine whether a statute is clear or ambiguous.[60]

In *Cardoza–Fonseca,* respondent challenged the Immigration Service's refusal to revoke a deportation order. Under immigration law there are two ways to block a deportation order. First, an alien may seek a mandatory withholding of a deportation order under section 243(h) of the Immigration and Naturalization Act. To obtain this relief, the alien must demonstrate that it is "more likely than not" that he would suffer persecution if returned to his country. Second, an alien may seek the discretionary grant of asylum under section 208(a) upon proving a "well-founded fear" of persecution upon deportation. The respondent made claims for relief under both sections and the immigration judge and the

derstanding of the world upon which the statute will operate.").

56. See sec. 13.7.1, supra. See also, Lyng v. Payne, 476 U.S. 926, 944, 106 S.Ct. 2333, 2344, 90 L.Ed.2d 921 (1986), rehearing denied 478 U.S. 1031, 107 S.Ct. 11, 92 L.Ed.2d 766 (1986) (Stevens, J., dissenting); Hall v. Lyng, 828 F.2d 428 (8th Cir.1987) (interpreting on basis of general purposes of statute); Barnett v. Weinberger, 818 F.2d 953 (D.C.Cir.1987) (same).

57. 470 U.S. at 134, 105 S.Ct. at 1112.

58. 470 U.S. at 137, 105 S.Ct. at 1113. For a recent Supreme Court case in which *Chevron* was noticeable by its absence, but the Court split 5–4 over whether the statute in contention was unambiguous, see Sullivan v. Stroop, 496 U.S. 478, 110 S.Ct. 2499, 110 L.Ed.2d 438 (1990). For a discussion of *Chevron* in the context of a statute found clear by one judge, but ambiguous by the majority, see NRDC v. EPA, 804 F.2d 710 (D.C.Cir.1986).

59. 480 U.S. 421, 107 S.Ct. 1207, 94 L.Ed.2d 434 (1987). See also, De Osorio v. INS, 10 F.3d 1034 (4th Cir.1993).

60. *See, e.g.,* Fisher v. I.N.S., 37 F.3d 1371, 1382 (9th Cir.1994) (the court refused to apply *Chevron* in interpreting how to apply certain refugee statutes).

Board of Immigration Appeals denied both claims. In so doing, they applied the "more likely than not" standard in both denials. INS contended that both the "more likely than not" standard and the "well-founded fear" standard were identical and argued that *Chevron* required judicial deference to this interpretation.

The Supreme Court rejected both the deference argument and the agency's construction of the statutes. Writing for the majority, Justice Stevens noted that "[t]he question whether Congress intended the two standards to be identical is a pure question of statutory construction for the courts to decide." Finding clear intent in this case, the court determined that Congress intended the two standards to be different. More important, the Court implied that whenever such a "pure question of statutory construction" is present, the Court must use "the traditional tools of statutory construction" to divine an answer.[61]

This approach to these issues is more in accord with pre-*Chevron* review doctrine. If the language of *Cardoza–Fonseca* is taken seriously, a court need only defer to an agency's interpretation when the "traditional tools of statutory construction" yield no answer to the "pure question of statutory construction." This is counter to the commonly held view that *Chevron* suggests a more narrow inquiry; namely, once an ambiguity is found in the statutory text, deference is in order.[62] Indeed, the majority's more expansive reading of *Chevron* prompted Justice Scalia to file a concurrence in which he agreed with the result reached by the Court but strongly differed with the majority's interpretation of *Chevron*. Justice Scalia argued that the majority's interpretation of *Chevron* is "flatly inconsistent with [the Court's] well established interpretation."[63] Suggesting that the majority view would make "deference a doctrine of desperation," Scalia argued that such an approach "authoriz[es] courts to defer only if they would otherwise be unable to construe the enactment at issue."[64]

61. *Cardoza–Fonseca* also departed from *Chevron* by holding that a recent reinterpretation by an agency would receive less deference if it reversed a prior policy or statutory interpretation (relying in part on Watt v. Alaska, 451 U.S. 259, 101 S.Ct. 1673, 68 L.Ed.2d 80 (1981)). For a discussion of the relevance of consistent agency interpretation in determining the level of judicial deference, see infra sec. 13.8.3.

62. For an attempt to reconcile Cardoza–Fonseca with *Chevron*, see Michael Henry, Deference Running Riot: Separating Interpretation and Lawmaking Under Chevron, 6 Admin. L.J. 187 (1992) (arguing that there are different types of ambiguity involved and that those that do not involve the development of a factual record or the application of law to facts is a pure question of law to be resolved by courts).

63. 480 U.S. at 454, 107 S.Ct. at 1225.

64. Id. But see *MCI Telecommunications Corp. v. American Tel. & Tel. Co.*, 512 U.S. 218, 114 S.Ct. 2223, 129 L.Ed.2d 182 (1994) (concluding the statutory term "modify" connotes only moderate change, the court overturned FCC regulations that dramatically changed the rules for certain tariffs. Some lower courts have interpreted *Chevron* in a manner consistent with the interpretation Justice Scalia takes issue with in this case). See, e.g., Union of Concerned Scientists v. U.S. Nuclear Regulatory Com'n, 824 F.2d 108, 113 (D.C.Cir.1987), appeal after remand 880 F.2d 552 (1989). For an interpretation of *Cardoza–Fonseca* more in accord with *Chevron*, see Farina, supra note 181 at 460. See also, NLRB v. United Food and Commercial Workers Union, 484 U.S. 112, 132, 108 S.Ct. 413, 426, 98 L.Ed.2d 429 (1987) (Scalia, J., concurring).

It is interesting to note that Chief Judge Wald has stated that "*Cardoza–Fonseca* re-

The Supreme Court applied a more sympathetic reading of *Chevron* in *K Mart Corporation v. Cartier, Inc.*[65] This case involved custom service regulations interpreting the Tariff Act of 1930. Specifically it involved section 525 of the Act[66] which prohibits the importation of "any merchandise of foreign manufacture" bearing a trademark owned by an American individual or corporation, and registered at the Patent and Trademark Office. The custom service regulation provided an exemption from § 526 permitting the importation of goods produced oversees by the "same person" who holds the U.S. trademark or by a person who is "subject to common control" with the U.S. trademark holder.[67] It provided an additional exemption where the foreign manufacturer receives authorization from the U.S. trademark holder to use its trademark. The case hinged upon the meaning of "merchandise of foreign manufacture". The majority found that statutory phrase to be ambiguous. Applying *Chevron,* it then held that the Custom services interpretation was reasonable as to one exemption, but unreasonable as to the other. Part IIA of Justice Kennedy's opinion set forth the majority's understanding of *Chevron.* He was joined by Justices Scalia, O'Connor, Blackmun, White and the Chief Justice:

> "In determining whether a challenged regulation is valid, a reviewing court must first determine if the regulation is consistent with the language of the statute.... In ascertaining the plain meaning of the statute, the court must look to the particular statutory language at issue, as well as the language and design of the statute as a whole. If the statute is silent or ambiguous with respect to the specific issue addressed by the regulation, the question becomes whether the agency regulation is a permissible construction of the

inforces an understandable reluctance on the part of judges to cede more authority than is demanded by the Supreme Court in the area of statutory construction where judges are so clearly equipped to function and historically have been allowed to do so." See Patricia M. Wald, "The Contribution of the D.C. Circuit To Administrative Law", speech to D.C. Bar (Oct., 1987) transcribed in 40 Admin.L.Rev. 507 (Fall, 1988). Some lower court cases have relied considerably on *Cardoza–Fonseca.* See, e.g. International Union, UAW v. Brock, 816 F.2d 761 (D.C.Cir.1987). The D.C. Circuit relied on *Chevron* and *Cardoza–Fonseca* to invalidate a Labor Department interpretation of the term "employment" in section 231 of the Trade Act of 1974. The Trade Act provides assistance to workers displaced by foreign competition provided they meet certain eligibility requirements. One such requirement is that they must have been employed for at least 26 weeks out of the last 52 before the aid is sought. The Labor Department interpreted the term "employment" to exclude periods of sick leave, vacation leave, and leaves of absence.

The court invalidated this interpretation, terming it a "pure question of statutory construction" under *Cardoza–Fonseca* and applying the "traditional tools" of statutory construction. In invalidating the agency interpretation the court relied on (1) the "ordinary meaning" of the term employment; (2) the "mood of [Congressional] largess" as evidenced by the legislative history; and (3) the illogic of the secretary's view. This court, operating under the *Chevron* framework, felt no need to defer in light of its ability to construe the statute. See also, Seldovia Native Association, Inc. v. Lujan, 904 F.2d 1335 (9th Cir.1990); City of Boston v. Department of HUD, 898 F.2d 828 (1st Cir.1990) ("[C]ongressional intent can be determined under traditional canons of analysis.... We, therefore, do not defer to HUD's inconsistent interpretation ... ").

65. 486 U.S. 281, 108 S.Ct. 1811, 100 L.Ed.2d 313 (1988).

66. 19 U.S.C.A. § 1526.

67. Id. at 289, 108 S.Ct. at 1063.

statute. If the agency regulation is not in conflict with the plain language of the statute, a reviewing court must give deference to the agency's interpretation of the statute."[68]

The majority thus eschewed any use of legislative history in construing the meaning of the text of the statute before it. Ambiguity or clarity must be found within the four corners of the statute. This does not preclude reference to statutory purposes found in the statute or the design of the statute as a whole. Such an approach, however, goes no further in determining whether Congress was clear or ambiguous in its directives to the agency.[69] In short, the court's recent opinions have not been entirely clear on just how *Chevron* is to be interpreted. Courts do, however, increasingly seem to limit their independent judicial analysis of the issues involved only to the statutory text.[70] In so doing, there often is considerable room for disagreement over what is clear and what is ambiguous. As Chief Judge Wald has observed:

> How comfortably can a judge conclude that one argument is superior to all others, based on his best analysis of statutory language and legislative history, yet defer to an inferior reading because an agency has taken that position? Even if *Chevron* commands such a mental feat, how can a court resist labeling a vastly "superior" interpretation "clear congressional intent" and calling all other positions "unreasonable"? Since our circuit spends more time interpreting

68. K Mart Corporation v. Cartier, Inc., 486 U.S. at 291, 292, 108 S.Ct. at 1817.

69. Justices Brennan, Marshall and Stevens dissented in part. They extensively reviewed the legislative history of the Tariff Act of 1930 and reached the conclusion that both regulations were reasonable interpretations. They also noted the special deference the court traditionally owed towards longstanding administrative interpretations. See also, Sullivan v. Zebley, 493 U.S. 521, 110 S.Ct. 885, 107 L.Ed.2d 967 (1990) (Court voids regulations they found to be "manifestly contrary to the statute"); Compare Dole v. United Steelworkers of America, 494 U.S. 26, 110 S.Ct. 929, 108 L.Ed.2d 23 (1990), superseded by statute as stated in Matter of Rhone-Poulenc AG Co., 1996 WL 691425 (E.P.A.1996) (relying on a *Cardoza–Fonseca* approach to *Chevron*) with Sullivan v. Everhart, 494 U.S. 83, 110 S.Ct. 960, 108 L.Ed.2d 72 (1990), on remand 901 F.2d 838 (10th Cir.1990) (relying on an approach to *Chevron* that focuses only on statutory text and defers when ambiguity is found).

Recently, the Court did briefly explore legislative history when it applied a *Chevron* approach in the area of family planning in Rust v. Sullivan, 500 U.S. 173, 111 S.Ct. 1759, 114 L.Ed.2d 233 (1991). *See also*, National Credit Union Administration v. First Nat'l Bank and Trust Co., 522 U.S. 479, 118 S.Ct. 927, 936, 140 L.Ed.2d 1 (1998) (where the Court briefly mentioned legislative history in a footnote but, nonetheless, relied on this legislative history in their final determination as to the proper meaning to be given the statute in question); AT & T Corp. v. Iowa Utilities Board, 525 U.S. 366, 119 S.Ct. 721, 142 L.Ed.2d 835 (1999) (this case is another example of the split on the Court over what tools to use in the interpretation of challenged statues, here the Court was divided over the question whether or not the FCC interpreted its authority under the Telecommunications Act of 1996 in a manner consistent with Chevron).

70. See, e.g., PBGC v. LTV Corp., 496 U.S. 633, 110 S.Ct. 2668, 110 L.Ed.2d 579 (1990), on remand 122 B.R. 863 (S.D.N.Y. 1990) (Where the Court explicitly rejected legislative history that contradicted its textual analysis of the statute involved: "Moreover, and more generally, the language of a statute—particularly language expressly granting an agency broad authority—is not to be regarded as modified by examples set forth in the legislative history. An example, after all, is just that: an illustration of a statute's operation in practice. It is not . . . a definitive interpretation of a statute's scope." Id. at 597).

statutes then "almost anything else, the degree of deference we give to agencies" interpretations is a prime determinant of outcomes. Lately, ... our Court seems to be inching back towards a more balanced stance allowing for greater space for judicial legal interpretation and moving away from complete deference to the agency.[71]

§ 13.7.4 Chevron, Context and Textualism

The *Chevron* doctrine has continued to evolve as Supreme Court Justices and judges differ in their views on when and how to apply the *Chevron* doctrine as well as the proper deference to be accorded agency decisions once it has been determined that the *Chevron* approach should be used.[72] These differences have been exacerbated, especially at the Supreme Court level, by the emergence of an approach to statutory construction that some commentators have labeled textualism. A textualist approach to interpretation is not necessarily devoid of context, but the context involved usually is limited to the face of the statute under consideration. As Judge Wald has written, "[t]extualism is a mode of statutory interpretation that relies on text and dictionaries to determine the meaning of statutory provisions and eschews reference to legislative history."[73] As one commentator has noted, a judge using this interpretive methodology seeks to determine "what an ordinary reader of a statute would have understood the words to mean at the time of enactment, not what the intentions of the enacting legislators were."[74] As a result, legislative history is essentially eliminated as a tool of statutory construction, particularly when the court is engaged in step one of the *Chevron* analysis—determining whether Congress spoke to the precise question at issue.[75]

71. Wald, The D.C. Circuit: Here and Now, 55 Geo.Wash.L.Rev. 718, 727 (1987). But see Shuck & Elliott, supra note 183, arguing that *Chevron* has very definitely increased judicial deference to agency interpretations in the federal courts, generally.

72. *See*, Richard J. Pierce, Jr., *The Supreme Court's New Hypertextualism: An Invitation to Cacophony and Incoherence in the Administrative State*, 95 Colum. L. Rev. 749, 750 (1995) (arguing that "[The Supreme Court's] post-Chevron jurisprudence is so confused that it is difficult to determine what remains of the original, highly deferential test). This inconsistency in applying the test is largely attributable to post-chevron changes in the choice of 'traditional tools of statutory construction,' a phrase the Chevron Court used in a footnote to describe the manner in which courts should apply the first part of the test. As the Court has changed the mix of 'tools' it uses and the ways in which it uses those tools, it has gradually ceased to apply step two of the Chevron test to uphold an agency construction of ambiguous statutory language, because it rarely acknowledges the existence of ambiguity." There appears to be more consistency at the appellate level. For an empirical study of all Court of Appeals decisions from 1995–1996 that cited *Chevron*, see Orin s. Kerr, Shedding Light on *Chevron*: An Empirical study of the *chevron* Doctrine in the U.S. Courts of Appeals, 15 Yale J. on reg. 1 (1998) (agency interpretations upheld 73% of the time. Of those overturned, 53% failed step one of the *Chevron* test and 18% failed step two, i.e., their application of the statutory term was upheld to be unreasonable).

73. 72 Wald, Judicial Review In Midpassage: The Uneasy Partnership Between Courts And Agencies Plays On, 32 Tulsa L.J. 221, 241 (1996).

74. Thomas W. Merrill, *Textualism and the Future of the Chevron Doctrine*, Wash. U. L.Q. 351 (1994) (discussing Chevron and the rise of textualism on the present Court as well as its effects on the way the Supreme Court interprets statutes).

75. For a case debating the uses and misuses of legislative history, see Bank One

Justice Scalia has been the primary proponent of the textualist approach on the Supreme Court. Writing for the majority in *MCI Telecommunications Corp. v. American Telephone and Telegraph Co.*,[76] for example, Justice Scalia used dictionary definitions to interpret the word "modify" as it is used in the Communications Act of 1934.[77] He concluded that this word clearly connotes moderate change, not the kind of sweeping change embodied in the FCC's regulations whose legality was at issue in this case. The Court struck them down, noting that the end result of the new FCC regulations represented "a whole new regime of regulation (or of free-market competition), which may well be a better regime but is not the one that Congress established."[78]

Courts also refer to "the traditional tools of statutory construction,"[79] which include the use of the overall context of the statute question—its text, purpose, legislative history and substantive background considerations. Just what tools will be used or what constitutes the context of a statutory term is not always clear, but the farther one gets from just the text of the statute, the farther one gets from a relatively pure form of textualism. Even when the context invoked to explain a statutory term excludes legislative history, it can include other provisions of the statue in question, its overall structure and internal logic,[80] as well as, on occasion, other related Congressional actions or inactions.[81] In *Food and Drug Administration v. Brown & Williamson Tobacco Corp.*,[82] the Court reviewed the Food and Drug Administration's (FDA) regulations of tobacco under the Federal Food, Drug and Cosmetic Act (FDCA).[83] Its search for the meaning of the statutory terms "drug" and "drug delivery devices" was so broad as to, in effect, utilize more traditional tools of statutory construction, including prior legislative actions and inactions if not legislative history, per se. Two factors may have accounted for the departure from a relatively strict textualist approach used in some of the previous cases. First, this case represented an attempt by the FDA to expand its own jurisdiction, in a context in which it had resisted doing so for many years. Interpretive issues that

Chicago, N.A. v. Midwest Bank & Trust Co., 516 U.S. 264, 116 S.Ct. 637, 133 L.Ed.2d 635 (1996); but see Atlantic Mutual Ins. Co. v. Commissioner of Internal Revenue, 523 U.S. 382, 118 S.Ct. 1413, 140 L.Ed.2d 542 (1998) (Justice Scalia's opinion opposes the use of legislative history and Justice Stevens supports its use in some contexts).

76. 512 U.S. 218, 114 S.Ct. 2223, 129 L.Ed.2d 182 (1994).

77. Specifically, § 203(b)(2) gives the FCC the authority to "modify any requirement".

78. 512 U.S. at 234. *See also*, Whitman v. American Trucking Association, Inc. 531 U.S. 457, 121 S.Ct. 903, 149 L.Ed.2d 1 (2001) (Justice Scalia, writing for the majority, held that both the EPA's interpretation of the Clean Air Act and that of the D.C. Circuit Court of Appeals were incorrect: their reading "goes beyond the limits of what is ambiguous and contradicts what in our view is quite clear."); National Credit Union Admin. v. First Nat. Bank & Trust Co., 522 U.S. 479, 118 S.Ct. 927, 140 L.Ed.2d 1 (1998).

79. Chevron, U.S.A., Inc. v. Natural Resources Defense Council, 467 U.S. 837, n. 9, 104 S.Ct. 2778, 81 L.Ed.2d 694 (1984).

80. See. e.g., Third Nat'l Bank v. Impac Ltd., 432 U.S. 312, 322–23, 97 S.Ct. 2307, 53 L.Ed.2d 368 (1977).

81. See, e.g., Federal Housing Administration v. The Darlington, Inc., 358 U.S. 84, 90–92, 79 S.Ct. 141, 3 L.Ed.2d 132 (1958).

82. 529 U.S. 120, 120 S.Ct. 1291, 146 L.Ed.2d 121 (2000).

83. 21 U.S.C. §§ 301–395 (1994).

can result in expanding an agency's jurisdiction can evoke a closer judicial look at congressional intent than what a plain meaning or textualist approach might suggest. More important, the policy issues involved in this case were so sensitive that the majority may very well have assumed that only Congress could address them and that it must do so directly. As Professor William Popkin has noted, "the Court seems to conclude that the power to regulate cigarettes is too controversial to be achieved by an agency on the basis of uncertain legislative signals, at least where there are signs of periodic legislative review of the issue (that is, no legislative inertia)."[84]

Specifically, the FDA's regulations sought to reduce smoking by children and adolescents. Writing for the majority of the Court, Justice O'Connor agreed that the thousands of premature deaths caused each year by tobacco presented "one of the most troubling public health problems facing our Nation;"[85] however, the magnitude of the problem did not mean the agency had the power to deal with it. By a five to four vote, the Court invalidated FDA regulations concerning the sale of cigarettes to minors and concluded that Congress did authorize the FDA to regulate tobacco.

At issue in this case was the meaning of the statutory terms "drugs" and "devices" in FDCA. FDA took the position that nicotine was a "drug" and that cigarettes and smokeless tobacco were "drug delivery devices," thereby granting them the jurisdiction to regulate tobacco products.[86] The Court invoked *Chevron* to guide its analysis of the agency's interpretation of the Act. In so doing, the Court noted that in determining "whether Congress has specifically addressed the question at issue, a reviewing court should not confine itself to examining a particular statutory provision in isolation."[87] In concluding that FDA's interpretation of "drug" was not acceptable, the Court stated that it was necessary to look at the FDCA as a "symmetrical and coherent regulatory scheme,"[88] noting that safety was the essential purpose of the Act. To achieve this purpose and to be consistent with the overall regulatory scheme of the Act, the Court concluded that if, indeed, nicotine was a drug covered by this Act, the agency would have to have banned the use of tobacco and removed it from the market, not just regulate its use by minors.[89] Put in this light, it was clear that Congress never intended in this Act to give the FDA such power. This was true, not only because of the regulatory structure of this Act, but because in other legislative action, Congress specifically foreclosed the removal of tobacco products from the markets. Congress had enacted six separate pieces of legislation since 1965 addressing the problem of tobacco use and human health and,

84. William Popkin, Materials on Legislation: Political Language and the Political Process (Foundation Press, 2000).

85. 120 S.Ct. at 1296.

86. See generally, Cass R. Sunstein, Is Tobacco a Drug— Administrative Agencies as Common Law Courts, 47 Duke L. J. 1013 (1998).

87. 120 S.Ct at 1300–301

88. Id. at 1301 (quoting Gustafson v. Alloyd Co., 513 U.S. 561, 569, 115 S.Ct. 1061, 131 L.Ed.2d 1 (1995)).

89. Id. at 1302.

against this backdrop, never once did it even suggest the FDA had the power it claimed in this case.[90] As the Court noted, "Taken together, these actions by Congress over the past 35 years preclude an interpretation of the FDCA that grants the FDA jurisdiction to regulate tobacco products."[91] In effect, the Court held, when Congress passed the FDCA in 1938 it did not intend the FDA to exercise jurisdiction over tobacco.[92]

This conclusion, however, would appear to contradict the plain language of the statute. In dissent, Justice Breyer argued that tobacco products fell within the statutory definition of "drugs" over which the FDA clearly had authority[93] and that the regulation of tobacco products was consistent with the broad purpose of the FDCA to protect public health.[94] The majority, however, turned to an even broader Congressional context by considering other legislative action as well as Congressional silence. Rather than defer to the agency, the majority concluded that it would be unlikely that Congress would implicitly delegate to the agency so important a policy decision as the use of tobacco. Indeed, the statute itself dealt only with products that "were safe for [their] intended use."[95] Congress would not have implicitly delegated regulatory authority over products such as tobacco that had no safe use.[96] Even if the Act itself was ambiguous, subsequent Congressional acts showed that FDA jurisdiction over tobacco never was intended.[97]

Textualism in its purest form may have reached its high water mark in the 1990's. A variety of factors, including the controversial nature of the issues involved, the nature of the proceedings used to promulgate the agency's decision, as well as the timing of that decision, and the institutional competence of the decision makers are all factors that may come into play as courts decide when and how to apply *Chevron* in a variety of factual contexts.[98]

§ 13.8 JUDICIAL DEFERENCE TO AGENCY INTERPRETATIONS OF LAW

If a reviewing court is satisfied that there is no clear congressional intent respecting the precise question at issue, a reasonableness test applies to the agency's interpretation of the statute involved. As the majority in *Chevron* noted, "the court may not substitute its own construction for a reasonable interpretation" by the agency.[1] This is the

90. Id. at 1303–304.

91. Id. at 1312.

92. Id.

93. Id. at 1316.

94. Id.

95. Id. at 1306.

96. Id.

97. Id. at 1313.

98. See, e.g., Christensen v. Harris County, 529 U.S. 576, 120 S.Ct. 1655, 146 L.Ed.2d 621 (2000), discussed *infra* at § 13.8.5 See generally, §§ 13.8.1–13.8.5.

§ 13.8

1. Chevron, U.S.A., Inc. v. NRDC, Inc., 467 U.S. 837, 844, 104 S.Ct. 2778, 2782, 81 L.Ed.2d 694 (1984). See also, Japan Whaling Ass'n v. American Cetacean Soc., 478 U.S. 221, 233–34, 106 S.Ct. 2860, 2867–68, 92 L.Ed.2d 166 (1986); United States v. Fulton, 475 U.S. 657, 666–67, 106 S.Ct. 1422, 1427–28, 89 L.Ed.2d 661 (1986); Hillsborough County, Fla. v. Automated Medical Lab., Inc., 471 U.S. 707, 714, 105 S.Ct. 2371, 2375, 85 L.Ed.2d 714 (1985), on remand 767 F.2d 748 (1985); Chemical Manufactures Ass'n v. NRDC, 470 U.S. 116,

case, even if the Court would have reached a different conclusion in a judicial setting.[2] Reasonableness review usually involves "the agency's textual analysis (broadly defined, including where appropriate resort to legislative history) and ... the compatibility of that inquiry with the congressional purposes informing the measure."[3] Though it may be argued that an agency interpretation must be accepted by a reviewing court if it is deemed reasonable,[4] courts continue to discuss reasonableness questions in terms of degrees of deference.[5]

This section will examine various legal contexts and agency lawmaking formats and the extent to which these contexts and formats encourage a court to defer to an agency's interpretation of law even if the interpretation in question may theoretically be entitled to independent judicial review.[6] These contexts include statutory provisions, institutional factors such as agency expertise,[7] the timing,[8] clarity,[9] and apparent thoroughness of an agency's decision[10] as well as the procedural format used by the agency when it interprets the law.

125–25, 105 S.Ct. 1102, 1107, 84 L.Ed.2d 90 (1985).

2. See Council of Commuter Organizations v. Thomas, 799 F.2d 879, 886 (2d Cir.1986).

3. AT&T Corp. v. Iowa Utilities Bd., 525 U.S. 366, 392, 119 S.Ct. 721, 142 L.Ed.2d 835 (1999); Continental Air Lines, Inc. v. DOT, 843 F.2d 1444, 1449 (D.C.Cir. 1988). For reasonableness cases in general, see International Union, UMW v. FMSHRC, 840 F.2d 77, 81 (D.C.Cir.1988); NRDC v. Thomas, 805 F.2d 410, 420 (D.C.Cir.1986); FAIC Securities, Inc. v. United States, 768 F.2d 352, 361 (D.C.Cir. 1985). See also, Rust v. Sullivan, 500 U.S. 173, 111 S.Ct. 1759, 114 L.Ed.2d 233 (1991).

4. See Starr, Judicial Review in the Post–Chevron Era, 3 Yale J. on Reg. 283, 296 (1986).

5. See, e.g., Chevron v. NRDC, 467 U.S. at 844, 104 S.Ct. at 2782 (Justice Stevens speaks of the "considerable weight" courts should give to an agency construction); Massachusetts v. O'Leary, 925 F.Supp. 857, 862–63 (1996); Lukhard v. Reed, 481 U.S. 368, 381, 107 S.Ct. 1807, 1815, 95 L.Ed.2d 328 (1987); FDIC v. Philadelphia Gear Corp., 476 U.S. 426, 437, 106 S.Ct. 1931, 1938, 90 L.Ed.2d 428 (1986), on remand 795 F.2d 903 (10th Cir.1986); Montana v. Clark, 749 F.2d 740, 745 (D.C.Cir. 1984), cert. denied 474 U.S. 919, 106 S.Ct. 246, 88 L.Ed.2d 255 (1985). For a discussion of the role that procedural contexts should play in the weight accorded agency interpretations of law, see Anthony, Which Agency Interpretations Should Bind the Courts and the Public?, 7 Yale J. on Reg. 1, 33 (1990). For an article arguing that judicial deference to agency interpretation of statutes impermissibly weakens the historical and justifiable influence of the judicial branch over the political process, see Jonathan T. Molot, The judicial Perspective in the Administrative State: Reconciling Modern Doctrines of Deference with the Judiciary's Structural Role, 53 Stan. L.Rev. 1 (2000).

6. See generally, Gellhorn and Verkuil, Controlling Chevron–Based Delegations, 20 Cardozo L.Rev. 989 (1999); Note, Coring the Seedless Grape: Reinterpretation of Chevron v. NRDC, 87 Colum.L.Rev. 986, 997–1002 (1987); Diver, Statutory Interpretation in the Administration State, 133 U.Pa.L.Rev. 549 (1985); Woodward and Levin, In Defenses of Deference: Judicial Review of Agency Action, 31 Admin.L.Rev. 329 (1979).

7. Massachusetts v. U.S. Dept. of Education, 837 F.2d 536, 543 (1st Cir.1988). See also, NLRB v. Curtin Matheson Scientific, Inc., 494 U.S. 775, 110 S.Ct. 1542, 108 L.Ed.2d 801 (1990), on remand 905 F.2d 871 (5th Cir.1990); National Medical Enterprises, Inc. v. Sullivan, 916 F.2d 542 (9th Cir.1990), cert. denied 500 U.S. 917, 111 S.Ct. 2014, 114 L.Ed.2d 100 (1991).

8. NLRB v. United Food and Commercial Workers Union, 484 U.S. 112, 124 n. 20, 108 S.Ct. 413, 421 n. 20, 98 L.Ed.2d 429 (1987), on remand 840 F.2d 171 (3d Cir. 1988).

9. Barnett v. Weinberger, 818 F.2d 953 (D.C.Cir.1987).

10. Id.

§ 13.8.1 The Role of Congress

In some instances, Congress itself makes clear that it wants the agency to be the primary interpreter of its own enabling statute. In *Social Security Board v. Nierotko,*[11] for example, the Supreme Court suggested that Congress could delegate interpretive as well as legislative power to an agency. In that case, the Court held that the Social Security Board did not have the power to exclude a worker's back pay from his "wages" for the purpose of calculating benefits. In so doing, however, the Court noted:

> [When an Administrator] interprets a statute so as to make it apply to particular circumstances, it acts as a delegate to the legislative power. Congress might have declared that "back pay" awards under the Labor Act should or should not be treated as wages. Congress might have delegated to the Social Security Board to determine what compensation paid by employers to employees should be treated as wages. Except as such interpretive power may be included in the agencies' administrative function, Congress did neither.[12]

Congress can, in effect, designate the agency as a primary interpreter of the statute involved.[13] Short of an explicit delegation of law making power, a congressional decision to vest rulemaking power in an agency is often a decisive factor in a court's decision to defer when an agency uses this procedural format to make law.[14] This does not, however, mean that the agency's power in this regard is unlimited. It can be overturned, but only if the Secretary exceeded his statutory authority or if the regulation is "arbitrary, capricious, or an abuse of discretion, or otherwise not in accordance with law."[15]

The agency did exceed its authority in *Addison v. Holly Hill Fruit Products, Inc.*[16] The Court was asked to review an administrative interpretation of an exemption provision in the Fair Labor Standards Act. This Act required employers to pay a fixed minimum wage, but exempted, among others, employers whose employees were engaged in the canning of agricultural products. Specifically, the exemption applied to those "within the area of production (as defined by the Administrator),

11. 327 U.S. 358, 66 S.Ct. 637, 90 L.Ed. 718 (1946).

12. Id. at 369, 66 S.Ct. at 643.

13. See Monaghan, Marbury and the Administrative State, 83 Colum.L.Rev. 1 (1983).

14. See, e.g., Massachusetts v. Secretary of HHS, 749 F.2d 89 (1st Cir.1984), cert. denied 472 U.S. 1017, 105 S.Ct. 3478, 87 L.Ed.2d 613 (1985); Mourning v. Family Publications Service, Inc., 411 U.S. 356, 369, 93 S.Ct. 1652, 1660, 36 L.Ed.2d 318 (1973); Chrysler Corp. v. Brown, 441 U.S. 281, 308, 99 S.Ct. 1705, 1720, 60 L.Ed.2d 208 (1979), on remand 611 F.2d 439 (3d Cir.1979); National Petroleum Refiners Ass'n v. FTC, 482 F.2d 672 (D.C.Cir.1973), cert. denied 415 U.S. 951, 94 S.Ct. 1475, 39 L.Ed.2d 567 (1974); National Nutritional Foods Ass'n v. Weinberger, 512 F.2d 688 (2d Cir.1975), cert. denied 423 U.S. 827, 96 S.Ct. 44, 46 L.Ed.2d 44 (1975). But see, Pension Benefit Guaranty Corp. v. LTV Corp., 496 U.S. 633, 110 S.Ct. 2668, 110 L.Ed.2d 579 (1990), on remand 122 B.R. 863 (S.D.N.Y.1990) (Court grants *Chevron* deference to an agency interpretation made under very informal circumstances).

15. 5 U.S.C.A. § 706(A).

16. 322 U.S. 607, 64 S.Ct. 1215, 88 L.Ed. 1488 (1944), rehearing denied 323 U.S. 809, 65 S.Ct. 27, 89 L.Ed. 645 (1944).

engaged in . . . canning of agricultural . . . commodities that are obtained by the establishment where he is employed from farms in the immediate locality and the number of employees in such establishment does not exceed seven."[17]

When the case reached the Supreme Court, the Court had to decide whether "the Administrator could lawfully include in the definition of 'area of production' the condition that the number of employees in the establishment not exceed seven."[18] In reviewing the Administrator's determination, the Court noted that the phrase "area of production" encompasses a "variety of agricultural conditions and industries throughout the country" and thus, "the bounds of these areas could not be defined by Congress itself." The Court continued:

> Neither was it deemed wise to leave such economic determinations to the contingencies and inevitable diversities of litigation. And so Congress left the boundary-making to the experienced and informed judgment of the Administrator. Thereby Congress gave the Administrator appropriate discretion to assess all the factors relevant to the subject matter, that is, the fixing of minimum wages and maximum hours.

The fact that Congress did this did not mean that anything the Administrator did was acceptable, but, in the words of the Court:

> In delineating the area the Administrator may properly weigh and synthesize all such factors. So long as he does that and no more, judgment belongs to him and not to the courts.

In this case, however, the Court determined that Congress did not intend to discriminate between larger and smaller establishments. The Court, therefore, reversed the agency's interpretation of its mandate. The Court was prepared to defer, provided the agency used the proper statutory factors in rendering its interpretation of the statute. The fact that Congress delegated its rulemaking authority to the Administrator would, under normal circumstances, be reason enough for judicial deference. In this case, however, the agency went beyond its powers in formulating its rule in granting these kinds of exemptions.[19]

Congressional inaction in the light of long standing agency interpretations of its law can be another factor militating in favor of judicial deference. In *Bob Jones University v. U.S.*,[20] for example, the IRS denied tax exempt status to a private school because of its racially discriminatory practices. The Court upheld the IRS interpretation noting that "nonaction by Congress is not often a useful guide, but the nonaction

17. Id. at 611, 64 S.Ct. at 1218.

18. Id.

19. Of course, the power of an agency to engage in rulemaking in the first place must be established before a court will defer to its interpretation. See, e.g., Federal Communications Commission v. National Citizens Committee for Broadcasting, 436 U.S. 775, 98 S.Ct. 2096, 56 L.Ed.2d 697 (1978); United States v. Vogel Fertilizer Co., 455 U.S. 16, 102 S.Ct. 821, 70 L.Ed.2d 792 (1982).

20. 461 U.S. 574, 103 S.Ct. 2017, 76 L.Ed.2d 157 (1983).

here is significant."[21] Though thirteen bills attempting to overthrow the IRS's interpretation of the relevant section had failed, numerous amendments to that section had, in fact, been passed. None, however, modified IRS' interpretation: "In view of its prolonged and acute awareness of so important an issue, Congress' (sic) failure to act on the bills proposed on this subject provides added support for concluding that Congress acquiesced in the IRS rulings of 1970 and 1971."[22]

Similarly, in *Zemel v. Rusk,*[23] the petitioner desired to visit Cuba after the United States had broken diplomatic relations with that country. He claimed that the Secretary of State's restrictions on travel to Cuba were not valid. The Supreme Court responded that a history of executive interpretations of the 1926 Passport Act "would be of relevance to our construction of the Act."[24] The Court also pointed out that in "some circumstances, Congress' failure to repeal or revise in the face of such administrative interpretation has been held to contribute persuasive evidence that that interpretation is the one intended by Congress."[25] The Court went on to say that this particular circumstance was even more compelling, for "despite 26 years of executive interpretation of the 1926 Act as authorizing the imposition of area restriction, Congress in 1952, though it once again enacted legislation relating to passports, left completely untouched the broad rulemaking authority granted in the earlier Act."[26]

In addition to judicial deference due to specific directions from Congress or inaction in the face of long standing agency interpretations we have also noted the deference *Chevron* requires when Congress has been silent or ambiguous concerning its intentions on a particular issue.[27] Some courts have explained that in such circumstances a "sensible legislator" would want its silence construed by agencies, not courts.

In *Mayburg v. Secretary of Health and Human Services,*[28] for example, Judge Breyer noted that courts "might defer" by asking what a "sensible legislator would have expected given the statutory circumstances."[29] For Judge Breyer,

> [t]he less important the question of law, the more interstitial its character, the more closely related to everyday administration or substantive expertise, the less likely it is that Congress (would have)

21. 461 U.S. at 600, 103 S.Ct. at 2032.

22. 461 U.S. at 600–01, 103 S.Ct. at 2032–34. For a discussion of the role of Congress an dits interplay with Chevron, see Herz, Deference Running Riot: Separating Interpretation and Lawmaking Under Chevron, 6 Admin.L.J. Am.U. 187 (1992).

23. 381 U.S. 1, 85 S.Ct. 1271, 14 L.Ed.2d 179 (1965), rehearing denied 382 U.S. 873, 86 S.Ct. 17, 15 L.Ed.2d 114 (1965).

24. 381 U.S. at 11, 85 S.Ct. at 1278.

25. Id.

26. 381 U.S. at 12, 85 S.Ct. at 1278. See also, United States v. Riverside Bayview Homes, Inc., 474 U.S. 121, 134–39, 106 S.Ct. 455, 463–65, 88 L.Ed.2d 419 (1985). See also Food and Drug Administration v. Brown & Williamson Tobacco Corp., discussed *supra*, §§ 13.7.4.

27. See sec. 13.7.2, supra.

28. 740 F.2d 100 (1st Cir.1984).

29. Id. at 106.

"wished" or "expect" the courts to remain indifferent to the agency's views.[30]

In the case at bar, the Court found that the interpretative issues were central to the statutory scheme and that nothing suggested "any specific congressional intent to place the power to construe this statutory term primarily in the agency's hands."[31]

In *Montana v. Clark,*[32] the Court dealt with a Department of Interior interpretation of its own regulation implementing the Surface Mining Control and Reclamation Act. That Act "expressly recognized that the jurisdictional status of Indian lands was too uncertain to permit effective allocation of regulatory authority for those regions."[33] Nevertheless, as the Court noted, "over seven years have now passed and the promise of congressional clarification remains unfulfilled."[34] In the meantime, the Secretary had to devise rules to collect fees for and administer the reclamation fund. Given this "remarkably mixed message," the Court concluded that "pending congressional clarification, Congress afforded the Secretary substantial discretion" and that deference was appropriate.[35]

In short, the court could infer what it thought a sensible legislator must have intended, given the circumstances. When it comes to answering the question why courts defer, Judge Breyer has suggested that essentially two answers can be given:

> "One answer rests upon an agency's better knowledge of congressional intent. The other rests upon Congress' intent that courts give an agency legal interpretations special weight, an intent (where Congress is silent) courts may impute on the basis of various 'practical' circumstances."[36]

§ 13.8.2 Timing Issues

Closely related to the inferences that may be drawn from congressional action, inaction, silence or ambiguity, are a variety of matters concerning timing. Timing issues can, on occasion, highlight the relationship of the agency's interpretation to that presumed to have been intended by Congress. For example, if an agency's construction of its statute is contemporaneous with the passage of the statute, deference usually is accorded that interpretation.

30. Id. See also, cases cited by the Court, International Brotherhood of Teamsters v. Daniel, 439 U.S. 551, 566 n. 20, 99 S.Ct. 790, 800 n. 20, 58 L.Ed.2d 808 (1979); Constance v. Secretary of Health and Human Services, 672 F.2d 990, 995–96 (1st Cir.1982); L. Jaffe, "Judicial Control of Administrative Action", 560–64 (1965).

31. 740 F.2d at 107. See also, Gellhorn, Justice Breyer on Statutory Review and Interpretation, 8 Admin. L.J. Am. U. 755 (1995).

32. 749 F.2d 740 (D.C.Cir.1984), cert. denied 474 U.S. 919, 106 S.Ct. 246, 88 L.Ed.2d 255 (1985).

33. Id. at 746.

34. Id.

35. Id.

36. Breyer, Judicial Review, Questions of Law and Policy, 38 Admin.L.Rev. 363, 372 (1986).

In *Norwegian Nitrogen Products Co. v. United States,*[37] a Norwegian nitrite manufacturer complained that it had not received a fair hearing because the domestic cost of manufacture had not been disclosed, as a trade secret, during the proceedings to determine whether to impose a duty on that material.[38] The Court upheld the agency's construction of whether the party had been heard as required by the statute. The Court reasoned that after the Tariff Act of 1922 was enacted, an investigation was held into the procedures and methods of the Commission, including the hearings process. Despite a majority report suggesting that the provisions be repealed, the Commission was continued as is shown by the Tariff Act of 1930. The Court mentioned the presumption of validity of administrative practice and added that "the practice has peculiar weight when it involves a contemporaneous construction of a statute by the men charged with the responsibility of setting its machinery in motion, of making its parts work efficiently and smoothly when they are yet untried and new."[39]

Similarly, in *Sunray Mid–Continent Oil Co. v. FPC,*[40] the petitioner sought a certificate of public convenience and necessity under the Natural Gas Act[41] in order to sell natural gas in interstate commerce. It requested a certificate limited to the period of the sales contract, and the Federal Power Commission refused to grant it. The court upheld the Commission largely because "this ruling was made by Commissioners who had been in office during the passage of the Act . . . The ruling has been followed, and we think this contemporaneous and consistent construction . . . is to be afforded weight in the construction we make."[42]

37. 288 U.S. 294, 53 S.Ct. 350, 77 L.Ed. 796 (1933); see also, Unbelievable, Inc. v. NLRB, 118 F.3d 795, 804 (D.C.Cir. 1997); NLRB v. Beverly Enterprises–Massachusetts, Inc., 174 F.3d 13, 22 (1st Cir. 1999); NLRB v. New Jersey Bell Telephone Co., 936 F.2d 144, 147 (3d Cir.1991); NLRB v. United Food and Commercial Workers Union, 484 U.S. 112, 123 n. 20, 108 S.Ct. 413, 421 n. 20, 98 L.Ed.2d 429 (1987), on remand 840 F.2d 171 (3d Cir.1988); Chula Vista City School Dist. v. Bennett, 824 F.2d 1573, 1580 (Fed.Cir.1987), cert. denied 484 U.S. 1042, 108 S.Ct. 774, 98 L.Ed.2d 861 (1988).

38. The Norwegians themselves had also refused to disclose their costs.

39. 288 U.S. at 315, 53 S.Ct. at 358.

40. 364 U.S. 137, 80 S.Ct. 1392, 4 L.Ed.2d 1623 (1960), rehearing denied 364 U.S. 856, 81 S.Ct. 32, 5 L.Ed.2d 80 (1960).

41. 52 Stat. 821, (codified as amended at 15 U.S.C.A. § 717).

42. 364 U.S. at 154, 80 S.Ct. at 1402. See also Alcoa v. Central Lincoln Peoples' Utility Dist., 467 U.S. 380, 390, 104 S.Ct. 2472, 2479, 81 L.Ed.2d 301 (1984) (longstanding administrative constructions are preferred); Leary v. United States, 395 U.S. 6, 25–26, 89 S.Ct. 1532, 1542–43, 23 L.Ed.2d 57 (1969), appeal after remand 431 F.2d 85 (5th Cir.1970); Alexander v. Cosden Pipe Line Co., 290 U.S. 484, 498, 54 S.Ct. 292, 297, 78 L.Ed. 452 (1934); Vulcan Power Co. v. Bonneville Power Admin., 89 F.3d 549, 550 (9th Cir.1996).

In Lowe v. SEC, 472 U.S. 181, 105 S.Ct. 2557, 86 L.Ed.2d 130 (1985), on the other hand, the petitioner's registration as an investment advisor was revoked by the SEC after a conviction for assorted investment offenses. The SEC later claimed that the petitioner violated the Investment Advisors Act of 1940 by publishing a newsletter containing investment advice. The Court refused to defer to the agency opinion, partly due to First Amendment considerations, but also because the petitioner, in their view, was entitled to a statutory exemption. The court held that the reformulation of this exemption "was not drafted until 1977–37 years after the passage of the Act—and therefore it was not entitled to the deference due a contemporaneous construction of the Act." 472 U.S. at 207 n. 52, 105 S.Ct. at 2571 n. 52. For a detailed examination of this case, see Aman, *SEC v.*

Courts also often give considerable weight to agency interpretations when the agency itself has helped draft the statute.[43] In *Howe v. Smith,*[44] for example, a prisoner was transferred from a Vermont state prison to a federal prison because there was no provision for long term high security prisoners in the state. The prisoner brought an action on the ground that the federal officials lacked statutory authority to confine him. The Court noted that in addition to thirty years of consistent administration of the statute in question, "the Bureau's interpretation of the statute merits greater than normal weight because it was the Bureau that drafted the legislation and steered it through Congress with little debate."[45]

§ 13.8.3 Consistency of Interpretation

Closely related to the timing issues discussed above is the degree to which an agency has been consistent in its own construction of a statute over time. If the agency has maintained its interpretive position consistently, that consistency may encourage judicial deference[45.5] even if the statutory issue in question has not arisen very frequently. In *Haig v. Agee,*[46] for example, the Secretary of State promulgated regulations in 1966 concerning revocation of the passports of American citizens who "are likely to cause serious damage to the national security or the foreign policy of the United States." The power to do so stemmed from Passport Acts of 1856 and 1926 which implicitly left this power in the hands of the Executive, who delegated the power to the Secretary of State. Agee was a former CIA operative who, since leaving the Agency, was accused of seeking to expose CIA operations and agents. After revocation of his passport, "Agee argue(d) that the only way the Executive can establish implicit Congressional approval is by proof of longstanding and consistent enforcement of the claimed power."[47] The Court disagreed: "The Secretary has construed and applied its regulations consistently, and it would be anomalous to fault the Government be-

Lowe, Professional Regulation and the First Amendment, 1985 Sup.Ct.Rev. 93.

43. See also United States v. American Trucking Ass'ns, 310 U.S. 534, 549, 60 S.Ct. 1059, 1067, 84 L.Ed. 1345 (1940), rehearing denied 311 U.S. 724, 61 S.Ct. 53, 85 L.Ed. 472 (1940); Hassett v. Welch, 303 U.S. 303, 310–11, 58 S.Ct. 559, 563, 82 L.Ed. 858 (1938); Shapiro v. United States, 335 U.S. 1, 12 n. 13, 68 S.Ct. 1375, 1381 n. 13, 92 L.Ed. 1787 (1948), rehearing denied 335 U.S. 836, 69 S.Ct. 9, 93 L.Ed. 388 (1948).

44. 452 U.S. 473, 101 S.Ct. 2468, 69 L.Ed.2d 171 (1981); see also, Blango v. Thornburgh, 942 F.2d 1487, 1490 (10th Cir. 1991).

45. 452 U.S. at 485, 101 S.Ct. at 2476.

45.5 See, e.g., Pattern Makers' League v. NLRB, 473 U.S. 95, 115, 105 S.Ct. 3064, 3076, 87 L.Ed.2d 68 (1985); see also, NLRB v. United Food and Commercial Workers Union, 484 U.S. 112, 124 n. 20, 108 S.Ct. 413, 421 n. 20, 98 L.Ed.2d 429 (1987), on remand 840 F.2d 171 (3d Cir.1988); Bowen v. American Hospital Ass'n, 476 U.S. 610, 645 n. 34, 106 S.Ct. 2101, 2122 n. 34, 90 L.Ed.2d 584 (1986); Unbelievable, Inc. v. N.L.R.B., 118 F.3d 795, 804 (D.C.Cir.1997). But see Chevron, U.S.A., Inc. v. NRDC, 467 U.S. 837, 104 S.Ct. 2778, 81 L.Ed.2d 694 (1984). In Healea v. Bowen, 871 F.2d 48 (7th Cir.1988), the Seventh Circuit accorded the Secretary of Health and Human Services' regulation less deference because it reversed a nine-year-old policy, but nevertheless upheld the new rule after determining that it was a permissible construction of the statute.

46. 453 U.S. 280, 101 S.Ct. 2766, 69 L.Ed.2d 640 (1981).

47. 453 U.S. at 301, 101 S.Ct. at 2779.

cause there were so few occasions to exercise the announced policy and practice."[48]

Similarly, *Saxbe v. Bustos*[49] involved an administrative construction of the Immigration and Naturalization Act[50] that classified a worker who lives in Canada or Mexico and commutes to work in the United States either daily or seasonally "as one variety of 'special immigrant' an immigrant 'lawfully admitted for permanent residence who is returning from a visit abroad.'"[51] The United Farm Workers objected to the benefits given to alien workers of this classification, such as those that allow them to leave the country temporarily, re-enter without regard to quotas, and dispense with visas or other formal documentation.[52] The Court upheld the agency interpretation: "Our conclusion reflects the administrative practice, dating back at least to 1927 when the Bureau of Immigration was part of the Department of Labor.[53] . . . This longstanding administrative practice is entitled to great weight, particularly where, as here, Congress has revisited the Act and left the practice untouched. Such a history of administrative construction and congressional acquiescence may add a gloss or qualification to what on its face is unequalled statutory language."[54]

48. 453 U.S. at 303, 101 S.Ct. at 2780. In Udall v. Tallman, 380 U.S. 1, 85 S.Ct. 792, 13 L.Ed.2d 616 (1965), rehearing denied 380 U.S. 989, 85 S.Ct. 1325, 14 L.Ed.2d 283 (1965) the Court pointed out that "the Secretary's interpretation had, long prior to respondent's applications, been a matter of public record and discussion. The agreement worked out with the House Committee on Merchant Marine and Fisheries in 1956, and the approval of the Swanson River leases pursuant thereto, though probably constituting no 'legislative ratification' in any formal sense, served to demonstrate the notoriety of the Secretary's construction, and thereby defeat any possible claim of detrimental reliance upon another interpretation." 380 U.S. at 17–18, 85 S.Ct. at 801–02.

49. 419 U.S. 65, 95 S.Ct. 272, 42 L.Ed.2d 231 (1974).

50. Sec. 101(a)(27)(B), 66 Stat. 169, as amended, 79 Stat. 916, 8 U.S.C.A. § 1101(a)(27)(B).

51. 419 U.S. at 66, 95 S.Ct. at 274.

52. 8 U.S.C.A. § 1181(b).

53. 419 U.S. at 73, 95 S.Ct. at 278.

54. 419 U.S. at 74, 95 S.Ct. at 279. See also Pattern Makers' League v. NLRB, 473 U.S. 95, 105 S.Ct. 3064, 87 L.Ed.2d 68 (1985). The Court stated that there were two strong reasons it should defer to the Board's decision: "First, in related cases this Court has invariably yielded to Board decisions on whether fines imposed by a union 'restrain or coerce' employees. Second, the Board consistently has construed Sec. 8(b)(1)(A) as prohibiting the imposition of fines on employees who have tendered resignations invalid under a union constitution." 473 U.S. at 115, 105 S.Ct. at 3076. Justice White's concurrence in *Pattern Makers'* suggests the ultimate in deference: "[T]here is nothing in the legislative history to indicate that the Board's interpretation is the only acceptable construction of the Act, and the relevant sections are also susceptible to the construction urged by the union in this case. Therefore, were the Board arguing for that interpretation of the Act, I would accord its view appropriate deference." 473 U.S. at 117, 105 S.Ct. at 3076.

See also, NLRB v. Bell Aerospace Co., 416 U.S. 267, 94 S.Ct. 1757, 40 L.Ed.2d 134 (1974). In that case, the Board held that managerial employees, if not susceptible to conflicts of interest in labor relations, could unionize. In reversing the Board's determination, the Court held that "a court may accord great weight to the longstanding interpretation placed on a statute by an agency charged with its administration." Id. at 275, 94 S.Ct. at 1762. The Court cited a series of decisions by the Board from 1947 to 1970 that held, with one exception, that managerial employees were not covered by the National Labor Relations Act. Id. at 288 n. 14, 94 S.Ct. at 1768 n. 14.

Inconsistency *per se* does not automatically negate judicial deference. If there has been a considered change, as in *NLRB v. Action Automotive, Inc.*,[55] a court may still defer if the agency has adequately explained its decision.[56] In *Action Automotive,* for example, the wife of one of the company's owners and the mother of all three owners were employed as a part-time clerk and a full-time cashier, respectively. The NLRB sustained a union challenge to the validity of the wife and the mother's votes in a representation election held among the company's employees, despite the fact that neither woman enjoyed any exceptional job-related benefits. In reversing the court of appeals, the Supreme Court enumerated a number of other factors that the Board might weigh besides job benefits when determining valid voters. The Court commented that "the policy regarding family members, although not defined by bright-line rules, is a reasonable application of its 'community of interest' standard."[57] The court added that "the Board's policy is not undermined by the fact that it has modified and refined its position; an agency's day to day experience with problems is bound to lead to adjustments."[58] Thus, an agency can have a valid excuse for inconsistent interpretations if it varies its stance for well defined reasons.[59]

When courts conclude that the agency has been inconsistent and it has not given a considered reason for its change of position, however, they rarely defer. In *International Brotherhood of Teamsters v. Daniel*[60] for example, the Court was required to decide whether a compulsory pension plan that was funded solely by employers was a "security"[61] and

55. 469 U.S. 490, 495 n. 4, 105 S.Ct. 984, 988 n. 4, 83 L.Ed.2d 986 (1985).

56. See also, Massachusetts v. Lyng, 893 F.2d 424 (1st Cir.1990).

57. 469 U.S. at 496, 105 S.Ct. at 988.

58. Id. at 495 n. 4, 105 S.Ct. at 988 n. 4.

59. Chevron, U.S.A., Inc. v. Natural Resources Defense Council, Inc., can also be seen in this light. 467 U.S. 837, 104 S.Ct. 2778, 81 L.Ed.2d 694 (1984), discussed supra in sec. 13.7.2. In *Chevron* the Court ruled that the varying legal interpretations in this case "convinces us that the agency primarily responsible for administering this important legislation has consistently interpreted it flexibly and not in a sterile vacuum, but in the context of implementing policy decisions in a technical and complex arena." Id. at 863, 104 S.Ct. at 2792. Rather than viewing inconsistency on the agency's part as a hindrance to deference, the Court found that "the agency, to engage in formal rulemaking, must consider varying interpretations and the wisdom of its policy on a continuing basis." Id. The Court also suggested that inconsistency can be a virtue: "the fact that the agency has adopted different variations in different contexts adds force to the argument that the definition itself is flexible, particularly since Congress itself has never indicated any disapproval of a flexible reading of the statute." Id. at 864, 104 S.Ct. at 2792.

In Andrus v. Sierra Club, 442 U.S. 347, 99 S.Ct. 2335, 60 L.Ed.2d 943 (1979), the Sierra Club, contended that the Secretary of the Interior and the Office of Management and Budget were required to submit Environmental Impact Statements (EIS) to accompany proposed budget cutbacks at the National Wildlife Refuge System. This had been the interpretation of the Council on Environmental Quality in regard to the National Environmental Policy Act of 1969. The Court upheld the new interpretation that did not require an EIS to be filed in such a case: "CEQ's reversal of interpretation occurred during the detailed and comprehensive process, ordered by the President, of transforming advisory guidelines into mandatory regulation applicable to all federal agencies." Id. at 358, 99 S.Ct. at 2341.

60. 439 U.S. 551, 99 S.Ct. 790, 58 L.Ed.2d 808 (1979).

61. Section 2(1) Securities Act of 1933, Sec. 3(a)(10) Securities Exchange Act of 1934.

whether there had been a "sale"[62] under the Securities Acts. The Court found that the pension plan in question was not subject to either of the Securities Acts, despite arguments in the SEC's *amicus curiae* brief that deference was due to a longstanding and consistent agency interpretation of the statute: "it is clear here that the SEC's position is neither longstanding nor even arguable within the outer limits of its authority to interpret these Acts.[63] As far as we are aware, at no time before this case arose did the SEC intimate that the antifraud provisions of the Securities Acts nevertheless applied to non-contributory pension plans."[64]

Inconsistency also undercut the deference the court was willing to give the agency in *Morton v. Ruiz.*[65] That case involved a controversy over the denial of general assistance to the Papago Indians under the Snyder Act by the Bureau of Indian Affairs. The conflict was over whether the Act authorized assistance for those "on or near" the reservation (the respondents were near) or only to those "on" the reservation. The Court rejected the argument that the agency approach was entitled to deference because "the BIA, through its own practices and representations, has led Congress to believe that these appropriations covered Indians 'on or near' the reservations and it is too late now to argue that the words 'on reservations' in the Manual mean something different from 'on or near' when, in fact, the two have been continuously equated by the BIA to Congress."[66]

If the inconsistency on the part of the agency appears to be egregious, the court may assign no weight at all to the agency's views.[67] Where the inconsistency involved results from different interpretations by two separate agencies, courts have sometimes been reluctant to give any deference to one or the other interpretation.[68] Even if the agency has been consistent over the long term, weight may not be given to their

62. Section 2(3) Securities Act of 1933, Sec. 3(a)(14) of the Securities Exchange Act of 1934.

63. 439 U.S. at 566, 99 S.Ct. at 800.

64. 439 U.S. at 569, 99 S.Ct. at 801.

65. 415 U.S. 199, 94 S.Ct. 1055, 39 L.Ed.2d 270 (1974).

66. 415 U.S. at 237, 94 S.Ct. at 1075.

67. See, e.g., Secretary of the Interior v. California, 464 U.S. 312, 321 n. 6, 104 S.Ct. 656, 661 n. 6, 78 L.Ed.2d 496 (1984), on remand 729 F.2d 614 (9th Cir.1984) ("Under normal circumstances NOAA's understanding of the meaning of CZMA Section 307(c)(1) would be entitled to deference by the courts. But in construing Sec. 307(c)(1) the agency has walked a path of such tortured vacillation and indecision that no help is to be gained in that quarter."); see also, United Housing Foundation, Inc. v. Forman, 421 U.S. 837, 95 S.Ct. 2051, 44 L.Ed.2d 621 (1975), rehearing denied 423 U.S. 884, 96 S.Ct. 157, 46 L.Ed.2d 115 (1975) ("in this case the SEC's position flatly contradicts what appears to be a rather careful statement of the Commission's views in a recent release," adding "in view of this unexplained contradiction in the Commission's position we accord no special weight to its views.").

68. See, e.g., North Haven Board of Education v. Bell, 456 U.S. 512, 522 n. 12, 102 S.Ct. 1912, 1918 n. 12, 72 L.Ed.2d 299 (1982); see also, General Electric Co. v. Gilbert, 429 U.S. 125, 97 S.Ct. 401, 50 L.Ed.2d 343 (1976), superseded by statute as stated in EEOC v. Horizon/CMS Healthcare Corp., 220 F.3d 1184 (10th Cir.2000) (The Court found that "the administrative interpretation of Title IX (of the Education Amendment of 1972) has changed, and a split has occurred between the federal agencies responsible for promulgating Title IX regulations.").

views if the court concludes that the agency did not give the ruling "thorough consideration."[69]

§ 13.8.4 Reliance

Public reliance on agency interpretations can also encourage judicial deference to agency interpretations. In *Udall v. Tallman,*[70] for example, oil lands in Alaska were leased on a first come, first serve basis. The lessees filed their application first, before the lands were opened up and their lease was granted. Respondents filed after the lands were opened up and were informed that the lands had already been leased. They brought an action in district court. After a summary judgment in favor of the Secretary of the Interior, they appealed. The appellate court reversed, holding that since they were the first to file after the lands were opened up, they were entitled to the lease. The Supreme Court reversed again, however, noting: "While [the leases] have been developed in reliance upon the Secretary's interpretation, respondents do not have a claim to have relied to their detriment upon a contrary construction. The Secretary's interpretation may not be the only one permitted by the language of the orders, but it is quite clearly a reasonable interpretation; courts must therefore respect it."[71]

A related consideration is whether the agency's interpretation involves a matter of "public controversy" that should have attracted congressional attention. In *United States v. Rutherford,*[72] the Food and Drug Administration, on remand from the District Court, determined that an alleged cancer drug, Laetrile, was a "new drug."[73] Since the agency also found that the drug was not protected by a grandfather clause it was not to be distributed without "full reports of investigations which have been made to show whether such a drug is safe for use, and whether such a drug is effective in use."[74] The Court of Appeals held that "an implied exemption from the Act was justified because the safety and effectiveness standards set forth in Sec. 201(p)(1) could have 'no reasonable application' to terminally ill patients."[75] The Supreme Court disagreed because the legislative intent and past FDA policy mandated that the terminally ill were not to be excepted from the Act. In agreeing with the agency's analysis, the court suggested that "deference is particularly appropriate where, as here, an agency's interpretation involves

69. See, e.g. SEC v. Sloan, 436 U.S. 103, 98 S.Ct. 1702, 56 L.Ed.2d 148 (1978); see also, Burlington Truck Lines, Inc. v. United States, 371 U.S. 156, 167, 83 S.Ct. 239, 245, 9 L.Ed.2d 207 (1962); c.f. Securities Industry Ass'n v. Board of Governors, 468 U.S. 207, 217, 104 S.Ct. 3003, 3009, 82 L.Ed.2d 158 (1984). However, even where a ruling reverses a long-standing policy, and is given less deference because of this, the ruling may still be upheld. See Healea v. Bowen, 871 F.2d 48 (7th Cir.1988).

70. 380 U.S. 1, 85 S.Ct. 792, 13 L.Ed.2d 616 (1965).

71. 380 U.S. at 4, 85 S.Ct. at 795; see also Train v. NRDC, 421 U.S. 60, 95 S.Ct. 1470, 43 L.Ed.2d 731 (1975).

72. 442 U.S. 544, 99 S.Ct. 2470, 61 L.Ed.2d 68 (1979), on remand 616 F.2d 455 (10th Cir.1980).

73. Sec. 201, 21 U.S.C.A. § 355.

74. Sec. 505, 21 U.S.C.A. § 355.

75. 442 U.S. at 554–55, 99 S.Ct. at 2476–77.

issues of considerable public controversy, and Congress has not acted to correct any misperception of its statutory objective."[76]

§ 13.8.5 Procedural Format Used by Agency

If an agency is not exercising its interpretive powers pursuant to rulemaking authority explicitly granted by Congress, the presumption of correctness that accompanies its interpretations cannot automatically be invoked. Courts thus have more discretion to defer or not defer in the context of agency interpretative rules.[77] In *Skidmore v. Swift & Co.,*[78] for example, the Court reviewed an Administrator's interpretations of the Fair Labor Standards Act. Seven firemen brought an action in Federal Court seeking compensation for the fact that they had to stay in the fire hall on Company premises three and a half to four nights a week. This involved no task, except to answer any alarms that might arise. The men used their time as they saw fit, but they were required to stay in or close to the fire hall and be ready to respond, if needed. The issue presented to the Court was whether this constituted "work" for purposes of the statute involved.

As the Court noted, this was not a case in which Congress utilized "the services of an administrative agency to find facts and to determine in the first instance whether particular cases fall within or without the Act."[79] Nevertheless, the Administrator (Secretary of Labor) was expected to think about issues such as these. Indeed, he set forth his views of the application of the Act under various circumstances in an interpretive bulletin and in various informal findings. None of these documents or statements had the force of law; nor, as the Court noted, were they developed in the context of adversary hearings:

> "The rulings of this Administrator are not reached as a result of hearing adversary procedures in which he finds facts from evidence and reaches conclusions of law from findings of fact. They are not, of course, conclusive, even in cases with which they directly deal, much less in those in which they apply only by analogy. They do not constitute an interpretation of the Act or a standard for judging factual situations which binds a district court's processes. . . ."[80]

The Court, nevertheless, went on to note that "the administrator's policies are made in pursuance of official duty, based upon more specialized experience and broader investigations and information than is likely to come to a judge in a particular case."[81] The Court thus found the Administrator's views rejecting the petitioner's requests for overtime

76. 442 U.S. at 554, 99 S.Ct. at 2476.

77. The Majority's approach in *Chevron v. NRDC,* sec. 13.7.2, supra, however, did not discuss the legislative-interpretation rule distinction. See 467 U.S. at 837, 104 S.Ct. at 2778. For an excellent discussion of the importance of the procedural format used to interpret the law, see Anthony, supra note 242.

78. 323 U.S. 134, 65 S.Ct. 161, 89 L.Ed. 124 (1944).

79. 323 U.S. at 137, 65 S.Ct. at 163.

80. Id. at 139, 65 S.Ct. at 164.

81. Id.

persuasive in this case. They were not binding, but the Court noted that the Administrator's rulings and interpretations in this area were entitled to respect, depending upon a variety of factors: "The weight of such a judgment in a particular case will depend upon the thoroughness evident in its consideration, the validity of its reasoning, its consistency with earlier and later pronouncement, and all those factors which give it power to persuade, if lacking power to control.... "[82]

The Supreme Court recently split on its reading of *Chevron* in *Skidmore* situations, where the administrative action in question is not necessarily a product of formal adjudication or public notice-and-comment procedures. In *Christensen v. Harris County*,[83] the various Supreme Court opinions suggest serious differences about the meaning of *Chevron* when applied to different types of agency decision-making. The Court dealt with an interpretation in an opinion letter, not unlike "interpretations contained in policy statements, agency manuals, and enforcement guidelines."[84] The majority opinion in that case held that "interpretations contained in formats such as opinion letters are 'entitled to respect' under our decision in *Skidmore v. Swift*, ... but only to the extent that those interpretations have the 'power to persuade'."[85] Justice Scalia disagreed. He argued that *Skidmore* was irrelevant after *Chevron* because the holding of that case was based on a broad theory of deference, unlike *Skidmore*.[86] Nevertheless, Justice Scalia reached the same result, under *Chevron*, that the majority reached applying *Skidmore*. Like the majority, he did not believe the statute or the regulations could prohibit the employer's action.[87]

Justice Stevens, in dissent joined by Justices Ginsberg and Breyer, relied on *Skidmore* as did Justice Breyer in a separate dissent, also joined by Justice Ginsburg. Justice Breyer argued that "*Skidmore* made clear that courts may pay particular attention to the views of an expert agency where they represent 'specialized experience', even if they do not constitute an exercise of delegated law making authority."[88] *Chevron*, on the other hand, "focused upon an additional separate legal reason for deferring to certain agency determinations, namely that Congress had delegated to the agency the legal authority to make those determinations."[89]

82. Id. at 140, 65 S.Ct. at 164. See also, General Electric Co. v. Gilbert, 429 U.S. 125, 141–45, 97 S.Ct. 401, 50 L.Ed.2d 343 (1976), superseded by statute as stated in EEOC v. Horizon/CMS Healthcare Corp., 220 F.3d 1184 (10th Cir.2000); Morton v. Ruiz, 415 U.S. 199, 231–37, 94 S.Ct. 1055, 1072–75, 39 L.Ed.2d 270 (1974).

83. 529 U.S. 576, 120 S.Ct. 1655, 146 L.Ed.2d 621 (2000).

84. Id. at 1662.

85. Id. at 1663.

86. Id. at 1664. Justice Scalia also cited a number of cases in which *Chevron* rather than *Skidmore* applied. See INS v. Aguirre–Aguirre, 526 U.S. 415, 425, 119 S.Ct. 1439, 143 L.Ed.2d 590 (1999); NationsBank of North Carolina, N.A. v. Variable Annuity Life Insurance Co., 513 U.S. 251, 256–57, 115 S.Ct. 810, 130 L.Ed.2d 740 (1995); Pension Benefit Guaranty Corp. v. LTV Corp., 496 U.S. 633, 647–48, 110 S.Ct. 2668, 110 L.Ed.2d 579 (1990); Young v. Community Nutrition Institute, 476 U.S. 974, 978–79, 106 S.Ct. 2360, 90 L.Ed.2d 959 (1986).

87. Christensen v. Harris County, 120 S.Ct. at 1664.

88. Id. at 1667.

89. Id. at 1668–69.

§ 13.9 JUDICIAL REVIEW OF AGENCY PROCEDURES

Another kind of question of law involves the procedures used or not used by an agency when exercising its powers. Section 706(2)(D) provides that courts may set aside agency actions that are "without observance of procedure required by law."[1] Courts have generally held that these procedural errors must, in fact, be prejudicial.[2] There generally is also a presumption of regularity that applies when agency procedures are challenged.[3] Nevertheless, agency failure to abide by the procedural requirements of the APA,[4] its own enabling act[5] or its own regulations may authorize judicial reversal.[6]

Courts have on occasion required more procedure than the APA explicitly requires in an effort to assure not only fair procedures at the agency level, but meaningful review in court. Interpreting the APA or other relevant procedural provisions so as to require decision-making procedures beyond what those provisions themselves required was

§ 13.9

1. 5 U.S.C.A. § 706(2)(D).

2. See, e.g., Small Refiner Lead Phase—Down Task Force v. US EPA, 705 F.2d 506, 521 (D.C.Cir.1983) ("The APA's prejudicial error rule ... requires only a *possibility* that the error would have resulted in some change in the final rule."); Weyerhaeuser Co. v. Costle, 590 F.2d 1011, 1031 n. 27 (D.C.Cir.1978).

3. See, e.g., United States v. Morgan, 313 U.S. 409, 421, 61 S.Ct. 999, 1004, 85 L.Ed. 1429 (1941); Schweiker v. McClure, 456 U.S. 188, 195, 102 S.Ct. 1665, 1669, 72 L.Ed.2d 1 (1982), superseded by statute as stated in Diagnostic Cardioline Monitoring of New York, Inc. v. Shalala, 2000 WL 1132273 (E.D.N.Y.2000); Withrow v. Larkin, 421 U.S. 35, 47, 95 S.Ct. 1456, 1464, 43 L.Ed.2d 712 (1975), on remand 408 F.Supp. 969 (E.D.Wis.1975).

4. For examples of agency failure to abide by the procedural requirements of the APA, see United States Dept. of Labor v. Kast Metals Corp., 744 F.2d 1145, 1149 (5th Cir.1984) ("an agency cannot out flank ... the APA's rulemaking framework by definitional fiat"); Community Nutrition Institute v. Butz, 420 F.Supp. 751, 754 (D.D.C. 1976) ("[w]hen a regulatory agency exercises its statutory authority to set standards and prescribe conduct, as in the case here, it must do so in accordance with the substantive rulemaking provisions of the APA"); Texaco, Inc. v. FPC, 412 F.2d 740 (3d Cir.1969) (FPC's action did not fall under "minor" or "emergency" exception to notice requirement. Its action was, therefore, set aside). See also N.L.R.B. v. Wyman–Gordon Co., 394 U.S. 759, 89 S.Ct. 1426, 22 L.Ed.2d 709 (1969); United States v. Frontier Airlines, Inc., 563 F.2d 1008 (10th Cir.1977) (Held: FAA did not meet burden of showing that it acted within authority. FAA did not follow the APA.); PPG Industries, Inc. v. Costle, 659 F.2d 1239 (D.C.Cir.1981) (EPA failed to meet notice requirement of APA); Appalachian Power Co. v. Train, 566 F.2d 451, 457 (4th Cir. 1977) (inadequate publication); Ford Motor Co. v. United States, 567 F.2d 661 (6th Cir.1977) (same); Marathon Oil Co. v. EPA, 564 F.2d 1253, 1271–72 (9th Cir.1977) (nondisclosure of data).

5. For examples of agency failure to abide by its own enabling act, see Doraiswamy v. Secretary of Labor, 555 F.2d 832 (D.C.Cir.1976) ("An administrative agency is bound not only by the precepts of its governing statute but also by those incorporated into its own regulations."); Atchison, Topeka, and Santa Fe Railway Company, et al. v. ICC, 607 F.2d 1199 (7th Cir.1979) (no statutory authority was found for "tariff" publication of operating schedules); City of Santa Clara v. Andrus, 572 F.2d 660 (9th Cir.1978), cert. denied 439 U.S. 859, 99 S.Ct. 176, 58 L.Ed.2d 167 (1978) ("Administrative actions taken in violation of statutory authority or requirement are of no effect."); Office of Consumers' Counsel v. FERC, 655 F.2d 1132 (D.C.Cir.1980).

6. For examples of agency failure to abide by its own regulations, see *Doraiswamy,* supra note 332; Nader v. NRC, 513 F.2d 1045 (D.C.Cir.1975) (NRC's order invalid since it did not comply with its own regulations); Morton v. Ruiz, 415 U.S. 199, 94 S.Ct. 1055, 39 L.Ed.2d 270 (1974) ("Where the rights of individuals are affected, it is incumbent upon agencies to follow their own procedures.").

roundly condemned by the Supreme Court in *Vermont Yankee v. NRDC.*[7] Yet, that case itself suggested that, in some instances, additional procedural care on the part of an agency may be necessary to assure "meaningful judicial review." Determining when a procedural requirement is statutorily based or, in fact, represents the application of administrative common law is by no means an easy judicial task.[8]

§ 13.9.1 The Hard Look Doctrine and Agency Procedure: Judicial Innovation and Administrative Common Law

Section 553(c) of the APA requires that there be "a concise general statement" of the "basis and purpose" of rules promulgated pursuant to this provision. As we shall see,[9] the failure to comply with section 553(c) can be seen as a procedural as well as a substantive requirement. Just how good a reason must be given to satisfy this requirement is frequently in contention when courts review the merits of agency rules.[10]

In 1976 Judges Leventhal and Bazelon engaged in a famous debate in *Ethyl Corp. v. EPA.*[11] Judge Bazelon argued that "technically illiterate" judges should not get involved in the substance of agency decisions.[12] His solution to the need for courts to supervise agency decisionmaking reasoned decisionmaking was purely procedural: "in cases of great technological complexity, the best way for courts to guard against unreasonable or erroneous administrative decisions is not for the judges themselves to scrutinize the technical merits of each decision. Rather, it

7. For a discussion of this case and its significance see chapter 2, sec. 2.2.2, supra. See also, Scalia, *Vermont Yankee:* The APA, the D.C. Circuit and the Supreme Court, 1978 Sup.Ct.Rev. 345; Stewart, The Development of Administrative and Quasi-Constitution Law in Judicial review of Environmental Decision-making: Lessons from the Civil Rights Act, 62 Iowa L.Rev. 713, 731–733 (1977); Byse, *Vermont Yankee* and the Evolution of Administrative Procedure: A somewhat Different View, 91 Harv.L.Rev. 1823, 1828–1829 (1978).

Courts have used the *Vermont Yankee* decision in order to dismiss plaintiff's claim that administrative common law does exist: see Granville House, Inc. v. Department of Health, Educ. and Welfare 772 F.2d 451, 457 (8th Cir.1985); National Classification Committee and National Motor Freight Traffic Association, Inc. v. I.C.C., 765 F.2d 1146 (D.C.Cir.1985); Baylor University Medical Center v. Heckler, 758 F.2d 1052 (5th Cir.1985); Bedford County General Hospital v. Heckler, 757 F.2d 87 (6th Cir. 1985).

8. See generally, Howarth, Informal Agency Rulemaking and the Courts: A Theory for Procedural Review, 61 Wash.U.L.Q. 891 (1984).

9. See sec. 13.10.4, infra.

10. See sec. 13.10.6, infra for detailed discussion of the substance of the reasons agencies give to justify their rules. For cases reversing an agency decision for failure to explain their decisions adequately, see, e.g., Hooker Chemicals & Plastics Corp. v. Train, 537 F.2d 639, 642 (2d Cir.1976); American Petroleum Institute v. EPA, 661 F.2d 340, 357 (5th Cir.1981); National Renderers Ass'n v. EPA, 541 F.2d 1281, 1287 (8th Cir.1976) (failure to explain costs); Appalachian Power Co. v. Train, 545 F.2d 1351, 1364 n. 31 (4th Cir.1976) (failure to explore benefits); CPC International Inc. v. Train, 540 F.2d 1329, 1339 n. 12 (8th Cir. 1976), cert. denied 430 U.S. 966, 97 S.Ct. 1646, 52 L.Ed.2d 357 (1977) (indecipherable date); Marathon Oil Co. v. EPA, 564 F.2d 1253, 1271–72 (9th Cir.1977) (nondisclosure of data); Tanners' Council of America, Inc. v. Train, 540 F.2d 1188, 1193 (4th Cir.1976) (lack of hard analysis).

11. 541 F.2d 1, 66–69 (D.C.Cir.1976), cert. denied 426 U.S. 941, 96 S.Ct. 2662, 49 L.Ed.2d 394. See also, Friends of the Earth v. U.S. Atomic Energy Commission, 485 F.2d 1031, 1032–35 (D.C.Cir.1973).

12. 541 F.2d at 66–67.

is to establish a decision-making process that assures a reasoned decision that can be held up to the scrutiny of the scientific community."[13]

Judge Leventhal disagreed. He argued that substantive review was, in fact, necessary if judges were to carry out their statutory and constitutional duties: "The substantive review of administrative action is modest, but it cannot be carried out in a vacuum of understanding. Better no judicial review at all than a charade that gives the imprimatur without the substance of judicial confirmation that the agency is not acting unreasonably."[14] Judge Leventhal went on to emphasize that he was not advocating wholesale substitution of judicial judgments for that of the agency. He concluded, however, that: "on issues of substantive review, on conformance to statutory standards and requirements of rationality, the judges must act with restraint. Restraint, yes, abdication, no."[15]

This debate took place during an era of judicial activism that centered largely on the review of new environmental regulations, particularly those implementing the Clean Air Act of 1970. In *Kennecott Copper Corp. v. EPA,*[16] the court, noting that it was " 'in a real sense part of the total administrative process,' "[17] considered a challenge to an EPA rule setting national air quality standards limiting common industrial wastes such as sulfur oxides to 60 micrograms per cubic meter. In support of its rule, the Administrator cited a study previously published by the government, but one that referred to no figure lower than 85 micrograms per cubic meter. The government contended that its figure of 60 could be produced by the actual criteria used in that government report and that, in any event, 60 micrograms was within an acceptable margin of error.

The court stated that the agency was not required, in a proceeding governed by section 553 of the APA, to provide the same articulation required for orders or regulations issued after full, evidentiary hearings. Indeed, the court explicitly recognized that the agency had fully complied with section 553(c)'s requirement that there be a "concise general statement" of the basis and purpose of the regulation.[18] It also noted Congress' apparent desire to expedite the issuance of such rules. Nevertheless, the court concluded that "there are contexts of fact, statutory framework and nature of action, in which the minimum requirements of the Administrative Procedure Act may not be sufficient."[19] Thus, the court remanded the rule to the agency for further elaboration "[i]n the interest of justice ... and in aid of the judicial function, centralized in

13. Id.

14. Id. at 69.

15. Id. (In *Ethyl Corp.,* the court upheld an order of the Environmental Protection Agency requiring annual reductions in the lead content of leaded gasoline.).

16. 462 F.2d 846 (D.C.Cir.1972).

17. Id. at 849 (quoting Greater Boston Television Corp. v. FCC, 444 F.2d 841, 851–52 (D.C.Cir.1970), cert. denied 403 U.S. 923, 91 S.Ct. 2233, 29 L.Ed.2d 701 (1971)), stay denied, 405 U.S. 982, 92 S.Ct. 1242, 31 L.Ed.2d 449 (1972).

18. Id. at 850.

19. Id.

this court, [and] of expeditious disposition of challenges to standards. . . ."[20] On remand, the agency revised its standard.[21]

The court's involvement in Clean Air Act cases escalated in *International Harvester Co. v. Ruckelshaus.*[22] In that case, three major automobile manufacturers challenged an EPA decision denying them a one year suspension of the Clean Air Act emission standards promulgated by the agency. The auto makers prevailed because the court concluded that the agency's technical methodology for measuring emission standards should have been subject to comment by industry. Failure to open up this aspect of the decision to public comments, the court held, undermined an informed decision-making process. To correct this, the court not only reversed and remanded the case to the agency, but it specified that the parties were to be given an opportunity to comment on matters not previously set out for the public by EPA. In addition, they were to have a chance to cross-examine agency officials concerning the old and the new materials.[23]

In *Portland Cement Ass'n v. Ruckelshaus,*[24] another important Clean Air Act case, the D.C. Circuit went further, mandating additional agency procedures. The court required the agency not only to reopen its rulemaking proceedings and to give manufacturers the opportunity to see and comment upon certain evidence involving agency test results and procedures, but it also required an agency response to petitioners complaints about methodology. The agency had failed to allow parties to comment on EPA's methodology, even though the agency had published some additional materials presumably supporting its rules governing the emission of cement dust.

The court invoked what it called a hard look approach, noting that: "This agency, particularly when its decisions can literally mean survival of persons or property, has a continuing duty to take a 'hard look' at the problems involved in its regulatory task, and that includes an obligation to comment on matters identified as potentially significant by the [earlier] court order remanding for further presentation."[25] The court was quick to add that not all comments required a response, but only those "significant enough to step over a threshold requirement of materiality. . . ."[26]

These kinds of procedural innovations were eventually incorporated into the legislation governing the EPA. The 1977 amendments to the

20. Id.

21. For an interesting discussion by one of the EPA's attorneys supporting the additional procedure required by the D.C. Circuit, see Pedersen, Formal Records and Informal Rulemaking, 85 Yale L.J. 38 (1975).

22. 478 F.2d 615 (D.C.Cir.1973).

23. Id. at 649.

24. 486 F.2d 375 (D.C.Cir.1973), cert. denied 417 U.S. 921, 94 S.Ct. 2628, 41 L.Ed.2d 226 (1974).

25. Id. at 394.

26. Id. at 394. On remand the Administrator reaffirmed the regulation and added a more complete response. This rule was later upheld in Portland Cement Ass'n v. Train, 513 F.2d 506 (D.C.Cir.1975), cert. denied 423 U.S. 1025, 96 S.Ct. 469, 46 L.Ed.2d 399 (1975), rehearing denied 423 U.S. 1092, 96 S.Ct. 889, 47 L.Ed.2d 104 (1976).

Clean Air Act essentially codified many of the D.C. Circuit's rulemaking innovations.[27] This kind of creative judicial supervisory role was at the heart of the dispute in *Vermont Yankee Nuclear Power Corp. v. NRDC.*[28] In that case, the Supreme Court, in no uncertain terms, made clear that if procedures other than those required by the APA were necessary, mandating that these new procedures be used was the job of Congress, not the D.C. Circuit Court of Appeals. *Vermont Yankee* was thus a judicial attempt to put an end to the development of administrative common law.[29] Implicitly, cases such as *Portland Cement, Kennecott Copper,* and *International Harvester* rest either on the assumption that courts can create a kind of administrative common law or that such additional procedural requirements were, in fact, constitutionally based. In *Ethyl Corp. v. EPA,*[30] Judge Leventhal had argued that:

> [i]n the case of legislative enactments, the sole responsibility of the courts is constitutional due process review. In the case of agency decision-making the courts have an additional responsibility set by Congress. Congress has been willing to delegate its legislative powers broadly—and courts have upheld such delegation—because there is court review to assure that the agency exercises the delegated power within statutory limits, and that it fleshes out objectives within those limits by an administration that is not irrational or discriminatory.[31]

This substantive basis for closer judicial review survived the Court's decision in *Vermont Yankee;* however, the ability of courts to control agency discretion solely by the imposition of procedures not found in the APA, the agency's enabling act, its own regulations or mandated by the Constitution clearly did not.

§ 13.10 JUDICIAL REVIEW OF AGENCY POLICY

This section examines the scope of judicial review of agency policy decisions. These decisions can be made in the context of formal adjudica-

27. See, e.g., 2 William H. Rodgers, Jr., Environmental Law, Air and Water, 36–45 (1986).

28. 435 U.S. 519, 98 S.Ct. 1197, 55 L.Ed.2d 460 (1978), on remand 685 F.2d 459 (D.C.Cir.1982). This case is discussed in detail in chapter 2, sec. 2.2, supra.

29. The opinion, itself, however, leaves open the possibility that the agencies themselves may have additional procedures to assure meaningful judicial review. See, e.g., Independent United States Tanker Owners Committee v. Lewis, 690 F.2d 908 (D.C.Cir. 1982); Illinois v. United States, 666 F.2d 1066 (7th Cir.1981), appeal after remand 698 F.2d 888 (1983); Lead Industries Ass'n v. EPA, 647 F.2d 1130 (D.C.Cir.1980), cert. denied 449 U.S. 1042, 101 S.Ct. 621, 66 L.Ed.2d 503 (1980); National Lime Ass'n v. EPA, 627 F.2d 416 (D.C.Cir.1980). See also Howarth, supra note 335, at 892, noting that some lower courts have ignored the spirit of *Vermont Yankee,* citing, e.g., Connecticut Light and Power Co. v. NRC, 673 F.2d 525 (D.C.Cir.1982) cert. denied, 459 U.S. 835, 103 S.Ct. 79, 74 L.Ed.2d 76 (1982); National Lime Ass'n v. EPA, 627 F.2d 416 (D.C.Cir.1980); East Texas Motor Freight Lines, Inc. v. United States, 593 F.2d 691 (5th Cir.1979); Weyerhaeuser Co. v. Costle, 590 F.2d 1011 (D.C.Cir.1978). See generally, Note, Counter Revolution in the Federal Courts of Appeals—The Aftermath of *Vermont Yankee,* 15 U.Rich.L.Rev. 723–730 (1981).

30. 541 F.2d 1 (D.C.Cir.1976), cert. denied 426 U.S. 941, 96 S.Ct. 2662, 49 L.Ed.2d 394 (1976).

31. Id. at 68 (footnotes omitted).

tory or rulemaking proceedings; they also may be the result of hybrid rulemaking proceedings,[1] informal proceedings such as those pursuant to section 553 of the APA or even more informal agency action that falls outside of the procedural ambit of either APA rulemaking or adjudication. Courts usually apply the arbitrary and capricious standard of review found in section 706(2)(A) of the APA when assessing the reasonableness of such decisions. In most cases, there is a presumption that the agency has been reasonable in carrying out its statutory duties. Those challenging the substance of an agency's decision have the burden of showing it to be unreasonable or, in effect, "arbitrary, capricious and an abuse of discretion."

This section will focus, in particular, on judicial review of agency policies made in the context of informal or hybrid rulemaking proceedings. As we shall see, courts have, over time, judicialized the processes by which such policies are made by, in effect, requiring an administrative record for purposes of judicial review as well as, in some cases, a reasonably detailed explanation of why an agency has adopted the policies in question.

§ 13.10.1 Pre–APA Judicial Review of Agency Rules

When courts reviewed agency policy judgments prior to the APA, they treated them very much the way they might treat a piece of legislation challenged as unreasonable on constitutional grounds. There was no expectation that the legislation involved be based on a record. In most cases the proponent of the legislation need only show that there was a rational basis for the legislation. Post hoc rationalizations were acceptable.[2]

Pacific States Box & Basket Co. v. White[3] typified the deferential kind of judicial approach taken to the review of agency rules. In that case, the Pacific Box Company challenged an Oregon regulation prescribing uniform container sizes for strawberries and raspberries. The regulation was promulgated by the Oregon Department of Agriculture prior to any federal or state version of the APA. Pacific Box challenged the regulation primarily on substantive due process grounds.[4] To meet this challenge, legislation had to meet a minimum rationality requirement. Specifically, a challenger would have to rebut a presumption of the existence of any set of facts which might support the legislative action:

> "When such legislative action 'is called in question, if any state of facts reasonably can be conceived that would sustain it, there is a presumption of the existence of that state of facts, and one who

§ 13.10

1. See chapter 2, sec. 2.2, supra.

2. For an example of this kind of judicial deference to legislation dealing with economic issues after the demise of *Lochner v. N.Y.*, see, e.g. Williamson v. Lee Optical, 348 U.S. 483, 75 S.Ct. 461, 99 L.Ed. 563 (1955), rehearing denied 349 U.S. 925, 75 S.Ct. 657, 99 L.Ed. 1256 (1955).

3. 296 U.S. 176, 56 S.Ct. 159, 80 L.Ed. 138 (1935).

4. Appellants also made an equal protection claim and a commerce clause claim. 296 U.S. at 180, 56 S.Ct. at 161.

assails the classification must carry the burden of showing by a resort to common knowledge or other matters which may be judicially noticed, or to other legitimate proof, that the action is arbitrary.' "[5]

The unique question posed by this case, however, was whether administrative regulations as opposed to legislation, must meet this or an even stronger standard. Justice Brandeis, writing for the Court, held that the tests were identical: "[T]he presumption of the existence of facts justifying its specific exercise attaches alike to statutes, to municipal ordinances, and to orders of administrative bodies."[6]

After enactment of the APA, courts continued to defer to agency judgments about policy issues, but the agency itself had to explain the reasons behind its policies. It was important that the reasons given be those of the agency[7] and that they be something other than "post-hoc rationalizations." This was a significant step beyond the approach taken in *Pacific States.* These basic principles and the approaches to judicial review of agency action as opposed to legislation were formally established in the *Chenery* cases.

The first time *SEC v. Chenery Corp.*[8] reached the Supreme Court, the Court dealt with an agency decision that set aside a particular corporate reorganization on grounds that certain common law judicial precedents did not allow it. The Supreme Court did not necessarily disagree with the result reached by the SEC,[9] but it held that this result could not be justified on the grounds asserted by the agency. The case was reversed and remanded to the agency. On remand, the SEC again refused to approve the proposed reorganization. This time, however, it did not rely on judicial precedents, but its own interpretation of its governing statute.[10]

The case was appealed again and the Supreme Court reviewed it once more. In *Chenery II,* the Court explained its view of the role of the administrative process and the respective roles that courts and agencies should play. In the Court's view, a fundamental rule of administrative law was that a reviewing court must judge the propriety of an agency's action solely by the grounds invoked by the agency. Were it to agree with the agency's results, but then substitute a rationale supporting those results that it believed was more appropriate, it would "propel the court

5. 296 U.S. at 185, 56 S.Ct. at 163.

6. 296 U.S. at 186, 56 S.Ct. at 164.

7. See SEC v. Chenery Corp., 332 U.S. 194, 67 S.Ct. 1575, 91 L.Ed. 1995 (1947).

8. This case reached the Supreme Court twice in SEC v. Chenery Corp., 318 U.S. 80, 63 S.Ct. 454, 87 L.Ed. 626 (1943) (*Chenery I*) and 332 U.S. 194, 67 S.Ct. 1575, 91 L.Ed. 1995 (1947) (*Chenery II*). For a brief discussion of the relationships of these cases to the hard look doctrine discussed infra, see Garland, Deregulation and Judicial Review, 98 Harv.L.Rev. 505, 526 (1985).

9. *Chenery I,* the Court reviewed the SEC's decision under the Public Utility Holding Company Act approving a voluntary reorganization plan on the condition that preferred stock purchased pursuant to the reorganization plan could only be sold at cost plus four per cent rather than the usual procedure allowance providing for conversion of preferred stock into common stock.

10. *Chenery II,* 332 U.S. at 199, 67 S.Ct. at 1578.

into the domain which Congress has set aside exclusively for the administrative agency."[11] Despite Justice Jackson's sense of exasperation expressed in dissent,[12] the Court went on to emphasize that:

> If the administrative action is to be tested by the basis upon which it purports to rest, that basis must be set forth with such clarity as to be understandable. It will not do for a court to be compelled to guess at the theory underlying the agency's action; nor can a court be expected to chisel that which must be precise from what the agency has left vague and indecisive. In other words, "We must know what a decision means before the duty becomes ours to say whether it is right or wrong."[13]

In taking this approach to agency decision-making, however, the courts in the *Chenery* cases did not necessarily demand a good explanation or the best explanation an agency could offer. Rather, courts simply demanded a rational agency explanation that would help show that the agency's action was within its statutory powers.[14]

§ 13.10.2 The APA and Degrees of Rationality

The reasons an agency gives for its policy judgments need not be the best reasons or even relatively good reasons, as far as the courts are concerned. Agency actions usually are upheld in the face of rationality challenges as long as the agency gives a reason for its actions. In the usual case, courts seldom invalidate federal agency decisions under the arbitrary and capricious standard[15] because they disagree with the reasons an agency gives for its actions.[16] This is because, courts emphasize,

11. 332 U.S. at 196, 67 S.Ct. at 1577.

12. Justice Jackson, somewhat incredulously, noted that the Court had now "sustain[ed] the identical administrative order which only recently it held invalid." 332 U.S. at 209, 67 S.Ct. at 1760. He went on to remark: "I give up. Now I realize fully what Mark Twain meant when he said, 'The more you explain it, the more I don't understand it.' " Id. at 214, 67 S.Ct. at 1762.

13. Id. at 196–97, 67 S.Ct. at 1577–78, (citing United States v. Chicago, M., St.P. & P.R. Co., 294 U.S. 499, 511, 55 S.Ct. 462, 467, 79 L.Ed. 1023 (1935)).

14. See also Bowman Transp., Inc. v. Arkansas–Best Freight System, Inc., 419 U.S. 281, 285–86, 95 S.Ct. 438, 442, 42 L.Ed.2d 447 (1974), rehearing denied 420 U.S. 956, 95 S.Ct. 1340, 43 L.Ed.2d 433 (1975); Atchison, T. & S.F. Ry. Co. v. Wichita Bd. of Trade, 412 U.S. 800, 807–08, 93 S.Ct. 2367, 2375, 37 L.Ed.2d 350 (1973); Colorado Interstate Gas Co. v. Federal Power Com'n, 324 U.S. 581, 595, 65 S.Ct. 829, 836, 89 L.Ed. 1206 (1945). Eventually, courts also required this explanation to be contemporaneous with the agency's decision, and not simply a post-hoc rationalization. See, e.g., American Textile Mfrs. Institute v. Donovan, 452 U.S. 490, 539, 101 S.Ct. 2478, 2505, 69 L.Ed.2d 185 (1981); Camp v. Pitts, 411 U.S. 138, 143, 93 S.Ct. 1241, 1244, 36 L.Ed.2d 106 (1973); Citizens to Preserve Overton Park, Inc. v. Volpe, 401 U.S. 402, 419, 91 S.Ct. 814, 825, 28 L.Ed.2d 136 (1971); American Trucking Ass'n, Inc. v. United States, 688 F.2d 1337, 1346 (11th Cir.1982), cert. denied 467 U.S. 1240, 104 S.Ct. 3509, 82 L.Ed.2d 819 (1984).

15. See, e.g., Bowman Transportation, Inc. v. Arkansas–Best Freight System, Inc., 419 U.S. 281, 95 S.Ct. 438, 42 L.Ed.2d 447 (1974), rehearing denied 420 U.S. 956, 95 S.Ct. 1340, 43 L.Ed.2d 433 (1975). See also National Small Shipments Traffic Conference, Inc. v. Civil Aeronautics Board, 618 F.2d 819, 826 (D.C.Cir.1980).

16. See Citizens to Preserve Overton Park, Inc. v. Volpe, 401 U.S. 402, 416, 91 S.Ct. 814, 824, 28 L.Ed.2d 136 (1971) ("[a]lthough this inquiry into the facts is to be searching and careful, the ultimate standard of review is a narrow one. The court is not empowered to substitute its judgment for that of the agency"); Duke Power Co. v.

that it is not their function to substitute their own judgment for that of the agency.[17]

On occasion, however, agency policy decisions challenged as arbitrary and capricious are particularly confused or misguided.[18] The application of the arbitrary and capricious standard, particularly in the context of hybrid rulemaking procedures, also has given rise to variants of the so-called hard-look doctrine. As we shall see below, in certain cases courts have demanded that the agency give more than a reason, but, in effect, a good reason before they uphold its actions.[19] Short of the hard-look cases, however, rationality review of administrative action can result in closer judicial scrutiny of agency policy judgments than in the past.[20] Even in cases that uphold agency policy determinations, the level of judicial scrutiny often requires not just a reason, but an understandable, coherent reason. This is not necessarily a reflection on any greater activism on the part of the court. It often has more to do with the complicated nature of the decisions made by the agency.

In *Baltimore Gas and Elec. Co. v. Natural Resources Defense Council, Inc.*,[21] for example, the Supreme Court unanimously upheld a rule promulgated by the Nuclear Regulatory Commission and attacked as arbitrary, capricious, and an abuse of discretion. The complicated nature of the rule involved, however, resulted in an approach to judicial review that was far from pro-forma. The rule in question required that NRC licensing boards, when considering license applications for new nuclear plants, not give any negative environmental weight to the risks of radiation escape from long-term spent fuel storage. In assessing the rationality of the Commission's rule, the Court noted that it was "crucial

NRC, 770 F.2d 386, 390–91 (4th Cir.1985); United States v. Garner, 767 F.2d 104, 116 (5th Cir.1985); Scenic Hudson Preservation Conference v. FPC, 453 F.2d 463, 468 (2d Cir.1971), cert. denied 407 U.S. 926, 92 S.Ct. 2453, 32 L.Ed.2d 813 (1972).

17. See, e.g., Levin, Scope of Review Doctrine Restated: An Administrative Law Section Report, 38 Admin.L.Rev. 239, 254 (1986) (citing Dugan v. Ramsay, 727 F.2d 192 (1st Cir.1984)); Conway v. Watt, 717 F.2d 512 (10th Cir.1983); National Ass'n of Independent Television Producers and Distributors v. FCC, 516 F.2d 526, 534–35 (2d Cir.1975); Robert E. Derecktor of R.I., Inc. v. Goldschmidt, 506 F.Supp. 1059, 1065–66 (D.R.I.1980).

18. See, e.g., Dugan v. Ramsay, 727 F.2d 192 (1st Cir.1984); Conway v. Watt, 717 F.2d 512 (10th Cir.1983); National Association of Independent Television Producers and Distributors v. FCC, 516 F.2d 526, 542–43 (2d Cir.1975) (cited in, Levin, supra note 375, at 254). See also, Motor Vehicle Mfrs. Ass'n v. State Farm Mutual Auto. Ins., 463 U.S. 29, 43, 103 S.Ct. 2856, 2867, 77 L.Ed.2d 443 (1983), appeal after remand 802 F.2d 474 (D.C.Cir.1986), cert. denied 480 U.S. 951, 107 S.Ct. 1616, 94 L.Ed.2d 800 (1987).

19. See sec. 13.10.5, infra.

20. See, e.g., National Ass'n of Independent Television Producers and Distributors v. FCC, 516 F.2d 526 (2d Cir.1975); National Tire Dealers & Retreaders Ass'n, Inc. v. Brinegar, 491 F.2d 31 (D.C.Cir. 1974); see also, Aqua Slide 'N' Dive Corp. v. Consumer Product Safety Com'n, 569 F.2d 831 (5th Cir.1978); Home Box Office, Inc. v. FCC, 567 F.2d 9 (D.C.Cir.1977), cert denied, 434 U.S. 829, 98 S.Ct. 111, 54 L.Ed.2d 89 (1977); Health Systems Agency of Oklahoma, Inc. v. Norman, 589 F.2d 486 (10th Cir.1978); Hurley v. United States, 575 F.2d 792 (10th Cir.1978); Process Gas Consumers Group v. U.S. Dept. of Agriculture, 694 F.2d 728, 761–62 (D.C.Cir.1981), vacated in part on rehearing, 694 F.2d 778 (D.C.Cir. 1982); American Academy of Pediatrics v. Heckler, 561 F.Supp. 395 (D.D.C.1983).

21. 462 U.S. 87, 103 S.Ct. 2246, 76 L.Ed.2d 437 (1983).

to place the zero-release assumption in context."[22] This required the evaluation of three interrelated factors—the limited purpose for which the zero assumption applied, the fact that it was but a single figure in an entire table, and that "a reviewing court must remember that the Commission is making predictions, within its area of special expertise, at the frontiers of science."[23] With these factors as background, the Court was able to conclude that the Commission's decision was within the bounds of reasoned decisionmaking. Though it gave the benefit of the doubt to the Commission and took a deferential approach to the agency's ultimate conclusions, the complicated nature and importance of the issues involved demanded relatively close judicial analysis of the various and complicated interrelationships of the agency issues involved.

Increasingly, courts' closer examination of agency judgments and their demand for a clear statement of the basis and purpose of the agency action involved have led to reversals of agency actions.[24] Many of these cases have involved use of a variant of the hard look or reasoned decisionmaking doctrine.[25] But courts have also reversed agency policy decisions as violative of only the arbitrary and capricious standard of the APA, without any explicit invocation of the hard look doctrine or use of a substantial evidence standard found in hybrid rulemaking statutes.[26]

22. 462 U.S. at 101, 103 S.Ct. at 2254.

23. 462 U.S. at 103, 103 S.Ct. at 2255.

24. See, e.g., United States v. Garner, 767 F.2d 104, 116–18 (5th Cir.1985); Maryland People's Counsel v. FERC, 761 F.2d 768 (D.C.Cir.1985); International Broth. of Teamsters v. United States, 735 F.2d 1525 (D.C.Cir.1984); National Lime Ass'n v. EPA, 627 F.2d 416, 431 (D.C.Cir.1980); Central Florida Enterprises, Inc. FCC, 598 F.2d 37, 50 (D.C.Cir.1978), cert. dismissed 441 U.S. 957, 99 S.Ct. 2189, 60 L.Ed.2d 1062 (1979); National Propane Gas Ass'n v. U.S. Dept. of Transp., 43 F.Supp.2d 665 (N.D.Tex.1999). See also National Ass'n of Independent Television Producers and Distributors v. FCC, 516 F.2d 526 (2d Cir. 1975); National Tire Dealers & Retreaders Ass'n, Inc. v. Brinegar, 491 F.2d 31 (D.C.Cir.1974); Columbia Broadcasting System, Inc. v. FCC, 454 F.2d 1018 (D.C.Cir. 1971). See, Shapiro and Levy, Heightened Scrutiny of the Fourth Branch: Separation of Powers and the Requirement of Adequate Reasons for Agency Decisions, 1987 Duke L.J. 387 (1987).

25. See sec. 13.10.5 infra. See, e.g., Greater Boston Television Corp. v. FCC, 444 F.2d 841, 852 (D.C.Cir.1970), cert. denied 403 U.S. 923, 91 S.Ct. 2233, 29 L.Ed.2d 701 (1971), stay denied, WHDH, Inc. v. FCC, 405 U.S. 982, 92 S.Ct. 1242, 31 L.Ed.2d 449 (1972); Independent Air, Inc. v. DOT, 767 F.2d 1488 (11th Cir.1985).

26. See, e.g., National Association of Independent Television Producers and Distributors v. FCC, 516 F.2d 526 (2d Cir. 1975). For other cases reversing agency action as arbitrary, capricious, and an abuse of discretion, see Jen Hung Ng v. INS, 804 F.2d 534 (9th Cir.1986); Motor Vehicle Mfrs. Ass'n of the United States, Inc. v. EPA, 768 F.2d 385 (D.C.Cir.1985), cert denied 474 U.S. 1082, 106 S.Ct. 852, 88 L.Ed.2d 892 (1986); National Tire Dealers & Retreaders Ass'n, Inc. v. Brinegar, 491 F.2d 31 (D.C.Cir.1974); CBS, Inc. v. FCC, 454 F.2d 1018 (D.C.Cir.1971). For other cases that take more of a hard look approach, see sec. 13.10.6, infra. See also Process Gas Consumers Group v. U.S. Dept. of Agriculture, 694 F.2d 728, 761–62 (D.C.Cir. 1981), opinion vacated in part on rehearing, 694 F.2d 778 (D.C Cir. 1982); Health Systems Agency of Oklahoma, Inc. v. Norman, 589 F.2d 486 (10th Cir.1978); Hurley v. United States, 575 F.2d 792 (10th Cir. 1978), appeal after remand 624 F.2d 93 (1980); Aqua Slide 'N' Dive Corp. v. Consumer Product Safety Commission, 569 F.2d 831 (5th Cir.1978); Home Box Office, Inc. v. FCC, 567 F.2d 9 (D.C.Cir.1977), cert. denied 434 U.S. 829, 98 S.Ct. 111, 54 L.Ed.2d 89 (1977); American Academy of Pediatrics v. Heckler, 561 F.Supp. 395 (D.D.C.1983); Arlington Hospital v. Schweiker, 547 F.Supp. 670 (E.D.Va.1982); Robert E. Derecktor of Rhode Island Inc. v. Goldschmidt, 506 F.Supp. 1059 (D.R.I. 1980); Community Nutrition Institute v. Bergland, 493 F.Supp. 488 (D.D.C.1980).

Even in cases that ultimately uphold an agency's decision, the influence of a modified rational basis approach can be seen in the courts' description of what the agency must show in order to prevail. In *Shoreham Cooperative Apple Producers Ass'n, Inc. v. Donovan,*[27] for example, various apple producers challenged a Department of Labor rule setting forth a new procedure for computing the wage rate at which immigrant labor may be hired. Although the challengers demonstrated some clear flaws with the new method, the court found that the agency's decision was rational. It had considered the objections and had given reasons for what it did. The "DOL was not required ... to rebut every alleged flaw with empirical data."[28] Yet, the court did note that it must "supply a *detailed* and rational explanation of its decision to adopt" the rule.[29] As we shall see below, courts' requirements of reasoned decision-making can increase, substantially, the amount of judicial scrutiny provided in individual cases.[30] To better understand the rhetorical and substantive basis for closer judicial scrutiny of agency policy determinations, it is useful to examine first an important precedent for purposes of such review, *Citizens to Preserve Overton Park, Inc. v. Volpe.*[31]

§ 13.10.3 The Scope of Judicial Review of Informal Agency Policy Judgments: *Citizens to Preserve Overton Park Inc. v. Volpe*

Agencies make policy in a variety of procedural contexts. As we have discussed in Chapter 9, agencies perform most of their tasks informally.[31] While most of these decisions do not produce justiciable results, informal agency action is not necessarily immune from review. *Citizens to Preserve Overton Park, Inc. v. Volpe,*[32] for example, authorized judicial review of certain kinds of informal agency actions thought to have been immune from review. In so doing, the Court in *Overton Park* has had substantial influence on the scope of judicial review in subsequent rulemaking cases, even though *Overton Park* itself involved judicial review of informal agency action. The case merits our close attention.

In *Overton Park,* Secretary of Transportation Volpe approved the construction of a six lane interstate highway through Overton Park in Memphis, Tennessee. He thus authorized federal funds for the project even though the Federal–Aid Highway Act of 1968 required that he not approve such construction if a "feasible and prudent" alternate route existed.[33] That act also required that all possible planning be undertaken to minimize harm to the park.[34] The Secretary did not provide any

27. 764 F.2d 135 (2d Cir.1985).

28. Id. at 142.

29. Id. (emphasis added). See also Air Line Pilots Ass'n International v. Department of Transportation, 791 F.2d 172 (D.C.Cir.1986).

30. See sec. 13.10.5, infra.

31. 401 U.S. 402, 91 S.Ct. 814, 28 L.Ed.2d 136 (1971).

31. See chapter 9, sec. 9.1, supra.

32. 401 U.S. 402, 91 S.Ct. 814, 28 L.Ed.2d 136 (1971).

33. 401 U.S. at 404–05, 91 S.Ct. at 817–18.

34. Id. at 405, 91 S.Ct. at 818.

reasons or findings in support of his decision. His action was challenged by a number of private citizens and local and national environmental groups. Their main procedural contention was that the Secretary should be required to make formal findings showing that he had acted in accord with the statute. They also challenged the merits of Secretary Volpe's decision.[35]

The challengers lost in both the District Court and the Court of Appeals.[36] The Supreme Court, however, ruled that Congress clearly intended that "protection of parkland was to be given paramount importance."[37] It further stated: "If the statutes are to have any meaning, the Secretary cannot approve the destruction of parkland unless he finds that alternative routes present unique problems."[38]

Though the Court did not require formal findings of fact, it did hold that the Secretary's action could properly be reviewed for arbitrariness, stating that it "must consider whether the decision was based on a consideration of the relevant factors and whether there has been a clear error of judgment."[39]

The Court additionally noted that even though the "inquiry into the facts is to be searching and careful, the ultimate standard of review is a narrow one."[40] But along the way, the Court used a variety of other standards as well to describe the scope of review a court must utilize. The court must "engage in a substantial inquiry."[41] Nevertheless, we are also told that the Secretary's decision is "entitled to a presumption of regularity."[42] Yet, "that presumption is not to shield his action from a thorough, probing, in-depth review."[43] There is language in this opinion to satisfy a variety of scope of review positions, from narrow to searching. The Court ultimately concluded that even though no formal findings were required, the Secretary had to provide additional information to substantiate his decision. It held that the Secretary's decision had to be evaluated (1) on the basis of the "record" before the agency at the time of the decision; (2) by testimony given by the Secretary if necessary; and (3) on the basis of any formal findings the Secretary chooses to make.[44] In short, an inquiry into whether Volpe had acted in an arbitrary or capricious manner had to be centered on rationalizations either provided or easily inferred from whatever "record" existed at the time the decision was made.

The *Overton Park* decision can be viewed in three separate ways: (1) as a failure of the Secretary to follow clear congressional intent; (2) as a failure to meet the arbitrary and capricious standard of judicial review; and (3) as a failure to generate some form of record by which courts

35. Id. at 408, 91 S.Ct. at 819.

36. Citizens to Preserve Overton Park, Inc. v. Volpe, 432 F.2d 1307 (6th Cir.1970).

37. 401 U.S. at 412–13, 91 S.Ct. at 821–22.

38. Id. at 413, 91 S.Ct. at 822.

39. Id. at 416, 91 S.Ct. at 824.

40. Id.

41. Id. at 415, 91 S.Ct. at 823.

42. Id.

43. Id.

44. Id. at 420, 91 S.Ct. at 825.

could adequately review the agency's decision. Depending on which of these aspects of the opinion is emphasized, *Overton Park* has more or less to say about the arbitrary and capricious standard of judicial review.

One way to read this decision is to emphasize the first aspect of the case and argue that the primary issue in the case was whether Secretary Volpe had failed to give consideration to factors clearly set forth by statute. This issue raises a question of law. The language in the opinion that suggests "close scrutiny" may, therefore, be read as applying to questions of law and thus, requiring essentially *de novo* judicial review.[45] Emphasizing the questions of law present in this case would also explain the strong language employed by the Court at other points in the opinion. This language should not, therefore, necessarily be read as an attempt to re-define the arbitrary and capricious standard. It is, in fact, a response to the legal issues posed in this case.

An emphasis on the second aspect of this opinion, however, would lead to the opposite conclusion. *Overton Park* arguably did have something to say about defining the arbitrary and capricious standard. For those who favor strong review, there is the "clear error," and "searching and careful" language used by the Court.[46] On the other hand, for those favoring a more restrained judicial approach, there is the language stating that the inquiry is a "narrow" one.[47] Both rhetorical strands of this case have been used in subsequent cases challenging the rationality of agency action under the arbitrary and capricious standard.

The third aspect of the *Overton Park* opinion is its assumption that an agency record was in existence at the time Secretary Volpe made his decision. This, in turn, implied that informal agency action of this sort should be based on a record. Carrying this assumption over to judicial review of agency rules, as many courts have done, arguably strains what the drafters of the APA intended in such cases.[48] The APA says very

45. See generally sec. 13.7, supra.

46. "[T]he court must consider whether the decision was based on a consideration of the relevant factors and whether there has been a clear error of judgment." 401 U.S. at 416, 91 S.Ct. at 824. "[T]his inquiry into the facts is to be searching and careful." Id. But see, NAACP v. FCC, 682 F.2d 993, 998 n. 4 (D.C.Cir.1982) (court specifically states that the "clear error of judgment" language in *Overton Park* was not to be equated with "clearly erroneous" standard in Rule 52 of the FRCP).

47. "[T]he ultimate standard of review is a narrow one." 401 U.S. at 416, 91 S.Ct. at 824.

48. Yet, it should be noted that prior to *Overton Park,* as early as 1968, 5 U.S.C.A. § 553(c) was being invoked to demand an apparently more detailed agency explanation: "We do not expect the agency to discuss every item of fact or opinion included in the submissions made to it in informal rule making. We do expect that, if the judicial review which Congress has thought it important to provide is to be meaningful, the 'concise general statement of ... basis and purpose' mandated by [5 U.S.C.A. § 553(c)] will enable us to see what major issues of policy were ventilated by the informal proceedings and why the agency reacted to them as it did." Automotive Parts & Accessories Ass'n v. Boyd, 407 F.2d 330, 338 (D.C.Cir.1968).

For other cases arguably expanding the APA concise statement requirement in informal rulemaking, see United States v. Nova Scotia Food Products Corp., 568 F.2d 240 (2d Cir.1977); Portland Cement Ass'n v. Ruckelshaus, 486 F.2d 375 (D.C.Cir. 1973), cert. denied 417 U.S. 921, 94 S.Ct. 2628, 41 L.Ed.2d 226 (1974); Kennecott Copper Corp. v. EPA, 462 F.2d 846 (D.C.Cir.1972). See sec. 13.9.1, supra.

little about informal action and nothing about the kind invoked in *Overton Park.* As far as informal rulemaking is concerned, the APA simply states that an agency, upon promulgation of new rules "shall incorporate in the rules adopted a concise general statement of their basis and purpose."[49] By remanding for the generation of a record in the context of such informal agency action, *Overton Park* became an important precedent enabling courts to demand a *de facto* record requirement in informal adjudicatory and informal rulemaking settings.[50]

Informal rulemaking under § 553 is a far cry from formal APA adjudication or rulemaking. Section 556(3) makes very clear that formal rules and orders promulgated pursuant to this provision must be based on a record. Section 553 sets forth no such requirement. In fact, one might assume that a crucial difference between formal and informal proceedings is the existence of a record in formal proceedings. Increasingly, however, courts have tended to review informal rulemaking on the basis of a record as well.[51] Most § 553 proceedings do generate a body of data that could be called a record, and against which the rationality of the agency's decision can be tested. Comments are filed and agency studies often are undertaken. It is, however, precisely in such policy oriented proceedings that the expertise of the agency comes in to play. Staff members can and usually do consult widely on such issues and agency heads are expected to exercise political judgment and technical expertise. Many of these kinds of consultations and judgments are not a part of the record proper, but may and should affect the outcome. In addition, the administrative burden of assembling the entire factual justification for a rule can be enormous and significantly undercut the efficiency of the rulemaking process.[52] As rulemaking became a more and more significant source of agency law making in the 1970's and 1980's, however, increased judicialization of the rulemaking process has occurred.[53] *Overton Park's* strong language regarding the scope of judicial review has significantly altered the way in which courts review informal agency proceedings. Quite apart from the question of whether informal rules must be based exclusively on a record, courts have become much more demanding when it comes to the clarity, persuasiveness and

49. 5 U.S.C.A. § 553(c).

50. Subsequently, the Supreme Court affirmed the *de facto* record requirement for informal agency actions in Camp v. Pitts, 411 U.S. 138, 93 S.Ct. 1241, 36 L.Ed.2d 106 (1973) discussed in detail supra in chapter 9, sec. 2. The Supreme Court also appeared to approve this same approach for judicial review of informal rulemaking in Vermont Yankee Nuclear Power Corp. v. Natural Resources Defense Council, Inc., 435 U.S. 519, 98 S.Ct. 1197, 55 L.Ed.2d 460 (1978), on remand 685 F.2d 459 (D.C.Cir.1982).

51. See Auerback, Informal RuleMaking: A Proposed Relationship Between Administrative Procedures and Judicial Review 72 NW.U.L.Rev. 15, 22–30 (1977); see also, Pedersen, Formal Records and Informal Rulemaking, 85 Yale L.J. 38 (1975). For a discussion of various exceptions to the exclusivity record in informal rulemaking proceedings see Starn and Wald, Setting No Records: The Failed Attempt to Limit the Record in Review of Administrative Action, 36 Admin.L.Rev. 333, 343–44 (1984).

52. For a good discussion of why a general requirement that rules be reviewable on a record, see, Auerbach, Administrative Rulemaking in Minnesota, 63 Minn. L.Rev. 151 (1979).

53. This trend has been accelerated by the many statutes that include hybrid rulemaking provisions and a substantial evidence standard of judicial review.

thoroughness of the agency's statement of the "basis and purpose" of the rule involved. At times the court will remand so that the agency can show more clearly that it has, in fact, engaged in reasoned decisionmaking. At other times, the court specifically invokes a particularly strong version of reasoned decisionmaking, the hard look doctrine. We shall examine this doctrine in detail. As we shall see, it was developed in the context of adjudicatory proceedings, but variants of the hard look or reasoned decisionmaking doctrines are now commonly applied by courts when reviewing informal and hybrid rulemaking as well.

§ 13.10.4 The Hard Look Doctrine—Judicial Review of Agency Change

The case in which the modern version of the hard look doctrine was first applied is *Greater Boston Television Corp. v. FCC.*[54] This case suggests a purely procedural trigger for the hard look approach, one which transcends the various substantive contexts that can also help trigger close judicial review.[55] When an agency changes its policy direction—i.e., when it produces a result that goes in a 180 degree opposite direction—the hard look doctrine often is invoked. The underlying premise of the hard look doctrine is that the process of agency reasoning produces wise policies that further the agency's statutory goals and, therefore, enhance its legitimacy. This emphasis on the agency's need to display a reasoned approach to its tasks, particularly when significant changes in policy are in order, strongly resembles common law methodology. Like the common law, changes in agency law are expected to occur gradually, to be adaptable to pre-existing legal frameworks and to represent, in effect, a form of regulatory progress.[56] Sudden changes in policy are permitted, but only if they are adequately explained and supported so that the court is confident that they were carefully considered. Change is thus expected to be the product of reasoned analysis brought to bear on accumulated experience and not just the result of a new set of political forces or regulatory appointees. Thus this form of the hard look doctrine assumes a kind of rationality and deliberative approach to administrative change that is measured by and pays close attention to *stare decisis.*

Greater Boston Television Corp. v. FCC[57] clearly demonstrates the common law-like aspects of this doctrine. That case involved an appeal of an FCC order that awarded a television operating license to Boston Broadcasters, Inc. after nearly sixteen years of administrative compara-

54. 444 F.2d 841 (D.C.Cir.1970), cert. denied 403 U.S. 923, 91 S.Ct. 2233, 29 L.Ed.2d 701 (1971); stay denied WHDH, Inc. v. FCC, 405 U.S. 982, 92 S.Ct. 1242, 31 L.Ed.2d 449 (1972); see generally Leventhal, Environmental Decisionmaking and the Role of the Courts, 122 U.Pa.L.Rev. 509, 511 (1974).

55. See Aman, Administrative Law in a Global Era: Progress, Deregulatory Change, & The Rise of the Administrative Presidency, 73 Cornell L.Rev. 1101, 1131–41 (1988). This and the following section draw heavily from this article.

56. See Aman, supra note 414, at 1145.

57. 444 F.2d 841 (D.C.Cir.1970), cert. denied 403 U.S. 923, 91 S.Ct. 2233, 29 L.Ed.2d 701 (1971), stay denied WHDH, Inc. v. FCC, 405 U.S. 982, 92 S.Ct. 1242, 31 L.Ed.2d 449 (1972).

tive licensing proceedings.[58] The court affirmed the FCC's ruling on appeal only after elaborating what it called the need for the agency to take a "hard look" at the issues.[59] In so doing, the court set forth both the circumstances under which a hard look test might be appropriate as well as the requirements of such an approach.

According to the court in *Greater Boston,* a hard look approach is required when certain danger signals become apparent. Foremost among these danger signals is a perceived reversal in policy direction. Specifically, Judge Leventhal noted:

> Judicial vigilance to enforce the Rule of Law in the administrative process is particularly called upon where ... the area under consideration is one wherein the Commission's policies are in flux. An agency's view of what is in the public interest may change, either with or without a change in circumstances. But an agency changing its course must supply a reasoned analysis indicating that prior policies and standards are being deliberately changed, not casually ignored, and if an agency glosses over or swerves from prior precedents without discussion it may cross the line from the tolerably terse to the intolerably mute.[60]

58. Initially, this license had been awarded to a competitor of Boston Broadcasting station WHDH. While this decision was on appeal, "it came to the court's attention that the Commission's award might be subject to an infirmity by virtue of improper *ex parte* contacts with the Chairman of the Commission." 444 F.2d at 844. This possibility triggered another round of evidentiary hearings, at the end of which the Commission again awarded the license to WHDH, but only for 4 months, instead of the customary three year period. The Commission was unsure of the extent of the *ex parte* contacts and how they should affect the Commission's decision. When WHDH filed for a renewal three months later, the Commission began another round of comparative license hearings. Meanwhile, both WHDH and Greater Boston appealed the grant of this 4—month license. During this appeal, Mr. Robert Choate of WHDH, the person who had initiated the improper ex parte contacts, died. The court remanded the case to determine what effect, if any, his death should have on the licensing proceedings. The court also authorized the Commission to combine the renewal proceedings with these remanded proceedings. This consolidated comparative proceeding began in May, 1964. After further comparative hearings, the hearing examiner placed primary emphasis on the actual operating record of WHDH under its temporary authorizations of the preceding nine years and granted it a three year license. The Commission, however, reversed this decision in what turned out to be a very controversial opinion.

The television industry was upset and began to organize its forces to seek legislative reversal of this decision. It feared that Commission policy would now place all license holders on equal footing with new applicants every time their three-year licenses came up for renewal. The Commission, on rehearing, however, added a paragraph to clarify that this was not an ordinary renewal case. 444 F.2d at 849. WHDH's license had been granted for the most part under temporary authorizations. It did not receive an operating license until 1962 and then it was only for four months. It was, in fact, the Commission's concern with the "inroads made by WHDH upon the rules governing fair and orderly adjudication," 444 F.2d at 845, (citing Commission decision), that resulted in its decision to subject this particular license holder to a comparative hearing on its application for renewal.

59. 444 F.2d at 851 (the "supervisory function calls on the court to intervene not merely in case of procedural inadequacies, or bypassing of the mandate in the legislative chapter, but more broadly if the court becomes aware, especially from a combination of danger signals, that the agency has not really taken a 'hard look' at the salient problems, and has not genuinely engaged in reasoned decisionmaking." Id. (footnote omitted)).

60. Id. at 852.

The fact that this approach to judicial review calls for a "reasoned analysis" inevitably implies a substantive as well as a procedural component to the doctrine. Although the court did not clearly explain how good a reason an agency must give if it does decide to change course, the opinion strongly implies that not just any reason will do. Indeed, the kind of reasoning the court envisioned is that which

> promotes results in the public interest by requiring the agency to focus on the values served by its decision, and hence releasing the clutch of unconscious preference and irrelevant prejudice. It furthers the broad public interest of enabling the public to repose confidence *in the process* as well as the judgments of its decision-makers.[61]

In this sense, process and substance are intertwined. The process of reasoned decision-making will presumably yield substantive reasons which the public (through the courts) will at least recognize as good reasons, though not necessarily reasons with which all might agree. By ensuring that agencies publicly articulate their rationales, courts thereby encourage results worthy of judicial deference and public approval. The reasoning process is thus a meaningful means to a more acceptable end. In this sense, it cannot be divorced from the product it produces.

But just how good a reason an agency must give and how much deference a court is willing to give to that reason are matters of degree. If the court has a primarily procedural cast of mind, it may, in the face of a reason with which it may not agree, reluctantly conclude that Congress ultimately wanted the agency to make the substantive decision involved, albeit in a manner capable of explanation to a court. A pure process approach would find virtually any reason acceptable as long as the agency's action is within its statutory powers.[62] At the other end of the spectrum, a more substantive judicial approach would in effect, require that the agency give not just a plausible reason for its action, but a persuasive reason.[63]

The more demanding a court becomes in assessing the relationship of an agency's reason to the Congressional purposes behind its statutory powers or to the agency's own stated purposes in the rule it proposes, the more substantive judicial review can become.[64] Indeed, an analysis of the reasonableness of a policy decision can begin to approximate an *ultra vires* review.[65] If the action is outside the agency's legal powers, no one

61. Id. at 852 (emphasis added) (footnote omitted).

62. See, e.g., Justice Rehnquist's dissent in *State Farm Mutual* discussed in sec. 13.10.5, infra.

63. See, e.g., Justice White's discussion of the Department of Transportation's reasons to eliminate the automatic seatbelt option, sec. 13.10.5, infra.

64. In deregulatory settings, some reviewing courts have demanded that an agency explain the connection between the policy they seek to reverse and the congressional intent they seek to further. See generally, Garland, supra note 366, at 527, n. 112 (citing International Bhd. of Teamsters, Chauffeurs, Warehousemen and Helpers of America v. United States), 735 F.2d 1525, 1531–32 (D.C.Cir.1984); Action on Smoking and Health v. CAB, 699 F.2d 1209, 1216–17 (D.C.Cir.1983); Wheaton Van Lines, Inc. v. ICC, 671 F.2d 520, 527–28 (D.C.Cir.1982).

65. Cf. Office of Consumers' Counsel v. FERC, 655 F.2d 1132, 1147–48 (D.C.Cir. 1980) with Public Utilities Commission of Colo. v. FERC, 660 F.2d 821, 826–27

objects when courts take a hard look and substitute their legal judgment for that of the agency;[66] however, problems arise when the policy advocated by an agency is at least technically within its powers, but philosophically at odds with what Congress presumably intended or what a Court thinks Congress may have intended when it passed the legislation in question. Demanding better reasons when, in fact, there is disagreement with the actual substance of an agency's decision may make the courts the ultimate arbiters of *wise* policy choices. What is wise is, in effect, defined by what a court may think Congress itself would have wanted at the time it passed the legislation involved or, quite simply, what a judge thinks is wise.

Although hard look review usually shifts decision-making power from agencies to courts, Judge Leventhal did not see this doctrine in power terms. Nor did he see it necessarily as a substantive doctrine. Leventhal viewed it as part of a decision-making process, a process in which courts played an integral part. He saw judicial involvement of this sort as necessary for the good of the administrative process in general and agencies in particular.[67]

Quite apart from a hard look by agencies, and the partnership rationale advocated by Judge Leventhal, a closer or hard look by courts themselves may also result. Courts have often taken a substantive hard look at agency policy decisions by challenging directly the agency's own reasoning for issuing a rule,[68] or by pointing to some specific alternative approaches or relevant factors that the agency perhaps should have taken or at least explained.[69] Predicting whether a court will accept or reject an agency's reasoning can be very difficult,[70] but it has become

(D.C.Cir.1981), cert. denied 456 U.S. 944, 102 S.Ct. 2009, 72 L.Ed.2d 466 (1982).

66. See, e.g., Weyerhaeuser Co. v. Costle, 590 F.2d 1011 (D.C.Cir.1978).

67. Thus, Judge Leventhal argued that

> "agencies and courts together constitute a 'partnership' in furtherance of the public interest, and are 'collaborative instrumentalities of justice.' The court is in a real sense part of the total administrative process, and not a hostile stranger to the office of first instance. This collaborative spirit does not undercut, it rather underlines the court's rigorous insistence on the need for conjunction of articulated standards and reflective findings."

444 F.2d at 851–52 (citing Niagara Mohawk Power Corp. v. FPC, 379 F.2d 153, 160 n. 24 (D.C.Cir.1967) and United States v. Morgan, 313 U.S. 409, 422, 61 S.Ct. 999, 1004, 85 L.Ed. 1429 (1941)).

This rationale is similar to that provided by Judge Frank at the height of the post New Deal deference era. Urging, in dissent, that the court overturn a certain ICC order, Judge Frank argued: "To condone the Commission's conduct here is to give aid and comfort to the enemies of the Administrative process, by sanctioning administrative irresponsibility; the friends of that process should be the first to denounce its abuses." Old Colony Bondholders v. New York, N.H. & H.R. Co., 161 F.2d 413, 451 (2d Cir.1947), cert. denied 331 U.S. 858, 67 S.Ct. 1754, 91 L.Ed. 1865 (Frank, J. dissenting).

68. See, e.g., Justice White's majority opinion in *State Farm Mutual* discussed in sec. 13.10.5, infra.

69. See, e.g., Scenic Hudson Preservation Conference v. FPC, 354 F.2d 608, 612 (2d Cir.1965), cert. denied 384 U.S. 941, 86 S.Ct. 1462, 16 L.Ed.2d 540 (1966); see also Brae Corp. v. United States, 740 F.2d 1023, 1049–51 (D.C.Cir.1984), cert. denied 471 U.S. 1069, 105 S.Ct. 2149, 85 L.Ed.2d 505; International Ladies' Garment Workers' Union v. Donovan, 722 F.2d 795, 822–26 (D.C.Cir.1983); Maryland People's Counsel v. FERC, 761 F.2d 768, 774–79 (D.C.Cir. 1985).

70. See, e.g., Small Refiner Lead Phase—Down Task Force v. EPA, 705 F.2d 506, 541 (D.C.Cir.1983).

increasingly clear that courts will, on occasion, go beyond simply requiring that reasons be given and in effect demand that those reasons be good reasons.[71]

The leading Supreme Court case dealing with reasoned decisionmaking and the hard look approach is *Motor Vehicle Mfrs. Ass'n v. State Farm Mutual Auto. Ins. Co.*[72] Because of the importance of this case, both as a precedent and as a summary of the various approaches judges may take when reviewing the rationality of agency policy judgments, we shall examine it in detail.

§ 13.10.5 *Motor Vehicle Manufacturers Assoc. v. State Farm Mutual*

In *Motor Vehicle Manufacturers Ass'n v. State Farm Mutual,*[73] plaintiffs challenged a Department of Transportation decision rescinding a mandatory passive restraint rule adopted during the Carter Administration. The Carter rule, allowing either automatic seatbelts or airbags, required all cars to be fitted with passive restraints by 1984. Shortly after the 1980 election, this rule was rescinded. In rescinding this rule, the agency reasoned as follows. In 1977 when the rule was first issued, the agency had assumed that airbags would be installed in 60% of all new cars and automatic seatbelts in 40%. But by 1981 it became apparent that automobile manufacturers planned to install automatic

71. See, e.g., National Lime Ass'n v. EPA, 627 F.2d 416, 451 n. 126 (D.C.Cir. 1980); Baton Rouge Marine Contractors, Inc. v. Federal Maritime Com'n, 655 F.2d 1210, 1215–18 (D.C.Cir.1981). The legal language to which a substantive or a procedural hard look approach is tied usually remains the "arbitrary and capricious" clause of the Administrative Procedure Act (APA). 5 U.S.C.A. § 706(2)(A). Sometimes, this language is buttressed by provisions in the agency's own enabling act that give a court an opportunity to claim that Congress intended, in effect, to read a sliding scale approach into the APA. Hybrid rulemaking statutes calling for the application of a substantial evidence test to a policy making determination often are implicitly or explicitly used as authority for a more substantive judicial look at agency decisions. See Garland, Deregulation and Judicial Review, supra note 366, at 533–35. See, e.g., Recording Industry Ass'n v. Copyright Royalty Tribunal, 662 F.2d 1, 8 (D.C.Cir.1981); Weyerhaeuser Co. v. Costle, 590 F.2d 1011, 1027 (D.C.Cir.1978). Quite apart from hybrid rulemaking statutes, the nature of the agency itself, of course, may also affect the way in which a court will review its regulations. Some agencies arguably have interests that are at odds with the public interest goals of the statutes involved. A self-interested governmental entity may, in its single-mindedness, be as likely to disregard broader public values as any regulated private entity. In cases such as these, courts have acted, in effect, as super agencies serving as the ultimate guardians of the public interest. Thus, courts themselves have taken a hard look and often found the agency's actions inadequate. See Calvert Cliffs' Coordinating Committee, Inc. v. AEC, 449 F.2d 1109 (D.C.Cir.1971). See Aman, supra note 414, at 1141–43. This presumably avoids the *Vermont Yankee* problem of having an appellate court procedurally gloss the APA in ways that Congress arguably did not intend when it passed the APA in 1946. But see, Public Systems v. FERC, 606 F.2d 973, 983–84, 986 (D.C.Cir.1979) (Robb, J. dissenting).

72. 463 U.S. 29, 103 S.Ct. 2856, 77 L.Ed.2d 443 (1983). See also Allied–Signal Aerospace Co. v. U.S., 28 F.3d 1188 (Fed. Cir.1994), cert. denied, 513 U.S. 1077, 115 S.Ct. 722, 130 L.Ed.2d 628 (1995) (discussing various types of situations to which the Motor Vehicle analysis applies).

73. In the D.C. Circuit, the case was captioned State Farm Mutual Automobile Ins. Co. v. Department of Transportation, 680 F.2d 206 (D.C.Cir.1982), judgment vacated, 463 U.S. 29, 103 S.Ct. 2856, 77 L.Ed.2d 443 (1983).

seatbelts in approximately 99% of the new cars. The agency assumed, however, that the overwhelming majority of such seatbelts could and presumably would be easily and permanently detached. If this did occur, and President Reagan's Department of Transportation thought it highly likely, the life-saving potential of the automatic seatbelt would be completely undercut. The prospects for seatbelt use would be no better than the current use of manual restraints. Thus, DOT found no real basis for reliably predicting any significant increase in safety. Given the great expense of implementing the passive restraint rule and the minimal benefits anticipated under such circumstances, the agency rescinded the rule.

For many reasons this turned out to be a relatively easy case to decide against the agency. Not a single judge on the D.C. Circuit nor a single Justice voted to uphold the agency's decision. Although they all found fault with the agency's reasoning, or the lack thereof, three very different judicial approaches and scopes of review emerged. Underlying these approaches are three different judicial conceptualizations of the administrative process and the relationship of courts to that process. Both the procedural and substantive strands of the hard look doctrine converged in Judge Mikva's majority opinion for the D.C. Circuit.[74] Judge Mikva applied what he characterized as "thorough probing, in depth review."[75] Such review required the court to determine "whether the agency has engaged in reasoned decisionmaking, making actual judgments concerning the significance of the evidence in the record and supporting its decision with 'reasoned analysis'."[76]

In supporting this decision to take a hard look, Mikva first noted that the recision meant a "sharp change in policy" and that this was, itself, a "danger signal." However, this "policy change" approach was developed by Judge Leventhal in the context of an adjudicatory proceeding. To justify the use of the adjudicatory version of the hard look doctrine in the legislative context in which he now sought to apply it, Judge Mikva wrote:

> The answer to this question lies in the fact that an agency is not a legislature. Congress delegates rulemaking power in the anticipation that agencies will perform particular tasks.... Even when there is no claim that the agency has exceeded its jurisdiction, as there is not in this case, sudden and profound alterations in an agency's policy constitute "danger signals" that the will of Congress is being ignored.[77]

Judge Mikva relied on the legislative history of the Motor Vehicle Safety Act and congressional inaction in the face of various legislative attempts to modify the airbags rule. Judge Mikva noted that this rule

74. 680 F.2d at 228–229.

75. Id. at 228.

76. Id. at 229 (citing City of Charlottesville v. FERC, 661 F.2d 945, 951 n. 35 (D.C.Cir.1981), appeal after remand 774 F.2d 1205 (1985), cert. denied 475 U.S. 1108, 106 S.Ct. 1515, 89 L.Ed.2d 914 (1986)).

77. Id. at 221 (footnote omitted).

had caused a great deal of debate in Congress, but Congress chose not to act. Though Congressional inaction of this kind can speak in many ways, Judge Mikva (a former congressman) interpreted it as a kind of congressional approval for the passive restraint rule, and an implicit expression of the will of Congress. With this view of the legislative process surrounding the administrative process, Judge Mikva went on to reiterate Judge Leventhal's essentially procedural concept of the relationships of courts to agencies: "courts, administrative agencies, and Congress are partners, not adversaries. Courts do not substitute judgment for that of the agency, but ensure that agencies exercise their judgment only in accordance with the will of Congress."[78] Even though Congress had not acted affirmatively here, it had not acted negatively and against this backdrop of legislative history, Judge Mikva demanded that any proposed recision be accompanied by "clear and convincing reasons."[79]

The Supreme Court, speaking through Justice White, also found the agency's action arbitrary and capricious. In so doing it rejected the court of appeals' approach to the scope of judicial review as well as its attempt to intensify that scope based on a reading of legislative non-events. If anything, the Supreme Court found that perhaps the opposite conclusion regarding Congressional support for passive restraint could be drawn from the Congressional debates relied upon by Judge Mikva. At best, the Court regarded such non-action as irrelevant. It did, however, agree with the D.C. Circuit that "an agency changing its course by rescinding a rule is obligated to supply a reasoned analysis for the change beyond that which may be required when an agency does not act in the first instance."[80] The majority stated, however, that agency decisions to deregulate would not receive stronger review than other changes in agency policy.[81]

Even so, the majority applied its reasonableness test to the rulemaking record before it with an intensity that resembled the analysis of the D.C. Circuit. Since the agency gave no reason whatsoever for abandoning the airbag option, the degree of scrutiny was not really put to the test. Even the dissent was in agreement that the agency's failure to offer any reasons for abandoning the airbag option could not satisfy the arbitrary and capricious standard. But the majority did not stop with its discussion of the airbags option. It went even further in concluding that the agency failed to give reasons for not even mentioning non-detachable seatbelts as an alternative.[82] The majority thus took a substantive hard look at the

78. Id. at 242.

79. Id. at 229.

80. 463 U.S. at 42, 103 S.Ct. at 2866.

81. In the words of the Court, this did not "alter the standard of judicial review established by law." Id. at 42, 103 S.Ct. at 2866. "We will ... 'uphold a decision of less than ideal clarity if the agency's path may reasonably be discerned.' " Id. at 43, 103 S.Ct. at 2867 (citing Bowman Transp., Inc. v. Arkansas–Best Freight System, Inc., 419 U.S. 281, 286, 95 S.Ct. 438, 442, 42 L.Ed.2d 447 (1974)). The Court even went so far as to suggest that "the removal of a regulation may not entail the monetary expenditures and other costs of enacting a new standard, and, accordingly, it may be easier for an agency to justify a deregulatory action." Id. at 42, 103 S.Ct. at 2866.

82. Id. at 55, 103 S.Ct. at 2873.

agency's evidence for its conclusion that detachable passive belts would not work and found it wanting.[83] It rejected the agency's pessimistic interpretation of the cost benefit data in the record and resolving all doubts in favor of increasing safety, the Court found that this data supported the passive restraint rule.[84]

Writing for four members of the Court, Justice, later Chief Justice, Rehnquist filed a separate opinion, concurring in part and dissenting in part. The crucial paragraph in Justice Rehnquist's opinion states:

> The agency's changed view of the standard seems to be related to the election of a new President of a different political party. It is readily apparent that the responsible members of one administration may consider public resistance and uncertainties to be more important than do their counterparts in a previous administration. A change in administration brought about by the people casting their votes is a perfectly reasonable basis for an executive agency's reappraisal of the costs and benefits of its programs and regulations. As long as the agency remains within the bounds established by Congress, it is entitled to assess administrative records and evaluate priorities in light of the philosophy of the administration.[85]

Justice Rehnquist thus also advocated a reasonableness test, but implied strongly that what was required was *a* reason, not necessarily a reason that a court thought was a good reason. The agency, however, could not meet even this minimalist approach. Since the agency gave no reasons at all for dismissing the use of mandatory airbags, even Justice Rehnquist had to agree that literally no rational basis existed for the decision. It was, in Justice Rehnquist's view, wrong to go further. Indeed, the agency's reasons regarding detachable automatic seatbelts were fully acceptable and the fact they failed to consider the alternative of non-detachability was, in the dissent's view, irrelevant.[86]

83. The Agency was quick to conclude that the use of detachable passive belts could not reliably predict "even a five-percentage point increase as the minimum level of expected usage increase." Id. at 51, 103 S.Ct. at 2871 (citing Notice 25), 46 Fed.Reg. 53423 (1981). Justice White disagreed with this assessment.

84. The Court noted that "the safety benefits of wearing seatbelts are not in doubt, and it is not challenged that were those benefits to accrue, the monetary costs of implementing the Standard would be easily justified." Id. at 52, 103 S.Ct. at 2871. The Court thus rejected the agency's view of the evidence of likely usage of automatic belts and found that at best, "the agency's view of the field tests on passive restraints indicates only that there is no reliable real-world experience that usage rates will substantially increase." Id. at 53, 103 S.Ct. at 2872. On the other hand, as the Court pointed out, "inertia—a factor which the agency's own studies have found significant in explaining the current low usage rates for [manual] seatbelts—works in *favor* of, not *against*, use of the protective device." Id. at 54, 103 S.Ct. at 2872 (footnote omitted) (emphasis in original). The Court did not denigrate the agency's concern over the costs of passive restraints, but directed that "NHTSA should bear in mind that Congress intended safety to be the pre-eminent factor under the [Motor Vehicle Safety] Act." Id. at 55, 103 S.Ct. at 2873.

85. Id. at 59, 103 S.Ct. at 2875 (footnote omitted).

86. For a Supreme Court case in which the Court relied heavily on *State Farm,* see Bowen v. American Hospital Ass'n, 476 U.S. 610, 106 S.Ct. 2101, 90 L.Ed.2d 584 (1986).

§ 13.10.6 Reasoned Decisionmaking—A Summary

The hard look or reasoned decisionmaking approach taken by the majority in *State Farm* is very much alive in the lower courts.[87] Though seldom invoked in so many words, the judiciary's demand for "reasoned decision-making" is now a permanent part of the regulatory landscape. As Chief Judge Wald has pointed out with regard to the D.C. Circuit: "under a third of the agency cases reversed in 1987 (67 out of 222), were reversed because the agency's rationale was inadequate." Indeed, "the most common deficiency" was "the agency's failure to explain 'departure from prior precedent.' "[88]

Courts also remand agency decisions for further action when no reason is given by the agency for its decision[89] or if the agency has failed to take into account all relevant considerations.[90] Similarly an agency

87. See, e.g., Professional Pilots Federation v. F.A.A., 118 F.3d 758 (D.C.Cir. 1997), cert. denied, 523 U.S. 1117, 118 S.Ct. 1794, 140 L.Ed.2d 936 (1998), rehearing denied, 524 U.S. 968, 119 S.Ct. 5, 141 L.Ed.2d 766 (1998); Public Citizen v. Steed, 733 F.2d 93 (D.C.Cir.1984); International Ladies' Garment Workers' Union v. Donovan, 722 F.2d 795 (D.C.Cir.1983): but see New York Council, Association of Civilian Technicians v. Federal Labor Relations Authority, 757 F.2d 502 (2d Cir.1985), cert. denied 474 U.S. 846, 106 S.Ct. 137, 88 L.Ed.2d 113 (1985); Coalition for Environment v. NRC, 795 F.2d 168, 174 n. 5 (D.C.Cir.1986).

88. Wald, The Contributions of the D.C. Circuit to Administrative Law, 40 Admin.L.Rev. 507, 528 (1988).

89. See New England Coalition on Nuclear Pollution v. NRC, 727 F.2d 1127, 1130–31 (D.C.Cir.1984), appeal after remand 795 F.2d 168 (1986); Sierra Club v. Gorsuch, 715 F.2d 653, 660–61 (D.C.Cir. 1983) ("[i]f there is reasoned decisionmaking lurking behind such agency behavior, it is yet to be articulated. For agency behavior to be upheld, it must not only be explainable; it must also be explained"); Environmental Defense Fund, Inc. v. EPA, 465 F.2d 528, 539 (D.C.Cir.1972).

But cf. Center for Auto Safety v. Peck, 751 F.2d 1336, 1361 (D.C.Cir.1985) ("we must be implacably skeptical of belated recognition at the appellate stage that elements of scientific analysis unchallenged during a contested proceeding are incomprehensible without further explanation") (Scalia, J.).

90. See Citizens to Preserve Overton Park, Inc. v. Volpe, 401 U.S. 402, 416, 91 S.Ct. 814, 824, 28 L.Ed.2d 136 (1971); United States v. Garner, 767 F.2d 104, 116–18 (5th Cir.1985); Maryland People's Counsel v. FERC, 761 F.2d 768, 774–79 (D.C.Cir. 1985); Center for Auto Safety v. Peck, 751 F.2d 1336, 1373 (D.C.Cir.1985) ("[a]lthough the ultimate scope [of review] may be narrow, the depth must be sufficient for us to be able to comprehend the agency's handling of the evidence cited or relied upon. The purpose of this in-depth review is to educate ourselves so that we can properly perform our reviewing function: determining whether the agency's conclusions are 'rationally supported' ") (Wright, J., dissenting); Brae Corp. v. United States, 740 F.2d 1023, 1049–51 (D.C.Cir.1984), cert. denied 471 U.S. 1069, 105 S.Ct. 2149, 85 L.Ed.2d 505 (1985); International Broth. of Teamsters v. United States, 735 F.2d 1525 (D.C.Cir.1984); Farmers Union Cent. Exchange, Inc. v. FERC, 734 F.2d 1486, 1510–11 (D.C.Cir.1984), cert. denied 469 U.S. 1034, 105 S.Ct. 507, 83 L.Ed.2d 398 (1984) (FERC acted arbitrarily and capriciously in failing to examine or consider any steps short of total deregulation of oil pipeline rates); International Ladies' Garment Workers' Union v. Donovan, 722 F.2d 795, 822–26 (D.C.Cir.1983); Action on Smoking and Health v. CAB, 699 F.2d 1209, 1217 (D.C.Cir.1983) ("to uphold the agency's action, it must be shown that the [agency] rationally considered the relevant evidence"); Telocator Network v. FCC, 691 F.2d 525, 545 (D.C.Cir.1982); Ritter Transportation, Inc. v. ICC, 684 F.2d 86, 88 (D.C.Cir.1982), cert. denied 460 U.S. 1022, 103 S.Ct. 1272, 75 L.Ed.2d 494 (1983); Baton Rouge Marine Contractors, Inc. v. FMC, 655 F.2d 1210, 1215–18 (D.C.Cir.1981); American Public Gas Ass'n v. FPC, 567 F.2d 1016, 1029–30 (D.C.Cir.1977), cert. denied 435 U.S. 907, 98 S.Ct. 1456, 55 L.Ed.2d 499 (1978); Action for Children's Television v. FCC, 564 F.2d 458, 478–79 (D.C.Cir.1977); Rodway v. USDA, 514 F.2d

may be required to engage in more reasoned decisionmaking if its decisional rationale has failed to consider relevant alternatives.[91]

As we have already seen, courts are particularly willing to remand agency findings for more reasoned decisionmaking in cases where an agency discontinues a previous policy approach.[92] A court's decision to

809, 817 (D.C.Cir.1975) (agency must respond in a reasoned manner to "explain how the agency resolved any significant problems raised by the comments, and to show how that resolution led the agency to the ultimate rule"); Portland Cement Ass'n v. Ruckelshaus, 486 F.2d 375, 402 (D.C.Cir. 1973), cert. denied 417 U.S. 921, 94 S.Ct. 2628, 41 L.Ed.2d 226 (1974); International Harvester Co. v. Ruckelshaus, 478 F.2d 615, 651 (D.C.Cir.1973) ("agency [must] set forth with clarity the grounds for its rejection of opposing views") (Bazelon, J., concurring); Scenic Hudson Preservation Conference v. FPC, 354 F.2d 608, 612 (2d Cir. 1965), cert. denied 384 U.S. 941, 86 S.Ct. 1462, 16 L.Ed.2d 540 (1966).

See also Public Citizen Health Research Group v. Tyson, 796 F.2d 1479, 1507 (D.C.Cir.1986) (under substantial evidence test, OSHA's refusal to adopt a short term exposure limit (STEL) was not supported by substantial evidence on the record as a whole since OSHA "entirely failed to consider an important aspect of the problem" (quoting *State Farm,* 463 U.S. at 43, 103 S.Ct. at 2867)).

But cf. Center for Auto Safety v. Peck, 751 F.2d 1336, 1355 n. 15 (D.C.Cir.1985) ("we cannot agree that the failure to factor insignificant health and safety effects into the agency's cost-benefit analysis constituted a failure 'to consider an *important* aspect of the problem' "(quoting *State Farm,* 463 U.S. at 43, 103 S.Ct. at 2867) (emphasis in original)) (Scalia, J.).

91. See U.S. v. O'Hagan, 521 U.S. 642, 117 S.Ct. 2199, 138 L.Ed.2d 724 (1997); Motor Vehicle Mfrs. Ass'n v. State Farm Mutual Automobile Ins. Co., 463 U.S. 29, 43, 103 S.Ct. 2856, 2867, 77 L.Ed.2d 443 (1983), appeal after remand 802 F.2d 474 (D.C.Cir.1986) (options ignored by the agency could not be characterized as "unknown or uncommon"); Public Citizen v. Steed, 733 F.2d 93, 104–05 (D.C.Cir.1984); International Ladies' Garment Workers' Union v. Donovan, 722 F.2d 795, 815 (D.C.Cir.1983) ("such an 'artificial narrowing of options' is antithetical to reasoned decisionmaking and cannot be upheld") (quoting Pillai v. CAB, 485 F.2d 1018, 1027 (D.C.Cir.1973)); Specialty Equipment Market Ass'n v. Ruckelshaus, 720 F.2d 124, 138–40 (D.C.Cir.1983); Office of Communication of United Church of Christ v. FCC, 707 F.2d 1413, 1442 (D.C.Cir.1983) (court refused to accept the FCC's "conclusory assurances" and vacated because "the Commission has failed to give adequate consideration to the vital information role that the logging requirements presently serve in the overall scheme of the Communications Act"); Cincinnati Gas & Elec. Co. v. EPA, 578 F.2d 660, 664 (6th Cir.1978), cert. denied 439 U.S. 1114, 99 S.Ct. 1017, 59 L.Ed.2d 72 (1979); National Citizens Committee for Broadcasting v. FCC, 567 F.2d 1095, 1115 (D.C.Cir.1977) (agency considerations "should [not] be limited to comparison of only two alternatives"), cert. denied 436 U.S. 926, 98 S.Ct. 2820, 56 L.Ed.2d 769 (1978).

But see *State Farm,* 463 U.S. at 51, 103 S.Ct. at 2871 (Court pointedly avoided making reasoned decisionmaking "broadly require an agency to consider all policy alternatives in reaching decision").

92. See Motor Vehicle Mfrs. Ass'n v. State Farm Mutual Automobile Ins. Co., 463 U.S. 29, 103 S.Ct. 2856, 77 L.Ed.2d 443 (1983), appeal after remand 802 F.2d 474 (D.C.Cir.1986), cert. denied 480 U.S. 951, 107 S.Ct. 1616, 94 L.Ed.2d 800 (1987); Atchison, T. & S.F.R. Co. v. Wichita Bd. of Trade, 412 U.S. 800, 807–08, 93 S.Ct. 2367, 2375, 37 L.Ed.2d 350 (1973) (there is "a presumption that [pre-existing] policies will be carried out best if the settled rule is adhered to"); Action for Children's Television v. FCC, 821 F.2d 741, 746 (D.C.Cir. 1987) ("the Commission's barebones incantations of two abbreviated rationales cannot do service as the requisite 'reasoned basis' for altering its long-established [15 year-old] policy"); National Black Media Coalition v. FCC, 775 F.2d 342, 355 (D.C.Cir. 1985) (it is "a clear tenet of administrative law that if the agency wishes to depart from its consistent precedent it must provide a principled explanation for its change of direction"); Delmarva Power & Light Co. v. FERC, 770 F.2d 1131, 1142 & n. 9 (D.C.Cir. 1985) ("review of the reasonableness of an administrative adjudication includes consideration of the administrator's consistency in deciding similar cases") (quoting Department of the Treasury v. FLRA, 707 F.2d 574, 581 n. 25 (D.C.Cir.1983)); Independent Air, Inc. v. DOT, 767 F.2d 1488, 1491 (11th

require more reasoned decisionmaking may also result from its perception of politically motivated agency action. A court may also be more willing to require more reasoned decisionmaking when serious or publicly harmful consequences of the agency issues under consideration are likely.[93]

§ 13.11 JUDICIAL REVIEW OF AGENCY INACTION

Thus far we have examined the application of APA standards of judicial review to agency actions. This section will now examine the standards when applied to agency decisions not to act.

The APA definition of "agency action" includes a "failure to act."[1] It also provides that an individual may petition an agency directly, requesting the agency to issue, amend or repeal a rule[2] or possibly to begin an action in court, requesting the court to compel certain agency action.[3] If the petitioning process proves unsuccessful, the individual may

Cir.1985); Airmark Corp. v. FAA, 758 F.2d 685, 691–92 (D.C.Cir.1985); Advanced Micro Devices v. CAB, 742 F.2d 1520, 1542 (D.C.Cir.1984); United States Satellite Broadcasting Co. v. FCC, 740 F.2d 1177, 1187 (D.C.Cir.1984); Brae Corp. v. United States, 740 F.2d 1023, 1038 (D.C.Cir.1984) ("agency must explain why the original reasons for adopting the rule or policy are no longer dispositive"), cert. denied 471 U.S. 1069, 105 S.Ct. 2149, 85 L.Ed.2d 505 (1985); International Broth. of Teamsters, Chauffeurs, Warehousemen and Helpers of America v. United States, 735 F.2d 1525, 1531–32 (D.C.Cir.1984); International Ladies' Garment Workers' Union v. Donovan, 722 F.2d 795, 813 (D.C.Cir.1983) (rescission of a 40–year old regulation restricting the home employment of workers in the knitted outer-wear industry found to be arbitrary and capricious); Black Citizens for a Fair Media v. FCC, 719 F.2d 407, 417 n. 25 (D.C.Cir.1983), cert. denied 467 U.S. 1255, 104 S.Ct. 3545, 82 L.Ed.2d 848 (1984) ("a change [in policy] is another factor to scrutinize, not a warrant for employing a different standard of review. Our scrutiny is heightened in that it includes this additional factor"); Action on Smoking and Health v. CAB, 699 F.2d 1209, 1216–17 (D.C.Cir. 1983) (these requirements "merely ensure that those changes reflect reasoned consideration of competing objectives and alternatives"); Wheaton Van Lines, Inc. v. ICC, 671 F.2d 520, 527–28 (D.C.Cir.1982); Natural Resources Defense Council, Inc. v. SEC, 606 F.2d 1031, 1049 n. 23 (D.C.Cir.1979); Greater Boston Television Corp. v. FCC, 444 F.2d 841, 852 (D.C.Cir.1970) ("an agency changing its course must supply a reasoned analysis indicating that prior policies and standards are being deliberately changed, not casually ignored"), cert. denied 403 U.S. 923, 91 S.Ct. 2233, 29 L.Ed.2d 701 (1971), stay denied, 405 U.S. 982, 92 S.Ct. 1292, 31 L.Ed.2d 449 (1972). New Castle County Airport Com'n v. CAB, 371 F.2d 733, 735 (D.C.Cir.1966), cert. denied 387 U.S. 930, 87 S.Ct. 2052, 18 L.Ed.2d 991 (1967). See also Farmers Union Cent. Exchange, Inc. v. FERC, 734 F.2d 1486, 1500 (D.C.Cir.1984), cert. denied 469 U.S. 1034, 105 S.Ct. 507, 83 L.Ed.2d 398 (1984) ("FERC's *adherence* to the *old* ICC rate base method also demands a reasoned justification") (emphasis added).

But cf. Center for Auto Safety v. Peck, 751 F.2d 1336, 1349 (D.C.Cir.1985) (an agency's justification for a change in policy "need not consist of affirmative demonstration that the status quo is wrong; it may also consist of demonstration, on the basis of careful study, that there is no cause to believe that the status quo is right, so that the existing rule has no rational basis to support it").

93. See, e.g., Center for Auto Safety v. Dole, 828 F.2d 799, 801–03 (D.C.Cir.1987) (in conducting review of National Highway Transportation Safety Administrator's finding on likelihood of safety-related defect in automobile, court must examine not merely statement of reasons given by Administrator but also evidence compiled in technical review on which agency relied in making its decision).

§ 13.11

1. 5 U.S.C.A. § 551(13).

2. 5 U.S.C.A. § 553(e).

3. 5 U.S.C.A. § 706. A court may review an agency's refusal to act under APA

seek judicial review of the agency's denial of petition. Some agency inaction is barred from judicial review if the inaction "is committed to agency discretion by law."[4] In *Citizens to Preserve Overton Park, Inc. v. Volpe*[5] the Supreme Court noted that "[t]he legislative history of the [APA] indicates that [§ 701(a)(2)] is applicable in those rare instances where 'statutes are drawn in such broad terms that in a given case there is no law to apply.' "[6] *Overton Park* involved application of § 701(a)(2) with regard to agency *action*. The leading case applying § 701(a)(2) to agency *inaction* is *Heckler v. Chaney.*[7]

Chaney involved a suit by death row inmates to require the Food and Drug Administration (FDA) to take enforcement action against prison officials. The officials, acting pursuant to state statutes, were performing human executions by means of injection with a drug the inmates claimed FDA had not approved for such use. The inmates presented evidence that the lethal injections "pose a substantial threat of torturous pain" rather than the intended quick and painless death.

According to the Food, Drug and Cosmetic Act (FDCA), the Commissioner of FDA must assure that all "new drugs" are "safe and effective" for use under conditions prescribed, recommended, or suggested on the official labeling. If the drug's labeling does not bear adequate warnings against unapproved use or methods of administration sufficient to protect its users, the drug is "misbranded." The inmates claimed that since the drug did not effect executions quickly and painlessly that the drug was misbranded. They wanted FDA to change the labeling, to notify prison officials that the drug was not approved for use in lethal injections, and to prosecute persons who continued to use the drug in an unapproved fashion.

The Commissioner replied by letter, refusing to take any of the action requested, asserting that (1) FDA could not regulate the state-sanctioned use of the drugs, and (2) even if it could, it would not pursue enforcement. The reasons for the second ground of refusal were (a) the case law was unclear on this issue, and (b) FDA had a policy of not enforcing its regulations where violations did not pose "serious danger to the public health."

When FDA refused to take action, the inmates filed suit in the United States District Court for the District of Columbia.[8] The District Court granted summary judgment to FDA, holding that "decisions of executive departments and agencies to *refrain* from instituting investigations and enforcement proceedings are essentially unreviewable by the

§ 706(1), which gives courts the power to "compel agency action unlawfully withheld or unreasonably delayed."

4. 5 U.S.C.A. § 701(a)(2).

5. 401 U.S. 402, 91 S.Ct. 814, 28 L.Ed.2d 136 (1971).

6. Id. at 410, 91 S.Ct. at 820 (1971) (quoting S.Rep. No. 752, 79th Cong., 1st Sess. 26 (1945)).

7. 470 U.S. 821, 105 S.Ct. 1649, 84 L.Ed.2d 714 (1985). For an analysis of section 701(a)(2) and unreviewability in general, see Levin, Understanding Unreviewability In Administrative Law, 74 Minn.L.Rev. 689 (1990).

8. Chaney v. Schweiker, Civ. No. 81–2265 (D.C.1982).

courts."[9] The court of appeals found that an FDA policy statement, having the force of a rule and interpreting the relevant statute, "obligated" FDA thoroughly to investigate where the unapproved use of an approved drug became "widespread" or "endanger[ed] the public health."[10] The court found this policy statement constituted "law to apply," thus contradicting the District Court's conclusion that FDA's refusal to enforce was committed to agency discretion by law. The court then went on to find the Commissioner had failed to support with any evidence his claim that no serious danger to the public health resulted from the use of drugs in lethal injections. Since the Commissioner's refusal to enforce was based upon this claim, the court found the refusal to be "arbitrary, capricious and without authority of law."[11]

The Supreme Court reversed, holding that "tradition, case law, and sound reasoning" required the Court to deny judicial review of FDA's decision not to enforce in this case.[12] After citing prior cases, which the Court said established the proposition that "an agency's decision not to prosecute or enforce ... is a decision generally committed to an agency's absolute discretion,"[13] the Court provided four reasons why such decisions are unsuited for judicial review. First, "an agency decision not to enforce often involves a complicated balancing of a number of factors which are peculiarly within its expertise,"[14] such as the use of limited resources, agency enforcement priorities and the likelihood of success of a particular action. Second, agency refusals to act do not involve the exercise of "*coercive* power over an individual's liberty or property rights,"[15] the areas courts are often called upon to protect. Third, while agency action provides a "focus for judicial review,"[16] agency inaction does not provide such a focus. Fourth, an agency's refusal to enforce "shares to some extent the characteristics of the decision of a prosecutor in the Executive Branch not to indict—a decision which has long been regarded as the special province of the Executive Branch."[17]

The Court thus held that when an agency refuses to take enforcement steps, "the presumption is that judicial review is not available."[18] This presumption, however, can be rebutted when Congress has provided the Court with "law to apply:" when Congress "has indicated an intent to circumscribe agency enforcement discretion, and has provided meaningful standards for defining the limits of that discretion."[19] The Court found no such guidelines in the enforcement provisions of the FDCA. The Court further found that the policy statement the court of appeals relied upon was vague and contradicted by a FDA regulation, and thus not sufficient to rebut the presumption of unreviewability. Given the

9. Id. at App. to Pet. for Cert. 74a (emphasis in original).

10. Chaney v. Heckler, 718 F.2d 1174, 1186 (D.C.Cir.1983) (citing 37 Fed.Reg. 16,-504 (1972)).

11. Id. at 1189.

12. Heckler v. Chaney, 470 U.S. 821, 105 S.Ct. 1649, 84 L.Ed.2d 714 (1985).

13. Id. at 831, 105 S.Ct. at 1655.

14. Id.

15. Id. at 832, 105 S.Ct. at 1656.

16. Id.

17. Id.

18. Id. at 831, 105 S.Ct. at 1655.

19. Id. at 834, 105 S.Ct. at 1657.

presumption of unreviewability, and plaintiffs' inability to rebut that presumption, the Court held that "FDA's decision not to take the enforcement actions requested ... is therefore not subject to judicial review under the APA."[20]

Courts have considered application of *Chaney* in various contexts. For purposes of discussion, the case law is best divided into the following areas of inquiry: (1) to what types of inaction does the presumption of unreviewability apply; (2) what constitutes "meaningful standards" sufficient to rebut the presumption; and (3) what standard of review do courts apply when review of agency inaction is possible.

§ 13.11.1 To What Types of Inaction Does the Presumption of Unreviewability Apply—Enforcement Decisions

Since *Chaney,* courts have applied the *Chaney* presumption of non-renewability to enforcement cases.[21] Courts have considered "enforcement" to include a settlement agreement between the agency and the potential subject of enforcement actions;[22] the withdrawal at an administrative hearing of a citation charging an employer with violating the Occupational Safety and Health Act;[23] denial of a petition to reopen an enforcement investigation;[24] denial of a petition to reopen a prior case for clarification;[25] refusal to provide legal counsel to a government employee;[26] and denial of Extended Voluntary Departure status to illegal aliens, which status would act as a temporary suspension of enforcement of the Immigration and Nationality Act against the aliens by the Attorney General.[27]

The *Chaney* Court itself explicitly stated that *Chaney* did not involve (1) an agency claim of lack of jurisdiction;[28] (2) a claim that the agency

20. Id. at 837, 105 S.Ct. at 1659.

21. See, e.g., Crowley Caribbean Transport, Inc. v. Pena, 37 F.3d 671 (D.C.Cir.1994); International Union, United Automobile, Aerospace & Agricultural Implement Workers of America v. Brock, 783 F.2d 237 (D.C.Cir.1986), on remand 678 F.Supp. 4 (D.D.C.1988), judgment reversed 869 F.2d 616 (D.C.Cir.1989) [hereinafter *UAW v. Brock*]; Community Nutrition Institute v. Young, 818 F.2d 943 (D.C.Cir. 1987).

22. See, e.g., Schering Corp. v. Heckler, 779 F.2d 683 (D.C.Cir.1985) (The court characterized the agreement as a formalization of FDA's decision not to enforce for a specified time, and that this decision "simply represents the *quid pro quo* that the agency found necessary to procure Tri–Bio's abandonment of its declaratory judgment claim." Id. at 687).

23. Cuyahoga Valley Ry. Co. v. United Transportation Union, 474 U.S. 3, 106 S.Ct. 286, 88 L.Ed.2d 2 (1985), on remand 783 F.2d 58 (6th Cir.1986).

24. Center for Auto Safety v. Dole, 846 F.2d 1532 (D.C.Cir.1988).

25. Interstate Commerce Com'n v. Brotherhood of Locomotive Engineers, 482 U.S. 270, 107 S.Ct. 2360, 96 L.Ed.2d 222 (1987).

26. Falkowski v. Equal Employment Opportunity Com'n, 764 F.2d 907 (D.C.Cir. 1985), rehearing denied 783 F.2d 252 (1986) (Department of Justice's refusal to represent employee in suit against her by a subordinate employee considered "in many ways analogous to deciding whether to enforce a statute." Id. at 911).

27. Hotel & Restaurant Employees Union, Local 25 v. Attorney General, 804 F.2d 1256 (D.C.Cir.1986). See also Lorion v. NRC, 785 F.2d 1038 (D.C.Cir.1986).

28. 470 U.S. at 833 n. 4, 105 S.Ct. at 1656 n. 4.

abdicated its statutory responsibilities;[29] or (3) a claim that the agency violated constitutional rights.[30] Courts have also rejected attempts to extend the reasoning of *Chaney* to claims of unreasonable delay by the agency;[31] (5) a claim that an agency's statutory interpretation is erroneous;[32] or (6) a claim that the agency action taken is contrary to law.[33]

§ 13.11.2 What Constitutes "Meaningful Standards" Sufficient to Rebut the Presumption of Unreviewability

Chaney considered both FDA's enabling statute, which held no restrictions on FDA's actions, and a policy statement, which the Court found the agency had not officially adopted and which therefore did not bind FDA. The Court did not say whether a policy statement, if adopted, or any other possible sources of "law" would bind the agency, i.e. provide "law to apply." The *Chaney* Court did, however, discuss an example of where an enabling statute *did* provide meaningful standards in the enforcement context when it distinguished *Dunlop v. Bachowski.*[33.5]

In *Bachowski* a union employee filed a complaint with the Department of Labor (DOL), under the Labor–Management Reporting and Disclosure Act, 29 U.S.C.A. § 481 et seq. (LMRDA), requesting the Secretary file suit to set aside a union election. When the Secretary refused to file suit, the employee brought suit in federal court. The Supreme Court held that LMRDA § 402[34] required the Secretary to investigate any complaints brought and that the Secretary's decision not to file suit was subject to judicial review. Section 402 reads in part "the Secretary shall investigate such complaint and, if he finds probable cause to believe that a violation ... has occurred ... he shall ... bring a civil action ... "[35] The Court in *Chaney* noted that this section "quite clearly withdrew discretion from the agency and provided guidelines for the exercise of its enforcement power." The mandatory language of § 482 is sufficient to allow a court to question the Secretary's refusal to act.

Courts have continued to allow judicial review after *Chaney* in suits challenging the Department of Labor's decision not to enforce under LMRDA § 402.[36]

29. Id.

30. 470 U.S. at 838, 105 S.Ct. at 1659. See also, Webster v. Doe, 486 U.S. 592, 108 S.Ct. 2047, 100 L.Ed.2d 632 (1988), on remand 859 F.2d 241 (D.C.Cir.1988), where the Court allows review of plaintiff's constitutional claim although a related firing decision by the Director of CIA is found unreviewable.

31. Cutler v. Hayes, 818 F.2d 879 (D.C.Cir.1987).

32. *UAW v. Brock,* supra note 473.

33. Farmworker Justice Fund, Inc. v. Brock, 811 F.2d 613 (D.C.Cir.1987), vacated as moot 817 F.2d 890 (1987).

33.5 421 U.S. 560, 95 S.Ct. 1851, 44 L.Ed.2d 377 (1975), on remand 405 F.Supp. 1227 (W.D.Pa.1975).

34. 29 U.S.C.A. § 482.

35. Id.

36. Petersen v. Dole, 956 F.2d 1219 (D.C.Cir.1992); Shelley v. Brock, 793 F.2d 1368 (D.C.Cir.1986) (on facts similar to *Bachowski* 's, the court noted *Chaney*'s inapplicability); Doyle v. Brock, 821 F.2d 778 (D.C.Cir.1987) ("It is well settled that the

An agency's own regulations and guidelines can also provide meaningful standards or law to apply. In *Center for Auto Safety v. Dole*[37] for example, citizens petitioned the National Highway Traffic Safety Administration (NHTSA) to reopen an enforcement investigation against an auto manufacturer. When NHTSA denied the petition, the citizens brought suit. The court held that the *Chaney* presumption of nonreviewability did not apply. In deciding that the court could look to agency regulations as well as the enabling statute, the court reasoned:

> "We have previously held that regulations promulgated by an administrative agency in carrying out its statutory mandate can provide standards for judicial review of agency action. Such self-imposed constraints may supply the 'law to apply' ... to overcome the presumption against reviewing administrative agency inaction, including nonenforcement decisions. When an agency chooses to so fetter its discretion, the presumption against reviewability recognized in Chaney must give way."[38]

The court found that the regulations did not "limit the agency's discretion in a way that enable[d the court] to conduct a meaningful review of the agency's compliance."[39] The regulations directed the agency to reopen the investigation "if, after a 'technical review,' it finds that 'there is a reasonable possibility that the requested order will be issued at the conclusion of the appropriate proceeding.' "[40] The court found the regulation allowed the agency to consider other factors, in addition to safety, such as enforcement priorities and available resources, in making a determination of "reasonable possibility," and that the weight given these factors is still sufficiently within the agency's discretion so as to preclude meaningful review.[41]

decision of the Secretary not to file suit is subject to judicial review...." Id. at 782).

In *UAW v. Brock,* supra note 473, however, the court found another provision of the LMRDA did not rebut the *Chaney* presumption of nonreviewability. In *UAW* plaintiffs challenged the Secretary's refusal to bring civil actions against employers allegedly violating reporting requirements contained in LMRDA § 203 (29 U.S.C.A. § 433). The provision allowing enforcement of § 203, 29 U.S.C.A. § 440, reads " ... the Secretary may bring a civil action ... " The court found this language "does not mandate that the Department take enforcement action against each and every violation." Further, nothing else in the statute "or any other source" provided guidelines or enforcement priorities.

37. 846 F.2d 1532 (D.C.Cir.1988).

38. Id. at 1543 (emphasis added).

39. Id. at 1535.

40. Id. at 1534.

41. See also Hill v. Group Three Housing Development Corp., 799 F.2d 385 (8th Cir.1986) (Court found plaintiffs failed to point to limits on HUD's discretion in the statute, agency regulations or HUD Handbook guidelines); Massachusetts Public Interest Research Group, Inc. v. United States Nuclear Regulatory Com'n, 852 F.2d 9 (1st Cir.1988) ("We agree with the District of Columbia Circuit that agency regulations *may* provide a standard to apply within the meaning of *Chaney.*" The court went on to consider agency regulations, policy statements and informal standards.).

The District of Columbia Court of Appeals avoided deciding whether an agency's regulations and precedent could provide meaningful standards in Lorion v. NRC, 785 F.2d 1038 (D.C.Cir.1986). To avoid the difficult question of whether these sources could allow for review, the court decided that on the merits of plaintiff's claim plaintiff would not succeed, and therefore there was no need to decide the reviewability issue.

While an adopted regulation clearly binds an agency by its terms, less statute-like pronouncements, such as policy statements and internal standards used by the agency, may or may not have the force of "law" to qualify as "law to apply" sufficient to rebut the *Chaney* presumption. In *Padula v. Webster*[42] the District of Columbia Court of Appeals described a test for determining whether an agency's policy statements will bind the agency.[43] "In determining whether an agency's statements constitute 'binding norms,' we traditionally look to [(1)] the *present effect* of the agency's pronouncements."[44] To have a present binding effect, a statement must (a) not be merely prospective, and (b) impose obligations on the agency and provide rights to others. The court also looks to [2] "whether the agency's statements leave the agency free to exercise its discretion."[45] This involves considering whether the statement (a) imposes significant restraints on the agency's discretion, and (b) is intended by the agency to be binding. To determine agency intent, look to the statement's language, context, and any other available extrinsic evidence. If the agency's statement affects the agency and others and is not intended to leave the agency free to exercise its discretion, then the agency's statement is binding and constitutes "law to apply."

§ 13.11.3 What Standard of Review Do Courts Apply to Agency Inaction

Even if a court concludes that it will review some aspect of an agency enforcement decision, the scope of review is generally very narrow. In *Shelley v. Brock*[46] for example, the court stated that the standard for reviewing agency decisions not to enforce under LMRDA § 402 is "quite deferential." Quoting *Dunlop v. Bachowski,* the court noted that "the statute [LMRDA section 402] relies upon the special knowledge and discretion of the Secretary for the determination of both the probable violation and the probable effect."[47] The Secretary must provide a statement of reasons supporting his decision with a "rational and defensible basis,"[48] and including "specific reference to the terms of the authority vested in [the Secretary] by the Act."[49] The court may consider only the statement of reasons in making its determination whether the Secretary's decision is "so irrational as to constitute the decision arbitrary and capricious."[50] Only in the "rare case" can the court look further than the statement of reasons.

The court in *Doyle v. Brock*[51] applied the same standard of review as in *Shelley.* The Secretary's statement of reasons must be "founded on

42. 822 F.2d 97 (D.C.Cir.1987).

43. *Padula* involved a request for judicial review of the FBI's refusal to hire the plaintiff. The court found the FBI's hiring decisions to be committed to agency discretion because the court could find no judicially manageable standards in statutes, regulations or policy statements.

44. Id. at 100 (emphasis added).

45. Id.

46. 793 F.2d 1368 (D.C.Cir.1986).

47. Id. at 1372 (quoting 421 U.S. at 571, 95 S.Ct. at 1859).

48. Id. at 1373 (quoting 421 U.S. at 573, 95 S.Ct. at 1861).

49. Id.

50. Id. at 1372 (quoting 421 U.S. at 573, 95 S.Ct. at 1861).

51. 821 F.2d 778 (D.C.Cir.1987).

grounds permitted by the statute or case law."[52] The court may consider only the statement of reasons in determining whether the Secretary's decision is "so irrational as to constitute the decision arbitrary and capricious."[53]

Similarly, courts generally provide a narrow scope of review when an agency's refusal to promulgate a new rule is in contention. In *American Horse Protection Association, Inc. v. Lyng,*[54] for example, the court took a deferential standard of review to the Department of Agriculture's refusal to initiate rulemaking proceedings:

> "[A]n agency's refusal to institute rulemaking proceedings is at the high end of the range [of deference accorded to the agency under arbitrary and capricious review].... Such a refusal is to be overturned 'only in the rarest and most compelling of circumstances' ... which have primarily involved 'plain errors of law, suggesting that the agency has been blind to the source of its delegated power.' "[55]

The Secretary must consider relevant factors, explain facts and policy concerns relied on, and rely only upon facts which have some basis in the record.[56] The court should consider " 'the petition for rulemaking, comments pro and con ... and the agency's explanation of its decision to reject the petition.' "[57] The court "must consider whether the agency's decisionmaking was 'reasoned,' "[58] i.e., whether "arbitrary, capricious, an abuse of discretion, or otherwise not in accordance with law."[59] The court will look more closely at a refusal denying "modification of a rule [when the petition alleges] a radical change in [the rule's] factual premises."[60]

52. Id. at 783 (quoting *Shelley* at 1374).

53. Id. at 782 (quoting 421 U.S. at 573, 95 S.Ct. at 1861).

54. 812 F.2d 1 (D.C.Cir.1987), on remand 681 F.Supp. 949 (D.D.C.1988).

55. 812 F.2d at 4–5 (citing ITT World Communications, Inc. v. FCC), 699 F.2d 1219, 1245–46 (D.C.Cir.1983), reversed on other grounds 466 U.S. 463, 104 S.Ct. 1936, 80 L.Ed.2d 480 (1984); WWHT, Inc. v. FCC, 656 F.2d 807, 818 (D.C.Cir.1981); State Farm Mutual Automobile Insurance Co. v. Department of Transportation, 680 F.2d 206, 221 (D.C.Cir.1982), vacated on other grounds 463 U.S. 29, 103 S.Ct. 2856, 77 L.Ed.2d 443 (1983), appeal after remand 802 F.2d 474 (D.C.Cir.1986), cert. denied 480 U.S. 951, 107 S.Ct. 1616, 94 L.Ed.2d 800 (1987) (1983); General Motors Corp. v. NHTSA, 898 F.2d 165 (D.C.Cir.1990) (agency's refusal to institute rulemaking is subject to the arbitrary and capricious standard, but that review is "especially narrow").

56. 812 F.2d at 5.

57. Id. (quoting *WWHT,* 656 F.2d at 817–18).

58. Id.

59. 5 U.S.C.A. § 706(2)(A).

60. Id. at 5 (citing Geller v. FCC, 610 F.2d 973 (D.C.Cir.1979), summarized in *WWHT,* 656 F.2d at 819, as holding that "an agency may be forced by a reviewing court to institute rulemaking proceedings if a significant factual predicate of a prior decision on the subject ... has been removed").

Chapter 14

MONEY DAMAGES

Table of Sections

As regards money damages for wrongful agency action, the distinction that must be kept in mind is between (1) official liability, which is the public official's personal liability for his wrongful acts, and (2) the liability of government itself, by money paid out of the public treasury. Government and the public fisc are protected against damage actions by the strong doctrine of sovereign immunity. Public officials, as they might pay out of pocket for their wrongs, do not enjoy quite the same degree of protection.

Indeed, the origins of judicial review of agency action in significant part lay in common law actions against public officials.[1] These actions represented an application of private law, the law that pertains to all of us in our relations one with another, to these officials. As said by Dicey, "every official, from the Prime Minister down to a constable or a collector of taxes, is under the same responsibility for every act done without legal justification as any citizen."[2] Accordingly, in *Miller v. Horton* when public officials, who were authorized by statute to dispose

1. See chap. 12, sec. 12.2.

2. A. Dicey, The Law of the Constitution 114 (8th Ed.1915). Dicey extrapolated this standard of official liability from case law. The thread that ran through these cases, as Dicey saw it, was the principle of generality of law, which he expressed as follows: "It means, again, equality before the law, or the equal subordination of all classes to the ordinary law of the land administered by the ordinary Law Courts" Id. At 120. Regarding this principle of generality, see chap. 3, sec. 3.1, supra.

of domestic animals with contagious diseases but instead mistook a healthy horse for a diseased horse and then killed it, the court, per Justice Holmes, found them liable to the owner for damages.[3]

But then, as Dicey also said, a public official might avoid liability on the grounds of "legal justification," that is, by whether the act of which a private party complains was authorized by public law. If the horse in *Miller v. Horton* had in fact been diseased within the meaning of the public act under which the officials acted, then its destruction would certainly have been under a "legal justification" that defeated a tort action against the officials. But without such justification an official is open to liability: He is, as the courts have said, "stripped of his official or representative character and ... subjected in his person to the consequences of his individual conduct."[4] And so it was in *Miller v. Horton*.

In this relation of "legal justification," a suit for damages, as well as being a means of compensation for injury inflicted, is a means for reviewing the legality of agency action. As a form of review, the suit tests whether the action in question is an appropriate exercise of public authority. But purely as a means of gaining judicial review of agency action, this sort of tort action, has, over time, withered. It has been supplanted by general forms of review as provided in the Administrative Procedure Act or by special statutory review as a legislature might provide for a specific agency.[5] Under these generous review provisions, actions to set aside an agency rule or order, or for declaratory and injunctive relief, have today become the usual mode for correcting agency action.

At times, however, these modern forms of review may not be an adequate surrogate for money damages. They fail to provide compensation. Otherwise, the range of agency actions covered by these forms of review may *not* be entirely coextensive with the range of actions subject to review respecting money damages. Also, a suit for money damages offers a different forum, the civil jury. Consequently, action for damages remain important in administrative law.

3. 152 Mass. 540, 26 N.E. 100 (1891). The defendants were members of a municipal health board authorized by statute to destroy "in all cases of ... glanders" infected domestic animals, and these officials killed a man's horse because they thought it had glanders. He sued them, and a jury found that the horse, in fact, did not have the disease. On appeal, Justice Holmes, saying that "the statute means no more than it says, and is intended to authorize the killing of actually infected horses only," found that the board members were liable in damages for their error.

4. Ex parte Young, 209 U.S. 123, 160, 28 S.Ct. 441, 52 L.Ed. 714 (1908). See Larson v. Domestic & Foreign Commerce Corp., 337 U.S. 682, 689, 69 S.Ct. 1457, 93 L.Ed. 1628 (1949) ("where the officer's powers are limited by statute, his actions beyond those limitations are considered individual and not sovereign actions."). See also Bates v. Clark, 95 U.S. (5 Otto) 204, 24 L.Ed. 471 (1877) (A federal statute directed seizure of alcoholic beverages in Indian country). The seizure in question, however, was not made in Indian country; thus, the objection "fatal" to defendants' claims of legal justification was that "in that locality [the seizing officers] were utterly without any authority in the premises." Consequently, they were liable in damages.

5. Regarding modern forms of judicial review, see chap. 12, sec. 12.2.

§ 14.1 GOVERNMENT LIABILITY AND SOVEREIGN IMMUNITY

Under "official liability," an injured person may bring an action in damages against the responsible official. The injured person might, however, consider another action: he might consider suing the principal, i.e., the government, as well as the agent (the public official). In private law, the principal is indeed liable for the acts of an agent, according to the common law doctrine of respondeat superior. Thus, enterprise liability, the liability of an employer for the acts of its employees, is the norm in private law. Enterprise liability, however, is not necessarily the case when the principal is the government. "Sovereign immunity," the immunity of government from suit, is fixture of American law. And this immunity is absolute, precluding liability on the part of government for the acts of its officials, *unless the government waives its immunity.*

Sovereign immunity may be waived, but only by a legislative act. This waiver may be by a *private* bill pertaining to specific individuals and circumstances.[1] More generally, Congress may waive immunity by a public law, and in some important instances Congress has by such laws waived the immunity that the federal government would otherwise enjoy. In a modern development, Congress has by such a waiver established a relatively new system of enterprise liability, wherein the principle, the federal government, has indeed assumed the liability for the wrongful acts of its officials (with the significant exception of such "constitutional torts" as may be committed by these officials). This development was by a 1988 amendment (the "Westfall Act") to the Federal Tort Claims Act.

The Federal Torts Claims Act and the Tucker Act (largely for contract claims) are important waivers of sovereign immunity. These acts are discussed in the immediately following sections. Another significant waiver, which does *not* include money damages proper but does include equitable, non-compensatory, transfers of money, is that of § 702 of the Administrative Procedure Act. This waiver (which is for declaratory and injunctive relief and equitable relief in general) is discussed at § 12.1.

§ 14.1.1 The Westfall Act And Respondeat Superior

As we said, the principle of respondeat superior does not apply to government so as to make it liable for the wrongs of its employees. However, in 1988 Congress revised this state of affairs, by establishing a statutory system of government liability for the ordinary torts of its employees and officials. This was by means of an amendment to the

§ 14.1

1. In fact, the private-bill pressure—the politics and the workload—on Congress has been a reason for Congress to waive immunity broadly, in general classes of cases such as contract claims and torts. See United States v. Mitchell, 463 U.S. 206, 212–13, 103 S.Ct. 2961, 77 L.Ed.2d 580 (1983).

Federal Torts Claim Act. This amendment is itself known as the Westfall Act.

By means of the Federal Tort Claims Act ("FTCA"), the federal government has to an extent waived the immunity of, and provided for money damages against, the federal government for injuries caused by certain "negligent or wrongful" acts of its officials.[2] But under the FTCA, an action might also be brought against the official who had committed the wrong. With the Westfall Act, the FTCA was amended to provide for the substitution of the United States as the party defendant in such tort actions (excepting constitutional torts) as they might be brought against federal officials.

This move was inspired by the Supreme Court decision in *Westfall v. Erwin*,[3] where the Court, in trying to balance the needs of injured parties against the occasional unfairness, and the detriment to energetic public action, of damages paid for by public officials, pointedly stated that Congress was in the best position to make that balance and that "Legislated standards governing the immunity of federal employees involved in state-law tort actions would be useful." The Westfall Act was Congress's response to that suggestion.

As provided by the Act,

> "The remedy against the United States provided by [the FTCA] for injury or loss of property, or personal injury or death arising or resulting from the negligent or wrongful act or omission of any employee of the Government while acting within the scope of his office or employment is exclusive of any other civil action or proceeding for money damages. . . ."[4]

Upon certification by the Attorney General that an employee acted "within the scope of his office or employment," that employee is dropped from a tort action against him and the United States substituted as the party defendant.[5] By this means, the employee is relieved of liability in damages and other costs such as attorney fees. Just so, the Westfall Act establishes a scheme of enterprise liability on the part of government.

As the United States assumes the liabilities of its employees, it comes into all the defenses that an employee might have asserted as well as those defenses available to the United States under the FTCA. In this latter respect, the Westfall Act provides that a suit "shall proceed in the same manner as any action the United States filed pursuant to [the FTCA] and shall be subject to the same limitations and exceptions to

2. 28 U.S.C. §§ 1346(b), 2671 et seq. Money damages as provided for by this Act do *not* include punitive damages. 28 U.S.C. § 2674.

3. 484 U.S. 292, 108 S.Ct. 580, 98 L.Ed.2d 619 (1988).

4. Formally known as the Employees Liability Reform and Tort Compensation Act of 1988, Pub.L. 100–694, 102 Stat. 4564 (1988), codified at 28 U.S.C. § 2679(b)(1).

5. This attorney general certification, which is often a key element in determining the liability of a public official, is not conclusive, not with respect to the courts. Instead, courts may review and correct this determination. Gutierrez de Martinez v. Lamagno, 515 U.S. 417, 115 S.Ct. 2227, 132 L.Ed.2d 375 (1995).

those actions."[6] This "same limitations and exceptions" proviso limits somewhat the remedies previously available to persons injured by official actions. This point is made, and illustrated, by the Supreme Court decision in *United States v. Smith.*[7]

A medical malpractice action had been brought against a military physician for acts done in Italy. Upon certification that the acts were done in the course of government employment, the doctor was dropped from the case and the United States substituted as defendant. The United States then asserted a defense available to it under the FTCA, which was that that Act did not waive governmental immunity for acts done abroad.[8] The district court then dismissed the action. The district court decision was, however, reversed by the Ninth Circuit court of appeals. That court reasoned that the Westfall Act relieved an employee, such as the physician, of personal liability only when there is in fact a remedy against the federal government. Accordingly, that court reinstated the original action against physician. The Supreme Court, though, reversed the Ninth Circuit, reinstated the United as the defendant, and then dismissed the action inasmuch as the FTCA did not admit of a claim based on torts committed on foreign soil. The Court explained that " 'limitations and exceptions language' ... persuades us that Congress recognized that the required substitution of the United States as the defendant in tort suits filed against government employees would sometimes foreclose a tort plaintiff's recovery altogether."

So as to more better understand the FTCA and its limitations and exceptions, we now turn to that Act.

§ 14.1.2 The Federal Tort Claims Act

The FTCA establishes governmental liability "for injury or loss of property, or personal injury or death caused by the negligent or wrongful act or omission of any federal employee acting within the scope of his office or employment in circumstances where the United States, if a private person, would be liable to the claimant in accordance with the law of the place where the act or omission occurred."[9]

This assumption of liability for the "negligent or wrongful act or omission of any federal employee" is limited in some important respects. It applies only where "a private person, would be liable to the claimant in accordance with the law of the place where the act or omission occurred."[10] Being limited to circumstances where a private person would be liable, the assumption of liability is not for wrongs peculiar to government, such as acts in violation of the Constitution.[11] Also, as the

6. 28 U.S.C. § 2679 (d)(4).

7. 499 U.S. 160, 111 S.Ct. 1180, 113 L.Ed.2d 134 (1991).

8. 28 U.S.C. § 2680(k).

9. 28 U.S.C. § 1346(b). Money damages as provided for by this Act do *not* include punitive damages. 28 U.S.C. § 2674.

10. 28 U.S.C. § 1346(b).

11. This implication is made specific by the Westfall Act at 28 U.S.C. § 2679(b)(1). Some constitutional violations, however, may also amount to wrongs under private law. For instance, an invasion of privacy as

Act refers to "the law of the place where the act or omission occurred," the Act apparently excludes acts wrongful under federal law (as opposed to acts wrongful under state law) from its waiver of immunity. Where a FTCA action was filed against a federal inspector for his alleged negligence in correcting unsafe working conditions as identified by the Occupational Safety and Health Act, the action was dismissed because "the duties required of OSHA officers are federally imposed and have no counterparts cognizable under [state] law."[12]

The FTCA is further limited in that it largely (albeit not completely) pertains to torts sounding in negligence. The Act does refer to "wrongful" as well as negligent acts. But as the FTCA was originally interpreted, these "wrongful" acts were mostly limited to actions in trespass.[13] Also, a number of wrongful acts, those consisting of intentional torts (for instance, defamation) were identified by the Act and then specifically excluded from its coverage.[14] In 1974, however, the FTCA was amended to extend government liability to a certain range of intentional acts. This range consisted of acts committed by federal "investigative or law enforcement officers." These acts included assault, battery, false imprisonment, false arrest, abuse of process, or malicious prosecution.[15]

Finally, the Act's establishment of government liability is significantly limited in that it does not include the discretionary acts of government officials. The Act excludes "Any claim based upon ... the exercise or performance or the failure to exercise or perform a discretionary function or duty on the part of a federal agency or an employee of the Government, whether or not the discretion involved be abused."[16] The scope of this "discretionary act" exemption has been the subject of a large amount of litigation. Generally speaking, this exemption is meant to preclude tort liability for judgments about public policy, as opposed to liability for ordinary negligence. In this respect, the exemption protects "governmental actions based on considerations of public policy" and "prevent[s] judicial second guessing of legislative and administrative decisions grounded in social, economic, and political policy through the

protected by the Constitution might be construed as a trespass under private law.

12. Davis v. United States, 536 F.2d 758 (8th Cir.1976). But see United States v. Muniz, 374 U.S. 150, 83 S.Ct. 1850, 10 L.Ed.2d 805 (1963), where the Court, in connection with an action brought by federal prisoners against their federal keepers, held that the Act did not import state law doctrines of immunity. The Court did, however, make it clear that standards of due care were to be drawn from state law. Id. at n. 27.

13. See Dalehite v. United States, 346 U.S. 15, 45, 73 S.Ct. 956, 97 L.Ed. 1427 (1953).

14. 28 U.S.C. § 2680(h).

15. Pub.L. No. 93–253, § 2, 88 Stat. 50. The law was passed in response to Bivens v. Six Unknown Named Agents of Federal Bureau of Narcotics, 403 U.S. 388, 91 S.Ct. 1999, 29 L.Ed.2d 619 (1971), which established official liability for constitutional torts. See sec. 14.2.1, supra. While this amendment to the FTCA might have been seen as establishing an exclusive liability, on the part of government as opposed to government officials, for these constitutional torts, and thereby (as an exclusive remedy) eliminating official liability under *Bivens*, the Supreme Court has refused to read the amendment as establishing such an exclusive remedy. Carlson v. Green, 446 U.S. 14, 100 S.Ct. 1468, 64 L.Ed.2d 15 (1980).

16. 28 U.S.C.A. § 2680(a).

medium of an action in tort."[17] Accordingly, whether an action is "discretionary" so as not to be subject to tort liability often involves a two-part inquiry. First, the courts ask whether the action complained of "involves the element of judgment." Second, they ask whether that judgment is of "the kind that the discretionary function exception was designed to shield."[18]

The question of whether the action complained of involves the "element of judgment" is usually expressed in terms of a "permissible policy judgment."[19] By this expression, the courts try to understand whether an official action was so dictated by statute that the official had no room for policy judgments. In *Berkovitz v. United States,* a child had contacted polio from a federally licensed polio vaccine. The parents then sued, under the FTCA, for damages.[20] In part, the plaintiff alleged that the federal Division of Biologic Standards had licensed the polio vaccine on the basis of inadequate data, that is, without the benefit of data as required by statute and regulations. Such a failure to comply with a specific statutory directive, the Court found, was not "a permissible policy judgment." The Court explained:

> The [Division of Biologic Standards] has no discretion to issue a license without first receiving the required test data; to do so would violate a specific statutory and regulatory directive. Accordingly, to the extent that [plaintiffs'] licensing claim is based on a decision of the [Division of Biologic Standards] to issue a license without having received the required test data, the discretionary function exception imposes no bar.[21]

The second element, whether a judgment is of "the kind that the discretionary function exception was designed to shield," is illustrated by the Supreme Court decision is *United States v. Gaubert.*[22] The Federal Home Loan Bank Board ("FHLBB") had assumed a role in the management of a failing savings and loan bank. Thereafter, shareholders of that institution charged that the FHLBB had been negligent in its supervi-

17. United States v. S.A. Empresa (Varig Airlines), 467 U.S. 797, 813–14, 104 S.Ct. 2755, 81 L.Ed.2d 660 (1984), United States v. Gaubert, 499 U.S. 315, 323, 111 S.Ct. 1267, 113 L.Ed.2d 335 (1991).

18. United States v. Gaubert, 499 U.S. 315, 322–23, 111 S.Ct. 1267, 113 L.Ed.2d 335 (1991); Appley Brothers v. United States, 164 F.3d 1164 (8th Cir.1999).

19. Berkovitz v. United States, 486 U.S. 531, 539, 108 S.Ct. 1954, 100 L.Ed.2d 531 (1988).

20. 486 U.S. 531, 108 S.Ct. 1954, 100 L.Ed.2d 531 (1988).

21. On similar grounds ("Because [plaintiffs] may yet show, on the basis of materials obtained in discovery or otherwise, that the conduct challenged here did not involve the permissible exercise of policy discretion,") the Court also sustained the plaintiff's count respecting the agency's alleged failure to inspect certain lots of vaccine.

Respecting the licensing of the vaccine, the plaintiffs had another, but not clearly stated, allegation. The allegation had something to do with whether the Division of Biologic Standards was correct in its judgment to license the vaccine. Here, the court ruled that in any event "application of the discretionary function exception" depended on whether the responsible agency officials "appropriately exercise policy judgment in determining that a vaccine product complies with the relevant safety standards," which was a question to be decided on remand.

22. 499 U.S. 315, 111 S.Ct. 1267, 113 L.Ed.2d 335 (1991).

sion of the bank and sued for damages under the Federal Tort Claims Act. The United States contended that it was exempt from liability by virtue of the discretionary functions provisions of the Act. The Court found that the FHLBB's involvement in bank management were not so precisely dictated by statute that they could not be said to be policy judgments by the agency. But by itself, that finding did not resolve the issue. There remained the question of whether "that judgment is of the kind that the discretionary function exception was designed to shield."

The judgments that the "exception was meant to shield" were those involving "governmental actions and decisions based on considerations of public policy." Allegations of FHLBB negligence at higher levels, such as in advising the savings and loan bank to place subsidiaries in bankruptcy or in causing it to hire a certain financial consultant, were about judgments based "on public policy considerations." These allegations, therefore, were shielded by the discretionary functions exception. The shareholders also contended that "day-to-day" decisions concerning [the bank's] affairs did not implicate social, economic, or political policies. The Court disagreed with that assessment. While these regulatory activities reached down to an "operational" level, these activities and the judgment entailed in them were part of a general policy of "protecting the savings and loan industry at large." As such, these judgments were policy judgments shielded from liability.[23]

§ 14.1.3 The Tucker Act

The Tucker Act was passed in 1887. As against the federal government, it waives sovereign immunity for claims "founded either upon the Constitution, or an Act of Congress, or any regulation of an executive department, upon any express or implied contract with the United States or for liquidated or unliquidated damages in cases not sounding in tort."[24] Because the bulk of actions brought under the Tucker Act comes under its waiver for express or implied contracts, the Act is usually thought of as a waiver respecting government contracts.

By its terms, however, the Tucker Act includes non-contractual claims, claims "founded either upon the Constitution, or an Act of Congress, or any regulation of an executive department." This language, in and of itself, would seem broadly to waive governmental immunity for claims other than contract claims, for claims based on personal injury caused by acts in violation of constitutional or statutory law. The waiver, however, is more limited than it seems. Because the Tucker Act also says it does not extend to cases "sounding in tort," its waiver of immunity has never been taken as providing jurisdiction for personal injuries

23. The lower court had distinguished between "policy functions" and "operational" activities, and found that the latter were not protected by the discretionary function exception. 499 U. S. at 321. The Supreme Court, continuing it practice of assessing liability not by the status of the actor but by his function, rejected that distinction.

24. Tucker Act, Act of Mar. 3, 1887, ch. 359, 24 Stat. 505, and codified in various sections of Title 28 of the United States Code. The part quoted above is 28 U.S.C.A. § 1491.

caused by the wrongful acts of federal officials.[25] The claims that the "non-contractual" provisions of the Tucker Act do refer to have been described as being comprised of "two somewhat overlapping classes." These classes are where:

> [1] the plaintiff has paid money over to the Government, directly or in effect, and seeks return of all or part of that sum; and [2] . . . money has not been paid but the plaintiff asserts that he is nevertheless entitled to payment from the treasury.[26]

The first class of claims should include tax refund suits or other such actions " 'to recover an illegal exaction [of money] made by officials of the government.' "[27] In the second class of claims, where the plaintiff asserts that he is "entitled to payment from the treasury," the plaintiff must assert "that the particular provision of law relied upon grants the claimant, expressly or by implication, a right to be paid a certain sum."[28] An instance of the "right to be paid a certain sum" is that of a taking without just compensation.[29] For claims under statutory law, the "right to be paid a certain sum" was explained in *United States v. Mitchell.*[30]

In *Mitchell,* the Quinault Indians had alleged that the Department of Interior, in acting as a fiduciary for them in managing certain tribal timberlands, had violated this relation of trust by mismanaging the timberlands. The Indians sought money damages from the government, and for these damages a waiver of governmental immunity was of course necessary. The Court found this necessary waiver in the Tucker Act, as the Act included claims founded upon "an Act of Congress, or any regulation of an executive department." The Court, however, said that a "second step," rather a substantive step, was necessary: the relevant statutes and regulations, those pertaining to the trustee status of the Department of Interior, had to establish a claim against the government. These two steps were described by Justice Marshall, who wrote for a majority of the Court, as "analytical distinct":

> In this case . . . there is simply no question that the Tucker Act provides the United States' consent to suit for claims founded upon statutes or regulations that create substantive rights to money damages. If a claim falls within this category, the existence of a waiver of sovereign immunity is clear. The question in this case is thus analytically distinct: whether the statute or regulations at issue can be interpreted as requiring compensation.[31]

25. E.g. Basso v. United States, 239 U.S. 602, 36 S.Ct. 226, 60 L.Ed. 462 (1915).

26. Id.

27. Eastport Steamship Corp. v. U.S., 372 F.2d 1002, 1008 (Ct.Cl.1967).

28. Id. at 1007.

29. United States v. Causby, 328 U.S. 256, 66 S.Ct. 1062, 90 L.Ed. 1206 (1946).

30. 463 U.S. 206, 103 S.Ct. 2961, 77 L.Ed.2d 580 (1983).

31. 463 U.S. at 219, 103 S.Ct. at 2969. In this case, the majority had first of all undertaken, as it said, to dispel once and for all the notion that the Tucker Act merely provided jurisdiction to hear cases within its terms instead of waiving immunity for these cases. In this regard, the Court, as flatly as it could, stated that

> [T]his Court [has] employed language suggesting that the Tucker Act does not effect a waiver of sovereign immunity. Such

According to the majority, the pertinent statutory provisions did indeed establish a relation of trust between the federal government and the plaintiffs. Therefore these provisions provided a substantive basis for a claim of breach of trust. While these statutes did not themselves provide for compensation for a breach of trust, such an action was implied by reference to private law and to the fact that under private law "It is well established that a trustee is accountable in damages for breaches of trust."

§ 14.2 LIABILITY OF PUBLIC OFFICERS

If only for deeper pockets, a person injured by official action might prefer damages from the government. But unless it can be brought under some waiver, this suit will be blocked by sovereign immunity. But sovereign immunity does not block all avenues and actions for damages for the wrong committed. As we said, the official that committed the wrong may himself be liable in damages. This has been the rule, at least from *Dr. Bonham's Case* on down to the present.

The liability of public officials may rise out of a number of sources. It can result from an invasion of rights—of property, contract, or tort—established under the common law. For instance, if an official makes an unlawful search of a person's property, that official may be liable for damages sounding in trespass or privacy. Apart from the common law, official liability can be based on invasion of rights created by statute. Also, in an area of considerable expansion over the past several years, public officials may be liable in damages for violations of rights protected by the Constitution.

As we have seen, the age-old rule of official liability for ordinary torts has, for federal officials, largely been eliminated by means of the Westfall Act. The extent to which state legislatures similarly substitute governmental liability for official liability in these common-law tort situations will vary from state to state. However, state and federal officials alike remain personally liable in damages for acts in violation of constitutional law. Therefore, the first matter we will discuss is this section is the creation and expansion of "constitutional torts." The other matter is the continuing development of an immunity, an "official immunity," for public officials sued for damages. Both of these things—an official liability and a concomitant official immunity—are products of the courts. Consequently, our discussion of them is about case law, which unfortunately has not unfolded so evenly.

§ 14.2.1 Official Liability And Constitutional Torts

The liability of a public official is for acts done without "legal justification." The legal justification that would excuse, say a trespass by

language was not necessary to the decision in either case.... Without in any way questioning the result in either case, we conclude that this isolated language should be disregarded. If a claim falls within the terms of the Tucker Act, the United States has presumptively consented to suit.

463 U.S. at 216, 103 S.Ct. at 2967.

Given the broad and ambiguous range of constitutional rights, *Monroe v. Pape* and *Bivens* have resulted in a significantly enlarged exposure of public officials to damages actions.[11] The trend has been to increase the exposure. In *Monell v. Department of Social Services,* the Supreme Court reversed a previous position and held that municipalities were subject to damages under Sec. 1983.[12] In *Carlson v. Green,* the Court held that the availability of a recovery from the federal government under the Federal Tort Claims Act did not preclude a constitutional tort action against an official on the same violation.[13]

This rise of constitutional torts makes possible a fuller relief to the victims of unlawful official action. At the same time, however, in their indeterminate range these torts have significantly enlarged the liabilities of officials trying to do their duty. In turn, the courts have tried to limit this exposure. In some small extent, the courts have done so by placing a limit on the *substantive* range of constitutional torts. This limit, as set by the Supreme Court, is that in constitutional torts official liability does not include actions based on a lack of due care. Instead, the tort must be intentional.[14] In a larger extent, the courts have tried to protect public

gress could develop. Also, a better route might be to waive sovereign immunity, as only Congress can," so as "to pay damages out of the public treasury rather than the official's pockets." Id. at 422, 91 S.Ct. at 2017. Waiving sovereign immunity would alleviate the deterrence to vigorous official action as caused by a personal liability for such action. In *Bivens,* this deterrence was described by Justice Blackmun as follows:

> Whenever a suspect imagines, or chooses to assert, that a Fourth Amendment right has been violated, he will now immediately sue the federal officer in federal court. This will tend to stultify proper law enforcement and to make the day's labor for the honest and conscientious officer even more onerous and more critical.

Id. at 430, 91 S.Ct. at 2021.

11. The expansion of such actions is indicated by the fact that in 1961, the year of *Monroe v. Pape,* only 296 civil rights actions were filed against state officials under Sec. 1983, whereas in 1986 there were over 40,000. For a statistical study of these actions, see Eisenberg & Swab, The Reality of Constitutional Tort Litigation, 72 Corn. L.Rev. 101 (1987).

12. 436 U.S. 658, 98 S.Ct. 2018, 56 L.Ed.2d 611 (1978).

13. 446 U.S. 14, 100 S.Ct. 1468, 64 L.Ed.2d 15 (1980). This case involved a claim for damages for violation of the eighth amendment right against cruel and unusual punishment. The decedent had died after prison officials allegedly failed to assure proper medical care. The Court approved the claim for damages, notwithstanding the fact that following *Bivens,* Congress had amended the Federal Tort Claims Act to provide for relief, via money damages paid out of the public treasury, for various forms of police misconduct. 28 U.S.C. § 2680(h). In finding that this new relief under the Federal Torts Claim Act did not bar a *Bivens* type constitutional tort remedy, the Court was guided by considerations of the most effective deterrent of misconduct by public officials. Inasmuch as the official pays out of his or her own pocket book and is subject to punitive as well as compensatory damages, the *Bivens* action is likely the more effective deterrent.

14. Daniels v. Williams, 474 U.S. 327, 106 S.Ct. 662, 88 L.Ed.2d 662 (1986). In this case an inmate at a city jail brought a Sec. 1983 action against prison officials in which he claimed that he had tripped and fallen on an object negligently left on a stairway by a deputy. His argument was that this negligence amounted to a taking of liberty without due process of law. The Court, however, held that allegations of a lack of due care did not establish a cause of action under due process. In so holding, it overruled its decision in Parratt v. Taylor, 451 U.S. 527, 101 S.Ct. 1908, 68 L.Ed.2d 420 (1981), "to the extent that [that decision] states that a mere lack of due care by a state official may 'deprive' an individual of life, liberty or property under the fourteenth amendment." 474 U.S. at 330–31, 106 S.Ct. at 664–65.

employees, when they are simply trying to do their duty, in another way. In this other way, the courts have created a doctrine of "official immunity" that is offered as an off-set to the doctrine of official liability.

§ 14.3 OFFICIAL IMMUNITY: HISTORY AND POLICIES

There is considerable appeal in holding public officials liable for wrongs they commit. Under private law, compensation is the rule for injury wrongfully inflicted, and fairness seems to dictate extending this rule to government acts. Also, official liability for bad acts should deter governmental lawlessness in the first place.

Nonetheless, the good sense in strict liability of public official is open to question. It may be unfair to hold an official liable in damages as she in good faith tries to perform the hard tasks that the public demands.[1] These tasks require difficult judgments, and these judgments often bear down on people in such a way as both to offend them and to make them likely plaintiffs. The teacher who disciplines, the policeman who searches and arrests, these officials and many others like them have to make difficult judgments that are painful to those subject to them. And these people may be disposed to retaliate through litigation. The Supreme Court has said as much, as it spoke about retaliatory litigation as provoked by vigorous public action:

> While there is not likely to be anyone willing and legally able to seek damages from the officials if they do not authorize the administrative proceeding . . . , there is a serious danger that the decision to authorize proceedings will provoke a retaliatory response. An individual targeted by an administrative proceeding will react angrily and may seek vengeance in the courts.

The Court added that "A corporation will muster all of its financial and legal resources in an effort to prevent administrative sanctions. 'When millions may turn on regulatory decisions, there is a strong incentive to counterattack.' "[2]

So, along with possibility of injustice to the individual official, official liability may also diminish the general public welfare. For instance, in *Miller v. Horton*[3] where health officials had mistakenly thought the plaintiff's horse had glanders, the damages these officials had to pay might cause them to be hesitant, too hesitant, the next time they had to deal with a diseased animal. The deterrence to vigorous official action is not just the amount of damages that officials may have to pay. It also includes litigation costs such as legal fees, time, embar-

§ 14.3

1. "[T]he injustice, particularly in the absence of bad faith, of subjecting to liability an officer who is required, by the legal obligations of his position, to exercise discretion . . ." has been much a part of Supreme Court decisional law on official liability. Scheuer v. Rhodes, 416 U.S. 232, 240, 94 S.Ct. 1683, 1688, 40 L.Ed.2d 90 (1974), appeal after remand 570 F.2d 563 (6th Cir. 1977).

2. Butz v. Economou, 438 U.S. 478, 515, 98 S.Ct. 2894, 2915, 57 L.Ed.2d 895 (1978), on remand 466 F.Supp. 1351 (S.D.N.Y.1979), affirmed 633 F.2d 203 (2d Cir.1980).

3. 152 Mass. 540, 26 N.E. 100 (1891).

rassment, and so forth. And unlike the employee in private litigation—where the employer is likely to be joined as a defendant and absorb some of the costs—the public official often stands alone: joining his employer is barred by sovereign immunity.[4]

Consequently, the potential of official liability is that of a range of public action that is not as vigorous as it ought to be: police may not be enthusiastic law enforcers, parole boards may refuse to parole, public employers may overlook malingerers, teachers may not make hard disciplinary choices. The diminishment of public action may not be just a reluctance to take action, it may as well be an increased formality and awkwardness in that action as the official shields himself with layers of documentation and decisional processes.[5] Accordingly, the courts have been mindful of the downside to official liability. As we said, this concern has moved them in the direction of an "official immunity" that the official might plead as a defense against such liability.

The Constitution itself provides an immunity only to members of Congress in relation to speech or debate in legislative actions.[6] And so, the larger range of immunity, for public officials in general, is wholly the product of the courts. In the courts, immunity appears to have first been created for judges and those involved in the judicial process.[7] Then it expanded, to include agency officials.

In 1845 in *Kendall v. Stokes,* the Postmaster General was sued for erroneously suspending payments to a creditor of the Post Office.[8]

4. Federal officials, however, do not stand completely alone. The practice of the Justice Department is to provide an attorney to defend them when they are acting within the scope of their authority. Bermann, Integrating Governmental and Officer Tort Liability, 77 Colum.L.Rev. 1175, 1192 (1977).

5. For a good discussion of deterrence to vigorous public action, and, indeed, a good discussion of the range of competing interests in this area of official liability, see P. Schuck, Suing Government: Citizen Remedies for Official Wrongs (1983).

6. U.S. Const. Art. I, § 6. This provision is that congressmen "shall in all cases, except treason, Felon, And Breach of Peace, be privileged from Arrest during their Attendance at the Session of their respective Houses, and in going to and returning from the same; and for any Speech or Debate in Either House, they shall not be questioned in any other place." As explained by Justice Harlan, this immunity is rooted in separation of powers considerations: "There is little doubt that the instigation of criminal charges against critical or disfavored legislators by the executive in a judicial form was the chief fear prompting the long struggle for parliamentary privilege in England and, in the context of the American system of separation of powers, is the predominant thrust of the Speech and Debate Clause." United States v. Johnson, 383 U.S. 169, 182, 86 S.Ct. 749, 756, 15 L.Ed.2d 681 (1966).

7. Bradley v. Fisher, 80 U.S. (13 Wall.) 335, 20 L.Ed. 646 (1872). In 1872, judicial immunity was seen as ancient law, as the "settled doctrine of the English courts for many centuries, and has never been denied, that we are aware of, in the courts of this country." 13 Wall. at 347. This immunity, however, was also supported by logic. If a civil action for damages could be maintained it would cut against "independence without which no judiciary can either be respectable or useful." Id. Thus the judiciary gained an absolute immunity "whilst exercising their judicial functions within the general scope of their jurisdictions." 13 Wall. at 354. This immunity was extended to other officers of government involved in the judicial process, and for the same reason, so that they can vigorously carry out their public function. Yaselli v. Goff, 12 F.2d 396 (2d Cir.1926), affirmed per curiam 275 U.S. 503, 48 S.Ct. 155, 72 L.Ed. 395 (1927). For an extension of the absolute immunity of the judiciary to agency officials involved in similar functions, see Butz v. Economou, 438 U.S. 478, 98 S.Ct. 2894, 57 L.Ed.2d 895 (1978).

8. 44 U.S. (3 How.) 87, 11 L.Ed. 506 (1845). Under this case, perhaps only high

Suspending such payments was, however, among the normal duties of this office. In this duty, the Postmaster General had acted "from a sense of public duty, and without malice" and had simply erred in the exercise of the discretion bestowed upon him. The Court, therefore, held that "a public officer, acting to the best of his judgment and from a sense of duty, in a matter of account with an individual [is not] liable in an action for an error of judgment."

Today, we refer to the immunity as thus established as "qualified immunity." Under it, public officials are immune from damages, for (1) discretionary actions (2) done in good faith, and (3) in the course of their official duties.[9]

The qualified immunity of *Kendall v. Stokes* was, however, soon seen as not enough. Under it the public official might still be subject to considerable litigation costs, because his good faith remained open to the scrutiny of judge and jury. Consequently, in its 1896 decision in *Spalding v. Vilas,* the Court recognized a greater immunity, an "absolute immunity."[10]

Spalding v. Vilas involved a defamation action brought, again, against the Postmaster General. This time, however, the wrong in question could not be assigned to a good-faith error in judgment, inasmuch as the Postmaster General was alleged to have *maliciously* published false information about the plaintiff. The Court, however, again dismissed the suit, this time on the grounds that the Postmaster General had a form of immunity greater than a merely qualified immunity. The Postmaster General was, the Court held, *absolutely* immune from suit so long as he "did not exceed his authority nor pass the line of his duty."[11] The head of an Executive Department, the Court explained, "should not have to work under an apprehension that his motives might become the subject of a civil litigation."

officials gained immunity, considering that the case involved a cabinet-level official. But see Wilkes v. Dinsman, 48 U.S. (7 How.) 89, 131, 12 L.Ed. 618 (1849) (immunity appears to have been extended to a military officer).

9. Initially, the courts were strict in their insistence on the act in question being within the limits assigned by statute, and unwilling to tolerate mistakes as to statutory limits. As the Supreme Court said in its review in Butz v. Economou, 438 U.S. 478, 489, 98 S.Ct. 2894, 2902, 57 L.Ed.2d 895 (1978), of the history of official liability, "the immunity of federal officials began as a means of protecting them in the execution of their federal statutory duties from criminal or civil actions based on state law.... A federal official who acted outside of his federal statutory authority would be held strictly liable for his trespassory acts." An instance of the strict insistence on the official's acting within the scope of his statutory authority is provided by Bates v. Clark, 95 U.S. (5 Otto) 204, 24 L.Ed. 471 (1877). In this case a federal statute directed seizure of alcoholic beverages in Indian country. The seizure in question, however, was not made in Indian country; thus, the objection "fatal" to defendants' claims of legal justification was that "in that locality [the seizing officers] were utterly without any authority in the premises."

10. 161 U.S. 483, 16 S.Ct. 631, 40 L.Ed. 780 (1896).

11. 161 U.S. at 499. In issuing the communication in question, the Postmaster General, the Court found, had acted within his duty. The allegedly defamatory information had circulated among postmasters.

§ 14.3.1 Official Immunity: Modern Doctrine

The scheme of personal immunity for modern administrative officials involves choices between qualified and absolute immunity. Presently, the rule seems to be that of a qualified immunity for public officials, with absolute immunity provided only for "special functions".[12] Initially, though, the Supreme Court appeared to favor a norm of absolute liability.

One of the more eloquently reasoned decisions in favor of absolute immunity is that of Judge Learned Hand in *Gregoire v. Biddle.*[13] As a supposed enemy alien, the plaintiff had been arrested and detained on Ellis Island during World War II. He had been detained in spite of a finding, reaffirmed by the Enemy Alien Review Board, that he was not a German alien. For this detention he sued two successive Attorneys General, two successive Directors of the Enemy Alien Control Unit at Justice, and the district Director of Immigration at Ellis Island.

While the court assumed that defendants had acted "maliciously and willfully," it nonetheless found the complaint deficient inasmuch as the defendants were absolutely immune from suit. Judge Hand's explanation of this holding, for preferring an absolute immunity over a qualified immunity protecting only good faith actions, was as follows:

> It does indeed go without saying that an official, who is in fact guilty of using his powers to vent his spleen upon others, or for any other personal motive not connected with the public good, should not escape liability for the injuries he may so cause; and, if it were possible in practice to confine such complaints to the guilty, it would be monstrous to deny recovery. The justification for doing so is that it is impossible to know whether the claim is well founded until the case has been tried, and that to submit all officials, the innocent as well as the guilty, to the burden of a trial and to the inevitable danger of its outcome, would dampen the ardor of all but the most resolute, or the most irresponsible, in the unflinching discharge of their duties. Again and again the public interest calls for action which may turn out to be founded on a mistake, in the face of which an official may later find himself hard put to satisfy a jury of his good faith.

In its 1959 decision in *Barr v. Matteo,*[14] the Supreme Court endorsed this reasoning and seemed to establish absolute immunity as the rule for federal officials. In this case, middle-level officials had sued their boss, the head of the Office of Rent Stabilization, for libel in a certain press release.[15] These plaintiffs charged that the "publication and terms [of the

12. The exceptions, as we discuss them below, are for "officials whose special functions require full exemption from liability," infra sec. 14.3.1, and for federal officials charged with common law torts, infra sec. 14.3.1.

13. 177 F.2d 579, 581 (2d Cir.1949).

14. 360 U.S. 564, 79 S.Ct. 1335, 3 L.Ed.2d 1434 (1959).

15. The press release concerned the plaintiffs' involvement in a plan, then in question on the floor of the Senate, to use agency funds for certain salary arrangements.

release] had been actuated by malice on the part of the [defendant]." The trial court denied defendant's claim of immunity and submitted the matter to a jury, which found for the plaintiffs. On appeal to the Supreme Court, the sole issue was the proper level of immunity: was it qualified, which would allow the judgment to stand (inasmuch as malice negated good faith), or absolute, which would overturn it?[16]

A divided Court opted for absolute immunity. The policy grounds, as assessed in an opinion by Justice Harlan, were much the same as those of Judge Hand in *Gregoire v. Biddle.* As said by Justice Harlan, immunity would be " 'of little value [to officials] if they could be subjected to the cost and inconvenience and distractions of a trial upon a conclusion of the pleader, or to the hazard of a judgment against them based upon a jury's speculation as to motives.' "[17]

* * *

The immunity conferred by *Barr v. Matteo* pertained only to federal officials. Immunity for state officials sued for violation of federally-protected rights under the Civil Rights Acts, was, however, forthcoming.[18] But unlike federal officials, the immunity available to state officials was found to be a qualified rather than an absolute immunity.

In *Scheuer v. Rhodes,* the estates of three students killed by the Ohio National Guard at Kent State University brought an action in damages under Sec. 1983 of the Civil Rights Acts.[19] This action was against the governor, officers and enlisted men in the Ohio National Guard, and the president of Kent State University. The contention was that the civil disturbance at Kent State had been suppressed in an unconstitutional manner.[20]

The various defendants all claimed an absolute immunity as provided in *Barr v. Matteo.* The Court, however, saw *Barr v. Matteo* as different from the case at hand in some significant respects. *Barr v. Matteo* had been a common law action. The case at hand, however, involved an alleged constitutional violation, and it was brought under Sec. 1983 of

16. Inasmuch as the court below had found that a jury might reasonably find malice on the part of the defendant, qualified immunity would not have protected him against the verdict.

17. Id. at 575, 79 S.Ct. at 1341, quoting Tenney v. Brandhove, 341 U.S. 367, 377, 71 S.Ct. 783, 788, 95 L.Ed. 1019 (1951), rehearing denied 342 U.S. 843, 72 S.Ct. 20, 96 L.Ed. 637 (1951). As well, the Court relied upon the "admirably expressed" rationale of Judge Learned Hand, 360 U.S. at 571, 79 S.Ct. at 1339. The Court's own assessment was that the fear of damage suits as well as the time and energy they would consume "might appreciably inhibit the fearless, vigorous, and effective administration of policies of government." Id.

18. The general authority of federal courts to find an immunity for state officials was that "The purpose of [the Civil Rights Acts] was not to abolish the immunities available at common law." Pierson v. Ray, 386 U.S. 547, 554, 87 S.Ct. 1213, 18 L.Ed.2d 288 (1967).

19. 416 U.S. 232, 94 S.Ct. 1683, 40 L.Ed.2d 90 (1974).

20. The "essence" of the various complaints was that the defendants " 'intentionally, recklessly, willfully and wantonly' caused an unnecessary deployment of the Ohio National Guard on the Kent State campus and, in the same manner, ordered the Guard members to perform allegedly illegal actions which resulted in the deaths of plaintiffs' decedents." Id. at 235, 94 S.Ct. at 1686.

the Civil Rights Acts. The Court thought that to extend the absolute immunity of *Barr v. Matteo* to Sec. 1983 would gut that statute as it provided for damages, and in doing so nullify the intent of Congress. Because Sec. 1983 was directed to the " 'misuse of power, possessed by virtue of state law,' " state officials "as a class, could not be totally exempt, by virtue of some absolute immunity, from liability under its terms."

Consequently, the Court approved only a "qualified immunity" for the whole class, including the governor, of state officials. This immunity was afforded if there were "existence of reasonable grounds for the belief formed at the time and in light of all the circumstances, coupled with good-faith belief," respecting "acts performed in the course of official conduct."[21]

Following *Scheuer v. Rhodes,* the system of immunity was that of qualified immunity for state officials sued under federal law and, apparently, absolute immunity for federal officials (under *Barr v. Mateo*). This system, however, was adjusted—with a uniformity in standards for state and federal officials being one of the ends—in *Butz v. Economou.*[22]

In *Butz v. Economou,* the Department of Agriculture had issued a complaint against a registered dealer in commodities futures, alleging that he had failed to maintain minimum financial requirements as prescribed by the Department. After a departmental hearing, the complaint was sustained. While this departmental action was in process, the broker filed an action in federal court for damages, based on alleged due process violations, against several department officials. These officials, the plaintiff claimed, had initiated the process against him in retaliation for his criticism of the Department's Commodities Exchange Authority. The officials whom he sued included the Secretary of Agriculture, the hearing officer and the judicial officer (who had presided over the hearing and departmental appeal of the hearing), the prosecuting agency attorney, and various other agency attorneys.

The court of appeals found that the federal defendants were entitled to only the "qualified 'good faith, reasonable grounds' immunity" that had been approved, albeit for state officials, in *Scheuer v. Rhodes.* These defendants, however, claimed that as federal officials they were entitled to absolute immunity under *Barr v. Matteo,* and they appealed on that ground. Consequently, the single question before the Supreme Court was whether the individual defendants in the case were entitled to absolute

21. Otherwise, in reference to the findings that would be required on remand, the Court referred to "whether the Governor and his subordinate officers were acting within the scope of their duties ... and discretion under Ohio law; whether they acted in good faith both in proclaiming an emergency and as to the actions taken to cope with the emergency so declared," and whether "the lesser officers and enlisted personnel of the Guard acted in good faith obedience to the orders of their superiors." This substantive description, of the grounds for qualified immunity, did not last: it exposed public officials to more litigation costs than the Court was willing to tolerate. See sec. 14.3.3, infra.

22. 438 U.S. 478, 98 S.Ct. 2894, 57 L.Ed.2d 895 (1978), on remand 466 F.Supp. 1351 (S.D.N.Y.1979), affirmed 633 F.2d 203 (2d Cir.1980).

immunity. The Court held that generally they were not, that generally they could claim only a qualified immunity.

The Court was moved by two concerns, one of which was a regard for constitutional rights. The majority thought that absolute immunity would "seriously erode the protection provided by basic constitutional guarantees."[23] This regard for constitutional rights was brought into play inasmuch as the plaintiff in *Butz* had alleged that agency procedures violated due process.

The other concern of the Court was with differing standards of immunity for state and federal officials, especially in the realm of constitutional rights. The majority in *Butz* thought that the standard should be the same for both. It asserted that "surely *federal* officials should enjoy no greater zone of protections when they violate *federal* constitutional rules than do *state* officers." This proposition of a similar immunity is not, however, self-evident. The action in damages against state officials was created by Congress, out of a special concern (for securing impartial protection of federal rights). No such congressional action and no similar concern are present in the case of federal officials.[24] Nonetheless, a majority of the Court, on the bases of a high place of constitutional rights and a single measure of immunity for state and federal officials, held that "in a suit for damages arising from unconstitutional action, federal executive officials exercising discretion are entitled only to the qualified immunity specified in *Scheuer*."

There is, however, an exception to this baseline of qualified immunity, a "special functions" exemption that is the subject of the next section.

§ 14.3.2 The "Special Functions" Claim to Absolute Immunity

As said in *Butz v. Economou,* "Although a qualified immunity from damages liability should be the general rule for executive officials charged with constitutional violations, our decisions recognize that there are some officials whose special functions require a full exemption from liability."[25] This is to say that rather than qualified immunity, absolute immunity may be had by "officials whose special functions require a full exemption from liability." Presently, this "special functions" category

23. In this respect, the court stated, "To create a system in which the Bill of Rights monitors more closely the conduct of state officials than it does that of federal officials is to stand the constitutional design on its head."

24. Hence, as Chief Justice Rehnquist argued in dissent, differing standards of immunity for state and federal officials (qualified for state officials, absolute for federal officials) was not anomalous. Rehnquist, in relation to the different situation of federal officials, explained that the federal government might itself assume financial responsibility for its wrongs and that it "can internally supervise and check its own officials." On the other hand, in relation to the state actions,

> The Federal Government is not so situated that it can control state officials or strike this same balance.... Hence the necessity of sec. 1983 and the differing standards of immunity.

438 U.S. at 525, 98 S.Ct. at 2920.

25. 438 U.S. 478, 508, 98 S.Ct. 2894, 57 L.Ed.2d 895 (1978).

consists of two classes, those involved in judicial functions and the President. This category seems unlikely to get larger.

Agency officials involved in judicial functions are the bigger class of officials eligible for absolute immunity under the special functions exemption. In *Butz v. Economou,* the plaintiff had sued the agency officials who had participated in the hearing against him. These officials included the hearing officer and the officer who had presided over a departmental appeal of that hearing, the agency attorney who had prosecuted the administrative proceeding, and agency attorneys who had presented evidence at the departmental hearing. The Court found all these officials, because they were associated with a judicial function within the agency, eligible for the "special functions" category of absolute immunity.

This immunity was established by reference to the absolute immunity that courts have, and the Court surveyed both the logical and historical bases of that immunity.[26] From the standpoint of logic, the Court noted that certain "safeguards" were built into the court process and that these safeguards mitigated the need for judicial liability for misdeeds. These safeguards included the "insulation of the judge from the political influence, the importance of precedent in resolving controversies, the adversary nature of the process, and the correctibility of error on appeal." These safeguards pertained not just to judges, but to other participants in the process. The Court explained that "Advocates are restrained not only by their professional obligations but by the knowledge that their assertions will be contested by their adversaries in open court," "Jurors are carefully screened to remove all possibility of bias," and "Witnesses are, of course, subject to the rigors of cross-examination and the penalty of perjury." Consequently, absolute immunity had not, as the Court noted, been limited to judges. Instead, it had been extended to other participants in the judicial process, to prosecutors, jurors, and witnesses so that they might vigorously carry out their role in that process.

But should this immunity, to the various participants in the judicial process in courts, be extended to agency adjudication? In *Butz v. Economou* the Court said yes, because of what it saw as functional similarities between courts and agency adjudication. The majority in *Butz* explained that "Judges have absolute immunity not because of their particular location within the Government but because of the special nature of their responsibilities," and "Adjudication within a federal administrative agency shares enough of the characteristics of the judicial process that those who participate in such adjudication should also be immune from suits for damages." Therefore, the Court held that all the departmental officials involved in the adjudicatory process against the plaintiff were, on special functions grounds, entitled to absolute immunity. In *Butz,*

26. In relation to history, the Court noted that absolute immunity had been " 'the settled doctrine of the English courts for many centuries, and has never been denied, that we are aware of, in the courts of this country.' " 438 U.S. at 508, 98 S.Ct. at 2912.

These officials included the hearing officer, "agency official[s] performing certain functions analogous to those of a prosecutor," and "agency attorney[s] who arranged for the presentation of evidence on the record."

After *Butz v. Economou,* the special functions exception, and the absolute immunity that attends it, was extended to the President, and stopped there. In *Nixon v. Fitzgerald,* the plaintiff claimed that his job as a management analyst with the Defense Department had been eliminated in retaliation for his testimony before Congress about cost overruns in defense contracts.[27] Consequently, he brought an action for damages against President Nixon, in which he claimed that Nixon had eliminated his job because of his whistle-blowing, and had done so in violation of the first amendment and federal statutes.

Although *Scheuer v. Rhodes* had held that state governors could claim only a "good faith" qualified immunity, the Court refused to limit the President, because of the importance and singularity of his office, to that form of immunity. As explained by the Court, "Because of the singular importance of the President's duties, diversion of his energies by concern with private lawsuit would raise unique risks to the effective functioning of government." Also, the Court reasoned that the volume of hard decisions and "the sheer prominence" of the presidency would expose that office to an inordinately large amount of civil litigation.[28]

But in the companion case of *Harlow v. Fitzgerald,* the Court refused to widen the special functions exemption to include presidential aides.[29] These aides had argued that presidential policy is made and executed through the Whitehouse staff and that they were therefore entitled to the special functions exemption of the President. The Court, however, found that this argument was foreclosed by *Butz v. Economou:* "Having decided in *Butz* that members of the Cabinet ordinarily enjoy only qualified immunity from suit, we conclude today that it would be equally untenable to hold absolute immunity an incident of the office of every Presidential subordinate based in the White House."[30]

* * *

27. 457 U.S. 731, 102 S.Ct. 2690, 73 L.Ed.2d 349 (1982).

28. The immunity afforded the President is, however, for only his, or her, actions done while in office. In Clinton v. Jones, 520 U.S. 681, 117 S.Ct. 1636, 137 L.Ed.2d 945 (1997), Mr. Clinton argued that the immunity should extend to actions (his alleged sexual harassment) done prior to his term in office. He contended that such litigation would "impose an unacceptable burden on the President's time and energy, and thereby impair the effective performance of his office." The Court, though, found against Mr. Clinton, and refuse to extend presidential immunity to acts done while out of office.

29. 457 U.S. 800, 102 S.Ct. 2727, 73 L.Ed.2d 396 (1982).

30. Id. at 809, 102 S.Ct. at 2733. In Mitchell v. Forsyth, 472 U.S. 511, 105 S.Ct. 2806, 86 L.Ed.2d 411 (1985), the Court rejected a claim by former Attorney General John Mitchell for absolute immunity in connection with a domestic wiretap he had authorized in "performing his national security function." In this regard, the Court noted that national security work did not present the same opportunities for "vexatious litigation" as did other areas and unlike other areas, such as the judicial process, there were no checks in place to otherwise prevent abuses of power.

Under the present special functions exemption, the measure of absolute liability is not the *status* of an official (whether the official is, for instance, a cabinet member). Instead, the measure is strictly functional, whether the act in question is a "function[ ] requir[ing] a full exemption from liability."[31] Presumably, if an administrative law judge does work that is not adjudicatory, he could not, in this other function, claim absolute immunity. The exception to this functional measure is the office of the President. The President, because of the singularity of his office, is in all functions and respects absolutely immune from civil damages for acts done while in office.[32]

§ 14.3.3 Redefinition Of The Substantive Basis Of Qualified Immunity

When in *Butz v. Economou* it established qualified immunity as the rule for public officials, the Court was mindful of the greater litigation costs associated with this lesser degree of immunity (and that these costs might stifle energetic enforcement of public policy). A majority of the Court were of the opinion that these costs could be contained by procedural options. As explained by Justice White:

> Insubstantial lawsuits can be quickly terminated by federal courts alert to the possibilities of artful pleading. Unless the complaint states a compensable claim for relief under the federal Constitution, it should not survive a motion to dismiss. Moreover, ... damages suits concerning constitutional violations need not proceed to trial, but can be terminated on a properly supported motion for summary judgment based on the defense of immunity.[33]

Four years later, in *Harlow v. Fitzgerald,* the Court found that this reliance on procedural safeguards had been too sanguine, and it took another step to diminish litigation costs and to provide officials with a better predictability respecting their exposure to personal damages.[34] This step was to redefine the substantive basis of qualified immunity. This basis was redefined so as (1) to provide a larger zone within which officials might act free of the threat of damages and (2) to make it easier to eliminate insubstantial suits at a pretrial phase.

31. 438 U.S. at 508, 98 S.Ct. at 2911.

32. With one caveat. Bowing to Congress's own competence in this area, in *Harlow v. Fitzgerald* the Court in a footnote stated:

> [W]e need not address directly the immunity question as it would arise if Congress expressly had created a damages action against the President of the United States.... Consequently, our holding today need only be that the President is absolutely immune from civil damages liability for his official acts in the absence of explicit affirmative action by Congress.

457 U.S. at 748 n. 27, 102 S.Ct. at 2700 n. 27.

33. 438 U.S. at 508, 98 S.Ct. at 2911.

34. 457 U.S. 800, 807, 102 S.Ct. 2727, 2732, 73 L.Ed.2d 396 (1982). In relation to its redefinition of qualified immunity, the Court again surveyed the social costs of official liability, and found them still quite significant. These costs included "distraction of officials from their governmental duties, inhibition of discretionary action, and deterrence of able people from public service." 457 U.S. at 816, 102 S.Ct. at 2737.

The substantive change was an adjustment to the "good faith" measure of qualified immunity. Whether the official had acted in good faith had usually been a question for the jury. However, this question involved a range of "experiences, values, and emotions" not readily assessable by a jury, or by anyone. Also, reserving good faith for jury determination meant that insubstantial claims could not be knocked out quickly on summary judgment. In the resultant full trial, officials were exposed to the full range of litigation costs. Moreover, in the inquiry invited by the good faith measure of immunity there was "often no end to the relevant evidence." This evidence included broad-ranging discovery and "deposing professional colleagues," all of which could be "disruptive of effective government."

The Court, therefore, undertook to shear qualified immunity of its good faith element. "Bare allegations of malice," the Court said, "should not suffice to subject government officials either to the cost of trial or to the burdens of broad reaching discovery." In place of the good faith test, the Court substituted a more objective, "reasonable person," measure. The substance of this measure was that "government officials performing discretionary functions generally are shielded from liability for civil damages insofar as their conduct does not violate clearly established statutory or constitutional rights of which a reasonable person would have known." This new measure, the Court said, should work as follows:

> On summary judgment, the judge appropriately may determine, not only the currently applicable law, but whether that law was clearly established at the time an action occurred. If the law at that time was not clearly established, an official could not reasonably be expected to anticipate subsequent legal developments, nor could he fairly be said to "know" that the law forbade conduct not previously identified as unlawful. Until this threshold immunity question is resolved, discovery should not be allowed.[35]

This more objective measure of qualified immunity, whether the defendant's conduct "violate[s] clearly established statutory or constitutional rights of which a reasonable person would have known," has been extended past federal officials, to include state officials sued under federal law.[36]

In application, however, this new measure has not been easy. The rights in question must be clearly established at the time the alleged violation occurred.[37] Unfortunately, reasonable people can often differ as to whether and when constitutional law is "clearly established." As said

35. 457 U.S. at 818, 102 S.Ct. at 2738. See Mitchell v. Forsyth, 472 U.S. 511, 530–35, 105 S.Ct. 2806, 2818–20, 86 L.Ed.2d 411 (1985), on remand 772 F.2d 894 (3d Cir. 1985), holding that Attorney General Mitchell was immune for a damages action for illegal domestic wiretaps in that the illegality of such wiretaps, when made in the national security, were not, at the time they were made, "clearly established" as illegal.

36. Davis v. Scherer, 468 U.S. 183, 104 S.Ct. 3012, 82 L.Ed.2d 139 (1984).

37. E.g., Mitchell v. Forsyth, 472 U.S. 511, 105 S.Ct. 2806, 86 L.Ed.2d 411 (1985).

by Chief Justice Rehnquist, "one need only look to the decisions of this Court—to our reversals, our recognition of evolving concepts, and our five-to-four split—to recognize the hazard of even informed prophecy as to what are 'unquestioned constitutional rights.' "[38] This ambiguity in constitutional rights no doubt continues the chilling effect on official action of an uncertain exposure to damages and as well some of the litigation costs (now about what is clearly established) that the Court in *Harlow v. Fitzgerald* had hoped to avoid.[39]

Another problem in the application of the *Harlow v. Fitzgerald* "clearly established" measure of immunity has to do with the level at which it operates. Does it pertain to general propositions of constitutional law, such as that one is entitled to notice and a fair hearing or that everyone is entitled to be secure in his home against unreasonable searches? Or does the clearly established measure instead apply more specifically, to categories of official conduct identified by the courts as violating these general propositions? In light of the Court's professed goal of providing bright-line measures of official liability, common sense suggests ruling out general propositions of constitutional law as the measure of liability because these propositions are usually too indeterminate to provide any sort of bright-line measure. Case law suggests the same.

In *Anderson v. Creighton,* an FBI agent was sued for damages in connection with an allegedly unlawful search of a home.[40] (The search was undertaken on the belief that a suspected bank robber might be found there.) The agent moved for summary judgment, and this motion was denied. In affirming this denial, the court of appeals, in relation to the agent's claim of immunity, ruled that the constitutional right in question ("the right of persons to be protected from warrantless searches of their homes unless the searching officers have probable cause and there are exigent circumstances") was "clearly established." Wheth-

38. Wood v. Strickland, 420 U.S. 308, 329, 95 S.Ct. 992, 1004, 43 L.Ed.2d 214 (1975).

39. An instance of this ambiguity, in the context of due process, is provided by Davis v. Scherer, 468 U.S. 183, 104 S.Ct. 3012, 82 L.Ed.2d 139 (1984). State officials had told a police officer that an outside job that he held put him in a conflict of interest and asked him to give up the job. When he did not do so, they fired him. He then sued these officials for damages, on the grounds that they had fired him without a hearing, in violation of his "clearly established" right to due process. The police officer, the trial court found, while understanding that his employers did not want him to keep the outside job, at the same time did not understand that they would fire him.

The case was heard by a district court and the court of appeals, and these courts found for the plaintiff. On appeal, the Supreme Court, while finding that due process had been violated, dividing five to three on whether the rights in issue were clearly established: the majority was of the opinion that these rights were not clearly established; the minority was of the opinion that they were. As the majority saw it, the lower courts were correct inasmuch as the state officials "had violated the most fundamental requirements of due process—meaningful notice and a reasonable opportunity to be heard." 468 U.S. at 200, 104 S.Ct. at 3022. The minority, however, noted that the patrolman had "been informed several times of the department's objection to the second employment and took advantage of several opportunities to present his reasons" and that Florida law also provided for a full post-termination evidentiary hearing. 468 U.S. at 192–93, 104 S.Ct. at 3018–19.

40. 483 U.S. 635, 107 S.Ct. 3034, 97 L.Ed.2d 523 (1987).

er "it was *not* clearly established that the circumstances with which Anderson was confronted did not constitute probable cause and exigent circumstances" was something that the court refused to consider.

For that refusal, the Supreme Court reversed the court of appeals. It did so because that court had applied the "clearly established" measure too abstractly, at too high a level of generality. At such a level of generality, "Plaintiffs would convert the rule of qualified *immunity* that our cases plainly establish into a rule of virtually unqualified *liability* simply by alleging violation of extremely abstract rights." Moreover, in terms of a premise of the "clearly-established" standard—a premise of predictability about what is or is not constitutional and what is not—the lower court had ruled incorrectly. The indeterminate level at which this court set the standard would make it "impossible for officials 'reasonably [to] anticipate when their conduct may give rise to liability for damages.' "

The clearly-established standard, the Court then held, should be applied in reference to a policeman's actual conduct, i.e., whether it was clearly established that a search in the sort of circumstances then facing the officer was unlawful. In this relation, the Court explained that "The contours of the right must be sufficiently clear that a reasonable official would understand that what he is doing violates that right."[41]

41. See also Gruenke v. Seip, 225 F.3d 290, 299 (3d Cir.2000) ("It is not sufficient that the right at issue be clearly established as a general matter. Rather, the question is whether a reasonable public official would know that his or her *specific conduct* violated clearly established rights)."

Chapter 15

EXECUTIVE CONTROL OF AGENCY DISCRETION

Table of Sections

Agencies exercise much of their power in ways that are generally not susceptible to meaningful judicial review. They set their own regulatory priorities, emphasizing some aspects of their regulatory powers while de-emphasizing others. They engage in a variety of informal regulatory actions ranging from informal adjudication to a kind of regulation by "raised eyebrow." More importantly, agencies play an important policy-making role and are part of the political process as a whole. As new administrations come to Washington and new individuals are appointed to head these various departments, they often have new and different perceptions of regulatory problems and issues that translate into different regulatory or deregulatory agendas, and consequently different allocations of budgetary resources within the agency.

In making these kinds of decisions, agencies are held politically accountable to the democratically elected branches of government in a number of ways. Not only do they depend on both branches for the budgets necessary to run their programs, but they are subject to a variety of direct and indirect political controls. The purpose of this chapter is to set forth the various ways in which agencies are held politically accountable to the executive branch. We shall focus first on the executive's role in attempting to control or influence the exercise of agency discretion.

§ 15.1 ADMINISTRATIVE AGENCIES AND THE EXECUTIVE BRANCH—INTRODUCTION

Executive power in general has increased enormously since the beginning of the Republic. This is not surprising. The Presidency is the only elected office with a national constituency. This fact, coupled with the magnitude of world events, inevitably seems to concentrate more and more responsibility in the Office of the President. As Justice Jackson astutely observed in *Youngstown Sheet & Tube Co. v. Sawyer*[1]:

> Executive Power has the advantage of concentration in a single head in whose choice the whole Nation has a part, making him the focus of public hopes and expectations. In drama, magnitude, and finality, his decisions so far overshadow any others that almost alone he fills the public eye and ear. No other personality in public life can begin to compete with him in access to the public mind through modern methods of communications. By his prestige as head of state and his influence upon public opinion he exerts a leverage upon those who are supposed to check and balance his power which often cancels their effectiveness.

Executive influence over the administrative process has also grown considerably, particularly over the last twenty years. This is due, in large part, to both the magnitude and the nature of the growth in the bureaucracy that has occurred since the early 1970's.[2] In his 1996 State of the Union Address, President Clinton declared: "The era of big Government is over."[3] Sixteen thousand pages of "unnec-

§ 15.1

1. 343 U.S. 579, 653–54, 72 S.Ct. 863, 879–80, 96 L.Ed. 1153 (1952) (concurring opinion).

2. "Between 1969 and 1979, Congress enacted and Presidents Nixon, Ford and Carter signed into law over 120 regulatory programs (by conservative count).... In 1960, there were 28 major federal regulatory agencies; in 1980 there were 56, and all but one of those were created after 1969. (The exception was the National Highway Traffic Safety Administration, established in 1966.) Between 1970 and 1980, the budgets for the federal regulatory agencies increased by 300% measured in real dollars." T. Lowi, The Constitution and the Regulation of Society 19–20 (paper on file with Cornell Law Review). Moreover, these new agencies were much more policy-oriented than the New Deal agencies that predated them. Rather than rely on case by case adjudication which has long been the hallmark of such agencies as the National Labor Relations Board or the Federal Power Commission (now the Federal Energy Regulatory Commission), agencies such as the Environmental Protection Agency, the Occupational Safety and Health Administration and the Consumer Products Safety Commission relied heavily on the rulemaking process. See Lowi, id. This, in part, accounts for another indicia of bureaucratic growth: "... [A]lthough many kinds of announcements are printed in the *Federal Register,* it is nevertheless indicative of the growth of regulation that the number of pages in the *Federal Register* increased from 14,479 in 1960 to just 20,000 in the whole decade of the 1960's, and then jumped by 300% to 60,000 pages in 1975. By the end of 1980, the number of pages had increased to 86,000." Id.

3. Address Before a Joint Session of the Congress on the State of the Union, Pub. Papers 79 (1996).

essary rules and regulations" had been eliminated from the federal bureaucracy, which shifted "more decisionmaking out of Washington, back to States and local communities;"[4] the Federal workforce had been reduced by 200,000 employees, which left the government with its smallest workforce in thirty years.[5] But streamlining governmental processes and reducing the size of the workforce is not synonymous with reducing public reliance on government functions. In some cases, the government has continued to perform key public functions, albeit with a smaller workforce. In other cases, states were left to fulfill functions formally performed by the federal government. And in other cases still, the government cut its workforce by contracting its functions out to private entities.[6] Therefore, while it is accurate to say that President Clinton reduced the size of the federal bureaucracy, it is not at all clear that public reliance on the types of services performed by the government was concomitantly reduced. The public relies on someone to provide prisons and collect taxes. In the last decade of the twentieth century, in particular, the private sector has become more involved and various public/private partnerships have flourished.[7]

Even with some of the cutbacks in the 1990's and a slowing of the overall rate of growth of the federal government, it is not possible for a President to be confident of his control of domestic policy by simply maintaining good relations with or control of Congress. The administra-

4. Id. at 85.

5. Id. During the Clinton–Gore administration, federal regulations overall were reduced and some agencies were downsized or eliminated. See, e.g., Executive Order 12, 861, 58 Fed. Reg. 48, 255 (1993) ("elimination of one-half of Executive Branch Internal Regulations' in order to streamline and improve customer service to the American People"); the Interstate Commerce Commission was abolished, and regulation in general became increasingly market-oriented, if not market based. See generally, Vice President Al Gore, Report of the National Performance Review, From Red Tape to Results: Creating a Government That Works Better and Costs less (Sept. 7, 1993) [hereinafter National Performance Review]. For a discussion of this report, see Jeffery s. Lubbers, Better Regulations: The National Performance Review's Regulatory Reform Recommendations, 1994 Duke L.J. 1165 (1994); Daniel P. Rodriquez, Management, Control, and the Dilemmas of Presidential Leadership in the Modern Administrative State, 1994 Duke L.J. 1180; Paul R. Verkuil, Is Efficient Government an Oxymoron?, 1994 Duke L.J. 1221.

6. For an excellent history of how the public sector has used the private sector to carry out its functions, see Daniel Guttman, Public Purpose and Private Service: The Twentieth Century Culture of Contracting Out and the Evolving Law of Diffused Sovereignty, 52 Admin. L. Rev. 85a (2000).

7. For an analysis that seeks to place the shift from governmental regulation to markets approaches in a global and comparative context, see Alfred C. Aman, Jr., The Globalizing State: A Future–Oriented Perspective on the Public/Private Distinction, Federalism, and Democracy, 31 Vand. J. Trans. L. 769 (1998). For analyses that focus primarily on the implications of these changes for administrative law, see Alfred C. Aman, Jr. Administrative Law For a New Century *in* The Province of Administrative Law (Michael Taggart, ed.) (Hart Pub., Oxford, 1997) pp. 90–117; Alfred C. Aman, Jr., Proposals For Reforming the Administrative Procedure Act: Globalization, Democracy and the Furtherance of a Global Public Interest, 6 Ind. J. Global Legal Stud. 397 (1999); Jody Freeman, Private Parties, Public Functions and the New Administrative Law, 52 Admin. L. Rev. 813 (2000); Jody Freeman, The Private Role In Public Governance, 75 NYU L. Rev. 543 (2000).

tive process itself has become an important and significant source of new policies and executive controls of that process has increased.

Given the tendency of most administrative agencies to view the world primarily from their own vantage point, greater executive coordination is necessary to minimize policy conflicts among agencies and to further a broader and perhaps more realistic perception of the public interest.

This coordinating executive role has been facilitated by the fact that Congress created regulatory structures in the 1970's that departed significantly from the independent commission model that typified the New Deal. The Environmental Protection Agency, for example, initially was headed by a single Administrator appointed by the President with advice and consent of the Senate. Now, this Administrator is a member of the cabinet. Moreover, Congress has delegated much of the responsibility for dealing with health and safety issues to cabinet level officials such as the Secretary of Labor.[8] Agencies headed by a cabinet level official are naturally more accountable to the President and more easily influenced by the policy preferences of the executive branch. Such individuals serve at the pleasure of the President. More important, the executive branch has institutionalized this influence through greater use of executive orders[9] and, in particular, a strengthening of the oversight role played by the Office of Management and Budget.[10]

There are many reasons why presidential control over the administrative process has been increasing. The President is in a good position to centralize and coordinate the regulatory process; he is electorally accountable, has a national constituency and is less likely to be as myopic as some single mission agencies can be.[11] He can also focus and energize an increasingly large and diverse bureaucracy and be involved in the early planning stages of regulatory policy.[12] There are, however, some constitutional statutory and institutional problems that can arise when executive oversight is too vigorous.[13]

The purpose of the following sections is twofold: (1) to set forth the broad constitutional framework within which executive power over the bureaucracy is exercised; and (2) to examine the legal issues that arise as the executive attempts directly to influence or control administrative discretion.

8. See, e.g., Occupational Safety and Health Act, 29 U.S.C.A. §§ 651–678.

9. See sec. 15.1.3, infra.

10. See sec. 15.1.2, infra.

11. See, Strauss and Sunstein, The Role of the President and OMB in Informal Rulemaking, 38 Admin.L.Rev. 181 (1986).

12. See Shane, Political Accountability in a system of Checks and Balances: The Case of Presidential Review of Rulemaking, 48 Ark.L.Rev. 161 (1995); see also McGarity, Special Issue of the Administrative State at a Crossroads: The APA at Fifty: The Expanded Debate Over the Future of the Regulatory State, 63 U.Chi.L.Rev. 1463 (1996) (an analysis of many administrative topics, including analysis on the presidential role in administrative action). See also Bruff, Presidential Management of Agency Rulemaking, 57 Geo.Wash.L.Rev. 533 (1989).

13. For an analysis of the evolution of executive power over administrative agencies and the constitutional issues that may arise, see Alfred C. Aman, Jr., Administrative Law In A Global Era (1992).

§ 15.1.1 Article II and Executive Management of the Bureaucracy

The Constitutional basis for executive control of the bureaucracy has always been vague and open-ended. Article II of the Constitution vests executive power in the presidency, but as Edward S. Corwin noted, "executive power" is a "term of uncertain content."[14] Article II speaks directly to issues that affect executive control of administrative agencies in four places. Article II,§ 2, cl. 2 gives the President the power to appoint "Officers of the United States" with the advice and consent of the Senate.[15] Article II,§ 2, cl. 1 requires "the Opinion, in writing" of certain heads of departments at the President's request.[16] Article II,§ 3, requires that "from time to time [the President shall] give to the Congress Information on the State of the Union."[17] It also requires that the President "take Care that the Laws be faithfully executed."[18] These provisions suggest a supervisory, perhaps even caretaker, presidential role,[19] but the appropriate extent of this supervisory role and its constitutional outer limit is, at best, unclear.

In relation to executive control of agencies, perhaps the most important of these provisions is the "take Care" clause of Article II. This clause received very little attention during the framing and ratification of the Constitution. As Professors Bruff and Shane have noted: "In all probability, it was generally understood as a ministerial obligation to enforce the laws and a prohibition against their suspension."[20] Nevertheless, this clause today provides the primary constitutional basis for the increasingly important supervisory role played by the president. Perhaps the foremost means of asserting presidential power over bureaucracies is the use of executive orders. Though this power has grown substantially, it is not without some limits. As the majority in *Youngstown Sheet and Tube v. Sawyer*[21] noted, the President's power to issue an executive order "must stem either from an act of Congress or from the Constitution itself."[22]

Although *Youngstown Sheet & Tube* defines the outer boundaries of executive power, courts generally have been willing to uphold executive power and executive orders issued pursuant to this power in a wide variety of contexts. If the President has the constitutional duty to ensure

14. Edward W. Corwin, The President: Office and Powers 3 (1957).

15. U.S. Const. Art. II,§ 2, cl. 2.

16. Id. at Art. II,§ 2, cl. 1.

17. Id. at Art. II,§ 3.

18. Id. For a superb analysis of this provision in the context of presidential non-enforcement, see Dawn E. Johnsen, Presidential Non–Enforcement of Constitutionally Objectionable Statutes, 63 Law and Contemporary Problems 101 (2000).

19. Strauss, The Place of Agencies in Government: Separation of Powers and the Fourth Branch, 84 Colum.L.Rev. 573, 598 (1984). For an alternative argument, see Cross, Executive Orders 12,291 and 12,498: A Test Case in Presidential Control of Executive Agencies, 4 J.Law & Pol. 483 (1988).

20. Peter M. Shane and Harold H. Bruff, The Law of Presidential Powers 395 (1988). See also, the documents excerpted in 4 The Founders' Constitution (P.B. Kurland & R. Lenner eds., 1987).

21. 343 U.S. 579, 72 S.Ct. 863, 96 L.Ed. 1153 (1952).

22. Id. at 585, 72 S.Ct. at 865.

that the laws are faithfully executed, it follows that, at the very least, he has the power to issue instructions to his officers to ensure that these tasks are carried out. Most executive orders thus deal primarily with matters internal to the federal bureaucracy—matters involving organization, personnel, budgetary problems and the like. But many executive orders do more than simply instruct officials what to do. They have, for example, been used to create public agencies, particularly during war time;[23] they have been used to institute wage and price controls[24] and even to implement the U.S. agreement with Iran to secure the release of our hostages in Iran.[25] Most recently, executive orders have been used to impose cost-benefit analyses on executive agencies,[26] or to emphasize the importance of federalism in federal regulation.[27] Many times executive orders seem to go beyond simply directing how a piece of legislation should be implemented. As Professor Mashaw has pointed out, "it seems clear that the executive order has been used in the last few decades in circumstances where legislation would certainly have been equally appropriate."[28]

One of the most important executive agencies used to carry out the directives of Presidential executive orders is the Office of Management and Budget (OMB). Given the importance of that office for executive influence over agency policy making, we shall examine it and some of the executive orders it administers in some detail.

§ 15.1.2 The Office of Management and Budget

The Office of Management and Budget had its beginnings in the Budget and Accounting Act of 1921.[29] That Act created the Bureau of the

23. See, e.g., Jerry L. Mashaw and Richard A. Merrill, Administrative Law—The American Public Law System 142 (2d ed. 1985). ("During World War I, for example, the War Trade Board, the Committee For Public Information, the U.S. Food Administration and the Grain Corporation were all established by Executive Order.").

24. See, e.g., Exec.Order No. 11,615, 36 C.F.R. Pt. 600; Fed. Procurement Wage & Price Control Program (1978) Exec.Order No. 12,092, 43 Fed.Reg. 511375 (1978).

25. See, e.g., Dames & Moore v. Regan, 453 U.S. 654, 101 S.Ct. 2972, 69 L.Ed.2d 918 (1981). In upholding the President's orders in this case, the Court pointed to what it considered to be the long history of congressional acquiescence in the presidential settlement of disputes involving foreign claims. It found no statutory authority for the President's action. For a similarly broad view of executive power based on congressional acquiescence rather than specific statutory authority, see United States v. Midwest Oil Co., 236 U.S. 459, 35 S.Ct. 309, 59 L.Ed. 673 (1915).

26. Exec.Order No. 12,291, 3 C.F.R. Pt. 127 (1982).

27. Exec.Order No. 12,612, 52 Fed. Reg. 41685 (Oct. 30, 1987).

28. Mashaw and Merrill, supra note 23, at 142. Professors Mashaw and Merrill note, for example, that in 1953 President Truman ordered the heads of all federal contracting agencies to incorporate, and enforce, nondiscrimination clauses in all government contracts. Exec.Order No. 10,479, 18 Fed.Reg. 4899 (1953). And President Kennedy issued a far-reaching executive order on non-discrimination in housing in 1962. Exec.Order No. 11,053, 27 Fed.Reg. 11527 (1962). Subsequent presidents have revised the non-discrimination requirements from time to time to extend discrimination prohibitions to sexual discrimination. Exec.Order No. 11,375, 32 Fed.Reg. 14303 (1967). See generally, Fleishman and Aufses, Law and Orders: The Problem of Presidential Legislation, 40 Law and Contemp.Prob. 135 (1976); Note, Presidential Legislation By Executive Order, 37 Univ. Colo.L.Rev. 105 (1964).

29. Pub.L. No. 67–13, cl. 18, 42 Stat. 20 (1921) (codified in scattered sections of 31 U.S.C.A.) For a discussion of it, see

Budget, thereby facilitating the President's ability to formulate a national budget. The Bureau of the Budget was viewed as a technical advisor, bipartisan and neutral in nature. Its functions grew in importance, but as late as 1970, it continued to maintain its image as essentially a neutral, technical advisory office.[30]

In 1970, however, President Nixon renamed the Bureau of the Budget the Office of Management and Budget (OMB), expanded its powers and changed some of its tasks and goals. In particular, the Office began to play the role of coordinator, attempting to ensure that various administrative policies and priorities were consistent with one another.[31] In addition, there was growing concern in the executive branch that, left on their own, agencies would spend too much money. To counteract these tendencies, centralized budget reviews and priorities were advocated.[32] These changes in direction transformed OMB into a more effective presidential device for controlling the policymaking direction of the bureaucracy, particularly executive agencies.

President Nixon was the first President to use OMB to review agency actions pursuant to a Presidential executive order. President Nixon's OMB instituted so-called "Quality of Life" reviews.[33] Under its provisions, the EPA was required to circulate proposed regulations among other agencies and to respond to their comments. In 1974, President Ford issued Executive Order 11,821, amended by E.O. 11,949. These orders required agencies to prepare so-called "inflation-impact statements" for all major regulations, defined as those having an impact in excess of $100 million.

Congress reacted to the changes in OMB's power and role by imposing new controls. In 1976, Congress passed legislation making the appointments of OMB Director and Deputy Director subject to Senate

Rosenberg, Presidential Control of Agency Rulemaking; An Analysis of Constitutional Issues that May Be Raised by Executive Order 12,291, 23 Ariz.L.Rev. 1199, 1217 (1981) [hereinafter Rosenberg, Presidential Control]; Rosenberg, Beyond the Limits of Executive Power: Presidential Control of Agency Rulemaking Under Executive Order 12,291, 80 Mich.L.Rev. 193, 221 (1981) [hereinafter Rosenberg, Beyond the Limits].

30. For a discussion of the growth of BOB and its gradual evolution into the OMB, see Fisher, Presidential Spending Power (1976).

31. See Reorganization Plan No. 2 of 1970, 3 C.F.R. Pt. 197 (1970), reprinted in 5 U.S.C.A.§ 824 and in 84 Stat. 2085 (1970), reprinted in 31 U.S.C.A.§ 16 app. at 1177. See generally, Rosenberg, Presidential Control, supra note 28, at 1218; Rosenberg, Beyond the Limits, supra note 29, at 220 (1981); DeMuth & Ginsburg, White House Review of Agency Rulemaking, 99 Harv. L.Rev. 1075 (1986).

32. "We all know that a government agency charged with the responsibility of defending the nation or constructing highways or promoting trade will invariably spend 'too much' on its goals. An agency succeeds by accomplishing the goals Congress set for it as thoroughly as possible—not by balancing its goals against other, equally worthy goals. This fact of agency life provides the justification for a countervailing administrative constraint in the form of a central budget office." DeMuth & Ginsberg, supra note 31, at 1081.

33. Office of Management & Budget Circular A–95. Although not taking the form of an executive order, it served much the same function as the later Ford, Carter, and Reagan executive orders. See Federal Regulation & Regulatory Reform, H.R.Doc. No. 134, 94th Cong., 2d Sess. (1976).

confirmation.[34] Also, OMB lost its final veto authority over independent regulatory agencies' information-gathering programs.[35] As a result, the General Accounting Office's power increased, giving it greater program evaluation functions and increased oversight responsibilities concerning potential Presidential impoundments of funds.[36] Congress also created a central budget evaluator of its own, the Congressional Budget Office,[37] thereby ending OMB's monopoly on the processing of agency budget requests. Finally, Congress severely reduced the President's authority to impound agency funds and consequently shape policy.[38] Congress, however, failed to divorce completely the presidency from the administrative process[39] and OMB retained substantial policy-making responsibilities.

President Carter further expanded OMB power in his attempt to control the bureaucracy by issuance of Executive Order 12,044.[40] Among other things, this order required that agencies set forth their rulemaking agenda in semiannual regulatory calendars, that they re-evaluate old rules, and that they conduct regulatory analysis of proposed rules having an economic impact of $100 million or more per year. President Carter later created a Regulatory Council to screen proposed rules and guard against duplication and established a Regulatory Analysis Review Group (RARG), composed of representatives of 36 executive and independent agencies. The primary responsibility of this group was to review carefully the regulatory analysis of fifteen to twenty of the most important rules proposed by certain agencies.

§ 15.1.3 Executive Orders 12,291 and 12,866

The efforts to influence the bureaucracy by Presidents Nixon, Ford and Carter provided the foundation for the more extensive controls imposed by President Reagan under Executive Order 12,291. Similar to the orders that preceded it, Order 12,291 required that agencies justify their major rules with a Regulatory Impact Analysis (RIA).[41] A "major" rule is one that is likely to result in an annual impact on the economy of $100 million or more, a major increase in costs or prices, or significant adverse effects on competition and other aspects of the economy in

34. 31 U.S.C.A.§ 16 (as amended by Pub.L. No. 93–250,§ 1, 88 Stat. 11 (1974)). Rosenberg, Presidential Control, supra note 29, at 1218. (1) Act of Mar. 2, 1974, Pub.L. No. 93–250, 88 Stat. 11 (codified as 31 U.S.C.A.§ 16). Rosenberg, Beyond the Limits, supra note 29, at 223.

35. Rosenberg, Presidential Control, supra note 29, at 1218–19.

36. Id. at 1219; Rosenberg, Beyond the Limits, supra note 29, at 224.

37. Rosenberg, Beyond the Limits, supra note 29, at 223; T. Lowi, The Personal President 186 (1985); Budget and Impoundment Control Act of 1974, Pub.L. No. 93–344, 88 Stat. 297 (codified in part at 31 U.S.C.A. §§ 1400–1407; 2 U.S.C.A. §§ 601–604).

38. Rosenberg, Beyond the Limits, supra note 29, at 224; Lowi, supra note 37, at 186; Budget and Impoundment Control Act of 1974, Pub.L. No. 93–344, 88 Stat. 297 (codified in part at 31 U.S.C.A.§ 1400–1407).

39. Lowi, supra note 37, at 186.

40. 3 C.F.R. Pt. 152 (1979) (revoked by Exec.Order No. 12,291, 3 C.F.R. Pt. 127 (1982)).

41. Exec.Order No. 12,291, § 3, 3 C.F.R. Pt. 128 (1981), reprinted in 5 U.S.C.A.§ 601 at 432. For an excellent analysis and description of OMB in action, see Bruff, supra note 12.

general.[42] This RIA must be forwarded to OMB and describe the potential costs and benefits of the proposed rule, as well as any alternative approaches that might achieve the same goals at a lower cost.[43] The RIA must be completed sixty days before issuing a Notice of Proposed Rulemaking[44] unless the rules are eligible for an exemption.[45]

Unlike its predecessors, Order 12,291 was not limited to seeking information or advising agencies. Section 2 of the Order imposes certain substantive requirements on agencies as well. Specifically, all agencies except "independent agencies" were required, "to the extent permitted by law," to include in their analysis a cost-benefit statement that certifies that "the potential benefits to society from the regulation outweigh the potential costs to society."[46] There is also a cost-effectiveness requirement that requires that the regulatory alternative chosen involve "the least net cost to society."[47] These cost-benefit analyses are not simply suggested as a guide. They are required: "Regulatory action shall not be undertaken"[48] unless these cost-benefit requirements are met.

In short, an RIA must contain a description of the rule's potential benefits and who will receive them, the costs and who shall pay them, and a description of alternative regulatory approaches that might achieve the same goal and why they were not chosen.[49] Order 12,291 does not explicitly define what a cost or a benefit is, nor how an agency should measure those costs and benefits. OMB has, however, prepared standards for the development of RIA's and it reviews all agency attempts to define and measure costs and benefits. OMB guidelines, for example, state that potential benefits should be "quantified in monetary terms" and that "the amount that people are willing to pay" is the "best measure" of a regulation's benefits.[50] This even applies to the value of benefits not directly traded in the marketplace, such as safety. More important, Order 12,291 requires that both proposed rules and even final rules be submitted to OMB before they are issued publicly. OMB can, in effect, veto rules before issuance, which effectively insulates much of OMB's input from judicial review.

42. Exec.Order No. 12,291, supra note 40, at§ 1(b).

43. The regulatory impact analysis required in Executive Order 12,291 is in many ways similar to the "regulatory flexibility analysis" required by the Regulatory Flexibility Act, 5 U.S.C.A. §§ 601–612. That Act requires agencies to consider the potential impact of their regulations on small businesses and other small entities and to consider regulatory alternatives. Review of agency rules is by the Chief Counsel for Advocacy of the Small Business Administration.

44. Exec.Order No. 12,291, supra note 40, at§ 3(c).

45. Section 8 exemptions cover regulations that respond to emergencies, conflict with deadlines imposed by court or statutory deadlines or are exempt by the Director of OMB.

46. Exec.Order No. 12,291, supra note 40, at§ 2(b).

47. Id.§ 2(d).

48. Id.§ 2(b).

49. Id.§ 3(d).

50. See The Role of Regulatory Impact Analysis, 1987–1988 Regulatory Program of the U.S.Gov't at xviii (benefit estimates) and xix (valuation of benefits). See also A Guide to Federal Agency Rulemaking 155 (Admin.Conf. of U.S., 2d ed. 1991).

Executive Order 12,291 was carefully drafted to avoid direct conflicts with statutes that rejected cost-benefit analyses.[51] As we have noted, it applies only "to the extent permitted by law"[52] and the order formally excludes independent regulatory agencies.[53] Independent agencies, however, may voluntarily engage in the kind of review advocated by OMB, though there is no legal requirement to do so.[54] Similarly, Executive Order 12,291 tries to deal with any actionable delays that its processes may cause. Section 8(a)(2) exempts "any regulation for which consideration or reconsideration under the terms of this Order would conflict with deadlines imposed by statute or by judicial order" from the procedures proscribed by the Order.[55] Despite this exception, some cases involving delay have found their way to the courts.[56]

Although what constitutes cost and how one may define benefit may change, this approach to executive oversight of administrative agency discretion has remained a standard feature of all administrations since the Reagan Administration.

Executive Order (EO) 12,866,[57] promulgated during the Clinton Administration, replaced EO 12,291, but did so without altering the

51. For a discussion of the extent to which agencies may use cost-benefit analysis in carrying out their statutory duties, see Industrial Union Department, AFL–CIO v. American Petroleum Institute, 448 U.S. 607, 100 S.Ct. 2844, 65 L.Ed.2d 1010 (1980) (the "Benzene" case where a plurality of the Supreme Court found that the statute involved impliedly required the existence of a "significant risk" before OSHA could act); American Textile Mfrs. Institute, Inc. v. Donovan, 452 U.S. 490, 101 S.Ct. 2478, 69 L.Ed.2d 185 (1981) (the "Cotton Dust" case) (the Supreme Court noted that when "Congress has intended that an agency engage in cost-benefit analysis, it has clearly indicated such intent on the face of the statute."); but see International Union, United Automobile, Aerospace and Agricultural Implement Workers v. OSHA, 938 F.2d 1310 (D.C.Cir.1991) (once a significant risk is found under OSHA, the agency may use cost-benefit analysis in interpreting its statute to determine what is economically and technologically feasible).

52. Exec.Order No. 12,291, supra note 40, at§ 2.

53. Id. § 1(d).

54. See, e.g., U.S. Regulatory Council, A Survey of Ten Agencies' Experience with Regulatory Analysis 7 (1981) (then Vice President Bush requesting the independent agencies to cooperate with the spirit of the Executive Order).

55. Exec.Order No. 12,291,§ 8(a)(2), 3 C.F.R. Pt. 127 (1981), reprinted in 5 U.S.C.A. § 601 at 434.

56. See, e.g., Environmental Defense Fund v. Thomas, 627 F.Supp. 566 (D.D.C. 1986); see generally, McGarity, Regulatory Analysis and Regulatory Reform, 65 Tex. L.Rev. 1243 (1987).

For a detailed discussion of the constitutionality of Executive Order 12,291, see A Symposium on Administrative Law: The Uneasy Constitutional Status of the Administrative Agencies, 36 Am.U.L.Rev. No. 2 (Winter 1987); DeMuth & Ginsburg, supra note 31; Morrison, OMB Interference With Agency Rulemaking: The Wrong Way to Write a Regulation, 99 Harv.L.Rev. 1059 (1986); see also Olson, The Quiet Shift of Power: Office of Management and Budget Supervision of Environmental Protection Agency Rulemaking Under Executive Order 12291, 4 Va.J.Nat.Res.L. 1 (1984); Sunstein, Cost–Benefit Analysis and the Separation of Powers, 23 Ariz.L.Rev. 1267 (1981).

57. 3 C.F.R. 638 (1993). For an analysis of Executive Order 12,866 and a comparison of it with earlier Reagan/Bush orders, see Colloquium, The Fifth Annual Robert C. Byrd Conference on the Administrative Process: The First Year of Clinton/Gore: Reinventing Government or Redefining Reagan/Bush Initiatives?, 8 Admin.L.J. Am. U. 23 (1994); Ellen Siegler, Executive Order 12,866: An Analysis of the New Executive Order on Regulatory Planning and Review, 24 Envtl. L. Rep. 10,070 (1994). For a discussion of the similarities between Regan/Bush and Clinton/Gore regulatory initiatives and some of the reasons for those similarities, see Alfred C. Aman, Jr., A

approach to executive oversight in set forth EO 12,291. EO 12,866 pursues the same goals of regulatory efficiency and accountability. As in EO 12,291, executive oversight and regulatory cost consciousness dominate the Clinton EO approach to regulatory issues. EO 12,866 requires agencies to develop only necessary regulations,[58] to do so in a cost-effective manner, and "to select those approaches that maximize net benefits." Unlike EO 12,291, the Clinton EO specifically requires the consideration of equity[59] rather than outright deregulation. It encourages the use of the market incentives to achieve regulatory goals, rather than the use of direct regulation.[60]

There are other content differences between this order and EO 12,291. The regulations somewhat broaden the nature of the cost-benefit analysis by recognizing certain limits of relying solely on quantitative analysis.[61] EO 12,886 also clearly puts the White House formally in charge of the regulatory process. All disputes between OIRA and rule-making agencies are to be resolved by the Vice President or President.[62]

§ 15.1.4 The Paperwork Reduction Act and the Office of Information and Regulatory Affairs

The Office of Information and Regulatory Affairs (OIRA) within OMB was created by the Paperwork Reduction Act of 1980 (PRA).[63] That Act sought "to minimize federal paperwork burden on individuals, small business and State and local government, ... to minimize the cost of information collection to the Federal Government, ... and to maximize its usefulness" to the federal government of the information collected.[64] This Act established the Office of Information and Regulatory Affairs (OIRA) in OMB and authorizes it to review agency rules that contain information collection requirements.[65] In so doing, OIRA required agencies to justify the record-keeping procedures it imposed on regulated entities and to show these procedures were the least burdensome possible, did not duplicate other federal requirements and provided useful information.[66]

Global Perspective on current Regulatory Reforms: Rejection, Relocation, or Reinvention?, 2 Ind. J. Global Legal Stud. 429 (1993). See also, Robert W. Hahn et al, Empirical Analysis: Assessing Regulatory Impact Analyses: The Failure of Agencies to Comply with Executive Order 12,866 (LR3), 23 Harv.J.L & Pub. Pol'y 859 (2000).

58. 3 C.F.R. 638 (1993).

59. Id.

60. Id.

61. Id.

62. See Richard H. Pilden and Cass Sunstein, 62 U.Chi.L.Rev. 1 (1993).

63. 44 U.S.C.A. §§ 3501–3520. That Act was updated in 1995: Pub. L. No. 104–13, 109 Stat. 163 (codified at 44 U.S.C. § 3501–3520). For a recent analysis of the 1995 Act, see Jeffrey S. Lubbers, Paperwork ReDux: The (Stronger) Paperwork Reduction Act of 1995, 49 Admin.L.Rev. 111 (1997).

64. 44 U.S.C.A. § 3501.

65. This review of agency "information collection requirements" does not include disclosure to third parties, but only disclosures to the government; see Dole v. United Steelworkers of America, 494 U.S. 26, 110 S.Ct. 929, 108 L.Ed.2d 23 (1990), superseded by statute as stated in Matter of Rhone-Poulenc AG Co., 1996 WL 691425 (E.P.A. 1996).

66. See 5 C.F.R. § 1320.4(b).

Review of rules by OIRA personnel, known as "desk officers," is generalist in nature. This is because of the nature of the task at hand. Because OIRA reviews all rules of covered agencies, the volume of work alone precludes detailed analysis. OIRA desk officers, however, also provide OMB review, pursuant to Executive Order 12,866, of agency rules that do not contain a paperwork reduction request. They use the same general criteria: whether the agency action rule is justified by the benefits it provides and whether its burdens have been minimized.[67]

The main purposes of OIRA are to allow the executive to pursue its policy goals in an efficient manner, and to require cost conscious decisionmaking by agencies. OIRA personnel may discover analytic inconsistencies in agency rules that might prove embarrassing in a court challenge of the agency's rules. Although OIRA's principal officers do not expect expertise or in depth research from the desk officers who review the rules, OIRA personnel do, in effect, constitute a group of "superanalysts" who review agencies' analyses and seek improvements in their regulatory techniques.[68]

Agencies retain the authority to promulgate rules without OIRA's consent. It is rare, however, for an agency to appeal an adverse OIRA decision, or to publish a rule in light of OIRA opposition, given the potential for worsened relations with, or retribution by, OMB.[69] OIRA may thus impede agencies' responsibilities delegated by law through delays which cause agencies to miss statutory deadlines. In *Environmental Defense Fund v. Thomas*,[70] for example, EPA had already missed its statutory deadline to promulgate rules dealing with hazardous wastes in underground storage tanks. Despite the missed statutory deadlines, OIRA persuaded EPA to alter its approach to these hazardous waste issues. As a result, EPA published its rules four months after the statutory deadline. Finding that the executive order's exemption for rules under deadline "[a]pparently ... simply ignored," the court held that OMB review must terminate in time to allow deadlines to be met.[71]

The potential for undue interference with agency policy making through OIRA review was brought to light in the context of asbestos regulation. Under Section 9 of the Toxic Substances Control Act,[72] EPA may defer to the Occupational Safety and Health Administration (OSHA) and the Consumer Product Safety Commission (CPSC) for asbestos regulation. After five years of preparation, EPA sent to OIRA two proposed regulations to control asbestos. EPA's rules would have

67. Bruff, supra note 12, at 557–560. See also, Shane, Political Accountability in a System of Checks and Balances: The Case of Presidential Review of Rulemaking, 48 Ark.L.Rev. 161, 190, 209–211 (1995).

68. Id.

69. Id. at 567.

70. 627 F.Supp. 566 (D.D.C.1986).

71. Id. at 569–71. See also, *Natural Resources Defense Council v. EPA*, 966 F.2d 1292 (9th Cir.1992) (factors argued by EPA to justify missing a dealing does not grant EPA authority to ignore unambiguous deadlines set by congress) citing *Delaney v. EPA*, 898 F.2d 687, 691 (9th Cir.1990), *cert denied*. Congress set theme and expected compliance. See also, 132 Cong. Rec. 32,-381–82 (remarks of Senator Stafford) ("deadlines are not aspirational").

72. 15 U.S.C.A. § 1608.

banned four product categories and phased out production of several others.[73] OIRA disagreed with EPA's proposed rules and pressed the agency to invoke Section 9 of the Toxic Substances Control Act. After months of refusing to accede to OIRA's request, EPA reversed course and deferred under Section 9. The only apparent legal support for its decision was an OMB memorandum mandating deferral. EPA eventually reconsidered its decision and published its initial proposed rules but only because of an enraged EPA staff and Congress.[74]

Another example where an agency suddenly changed a considered position in response to OIRA and OMB pressure occurred in the regulation of ethylene oxide, a suspected carcinogen used in the sterilization of hospital instruments. The final rule contemplated by OSHA set a Permanent Exposure Limit and Short Term Exposure Limit ("STEL"), each of which OSHA claimed was economically feasible. OIRA responded that the STEL set by OSHA was inadequately supported by health effects data and would not be cost-effective. OSHA reconsidered its rule and, with a judicial deadline drawing near, submitted a rule which simply deleted the STEL and any reference to it. In Public Citizen Health Research Group v. Tyson,[75] the D.C. Circuit upheld OSHA's permanent exposure limit but remanded the short term limit portion of the rule to the agency. Four years after the initial court deadline, OSHA finally issued a short term exposure limit regulation.[76]

The OIRA review process thus presents an opportunity for OMB to engage in substantive policy decisionmaking. In United Steelworkers of America v. Pendergrass,[77] the Third Circuit considered the scope of the Paperwork Reduction Act in light of this fact.[78] In this case, OIRA had disapproved OSHA's proposed requirements that chemical manufacturers' exchange information sheets disclosing hazards to workers at multi-employer worksites, and provide certain exemptions from duplicative labeling of potentially hazardous materials in the workplace. The court held that such third-party information disclosure was not regulated under the act, and noted the act's disclaimer of any intent to displace decisions delegated to agencies by law through an increase of OMB authority over agency substantive policy decisions. The Supreme Court affirmed Pendergrass *in* Dole v. United Steelworkers,[79] holding that "the Paperwork Reduction Act does not give OMB the authority to review agency rules mandating disclosure by regulated entities to third par-

73. See 51 Fed.Reg. 3738 (1986).

74. See EPA's Asbestos Regulations: Hearing before the Subcomm. on Oversight and Investigations of the House Energy and Commerce Comm., 99th Cong., 1st Sess. (1985); EPA's Asbestos Regulations: Report on a Case Study on OMB's Interference in Agency Rulemaking 1–5 (Comm.Print 1985).

75. 796 F.2d 1479 (D.C.Cir.1986).

76. 53 Fed.Reg. 11,414 (1988).

77. 855 F.2d 108 (3d Cir.1988), cert. denied, 494 U.S. 1003, 110 S.Ct. 1295, 108 L.Ed.2d 472 (1990).

78. The court's concern over OIRA's indirect effects on agency substantive policy thus "suggests that OIRA and the courts may struggle over the relationship between paperwork functions and cost-benefit review." Bruff, supra note 12, at 576.

79. 494 U.S. 26, 110 S.Ct. 929, 108 L.Ed.2d 23 (1990), superseded by statute as stated in Matter of Rhone-Poulenc AG Co., 1996 WL 691425 (E.P.A.1996).

ties."[80] The 1995 amendments to the Paperwork Reduction Act, however, overruled this interpretation of the Act.[81] Agency rules that require businesses or individuals to maintain information for third parties or the public are now covered.[82]

§ 15.2 EXECUTIVE PARTICIPATION IN INFORMAL RULEMAKING PROCESSES

Most OMB review occurs before any proposed agency rules have been submitted to the public for notice and comment. Certain policy issues can easily be dealt with behind the scenes. Once an informal rulemaking process is publicly underway, however, questions arise concerning the appropriate role the executive branch can or should play at this stage of the process.[1] Can the executive branch, for example, engage in ex parte contacts designed to influence the outcome of the rulemaking process? This question raises a number of issues that go to the heart of the executive branch's relationship to the administrative process, issues where the APA offers little or no guidance. Section 553, for example, makes no mention of ex parte contacts, and judicial imposition of such a rule may raise Vermont Yankee-*like concerns.*[2]

The leading case on executive *ex parte* contacts is *Sierra Club v. Costle.*[3] This case involved both substantive and procedural attacks on certain new source performance standards for coal-fired power plants

80. Id. at 42, 110 S.Ct. at 938.

81. The key language is the addition of "or requiring disclosure to third parties or the public" to the definition of "collection of information".

82. Id.

§ 15.2

1. See generally, Peter L. Strauss, Presidential Rulemaking, 72 Chicago–Kent L.Rev. 965 (1997); Young, Judicial review of Informal Agency Action on the Fiftieth Anniversary of the APA: The Alleged Demise and Actual Status of Overton Park's Requirement of Judicial Review "On the Record," 10 Admin.L.J. Am.U. 179 (1996); Shane, Political Accountability in a System of Checks and balances: The Case of Presidential Review of Rulemaking, 48 Ark. L.Rev. 161 (1995); Strauss & Sunstein, The Role of the President in Informal Regulation: Incorporating the Administrative Process, 38 Admin.L.Rev. 181, (1986); Croley, Theories of Regulation: Incorporating the Administrative Process, 98 Colum.L.Rev. 1 (1998). See also, Symposium on Presidential Control of Rulemaking, 56 Tul.L.Rev. 811 (1982); Verkuil, Jawboning Administrative Agencies: Ex Parte Contacts by the White House, 80 Colum.L.Rev. 943 (1980).

2. It has been argued that without such Congressional action, Vermont Yankee Nuclear Power Corp. v. NRDC, 435 U.S. 519, 98 S.Ct. 1197, 55 L.Ed.2d 460 (1978), precludes reviewing courts from requiring agencies to adhere to procedures not currently in the Administrative Procedure Act. See Verkuil, supra note 83, at 976; Rosenberg, Beyond the Limits of Executive Power: Presidential Control of Agency Rulemaking Under Executive Order 12,291, 80 Mich.L.Rev. 193, 235 (1982); Gray, Presidential Involvement in Informal Rulemaking, 56 Tul.L.Rev. 863, 868 (1982). But see, *Ammex, Inc. v. United States*, 62 F.Supp. 2d 1148 (Ct. Int'l Trade 1999) (if agency considered, even indirectly, any international documents, those documents should be included in the record; when a party demonstrates there is a reasonable basis that considered materials are not in the record, there can be limited discovery to complete the record, assuming that a party shows there is a reasonable basis.)

3. 657 F.2d 298 (D.C.Cir.1981). See also, *Portland Audubon Soc'y v. Oregon Lands Coalition*, 984 F.2d 1534 (9th Cir. 1993); Action for Children's Television v. F.C.C., 564 F.2d 458 (D.C.Cir.1977); Home Box Office, Inc. v. F.C.C., 567 F.2d 9 (D.C.Cir.1977), cert. denied 434 U.S. 829, 98 S.Ct. 111, 54 L.Ed.2d 89 (1977); Sangamon Valley Television Corp. v. United States, 269 F.2d 221 (D.C.Cir.1959).

promulgated by the Environmental Protection Agency. These standards were issued pursuant to the Clean Air Act, and were intended to reduce sulfur dioxide and particulate emissions from new facilities by utilizing "scrubber" technology. After rejecting a variety of substantive challenges to these rules, the court focused specifically on the procedural issues raised. Foremost among these was the claim that off-the-record meetings between President Carter and EPA officials, after the public comment period had closed, had unduly influenced the agency's decision. Failure to docket these conversations, the plaintiffs argued, effectively prevented interested parties from rebutting the President's input, and blocked any opportunity for meaningful judicial review.

The court found that the facts revealed "a single undocketed meeting . . . attended by the President, White House staff, other high ranking members of the Executive Branch, as well as EPA officials, and which concerned the issues and options presented by the rulemaking."[4] It then considered two separate issues. First, it considered whether executive contacts were permissible before, during, or after the comment period. In holding that such communications were permissible, the court relied extensively on the President's Article II powers over executive agencies. Specifically, the court emphasized the fact that "[i]n the particular case of EPA, Presidential authority is clear since it has never been considered an 'independent agency,' but always part of the Executive Branch."[5] More fundamentally, the court emphasized that under our Constitution, all executive power "rests exclusively with the President."[6] Particularly given the broad national economic implications of the regulations involved in this case, and the complicated tradeoffs among cost, environmental, and energy considerations, the court concluded that "[o]ur form of government simply could not function effectively or rationally if key executive policymakers were isolated from each other and from the Chief Executive. Single mission agencies do not always have the answers to complex regulatory problems."[7]

This approach to the issue was consistent with recognition of the importance of agency expertise. Implicit in any policymaking process is the assumption that various policy alternatives will be produced. Producing viable alternatives is the job of the agency experts, but choosing among these alternatives is a political decision, one in which the President can and should be involved. If Congress did not wish the executive to be so involved it could have said so. The Clean Air Act, however, did not "explicitly treat the issue of post-comment period meetings with

4. 657 F.2d at 404.

5. 657 F.2d at 405–06. Most commentators agree that the President has less authority to intervene in non-Executive agency rulemaking. See Cutler, The Case For Presidential Intervention In Regulatory Rulemaking By the Executive Branch, 56 Tul.L.Rev. 830, 838 (1982), Verkuil; supra note 83, at 961, 979. See also Recommendation 80–6: Intragovernmental Communications in Informal Rulemaking Proceedings, Recommendations and Reports 27 (Admin.Conf. of the U.S. 1980) which recommends a model for Presidential intervention in rulemaking but explicitly limits its application to Executive departments and agencies.

6. 657 F.2d at 405.

7. Id. at 406.

individuals outside EPA,"[8] and the court was not about to infer any such ban.

A second procedural issue remained. Even assuming the legality of *ex parte* executive communications after the close of the comment period, should not both the fact and the substance of these comments be provided for in the rulemaking record? The court answered no, concluding that "[t]he purposes of full-record review ... do not require that courts know the details of every White House contact, including a Presidential one, in this informal rulemaking setting."[9] In so doing, the court emphasized that "any rule issued here with or without White House assistance must have the requisite *factual support* in the rulemaking record, and under this particular statute the Administrator may not base the rule in whole or in part on any '*information or data*' which is not in the record, no matter what the source."[10] Yet, the court also recognized that it "is always possible that undisclosed Presidential prodding may direct an outcome that *is* factually based on the record, but different from the outcome that would have obtained in the absence of Presidential involvement."[11] Thus the Court did not believe "that Congress intended that the courts convert informal rulemaking into a rarified technocratic process, unaffected by political considerations or the presence of Presidential power."[12]

§ 15.3 THE APPOINTMENT POWER

The President is the chief administrator of the executive branch. In this role, he is responsible for the appointment and removal of those officers who serve in the various agencies. The ability to appoint and remove such decision-makers is yet another means by which the executive can exert some control over the bureaucracy; however, neither the President's power of appointment nor his power of removal is absolute.

The Appointments Clause distinguishes between "officers of the United States" and "inferior officers."[1] It requires that "Officers of the

8. Id. at 400. The Court refused to extend its ruling in Home Box Office, Inc. v. FCC, 567 F.2d 9 (D.C.Cir.1977), cert. denied 434 U.S. 829, 98 S.Ct. 111, 54 L.Ed.2d 89 (1977), to the facts in this case. For a discussion of ex parte contacts in adjudicatory contexts, see chapter 9, sec. 9.5.3 supra.

9. 657 F.2d at 407.

10. Id. at 407–08 (emphasis in original) (footnote omitted). One commentator has challenged this rationale, claiming that it confuses the question of whether there is some evidence in the record to sustain the agency's decision with the concern that the agency considered irrelevant information that affected the outcome, thereby rendering its formal justification "purely cosmetic." Morrison, Presidential Intervention in Informal Rulemaking: Striking the Proper Balance, 56 Tul.L.Rev. 879, 898 (1982). Another commentator has added that while the court relies on Art. II to justify presidential participation, the nondisclosure arguments rest only on the questionable assumption that an on-the-record requirement would adversely affect the President's policy-making authority. Rosenberg, supra note 84, at 242.

11. 657 F.2d at 408 (emphasis in original).

12. Id. at 408.

§ 15.3

1. U.S.Const. art. II, § 2, cl. 2, simply states that the President:

shall nominate, and by and with the Advice and Consent of the Senate, shall appoint Ambassadors, other Public Min-

United States" be appointed by the President with the advice and consent of the Senate. Inferior officers, however, may be appointed by the President alone, by heads of departments, or by the judiciary. This distinction between "Officers of the United States" and inferior officers, and the different appointment procedures that apply, naturally raises the issue of how one determines the kind of officer being appointed. The Supreme Court addressed this issue in *Morrison v. Olson*,[2] holding that an individual appointed as an "independent counsel" pursuant to the Ethics in Government Act of 1978 was an "inferior officer." In so doing, the Court relied heavily on Buckley v. Valeo,[3] another leading Supreme Court case dealing with this same issue. We shall examine each of these cases in turn.

Buckley v. Valeo involved, *inter alia,* a challenge to the constitutionality of the mode of appointment of Commissioners to an eight member Federal Election Commission established by the Federal Election Campaign Act of 1971.[4] That Commission was composed of six voting members, two appointed by the President, two appointed by the President *pro tempore* of the Senate, and two appointed by the Speaker of the House of Representatives. All six were subject to confirmation by a majority of both Houses of Congress. The Court held that constituting the Commission in this manner violated the Appointments Clause, noting that the "fair import [of that clause] is that any appointee exercising significant authority pursuant to the laws of the United States is an "Officer of the United States," and must, therefore, be appointed in the manner prescribed by § 2, cl. 2, of that Article.[5] The Court concluded that these Commissioners did, indeed, exercise "significant authority pursuant to the laws of the United States,"[6] and thus were in fact, "Officers of the United States."[7] In so doing, however, the Court was at best unclear

isters and Consuls, Judges of the Supreme Court, and all other Officers of the United States, whose Appointments are not herein otherwise provided for, and which shall be established by Law; but the Congress may by Law vest the Appointment of such inferior officers, as they think proper, in the President alone, in the Courts of Law, or in the Heads of Departments.

As one commentator has noted "[t]hese few words have raised innumerable questions in the minds of judges and constitutional scholars. For example, who are 'Officers of the United States'? Who are 'inferior Officers'? Are the 'Heads of Departments' Officers, inferior Officers, or neither? Is the category 'all other Officers of the United States' inclusive of the public officials referred to as inferior Officers?" Burkoff, Appointment and Removal Under the Federal Constitution: The Impact of *Buckley v. Valeo*, 22 Wayne L.Rev. 1335, 1337 (1976) (footnotes omitted).

2. 487 U.S. 654, 108 S.Ct. 2597, 101 L.Ed.2d 569 (1988), on remand 857 F.2d 801 (D.C.Cir.1988).

3. 424 U.S. 1, 96 S.Ct. 612, 46 L.Ed.2d 659 (1976).

4. Federal Election Campaign Act of 1971, Pub.L. No. 93–443, § 310, 88 Stat. 1272, 1280 (1974) (current version codified at 2 U.S.C.A. § 437(c)).

5. 424 U.S. at 126, 96 S.Ct. at 685.

6. Id.

7. Thus, the appointment processes used by Congress were unconstitutional. Commissioners must be appointed by the President with advice and consent of the Senate. As to the definition of "inferior officers of the United States," the *Buckley* Court quoted with approval the traditional statements found in United States v. Germaine, 99 U.S. (9 Otto) 508, 509–10, 25 L.Ed. 482 (1878). See Buckley v. Valeo, 424 U.S. at 125, 96 S.Ct. at 685. The Court also defines inferior officers of the United

when it came to explaining the criteria it used to conclude that these Commissioners were "Officers of the United States." The Court did not go so far as to state that some of the Commission's powers were core executive functions, but it did differentiate among the Commission's activities and found that some of them were more appropriate for the executive, rather than the legislative branch.

Foremost among the Commission's executive powers was its enforcement authority. In concluding that these Commissioners were "Officers of the United States," the Court placed considerable weight on the fact that the Commissioners had the power to bring lawsuits, the "ultimate remedy for a breach of the law."[8] The Court emphasized that this "discretionary power to seek judicial relief . . . cannot possibly be regarded as merely in aid of the legislative function of Congress".[9] The Constitution entrusts the President to "take care that the laws are faithfully executed."[10] A Commission that exercises these as well as investigative and informative functions must, therefore, be composed of "persons who are Officers of the United States".[11] The Court in *Buckley v. Valeo* thus concluded that whether an appointee is an officer of the United States or an inferior officer turns on a substantive evaluation of the appointee's duties, powers, and the extent of his independence from

States. Id. at 126 n. 162, 96 S.Ct. at 685 n. 162. And indeed, it is important to note that the appointment process used in this case would satisfy neither the constitutional appointment requirements of "inferior officers" nor "Officers of the United States." Even if these were inferior officers, they could not have been appointed by the President *pro tempore* of the Senate or the Speaker of the House. Arguably, appointment by Congress requires more than just action by these two individuals.

8. 424 U.S. at 138, 96 S.Ct. at 691.

9. Id.

10. U.S. Const. Art. II, § 3.

11. 424 U.S. at 140, 96 S.Ct. at 692. On the other hand, the Court also noted that "[i]nsofar as the powers confided in the Commission are essentially of an investigative and informative nature, . . . there can be no question that the Commission as presently constituted may exercise them." Id. at 137, 96 S.Ct. at 690.

The close judicial scrutiny that the Court applied to this Commission and its makeup arguably represented a departure from the case law that preceded *Buckley*. See, e.g., United States v. Hartwell, 73 U.S. (6 Wall.) 385, 18 L.Ed. 830 (1867); United States v. Germaine, 99 U.S. (9 Otto) 508, 25 L.Ed. 482 (1878); United States v. Moore, 95 U.S. (5 Otto) 760, 24 L.Ed. 588 (1877); United States v. Mouat, 124 U.S. 303, 8 S.Ct. 505, 31 L.Ed. 463 (1888); Ex parte Reed, 100 U.S. (10 Otto) 13, 25 L.Ed. 538 (1879); United States v. Smith, 124 U.S. 525, 8 S.Ct. 595, 31 L.Ed. 534 (1888); Burnap v. United States, 252 U.S. 512, 40 S.Ct. 374, 64 L.Ed. 692 (1920); Auffmordt v. Hedden, 137 U.S. 310, 11 S.Ct. 103, 34 L.Ed. 674 (1890). Those earlier cases, as one commentator has pointed out, "attached no inherent consequences to the lack of Officer status." Burkoff, supra note 95, at 1361. Indeed, the courts traditionally chose "to *avoid* rather than *decide* the issue by deferring unabashedly to congressional practice." Id. at 1363 (emphasis in original). See Go–Bart Importing Co. v. United States, 282 U.S. 344, 51 S.Ct. 153, 75 L.Ed. 374 (1931); Myers v. United States, 272 U.S. 52, 47 S.Ct. 21, 71 L.Ed. 160 (1926); Burnap v. United States, 252 U.S. 512, 40 S.Ct. 374, 64 L.Ed. 692 (1920); Rice v. Ames, 180 U.S. 371, 21 S.Ct. 406, 45 L.Ed. 577 (1901); United States v. Smith, 124 U.S. 525, 8 S.Ct. 595, 31 L.Ed. 534 (1888); United States v. Mouat, 124 U.S. 303, 8 S.Ct. 505, 31 L.Ed. 463 (1888); Ex parte Siebold, 100 U.S. (10 Otto) 371, 25 L.Ed. 717 (1879); United States v. Germaine, 99 U.S. (9 Otto) 508, 25 L.Ed. 482 (1878); United States v. Hartwell, 73 U.S. (6 Wall.) 385, 18 L.Ed. 830 (1867); Ex parte Hennen, 38 U.S. (13 Pet.) 230, 10 L.Ed. 138 (1839); McGrath v. United States, 275 Fed. 294 (2d Cir.1921); Collins v. United States, 14 Ct.Cl. 568 (1879). But see Springer v. Philippine Is-

control by superiors.[12] Neither the appointee's title nor the determination made by Congress as to how he should be appointed is dispositive; however, it is not at all clear when the officer is engaged in "the performance of a significant governmental duty exercised pursuant to a public law."[13]

Morrison v. Olson[14] involved a variety of challenges to the constitutionality of the independent counsel provisions of the Ethics in Government Act.[15] That Act provided for the appointment of an independent counsel in certain situations when high executive officials were suspected of violation of federal laws. The constitutional challenges in this case included claims that the independent counsel was an "Officer of the United States" and that the method of appointment provided by the Act violated the Appointments Clause.

Specifically, it was contended that the independent counsel could only be appointed by the President with advice and consent of the Senate. The Ethics in Government Act provided otherwise. The Act required that the Attorney General take certain actions upon receipt of information that he determined is "sufficient to constitute grounds to investigate whether any person [covered by the Act] may have violated any Federal criminal law."[16] After this investigation was complete or after the passage of ninety days, the Attorney General then had to file a report with the Special Division of the United States Court of Appeals for the District of Columbia. The Court had no power of its own to appoint an independent counsel, but if the Attorney General determined that there were "reasonable grounds to believe that further investigation or prosecution is warranted," then he "shall apply to the division of the court for the appointment of an independent counsel" and that court shall appoint "an appropriate independent counsel and shall define that independent counsel's prosecutorial jurisdiction."[17]

The Court had little difficulty with the argument that the independent counsel was an "Officer of the United States." Noting that the line between "inferior" and "principal" officers was far from clear, the Court focused on several factors. First, the independent counsel could be

lands, 277 U.S. 189, 48 S.Ct. 480, 72 L.Ed. 845 (1928).

12. 424 U.S. at 126 and n. 162, 96 S.Ct. at 685 and n. 162. See also id. at 269–70 (White, J., concurring in part and dissenting in part).

13. Id. at 141, 96 S.Ct. at 692.

14. 487 U.S. 654, 108 S.Ct. 2597, 101 L.Ed.2d 569 (1988), on remand 857 F.2d 801 (1988).

15. 28 U.S.C. §§ 49, 591 et. seq. (supp. 1988). This statute was reenacted in 1994 by the Independent Counsel Reauthorization Act of 1994, which was to be in place for five years. At the end of that time, Congress allowed the Act to expire. The application of the Act by the Independent Counsel's office was criticized before and after the Clinton impeachment. See, e.g., Norman Orenstein, This Law is a Turkey, Wash. Post, Dec. 14, 1997, at C7; Bruce L. Moyer, Congressional Dissatisfaction with Independent Counsel Law Grows, 45 Fed. Law 10 (1998). Many members of Congress introduced legislation to reform the Act, but none made it out of committee. See, e.g., S. 2075, 105th Cong. (1998) (providing expedited review of Executive privilege claims); Independent Counsel Limited Powers Act, J.R. 3464, 105th Cong. (1998) (altering the Independent Counsel's jurisdiction, authority to appoint an independent counsel, and crimes subject to investigation).

16. 28 U.S.C.A. § 49.

17. 487 U.S. at 661, 108 S.Ct. at 2603.

removed for cause by the Attorney General. "The fact that she can be removed," the court reasoned, "indicates that she is in some degree 'inferior' in rank and authority."[18] Second, the Court focused on the limited nature of the independent counsel's duties. She was appointed to prosecute only one case; her investigative and prosecutorial powers did not include any "authority to formulate policy for the Government or the Executive Branch, nor did it give appellant any administrative duties outside of those necessary to operate her office."[19] Her jurisdiction was limited in ways determined by the Special Division and her appointment terminated when the case was concluded. She had no ongoing responsibilities. The Court easily concluded that this kind of official was clearly an inferior officer.[20]

There were three other related issues as well. Even if the independent counsel was not an "Officer of the United States," petitioners contended that this kind of official could not, in any event, be appointed by the judiciary. Moreover, the restrictions on removal violated the President's constitutional duty to "take care that the laws be faithfully executed." Underlying all of these arguments was a conception of the separation of powers that suggested an independent constitutional source of limitations on the use of the appointment and removal powers. We examine these issues in the next section. *Edmond v. United States*[21] used a more focused approach to resolve the issue of whether a particular official was a principal or an inferior officer. This case involved a challenge to the Secretary of Transportation's Appointment of civilian members of the Coast Guard Court of Criminal Appeals, a military court. Writing for eight Justices, Justice Scalia concluded these appointees were inferior officers, emphasizing that they were under the supervision of a higher ranking officer. Justice Souter concurred in the outcome of the case, but questioned whether a relationship with a higher ranking official alone was enough to make this person an "inferior officer."[22]

§ 15.3.1 Appointing Inferior Officers

The Appointments Clause specifies how "inferior Officers" are to be appointed. It provides that "the Congress may by Law vest the Appointment of such inferior Officers, as they think proper, in the President alone, in the Courts of Law, or in the Heads of Departments."[23] The language of this clause gives Congress wide discretion when it comes to determining just how these appointments should be made; however, as the Court pointed out in *Morrison,* this discretion is not unlimited.

18. Id. at 670, 108 S.Ct. at 2608.

19. Id. at 670–73, 108 S.Ct. at 2608–09.

20. The Court cited a number of cases as consistent with this conclusion. See United States v. Eaton, 169 U.S. 331, 18 S.Ct. 374, 42 L.Ed. 767 (1898); Ex parte Siebold, 100 U.S. (10 Otto) 371, 25 L.Ed. 717 (1880); Go–Bart Importing Co. v. United States, 282 U.S. 344, 352–53, 51 S.Ct. 153, 156–57, 75 L.Ed. 374 (1931); United States v. Nixon, 418 U.S. 683, 694, 696, 94 S.Ct. 3090, 3100, 3102, 41 L.Ed.2d 1039 (1974).

21. 520 U.S. 651, 117 S.Ct. 1573, 137 L.Ed.2d 917 (1997).

22. Id.

23. U.S. Const. Art. II, § 2, cl. 2.

Interbranch appointments, for example, can raise significant separation of powers considerations. The judiciary could not, for example, appoint key officials in the State Department. In 1839, the Court in *Ex parte Hennen*,[24] noted that the appointive power was "no doubt intended to be exercised by the department of the government to which the officer to be appointed most appropriately belonged."[25] Forty years later, however, in *Ex parte Siebold*,[26] the Court upheld a statute placing the appointment of election commissioners in the Court of Appeals. In so doing, the Court noted that the appointment of inferior officers should usually be vested "in that department of the government, executive or judicial, or in that particular executive department to which the duties of such officers appertain."[27] Yet, there was, in fact, "no absolute requirement to this effect in the Constitution; and, if there were, it would be difficult in many cases to determine to which department an office properly belonged."[28] The Court emphasized that the practical answer to the question of who should make the determination was Congress,[29] but went on to note that if it were to review Congress's decision, it must nevertheless remain alert to any "incongruity" between the appointing body and the officer's duties.[30]

The Court in *Morrison* recognized that, outside of *Ex parte Hennen* and *Ex parte Siebold,* "there is very little, if any, express discussion of the propriety of interbranch appointments in our decisions, and we see no reason now to depart from the holding of *Siebold* that such appointments are not proscribed by the excepting clause."[31] The Court found no support in the sparse history of that clause to indicate that Congress did not have the discretion to make interbranch appointments. In the contexts of the *Morrison* case, the Court concluded that Congress had not violated any separation of powers principles, because the appointment of the independent counsel by the judiciary did not have the potential to "impair the constitutional functions assigned to one of the branches."[32]

The Court also raised and rejected another possible objection to interbranch appointments: " 'incongruity' between the functions normally performed by the courts and the performance of their duty to appoint."[33] In *Morrison,* the Court found no such incongruity, noting

24. 38 U.S. (13 Pet.) 225, 10 L.Ed. 136 (1839) (upholding the District Court's authority to appoint and remove a court clerk).

25. Id. at 258.

26. 100 U.S. (10 Otto) 371, 25 L.Ed. 717 (1879).

27. Id. at 397.

28. Id.

29. Id. at 397–98. ("[a]nd, looking at the subject in a practical light, it is perhaps better that it should rest there, than the country should be harassed by the endless controversies to which a more specific direction on this subject might have given rise").

30. Id. at 398.

31. 487 U.S. at 674, 108 S.Ct. at 2610. See also, *U.S. v. Hilario*, discussed supra, 218 F.3d 19 (1st Cir.2000) (because the classification of US attorneys is that of inferior officers, "congress as a theoretical matter can entrust their appointment to the president, the head of a department, or the courts of law, without requiring Senate confirmation").

32. Id. at 676, 108 S.Ct. at 2611.

33. Id.

that courts have often been involved in appointing attorneys to act as prosecutors.[34] The Court thus rejected, at least implicitly, the argument that all executive power must be vested solely in the executive.[35] A similar assumption underlies its approach to the issues involving removal of an independent counsel.

In addition to limitations on interbranch appointments, the Court has recently explored the boundaries of the terms "Courts of Law" and "Heads of Departments" in *Freytag v. Commissioner of Internal Revenue*.[36] In that case, the Court noted that the Appointments Clause was intended to "ensure that those who wielded [appointment power] were accountable to political force and the will of the people."[37] If an inferior officer is not appointed directly by the President, Congress may not assign appointment authority unless the agency to which that officer has been appointed may properly be categorized as either a "Court of Law" or a "Department."

34. The Court cited Young v. United States ex rel. Vuitton et Fils S.A., 481 U.S. 787, 107 S.Ct. 2124, 95 L.Ed.2d 740 (1987); Go–Bart Importing Co. v. United States, 282 U.S. 344, 51 S.Ct. 153, 75 L.Ed. 374 (1931); United States v. Solomon, 216 F.Supp. 835 (S.D.N.Y.1963).

For interesting analyses of this issue during the hearings before passage of this Act, see Special Prosecutor and Watergate Grand Jury Legislation: Hearings Before the Subcomm. on Criminal Justice of the House Comm. on the Judiciary, 93d Cong., 1st Sess. 208–09 (1973). ("It is unnecessary to consider here whether this provision would permit Congress to place in the courts the power to appoint officials unconnected with the courts. For a prosecuting attorney, like all members of the bar, is an officer of the court. In the criminal process he is as integral as the judge to the work of the courts.") (statement of Daniel J. Meador); Special Prosecutor: Hearings Before the Senate Comm. on the Judiciary, 93d Cong., 1st Sess. (Part 1) 325 (1973). ("It is a matter within the discretion of Congress as to where the assignment of prosecutorial functions should rest. It is quite true that they did rest that function in an officer inferior to the President, but I don't think they are compelled to do so. I don't think either the history as [sic] the time of the adoption of the Constitution, or the history since, suggests that the performance of the judicial function, of which the prosecutor is such an indispensable adjunct, is one that must fall within the control of the executive branch or the President himself.") (statement of Philip B. Kurland). See also Rice v. Ames, 180 U.S. 371, 21 S.Ct. 406, 45 L.Ed. 577 (1901) (finding Congress constitutionally vested the courts with the power to appoint commissioners); Hobson v. Hansen, 265 F.Supp. 902 (D.D.C.1967) (finding constitutional a statute vesting appointment power of the District of Columbia Board of Education in the D.C. District Court); United States v. Solomon, 216 F.Supp. 835 (S.D.N.Y.1963) (upholding the precursor to 28 U.S.C.A. § 546, authorizing court appointment of interim U.S. attorneys); Go–Bart Importing Co. v. United States, 282 U.S. 344, 51 S.Ct. 153, 75 L.Ed. 374 (1931).

35. But see Scalia, J. in dissent, arguing that Art. II, § 1, cl. 1 of the Constitution providing that the executive power shall be vested in a President "does not mean *some of* the executive power, but *all of* the executive power." 487 U.S. at 705, 108 S.Ct. at 2626 (Scalia, J., dissenting) (emphasis in original).

36. 501 U.S. 868, 111 S.Ct. 2631, 115 L.Ed.2d 764 (1991). For discussions of this case, see Geier, The Tax Court, article III, and the Proposal Advanced by the Federal Courts Study Committee: A Study in Applied Constitutional Theory, 76 Cornell L.Rev. 985 (1991) (critiquing the effectiveness and the constitutionality of special trial judges); see also McNeil, The Administrative Hearing Officer and the National Appeals Division of the U.S. Dep't of Agriculture: A Brief History, A Contemporary Perspective, and Some Thoughts For The Future, 19 J. NAALJ 75, 81–84 (1999) (noting the danger of executive or congressional appointment of special trial judges (article III judges) on the constitutional doctrine of separation of powers); Schwarts, A Decade of Administrative Law: 1987–1996, 32 Tulsa L.J. 493, 500–502 (1997) (explaining the Freytag decision and discussing the ramifications of Scalia's concurrence in light of the majority opinion).

37. Id.

Freytag concerned the appointment of special trial judges by the Chief Judge of the U.S. Tax Court. Congress created the Tax Court pursuant to its authority under Article I. It also empowered the Chief Judge to appoint trial judges to preside over any proceeding properly before the Tax Court and, in certain specified types of cases, to issue opinions. After unanimously concluding that such special trial judges were inferior officers rather than employees, the Court split on how appropriately to categorize the Tax Court. Justice Blackmun, writing for a majority of five, concluded that the Tax Court exercised judicial power similar to Article III courts of law. He expressed concern about an overly inclusive definition of what kinds of agencies fell under the rubric of "Department," suggesting that these be limited to Cabinet-level entities, "expressly 'created' and 'giv[en] ... the name of a department' by Congress."[38] Noting that the Tax Court's decisions are not subject to review in either the Executive or Legislative Branches, the majority concluded that "[t]he Tax Court's exclusively judicial role distinguishes it from other non-Article III tribunals that perform multiple functions and provides the limit on the diffusion of appointment power that the Constitution demands."

Justice Scalia, however, argued that "Courts of Law" meant only Article III courts, which enjoyed the full panoply of protections afforded an independent branch of government.[39] Article I courts could not exercise true judicial power, but are instead executive in nature. Thus, in his view, the Tax Court should properly be categorized as a department for purposes of the Appointments Clause.

§ 15.4 THE POWER TO REMOVE

The Constitution speaks directly to the *appointment* of officials. With the exception of the impeachment provisions,[1] however, there is no constitutional text that deals with the *removal* of certain officials. While it has long been recognized that cabinet level officers such as the

38. Id. at 886, 111 S.Ct. at 2642 (quoting from United States v. Germaine, 99 U.S. (9 Otto) 508, 510–11, 25 L.Ed. 482 (1879)). The title of an agency, however, is not dispositive. The dissent argues the majority's designation of which agencies may be considered departments for Appointments Clause analysis is fraught with ambiguity. In footnote 4 of the opinion, Justice Blackmun suggests other agencies lacking the "Department" designation may yet be considered a department for Appointments Clause purposes: "We do not address here any question involving the appointment of an inferior officer by the head of one of the *principal* [emphasis added] agencies, such as the Federal Trade Commission, the Securities Exchange Commission, the Federal Energy Regulatory Commission, the Central Intelligence Agency, and the Federal Reserve Bank of St. Louis."

39. "[T]he Judicial Branch was separated from Congress not merely by a paper assignment of functions, but by endowment with the means to resist encroachment—foremost among which, of course, are life tenure (during 'good behavior') and permanent salary." 501 U.S. at 907, 111 S.Ct. at 2054.

Justice Scalia further argues that "there is nothing 'inherently judicial' about 'adjudication.' To be a federal officer and to adjudicate are necessary but not sufficient conditions for the exercise of federal judicial power ..."

§ 15.4

1. See U.S. Const. Art. I, § 2, cl. 5; Art. I, § 3, cl. 6; Art. II, § 4.

Secretaries of State, Treasury, or Defense serve at the pleasure of the President, it is not as clear whether inferior officers or other "Officers of the United States" are subject to unconditional Presidential removal powers. Congress has often sought to insulate certain officials from the executive by granting them a term of years and conditioning their removal during that term on "inefficiency, neglect of duty, or malfeasance in office."[2] This kind of insulation from removal is usually the key defining characteristic of an independent commission.

The independent commission is, in many ways, an invention of the Progressive Era. An independent commission attempts to assure a neutral, expert approach to regulatory issues, one that is above the political fray. The tenure that commission members are statutorily granted is intended to isolate them from politics in general and the President in particular.[3] While the desire for this kind of independence is understandable, independent commissions have never fit comfortably within our tripartite system of government. Their combination of legislative, executive and judicial powers, coupled with their relative independence from the executive branch, has been a source of conflict and constitutional litigation for well over one hundred years. In resolving issues dealing with various aspects of the independent nature of regulatory commissions, particularly those involving the appointment and especially the removal of commission members, courts have, over time, developed a number of separation of powers theories and approaches. The issues and constitutional approaches were particularly important during Franklin Roosevelt's administrations and the establishment of the New Deal. The analytical difficulties of the courts during that era, coupled with a new skepticism concerning the role of federal regulation in general and independent commissions in particular, has resulted in greatly increased interest in these issues in the 1970s and 1980s. The end result has been a series of important separation of powers cases that, at least indirectly, re-examine the constitutionality of independent agencies in our federal structure and do so with a variety of constitutional approaches to these issues.

§ 15.4.1 The Power to Remove—The Early Cases

In *Myers v. United States,*[4] the Supreme Court confronted a removal

2. See, e.g., the Federal Trade Commission Act, 15 U.S.C.A. §§ 41–58. Most independent commissions have such provisions, but not all. It is interesting to note, for example, that though the SEC and the FCC are usually thought of as independent regulatory commissions, they provide no such formal, statutory protection for their commissioners.

3. See generally Symposium: The Independence of Independent Agencies, 1988 Duke L.J. 215 (1988). See also Hall and Rayos, Independent Counsel Investigations, 36 Am. Crim. L.Rev. 809 (1999); Gormley, An Original Model of the Independent Counsel Statute, 97 Mich. L.Rev. 601, 614–616 (1998).

4. 272 U.S. 52, 47 S.Ct. 21, 71 L.Ed. 160 (1926). For discussions of *Myers v. United States,* on which this section heavily relies, see Aman, Introduction to Symposium: *Bowsher v. Synar,* 72 Cornell L.Rev. 421, 423–24 (1987); see also Manning, Symposium: The Independent Counsel Statute: Reading "Good Cause" In Light Of Article II, 83 Minn. L.Rev. 1285 (1999); Humphrey's Executor v. United States, 295 U.S. 602, 55 S.Ct. 869, 79 L.Ed. 1611 (1935).

issue for the first time.[5] This issue was raised by a statute that sought to condition the removal of an inferior officer on the advice and consent of the Senate. On July 21, 1917, President Wilson appointed Mr. Myers postmaster of the first class in Portland, Oregon, for a term of four years. On January 20, 1920, Wilson demanded his resignation, but Myers refused to resign. On February 2, 1920, he was removed from office by order of the Postmaster General, acting under the direction of the President. Myers protested his removal until the end of his term, and pursued no other occupation and drew compensation for no other service during this time. He brought suit for his salary from the date of his removal to the end of the term, filing a claim for $8,838.71 in the Court of Claims. The Court ultimately ruled against Myers, and he appealed to the Supreme Court.[6]

Chief Justice Taft, no stranger to the powers and responsibilities of the Presidency, framed the issue in the case expansively:

> This case presents the question whether under the Constitution the President has the exclusive power of removing executive officers of the United States whom he has appointed by and with the advice and consent of the Senate.[7]

Writing for the majority, Chief Justice Taft gave an equally expansive answer. In his view all legislative power was granted to the legislature; all executive power to the executive; and all judicial power to one Supreme Court and such inferior courts as Congress might establish. Thus, "[f]rom this division on principle, the reasonable construction of the Constitution must be that the branches should be kept separate in all cases in which they were not expressly blended, and the Constitution should be expounded to blend them no more than it affirmatively requires."[8]

The Court also reasoned that "[t]he history of the clause by which the Senate was given a check upon the President's power of appointment makes it clear that it was not prompted by any desire to limit removals."[9] For Chief Justice Taft, "[t]he power to prevent the removal of an

5. The first major removal case never came to court. It involved the attempt to impeach President Andrew Johnson for defying the Tenure of Office Act of 1867. Despite the provisions of that Act, President Johnson removed Secretary of War Stanton without the approval of the Senate. The House then voted to impeach Johnson, but the Senate failed to convict him by one vote. See Peter M. Shane & Harold H. Bruff, The Law of Presidential Power 290 (1988).

6. The statute under which Myers was appointed provided that:

> Postmasters of the first, second and third classes shall be appointed and may be removed by the President by and with the advice and consent of the Senate and shall hold their offices for four years unless sooner removed or suspended according to law.

19 Stat. 80, 81, c. 179 (1876). President Wilson had neither asked nor received the Senate's consent to his removal of Myers.

7. 272 U.S. at 106, 47 S.Ct. at 22.

8. Id. at 116, 47 S.Ct. at 25.

9. Id. at 119, 47 S.Ct. at 26. The First Congress of the United States considered the President's removal power during a debate on bills establishing Executive Branch departments. In the so-called "Decision of 1789," Congress determined that the removal authority over such officials belongs to the President alone. See id. at 111–32, 47 S.Ct. at 23–30.

officer who has served under the President is different from the authority to consent to or reject his appointment."[10] There was thus no need to maintain any kind of parity when it came to removing officials. Emphasizing the Executive Power of the President to "take Care that the Laws be faithfully executed," the majority concluded that the President "may properly supervise and guide their construction of the statutes under which they act in order to secure that unitary and uniform execution of the laws which Article II of the Constitution evidently contemplated in vesting general executive power in the President alone."[11]

The expansive power granted to the President in the removal of public officers such as Myers was reconsidered and considerably narrowed in *Humphrey's Executor v. United States.*[12] President Roosevelt had attempted to remove William E. Humphrey, a commissioner of the Federal Trade Commission. The Federal Trade Commission Act provided that a Commissioner was subject to removal for "inefficiency, neglect of duty, or malfeasance in office."[13] President Roosevelt's disapproval of Commissioner Humphrey was not, however, based on any of these factors, but rather his dislike for Humphrey's policy positions. Being a Hoover appointee, Humphrey was out of step with the views and goals of the new Roosevelt Administration.[14]

Writing for a unanimous Court, Justice Sutherland upheld the congressional limitation on removal and narrowed the holding of *Myers* considerably. First, the Court noted that *Myers* dealt with "purely executive officers" but did not "include an officer who occupies no place in the executive department and who exercises no part of the executive power vested by the Constitution in the President."[15] The Court characterized the Federal Trade Commission's responsibilities and activities as in part quasi-legislative and in part quasi-judicial.[16] Thus, "[s]uch a body cannot in any proper sense be characterized as an arm or an eye of the

10. Id. at 121, 47 S.Ct. at 26.

11. Id. at 135, 47 S.Ct. at 31. In dicta, the Court recognized that "there may be duties so peculiarly and specifically committed to the discretion of a particular officer as to raise a question whether the President may overrule or revise the officer's interpretation of his statutory duty in a particular instance." There then "may be duties of a quasi-judicial character imposed on executive officers and members of executive tribunals whose decisions after hearing affect interests of individuals, the discharge of which the President can not in a particular case properly influence or control." Id. Nevertheless, even such exceptions did not permanently impair the power of the President to remove such an official. He could consider the decision after its rendition as a reason for removing the officer, on the ground that "the discretion regularly entrusted to that officer by statute has not been on the whole intelligently or wisely exercised." Id.

12. 295 U.S. 602, 55 S.Ct. 869, 79 L.Ed. 1611 (1935).

13. The Federal Trade Commission Act, ch. 311, 38 Stat. 717 (codified as amended at 15 U.S.C.A. § 41).

14. President Roosevelt's letter asking for Commissioner Humphrey's resignation stated that "the aims and purposes of the Administration with respect to the work of the Commission can be carried out most effectively with personnel of my own selection." 295 U.S. at 618, 55 S.Ct. at 870 (quoting Letter from President Franklin D. Roosevelt to William E. Humphrey (July 25, 1933)). It disclaimed "any reflection upon the commissioner personally or upon his services." Id. at 618, 55 S.Ct. at 870.

15. Id. at 628, 55 S.Ct. at 874.

16. Id.

executive."[17] Congress's desire to condition the removal of such commissioners was thus clearly constitutional.

The Court, nevertheless, recognized that not all of the Federal Trade Commission's activities could fit neatly under the legislative or judicial rubrics. The Commission's investigatory powers certainly posed a problem for the Court, which it dealt with in two ways. First, the Court concluded that if the powers were executive, they were of sufficiently lesser consequence than the Commission's primarily legislative and judicial tasks. Thus, they did not warrant full executive control.[18] Second, the Court concluded that such executive tasks constituted executive functions, not executive powers. An executive function, as opposed to an executive power, was one carried out primarily in the "discharge or effectuation" of quasi-legislative and quasi-judicial activities. The Court's reasoning thus reflects a proportionate approach to the determination of the *overall* function of an agency. If an agency's tasks were primarily legislative or judicial, the Court was willing to view its executive duties as secondary activities. This kind of analysis has never been fully accepted and, as we shall see, it conflicts directly with the theory of a unitary executive.[19] The *Humphrey's* Court itself recognized that it had established a grey area between the purely executive officers of *Myers,* who serve at the will of the President, and "our present decision that such power does not extend to an office such as that here involved."[20] The *Humphrey's* Court, however, was content to "leave such cases ... for future consideration and determination as they may arise."[21]

17. Id. The crucial paragraph in the opinion is as follows:

> The Federal Trade Commission is an administrative body created by Congress to carry into effect legislative policies embodied in the statute in accordance with the legislative standard therein prescribed, and to perform other specified duties as a legislative or as a judicial aid. Such a body cannot in any proper sense be characterized as an arm or an eye of the executive. Its duties are performed without executive leave and, in the contemplation of the statute, must be free from executive control. In administering the provisions of the statute in respect of "unfair methods of competition"—that is to say in filling in and administering the details embodied by that general standard—the commission acts in part quasi-legislatively and in part quasi-judicially. In making investigations and reports thereon for the information of Congress under § 6, in aid of the legislative power, it acts as a legislative agency. Under § 7, which authorizes the commission to act as a master in chancery under rules prescribed by the court, it acts as an agency of the judiciary. To the extent that it exercises any executive function—as distinguished from executive power in the constitutional sense—it does so in the discharge and effectuation of its quasi-legislative or quasi-judicial powers, or as an agency of the legislative or judicial departments of the government. Id.

18. Id.

19. See e.g., Synar v. United States, 626 F.Supp. 1374, 1401 (D.D.C.1986) ("congressional removal power cannot be approved with regard to an officer who actually participates in the execution of the laws"), affirmed sub nom. Bowsher v. Synar, 478 U.S. 714, 106 S.Ct. 3181, 92 L.Ed.2d 583 (1986). See also Morrison v. Olson, 487 U.S. 654, 685, 108 S.Ct. 2597, 2616, 101 L.Ed.2d 569 (1988) ("[u]nlike both *Bowsher* and *Myers,* this case does not involve an attempt by Congress itself to gain a role in the removal of executive officials other than its established powers of impeachment and conviction"); but see id. at 685, 108 S.Ct. at 2616. ("Since the statute vests some purely executive power in a person who is not the President of the United States it is void") (Scalia, J., dissenting).

20. 295 U.S. at 632, 55 S.Ct. at 875.

21. Id.

The Court returned to these issues over twenty years later in *Wiener v. United States.*[22] Commissioner Wiener served on the War Claims Commission, having been appointed by President Truman in 1950. President Eisenhower sought to remove the Commissioner six months before the end of his term for essentially policy reasons, similar to President Roosevelt's dismissal of Commissioner Humphrey.[23] Unlike the Federal Trade Commission Act, however, the War Claims Act said nothing about Presidential removal. In deciding the limits of a President's removal power in such a situation, the Court proposed a functional theory of separation of powers. Justice Frankfurter, writing for the majority, stated:

> the most reliable factor for drawing an inference regarding the President's power of removal ... is the nature of the function that Congress vested in the War Claims Commission. What were the duties that Congress confided to this Commission? And can the inference fairly be drawn from the failure of Congress to provide for removal that these Commissioners were to remain in office at the will of the President?[24]

After reviewing the legislative history of the War Claims Act, Justice Frankfurter concluded that the Act "precluded the President from influencing the Commission in passing on a particular claim."[25] It thus clearly followed that Congress also "did not wish to have hang over the Commission the Damocles' sword of removal by the President for no reason other than that he preferred to have on that Commission men of his own choosing."[26] For Justice Frankfurter, the adjudicatory functions of the Commission and "the intrinsic judicial character of the task with which the Commission was charged" were dispositive.[27]

The Court's analyses of the issues in *Myers, Humphrey's* and *Wiener* clearly left much to be desired. *Myers* painted with so broad a brush as to require the narrowing that took place in *Humphrey's.* But that case created an essentially unworkable distinction between executive functions and executive powers. *Wiener,* while instructive, focused on adjudication, where an easier case for independence from the executive branch could be justified than in the policy arena, where agency power continued to grow enormously, especially during the decade of 1970–1980. Yet, independent commissions were able to exist, albeit uneasily, within our constitutional framework. It was nearly fifty years later that these questions returned once again, triggered, perhaps in large part, by the implications of the Supreme Court's rhetoric and analysis of the issues presented in *Immigration and Nationalization Service v. Chadha.*[28]

22. 357 U.S. 349, 78 S.Ct. 1275, 2 L.Ed.2d 1377 (1958).

23. "I regard it as in the national interest to complete the administration of the War Claims Act of 1948 ... with personnel of my own selection". Id. at 350, 78 S.Ct. at 1276.

24. Id. at 353–54, 78 S.Ct. at 1278–79.

25. Id. at 356, 78 S.Ct. at 1279.

26. Id.

27. Id. at 355, 78 S.Ct. at 1279.

28. 462 U.S. 919, 103 S.Ct. 2764, 77 L.Ed.2d 317 (1983).

§ 15.4.2 *INS v. Chadha*

Immigration and Naturalization Service v. Chadha[29] was concerned with the validity of § 244(c)(2) of the Immigration and Nationality Act (Act).[30] This Act authorized either House of Congress, acting alone, to invalidate a decision of the executive branch to allow a deportable alien to remain in the U.S. The Supreme Court held this one-house veto provision to be unconstitutional, but it did so with an opinion so sweeping that it cast into serious doubt a variety of other legislative veto provisions as well.

Chadha was an East Indian born in Kenya and holding a British passport. He overstayed his student visa. When ordered to show cause why he should not be deported, Chadha obtained an adjournment of his deportation hearing so that he could apply for a suspension of the deportation order pursuant to § 244(a)(1) of the Act.[31] After successfully meeting the Act's requirements of seven years' continuous presence in the U.S., good moral character, and the likelihood of extreme hardship if deported, Chadha obtained a suspension of his deportation from an Immigration Judge on June 25, 1974. The report of the suspension was given to Congress by the Attorney General, in accordance with § 244(c)(1) of the Act.[32] A year and a half later, the House of Representatives passed a resolution expressing its disapproval of the suspension of Chadha (and five others). There was no debate nor any recording of the voice vote on the resolution. Since this resolution was not considered to be legislation by the House, it was not sent to the Senate for passage and then to the President for his signature. The Immigration Naturalization Service ordered Chadha deported on November 8, 1976. Chadha's appeal to the Board of Immigration Appeals, arguing that § 244(c)(2) was unconstitutional, was dismissed for lack of jurisdiction over constitutional questions. His appeal to the Ninth Circuit, however, was successful. That court held that section 244(c)(2) was unconstitutional and ordered the Attorney General "to cease and desist from taking any steps to deport [Chadha] based upon the resolution enacted by the House of Representatives."[33] The Supreme Court agreed and affirmed the decision.

There were, however, many ways to resolve the issues presented by this case. The majority of the Court chose a very broad constitutional approach to the case, foreclosing litigation over legislative veto provisions in other, arguably less questionable, constitutional circumstances.[34]

29. 462 U.S. 919, 103 S.Ct. 2764, 77 L.Ed.2d 317 (1983).

30. Codified at 8 U.S.C.A. § 1254(c)(2).

31. 8 U.S.C.A. § 1254(a)(1).

32. 8 U.S.C.A. § 1254(c)(1).

33. Chadha v. INS, 634 F.2d 408, 436 (9th Cir.1980) (quoted in 462 U.S. at 928, 103 S.Ct. at 2772).

34. See 462 U.S. at 970–74, 103 S.Ct. at 2794–96 (White, J., dissenting). (Justice White notes that "during the 1970s the legislative veto was important in resolving a series of major constitutional disputes between the President and Congress over claims of the President to broad impoundment, war and national emergency powers."). See also, legislative veto to provisions in the energy area, 462 U.S. at 971 n. 8, 103 S.Ct. at 2795 n. 8; the educational field, 462 U.S. at 972, 103 S.Ct. at 2795;

Writing for the majority, Chief Justice Burger began by treating the House veto as an essentially legislative act. The Court reasoned that "the House took action that had the purpose and effect of altering the legal rights, duties, and relations of persons ... all outside the Legislative Branch."[35] As far as the majority was concerned, this Act was therefore legislative in character. As such, it was subject not only to the bicameral requirements of the Constitution, but also to presentation to the President for his approval or veto.[36]

Though the Court recognized that the branches of government are not " 'hermetically sealed' from one another,"[37] its approach put a premium on the consequences that flowed from labeling the action of one House as legislative. The Court noted several narrowly prescribed areas authorizing "either House of Congress to act alone and outside of its prescribed bicameral legislative role,"[38] and this was not one of them. The one House veto in this case was tantamount to an amendment of the statute involved a result and that could be accomplished only in the usual way: by vote of the House and Senate and the signature of the President.[39] While the majority may have reached the correct result, its analysis proves too much.[40] The opinion's implicit emphasis on the labels of legislative, executive or judicial provided the rhetorical ammunition for a variety of cases seeking judicial reassessment of the constitutionality not only of the great number of statutes that have incorporated some kind of legislative veto mechanism, but of regulatory statutes in general that sought to delegate legislative, executive and judicial power, and various combinations thereof, to the unelected officials that run the various federal agencies.

Other decisionmaking routes were available to the Court that would not nearly have been so sweeping in their scope and effect on other forms of legislative control of the administrative process.[41] Justice Powell's concurrence, for example, would have invalidated the congressional action because it "assumed a judicial function in violation of the principle of separation of powers." His approach was tailored to the facts of the case, which Justice Powell viewed as involving adjudication, not legislation. The constitutional issue arose because Congress's review of the decision to allow Chadha to remain in the U.S. was more appropriate

and the trade regulation area, 462 U.S. at 972 n. 9, 103 S.Ct. at 2795.

35. 462 U.S. at 952, 103 S.Ct. at 2784.

36. Id. at 946, 103 S.Ct. at 2781.

37. Id. at 951, 103 S.Ct. at 2784.

38. Id. at 955, 103 S.Ct. at 2786.

39. Id. at 956–58, 103 S.Ct. at 2786–88.

40. See Strauss, Was There a Baby in the Bathwater? A Comment on the Supreme Court's Legislative Veto Decision, 1983 Duke L.J. 789, 794–795 (1983). Professor Strauss notes that "the Chief Justice's opinion for the majority turns on a charterization of the House resolution as 'legislative action'." Id. at 794. But in determining what is and what is not legislative, the Court sets forth an approach that "depends on the identity of the actor and whether the actor meant its actions to have force." Id. The Court thus eschews any analysis of the character of the action itself—i.e., whether it is legislative or judicial—and it asserts as its primary guideline whether the action taken by a particular actor was intended to alter legal rights. Since the legislature acted in *Chadha* and it intended its actions to alter Chadha's legal rights, it was legislative action.

41. Id.

for a court.[42] This was confirmed for him by examination of the Congressional Record, where there were remarks by the Chairman of the Judiciary Subcommittee on Immigration, Citizenship, and International Law explaining that "it is the opinion of the committee that [Chadha's and others'] deportation should not be suspended."[43] To Justice Powell this was "[o]n its face clearly adjudicatory."[44]

In a lengthy dissent, Justice White lamented the demise of legislative veto provisions, which he numbered at more than 200. He saw the legislative veto as a practical solution to the problem of control of the power granted agencies pursuant to congressional delegations.[45] He gave a detailed review of the various types of legislative vetoes enacted by Congress, and argued that the majority should have restricted itself to a consideration of § 244(c)(2) on narrow separation-of-powers grounds. Justice White's approach and conclusions were thus in direct conflict with the majority's position that a legislative veto amounted to legislation pure and simple: "The power to exercise a legislative veto is not the power to write new law without bicameral approval or Presidential consideration. The veto must be authorized by statute and may only negative what an Executive department or independent agency has proposed. On its face, the legislative veto no more allows one House of Congress to make law than does the Presidential veto confer such power on the President."[46] The core of his dissent was that the majority radically overreached with its opinion, ignoring the requirements of the modern administrative state, and denying to Congress what Chief Justice Marshall called the power to "avail itself of experience, to exercise its reason, and to accommodate its legislation to circumstances."[47]

Quite apart from, in effect, declaring all legislative vetoes unconstitutional, the rhetoric of the majority's opinion in *Chadha* reopened, once again, the removal issues involved in *Myers, Humphrey's* and *Wiener*. The majority's approach in *Chadha* became an important part of the Court's analyses in *Bowsher v. Synar,* which we shall now examine.

§ 15.4.3 The Removal Power Revisited—*Bowsher v. Synar*

Congress passed the *Balanced Budget and Emergency Deficit Con-*

42. 462 U.S. at 963–66, 103 S.Ct. at 2790–92. Justice Powell's primary concern was for the fairness of the procedures that applied or, as in this case, did not apply to Chadha. The fact that a court was not involved in such an adjudicatory matter emphasized this lack of fairness.

43. Id. at 964, 103 S.Ct. at 2790 (quoting 121 Cong.Rec. 40,800 (1975)).

44. 462 U.S. at 964, 103 S.Ct. at 2790.

45. Id. at 967, 103 S.Ct. at 2792.

46. Id. at 980, 103 S.Ct. at 2799.

47. McCulloch v. Maryland, 17 U.S. (4 Wheat.) 316, 415–16, 4 L.Ed. 579 (1819), quoted in 462 U.S. at 984, 103 S.Ct. at 2801. Professor Strauss argues that the Court (and the litigants) failed to distinguish between use of legislative vetoes in "political" settings of continuing dialogue between the legislative and executive branches—where he considers the case for legislative veto strongest—and regulatory contexts, where the President is not ordinarily involved, other avenues of review are available, and the potential for abuse by Congress is greater. See generally, Strauss, supra note 171.

trol Act of 1985,[48] popularly known as the "Gramm–Rudman–Hollings Act," on December 12, 1985. The purpose of the Act is to eliminate the federal budget deficit by requiring, under certain circumstances, across the board cuts in federal spending. These "automatic" reductions are to be accomplished in the following way. Each year, the Directors of the Office of Management and Budget (OMB) and the Congressional Budget Office (CBO) are independently to estimate the size of the federal budget deficit for the coming year. If that deficit exceeds the maximum targeted deficit for that fiscal year by a particular amount, the OMB and CBO Directors are to calculate independently, on a program by program basis, the budget reductions necessary to meet the maximum permissible deficit. They then report jointly their deficit and budget estimates to the Comptroller General. The Comptroller General then reviews these reports (which may differ both in their approaches to the calculations and the actual numbers at which they arrive) and then reports his conclusions to the President.[49] The President issues a sequestration order mandating the spending reductions specified by the Comptroller General.[50] At this point, Congress has an opportunity to act by cutting the

48. Pub.L. 99–177, 99 Stat. 1038 (codified as amended at 2 U.S.C.A. §§ 900–922).

49. Section 251(b) of the Act stated, specifically:

> (1) REPORT TO BE BASED ON OMB—CBO REPORT. The Comptroller General shall review and consider the report issued by the Directors for the fiscal year and, with due regard for the data, assumptions, and methodologies used in reaching the conclusions set forth therein, shall issue a report to the President and the Congress on August 25 of the calendar year in which such fiscal year begins (or on January 20, 1986, in the case of the fiscal year 1986), estimating the budget base levels of total revenues and total budget outlays for such fiscal year, identifying the amount of any deficit excess for such fiscal year (adjusted in accordance with subsection (a)(3)(A)(ii), in the case of fiscal year 1986), stating whether such deficit excess (or adjusted deficit excess, in the case of fiscal year 1986) will be greater than $10,000,000,000 (zero in the case of fiscal years 1986 and 1991), specifying the estimated rate of real economic growth for such fiscal year, for each quarter of such fiscal year, and for each of the last two quarters of the preceding fiscal year, indicating whether the estimate includes two or more consecutive quarters of negative economic growth, and specifying (if the excess is greater than $10,000,000,000, or zero in the case of fiscal years 2986 and 1991), by account, for non-defense programs and by account and programs, projects, and activities within each account, for defense programs, the base from which reductions are taken and the amounts and percentages by which such accounts must be reduced during such fiscal year in order to eliminate such deficit excess (or adjusted deficit excess, in the case of fiscal year 1986). Such report shall be based on the estimates, determinations, and specifications of the Directors and shall utilize the budget base, criteria, and guidelines set forth in subsection (a)(6) and in sections 255, 256, and 257. . . .

99 Stat. at 1068.

50. Section 252 of the Act states: (a) ISSUANCE OF INITIAL ORDER.

> (1) IN GENERAL. On September 1 following the submission of a report by the Comptroller General under section 251(b) which identifies an amount greater than $10,000,000,000 (zero in the case of fiscal years 1986 and 1991) by which the deficit for a fiscal year will exceed the maximum deficit amount for such fiscal year (or on February 1, 1986, in the case of the fiscal year 1986), the President, in strict accordance with the requirements of paragraph (3) and section 251(a)(3) and (4) and subject to the exemptions, exceptions, limitations, special rules, and definitions set forth in sections 255, 256, and 257, shall eliminate the full amount of the deficit excess (as adjusted by the Comptroller General in such report in accordance with section 251(a)(3)(A)(ii), in the case of fiscal

budget itself in a manner that would obviate the need for this order. If Congress fails to act, however, the sequestration order becomes effective and across-the-board spending reductions must be made.

This statute was challenged almost immediately in district court and a three-judge court struck down the law as unconstitutional. The district court held that the role of the Comptroller General in the deficit reduction process violated separation of powers principles. In reaching this conclusion, the district court took a number of interesting approaches to the problems discussed above.

After reviewing all of the Supreme Court cases that dealt with the removal power thus far, the court concentrated on *Humphrey's Executor,* taking aim at what it called "the political science preconceptions characteristic of its era and not of the present day."[51] The court went on to note that:

> It is not as obvious today as it seemed in the 1930's that there can be such things as genuinely "independent" regulatory agencies, bodies of impartial experts whose independence from the President does not entail correspondingly greater dependence upon the committees of Congress to which they are then immediately accountable; or, indeed, that the decisions of such agencies so clearly involve scientific judgment rather than political choice that it is even theoretically desirable to insulate them from the democratic process.[52]

Quite apart from casting substantial doubt on the policy justifications for independent agencies, the district court expressed serious concern with the overall constitutionality of the so-called headless fourth branch.

> It has ... always been difficult to reconcile *Humphrey's Executor's* "headless fourth branch" with a constitutional text and tradition

year 1986) by issuing an order that (notwithstanding the Impoundment Control Act of 1974)?

(A) modifies or suspends the operation of each provision of Federal law that would (but for such order) require an automatic spending increase to take effect during such fiscal year, in such a manner as to prevent such increase from taking effect, or reduce such increase, in accordance with such report; and

(B) eliminates the remainder of such deficit excess (or adjusted deficit excess, in the case of fiscal year 1986) by sequestering new budget authority, unobligated balances, new loan guarantee commitments, new direct loan obligations, and spending authority as defined in section 401(c)(2) of the Congressional Budget Act of 1974, and reducing obligation limitations, in accordance with such report....

Id. at 1072. See also § 252(a)(5): The order must provide for reductions in the manner specified in section 251(a)(3), must incorporate the provisions of the report submitted under section 251(b), and must be consistent with such report in all respects. The President may not modify or recalculate any of the estimates, determinations, specifications, bases, amounts, or percentages set forth in the report submitted under section 251(b) in determining the reductions to be specified in the order with respect to programs, projects, and activities, or with respect to budget activities, within an account, with the exception of the authority granted to the President for fiscal year 1986 with respect to defense programs pursuant to paragraph (2)(C). Id. at 1074.

51. Synar v. U.S., 626 F.Supp. 1374, 1398 (D.D.C.1986).

52. Id.

establishing three branches of government.... [53]

The court also noted that there had been some changes since *Humphrey's* had been decided. Specifically, the court focused on *INS v. Chadha* and noted that, at a minimum, "some of the language of the majority opinion in *Chadha* does not lie comfortably beside the central revelation of *Humphrey's Executor* that an officer such as a Federal Trade Commissioner 'occupies no place in the executive department,' and that an agency which exercises only 'quasi-legislative or quasi-judicial powers' is 'an agency of the legislative or judicial departments of the government.' "[54]

But the district court ultimately chose a narrower ground for its decision, noting that "[t]he Supreme Court's signals are not sufficiently clear ... to justify our disregarding the rationale of *Humphrey's Executor*.... "[55] Relying solely on *Humphrey's* the court found the Balanced Budget Act unconstitutional. For the court, the case at bar presented an official who was neither a "purely executive officer" nor an officer such as that in *Humphrey's*. The Comptroller General fell precisely within the no-man's land described in *Humphrey's*. He exercised some powers that were unquestionably legislative, but the Court found that his powers under the automatic deficit reduction process were neither exclusively legislative nor judicial.[56]

Noting that the Comptroller General was removable only by Congress, the lower court was "confident ... that congressional removal power cannot be approved with regard to an officer who actually participates in the execution of the laws."[57] The lower court also suggested that this case could be decided on broader grounds: "[w]e think it at least questionable whether the power would be approved even with respect to officers of the United States who exercise only 'quasi-legislative' powers in the *Humphrey's Executor* sense—since it would dramatically reduce the value of the right to appoint such officers which the Constitution has assured to the Executive or to the Courts of Law, a right that the Supreme Court has regarded as an important element of the balance of powers, prompted by the founders' often expressed fear 'that the Legisla-

53. Id.

54. Id. at 1399 (quoting *Humphrey's*, 295 U.S. at 628, 55 S.Ct. at 874).

55. Id.

56. Id. at 1399–1400. "Under subsection 251(b)(1), the Comptroller General must specify levels of anticipated revenue and expenditure that determine the gross amount which must be sequestered; and he must specify which particular budget items are required to be reduced by the various provisions of the Act ... and in what particular amounts. The first of these specifications requires the exercise of substantial judgment concerning present and future facts that affect the application of the law—the sort of power normally conferred upon the executive officer charged with implementing a statute. The second specification requires an interpretation of the law enacted by Congress, similarly a power normally committed initially to the Executive under the Constitution's prescription that he 'take Care that the Laws be faithfully executed.' Art. II, § 3. *And both of these specifications by the Comptroller General are, by the present law, made binding upon the President in the latter's application of the law.* Act § 252(a)(3).... In our view, these cannot be regarded as anything but executive powers in the constitutional sense." Id. at 1400 (emphasis in original).

57. Id. at 1401.

tive Branch of the National Government will aggrandize itself at the expense of the other two branches.' "[58] The Supreme Court majority, in affirming this decision, did not take this bait. It affirmed on the relatively narrow grounds staked out by the lower court, and rejected any implication that it intended to reach the issue of the constitutionality of independent agencies in general.[59] It later reaffirmed this holding in *Morrison v. Olson*.[60]

§ 15.4.4 The Supreme Court's Opinion in *Bowsher v. Synar*

Writing for the majority, Chief Justice Burger had little trouble getting to the merits of the case.[61] The majority used this case as an opportunity to reiterate the separation-of-powers approach previously used by the Court in *INS v. Chadha*[62] and *Buckley v. Valeo*.[63]

Quoting from *Buckley* and *Chadha*, the *Bowsher* Court set forth its separation of powers premises:

> The dangers of congressional usurpation of Executive Branch functions have long been recognized. "The debates of the Constitutional Convention, and the Federalist Papers, are replete with expressions of fear that the Legislative Branch of the National Government will aggrandize itself at the expense of the other two branches." *Buckley v. Valeo*. Indeed, we also have observed only recently that "[t]he hydraulic pressure inherent within each of the separate Branches to exceed the outer limits of its power, even to accomplish desirable objectives, must be resisted."[64]

In light of these pressures, the Court reasoned that if the Comptroller General exercised executive powers and only Congress could remove him, then this would be tantamount to a congressional veto and violative of the principles set forth in *Chadha*. In equating Congressional removal with a legislative veto, the Court reasoned that "Congress could simply remove, or threaten to remove, an officer for executing the laws in any fashion found to be unsatisfactory to Congress."[65] This, the Court said, was precisely what *Chadha* disallowed. Like the lower court, the Supreme Court majority had little difficulty finding that the Comptroller General exercised executive power that under the Constitution could not

58. Id. (quoting Buckley v. Valeo, 424 U.S. 1, 129, 96 S.Ct. 612, 687, 46 L.Ed.2d 659 (1976)).

59. *Bowsher*, 478 U.S. at 725 n. 4, 106 S.Ct. at 3187 n. 4 ("an affirmance in this case [does not] require [ ] casting doubt on the status of 'independent' agencies because no issues involving such agencies are presented here").

60. See chapter 14, sec. 14.4.5, supra.

61. The Court gave short shrift to the various standing arguments that were advanced 478 U.S. at 721, 106 S.Ct. at 3185 and, given its disposition on the separation-of-powers arguments that were made, the majority did not have to reach the delegation questions raised by the Act. Id. at 724–26.

62. 462 U.S. 919, 103 S.Ct. 2764, 77 L.Ed.2d 317 (1983).

63. 424 U.S. 1, 96 S.Ct. 612, 46 L.Ed.2d 659 (1976).

64. *Bowsher*, 478 U.S. at 727, 106 S.Ct. at 3188 (citations omitted).

65. Id. at 726, 106 S.Ct. at 3188.

be so completely controlled by Congress.[66] Justices Stevens and Marshall concurred in the result,[67] Justices White and Blackmun each dissented.[68]

The majority took what has been described as a "formalistic" separation-of-powers approach.[69] It examined the activities of the Comptroller General, determined whether they were best characterized as executive, legislative, or judicial. It then examined the place of the Comptroller General in our administrative structure in order to determine whether he was properly under the control of the relevant branch. Justice Stevens' concurring opinion rejected this approach, which in his view was too dependent on "a labeling of the functions assigned to the Comptroller General as 'executive powers.' "[70] Indeed, "[o]ne reason that the exercise of legislative, executive, and judicial powers cannot be categorically distributed among three mutually exclusive branches of Government is that governmental power cannot always be readily characterized with only one of those three labels."[71] For Stevens, the Comptroller is and always has been an agent of Congress, easily distinguishable from independent administrative agencies.[72] Justice Stevens nevertheless recognized that the Comptroller General had some obligations to the Executive, but these alone could not change his status:

> Obligations to two Branches are not ... impermissible and the presence of such dual obligations does not prevent the characterization of the official with the dual obligations as part of one branch.[73]

As an agent of Congress, the Comptroller General's duties under the Act were "anything but ministerial."[74] For Justice Stevens, this official was, in fact, "vested with the kind of responsibilities that Congress was elected to discharge itself under the fallback provision that will become effective if and when § 251(b) and § 251(c)(2) are held invalid."[75] Thus, like the majority, Justice Stevens also relied heavily on *INS v. Chadha,* but not for the proposition that Congressional removal was tantamount to a veto power, an equation which Justice Stevens and White rejected, but for the proposition that Congress cannot do indirectly what it cannot do directly. To make binding national policy, Congress must pass a bill

66. Id. at 732–34, 106 S.Ct. at 3191.

67. Id. at 736, 106 S.Ct. at 3193.

68. Id. at 759, 776, 106 S.Ct. at 3205, 3214.

69. See Strauss, The Place of Agencies in Government: Separation of Powers and the Fourth Branch, 84 Colum.L.Rev. 573 (1984); Strauss, Formal & Functional Approaches to Separation of Powers Questions—A Foolish Inconsistency?, 72 Cornell L.Rev. 488 (1987).

70. 478 U.S. at 757, 106 S.Ct. at 3204 (Stevens, J., concurring).

71. Id. at 749, 106 S.Ct. at 3199.

72. Justice Stevens noted that: "Rather than an independent agency, the Comptroller General and the GAO are functionally equivalent to congressional agents such as the Congressional Budget Office, the Office of Technology Assessment, and the Library of Congress' Congressional Research Service. As the statutory responsibilities make clear, like those congressional agents, the Comptroller General and General Accounting Office function virtually as a permanent staff for Congress." Id. at 746 n. 11, 106 S.Ct. at 3198 n. 11.

73. Id. at 746, 106 S.Ct. at 3198.

74. Id. at 748, 106 S.Ct. at 3199.

75. Id.

through both houses, and have it signed by the President or have two-thirds of each house override a Presidential veto. It could not, in effect, delegate this power to one of its agents and thereby sidestep the constitutional processes by which a bill becomes a law.[76]

Justice White, in his dissent, also rejected what he called the majority's "distressingly formalistic view of separation of powers."[77] He saw this case as having been decided on a triviality. There was no evidence whatsoever that the Comptroller General was, in fact, subservient to Congress. Moreover, he could not be removed at will, but only for certain stated causes. As White pointed out, the majority did *not* take the position that the Comptroller General must be removable at the will of the President. Rather, the majority objected to the fact that the President seemed to have played no role. But this too, according to Justice White, was inaccurate. Not only must Congress remove the Comptroller General for cause, but by a joint resolution. A joint resolution requires passage of both houses of Congress *and* it must be presented to the President for his signature. This not only satisfies the *Chadha* case upon which the majority relied so heavily, but makes clear that the President *does* have a role to play in the removal process.

By far, however, the most important aspect of Justice White's dissent is his alternative, approach to separation of powers issues, one that was willing to rely on the ability of the legislative and executive branches to protect themselves during the legislative process:

> The wisdom of vesting "executive" powers in an officer removable by joint resolution may indeed be debatable—as may be the wisdom of the entire scheme of permitting an unelected official to revise the budget enacted by Congress—but such matters are for the most part to be worked out between the Congress and the President through the legislative process, which affords each branch ample opportunity to defend its interests. The Act vesting budget-cutting authority in the Comptroller General represents Congress' judgment that the delegation of such authority to counteract ever-mounting deficits is "necessary and proper" to the exercise of the powers granted the Federal Government by the Constitution; and the President's approval of the statute signifies his unwillingness to reject the choice made by Congress.[78]

Justice White was thus willing to defer to political realities. Indeed, "[u]nder such circumstances, the role of this Court should be limited to determining whether the Act so alters the balance of authority among the branches of government as to pose a genuine threat to the basic division between the lawmaking power and the power to execute the

76. Id. at 755, 106 S.Ct. at 3203. (If Congress were free to delegate its policy-making authority to one of its components, or to one of its agents, it would be able to evade "the carefully crafted restraints spelled out in the Constitution." (quoting INS v. Chadha, 462 U.S. at 959, 103 S.Ct. at 2788)).

77. Id. at 759, 106 S.Ct. at 3205 (White, J., dissenting).

78. Id. at 776, 106 S.Ct. at 3214.

law."[79] Justice White saw no such threat and viewed the majority's concern with removal as being "of minimal practical significance and ... no substantial threat to the basic scheme of separation of powers."[80]

As far as independent commissions are concerned, the significance of the opinions in *Bowsher* is that *Humphrey's Executor* remained a viable precedent. As the majority noted in footnote four of its opinion:

> The statutes establishing independent agencies typically specify either that the agency members are removable by the President for specified causes, ... or else do not specify a removal procedure.... This case involves nothing like these statutes, but rather a statute that provides for direct congressional involvement over the decision to remove the Comptroller General.[81]

Nevertheless, the majority took an approach to separation of powers issues that kept open the possibility that an independent commission engaged primarily in executive functions may, indeed, be unconstitutional. That issue was very much involved in *Morrison v. Olson.*[82]

§ 15.4.5 *Morrison v. Olson*

The primary issue presented to the Court in *Morrison v. Olson* was whether Congress could restrict the removal of an independent counsel charged solely with the duty to prosecute. Petitioners characterized that duty as a core executive function and argued that Congress could not in any way restrict the executive's control over such a person.

Writing for the majority in *Morrison,* Chief Justice Rehnquist rejected this argument.[83] "Unlike both *Bowsher* and *Myers,* this case does not involve an attempt by Congress itself to gain a role in the removal of executive officials other than its established powers of impeachment and conviction. The act instead puts the removal power squarely in the hands of the Executive Branch; an independent counsel may be removed from office, 'only by the personal action of the Attorney General, and

79. Id.

80. Id. at 759, 106 S.Ct. at 3205. Justice Blackmun also dissented, agreeing with Justice White that it was unrealistic to assume that the Comptroller General was subservient to Congress. On the other hand, he agreed with the majority to the extent that he believed "an attempt by Congress to participate *directly* in the removal of an executive officer ... might well violate the principle of separation of powers by assuming for Congress part of the President's constitutional responsibility to carry out the laws." Id. at 777, 106 S.Ct. at 3214 (Blackmun, J., dissenting) (emphasis in original). Justice Blackmun, however, concluded that question need not be decided because the plaintiffs were not entitled to the relief they sought. Specifically, they should be challenging the constitutionality of the removal provision in the 1921 act, a challenge for which "it is far from clear they would have standing." In the case at bar, what was challenged was the constitutionality of the automatic budget reduction provisions of the Deficit Control Act. According to Justice Blackmun, it was not appropriate for the Supreme Court to invalidate "legislation of this magnitude in order to preserve a cumbersome, 65–year–old removal power that has never been exercised and appears to have been all but forgotten until this litigation." Id. at 778, 106 S.Ct. at 3215.

81. Id. at 725 n. 4, 106 S.Ct. at 3187 n. 4.

82. 487 U.S. 654, 108 S.Ct. 2597, 101 L.Ed.2d 569 (1988), on remand 857 F.2d 801 (D.C.Cir.1988).

83. 487 U.S. at 685, 108 S.Ct. at 2616.

only for a good cause.' "[84] While emphasizing the role of the executive in initiating the removal of an independent counsel, the majority downplayed the fact that Congress was also involved, having statutorily conditioned that removal on "good cause." It was Justice Scalia, in dissent, who noted that "limiting removal power to 'good cause' is an impediment to, not an effective grant of, presidential control."[85]

While the majority reaffirmed the result in *Humphrey's Executor,* it shifted the emphasis from a labeling approach used in *Humphrey's* to a more deferential separation of powers approach. Rather than characterizing the activities involved as quasi-legislative or quasi-judicial or quasi-executive, the majority stated that "the real question is whether the removal restrictions are of such a nature that they impede the President's ability to perform his constitutional duty, and the functions of the officials in question must be analyzed in that light."[86]

In resolving that issue, the majority used what the dissent disparagingly called a "balancing test,"[87] one that did not specify the criteria or the respective weight to be given to the criteria it used when engaging in such a balancing approach. The majority simply concluded that "this case does not involve an attempt by Congress to increase its own powers at the expense of the Executive Branch."[88] For the majority in this case, neither Congress's nor the judiciary's role in the appointment or removal of the independent counsel was enough to impede the President's ability to perform his constitutional duty.

This deferential approach—deferential to the bargain struck by Congress and the Executive when this legislation was passed—was a far cry from the more expansive view of executive power taken in Justice Scalia's dissent, and the more demanding separation of powers approach used by the majority of the Supreme Court in *Bowsher* and *Chadha.* In a fiery dissent, Justice Scalia took an approach premised on two basic assumptions: (1) Article II vested *all* executive power in the Executive Branch, and (2) the independent counsel's duties constituted core executive functions. As such, they could only be exercised by an individual fully within the control of the President. Many of the broader arguments made by the lower court's opinion in *Bowsher* now came to rest in his dissent in *Morrison.*

Quite apart from the board constitutional theory upon which Justice Scalia based his dissent, he prophetically foresaw the kinds of abuses this kind of prosecutorial power can create that many observers ultimately recognized in the aftermath of the Clinton impeachment proceedings. Specifically, Justice Scalia noted:

> "The mini-Executive that is the independent counsel, however, operating in an area where so little is law and so much is discretion,

84. 487 U.S. at 686, 108 S.Ct. at 2616 (quoting Ethics in Government Act of 1978, 28 U.S.C.A. §§ 49, 596(a)(1)).

85. 487 U.S. at 706, 108 S.Ct. at 2627 (Scalia, J., dissenting).

86. Id. at 691, 108 S.Ct. at 2619.

87. Id. at 710, 108 S.Ct. at 2629.

88. Id. at 692, 108 S.Ct. at 2620.

is intentionally cut off from the unifying influence of the Justice Department, and from the perspective that multiple responsibilities provide. What would normally be regarded as a technical violation (there are no rules defining such things), may in her small world assume the proportions of an indictable offense. What would normally be regarded as an investigation that has reached the level of pursuing such picayune matters that it should be concluded, may to her be an investigation that ought to go on for another year. How frightening it must be to have your own independent counsel and staff appointed, with nothing else to do but to investigate you until investigation is no longer worthwhile—with whether it is worthwhile not depending upon what such judgments usually hinge on, competing responsibilities. And to have that counsel and staff decide, with no basis for comparison, whether what you have done is bad enough, willful enough, and provable enough, to warrant an indictment. How admirable the constitutional system that provides the means to avoid such distraction. And how unfortunate the judicial decision that has permitted it.''[89]

In 1999, Congress allowed the Independent Counsel Act to expire.[90]

The separation of powers approach used in *Morrison* was reaffirmed by the same eight-to-one vote a year later in *Mistretta v. United States.*[91] This case involved a challenge to the constitutionality of the Sentencing Reform Act of 1984, specifically the Sentencing Commission established by that Act. That Commission was located in the judicial branch. The gravamen of the plaintiffs' complaint focused on what they contended to be the undermining effects on Article III judges that commission had. The case thus presented separation of powers issues that could easily have triggered the closer judicial scrutiny of such questions that characterized *Bowsher* and *Chadha.* The Court's approach in *Mistretta,* however, represented a "flexible understanding of separation of powers," and "recognized Madison's teaching that the greatest security against tyranny—the accumulation of excessive authority in a single branch—lies not in a hermetic division between the Branches, but in a carefully crafted system of checked and balanced power within each Branch."[92] The Court found no such aggrandizement in this case, nor did it believe the integrity of the judiciary to be undermined by requiring Article III judges to sit on a sentencing Commission located in the Judicial Branch and to promulgate various sentencing policy guidelines. The Court emphasized that the Commission did not exercise judicial power[93] and the President's

89. Id. at 732, 108 S. Ct. at 2640.

90. See note 109, supra. See generally, Anthony Sarno, Jr., The Economic Costs of Independent Counsel Investigations, 5 Wid. L. Symp. J. 339 (2000); Orrin G. Hatch, The Independent Counsel Statute and Questions About its Future, 62 law & Contemp. Prob. 145 (1999); Benjamin J. Priester, Paul G. Rozelle, & Mirah A. Horowitz, The Independent Counsel Statute: A Legal History, 62 Law & Contemp. Prob. 5 (1999); Stephan O. Kline, Heal It, Don't Bury It! Testimony on Reauthorization of the Independent Counsel Act, 1999 Det. C.L. Rev. 51.

91. 488 U.S. 361, 109 S.Ct. 647, 102 L.Ed.2d 714 (1989).

92. 488 U.S. at 381, 109 S.Ct. at 659.

93. Id. at 387 n. 14, 109 S.Ct. at 662 n. 14.

relationship to it was "functionally no different from what it would have been had Congress not located the Commission in the Judicial Branch."[94] The Court's unwillingness to use the separation-of-powers approach used in *Bowsher* or *Chadha* suggests that constitutionality of independent agencies may, once again, be only an academic topic of discussion.

Two years later, however, the tension between these two approaches—judicial deference to administrative solutions crafted by both the executive and legislative branches, and a more formalistic separation of powers analysis—came to the fore again in *Metropolitan Washington Airports Authority v. Citizens for Abatement of Aircraft Noise, Inc.*[95] The Court struck down, on separation of powers grounds, a Congressional Board of Review with oversight responsibility for National and Dulles Airports. In 1987, Congress and the Department of Transportation approved a plan to cede control to a specially created regional body, the Metropolitan Washington Airports Authority (MWAA), chartered by the State of Virginia and the District of Columbia. Concern for the need to protect the continuing federal interest in the operation of National Airport in particular, with its close proximity to Capitol Hill, led Congress to require, as a condition of the transfer, the creation of a Board of Review with the power to veto the actions of the MWAA's Board of Directors. Membership on the Board of Review was restricted to Members of Congress also serving on aviation related congressional committees. They were to act "in their individual capacities."

Despite the acquiescence of the State of Virginia and the District of Columbia to such continuing federal oversight, and even absent any reservations on the part of the Executive Branch, Justice Stevens, writing for the Court, found this element of control retained by Congress to constitute legislative action that did not conform to the precepts of Article I. Citing *Chadha,* he noted that "the maintenance of federal control over the airports ... is invalid, not because it invades any state power, but because Congress' continued control violates the separation of powers principle, the aim of which is to protect not the States but the whole people from improvident laws."[96] The majority dismissed the idea that the members of the Board of Review served in their personal rather than legislative capacities. Only members of Congress with legislative responsibility for the regulation of air transportation could sit on the Board of Review. Furthermore, the floor debate in the House of Representatives during consideration of the transfer legislation suggested that the Board was intended all along to enable Congress to control decisions affecting the two airports without the normal constraints on legislative activity. Thus, not only was Congress exercising executive power, but it was doing so outside the bicameralism and presentment requirements of Article I.

94. Id. at 378, 109 S.Ct. at 658.

95. 501 U.S. 252, 111 S.Ct. 2298, 115 L.Ed.2d 236 (1991).

96. Id. at 271, 111 S.Ct. at 2309 (citing *Chadha,* 462 U.S. at 951, 103 S.Ct. at 2784).

In dissent, Justice White took issue with the majority's approach to this case. Joined by Chief Justice Rehnquist and Justice Marshall, he preferred a more pragmatic *Mistretta* analysis, noting that neither Virginia nor the District of Columbia objected to the arrangement, and that the executive branch filed briefs on behalf of the MWAA. White characterized the transfer as "another innovative and otherwise lawful governmental experiment," and emphasized the federal government's authority to place conditions upon the conveyance of its property to a state created body.[97] He challenged the majority's skepticism as to the ability of members of Congress to serve in their individual capacity to safeguard the interests of nationwide travelers, and their equation of this to a federal interest giving rise to separation-of-powers scrutiny. According to Justice White, any unconstitutional consequences of this arrangement involve "pure speculation" and are, therefore, outside the Court's purview.

§ 15.4.6 *Clinton v. City of New York*

Presidents have long sought the power to reject particular provisions of legislative acts.[98] *Clinton v. City of New York*[99] addressed the constitutionality of an act designed to provide this power, the Line Item Veto Act (Act) of 1996.[100] That Act sought to give the President the power to cancel the funding for certain limited types of provisions that already had been signed into law. In many ways, this case proved to be the mirror image of *INS v. Chadha.*[101] *Chadha* held that once Congress delegated power to the executive branch, Congress could not repeal or amend that legislation without approval of both houses of Congress and the signature of the President. Similarly, in *Clinton*, the Court held, the President could not unilaterally repeal or amend a law.[102] Unlike the usual veto power exercised by the President, in which bills are rejected *in toto*, this Act allowed for only parts of bills to be vetoed or, in effect,

97. The dissent cites the Property Clause in Article IV, Sec. 3, Clause 2 of the U.S. Constitution, finding additional authority in South Dakota v. Dole, 483 U.S. 203, 107 S.Ct. 2793, 97 L.Ed.2d 171 (1987). In *Dole,* the Court held that Congress could condition a grant of federal highway funds to a State on that State adopting a drinking age no lower than 21, regardless of whether Congress would be able to directly mandate the same result. So long as the federal government did not use its spending power to "induce the States to engage in activities that would themselves be unconstitutional . . . ," any condition on the receipt of federal property would apparently pass muster. Id. at 284, 111 S.Ct. at 2316 (quoting 483 U.S. at 210–11, 107 S.Ct. at 2797–98).

The added element of federal/state issues in the *MWAA* case makes direct comparison with other separation of powers cases problematic. Unlike in *Morrison* or *Mistretta,* where one might arguably be hard pressed to identify a disadvantaged party, the plaintiffs in *MWAA* alleged the very tangible harm of high levels of aircraft noise. This additional element may have tipped the balance in favor of returning to the strict formalistic approach of *Bowsher* and *Chadha.* Both of the latter cases were frequently cited in the majority's opinion.

98. See generally, Michael J. Gerhardt, The Bottom Line on the Line–Item Veto Act of 1996, 6 Cornell J. L. & Pub. Pol'y 233 (1997).

99. 524 U.S. 417, 118 S.Ct. 2091, 141 L.Ed.2d 393 (1998).

100. 2 U.S.C. §§ 691–692 (Supp. II 1996).

101. 462 U.S. 919, 103 S.Ct. 2764, 77 L.Ed.2d 317 (1983). See § 15.4.2, supra.

102. 118 S.Ct. at 2095.

"cancelled". The majority of the Court held that such cancellations were tantamount to "Presidential amendments" of bills, and as such, were subject to the requirements of Article I, § 7 of the Constitution.[103]

The procedural history of the case is complex. The Line Item Veto Act first became effective on January 1, 1997, and its constitutionality was immediately challenged by six members of Congress. The District Court for the District of Columbia held the Act unconstitutional.[104] A direct, expedited appeal was granted by the Supreme Court. The Court held that the members of Congress had not "alleged a sufficiently concrete injury to have established Article III standing."[105] The case was then remanded to the District Court and dismissed for lack of jurisdiction.[106]

Within two months of the Court's decision, the President exercised his authority under the Act, and canceled provisions in two pieces of legislation. He canceled § 4722(c) of the Balanced Budget Act of 1997 (BBA),[107] and § 968 of the Taxpayer Relief Act of 1997 (TRA).[108] Two parties claimed injuries: one because of the cancellation of the BBA provision, and the other based on the cancellation of the TRA provision. The case was again brought before the District Court, which, for a second time, held that the Act was unconstitutional.[109] Again, the Supreme Court heard the case on expedited appeal. This time the Court agreed that the plaintiffs had standing and it reached the merits of the case, concluding the Act was unconstitutional.

The Line Item Veto Act authorized the President to "cancel in whole" three types of provisions.[110] These were: (1) any dollar amount of discretionary budget authority, (2) any item of new direct spending, and (3) any limited tax benefit.[111] The first set of plaintiffs, the City of New York and various health care concerns, brought suit based on the provision canceled in the BBA, which was an item of "new direct spending." The second set of plaintiffs, a cooperative of Idaho potato growers and an individual member of that cooperative, filed suit based on the provisions canceled in the TRA, which was a form of "limited tax relief."[112]

The first set of plaintiffs were injured in the following way. The Federal government, pursuant to the Social Security Act, subsidizes medical care for the indigent by transferring huge sums of money to the states. In 1991, Congress provided that these state subsidies were to be reduced by the amount of certain taxes imposed by the states on health

103. Id.

104. Byrd v. Raines, 956 F.Supp. 25 (D.D.C.1997).

105. Raines v. Byrd, 521 U.S. 811, 117 S.Ct. 2312, 138 L.Ed.2d 849 (1997).

106. Id.

107. Pub. L. No. 105–33, § 4722(c), 111 Stat. 251, 515 (1997).

108. Pub. L. No. 105–34, § 968, 111 Stat. 788, 895 (1997).

109. 985 F.Supp. 168 (D.D.C.1998).

110. Pub. L. No. 104–130 § 1021(a), 110 Stat. 1200 (1996).

111. Pub. L. No. 104–130 § 1021(a)(1)–(3), 110 Stat. 1200 (1996).

112. 985 F.Supp. 168 (D.D.C.1998).

care institutions.[113] New York was therefore required to return hundreds of millions of dollars to the federal government. It requested a waiver from the Health and Human Services Agency (HHS). When the HHS failed to rule on the waiver request, New York sought congressional assistance. It received it in the form of an amendment to the BBA, which freed New York State of its obligation to refund money to the federal government it had received in connection with the Medicaid program.

President Clinton vetoed this provision in the BBA, pursuant to his authority under the Line Item Veto Act. It was clearly an "item of new direct spending." This again left the state of New York dependent on a favorable ruling from the HHS on its waiver request. Had the HHS denied the waiver, the New York City Health and Hospitals Corporation (NYCHHC) would have been forced to reimburse the state for some of the monies the state would be returning to the federal government. The Court found the contingent liability suffered by the NYCHHC to be an "immediate injury," enough to give the city and the health care institutions standing to bring their suit.[114]

The second plaintiff, Snake River Potato Growers, Inc. (Snake River), was injured by the President's action in a more direct fashion. Snake River was a cooperative formed to assist Idaho potato farmers, in part by acquiring processing plants to reduce its members' post-harvest expenditures. Prior to the drafting of Section 968 of the TRA, it was possible for a corporation to structure the acquisition of another corporation, including a food processing company, without the seller realizing a gain subject to the capital gains tax. Section 968 did not eliminate that possibility. Rather, it allowed cooperatives, for the first time, to structure their acquisitions as any corporation might. It thus put them on equal ground with so-called "standard" corporations. Companies now had the same tax incentives to sell to cooperatives as they previously had to sell to other corporations. This provision of the Act clearly provided a "limited tax benefit."

When President Clinton canceled Section 968, pursuant to his authority under the Line Item veto Act, Snake River was in the midst of negotiations to purchase an Idaho-based potato processor. After the cancellation, the negotiations collapsed. Snake River planned to pursue other acquisition efforts, but only if the cancellation were reversed, and it could again offer the capital gains tax deferment to potential sellers. The Court found that the cancellation inflicted a "sufficient likelihood of economic injury," and that was enough to establish standing.[115]

Writing for the majority, Justice Stevens began his analysis of the merits of the Line Item Veto Act by noting that the canceled statutory provisions all were passed in accordance with all of the requirements of Article I, § 7 of the Constitution.[116] They passed both houses of Congress and were signed by the President. He then examined the strict procedur-

113. Id. at 171–72.

114. 118 S.Ct. at 2091.

115. Id. at 2100.

116. Id. at 2103.

al requirements imposed on the President by the Act, all of which were "meticulously followed" when he canceled the provisions in question.[117] Although the statute provided for a congressional override of a cancellation under the Act—aptly called a "disapproval bill"—Congress did not exercise this option for either of these cancellations.[118] The Court also noted that a disapproval bill, which the Act required to be passed by a majority of both houses, could be vetoed by the President, like any other congressional bill.[119]

Directly addressing the canceled provisions, the majority of the Court stated that the President's action prevented the provisions from having "legal force and effect."[120] This, they concluded, was tantamount to a "Presidential amendment;" citing *Chadha*, the Court held that this was in direct conflict with Article I of the Constitution.[121] The decision to repeal a part, but not all of the Act in question, was tantamount to an amendment of the statute involved. As far as the Court was concerned, neither Article I, nor Article II gave the President authority for such unilateral action. The most the President could do was to initiate and influence legislative proposals.[122] The Court then distinguished the standard Presidential veto from the type of veto at issue here, noting that an Article I veto takes place *before* a bill becomes law; however, under the Line Item Veto Act, the veto takes place *after* the bill has become law. Second, an Article I veto is of the entire bill; under the Line Item Veto Act, the veto applies to only a part of the bill.[123]

The Court went on to interpret what it termed the "constitutional silence" on the issue of a President repealing or amending a statute as a direct prohibition of such action.[124] Relying explicitly on *Chadha*, the majority spoke of the "finely wrought" procedure the Framers designed to enact legislation, arguing that unilateral repeals or amendments by the President would upset that procedure.[125]

In opposition, the government had argued, in effect, that the President was merely exercising discretionary authority explicitly provided by Congress.[126] As such, the President's actions were the same as if he simply had declined to spend certain money that had been appropriated, or declined to implement certain tax measures.[127] The majority of the Court rejected these arguments, noting that the power provided the President under this Act authorized the rejection rather than the implementation of a legislative judgment; it was not contingent on changed conditions, and was wholly permissive.[128] Moreover, the Court said, many of the statutes that allowed some Presidential discretion dealt with foreign affairs—an area where the President has traditionally enjoyed

117. Id. at 2102.
118. Id.
119. Id. at 2102–103
120. Id. at 2103.
121. Id. at 2103–104.
122. Id. at 2103.
123. Id.
124. Id.
125. Id. at 2104.
126. Id.
127. Id.
128. Id. at 2105–06.

much leeway.[129] Finally, the Court summarily rejected the notion that a congressional blessing was enough to save the Act. "Congress cannot alter the procedures set out in Article I, § 7, without amending the Constitution."[130]

The Court concluded by emphasizing that this case and its holding was focused on only one issue: the Act violated the Presentment Clause.[131] Citing *Chadha*, the Court found impermissible the disruption to the "finely wrought" procedure "commanded by the Constitution."[132] This was a direct rejection of the District Court's alternative holding, that found the Act to be in violation of Separation Powers as well.[133] Indeed, the majority of the Court noted that its holding was narrow, and was the inevitable result of finding that the procedures authorized by the Act were not authorized by the Constitution.[134]

Justice Kennedy concurred in the majority opinion, but based his conclusions on what he perceived to be the important connections present in this case between separation of powers principles and personal freedom. He concluded that an act, such as the Line Item Veto Act, that expanded presidential authority too greatly would clearly "threaten the liberties of individual citizens."[135]

Justice Scalia concurred in part and dissented in part. He concurred with the majority on the issue of standing, but only with regard to the first set of plaintiffs—i.e., the City of New York and the health care institutions.[136] He then analyzed the case presented by the New York appellees. Unlike the majority, he did not find the President's exercise of power under the Act in violation of the Presentment Clause.[137] Justice Scalia focused not on the President's power to veto parts of a bill, but rather on the cancellation power. He noted that the Presentment Clause does, indeed, prevent the President from canceling a law that Congress has not authorized him to cancel; however, the Courts have long accepted that the President can cancel a law which, by its own terms, authorizes the President to do so.[138] The Presentment Clause, he argued, no more prohibits the President from reducing congressional dispositions than it prevents him from augmenting those dispositions, provided the statute authorizes such reduction or augmentation.[139]

If these reductions or augmentations caused a constitutional problem, the problem was not due to the Presentment Clause, but rather the non-delegation doctrine.[140] For Justice Scalia, the real issue in this case

129. Id. at 2106.

130. Id. at 2107.

131. Id. at 2108.

132. Id. at 2107.

133. Id. at 2108.

134. Id.

135. Id.

136. He did not find that the second plaintiffs, Snake River, had any standing—either constitutionally statutorily based. Before addressing the merits, Justice Scalia made another procedural observation: he would have accepted the notice for expedited appeal as a petition for writ of certiorari, and he would have granted cert. Id.

137. 118 S.Ct. at 2115–16.

138. Id. at 2120.

139. Id. at 2118.

140. 118 S.Ct. at 2116.

was not whether the Presentment Clause has been violated, but whether Congress went too far in its delegation of authority to another branch, in this case the Executive Branch.[141] This case was not the mirror image of *Chadha*, but was similar to *Bowsher v. Synar*.[142] Although the President's discretionary power here was greater than that of the comptroller General in *Bowsher*, it was "no broader than the discretion traditionally granted the president in his execution of spending laws."[143]

In short, Justice Scalia maintained that there was no difference in granting power to the President to cancel an item of spending, or granting him authority to spend money at his discretion: it conferred the same degree of power.[144] The case came down only to semantics. A statute authorizing the President to "decline to spend" appropriated monies would have been constitutional, but because the authorization was to "cancel", it failed.[145] Justice Scalia's dissent acknowledged that there was a difference, but it was merely technical and not dispositive of this case.[146] The Presentment Clause was not implicated by the Line Item Veto Act, and the non-delegation doctrine was not violated by such technicalities.[147]

Justice Breyer also concurred in part and dissented in part.[148] He agreed that the plaintiffs had standing;[149] however, he maintained that the Act did not violate any specific constitutional provision, nor did it pose a Separation of Powers problem. Justice Breyer's opinion focused on three primary considerations.

First, the Act had as its purpose a proper objective—namely, Congress wanted to give the President the power to give effect to some, but not all, of the provisions in a massive appropriations bill.[150] He noted that at the nation's founding, this same end could have been accomplished by a different means: the appropriations were so few in number, they could have been written into separate bills, one for each item of spending.[151] This would have allowed the President to pick which, if any, of the bills (and hence items), he wanted to become law. Thus, the question for Justice Breyer was: is it permissible for Congress to choose a new means of accomplishing what it could have done by other means?[152] The complexity of modern appropriations bills is such that the means available to the first Congress was no longer practicable, he argued, though technically it would not have been unconstitutional.[153]

The second consideration for Justice Breyer was that the case primarily involved the structural provisions of the Constitution, which, as he noted, were "generally phrased."[154] These provisions delegate all

141. Id.

142. Id.

143. Id.

144. Id. at 2117.

145. Id.

146. Id. at 2118.

147. Id.

148. Id.

149. Id.

150. Id.

151. Id.

152. Id. at 2119.

153. Id.

154. Id.

legislative power to Congress, and all executive power to the President. Despite the seemingly distinct lines drawn by these words, the Court had given them a generous interpretation. Quoting Justice Marshall's famous passage from *McCulloch v. Maryland*,[155] Justice Breyer called attention to the Framers' vision which was based on pragmatic considerations, and allowed the Court to accept "necessary institutional innovation."[156] The Court in this case was not called on to referee a dispute between the other two branches of government, Justice Breyer thus noted a third important consideration. The majority clearly recognized that the other two branches of government reached a consensus. In his view, under such circumstances, the Court should interfere "[only] for the most compelling constitutional reasons."[157]

In short, Justice Breyer took exception with the majority's conclusion that the President, by exercising his authority under the Act, had somehow repealed or amended a law. Justice Breyer saw the President's action not as changing a law, but rather as *following* the law, thereby exercising the legal authority granted to him by Congress.[158]

155. Id.

156. Id.

157. Id.

158. Id. at 2120.

Chapter 16

LEGISLATIVE CONTROL OF AGENCY DISCRETION

Table of Sections

Congress has a variety of ways of exercising its oversight functions.[1] First, along with the executive branch, Congress is involved in the appointments process. Agency heads and other "officers of the United States" are appointed by the President with advice and consent of the Senate. Congress also has the "power of the purse" and agencies must regularly submit their operating budgets to Congress. In addition, Congress may compel an agency to report to it regularly by means of committee or subcommittee hearings or more formal, filed reports. These reports and hearings can also encourage informal contacts between agency and congressional staffs that provide another form of congressional feedback and oversight.

Congress also exercises various forms of statutory control. Congress delegates power to agencies by the statutes it drafts. An agency's enabling regulatory statute defines the scope of the agency's authority and Congress sets forth the procedures that an agency must use in exercising its authority and it establishes the agency's structure. That structure, as we shall see, can better facilitate executive control of agency policy making or give Congress a greater day-to-day role. In addition, Congress can exercise other forms of statutory control of agency discretion. Generic procedural statutes such as the National Environmental Policy ACT (NEPA),[2] the Paperwork Reduction Act[3] and

1. For summary and analysis of these various oversight techniques, see C. Forman, Congress and Social Regulation In the Reagan Era in The Reagan Regulatory Strategy 189 (G. Eads and M. Fix eds. 1983).

2. 42 U.S.C.A. §§ 4321–4361.

the Regulatory Flexibility Act[4] are designed to improve the quality of agency decisions across the board; the Unfunded Mandates Act also triggers various regulatory review proceedings and is designed to limit the costs imposed on state and local governments.[5] Certain provisions within regulatory enabling acts are an attempt to control agency decisionmaking processes in specific contexts. For example, the Resource Conservation and Recovery Act (RCRA) requires the EPA to issue its regulations within a specified time period. If this does not occur, a congressionally-specified result goes into effect.[6] In addition, throughout the 1980's and 1990's, Congress and agencies have increasingly relied on market incentives and market-oriented agency structures to guide the exercise of agency discretion and legislation that encourages agencies to do the same when carrying out their regulatory duties.[7] We shall examine these various forms of Congressional oversight in some detail.

§ 16.1 AGENCY STRUCTURE

Congress can and does create a variety of agency forms and structures, each with different implications for the relationship of that agency to Congress and the Executive Branch. Agencies may, for example, be composed of several members, each appointed for a term of years and removable only for cause. Such agencies are usually referred to as independent commissions and, as such, are more amenable to Congressional control than Executive control.[1] Agencies, such as the Department of Labor, can also be executive agencies, a part of the President's cabinet, and clearly more subject to his direct control. The heads of these agencies are cabinet officials and they serve at the pleasure of the President. They are much more susceptible to the policy predilections of the executive branch. Still other agencies may be executive agencies, but not be at the cabinet level. Finally, there are variations on these themes. The Department of Energy, for example, consists of a cabinet level agency, headed by the Secretary of Energy and an independent commission called the Federal Energy Regulatory Commission. Or there may be an executive agency headed by a single head, such as the Occupational Safety and Health Administration which is situated in an executive cabinet level agency, the Department of Labor. These various structures arguably give Congress or the Executive more or less day to day control over the activities of these agencies.[2]

3. 42 U.S.C.A. §§ 3501–3520.

4. 5 U.S.C.A. §§ 601–612.

5. These Acts are discussed more fully *infra* at § 16.2.1.

6. 42 U.S.C.A. § 6924(d)(1). See ACUS, A Guide To Federal Agency Rulemaking 16 (2nd ed. 1991); see generally, Abbott, The Case Against Federal Statutory and Judicial Deadlines, 39 Admin.L.Rev. 171 (1987).

7. See, e.g., Alfred C. Aman, Jr., A Global Perspective on Current Regulatory Reforms: Rejection, Relocation, or Reinvention? 2 Ind. J. Global Legal Stud. 429 (1995).

§ 16.1

1. For a collection of articles on the role of independent agencies in modern society, see Symposium; The Independence of Independent Agencies, 1988 Duke L.J. 215 (1988).

2. Id.

Independent agencies serve under Congress and have been described as the agents of Congress.[3] These agencies derive their independence from the President from at least three statutory techniques. A commissioner of an independent agency (1) is selected through a bipartisan procedure, (2) serves for a fixed term, and (3) can only be removed from office for express causes. The President is usually required to appoint some of the commissioners of an independent agency from the party out of power or from among those who are politically independent, thereby further isolating, at least to some extent, the agency from executive political pressure. A commissioner also usually serves a term of years that generally extends beyond the President's four-year term of office, providing additional political independence for the agency.[4] Finally, the President can only remove an agency official for designated causes preventing removal of the official for purely political reasons.[5] Congress retains control over the agency through the confirmation process in which the Senate can condition its approval on the assurances of certain promises by the nominee or reject the nomination altogether.

Independent agencies are collegial bodies, typically organized as commissions or boards.[6] Independent agencies bear many similarities to the appellate courts, our most respected collegial bodies.[7] Their decisionmaking process tends to be consensual and may show more concern with fairness and accuracy than with efficiency. The process of group decisionmaking often results in compromises rather than extreme positions, and helps to achieve consistent results in difficult factual situations.[8]

3. See 5 Senate Comm. on Gov't Affairs, Study on Federal Regulation: Regulatory Organization, S.Doc. No. 19, 95th Cong., 1st Sess. 31 (1977). Senator Hart is quoted in the Senate study: "The commissions, if I may risk an oversimplification, are ours." Id.

4. The length of the term varies depending on the agency. FCC Commissioners, for example, serve five years, while Federal Reserve Board members serve fourteen years. See 47 U.S.C.A. § 154(c) and 12 U.S.C.A. § 241. For discussion of the independence of the Federal Reserve Board and the statutory bases of that independence, see Aman, Bargaining For Justice: An Examination of the Use and Limits of Conditions by the Federal Reserve Board, 74 Iowa L.Rev. 837 (1988).

5. See Humphrey's Executor v. United States, 295 U.S. 602, 55 S.Ct. 869, 79 L.Ed. 1611 (1935). A representative removal clause is as follows: "[A]ny commissioner may be removed by the President for inefficiency, neglect of duty, or malfeasance in office." 15 U.S.C.A. § 41 (FTC).

6. For an excellent analysis of the motivations Congress may have in choosing to regulate one area through an independent agency and another through an executive agency, see Verkuil, The Purposes and Limits of Independent Agencies, 1988 Duke L.J. 257 (1988). There is no definitive listing of "official" independent agencies. One list is contained in the Unified Agenda of Federal Regulations and it shows 14 independent agencies: Commodity Futures Trading Commission, Consumer Product Safety Commission, Farm Credit Administration, Federal Communications Commission, Federal Deposit Insurance Corporation, Federal Energy Regulatory Commission, Federal Home Loan Bank Board, Federal Maritime Commission, Federal Reserve System, Federal Trade Commission, Interstate Commerce Commission, National Credit Union Administration, Nuclear Regulatory Commission, and Securities and Exchange Commission. See also 44 U.S.C.A. § 3502(10) (listing 16 independent agencies).

7. Martin M. Shapiro, Courts—A Comparative and Political Analysis 111—15 (1981).

8. A study of three-person Administrative Law Judge panels revealed that their decisions showed less variability than single ALJ's. See Jerry L. Mashaw et al., Social Security Hearings and Appeals 20–29 (1978).

Commissions have jurisdiction only over a limited subject matter, often of a highly technical nature. Independent agencies can develop an expertise with the subject matter that enables them to carry out their adjudicatory functions in an informed and cost-efficient manner. A generalist judge with a crowded docket simply does not have the time or resources to develop the expertise needed to adjudicate controversies in many technical areas. Where political independence, collegial decision-making, and subject matter expertise are required, Congress regulates the field through an independent agency.

Congress also creates free-standing executive agencies to direct implementation of broad programs, such as protection of the environment through the Environmental Protection Agency (EPA). Areas that call for quick, decisive action are better managed by single deciders who can act and be held politically accountable for their actions.[9] The executive agency head is appointed by the President, serves for whatever term desired by the President, and can be removed from office by the President for any reason. These features make the executive agency much less susceptible to Congressional influence and more amenable to executive control. The executive agency is, perhaps, best suited to policymaking through decisions made by an individual in contrast to the independent agency, which is particularly suited to adjudication through collegial decisionmaking.

Another type of agency structure consists of an independent agency linked to an executive agency. An example of this split-function design exists in the Occupational Safety and Health Administration (OSHA). The Department of Labor, an executive department, administers OSHA, which has responsibility for establishing and enforcing health and safety standards.[10] A three member independent agency, the Occupational Safety and Health Review Commission, adjudicates disputes arising from OSHA's standards enforcement. This innovative structure is designed to place the policymaking, prosecution, and adjudication functions directly with the Secretary of Labor.[11] The split-function structure was also used when the independent Federal Energy Regulatory Commission was placed within the Department of Energy.[12] The advantage of the split-function approach is that it legitimizes the adjudicatory function by maintaining a degree of independence *within* an agency having a significant degree of executive control. The major disadvantage is that turf battles can occur between the Secretary and the Commission, because

9. See U.S. Comm'n on Org. of the Executive Branch of Gov't, Comm. on Indep. Regulatory Comm'ns, A Report with Recommendations (1949) ("The very qualities which make these agencies valuable for regulation, especially group deliberation and discussion, make them unsuited for executive and operating responsibilities.").

10. 29 U.S.C.A. § 651–678.

11. See H.R. 843, 90th Cong., 1st Sess., introduced, 113 Cong.Rec. 112 (1967).

12. See Aman, Institutionalizing the Energy Crisis: Some Structural and Procedural Lessons, 65 Cornell L.Rev. 491 (1980). Professor Aman observes that the split-function arrangement replaces the old problem of interagency fragmentation with a new problem of interagency fragmentation. See also Byse, The Department of Energy Organization Act: Structure and Procedure, 30 Admin.L.Rev. 193 (1978).

while the Secretary retains responsibility for rulemaking, the rules themselves must be interpreted in adjudication before the Commission.[13] Commentators have observed that these battles appear inherent in the split-function arrangement.[14]

It is, of course, important not to overemphasize the independence of collegial commissions or the responsiveness of executive agencies to presidential directives. As some commentators have noted the political process establishes control mechanisms over a government agency that are very similar regardless of what form Congress chooses.[15] A President enjoying great popular support can exercise significant influence over an independent regulatory agency through the nomination and budget processes as well as through informal channels.[16]

Independent agencies are not, of course, completely free of the executive branch. The administration in power is also able to control independent agencies through the Department of Justice. Most independent agencies do not have their own litigating authority and must rely on the Justice Department to represent them. The President directly controls the Justice Department and can therefore indirectly control the litigation strategy of the independent agency. The Justice Department

13. See Donovan v. A. Amorello & Sons, Inc., 761 F.2d 61 (1st Cir.1985); see also Donovan v. Daniel Marr & Son Co., 763 F.2d 477 (1st Cir.1985) (supporting but qualifying the Secretary of Labor's authority). But see Brennan v. Gilles & Cotting, Inc., 504 F.2d 1255 (4th Cir.1974) (favoring OSHRC's interpretation of a rule over OSHA's). See generally, Johnson, The Split—Enforcement Model: Some Conclusions from the OSHA and MSHA Experiences, 39 Admin.L.Rev. 315 (1987).

14. Johnson, supra note 20, at 340, 347.

15. See Foote, Independent Agencies Under Attack: A Skeptical View of the Importance of the Debate, 1988 Duke L.J. 223 (1988). Professor Foote argues that informal mechanisms of control throughout the entire political environment break down the independence of independent agencies to make them functionally similar to executive agencies. Id. at 232–36. See also Robinson, Independent Agencies: Form and Substance in Executive Prerogative, 1988 Duke L.J. 238 (1988). Professor Robinson observes that the President has the ability to influence the policy of an independent agency, directly and indirectly, through appointment of members, budgetary controls, and powers of persuasion. Id. at 245–46. See also Morrison, How Independent are Independent Regulatory Agencies?, 1988 Duke L.J. 252 (1988). Morrison maintains that the difference between an independent agency and an executive agency is not substantial considering that the executive branch controls the independent agency's appointments, budget, and litigating authority. Id. at 252–54.

16. For example, Congress conferred upon the Consumer Product Safety Commission (CPSC) independent status so that it could be free from political pressures in making policies and rules to protect consumers from unsafe products. See Michael D. Reagan, Regulation: The Politics of Policy 49 (1987). Even though the CPSC nominally enjoys independent status, the Reagan administration was able to exercise considerable control over that agency. CPSC's staff was cut by more than forty percent and its budget by almost a quarter. Waldman, Kids in Harm's Way, Newsweek, Apr. 18, 1988, at 47–48. Although a commissioner serves for a fixed term, if he perceives that the President or his policies will outlast the length of that term, he may be inclined to adopt the administration's viewpoint concerning the proper role of the agency so that he might better position himself for the next round of nominations by the executive. The extent to which this factor played a role in setting the tone at the CPSC is unclear, but after the Reagan administration tried to abolish the agency, there were reports of conflicts among the commissioners. Their decisions were either not forthcoming or excessively delayed. One disgruntled staffer reported: "The signal from above appears to be that we really don't want you to do anything, so you kind of just sit back and you don't push for anything." Id.

can decide, without obtaining agreement from the agency, which cases to pursue and how to present the issues consistently with the President's political views.

In the case of an executive agency, however, the President's ability to replace the agency head can be reduced by political realities. As Professor Strauss has noted: "Even in executive agencies, the layer over which the President enjoys direct control of personnel is very thin and political factors may make it difficult for him to exercise even those controls to the fullest. An administrator with a public constituency and mandate . . . cannot be discharged—and understands that he cannot be discharged—without substantial political cost."[17] The view that regulatory agencies, regardless of their formal structure, are influenced by many factors, including Congress, the President, the courts, economic conditions, the composition of agency staffs, private interest groups, and public opinion is supported by mounting empirical evidence.[18]

§ 16.1.1 Federal Corporations: A Public–Private Agency Structure

An increasingly common approach to regulatory reform throughout the 1980's and 1990's was to leave certain public functions in the public sector, but to use federal corporations, essentially a private sector structural model, for the supervision and delivery of those services.[19] Some federal corporations are wholly federal and others consist of various mixes of public and private power.[20]

Federal corporations have long provided a structural framework for this kind of a public/private approach. The federal government's authority to charter corporations is well established and authorised by the Necessary and Proper Clause of the Constitution.[21] The United States Postal Service, the Federal Aviation Administration (FAA), the Federal

17. Strauss, The Place of Agencies in Government: Separation of Powers and the Fourth Branch. 84 Colum.L.Rev. 573, 590 (1984) (footnotes omitted).

18. See, e.g., Moe, Control and Feedback in Economic Regulation: The Case of the NLRB, 79 Am.Pol.Sci.Rev. 1094, 1095 (1985); The Politics of Regulation (James Q. Wilson ed. 1980); Martha Derthick & Paul J. Quirk, The Politics of Deregulation (1985).

19. See A. Michael Fromkin, Reinventing The Government Corporation, 1995 U. Ill. L.Rev. 543 (1995). This section relies heavily on Alfred C. Aman, Jr., Administrative Law for a New Century, in The Province of Administrative Law (M. Taggart, ed.) (Hart Pub., Oxford 1997) pp. 103–105.

20. Some of these constructs, for example, take the form of "mixed-ownership government corporations". Examples of such corporations are: Amtrak; the Central Bank for Cooperatives; the Federal Deposit Insurance Corporation; the Federal Home Loan Banks; the Federal Intermediate Credit Banks; the Federal Land Banks; the National Credit Union Administration Central Liquidity Facility; the Regional Banks for Cooperatives; the Rural Telephone Bank when the ownership, control, and operation of the bank are converted under § 410(a) of the Rural Electrification Act of 1936 (7 U.S.C. 950(a)); the United States Railway Association; the Financing Corporation; the Resolution Trust Corporation; and the Resolution Funding Corporation.

21. See *McCulloch v. Maryland*, 17 U.S. (4 Wheat.) 316, 4 L.Ed. 579 (1819), see also *Osborn v. Bank of the United States*, 22 U.S. (9 Wheat.) 738, 6 L.Ed. 204 (1824). The *Osborn* Court echoed the *McCulloch* Court's reasoning. See also A.M. Froomkin, "Reinventing the Government Corporation" [1995], supra note 26 at 551.

Railway Administration, and the Overseas Private Investment Corporation (OPIC) are just a few examples of the federal government's use of private models for delivering public services.[22]

These federal corporations take various forms and the relative mix of private and public power affect the application of the state action doctrine. The state action doctrine looms large in determining the extent to which administrative law or constitutional law will apply to these entities. If the federal government can simply avoid constitutional protections by corporatising governmental agencies, form will clearly have triumphed over substance. The court concluded that this should not be the case in *Lebron v. National Railroad Passenger Corporation*.[23] In *Lebron*, the Court held that Congress' decision that Amtrak was a private entity was not determinative for the courts when asked to decide whether the state action doctrine applied.[24] The Supreme Court held that a "corporation is an agency of the government, for purposes of constitutional obligations of the government rather than 'privileges of the government', when the state has specifically created that corporation for the furtherance of a governmental objective and does not merely hold some shares but rather controls the operation of the corporation through its appointees".[25] Recalling its stance as to the status of the Reconstruction Finance Corporation, the Court went on to note that the fact "that . . . Congress chose to call it a corporation does not alter its characteristics so as to make it something other than what it actually is. . . ."[26]

The conclusion that Amtrak is "an agency or instrumentality of the United States for the purpose of individual rights guaranteed against the Government by the Constitution", is founded on the history of government-created and controlled corporations. As the Court noted:[27]

> a remarkable feature of the heyday of those corporations, in the 1930s and 1940s, was that, even while they were praised for their status "as agencies separate and distinct, administratively and financially and legally, from the government itself, which has facili-

22. Other examples of wholesale government cooperation of private sector models are plentiful. These entities are called "wholly-owned government corporations", 31 U.S.C.A. § 9101(3), and include the following: the Commodity Credit Corporation; the Community Development Financial Institutions Fund; the Export–Import Bank of the United States; the Federal Crop Insurance Corporation; Federal Prison Industries Incorporated; the Corporation for National and Community Service (Americorps); the Government National Mortgage Association; the Pennsylvania Avenue Development Corporation; the Pension Benefit Guaranty Corporation; the Rural Telephone Bank until the ownership, control, and operation of the Bank are converted under § 410(a) of the Rural Electrification Act of 1936 (7 U.S.C. 950(a)); the Saint Lawrence Seaway Development Corporation; the Secretary of Housing and Urban Development when carrying out duties and powers related to the Federal Housing Administration Fund; the Tennessee Valley Authority; the Uranium Enrichment Corporation; the Panama Canal Commission; and the Alternative Agricultural Research and Commercialization Corporation.

23. 513 U.S. 374, 115 S.Ct. 961, 130 L.Ed.2d 902 (1995) (hereafter referred to as *Lebron*).

24. Ibid., 971.

25. Ibid., 974.

26. Idem.

27. Idem (quoting from Pritchett, "The Government Corporation Control Act of 1945" (1946) 40 *Am Pol Sci Rev* 495).

tated their adoption of commercial methods of accounting and financing, avoidance of political controls, and utilization of regular procedures of business management", it was fully acknowledged that they were a "device" of "government", and constituted "federal corporate agencies" apart from "regular government departments".

Lebron may be the new day, but it is important to note that the courts have not always been so accommodating when it comes to seeing through the "private veil" of the corporate form. Courts have held that the Legal Services Corporation, the Corporation for Public Broadcasting and Communications Satellite Corporation (COMSAT) are all essentially private concerns.[28]

§ 16.2 POLITICAL CONTROLS

Perhaps the most visible and most effective means through which Congress can exert influence over administrative agencies is through the appropriations process. Budgetary hearings in both houses of Congress are opportunities for members of the appropriations committees to review agency performance, and affect future agency policy by changing the levels of funds appropriated for certain purposes.[1]

The appropriations process is particularly important to administrators, for the threat of congressional displeasure and the possible cutting of funds can influence agency policymaking, even when an agency's appropriation is not up for review. Congress can use the appropriations process to express displeasure with agency actions; it can limit statutory jurisdiction by forbidding expenditures for certain purposes, or reward agencies that successfully pursue congressional interests.[2]

These decisions, which can and often do have the effect of making certain agency programs obsolete, are easily made without any ostensible change to the existing statutes. Congress can, however, also use the appropriations process to amend the statutory laws under which an agency operates. Members of Congress can include limiting language in

28. See, e.g., *Network Project v. Corporation for Public Broadcasting*, 4 Media L. Rep. (BNA) 2399, 2403–8 (D.D.C.1979); *Texas Rural Legal Aid Inc. v. Legal Services Corp.*, 940 F.2d 685, 699 (D.C.Cir. 1991); *Warren v. Government National Mortgage Association*, 611 F.2d 1229, 1232–5 (8th Cir.1980), cert. denied, 449 U.S. 847, 101 S.Ct. 133, 66 L.Ed.2d 57 (1980). See also *Jackson v. Culinary School of Washington*, 788 F.Supp. 1233, 1265 (D.D.C. 1992) (holding that the Federal Student Loan Guaranty Association is "not a governmental entity" because Congress designated the corporation "private").

§ 16.2

1. See Richard F. Fenno, Jr., The Power of the Purse (1966). See also 2 Senate Comm. On Govt Operations, Study of Federal Regulation: Congressional Oversight of Regulatory Agencies, S.Doc. No. 26, 95th Cong., 1st Sess. 31–33 (1977).

2. See Weingast and Moran, The Myth of the Runaway Bureaucracy, Regulation, May/June 1982 at 33. There is an "invisible congressional hand" through which appropriations subcommittees channel budgetary rewards to agencies. For a criticism of the idea that budgetary oversight is effective to control agency decisions see Clarkson & Murris, Containing the F.T.C., 35 Miami L.Rev. 77, 93 (1980).

the small print of the appropriations bill, which will become law unless a member challenges it on the House or Senate floor. Often this small print imposes substantial conditions upon the use of appropriated funds which were not previously restricted by law.

After passing the authorizing legislation for an agency and appropriating funds to it, Congress can still monitor the performance of an agency through the process of congressional oversight. Oversight is an important test of the political acceptability of regulation. Statutory standards usually do not provide precise notice of the policy which will emerge from the agency and many people who never had the chance to affect the formulation of the legislation may be affected by its implementation.

Many statutes specifically provide for periodic oversight hearings by Congress.[3] In addition, a congressional committee or subcommittee can call an oversight hearing at any time to enquire into a particular agency's policies and programs. Such hearings are particularly valuable to members of Congress because they provide legislators a visible opportunity to press for regulatory initiatives which can affect the public interest.[4] They are especially effective when undertaken by committees which focus on specific areas of policy, such as the Agriculture or Labor committees. Such committees can direct their large staff resources towards the review of existing policies and the formulation of coherent policy initiatives. Agencies can expect vigorous questioning from committee members, who often are under pressure from their own constituencies to make changes in existing programs.[5]

Oversight is also a means through which Congress can effect changes in an agency's directives without amending the statute which established the agency. (Such amendment is usually very difficult considering the politically turbulent nature of Congress.) Although congressional rhetoric often portrays oversight as a means to enforce the original intent of its statutes, in reality the result is often quite different. Changes in constituent pressures and in the political compositions of Congress between the passage of the legislation and the present will

3. For example, see 42 U.S.C.A. § 9651(h)(3) (congressional oversight hearings to ensure EPA compliance with regulations); 49 U.S.C.A.App. § 2520 (congressional oversight provision for Department of Transportation).

4. One prominent example of this is the history of airline deregulation. See Levine, Revisionism Revised—Airline Deregulation and the Public Interest, 44 Law & Contemp.Probs. 179 (Winter 1981). Some authors however are concerned about this trend, saying that it has decreased the overall effectiveness of oversight. Unless an oversight activity reveals a scandalous situation with an opportunity for favorable publicity, members of Congress consider it to be dull and potentially troublesome. There is no incentive for members to do this type of oversight work; thus it is rarely done. See Bernard Rosen, Holding Government Bureaucracies Accountable (1982); Aberbach, Changes in Congressional Oversight, 22 Am.Behav.Scientist 493 (1979).

5. This is particularly so because Congressional Committees have a tendency to be self-selected, with members choosing to sit on committees that decide policies of direct interest to their constituencies. See Weingast, Regulation, Reregulation and Deregulation: The Political Foundations of Agency Clientele Relationships, 44 Law & Contemp.Probs. 147 (Winter 1981). See also David R. Mayhew, Congress: The Electoral Connection at 89–90 (1974).

influence the oversight process. The policies implemented by an agency will often be different than those envisioned by the Congress that originally authorized the agency programs.[6]

In addition to the formal oversight device of a committee hearing, there exist less formal ways through which individual members of Congress can exert influence over agency policymaking. One method used by every member of Congress is intervention in matters pending before an administrative agency, usually made on behalf of constituents.[7] The nature of these inquiries, made by members of Congress and their staffs to agency personnel, can range from status reports on an individual's request currently before the agency, to complaints regarding the substance or procedures of the current regulatory scheme. While this type of activity will not usually lead to substantive changes in a particular agency's regulatory scheme, it can lead to an accelerated decision on a particular party's claim before that agency, or an informal review of procedures by agency officials who are aware of the potential power which an individual member of Congress may hold.[8]

The judiciary is generally reluctant to interfere with congressional oversight. Courts have, however, set rudimentary ground rules for oversight devices such as hearings and informal pressure from individual members. In *Pillsbury Co. v. FTC*,[9] the court, distinguishing between an agency's legislative and judicial functions, held that a Congressional investigation could not "focus ... directly and substantially upon the mental decisional processes of a Commission in a case which is pending before it."[10] While Congress has the right to inquire into almost the entire range of an agency's activities, this right must be limited when it interferes with an individual's right to a fair and impartial trial before an agency's adjudicatory tribunal.

In response to mounting concern over the possible negative effect of pressures placed upon an agency by an individual member of Congress or by a small group of members, the courts have attempted to set standards

6. On the overall nature of informal oversight see Bruff, Legislative Formality, Administrative Rationality, 63 Tex.L.Rev. 207 (1984).

7. See generally, Walter Gellhorn, When Americans Complain (1966).

8. See Weingast & Moran, Bureaucratic Discretion or Congressional Control—Regulatory Policymaking at the FTC, 91 J.Pol.Econ 765 (1983). Weingast and Moran believe that regulatory agencies are remarkably sensitive to even small changes in the imposition of preferences, especially when made by members of the oversight committee or subcommittee to which that agency must respond. They argue that the mechanics of congressional influence are both subtle and indirect, so much that even careful observers may not perceive their operation. See also Weingast & Moran, The Myth of the Runaway Bureaucracy—The Case of the FTC, Regulation, May–June 1982, at 33.

Other scholars have doubts about the effects which constituent complaints have on the correction of administrative problems. See Klonoff, The Congressman as Mediator Between Citizens and Government Agencies: Problems and Prospects 16 Harv.J.Legis, 701, 712–713 (1979). Klonoff argues that while the quantity and variety of complaints received by congressional offices are a rich source of information upon which to base legislative reforms of agencies, members of Congress rarely perceive and almost never act upon the larger agency problems implied in citizens allegation.

9. 354 F.2d 952 (5th Cir.1966).

10. Id. at 964 (emphasis in original).

for overturning administrative rulemaking on the grounds of Congressional pressure. Addressing this issue, the D.C. Circuit, in *Sierra Club v. Costle*,[11] articulated a two part standard: first, the claimant must prove that the content of the pressure upon agency officials was designed to force him to base his decision upon factors not made relevant by Congress in the applicable statute, and second, he must prove that the official's decision was affected by these extraneous considerations.[12] Thus, it is proper for a Member of Congress to represent vigorously the interests of his or her constituents before an administrative agency engaged in general rulemaking so long as he or she does not frustrate the intent of Congress as a whole or undermine applicable procedural rules.

§ 16.2.1 Statutory Techniques by Which Congress Controls Agency Discretion

Over the years Congress has also passed numerous statutes which are designed to affect the substance of agency decisions, through the implementation of generic procedural requirements. One of these statutes is the National Environmental Policy Act of 1969 *(NEPA)*.[13] That Act was a response to a growing national concern over the state of the environment. It sets forth procedural requirements to assure that agencies will consider substantive environmental values in the formulation and implementation of policy. The core of the Act is a requirement that an agency must prepare an environmental impact report before taking any major administrative action. This report must identify the possible effects of the proposed actions on the environment, and evaluate possible alternatives. Although NEPA does not say that all actions which are hazardous to the environment must be avoided, it has the effect of increasing administrative awareness of the environment, and often fosters rethinking of government actions.[14]

Another statute through which Congress is able to influence administrative policy through procedural means is the *Regulatory Flexibility Act of 1980* (RFA), amended in 1996.[15] Throughout the mid to late seventies Congress became increasingly concerned about the impact that

11. 657 F.2d 298 (D.C.Cir.1981)

12. See also D.C. Federation of Civic Associations v. Volpe, 459 F.2d 1231 (D.C.Cir.1971), cert. denied 405 U.S. 1030, 92 S.Ct. 1290, 31 L.Ed.2d 489 (1972). If, in the process of making an adjudicatory decision, an agency official takes into consideration factors which Congress could not have intended to make relevant (such as congressional pressures on unrelated issues), then his decision will be remanded since it was made on an impermissible premise. The court emphasized that judicial invalidation has been and will continue to be very rare, limited solely to questions pending in formal adjudications before an agency.

13. Pub.L. No. 91–190, 83 Stat. 852 (1970) (codified as amended at 42 U.S.C.A. § 4321 (Supp.1992)).

14. See F. Anderson, NEPA in the Courts: A Legal Analysis of the National Environmental Policy Act (1973) (a discussion of NEPA's procedural requirements and operational impact). See also, Cramton & Berg, On Leading a Horse to Water: NEPA and the Fed Bureaucracy, 71 Mich. L.Rev. 511 (1971) (NEPA's goals are framed in broad constitutional terms and its procedural directives leave much room for agency adaption).

15. 5 U.S.C. § 601–12.

regulation, especially environmental and health regulation, was having upon small businesses. These regulations often had a disproportionately greater economic effect on small businesses, hurting their competitive positions. Under the RFA an agency must study the economic effect which proposed actions will have on small businesses, as well as review and re-evaluate regulations. By requiring that agencies consider a rule's impact on small businesses, this statute effectively slows down the development of new initiatives and fosters the development of alternative actions.[16]

The 1980 Regulatory Flexibility Act (RFA),[17] amended in 1996, requires that whenever agencies engage in rulemaking they consider the special circumstances and problems of small entities. In 1996, the Act was extended to Internal Revenue Service (IRS) interpretive rules that regulate information collection from small entities. Each time the agency promulgates an information collection rule, it must prepare a regulatory flexibility analysis that describes the likely effect of the rule on small entities. The RFA is subject to public comment, as is the rule. The Act originally prohibited judicial review of RFAs except as part of the rulemaking record.[18] In 1996, however, Congress amended the Act by providing judicial review to small entities adversely affected by these requirements.[19]

The Unfunded Mandates Reform Act of 1995[20] also triggers regulatory review. This legislation requires Congress and federal agencies (except independent agencies) to give special consideration to all legislation and regulations likely to impose mandates on state, local, and tribal entities.[21] Agencies, in particular, are required to prepare a regulatory analysis for any rulemaking likely to impose costs in excess of $100 million on the private sector.[22] The Act codifies many of the provisions of Executive Order 12,866.[23] The provisions of the Act, however, are subject to very limited judicial review.[24] Nevertheless, the Act requires identification of and limits to the high and often hidden costs that federal mandates can impose on state and local governments.[25]

16. See Stewart, The New Regulatory Flexibility Act, 67 A.B.A.J. 66 (Jan 1981); Verkuil, A Critical Guide to the Regulatory Flexibility Act, 1982 Duke L.J. 213 (1982) (the RFA also gives opportunities for outside parties to introduce considerations that may have been overlooked when the rules were initially adopted).

17. 5 U.S.C. § 601–12, amended by Pub. L. No. 104–121, Title II, §§ 241–245, 100 Stat, 864.

18. Pub. L. No. 96–354, 94 Stat. 1165.

19. Pub. L. 104–121, 110 Stat. 865, codified at 5 U.S.C § 611. See Associated Fisheries of Maine, Inc. v. Daley, 127 F.3d 104 (1st Cir.1997) (applying a reasonableness standard to the agency rule).

20. Pub. L. No. 104–4, 109 Stat. 48, codified at 2 U.S.C. § 1501–71.

21. 2 U.S.C. § 1501.

22. 2 U.S.C. § 1532.

23. Cf. 3 C.F.R. 638 (1993).

24. 2 U.S.C. § 1571.

25. H.R. Rep. No. 104–76, at 26 (1995). See generally, R. Adler, Unfunded Mandates and Fiscal Federalism: A Critique, 50 Vand. L.Rev. 1137 (1997); D. Cole & C. Comer, Rhetoric, Reality, and the Law of Unfunded Federal Mandates, 8 Stan. L. & Pol'y Rev. 103 (1997); S. Leckrone, Note, Turning Back the Clock: The Unfunded Mandates Reform Act of 1995 and Its Effective Repeal of Environmental Legislation, 71 Ind. L.J. 1029 (1996).

§ 16.2.2 Market Controls

The government frequently is now expected to look like, as well as perform, in a manner consistent with private sector models. This is particularly true for the various commercial activities that the government carries out, but the dominance of the market and market models is not so limited.[26] Market discourses have also been used frequently to structure various non-commercial regulatory approaches and incentives, such as the use of market approaches in the amendments to the Clean Air Act.[27]

Legislative deregulation or privatization is to be distinguished from the use of market incentives and market regulatory approaches as a substitute for so-called command and control regulation. Perhaps the most extensive U.S. example of this approach is the use of market regulation by the Environmental Protection Agency (EPA).[28] Rather than trying to mandate precisely how certain industries might lower

26. In the first National Performance Review (NPR), published in September 1993, the Gore Commission outlined both the state of the United States government and a plan to "reinvent" the government so that it might better serve people. In this report the Administration stated that its goals were to create a government "that makes sense"; "gets results"; "puts customers first"; and "gets its money's worth". To that end, it directed all agency heads to: "cut obsolete regulations"; "reward results, not red tape"; "get out of Washington and create grassroots partnerships"; and "negotiate, don't dictate". Since issuing the first report, the Administration has published two updates, the latest of which proclaims boldly that "The Era of Big Government is Over". vice President Al Gore, Report of the National performance Review, From Red Tape to Results: Creating a Government That Works Better and Costs Less (Sept. 7, 1993) [hereinafter National Performance Review]. For a discussion of this report, see Jeffery s. Lubbers, Better Regulations: The National Performance Review's Regulatory Reform Recommendations, 1994 Duke L.J. 1165 (1994); Daniel P. Rodriquez, Management, Control, and the Dilemmas of Presidential Leadership in the Modern Administrative State, 1994 Duke L.J. 1180; Paul R. Verkuil, Is Efficient Government an Oxymoron?, 1994 Duke L.J. 1221.

The Government Performance and Results Act of 1993 (GPRA), Pub. L. No. 103–62, 107 Stat. 285 (1993) (codified in scattered sections of 5 U.S.C., 31 U.S.C., and 39 U.S.C.). See generally S. Rep. No. 58, 103d Cong. (1993), *reprinted in* 1993 U.S.C.C.A.N. 327, requires performance-based budgeting by the government in pursuit of improving Federal program effectiveness and "public accountability by promoting a new focus on results, service quality, and customer satisfaction," GPRA § 2(b)(3), 107 Stat. at 285. In the spirit of reinventing government, the GPRA incorporates Total Quality management business principles into administrative agency operations. For a list of articles that analyze the GPRA and the reinvention of government in the environmental sector, see Rena I. Steinzor, devolution and the Public Health, 24 Harv. Envtl. L. Rev. 351, 351, n.1 (2000). For up-to-date information and people and organizations working towards results-oriented government, see National Partnership for reinventing Government (updated March 17, 2000) <http://www.npr.gov/initiati/mfr/>.

27. See Clean Air Act Amendments of 1990, Pub. L. No. 101–549 (1990).

28. See generally Bruce A. Ackerman & Richard B Stewart, Reforming Environmental Law, 37 Stan. L. Rev. 1333, 1341 (1985):

> Our basic reform would respond to these deficiencies by allowing polluters to buy and sell each other's permits—thereby creating a powerful financial incentive for those who can clean up most cheaply to sell their permits to those whose treatment costs are highest.

See also Marshall J. Breger et al., Providing Economic Incentives In Environmental Regulation, 8 Yale J. on reg. 463, 468–69 (1991) ("I am persuaded that the endless proliferation of command-and-control regulations is not, in general, a workable or appropriate long-run way of dealing with this problem").

their pollution levels, the EPA seeks to provide market incentives to achieve such goals. For example, a market for pollution reduction might be created by selling pollution permits. Those industries capable of lowering their pollution below mandated levels can receive compensation from those companies unable to meet their goal.[29] Using the market in this way is a form of deregulation in that it provides more compliance alternatives to the regulated entities, and more flexibility for regulated entities in determining how best to achieve their goals. Such approaches usually are less costly to implement and enforce.

Other forms of market-based regulations include greater reliance on taxes, rather than regulation, even market-based regulation. The imposition of higher costs on certain actors forces them to internalize external costs. User fees can also have regulatory effects. User fees can also serve several other important purposes, beyond simply raising revenues. These purposes include encouraging more efficient allocation of services between government and the private sector as well as encouraging privatization of governmental activities.[30] The expected distributional effect of fee-based governmental service is that less of a service will be demanded so that the decision to reject or employ a user fee is best viewed as based on a desire to induce a socially-optimal amount of the underlying good or service. Setting user fees thus allows government to have an effect on the market without direct regulation.[31]

The collection and dissemination of information can also play a major regulatory role. When airfares were deregulated and the service level of some airlines subsequently seemed to drop rather than improve, the Department of Transportation required reports from the airlines regarding lost luggage, on-time arrivals, and the like.[32] Providing consumers with information concerning their effectiveness was, thus, an effective but non-directive form of regulation.

§ 16.3 THE LEGISLATIVE VETO AND BEYOND

Prior to the Supreme Court's decision in *INS v. Chadha*,[1] one house and two house vetoes were a common method by which Congress sought to control agency rulemaking.[2] Though the Court's opinion in *Chadha* dealt only with a one-house veto of the suspension of a deportation order by the Attorney General subsequent Supreme Court decisions have applied *Chadha* to two-house vetoes as well as agency rules.[3] Various

29. Id.

30. Clayton P. Gillette & Thomas D. Hopkins, Federal User Fees: A Legal and Economic Analysis, 67 B.U. L. Rev. 795, 799 (1987).

31. Id. at 801.

32. U.S. Department of Transportation, Secretary's Task Force on Competition in the U.S. Domestic Airline Industry (1990).

§ 16.3

1. 462 U.S. 919, 103 S.Ct. 2764, 77 L.Ed.2d 317 (1983), discussed in chapter 15, sec. 15.4.2, supra.

2. See generally, Bruff and Gellhorn, Congressional Control of Administrative Regulation: A Study of Legislative Vetoes, 90 Harv.L.Rev. 1369 (1977).

3. Process Gas Consumers Group v. Consumer Energy Council, 463 U.S. 1216, 103 S.Ct. 3556, 77 L.Ed.2d 1402 (1983), aff'g Consumers Union v. FTC, 691 F.2d

alternatives to the veto have become more popular. One of these alternatives is sunset legislation.[4] Another is the use of joint resolutions either to disapprove agency actions or to conditionally approve them in advance. Similarly, Congress can order agencies to "report and wait" before implementing new regulations, giving Congress a chance to intervene with legislation, if need be. Given the demise of the legislative veto, the political, statutory and structured controls discussed above now take on even greater significance.

In 1996 a new chapter was added to Title 5 of the U.S. Code, and like the RFA and the Paperwork Reduction Act of 1980, Chapter 8 directly affects agency procedures.[5] The title of the chapter is *Congressional Review of Agency Rulemaking*. For purposes of the Chapter, a rule is defined the same as it is in § 551(4) of the APA, with a number of exceptions. Most notable among the exceptions are "internal" rules—i.e., rules that don't substantially affect non-agency parties—and rules that concern monetary policy, promulgated by the Federal Reserve or the Federal Open Market Committee.[6] Although the definition of the "rule" is broad, the focus of the legislation is aimed at "major rules". A major rule is defined as one having a significant impact on the economy, particularly one whose annual economic effect is likely to be more than $100 million.

Under the statute, agencies are required to submit to both Houses of Congress and the comptroller General, a report containing information that can be used to evaluate the proposed rule. This report includes: a cost-benefit analysis of the rule, if any, a regulatory flexibility analysis, and an analysis pursuant to the Unfunded Mandates Reform Act of 1995.[7] After submission of the report, a non-major rule can take effect "as otherwise provided by law"—i.e., the only delay is in providing the report.[8] It should be noted however, that the statute does provide for a congressional disapproval procedure, manifest in the form of a joint resolution, and this could invalidate a rule that had previously become effective.[9] The President does have the power to veto the joint resolution, with Congress having the opportunity to override the veto.[10] When a report for a major rule is submitted, Congress has up to sixty calendar days to submit a joint resolution, with allowances for days not in session. Moreover, if the report is submitted with less than sixty session days remaining in the Senate (legislative days in the House), the review can carry into the next session of Congress.

575 (D.C.Cir.1982) (two-house veto of FTC rules held unconstitutional); Process Gas Consumers Group v. Consumer Energy Council of America, 463 U.S. 1216, 103 S.Ct. 3556, 77 L.Ed.2d 1402 (1983), aff'd Consumer Energy Council of America v. FERC, 673 F.2d 425 (D.C.Cir.1982) (agency rules veto struck down). For a discussion of the *Chadha* decision, see Strauss, Was There a Baby in the Bathwater? A Comment on the Supreme Court's Legislative Veto Decision, 1983 Duke L.J. 789 (1983).

4. See Behn, The False Dawn of the Sunset Laws, 49 The Public Interest 103 (1977).

5. 5 U.S.C. §§ 801–808.

6. 5 U.S.C. § 807.

7. 5 U.S.C. § 801(a)(1)(B).

8. 5 U.S.C. § 801(a)(4).

9. 5 U.S.C. § 802.

10. 5 U.S.C. § 801(a)(3)(B).

One of the most obvious benefits of the statute is to make Congress more accountable for some of the actions undertaken by agencies. Whether this benefit will be outweighed by the increased administrative burden, remains subject to debate.[11]

11. See Daniel E. Troy, New Congressional Review Procedures of Agency Rules, 21–SUM Admin. & Reg. L. New 4 (1996) (noting that the increased congressional accountability may justify the additional administrative burden); but see Daniel Cohen and Peter L. Strauss, Congressional Review of Agency Regulations, 49 Admin. L.Rev. 95 (1997) (concluding that agencies may take steps to limit their exposure to the congressional review process, which would cause a reduction in agency transparency and accessibility; the overall effect of the review process being increased costs with very little benefit gained).

Part Five

INFORMATION

Agencies need information to carry out their regulatory goals. They often obtain it from those they regulate. Some information is submitted voluntarily by regulated entities seeking governmental approvals of one sort or another. Other information may be obtained through the use of agency subpoenas in the context, for example, of agency enforcement proceedings. Still other kinds of information may result from statutorily mandated reporting requirements. The amount of information that the government can and does collect is vast. Particularly in the computerized age in which we live, privacy concerns now are even more serious. Moreover, there is the persistent question of whether information collected by one governmental agency for one purpose can then be transferred to another agency for a very different regulatory purpose. In addition, there is the concern that without citizen access to the information government has obtained, as well as openness in its decisionmaking processes, we may never be entirely sure that the government itself is acting properly. Inevitably, tensions arise between citizens' desire to know and various substantive regulatory contexts that arguably require a high degree of confidentiality. Increasingly, however, information obtained and held by the private sector also raises privacy questions.

Part Five examines the law that has developed to deal with these and other important information-related issues. To this end, chapters 17 and 18 focus on the Freedom of Information Act and the Privacy Act. Chapter 19 deals with the Government in the Sunshine Act and chapter 20 explores the legal issues that arise as the government seeks to acquire information from its citizens. These chapters essentially focus on four broad questions: (1) What rights do we as citizens have to information collected and retained by various governmental agencies? (2) What right does the government have to obtain information from its citizens? (3) How open to the public must governmental decisionmaking processes be? In addition, (4) to what extent does the use of technology by the private sector, enabling it to buy and sell information involving individuals, raise new privacy concerns?

Chapter 17

CITIZENS' ACCESS TO GOVERNMENTALLY HELD INFORMATION

Table of Sections

---

§ 17.1 OVERVIEW—OPEN GOVERNMENT

In the late 1960's and throughout the 1970's, Congress passed a number of Acts aimed at increasing the openness with which agencies carried out their regulatory responsibilities. The most important of these was the Freedom of Information Act (FOIA), passed in 1966.[1] It, and its subsequent amendments,[2] establish a liberal disclosure policy regarding public access to information obtained, generated and held by the government. "Any person" is entitled to request and receive identifiable records held by an agency, unless the records in question fall within one of the Act's nine exemptions.[3] Disclosure is the norm. A requester's motives or her relation to the information she seeks to acquire are irrelevant.[4] An agency's refusal to disclose requested information is subject to *de novo* judicial review and the government has the burden of proving that the information it seeks to withhold is, in fact, exempt from disclosure.[5]

In 1972, Congress passed the Federal Advisory Committee Act (FACA)[6] designed to ensure greater openness with regard to the various boards of experts and advisors which agencies sometimes rely upon for advice. FACA attempts to ensure that the use of such private advisory bodies does not result in private solutions for public matters. Thus, the Act provides, among other things, that advisory board meetings be noticed and take place in public. It also attempts to ensure that there be a wide cross-section of interests represented on the Board.

FACA was the forerunner of the Government in the Sunshine Act passed by Congress in 1976.[7] Just as the Freedom of Information Act established a norm of disclosure for agency records and files, the Sunshine Act established a norm of openness for agency deliberations. The Act requires that most meetings of multimember commissions be noticed in advance and held in public. The title of the Act is derived from a statement by Justice Brandeis and it reflects its basic premises: "Publicity is justly commended as a remedy for social and industrial diseases. Sunlight is said to be the best of disinfectants; electric light the most efficient policeman."[8]

Congress passed the Federal Privacy Act[9] in 1974. Unlike FOIA, FACA and the Sunshine Act, the Privacy Act is more directly concerned with individuals. The basic premise of the Act is that the federal government's ability to use sophisticated information technology, such as computer data banks, greatly magnifies the potential for the harm that can result to individual privacy interests. The Act relies on openness to

§ 17.1

1. Pub.L. No. 89–487, 80 Stat. 250 (1966) (codified as amended at 5 U.S.C.A. § 552).

2. The Act was amended significantly in 1974, Pub.L. No. 93–502, 88 Stat. 1561; in 1976, Pub.L. No. 94–409, 90 Stat. 1241; in 1986, Pub.L. No. 99–570, 100 Stat. 3207 (1986); and in 1996, Pub L No. 104–231, 110 Stat. 3049. See sec. 17.2.1 infra.

3. 5 U.S.C.A. § 552(a)(3). For a detailed discussion of the current Act and its exemptions, see sections 17.4–17.4.9 infra.

4. 5 U.S.C.A. § 552(a)(4)(B).

5. Id.

6. Pub.L. No. 92–463, 5 U.S.C.A.App. I. For a discussion of that Act, see Public Citizen v. U.S. Dept. of Justice, 491 U.S. 440, 109 S.Ct. 2558, 105 L.Ed.2d 377 (1989).

7. Pub.L. No. 94–409, 390 Stat. 1241 (1976) (codified as amended at 5 U.S.C.A. § 552(b)).

8. Louis Brandeis, *What Publicity Can Do*, Harper's Weekly at 10 (Dec. 20, 1913).

9. Pub.L. No. 93–579, 88 Stat. 1896 (1974) (codified as amended at 5 U.S.C.A. § 552(a)).

ameliorate this potential harm. It enables individuals to determine what records pertaining to them are being collected, maintained and used by federal agencies. It seeks to prevent the use of records obtained for one purpose to then be used for an entirely different purpose, without individual consent. And it also seeks to enable individuals to gain access to information pertaining to them and to correct or amend those records if they are wrong.[10]

The remainder of this part will examine the FOIA, Privacy and Government in the Sunshine Acts in detail. The common assumption underlying all of this legislation is that open government leads to better government. Open government is in accord with our basic principles of democracy and the need for citizens to know how their government, in fact, functions. This enables the citizenry to make proper evaluations of the wisdom of governmental uses of power. It also, however, is in accord with a healthy sense of distrust of governmental power as well and the need to control agency discretion to ensure that the law is administered properly. In this sense, open government and the publicity that goes along with it provides not only valuable information but a means of effectively constraining government and thus protecting citizens from any potential abuses of governmental power that may exist. Of course, as we shall now see, there are other important interests at stake that often militate in favor of governmental confidentiality, such as when national security interests or the trade secrets of a corporation are at stake. Most of the above statutes thus provide for a number of exemptions to their basic goals of openness and disclosure. Balancing these various policy interests and goals has given rise to a good deal of litigation and case law, especially under the Freedom of Information Act.

§ 17.2 THE 1966 FREEDOM OF INFORMATION ACT—BACKGROUND

In 1953, Harold L. Cross published *The People's Right to Know*.[1] It was a response to a study undertaken for the American Society of Newspaper Editors. It argued that regulators at federal, state and local levels hid the facts of government and set forth the laws which appeared to authorize such secrecy.[2] Cross' exposé spurred a series of Congressional investigative hearings on agency operations, revealing a pattern of routine bureaucratic secrecy concerning matters directly affecting the public. Members of Congress decried the "paper curtain" then shrouding Washington.[3] The political process of creating the necessary consciousness to change this state of affairs thus began.

10. 5 U.S.C.A. § 552(a).

§ 17.2

1. H. Cross, The People's Right to Know (1953).

2. Id. at 1–13.

3. There was a growing perception of a prevailing "it's none of your damned business" attitude among the federal agencies. Some members even claimed that the Pentagon had classified the fact that water runs downhill. H.R.Rep. No. 86–2084, at 81–83 (1960).

In 1958, Congress amended an ancient "housekeeping law," by which the first Congress had given department heads broad authority to establish rules to protect the property and papers of their departments,[4] and under which modern agencies claimed authority to withhold files from the public. The one-sentence amendment simply read: "This section does not authorize withholding information from the public or limiting the availability of records to the public."[5]

This change was not effective. Federal agencies resorted to section 3 of the 1946 Administrative Procedure Act (APA) to justify nondisclosure. The "Public Information" provision of that Act stated that all public records were open for inspection unless they were held to be confidential "for good cause." Agencies became adept at finding "good cause" for withholding information; moreover, section 3 limited access to "persons properly and directly concerned" with the subject matter sought.[6]

Repeated efforts to pass a comprehensive information reform bill finally resulted in the Freedom of Information Act, which amended section 3 of the APA in 1967.[7] The 1966 Freedom of Information Act declared that "any person" could request government information. The new section 552 replaced the previous section's three vague qualifiers with nine specific categories of exemptible information, and it created a judicial remedy if the agency improperly withheld information. When a dispute arose over the appropriateness of a request seeking information from an agency, the Act guaranteed a right of *de novo* judicial review in the Federal District Courts.[8] Despite his personal opposition to the Act, President Lyndon Johnson signed the bill into law "with a deep sense of pride that the United States is an open society in which the people's right to know is cherished and guarded."[9]

In reality, President Johnson had little to fear from the new bill. It was, as one commentator noted, a "weak and complicated law, weakened

4. That law read: "The head of each department is authorized to prescribe regulations, not inconsistent with law for the government of his department, the conduct of its officers and clerks, the distribution and performance of its business, and the custody, use, and preservation of the records, papers, and property appertaining to it." Rev. Stat. 161 (1875) (codified as amended at 5 U.S.C.A. § 301 (1994)).

5. Pub.L. No. 85–619, 72 Stat. 547 (1958).

6. Pub.L. No. 79–404, § 3, 60 Stat. 238 (1946). The Republican Policy Committee noted in 1966 that "requirements for disclosure in the present law [APA § 3] are so hedged with restrictions that it has been cited as the statutory authority for 24 separate classifications devised by Federal agencies to keep administrative information from public view." 112 Cong.Rec. 10,950 (1966) (statement of Rep.Rhodes).

7. Pub.L. No. 90–23, 81 Stat. 54 (1967).

8. "Upon complaint, the district court of the United States in the district in which the complainant resides, or has his principal place of business, or in which the agency records are situated shall have jurisdiction to enjoin the agency from the withholding of agency records and to order the production of any agency records and to order the production of any agency records improperly withheld from the complainant. In such cases the court shall determine the matter de novo and the burden shall be upon the agency to sustain its action." Pub.L. No. 89–487, 80 Stat. 250 (1966).

9. Subcomm. on Administrative Practice and Procedure of the Sen. Comm. on the Judiciary, 93rd Congress, Freedom of Information Act Source Book: Legislative Materials, Cases, Articles 1 (Comm. Print 1974).

further by the Justice Department's emasculation of the House report . . . [and] further weakened by the [Justice Department's] memorandum explaining the statute and weakened even further by agency regulations implementing it."[10] As part of the political bargain to secure passage of the Act, the Justice Department was permitted to draft portions of the House report. Later, upon resort to the legislative history of the Act, reviewing courts were faced with a choice between the Senate report, which favored disclosure, and a much more restrictive House report.[11] The Justice Department's memorandum interpreting the Act[12] "reflect[ed] the point of view of the agencies, all of whom opposed the enactment."[13]

Because of the confusion over the meaning of the 1966 Act, its reluctant implementation by the federal regulatory agencies and the Department of Justice, as well as the staying power of "the old secrecy culture, bred by experience during the recent world conflict and by Cold War fear,"[14] the Act achieved few of the results its sponsors envisioned. The original FOIA has since been described as "a relatively toothless beast, sometimes kicked about shamelessly by the agencies."[15]

The federal judiciary decreed that disclosure was to be "the guiding star . . . in construing the Act."[16] Where Congress was silent as to the means of implementing and monitoring agency disclosure, the courts fashioned practical procedures to fill the gaps. There were several examples of judicial attempts to deal with the inadequacies of the 1966 Act, prior to Congressional amendments in 1974.

In *Vaughn v. Rosen*,[17] for example, the D.C.Circuit established a document indexing requirement which remains the norm in FOIA litigation today. In *Vaughn*, a law professor sought FOIA disclosure of certain Civil Service Commission (CSC) reports. The CSC denied the request, and alluded to three different FOIA exemptions in a conclusory affidavit justifying nondisclosure. The Court ruled that the conclusory affidavits

10. See Archibald, The FOIA Revisited, 39 Pub.Admin.Rev. 311, 315 (1979).

11. See Davis, The Information Act: A Preliminary Analysis, 34 U.Chi.L.Rev. 761, 762–63 (1967). According to Professor Davis, all pre–1976 judicial opinions that rest upon the House Report may now be unreliable authorities since nearly all FOIA interpretations utilize legislative history. 1 Kenneth Culp Davis, Administrative Law Treatise 314, (2d ed. 1978) [hereinafter Davis, Treatise].

12. U.S. Dept. of Justice Attorney General's Memorandum on the Public Information Section of the APA (Washington: U.S. Gov't. Printing Office, 1967).

13. Davis, Treatise, supra note 21, at 68. Professor Davis has deplored the abuse of the 1966 Act's rigged legislative history. His 1971 analysis of FOIA was very critical: "Congress wound up with a rather shabby product," due largely to inattention and indifference. "Congress has not only legislated badly but has taken pains to prevent the courts from correcting its ineptitudes." Id. at 85. He concluded that Congress was ill-equipped to oversee the Act, and recommended instead centralized administrative oversight.

14. Relyea, Introduction: The FOIA a Decade Later, 39 Pub.Admin.Rev. 310 (1979).

15. Scalia, The FOIA Has No Clothes, Regulation, March/April 1982, at 15.

16. Consumers Union v. Veterans Administration, 301 F.Supp. 796, 800 (S.D.N.Y.1969), dismissed 436 F.2d 1363 (2d Cir.1971).

17. 484 F.2d 820 (D.C.Cir.1973), cert. denied, 415 U.S. 977, 94 S.Ct. 1564, 39 L.Ed.2d 873 (1974).

failed to demonstrate the relevance of a claimed exemption. Faced with the prospect of painstakingly reviewing the requested documents themselves, the *Vaughn* court noted that while "[s]uch an investment of judicial energy might be justified to determine some issues ... [t]he burden [of document review] has been placed specifically by statute on the Government."[18] The Court therefore remanded the case to the court below, ordering the agency to provide a detailed justification of its decision to withhold a document.[19] In essence, the Court required the agency to "subdivide the document[s] under consideration into manageable parts cross-referenced to the relevant portion of the Government's justification."[20] Out of "[r]espect for the enormous document-generating capacity of government agencies," the *Vaughn* court also gave the trial court discretion to designate a special master to examine documents and evaluate an agency's contention of exemption.[21]

These elaborate indexing requirements facilitated both *in camera* and appellate review, making it more difficult for agencies to justify nondisclosure. Because most FOIA disputes are resolved upon motions for summary judgment,[22] *Vaughn* indices are often prepared by agencies as a necessary part of FOIA litigation.[23]

Likewise, the judiciary first imposed the requirement that agencies release segregable nonexempt portions of documents that were partially exempt under FOIA.[24] Although this procedure often results in the requester's receiving documents that have been partially blacked-out, it is in keeping with FOIA's presumption favoring disclosure. As with the *Vaughn* indexing requirement, agencies found it more difficult to justify wholesale nondisclosure.[25]

18. 484 F.2d at 825.

19. Id. at 826.

20. Id. at 827.

21. Id. at 828.

22. See generally Windels, Marx, Davies & Ives v. Dep't of Commerce, 576 F.Supp. 405, 406–11 (D.D.C.1983). See also the sample *Vaughn* motion and memo in American Civil Liberties Union, Litigation Under the Federal Freedom of Information Act, app. F at A–110–12 (Allan Robert Adler ed., 15th ed. 1990).

23. *Vaughn* indices are discussed further at sec. 17.3.4 infra.

24. EPA v. Mink, 410 U.S. 73, 91, 93 S.Ct. 827, 837, 35 L.Ed.2d 119 (1973), superseded by statute as stated in Halpern v. FBI, 181 F.3d 279 (2d Cir.1999). Congress adopted the requirement as an express part of the statute in the 1974 amendment to FOIA. Pub.L. No. 93–502, 88 Stat. 1561 (codified at 5 U.S.C.A. § 552(b)).

25. Such attention to detail is not without its price. To ensure that legitimately exempt materials are not released, agency personnel familiar with the matter—i.e., active agency personnel pulled from the field, as opposed to supplementary or clerical employees—must themselves review and redact the pertinent documents. There are rare exceptions to this requirement. For example, the Central Intelligence Agency Information Act of 1984 § 2(a), 50 U.S.C. § 431 (1998), "provides a blanket exemption from FOIA requirements for most CIA operational files in order 'to relieve the Central Intelligence Agency from an unproductive [FOIA] requirement to search and review certain CIA operational files.' No counterpart statute providing for such a broad exemption from disclosure exists for other agencies." McNamera v. United States Dep't of Justice, 974 F.Supp. 946, 954 (W.D.Tex.1997) (citations omitted). See also Lisa A. Krupicka & Mary E. LaFrance, Note, Developments Under the Freedom of Information Act—1984, 1985 Duke L.J. 742 (1985).

The original Act's shortcomings were apparent in two other decisions: *Frankel v. Securities and Exchange Commission*[26] and *Environmental Protection Agency v. Mink*.[27] In *Frankel,* plaintiffs instituted a FOIA suit to compel the SEC to release a report on a nonpublic investigation of the Occidental Petroleum Corporation. Plaintiffs were Occidental shareholders contemplating a suit against the corporation's directors for securities laws violations. The SEC denied the request, claiming an exemption under the investigatory files section[28] of FOIA. Despite the fact that the investigation had ended, the Court ruled that the then-existing investigatory files exemption was broad enough to protect the report from disclosure; if an agency's investigatory files were obtainable without limitation after the investigation was concluded, future law enforcement efforts by the agency could be seriously hindered.[29]

EPA v. Mink highlighted another apparent weakness in the original Act. Congresswoman Mink and thirty-two other Representatives filed a FOIA request with the Environmental Protection Agency, seeking release of recommendations made to President Nixon regarding the advisability of underground nuclear testing scheduled to take place in Amchitka Island, Alaska. The EPA contended that the documents had been classified Top Secret or Secret pursuant to an Executive Order,[30] and were therefore exempt from disclosure under section 552(b)(1), the national security exemption. The Court upheld the EPA's claim, ruling that the documents' top secret classification pursuant to an Executive Order, made them *per se* nondisclosable,[31] and that *de novo* review was ended upon resolution of the classification issue. Exemption (b)(1) did not authorize *in camera* inspection of classified documents "at the insistence of any objecting citizen." Rather, "Congress chose to follow the Executive's determination in these matters and that choice must be honored."[32]

Justice Douglas vigorously dissented, noting that "[t]he Executive Branch now has *carte blanche* to insulate information from public scrutiny whether or not that information bears any discernible relation to the interests sought to be protected by subsection (b)(1) of the Act."[33] Even Justice Stewart's concurring opinion was admonitory:

One would suppose that a nuclear test that engendered fierce controversy within the Executive Branch . . . would be precisely the kind of event that should be opened to the fullest possible disclosure consis-

26. 460 F.2d 813 (2d Cir.1972), cert. denied 409 U.S. 889, 93 S.Ct. 125, 34 L.Ed.2d 146 (1972).

27. 410 U.S. 73, 93 S.Ct. 827, 35 L.Ed.2d 119 (1973), superseded by statute as stated in Halpern v. FBI, 181 F.3d 279 (2d Cir.1999).

28. The 1966 version of § 552(b)(7) exempted "investigatory files compiled for law enforcement purposes except to the extent available by law to a party other than an agency."

29. 460 F.2d at 817.

30. 410 U.S. at 81, 93 S.Ct. at 833. (See generally Exec. Order No. 10,501 3 C.F.R. Pt. 979 (1953)).

31. 410 U.S. at 82–83, 93 S.Ct. at 834.

32. Id. at 81, 93 S.Ct. at 833.

33. Id. at 110, 93 S.Ct. at 847.

tent with legitimate interests of national defense.... But in enacting § 552(b)(1), Congress chose, instead, to decree blind acceptance of Executive fiat.[34]

The Court's opinion in *Mink* became an important factor militating in favor of FOIA reform in 1974.

§ 17.2.1 The 1974 Amendments to FOIA

Following a 1972 Library of Congress study of the administration of the FOIA,[35] investigative subcommittees in the House and the Senate held extensive hearings. Congress then proposed a series of amendments that unequivocally and specifically mandated agency disclosure.[36] The amendments were debated and finalized amid the governmental furor over the Watergate investigations, and were in conference committee when President Nixon resigned from the presidency.[37] Executive obstinacy and resistance to the proposals left the agencies' viewpoints underrepresented in the traditional legislative process, and the FOIA reform bill passed both Houses.[38]

The 1974 amendments added specific language and conditions to the original FOIA, in order to curtail opportunities for "discretionary" nondisclosure. Exorbitant search and copying costs were outlawed, and replaced by uniform fee schedules charging only *direct* costs, with provisions for waiver of the fee if the information sought "benefits the general public." The Act's pro-disclosure attitude was reaffirmed by provisions for the award of attorney's fees to requesting plaintiffs who substantially prevail. The amended Act also authorized disciplinary legal action against any official found to have "arbitrarily and capriciously"

34. Id. at 94–95, 93 S.Ct. at 839–40.

35. Archibald, supra note 20, at 316; see also 118 Cong.Rec. 9949 (March 21, 1972).

36. Ferguson, FOIA: A Time for Change?, 1983 Det.C.L.Rev. 171, 182–83. While there is little doubt that the 1966 FOIA needed revisions, one commentator has suggested that the reforms Congress proposed did not necessarily represent a careful balancing of the conflicting and complex considerations involved:

> The "74 amendments ... can in fact only be understood as the product of the extraordinary era that produced them—when 'public interest law,' 'consumerism,' and 'investigative journalism' were at their zenith, public trust in the government at its nadir, and the executive branch and Congress functioning more like two separate governments than two branches of the same."

Scalia, supra note 25, at 15.

37. Archibald, supra note 20, at 316.

38. See 1974 FOIA Source Book, supra note 19, at 366, 396–397 (1974). It was ironic that, "barely two months after taking office as a result of the Watergate coverup, [an unelected] President Ford felt he had to veto a bill that proclaimed 'Freedom of Information' in its title." Scalia, supra note 25, at 16. See also, Public Papers of the Presidents: Gerald R. Ford—1974 at 374–376; 1974 FOIA Source Book, supra note 19, at 481. President Ford vetoed the FOIA amendment out of three concerns: the need for *in camera* review of classified documents, the need for flexibility with respect to investigatory files, and the need for flexibility with regard to the 10 day determination period. FOIA Source Book at 484–85. A further indication of the nation's mood was the ease with which President Ford's veto was overridden. The House vote was 371–31, with 32 not voting. The Senate vote was 65–27, with 8 not voting. The executive bureaucracy had abused the people's trust. With the 1974 amendments, a piqued Congress made FOIA a significant disclosure statute. See 1974 FOIA Source Book supra note 19, at 403–480, for public and congressional reactions to President Ford's veto.

withheld requested records. The Amendment effectively overruled *Mink* by requiring that information withheld under Exemption 1 be "properly" classified under criteria established by an Executive Order in the interest of national defense or foreign policy, thus inviting *in camera* review by the courts and less deference to the Executive. *Frankel* was likewise overruled by restricting the scope of Exemption (b)(7)[39] to one of six specific investigatory law enforcement concerns.

As in the original Act, the *agency* bore the burden of proof for non-disclosure. The Amendment also added provisions mandating the release of "reasonably segregable portions" of properly exempt documents and requiring each agency to submit annual FOIA compliance reports to Congress. The Attorney General was to file an annual report cataloging FOIA cases and Department of Justice efforts to encourage agencies' adherence to FOIA.[40]

The 1974 amendments gave practicable and enforceable life to the 1966 FOIA mandate, making it much more difficult for the agencies to avoid their legal duty to search and disclose. In particular, the strict time limits for agency responses to requests and the narrowing of the withholding exemptions encouraged agency compliance and disclosure.[41] The 1996 Amendments to FOIA change some of these provisions. We shall examine them in detail in § 17.2.3.

§ 17.2.2 The 1976 and 1986 Amendments

The 1976 amendments to FOIA were enacted as a rider to the Sunshine Act,[42] in large part, as a response to the Supreme Court's decision in *Administrator, Federal Aviation Administration v. Robert-*

39. For text of 5 U.S.C.A. § 552(b)(7), see sec. 17.4.7, infra.

40. See generally, 5 U.S.C.A. § 552, Explanatory Notes (1990).

41. But increased agency compliance to FOIA demands has also served to highlight unforeseen costs, uses, and side-effects of the Act's ambitious goals.

A 1974 House Report found that "potential costs directly attributable to [the 1974 FOIA Amendments] should, for the most part, be absorbed within the operating budgets of the agencies ... with existing staff, so that significant amounts of additional funds will not be required." See House Comm. on Gov't Operations, Amending FOIA, H.R.Rep. No. 876, 93d Cong., 2d Sess. 9 (1974), reprinted in FOIA Source Book, supra note 19, at 129. The committee also estimated that "additional costs that may be required by this legislation should not exceed $50,000 in fiscal year 1974 and $100,000 for each of the succeeding five fiscal years." Id. at 130. Disparate and incomplete agency FOIA accounting methods make actual cost assessments nearly impossible, but the Committee's estimates seem to have been unrealistically low. The Department of Justice estimated 1980 FOIA costs to the agencies to be "at least $57 million ... of which only 3% or 4% was recovered from requesters." See FOIA: Hearings on S. 587, S. 1235, S. 1247, S. 1730, and S. 1751 Before the Subcomm. on the Constitution of the Senate Comm. on the Judiciary, 97th Cong., 1st Sess. 662 (1981) (U.S.G.P.O.1982) (materials submitted by Attorney General). A single request for CIA documents cost the public some $400,000 to process. Id. at 663. The Office of Management and Budget estimated 1980 FOIA costs at $250 million. O'Reilly, Who's on First?, 10 J.Leg. 95, 103 n. 61 (1983). But cf. FOIA: Hearings on S. 587, S. 1235, S. 1247, S. 1730, and S. 1751, supra, at 785–787 (statement of Jack Landau) (responding that 1980 FOI costs were less than 5% of the more than $1 billion which the government spends annually on public affairs offices, parades, and "propaganda").

42. 5 U.S.C.A. § 552(b). For a discussion of the Sunshine Act, see chap. 19, infra.

son.[43] In 1970 the Center for the Study of Responsive Law requested that the FAA make available certain analyses concerning the operation and maintenance performance of commercial airlines, so-called SWAP reports.[44] At the urging of the airlines, the FAA refused the request, claiming that the documents were protected from disclosure by then-FOIA Section 552(b)(3), covering matters that were "specifically exempt from disclosure by statute." The statute cited by the FAA was its own charter, section 1104 of the Federal Aviation Act of 1958. Section 1104 authorizes the FAA, upon receipt of a written objection to disclosure, to order such information withheld when, in the FAA's judgment, disclosure would adversely affect the interests of the objecting party and is not required in the interest of the public. The FAA reasoned that "non-public submissions ... encourage a spirit of openness on the part of airline management which is vital to the promotion of aviation safety—the paramount consideration of airlines and government alike in this area."[45]

The Supreme Court reversed the D.C. Circuit, which had viewed the FOIA as intending to eliminate broad discretionary authority and thus denied the documents Exemption 3 status. The Supreme Court declared that the reports were indeed exempt from disclosure, noting that Exemption 3 contained no built-in standard, and that the FOIA's legislative history showed that Congress did not intend to modify the numerous statutes "which restrict public access to specific Government records."[46] The Court refused to read the FOIA as repealing by implication all existing statutes[47] and thus affirmed the FAA's withholding authority.

The 1976 amendment sought to resolve the issue by narrowing Exemption 3 to cover matters:

> specifically exempted from disclosure by statute (other than section 552(b) of this title), provided that such statute (A) requires that the matters be withheld from the public in such a manner as to leave no discretion on the issue, or (B) establishes particular criteria for withholding or refers to particular types of matters to be withheld.[48]

The Amendment has been effective against overly-broad discretionary withholding, but in some areas, conflicting statutes continue to override FOIA's goal of across-the-board disclosure. Such statutorily-authorized categorical exemptions, by which Congress predetermines that certain types of information should not be subject to FOIA review or disclosure, have enabled the government to restrict, albeit indirectly, the dissemination of information without violating the letter of FOIA.[49]

43. 422 U.S. 255, 95 S.Ct. 2140, 45 L.Ed.2d 164 (1975), superseded by statute as stated in Public Citizen, Inc. v. F.A.A., 988 F.2d 186 (D.C.Cir.1993).

44. Id. at 257, 95 S.Ct. at 2143.

45. Id. at 259, 95 S.Ct. at 2144.

46. Id at 265, 95 S.Ct. at 2147.

47. Id at 266, 95 S.Ct. at 2147–48.

48. 5 U.S.C.A. § 552(b)(3) (the reference to section 552(b) is to the Government in the Sunshine Act).

49. See, e.g., The Intelligence Authorization Act for Fiscal Year 2000, Pub. L. No. 106–120, 113 Stat. 1606, which exempts from FOIA the activities, records, and proceedings of the National Commission for the Review of the National Reconnaissance

Congress held hearings on proposed FOIA reforms in 1981, but failed to reach a consensus.[50] After further hearings in the spring of 1983,[51] Senate Bill 774 passed the Senate by voice vote after minimal debate.[52] But a similar measure was buried in the House Government Operations Subcommittee. In 1986, however, Congress again amended FOIA. The FOIA Reform Act became law on October 27, 1986 as part of the Anti–Drug Abuse Act of 1986.[53] It broadened Exemption 7 (law enforcement information), added new law enforcement record exclusions, and created a new fee and fee waiver structure.[54]

Political and Congressional attitudes have moved away from the "disclosure at any cost" mindset which prevailed a decade ago.[55] Congress has also enacted other minor laws—one exempting many CIA files from FOIA request,[56] another ending the expedited treatment of FOIA cases on the federal docket[57] another exempting from FOIA requests certain meat packers' reports to the Department of Agriculture[58] and still another expediting the processing of FOIA requests for Nazi war criminal records[59]—that exemplify Congress' willingness to at least tinker with FOIA.

§ 17.2.3 The 1996 Amendments

The 1996 amendments to the Freedom of Information Act (FOIA)[60] require agencies to disseminate government information by the Internet or by other electronic means. Congress intended the amendments to decrease the number of agency backlogs of FOIA requests.[61] Prior to

Office (the NRO designs, builds, and operates spy satellites for the CIA and Department of Defense).

50. In July, 1981, the Senate Subcommittee on the Constitution held extensive hearings on a number of FOIA reform bills. See Freedom of Information Act: Hearings on S. 587, S. 1235, S. 1247, S. 1730, and S. 1751 Before the Subcomm. on the Constitution of the Senate Comm. on the Judiciary, 97th Cong., 1st Sess. (1981) (two volumes). Presiding over the hearings was Sen. Orrin G. Hatch of Utah, who declared that "since the enthusiastic rewrite of the [A]ct in 1974, it has at times frustrated rather than fulfilled its basic mission of insuring Government efficiency and informing voters." Id. at 2. The resultant bill proposed to extend time limits for agency compliance, broaden the withholding exemptions, and restructure the fee system. The bill was reported, but never made it to the floor.

51. See The FOIA Reform Act: Hearings on S. 774 Before the Subcomm. on the Constitution of the Senate Comm. on the Judiciary, 98th Cong., 1st Sess. (1983).

52. 1984 Cong.Q.Weekly Rep. 511 (March 3, 1984).

53. Pub.L. No. 99–570, 100 Stat. 3207 (1986).

54. 5 U.S.C.A. § 552(b)(7), (c) and (a)(4)(A). These changes are dealt with in detail in sections 17.3.5 and 17.3.7, infra.

55. See generally, Scalia, supra note 25.

56. Central Intelligence Agency Information Act, Pub.L. No. 98–447, 98 Stat. 2209 (Oct. 15, 1984).

57. See Pub.L. No. 98–620, Title IV, Federal Courts Improvements, §§ 401, 402(2), 98 Stat. 3356–57, (Nov. 11, 1984), reprinted in 2 U.S.C.C.A.N. 3356 (1984) (replacing various "expedited treatment" statutes with each courts' authority over its own docket. Expedited treatment is to be granted in the discretion of the court upon a factual showing of "good cause.").

58. Livestock Mandatory Reporting Act of 1999, H.R. 1906, 106th Cong.

59. Nazi War Crimes Disclosure Act, S. 1379, 105th Cong. § 4(a) (1998).

60. Electronic Freedom of Information Act Amendments of 1996, Pub. L. No. 104–231, 110 Stat. 3048 (codified at 5 U.S.C.A. § 552 (Supp. 2000)).

61. H.R. Rep. No. 104–795, at 11, 13–14 (1996), *reprinted in* 1996 U.S.C.C.A.N. 3448, 3454, 3456–57; Statement by Presi-

passing the 1996 amendments, Congress recognized that to decrease the backlog of FOIA requests it would have to resolve certain legal conflicts created by computer technology. Whether FOIA extended to electronic records was foremost among these conflicts.[62] For years, the U.S. Attorney

General had said that FOIA applied to electronic records,[63] but it was not certain how many agency heads shared this opinion.[64] Although the conflicts created by FOIA's purported relationship to electronic media were generally hypothetical,[65] Congress had to resolve these conflicts if "Electronic FOIA" (E–FOIA) were to succeed.

The roots of these legal conflicts extend fifty years back to when the federal government first embarked upon transforming itself from a paper bureaucracy to an electronic bureaucracy. In 1955, when Congress started to debate public access to government information, the federal government owned only forty-five computers.[66] By the early 1990s, it was not uncommon for an agency's personal computers to outnumber its employees,[67] and by the mid–1990s, more than 800 Federal sites had been established on the World Wide Web.[68] The transformation of the federal government from a paper bureaucracy to an electronic bureaucracy received help from the Paperwork Reduction Act of 1980,[69] the purpose of which was "to ensure that automatic data processing and telecommunications technology [were] acquired and used by the Federal Government [to reduce] the information processing burden for the Federal Government. . . ."[70]

dent William J. Clinton Upon Signing H.R. 3802, Pub. Papers 1743 (Oct. 12, 1996). The Federal Bureau of Investigation, for example, faced a four-year backlog of FOIA requests in 1996. H.R. Rep. No. 104–795, at 11 (1996), *reprinted in* 1996 U.S.C.C.A.N. 3448, 3454.

62. Other conflicts included whether the additional computer programming required to retrieve certain electronic documents was itself a record under FOIA, what constituted a "reasonable effort" on the part of the agency searching for electronic records, and when access to electronic records should be guaranteed. Office of Technology Assessment, Informing the Nation 207 (1988).

63. *"The Electronic Freedom of Information Improvement Act," Hearing Before the Subcomm. on Technology and the Law of the Senate Comm. on the Judiciary on S. 1940*, 102nd Cong. 11 n.1 (1992) (hereinafter *Hearing on S. 1940*) (statement of Steven R. Schlesinger, deputy director, Office of Policy and Communications, DOJ).

64. One DOJ survey revealed that more than two-thirds of 83 department and agency heads did not believe that agency software was a record under FOIA, 76% did not believe that FOIA required them to create new computer programs to search electronic records, and nearly 59% did not believe that FOIA required them to provide a record in electronic format if the record already existed in another format. DOJ, DOJ Report on "Electronic Records" Issues Under the Freedom of Information Act 5–6 (1990), *reprinted in Hearing on S.1940, supra* note 73, at 36–37 (1992).

65. Only a fraction of any agency's FOIA requests had, by that time, implicated electronic records. *Hearing on S.1940, supra* note 73, at 92 (testimony of Daniel Metcalf, co-director, Office of Information and Privacy, DOJ).

66. H. Rep. No. 104–795, at 11 (1996), *reprinted in* 1996 U.S.C.C.A.N. 3448, 3454.

67. In 1995, the General Services Administration reported that it had more than 16,000 employees—and more than 19,000 personal computers. S. Rep. No. 104–272, at 8 (1996).

68. *Id.*

69. Pub. L. No. 96–511, 109 Stat. 163 (1980).

70. *Id.*

The U.S. Patent and Trademark Office (PTO) was one of the first agencies to exploit computer technology pursuant to the Paperwork Reduction Act. In the early 1980s, the PTO contracted with a private vendor to convert the agency's paper records into electronic records. The contract, however, required the PTO to deny FOIA requests for any agency electronic records.[71] This contract provision troubled Congress, which wondered whether the public's FOIA access to electronic records would be compromised if more agencies followed the PTO's example.[72] In 1985, the House of Representatives began hearings on the legal conflicts created by agency electronic records.[73] Many members of Congress soon concluded that technological changes had made FOIA obsolete;[74] the question then was whether FOIA provided access to records or access to information.[75]

In the meantime, agencies suffered increasing backlogs of FOIA requests for paper records, which prompted the 1996 amendments to FOIA. If the 1996 amendments were successfully to remove the causes of agency delays in processing FOIA requests, then Congress had to remove the legal barriers to electronically processing those requests. Thus, Congress explicitly defined an "agency record" as "any information that would be an agency record . . . when maintained by an agency in any format, including an electronic format."[76] This definition of an agency record overruled cases such as *SDC Development Corp. v. Mathews*,[77] in which the court found that an agency-created computer database of research abstracts was not an agency record. In addition to clarifying the definition of "agency record," the 1996 amendments included numerous administrative innovations: the multitrack processing of requests was added to FOIA,[78] agencies were allowed to negotiate response times outside the new 20-day limit[79] in "unusual circumstances,"[80] and the "exceptional circumstances" clause (under which a court may extend an agency's response time) was clarified.[81] Moreover, implicit within the

71. *"Electronic and Dissemination of Information by Federal Agencies," Hearings Before the Subcomm. on Government Information, Justice and Agriculture of the House Comm. on Government Operations*, 99th Cong. 126 (1985) (report by the American Librarian Association).

72. 130 Cong. Rec. H5527–29 (daily ed. March 14, 1984) (statement of Rep. English).

73. An investigation found "a risk that agencies may be able to exert greater control over information in electronic information systems than is possible with data maintained in traditional, hard-copy formats." H.R. Rep. No. 99–560, at 1–2 (1986).

74. *"Federal Information Dissemination Policies and Practices," Hearing Before the Subcomm. on Government Information, Justice, and Agriculture of the House Comm. on Government Operations*, 101st Cong. 1–2 (1989) (statement of Rep. Wise).

75. Office of Technology Assessment, *supra* note 72, at 208.

76. 5 U.S.C.A. § 552(f)(2) (Supp. 2000).

77. 542 F.2d 1116 (9th Cir.1976).

78. 5 U.S.C.A. § 552(a)(6)(D) (Supp. 2000).

79. 5 U.S.C.A. § 552(a)(6)(A) (Supp. 2000).

80. 5 U.S.C.A. § 552(a)(6)(B) (Supp. 2000).

81. 5 U.S.C.A. § 552(a)(6)(C) (Supp. 2000). *See generally* Open America v. Watergate Special Prosecution Force, 547 F.2d 605 (D.C.Cir.1976) (holding that that an unforeseen 3,000 percent increase in FOIA requests in one year, which created a massive backlog in an agency with insufficient resources to process the requests in a timely manner, constituted "exceptional circumstances.").

amendments is the assumption that "agency regulations may permit the aggregation of requests by the same requestor, or requestors that an agency reasonably believes are acting in concert."[82] The amendments also require agencies to promulgate regulations that authorize expedited access to requestors who show a "compelling need" for a speedy response.[83]

Additional innovations designed to facilitate FOIA requests included a requirement that agencies make their opinions and policy statements available via the Internet or other by electronic means.[84] Agencies must also provide copies of previously released records on a popular topic, such as the assassinations of public figures, via the Internet or by other electronic means.[85] Finally, the 1996 amendments require agencies to provide information in its requested form, which includes when records are requested in an electronic format and the agency can readily reproduce the records in that form.[86] The 1996 amendments therefore overrule *Dismukes v. Department of the Interior*, which held that an agency "has no obligation under the FOIA to accommodate plaintiff's preference [but] need only provide responsive, nonexempt information in a reasonably accessible form."[87]

The 1996 amendments were passed during a period of decline in FOIA litigation. From Sept. 30, 1993 to Sept. 30, 1999, the number of FOIA cases commenced in U.S. district courts went from 573[88] to 352[89]—more than a thirty-eight percent decrease. By Sept. 30, 1999, the number of FOIA cases commenced in U.S. district courts during the prior twelve months had declined more than eleven percent,[90] and only thirty-one FOIA cases had been pending three or more years in U.S. district courts.[91] A probable factor in the slowing of new FOIA litigation was President Clinton's Executive Order 12,958 (April 17, 1995), which so far has led to the declassification of more than 600 million pages of historical documents.[92]

82. H.R. Rep. No. 104–795, at 25 (1996), *reprinted in* 1996 U.S.C.C.A.N. 3448, 3468.

83. 5 U.S.C.A. § 552(a)(6)(E)–(F) (Supp. 2000).

84. 5 U.S.C.A. § 552(a)(2)(E) (Supp. 2000).

85. 5 U.S.C.A. § 552 (a)(2)(D) (Supp. 2000). The Federal Bureau of Investigation web site, for example, features an "Electronic Reading Room" where popularly requested FOIA documents are displayed. See FBI, FOIA Electronic Reading Room (visited Aug. 8, 2000) <http://foia.fbi.gov/>.

86. 5 U.S.C.A. § 552(a)(3) (Supp. 2000).

87. 603 F.Supp. 760, 763 (D.D.C.1984).

88. Administrative Office of the United States Courts, Judicial Business of the United States Courts, 1998 Annual report of the Director 147 tbl.C–2A (1999).

89. Administrative Office of the United States Courts, Judicial Business of the United States Courts, 1999 Annual report of the Director 141 tbl.C–2A (2000).

90. *Id.*

91. *Id.* at 65 tbl.S–11.

92. *See* Vernon Loeb, *Declassification Let A Few Secrets Slip*, Wash. Post, Jan. 27, 2000, at A25.

§ 17.3 PRELIMINARY, PRACTICAL, AND PROCEDURAL ASPECTS OF FOIA—THE STRUCTURE OF THE ACT

FOIA is divided into seven subsections. Subsection (a)(1) requires automatic publication in the Federal Register of matters such as descriptions of agency organization, functions, procedures, substantive rules and statements of general policy. Subsection (a)(2) requires agencies to "make available for public inspection and copying" materials such as final opinions rendered in the adjudication of cases, policy statements and interpretations not published in the Federal Register, administrative staff manuals or instructions "unless the materials are promptly published and copies offered for sale", and copies of records released in response to FOIA requests that the agency determines have been or will likely be the subject of additional requests, as well as an index of these previously released records. The 1996 amendments direct these records to be made available by computer telecommunications or other electronic form if the agency does not have the means to put the information on-line. To protect personal privacy, an agency may delete identifying details from these materials, but must indicate the extent of any deletion. Agencies must also compile and publish indices of these materials in order to facilitate public access.

Subsections (a)(1) and (a)(2) guarantee at least constructive notice to the public of agencies' regulations and operations, along with the procedures necessary to initiate agency action or responses.[1] An agency's failure to satisfy the notification requirements of either subsection can invalidate related agency action.[2] Conversely, although an agency's failure to respond to a FOIA request within the statutory time frame constitutes the exhaustion of administrative remedies necessary for the requester to seek *de novo* judicial review,[3] failure to heed an agency's previously-published procedures for making FOIA requests may stop the requester from seeking judicial relief.[4]

§ 17.3

1. See, e.g., Schwaner v. Department of the Air Force, 698 F.Supp. 4 (D.D.C.1988), rev'd on other grounds, 898 F.2d 793 (D.C.Cir.1990); see also Welch v. United States, 750 F.2d 1101, 1111 (1st Cir.1985) (purposes of subsections (a)(1) and (a)(2) are to provide public notice and guidance).

2. See, e.g., Vigil v. Andrus, 667 F.2d 931, 938 (10th Cir.1982); Anderson v. Butz, 550 F.2d 459, 462 (9th Cir.1977). But see United States v. Hall, 742 F.2d 1153, 1155 (9th Cir.1984) (no invalidation if complaining party had actual and timely notice of unpublished agency policy); Zaharakis v. Heckler, 744 F.2d 711, 714 (9th Cir.1984) (no invalidation if complainant unable to show she was adversely affected by the lack of publication).

3. 5 U.S.C.A. § 552(a)(6)(C). But cf. Open America v. Watergate Special Prosecution Force, 547 F.2d 605, 615–16 (D.C.Cir.1976) (absent exceptional urgency on part of requester, agency deemed to be complying with FOIA, notwithstanding passage of the statutory deadline, if it is exercising "due diligence" while processing requests in the order in which they are received); Spannaus v. U.S. Department of Justice, 824 F.2d 52, 58 (D.C.Cir.1987) (statute of limitations started to run when the agency failed to comply with the FOIA request within ten working days, and not when all administrative appeals were completed).

4. See, e.g., Brumley v. U.S. Department of Labor, 767 F.2d 444, 445 (8th Cir. 1985) (plaintiff's disclosure suit dismissed for failure to exhaust administrative reme-

Subsection (a)(3) is the center of the Act. Except with respect to records made available pursuant to subsections (a)(1) and (a)(2), "each agency," upon receipt of a request for records "which reasonably describes such records" and is made in accordance with the agency's published procedures, must make the requested records promptly available "to any person in any form or format requested by the person if the record is readily reproducible by the agency in that form or format." Moreover, an agency must make "reasonable efforts to search for the record in electronic format." Subsection (a)(4) limits the fees that agencies can charge for a request,[5] authorizes *de novo* judicial review of an agency's decision to withhold requested records,[6] and prescribes fairly stringent deadlines by which agencies must respond to requests. In the event that a court finds that records have been withheld improperly, there are conditional provisions for plaintiffs' recovery of attorney fees[7] and disciplinary action against responsible agency personnel.[8]

Subsection (b) defines nine types of information that are exempt from disclosure under the Act. The last sentence of subsection (b),

dies where agency's delayed response resulted in part from plaintiff's failure to make his request in accordance with published routing procedures).

5. Fees are limited to "reasonable standard charges ... for recovery of only the [agency's] direct costs of ... search for duplication," but documents must be furnished "without any charge or at a charge reduced below the fee established ... if disclosure of the information is in the public interest." 5 U.S.C.A. § 552(a)(4)(A). Depending on the scope of the search, search and copying costs can be substantial, and often vary from agency to agency. See, e.g.,28 C.F.R. § 16.11 (1999). The agency's discretionary determination of whether a request qualifies for a fee waiver—i.e., is "in the public interest"—may thus dictate the viability of a request. See, e.g., Ely v. U.S. Postal Service, 753 F.2d 163, 165 (D.C.Cir.1985), cert. denied 471 U.S. 1106, 105 S.Ct. 2338, 85 L.Ed.2d 854 (1985) (requester's indigency alone insufficient to warrant waiver of fees).

6. The general rule under FOIA is that administrative remedies must be exhausted prior to judicial review. See, e.g., Tuchinsky v. Selective Service System, 418 F.2d 155, 158 (7th Cir.1969); Weisberg v. U.S. Department of Justice, 745 F.2d 1476, 1497 (D.C.Cir.1984), affirmed in part and remanded, 848 F.2d 1265 (D.C.Cir.1988); however, the Act gives requesters the right to seek immediate judicial review, even where the requester has not filed an administrative appeal, when the agency does not respond to a *properly-made* request within the statutory time limits (20 business days, absent "unusual circumstances") set forth in § 552(a)(6). Practically speaking, this constructive exhaustion provision has been diluted by the D.C. Circuit's holding in Open America v. Watergate Special Prosecution Force, 547 F.2d 605, 615–16 (D.C.Cir.1976) (notwithstanding its failure to respond by statutory deadline, agency deemed to be complying with FOIA if exercising "due diligence" under the circumstances).

7. Courts are authorized to award "attorney fees and other litigation costs reasonably incurred" to a FOIA complainant who has "substantially prevailed." Whether a plaintiff has "substantially prevailed" is a question of fact that involves both causation and equities. See, e.g., Weisberg v. U.S. Department of Justice, 745 F.2d 1476, 1494–1500 (D.C.Cir.1984), affirmed in part and remanded, 848 F.2d 1265 (D.C.Cir. 1988).

8. Where a court orders disclosure of improperly withheld records *and* assesses attorneys fees and costs against the government *and* issues a written finding that agency personnel may have acted arbitrarily and capriciously, the Special Counsel of the Merit System Protection Board must initiate an investigation and take appropriate action. 5 U.S.C.A. § 552(a)(4). However, no court to date has issued the written finding that is a prerequisite for such sanctions. See, e.g., Perry v. Block, 684 F.2d 121, 122 (D.C.Cir.1982) (despite a "regrettable [2-year] saga of carelessness and delay," court refused to issue a sanction, in part because the records sought were not technically disclosed pursuant to court order).

mandates the release of reasonably segregable portions of any requested record "after deletion of the portions which are exempt." This provision was added as part of the 1974 amendments and it prevents agencies from classifying entire categories of records as exempt.[9] At the same time, it imposes a significant burden on the agencies, who must often pull from the field personnel most familiar with the subject matter to review and redact large volumes of documents so as to avoid disclosure of legitimately exempt information.[10] The ease with which computers can redact information makes it impossible to tell how much information has, in fact, been redacted. The 1996 amendments, therefore, require agencies to identify the location of deletions and show the amount of deleted material at the place on the record where the deletion was made.[11]

Subsection (c) allows an agency to exempt information related to a pending criminal investigation, information that identifies informants, and FBI records that pertain to foreign intelligence and international terrorism.[12] Subsection (d) states that FOIA does not authorize agencies to withhold information from Congress.[13] Subsection (e) requires annual reports to Congress from each agency regarding its FOIA operations, and an annual report from the Attorney General regarding FOIA litigation and the Department of Justice's efforts (through the Office of Information and Privacy) to encourage agency compliance with FOIA.[14] The 1996 amendments, which completely restructured existing provisions in subsection (e),[15] require that the Attorney General's report and all agency FOIA reports be made available on-line. Also, the reports are required to be more useful to the public by answering basic questions, such as how to make a FOIA request.[16]

Subsection (f) defines the term "agency" so as to subject nearly all executive branch entities to FOIA.[17] FOIA's mandate does not, however, extend to records maintained by Congress, by the courts or by state governments.[18] Nor does FOIA apply to entities that "are neither char-

9. See Irons v. Gottschalk, 548 F.2d 992 (D.C.Cir.1976) cert. denied sub nom. Irons v. Parker, 434 U.S. 965, 98 S.Ct. 505, 54 L.Ed.2d 451 (1977) (existence of some exempt information does not justify nondisclosure of the entire record).

10. In regard to certain types of requested information—such as that pertaining to intelligence-gathering operations or matters of national security—this painstaking process of review can result in the release of heavily-redacted documents of little or no practical value to anyone. Such concerns prompted Congress to exempt CIA operational files from FOIA's "release of segregable portions" requirement. See Central Intelligence Information Act, Pub.L.No. 98–477, 98 Stat. 2209 (1984).

11. 5 U.S.C. § 552(a)(6)(F).

12. 5 U.S.C. § 552(c).

13. FOIA's exemptions cannot be used to justify withholding from Congress as a body or from one of its committees; individual members of Congress, however, have only the right of access guaranteed to "any person" under subsection (a)(3). See H.R.Rep. No. 1497, 89th Cong., 2d Sess. 11–12 (1966).

14. 5 U.S.C.A. § 552(e)(1).

15. 5 U.S.C.A. § 552(e)(2)-(3).

16. 5 U.S.C.A. § 552(g).

17. See 5 U.S.C.A. § 551(1).

18. See, e.g., Goland v. CIA, 607 F.2d 339, 348 (D.C.Cir.1978), vacated in part and reh'g denied 607 F.2d 367 (D.C.Cir.1978), cert. denied, 445 U.S. 927, 100 S.Ct. 1312, 63 L.Ed.2d 759 (1980) (Congress); Warth v. Department of Justice, 595 F.2d 521, 523 (9th Cir.1979) (courts); Davidson v. State of

tered by the Federal Government nor controlled by it."[19] The proliferation in recent years of quasi-governmental advisory boards, investigative commissions and corporate entities serving particular public interests has resulted in a spate of FOIA litigation concerning this threshold issue.[20] For example, units of the Executive Office and other bodies whose sole function is to advise and assist the President are not considered "agencies" subject to FOIA, while entities whose functions are not so limited must respond to FOIA requests.[21] In determining whether an entity is an agency for the purpose of FOIA, courts usually assess a variety of considerations, typically including the origin of the entity, the manner in which its members were appointed, whether the body has rulemaking authority, whether its employees are deemed federal employees, and the amount of government supervision of day-to-day operations.[22]

The 1996 amendments also made it explicit under subsection (f) that a "record" for the purposes of FOIA includes electronically stored information. The policy is broad and does not discriminate against different types of storage media. The form in which an agency's data are stored, therefore, cannot improve agency attempts to evade disclosure.[23] The 1996 amendments also added a subsection (g), which requires agencies to make available a guide for requesting records from the agency. It is anticipated that such guides will be made available by electronic means.[24]

§ 17.3.1 Definition of an "Agency Record"

The Supreme Court has stated that FOIA "does not obligate agencies to create or retain documents; it only obligates them to provide

Georgia, 622 F.2d 895, 897 (5th Cir.1980) (state government).

19. H.R.Rep. No. 1380, 93d Cong., 2d Sess. 15 (1974).

20. See, e.g., Rushforth v. Council of Economic Advisers, 762 F.2d 1038, 1043 (D.C.Cir.1985) (President's Council of Economic Advisers not a federal "agency" for purposes of FOIA); Forsham v. Harris, 445 U.S. 169, 179–80, 100 S.Ct. 977, 983–84, 63 L.Ed.2d 293 (1980) (private grantee of federal agency not subject to FOIA); Ehm v. National Railroad Passenger Corp., 732 F.2d 1250, 1252–55 (5th Cir.1984), cert. denied, 469 U.S. 982, 105 S.Ct. 387, 83 L.Ed.2d 322 (1984) (Amtrak not a federal agency for purposes of Privacy Act; subject to FOIA only because of express statutory reference); see also, Sweetland v. Walters, 60 F.3d 852, 855 (D.C.Cir.1995) (President's Executive Residence is not a federal agency for the purpose of FOIA); Dong v. Smithsonian Inst., 125 F.3d 877, 883 (D.C.Cir.1997), cert. denied, 524 U.S. 922, 118 S.Ct. 2311, 141 L.Ed.2d 169 (1998) (Smithsonian Institution is not a federal agency for the purpose of the Privacy Act); Armstrong v. Executive Office of the President, 90 F.3d 553, 555–56 (D.C.Cir.1996) (National Security Council not an agency within the meaning of FOIA). The Irwin memorial line of cases includes Dong v. Smithsonian.

21. See *Rushforth,* supra note 122, 762 F.2d at 1043; Sweetland v. Walters, supra note 122, 60 F.3d 852 at 855.

22. See, e.g., Ehm v. National Railroad Passenger Corporation, 732 F.2d 1250, 1255 (5th Cir.1984), cert. denied, 469 U.S. 982, 105 S.Ct. 387, 83 L.Ed.2d 322 (1984).

23. This portion of the Act effectively overrules SDC Dev. Corp. v. Mathews, 542 F.2d 1116 (9th Cir.1976) (finding that an agency-created database was library material exempt from FOIA requests under the Records Disposal Act's library material exclusion provision).

24. H.R. Rep. No. 104–795, 104th Cong., 2d Sess., 30 (1996).

access to those which it in fact has created and retained."[25] While the 1996 amendments expanded the definition of "agency record" to include records in "an electronic format,"[26] Congress did not intend the provision to "broaden the concept of agency record."[27] Assuming that the materials in question have been "created and retained," their further classification as "agency records" is critical to the party seeking access because the federal courts' authority to compel disclosure is limited by the terms of the Act. "Federal jurisdiction under [Section 552(a)(4)(B) of FOIA] is ... premised upon three requirements: a 'showing that an agency has (1) "improperly"; (2) "withheld"; (3) "agency records." ' "[28] Unfortunately, FOIA, "for all its attention to the treatment of 'agency records' never defines that crucial phrase.... [Moreover,] ... the legislative history yields insignificant insight into Congress' conception of the sorts of materials the Act covers."[29] Courts seeking to determine whether requested documents are "agency records" subject to FOIA must still treat the matter as a threshold question of fact. The relevant factors are whether the documents were (1) in the agency's control, (2) generated within the agency, (3) placed into the agency's files, and (4) used by the agency "for any purpose."[30]

Two D.C. Circuit Court of Appeals opinions—*Wolfe v. Department of Health and Human Services*[31] and *Grand Central Partnership v. Cuomo*[32]—provide comprehensive discussions of the factors and precedents relevant to the "agency record" determination. Neither "use" nor "control" of the documents is alone sufficient to establish their character for purposes of FOIA; by necessity, courts have fashioned a totality of the circumstances approach.[33] Using a broad based approach that focused on possession, agency discretion to disclose as well as the agency's own use of or reliance on the records in contention, the D.C. Circuit in *Tax Analysts v. U.S. Department of Justice*[34] held that federal district court

25. Kissinger v. Reporters Committee for Freedom of Press, 445 U.S. 136, 152, 100 S.Ct. 960, 969, 63 L.Ed.2d 267 (1980); see also Forsham v. Harris, 445 U.S. 169, 182, 100 S.Ct. 977, 985, 63 L.Ed.2d 293 (1980).

26. 5 U.S.C.A. § 552(f)(2) (Supp. 2000).

27. H.R. Rep. No. 104–795, at 20 (1996), reprinted in 1996 U.S.C.C.A.N. 3448, 3463.

28. Bureau of National Affairs, Inc. v. U.S. Department of Justice, 742 F.2d 1484, 1488 (D.C.Cir.1984), (quoting Kissinger v. Reporters Committee for Freedom of Press, 445 U.S. 136, 150, 100 S.Ct. 960, 968, 63 L.Ed.2d 267 (1980)).

29. McGehee v. Central Intelligence Agency, 697 F.2d 1095, 1106 (D.C.Cir.1983), modified in other respects 711 F.2d 1076 (1983).

30. Bureau of National Affairs, Inc. v. U.S. Department of Justice, supra note 130, at 1489–90 (citing Kissinger v. Reporters Committee for Freedom of Press, 445 U.S. 136, 157, 100 S.Ct. 960, 972, 63 L.Ed.2d 267 (1980)).

31. 711 F.2d 1077 (D.C.Cir.1983) (although physically located at HHS offices, presidential transition team records were neither created by an agency nor "obtained" by HHS, and were therefore beyond the reach of FOIA).

32. 166 F.3d 473 (2d Cir.1999); 742 F.2d 1484, 1495–96 (D.C.Cir.1984) (except for daily agendas distributed within the agency, appointment calendars and telephone logs of agency officials held not agency records).

33. Cf. Note, A Control Test for Determining "Agency Record" Status Under FOIA, 85 Colum.L.Rev. 611, 627 (1985).

34. 845 F.2d 1060 (D.C.Cir.1988), affirmed 492 U.S. 136, 109 S.Ct. 2841, 106 L.Ed.2d 112 (1989). See also Payne Enter-

tax opinions were agency records subject to disclosure by the Department of Justice.[35]

The jurisdictional "agency record" classification becomes even more difficult when documents created by an entity exempt from FOIA are sought from an agency that is not exempt. In *Forsham v. Harris,*[36] the Court dealt with the question of whether records produced by a private grantee pursuant to a federal grant were agency records. The Court noted that "[r]ecords of a nonagency certainly could become records of an agency as well,"[37] but merely operating under the funding auspices of a federal agency was not enough to convert the nonagency's work product into an agency record. For the Court, "an agency must first either create or obtain a record as a prerequisite to its becoming an 'agency record' within the meaning of the FOIA."[38] The Court implied that what constituted the creation or the obtaining of agency records was not to be broadly construed and it rejected arguments to the effect that agency access to privately produced records or even agency use of a nonagency's findings would necessarily transform this work product into an agency record.

In *Kissinger v. Reporters Committee for Freedom of the Press,*[39] the Court dealt with the related issue of whether agency records obtained or created by an agency subject to FOIA and then transferred to a nonagency remain accessible under FOIA. The Court noted that for FOIA to apply, it must be shown that the agency remained in "possession or control"[40] of the records. In *Kissinger,* the Court concluded that certain records created by the Secretary of State and subsequently transferred to a nonagency were no longer in that agency's control and thus, not subject to FOIA. In so deciding, the Court relied heavily on the importance of agency control.[41] The Ninth Circuit proposed a two-part test to

prises, Inc. v. United States, 837 F.2d 486, 494 (D.C.Cir.1988) (contract bid abstracts sought by commercial company were agency records subject to disclosure); Tax Analysts v. U.S. Dep't of Justice, 913 F.Supp. 599 (D.D.C.1996), aff'd without opinion by 107 F.3d 923 (D.C.Cir.1997), cert. denied by 522 U.S. 931, 118 S.Ct. 336, 139 L.Ed.2d 260 (1997) (West-provided electronic database not an agency record under FOIA where the right to use data was contractually restricted).

35. 845 F.2d at 1067–69. The court noted, however, that "not everything in an agency library ... is an 'agency record' subject to disclosure under the Act." Id. at 1069.

36. 445 U.S. 169, 100 S.Ct. 977, 63 L.Ed.2d 293 (1980).

37. Id. at 181, 100 S.Ct. at 985.

38. Id. at 182, 100 S.Ct. at 985. See also Marzen v. Department of HHS, 825 F.2d 1148 (7th Cir.1987) (agency records do not include records obtained by a governmental agency without legal authority to do so).

39. 445 U.S. 136, 100 S.Ct. 960, 63 L.Ed.2d 267 (1980).

40. Id. at 152, 100 S.Ct. at 969.

41. *Kissinger* notes that "[w]e simply decline to hold that the physical location of the notes of telephone conversations renders them 'agency records'. The papers were not in the control of the State Department at any time. They were not generated in the State Department. They never entered the State Department's files, and they were not used by the Department for any purpose." 445 U.S. at 157, 100 S.Ct. at 972. Commenting on this aspect of the decision, the Ninth Circuit stated that it did not read the Court's "recitations to be a checklist of factors used to assess whether documents constitute agency records." The Ninth Circuit added that in any event, this list offers little guidance "since these factors cannot all be accorded equal weight and are in many situations, overlapping." Berry v. De-

resolve such issues: documents prepared by nonagencies may nevertheless become agency records if (1) they are "in the possession of an agency and (2) prepared substantially to be relied upon in agency decisionmaking."[42]

§ 17.3.2 FOIA Requests

A FOIA request can be made by "any person."[43] The Administrative Procedure Act[44] defines person as including individuals (including foreign citizens),[45] partnerships, corporations, associations, and foreign, state, or local governments. Those who flout the law, however, such as fugitives from justice,[46] are denied access under FOIA. Nevertheless, "FOIA grants a right which is virtually unprecedented anywhere else in the world: the right to obtain government documents just for the asking."[47]

FOIA requests can be made for any reason; no showing of relevancy or purpose is required. Persons seeking information under FOIA do not have to state a reason for their request.[48] In practice, however, a requester's particular needs and purposes may be relevant to certain procedural aspects of FOIA, such as expedited treatment, waiver or reduction of search and copying fees, discretionary release, or the award of attorney's fees and costs to a successful FOIA plaintiff.

In regard to the form of FOIA requests, the Act requires that requests "reasonably describe"[49] the records sought and that they be submitted in accordance with the relevant agencies' published procedur-

partment of Justice, 733 F.2d 1343, 1348–49 (9th Cir.1984), on remand 612 F.Supp. 45 (D.Ariz.1985)

42. Berry v. Department of Justice, 733 F.2d 1343, 1349 (9th Cir.1984), on remand 612 F.Supp. 45 (D.Ariz.1985). See also, Note, supra note 135; Note, The Definition of Agency Records Under the Freedom of Information Act, 31 Stan.L.Rev. 1093 (1979); Note, Agency Records Under the Freedom of Information Acts: An Analysis of *Forsham v. Califano,* 13 Ga.L.Rev. 1040 (1979).

43. 5 U.S.C.A. § 552(a)(3).

44. See id. § 551(2).

45. The propriety of foreign citizens' access to U.S. government documents via FOIA has been questioned. See, e.g., Senate Comm. on the Judiciary, S.Rep. No. 221, 98th Cong., 1st Sess. (1983) (S.774, the Freedom of Information Reform Bill, passed the Senate in early 1984; among other things, the bill would have prohibited FOIA requests by foreign nationals. The 98th Congress adjourned, however, without House action on the proposed reform bill.).

46. See, e.g., Doyle v. U.S. Department of Justice, 494 F.Supp. 842, 843 (D.D.C. 1980), affirmed 668 F.2d 1365 (D.C.Cir. 1981), cert. denied 455 U.S. 1002, 102 S.Ct. 1636, 71 L.Ed.2d 870 (1982) (fugitive from justice held not entitled to enforcement of FOIA's access provisions because persons who have thus removed themselves from the jurisdiction of the courts cannot reasonably expect judicial aid in obtaining government records); see also, Javelin International Ltd. v. Department of Justice, 2 G.D.S. ¶ 82,141 at 82,479 (D.D.C.1981) (access denied where FOIA plaintiff was acting as agent for fugitive from justice).

47. Wald, FOIA: A Short Case Study in the Perils and Paybacks of Legislating Democratic Values, 33 Emory L.J. 649, 657 (1984).

48. See H.R. Rep. No. 106–50, at 3 (1999) ("Those seeking information are no longer required to show a need for information. Instead, the 'need to know' standard has been replaced by a 'right to know' doctrine.") See also NLRB v. Sears, Roebuck & Co., 421 U.S. 132, 143 n. 10, 95 S.Ct. 1504, 1513 n. 10, 44 L.Ed.2d 29 (1975) (FOIA requester's basic rights to access "are neither increased nor decreased" by virtue of requester's greater interest in the records than that of an average member of the general public).

49. See 5 U.S.C.A. § 552(a)(3)(A).

al regulations.[50] A description of a requested record is sufficient if it enables a professional agency employee familiar with the subject area to locate the record with "a reasonable amount of effort."[51] In addition, agencies must make "reasonable efforts" to search for electronic records.[52]

Given the breadth of the phrase "any person," standing is rarely a problem in the FOIA context. While the general rule under FOIA is that administrative remedies must be exhausted prior to judicial review,[53] the Act gives requesters the unqualified right to seek immediate judicial review—even where the requester has not filed an administrative appeal—when the agency does not respond to a properly-made request within the statutory time limit (twenty business days, absent "unusual circumstances").[54] In practice, however, courts have looked askance at the Act's constructive exhaustion provision. The D.C. Circuit has held that, notwithstanding an agency's failure to dispose of a FOIA request within the statutory period, the agency is deemed to be complying with FOIA if it is exercising good faith and "due diligence" by processing requests in the order in which they are received, so long as the agency is not "lax overall in meeting its obligations under the Act with all available resources."[55] The adequacy of an agency's search in response to a FOIA request is determined by a "reasonableness" test that can vary from case to case.[56] Thus, although FOIA plaintiffs enjoy a statutory presumption of immediate judicial recourse,[57] they have a concomitant

50. See, e.g., Brumley v. U.S. Department of Labor, 767 F.2d 444, 445 (8th Cir. 1985) (suit dismissed for failure to exhaust administrative remedies where agency's delayed response resulted in part from plaintiff's failure to make his request in accordance with published routing procedures); Marks v. U.S. Department of Justice, 578 F.2d 261, 263 (9th Cir.1978).

51. H.R.Rep. No. 876, 93d Cong., 2d Sess. 6 (1974), reprinted in 1974 U.S.C.C.A.N. 6271. See, e.g., Krohn v. Department of Justice, 628 F.2d 195, 198 (D.C.Cir.1980) (plaintiff's request too vague to satisfy statutory requirements); McGehee v. C.I.A., 697 F.2d 1095, 1102 n. 28 (D.C.Cir.1983), modified in other respects 711 F.2d 1076 (1983).

52. 5 U.S.C.A. § 552(a)(3)(C)(Supp. 2000)

53. Weisberg v. U.S. Department of Justice, 745 F.2d 1476, 1497 (D.C.Cir.1984), affirmed in part and remanded, 848 F.2d 1265 (D.C.Cir.1988); Tuchinsky v. Selective Service System, 418 F.2d 155, 158 (7th Cir. 1969). See Taylor v. United States Treasury Dep't, IRS, 127 F.3d 470 (5th Cir.1997).

54. See 5 U.S.C.A. § 552(a)(6).

55. Open America v. Watergate Special Prosecution Force, 547 F.2d 605, 615 (D.C.Cir.1976). In general, however, courts are reluctant to impose penalties when agencies release data only after a lawsuit is filed. See Church of Scientology of California v. Harris, 653 F.2d 584, 587 (D.C.Cir. 1981) (FOIA litigant was eligible for § 552(a)(4)(E) award of attorney fees when it "substantially prevailed" in its suit by forcing the release of two-thirds of requested documents); see also Cox v. U.S. Department of Justice, 601 F.2d 1, 6 (D.C.Cir. 1979) (Party seeking fees absent a court order must show necessity of prosecution and its nexus with agency surrender of information).

56. See Weisberg v. U.S. Department of Justice, 705 F.2d 1344, 1351 (D.C.Cir. 1983); H.R.Rep. No. 876, 93rd Cong., 2d Sess. 6 (1974), reprinted in 1974 U.S.C.C.A.N. 6271; see also Hill v. U.S. Air Force, 795 F.2d 1067, 1069 n. 2 (D.C.Cir. 1986).

57. But cf. Vaughn, Administrative Alternatives and the Federal Freedom of Information Act, 45 Ohio St.L.J. 185 (1984) (deploring the cost disincentives, sluggishness and practical ineffectiveness of judicial review as a FOIA enforcement mechanism). "Confronted with delay in agency response, the costs of seeking judicial review, and the court' treatment of agency delay, requesters are left to bargain with agencies over re-

duty to frame their requests with sufficient specificity so that these requests are not unreasonably burdensome.

§ 17.3.3 Agencies' Duties Under FOIA

One of the Act's salutary effects on the federal bureaucracy has been its implicit requirement of responsible records management. After thirty-five years of FOIA-mandated access, including documents in electronic format, agencies have been forced to develop workable procedures for categorizing, indexing, storing and retrieving government-generated documents. Hence, retrieval and access under FOIA have become faster and more efficient. Indeed, developing information technology has rectified many of the Act's practical shortcomings,[58] as well as create unforeseen problems.[59]

As noted earlier, FOIA requires each agency to "currently publish in the Federal Register for the guidance of the public" descriptions of its structure and operating procedures, its substantive rules and interpretations, and the methods by which the public can obtain further information from the agency.[60] Final orders, opinions, statements of policy and non-exempt staff manuals not appearing in the Federal Register must be "made available for public inspection and copying" and indexed periodically in a form available to the public,[61] including by computer telecommunication. The Act warns that failure to comply with either the publication or "available to the public" requirements can result in the invalidation of related agency action.[62]

Until a request is properly received (i.e., filed in accordance with published procedures) by the proper component of the agency, there is no obligation on the agency to search, to meet time deadlines or to release documents.[63] Upon receipt of a proper FOIA request, an agency must inform the requester of its decision to grant or deny access to the requested records within twenty working days; access to disclosable records should be granted "promptly" thereafter.[64] Response time limits may be extended when the agency must examine an inordinate number of requested documents, when the records must be collected from separate offices, or when the agency must consult with another agency or component.[65] Congress also intended to allow the aggregation of re-

lease of the requested information. While requesters believe that agencies will eventually release all or a substantial part of the information, little is gained by seeking judicial review, and agencies have no incentive to invent methods for more rapid compliance." Id. at 189. See also H.R. Rep. No. 104–795, at 23 (1996), reprinted in U.S.C.C.A.N. 3448, 3466 (citing "agency delays in responding to FOIA requests" as the "single most frequent complaint" about FOIA).

58. "See U.S. Dep't of Justice, FOIA Report for FY 1999, at 23 (visited Sept. 23, 2000) <http://www.usdoj.gov.oip/annual_report/1999/99contents.htm>."

59. See chapter 19, sec. 19.1 infra.

60. See 5 U.S.C.A. § 552(a)(1).

61. See id. § 552(a)(2).

62. See, e.g., Vigil v. Andrus, 667 F.2d 931, 938 (10th Cir.1982); Anderson v. Butz, 550 F.2d 459, 462 (9th Cir.1977).

63. See, e.g., Brumley v. U.S. Department of Labor, 767 F.2d 444 (8th Cir.1985).

64. See 5 U.S.C.A. § 552(a)(6)(A)(i); § 552(a)(6)(C).

65. See id. § 552(a)(6)(B). Courts are divided whether a back-log in processing requests is sufficient cause to justify exceed-

quests.[66]The 1996 amendments provided that agencies could promulgate regulations for multitrack processing of FOIA requests.[67] To promote cooperation between a requestor and an agency[68], the 1996 amendments also added a provision that allows a requestor to limit the scope of a request if such modification will expedite processing the request. Refusal to modify the scope of a request may be considered as a factor when determining whether "exceptional circumstances" exist.[69]Administrative appeals must be decided within twenty days.[70]

Because FOIA places the burden of proof squarely upon the government,[71] a defendant agency in a FOIA dispute must prove either that the requested documents are wholly exempt from disclosure or, alternatively, that such records have not been found or identified.[72] The agency must therefore demonstrate that it has conducted a "search reasonably calculated to uncover all relevant documents;"[73] the inquiry "is not whether there might exist any other documents possibly responsive to the request, but rather whether the *search* for those documents was *adequate*."[74] In demonstrating the adequacy of its search, an agency may "rely upon reasonably detailed, nonconclusory affidavits submitted in good faith."[75] Courts are usually sympathetic to the agencies' time, budget and personnel constraints; to the extent possible, requesters are expected to focus their queries.[76]

ing the time limit. Open America v. Watergate Special Prosecution Force, 547 F.2d 605, 615–16 (D.C.Cir.1976). Cf. Exner v. FBI, 542 F.2d 1121, 1123 (9th Cir.1976). The 1996 amendments make clear, however, that predictable agency backlogs do not justify exceeding the time limit. 5 U.S.C.A. § 552(a)(6)(C)(ii) (Supp. 2000).

66. H.R. Rep. No. 104–795, at 25 (1996), reprinted in 1996 U.S.C.C.A.N. 3448, 3468.

67. 5 U.S.C.A. § 552(a)(6)(D) (Supp. 2000).

68. H.R. Rep. No. 104–795, at 23 (1996), reprinted in 1996 U.S.C.C.A.N. at 3448, 3466.

69. 5 U.S.C.A. § 552(a)(6)(B)(ii) (Supp. 2000).

70. See 5 U.S.C.A. § 522(a)(6)(A)(ii).

71. Id. § 552(a)(4)(B). The 1996 amendments make clear, however, that the courts will accord "substantial weight" to an agency's affidavit concerning the technical feasibility of searching for electronic records or producing records in electronic format. Id. (Supp. 2000).

72. National Cable Television Ass'n, Inc. v. FCC, 479 F.2d 183, 186 (D.C.Cir. 1973).

73. Weisberg v. U.S. Department of Justice, 705 F.2d 1344, 1351 (D.C.Cir.1983) (*Weisberg I*).

74. Weisberg v. U.S. Department of Justice, 745 F.2d 1476, 1485 (D.C.Cir.1984) (*Weisberg II*), affirmed in part and remanded, 848 F.2d 1265 (D.C.Cir.1988) (citing *Weisberg I,* 705 F.2d at 1351 and Perry v. Block, 684 F.2d 121, 128 (D.C.Cir.1982) (per curiam) (emphasis in original)).

75. Id. at 1485 (citations omitted).

76. See, e.g., id. at 1485–89 (where FBI had already released 60,000 pages of documents in response to plaintiff's 28–paragraph FOIA request [id. at 1480, n. 5], Court rejected plaintiff's claim that agency unreasonably failed to search individual files related to the request and failed to reprocess materials released pursuant to plaintiff's previous FOIA request). See also Goland v. CIA, 607 F.2d 339, 353 (D.C.Cir. 1978) (production of records not previously segregated required only where material can be identified with reasonable effort), vacated in part and reh'g denied, 607 F.2d 367 (D.C.Cir.1979), cert. denied, 445 U.S. 927, 100 S.Ct. 1312, 63 L.Ed.2d 759 (1980); Marks v. U.S. Department of Justice, 578 F.2d 261, 263 (9th Cir.1978) (no duty to search FBI field offices where requester directed request only to FBI Headquarters and did not specify which field office he wanted searched); Biberman v. FBI, 528 F.Supp. 1140, 1144 (S.D.N.Y.1982) ("it has frequently been held that a general FOIA request to headquarters does not 'reason-

Courts have also long held that an agency is under no duty to *create* files or documents in order to fill a FOIA request for information: FOIA "only requires disclosure of certain documents which *the law* requires the agency to prepare or which the agency has decided for its own reasons to create."[77] Nor is an agency required to reorganize its files in response to a plaintiff's request in the form in which it was made.[78]

§ 17.3.4 Summary Judgment, *Vaughn* Indices, and *In Camera* Review

In some respects, the adversarial system is ill-suited for the resolution of FOIA disputes. Practically speaking, the plaintiff-requester is at a distinct disadvantage. In the typical situation, the requester cannot be sure of either the contents or the volume of government-held documents relevant to his request. Although FOIA addresses this problem by placing the burden of justifying nondisclosure on the government,[79] the agency cannot be expected to display the disputed documents in an open courtroom so as to justify withholding them; to do so would be to divulge—at least to the parties, if not to the public—the very information which the agency claims is exempt from disclosure under FOIA. Moreover, federal courts have neither the time nor the inclination to preside over adversarial arguments as to the character of each of the often hundreds or thousands of withheld documents pertaining to the plaintiff's request.[80] By necessity, then, FOIA plaintiffs must rely on the integrity and competence of the agency and its personnel.

Nearly all FOIA cases are adjudicated in the context of motions for summary judgment.[81] The agency usually seeks to sustain its burden of justifying nondisclosure through submission of detailed affidavits which describe the agency's search technique and which identify the documents at issue and explain why they fall under one or more of FOIA's

ably describe' a search of numerous field offices.") ... But note In re U.S. Department of Defense, 848 F.2d 232, 237 (D.C.Cir.1988), cert. denied 488 U.S. 820, 109 S.Ct. 62, 102 L.Ed.2d 40 (1988) (court rejected DOD's petition to prevent appointment of special master to review FOIA request to produce 14,000 pages of classified documents generated from 1980 aborted attempt to rescue hostages in Iran) ("Judge Oberdorfer specifically said that he did not consider random sampling appropriate in this case [to verify accuracy of unclassified and classified document indices], deciding instead that the alternative technique of *representative* sampling was required ... By contrast, random sampling, like the 1% sampling strategy used in *Weisberg,* although appropriate in many cases, may overlook distinctive documents or accidentally shield patently unexceptional documents from FOIA release.") (footnote omitted).

77. NLRB v. Sears, Roebuck & Co., 421 U.S. 132, 162, 95 S.Ct. 1504, 1522, 44 L.Ed.2d 29 (1975); accord, Krohn v. Department of Justice, 628 F.2d 195, 197–98 (D.C.Cir.1980).

78. Irons v. Schuyler, 465 F.2d 608, 615 (D.C.Cir.1972), cert. denied sub nom. Irons v. Commissioner of Patents, 409 U.S. 1076, 93 S.Ct. 682, 34 L.Ed.2d 664 (1972).

79. See 5 U.S.C.A. § 552(a)(4)(B).

80. See Vaughn v. Rosen, 484 F.2d 820, 824–26 (D.C.Cir.1973), cert. denied 415 U.S. 977, 94 S.Ct. 1564, 39 L.Ed.2d 873 (1974).

81. See Fed.R.Civ.P. 56(c), which provides in pertinent part that "judgment shall be rendered forthwith if the pleadings, depositions, answers to interrogatories, and admissions on file, *together with the affidavits, if any,* show that there is no genuine issue as to any material fact." (emphasis added).

exemptions. Summary judgment may be granted solely on the basis of agency affidavits if they are clear, specific, and reasonably detailed, if they describe the withheld information in a factual and non-conclusory manner, and if there is no contradictory evidence on the record or evidence of agency bad faith.[82] If all of these requirements are met, such affidavits are usually accorded substantial weight by the courts.[83]

Moreover, courts have consistently held that a requester's opinion disputing the risk created by disclosure is not sufficient to preclude summary judgment for the agency, when the agency possessing the relevant expertise has provided sufficiently detailed affidavits.[84]

To counterbalance this necessary reliance on agency assertions, courts (or plaintiff, upon motion)[85] can and often do demand from the withholding agency a so-called *Vaughn* index. First prescribed by the D.C.Circuit in 1973,[86] a *Vaughn* index is an itemized index which correlates each withheld document (or part thereof) with a specific FOIA exemption and the relevant part of the agency's refusal justification.[87] *Vaughn* indices are routinely prepared in cases involving a large number of disputed documents.[88] They are useful at either the trial court level or upon appeal,[89] but they are not required at the administrative level.[90]

82. Quinon v. FBI, 86 F.3d 1222, 1227 (D.C.Cir.1996); Minier v. CIA, 88 F.3d 796 (9th Cir.1996) ("Bad faith" requires a showing of tangible evidence, not mere allegations).

83. Note that the D.C. Circuit distinguishes according "substantial weight" from granting "deference" to agency affidavits. In cases related to national security (Exemption 1 cases), the court typically gives special deterrence to agency affidavits. See, e.g., CIA v. Sims, 471 U.S. 159, 179, 105 S.Ct. 1881, 1893, 85 L.Ed.2d 173 (1985) ("The decisions of the Director [of the CIA], who must of course be familiar with 'the whole picture,' as judges are not, are worthy of great deference given the magnitude of the national security interests and potential risks at stake. It is conceivable that the mere explanation of why information must be withheld can convey valuable information to a foreign intelligence agency."). See also Gardels v. CIA, 689 F.2d 1100, 1104 (D.C.Cir.1982); Taylor v. Department of the Army, 684 F.2d 99, 106–07 (D.C.Cir.1982). In non-national security related cases, the court awards substantial weight to affidavits. See, e.g., Alyeska Pipeline Service Company v. EPA, 856 F.2d 309, 315 (D.C.Cir.1988) ("In this circuit, however, we have not found it appropriate to extend any special deference beyond the Exemption 1 context ... The affidavits of both parties are to be given the weight they are due on the basis of their contents. We have held that EPA's affidavit discharged its burden and that no genuine issue of material fact was presented."). See also Washington Post Co. v. U.S. Department of State, 840 F.2d 26, 31 (D.C.Cir.1988), vacated by, on reh'g at 898 F.2d 793 (D.C.Cir.1990).

84. See Alyeska Pipeline Service Company v. EPA, 856 F.2d 309, 313–14 (D.C.Cir.1988) ("If FOIA parties could routinely block summary judgment in this fashion [by simply drawing a conflicting conclusion of the impact of disclosure from the same set of facts] many unmeritorious FOIA cases could not be disposed of prior to a trial."); see also Gardels v. CIA, 689 F.2d 1100, 1106 n. 5 (D.C.Cir.1982); Windels, Marx, Davies & Ives v. Department of Commerce, 576 F.Supp. 405, 410–11 (D.D.C. 1983).

85. Vaughn v. Rosen, 484 F.2d 820 (D.C.Cir.1973), cert. denied 415 U.S. 977, 94 S.Ct. 1564, 39 L.Ed.2d 873 (1974).

86. Id. See sec. 17.2 supra.

87. Id. at 827. See, e.g., Conoco Inc. v. U.S. Department of Justice, 687 F.2d 724, 730–32 (3d Cir.1982) (appendix containing court approved detailed description of one document).

88. See, e.g., Wightman v. Bureau of Alcohol, Tobacco & Firearms, 755 F.2d 979, 981 n. 1 (1st Cir.1985).

89. *Vaughn,* 484 F.2d at 824–25.

90. See Mead Data Central, Inc. v. U.S. Department of the Air Force, 566 F.2d 242, 251 (D.C.Cir.1977) (objectives of *Vaughn*

Using a *Vaughn* index, a court can conduct an *in camera* review of randomly-selected withheld documents so as to assess the agency's otherwise unmonitored characterization of its records. The index enables the court to ascertain whether the agency has in fact disclosed "reasonably segregable portions" of otherwise exempt records, as required by the Act.[91] More importantly, it ensures that the administrative burdens associated with FOIA documents are borne by the agencies, not the courts. Depending on the volume of documents involved, an agency's compilation of an adequate *Vaughn* index can be a painstaking and tedious affair. Practically speaking, the mere prospect of a court-mandated *Vaughn* procedure may provide the agencies with far more incentive to disclose than does FOIA's statutory presumption of disclosure.[92] If the index is not sufficiently detailed, the court may remand and require a more detailed index.[93]

The *Vaughn* index has thus evolved into an extremely effective tool with which to resolve FOIA cases.[94] At the very least, these indices guarantee that agencies will review withheld documents with the knowledge that FOIA's mandate is indeed enforceable. Moreover, "[s]uch detailed summaries permit the party seeking disclosure to knowingly argue for the release of the disputed information, and permit effective appellate review."[95]

A corollary to the *Vaughn* indices and agency affidavits is FOIA's provision for judicial *in camera* inspection of withheld documents,[96] under which the court has authority to peruse the documents themselves

requirements are applicable to intra-agency proceedings, but failure to follow during administrative review of FOIA request is not reversible error).

91. See 5 U.S.C.A. § 552(b).

92. See, e.g., Union of Concerned Scientists v. NRC, 824 F.2d 1219, 1221 (D.C.Cir.1987) (in exchange for release of 2000 partial pages of 4000 originally sought, requesters agreed to limit litigation to seven primary documents and accept a *Vaughn* index for only that information). See also Weisberg v. U.S. Department of Justice, 745 F.2d 1476, 1482–83 (D.C.Cir. 1984), affirmed in part and remanded, 848 F.2d 1265 (D.C.Cir.1988) (in return for FBI's promise to release 15,000 pages of documents, plaintiff promised not to file a *Vaughn* motion).

93. See King v. U.S. Department of Justice, 830 F.2d 210 (D.C.Cir.1987); Campbell v. U.S. Dep't of Justice, 164 F.3d 20 (D.C.Cir.1998).

94. See e.g., Alyeska Pipeline Service Company v. EPA, 856 F.2d 309, 312 (D.C.Cir.1988) (general and conclusory statements with proper justifications is acceptable under Exemption 7 case law); NLRB v. Robbins Tire & Rubber Co., 437 U.S. 214, 223–24, 98 S.Ct. 2311, 2317–18, 57 L.Ed.2d 159 (1978) (generic explanations, focusing on types of records and harms to investigations resulting from disclosure, permitted under Exemption 7(A)); Antonelli v. FBI, 721 F.2d 615, 617–19 (7th Cir.1983), cert. denied 467 U.S. 1210, 104 S.Ct. 2399, 81 L.Ed.2d 355 (1984) (no *Vaughn* index required in third-party request for records where agency would neither confirm nor deny existence of records on particular individuals absent showing of public interest in disclosure); Ely v. FBI, 781 F.2d 1487 (11th Cir.1986) (showing of public interest must be more than an *ipse dixit* assertion of privilege—"the government must first offer evidence, either publicly or in camera, to show that there is a legitimate claim of privilege.") Id. at 1492; Weisberg v. U.S. Department of Justice, 745 F.2d 1476, 1483 (D.C.Cir.1984), affirmed in part and remanded, 848 F.2d 1265 (D.C.Cir. 1988) (*Vaughn* index ordered for every 200th document).

95. Ingle v. Department of Justice, 698 F.2d 259, 263–64 (6th Cir.1983).

96. 5 U.S.C.A. § 552(a)(4)(B).

in order to ascertain their exempt status.[97] Recognizing that judges are often in no position to assess the importance and ramifications of sensitive documents,[98] most courts have taken the position that *in camera* inspection is to be the exception, not the rule.[99] Where an agency meets its burden by means of sufficiently detailed affidavits, *in camera* review may be deemed unnecessary and inappropriate.[100]

§ 17.3.5 Agency Fees, Agency Waivers and Attorney Fees

The 1986 FOIA Reform Act revised FOIA's fee and fee waiver provisions by establishing a three-tiered fee structure. Agencies are allowed to charge for document review, in addition to search[101] and duplication costs for records requested for commercial use. Agencies can charge only duplication but not search fees for noncommercial requests by educational or noncommercial scientific institutions or the news media. Charges on all other requests are limited to search and duplication costs. FOIA also authorizes agencies to waive or reduce customary charges for document searches and duplication[102] when agencies determine that such action "is in the public interest because it is likely to contribute significantly to public understanding of the operations or activities of the government and is not primarily in the commercial interest of the requester."[103] The Department of Justice has issued guidelines to carry out these provisions.[104] Whenever the public interest goals of the statute are outweighed by any commercial or personal benefit to the requester, a fee waiver is inappropriate.[105]

De novo judicial review is appropriate in any action challenging the failure to grant a fee waiver, provided that the court's review is limited to the record before the agency.[106] Courts also generally agree that indigency alone, without any showing of public benefit, is insufficient to warrant a fee waiver.[107] Generally speaking, bona fide public interest

97. See generally Comment: In Camera Inspections Under the FOIA, 41 U.Chi. L.Rev. 557 (1974).

98. See, e.g., CIA v. Sims, 471 U.S. 159, 179, 105 S.Ct. 1881, 1893, 85 L.Ed.2d 173 (1985) ("The decisions of the Director [of the CIA], who must of course be familiar with 'the whole picture,' as judges are not, *are* worthy of great deference . . .") (emphasis added).

99. See Ingle v. Department of Justice, 698 F.2d 259, 266 (6th Cir.1983).

100. See Brinton v. Department of State, 636 F.2d 600, 606 (D.C.Cir.1980), cert. denied 452 U.S. 905, 101 S.Ct. 3030, 69 L.Ed.2d 405 (1981).

101. The 1996 amendments define a "search" as locating records or information "manually or by automated means," 5 U.S.C. § 552(a)(3)(D).

102. See generally Bonine, Public Interest Fee Waivers Under the FOIA, 1981 Duke L.J. 213; S. Rep. No. 93–854, at 10–12 (1974) (discussing policy of search and copy fees).

103. 5 U.S.C.A. § 552(a)(4)(A)(iii).

104. 28 C.F.R. § 16.11 (1999). See also Uniform Freedom of Information Act Fee Schedule and Guidelines, 52 Fed.Reg. 10012, 10017 (March 27, 1987) (The OMB based fee determinations depend on the identity of requester. Commercial users pay all costs of search and reproduction, while educational and non-commercial scientific institutions, representatives of the news media, and all others receive varying discounts).

105. See Ely v. U.S. Postal Service, 753 F.2d 163, 165 (D.C.Cir.1985), cert. denied 471 U.S. 1106, 105 S.Ct. 2338, 85 L.Ed.2d 854 (1985).

106. 5 U.S.C.A. § 552(a)(4)(A)(vii).

107. See, e.g., Ely supra note 207 at 165.

requesters (e.g., scholars, historians and researchers) usually qualify for a fee waiver or reduction.[108]

In regard to the more substantial costs of suing the government for disclosure of records requested under FOIA, the Act authorizes the trial court to award reasonable attorney fees and litigation costs if the plaintiff "substantially prevails."[109] In determining whether such an award is appropriate, courts embark on a two-step inquiry: first, is the plaintiff eligible for an award of fees and/or costs, and if so, is the plaintiff entitled to them?

To be eligible, a plaintiff must "substantially prevail," i.e., she must show that the prosecution of the suit was reasonably necessary to obtain the information sought and that a causal connection existed between the suit and the agency's disclosure of the requested documents.[110] But the mere fact that documents were released after the filing of the suit does not necessarily mean that the plaintiff substantially prevailed; to be eligible, the plaintiff must *prove* that the filing of the lawsuit caused the release of the documents.[111]

Even if a plaintiff meets the eligibility test, a court must exercise its discretion in deciding whether the plaintiff is entitled to an award. There are four criteria for this inquiry: (1) the public benefit derived from the case; (2) the commercial benefit to the complainant; (3) the nature of the complainant's interest in the records sought; and (4) whether the government's withholding had a reasonable basis in law.[112] If a court decides to make a fee award, it must first determine the appropriate fee amount by multiplying the number of hours reasonably expended by a reasonable hourly rate; this "lodestar" may then be adjusted up or down depending among other factors, such as the skill of counsel and the difficulty of the case.[113] The award of attorney fees is the exception, not the rule.

Another issue under FOIA is whether a *pro se* litigant who "sub-

108. See, e.g., Weisberg v. U.S. Department of Justice, 745 F.2d 1476, 1483 n. 10 (D.C.Cir.1984), affirmed in part and remanded, 848 F.2d 1265 (D.C.Cir.1988) (author investigating assassination of Martin Luther King entitled to a fee waiver in regard to 60,000 pages of disclosed documents).

109. 5 U.S.C.A. § 552(a)(4)(E).

110. See, e.g., Cox v. U.S. Department of Justice, 601 F.2d 1, 6 (D.C.Cir.1979) (citing Vermont Low Income Advocacy Council, Inc. v. Usery, 546 F.2d 509, 513 (2d Cir. 1976)); Miller v. U.S. Department of State, 779 F.2d 1378 (8th Cir.1985) (claimant will have substantially prevailed, even if she did not receive favorable judgment, if she can prove the suit was necessary to obtain the release of documents and the suit caused such release).

111. See, e.g., Murty v. Office Of Personnel Management, 707 F.2d 815, 816 (4th Cir.1983) ("telephone call of inquiry as to what has happened to his request . . . would have produced the same result as the law suit"); Weisberg v. U.S. Department of Justice, 745 F.2d 1476, 1494–99 (D.C.Cir.1984), affirmed in part and remanded, 848 F.2d 1265 (D.C.Cir.1988).

112. Fenster v. Brown, 617 F.2d 740, 742 (D.C.Cir.1979).

113. See Copeland v. Marshall, 641 F.2d 880, 891–94 (D.C.Cir.1980) (*en banc*); Weisberg v. U.S. Department of Justice, 745 F.2d 1476, 1499–1500 (D.C.Cir.1984), affirmed in part and remanded, 848 F.2d 1265 (D.C.Cir.1988).

stantially prevails'' is entitled to an award of attorney fees.[114] Most courts which have considered the question have held that FOIA does not contemplate an award of fees to *pro se* litigants.[115] The D.C. Circuit, however, has approved the award of attorney fees to *pro se* litigants.[116]

§ 17.3.6 §§ 552(c)(2) and (c)(3)

There is almost no case law interpreting § 552(c). What little exists at the Circuit court level involves an interpretation of § 552(c)(2) in relation to a so-called ''Glomar response,'' after Phillippi v. Central Intelligence Agency.[117] A Glomar response is when an agency, for reasons of security, refuses to confirm or deny the existence of records.[118] Sec. 552(c)(3) was referred to in dicta that pertained to whether the FBI was an agency for the purpose of FOIA.[119] The DOJ argued that the FBI was not an agency for the purpose of FOIA; the Court refused to reach the merits of the argument as it was raised for the first time on appeal. The Court did note that FOIA appears to contemplate the FBI as subject to its provisions under 5 U.S.C. § 552(c)(3).

§ 17.4 FOIA CASELAW: THE NINE EXEMPTIONS

The following sections present an overview of the caselaw related to subsection (b) of FOIA,[1] which designates nine exemptions from the Act's disclosure requirements.[2] The Department of Justice policy for the

114. See generally Note, Attorney fees, Freedom of Information, and *pro se* Litigants: *Pro Se* Prohibitions Frustrate Policies, 26 Wm. & Mary L. Rev. 349–73 (1985).

115. Aronson v. U.S. Dep't of Housing and Urban Development, 866 F.2d 1, 4 (1st Cir.1989) (noting that all circuits except D.C. have held that a non-lawyer pro se litigant is not entitled to attorney fees).

116. See Cox, supra note 212, 601 F.2d at 5–6. Cf. Blazy v. Tenet, 194 F.3d 90, 95 (D.C.Cir.1999) (error for district court to use FOIA analysis to decide whether pro se Privacy Act claimant was entitled to attorney fees).

117. 546 F.2d 1009 (D.C.Cir.1976).

118. See Benavides v. Drug Enforcement Admin., 968 F.2d 1243, 1248 (D.C.Cir. 1992) (Congress did not intend to authorize use of a Glomar response under § 552(c)(2) when an informant's status has been ''officially confirmed''), modified on reh'g, in part, by 976 F.2d 751, 753 (D.C.Cir.1992) (not authoritatively found whether § 552(c)(2) requires a Glomar response or a ''no records have been found'' response).

119. See Peralta v. U.S. Attorney's Office, 136 F.3d 169 (D.C.Cir.1998) (a classic ''who's on first'' tale of bureaucratic snafu's that opens with the following line from the Court: ''In order to make sense of this case, we note preliminarily that the parties and the district court lost track of the identity of the 'defendant' in this litigation'').

§ 17.4

1. For more detailed listings of current FOIA issues and caselaw under both the exemptions and the procedural periphery of the Act, see U.S. Dep't of Justice, Freedom of Information Act Guide & Privacy Act Overview [serial], available at http://www.usdoj.gov/oip/foi-act/htm; Guidebook to the Freedom of Information and Privacy Acts (2d ed., Franklin and Bouchard eds. 1986) [annual supplements]; Access Reports (biweekly commercial newsletter, available at http://www.accessreports.com); Privacy Times (biweekly commercial newsletter, available at http://www.privacytimes.com); FOIA Clearinghouse, http://www.citizen.org/litigation/litigation.htm; University of Missouri FOIA Project, http://web.Missouri.edu/_foiwww.

2. According to K.C. Davis, FOIA as interpreted by the courts is far superior to the Act as written. He also notes that the right at common law to inspect and copy public records is generally overlooked. See 1 Kenneth Culp Davis, Administrative Law Treatise 34–36 (2d ed. Supp. 1982).

application of any FOIA exemption is to encourage maximum responsible disclosure of agency material by application of a "foreseeable harm" standard.[3] For an exemption to apply to requested agency material, the agency must reasonably foresee that disclosure would be harmful to the agency interest protected by the exemption.[4]

§ 17.4.1 Exemption (b)(1): National Security Information

FOIA does not apply to matters that are:

"(A) specifically authorized under criteria established by an Executive order to be kept secret in the interest of national defense or foreign policy and (B) are in fact properly classified pursuant to such Executive order;"[5]

Congress amended the national security exemption in 1974, thereby overruling *EPA v. Mink*,[6] discussed previously,[7] and authorizing judicial *in camera* review of classified documents. The 1974 FOIA amendments sought to minimize automatic deference to the Executive.

The current judicial approach to Exemption 1 claims, as outlined in *King v. U.S. Department of Justice*,[8] allows the agency significant discretion in determining what is and what is not covered by Exemption 1. As in all FOIA cases of contested exemptions, the district court must review *de novo* any claim advanced,[9] and the agency must bear the burden of justifying its decision to withhold the information.[10] Congress intended the courts to accord substantial weight to an agency's affidavit concerning the details of the classification of the disputed record.[11] For a district court to award summary judgment to an agency claiming an Exemption 1 withholding: (1) the affidavits must describe the documents in enough detail and with sufficient specificity to demonstrate that material withheld is logically within the domain of the exemption claimed,[12] and (2) the affidavits must be controverted neither by contrary record evidence nor impugned by bad faith on the part of the agency.[13] The affidavits cannot support summary judgment if they are "conclusory, merely reciting statutory standards, or if they are too vague or sweeping."[14]

The standard of review to which the court subjects the documents in its *de novo* review of the agency decision is unclear in light of the congressional mandate to accord great weight to the affidavits of the

3. See U.S. Dep't of Justice, Freedom of Information Act Guide & Privacy Act Overview 116 (2000).

4. Id.

5. 5 U.S.C.A. § 552(b)(1).

6. 410 U.S. 73, 93 S.Ct. 827, 35 L.Ed.2d 119 (1973), superseded by statute as stated in Halpern v. FBI, 181 F.3d 279 (2d Cir.1999).

7. See sec. 17.2 supra.

8. 830 F.2d 210 (D.C.Cir.1987) (Exemption 1 categorization by FBI of files kept on civil rights lawyer who died in 1952 remanded to district court for further examination).

9. 5 U.S.C.A. § 552(a)(4)(B).

10. Id.

11. Cf. Halpern v. FBI, supra note 227 (noting the tension between de novo review and deference to an agency affidavit).

12. King v. U.S. Dep't of Justice, 830 F.2d 210, 217 (D.C.Cir.1987).

13. Id. at 217.

14. Id. (internal quotation marks omitted, citation omitted).

agency.[15] In reviewing Exemption 1 claims, courts generally accord the agency broad discretion in determining just what is and what is not exempt in section (b)(1). Courts tend to give "utmost" deference to agency classification,[16] or require only a "reasonable" basis for finding potential harm in disclosure.[17]

Exemption 1 cases typically involve access to classified affidavits and the adequacy of an agency's response to a FOIA request. In disputes over especially sensitive classified information, the court normally allows the agency to submit an *in camera* affidavit. Such a situation arises when an agency asserts that it cannot even admit to the existence of the records sought without incurring a breach of security. The court in *Phillippi v. CIA*[18] followed this "neither confirm nor deny" procedure where the plaintiff sought CIA records in order to confirm rumors that the United States had hired the Glomar Explorer to attempt to salvage a sunken Russian submarine. In situations requiring a "Glomar denial," plaintiff's counsel is generally excluded from the *in camera* review of the classified affidavits;[19] however, the court has required the agency to release segregable portions of the affidavit.[20]

Exemption 1 litigation is often protracted by demands that the agency release "reasonably segregable" declassified portions[21] of the protected documents, a burden resisted by most agencies.[22] Those seeking release contend that the agencies have hidden public information behind overly-broad claims of exemption, while the agencies argue that such segregation is a time-consuming waste of expert agency staff and a process that allows anti-U.S. requesters to piece together related segments as clues to classified activity.[23] In 1984, Congress addressed these concerns by exempting certain CIA operational files from FOIA requests.[24]

15. See Robert P. Deyling, Judicial Deference and De Novo Review in Litigation Over National Security Information Under the FOIA, 37 Vill. L. Rev. 67 (1992). The courts tend to use a 2-pronged approach similar to that developed by the 2nd Circuit. On the one hand, when the agency affidavit lacks sufficient specificity or smacks of bad faith, the court applies de novo review. On the other hand, when the agency affidavit is sufficiently detailed, the district court "should restrain its discretion to order in camera review." Halpern v. FBI, supra note 227, at 292.

16. Taylor v. Department of the Army, 684 F.2d 99, 104 (D.C.Cir.1982).

17. Ray v. Turner, 587 F.2d 1187, 1193 (D.C.Cir.1978).

18. 546 F.2d 1009 (D.C.Cir.1976).

19. See Arieff v. U.S. Department of Navy, 712 F.2d 1462, 1470 n. 2 (D.C.Cir. 1983).

20. Hayden v. National Security Agency,608 F.2d 1381, 1387 (D.C.Cir.1979), cert. denied, 446 U.S. 937, 100 S.Ct. 2156, 64 L.Ed.2d 790 (1980) (Jane Fonda and Tom Hayden denied access to NSA Intelligence Files on them) (segregable provision of FOIA applies to classified affidavits).

21. 5 U.S.C.A. § 552(b).

22. See, e.g., Agee v. CIA, 517 F.Supp. 1335, 1342 n. 5 (D.D.C.1981) (agency spent $400,000 to review documents sought by former agent writing an exposé).

23. See CIA v. Sims, 471 U.S. 159, 178–80, 105 S.Ct. 1881, 1892–93, 85 L.Ed.2d 173 (1985).

24. Central Intelligence Agency Information Act, Pub.L. No. 98–477, 98 Stat. 2209 (1984). Because it restricts access to CIA files which were in large part already individually exempt under FOIA, the law is primarily a cost-saving measure which rarely restricts access to information. See, e.g., Hunt v. CIA, 981 F.2d 1116 (9th Cir.1992).

During the Cold War, the Executive branch, the CIA, and the Attorney General had persistently called on Congress to broaden the national security exemption.[25] With the end of the Cold War, however, members of Congress began to rethink the U.S. government's "culture of secrecy."[26] Congress found that the Cold War had created an "extensive secrecy system ... which limited public access to information and reduced the ability of the public to participate with full knowledge in the process of governmental decisionmaking."[27] In 1992, nearly 6.4 million documents were classified; in the meantime, the private sector spent $14 billion yearly to implement government regulations to protect classified information.[28] It was with these facts in mind that Congress established the two-year Commission on Protecting and Reducing Government Secrecy to study government practices relating to classified information.[29] The Commission recommended, among other things, that Congress create "a stable and reliable" statutory system for document classification and document declassification to replace the five-decade-old discretionary classification system created by executive orders.[30] In spite of the Commission's call for less government secrecy, however, agency affidavits that are not conclusory still suffice to satisfy the burden of proof in disputes over classified materials.[31]

Supreme Court decisions confirm, albeit tangentially, that the judiciary is reluctant to substitute its judgment in place of an agency's expertise or insights, especially when the CIA is involved. In *CIA v. Sims,*[32] for example, the Court stated that "it is the responsibility of the Director of Central Intelligence, not that of the judiciary, to weigh the variety of complex and subtle factors in determining whether disclosure of information may lead to an unacceptable risk of compromising the Agency's intelligence gathering process."[33] Although the *Sims* decision technically addressed the ambit of the term "intelligence source" and the scope of the National Security Act of 1947 authorizing the CIA to withhold information pursuant to Exemption 3 of FOIA, the tone and language of the Court's opinion was reminiscent to the Court's tone in *EPA v. Mink*.[34]

25. See generally Harold C. Relyea, Modifying the FOIA: Ideas and Implications, reprinted in FOI Trends in the Information Age 56, 57–61, 70–77 (Tom Riley & H. Relyea eds., 1983).

26. S. Doc. No. 105–2, at XXXI (1997) (Foreword by Sen. Moynihan to the Report of the Commission on Protecting and Reducing Government Secrecy).

27. 1994 Protection and Reduction of Government Secrecy Act, Pub. L. No. 103–238, 108 Stat. 525.

28. Id.

29. Id. The creation of the Commission was only the second time in 80 years that Congress had studied the policies behind government secrecy. S. Doc. No. 105–2 at XXXII (1997). The first time was with the 1955 Wright Commission. Id.

30. Id. at XXII.

31. See, e.g., Public Citizen, Inc. v. Dep't of State 100 F.Supp.2d 10, 25 (D.D.C. 2000) (citing Stein v. Dep't of Justice, 662 F.2d 1245, 1253 (7th Cir.1981)). Cf. Rosenfeld v. U.S. Dep't of Justice, 57 F.3d 803, 807 (9th Cir.1995) (deference to agency classification decision not warranted when agency fails to show "with particularity" why Exemption 1 is appropriate).

32. 471 U.S. 159, 105 S.Ct. 1881, 85 L.Ed.2d 173 (1985).

33. Id. at 180, 105 S.Ct. at 1893–94.

34. 410 U.S. 73, 93 S.Ct. 827, 35 L.Ed.2d 119 (1973), superseded by statute

In 1995, President Clinton issued Executive Order 12,958, which significantly facilitated declassification of government information, especially of older records.[35] The Executive Order, with exceptions, limits the duration on new classification actions, automatically declassified information that is twenty-five years old or older,[36] and authorizes agencies to apply a balancing test between the public interest and national security for declassification decisions. In spite of Executive Order 12,958 reversing the Reagan–Bush Administrations' trend toward greater government secrecy, some members of Congress have criticized the executive order classification system for being too permissive in its grant of classification authority. These critics cite the fact that during the Clinton Administration, twenty officials who had the authority to classify information as "Top Secret" delegated that authority to nearly 1,400 persons. From those 1,400 persons, two million government employees and one million government contractors derived their own authority to classify documents.[37]

§ 17.4.2 Exemption (b)(2): Internal Rules and Practices

FOIA's disclosure mandate does not apply to matters "related solely to the internal personnel rules and practices of an agency."[38]

Although there was some confusion in the 1960s and 1970s whether Exemption 2 pertained to agency personnel practices or to agency general practices,[39] the U.S. Court of Appeals for the District of Columbia Circuit settled the issue in *Founding Church of Scientology, Inc. v. Smith* by creating an Exemption 2 test. First, the withheld agency material must fall within the "internal personnel rules and practices of an agency" language of the statute.[40] Second, the withheld material must

as stated in Halpern v. FBI, 181 F.3d 279 (2d Cir.1999), discussed in sec. 17.2 supra. See also CIA v. Holy Spirit Association, 455 U.S. 997, 102 S.Ct. 1626, 71 L.Ed.2d 858 (1982) (memo decision) (vacating that portion of D.C. Circuit's affirmation of a district court's ruling that CIA affidavits were impermissibly conclusory and "overly broad").

35. Exec. Order No. 12,958, 3 C.F.R. 333 (1995–2000), reprinted in 50 U.S.C.A. § 435 note at 124–35 (Supp. 2000).

36. In 1995, there were more than 1.5 billion pages of classified government documents 25 years old or older. S.Doc. No. 105–2, at XXXIV (1997). President Clinton's Executive Order mandated the creation of a government declassification electronic database for material older than 25 years that falls under the Order's automatic declassification provision. See Exec. Order No. 12,958 § 3.4(a).

37. Id. at XXVII. In 1995, there were 3.6 million classification actions; 400,000 were "Top Secret." Id.

38. 5 U.S.C.A. § 552(b)(2).

39. See S. Rep. No. 89–813 (1965) (giving a narrow interpretation of Exemption 2); H.R. Rep. No. 89–1497 (1966) (giving a brood interpretation of Exemption 2). Cf. Department of Air Force v. Rose, 425 U.S. 352, 96 S.Ct. 1592, 48 L.Ed.2d 11 (1976) (finding the Senate Report to be more authoritative than the House Report without resolving the issue whether Exemption 2 covered agency personnel practices or general agency practices).

40. Founding Church of Scientology, Inc. v. Smith, 721 F.2d 828, 831 n. 4 (D.C.Cir.1983). Later questions arose whether the phrase "internal personnel rules and practices" modified "of an agency," which would be a narrow construction of the exemption, or whether "and practices of an agency" was a separate element from "internal personnel rules," which would be a broad construction of the exemption. See Abraham & Rose, P.L.C. v. United States, 138 F.3d 1075, 1080 (6th Cir.1998) (stating that Exemption 2 only covers agency infor-

relate to "trivial administrative matters of no genuine public interest."[41] If these two elements are satisfied, then exemption is automatic.[42] On the other hand, if withholding the material would frustrate a legitimate public interest, then the material must be released—unless the agency can show that such disclosure would "risk circumvention of lawful agency regulation."[43]

The test created in *Founding Church of Scientology* has evolved into a "low (b)(2)" exemption and a "high (b)(2)" exemption.[44] The low (b)(2) exemption covers agency personnel rules, internal agency practices, and matters sufficiently related to such rules or practices. Included within the scope of the low (b)(2) exemption are "trivial administrative data such as file numbers, mail routing stamps, initials, data processing notations, and other administrative markings."[45] High (b)(2) exemptions cover "predominately internal documents the disclosure of which would likely circumvent agency regulations and statutes."[46] Included within the scope of high (b)(2) exemptions are records that would reveal an informant's identity,[47] records that would reveal "sensitive administrative instructions,"[48] and information that would reveal prison procedures.[49]

An agency that invokes the low (b)(2) must satisfy two elements. First, the agency must show "that the requested information sought to be sheltered from disclosure relates predominantly to [the] agency's internal 'rules and practices' for personnel"[50] or sheds "significant light" on a "rule or practice."[51] Second, the agency must show that "that the public has no genuine or legitimate interest in the requested informa-

mation about "internal 'rules and practices' for personnel"); Audubon Soc'y v. United States Forest Serv., 104 F.3d 1201, 1204 (10th Cir.1997) (holding that Exemption 2 only applies to documents related to agency "personnel practices").

41. Founding Church of Scientology, Inc. v. Smith, 721 F.2d at 831 n.4.

42. Id.

43. Id.

44. See Coleman v. FBI, 13 F.Supp. 2d 75, 78 (D.D.C.1998).

45. Id. But see Manna v. United States Dep't of Justice, 832 F.Supp. 866, 880 (D.N.J.1993), affirmed, 51 F.3d 1158 (3d Cir.1995), cert. denied, 516 U.S. 975, 116 S.Ct. 477, 133 L.Ed.2d 405 (1995) (denying Exemption 2 status to documents, the internal markings of which the DEA "failed to describe or explain").

46. Coleman v. FBI, 13 F.Supp.2d at 78.

47. See Blanton v. United States Dep't of Justice, 63 F.Supp.2d 35, 43 (D.D.C. 1999).

48. See Institute for Policy Studies v. Department of Air Force, 676 F.Supp. 3, 5 (D.D.C.1987).

49. See Kuffel v. United States Bureau of Prisons, 882 F.Supp. 1116, 1123 (D.D.C. 1995).

50. Abraham & Rose, P.L.C. v. United States, 138 F.3d 1075, 1080 (6th Cir.1998).

51. Schwaner v. Department of Air Force, 898 F.2d 793, 797 (D.C.Cir.1990). See also Audubon Soc'y v. United States Forest Serv., supra note 261, at 1204 (finding that habitat maps of a "threatened" species under the Endangered Species Act are not sufficiently related to agency internal rules and practices to fall under Exemption 2). The courts have held that government lists, by themselves, do not shed sufficient light on agency practices to fall under Exemption 2. See DeLorme Publ'g Co. v. NOAA, 917 F.Supp. 867, 876 (D.Me. 1996) (finding that lists only reveal that an agency is in the practice of collecting information). Moreover, information that only potentially sheds light on an agency practice does not fall under Exemption 2. See Abraham & Rose, P.L.C, supra note 271, at 1081.

tion."[52] An agency that invokes the high (b)(2) exemption must satisfy three elements: first, the agency must show that the requested information "relates to the 'internal personnel rules and practices' of the agency; second, that the requested material is 'predominantly internal';[53] and third, that 'disclosure would risk circumvention of federal statutes or regulations.'[54] Under the 'anti-circumvention' element of the high(b)(2) exemption, the interest of the public in the requested information is immaterial."[55] This aspect of Exemption 2 therefore relies on the "foreseeable harm" standard.[56] Nevertheless, an agency may be required to determine whether any "reasonably segregable" portion of the information can be disclosed without harm.[57] The courts have held that the passage of time does not affect the releasability of agency information.[58]

§ 17.4.3 Exemption (b)(3): Exemption by Statute

Under FOIA, an agency may refuse to release information if the information is "specifically exempted from disclosure by statute (other than § 552b of this title) [The Privacy Act], provided that such statute (A) requires that the matters be withheld from the public in such a manner as to leave no discretion on the issue, or (B) establishes particular criteria for withholding or refers to particular types of matters to be withheld."[59] Courts employ a two step approach in reviewing Exemption

52. See Abraham & Rose, P.L.C., supra note 271, at 1080 n.4. This "public interest" threshold is a low one. See Founding Church of Scientology, Inc., supra note 262, at 830–31 n.4. See also Church of Scientology v. IRS, 816 F.Supp. 1138, 1149 (W.D.Tex.1993) (holding that the "public is entitled to know how IRS is allocating" employee travel advances). But see Voinche v. FBI, 46 F.Supp.2d 26, 30 (D.D.C.1999) (finding that telephone number of FBI Public Corruption Unit telephone numbers are a "trivial administrative matter of no genuine public interest").

53. Crooker v. Bureau of Alcohol, Tobacco & Firearms, 670 F.2d 1051, 1053 (D.C.Cir.1981). The courts usually show great deference to law enforcement activities as "purely internal;" agency activities. See, e.g., Wiesenfelder v. Riley, 959 F.Supp. 532 (D.D.C.1997). Cf. Maricopa Audubon Soc'y v. United States Forest Serv., 108 F.3d 1082 (9th Cir.1997) (finding that agency maps of endangered species habitats failed the test of "predominant internality); Audubon Soc'y v. United States Forest Serv., 104 F.3d 1201 (10th Cir.1997) (same)".

54. Audubon Soc'y v. United States Forest Serv., 104 F.3d 1201, 1203 (10th Cir.1997).

55. See Voinche, supra note 273, at 328.

56. See discussion, supra § 17.4. See also Judicial Watch, Inc. v. United States Dep't of Commerce, 83 F.Supp.2d 105, 110 (D.D.C.1999) (finding that disclosure of government credit card numbers would create "an opportunity for misuse and fraud").

57. See, e.g., Schrecker v. United States Dep't of Justice, 74 F.Supp.2d 26, 32 (D.D.C.1999) (finding that FBI properly withheld from disclosure source codes for confidential informants and identifying data that were not "reasonably segregable").

58. See Buckner v. IRS, 25 F.Supp.2d 893, 899 (N.D.Ind.1998) ("Because DIF scores are investigative techniques . . . still used by the IRS in evaluating tax returns . . . the age of the scores is of no consequence" in evaluating the exempt status of the codes).

59. 5 U.S.C.A. § 552(b)(3). Rule 6(e) of the Federal Rules of Criminal Procedure falls within the ambit of Exemption 3(A) because the rule strictly regulates the disclosure of evidence and testimony before a Federal grand jury. See Church of Scientology Int'l v. United States Dep't of Justice, 30 F.3d 224, 235 (1st Cir.1994) (holding that grand jury exhibits "may be withheld simply on the basis of their status as exhibits"); McDonnell v. United States, 4 F.3d 1227, 1246 (3d Cir.1993) (same). The National Security Act of 1947 (50 U.S.C.A.

3 claims. First, the court determines whether the statute is a withholding statute by the standards set forth in Exemption (b)(3).[60] Secondly, the court then ascertains whether the information withheld falls within the boundaries of the non-disclosure statute.[61] The (b)(3) exemption does not provide a list of specific Federal statutes which would override FOIA's disclosure mandate. Rather, Congress chose to provide a generic exemption standard so that courts could decide what these statutory conflicts were on a case by case basis.

Exemption 3 is applicable only to Federal statutes; disclosure prohibitions in Executive orders and agency regulations do *not* trigger the exemption.[62] In *Baldrige v. Shapiro*[63] and *Consumer Products Safety Commission v. GTE Sylvania,*[64] the Supreme Court ruled that the Census Act and the Consumer Product Safety Act, respectively, were sufficiently specific to authorize withholding under Exemption 3 since the agencies had no discretion to release the records at issue. Other cases indicate that the more specific the conflicting statute, the more likely it is to acquire Exemption 3 status and to overcome the disclosure mandate of FOIA.[65] A related issue is whether post-FOIA statutes "displace" FOIA's broad presumption of disclosure. If a court accepts this displacement theory,[66] it can avoid the *de novo* review required by FOIA and resort instead to the less rigorous review standards contained in the Administrative Procedure Act.[67] The validity of this displacement theory is in considerable doubt.[68] A court may, however, accept the

§ 403–3(c)(6) (West Supp. 2000)), which requires the Director of the CIA to protect "intelligence sources and methods," refers to particular types of matters to be withheld and so falls within the scope of Exemption 3(B). See Frugone v. CIA, 169 F.3d 772, 774–75 (D.C.Cir.1999) (finding that CIA properly used a Glomar response despite claims that another agency had already confirmed the information).

60. CIA v. Sims, 471 U.S. 159, 167, 105 S.Ct. 1881, 1887, 85 L.Ed.2d 173, 182 (1985); See also Reporters Committee for Freedom of the Press v. U.S. Department of Justice, 816 F.2d 730, 735 (D.C.Cir.1987), remanded 831 F.2d 1124 (1987), rev'd, 489 U.S. 749, 109 S.Ct. 1468, 103 L.Ed.2d 774 (1989); Essential Info, Inc. v. USIA, 134 F.3d 1165, 1168 (D.C.Cir.1998) (holding that a statute that prohibits "dissemination" and "distribution" of information qualifies as a "nondisclosure" statute).

61. Irons & Sears v. Dann, 606 F.2d 1215, 1219 (D.C.Cir.1979), cert. denied sub nom. Irons & Sears v. Commissioner of Patents & Trademarks, 444 U.S. 1075, 100 S.Ct. 1021, 62 L.Ed.2d 757 (1980).

62. See Washington Post Co. v. U.S. Dept. of HHS, 690 F.2d 252, 273 (D.C.Cir. 1982), on remand 603 F.Supp. 235 (D.D.C. 1985) (Tamm, J., dissenting); Founding Church of Scientology v. Bell, 603 F.2d 945, 952 (D.C.Cir.1979).

63. 455 U.S. 345, 102 S.Ct. 1103, 71 L.Ed.2d 199 (1982).

64. 447 U.S. 102, 100 S.Ct. 2051, 64 L.Ed.2d 766 (1980).

65. See, e.g., Church of Scientology v. IRS, 484 U.S. 9, 15–16, 108 S.Ct. 271, 274–75, 98 L.Ed.2d 228 (1987) (IRC § 6103); Essential Info. v. United States Info. Agency, 134 F.3d 1165 (D.C.Cir.1998) (Smith–Mundt Act); Irons and Sears v. Dann, 606 F.2d 1215 (D.C.Cir.1979), cert. denied, sub nom. Irons & Sears v. Commissioner of Patents and Trademarks, 444 U.S. 1075, 100 S.Ct. 1021, 62 L.Ed.2d 757 (1980) (Patents Act).

66. United States v. First National State Bank of New Jersey, 616 F.2d 668, 672 n. 6 (3d Cir.1980), cert. denied sub nom. Levey v. U.S., 447 U.S. 905, 100 S.Ct. 2987, 64 L.Ed.2d 854 (1980) (citing *Zale* with approval in dictum).

67. 5 U.S.C.A. § 701 et seq.

68. See Washington Post Co. v. U.S. Department of State, 685 F.2d 698, 703–04 n. 9 (D.C.Cir.1982), reh'g en banc denied, 685 F.2d 706 (D.C.Cir.1982), cert. granted 464 U.S. 812, 104 S.Ct. 65, 78 L.Ed.2d 80

displacement theory where a statute provides a comprehensive scheme to access information.[69]

In an issue that has particular bearing on FOIA exemption (b)(4), most courts have ruled that the Trade Secrets Act,[70] which prohibits the unauthorized disclosure of certain economic information, is *not* an Exemption 3 statute authorizing non-disclosure.[71] These courts generally rely on the House Committee Report to the 1976 FOIA amendments,[72] which suggests that the Trade Secrets Act is outside the ambit of Exemption 3, and that disclosure is therefore the rule. Despite the importance of the question, the Supreme Court has sidestepped the issue;[73] however, in *CNA Financial Corp. v. Donovan,*[74] the D.C. Circuit explicitly declared that the Trade Secrets Act failed to satisfy the requirements of Exemption 3.[75] On the other hand, the National Defense Authorization Act for Fiscal Year 1997[76] may protect certain confidential business information. The Act protects from disclosure the proposal of an unsuccessful offeror that bids for a government contract.[77] Moreover, the proposal of a successful offeror is also protected if the proposal is not "set forth or incorporated by reference" in the final contract.[78]

At one time, the most notable controversy over Exemption 3 involved the reconciliation of the 1974 Federal Privacy Act with FOIA. The Federal Privacy Act[79] seeks to protect against the unauthorized release of government-held information pertaining to an individual. A portion of

(1983), vacated and remanded, 464 U.S. 979, 104 S.Ct. 418, 78 L.Ed.2d 355 (1983). (holding that information could not be withheld pursuant to statutes that were passed after FOIA but nevertheless did not satisfy the Exemption 3 requirement). See also Church of Scientology v. IRS, 792 F.2d 146, 149 (D.C.Cir.1986), aff'd, 484 U.S. 9, 108 S.Ct. 271, 98 L.Ed.2d 228 (1987) (implicit "displacement" of the FOIA may be found only where a statute establishes rules and procedures, duplicating the FOIA, for the public to obtain access to documents produced under the statute).

69. See, e.g., Gersh & Danielson v. EPA, 871 F.Supp. 407, 410 (D.Colo.1994) (holding that the Clean Water Act disclosure provisions trump FOIA exemptions). But see Minier v. CIA, 88 F.3d 796, 802 (9th Cir.1996) (finding the comprehensive disclosure scheme of the President John F. Kennedy Assassination Records Collection Act was not intended to prevent the CIA from claiming "proper FOIA exemptions"); Winterstein v. United States Dep't of Justice, 89 F.Supp.2d 79, 82–83 (D.D.C.2000) (stating that the Nazi War Crimes Disclosure Act does not control FOIA requests except where Congress excluded particular records from disclosure).

70. 18 U.S.C.A. § 1905.

71. Westchester General Hospital, Inc. v. Department of HEW, 464 F.Supp. 236, 242 (M.D.Fla.1979).

72. See House Comm. on Gov't Operations, H.R.Rep. No. 880, 94th Cong., 2d Sess., pt. 1, at 23 (1976).

73. See Chrysler Corp. v. Brown, 441 U.S. 281, 319 n. 49, 99 S.Ct. 1705, 1726 n. 49, 60 L.Ed.2d 208 (1979).

74. 830 F.2d 1132 (D.C.Cir.1987), cert. denied 485 U.S. 977, 108 S.Ct. 1270, 99 L.Ed.2d 481 (1988).

75. Id. at 1137–43. See also, Mudge Rose Guthrie Alexander & Ferdon v. U.S. International Trade Commission, 846 F.2d 1527 (D.C.Cir.1988) where the D.C. Circuit distinguished *Donovan* and held that section 777 of the Tariff Act did satisfy Exemption 3's requirements. Unlike the Trade Secrets Act, Section 777 was narrow, applied only to a single agency and protected information specifically labeled as "proprietary." Id. at 1530–31.

76. Pub. L. No. 104–201, § 821, 110 Stat. 2422 (codified as amended at 10 U.S.C. § 2305(g) (1994 & Supp. IV 1998) and at 41 U.S.C. § 253b(m) (1994 & Supp. III 1997)).

77. Id.

78. Id.

79. 5 U.S.C.A. § 552a.

that Act authorizes certain agency heads to exempt entire systems of records from disclosure. Another portion strictly limits those requesters who may receive information concerning an individual without the individual's consent.[80] Under an earlier view, the Privacy Act was an individual's sole avenue of inquiry in requesting information on herself; if a section of the Privacy Act exempted the information she requested from disclosure, her inquiry was effectively ended. The agency did not have to honor her subsequent FOIA request for the same material, due to the Privacy Act's status as a valid (b)(3) exempting statute. The problem with this position was that a third party requester, utilizing the disclosure-oriented FOIA, might be able to obtain information on an individual that was inaccessible to the individual herself. The Department of Justice and at least two circuits adopted this approach.[81]

An opposing school of thought maintained that the Privacy Act was *not* a FOIA (b)(3) exempting statute, and that the Privacy Act and the FOIA were distinct governing statutes, each requiring a separate inquiry. In adhering to this view, the ABA's Administrative Law Section[82] and two circuit courts[83] concluded that an individual should have as much access to her own files as possible, whether it be via the Privacy Act, the FOIA or both. The problem that then arose was that an individual requester who obtained information under FOIA was ostensibly prohibited from disclosure under the Privacy Act. In a broad request, which statute was to control?

The Supreme Court granted *certiorari* to resolve the conflict, but Congress stepped in. As part of the CIA Information Act,[84] Congress amended the final paragraph of the Privacy Act to provide that "[n]o agency shall rely on any exemption in this section [of the Privacy Act] to withhold from an individual any record which is otherwise accessible to such individual under the provision of [FOIA]."[85] The single-sentence amendment mooted the issue before the Supreme Court[86]—and repudiated the Justice Department's constrictive view of the interplay between the two Acts.

80. See chapter 18 infra for a detailed discussion of this Act.

81. See Painter v. FBI, 615 F.2d 689 (5th Cir.1980); Terkel v. Kelly, 599 F.2d 214 (7th Cir.1979), cert. denied, sub nom. Terkel v. Webster, 444 U.S. 1013, 100 S.Ct. 662, 62 L.Ed.2d 642 (1980); Shapiro v. DEA, 721 F.2d 215 (7th Cir.1983), cert. granted, 466 U.S. 926, 104 S.Ct. 1706, 80 L.Ed.2d 179 (1984), mooted & vacated, 469 U.S. 14, 105 S.Ct. 413, 83 L.Ed.2d 242 (1984).

82. Administrative Law News (Spring 1984) (American Bar Ass'n. Publication).

83. See Greentree v. U.S. Customs Service, 674 F.2d 74 (D.C.Cir.1982); Porter v. U.S. Department of Justice, 717 F.2d 787 (3d Cir.1983); Provenzano v. U.S. Department of Justice, 717 F.2d 799 (3d Cir.1983), reh'g denied 722 F.2d 36 (3d Cir.1983), cert. granted, 466 U.S. 926, 104 S.Ct. 1706, 80 L.Ed.2d 179 (1984), mooted & vacated, 469 U.S. 14, 15, 105 S.Ct. 413, 414, 83 L.Ed.2d 242 (1984).

84. Pub.L. No. 98–477, 98 Stat. 2209 (1984).

85. Id. Section 2(c), 98 Stat. at 2211–12. But note that when the Privacy Act applies, it authorizes disclosure only when no FOIA exemptions apply.

86. U.S. Department of Justice v. Provenzano, 469 U.S. 14, 15, 105 S.Ct. 413, 414, 83 L.Ed.2d 242 (1984), on remand 755 F.2d 922 (1985) (per curiam) (issue mooted, judgments below vacated and remanded for reconsideration under new statute).

§ 17.4.4 Exemption (b)(4): Trade Secrets

Also exempt from disclosure under FOIA are "trade secrets and commercial or financial information obtained from a person [that is] privileged or confidential."[87]

There is no clear definition of "trade secrets." Although the term arguably encompasses virtually any information that provides anyone a competitive advantage, the D.C. Circuit has defined the phrase more narrowly, as "a secret, commercially valuable plan, formula, process or device that is used for the making, preparing, compounding, or processing of trade commodities and that can be said to be the end product of either innovation or substantial effort."[88] The same court also required that there be a "direct relationship" between the trade secret and the productive process.[89] As we have seen, the Trade Secrets Act[90] is not a valid Exemption (b)(3) withholding statute.[91] The D.C. Circuit, however, has held that Exemption 4 and the Trade Secrets Act are coextensive.[92]

The majority of Exemption 4 cases focus on whether the information sought falls within the second category of the exemption. To do so, the information must be commercial or financial *and* obtained from a person *and* be privileged[93] or confidential.[94]

If information relates to business or trade—e.g., business sales statistics, research data, technical designs, customer and supplier lists, profit and loss data, overhead or operating costs, financial status or reports—courts have little difficulty in considering it "commercial or financial."[95] Exemption 4 protection has, however, been denied for information about the general physical characteristics or performance of

87. 5 U.S.C.A. § 552(b)(4).

88. Public Citizen Health Research Group v. FDA, 704 F.2d 1280, 1288 (D.C.Cir.1983). See also Anderson v. Department of HHS, 907 F.2d 936, 944 (10th Cir.1990) ("We agree with the D.C. Circuit's narrow definition because we believe that it is more consistent with the policies behind the FOIA than the broad Restatement definition. Of the arguments put forth by that court in support of its construction, we find most compelling the observation the adoption of the Restatement definition of 'trade secrets' would render superfluous the 'commercial or financial information' prong of Exemption 4 because there would be no category of information falling within the latter but outside the former. Like the D.C. Circuit, we are reluctant to construe the FOIA in such a manner.").

89. Id.

90. 18 U.S.C.A. § 1905.

91. See CNA Financial Corp. v. Donovan, 830 F.2d 1132, 1137–43 (D.C.Cir.1987), cert. denied sub nom. CNA Financial Corp. v. McLaughlin, 485 U.S. 977, 108 S.Ct. 1270, 99 L.Ed.2d 481 (1988).

92. Id. at 1144. See Chrysler Corp. v. Brown, 441 U.S. 281, 317–19 and n. 49, 99 S.Ct. 1705, 1725–26 and n. 49, 60 L.Ed.2d 208 (1979).

93. See Washington Post Co. v. Department of HHS, 795 F.2d 205, 208 (D.C.Cir.1986), appeal after remand 865 F.2d 320 (1989) (J. Scalia) (agency waived its right to raise "privilege" defense on remand by not doing so at the outset of the case).

94. See, e.g., Gulf & Western Industries, Inc. v. United States, 615 F.2d 527, 529 (D.C.Cir.1979); Consumers Union v. VA, 301 F.Supp. 796, 802 (S.D.N.Y.1969), appeal dismissed as moot 436 F.2d 1363 (2d Cir.1971).

95. See, e.g., Lepelletier v. FDIC, 977 F.Supp. 456, 459 (D.D.C.1997) (finding that the identities of businesses that have unclaimed deposits are financial information), aff'd in part, rev'd in part & remanded on other grounds, 164 F.3d 37 (D.C.Cir.1999).

a product or formula when the requested information would not reveal the formula itself.[96] Protection for financial information extends to persons as well as corporations and business entities.[97] There is some authority to the effect that information from nonprofit entities is not "commercial or financial" within the meaning of Exemption 4.[98]

The second of Exemption 4's specific criteria—that the information be "obtained from a person"—is satisfied in virtually all circumstances, owing to the Act's broad definition of "person" derived from the APA.[99] Information created by the federal government is not usually information "obtained from a person" unless the information is a summary or reformulation of information supplied by a source outside the government.[100]

The third criterion of Exemption 4's standard—that the information also be "privileged[101] or confidential"—has been heavily litigated. *National Parks and Conservation Association v. Morton,*[102] remains the standard for Exemption 4 "confidentiality" determinations. In *National Parks,* plaintiff's FOIA request asked for information and agency records concerning the concession operations of the National Park Service. The court below had granted the defendant Secretary of the Interior's motion for summary judgment, ruling that the concession records were "confidential" and exempt under Section (b)(4). The D.C. Circuit reversed and remanded, devising a two-part test:

96. See Animal Legal Defense Fund, Inc. v. Department of the Air Force, 44 F.Supp.2d 295, 303 (D.D.C.1999) (denying summary judgment when agency only stated that requested information contained commercial information but did not describe the documents, which would have allowed the accuracy of the claim to be tested).

97. Washington Post Co. v. Department of HHS, 690 F.2d 252, 266 (D.C.Cir. 1982), on remand 603 F.Supp. 235 (D.D.C. 1985), rev'd 795 F.2d 205 (D.C.Cir.1986), appeal after remand, 865 F.2d 320 (1989).

98. See Washington Research Project, Inc. v. Department of HEW, 504 F.2d 238, 244–45 (D.C.Cir.1974), cert. denied 421 U.S. 963, 95 S.Ct. 1951, 44 L.Ed.2d 450 (1975); cf. American Airlines, Inc. v. National Mediation Board, 588 F.2d 863, 870 (2d Cir. 1978) (profit/nonprofit distinction gives "much too narrow a construction" to Exemption 4's language). But see Critical Mass Energy Project v. NRC, 975 F.2d 871, 880 (D.C.Cir.1992) (en banc) (finding that the safety reports of a nuclear power plant nonprofit consortium are "commercial in nature").

99. See, e.g., Nadler v. FDIC, 92 F.3d 93, 95 (2d Cir.1996) (quoting APA definition of "person"); Stone v. Export–Import Bank, 552 F.2d 132, 136–37 (5th Cir.1977), cert. denied 434 U.S. 1012, 98 S.Ct. 726, 54 L.Ed.2d 756 (1978) (foreign government); Lepelletier v. FDIC, 977 F.Supp. 456, 459 (D.D.C.1997) (banks), aff'd in part, rev'd in part & remanded on other grounds, 164 F.3d 37 (D.C.Cir.1999). Comstock International (U.S.A.), Inc. v. Export–Import Bank, 464 F.Supp. 804, 806 (D.D.C.1979) (corporation).

100. See Philadelphia Newspapers, Inc. v. Department of HHS, 69 F.Supp.2d 63, 67 (D.D.C.1999) (finding that an agency audit is not "a summary or reformulation of information supplied by a source outside the government" and that a government analysis is not "obtained from a person" under Exemption 4).

101. See Sharyland Water Supply Corp. v. Block, 755 F.2d 397, 400 (5th Cir. 1985) (held that "privileged" refers "only to privileges created by the Constitution, statute or the common law"), cert. denied 471 U.S. 1137, 105 S.Ct. 2678, 86 L.Ed.2d 697 (1985); see Note, Developments Under the FOIA—1985, 1986 Duke L.J. 384 (1986).

102. 498 F.2d 765 (D.C.Cir.1974), appeal after remand, 547 F.2d 673 (1976).

> Commercial or financial matter is "confidential" for purposes of the [(b)(4)] exemption if disclosure of the information is likely to have either of the following effects: (1) to impair the Government's ability to obtain necessary information in the future; or (2) to cause substantial harm to the competitive position of the person from whom the information was obtained.[103]

The test articulated in *National Parks* has come to be known as the "impairment prong" and the "competitive harm prong." Under the impairment prong, an agency must show that the requested information was voluntarily provided to the government and that the submitting party would not provide such information in the future if the information were subject to public disclosure.[104] The competitive harm prong is intended to limit the use of proprietary information by competitors.[105] Under this prong, a submitter is allowed to testify about possible competitive harm that disclosure would cause.[106] Actual competitive harm need not be shown to satisfy the competitive harm prong. Rather, all that must be shown is "actual competition and a likelihood of substantial competitive injury."[107] Although some courts have suggested that each prong requires a balancing of the degree of harm against public interest in disclosure,[108] the U.S. Court of Appeals for the District of Columbia recently rejected an Exemption 4 balancing test as "inconsistent with the 'balance of private and public interests' the Congress [already] struck in Exemption 4.[109] Since Exemption 4 is to benefit the supplier of information, the confidentiality test in Exemption 4 already provides the appropriate balance between competing interests."[110]

103. Id. at 770. Whether government concerns other than its ability to obtain information might trigger Exemption 4 is unclear. Recent cases suggest that government interest in agency efficiency will suffice. See Critical Mass Energy Project v. NRC, 830 F.2d 278 (D.C.Cir.1987), on remand 731 F.Supp. 554 (D.D.C.1990), rev'd 931 F.2d 939 (D.C.Cir.1991), vacated 942 F.2d 799 (1991); see also 9 to 5 Organization for Women Office Workers v. Board of Governors of Federal Reserve System, 721 F.2d 1 (1st Cir.1983).

104. See Bowen v. FDA, 925 F.2d 1225, 1228 (9th Cir.1991) (protecting information related to government cyanide-tampering investigations); Gilmore v. United States Dep't of Energy, 4 F.Supp.2d 912, 923 (N.D.Cal.1998) (protecting video conferencing software because "corporations will be less likely to enter into joint ventures with the government to develop technology if that technology can be distributed freely").

105. See Public Citizen Health Research Group v. FDA, 704 F.2d 1280, 1291 n. 30 (D.C.Cir.1983). But see McDonnell Douglas Corp. v. NASA, 180 F.3d 303, 306–07 (D.C.Cir.1999) (accepting the claim that the disclosure of government contract prices would harm the contractor by making *customers* of the contractor more competitive).

106. See Executive Order No. 12,600, 52 Fed. Reg. 23,781 3 C.F.R. 235 (1987) (agencies now required to notify submitters of confidential records when those records are requested under FOIA).

107. CNA Fin. Corp. v. Donovan, 830 F.2d 1132, 1152 (D.C.Cir.1987). See also Frazee v. United States Forest Serv., 97 F.3d 367, 371 (9th Cir.1996); GC Micro Corp. v. Defense Logistics Agency, 33 F.3d 1109, 1113 (9th Cir.1994).

108. See, e.g., Washington Post Co. v. United States Dep't of Health & Human Services, 690 F.2d 252, 269 (D.C.Cir.1982).

109. Public Citizen Health Research Group v. FDA, 185 F.3d 898, 904 (D.C.Cir. 1999).

110. Id.

§ 17.4.5 Exemption (b)(5): Intra and Inter Agency Memoranda

The fifth exemption of FOIA permits an agency to withhold "inter-agency or intra-agency memoranda or letters which would not be available by law to a party other than an agency in litigation with the agency."[111]

Exemption 5 is generally construed to "exempt those documents, and only those documents, normally privileged in the civil discovery context."[112] Its three main components are the deliberative process privilege (executive privilege), the attorney work-product privilege and the attorney-client privilege.[113] Under Exemption 5, the threshold issue is whether a record is the type covered by the statutory language "inter-agency or intra-agency memorandums."[114] The courts have construed the scope of Exemption 5 broadly to include documents created outside of an agency.[115] On the other hand, whether Exemption 5 covers documents created during a settlement conference between the government and an adverse party remains unresolved,[116] although recently there has developed a "settlement negotiation" privilege outside of the FOIA.[117]

The initial determination of the court is whether what is involved can be characterized as "an intra-agency or inter-agency document." While civil discovery privileges are applied to Exemption 5 "by way of rough analogies,"[118] discovery and FOIA privileges raise quite different issues,[119] largely because of the vagaries inherent in assessing potential

111. 5 U.S.C.A. § 552(b)(5).

112. NLRB v. Sears, Roebuck & Co., 421 U.S. 132, 149, 95 S.Ct. 1504, 1516, 44 L.Ed.2d 29 (1975); see also FTC v. Grolier, Inc., 462 U.S. 19, 26, 103 S.Ct. 2209, 2214, 76 L.Ed.2d 387 (1983) ("The test under Exemption 5 is whether the documents would be 'routinely' or 'normally' dismissed upon a showing of relevance.").

113. The Supreme Court also extended Exemption 5 to include confidential factual statements made to air crash investigators (United States v. Weber Aircraft, Corp., 465 U.S. 792, 798, 104 S.Ct. 1488, 1492, 79 L.Ed.2d 814 (1984); Machin v. Zuckert, 316 F.2d 336 (D.C.Cir.1963), cert. denied 375 U.S. 896, 84 S.Ct. 172, 11 L.Ed.2d 124 (1963)) and confidential commercial information protected by Fed.R.Civ.P. 26c(7) (Federal Open Market Committee v. Merrill, 443 U.S. 340, 360, 99 S.Ct. 2800, 2812, 61 L.Ed.2d 587 (1979)). But see Burka v. Department of HHS, 87 F.3d 508, 517 (D.C.Cir.1996) (ruling that agency must show that discovery material is protected for reasons similar to FOIA material before court will deem the information privileged).

114. See United States Dep't of Justice v. Julian, 486 U.S. 1, 11 n. 9, 108 S.Ct. 1606, 100 L.Ed.2d 1 (1988) (Scalia, J., dissenting) (stating that "the most natural meaning of the phrase 'intra-agency memorandum' is a memorandum that is addressed both to and from employees of a single agency-as opposed to an 'inter-agency memorandum,' which would be a memorandum between employees of two different agencies").

115. See, e.g., General Electric Co. v. EPA, 18 F.Supp.2d 138, 142 (D.Mass.1998) (exempting state agency data sent to a federal agency at the request of the federal agency).

116. See U.S. Dep't of Justice, Freedom of Information Act Guide & Privacy Act Overview 234–35 (2000) [hereinafter FOIA Guide].

117. See, e.g., Butta–Brinkman v. FCA Int'l, 164 F.R.D. 475, 477 (N.D.Ill.1995). But See Burka v. HHS, supra note 334, at 517.

118. EPA v. Mink, 410 U.S. 73, 86, 93 S.Ct. 827, 836, 35 L.Ed.2d 119 (1973), superseded by statute as stated in Halpern v. FBI, 181 F.3d 279 (2d Cir.1999).

119. See, e.g., Playboy Enterprises, Inc. v. Department of Justice, 677 F.2d 931, 936 (D.C.Cir.1982).

effects of disclosure on the decisionmaking process. In practice, courts tend to interpret Exemption 5 broadly to include documents generated by consultants and documents produced pursuant to agency initiative.[120]

The deliberative process privilege is invoked to "prevent injury to the quality of agency decisions."[121] Ideally, Exemption 5 serves to encourage open and frank discussion between agency superiors and subordinates, to protect against premature disclosure of unadopted policies, and to guard against public confusion generated by disclosed but ultimately unrelied-upon rationales.[122] Such a "deliberative process" communication or document must be predecisional[123] and part of the decisionmaking process;[124] statements of policy and final decisions which have force of law *cannot* be withheld under Exemption 5.[125] A persistent and unsettled Exemption 5 deliberative process issue is the distinction between facts and decisional process material. "Facts" are "generally available for discovery,"[126] but may be withheld if "inextricably intertwined" with deliberative material, or "if the manner of selecting or presenting those facts would reveal the deliberative process."[127]

120. See Ryan v. Department of Justice, 617 F.2d 781, 790 (D.C.Cir.1980); Soucie v. David, 448 F.2d 1067, 1078 n. 44 (D.C.Cir.1971). See also, U.S. Department of Justice v. Julian, 486 U.S. 1, 13, 108 S.Ct. 1606, 1614, 100 L.Ed.2d 1 (1988) (presentence reports not exempt under (b)(5)).

121. NLRB v. Sears, Roebuck & Co., supra note 150, at 151.

122. See, e.g., Russell v. Department of the Air Force, 682 F.2d 1045, 1048 (D.C.Cir. 1982); Coastal States Gas Corp. v. DOE, 617 F.2d 854, 866 (D.C.Cir.1980).

123. Jordan v. U.S. Department of Justice, 591 F.2d 753, 774 (D.C.Cir.1978). See also City of Va. Beach v. United States Dep't of Commerce, 995 F.2d 1247, 1254 (4th Cir.1993) (protecting documents that contained analyses of the future effect of a past decision); North Dartmouth Properties, Inc. v. Department of HUD, 984 F.Supp. 65, 69 (D.Mass., 1997) (holding that an e-mail message created after the agency decision was predecisional and protected under Exemption 5 because the e-mail only restated agency predecisional deliberations and the author's recommendations). But see Burkins v. United States, 865 F.Supp. 1480, 1501 (D.Colo.1994) (holding that otherwise predecisional memoranda lost Exemption 5 protection where a final report incorporated the memoranda). Cf. Greyson v. McKenna & Cuneo, 879 F.Supp. 1065, 1069 (D.Colo.1995) (concluding that the phrase "the evidence shows" is not enough to infer the adoption of predecisional documents).

124. Vaughn v. Rosen, 523 F.2d 1136, 1144 (D.C.Cir.1975).

125. See, e.g., Tax Analysts v. IRS, 117 F.3d 607, 617 (D.C.Cir.1997) (holding that non-binding IRS field service advice memoranda are not predecisional documents, because they are "statements of an agency's legal position"). Cf. A. Michael's Piano, Inc. v. FTC, 18 F.3d 138, 147 (2d Cir.1994), cert. denied, 513 U.S. 1015, 115 S.Ct. 574, 130 L.Ed.2d 490 (1994) (finding that a staff attorney's recommendations were predecisional because attorney had no authority to close investigation).

126. EPA v. Mink, 410 U.S. at 87–88, 93 S.Ct. at 836.

127. Ryan v. Department of Justice, 617 F.2d at 790; Montrose Chemical Corp. v. Train, 491 F.2d 63, 71 (D.C.Cir.1974); Mead Data Central, Inc. v. U.S. Dept. of Air Force, 566 F.2d 242, 256–57 (D.C.Cir.1977). Contra Playboy Enterprises, Inc. v. Department of Justice, 677 F.2d 931, 935 (D.C.Cir. 1982) ("report does not become a part of the deliberative process merely because it contains only those facts which the person making the report thinks material"). See also Paisley v. CIA, 712 F.2d 686 (D.C.Cir. 1983) (overview of Exemption 5 regarding a widow's request for documents relating to her murdered CIA-employed husband), modified in other respects, 724 F.2d 201 (1984); ITT World Communications, Inc. v. FCC, 699 F.2d 1219, 1239 (D.C.Cir.1983) (burden on agency to show that deliberative facts are "inextricably intertwined"), rev'd on other grounds, 466 U.S. 463, 104 S.Ct. 1936, 80 L.Ed.2d 480 (1984).

The Freedom of Information Act has long had a significant impact on the rulemaking process by providing access to potential litigants of aspects of the rulemaking record that might not otherwise be public. The D.C. Circuit in *Wolfe v. Department of Health and Human Services*[128], however, recently adopted a very broad definition of material eligible to be withheld as part of the deliberative process. In so doing, the court has now somewhat restricted the ability of the public to gain access to certain aspects of the rulemaking process, particularly when the information sought "reflects [plaintiff'] dissatisfaction with the results of the development of formal presidential oversight of executive branch rulemaking."[129] Citing *Mead Data Central, Inc. v. U.S. Department of the Air Force,*[130] the court stated: "Exemption Five is intended to protect the deliberative process of government and not just deliberative material."[131] In so doing, the court expanded the scope of information exempt from FOIA requests in refusing to grant FOIA access to regulatory logs dealing with the status of regulatory actions awaiting approval from the FDA, HHS and OMB. Plaintiffs in this litigation sought this material "to be able to identify, in general, which regulatory actions have been proposed by FDA and to know how long regulatory actions initiated by FDA are spending at each stopping point along the approval route from FDA to HHS to OMB and back to HHS. . . ."[132] They suspected that OMB was blocking FDA health regulations and they wished to publicize this fact. The court, *en banc,* however, rejected this request, taking into account plaintiffs' motives and ruling that the dates on which certain regulatory proposals were transmitted between the agencies constituted predecisional and deliberative material.[133]

The fact-deliberative process approach was at issue in *Mapother v. Department of Justice,*[134] a case which illustrates the breadth of the deliberative process exemption. In *Mapother*, the DOJ appealed a U.S. district court ruling ordering the DOJ to disclose the "Waldheim Report" and all source documents and materials that were relied on to prepare that report. The Report was prepared for the U.S. Attorney General by the DOJ and it set forth, in detail, the wartime activities of former Secretary–General of the United Nations and former President of Austria, Kurt Waldheim. Evidence showed that Waldheim may have participated in Nazi war crimes, and the Attorney General used the Report as a basis for barring Waldheim from entering the United States. The D.C. Circuit found that since the bulk of the evidence in the Report

128. 839 F.2d 768 (D.C.Cir.1988) (en banc).

129. Id. at 770.

130. 566 F.2d 242 (D.C.Cir.1977).

131. 839 F.2d at 773.

132. Id. at 770.

133. Id. at 775. The majority applied a broad rule encompassing all phases of the deliberative process. The dissent, however, vigorously opposed the application of Exemption 5 to the material requested: "(The majority's) opinion must be given a narrow reading, if it is not to work a major disruption in circuit law under FOIA . . . I believe that it is inappropriate, in the context of FOIA's overriding policy in favor of disclosure, for today's majority to shield a whole category of information based on the mere speculation that, under some circumstances, *some* of it might be legitimately exempt." Id. at 776–78.

134. 3 F.3d 1533 (D.C.Cir.1993).

"was assembled through an exercise of judgment in extracting pertinent material from a vast number of documents for the benefit of an official called upon to take discretionary action," the Report fell within the deliberative process privilege.[135] On the other hand, the court also held that a mere chronology of Waldheim's military career was not, in and of itself, deliberative. It was simply "a comprehensive collection of the essential facts" that "reflect[ed] no point of view."[136]

The attorney work-product privilege, which is construed broadly,[137] cannot be invoked until "some articulable claim, likely to lead to litigation,"[138] has arisen. To invoke the privilege, litigation need not be commenced as long as there are specific identifiable claims that make litigation probable.[139] Also, Rule 26(b)(3) of the Federal Rules of Civil Procedure allows the privilege to protect documents prepared "by or for another party or by or for that other party's representative."[140] Furthermore, the work-product privilege applies when the information has been shared with a party that shares a common interest with the agency,[141] even after the document has become the basis for a final agency decision.[142] Finally, broad attorney work-product protection is also afforded to factual materials.[143] The burden is on the agency to show that the

135. Id. at 1539. The court distinguished an earlier case in which it had held that a "report does not become part of the deliberative process merely because it contains only those facts which the person making the report thinks material." Contra Playboy Enterprises, Inc. v. Department of Justice, 677 F.2d 931, 935 (D.C.Cir.1982). Playboy Enterprises, said the court, involved a report created only to inform the Attorney General of facts that he would make available to Members of Congress, as opposed to the present report, which was created to inform a decision he would have to make.

136. Mapother, 3 F.3d at 1539–40. Nevertheless, the scope of the deliberative process exemption can restrict the ability of the public to access certain rulemaking information. Recently, however, there has emerged a policy component to analysis under the deliberative process exemption that may favor the release of purely factual data where an agency can shoe no strong policy consideration in a decision to withhold the information. See Ethyl Corp. v. EPA, 25 F.3d 1241, 1248–49 (4th Cir.1994) (holding that "privilege does not protect a document which is merely peripheral to actual policy formulation"); Petroleum Info. Corp. v. United States Dep't of Interior, 976 F.2d 1429, 1435 (D.C.Cir.1992).

137. See FOIA Guide, supra note 337, at 259.

138. Coastal States Gas Corp. v. DOE, 617 F.2d 854, 865 (D.C.Cir.1980).

139. See Blazy v. Tenet, 979 F.Supp. 10, 24 (D.D.C.1997), affirmed, 1998 WL 315583 (D.C.Cir.1998) (stating that pre-litigation communication between agency employee review panel and agency attorney whether to retain plaintiff employee demonstrated that the agency "was concerned about potential litigation"). Cf. A. Michael's Piano, Inc. v. FTC, 18 F.3d 138, 146–47 (2d Cir.1994), cert. denied, 513 U.S. 1015, 115 S.Ct. 574, 130 L.Ed.2d 490 (1994) (exempting documents "related to possible settlements" of litigation); Feshbach v.SEC, 5 F.Supp.2d 774, 783 (N.D.Cal.1997) (protecting preliminary law enforcement documents created "based upon a suspicion of specific wrongdoing and represent[ing] an effort to obtain evidence and to build a case against the suspected wrongdoer").

140. See Durham v. United States Dep't of Justice, 829 F.Supp. 428, 432–33 (D.D.C.1993) (protecting material prepared by government personnel under direction of the prosecuting attorney).

141. See United States v. Gulf Oil Corp., 760 F.2d 292, 295–96 (Temp. Emer. Ct. App. 1985)

142. See Federal Trade Commission v. Grolier Inc., 462 U.S. 19, 103 S.Ct. 2209, 76 L.Ed.2d 387 (1983).

143. Id. See also Tax Analysts v. IRS, 117 F.3d 607, 620 (D.C.Cir.1997) (holding that district court erred when it limited protection to "the mental impressions, conclusions, opinions, or legal theories of an

privilege applies.[144]

Courts also construe Exemption 5's attorney-client privilege in a likewise liberal manner, based primarily on the rationale that agency personnel at all levels will more likely communicate with an attorney without fear of disclosure[145] particularly if confidentiality is maintained throughout.[146]

Also protected from discovery "for good cause shown" are trade secrets or commercially valued information which is part of a government-generated preliminary study or contract proceeding. The idea is to prevent disclosure of information which would put the government at a competitive disadvantage in the contract process.[147] Another issue is whether documents or statements submitted to an agency by persons independent of the agency are transformed into an "intra-agency memo" by virtue of their inclusion in the internal agency reports.[148]

attorney"); Norwood v. FAA, 993 F.2d 570, 576 (6th Cir.1993) (holding that work-product privilege protects factual and deliberative documents); May v. IRS, 85 F.Supp.2d 939 (W.D.Mo.1999) (protecting "the factual basis for [a] potential prosecution and an analysis of the applicable law"); Rugiero v. United States Dep't of Justice, 35 F.Supp.2d 977, 984 (E.D.Mich.1998) (holding that "factual and deliberative work product are exempt from release under FOIA") (appeal pending); Manchester v. DEA, 823 F.Supp. 1259, 1269 (E.D.Pa. 1993), affirmed, 40 F.3d 1240 (3d. Cir.1994) (holding that segregation is not required when "factual information is incidental to, and bound with, privileged" information).

144. See Kronberg v. United States Dep't of Justice, 875 F.Supp. 861, 869 (D.D.C.1995).

145. See Brinton v. Department of State, 636 F.2d 600, 604 (D.C.Cir.1980), cert. denied 452 U.S. 905, 101 S.Ct. 3030, 69 L.Ed.2d 405 (1981); Schlefer v. United States, 702 F.2d 233, 245 (D.C.Cir.1983). Cf. Barnes v. IRS, F.Supp.2d 896, 901 (S.D. Ind. 1998) (protecting material "prepared by an IRS attorney in response to a request by a revenue officer to file certain liens pursuant to collection efforts against the plaintiffs"); NBC v. SBA, 836 F.Supp. 121, 124–25 (S.D.N.Y.1993) (holding that privilege covers "professional advice given by attorney that discloses" information given by client).

146. See Coastal States Gas Corp. v. DOE, 617 F.2d 854, 863 (D.C.Cir.1980); Mead Data Central, Inc. v. U.S. Department of the Air Force, 566 F.2d 242, 254 (D.C.Cir.1977). Voluntary, careless, or irresponsible releases of documents in previous instances will raise the issue of a waiver of the privilege. See, e.g., Cooper v. Department of the Navy, 558 F.2d 274, 278 (5th Cir.1977), appeal after remand, 594 F.2d 484 (1979), cert. denied, 444 U.S. 926, 100 S.Ct. 266, 62 L.Ed.2d 183 (1979) (prior disclosure of aircraft accident investigation reported to aircraft manufacturer did not constitute waiver); Erb v. U.S. Department of Justice, 572 F.Supp. 954, 956 (W.D.Mich. 1983) (prior "limited disclosure" by FBI to defense attorney and prosecutor held not a waiver); but cf. Shermco Industries, Inc. v. Secretary of the Air Force, 613 F.2d 1314, 1320 (5th Cir.1980); State of North Dakota ex rel. Olson v. Andrus, 581 F.2d 177, 182 (8th Cir.1978).

147. See, e.g., Federal Open Market Committee of Federal Reserve System v. Merrill, 443 U.S. 340, 99 S.Ct. 2800, 61 L.Ed.2d 587 (1979), on remand, 516 F.Supp. 1028 (D.D.C.1981) (holding that Federal Reserve Board was entitled to purposely delay for one month the release of market-impacting financial information—"the sensitivity of commercial secrets involved, and the harm that would be inflicted on the Government by premature disclosure should continue to serve as relevant criteria." Opinion includes a general discussion of Exemption 5's different privileged categories.).

In a related vein, the Supreme Court has held that Exemption 5 also incorporates the civil discovery privilege protecting witness' statements generated during governmental investigations. See United States v. Weber Aircraft Corp., 465 U.S. 792, 802, 104 S.Ct. 1488, 1494, 79 L.Ed.2d 814 (1984) (suggesting that Exemption 5 may be read expansively to include other established privileges as they arise).

148. Van Bourg, Allen, Weinberg & Roger v. NLRB, 751 F.2d 982, 985 (9th

An important area of Exemption 5 caselaw has been the extent to which public availability (in some form) affects an agency's duty to disclose agency records.[149] The Court of Appeals for the District of Columbia Circuit attempted to clarify this issue in *Tax Analysts v. U.S. Department of Justice.*[150] The requester in *Tax Analysts* was the publisher of a nonprofit tax magazine that was suing to gain weekly access under FOIA to Justice Department files containing federal district court tax opinions. Although many of the files were available in various district courts, the Justice Department had the advantage of holding all of the requested opinions in a central clearinghouse. For efficiency reasons, *Tax Analysts* requested access to the opinions stored in this clearinghouse. The district court granted summary judgment to the government, holding the information was not "improperly withheld"[151] under Exemption 5 because the opinions were already publicly available.[152] The Court of Appeals reversed, holding that the tax cases are agency records,[153] and that they must be made available to the requester by the department itself.[154] With respect to the issue of alternative public availability with respect to the agency's duty to disclose, the court ruled firmly in favor of the requester.[155] "[I]n response to a FOIA request, an

Cir.1985) (statements by witnesses who are not agency employees, and are not prepared by the agency as internal documents or for use in litigation, are not "internal agency" documents); NAACP Legal Defense and Educational Fund, Inc. v. U.S. Department of Justice, 612 F.Supp. 1143, 1146 (D.D.C. 1985) (information acquired by the withholding agency from sources independent of the agency is not exempt). Cf. Badhwar v. U.S. Department of the Air Force, 615 F.Supp. 698, 702 (D.D.C.1985), aff'd, 829 F.2d 182 (D.C.Cir.1987) (upheld exemption of statements of military air accident witnesses, focusing on the agency's use and not the source of the statements). See Durns v. Bureau of Prisons, 804 F.2d 701 (D.C.Cir. 1986), reh'g en banc denied 806 F.2d 1122 (1986) (agency copies of presentence reports prepared by and for employees of the judiciary satisfy Exemption 5).

149. Earlier cases have held that the government is under no duty to disclose the agency record if the same information is available in an alternative form. See, e.g., Lead Industries Ass'n, Inc. v. OSHA, 610 F.2d 70, 86 (2d Cir.1979); SDC Dev. Corp. v. Mathews, 542 F.2d 1116, 1120 (9th Cir. 1976).

150. 845 F.2d 1060 (D.C.Cir.1988). The court reversed a lower court opinion which held that because the requested tax opinions were publicly available elsewhere (in the various district courts across the country) the government was not "improperly withholding" them.

151. 5 U.S.C.A. § 552(a)(4)(B) confers jurisdiction to the court under FOIA only when "agency records" are "improperly withheld."

152. Tax Analysts v. U.S. Department of Justice, 643 F.Supp. 740, 743–44 (D.D.C. 1986).

153. Tax Analysts v. U.S. Department of Justice, 845 F.2d at 1067–68. Although the court held the only issue in the case was whether the records were "improperly withheld" it did first address the "agency records" question. The court accepted the *Kissinger* test for determining agency records (possession, agency's use or reliance on records, and discretion to disclose) but made a distinction between control over content and control over the document itself: "every court decision received by the Department of Justice is by any means an 'agency record' subject to disclosure under the Act. Only those tax decisions requested by Tax Analysts that have been [1] incorporated into Department files, [2] are relied upon by Tax Division attorneys in their work, and [3] remain unencumbered by judicial limitations on dissemination, constitute disclosable 'agency records.'" Id. at 1069.

154. Id. at 1062.

155. For a discussion of *Tax Analyst*'s impact on the disclosure of court opinions, see, e.g., Field, Improved Court Opinion Disclosures Likely, 39 Tax Notes 562 (1988); Field, Court Opinions from the DOJ: A Slippery Slope?, 43 Tax Notes 526 (1989).

agency must itself make disclosable agency records available to the public and may not, on grounds of administrative convenience, avoid this statutory duty by pointing to another public source for the information."[156]

§ 17.4.6 Exemption (b)(6): Privacy Protection

FOIA also authorizes agencies to withhold "personnel and medical files and similar files the disclosure of which would constitute a clearly unwarranted invasion of personal privacy."[157] In *Department of the Air Force v. Rose,*[158] the Supreme Court declared that "the primary concern of Congress in drafting Exemption 6 was to provide for the confidentiality of personal matters."[159] Consequently, judicial review of Exemption 6 claims focuses not on the physical nature of the information, but rather on the information itself and the impact it will have on the privacy of the individual.[160]

In Exemption 6 cases, the court must first find that the requested information falls within the category of "personnel and medical files and similar files."[161] The information must be able to identify a *specific* individual. If the information pertains to a group out of which no individual can be identified, Exemption 6 does not protect the information—unless the requested information can be attributed to all members of the group.[162] Hence, neither corporations nor associations necessarily possess protectable privacy interests,[163] although "personal financial information is protected, including information about small businesses when the individual and corporation are identical."[164] But where the individual and corporation are identical, the individual's expectation of

156. 845 F.2d at 1067. See also Burka v. United States Dep't of Health and Human Services, 87 F.3d 508 (D.C.Cir.1996) (following Tax Analysts where HHS had already published some research about smoking-related behavior).

157. 5 U.S.C.A. § 552(b)(6). For reform proposals, see sec. 14.2 supra.

158. 425 U.S. 352, 96 S.Ct. 1592, 48 L.Ed.2d 11 (1976).

159. Id. at 376 n. 14, 96 S.Ct. at 1606 n. 14. But see Norwood v. FAA, 993 F.2d 570, 575 (6th Cir.1993) (holding that only items such as names and social security numbers, which "by themselves" would identify an individual, could be withheld) modified, No. 92–5820 (6th Cir. July 9, 1993) (stating that there might be occasions in which an agency could justifiably withhold information other than "those items which 'by themselves' would identify the individuals," but that the FAA "made no such particularized effort, relying generally on the claim that 'fragments of information' might be able to be pieced together into an identifiable set of circumstances") reh'g denied (6th Cir. Aug. 12, 1993).

160. See New York Times Co. v. NASA, 852 F.2d 602 (D.C.Cir.1988) (voice recording of shuttle launch containing non-personal information previously released to media held not exempt under (b)(6)); see also Wine Hobby USA, Inc. v. IRS, 502 F.2d 133 (3d Cir.1974); Rural Housing Alliance v. U.S. Department of Agriculture, 498 F.2d 73 (D.C.Cir.1974); Howard Johnson Co. v. NLRB, 618 F.2d 1 (6th Cir.1980).

161. 5 U.S.C. § 552(b)(6).

162. See, e.g., Na Iwi O Na Kupuna v. Dalton, 894 F.Supp. 1397, 1413 (D.Haw. 1995) (involving records about a large group of Native Hawaiian human remains).

163. See Sims v. CIA, 642 F.2d 562, 572 n. 47 (D.C.Cir.1980), vacated on other grounds (Exemption 3), 471 U.S. 159, 105 S.Ct. 1881, 85 L.Ed.2d 173 (1985); National Parks & Conservation Ass'n v. Kleppe, 547 F.2d 673, 685 n. 44 (D.C.Cir.1976).

164. Providence Journal Co. v. FBI, 460 F.Supp. 778, 785 (D.R.I.1978), rev'd on other grounds, 602 F.2d 1010 (1st Cir. 1979). See also National Parks, 547 F.2d at 685–86.

privacy is diminished as to matters in which she is acting in a business capacity.[165]

Where privacy interests *are* implicated, determination of whether disclosure would be a "*clearly* unwarranted invasion of personal privacy" requires a balancing of the public interest in disclosure against the privacy interests which might be invaded.[166] First, it must be shown that a protectable privacy interest exists and would be threatened by disclosure.[167] If such a privacy interest is found to exist, the public interest in disclosure must be weighed against the privacy interest.[168] If no public interest exists, the information should be protected.[169] Likewise, if the privacy interest outweighs the public interest, the information should be withheld.[170] Otherwise, the information should be released.[171] Typical privacy interests falling easily under Exemption 6 include marital status, religious affiliation, medical information, welfare payments, legitimacy of children, reputation and the like.[172]

The Supreme Court's 1989 landmark FOIA decision in *United States Department of Justice v. Reporters Committee for Freedom of the Press*[173] affects the application of Exemption 6 in all cases. *Reporters Committee* involved media requests for any FBI criminal history records ("rap sheets") about persons alleged to have been involved in organized crime and illegal acts with a corrupt Congressman.[174] The Court held that the rap sheets were protected under Exemption 7(C), and established five principles that govern analysis under Exemptions 6 and 7(C). First, substantial privacy interests can exist in personal information even if the data were at one time publicly available, but currently are not; if such data "were 'freely available,' there would be no reason to invoke the FOIA to obtain access to" them.[175] Second, the identity of a FOIA requester cannot be a factor when deciding what should be released

165. See. e.g., Oregon Natural Desert Ass'n v. United States Dep't of the Interior, 24 F. Supp. 2d 1088, 1089 (D.Or.1998) (finding that cattle owners who violated federal grazing laws have "diminished expectation of privacy" in their names when the information is related to commercial interests); Washington Post Co. v. USDA, 943 F.Supp. 31, 34–36 (D.D.C.1996) (finding that farmers who received cotton price subsidies have only minimal privacy interest in their home addresses when they use their homes to run their business). But see Campaign for Family Farms v. Glickman, 200 F.3d 1180, 1187–89 (8th Cir.2000) (holding that pork producers had a privacy interest in their identities on a petition to abolish mandatory marketing contributions because release of information "would vitiate petitioner' privacy interest in secret loans made by Farmers Home Administration to individual borrowers"), summary affirmance granted, No. 99–5365, 2000 WL 520724, at 11 (D.C.Cir. Mar.7, 2000).

166. Department of the Air Force v. Rose, 425 U.S. 352, 372, 96 S.Ct. 1592, 1604, 48 L.Ed.2d 11 (1976).

167. See Norwood v. FAA, 993 F.2d at 573–76.

168. Id. at 573.

169. See Lepelletier v. FDIC, 164 F.3d 37, 46–49 (D.C.Cir.1999).

170. Id.

171. Id.

172. See, e.g., Rural Housing Alliance v. U.S. Dept. of Agriculture, 498 F.2d 73, 77 (D.C.Cir.1974); Church of Scientology v. Department of Defense, 611 F.2d 738, 745–47 (9th Cir.1979).

173. 489 U.S. 749, 109 S.Ct. 1468, 103 L.Ed.2d 774 (1989).

174. 489 U.S. at 757.

175. Id. at 764.

under FOIA.[176] Third, the public interest in the information depends "on the nature of the requested document and its relationship to" the public interest in general.[177] Fourth, the public interest in general under FOIA privacy exemptions is in shedding light "on an agency's performance of its statutory duties."[178] Fifth, under Exemption 7(C), agencies may decide that "as a categorical matter," certain types of information are always protectable under an exemption, "without regard to individual circumstances."[179]

Considerable caselaw has developed with respect to Exemption 6 privacy challenges to requests for mailing lists.[180] Generally, courts have found a "minimal invasion of privacy effected by disclosure"[181] and have applied a "public interest" versus privacy interests balancing test in favor of the requester. The courts have carved out narrow exemptions to this general rule only where something in addition to names and addresses is requested[182] or where the union requester was different than the workers' certified union representative.[183]

§ 17.4.7 Exemption (b)(7): Law Enforcement Purposes

FOIA also gives the various agencies the right to withhold:

> records or information compiled for law enforcement purposes, but only to the extent that the production of such law enforcement records or information (A) could reasonably be expected to interfere with enforcement proceedings, (B) would deprive a person of a right to a fair trial or an impartial adjudication, (C) could reasonably be expected to constitute an unwarranted invasion of personal privacy, (D) could reasonably be expected to disclose the identity of a

176. Id. at 771.

177. Id. at 772.

178. Id. at 773–75. See also O'Kane v. United States Customs Serv., 169 F.3d 1308, 1310 (11th Cir.1999) (affirming that the Electronic Freedom of Information Act Amendments of 1996 do not overrule the Reporters Committee definition of public interest) (per curiam).

179. 489 U.S. at 780.

180. See, e.g., Army Times Publishing Co. v. Department of the Army, 684 F.Supp. 720 (D.D.C.1988) (court rejected a challenge to the disclosure of names, addresses, rank and current assignment of active duty Army personnel); Southern Utah Wilderness Alliance, Inc. v. Hodel, 680 F.Supp. 37 (D.D.C.1988) (court rejected a challenge to the disclosure of the names and addresses of national park visitors); United States Dept. of Navy v. Federal Labor Relations Authority, 840 F.2d 1131 (3d Cir.1988), cert. dismissed 488 U.S. 881, 109 S.Ct. 632, 102 L.Ed.2d 170 (1988) (Navy Yard ordered to release to union representatives the names and addresses of workers); United States Dept. of Agr. v. Federal Labor Relations Authority, 836 F.2d 1139 (8th Cir.1988), vacated, 488 U.S. 1025, 109 S.Ct. 831, 102 L.Ed.2d 964 (1989), on remand, 876 F.2d 50 (8th Cir.1989) (Agriculture Department order to release names and addresses of employees to union representative. However, those employees who objected to the release of their name could take their name off the list.).

181. United States Dept. of Navy v. Federal Labor Relations Authority, 840 F.2d 1131, 1137 (3d Cir.1988), cert. denied, 488 U.S. 881, 109 S.Ct. 632, 102 L.Ed.2d 170 (1988).

182. See, e.g., International Broth. of Elec. Workers Local Union No. 5 v. United States Dept. of Housing and Urban Dev., 852 F.2d 87, 92 (3d Cir.1988) (court granted release of names and addresses of employees but cited significant privacy interests in refusing release of social security numbers).

183. See Local 3, Intern. Broth. of Elec. Workers v. NLRB, 845 F.2d 1177, 1181 (2d Cir.1988).

confidential source, including a state, local, or foreign agency or authority or any private institution which furnished information on a confidential basis, and, in the case of a record or information compiled by a criminal law enforcement authority in the course of a criminal investigation or by an agency conducting a lawful national security intelligence investigation, information furnished by a confidential source (E) would disclose techniques and procedures for law enforcement investigations or prosecutions or would disclose guidelines for law enforcement investigations or prosecutions if such disclosure could reasonably be expected to risk circumvention of the law, or (F) could reasonably be expected to endanger the life or physical safety of any individual.[184]

The original version of Exemption 7[185] exempted all investigatory files.[186] In 1974, Congress narrowed the scope of Exemption 7[187] with six criteria (analyzed *infra*) that required a two-step analysis: first, the record had to be an "investigatory record compiled for law enforcement purposes," and second disclosure of the record had to threaten one of the six enumerated harms.[188] In 1986, Congress amended Exemption 7 again, broadening the protection given to law enforcement records[189] by exempting all "records or information compiled for law enforcement purposes."[190] It also lowered the standard by which an agency must show harm, from "would" cause harm to "could" cause harm.[191] Because few courts have analyzed the threshold standard created by the 1986 amendments, it is useful to study cases in which courts analyze the language of the pre–1986 Exemption 7 language.[192] Law enforcement records that qualified for Exemption 7 protection prior to the 1986 amendments will likely still qualify for protection.[193]

To determine whether a document was "compiled for law enforcement purposes" under Exemption 7, courts distinguish between agencies that have mixed law enforcement and administrative duties, and agencies that only have law enforcement duties. A mixed-function agency usually must to show that the requested records pertain to the enforce-

184. 5 U.S.C.A. § 552(b)(7).

185. Pub. L. No. 90–23, 81 Stat. 54, 55 (1967) (subsequently amended).

186. See, e.g., Weisberg v. United States Dep't of Justice, 489 F.2d 1195, 1198–1202 (D.C.Cir.1973), superseded by statute/Rule as stated in National Public Radio v. Bell, 431 F.Supp. 509 (D.D.C. 1977).

187. Pub. L. No. 93–502, 88 Stat. 1561, 1563 (1974) (subsequently amended).

188. See FBI v. Abramson, 456 U.S. 615, 622, 102 S.Ct. 2054, 72 L.Ed.2d 376 (1982).

189. Freedom of Information Reform Act of 1986, Pub. L. No. 99–570, § 1802, 100 Stat. 3207, 3207–48 (1986). See United States Dep't of Justice v. Reporters Comm. for Freedom of the Press, 489 U.S. 749, 756 n. 9, 109 S.Ct. 1468, 103 L.Ed.2d 774 (1989) (recognizing that the 1986 amendments "represents a congressional effort to ease considerably a Federal law enforcement agency's burden in invoking [Exemption 7]"); Hopkinson v. Shillinger, 866 F.2d 1185, 1222 n. 27 (10th Cir.1989), cert. denied, 497 U.S. 1010, 110 S.Ct. 3256, 111 L.Ed.2d 765 (1990) ("The 1986 amendment[s] broadened the scope of exemption 7's threshold requirement.").

190. See § 1802, 100 Stat. at 3207–48.

191. Id.

192. United States Dep't of Justice, Freedom of Information Act Guide & Privacy Act Overview 336 (2000).

193. Id.

ment of a statute or regulation within the authority of the agency[194] and that the records were compiled for "adjudicative or enforcement purposes."[195] Information that an agency did not initially obtain or create for law enforcement purposes may still qualify for exemption if the information is later compiled for a valid law enforcement purpose, but before "the Government invokes the Exemption."[196]

The Circuit courts have taken two approaches to applying the Exemption 7 test. A *per se* rule is applied to all criminal law enforcement agency "investigative" records by the First,[197] Second,[198] Sixth,[199] and Eighth Circuit[200] Courts of Appeal, whereas other Circuits require an agency to show a specific nexus between the records and a proper law enforcement purpose.[201] To decide whether the Exemption 7 threshold has been met, the Court of Appeals for the District of Columbia applies a two-part test that is a hybrid of the aforementioned tests: (1) whether the agency investigation is related to federal law enforcement or to national security; and (2) whether there is a rational nexus between the investigation and the agency law enforcement duties.[202]

194. See Church of Scientology Int'l v. IRS, 995 F.2d 916, 919 (9th Cir.1993); Lewis v. IRS, 823 F.2d 375, 379 (9th Cir.1987); Birch v. United States Postal Serv., 803 F.2d 1206, 1210–11 (D.C.Cir.1986); Church of Scientology v. United States Dep't of the Army, 611 F.2d 738, 748 (9th Cir.1979); Irons v. Bell, 596 F.2d 468, 473 (1st Cir. 1979). See also Philadelphia Newspapers, Inc. v. Department of HHS, 69 F.Supp.2d 63, 67 (D.D.C.1999) (holding that investigative records of alleged Medicare fraud were compiled for law enforcement purposes).

195. See Becker v. IRS, 34 F.3d 398, 407 (7th Cir.1994) (holding that IRS has "law enforcement purpose in investigating potential illegal tax protester activity"); Church of Scientology, 995 F.2d at 919 (finding that IRS Exempt Organizations Division "performs law enforcement function by enforcing provisions of the federal tax code"); Rural Hous. Alliance v. United States Dep't of Agriculture, 498 F.2d 73, 80 (D.C.Cir.1974).

196. John Doe Agency v. John Doe Corp., 493 U.S. 146, 153, 110 S.Ct. 471, 107 L.Ed.2d 462 (1989). See also KTVY–TV v. United States, 919 F.2d 1465, 1469 (10th Cir.1990); Kansi v. United States Dep't of Justice, 11 F.Supp.2d 42, 44 (D.D.C.1998); Butler v. Department of the Air Force, 888 F.Supp. 174, 179–80, 182 (D.D.C.1995), affirmed, 116 F.3d 941 (D.C.Cir. 1997).

197. Curran v. Department of Justice, 813 F.2d 473, 475 (1st Cir.1987) (holding that law enforcement agency investigatory records are "inherently" created for law enforcement purposes); Irons, 596 F.2d at 474–76 (same).

198. Halpern v. FBI, 181 F.3d 279, 296 (2d Cir.1999) (holding that purpose of investigation is not subject to judicial review when records are compiled for law enforcement investigation); Ferguson v. FBI, 957 F.2d 1059, 1070 (2d Cir.1992); Williams v. FBI, 730 F.2d 882, 884–85 (2d Cir.1984) (ruling that law enforcement agency records are given "absolute protection" even when "records were compiled in the course of an unwise, meritless or even illegal investigation");

199. Detroit Free Press, Inc. v. Department of Justice, 73 F.3d 93, 96 (6th Cir. 1996) (holding that mug shots protected under Exemption 7).

200. Miller v. USDA, 13 F.3d 260, 263 (8th Cir.1993); Kuehnert v. FBI, 620 F.2d 662, 666 (8th Cir.1980).

201. See, e.g., Davin v. United States Dep't of Justice, 60 F.3d 1043, 1056 (3d Cir.1995) (applying two-pronged rational nexus test); Rosenfeld v. United States Dep't of Justice, 761 F.Supp. 1440, 1445–48 (N.D.Cal.1991), aff'd in pertinent part, rev'd in part & remanded, 57 F.3d 803 (9th Cir.1995); Friedman v. FBI, 605 F.Supp. 306, 321 (N.D.Ga.1981).

202. Pratt v. Webster, 673 F.2d 408, 420–21 (D.C.Cir.1982). See also Campbell v. United States Dep't of Justice, 164 F.3d 20, 32 (D.C.Cir.1998); Summers v. Department of Justice, 140 F.3d 1077, 1083 (D.C.Cir. 1998); Quiñon v. FBI, 86 F.3d 1222, 1228–29 (D.C.Cir.1996); Computer Prof'ls for Soc. Responsibility v. United States Secret Serv., 72 F.3d 897, 902, 904 (D.C.Cir.1996); King v. United States Dep't of Justice, 830 F.2d

(1) Subsection 7(A): disclosure which "could reasonably be expected to interfere with enforcement proceedings."

An agency that invokes Exemption 7(A) must show: (1) that a law enforcement proceeding is pending[203] or prospective[204] and (2) that releasing the information could reasonably be expected to cause some specific harm.[205] Although Exemption 7(A) is not intended to "endlessly protect material simply because it [is] in an investigatory file,"[206] it remains applicable during long-term investigations.[207] Even after an enforcement proceeding concludes, Exemption 7(A) may be appropriate.[208] The courts have broadly interpreted the "law enforcement proceedings"[209] to which Exemption 7(A) applies.[210]

(2) Subsection 7(B): disclosure that "would deprive a person of the right to a fair trial or an impartial adjudication."

Under the test created by the District of Columbia Circuit Court of Appeals in *Washington Post Co. v. United States Dep't of Justice*, to successfully invoke Exemption 7(B), an agency must show: "(1) that a trial or adjudication is pending or truly imminent; and (2) that it is more probable than not that disclosure of the material sought would seriously

210, 229 (D.C.Cir.1987); Wichlacz v. United States Dep't of Interior, 938 F.Supp. 325, 330 (E.D.Va.1996), affirmed, 114 F.3d 1178 (4th Cir.1997); Western Journalism Ctr. v. Office of the Indep. Counsel, 926 F.Supp. 189, 191 (D.D.C.1996), affirmed, 1997 WL 195516 (D.C.Cir.1997).

203. See, e.g., NLRB v. Robbins Tire & Rubber Co., 437 U.S. 214, 224, 98 S.Ct. 2311, 57 L.Ed.2d 159 (1978); Campbell v. Department of HHS, 682 F.2d 256, 259 (D.C.Cir.1982); Scheer v. United States Dep't of Justice, 35 F.Supp.2d 9, 13 (D.D.C. 1999); Western Journalism Ctr. v. Office of the Indep. Counsel, 926 F.Supp. 189, 192 (D.D.C.1996), affirmed, 1997 WL 195516 (D.C.Cir.1997), ; Butler v. Department of the Air Force, 888 F.Supp. 174, 183 (D.D.C. 1995), affirmed, 116 F.3d 941 (D.C.Cir. 1997).

204. See, e.g., Manna v. United States Dep't of Justice, 51 F.3d 1158, 1165 (3d Cir.1995), cert. denied, 516 U.S. 975, 116 S.Ct. 477, 133 L.Ed.2d 405 (1995); Scheer, 35 F.Supp.2d at 13; General Elec. Co. v. EPA, 18 F.Supp.2d 138, 144 (D.Mass.1998); Kay v. FCC, 976 F.Supp. 23, 38 (D.D.C. 1997), affirmed, 172 F.3d 919 (D.C.Cir. 1998); Foster v. United States Dep't of Justice, 933 F.Supp. 687, 692 (E.D.Mich.1996); Cudzich v. INS, 886 F.Supp. 101, 106 (D.D.C.1995).

205. See, e.g., Miller v. USDA, 13 F.3d 260, 263 (8th Cir.1993); Crooker v. Bureau of ATF, 789 F.2d 64, 65–67 (D.C.Cir.1986); Grasso v. IRS, 785 F.2d 70, 77 (3d Cir. 1986); Scheer, 35 F.Supp.2d at 13–14; American Civil Liberties Union Found. v. United States Dep't of Justice, 833 F.Supp. 399, 407 (S.D.N.Y.1993).

206. Robbins Tire, 437 U.S. at 230. See also Solar Sources, Inc. v. United States, 142 F.3d 1033, 1037 (7th Cir.1998); Dickerson v. Department of Justice, 992 F.2d 1426, 1431 (6th Cir.1993), cert. denied, 510 U.S. 1109, 114 S.Ct. 1049, 127 L.Ed.2d 372 (1994); Kay, 976 F.Supp. at 37–38.

207. See, e.g., Dickerson, 992 F.2d at 1432 (affirming conclusion that FBI investigation into 1975 disappearance of Jimmy Hoffa was ongoing and therefore still "prospective").

208. See Solar Sources, 142 F.3d at 1040 (finding Exemption 7(A) applicable when charges are pending against additional defendants); Kansi v. United States Dep't of Justice, 11 F.Supp.2d 42, 45 (D.D.C.1998) (finding Exemption 7(A) appropriate in post-conviction motions); Cudzich, 886 F.Supp. at 106–07 (holding Exemption 7(A) applicable when additional charges are pending against the original defendant).

209. 5 U.S.C. § 552(b)(7)(A) (1994 & Supp. IV 1998).

210. See United States Dep't of Justice v. Reporters Comm. for Freedom of the Press, 489 U.S. 749, 777–78 n. 22, 109 S.Ct. 1468, 103 L.Ed.2d 774 (1989); Manna, 51 F.3d at 1164 n.5; Curran v. Department of Justice, 813 F.2d 473, 474 n. 1 (1st Cir. 1987).

interfere with the fairness of those proceedings."[211] In *Washington Post Co.* the issue was whether the disclosure of a pharmaceutical company internal report that had been given to the Justice Department for a grand jury investigation would deprive the company of a fair and impartial pending civil trial.[212] Exemption 7(B) most likely would be invoked in ongoing law enforcement proceedings. But Exemption 7(A), invoked to protect agency law enforcement interests, would also protect defendants to the prosecution. Hence, Exemption 7(B) is rarely invoked.[213]

(3) Subsection 7(C): disclosure that "could reasonably be expected to constitute an unwarranted invasion of personal privacy."

Courts have consistently interpreted Exemption 7(C) more broadly than Exemption 6 (see discussion of *United States Department of Justice v. Reporters Committee for Freedom of the Press*[214] and Exemptions 6 & 7(C), *supra*, at § 17.4.6). Specifically, under Exemption 7(C), agencies may decide that "as a categorical matter," certain types of information are always protectible under an exemption, "without regard to individual circumstances."[215] The language of Exemption 7(C), in contrast to that of Exemption 6, lowers the burden of proof to justify withholding by omitting the word "clearly" from the language of Exemption 7(C).[216] Under Exemption 7(C), once a privacy interest has been identified and analyzed for significance, it is balanced against the public interest that would be served by disclosure.[217] Under *Reporters Committee*, the public interest is to "shed light on an agency's performance of its statutory duties."[218]

(4) Subsection 7(D): such release as "could reasonably be expected to [a] disclose the identity of a confidential source including a State, local or foreign agency or authority or any

211. Washington Post Co. v. United States Dep't of Justice, 863 F.2d 96, 102 (D.C.Cir.1988).

212. Id. at 99.

213. See United States Dep't of Justice, Freedom of Information Act Guide & Privacy Act Overview 372 (2000).

214. 489 U.S. 749, 109 S.Ct. 1468, 103 L.Ed.2d 774 (1989).

215. Id. at 780. See also Fiduccia v. United States Dep't of Justice, 185 F.3d 1035, 1047–48 (9th Cir.1999); Nation Magazine v. United States Customs Serv., 71 F.3d 885, 896 (D.C.Cir.1995); Center to Prevent Handgun Violence v. United States Dep't of the Treasury, 981 F.Supp. 20, 23 (D.D.C.1997); McNamera v. United States Dep't of Justice, 974 F.Supp. 946, 957–60 (W.D.Tex.1997). But see Kimberlin v. Department of Justice, 139 F.3d 944, 948 (D.C.Cir.) (rejecting categorical nondisclosure and suggesting a case-by-case balancing test between "rank of public official involved and the seriousness of misconduct alleged"), cert. denied, 525 U.S. 891, 119 S.Ct. 210, 142 L.Ed.2d 173 (1998); Davin v. United States Dep't of Justice, 60 F.3d 1043, 1060 (3d Cir.1995) (holding that "government must conduct a document by document fact-specific balancing").

216. See Department of Air Force v. Rose, 425 U.S. 352, 378–79 n. 16, 96 S.Ct. 1592, 48 L.Ed.2d 11 (1976).

217. See Schiffer v. FBI, 78 F.3d 1405, 1410 (9th Cir.1996); Computer Prof'ls for Soc. Responsibility v. United States Secret Serv., 72 F.3d 897, 904 (D.C.Cir.1996); Massey v. FBI, 3 F.3d 620, 624–25 (2d Cir. 1993); Church of Scientology Int'l v. IRS, 995 F.2d 916, 921 (9th Cir.1993); Thomas v. Office of United States Attorney, 928 F.Supp. 245, 250 (E.D.N.Y.1996); Church of Scientology v. IRS, 816 F.Supp. 1138, 1160 (W.D.Tex.1993).

218. 489 U.S. at 773.

private institution which furnished information on a confidential basis, and, [b] in the case of a record or information compiled by criminal law enforcement authority in the course of a criminal investigation or by an agency conducting a lawful national security intelligence investigation, information furnished by a confidential source."

Of all FOIA law enforcement exemptions, Exemption 7(D) affords perhaps the broadest protection[219] by ensuring that "confidential sources are not lost through retaliation against the sources for past disclosure or because of the source' fear of future disclosure."[220] Exemption 7(D) protects sources' identities when they provide information under an express promise of confidentiality[221] or "under circumstances from which such an assurance could be reasonably inferred."[222] The first clause of Exemption 7(D), thus, protects an informant's name and address,[223] and any information that would "tend to reveal" the source's identity.[224] Nevertheless, not all sources who furnish information to a criminal investigation are presumed confidential.[225] Rather, source confidentiality must be decided case-by-case,[226] and the presumption of confidentiality should not be applied automatically to cooperating law enforcement agencies.[227]

"Sources" can include citizens who offer unsolicited allegations of misconduct,[228] citizens who answer law enforcement agency inquiries,[229] medical personnel,[230] commercial or financial institutions,[231] state and local law enforcement agencies,[232] and foreign law enforcement agencies.[233] "Confidential" indicates that the source furnished the informa-

219. United States Dep't of Justice, Freedom of Information Act Guide & Privacy Act Overview 404 (2000).

220. Brant Constr. Co. v. EPA, 778 F.2d 1258, 1262 (7th Cir.1985). See also Ortiz v. Department of HHS, 70 F.3d 729, 732 (2d Cir.1995), cert. denied, 517 U.S. 1136, 116 S.Ct. 1422, 134 L.Ed.2d 546 (1996); McDonnell v. United States, 4 F.3d 1227, 1258 (3d Cir.1993).

221. See Rosenfeld v. United States Dep't of Justice, 57 F.3d 803, 814 (9th Cir.1995); Jones v. FBI, 41 F.3d 238, 248 (6th Cir.1994); McDonnell, 4 F.3d at 1258.

222. S.Rep. No. 93–1200, 93d Cong. at 13 (1974).

223. See, e.g., Ferreira v. DEA, 874 F.Supp. 15, 16 (D.D.C.1995).

224. See Pollard v. FBI, 705 F.2d 1151, 1155 (9th Cir.1983); Billington v. Department of Justice, 69 F.Supp.2d 128, 138 (D.D.C.1999), affirmed in part, vacated in part, 233 F.3d 581 (D.C.Cir.2000); Putnam v. United States Dep't of Justice, 873 F.Supp. 705, 716 (D.D.C.1995); Ferreira, 874 F.Supp. at 16; Church of Scientology v. IRS, 816 F.Supp. 1138, 1161 (W.D.Tex. 1993).

225. United States Department of Justice v. Landano, 508 U.S. 165, 175, 113 S.Ct. 2014, 124 L.Ed.2d 84 (1993).

226. Id. at 179–80.

227. Id. at 176.

228. See, e.g., Brant Constr., 778 F.2d at 1263.

229. See, e.g., Providence Journal Co. v. United States Dep't of the Army, 981 F.2d 552, 565 (1st Cir.1992).

230. See, e.g., Putnam, 873 F.Supp. at 716.

231. See, e.g., Williams v. FBI, 69 F.3d 1155, 1158 (D.C.Cir.1995).

232. See, e.g., id. at 1160; Jones, 41 F.3d at 248; Ferguson v. FBI, 957 F.2d 1059, 1068 (2d Cir.1992); Peralta v. United States Attorney's Office, 69 F.Supp.2d 21, 35 (D.D.C.1999).

233. See, e.g., Billington v. Dep't of Justice, 69 F.Supp.2d 128, 138 (D.D.C. 1999), affirmed in part, vacated in part, 233 F.3d 581 (D.C.Cir.2000); Badalamenti v. Department of State, 899 F.Supp. 542, 549 (D.Kan.1995).

tion with the understanding that the agency "would not divulge the communication except to the extent the ... [agency] thought necessary for law enforcement purposes."[234] Under Exemption 7(D), "the question is not whether the requested *document* is of the type that the agency usually treats as confidential, but whether the particular *source* spoke with an understanding that the communication would remain confidential."[235] Because the applicability of Exemption 7(D) turns on the circumstances under which information is provided, and not the harm from disclosure, no balancing test is applied.[236]

The second clause of Exemption 7(D) affords broad protection to all information furnished by confidential sources to law enforcement authorities conducting criminal or lawful national security intelligence investigations.[237] The confidential source information covered by the second clause of Exemption 7(D) need not identify the source.[238]

(5) Subsection 7(E): disclosure which would reveal "techniques and procedures for law enforcement investigations or prosecutions, or would disclose guidelines for law enforcement investigations or prosecutions if such disclosure could reasonably be expected to risk circumvention of the law."

The first clause of Exemption 7(E) does not require an agency to show harm or the risk of circumvention of law from the disclosure of records or information covered by the exemption.[239] Instead, the exemption is designed to provide "categorical" protection of information.[240] For the exemption to apply, the technique or procedure must not be well known to the public.[241] On the other hand, commonly known procedures can be protected from disclosure when the reason for the usefulness of

234. Landano, 508 U.S. at 174. The Landano "necessary for law enforcement purposes" standard affirmatively resolved the conflict over whether Exemption 7(D) protection was available for sources who were advised that they might have to testify at trial. Cf. Van Bourg, Allen, Weinberg & Roger v. NLRB, 751 F.2d 982, 986 (9th Cir.1985) (no confidentiality) with Schmerler v. FBI, 900 F.2d 333, 339 (D.C.Cir.1990) (confidentiality).

235. Id. at 172 (emphasis added). See also Ortiz, 70 F.3d at 733; McDonnell, 4 F.3d at 1258; Providence Journal, 981 F.2d at 563; Ferguson, 957 F.2d at 1069.

236. See, e.g., Jones, 41 F.3d at 247; McDonnell, 4 F.3d at 1257; Nadler, 955 F.2d at 1487 n.8; Brant Constr., 778 F.2d at 1262–63.

237. See Ferguson, 957 F.2d at 1069; Kuffel v. United States Bureau of Prisons, 882 F.Supp. 1116, 1126 (D.D.C.1995).

238. See, e.g., Parker v. Dep't of Justice, 934 F.2d 375, 375 (D.C.Cir.1991).

239. United States Dep't of Justice, Freedom of information Act Guide & Privacy Act Overview 434 (2000) [hereinafter FOIA Guide]. But see Davin v. United States Dep't of Justice, 60 F.3d 1043, 1064 (3d Cir.1995) (requiring agency to show "that specific documents it has withheld contain secret information about techniques for recruiting informants [the disclosure of which] would risk circumvention of the law").

240. See American Civil Liberties Union Found. v. United States Dep't of Justice, 833 F.Supp. 399, 407 (S.D.N.Y.1993).

241. See H.R. Rep. No. 93–180, at 12 (1974), reprinted in 1974 U.S.C.C.A.N. 6267; Albuquerque Publ'g Co. v. United States Dep't of Justice, 726 F.Supp. 851, 858 (D.D.C.1989) (stating that agencies "should avoid burdening the Court with techniques commonly described in movies, popular novels, stories or magazines or television"). See also Rosenfeld v. United States Dep't of Justice, 57 F.3d 803, 815 (9th Cir.1995) (pretext telephone calls not protected); Public Employees for Envtl. Responsibility v. EPA, 978 F.Supp. 955, 963 (D.Colo.1997) (wiretapping not protected).

these procedures is not generally known.[242] Furthermore, courts have approved withholding information about many commonly known procedures—e.g., polygraph examinations[243]—because disclosure could impair the effectiveness of such procedures.[244] The second clause of Exemption 7(E) has a built-in standard of harm analogous to a "high" Exemption 2.[245] This clause protects law enforcement guideline information that the Court of Appeals for the District of Columbia Circuit found ineligible for withholding in *Jordan v. Department of Justice*.[246] Any "law enforcement guideline" is, thus, protected when disclosure "could reasonably be expected to risk circumvention of the law."[247]

(6) Subsection 7(F): disclosure "could reasonably be expected to endanger the life or physical safety of any individual."

Among those persons protected by Exemption 7(F) are law enforcement officers.[248] Moreover, courts have held that Exemption 7(F) protects the names of federal employees and third parties who may be unknown to the requester, but who are connected to particular law enforcement undertakings.[249] Although Exemption 7(F) duplicates the protection af-

242. See, e.g., Coleman v. FBI, 13 F.Supp.2d 75, 83 (D.D.C.1998) (protecting "manner and circumstances" but not the identities, of techniques "generally known to the public"); Delviscovo v. FBI, 903 F.Supp. 1, 3 (D.D.C.1995).

243. See, e.g., Blanton v. United States Dep't of Justice, 63 F.Supp.2d 35, 49–50 (D.D.C.1999); Coleman, 13 F.Supp.2d at 83; Perrone v. FBI, 908 F.Supp. 24, 28 (D.D.C. 1995).

244. See, e.g., Hale v. United States Dep't of Justice, 973 F.2d 894, 902–03 (10th Cir.1992) (disclosing the use of security devices could reduce their effectiveness); Billington v. Department of Justice, 69 F.Supp.2d 128, 140 (D.D.C.1999); Pray v. Dep't of Justice, 902 F.Supp. 1, 4 (D.D.C. 1995), affirmed in part, reversed in part, 1996 WL 734142 (D.C.Cir.1996) (releasing information about investigative techniques could enable criminals to neutralize the effectiveness of such techniques).

245. See FOIA Guide, supra note 1, at 441. (*See also* Exemption 2 discussion, *supra*, at § 17.4.2.)

246. 591 F.2d 753, 771 (D.C.Cir.1978) (en banc) (finding prosecution guidelines ineligible for protection).

247. See, e.g., PHE Inc. v. Department of Justice, 983 F.2d 248, 251 (D.C.Cir.1993)("[R]elease of FBI guidelines as to what sources of information are available to its agents might encourage violators to tamper with those sources of information and thus inhibit investigative efforts."); Voinche v. FBI, 940 F.Supp. 323, 331 (D.D.C.1996), affirmed, 1997 WL 411685 (D.C.Cir.1997), cert. denied, 522 U.S. 950, 118 S.Ct. 370, 139 L.Ed.2d 288 (1997) (upholding nondisclosure of FBI Criminal Intelligence Digest); Jimenez v. FBI, 938 F.Supp. 21, 27 (D.D.C.1996) (approving protection of Bureau of Prisons gang-validation criteria); Foster v. United States Dep't of Justice, 933 F.Supp. 687, 693 (E.D.Mich. 1996) (releasing techniques and guidelines used in undercover operations would diminish effectiveness of guidelines); Pully v. IRS, 939 F.Supp. 429, 437 (E.D.Va.1996) (releasing discriminant function scores would enable taxpayers to "flag" IRS computers). But see Church of Scientology v. IRS, 816 F.Supp. 1138, 1162 (W.D.Tex.1993) (holding that IRS did not show how releasing records about "harassment of Service employees ... could reasonably be expected to circumvent the law").

248. See, e.g., Bennett v. DEA, 55 F.Supp.2d 36, 41 (D.D.C.1999) (protecting DEA agents' names); Fedrick v. United States Dep't of Justice, 984 F.Supp. 659, 665 (W.D.N.Y.1997) (magistrate's recommendation) (same), adopted (W.D.N.Y. Oct. 28, 1997), aff'd sub nom. Fedrick v. Huff, 165 F.3d 13 (2d Cir.1998). But see Public Employees for Envtl. Responsibility v. EPA, 978 F.Supp. 955, 964 (D.Colo.1997) (finding no risk to agency investigators in disclosing EPA Inspector General guidelines).

249. See, e.g., Anderson v. United States Marshals Serv., 943 F.Supp. 37, 40 (D.D.C.1996) (protecting identity of individual when disclosure could endanger his safety); Foster v. United States Dep't of Justice, 933 F.Supp. 687, 693 (E.D.Mich. 1996) (protecting identities of confidential

forded under Exemption 7(C), Exemption 7(F) requires no balancing test.[250]

§ 17.4.8 Exemption (b)(8): Records of Financial Institutions

FOIA permits agencies to withhold information "contained in or related to examination, operating, or condition reports prepared by, on behalf of, or for the use of an agency responsible for the regulation or supervision of financial institutions."[251] There are two main purposes of Exemption 8: (1) to protect the security and stability of banks by withholding frank evaluations and (2) to promote employee-examiner cooperation. The courts tend to interpret Exemption 8 expansively;[252] in general entire documents relating to banks' conditions are exempt, with little need to show cause.[253]

§ 17.4.9 Exemption (b)(9): Records of Oil Exploration

Finally, FOIA specifically exempts from disclosure "geological and geophysical information and data, including maps, concerning wells."[254] Although few agencies have invoked Exemption 9 and few courts have interpreted it,[255] one court has held that the exemption only applies to "well information of a technical or scientific nature."[256]

informants when informants' lives would be endangered).

250. United States Dep't of Justice, Freedom of Information Act Guide & Privacy Act Overview 447 (2000).

251. 5 U.S.C. § 552(b)(8) (1994 & Supp. IV 1998). Courts have declined to restrict the scope of Exemption 8. See United States Dep't of Justice, Freedom of Information Act Guide & Privacy Act Overview 448 (2000) [hereinafter FOIA Guide]. See also Public Citizen v. Farm Credit Admin., 938 F.2d 290, 293–94 (D.C.Cir.1991) (construing the term "financial institutions" broadly and holding that it is not limited to "depository" institutions); Gregory v. FDIC, 631 F.2d 896, 898 (D.C.Cir. 1980) (finding that that Exemption 8 provides "absolute protection regardless of the circumstances underlying the regulatory agency's receipt or preparation of examination, operating or condition reports"); Feshbach v. SEC, 5 F.Supp.2d 774, 781 (N.D.Cal.1997) (holding that the term "financial institutions" includes "brokers and dealers of securities or commodities as well as self-regulatory organizations, such as the [National Association of Securities Dealers])"; Berliner, Zisser, Walter & Gallegos v. SEC, 962 F.Supp. 1348, 1352 (D.Colo. 1997) (ruling that an "investment advisor company" is a "financial institution" under Exemption 8).

252. See Gregory, 631 F.2d at 898; Berliner, 962 F.Supp. at 1353 (describing Exemption 8 "dual purposes" as "protecting the integrity of financial institutions and facilitating cooperation between [agencies] and the entities regulated by [them]").

253. FOIA Guide, supra note 472, at 450.

254. 5 U.S.C.A. § 552(b)(9) (1994 & Supp. IV 1998).

255. United States Dep't of justice, Freedom of Information Act Guide & Privacy Act Overview 454 (2000). See, e.g., Superior Oil Co. v. Federal Energy Regulatory Comm'n, 563 F.2d 191, 203–04 & n. 20 (5th Cir.1977) (non-FOIA case); Pennzoil Co. v. Federal Power Comm'n, 534 F.2d 627, 629–30 & n. 2 (5th Cir.1976) (non-FOIA case); National Broad. Co. v. SBA, 836 F.Supp. 121, 124 n. 2 (S.D.N.Y.1993) (mentioning Exemption 9). See generally Ecee, Inc. v. Federal Energy Regulatory Comm'n, 645 F.2d 339, 348–49 (5th Cir.1981) (holding that requirement that producers of natural gas submit confidential geological information was valid) (non-FOIA case).

256. Black Hills Alliance v. United States Forest Serv., 603 F.Supp. 117, 122 (D.S.D.1984) (withholding technical information about proposed uranium exploration drill holes).

§ 17.4.10 Exclusions

Three special protection provisions under subsection (c), referred to as record "exclusions," authorize federal law enforcement agencies to treat certain sensitive records "as not subject to the requirements of [the FOIA]."[257] An agency that applies one of the three record exclusions will simply inform the FOIA requester that no records responsive to his FOIA request exist.[258] The (c)(1) Exclusion authorizes federal law enforcement agencies to hide the existence of records of ongoing investigations or proceedings.[259] The (c)(2) Exclusion guards against identifying confidential informants in criminal proceedings.[260] The (c)(3) Exclusion guards certain FBI foreign intelligence, counterintelligence, and antiterrorism records.[261]

Just because an agency provides a "no records" response does not shield the agency from administrative or judicial review of the agency action.[262] The requestor may challenge the agency on grounds that the agency failed to perform a sufficiently detailed search.[263] Or, a requester may seek review to verify his suspicions that the information has been excluded under subsection (c) by asking a court to determine whether an exclusion, if one was used, was used appropriately.[264] Agencies, therefore, have prepared uniform procedures in advance to cope with administrative appeals and court challenges that seek review of the possibility that an exclusion was used.[265] Administrative appeal responses in these cases will not indicate whether the agency invoked an exclusion.[266] Moreover, agencies will routinely advise requestors that the standard agency policy is to refuse to confirm or deny that an exclusion was used in any particular case.[267] Thus, the standard government litigation policy in exclusion cases is to submit an in camera declaration about the FOIA request.[268] The government will then urge the court to issue a public decision that does not indicate whether the case at bar is an exclusion case, but rather states that "a full review of the claim was had and that, if an exclusion was in fact employed, it was, and remains, amply justified."[269]

§ 17.5 REVERSE FOIA SUITS

The Freedom of Information Act is replete with the word "shall," underscoring its heralded goal of *mandatory* information disclosure. But

257. 5 U.S.C. § 552(c)(1)–(3) (1994 & Supp. IV 1998).

258. United States Dep't of Justice, Freedom of Information Act Guide & Privacy Act Overview 455 (2000) [hereinafter FOIA guide].

259. Id. at 456.

260. Id. at 458.

261. Id. at 461. See also Exec. Order No. 12,958, 3 C.F.R. 333 (1996), reprinted in 50 U.S.C. § 435 note (Supp. II 1996) (classifying certain records for national security purposes).

262. FOIA Guide, supra note 475, at 463.

263. See, e.g., Oglesby v. United States Dep't of the Army, 920 F.2d 57, 67 (D.C.Cir. 1990).

264. FOIA Guide, supra note 475, at 463.

265. See id.

266. Id. at 464.

267. Id.

268. Id.

269. Id. at 465.

in regard to its exemptions (§ 552(b)), the Act is silent as to whether an agency "may" or "shall" refuse to disclose such exempt information.[1] A "reverse" FOIA action is one in which the submitter of information—usually a corporation or other business entity—seeks to enjoin an agency from releasing that information in response to a third-party FOIA request. In *Chrysler Corporation v. Brown,*[2] the Supreme Court held that those who submit information can bring suit to prevent its release.[3]

In compliance with Department of Labor federal contract regulations, Chrysler Corporation submitted various Affirmative Action reports and statistics regarding Chrysler's employment practice to the Defense Logistics Agency (DLA). In 1975, the DLA informed Chrysler that third parties had made FOIA requests for disclosure of Chrysler's job and hiring records at assembly plants in Delaware and Michigan. Chrysler brought suit in district court to enjoin the release of these records, arguing that disclosure (1) was barred by the FOIA, (2) was inconsistent with the Trade Secrets Act[4] and other "confidentiality statutes," and (3) would be in contravention of agency regulations, and therefore an abuse of discretion. The Supreme Court unanimously held that "Congress did not design the FOIA exemptions to be mandatory bars to disclosure."[5] Thus, even though certain requested material fell within one of FOIA's exemptions, the agency was not required to withhold it.[6] A decision to release the information, however, was subject to judicial review under section 706(2)(A) of the APA. A court could find that the agency's decision was "arbitrary, capricious, an abuse of discretion, or otherwise not in accordance with law."[7] This would be the case if, for example, the Trade Secrets Act protected the requested material. To release it under these circumstances would not be "in accordance with law." The Court in *Chrysler* established the right of parties to sue to prevent disclosure of material requested by others. It did not, however, resolve the issue of the

§ 17.5

1. CNA Fin. Corp. v. Donovan, 830 F.2d 1132, 1133 n. 1 (D.C.Cir.1987). See also Bartholdi Cable Co. v. FCC, 114 F.3d 274, 279 (D.C.Cir.1997); Cortez III Serv. Corp. v. NASA, 921 F.Supp. 8, 11 (D.D.C. 1996) (holding that in reverse FOIA actions "courts have jurisdiction to hear complaints brought by parties claiming that an agency decision to release information adversely affects them").

2. 441 U.S. 281, 99 S.Ct. 1705, 60 L.Ed.2d 208 (1979), on remand, 611 F.2d 439 (3d Cir.1979). For agency regulations dealing with this issue, see 28 C.F.R. § 16.7 (1980).

3. The Court noted: "The expanding range of federal regulatory activity and growth in the Government sector of the economy have increased federal agencies' demands for information about the activities of private individuals and corporations. These developments have paralleled a related concern about secrecy in Government and abuse of power. The [FOIA] was a response to this concern, but it has also had a largely unforeseen tendency to exacerbate the uneasiness of those who comply with governmental demands for information. For under the FOIA third parties have been able to obtain Government files containing information submitted by corporations and individuals who thought the information would be held in confidence...." 441 U.S. at 285, 99 S.Ct. at 1709.

4. 18 U.S.C.A. § 1905.

5. 441 U.S. at 293, 99 S.Ct. at 1713.

6. Accord, Campaign for Family Farms v. Glickman, 200 F.3d 1180, 1184 (8th Cir. 2000). See also Comdisco, Inc. v. GSA, 864 F.Supp. 510, 513 (E.D.Va.1994); Environmental Tech., Inc. v. EPA, 822 F.Supp. 1226, 1228 (E.D.Va.1993).

7. 5 U.S.C.A. § 706(2)(A). See, e.g., McDonnell Douglas Corp. v. Widnall, 57 F.3d 1162, 1164 (D.C.Cir.1995).

relationship of the Trade Secrets Act to Exemption 4 of FOIA. Subsequently, the D.C. Circuit has ruled that Exemption 4 and the Trade Secrets Act are coextensive, thereby making Exemption 4's bar against disclosure mandatory.[8]

Because of the sensitive nature of the information that may be involved, especially in Exemption 4 cases, there is always concern that FOIA will be used, not to further our knowledge about how government operates, but to provide information about the trade secrets of competitors. Executive Order Number 12600[9] attempts to deal with this issue in Exemption 4 cases. It requires that agencies that decide to release material that might be protected under Exemption 4,[10] must contact the company which submitted it and give them an opportunity to object.[11]

§ 17.5.1 FOIA Summary

Despite its critics, FOIA is inherent in our modern concept of citizens' access to information. With its nine exemptions, the Act attempts to achieve a rational balancing of the public's interest in information against the government's interest in effective and efficient operation.[12] In reality, however, by requiring *de novo* judicial review and placing the burden of proving exemption status on the agency, citizen access to information has been greatly facilitated. This is in accord with the basic purposes of the Act. FOIA springs from the popular distrust of government,[13] and from Congress' adversarial relationship with the Executive. In essence, FOIA is an attempt to regulate the regulators:

> There is no obligation in the Constitution compelling the American people to trust their government. And where a segment of the state enjoys no popular mandate for its actions, it should be willing to disclose the information responsibly, not only to enhance public

8. CNA Financial Corp. v. Donovan, 830 F.2d 1132, 1144 (D.C.Cir.1987), cert. denied 485 U.S. 977, 108 S.Ct. 1270, 99 L.Ed.2d 481 (1988). See also, Bartholdi, 114 F.3d at 281; McDonnell Douglas Corp. v. NASA, 895 F.Supp. 319, 322 n. 4 (D.D.C. 1995), vacated, 88 F.3d 1278 (D.C.Cir.1996). Submitters also challenge contemplated disclosures under other FOIA exemptions. See, e.g., Campaign for Family Farms, 200 F.3d at 1182 (Exemption 6); Bartholdi, 114 F.3d at 282 (Exemption 6); Na Iwi O Na Kupuna v. Dalton, 894 F.Supp. 1397, 1411–13 (D.Haw.1995) (Exemptions 3 and 6).

9. 52 Fed.Reg. 23781 (1987).

10. See generally Trifid Corp. v. National Imagery & Mapping Agency, 10 F.Supp.2d 1087, 1093 (E.D.Mo.1998) ("[A]gency's explanation of its decision may be 'curt' [if it] indicate[s] the determinative reason for the action taken").

11. But cf. McDonnell Douglas Corp. v. NASA, 895 F.Supp. 319, 323 (D.D.C.1995), vacated, 88 F.3d 1278 (D.C.Cir.1996) (finding that agency must "have the existing injunction modified or dissolved" because the agency "simply does not have the authority to require [submitter] to justify again and again why information, the disclosure of which has been enjoined by a federal court, should continue to be enjoined").

12. S.Rep. No. 813, 89th Cong., 1st Sess. 3 (1965) ("Success lies in providing a workable formula which encompasses, balances, and protects all interests, yet places emphasis on the fullest responsible disclosure.").

13. Id., at 10 ("A government by secrecy benefits no one. It injures the people it seeks to serve, it injures its own integrity and operation. It breeds mistrust, dampens the fervor of its citizens, and mocks their loyalty.").

knowledge of its activities, but also to cultivate a degree of trust (or to dispel distrust).[14]

FOIA can thus be viewed as a remarkable democratic achievement. Its self-appointed guardians, citizens and the investigative press, can point to hundreds of public interest stories made possible by FOIA requests.[15] FOIA disclosures have brought to light the Army's discreet investigation of the My Lai massacre,[16] improper IRS monitoring of political dissidents,[17] the Bay of Pigs debacle,[18] the Air Force's payment of defense contractors' lobbying costs,[19] CIA mind control experiments,[20] FBI smear campaigns,[21] information related to the Iran–Contra affair,[22] and transcripts of proceedings before the grand jury that indicted Alger Hiss for perjury in 1949.[23] Indeed, the mere existence of a judicially-enforced FOIA has encouraged many agencies voluntarily to release information on a regular basis.[24]

Critics of FOIA, however, assert that the democratic intentions of the Act have not been realized, and that in practice the Act has been abused by private interests and has spawned unintended side effects. For example, the Drug Enforcement Administration claims that 60% of the FOIA requests it receives are from imprisoned or known drug traffickers.[25] Some critics contend that FOIA's users are often organized crime figures and convicts who seek disclosure of law enforcement investiga-

14. Relyea, The FOIA and its Costs: A Brief Overview 2(1) Int'l J.Pub.Admin. 117, 126 (1980); see also Wald, The Freedom of Information Act: A Short Case Study in the Perils and Paybacks of Legislating Democratic Values, 33 Emory L.J. 649, at 654 (1984) ("If government is indeed a public trust, then information about the deeds of the trustees—those in power—must be available to the public, except when overriding concerns necessitate confidentiality.") (footnote omitted).

15. See, e.g., Public Citizen Litigation Group (Jan. 1998) <http://www.citizen.org/litigation/foic/foia_highlight.html> (listing numerous FOIA victories).

16. The Bureaucracy: Opening Up Those Secrets Time, April 14, 1975, at 28.

17. Eileen Shanahan, N.Y. Times, Nov. 18, 1974, at 1.

18. See Wald, supra note 504, at 661–664.

19. Sen. Edward Kennedy, Foreword: "Is the Pendulum Swinging Away from FOI?" 16 Harv.C.R.–C.L. L. Rev. 311 (1981).

20. See, CIA v. Sims, 471 U.S. 159, 105 S.Ct. 1881, 85 L.Ed.2d 173 (1985). See also Nicholas M. Horrack, Drugs Tested by CIA on Mental Patients, N.Y. Times, Aug., 3, 1977, at 1.

21. For example, see article concerning release of FBI files compiled under J. Edgar Hoover recording charges of sexual improprieties and preferences of public figures ("Censored Version Issued of Secret Hoover Files On Official's Misconduct," N.Y. Times, Nov. 24, 1976 at 15).

22. See, e.g., National Security Archive v. Office of Independent Counsel, 1992 WL 1352663 (D.D.C.1992).

23. See In re Petition of American Historical Association, 62 F.Supp.2d 1100 (S.D.N.Y.1999)

24. Sen. Jim Sasser, Oversight of the Administration of the Federal Freedom of Information Act: A Personal Report, November 1981, reprinted in Freedom of Information Trends in the Information Age 86, 113 (Tom Riley & Harold C. Relyea eds., 1983) (citing a correspondent's testimony before the Senate Subcomm. on Intergovernmental Relations of the Senate Comm. on Gov't Affairs, FOI Act Oversight Hearings, in 1980).

25. Freedom of Information Reform Act: Hearings Before the Subcomm. on the Constitution of the Senate Comm. on the Judiciary, 98th Cong., 1st Sess. 43 (1983) (statement of Jonathon C. Rose).

tions.[26] Regulated industries note that competitors routinely use FOIA requests to gain access to marketable trade secrets.[27] Government lawyers complain of being surprised and swamped by redundant FOIA "discovery" requests.[28]

With the fall of the Berlin Wall in 1989, the so-called American "culture of secrecy" [29]changed. During the 1990s, access to and declassification of government information was encouraged, reversing the 1980s trend of protecting any government document that could be linked in any way to national security. Information technology has played a crucial role in providing public access to government records and increasing the efficiency with which records are made available. The 1996 Electronic Freedom of Information Act amendments—which resulted in widespread dissemination of public documents via the World Wide Web—the massive declassification efforts of the federal government during the Clinton Administration, and the concomitant reduction in FOIA suits during the past few years are vindications of the openness and transparency upon which a free and democratic society rely. FOIA has been and continues to be a powerful tool in the quest to achieve the ideals of democracy.

26. Id., at 42–43. ("The FBI has found that 16% of the FOIA requests it receives are from known or suspected criminals."); see also Bonine, Public Interest Fee Waivers Under the Freedom of Information Act, 1981 Duke L.J. 213, n. 10 (1981).

27. Wald, supra note 504, at 666; O'Reilly, Regaining a Confidence: Protection of Business Confidential Data Through Reform of the Freedom of Information Act, 34 Admin.L.Rev. 263 (1982); Note, Protecting Confidential Business Information from Federal Agency Disclosure, 80 Colum.L.Rev. 109 (1981).

28. See Tomlinson, Use of FOIA for Discovery Purposes, 43 Md.L.Rev. 119 (1984). For reform proposals, see chapter 14, sec. 14.4 infra.

29. S. Doc. No. 105–2, at XXXI (1997) (Foreword by Sen. Moynihan to the Report of the Commission on Protecting and Reducing Government Secrecy).

Chapter 18

THE PRIVACY ACT

Table of Sections

§ 18.1 INTRODUCTION

Information technologies challenge the law to keep pace with new developments and new problems.[1] As technology continues to reveal new

§ 18.1

1. See, e.g., Michael Bartlett, Napster Boosts Internet Legal Issues, Billables, Newsbytes, Dec. 8, 2000 (visited Dec. 11, 2000) <http://www.newsbytes.com/news/00/159190.html> (reporting the effects of new technology on boosting business for law practitioners); Associated Press, Doctor Wins $675,000 Libel Verdict Based on Anonymous Net Posting, Dec. 10, 2000, available in LEXIS, News Group File, All (reporting the first award ever for Internet defamation); Jim Wolf, U.S. Embraces European Cybercrime Proposal, Reuters, Dec. 5, 2000, available in LEXIS, News Group, All (reporting that the United States has embraced a Council of Europe cybercrime convention); Jon Van, State's Attorney's Office Sues 2 Internet Firms Over Cookie Practices, Chi. Trib., Dec. 11, 2000, available in LEXIS, News Group, All (reporting that State has sued Internet firms over their intrusive consumer privacy practices). A substantial body of legal literature has grown that attempts to define the role of the law in relationship to emerging information technology. See, e.g., A. Michael Froomkin, Wrong Turn in Cyberspace: Using ICANN to Route Around the APA and the Constitution, 50 Duke L.J. 17 (2000) (arguing that the Department of Commerce use of a private nonprofit corporation to make rules on Internet domain names either violates the APA's requirement for notice and comment in rulemaking and judicial review, or violates the Constitution's nondelegation doctrine); Michael J. Madison, Complexity and Copyright in Contradiction, 18 Cardozo Arts & Ent LJ

uses for—and places a higher premium on[2]—personal information, the importance of control of that information intensifies. Information management law promises to be a growth industry, with significant international implications.

Privacy and disclosure laws are increasingly important as we move toward a more integrated global economy. The economic consequences for the United States due to increased barriers to transborder data flows would be significant because international communication is increasingly synonymous with international commerce. Groups of countries such as the Council of Europe have entered into mutual treaties and agreements which seek to ensure both the free flow of commercial information and the protection of individual privacy and trade secrets.[3] Relatively unre-

125 (2000) (discussing the effects of cyberspace on copyright law); Andrew L. Shapiro, The Disappearance 0f Cyberspace and the Rise of Code, 8 Seton Hall Const. L.J. 703 (1998) (arguing for the application of existing law to emerging information technology); Mark A. Lemley & David McGowan, Legal Implications of Network Economic Effects, 86 Calif. L. Rev. 479 (1998) (discussing the effects of, inter alia, computer networks on traditional law and economics theory); Jack L. Goldsmith, Against Cyberanarchy, 65 U. Chi. L. Rev. 1199 (1998) (arguing that personal jurisdiction over cyberspace activities will become functionally identical to personal jurisdiction over realspace activities); Henry H. Perritt, Jr., The Internet Is Changing International Law, 73 Chi.-Kent. L. Rev. 997 (1998); David G. Post, Pooling Intellectual Capital: Thoughts on Anonymity, Pseudonymity, and Limited Liability in Cyberspace, 1996 U. Chi. Legal F. 139. There is also a body of literature that is more skeptical about the progress or promise, or both, of the liberating effect of information technology on the law and vice versa. See, e.g., Neil Weinstock Netanel, Cyberspace Self-Governance: A Skeptical View from Liberal Democratic Theory, 88 Calif. L. Rev. 395 (2000) (arguing that the government must selectively regulate information technology to protect and promote liberal democratic ideals); see generally, Symposium: The Internet and the Sovereign State: The Role and Impact of Cyberspace on National and Global Governance, 5 Ind. J. Global Legal Stud. 415 (1998); Schwartz, Data Processing and Government Administration: Failure of the American legal Response to the computer, 43 Hastings L.J. 1321 (1992); Brownstein, Computer Communications Vulnerable As Privacy Laws Lag Behind Technology, Nat'l J., January 14, 1984, at 52. See also Nussbaum, The World After Oil 14–15 (1983): Though written in 1983, the following observations on information remain relevant today:

> Information will [soon] replace manufactured goods as the most valued commodity in the economy. By the middle of the 1980s, information processing will surpass car manufacturing as the largest industry in the country. And so inundated will society become with this data deluge that people with the skill to interpret and manage the flood for others will rise to the top of society and perhaps hold it hostage.... Even today, as the telecommunications revolution sweeps through the nation's offices and businesses, the very first questions anyone asks are "How safe is my computer?" "Can anyone look into my files?" "Who knows my secret password?" The years ahead will spawn an entire new wave of crime. Indeed, crimes of the 1990s will be radically different from today's concerns. Computer crime in particular—tapping into private electronic files—will soon become the most troublesome crime of the future. And it will trouble foreign governments and domestic corporations as much as the heads of households.

2. For an economic perspective on the value of privacy in relation to the benefits of information disbursement, see Posner et al., The Law and Economics of Privacy, 9 J.Legal Stud. 621–842 (1980).

3. See Directive 97/66 of the European Parliament and of the Council of 15, December 1997 Concerning the Processing of Personal Data and the Protection of Privacy in the Telecommunications Sector, 1998 O.J. (L 28) 1–8; Directive 95/46 of the European Parliament and of the Council of 24 October 1995 on the Protection of Individuals with Regard to the Processing of Personal Data and on the Free Movement of Such Data, 1995 O.J. © (93) 1. See also Council Resolution of 19 January 1999 on the Consumer Dimension of the Information Society, 1999 O.J. © (23) 1–3; Proposal

stricted transborder data flow is thus crucial to the domestic economies as well as the global economy. In the United States, domestic and international information and telecommunications policy is formulated, negotiated, and implemented by the National Telecommunications and Information Agency of the U.S. Department of Commerce.[4]

At the domestic level, agencies need information to plan and carry out their various regulatory duties. Each agency collects and catalogues the information it needs in its own fashion: the Internal Revenue Service via annual tax forms, the Federal Communications Commission through license applications, the law enforcement agencies through tips and investigations, Health and Human Services through financial eligibility forms, and so forth. Given the array of regulatory agencies, the aggregate amount of personal or financial information pertaining to individuals and held by the government is staggering.[5] Nonetheless, assuming that each agency sought only the information necessary for its particular administrative mission, and so long as individuals were mobile and information was stored in physically separate manual files that could not easily be retrieved or consolidated, "technological limitations and single inefficiency preserved a reasonable balance between the individual seeking various benefits without sacrificing privacy, and the government, which needed, and could compel the surrender of, vast amounts of personal data."[6] By the early 1970s, Congress recognized that this tenuous balance no longer existed.[7] With the increased use of efficient computer-based information systems, government agencies now have the capacity to compile, retrieve, analyze, and disseminate information with relative ease and rapidity. Notwithstanding each respective agency's legitimate need for certain types of personal information, the technological ability to combine scattered bits of data into a comprehensive personal dossier raised for some members of Congress almost Orwellian fears of an all-knowing and potentially intrusive bureaucracy.[8] Congress

for a Regulation of the European Parliament and of the Council on the Protection of Individuals with Regard to the Processing of Personal Data by the Institutions and Bodies of the Community and on the Free Movement of Such Data, COM(99) 337 final 1–62.

4. NTIA is the President's principal adviser on telecommunications and information policy issues and frequently works with other Executive Branch agencies to develop and present the Administration's position on these issues. NTIA established by Executive Order in 1976. E.O. 12,046, 3 C.F.R. (1978). Reprinted as amended in 47 U.S.C. § 305 note (1988). Congress codified NTIA's functions in the National Telecommunications and Information Administration Organization Act of 1992, Pub. L. No. 102–538, 106 Stat. 3533 (1992). (Codified at 42 U.S.C. §§ 901–927).

5. "In FY 1999, citizens spent an estimated 7.2 billion hours providing federal agencies the information needed to fulfill agency responsibilities." Office of Management and Budget, Information Collection Budget of the United States Government 79 (2000). In FY 2000, an estimated 7.4 billion hours will be spent by citizens providing needed information to federal agencies. Id. at 83 tbl.A.2.

6. Note, The Privacy Act of 1974: An Overview and Critique, 1976 Wash.U.L.Q. 667, 669 (1976) [hereinafter Note, The Privacy Act of 1974].

7. See Senate Comm. on Gov't Operations, Protecting Individual Privacy in Federal Gathering, Use and Disclosure of Information, S.Rep. No. 1183, 93d Cong., 2d Sess. 6 (1974), reprinted in Sourcebook, supra note 5, at 154, 159.

8. Americans today are scrutinized, measured, watched, counted and interrogated by more governmental agencies, law enforcement officials, social scientists and

sought to quiet those fears with the Privacy Act of 1974.[9]

Like the 1974 amendments to FOIA, the Privacy Act was drafted in the shadow of Watergate. Governmental improprieties that came to light during those hearings furthered the active distrust of government that developed during that era, and added to the pressure on Congress to enact some form of privacy legislation.[10]

The Senate and the House each passed materially different privacy bills,[11] and a series of informal meetings between House and Senate committee leaders produced a hurried compromise bill which was enacted without the benefit of a conference committee. As one commentator noted,

> [t]he consequence of this hasty and haphazard legislative process is an internally inconsistent statute with no reliable indication of congressional intent. The original committee reports are of limited value in interpreting the final statute. The only reliable legislative history consists of a rather skimpy staff analysis of the compromise amendments appearing in the Congressional Record. Consequently, courts are likely to have great difficulty interpreting the Act and vigorous enforcement may be impossible.[12]

poll takers than at any other time in our history. Probably in no nation on earth is as much individualized information collected, recorded and disseminated as in the United States.

"The information gathering and surveillance activities of the Federal Government have expanded to such an extent that they are becoming a threat to several of every American's basic rights, the rights of privacy, speech, assembly, association, and petition of Government. . . ."

> [I]f one reads Orwell and Huxley carefully, one realizes that "1984" is a state of mind. In the past, dictatorships always have come with hobnailed boots and tanks and machineguns, but a dictatorship of dossiers, a dictatorship of data banks can be just as repressive, just as chilling and just as debilitating on our constitutional protections.

120 Cong.Rec. 36,912 (quoting testimony of Prof. Arthur Miller); see also 120 Cong.Rec. at 36,904 (remarks of Sen. Goldwater); Id. at 36,647 (remarks of Rep. Alexander); Id. at 36,652 (remarks of Rep. Regula). Cf. Suzanne M. Thompson, The Digital Explosion Comes With a Cost: The Loss of Privacy, 4 J. Tech. L. & Pol'y 3, 38 (1999) ("The advanced technologies of the Information Age have changed the focus of data protection from government entities, who in the past have controlled the majority of personal information, to the private sector, which is now a major source for the widespread dissemination of personal data.").

9. Pub.L. No. 93–579, 88 Stat. 1896 (1974) (codified as amended at 5 U.S.C.A. § 552(a)).

10. For a concise and thoughtful account of the political events, the legal background, and congressional/public moods which led to the Privacy Act, see The Freedom of Information Reform Act: Hearings on S. 774 Before the Subcom. on the Constitution of the Senate Comm. on the Judiciary, 98th Cong., 1st Sess. 24–44 (1983) (statement of James H. Davidson).

11. S. 3418, H.R. 16373, 93d Cong., 2d Sess. (1974). The original Senate bill had more teeth. It provided for the establishment of a Federal Privacy Board, a virtually independent agency with the power to investigate and ensure other agencies' compliance with the Act. The original Senate version also called for the award of actual *and* punitive damages for "any" violation of the Act. The original House bill contained no provisions for oversight other than an annual report from the President; wary of exposing the agencies to undue liability, the original House bill provided for recovery of only "actual" damages upon a showing of a "willful, arbitrary or capricious" violation of the Act.

12. Note, The Privacy Act of 1974, supra note 6 (citing Analysis of House and Senate Compromise Amendments to the Federal Privacy Act, printed in 120 Cong. Rec. S 21,817 (1974) and 120 Cong.Rec. H 12,243 (1974)).

Despite the Privacy Act's incomplete and rather confusing legislative history, the Act has generated much less litigation[13] and has cost less to administer than might originally have been anticipated. In its haste to enact *some* sort of privacy legislation, Congress opted to settle for a compromise—a comprehensive statement of privacy policy which left the hard questions of enforcement[14] to the individual, to the courts and to future legislation.[15]

The Privacy Act, nevertheless, represents a statutory recognition of the fragile right of privacy in an administrative state which feeds on information. We shall now examine it in some detail. At the end of the chapter, we will briefly survey some legislation governing the private collection and use of personal data. Many of the concerns expressed, with regard to the governmental collection and use of data, are also involved when technology is used by the private sector.[16]

§ 18.1.1 An Overview of the Act

In passing the Privacy Act of 1974,[17] Congress declared that though, in its view, the right to privacy is a personal and fundamental right protected by the Constitution, increasing use of sophisticated information technology by the federal agencies has greatly magnified the potential harm to individual privacy that could result. It was, therefore, necessary and proper to regulate the collection and use of information by such agencies.[18] The Act's basic purpose is thus to provide for certain individual safeguards against invasions of privacy by the government.[19]

13. See H.R. Rep. No. 106–50, at 5 (1999).

14. Congress' decision to authorize a Privacy Protection Study Commission, Privacy Act of 1974, Pub.L. No. 93–579, § 5, 88 Stat. 1896, 1905 (1974), in lieu of a separate enforcement agency and a more tightly-written statute was part of the "wait and see" compromise which enabled the legislators to pass the end-of-session law without a joint conference committee. The tough issues were simply passed on to the Commission. See, e.g., Sourcebook, supra note 5, at 329, 949; O'Reilly, Who's On First?, supra note 14, at 99.

15. As will be seen infra, 1) lack of remedial incentive has resulted in relatively little use of the Act by individuals, 2) the courts have wrestled with the Act's scrambled legislative history with only limited success, and 3) at least some amendment to the statute appears to be necessary.

16. See § 18.8 infra. See generally, Alfred C. Aman, Jr., Information, Privacy and Technology: Citizens, Clients, or Consumers? in Freedom of Expression and Freedom of Information, Ch. 20 (Oxford Univ. Press, 2000) (Jack Beatson and Yvonne Cripps, eds.).

17. Pub.L. No. 93–579, 88 Stat. 1896. Sec. 3 of the Act is codified at 5 U.S.C.A. § 552a; for other sections, see 5 U.S.C.A. § 552a Notes (1984).

18. Id. § 2(a).

19. Specifically, id. § 2(b) states:

The purpose of the Act is to provide certain safeguards for an individual against an invasion of personal privacy by requiring Federal agencies, except as otherwise provided by law, to—

(1) permit an individual to determine what records pertaining to him are collected, maintained, used, or disseminated by such agencies;

(2) permit an individual to prevent records, pertaining to him obtained by such agencies for a particular purpose from being used or made available for another purpose without his consent;

(3) permit an individual to gain access to information pertaining to him in federal agency records, to have a copy made of all or any portion thereof, and to correct or amend such records; . . .

Section 5 of the Act establishes a seven-member Privacy Protection Study Commission (PPSC). The PPSC was given two years to assess virtually every aspect of federal information policy which might infringe upon personal privacy, and to make appropriate recommendations in a report to Congress and the President.[20] That report[21] recommended that Congress establish an independent entity to monitor, investigate and oversee vigorously the implementation and evolution of the Privacy Act.[22] Congress, however, has not chosen to establish a permanent, independent Privacy Board to actively administer the Act.

Section 6 of the Act designates the Office of Management and Budget as the overseer of the Act; the OMB is to develop and update guidelines to facilitate the agencies' compliance with the Act. Section 7 of the Act governs the use of individuals' social security numbers by federal, state and local governments. An individual cannot be denied any "right, privilege, or benefit" for his refusal to disclose his social security number, unless such disclosure is mandated by a federal statute. Furthermore, any federal, state or local government agency requesting an individual's social security number must inform the individual whether the disclosure is mandatory, under what statutory authority the number is sought, and what uses will be made of the disclosed number.[23] Subsequent legislation allowing or requiring collection of social security numbers for specific purposes, however, has weakened the force of section 7.[24]

The heart of the Privacy Act imposes restrictions on the collection, maintenance, use and dissemination of federal agency records. The Act prohibits the maintenance of "secret" record systems, ostensibly through a requirement that notice of new or changed systems of records be published in the Federal Register.[25] The Act gives individuals the

20. Personal Privacy in an Information Society: The Report of the Privacy Protection Study Commission (U.S.G.P.O., 1977).

21. Id.

22. Id. at 37.

23. See, e.g., Alcaraz v. Block, 746 F.2d 593 (9th Cir.1984) (use of social security numbers as condition of school meal programs); Wolman v. United States, 542 F.Supp. 84 (D.D.C.1982) (Selective Service's use of social security numbers did not violate the Privacy Act, given statutory authority); Doe v. Sharp, 491 F.Supp. 346 (D.Mass.1980); Greater Cleveland Welfare Rights Organization v. Bauer, 462 F.Supp. 1313 (N.D.Ohio 1978) (use of social security numbers on AFDC application upheld, with order for proper notice provisions); Doyle v. Wilson, 529 F.Supp. 1343 (D.Del.1982) (official immunity barred plaintiff's recovery of damages from court officers who made refund of traffic fine conditional upon plaintiff's disclosure of social security numbers).

24. See, e.g., 42 U.S.C.A. § 405 (authorizing use of social security numbers by states for any tax, general public assistance, driver's license or motor vehicle registration purposes); id. § 453(b) (authorizing use of social security numbers in draft registration).

25. 5 U.S.C.A. § 552a(e)(4). Originally, the Act required an annual publication in the Federal Register of each record system maintained by federal agencies. Finding that agency record systems had stabilized and that annual publication of all record systems was unduly expensive, Congress amended the publication requirement to apply only to new or changed record systems. Pub.L. No. 97–375, § 201(a), 96 Stat. 1821 (1982). Although the law continues to require the annual publication of a low-cost compilation of agency notices, 5 U.S.C.A. § 552a(f), use of the Federal Register as a means of notice to the general public has been roundly criticized as inadequate. In the first place, few members of the public

right to see and copy records about themselves maintained by federal agencies,[26] and to ask for correction of inaccurate, incomplete or irrelevant information contained therein.[27] Agencies are also required to keep an accounting of each disclosure outside the agency for five years, and to make that accounting available to the subject of the record upon request.[28]

Agencies can only collect information relevant and necessary to accomplish an agency function,[29] and must collect information to the "greatest extent practicable" from the subject himself.[30] The Act prohibits agencies from maintaining records describing how any individual exercises First Amendment rights unless such maintenance is expressly authorized by statute or pertinent to a legitimate law enforcement activity.[31]

Internally, records may be disclosed only to agency employees who have a need for the records in the performance of their duties.[32] Records may be disclosed externally (other than to the subject of the record) only if specifically permitted by the Act or if authorized in writing by the subject of the record.[33] The Act specifically permits disclosure of an individual's records without his consent to the Census Bureau, the National Archives, the Congress and the General Accounting Office; if required by FOIA; pursuant to court order; for statistical purposes; in compelling circumstances affecting health or safety; to a consumer reporting agency; for the civil and criminal law enforcement purposes of another agency; and for "routine" administrative use.[34] Routine uses must be established for each system of records by rule after 30 days for public notice and comment,[35] a procedure which ostensibly requires agencies to plan in advance and enunciate parameters for the disclosure of personal information. The broad "routine use" provision has generated considerable criticism and controversy.[36]

ever open the Federal Register, let alone sift through it for Privacy Act records notices. See, e.g., Oversight of the Privacy Act of 1974: Hearings Before a Subcomm. of the House Gov't Operations Comm., 98th Cong., 1st Sess.App. 7, at 585 (1983) (statement of the Director of Federal Register urging streamlined, less expensive publication); 1979 Annual Report of the President on the Implementation of the Privacy Act 10. Secondly, agencies have relied on the publication requirement as a procedural shield from later liability under the Act's more substantive provisions. "One of my chief concerns is that the bureaucracy, with the approval of OMB, has drained much of the substance out of the Act. As a result, the Privacy Act tends to be viewed as strictly a procedural statute ... agencies feel free to disclose personal information to anyone as long as the proper notices have been published in the Federal Register. No one seems to consider any more whether the Privacy Act prohibits a particular use of information." 1983 Oversight Hearings, supra, at 5 (opening statement of Chairman English).

26. 5 U.S.C.A. § 552a(d)(1).

27. Id. § 552a(d)(2)–(4).

28. Id. § 552a(c).

29. Id. § 552a(e)(1).

30. Id. § 552a(e)(2).

31. Id. § 552a(e)(7).

32. Id. § 552a(b)(1).

33. Id. § 552a(b).

34. Id. § 552a(b)(2)–(12).

35. Id. § 552a(e)(11).

36. See, e.g., Note, Narrowing the "Routine Use" Exemption to the Privacy Act of 1974, 14 U.Mich.J.L.Rev. 126 (1980); Note, The Privacy Act of 1974, supra note 6. Perhaps due to the inadequacy of the individual's civil remedies under the Act

The Act is as much a records management law as a privacy protection law. Agencies are required to maintain records used to make "any determination about an individual with such accuracy, relevance, timeliness, and completeness as is reasonably necessary to assure fairness to the individual in the determination."[37] Agencies are also required to establish "appropriate administrative, technical, and physical safeguards to insure security and confidentiality of records and to protect against any anticipated threats or hazards to their security or integrity which could result in substantial harm, embarrassment, inconvenience, or unfairness to any individual on whom information is maintained."[38] Agency rulemaking regarding privacy compliance and implementation is conducted pursuant to the informal notice and comment provisions of APA § 553.[39]

Enforcement of the Act is left to the initiative of the wronged or concerned individual. Provision is made for *de novo* review by the district court of an agency's alleged failure to release or correct self-information sought by an individual, or to otherwise comply with the requirements of the Act.[40] Although the court is empowered to order the release of wrongfully withheld records, there is no statutory provision for injunctive relief.[41] While there is a provision dealing with the award of "reasonable attorney fees and other litigation costs" to a complainant who has "substantially prevailed,"[42] courts applying such a discretionary standard in this and other contexts have been reluctant to saddle the government with costs in all but extreme situations. The Act purports to grant individual plaintiffs a right to "actual damages" of at least $1000,[43] but damages are only awarded upon the *individual's* proof that the agency "acted in a manner which was intentional or willful."[44] For damages greater than $1000, the plaintiff must prove "actual damages."[45] Although actual damages include out-of-pocket expenses, there is a split of authority whether the plaintiff can recover damages for physical and mental injury.[46] Injunctive relief is available only under

and the broadness of the routine use exception, there is a relative dearth of case law on the subject. See SEC v. Dimensional Entertainment Corp., 518 F.Supp. 773 (S.D.N.Y.1981) (disclosure of parole hearing transcript to SEC held to be routine use and a (b)(7) transfer); Burley v. DEA, 443 F.Supp. 619 (M.D.Tenn.1977).

37. 5 U.S.C.A. § 552a(e)(5).

38. Id. § 552a(e)(10).

39. Id. § 552a(f).

40. See generally id. § 552a(g).

41. See Parks v. U.S. Internal Revenue Service, 618 F.2d 677 (10th Cir.1980).

42. 5 U.S.C.A. § 552a(g)(2)(B).

43. Id. § 552a(g)(4).

44. Id.

45. Two courts, however, have gone as far as not to require "proven injuries." See Wilborn v. Department of HHS, 49 F.3d 597, 603 (9th Cir.1995) (declining to remand to district court for determination of damages because plaintiff only sought statutory minimum damages); Romero–Vargas v. Shalala, 907 F.Supp. 1128, 1134 (N.D.Ohio 1995) (holding that "emotional distress caused by the fact that the plaintiff's privacy has been violated is itself an adverse effect, and ... statutory damages can be awarded without an independent showing of adverse effects").

46. Cf. Dong v. Smithsonian Inst., 943 F.Supp. 69, 74–75 (D.D.C.1996) (awarding damages for injury to reputation), rev'd on grounds of statutory inapplicability, 125 F.3d 877 (D.C.Cir.1997) (ruling that "Smithsonian is not an agency for Privacy Act purposes"), cert. denied, 524 U.S. 922, 118 S.Ct. 2311, 141 L.Ed.2d 169 (1998), with Hudson v. Reno, 130 F.3d 1193, 1207

subsections (g)(1)(A) and (g)(1)(B), which require exhaustion. Injunctive relief is not available under subsections (g)(1)(C) or (g)(1)(D).[47] The Act also imposes criminal penalties on agency employees who flout the law's goals,[48] but again only upon a showing that such violations were knowing and willful.[49]

The Act also contains two mutually exclusive provisions[50] which permit the head of any agency to promulgate rules (with proper notice) whereby entire systems of records may be exempted from portions of the Privacy Act. These *en masse* records systems exemptions protect information in CIA,[51] Secret Service and law enforcement contexts;[52] federal security classification files and civil service testing materials; and military personnel records evaluating potential for promotion. The exemptions essentially permit the agencies to deny an individual access to or the right to amend even his own file if it is contained in such a system, reflecting a Congressional decision to subordinate individual privacy interests to national security, effective law enforcement and selected administrative functions. Most courts allow agencies to cite § 552a(j)(2) as a defense in access or amendment cases, often regardless of the records at issue or the stated reasons for the exemption.[53] The exempted

(6th Cir.1997) (affirming district court decision where plaintiff failed to show "actual damages" and stating that "actual damages under the Privacy Act do not include recovery for 'mental injuries, loss of reputation, embarrassment or other non-quantifiable injuries),' " cert. denied, 525 U.S. 822, 119 S.Ct. 64, 142 L.Ed.2d 50 (1998). See generally Chapman v. NASA (*Chapman II*), 736 F.2d 238 (5th Cir.1984), cert. denied, 469 U.S. 1038, 105 S.Ct. 517, 83 L.Ed.2d 406 (1984); Albright v. United States, 732 F.2d 181 (D.C.Cir.1984); Perry v. Block, 684 F.2d 121 (D.C.Cir.1982); DiMura v. FBI, 823 F.Supp. 45, 48 (D.Mass.1993). But see cf. Johnson v. Department of Treasure, IRS, 700 F.2d 971 (5th Cir.1983). See generally Note, Damages Under the Privacy Act of 1974: Compensation and Deterrence, 52 Fordham L.Rev. 611 (1984).

47. See Risley v. Hawk, 108 F.3d 1396, 1397 (D.C.Cir.1997) (per curiam); AFGE v. Department of HUD, 924 F.Supp. 225, 228 n. 7 (D.D.C.1996), rev'd on other grounds, 118 F.3d 786 (D.C.Cir.1997).

48. 5 U.S.C.A. § 552a(i).

49. See United States v. Trabert, 978 F.Supp. 1368 (D.Colo.1997) (finding defendant not guilty because prosecution did not prove "beyond a reasonable doubt that defendant 'willfully disclosed' protected material"). See generally In re Mullins (Tamposi Fee Application), 84 F.3d 1439, 1441 (D.C. Cir. 1996) (per curiam) (concerning application for reimbursement of attorney fees where Independent Counsel found no prosecution warranted under Privacy Act absent conclusive evidence of improper disclosure of information). The Act's constricted, low-stakes approach to civil damage awards does little to encourage individuals to initiate and sustain expensive litigation to enforce their rights under the Act. Private citizens thus have little incentive to run the gamut of deterrent civil remedies, the agencies are left to police themselves. See Note, supra note 45; Note, The Privacy Act of 1974, supra note 6.

50. 5 U.S.C.A. § 552a(j) and (k).

51. See Blazy v. Tenet, 979 F.Supp. 10, 23–25 (D.D.C.1997), affirmed, 1998 WL 315583 (D.C.Cir.1998).

52. See, e.g., Gowan v. United States Dep't of the Air Force, 148 F.3d 1182, 1189–90 (10th Cir.1998), cert. denied, 525 U.S. 1042, 119 S.Ct. 593, 142 L.Ed.2d 535 (1998) (Air Force Office of Special Investigations); Anderson v. United States Postal Serv., 7 F.Supp.2d 583, 586 n. 3 (E.D.Pa. 1998), affirmed, 187 F.3d 625 (3d Cir.1999) (Postal Inspection Service); Hatcher v. United States Dep't of Justice Office of Info. & Privacy Act, 910 F.Supp. 1,2–3 (D.D.C.1995) (United States Attorney's Office).

53. See, e.g., Anderson v. United States Marshals Serv., 943 F.Supp. 37, 39–40 (D.D.C.1996); Hatcher, 910 F.Supp. at 2–3 (D.D.C. 1995).

records systems, however, must still comply with certain portions of the Act, such as the proscription against collecting First Amendment data and the general requirements governing inter-agency disclosures and accurate collection, maintenance and accounting.[54]

The final parts of the Act make it applicable to (otherwise private sector) government contractors,[55] who for the purposes of the Act are regarded as agency employees; prohibit agencies from selling or releasing mailing lists of names and addresses, unless specifically authorized by law;[56] and mandate a biennial report from the President to the Congress on the administration and effectiveness of the Act.[57]

Finally, the Act states that no agency shall rely on a FOIA exemption to withhold from an individual any record which is otherwise accessible to him under the Privacy Act.[58] The converse to this issue—i.e., whether the Privacy Act is an individual's sole avenue of access to federally-held records pertaining to him or her[59]—has been the focus of a great deal of litigation over the interplay between FOIA and the Privacy Act.[60] Congress moved to resolve the issue with a 1984 amendment[61] to § 552a(a) which declares that "No agency shall rely on any exemption in this section to withhold from an individual any record which is otherwise accessible to such individual under the provisions of section 552 [FOIA] of this title." The amendment is designed to guarantee an individual the maximum access available to him or her under either or both the Privacy Act and FOIA—i.e., to insure that the Privacy Act is not regarded as an "exemption statute" for purposes of withholding materials sought pursuant to FOIA.[62] Perhaps ironically, the amendment was but a small part of the Central Intelligence Agency Information Act, the chief purpose of which is to exempt entire systems of CIA "operational files" from FOIA. Although the Act contains provisions for Privacy Act access by individuals seeking records on themselves, the head of the CIA is granted far greater discretion to withhold information from the public.[63]

54. 5 U.S.C. § 552a(e).

55. Id. § 552a(m).

56. Id. at § 552a(n).

57. Id. at § 552a(s).

58. Id. at § 552a.

59. See generally, Case Comment, *Greentree v. U.S. Customs Service:* A Misinterpretation of the Relationship between FOIA Exemption 3 and the Privacy Act, 63 B.U.L.Rev. 507 (1983); Note, Is the Privacy Act an Exemption 3 Statute and Whose Statute is it Anyway?, 52 Fordham L.Rev. 1334 (1984).

60. See, e.g., U.S. Dept. of Justice v. Provenzano, 469 U.S. 14, 105 S.Ct. 413, 83 L.Ed.2d 242 (1984), on remand, 755 F.2d 922 (3d Cir.1985) (question whether Privacy Act exemption is a withholding statute under FOIA held mooted by Congressional amendment); Shapiro v. DEA, 721 F.2d 215 (7th Cir.1983), vacated, 469 U.S. 14, 105 S.Ct. 413, 83 L.Ed.2d 242 (1984); Terkel v. Kelly, 599 F.2d 214 (7th Cir.1979), cert. denied, 444 U.S. 1013, 100 S.Ct. 662, 62 L.Ed.2d 642 (1980); Painter v. FBI, 615 F.2d 689 (5th Cir.1980). Contra Greentree v. U.S. Customs Service, 674 F.2d 74 (D.C.Cir.1982); Porter v. U.S. Dept. of Justice, 717 F.2d 787 (3d Cir.1983); Provenzano v. U.S. Dept. of Justice, 717 F.2d 799 (3d Cir.1983), reh'g denied, 722 F.2d 36 (1983), cert. granted, 466 U.S. 926, 104 S.Ct. 1706, 80 L.Ed.2d 180 (1984).

61. "Central Intelligence Agency Information Act," Pub.L. 98–477, 98 Stat. 2209 (1984).

62. See 5 U.S.C.A. § 552(b)(3).

63. See House Votes FOIA Exemption for CIA Files, 1984 Cong.Q. 2335.

§ 18.1.2 The Privacy Act: Caselaw

In contrast to FOIA, the Privacy Act has generated relatively little litigation. Greater public awareness of FOIA, the discouraging breadth of the "entire systems" exemptions within the Privacy Act, and the Act's enforcement and civil remedy provisions of section 552a have contributed to the relative lack of use of the Privacy Act. The Privacy Commission has cited other possible factors, such as agency preference for processing information requests under FOIA so as to avoid the Privacy Act's requirement that accountings be made of disclosures under that Act.[64]

§ 18.1.3 Threshold Concerns

The Privacy Act's coverage is limited to federal agencies[65] and government contractors.[66] Private corporations, state and local governments, and grantees who receive federal funds are *not* subject to the Act.[67] Unlike FOIA, which provides for disclosure to "any person,"[68] the Privacy Act is available only to individual citizens or alien residents of the United States:[69] noncitizens and corporate entities[70] are barred from utilizing either the access or remedy provisions of the Act.

64. 5 U.S.C.A. § 552a(c); Personal Privacy in an Information Society, supra note 21, at 509.

65. 5 U.S.C.A. § 552a(a)(1), (b), et seq. But see Alexander v. FBI, 971 F.Supp. 603, 606–07 (D.D.C.1997). Alexander, which continues to take a long complicated procedural path as this text goes to print, involves the incident popularly known as "Filegate." The Plaintiffs alleged that persons acting at the request of First Lady Hillary Rodham Clinton obtained the FBI files of employees who had worked for Presidents Reagan and Bush. The plaintiffs claimed that the files were improperly released and were used to cull embarrassing facts about the plaintiffs. Among other things, the plaintiffs alleged a violation of the Privacy Act by the White House for maintaining the files for no lawfully recognized purpose. The government moved to dismiss the count against the White House because the Office of Personnel Security (OPS) and the Office of Records Management (ORM), each units within the Executive Office of the President (EOP), were not agencies subject to the Privacy Act. The government premised its argument on the interpretation courts have given the word "agency" when applying the Freedom of Information Act (FOIA), which excludes "the President's immediate personal staff and units within the EOP whose sole function is to advise and assist the President." Id. at 606 (citing Kissinger v. Reporters Comm. for Freedom of the Press, 445 U.S. 136, 100 S.Ct. 960, 63 L.Ed.2d 267 (1980)). The court in Alexander, however, finding that no other court had applied the FOIA definition of "agency" to the EOP, declined to do so in this case. Alexander at 606. Moreover, the court found that FOIA was an access to information law, whereas the Privacy Act prevented invasions of privacy. Id. at 607. Alexander was criticized by Falwell v. Executive Office of the President, 113 F. Supp. 2d 967 (W.D.Va.2000), for being "[i]n contrast to the weight of precedent." Id. at 969 n.4.

66. Id. at § 552a(m) extends the Act's coverage to private-sector entities under contract with the federal government. See Henke v. U.S. Dept. of Commerce, 83 F.3d 1445 (D.C.Cir.1996).

67. See Ortez v. Washington County, State of Or., 88 F.3d 804 (9th Cir.1996). (Former county employee's claims against county and certain of its employees in their official capacities alleging violations of privacy act were properly dismissed because the statute applied only to federal government); also see Gilbreath v. Guadalupe Hosp. Foundation Inc., 5 F.3d 785 (5th Cir. 1993). (Release of medical records of federal employee's wife and sons would not violate Privacy Act as hospitals were not "agencies" of federal government within meaning of Act and Act expressly authorizes disclosure of information pursuant to order of court of competent jurisdiction.)

68. Id. § 552a(a)(2).

69. Id.

70. See Dresser Industries, Inc. v. United States, 596 F.2d 1231 (5th Cir.

The Privacy Act's definition of the type of information to which it applies is as follows:

> . . . the term "record" means any item, collection, or grouping of information about an individual that is maintained by an agency, including, but not limited to his education, financial transaction, medical history, and criminal or employment history and that contains his name, or the identifying number, symbol, or other identifying particular assigned to the individual, such as a finger or voice print or a photograph.[71]

Thus, as a threshold requirement, a plaintiff's suit must concern "records," "about an individual," which are part of a government-maintained "system of records." The courts of appeals have developed three different definitions for what a "record" is: a broad definition,[72] a more restricted definition,[73] and a narrowly construed definition.[74] Sign in/sign out sheets have been held not to be a "record" because not reflective of some quality of an individual,[75] while a videotape of agency employees discussing a change in job classification did constitute a "record" under the Act.[76] Private notes kept to refresh the memory have been held to be outside the scope of "records" subject to the Privacy Act, at least so long as they are kept private.[77] Whatever their content, records covered by the Act must also be part of a "system of records"[78] *and* retrievable by means of some personal identifier. Thus, daily reports requested by a plaintiff were not disclosable to him because, although they contained information pertaining to him, they were indexed and retrievable only under the name of an investigator.[79] Similarly, disclosure

1979), cert. denied, 444 U.S. 1044, 100 S.Ct. 731, 62 L.Ed.2d 730 (1980) (company may not sue under the Act on behalf of its employees).

71. 5 U.S.C.A. § 552a(a)(4).

72. See Quinn v. Stone, 978 F.2d 126 (3d Cir.1992) (holding that a record is "*any* information about an individual that is linked to that individual through an identifying particular" and not "limited to information which taken alone directly reflects a characteristic or quality"). See also Bechhoefer v. United States Dep't of Justice Drug Enforcement Admin., 209 F.3d 57 (2d Cir.2000) (adopting substantially the 3rd Cir. test). Cf. Williams v. Department of VA, 104 F.3d 670, 673–74 (4th Cir.1997) (finding that a record "substantially pertains" to an individual); Sullivan v. United States Postal Serv., 944 F.Supp. 191, 196 (W.D.N.Y.1996) (finding that an employment application is a record).

73. See Boyd v. Secretary of the Navy, 709 F.2d 684, 686 (11th Cir.1983) (per curiam) (stating a narrow test for "record").

74. See Tobey v. NLRB, 40 F.3d 469, 471–73 (D.C.Cir.1994) (finding that a "record" must contain "information that actually describes the individual in some way"); Fisher v. NIH, 934 F.Supp. 464, 466–67, 469–72 (D.D.C.1996), affirmed, 107 F.3d 922 (D.C.Cir.1996) (following Tobey).

75. See American Federation of Government Employees v. NASA, 482 F.Supp. 281 (S.D.Tex.1980).

76. Albright v. United States, 631 F.2d 915 (D.C.Cir.1980), on remand 558 F.Supp. 260 (D.D.C.1982), aff'd, 732 F.2d 181 (D.C.Cir.1984) ("As long as the tape contains a means of identifying an individual by picture or voice, it falls within the definition of a 'record' under the Privacy Act." Id. at 920).

77. See Bartel v. FAA, 725 F.2d 1403 (D.C.Cir.1984).

78. 5 U.S.C.A. § 552a(a)(5).

79. "[I]nformation pertaining to the requester . . . need not be disclosed unless the information is retrievable by means of the requester's own name or other personal identifier. That it can be easily retrieved in some other way by some other identifier is wholly beside the point." Smiertka v. U.S. Dept. of Treasury, 447 F.Supp. 221, 228

by other means of information contained in a retrievable record is not a *per se* violation of the Act; the record must actually be retrieved before such disclosure is barred.[80] Information which never makes it into a system of records from which it can be retrieved is not subject to Privacy Act requirements.[81] A requester can obtain access to a record pertaining to herself even if the record contains material about others.[82]

The Act's prohibition against maintenance of files pertaining to an individual's exercise of First Amendment rights,[83] however, appears to supersede these definitional requirements. Examining carefully the Act's legislative history, which stressed protection of First Amendment rights,[84] at least two courts have interpreted the strict "system of records" provisions to accommodate plaintiffs' assertions of a threat to First Amendment expression.[85]

(D.D.C.1978), remanded on other grounds, 604 F.2d 698 (D.C.Cir.1979). See also Tobey v. N.L.R.B., 40 F.3d 469, 309 U.S. App.D.C. 213 (1994); Grachow v. U.S. Customs Service, 504 F.Supp. 632 (D.D.C.1980).

80. See, e.g., Doyle v. Behan, 670 F.2d 535, 538 (5th Cir.1982) (phone conversation dealing with facts contained in file did not derive from retrieval of that file); Jackson v. Veterans Administration, 503 F.Supp. 653 (N.D.Ill.1980); Savarese v. U.S. Department of HEW, 479 F.Supp. 304 (N.D.Ga. 1979), aff'd mem. sub nom. Savarese v. Harris, 620 F.2d 298 (5th Cir.1980), cert. denied, 449 U.S. 1078, 101 S.Ct. 858, 66 L.Ed.2d 801 (1981).

81. See Kline v. Department of Health & Human Services, 927 F.2d 522 (10th Cir. 1991) (information in question had been derived from independent knowledge and nor from agency system of records, and was thus not covered by the Act). See also, Johnson v. U.S. Dept. of Air Force, 526 F.Supp. 679 (W.D.Okl.1980), aff'd, 703 F.2d 583 (Fed.Cir.1982) (petition circulated among co-workers and given to plaintiff's supervisor, who turned it over to plaintiff's union, held not to have been maintained in a system of records); Chapman v. NASA, 682 F.2d 526 (5th Cir.1982). But cf. Bartel v. FAA, 725 F.2d 1403 (D.C.Cir.1984).

82. See Voelker v. IRS, 646 F.2d 332 (8th Cir.1981). Agencies are required to promulgate rules concerning their procedures for disclosing personal information under the Privacy Act, 5 U.S.C. § 522a(f)(3) (1996). The United States Court of Appeals, District of Columbia Circuit, has decided that the procedural rules cannot give the record maintainer sole discretion in this regard. This, in effect, creates a substantive exemption from the Act's mandate to promulgate procedural rules. Benavides v. U.S. Bureau of Prisons, 995 F.2d 269, 301 U.S.App.D.C. 369 (1993).

83. 5 U.S.C.A. § 552a(e)(7).

84. See Albright v. United States, 631 F.2d 915 (D.C.Cir.1980) (*Albright I*), on remand, 558 F.Supp. 260 (D.D.C.1982), aff'd on other grounds, 732 F.2d 181 (D.C.Cir. 1984) (*Albright II*).

85. See *Albright I* and *Albright II* ("mere collection of such a record [videotape of employees-supervisor meeting], independent of the agency's maintenance, use, or dissemination of it thereafter [triggers (e)(7)]" 631 F.2d at 918); Clarkson v. IRS, 678 F.2d 1368 (11th Cir.1982), appeal after remand 811 F.2d 1396 (1987), cert. denied, 481 U.S. 1031, 107 S.Ct. 1961, 95 L.Ed.2d 533 (1987). See also Hobson v. Wilson, 737 F.2d 1, 64–65 (D.C.Cir.1984), cert. denied, 470 U.S. 1084, 105 S.Ct. 1843, 85 L.Ed.2d 142 (1985). The (e)(7) prohibition is not violated when a statute expressly authorizes the keeping of the record. See, e.g., Abernethy v. IRS, 909 F.Supp. 1562, 1570 (N.D.Ga.1995), affirmed, 108 F.3d 343 (11th Cir.1997), rehearing and suggestion for rehearing en banc denied, 116 F.3d 494 (11th Cir.1997); Hass v. United States Air Force, 848 F.Supp. 926, 930–31 (D.Kan. 1994). Nor is (e)(7) violated when the individual expressly authorizes the record. See Abernethy, 909 F. Supp. at 1570. There is also a law enforcement exemption to (e)(7), the strictest application of which in favor of First Amendment protection comes from the Court of Appeals for the Seventh Circuit. See Becker v. IRS, 34 F.3d 398, 408–09 (7th Cir.1994) (ordering IRS to expunge investigative information that could not "be helpful in future enforcement activity"). But see J. Roderick MacArthur Found. v. FBI, 102 F.3d 600, 603, 607 (D.C.Cir.1996), cert. denied, 522 U.S. 913, 118 S.Ct. 296, 139 L.Ed.2d 228 (1997) (criticizing Becker

§ 18.2 THE PRIVACY ACT AND FOIA

If no Privacy Act or FOIA exemptions apply, then the information should be disclosed. The Privacy Act's prohibition against non-consented disclosure of an individual's record outside the agency does *not* apply if such records are *required* to be released pursuant to FOIA.[1] Thus, if a person is guaranteed access to a file under FOIA (i.e., if none of the FOIA withholding exemptions are applicable), the disclosing agency need not obtain the Privacy Act-mandated consent of the individual named by the file[2]. If a FOIA exemption *is* applicable (i.e., if release is not "required" by FOIA), the Privacy Act should operate to prevent an agency's discretionary disclosure of such records without the consent of the individual.

If a Privacy Act exemption applies, an individual is not entitled to access her records under the Privacy Act, but may be able to gain access under FOIA. If both Privacy Act and FOIA exemptions apply, the record may be withheld. When an individual requests access to her own record (a first-party request), an agency must be able to invoke a Privacy Act and FOIA exemption to withhold that record. The rule that arises out of the confluence of the Privacy Act and FOIA is that all Privacy Act requests should be treated as FOIA requests. A first-party request, because it is also a FOIA request, requires an agency to search for records of the individual that are not maintained in a Privacy Act system of records. Only FOIA exemptions are relevant to these records. Privacy Act access provision and exemptions do not apply to any records not maintained in a system of records. An unresolved problem under the Privacy Act arises when an individual's file contains third-party information that would invade that third party's privacy, if released.[3]

Much of the early litigation[4] involving the Privacy Act and FOIA dealt with situations in which a person seeking access to his or her own records was told that those records were exempt from disclosure under the Privacy Act,[5] despite the fact that none of the FOIA exemptions applied. Given the more general, institutional exemptions of the Privacy Act,[6] as opposed to the subject-matter oriented exemptions of FOIA,[7] the issue presented by such requests was whether an individual was entitled to the maximum access afforded by *both* statutes, or whether the Privacy Act operated as the sole avenue of access to a person requesting his own

and finding that the Privacy Act does not require an agency to expunge records no longer pertinent to a current law enforcement activity).

§ 18.2

1. 5 U.S.C.A. § 552a(b)(2).

2. Bartel v. FAA, 725 F.2d 1403 (D.C.Cir.1984) (but agency must have actual FOIA request in hand before disclosing information). Cf. Cochran v. United States, 770 F.2d 949 (11th Cir.1985) (upheld disclosure in response to oral request from news media).

3. See Voelker v. IRS, 646 F.2d 332, 333–35 (8th Cir.1981).

4. See, e.g., U.S. Dept. of Justice v. Provenzano, 469 U.S. 14, 105 S.Ct. 413, 83 L.Ed.2d 242 (1984), on remand 755 F.2d 922 (3d Cir.1985).

5. E.g., under the "whole systems" exemptions applicable by regulation to CIA files, law enforcement records and selected federal personnel administrative records. 5 U.S.C.A. § 552a(j), (k).

6. Id.

7. Id. § 552(b).

file. The Justice Department took the latter position, arguing that the Privacy Act resulted in a *pro tanto* repeal of FOIA. As applied to individuals seeking *their own* records, the Privacy Act, in effect, qualified as a (b)(3) "exempting statute" under FOIA. Critics of the Justice Department's restrictive position insisted that such an approach was contrary to the spirit of the Privacy Act, and that the Justice Department's interpretation would conceivably grant a third party access to an individual's file (via FOIA), while the individual himself would be denied access under the Privacy Act; such individuals would thus be forced to circumvent the Privacy Act bar by resort to a straw FOIA request. A split between the Circuit Courts of Appeal finally resulted in the Supreme Court's granting of *certiorari* to decide the issue[8]—the first Privacy Act case ever to reach the Supreme Court.

Congress' passage of the CIA Information Act[9] in late 1984, however, mooted the question before the Court.[10] That Act, whose main purpose was to exempt "operational files" of the CIA from search and review pursuant to FOIA,[11] also amended the final paragraph of the Privacy Act, to prohibit an agency's reliance on a Privacy Act exemption to limit an individual's access to records "otherwise accessible" under FOIA.[12] The amended Act now provides an individual requester with the maximum information accessible under either or both Acts—no matter how the request is characterized.

Many of the current Privacy Act disputes which end up in court take on the character and caselaw of FOIA litigation. Because non-exempt disclosures pursuant to FOIA are not governed by the restrictions of the Privacy Act,[13] a reviewing court will first determine whether the information sought ought to have been disclosed under FOIA, usually by recourse to a *Vaughan* index or other agency justifications for withholding. If the material or subject matter sought cannot be withheld under a FOIA exemption, the court usually will order its disclosure without reaching the Privacy Act issues.[14] If a FOIA exemption does apply, however, the Privacy Act may compel its application and thus prevent the disclosure of information. In *U.S. Department of Defense v. FLRA*,[15] for example, a union sought the release of government employee home addresses from government agencies as part of negotiations involving a

8. U.S. Dept. of Justice v. Provenzano, 469 U.S. 14, 105 S.Ct. 413, 83 L.Ed.2d 242 (1984), on remand, 755 F.2d 922 (3d Cir. 1985).

9. Pub.L. No. 98–477, 98 Stat. 2209 (1984).

10. For a history of the conflict, see Susman, The Privacy Act and the Freedom of Information Act: Conflict and Resolution, 21 J. Marshall L.Rev. 703 (1988).

11. The Act purports to exempt from "unnecessary" search and review those files which were already clearly exempt under (b)(1); it specifically authorizes continued search and review of those same files upon request by an individual seeking information on himself, or upon request by Congress. Pub.L. No. 98–477 § 2(a). The Act was supported by *both* the Reagan Administration and the ACLU. 1984 Cong.Q. 2335.

12. Pub.L. No. 98–477, § 2(c), 98 Stat. 2209, 2211–12 (1984).

13. 5 U.S.C.A. § 552a(b)(2).

14. Litigation often involves Exemption (b)(6) of FOIA (Privacy Protection). See, e.g., Brown v. FBI, 658 F.2d 71 (2d Cir.1981).

15. 510 U.S. 487, 114 S.Ct. 1006, 127 L.Ed.2d 325 (1994).

collective bargaining agreement. The Supreme Court upheld the government's refusal to provide this information as an "unwarranted invasion of privacy" according to FOIA. The Court noted, that these addresses were, in fact, "records" covered by the Privacy Act. "Therefore, unless FOIA would require release of their addresses, their disclosure is 'prohibited by law,' and the agencies may not reveal them to the unions."[16] In effect, because exemption (b)(6) of the FOIA applied, FOIA did not require the release of this information and because of the Privacy Act, the agency had no discretion when it came to invoking this exemption.

§ 18.2.1 Privacy Act Disclosure and Exceptions

The Privacy Act basically prohibits the disclosure of personal records contained in a system of records without the consent of the record subject.[17] This prohibition is qualified by 12 exceptions. The broadest of these are disclosures pursuant to FOIA, discussed above, and the "routine use" exception.[18] There are two requirements for a routine use disclosure. First, an agency must publish all "routine uses" of personal information in the Federal Register upon establishment or revision.[19] Second, the routine use of a record must be "for purpose which is compatible with the purpose for which it was collected."[20] Despite

16. 510 U.S. at 494.

17. 5 U.S.C.A. § 552a(b). See Wilborn v. Department of Health and Human Services, 49 F.3d 597 (9th Cir.1995) (administrative law judge violated Privacy Act by including in an opinion a reference to discipline, which had been imposed upon an attorney while he was employed by the agency).

18. Id. § 552a(b)(3). "Routine use" is defined as "the use of such record for a purpose which is compatible with the purpose for which it was collected." Id. § 552a(a)(7).

19. Id. § 552a(e)(4)(D). An agency's definition of its routine use is given deference. See Department of the Air Force, Scott Air Force Base, Ill. v. FLRA, 104 F.3d 1396, 1402 (D.C.Cir.1997).

20. 5 U.S.C. § 552a(a)(7). See Britt v. Naval Investigative Serv., 886 F.2d 544, 547–50 (3d Cir.1989). Cf. United States Postal Serv. v. National Ass'n of Letter Carriers, 9 F.3d 138, 144 (D.C.Cir.1993). The compatibility requirement in law enforcement settings create situations where records are shared between agencies. This law enforcement routine use has yet to be successfully challenged. Cf. Nwangoro v. Department of the Army, 952 F.Supp. 394, 398 (N.D.Tex.1996). Also, litigation creates situations where the routine use of records includes filing them as public records with a court. See, e.g., Russell v. GSA, 935 F.Supp. 1142, 1145–46 (D.Colo.1996). Many types of information sharing among agencies qualifies as routine use. See, e.g., Pippinger v. Rubin, 129 F.3d 519, 531–32 (10th Cir. 1997) (disclosure of plaintiff's personnel information to various parties in litigation); Taylor v. United States, 106 F.3d 833, 836–37 (8th Cir.1997) (disclosure of federal taxpayer information to state tax officials); Mount v. United States Postal Serv., 79 F.3d 531, 534 (6th Cir.1996) (disclosure of plaintiff's medical information to union official); Jones v. Runyon, 32 F. Supp. 2d 873, 876 (N.D.W.Va.1998), affirmed, 173 F.3d 850 (4th Cir.1999) (disclosure to credit reporting service); Blazy v. Tenet, 979 F.Supp. 10, 26 (D.D.C.1997), affirmed, 1998 WL 315583 (D.C.Cir.1998) (CIA disclosure of information about employee to FBI); Magee v. United States Postal Serv., 903 F.Supp. 1022, 1029 (W.D.La.1995) (disclosure of employee's medical records to agency psychologist); Harry v. United States Postal Serv., 867 F.Supp. 1199, 1206–07 (M.D.Pa.1994), affirmed, 60 F.3d 815 (3d Cir.1995) (disclosure of employee documents). See also Gowan v. United States Dep't of the Air Force, 148 F.3d 1182, 1187, 1194 (10th Cir.1998) (disclosure of information about Members of Congress), cert. denied, 525 U.S. 1042, 119 S.Ct. 593, 142 L.Ed.2d 535 (1998). Routine use has also been invoked pursuant to the National Labor Relations Act. See, e.g., United States Postal Serv. v. National Ass'n of Letter Carriers, 9 F.3d 138, 141–46 (D.C.Cir.1993)

considerable criticism of the latter as a procedural cure-all enabling the agencies to do as they please with collected personal data,[21] the caselaw on the issue is undeveloped. Courts have generally upheld agency justifications of "routine use;"[22] however, the very breadth of the exception and the limited remedies obtainable under the Act limit the challenges to such uses. Federal agencies have cited the "routine use" exception to quell Privacy Act concerns over computer "matching" programs, in which different agencies pool and cross-reference unrelated databanks in search of fraud and double-dipping.[23] In 1998, President Clinton directed the OMB to clarify the routine use exception.[24]

§ 18.2.2 Exceptions to Disclosure—An Overview

Other exceptions to the prohibition on uncontested disclosure include those granted to employees of other agencies who need the records to perform their duties,[25] to law enforcement agencies for specific pur-

(holding that "if Postal Service could disclose the information under [its routine use] then it must disclose that information, because in the absence of a Privacy Act defense the arbitrator's award must be enforced"). Moreover, routine use has been invoked under the Federal Management Relations Statute. See Department of the Air Force v. FLRA, 104 F.3d 1396, 1399, 1401–02 (D.C.Cir.1997) (granting enforcement of a Federal Labor Relations Authority decision requiring Air Force to disclose to a union a disciplinary letter).

21. See Personal Privacy in an Information Society: The Report of the Privacy Protection Study Commission 517–19 (U.S.G.P.O., 1977); Note, Narrowing the "Routine Use" Exemption, 14 J.L. Reform 126 (1980); Note, The Privacy Act of 1974: An Overview and Critique, 1976 Wash. U.L.Q. 667, 685 (1976).

22. See, e.g., SEC v. Dimensional Entertainment Corp., 518 F.Supp. 773 (S.D.N.Y.1981) (disclosure of parole hearing transcript to SEC a routine use); Burley v. DEA, 443 F.Supp. 619 (M.D.Tenn.1977). Cf. Krohn v. Department of Justice, No. 78–1536, slip op. 6 (D.C.Cir. May 19, 1984) ("routine use" exception does not include information used "during appropriate legal proceedings"); Parks v. IRS, 618 F.2d 677 (10th Cir.1980) (not routine to distribute names and phone numbers of agents who declined to buy savings bonds during sales campaign to government employees); Doe v. Naval Air Station, 768 F.2d 1229 (11th Cir. 1985) (agency cannot give car registration data to police when such use is not included in agency's list of "routine uses").

23. See Kirchner, Privacy: A History of Computer Matching in Federal Government, Computerworld, Dec. 14, 1981, reprinted in Oversight of the Privacy Act of 1974: Hearings Before a Subcomm. of the House Comm. on Gov't Operations, 98th Cong., 1st Sess. 426 (1983). Other commentators are concerned about routine use and the potential for pooling patient genetic information stored in government mandated medical database. See Lisa L. Dahm, Using The DNA Profile as the Unique Patient Identifier in the Community Health Information Network: Legal Implications, 15 J. Marshall J. Computer & Info. L. 227 (1997); Sarah Gill, The Military's DNA Registry: An Analysis of Current Law and a Proposal for Safeguards, 44 Naval L. Rev. 175 (1997).

24. Memorandum on Privacy and Personal Information in Federal Records, 34 Weekly Comp. Pres. Doc. 870 (May 14, 1998).

25. Mount v. United States Postal Service, 79 F.3d 531 (6th Cir.1996) (Postal Service agents and employees with responsibility for making employment and/or disciplinary decisions regarding employee had a need to know about employee's medical records given questions surrounding employee's mental stability). Grogan v. IRS, 676 F.2d 692 (4th Cir.1982) (disclosure to IRS employees of a fellow employee's tax return for investigatory purposes upheld under (b)(1) on a "need to know" basis); see Hernandez v. Alexander, 671 F.2d 402 (10th Cir.1982); Beller v. Middendorf, 632 F.2d 788 (9th Cir.1980), cert. denied 452 U.S. 905, 101 S.Ct. 3030, 69 L.Ed.2d 405 (1981); Howard v. Marsh, 785 F.2d 645 (8th Cir.1986). Cf. Parks v. IRS, 618 F.2d 677 (10th Cir.1980) (lists of employees not contributing to fund-raiser not a valid (b)(1) disclosure).

poses,[26] for compelling health or safety reasons, pursuant to a court order[27], and for already published material[28] have not been heavily litigated. In order to ensure that privacy considerations are in fact considered, many courts have ruled that to be a valid exception to the Act, an order of a court of "competent jurisdiction"[29] must, in fact, be signed by the presiding judge; routinely-issued discovery subpoenas issued by the court clerk are not enough to establish the exception.[30]

§ 18.2.3 Access and Amendment

The Privacy Act allows an individual to gain access to "his record or to any information pertaining to him which is contained in the system," to review and copy such materials, and to "request amendment of a record pertaining to him."[31] The access provisions of the Act can in some cases contradict the "no disclosure without consent" mandate of section 552a(b). The most common situation occurs when an individual's file contains information regarding a third party. Although it often is standard agency practice to delete third party data from requested files, the Eighth Circuit has held that an agency may not withhold information

26. See SEC v. Dimensional Entertainment Corp., 518 F.Supp. 773 (S.D.N.Y. 1981); Burley v. DEA, 443 F.Supp. 619 (M.D.Tenn.1977).

27. Perry v. State Farm Fire & Casualty Co., 734 F.2d 1441 (11th Cir.1984), cert. denied 469 U.S. 1108, 105 S.Ct. 784, 83 L.Ed.2d 778 (1985) (when considering request to order disclosure, trial court should balance the need for disclosure against potential harm to the subject of that disclosure).

28. FDIC v. Dye, 642 F.2d 833 (5th Cir.1981) (release of information previously published is not a disclosure violation under the Privacy Act). cf. Pilon v. U.S. Dept. of Justice, 73 F.3d 1111, 315 U.S.App.D.C. 329 (1996) (Department of Justice's unauthorized release of protected agency record by faxing it to former employee was "disclosure" prohibited by Privacy Act, even though recipient came into contact with it in course of his duties).

29. 5 U.S.C.A. § 552a(b)(11).

30. See Doe v. DiGenova, 779 F.2d 74 (D.C.Cir.1985), on remand, 642 F.Supp. 624 (D.D.C.1986), aff'd in part, rev'd in part, 851 F.2d 1457 (D.C.Cir.1988); Stiles v. Atlanta Gas Light Co., 453 F.Supp. 798 (N.D.Ga.1978) (routine subpoenas issued during discovery do not qualify for exemption); Cf. Weahkee v. Norton, 621 F.2d 1080 (10th Cir.1980) (court-ordered discovery under Fed.R.Civ.P. 37 is exempt). See also In re Grand Jury Subpoenas Issued to U.S. Postal Service, 535 F.Supp. 31 (E.D.Tenn. 1981) (subpoena *duces tecum* ordering Postal Service to produce employee records for computer matching held to be outside the Privacy Act because grand jury not an "agency" but an investigative body).

Subsection (b)(11) provides no standard for issuing a court order, although courts have attempted to fashion one. See, e.g., Mason v. South Bend Community Sch. Corp., 990 F.Supp. 1096, 1097–99 (N.D.Ind. 1997) (determining that an agency's regulations did not authorize the release of records upon order of a court without an authorizing statute). Cf. Bosaw v. NTEU, 887 F.Supp. 1199, 1215–17 (S.D.Ind.1995) (issuing a court order); Ford Motor Co. v. United States, 825 F.Supp. 1081, 1083 (Ct. Int'l Trade 1993) (same). But cf. Lohrenz v. Donnelly, 187 F.R.D. 1, 8–9 (D.D.C.1999) (exercising jurisdiction over non-party agency in granting relief from an order without first finding that the court had jurisdiction). In some cases, it may be appropriate for a court to deny discovery requests. See Barnett v. Dillon, 890 F.Supp. 83, 88 (N.D.N.Y. 1995) (refusing to order disclosure of FBI records protected by Privacy Act).

31. 5 U.S.C.A. § 552a(d). See Mervin v. FTC, 591 F.2d 821 (D.C.Cir.1978) (party seeking amendment has burden of proof. The § 552a(g)(3) burden on the agency is limited to disclosure and does not apply to amending records). An individual's request should be processed under both the Privacy Act and FOIA. See Blazy v. Tenet, 979 F.Supp. 10, 16 (D.D.C.1997), affirmed, 1998 WL 315583 (D.C.Cir.1998); Freeman v. United States Dep't of Justice (FBI), 822 F.Supp. 1064, 1066 (S.D.N.Y.1993).

contained in a requester's record on the ground that the information concerns third parties and does not pertain to the requester.[32] That court's expansive reading of an individual's access rights, however, did not reach the question of whether the Act's general or specific exemptions, if invoked, would operate to deny access to "irrelevant" third party data.[33] It would seem that a "pertaining to the requester" standard regarding the inclusion of such third party information would placate the conflicting privacy concerns.

Frequent users of the Privacy Act are often agency and government employees who are (by virtue of their jobs) aware of the Act and its requirements. Thus, many of the amendment actions have involved changes sought in employment records or promotion/performance rating situations. Courts have tended to dismiss the claims of plaintiffs who appear to be resorting to the Act only to engage in a collateral attack on an adverse administrative decision.[34] Courts also do not permit actions against an agency seeking to alter documents that accurately reflected the agency's administrative finding, even though that finding is contestable.[35] Therefore, courts have generally held that only factual errors are subject to amendment.[36] The amendment remedy of the Act is thus applicable in practice only to proven factual errors and patently false or unsupported judgments and not to disagreements over which they might reasonably be differences of opinion. Moreover, the general and specific exemptions of the Act often serve to shield some types of data (e.g., law enforcement records) from the access requisite for amendment.

§ 18.2.4 Restrictions on Agency Collection and Maintenance of Data

Sections 552a(e)(1)–(12) of the Privacy Act impose specific restrictive requirements on agencies. Pursuant to these provisions, agencies are obliged to maintain only information on individual which is "relevant and necessary" to the agency's purpose;[37] collect information "to the

32. See Voelker v. IRS, 646 F.2d 332 (8th Cir.1981).

33. Cf. DePlanche v. Califano, 549 F.Supp. 685 (W.D.Mich.1982).

34. See White v. U.S. Civil Service Commission, 589 F.2d 713 (D.C.Cir.1978), cert. denied, sub nom. White v. Office of Personnel Management, 444 U.S. 830, 100 S.Ct. 58, 62 L.Ed.2d 39 (1979); Nagel v. Department of HEW, 725 F.2d 1438 (D.C.Cir.1984); Bashaw v. U.S. Dept. of Treasury, 468 F.Supp. 1195 (E.D.Wis.1979).

35. Douglas v. Agricultural Stabilization and Conservation Service, 33 F.3d 784 (7th Cir.1994).

36. See Turner v. Department of Army, 447 F.Supp. 1207 (D.D.C.1978); Blevins v. Plummer, 613 F.2d 767 (9th Cir. 1980); but c.f. R.R. v. Department of Army, 482 F.Supp. 770 (D.D.C.1980).

37. If a Privacy Act exemption applies, an individual is not entitled to access her records under the Privacy Act, but may be able to gain access under FOIA. If both Privacy Act and FOIA exemptions apply, the record may be withheld. When an individual requests access to her own record (a first-party request), an agency must be able to invoke a Privacy Act and FOIA exemption to withhold that record. The rule that arises out of the confluence of the Privacy Act and FOIA is that all Privacy Act requests should be treated as FOIA requests. A first-party request, because it is also a FOIA request, requires an agency to search for records of the individual that are not maintained in a Privacy Act system of records. Only FOIA exemptions are relevant to these records. Privacy Act access provision and exemptions do not apply to any records not maintained in a system of records. An

greatest extent practicable directly from the subject individual;"[38] inform each individual of the legal authority for seeking the data sought, and the purpose for which it is collected;[39] publish in the Federal Register detailed description of their systems of records and their respective "routine uses;"[40] make reasonable efforts to assure the accuracy, timeliness and relevance of records;[41] maintain no records describing an individual's exercise of First Amendment rights, *unless* expressly authorized by statute or by the individual or *unless* pertinent to an authorized law enforcement activity;[42] establish appropriate administrative, technical and physical safeguards to insure the security and confidentiality of records.[43]

Violations of these requirements are redressable only in actions for damages.[44] The lack of a provision for injunctive relief tends to limit the

unresolved problem under the Privacy Act arises when an individual's file contains third-party information that would invade that third party's privacy, if released.

38. See Dong v. Smithsonian Inst., 943 F.Supp. 69, 72–73 (D.D.C.1996) (holding that "concern over Plaintiff's possible reaction to an unpleasant rumor" did not justify the failure of the Smithsonian "to elicit information regarding alleged unauthorized trip directly from her"), rev'd on grounds of statutory inapplicability, 125 F.3d 877 (D.C.Cir.1997) (holding that "Smithsonian is not an agency for Privacy Act purposes"), cert. denied, 524 U.S. 922, 118 S.Ct. 2311, 141 L.Ed.2d 169 (1998). See also Jones v. Runyon, 32 F. Supp. 2d 873, 876 (N.D.W.Va.1998), affirmed, 173 F.3d 850 (4th Cir.1999); Magee v. United States Postal Serv., 903 F.Supp. 1022, 1028–29 (W.D.La.1995), affirmed, 79 F.3d 1145 (5th Cir.1996).

39. See United States Postal Serv. v. National Ass'n of Letter Carriers, 9 F.3d 138, 146 (D.C.Cir.1993); United States v. Wilber, 696 F.2d 79 (8th Cir.1982) (agencies not required to give notice of specific criminal penalty if taxpayer fails to pay tax).

40. See Pippinger v. Rubin, 129 F.3d 519, 524–28 (10th Cir.1997). Pippinger was about whether the IRS had complied with subsection (e)(4) in its use of a computer database called the "Automated Labor Employee Relations Tracking System" (ALERTS). The IRS used ALERTS to store all IRS employee disciplinary action. It contained limited information from two existing Privacy Act systems that the IRS had described in the Federal Register. Id. at 524–25. The court found that ALERTS was an "abstraction of certain individual records" from other records systems and so was not a new system of records that required description in the Federal Register, because only by the same users could access it for the same purposes as those published in the Federal Register for the original records system. Id. at 526–27.

41. See Edison v. Department of the Army, 672 F.2d 840 (11th Cir.1982) (the likelihood that inaccurate and incomplete records will cause harm must be balanced against the agency's resources and its ability to assure accurate and complete records). Records under this requirement need not be perfect. See, e.g., Buxton v. United States Parole Comm'n, 844 F.Supp. 642, 644 (D.Or.1994). In fact, one court has approved of records that contained disputed hearsay. See Graham v. Hawk, 857 F.Supp. 38, 40 (W.D.Tenn.1994), affirmed, 59 F.3d 170 (6th Cir.1995). Cf. Hass v. United States Air Force, 848 F.Supp. 926, 931 (D.Kan. 1994). But a violation of this requirement can give rise to civil damages. See Deters v. United States Parole Comm'n, 85 F.3d 655, 660–61 & n. 5 (D.C.Cir.1996). Courts, however, are reluctant to question an agency judgment call on whether to include information. See, e.g., Webb v. Magaw, 880 F.Supp. 20, 25 (D.D.C.1995) (finding that records were not created on a false assumptions but on a judgment call "based on a multitude of factors") (internal quotation marks omitted). Courts have also held that pure opinion and judgment is not subject to amendment. See, e.g., Reinbold v. Evers, 187 F.3d 348, 361 (4th Cir.1999).

42. See discussion supra in § 18.1.3.

43. 5 U.S.C.A. § 552a(e)(1)–(12). As long as information contained in agency's files is capable of being verified, the Privacy Act requires the agency to take reasonable steps to maintain the accuracy of the information to assure fairness to individuals. Sellers v. Bureau of Prisons, 959 F.2d 307, 294 U.S.App.D.C. 361 (1992).

44. See 5 U.S.C.A. § 552a(g)(1)(C)–(D) and (g)(4). See discussion of damages supra § 18.1.1.

number of actions brought to enforce the collection and maintenance rights granted by section 552a(e).

§ 18.3 FIRST AMENDMENT AND THE PRIVACY ACT

The most litigated provision of section 552a(e) of the Privacy Act is section (e)(7), which forbids the collection and maintenance of records describing an individual's exercise of her First Amendment rights. Alluding to the premium which the Congress placed on protection of First Amendment rights under the Privacy Act,[1] some courts have taken an expansive view of a plaintiff's rights under section (e)(7), holding that the strict "within a system of records" threshold requirement is inapplicable to First Amendment claims.[2] Courts have also sought to stretch the Privacy Act's remedy provisions to authorize expungement of illegally-held First Amendment records.[3]

Though the scope of a tenable First Amendment–Privacy Act claim may be relatively broad, there are serious obstacles to obtaining damages. A plaintiff must show (1) that the agency's violation was willful *and* (2) that he or she suffered an adverse effect as a result of that violation.[4] In addition, the qualifications tacked onto the proscription against First Amendment files in the Act itself severely limit its application. Records concerning First Amendment activities *may* be maintained if expressly authorized by statute or the individual, or if "pertinent to and within the scope of an authorized law enforcement activity."[5] Courts have tended to interpret the latter exception broadly, usually requiring only an articulable "relevance" between the objected-to First Amendment record and the law enforcement activity.[6] The "law enforcement activity" definition itself has been held to include the employer-employee relationship.[7] The law-enforcement exception thus tends to pre-empt

§ 18.3

1. See, e.g., Clarkson v. IRS, 678 F.2d 1368, 1373–76 (11th Cir.1982), appeal after remand 811 F.2d 1396 (1987), cert. denied 481 U.S. 1031, 107 S.Ct. 1961, 95 L.Ed.2d 533 (1987).

2. See Albright v. United States, 732 F.2d 181 (D.C.Cir.1984); Clarkson v. IRS, supra note 1.

3. Hobson v. Wilson, 737 F.2d 1, 64–66 (D.C.Cir.1984), cert. denied, 470 U.S. 1084, 105 S.Ct. 1843, 85 L.Ed.2d 142 (1985) (FBI's illegal Cointelpro monitoring of anti-war groups); Clarkson v. IRS, supra note 1. Edison v. Department of Army, 672 F.2d 840, 846–47 (11th Cir.1982).

4. See, e.g., Albright v. United States, supra note 2 (despite colorable First Amendment violation, plaintiff is not entitled to damages or attorney fees because no proof of willfulness or adverse effect).

5. 5 U.S.C.A. § 552a(e)(7). See also, supra note 85.

6. See Jabara v. Webster, 691 F.2d 272, 279–80 (6th Cir.1982), cert. denied, 464 U.S. 863, 104 S.Ct. 193, 78 L.Ed.2d 170 (1983) (investigations with respect to First Amendment activity permissible under the Act if "relevant to an authorized criminal investigation or to an authorized intelligence or administrative one"); Pacheco v. FBI, 470 F.Supp. 1091, 1108 n. 21 (D.P.R. 1979) (all FBI files within exception to (e)(7)); Patterson by Patterson v. FBI, 893 F.2d 595, 602–03 (3d Cir.1990), cert. denied 498 U.S. 812, 111 S.Ct. 48, 112 L.Ed.2d 24 (1990) (FBI's maintenance of records on elementary school student who received floods of international correspondence in connection with a school project were "relevant" to an authorized law enforcement activity of the agency. The court rejected the proposed rule that an agency must show a "substantial relationship" between the records and the enforcement activity.). Cf. Clarkson v. IRS, supra note 1.

7. Nagel v. U.S. Dept. of Health, Education and Welfare, 725 F.2d 1438, 1441–42 (D.C.Cir.1984) (memos in hospital administrator's file describing his misconduct at

many potential (e)(7) actions—assuming, of course, that the law enforcement activity itself is "authorized."[8]

§ 18.4 GENERAL AND SPECIFIC EXEMPTIONS TO THE PRIVACY ACT

The Privacy Act grants blanket exemptions to records maintained by the CIA and criminal law enforcement agencies,[1] and specific exemptions to such matter as classified records, Secret Service records, statistical data, and certain employment and promotion records.[2] Both the general and specific exemptions are only effective upon the agencies notice and promulgation of rules asserting the exempt status of the particular systems.[3] Although the exemptions purport to excuse such records only from the access and amendment provisions of the Act, thus leaving the ban on unconsented disclosures intact, blanket exemptions can also be used to shield those systems from the Privacy Act's civil remedy provisions.

Litigation under the blanket exemptions set forth in section 552a(j) has been understandably scarce.[4] The *per se,* institutional exclusion of CIA files under section (j)(1) makes any challenge difficult, if not impossible.[5] Section (j)(2)'s more generic exemption[6] necessitates a deter-

training sessions held to be within "law enforcement activity," in sense that they were properly retained pursuant to hospital's evaluation of appellant-employee's work performance and observation of hospital standards of conduct). Boyd v. Secretary of the Navy, 709 F.2d 684 (11th Cir.1983), cert. denied, 464 U.S. 1043, 104 S.Ct. 709, 79 L.Ed.2d 173 (1984). But cf. Albright v. United States, 631 F.2d 915 (D.C.Cir.1980), on remand 558 F.Supp. 260 (D.D.C.1982), aff'd, 732 F.2d 181 (D.C.Cir.1984) (unlawful for agency to secretly videotape employee grievance meeting).

8. See Hobson v. Wilson, 737 F.2d 1, 64–66 (D.C.Cir.1984), cert. denied 470 U.S. 1084, 105 S.Ct. 1843, 85 L.Ed.2d 142 (1985).

§ 18.4

1. 5 U.S.C.A. § 552a(j).

2. Id. § 552a(k).

3. See Ryan v. Department of Justice, 595 F.2d 954 (4th Cir.1979) (incomplete Department of Justice regulation left system open to damage remedy for unlawful disclosure).

4. See, e.g., Alford v. CIA, 610 F.2d 348, 348–49 (5th Cir.1980); Blazy v. Tenet, 979 F.Supp. 10, 23–25 (D.D.C.1997), affirmed, 1998 WL 315583 (D.C.Cir.1998).

5. "The head of any agency may promulgate rules, in accordance with the requirements (including general notice) of sections 553(b)(1)(2), and (3), (c), and (3) of this title, to exempt any system of records within the agency from any part of this section except subsections (b), (c)(1) and (2), (3)(4)(A) through (F), (e)(6), (7), (9), (10), and (11), and (i) if the system of records is—

(1) maintained by the Central Intelligence Agency..." 5 U.S.C.A. § 552a(j)(1).

6. The system of records may be exempted if it is "(2) maintained by an agency or component thereof which performs as its principal function any activity pertaining to the enforcement of criminal laws, including police efforts to prevent, control, or reduce crime or to apprehend criminals, and the activities of prosecutors, courts, correctional, probation, pardon, or parole authorities, and which consists of (A) information compiled for the purpose of identifying individual criminal offenders and alleged offenders and consisting only of identifying data and notations of arrests, the nature and disposition of criminal charges, sentencing, confinement, release, and parole and probation status; (B) information compiled for the purpose of a criminal investigation, including reports of informants and investigators, and associated with an identifiable individual; or (C) reports identifiable to an individual compiled at any stage of the process of enforcement of the criminal laws from arrest or indictment through release from supervision." Id. § 552a(j)(2).

mination not only that the exempted records are in the files of an agency whose "principal function" is law enforcement or the related court and correctional duties, but that they are also being used properly for valid law enforcement purposes.[7] Given the conflicting values of personal privacy and effective law enforcement, Congress opted for the latter.

Litigation under the more tailored, specific exemptions of section 552a(k) has dealt with the source-protecting exemptions for law enforcement and Federal civilian employment "background investigations."[8] Arguments that disclosure of confidential sources is necessary to ensure accurate and amendable records have been rejected by the courts.[9] In order to withhold source-sensitive law enforcement information as exempt, the agency must show that there was an express promise of confidentiality given in exchange for the information.[10] In the context of "investigatory material compiled solely for the purpose of determining suitability, eligibility, or qualifications for Federal civilian employment, military service, Federal contracts, or access to classified information," only information which would identify the source is exempt, provided there was an express promise of confidentiality.[11]

7. See, e.g., Gowan v. United States Dep't of the Air Force, 148 F.3d 1182, 1189–90 (10th Cir.1998), cert. denied, 525 U.S. 1042, 119 S.Ct. 593, 142 L.Ed.2d 535 (1998) (Air Force Office of Special Investigations qualified law enforcement authority) Binion v. U.S. Dept. of Justice, 695 F.2d 1189 (9th Cir.1983) (pardon file, though resulting from a civil proceeding, exempt as (j)(2) law enforcement record); Anderson v. United States Postal Serv., 7 F. Supp. 2d 583, 586 n. 3 (E.D.Pa.1998), affirmed, 187 F.3d 625 (3d Cir.1999) (United States Postal Inspection Service qualified law enforcement authority); Butler v. Department of the Air Force, 888 F.Supp. 174, 179 (D.D.C. 1995), affirmed, 116 F.3d 941 (D.C.Cir. 1997) (Air Force Office of Special Investigations qualified law enforcement authority); Nunez v. DEA, 497 F.Supp. 209 (S.D.N.Y. 1980) (DEA ruled to be a qualifying law enforcement authority).

8. Section 552a(k)(2) provides that a system of records may be exempted if it is "investigatory material compiled for law enforcement purposes, other than material within the scope of subsection (j)(2) of this section: *Provided, however,* that if any individual is denied any right, privilege, or benefit that he would otherwise be entitled by Federal law, or for which he would otherwise be eligible, such material shall be provided to such individual, except to the extent that the disclosure of such material would reveal the identity of a source who furnished information to the Government under an express promise that the identity of the source would be held in confidence, or, prior to the effective date of this section, under an implied promise that the identity of the source would be held in confidence." 5 U.S.C.A. § 552a(k)(2) (emphasis added). See Gowan v. United States Dep't of the Air Force, 148 F.3d at 1188–89; Viotti v. United States Air Force, 902 F.Supp. 1331, 1335 (D.Colo.1995).

9. See Hernandez v. Alexander, 671 F.2d 402 (10th Cir.1982).

10. See, Henke v. U.S. Dept. of Commerce, 83 F.3d 1445 (D.C.Cir.1996); Londrigan v. FBI, 670 F.2d 1164 (D.C.Cir.1981), appeal after remand 722 F.2d 840 (1983); Diamond v. FBI, 532 F.Supp. 216 (S.D.N.Y. 1981), aff'd, 707 F.2d 75 (2d Cir.1983), cert. denied, 465 U.S. 1004, 104 S.Ct. 995, 79 L.Ed.2d 228 (1984). But cf. Londrigan v. FBI (*Londrigan II*), 722 F.2d 840 (D.C.Cir. 1983) (strict requirements for confidentiality agreements made after the Act took effect but less strict for promises made before).

11. See May v. Department of the Air Force, 777 F.2d 1012 (5th Cir.1985); Volz v. U.S. Dept. of Justice, 619 F.2d 49 (10th Cir.1980), cert. denied, 449 U.S. 982, 101 S.Ct. 397, 66 L.Ed.2d 244 (1980) (records exempt even though source of the information was already known). See Croskey v. United States Office of Special Counsel, 9 F. Supp. 2d 8, 11 (D.D.C.1998), affirmed, 1999 WL 58614 (D.C.Cir.1999) (finding Office of Special Counsel report of why plaintiff had been fired was exempt from access and amendment provisions of Privacy Act pursuant to subsection (k)(2)); Viotti, 902 F. Supp. at 1335; Mittleman v. United

Two courts have heard subsection (k)(2) claims where individuals allegedly gave information in exchange for a promise of confidentiality then sued when their information was disclosed and their identities were insufficiently protected. In Sterling v. United States,[12] the District Court for the District of Columbia said that the plaintiff was "not barred from stating a claim for monetary damages merely because the record did not contain 'personal information' about him and was not retrieved through a search of indices bearing his name or other identifying characteristics."[13] In a later opinion, however, the court ruled in favor of the agency after the plaintiff failed to prove that the agency intentionally or willfully disclosed the plaintiff's identity.[14] In Bechhoefer v. United States Dep't of Justice,[15] on the other hand, the District Court for the Western District of New York was not persuaded by the Sterling court's analysis.[16] The court found that the disputed information in the case before it was not a record "about" the plaintiff and stated that subsection (k)(2) "does not prohibit agencies from releasing material that would reveal the identity of a confidential source," but rather "allows agencies to promulgate rules to exempt certain types of documents from mandatory disclosure under other portions of the Act."[17] The court also stated that the "plaintiff's reliance on § 552a(k)(2) [wa]s misplaced," and that subsection (k) was "irrelevant" to the plaintiff's wrongful disclosure claim.[18]

Another Privacy Act exemption, effective without rulemaking, would disallow individual access to "any information compiled in reasonable anticipation of a civil action or proceeding."[19] On the assumption that such information will eventually be disclosed at some stage in the litigation process, this exemption has been held to "afford the broad protection its broad terms imply."[20] Some courts have held that the

States Dep't of the Treasury, 919 F.Supp. 461, 469 (D.D.C.1995), aff'd in part & remanded in part on other grounds, 104 F.3d 410 (D.C.Cir.1997); Putnam v. United States Dep't of Justice, 873 F.Supp. 705, 717 (D.D.C.1995); Nemetz v. Department of Treasury, 446 F.Supp. 102 (N.D.Ill.1978); But see Doe v. U.S. Civil Service Commission, 483 F.Supp. 539 (S.D.N.Y.1980).

12. 798 F.Supp. 47, 49 (D.D.C.1992), affirmed, 1994 WL 88894 (D.C.Cir.1994).

13. Id.

14. Sterling v. United States, 826 F.Supp. 570, 571–72 (D.D.C.1993).

15. 934 F.Supp. 535, 538–39 (W.D.N.Y. 1996), vacated & remanded sub nom. Bechhoefer v. United States Dep't of Justice Drug Enforcement Admin., 209 F.3d 57 (2d Cir.2000)

16. Bechhoefer, 934 F. Supp. at 538–39.

17. Id.

18. Id. at 539.

19. 5 U.S.C.A. § 552a(d)(5).

20. Smiertka v. U.S. Dept. of Treasury, 447 F.Supp. 221 (D.D.C.1978), remanded on other grounds 604 F.2d 698 (D.C.Cir.1979). See also, Blazy v. Tenet, 979 F.Supp. 10, 24 (D.D.C.1997), affirmed, 1998 WL 315583 (D.C.Cir.1998) (construing broadly subsection (d)(5) to protect communications between CIA Office of General Counsel and Employee Review Panel). Subsection (d)(5) is not as broad as FOIA Exemption 5, 5 U.S.C. § 552(b)(5) (1994 & Supp. IV 1998), because it does not cover information compiled in anticipation of criminal prosecutions. Subsection (j)(2), however, may protect this sort of information. Also, subsection (d)(5) does not incorporate the deliberative process privilege or other Exemption 5 privileges. See, Savada v. DOD, 755 F.Supp. 6, 9 (D.D.C.1991). But see Blazy, 979 F. Supp. at 24 (stating incorrectly Exemption 5 and subsection (d)(5) allow and agency to withhold attorney work product information or information under the attorney-client or deliberative process

exemption extends beyond materials covered by the attorney work product privilege, and that the exemption (contrary to the above assumption) may be applicable even after the proceedings have ended.[21]

§ 18.5 PRIVACY ACT REMEDIES

The Privacy Act assesses criminal penalties (misdemeanor and $5000 fine) against any agency employee found to have knowingly and willfully disclosed records or maintained an unauthorized system of records in violation of the Act; a similar penalty can be levied against anyone who makes a request for records under false pretenses.[1] These sanctions are rarely invoked.[2] The Act also provides a complex scheme of different remedies[3] for different violations such as: if an agency fails to maintain accurate records, or to collect only necessary and relevant data, or to disclose personal records only with consent, or to otherwise comply with the Act and the individual suffers an adverse determination as to rights, qualifications, opportunities or benefits. If an agency refuses to amend a record on request, or denies an individual access to his files, a court can order amendment or disclosure, respectively, and in access cases, the burden of proof is on the agency; in amendment cases, however, it is on the plaintiff.[4]

privilege). Thus, deliberative information withheld under FOIA can be mandatorily disclosed under the Privacy Act. See Savada, 755 F. Supp. at 9.

21. Zeller v. United States, 467 F.Supp. 487 (E.D.N.Y.1979); Hernandez v. Alexander, 671 F.2d 402 (10th Cir.1982).

§ 18.5

1. 5 U.S.C.A. § 552a(i). For a discussion of the civil remedies under the Act, see generally Note, Damages Under the Privacy Act: Compensation and Deterrence, 52 Fordham L.Rev. 611 (1984).

2. See, e.g., United States v. Trabert, 978 F.Supp. 1368 (D.Colo.1997); In re Mullins (Tamposi Fee Application), 84 F.3d 1439, 1441 (D.C.Cir.1996) (per curiam).

3. 5 U.S.C.A. § 552a(g). Section 552a(g) provides in full as follows:

"(g)(1) Civil remedies.—Whenever any agency

"(A) makes a determination under subsection (d)(3) of this section not to amend an individual's record in accordance with his request, or fails to make such review in conformity with that subsection;

"(B) refuses to comply with an individual request under subsection (d)(1) of this section;

"(C) fails to maintain any record concerning any individual with such accuracy, relevance, timeliness, and completeness as is necessary to assure fairness in any determination relating to the qualifications, character, rights, or opportunities of, or benefits to the individual that may be made on the basis of such record, and consequently a determination is made which is adverse to the individual; or

"(D) fails to comply with any other provision of this section, or any rule promulgated thereunder, in such a way as to have an adverse effect on an individual.

"The individual may bring a civil action against the agency, and the district courts of the United States shall have jurisdiction in the matters under the provisions of this subsection . . ."

4. 5 U.S.C.A. § 552a(g)(1)(A)–(3)(A). R.R. v. Department of the Army, 482 F.Supp. 770 (D.D.C.1980); Hobson v. Wilson, 737 F.2d 1 (D.C.Cir.1984), cert. denied 470 U.S. 1084, 105 S.Ct. 1843, 85 L.Ed.2d 142 (1985) (court may order expunging of inaccuracies from the record); Brown v. FBI, 658 F.2d 71 (2d Cir.1981) (*de novo* review required and *in camera* examination of records allowed). Privacy Act remedies are exclusive; a violation of the Act does not provide relief for a defendant during a federal criminal prosecution. See United States v. Gillotti, 822 F.Supp. 984, 989 (W.D.N.Y. 1993) ("[T]he appropriate relief for a [Privacy Act] violation . . . is found in the statute and allows for damages as well as

Suits under the Act must be brought "within two years from the date on which the cause of action arises."[5] Conceivably, an individual could suffer an adverse determination based on records he or she was unaware of until well after the statute of limitations had run. The after-the-fact nature of privacy violations and the usual uncertainties over exhaustion of administrative remedies can make the two-year limit an abrupt procedural bar to remedy under the Act.[6]

Injunctive relief is available only to force the agency to give access to or allow amendments to an individual's records. A person seeking a court order halting improper disclosures is generally out of luck. Courts have consistently held that the Act's remedial scheme is the exclusive vehicle for redress of Privacy Act violations.[7]

In Privacy Act actions alleging infringement of First Amendment rights, however, courts have taken a more flexible approach. In at least three cases, appellate courts have stated that an order of expungement of records is, in proper circumstances, a permissible remedy for an agency's violation of the Privacy Act.[8] In such situations, courts are willing to look beyond the rigid confines of the Act's remedies: expungement of agency records can, in its own way, be a very effective form of injunctive relief.

Civil damages are available only for violations of the Act, which result in an "adverse effect."[9] Should a plaintiff succeed in demonstrat-

amendment or expungement of the unlawful records ... there is nothing in the statute itself, nor in any judicial authority, which suggests that its violation may provide any form of relief in a federal criminal prosecution"). Neither can a violation of the Privacy Act be invoked as a defense to refusing to comply with a summons. See Reimer v. United States, 43 F. Supp. 2d 232, 237 (N.D.N.Y.1999); Estate of Myers v. United States, 842 F.Supp. 1297, 1300–02 (E.D.Wash.1993). Nor can a violation of the Act serve as the basis for mandamus. Graham v. Hawk, 857 F.Supp. 38, 41 (W.D.Tenn.1994), affirmed, 59 F.3d 170 (6th Cir.1995).

5. 5 U.S.C.A. § 552a(g)(5). Only three decisions have analyzed the statute of limitations in the context of subsection (g)(5). See Biondo v. Department of the Navy, 928 F.Supp. 626, 632, 634–35 (D.S.C.1995), affirmed, 86 F.3d 1148 (4th Cir.1996); Burkins v. United States, 865 F.Supp. 1480, 1496 (D.Colo.1994); Mittleman v. United States Treasury, 773 F.Supp. 442, 448, 450–51 n. 7 (D.D.C.1991), summary affirmance granted, 76 F.3d 1240, 1242 (D.C.Cir.1996). The statute of limitations provision is strictly construed. See Griffin v. United States Parole Comm'n, 192 F.3d 1081, 1082 (D.C.Cir.1999); Mangino v. Department of the Army, 818 F.Supp. 1432, 1437 (D.Kan. 1993), affirmed, 17 F.3d 1437 (10th Cir. 1994).

6. See Hewitt v. Grabicki, 596 F.Supp. 297 (E.D.Wash.1984), aff'd, 794 F.2d 1373 (9th Cir.1986). Courts have held that the statute of limitations runs from the time the plaintiff knew or should have known of the Privacy Act violation. See, e.g., Armstrong v. United States Bureau of Prisons, 976 F.Supp. 17, 21 (D.D.C.1997), affirmed, 1998 WL 65543 (D.C.Cir.1998); Nwangoro v. Department of the Army, 952 F.Supp. 394, 397–98 (N.D.Tex.1996).

7. See Parks v. IRS, 618 F.2d 677 (10th Cir.1980); Edison v. Department of Army, 672 F.2d 840 (11th Cir.1982); Ryan v. Department of Justice, 595 F.2d 954 (4th Cir. 1979); Cell Associates, Inc. v. NIH, 579 F.2d 1155 (9th Cir.1978). Contra Florida Medical Ass'n, Inc. v. Department of HEW, 479 F.Supp. 1291 (M.D.Fla.1979).

8. Hobson v. Wilson, 737 F.2d 1, 64–65 (D.C.Cir.1984), cert. denied 470 U.S. 1084, 105 S.Ct. 1843, 85 L.Ed.2d 142 (1985); Clarkson v. IRS, 678 F.2d 1368, 1376–77 (11th Cir.1982), appeal after remand 811 F.2d 1396 (1987), cert. denied 481 U.S. 1031, 107 S.Ct. 1961, 95 L.Ed.2d 533 (1987); Albright v. United States, 631 F.2d 915, 921 (D.C.Cir.1980), on remand 558 F.Supp. 260 (D.D.C.1982), aff'd, 732 F.2d 181 (D.C.Cir.1984). See also, supra note 85.

9. 5 U.S.C.A. § 552a(g)(4). See generally Quinn v. Stone, 978 F.2d 126 (3d Cir. 1992) (Privacy Act's civil remedies section

ing a redressable "adverse effect," he must also prove that the agency's alleged violation of the Act was "intentional" or "willful."[10] Courts have rarely found agency conduct that meets these standards.[11]

§ 18.6 ATTORNEY FEES

The Privacy Act provides for an award of "reasonable attorney fees and other litigation costs" to any complainant who has "substantially prevailed" in either a suit for access or amendment or an action for damages.[1] The award of attorney fees and costs is left to the discretion of the court, which usually decides whether a party has "substantially prevailed" by considering whether the "prosecution of the action would reasonably be regarded as necessary to obtain the information" and whether "the action had a substantial causative effect on the delivery of the information."[2] In both FOIA and Privacy Act contexts, courts appear reluctant to award attorney fees and costs unless the plaintiff has *clearly* prevailed,[3] although individual case determinations make generalization

gives individual adversely affected by an agency violation of the Act a judicial remedy by which individual may seek damages, but limits right to sue by requiring an adverse effect as a standing requirement and by requiring allegation of causal connection between agency's violation of the Act and the adverse effect); Parks v. IRS, 618 F.2d 677, 682 (10th Cir.1980) (Union had no standing to sue in a representative capacity for damages suffered by its individual members); Edison v. Department of the Army, 672 F.2d 840, 843 (11th Cir.1982) (The Privacy Act requires a causal relationship between the allegedly erroneous record and an adverse determination based on that record); Wisdom v. Department of HUD, 713 F.2d 422 (8th Cir.1983), cert. denied, 465 U.S. 1021, 104 S.Ct. 1272, 79 L.Ed.2d 678 (1984) (violation of the Privacy Act is not enough to permit a recovery of damages. The individual must demonstrate that the violation had an adverse impact on him); Harper v. United States, 423 F.Supp. 192 (D.S.C.1976) (court denied taxpayer access to an IRS memorandum on him: "The December 1975 letters do not contain any information about the plaintiff which could reasonably be anticipated to cause an adverse inference about plaintiff or result in his harm. Furthermore, in his complaint plaintiff pleads no circumstances, however general or conclusory, which would support such an inference. Thus this court and defendants can only speculate as to the nature or causation of the harm which plaintiff alleges. Therefore, plaintiff has failed to plead adequately.... the 'adverse effect' required by the Privacy Act...." Id. at 196–97).

10. 5 U.S.C.A. § 552a(g)(4). See supra note 45.

11. See Perry v. Block, 684 F.2d 121 (D.C.Cir.1982) (despite "disjointed," "fitful," and "dilatory" response to requests, and notwithstanding fact that government released more documents after submitting an affidavit stating that all had been released, court affirmed district court's dismissal of plaintiff's claim for damages under the Privacy Act); Albright v. United States, 732 F.2d 181, 189 (D.C.Cir.1984); Chapman v. NASA, 736 F.2d 238, 242–43 (5th Cir.1984), cert. denied 469 U.S. 1038, 105 S.Ct. 517, 83 L.Ed.2d 406 (1984); Edison v. Department of Army, 672 F.2d 840, 846 (11th Cir.1982). Cf. Johnson v. Department of Treasury, IRS, 700 F.2d 971 (5th Cir.1983). See also, § 18.1.1, supra.

§ 18.6

1. See Reinbold v. Evers, 187 F.3d 348, 363 (4th Cir.1999) (holding that a plaintiff does not substantially prevail in an access case merely because the agency produces the records before suit is filed). Cf. Abernethy v. IRS, 909 F.Supp. 1562, 1567–69 (N.D.Ga.1995), affirmed, 108 F.3d 343 (11th Cir.1997), rehearing and suggestion for rehearing en banc denied, 116 F.3d 494 (11th Cir.1997) ("[T]he fact that records were released after the lawsuit was filed, in and of itself, is insufficient to establish Plaintiff's eligibility for an award of attorneys' fees").

2. See, e.g., Vermont Low Income Advocacy Council, Inc. v. Usery, 546 F.2d 509, 514 (2d Cir.1976).

3. See, e.g., Clarkson v. IRS, 678 F.2d 1368 (11th Cir.1982), appeal after remand 811 F.2d 1396 (1987), cert. denied 481 U.S. 1031, 107 S.Ct. 1961, 95 L.Ed.2d 533

difficult. Courts tend to look primarily at the validity of the statutory claim rather than the causative effect of litigation on agency document release in awarding or denying plaintiffs' costs. Courts have also held that pro se litigants are not eligible for an award of attorney fees.[4]

§ 18.7 THE COMPUTER MATCHING AND PRIVACY PROTECTION ACT OF 1988

Computer matching consists of side by side comparisons of different agencies' data banks and specific information collected about certain individuals.[1] The Computer Matching and Privacy Protection Act of 1988[2] was passed by Congress to address the continuing privacy concerns associated with government run computer matching programs.[3] The Act was largely precipitated by the lack of restraint displayed by federal agencies in performing computer matches.[4] By 1984 one HHS official estimated that the federal government had undertaken 2,000–3,000 matches, many of which are repeated regularly. The Act is designed to permit computer matching programs relating to the administration of

(1987); Barrett v. Bureau of Customs, 651 F.2d 1087 (5th Cir.1981), cert. denied 455 U.S. 950, 102 S.Ct. 1454, 71 L.Ed.2d 665 (1982). Cf. Perry v. Block, 684 F.2d 121 (D.C.Cir.1982); Johnson v. Department of Treasury, IRS, 700 F.2d 971 (5th Cir.1983).

4. See, e.g., Clarkson v. IRS, 678 F.2d 1368, 1371 (11th Cir.1982), appeal after remand, 811 F.2d 1396 (1987), cert. denied, 481 U.S. 1031, 107 S.Ct. 1961, 95 L.Ed.2d 533 (1987); Barrett v. Bureau of Customs, 651 F.2d 1087, 1089 (5th Cir.1981), cert. denied, 455 U.S. 950, 102 S.Ct. 1454, 71 L.Ed.2d 665 (1982). See also, Kay v. Ehrler, 499 U.S. 432, 111 S.Ct. 1435, 113 L.Ed.2d 486 (1991) (holding that a pro se attorney cannot recover attorney fees under fee-shifting provisions). Cf. Blazy v. Tenet, 194 F.3d 90, 94 (D.C.Cir.1999) (ruling that pro se plaintiff is not precluded from recovering outside counsel "consultations" fees). See also, id. at 95–97 (ruling that FOIA criteria for determining entitlement to attorney fees are inapplicable under the Privacy Act). Contra, Gowan v. United States Dep't of the Air Force, 148 F.3d 1182, 1194–95 (10th Cir.1998), cert. denied, 525 U.S. 1042, 119 S.Ct. 593, 142 L.Ed.2d 535 (1998); Reinbold v. Evers, 187 F.3d 348, 362 (4th Cir.1999) (citing Gowan with approval in dicta). Also, the Supreme Court has said that fee enhancement as compensation for the risk in a contingency fee arrangement is not available under statutes authorizing an award of reasonable attorney fees to a prevailing or substantially prevailing party. City of Burlington v. Dague, 505 U.S. 557, 561–66, 112 S.Ct. 2638, 120 L.Ed.2d 449 (1992).

§ 18.7

1. See generally Suzanne M. Thompson, The Digital Explosion Comes With a Cost: The Loss of Privacy, 4 J. Tech. L. & Pol'y 3, 37 (1999) (arguing that the Act falls short of its goals by not covering data gathered by private vendors); Thomas B. Kearns, Note, Technology and the Right to Privacy: The Convergence of Surveillance and Information Privacy Concerns, 7 Wm. & Mary Bill of Rts. J. 975 (1999) (arguing that advances in technology weaken protection under the Act); Patricia Mell, A Hitchhiker's Guide to Trans–Border Data Exchanges Between EU Member States and the United States Under the European Union Directive on the Protection of Personal Information, 9 Pace Int'l L. Rev. 147 (1997) (arguing that transfers of data between the EU and United States are inadequately protected by U.S. law); Adam Melita, Note, Much Ado About $26 Million: Implications of Privatizing the Collection of Delinquent Federal Taxes, 16 Va. Tax Rev. 699 (1997) (arguing that outsourcing government debt collection to private agencies will weaken protections under the Act).

2. Pub.L. 100–503, 102 Stat. 2513 (Oct. 18, 1988) (codified at 5 U.S.C.A. § 552a).

3. 5 U.S.C.A. § 552a(a)(8)(A). The typical purpose of a matching program is to assure compliance with the requirements for assistance under federal benefit programs or comparison of systems or personnel or payroll records.

4. See Betts, "Computer Matching Bill Would Protect Privacy," Computerworld, Sept. 5, 1988 at 2.

federal benefits or assistance programs and federal payroll operations.[5] Four general requirements are placed upon federal agencies participating in computer matching. First, the agency is required to enter into a formal written "matching agreement" with any entity to which the "source agency" intends to disclose information.[6] Second, the agency must verify any information retrieved from a match (colloquially referred to as a "hit") before any adverse action is taken against an individual as a result.[7] Third, the Act requires that federal agencies publish notice in the Federal Register that they are implementing or amending a computer matching program.[8] Finally, each agency participating in a computer matching program must establish a data integrity board to govern the implementation of the new regulations.[9]

Agencies wishing to run computer matching programs must first enter into a written matching agreement. The contents of such a proposed agreement are specified in the Act.[10] Any agreement must contain the following ten elements: (1) the purpose and legal authority for conducting the program; [11](2) the justification for the program and the anticipated results, including a specific estimate of any savings;[12] (3) a description of the records that will be matched and the projected starting and completion dates of the program;[13] (4) procedures for providing notice to applicants for and participants in federal benefit programs and applicants and holders of federal personnel positions, at the time of application and periodically thereafter, that any information provided may be subject to verification through matching programs;[14] (5) procedures for verifying information produced in the matching program;[15] (6) procedures for retention, use, and return of records;[16] (7) procedures for ensuring security of the records matched and the results of the matching program;[17] (8) prohibitions on duplication and redisclosure of records;[18] (9) information on assessments of accuracy of records to be used in the program;[19] (10) a specification that the Comptroller General may have access to all records of the receiving agency.[20] These provisions for "matching agreements" are at the core of the Act whose primary purpose is to regulate an area previously open to agency abuse. The Act also places an eighteen month time limit on any one matching agreement,[21] while providing for the possibility of a one year extension.[22]

5. See 5 U.S.C.A. § 552a(b)(13), (e)(12), (*o*)–(s), and (u).

6. Id. § 552a(*o*).

7. Id. § 552a(p)(1).

8. Id. § 552a(*o*)(2)(B).

9. Id. § 552a(u)(1), (2).

10. Id. § 552a(*o*)(1).

11. Id. § 552a(*o*)(1)(A).

12. Id. § 552a(*o*)(1)(B).

13. Id. § 552a(*o*)(1)(C).

14. Id. § 552a(*o*)(1)(D).

15. Id. § 552a(*o*)(1)(E).

16. Id. § 552a(*o*)(1)(F) and (I).

17. Id. § 552a(*o*)(1)(G).

18. Id. § 552a(*o*)(1)(H).

19. Id. § 552a(*o*)(1)(J).

20. Id. § 552a(*o*)(1)(K).

21. Id. § 552a(*o*)(2)(C).

22. Id. § 552a(*o*)(2)(D).

"(D) Within 3 months prior to the expiration of such an agreement pursuant to subparagraph (C), the Data Integrity Board of the agency may, without additional review, renew the matching agreement for a current, ongoing matching program for not more than one additional year if—

The Act also provides for public notice of 30 days before any new or amended government matching program may be implemented. Notice is through publication in the Federal Register.[23] Some privacy advocates argue this is a key weakness in the Act.[24]

Every agency participating in a matching program must establish a Data Integrity Board. The purpose of the Board is to govern the implementation of the Privacy Act.[25] As part of the Board's statutory duties, it must both review the agreement's justification and compliance with applicable laws and, additionally, make a cost-benefit assessment of all matching programs. The Board must review agency disposal and record keeping policies while serving as a clearinghouse for information on the accuracy of matching program records.[26] Most importantly, an agency Data Integrity Board is responsible for approving all the written matching agreements the agency enters into.[27] If the Board disapproves of a proposed match, a party to that proposed agreement may appeal to the Office of Management and Budget.[28] The OMB may reverse the Board if it finds the program to be lawful, cost-efficient and in the public interest.[29]

§ 18.8 PRIVACY, TECHNOLOGY AND THE PRIVATE SECTOR: CITIZENS AND CONSUMERS[1]

Just as technology has enhanced considerably the ability of the federal government to collect, share and use information about individuals, technological advances have resulted in enormous private databases as well. Indeed, early concerns about the burgeoning ability to computerize personal data resulted in an advisory committee of the U.S. Department of Health, Education and Welfare (HEW) recommending that a federal code of "fair information practices" be promulgated to encompass public *and* private computerized databases.[2] The code provided that

(i) such program will be conducted without any change; and

(ii) each party to the agreement certifies to the Board in writing that the program has been conducted in compliance with the agreement."

23. Id. § 552a(e)(12).

24. See, e.g., Note, The Computer Matching and Privacy Protection Act of 1988: Necessary Relief From the Erosion of the Privacy Act of 1974, 2 Software L.J. 283, 405–406 ("Congress has put its stamp of approval on the uncontested transfer of personal information by adopting minimally effective methods notifying the public.").

25. 5 U.S.C.A. § 552a(u)(1) and (2):

"(u) Data Integrity Boards.—(1) Every agency conducting or participating in a matching program shall establish a Data Integrity Board to oversee and coordinate among the various components of such agency the agency's implementation of this section. (2) Each Data Integrity Board shall consist of senior officials designated by the head of the agency; and shall include any senior official designated by the head of the agency as responsible for implementation of this section, and the inspector general of the agency, if any. The inspector general shall not serve as chairman of the Data Integrity Board."

26. Id. § 552a(u)(3)(A–C), (E–G).

27. Id. § 552a(u)(3)(A).

28. Id. § 552a(u)(5)(A).

29. Id.

§ 18.8

1. This section draws heavily on Alfred C. Aman, Jr., Information, Privacy, and Technology: Citizens, Clients or Consumers, § 18.1, *supra* note 17, at 342–46.

2. *See* Susan E. Gindin, *Lost and Found in Cyberspace: Information Privacy in the Age of the Internet*, 34 San Diego L. Rev. 1153, 1219 (1997).

no data systems would be maintained in secret, that individuals should have access to the information and be advised as to how it would be used, that information collected for one purpose would not be used for another purpose, that individuals must have a way to correct erroneous information, and that organizations collecting data must assure its accuracy and fair use.[3] Similar principles were incorporated into guidelines issued by the Organization for Economic Cooperation and Development in 1980.[4] These early recommendations remain today's core concepts of "choice and access," the twin "well-accepted fair information practices for all organizations in the computer age."[5]

U.S. Federal Trade Commission officials, when discussing consumer privacy, have used terms like "substantive fair information principles," which include "[n]otice, consent, access and security,"[6] and have shown some concern about the effects of inaccurate consumer information.[7] The Georgetown Internet Privacy Policy Survey (GIPPS) analyzed commercial web sites to find to what extent Web sites offered consumers "notice,[8] choice,[9] access,[10] or security,"[11] as well as "contact information

3. *Id.* at 1219.

4. *Id.*

5. Westin, *supra* note at A19. Representative Edward J. Markey (D–MA), in testimony during the Senate Banking Committee Hearing on Financial Privacy, asserted that "consumers should have a right to know when personal information is being collected about them, and get access to such information for review or correction." *Financial Privacy: Hearing on S.187 Before the Senate Comm. on Banking, Housing, and Urban Affairs*, 106th Cong. (1999) (statement of Rep. Edward J. Markey (D–MA)). Marc Rotenberg, Director of the Electronic Privacy Information Center, has said that a good privacy policy "should explain how and why personal information is being collected, how it will be used, and whether the individual can get access to the personal information. We think this is critical." Marc Rotenberg, Remarks at News Conference on Consumer Privacy (June 9, 1997), *available in* LEXIS, FDCH Political Transcripts. On the other hand, others advocate only control without access. America On Line's deputy director of law and public policy, and senior legal counsel, told the House Banking and Financial Services Committee Subcommittee on Financial Institutions and consumer Credit that AOL believed consumers have a right to know what information was being collected, how it would be used, and what choices consumers had in disclosing the information, yet never mentioned the consumer's rights to know exactly what the information was, or whether consumers should have a right to correct erroneous information. *See Internet Privacy*, *supra* note ? (remarks of Jill A. Lesser, Vice President Domestic Public Policy, America Online); *but see* remarks of Christine Varney, Hogan & Hartson ("[C]onsumers have a right to see the data that is held about them is accurate and ... one mechanism for checking accuracy is access"). *Id.*

6. *See Internet Privacy*, *infra* note 8 (remarks of FTC Commissioner Sheila Anthony).

7. *See* Bob Edwards, *Morning Edition* (National Public Radio broadcast, June 11, 1997).

8. "Notice ... was defined to include statements about what information is collected, how the information is collected, how the information collected will be used, whether the information will be reused or disclosed to third parties, and whether the site said anything about its use or non-use of Cookies." Mary J. Culnan, Georgetown Internet Privacy Policy Survey: Report to the Federal Trade Commission 9 (1999) [hereinafter GIPPS] (Visited November 13, 1999) <http://www.msb.edu/faculty/culnanm/GIPPS/mmrpt.PDF>.

9. "Choice ... was defined to include statements regarding choice offered about being contacted again by the same organization and choice about having non-aggregate personal information collected by the Web site disclosed to third parties." *Id.*

10. "Access ... was defined to include allowing consumers to review or ask questions about the information the site has collected and whether the sites disclosed how inaccuracies in personal information the site had collected were handled." *See* Culnan, *supra* note 20. *See also* Mary J.

a consumer could use to ask a question about the site's information practices or to complain to the company or another organization about privacy.''[12] Of the sites surveyed, less than fourteen percent contained all five elements: notice, choice, access, security, and contact information.[13] The findings prompted FTC Chairman Robert Pitofsky to express the Commission's concern over industry practices and consumer privacy; however, he reiterated the Commission's desire to let the market supply a solution to the problem through innovations such as privacy seals of approval.[14] Others are more specific. Gandy, for example, has called for the following five-part approach:

1. Collection of consumer data for expressly limited purposes,[15] and no collection of data from third parties.
2. Informing consumers about how data is collected and how it will be used.
3. The ability to access and correct information, with the data gatherer assuming responsibility for the accuracy of the information.
4. Assuring that data are not used for any but the stated purpose.
5. Informed consent from consumers prior to gathering data.[16]

The U.S. government favors voluntary compliance with industry standards. Even those who favor such an approach, however, confess that so far, the voluntary approach has not yielded satisfactory results. They advocate more entrepreneurship in adapting technology to the needs of consumers and data protection. A world of possibilities lies implicit in the particular computer code being used. Sophisticated methods have been devised to protect consumer privacy. For example, cryptographers have invented a method to transmit value over the Internet with digital tokens that are the equivalent of cash. Such an approach avoids the ''audit trail'' left by a credit card purchase; however, the technology nevertheless makes it possible that the record of digital cash purchases could be aggregated, and the consumer's spending habits thus profiled.

Still other commentators argue for government intervention, advocating that the government codify certain voluntary standards into law.[17]

CULNAN, PRIVACY AND THE TOP 100 WEB SITES: REPORT TO THE FEDERAL TRADE COMMISSION (1999) (Visited Nov. 13, 1999) <http://www.msb.edu/faculty/cul nanm/GIPPS/oparpt.PDF> (assessing notice, choice, access, security, and contact information for the top 100 commercial Web sites).

11. ''Security . . . was defined to include protecting information during transmission and during subsequent storage.'' *See* GIPPS, *supra* note 210.

12. *Id.*

13. *Id.*

14. *See Internet Privacy*, *supra* note 8 (remarks of FTC Chairman of Robert Pitofsky).

15. *See also* Spiros Simitis, *Reviewing Privacy in an Information Society*, 135 U. PA. L. REV. 707, 740–41 (arguing that data collectors should have an identifiable specific purpose for the data, and not collect data merely for anticipated future use).

16. *See* Gandy, *supra* note 11, at 136–37.

17. *See generally* David J. Klein, *Keeping Business out of the Bedroom: Protecting Personal Privacy Interests from the Retail*

"The regulation of the treatment of personal information would secure participation by citizens in the communications process. Moreover, in commercial speech cases, courts are willing to uphold regulations if the government can regulate the underlying economic activity."[18] Simitis adds that "[d]espite their different approaches to the problem, statutes, drafts, administrative procedures, court decisions, and reports of control agencies now offer a solid basis for identifying at least four essentials of an efficient processing regulation." These four essentials include recognizing the unique nature of data processing, limiting the use of data to the expressed purpose for which it was collected, continuous updating of data regulations, and "an independent authority to enforce data regulations."[19] Gindin proposes "fair information practice guidelines" that include federal guarantees of individual control over the collection and distribution of personal information, which would include the right to access and correct one's personal data.[20]

Lawmakers have begun to respond to such proposals by drafting legislation that would allow consumers access to their personal information from business entities. The Gramm–Leach–Bliley Act,[21] for example, places an affirmative and continue obligation on financial institutions to respect the privacy of customers and to protect the security and confidentiality of customer nonpublic personal information. Financial institutions are to give consumers the chance to opt out of such disclosure prior to the disclosure. In addition, the law restricts the power of financial institutions to share and reuse customer information, with exceptions made for agency and business situations where discloser of customer information is necessary.

In the 106th Congress, S.809, sponsored by Senator Conrad Burns (R–Mont.), would require Internet sites to give consumers the opportunity to look at information that had been collected about them, as well as limit disclosure of the information.[22] The Federal Trade Commission, however, which favors a voluntary free market approach, voted 3–1 not to endorse the bill.[23] Others have argued that conflicts between state and federal personal privacy laws could be resolved by applying a "quasi-FOIA standard to state law concerning consumer-business transac-

World, 15 J. MARSHALL J. COMPUTER & INFO L.391 (1997).

18. *See* Posadas de P.R. Assocs. v. Tourism Co. of P.R., 478 U.S. 328, 106 S.Ct. 2968, 92 L.Ed.2d 266 (1986) (holding that government power to regulate gambling gives it the power to regulate gambling advertisement).

19. *See* Simitis, *supra* note 15, at 737–38. Although such a regulatory agency would likely be challenged in the courts, the Supreme Court has held that "neither incorporated nor unincorporated associations can plead an unqualified right to conduct their affairs in secret. (Citations omitted)." *See also* California Bankers Ass'n v. Shultz, 416 U.S. 21, 65, 94 S.Ct. 1494, 39 L.Ed.2d 812 (1974). The Court added that a law enforcement interest could legitimately allow the government to require a bank to profile its customers. *Id.* at 66–67.

20. Gindin, *supra* note 204, at 1155, 1222.

21. See Pub.L.No. 106–102, 113 Stat. 1437 (1999) codified at 15 U.S.C. §§ 6801–27.

22. *Give Surfers Some Privacy*, THE TENNESSEAN, August 23, 1999, at 10A.

23. *Id.*

tions."[24] Yet another suggestion is for states to broaden the scope of the Restatement 2nd of Torts' privacy standard of appropriation to FOIA exemption six.[25] The reason is that without customer profiles, companies would be unable to realize the economic gain of reselling the profiles. At bare minimum, these scholars argue, states should require businesses to give consumers an opt-out opportunity.[26]

Such reasoning helps to bolster an argument that purely private entities, or private entities that contract with the government, should be subject to some sort of FOIA-like law, especially if the issue is one of control and voluntariness on the part of the consumer who must of necessity divulge personal information to such businesses.[27] Others are less confident in the state's ability to regulate private data acquisition.

> As U.S. lawyers we are most accustomed to thinking about the problems of data creation, dissemination, and access in certain delimited categories such as the First Amendment, intellectual property rules, the torts of invasion of privacy and defamation, and perhaps in the ambit of a few narrowly defined statutes such as the Privacy Act or the Fair Credit Reporting Act. These categories are valuable, but are collectively inadequate to the regulatory and social challenges posed by the information production, collection, and processing booms now under way.[28]

Simitis also notes the drawbacks of legislation inasmuch as legislation typically has failed to anticipate future technological exigencies.[29]

> The emphasis must shift to a context-bound allocation of information embodied in a complex system of both specific and substantive regulations. Yet, no matter how precise the rules, they nevertheless remain provisional measures because of the incessant advances in technology. Regulations on the collection and retrieval of personal data thus present a classic case of sunset legislation.[30]

Technology and the privacy concerns that accompany its use thus raises important issues for both the public and the private sectors.

24. *See generally* David J. Klein, *Keeping Business out of the Bedroom: Protecting Personal Privacy Interests from the Retail World*, 15 J. Marshall J. Computer & Info L. 391 (1997).

25. *Id.*

26. *Id.*

27. *See generally* John Hagel III & Marc Singer, Net Worth (1999). The authors argue that emerging technologies that give consumers more power over what information they disclose, at least on the Internet, afford an entrepreneurial opportunity for "infomediaires," third party data brokers to whom consumers would turn over their own electronic records of personal consumption habits to be compiled, collated, then peddled to business who see such information. The consumer would then reap the financial benefit of selling his or her personal data, and the infomediary would collect a commission or fee.

28. *See* Froomkin, *supra* note 1, at 399.

29. *See* Simitis, *supra* note 217, 230, at 741–42.

30. *Id* at 742.

Chapter 19

GOVERNMENT IN THE SUNSHINE ACT

Table of Sections

---

§ 19.1 INTRODUCTION

Declaring that "the public is entitled to the fullest practicable information regarding the decisionmaking processes of the Federal Government," Congress passed and President Ford signed the Government in the Sunshine Act in late 1976.[1] The Act requires that most meetings of agency members be open to the public,[2] and prohibits *ex parte* communications to and by agency personnel in formal adjudicatory or hearing situations.[3] The ban on *ex parte* communications is designed to preserve the authenticity of the administrative record for purposes of justification and review, and to insure fairness and due process in agency decisionmaking. The majority of the Act deals with the open meeting requirements. The underlying premise of the Act is that open meetings will lead to a greater public trust and confidence in government.

Although the federal Sunshine Act has been in effect since 1977, it has spurred little litigation,[4] and assessments of its overall impact on

§ 19.1

1. Pub.L. No. 94–409, § 2, 90 Stat. 1241 (1976). The popular title derives from Justice Brandeis' statement that, "Publicity is justly commended as a remedy for social and industrial diseases. Sunlight is said to be the best of disinfectants; electric light the most efficient policeman." Louis D. Brandeis, What Publicity Can Do, Harper's Weekly at 10 (Dec. 20, 1913).

2. Pub.L. No. 94–409, § 3, 90 Stat. 1241 (1976) (codified as amended at 5 U.S.C.A. § 552b).

3. Id. § 4 (codified as 5 U.S.C.A. § 557(d)). See also 5 U.S.C.A. § 556(d) (adverse decision may result from a party's violation of the *ex parte* prohibition).

4. See Mashaw & Merrill, Administrative Law: The American Public Law System 151 (4th ed. 1998).

federal agency decisionmaking and public perceptions have been, at best, inconclusive.[5]

§ 19.1.1 Overview of the Act

The Sunshine Act became effective in March, 1977.[6] The following will sketch[7] the outlines of the Act,[8] with reference to relevant case law.

The Act requires that "every portion of every meeting of an agency shall be open to public observation"[9] unless the subject matter is exempted. The ten categories of meetings which may be exempt—i.e., closed to the public—embrace subject matter similar to that exempted from FOIA:[10] national defense and foreign policy, trade secrets, criminal and law enforcement matters, sensitive financial information, information protected from disclosure by statute, matters which if disclosed would constitute a "clearly unwarranted" invasion of personal privacy, and so forth.[11] The Act then specifies procedures for the announcement of meetings, the closing of meetings deemed exempt, and the record to be kept to provide for public access to non-exempt portions of closed meetings. The Act also authorizes judicial review of alleged violations of the open meetings requirements.[12]

Subsection (a) of the Act defines the "agencies" and the "meetings" which are subject to the Sunshine Act's requirements. These definitional, threshold issues have been frequently addressed, if not clarified, by the federal courts.

All agencies headed by a collegial body of two or more members appointed by the President with the advice and consent of the Senate are

5. See, e.g. Special Committee, Administrative Conference of the United States, Report & Recommendation by the Special Committee to Review the Government in the Sunshine Act, 49 Admin. L.Rev. 421, 423 (1997) [hearing after, Sunshine Act Review Report] ("promotes inefficient practices within agencies which themselves contribute to the erosion of collegial decision-making"). See also, James T. O'Reilly and Gracia M. Berg, Stealth Caused by Sunshine: How Sunshine Act Interpretation Results in Less Information for the Public About the Decision–Making Process of the International Trade Commission, 36 Harv. Int'l.L.J. 425 (1995); David M. Welborn et al., Implementation and Effects of the Federal Government in the Sunshine Act (Washington, D.C.: Administrative Conference of the United States, 1984) [hereinafter Welborn, et al., Implementation and Effects of Sunshine].

6. 5 U.S.C.A. § 552b, Historical Note (1977).

7. For an analysis of state sunshine laws, see Teresa D. Pupillo, The Changing Weather Forecast: Government in the Sunshine in the 1990's—An Analysis of State Sunshine Laws, 71 Wash.L.Q. 1165 (1993). See also, Thomas, Courts and the Implementation of the Government in the Sunshine Act, 37 Admin.L.Rev. 259 (1985).

8. References to "the Act" in this section are to 5 U.S.C.A. § 552b. The prohibitions on *ex parte* communications, 5 U.S.C.A. § 557(d), will not be discussed. See notes 2 and 3, supra.

9. 5 U.S.C.A. § 552b(b).

10. Three of the ten exemptions are not similar to FOIA exemptions: if the meeting involves (1) accusing a person of a crime or censuring the person, (2) implementing proposed agency action which would be frustrated if known prematurely, or (3) agency's participation in formal rulemaking or litigation. The only important FOIA exemption not included is the one for inter/intra-agency memos since the Act is meant to open up deliberations.

11. 5 U.S.C.A. § 552b(c). Note that subsection (c)(3) disqualifies FOIA as a withholding statute *per se.* Cf. subsection (m).

12. Id. § 552b(d)–(m).

governed by the Act.[13] The term "agency" is adopted as defined in FOIA,[14] and includes any "subdivision" thereof authorized to act on behalf of the agency.[15] Despite the "subdivision" clause, the language of the Act does not appear to reach the decisionmaking sessions of lower-level agency members; thus, only the meetings of the relevant Board or Commission itself need be opened to the public.[16]

A common threshold issue is: what is an agency? In the two leading cases which deal with the Act's definition, the courts have confirmed the apparently limited scope of the Act. In *Symons v. Chrysler Corporation Loan Guarantee Board,*[17] a public interest group brought suit demanding that the Loan Guarantee Board's meetings be opened to the public. The Board was comprised of Presidentially-appointed heads of other agencies[18] who served on the Loan Guarantee Board in an *ex officio* capacity, at the behest of Congress. The Board argued that because none of its members had been appointed "to such position," *viz.,* the Loan Guarantee Board, by the President, it was not an agency subject to the Sunshine Act. The district court[19] had held that the Board *was* within the scope of the Act, stating that the Board's *ex officio* argument was based on a "crimped, unduly restrictive view of the statute."[20] In reversing the lower court's ruling, the D.C. Circuit adhered to the Act's literal definition of agency. The appellate court accepted the Board's contention that *ex officio* members were beyond the reach of the specific language of subsection 9(a) and that the Board was thus free to conduct its meetings behind closed doors.[21]

13. Id. § 552b(a)(1).

14. Id. § 552(e) defines "agency" as "any executive department, military department, Government corporation, Government controlled corporation, or other establishment in the executive branch of the Government (including the Executive Office of the President), or any independent regulatory agency." See Public Citizen v. Dept. of Justice, 111 F.3d 168, 170 (D.C.Cir.1997) (a former President is not an agency).

15. Id. § 552b(a)(1).

16. The gist of the Act is that "*Members* shall not jointly conduct or dispose of agency business other than in accordance with this section. Except as provided in subsection (c), every portion of every meeting of an agency shall be open to public observation." Id. § 552b(b). (emphasis added). By specifically alluding to "members", defined in subsection (a)(3) as individuals who belong to a collegial body heading an agency, the statute appears to apply only to meetings of agency heads themselves. Because agency policy and direction is frequently determined by regional and departmental meetings of subordinates, on whose reports agency heads rely, most of the actual administrative decision making process remains inaccessible to the public.

17. 670 F.2d 238 (D.C.Cir.1981). The Loan Board was created by Congress in 1980, and was authorized to make and guarantee loans to Chrysler Corporation, which was, at that time, facing bankruptcy.

18. The Secretary of the Treasury, the Chairman of the Federal Reserve Board, the Comptroller General, the Secretary of Labor, and the Secretary of Transportation.

19. Symons v. Chrysler Corporation Loan Guarantee Board, 488 F.Supp. 874 (D.D.C.1980), rev'd, 670 F.2d 238 (D.C.Cir. 1981).

20. Id. at 876.

21. The court also noted that, "if Congress had wanted to subject the Board to the provisions of the Act, it could have so provided when the Board was established." Congress had done just that when it established the Depository Institutions Deregulation Committee in 1980. See 670 F.2d at 244–45.

In *Hunt v. Nuclear Regulatory Commission,*[22] plaintiffs sought access to the *in camera* hearings of an NRC licensing board evaluating the safety of a steam system to be installed at the Black Fox nuclear power plant near Tulsa, Oklahoma. The NRC argued that the Sunshine Act did not apply to adjudicatory licensing hearings, and that the "subdivision" language of subsection (a)(1) referred only to subdivisions composed of members of the collegial body which headed the agency;[23] because no NRC commissioner served on the licensing board, the meetings could be held without reference to the Act. The Tenth Circuit upheld the NRC's literal interpretation of the Act's threshold provisions,[24] and refused to order the hearings opened to the public. Likewise, the United States District Court for the Northern District of California took a strict textualist approach to the definition of "agency" in Parravano v. Babbitt.[25] The plaintiffs argued that the U.S. Secretary of Commerce violated the Sunshine Act by meeting privately with the U.S. Secretary of the Interior to "discuss coordination of Indian in-river and ocean harvest fishing rates."[26] The court stated that the Sunshine Act defined an "agency" as an agency "that is headed by a 'collegial body composed of two or more individual members.' "[27] Accordingly, the court held that "[b]ecause the Department of Commerce is headed by a single person, not a collegial body, this provision does not apply."[28]

The second threshold issue is what constitutes a meeting: "[T]he deliberations of at least the number of individual agency members required to take action on behalf of the agency where such deliberations determine or result in the joint conduct or disposition of official agency business."[29] A meeting thus requires a quorum of agency members, an exchange of views or information (as opposed to one member giving a speech when other members are present), and "deliberations" concerning "official agency business" (as opposed to informal conversation touching on such matters).

The Court of Appeals for the District of Columbia too a pragmatic approach to the Sunshine Act definition of "agency" in Energy Research Foundation v. Defense Nuclear Facilities Safety Board.[30] Two environmental organizations had sought declaratory and injunctive relief requiring the Board to comply with the Sunshine Act. Congress created the Board in 1988 to act as an independent review body of Department of Energy (DOE) defense nuclear facilities. The Board was empowered to

22. 468 F.Supp. 817 (N.D.Okl.1979), aff'd, 611 F.2d 332 (10th Cir.1979), cert. denied, 445 U.S. 906, 100 S.Ct. 1084, 63 L.Ed.2d 322 (1980).

23. 5 U.S.C.A. § 552b(a)(1) states: "the term 'agency' means any agency, as defined in section 552(e) of the title, headed by a collegial body composed of two or more members, a majority of whom are appointed to such position by the President with the advice and consent of the Senate, *any subdivision thereof authorized to act on behalf of the agency.*" (emphasis added).

24. See also United States v. Rankin, 616 F.2d 1168 (10th Cir.1980) (mistaken good faith belief that Sunshine Act prohibited Atomic Licensing and Safety Board from closing an adjudicatory hearing not a legal defense for defendants, who chained themselves to the courtroom doors in an effort to block the *in camera* proceeding).

25. 837 F.Supp. 1034 (1993), affirmed, 70 F.3d 539 (9th Cir.1995), cert. denied, 518 U.S. 1016, 116 S.Ct. 2546, 135 L.Ed.2d 1066 (1996).

26. Id. at 1048.

27. Id. (citing § 552b(a)(1)).

28. 837 F.Supp. at 1048.

29. 5 U.S.C.A. § 552b(a)(2).

30. See 917 F.2d 581 (D.C.Cir.1990).

review and evaluate defense nuclear facility design, construction, and operating standards; to investigate defense nuclear facility practices or events that could affect public health and safety; and to make recommendations to the Secretary of Energy. The district court had used a "sole function test"[31] and legislative history to conclude that although the Board had powers "more expansive than a common advisory board," its sole function was nevertheless advisory.[32] Thus, the Board was not an agency under the Sunshine Act. The court of appeals, applying an "advice-plus" test,[33] reversed the district court. The court of appeals reasoned that even if it applied the Soucie "sole function test" (the appropriateness of which the court seemed to question in this case),[34] the Board was still an agency under the Sunshine Act. In addition to giving advice, said the court, the Board "investigates, evaluates and recommends and it has the additional authority to impose reporting requirements on the Secretary of Energy."[35] Moreover, the court could discern no Congressional intent to shield the Board from the Sunshine Act.[36]

The first Sunshine Act case to reach the Supreme Court resulted in an opinion and decision which reinforces the narrow scope of the Act's statutory language. In *Federal Communications Commission v. ITT World Communications, Inc.,*[37] Justice Powell and a unanimous Supreme Court interpreted the Act to define a "meeting" in such a way as not to "impair normal agency operations without achieving significant public benefit."[38] In this case, the FCC's Telecommunications Committee held "consultative process gatherings" (CPGs) with their European counterparts, hoping to discuss increased competition in the international communications markets. Representatives of the carriers were excluded from these and subsequent discussions. ITT and the other dominant carriers eventually[39] brought their cause to the District of Columbia Circuit Court of Appeals,[40] where they complained, *inter alia,* that their exclusion from the CPG's constituted an FCC violation of the Sunshine Act. The FCC argued that (1) there had been no formal delegation of authority to the Telecommunications Committee. Thus it lacked the authority necessary to qualify it as a section 551b(a)(1) "subdivision"; (2) the CPG's were informal but necessary background discussions, not section 552b(a)(2) meetings *per se;* and (3) foreign authorities would be disinclined to discuss international communications policy at a public meeting. The D.C. Court of Appeals rejected the FCC's arguments, holding that Telecommunications Committee members were indeed act-

31. Energy Research Foundation v. Defense Nuclear Facilities Safety Board, 734 F.Supp. 27, 29 (1990) (citing Soucie v. David, 448 F.2d 1067 (D.C.Cir.1971)).

32. Id.

33. 917 F.2d at 583–84.

34. Id. at 584 ("[T]he Soucie standard ... would place us in disagreement with Crooker v. Office of Pardon Attorney, 614 F.2d 825, 828 (2d Cir.1980).").

35. 917 F.2d at 585.

36. Id.

37. 466 U.S. 463, 104 S.Ct. 1936, 80 L.Ed.2d 480 (1984).

38. Id. at 468, 104 S.Ct. at 1940.

39. ITT had first initiated a rulemaking petition with the FCC and then filed a separate suit in the D.C. District Court before the case came before the Court of Appeals.

40. ITT World Communications, Inc. et al. v. FCC, 699 F.2d 1219 (D.C.Cir.1983).

ing on behalf of the agency, whether by implied delegation or official capacity;[41] that the background discussions did constitute "official agency business";[42] and that the presence of foreign authorities was not itself sufficient to overcome the Sunshine Act's presumption in favor of openness.[43] The D.C. Circuit's ruling that the FCC was bound by the Act represented not only a victory for ITT, but an expansive application and interpretation of the Act itself.

In a short opinion, Justice Powell and the Court reversed the D.C. CIRCUIT. According to the Court's rather pragmatic analysis, the consultative discussions were only background discussions "by which decisions already reached by the Commission could be implemented;"[44] while "integral ... [to the] policymaking process," they did not constitute "official agency business."[45] More importantly, the Court required an express delegation of authority to a "subdivision" in order for the latter to conduct agency business or a meeting susceptible to sunshine. Because the Telecommunications Committee's only delegated authority was to approve common carrier certifications, and since no such certifications were acted upon, there could not have been a "meeting" as defined by the Act.[46] Justice Powell noted that a more expansive view of the statute "would require public attendance at a host of informal conversations of the type Congress understood to be necessary for the effective conduct of agency business."[47]

§ 19.1.2 Exemptions to the Sunshine Act

While subsection (b) of the Sunshine Act—"every portion of every meeting of an agency shall be open to public observation"—prescribes openness,[48] subsection (c) provides ten exemptions to cover situations where the practical need for confidentiality outweighs the desire for openness. In recent years, agencies governed by the Act have relied on

41. Id. at 1241.

42. Id. at 1244.

43. Id. at 1244–45.

44. 466 U.S. at 470, 104 S.Ct. at 1941.

45. Id. at 470–73, 104 S.Ct. at 1941–42.

46. Id. at 473, 104 S.Ct. at 1942.

47. Id. For other cases dealing with the meaning of "meeting" in the Act, see Washington Association for Television and Children v. FCC, 665 F.2d 1264 (D.C.Cir.1981) (FCC's definition of "meeting" overly broad); Pacific Legal Foundation v. CEQ, 636 F.2d 1259 (D.C.Cir.1980) (agency could *not* limit open meeting requirement to those gatherings requiring a formal vote). The ABA's *amicus curiae* memorandum to the Supreme Court in the *ITT World* case noted that, "Under the [DC Circuit] court's decision, [agency] members may not meet with persons from outside the agency to discuss any matter within the official concern of the agency without complying with the provisions of the Sunshine Act. Such a result would have a pronounced (and deleterious) effect on the interaction between the agencies and the public ..." 466 U.S. at 473 n. 12, 104 S.Ct. at 1942, n. 12. For similar reasons, the D.C. Circuit has held that agency business conducted by means of notational voting (i.e., the circulation of written communications for review and approval/disapproval by each member) do not contravene the purposes of the Sunshine Act. Communications Systems, Inc. v. FCC, 595 F.2d 797 (D.C.Cir.1978).

48. See Philadelphia Newspapers, Inc. v. NRC, 727 F.2d 1195 (D.C.Cir.1984) (agency cannot close an entire meeting just because some of it will cover exempt information). But Railroad Commission of Texas v. United States, 765 F.2d 221 (D.C.Cir. 1985) (Sunshine Act does not require meeting be held to conduct agency business, only that if a meeting is held that it be open).

the exemptions to close roughly 40 percent of their meetings.[49] Agencies engaged in advisory and planning functions are more likely to conduct open meetings, whereas agency meetings dealing with financing and credit matters are rarely open to public observation.[50] Exemption (9) is the broadest exemption. It authorizes closing a meeting if premature disclosure would (a) induce speculation based on regulatory data concerning financial institutions or (b) "be likely to significantly frustrate implementation of a proposed agency action."[51] Exemption (10) pertains to subpoenas and adjudications,[52] and Exemption (4) deals with privileged trade secrets or commercial or financial information.[53] These Exemptions are cited most often to justify closure.[54] Cases alleging agency abuse of these exemptions in order to close a meeting are scarce.[55]

§ 19.1.3 Administrative Procedures Concerning Meetings

The Sunshine Act provides procedures aimed at ensuring the public maximum access to agency deliberations. A meeting can be closed pursuant to a subsection (c) exemption only upon the vote of a majority of the entire membership of the agency, taken well in advance of the

49. See Welborn, et al., Implementation and Effects of Sunshine, supra note 5 at 41–42.

50. Id. at 42–43.

51. 5 U.S.C.A. § 552b(c)(9)(A) and (B). See, e.g., Public Citizen v. National Economic Commission, 703 F.Supp. 113 (D.D.C.1989) (NEC failed to establish the applicability of Exemption 9(B) of the Sunshine Act that would permit its practice of closing entire meetings relating to budget options, deficit reduction, fiscal policy where they could have merely closed specific portions of meetings on a particularized basis). See also, O'Reilly and Berg, supra note 5.

52. Clark–Cowlitz Joint Operating Agency v. FERC, 788 F.2d 762 (D.C.Cir. 1986) (*en banc*) (protections of Exemption (10) do not end at conclusion of litigation).

53. 5 U.S.C.A. § 552b(c)(4).

54. Welborn, et al., Implementation and Effects of Sunshine, supra note 5, at 44.

55. See Philadelphia Newspapers, Inc. v. NRC, 727 F.2d 1195 (D.C.Cir.1984) (finding that exemption 10 was improperly invoked by the Nuclear Regulatory Commission to close a meeting on the Three Mile Island nuclear plant accident); Common Cause v. NRC, 674 F.2d 921 (D.C.Cir.1982) (strong public interest in predecisional process warrants opening of NRC budget meetings to public; Exemptions (2), (6), and (9)(b) did not justify closure); Time, Inc. v. U.S. Postal Service, 667 F.2d 329 (2d Cir. 1981) (Exemption (10) valid justification for closing U.S.P.S. Board of Governors' meeting concerning postal rate changes, because formal rulemaking necessitated "a determination on the record after opportunity for a hearing"); Wilkinson v. Legal Servs. Corp., 865 F.Supp. 891 (D.D.C.1994) (finding that Legal Services Cooperation did not justify its invocations of Exemptions 2, 9, and 10), rev'd in part on other grounds, 80 F.3d 535 (D.C.Cir.1996), cert. denied, 519 U.S. 927, 117 S.Ct. 295, 136 L.Ed.2d 214 (1996); Public Citizen v. National Economic Com., 703 F.Supp. 113 (D.D.C.1989) (finding invocation of Exemption 9 by the National Economic Commission unwarranted because although disclosure "may engender some speculation and may have some unknown and unquantifiable effect on various markets," the effect "must be balanced against the open society and unfettered public debate on important national issues upon which our democracy is founded," and "[t]he Commission's insistence on shielding the debate ... from public scrutiny ... chops the core of our democratic society"); A.G. Becker, Inc. v. Board of Governors of the Federal Reserve System, 502 F.Supp. 378 (D.D.C.1980) (despite inadequate notice, Exemptions (4), (8) and (10) properly relied upon to close meeting dealing with alleged illegal sale of commercial paper); See also BMY, Div. of HARSCO Corp. v. United States, 693 F.Supp. 1232, 1245 n. 9 (D.D.C.1988) (noting that Exemption 2 is not an exemption to APA publication requirements).

meeting in question. Moreover, upon voting to close a meeting, the agency must immediately publish in the *Federal Register* a record of the vote, a full written explanation of its decision to close the meeting, and a list of persons expected to attend the meeting and their affiliation.[56] In addition, counsel for the agency must publicly certify that, in his or her opinion, the meeting was properly closed pursuant to a relevant exemption.[57] Public notice of the meeting must be given (via publication in the *Federal Register*) at least one week in advance,[58] and must include the time and place of the meeting, its open or closed status, and an agency telephone number for further information.[59] A recorded transcript or detailed minutes must be kept of all meetings closed to the public, and copies of non-exempted portions of such transcripts must then be made available to the public.[60]

Federal district courts are empowered to enforce the requirements of the Sunshine Act "by declaratory judgment, injunctive relief, or other relief as may be appropriate."[61] "Any person" may allege a violation of the Act by an agency, so long as suit is brought prior to or within 60 days of the meeting at issue. The burden of proof is on the agency to justify its conduct. The court is authorized to examine *in camera* any transcript of the meeting, and invited to balance "orderly administration, . . . the public interest . . . [and] the interests of the parties"[62] in reaching its decision. The statute specifically envisions equitable relief, such as an order to release transcripts or an injunction against future closures.[63] Lacking other statutory sources of jurisdiction, however, the court cannot invalidate any substantive action taken or discussed by an agency found to have met in violation of the Act.[64] As with FOIA and the Privacy Act, it is in the court's discretion to award attorney fees to a party who "substantially prevails."[65]

In the few decisions that have been handed down, the courts have reinforced the Act's admonitory approach to enforcement. In *Pan Ameri-*

56. 5 U.S.C.A. § 552b(d)(1), (3). Note that subsection (d)(4) offers a somewhat streamlined procedure for an agency facing a series of exempt meetings.

57. Id. § 552b(f)(1).

58. See Coalition for Legal Services v. Legal Services Corp., 597 F.Supp. 198 (D.D.C.1984) (if agency business requires it, the one-week advance notice may be dispensed with in emergency situations).

59. 5 U.S.C.A. § 552b(e).

60. Id. § 552b(f)(1), (2). The agency is also required to keep such records for 2 years. Agencies have, by and large, complied with these procedures. See Welborn, et al., Implementation and Effects of Sunshine, supra note 5 at 37–41. See, e.g., A.G. Becker v. Board of Governors of the Federal Reserve System, 502 F.Supp. 378 (D.D.C. 1980) (inadequate notice); Northwest Airlines, Inc. v. EEOC, 24 FEP Cases 255 (D.D.C.1980) (failure to release transcript; utter disregard of meeting closing procedures); Pan American World Airways, Inc. v. CAB, 684 F.2d 31 (D.C.Cir.1982) (meeting improperly closed pursuant to foreign policy exemption).

61. 5 U.S.C.A. § 552b(h)(1).

62. Id.

63. Id.

64. "Nothing in this section authorizes any Federal court having jurisdiction solely on the basis [of this Act] to set aside, enjoin, or invalidate any agency action (other than an action to close a meeting or to withhold information under this section taken or discussed at any agency meeting out of which the violation of this section arose.)" Id. § 552b(h)(2).

65. Id. § 552b(i).

can World Airways, Inc. v. Civil Aeronautics Board,[66] for example, disgruntled airlines sought review of the CAB's decision to award the international air routes of bankrupt Braniff Airlines to American and Continental Airlines. Petitioners alleged, *inter alia,* that the CAB's decision was made without adequate notice at a hastily-called meeting which was improperly closed under the Sunshine Act's foreign policy exemption. With regard to the Sunshine Act claims, the D.C. Circuit found that the CAB's decision to close the meeting without explanation was "in patent violation of the law."[67] Because its jurisdiction over the case was not based solely on the Sunshine Act,[68] the court noted that it *did* have the authority to void the CAB's decision. After discussing subsection (h)(2) of the Act and its legislative history, however, the court concluded that though the agency's flagrant disregard for the Act had come "perilously close . . . to forcing us to set aside its action," an order to release the meeting's transcripts was a sufficient remedy.[69] Other cases confirm that release of transcripts[70] or judicial prohibition of future closings,[71] as opposed to invalidation of the offending agency's substantive action, are the prescribed and appropriate remedies for violations of the Sunshine Act.

§ 19.1.4 Relationship of Sunshine Act to Other Information Laws

The Sunshine Act does not expand or limit a person's rights under the FOIA.[72] Exemption 5 of the FOIA does, however, exempt predecisional memoranda.[73] The Sunshine Act does not, since it is meant to open up deliberations. Nothing in the Sunshine Act authorizes an agency to withhold materials otherwise accessible to an individual under the Privacy Act.[74] When an agency under the Sunshine Act meets with an advisory committee, it is not clear whether the Sunshine Act or the Federal Advisory Committee Act[75] applies. One commentator has concluded that both laws should apply.[76] Given the impact that private advisory groups might have on public policy, it is useful to examine this act in more detail.

The Federal Advisory Committee Act of 1972 (FACA)[77] was amended in 1976 to conform it to the requirements of the Sunshine Act for open

66. 684 F.2d 31 (D.C.Cir.1982).

67. Id. at 35.

68. Id. at 36, n. 10.

69. Id. at 36. The court's decision not to annul the CAB's decision also stemmed from its reluctance to "visit the sins of the CAB on the heads of American and Continental," and the reasonableness of the CAB's substantive decision. Id. at 37.

70. Braniff Master Executive Council of Air Line Pilots Ass'n v. CAB, 693 F.2d 220 (D.C.Cir.1982); Common Cause v. NRC, 674 F.2d 921 (D.C.Cir.1982).

71. Pacific Legal Foundation v. CEQ, 636 F.2d 1259 (D.C.Cir.1980); Common Cause v. NRC, 674 F.2d 921 (D.C.Cir.1982).

72. 5 U.S.C.A. § 552b(k).

73. Id. § 552b(5).

74. Id. § 552b(m).

75. Id. at Appendix I.

76. Marblestone, The Relationship Between the Government in the Sunshine Act and the Federal Advisory Committee Act, 362 Fed.B.J. 64 (1977).

77. Pub. L. No. 92–463, 86 Stat. 770 (1972).

meetings.[78] The Act is implemented by the General Services Administration (GSA).[79] Its primary concern is with the potential impact of private advisory committees on administrative agencies. These committees are made up of private citizens who are asked to provide agencies with advice and, in effect, to serve as sounding boards regarding particular issues or programs. Some committees are made up of scientific experts who might, for example, advise EPA on pesticide regulation. These committees are expected to be diverse and, indeed, many function in a political advisory way, depending upon the issues involved.[80] All such committees must be rechartered every two years, or simply be allowed to expire at that time.[81]

Under FACA, advisory committees must provide notice of their meetings and make them open to the public,[82] subject to the same exemptions that apply to the Sunshine Act.[83] These committees must keep minutes of their deliberations and these minutes must be accessible to the public.[84]

The FACA defines an "advisory committee" as "any committee, board, commission, council, Conference, panel, task force, or other similar group . . . which is (A) established by statute or reorganization plan, or (B) established or utilized by the President, or . . . (C) . . . by one or more agencies in the interest of obtaining advice or recommendations. . . . "[85] In *Public Citizen v. United States Dept. of Justice*[86] the Supreme Court held that FACA did not apply to an American Bar Association standing committee that provided advice to the Justice Department on potential judicial nominees, including presidential nominees to the Supreme Court. The Court construed FACA so as to avoid what the majority described as "formidable constitutional difficulties".[87] These would have arisen if the Court found that Congress had, through this legislation, attempted to control the processes by which the President secures advice concerning the exercise of his Article II appointment powers. The majority, thus, concluded that FACA was not intended to cover every situation in which the government consulted a private group.

78. Pub. L. No. 94–409, 90 Stat. 1240 (1976).

79. Exec. Order 12,024, 42 Fed. Reg. 61445 (1977).

80. 5 U.S.C. app. § 5(b)(2),(c).

81. Id. at § 14(a)(1).

82. Id. at § 10(a).

83. Id. at § 10(b).

84. Id. at § 10(b) and (c). See also Perrett and Wilkerson, Open Advisory Committees and the Political Process: The Federal Advisory Committee Act after two years, 63 Geo.L.J. 725 (1975).

85. 5 U.S.C. app. § 3(2).

86. 491 U.S. 440, 109 S.Ct. 2558, 105 L.Ed.2d 377 (1989).

87. 491 U.S. at 466. These constitutional difficulties rest specifically in a violation of the constitutional doctrine of separation of powers: "FACA cannot constitutionally be applied to the ABA Committee because to do so would violate the express separation of nomination and consent powers set forth in Article II of the Constitution and because no overriding congressional interest in applying FACA to the ABA Committee has been demonstrated; . . . the purposes of FACA are served through the public confirmation process and any need for applying FACA to the ABA Committee is outweighed by the President's interest in preserving confidentiality and freedom of consultation in selecting judicial nominees." Id. at 448 (citing the District Court opinion, 691 F.Supp. 483, 486 (D.D.C.1988)).

In this case, the committee in question was not the federal government's idea, nor did the government control or fund it.[88] Justice Kennedy, along with Justices Rehnquist and O'Connor, would have found the Act unconstitutional because, in their view, it did apply to the ABA and thus, sought to abridge the President's appointment powers.[89]

In *Association of American Physicians and Surgeons v. Clinton*[90] issues are also raised involving the scope of the FACA. Plaintiffs in this case challenged the confidential deliberations of President Clinton's Task Force on National Health Care Reform. They argued that FACA applied because one of its key participants was Hillary Rodham Clinton and she was not a federal employee. The Court, however, concluded that were they to submit private conversations between a President and his spouse, or convert a group of employees a spouse joined to an advisory committee subject to FACA, such a result could interfere with the President's constitutionally conferred executive powers. Once again the majority construed the FACA in such a way as to preclude this result.[91] One judge, in dissent, would have held the FACA unconstitutional as applied.[92]

§ 19.1.5 The Effects of Government in the Sunshine Act

Assessment of the impacts of sunshine on the Federal government is no easy task.[93] As some commentators have noted, "that the Sunshine Act has caused major changes in the internal decision-making processes of many agencies appears to be fairly certain. Its consequences for the substance, character and quality of agency decisions [are] less clear. One cannot know, obviously, the nature of the decisions that would have been made *sans* the act."[94] Nonetheless, some limited generalizations are possible.

While the Act has not resulted in widespread public participation in or attendance at agency meetings, it has been of benefit to the more particularistic "attentive publics" which have an interest in certain agencies'[95] actions. These groups—lobbyists, attorneys, journalists, public interest coalitions and representatives of the regulated industries—have used the Act's detailed notice procedures and open meetings to anticipate action on important issues and to understand the factors and personalities which shape decisions at a particular agency. In terms of successfully influencing agency decisions, "to the extent that there are winners, they appear to be those with the resources to closely follow

88. 491 U.S. at 443–44.

89. Id. at 468–69.

90. 997 F.2d 898 (D.C.Cir.1993).

91. 997 F.2d at 915–916.

92. Id. at 925. Judge Buckley noted: For an analysis of this Act, see Steven B. Croley and William F. Funk, The Federal Advisory Committee Act and Good Government, 14 Yale J. Reg. 452 (1997). For recent cases dealing with the scope of this Act, see Sofamor Danek Group, Inc. v. Gaus, 61 F.3d 929 (D.C.Cir.1995), cert. denied 516 U.S. 1112, 116 S.Ct. 910, 133 L.Ed.2d 841 (1996) (TBA); California Forestry Ass'n v. United States Forest Service, 102 F.3d 609 (D.C.Cir.1996).

93. See authorities in note 5, supra.

94. Welborn, et al., Implementation and Effects of the Federal Government in the Sunshine Act, supra note 5, at 71.

95. Id. at 54–55.

agency affairs. What they learn as a result of increased openness . . . is of real assistance in the advancement of their interests."[96]

Agency members' deliberations in public are likely to be more restrained and artificial when conducted in the spotlight of public scrutiny. Rather than appear uninformed at a meeting, an agency member might prefer to acquiesce on an issue, instead of demanding that the matter be explained and justified. Debate and critical analysis often may give way to posturing, politicking or silence. Respondents in an Administrative Conference study reported an increase in pre-meeting decisions, more reliance on staff-formulated position papers, and a greater willingness to dispose of matters via notation voting,[97] suggesting that frank discussion and constructive disagreement is less likely at open meetings. Indeed, the authors of the study point to the impairment of the collegial decisionmaking process as one of the most troublesome and counterproductive effects of the Act.[98]

The Sunshine Act has, however, shed more light on the agencies' executive actions, and there is little question that more information is now available to the public. But however one chooses to quantify such benefits, they must be weighed against the attendant costs. Besides its effects on the quality of collegial decisionmaking, the Act erects a series of procedural requirements which must be cleared prior to agency action.

It is, however, highly unlikely that Congress will significantly modify Act. If only symbolically, the Act has become a showpiece of administrative democracy and has acquired a charmed statutory life. As one Congressman noted during hearings on the legislation, "No one wants to be recorded [as] against 'Sunshine.' I understand that and recognize the political realities."[99]

96. Id. at 57.

97. Id. at 49–53, 82. The report suggests that "closed meetings are much more meaningful vehicles for decisionmaking than open ones . . . [at open meetings], some matters decided are not discussed, and when there is discussion it often appears to be for the record rather than for deliberative purposes." Id. at 63–67, 82–83.

98. Id. at 63–67, 82–83. For some proposed solutions to these problems, Sunshine Act Report, supra n. 5, 49 Admin. L.Rev. 421, 423 (1997), advocating "notation voting," thereby permitting more private meetings so long as detailed summaries of those meetings were provided and final votes were held in public.

99. Joint Comm. on Gov't Operations, Legis. Hist. of the Privacy Act of 1974: Source Book on Privacy, 94th Cong., 2d Sess. 819 (1976) (remarks of Rep. Moorhead).

Chapter 20

AGENCY ACQUISITION OF INFORMATION

Table of Sections

§ 20.1 INTRODUCTION

Effective and sensible federal regulation requires good information. For example, if only safe drugs are to be authorized, the FDA needs to know a great deal about new potential products. Similarly, if electricity rates are to be "just and reasonable," the Federal Energy Regulatory Commission must know a great deal about the cost of serving various classes of consumers as well as capital markets, rates of return, interest rates and the like. Good information is a necessary means to the successful accomplishment of regulatory ends.

Information, however, can also serve regulatory ends much more directly. Some agencies play an effective regulatory role simply by collecting relevant information and making that information accessible to the public. The Department of Transportation, for example, collects and disseminates information concerning the relative successes or failures of airline flight punctuality and baggage losses.[1] Similarly, other agencies such as the Department of Commerce or the Information Agency within the Department of Energy exist primarily to collect and disseminate data about certain industries.

Though information can be both a regulatory means and a regulatory end,[2] most information acquired by agencies is a means to other regulatory ends. Most of this information is provided voluntarily. Individuals or firms usually are willing to provide the information necessary in order to obtain a license or a government loan or to file a successful bank merger application to form or add to an existing bank holding company.

Conflict in this area, however, is inevitable. Sometimes, individuals or firms will assert statutory and constitutional rights in order to curb agency probing for additional information, particularly when they are trying to resist an agency's substantive regulatory attempts or simply reduce the regulatory costs imposed by the government's reporting requirements. When this occurs, agencies can and often do resort to one of three different approaches to obtain withheld information. They may obtain information by subpoenaing witnesses or documents; by invoking statutory authority requiring that records be regularly kept and reports routinely provided; or by engaging in physical, on-cite inspections to obtain the needed information. Each of these information-gathering techniques raises a number of legal issues, some statutory and some constitutional.

The power of administrative agencies to investigate and otherwise compel the disclosure of information from private individuals and firms is provided by statute.[3] These statutory grants of power are generally

§ 20.1

1. 14 C.F.R. §§ 234.1–234.12 (2000). For a discussion of the disclosure of information mandated by statutes and the role these statutes play as regulatory tools, see Cass Sunstein, Informational Regulation and Informational Standing: Akins and Beyond, 147 U.Pa.L.Rev. 613 (1999).

2. See, e.g., Shapiro v. United States, 335 U.S. 1, 8, 68 S.Ct. 1375, 1380, 92 L.Ed. 1787 (1948) ("The very language of § 202(a) [of the Emergency Price Control Act] discloses that the record-keeping and inspection requirements were designed not merely to 'obtain information for assistance in prescribing regulations or orders under the statute,' but also to aid 'in the administration and *enforcement* of this Act . . .' " (footnote omitted) (emphasis is in original)).

3. See, e.g., § 211(a) Fair Labor Standards Act (1938) which states that "[t]he Administrator or his designated representatives may investigate and gather data regarding the wages, hours, and other condi-

very broad, placing only the most limited kinds of restrictions on agency activities.[4] We shall examine this statutory authority first in the context of subpoenas and required reports, then in the context of physical inspections.

§ 20.2 ADMINISTRATIVE POWER TO OBTAIN INFORMATION THROUGH SUBPOENAS AND REQUIRED REPORTS—THE BASIC DOCTRINE

Agencies obtain information by issuance of administrative subpoenas, compelling parties to make documents and witnesses available, and by forcing disclosure of information through required reporting. Initially, courts were reluctant to give subpoena powers to agencies, citing the privacy interests of the parties and fourth amendment protections against unreasonable search and seizure. The onset of World War II, government regulation of war time production, and the eventual acceptance of an expanded federal regulatory role, gradually began to change the courts' perspective on these issues. Beginning in the 1940s, courts began to expand agencies' ability to gain access to information. Recognizing that the agencies' role was overseeing and enforcing compliance with congressional acts, not simply sanctioning violations, courts developed looser fourth amendment restrictions on administrative attempts to acquire information. This was a new legal direction for the courts and required modifying a number of earlier cases.

One of the earliest of these cases was *Kilbourn v. Thompson,*[1] which reflected judicial reservations about compelling disclosure of information. It involved an attempt by Congress to hold a non-cooperating witness in contempt. The Court, however, asserted its exclusive jurisdiction to determine whether a witness might be punished in this way. The Court

tions and practices of employment in any industry subject to this [Act] and may ... investigate such facts, conditions, practices, or matters as he may deem necessary or appropriate to determine whether any person has violated any provision of this [Act], or which may aid in the enforcement of the provisions of this [Act]." 29 U.S.C.A. § 211(a); see also Federal Trade Commission Act § 5, 15 U.S.C.A. § 45(a)(2) which empowers the Commission "to prevent persons, partnerships or corporations ... from using unfair methods of competition ... and unfair or deceptive acts or practices in or affecting commerce."

4. The Federal Trade Commission Act § 6, 15 U.S.C.A. § 46(a), is typical in its grant of power. This statute provides that the FTC has the power "To gather and compile information concerning, and to investigate from time to time the organization, business, conduct, practices, and management of any person, partnership, or corporation engaged in or whose business affects commerce, excepting banks, savings and loan institutions ... , federal credit unions.... , and common carriers subject to the Act to regulate commerce, and its relation to other persons, partnerships, and corporations." The power of the agencies to initiate investigations is also governed by statute and agency enacted regulations. For example, 16 C.F.R. § 2.1 (1989), which lays out the Rules of Practice for the Federal Trade Commission, provides that "Commission investigations and inquiries may be originated upon the request of the President, Congress, governmental agencies, or the Attorney General; upon referral by the courts; upon complaint by members of the public; or by the Commission upon its own initiative."

§ 20.2

1. 103 U.S. (13 Otto) 168, 26 L.Ed. 377 (1880).

held that "neither [House] possesses the general power of making inquiry into the private affairs of the citizen."[2] Justice Holmes took a similarly narrow view regarding the use of governmental power to coerce the disclosure of information. In *Harriman v. ICC,*[3] Holmes, in the majority opinion, held that the Interstate Commerce Commission's subpoena power only extended to investigations upon a complaint of specific violations. The I.C.C. did not have the power to compel witnesses to testify for the purpose of acquiring information to aid in the recommendation of legislation. "[T]he power to require testimony is limited, . . . to . . . cases where the sacrifice of privacy is necessary—those where the investigations concern a specific breach of the law."[4]

Justice Holmes also took a narrow approach to the interpretation of the subpoena powers of the Federal Trade Commission in 1924 in *FTC v. American Tobacco Co.*[5] In 1921, the Federal Trade Commission attempted to conduct an investigation into the domestic and export trade practices of two tobacco companies. Pursuant to a Senate resolution authorizing this investigation, the Commission issued subpoenas requesting all correspondence between the companies and its jobbers.[6] Holmes refused to enforce the subpoena because the agency made no showing that there was probable cause to believe that the Anti–Trust Act had, in fact, been violated. Nor did Holmes find any support for broad subpoena powers in the Senate resolution authorizing the investigation in the first place. He dismissed the possibility that Congress would have authorized a "fishing expedition" into the private affairs of citizens in the hopes of evincing evidence of a crime:[7]

2. Id. at 190.

3. 211 U.S. 407, 29 S.Ct. 115, 53 L.Ed. 253 (1908).

4. Id. at 419–20, 29 S.Ct. at 118–19 (1908). The decision in this case turned primarily on Holmes' reading of the I.C.C. empowering statutes, particularly Act of Feb. 4, 1887, ch. 104, 24 Stat. 379, 49 U.S.C.A. §§ 12, 13, 21 (recodified as 49 U.S.C.A. §§ 10311, 10321, 10326, 10505, 11501, 11502, 11701, 11703). He found Congress did not delegate the authority to subpoena witnesses for purposes other than investigations of breaches of law. Whether Congress itself has the authority to delegate a general subpoena power is not answered by the Court. Holmes, however, hints that such broad powers would violate citizens' privacy rights, due process and, consequently, perhaps even Congress itself does not have such authority.

In a dissenting opinion, Justice Day, joined by Justices Harlan and McKenna, first suggests that the purposes of administrative agencies are not only to investigate specific breaches of the law but also to investigate the manner in which interstate commerce business is conducted and managed. The dissent recognized that agencies needed the power to "prevent bad practices" and to afford them that power, the authorizing statutes must be interpreted broadly. Id. at 426, 29 S.Ct. at 121.

5. 264 U.S. 298, 44 S.Ct. 336, 68 L.Ed. 696 (1924).

6. The F.T.C. claimed authority to gather the requested information by virtue of § 6(a) of the Act of Sept. 26, 1914, ch. 311, 38 Stat. 717, 722, (codified as amended at 15 U.S.C.A. § 46) which provides that the Commission shall have power "to gather information concerning, and to investigate the business, conduct, practices and management of any corporation engaged in commerce . . . and its relation to other corporations and individuals." Id. at 304, 44 S.Ct. at 336 (quoted language is the Court's paraphrase of § 6(c)).

7. Id. at 306, 44 S.Ct. at 336–37. Again, as in *Harriman,* Holmes does not address the question of whether Congress could authorize such a "fishing expedition," but he does hint that such broad powers would violate the fourth amendment. Id. at 307, 44 S.Ct. at 338.

[T]he Commission claims an unlimited right of access to the respondents' papers with reference to the possible existence of practices in violation of [the F.T.C. Act]....

The mere facts of carrying on a commerce not confined within state lines and of being organized as a corporation do not make men's affairs public, as those of a railroad company now may be. Anyone who respects the spirit as well as the letter of the Fourth Amendment would be loath to believe that Congress intended to authorize one of its subordinate agencies to sweep all our traditions into the fire and to direct fishing expeditions into private papers on the possibility that they may disclose evidence of crime. We do not discuss the question whether it could do so if it tried, as nothing short of the most explicit language would induce us to attribute to Congress that intent....

The right of access given by the statute is to documentary evidence—not to all documents, but to such documents as are evidence. The analogies of the law do not allow the party wanting evidence to call for all documents in order to see if they do not contain it. Some ground must be shown for supposing that the documents called for do contain it.... Some evidence of the materiality of the papers demanded must be produced.[8]

Despite Holmes' warning against "fishing expeditions," the Court eventually began to loosen its grip on the agencies and their ability to gain access to information. In *Endicott Johnson Corp. v. Perkins*,[9] the Court upheld a subpoena issued in an enforcement proceeding, by the Secretary of Labor under the Walsh–Healy Public Contracts Act. The Court concluded that under the Act the Secretary was to make the final determination regarding who was covered by the statute. Coverage was no longer an issue to be decided by the courts in an enforcement action.[10] Additionally, the measure determining the validity of the information requested was relaxed. Justice Holmes' strict probable cause standard enunciated in *American Tobacco* gave way as the *Endicott Johnson* court declared that:

8. Id. at 305–06, 44 S.Ct. at 337 (citations omitted).

9. 317 U.S. 501, 63 S.Ct. 339, 87 L.Ed. 424 (1943). Under § 4 Walsh–Healy Public Contracts Act, 41 U.S.C.A. §§ 35–45, the Secretary of Labor was directed to administer the provisions of the Act and empowered to "make investigations and finding ... and prosecute any inquiry necessary to his functions." The subpoenas at issue requested payroll information relating to plants that were not included in the original contract agreements between Endicott Johnson and the government but which were allegedly manufacturing parts that were used in the production of the final goods for which the government contracted. Petitioner argued that those plants did not fall under the coverage of the Act and, therefore, the Secretary had no authority to investigate those plants.

10. "The matter which the Secretary was investigating and was authorized to investigate was an alleged violation of the Act and these contracts. Her scope would include determining what employees these contracts and the Act covered." Id. at 508, 63 S.Ct. at 343. The Court recognized that if the judiciary passed on the issue of coverage of the Act, the Secretary of Labor would be forced to determine who fell under the coverage of the Act before beginning the investigation. This, they felt, would be of "dubious propriety" and of "doubtful practicality." Id.

The evidence sought by the subpoena was not plainly incompetent or irrelevant to any lawful purpose of the Secretary in the discharge of her duties under the Act, and it was the duty of the District Court to order its production for the Secretary's consideration.[11]

Congress' authority to delegate such expansive investigative and information gathering powers to the agencies was affirmed by the express holding that the statute is "clearly within the limits of Congressional authority."[12] Because the opinion only addressed the authority of the Secretary of Labor under the Walsh–Healy Public Contracts Act, the Court limited its holding to those businesses covered by that Act.[13] This limitation was short-lived.

The Court in *Oklahoma Press Publishing Co. v. Walling*[14] not only extended the *Endicott Johnson* holding to investigations under the Fair Labor Standards Act, but it also set the modern standard for determining fourth amendment limitations on administrative subpoenas. The case involved a subpoena issued in an investigation by the Wage and Hour Administrator under the Fair Labor Standards Act.[15] The petitioner in that case resisted the agency's request for information on first, fourth and fifth amendment grounds. It also argued that the issue of coverage had to be determined before enforcement;[16] otherwise, enforc-

11. Id. at 509, 63 S.Ct. at 343.

12. Id. at 510, 63 S.Ct. at 344. In expanding the power of the agency to obtain the information it needed to proceed with its investigation, the *Endicott Johnson* Court acknowledged Congress' intention to have this agency play an active role in changing labor standards by noting that the purpose of the act "is to use the leverage of the Government's immense purchasing power to raise labor standards." Id. at 507, 63 S.Ct. at 342.

13. "[The Act] applies only to contractors who voluntarily enter into competition to obtain government business on terms of which they are fairly forewarned." Id. at 507, 63 S.Ct. at 342.

14. 327 U.S. 186, 66 S.Ct. 494, 90 L.Ed. 614 (1946). The Supreme Court reaffirmed the holding of this case in Donovan v. Lone Steer, Inc., 464 U.S. 408, 104 S.Ct. 769, 78 L.Ed.2d 567 (1984).

15. Section 11(a) of Fair Labor Standards Act (current version at 29 U.S.C.A. § 211(a)) states in part that "[t]he Administrator or his designated representatives may investigate and gather data regarding the wages, hours, and other conditions and practices of employment in any industry subject to this Act, and may . . . investigate such facts, conditions, practices, or matters as he may deem necessary or appropriate to determine whether any person has violated any provision of this Act, or which may aid in the enforcement of the provisions of this Act." Section 9 of the FLSA (which incorporates § 9 of the Federal Trade Commission Act) authorizes the Commission "to require by subpoena the attendance and testimony of witnesses and the production of all such documentary evidence relating to any matter under investigation." 29 U.S.C.A. § 209 (incorporating 15 U.S.C.A. § 49).

The subpoenas in question sought the production of specified records to determine whether petitioners were violating the Fair Labor Standards Act, including records relating to coverage of the Act.

16. The arguments put forth by petitioner based on the first amendment were easily dismissed by the Court, 327 U.S. at 192–94, 66 S.Ct. at 496–98. Because petitioner was a corporation, the fifth amendment protection against self-incrimination was held not available to it. For discussion on the fifth amendment in administrative subpoena cases, see sec. 20.3.2 infra. Finally, the Court relied on its holding in *Endicott Johnson Corp. v. Perkins* to find that the issue of coverage was to be determined by the Administrator of the Fair Labor Standards Act, not by the courts. The opinion discussed the relative weights to be given "the interests of men to be free from officious intermeddling", the expense and inefficiencies of examinations and the public interest in affording the Administrator the power to discharge his duties of enforcement and investigation, concluding that the

ing the subpoena might result in a "fishing expedition" violative of the fourth amendment. The Court held that literal application of the fourth amendment is not appropriate for subpoenas because no actual search and seizure took place.[17] Furthermore, in interpreting the authorizing statutes and legislative histories of the Act, the Court found that the very purpose of the subpoena and investigatory power granted to the agency was to discover and procure evidence of any possible violations, not merely to prove a pending charge or complaint.[18] These so called "fishing expeditions" were constitutional and, in fact, a necessary extension of Congress' power to create laws.[19]

The Court also examined certain fourth amendment protections against "constructive searches," to which the subpoenas were analogized. First, the Court addressed the limited privacy interests historically attributed to corporations.[20] In light of this restricted protection, the Court found that

> [T]he Fourth, if applicable, at the most guards against abuse only by way of too much indefiniteness or breadth in the things required to be "particularly described," if also the inquiry is one the demanding agency is authorized by law to make and the materials specified are relevant. The gist of the protection is in the requirement, expressed in terms, that the disclosure sought shall not be unreasonable.[21]

Unlike the issuance of a warrant for an actual search, to which the fourth amendment probable cause standard literally applies, a subpoena may be issued without a specific charge or complaint of violation of the law. Probable cause would be satisfied for enforcement of a subpoena if the court finds "that the investigation is authorized by Congress, is for a

Administrator should retain exclusive power over the issue of coverage in preliminary investigations. Id. at 211–14, 66 S.Ct. at 506–08.

17. "The short answer to the Fourth Amendment objections is that the records in these cases present no question of actual search and seizure, but raise only the question whether orders of court for the production of specified records have been validly made.... No officer or other person has sought to enter petitioners' premises against their will, to search them, or to seize or examine their books, records or papers without their assent ..." Id. at 195, 66 S.Ct. at 498.

18. The Court analogized the function of an administrative agency investigation to that of a grand jury. No probable cause standard will be imposed on the agency in its duty to determine if there has been a violation nor must it limit its inquiry to forecasts of the probable result of the investigation. However, the agency may "not act arbitrarily or in excess of [its] statutory authority." Id. at 216, 66 S.Ct. at 509.

19. In making this finding, the Court acknowledged Justice Holmes' contrary position taken in *American Tobacco.* In taking issue with the result that Holmes advocated, the Court stated that "if the [*American Tobacco* rationale] is followed here, the [lower court judgments upholding the subpoenas] must be reversed with the effect of cutting squarely into the power of Congress. For to deny the validity of the orders would be in effect to deny not only Congress' power to enact the provisions sustaining them, but also its authority to delegate effective power to investigate violations of its own laws, if not perhaps also its own power to make such investigations." Id. at 201, 66 S.Ct. at 502.

20. Id. at 202–08, 66 S.Ct. at 502–05. Courts recognize only a limited privacy right in corporations because they are entities created wholly by the state. Therefor the state is entitled to greater access to the corporation and knowledge of their conduct. Privacy rights of the corporation are addressed more thoroughly in later sections.

21. Id. at 208, 66 S.Ct. at 505.

purpose Congress can order, and the documents sought are relevant to the inquiry. Beyond this the requirement of reasonableness ... comes down to specification of the documents to be produced."[22]

The Court took the same approach when an agency demanded information from a company that was legally required to compile it. In *United States v. Morton Salt Co.*,[23] the Federal Trade Commission had ordered certain corporations to cease and desist from particular trade practices. Part of this order required that these companies file compliance reports with the Commission within ninety days. Subsequently, the Commission ordered respondents to file special reports to show continuing compliance with the decree. The companies objected.

In upholding the order for filing these special reports, the Court provided an extremely broad interpretation of the role of agencies in a law enforcement scheme and their inherent powers in fulfilling this role. Responding to petitioners' argument that the compliance reports were mere "fishing expeditions," the Court pointed out the difference between the role of the judiciary and the agencies in law enforcement proceedings and the mistaken confusion of the two in past cases. The Article III "case and controversy" limitation precluded the Court from conducting investigations before charges had been made. But, the Court reasoned, Congress had given agencies the authority to investigate and enforce its acts. This authority is not derived from judicial power and should not be so limited. The Court thus found that this power of "inquisition" granted to the agencies permitted them to "investigate merely on suspicion that the law is being violated, or even just because it wants assurance that it is not."[24]

Furthermore, the reporting requirement was found in no way to violate the fourth amendment proscription against unreasonable searches and seizures.[25] The Court determined that any privacy right

22. Id. at 209, 66 S.Ct. at 505. As to the relevancy and breadth portions of the test, the Court said that a workable formula could not be formulated as "adequacy or excess in the breadth of the subpoena are matters variable in relation to the nature, purposes and scope of the inquiry." Id. (footnote omitted).

23. 338 U.S. 632, 70 S.Ct. 357, 94 L.Ed. 401 (1950).

24. "Federal judicial power itself extends only to adjudication of cases and controversies and it is natural that its investigative powers should be jealously confined to these ends...."

We must not disguise the fact that sometimes, especially early in the history of the federal administrative tribunal, the courts were persuaded to engraft judicial limitations upon the administrative process. The courts could not go fishing and so it followed neither could anyone else. Administrative investigation fell before the colorful and nostalgic slogan "no fishing expeditions." ...

"The only power that is involved here is the power to get information from those who best can give it and who are most interested in not doing so.... [Agencies have] a power of inquisition ... which is not derived from the judicial functions. It is more analogous to the Grand Jury, which does not depend on a case or controversy for power to get evidence but can investigate merely on suspicion that the law is being violated, or even just because it wants assurance that it is not. When investigative and accusatory duties are delegated by statute to an administrative body, it, too, may take steps to inform itself as to whether there is probable violation of the law." Id. at 641–43, 70 S.Ct. at 362–65.

25. The Court had no difficulty in finding authority granted from Congress for the agencies to require special reports from reg-

protected by the fourth amendment had limited application to respondents. Corporations are artificial entities created by the state and thus are subject to greater scrutiny from the state for compliance with the laws under which they were created.

While they may and should have protection from unlawful demands made in the name of public investigation, corporations can claim no equality with individuals in the enjoyment of a right to privacy. They are endowed with public attributes. They have a collective impact upon society, from which they derive the privilege of acting as artificial entities. The Federal Government allows them the privilege of engaging in interstate commerce. Favors from government often carry with them an enhanced measure of regulation. Even if one were to regard the request for information in this case as caused by nothing more than official curiosity, nevertheless law-enforcing agencies have a legitimate right to satisfy themselves that corporate behavior is consistent with the law and the public interest.[26]

In short, the Court found that the Commission had stayed within the investigatory bounds of reasonableness both under the fourth amendment and under the F.T.C.'s own enabling act. The required reports fully satisfied all the elements of the test espoused in *Oklahoma Press*. The case thus authorized agency access to an extremely important source of information—statutorily required records and reports.

§ 20.3 RESTRICTIONS ON AGENCY ACCESS TO INFORMATION

Quite apart from the breadth of the Court's rationales for allowing agency access to information held by corporations—either by subpoena or required reports—there are also statutory and constitutional limitations. The Administrative Procedure Act requires that before a court can enforce an administrative subpoena or reporting requirement obtained "in accordance with law,"[1] it must take into account the protections of the fourth amendment and the established privileges to withhold evidence protected by the fifth amendment, and it may not exceed any specific legislative restriction or exception.

§ 20.3.1 The Fourth Amendment

The fourth amendment protects the "right of the people to be secure in their persons, houses, papers, and effects, against unreasonable searches and seizures." It further provides that "no Warrants shall issue, but upon probable cause, supported by Oath or affirmation, and particularly describing the place to be searched, and the persons or

ulated parties. The authority rests in § 6 of the Federal Trade Commission Act, 15 U.S.C.A. § 46(b), which grants power to the F.T.C. to require reports.

26. United States v. Morton Salt Co., 338 U.S. 632, 652, 70 S.Ct. 357, 368, 94 L.Ed. 401 (1950) (citations omitted).

§ 20.3

1. 5 U.S.C.A. § 555(d).

things to be seized."[2] The fourth amendment provides little or no protection to corporations seeking to resist disclosure pursuant to a subpoena duces tecum or a statutorily required reporting provision. As noted in *Morton Salt,*[3] courts recognize only a minimal privacy expectation in corporations. That they are artificial entities created by legislative fiat allows the government to scrutinize corporate behavior more closely for compliance with the laws of its creation.

In *California Bankers Association v. Shultz,*[4] the Court held that corporations have only a limited claim to privacy when it comes to agencies investigating their conduct. The case involved the Bank Secrecy Act of 1970 which prescribes certain bank recordkeeping requirements. These included keeping files of customer identities, making microfilm copies of checks and similar instruments, and keeping certain records of transactions involving sums over a given amount. The plaintiffs, which included several individual customers, the Security National Bank and the Bankers Association, based their challenge to these recordkeeping requirements on fourth amendment grounds. They claimed that a regulation which forces the bank to make and keep certain records is, in effect, an act of seizure of its own and its customers' private records. The Court dismissed the challenge on the behalf of the bank, finding that the bank's privacy interest in their records was limited. What limited right it had was not violated because the reporting requirements involved were not unreasonable.[5] The asserted customers' claim of a right to privacy in the records held by the bank similarly failed. The Court concluded that issuing a summons to a third party, the bank in this instance, was not a violation of the customers' privacy: "[I]t is difficult to see how the summoning of a third party, and the records of a third party, can violate the rights of [another]."[6] The Court followed the same reasoning in *United States v. Miller.*[7] It ruled that a client of a bank had no fourth amendment interest in the bank's records. Reversing a court of appeals decision, the Supreme Court held that the records that were subpoenaed did not fall into a constitutionally protected zone of privacy because they were the business records of the bank. As such, these records were about transactions to which the bank was a party; they were not the respondent's private records. In addition, the client had no protectable privacy interest in the records. The Court reasoned that although there had been

2. U.S. Const. amend. 4.

3. United States v. Morton Salt Co., 338 U.S. 632, 70 S.Ct. 357, 94 L.Ed. 401 (1950).

4. 416 U.S. 21, 94 S.Ct. 1494, 39 L.Ed.2d 812 (1974).

5. The regulations for the reporting by financial institutions of domestic financial transactions are reasonable and abridge no Fourth Amendment rights of such institutions because "neither incorporated nor unincorporated associations [have] an unqualified right to conduct their affairs in secret." Id. at 65, 94 S.Ct. at 1519 (citing *Morton Salt,* supra note 33). The Court went on to quote the test espoused in *Oklahoma Press* in determining the reasonableness of the reporting requirement. Id. at 67, 94 S.Ct. at 1520.

6. California Bankers Ass'n v. Shultz, 416 U.S. 21, 53, 94 S.Ct. 1494, 1513, 39 L.Ed.2d 812 (1974), (quoting Douglas, J., concurring, Donaldson v. United States, 400 U.S. 517, 537, 91 S.Ct. 534, 546, 27 L.Ed.2d 580 (1971)).

7. 425 U.S. 435, 96 S.Ct. 1619, 48 L.Ed.2d 71 (1976).

language in a prior case to the effect that "a 'search and seizure' become unreasonable when the Government's activities violate 'the privacy upon which [a person] justifiably relie[s],' " that same case also emphasized that "[w]hat a person knowingly exposes to the public ... is not a subject of fourth amendment protection."[8] Because "[a]ll of the documents attained, including financial statements and deposit slips, contain[ed] only information voluntarily conveyed to the banks and exposed to their employees in the ordinary course of business," the Court concluded that there was "no legitimate 'expectation of privacy' in their contents."[9]

The impact of this holding can be better understood when one considers how much information is "voluntarily" turned over to others, and the capacity of the government to store this information. Faced with increasing difficulty in enforcing internal revenue laws, the Internal Revenue Service (IRS) has begun using "state-of-the-art" computer technology in order to track down non-complying citizens.[10] "With more than twenty-five percent of its budget and manpower dedicated to computer operations, the IRS is one of the largest non-defense users of computers in the federal government. The Service presently has in force over forty mainframe computers at ten IRS service centers and the National Computer Center."[11]

In addition to access to information that government agencies collect, the IRS has access to thousands of private data banks, such as those belonging to banks, credit reporting agencies and commercial mailing list companies.[12] As noted above,[13] the Court essentially eliminated an individual's constitutional right to privacy in personal banking records. The facts in *United States v. Miller*[14] are, however, arguably distinguishable from the circumstances surrounding an IRS computer search. *Miller* involved a search of a customer's checks voluntarily placed into the public stream of commerce, whereas an IRS computer search of taxpayer information retained by government agencies involves a search of information obtained by the government through compulsion.[15] Quite apart from this distinction, the Court's opinion in *Whalen v. Roe*[16] recognizes the possible validity of a constitutionally based privacy claim

8. Id. at 442, 96 S.Ct. at 1623 (quoting, in part, from Katz v. United States, 389 U.S. 347, 353, 88 S.Ct. 507, 512, 19 L.Ed.2d 576 (1967)).

9. Id. at 442, 96 S.Ct. at 1623.

10. See, e.g., Comment, IRS Computer Data Bank Searches: An Infringement of the Fourth Amendment Search and Seizure Clause, 25 Santa Clara L.Rev. 153 (1985).

11. Id. at 155. "In order to implement its ambitious plan to track down noncompliers by computer, the Internal Revenue Service expects to spend nearly two billion dollars over the next six to eight years on state-of-the-art computer technology. With the combination of massive computer systems and access to thousands of data banks from which to draw personal information on millions of individuals, the IRS will have the capacity to conduct thorough computer searches of most citizens." Id. at 157, 158. The IRS has access to interagency data banks for the purpose of enforcing criminal laws.

12. Id. at 160.

13. See United States v. Miller, supra note 37.

14. Id.

15. Comment, supra note 40, at 174.

16. 429 U.S. 589, 97 S.Ct. 869, 51 L.Ed.2d 64 (1977).

when computerized data banks are involved. That case involved a constitutional challenge to a New York statute that authorized the state to record, in a centralized computer file, the names and addresses of all persons who were prescribed drugs by their physicians. The Court did not uphold the privacy based challenge to the statute; however, it did recognize that in some instances such a challenge might be successful.[17]

In a pair of cases dealing with drug testing, the Supreme Court upheld the constitutionality of drug testing of federal employees. In *National Treasury Employees Union v. Von Raab*,[18] the Court upheld federal regulations requiring a drug test as a condition to being appointed or promoted to jobs involving drug surveillance and interdiction.[19] In *Skinner v. Railway Labor Executives Association*,[20] the Court upheld regulations promulgated by the Federal Railroad Administration requiring railroads to test employees for drugs who might be involved in certain kinds of accidents.[21] In both cases, the regulations involved did not require probable cause. The Court balanced the privacy interests of the individuals involved with the interests of the government, concluding the government's interests were far more significant. In general, fourth amendment protections appear to be less rigorously applied in the course of administrative investigations than they are in the investigations of crimes. Put another way, the government has more power to obtain information to carry out its statutory duties than when it investigates an individual suspected of a crime. Of course, if information obtained by the government for regulatory purposes is then used for criminal purposes, constitutional problems may be involved.

Computer matching, "the exchange and searches of computer files to conduct investigations,"[22] also raises concerns about reasonable searches.[23] Even though computer matching has not been constitutional-

17. "We are not unaware of the threat to privacy implicit in the accumulation of vast amounts of personal information in computerized data banks or other massive government files. The collection of taxes, the distribution of welfare and social security benefits, the supervision of public health, the direction of our Armed Force, and the enforcement of the criminal laws require the orderly preservation of great quantities of information, much of which is personal in character and potentially embarrassing or harmful if disclosed.... Recognizing that in some circumstances that duty arguably has its roots in the Constitution, nevertheless New York's statutory scheme, and its implementing administrative procedures, evidence a proper concern with, and protection of, the individual's interest in privacy. We therefore need not, and do not, decide any question which might be presented by the unwarranted disclosure of accumulated private data—whether intentional or unintentional—or by a system that did not contain comparable security provisions. We simply hold that this record does not establish an invasion of any right or liberty protected by the Fourth Amendment." Id. at 605, 606, 97 S.Ct. at 879, 880 (footnotes omitted).

18. 489 U.S. 656, 109 S.Ct. 1384, 103 L.Ed.2d 685 (1989).

19. Id.

20. 489 U.S. 602, 109 S.Ct. 1402, 103 L.Ed.2d 639 (1989).

21. Id.

22. Sally E. Renskers, Comment, Trial by Certainty: Implications of Genetic "DNA Fingerprints," 39 Emory L.J. 309, 343 (1990).

23. See, e.g., Steven A. Bercu, Toward Universal Surveillance in an Information Age Economy: Can We Handle Treasury's New Police Technology?, 34 Jurim. J. 383 (1994) (citing concerns about Department of Treasury investigative computer technology); Matthew N. Kleiman, Comment, The

ly challenged,[24] it did play a key role in Jaffess v. Secretary, Dep't of Health, Education & Welfare.[25] In Jaffess, the plaintiff's veteran disability benefits were reduced after a computer matching program revealed that he was also receiving unreported social security benefits in violation of the law. The plaintiff sued for damages under the recently-passed Privacy Act; however, the district court ruled that the Act was inapplicable because it had not taken effective at the time the plaintiff filed his suit.[26] The court held that the computer matching of the plaintiff's veteran disability benefit records with his social security benefit records was lawful because Congress required the Department of Veterans Affairs to factor social security benefits into a grant of veteran disability benefits.[27] The court noted that the constitutional right of privacy did not include "the right of an individual to prevent disclosure by one governmental agency to another of matters obtained in the course of the transmitting agency's regular functions."[28]

On the other hand, the court acknowledged the concerns created by the power of technology to facilitate "interagency transfer of information within the federal government."[29] Moreover, the court did not suggest that

> a constitutional right of privacy might not be found to exist and appropriate relief granted in instances where the government is possessed of highly personal and confidential information which has been given under compulsion of law and with an expectation of privacy and where the disclosure of such information is unnecessary for the advancement or inconsistent with the fundamental purposes for which the data was obtained.[30]

Following Jaffess, then, agency computer matching violates the constitutional right to privacy when 1) the government obtains "highly personal and confidential information" 2) "under compulsion of law" 3) "with an expectation of privacy" and 4) disclosure is unnecessary for or inconsistent with the "fundamental purposes for which the data was obtained."

Commentators have argued that computer matching violates the Fourth Amendment protection against unreasonable searches because

Right to Financial Privacy Versus Computerized Law Enforcement: A New Fight in an Old Battle, 86 N.W.U. L.R. 1169 (1992) (same).

24. Cf. Samuel V. Schoonmaker, IV, Consequences and Validity of Family Law Provisions in the "Welfare Reform Act," 14 J. Am. Acad. Matrimonial Law. 3, 57 (1997) ("If a constitutional right to information privacy exists, it is contained in the First, Fourth, Fifth and Fourteenth Amendments to the Constitution of the United States.").

25. 393 F.Supp. 626 (S.D.N.Y.1975).

26. Id. at 628–29.

27. Id. at 629.

28. Id. (citations omitted).

29. Id. at 629–30.

30. Id. at 630. But see Whalen v. Roe, 429 U.S. 589, 605–6, 97 S.Ct. 869, 51 L.Ed.2d 64 (1977) ("We are not aware of the threat to privacy implicit in the accumulation of vast amounts of personal information in computerized databanks [and] therefore need not, and do not, decide any question which might be presented by the unwarranted disclosure of accumulated private data whether intentional or unintentional or by a system that did not contain comparable security provisions.").

computer matching requires no individualized suspicion.[31] Also, computer matching places the burden upon the suspect to prove that the computer records are inaccurate.[32] Computer matching may also violate Fifth Amendment due process by not providing notice to those whose records are affected,[33] or by depriving one of a property interest in one's personal information for public use without just compensation.[34] Additionally, some find computer matching objectionable because it places control over one's personal information in the hands of the State.[35] It is also possible that computer matching could chill free speech by coercing people to "modify their speech to meet social and legal standards."[36] Finally, it is suggested that computer matching violates the "compatibility principle," i.e., "that information collected for one purpose should not be transferred to another agency for other purposes."[37]

§ 20.3.2 The Fifth Amendment—Privileges to Withhold Requested Information

The fifth amendment protects a person from being "compelled in any criminal case to be a witness against himself."[38] Despite the language specifically providing the protection in criminal situations, the fifth amendment has long been recognized to apply in civil actions as well.[39] Likewise, compelling disclosure of documents or information has long been treated as equivalent to compelling a party to "be a witness against himself."[40] The privilege against self-incrimination, however, does not substantially limit agency attempts to obtain information necessary to enforce its regulations.

(a) Personal Nature of Fifth Amendment Protection

In large part, this is because the courts have consistently found that the privilege against self-incrimination is a strictly personal one and, thus, is not available to corporations or unincorporated associations.[41] In

31. Renskers, supra note 52, at 333–34.

32. Id. at 334.

33. Id.

34. See Schoonmaker, supra note 54, at 57.

35. Renskers, supra note 52, at 334 (citing to Lawrence Tribe, American Constitutional Law 1389 (2nd ed. 1988)).

36. See Schoonmaker, supra note 54, at 57.

37. Renskers, supra note 52, at 334. See generally, John Shattuck, In the Shadow of 1984: National Identification Systems, Computer–Matching, and Privacy in the United States, 35 Hast. L.J. 991 (1984).

38. U.S. Const. amend. 5. The courts have repeatedly emphasized that the fifth amendment protects only against revealing evidence that implicate the witness criminally. Compelling disclosure of information that is merely disgraceful or humiliating to the witness or which may jeopardize his reputation, job, etc. is not protected. See Smith v. United States, 337 U.S. 137, 69 S.Ct. 1000, 93 L.Ed. 1264 (1949).

39. Boyd v. United States, 116 U.S. 616, 6 S.Ct. 524, 29 L.Ed. 746 (1886) (a proceeding to forfeit a person's goods for prosecution, albeit in a civil action, is a criminal case within the meaning of the fifth amendment).

40. Id. at 634–35, 6 S.Ct. at 534–35.

41. See, e.g., Hale v. Henkel, 201 U.S. 43, 26 S.Ct. 370, 50 L.Ed. 652 (1906); United States v. Morton Salt Co., 338 U.S. 632, 70 S.Ct. 357, 94 L.Ed. 401 (1950); Wilson v. United States, 221 U.S. 361, 31 S.Ct. 538, 55 L.Ed. 771 (1911); United States v. White, 322 U.S. 694, 64 S.Ct. 1248, 88 L.Ed. 1542 (1944).

carving out this exception to the protection of the fifth amendment, the Court has reasoned that because a corporation is a creature of the state, the legislature should have unimpaired access to its records to insure that it is operating within the regulatory limits created by the state.[42] In one of the leading cases restricting the availability of the fifth amendment to corporations resisting enforcement of a subpoena the Court stated:

> "[a] corporation is a creature of the State.... Its powers are limited by law.... Its rights to act as a corporation are only preserved to it so long as it obeys the laws of its creation. There is a reserved right in the legislature to investigate its contracts and find out whether it has exceeded its powers.... While an individual may lawfully refuse to answer incriminating questions unless protected by an immunity statute, it does not follow that a corporation, vested with special privileges and franchises, may refuse to show its hand when charged with an abuse of such privileges."[43]

Nor does the privilege extend to the individual agent of the corporation who possesses the subpoenaed documents, even if those documents incriminate that individual. In *United States v. White,*[44] a representative of an unincorporated labor union was forced to turn over documents in his possession which tended directly to implicate his own criminality. The Court found that had he been holding these documents in a purely private capacity, the protections of the fifth amendment would be available. But the nature of his possession of the documents was as an agent of the association and the protection was held inapposite.[45] In *Braswell v. United States,*[46] the Court had the opportunity to broaden the corporate agent's protection in the wake of *Fisher v. United States*[47] and

42. Hale v. Henkel, 201 U.S. at 74–75, 26 S.Ct. at 379 (although an individual may lawfully refuse to answer incriminating questions unless protected by an immunity statute, a corporation is a creature of the state, and there is a reserved right in the legislature to investigate).

43. Wilson v. United States, 221 U.S. 361, 383–84, 31 S.Ct. 538, 545–46, 55 L.Ed. 771 (1911) (quoting Hale v. Henkel, 201 U.S. at 74–75, 26 S.Ct. at 379). This same principle is applied to other state created entities, regardless of size. In Bellis v. United States, 417 U.S. 85, 94 S.Ct. 2179, 40 L.Ed.2d 678 (1974) the Court found that a member of a three person partnership did not have the privilege available to him because the partnership had an institutional identity and the petitioner held the requested documents in the capacity of a representative of the partnership, not in a personal capacity. See generally Note, The Constitutional Rights of Associations to Assert the Privilege Against Self-incrimination, 112 U.Pa.L.Rev. 394 (1964).

44. 322 U.S. 694, 64 S.Ct. 1248, 88 L.Ed. 1542 (1944).

45. "[I]ndividuals, when acting as representatives of a collective group, ... assume the rights, duties and privileges of the artificial entity or association ... In their official capacity ... have no privilege against self-incrimination. And the official records and documents of the organization that are held by them in a representative rather than a personal capacity cannot be the subject of the personal privilege against self-incrimination, even though production of the papers might tend to incriminate them personally." Id. at 699, 64 S.Ct. at 1251.

46. 487 U.S. 99, 108 S.Ct. 2284, 101 L.Ed.2d 98 (1988). See generally, Ferrara et. al., SEC Enforcement Proceedings: Strategic Considerations for When the Agency Comes Calling, 51 Admin. L.Rev. 1143 (1999).

47. 425 U.S. 391, 96 S.Ct. 1569, 48 L.Ed.2d 39 (1976).

United States v. Doe.[48] The Court in *Doe* found that "[a]lthough the contents of a document may not be privileged, the act of producing the document may be."[49] However, the Court in *Braswell* failed to apply the act of production doctrine to the corporate custodian: "[T]he custodian's act of production is not deemed a personal act, but rather an act of the corporation. Any claim of Fifth Amendment privilege asserted by the agent would be tantamount to a claim of privilege by the corporation—which of course possesses no such privilege."[50]

The degree of protection enjoyed by the corporate custodian as an individual is far from certain. In an apparent attempt to protect the custodian in his or her individual capacity, the Court said that "[b]ecause the custodian acts as a representative, the act is deemed one of the corporation and not the individual. Therefore, . . . no evidentiary use of the 'individual act' [may be made] against the individual."[51] The Court stated that:

> The Government has the right . . . to use the corporation's act of production against the custodian. . . . And if the defendant held a prominent position within the corporation that produced the records, the jury may, just as it would had someone else produced the documents, reasonably infer that he had possession of the documents or knowledge of their contents. Because the jury is not told that the defendant produced the records, any nexus between the defendant and the documents results solely from the corporation's act of production and other evidence in the case.[52]

Consistent with the notion that the privilege against self-incrimination is a strictly personal one, courts generally will not sustain a claim of that privilege if the demanded items are not in the claimant's possession. Ownership of the information is less important in the context of the fifth amendment's protection than is actual possession. The privilege specifically protects against personal compulsion of self-incriminating information. In *Couch v. United States*,[53] the Court found that an accountant's client had no fifth amendment claim regarding documents subpoenaed from the accountant that the client had voluntarily turned over for the purpose of filing tax returns because the client lacked actual possession.[54]

48. 465 U.S. 605, 104 S.Ct. 1237, 79 L.Ed.2d 552 (1984).

49. Id. at 612, 104 S.Ct. at 1242.

50. *Braswell*, 487 U.S. at 110, 108 S.Ct. at 2291.

51. Id. at 118, 108 S.Ct. at 2295.

52. Id. (footnote omitted).

53. 409 U.S. 322, 93 S.Ct. 611, 34 L.Ed.2d 548 (1973).

54. "We do indeed believe that actual possession of documents bears the most significant relationship to Fifth Amendment protections against governmental compulsions upon the individual accused of crime." Id. at 333, 93 S.Ct. at 618. The Court did recognize, however, that in certain limited situations, the relinquishment of possession may be so temporary and insignificant as to leave the personal compulsions upon the accused substantially intact.

See also Fisher v. United States, 425 U.S. 391, 397, 96 S.Ct. 1569, 1574, 48 L.Ed.2d 39 (1976) (compelling the taxpayer's lawyer to produce documents for subpoena does not "compel" the taxpayer to do anything and does not compel the lawyer to be a witness against himself).

Just as the non-possessing owner may not claim a privilege as to documents subpoenaed from a third party, a third party may not claim the fifth amendment on behalf of the accused. The courts have emphasized that the privilege is a strictly personal one and may only be claimed by an individual who is actually being asked to disclose documents that will incriminate him or her personally. Recently, the Court has held that in situations where a third party is subpoenaed for information regarding another, the agency issuing the subpoena is under no obligation to notify the actual target of the investigation.[55]

(b) Public and Required Records Exempt From Fifth Amendment Protection

Records or documents that are considered public in nature are also exempt from protection under the fifth amendment. Documents, for example, that are part of the official records of a state or the federal government are the property of the government concerned and, as such, are not protected by the fifth amendment. This so-called public records exception was explained in *Davis v. United States.*[56] Here, the petitioner was the president of a corporation which maintained a gasoline filling station in New York City. The police obtained evidence that petitioner was violating gasoline rationing regulations by selling gasoline without coupons and at above-ceiling prices.[57] When the police arrested the petitioner, they demanded and, under protest, received the coupons covering the aggregate amount of sales. The Court held that the police officers' claim to the coupons was one of right because it did not deal "with *private* papers or documents, but with gasoline ration coupons which never became the private property of the holder but remained at all times the property of the Government and subject to inspection and recall by it."[58] Reiterating the distinction between private papers and public property in the custody of a citizen, the Court stated:

> But the physical custody of incriminating documents does not of itself protect the custodian against their compulsory production. The question still remains with respect to the nature of the documents and the capacity in which they are held.... Thus, in the case of public records and official documents, made or kept in the administration of public office, the fact of actual possession or of lawful custody would not justify the officer in resisting inspection, even though the record was made by himself and would supply the evidence of his criminal dereliction. If he has embezzled the public moneys and falsified the public accounts he cannot seal his official records and withhold them from the

55. SEC v. Jerry T. O'Brien, Inc., 467 U.S. 735, 104 S.Ct. 2720, 81 L.Ed.2d 615 (1984), on remand, 773 F.2d 1070 (9th Cir. 1985).

56. 328 U.S. 582, 66 S.Ct. 1256, 90 L.Ed. 1453 (1946), reh'g denied, 329 U.S. 824, 67 S.Ct. 107, 91 L.Ed. 700 (1946).

57. Petitioner was charged with a violation of § 2(a) of the Act of June 28, 1940, 54 Stat. 676 (originally codified as amended at 50 U.S.C.A. § 633, omitted as terminated pursuant to the provisions of 50 U.S.C.A. § 645).

58. 328 U.S. at 588, 66 S.Ct. at 1259 (emphasis is the Court's).

prosecuting authorities on a plea of constitutional privilege against self-incrimination.[59]

The Court, however, found that the distinction between property to which the government is entitled to possession and property to which it is not had repercussions beyond those indicated in *Wilson.* Thus, the Court in *Davis* held that "an owner of property who seeks to take it from one who is unlawfully in possession has long been recognized to have greater leeway than he would have but for his right to possession. The claim of ownership will even justify a trespass and warrant other steps otherwise unlawful."[60] Nonetheless, the Court did not intend to "suggest that officers seeking to reclaim government property may proceed lawlessly and subject to no restraints."[61] For instance, in the case at hand, the officers did not conduct a general exploratory search. Only the contraband coupons were demanded and seized. Additionally, the seizure was made on commercial premises during business hours.

In *Shapiro v. United States,*[62] the Court extended the *Davis* public records exception to private records required to be kept by law. In *Shapiro,* the petitioner was charged with having made sales in violation of regulations under the Emergency Price Control Act.[63] He was served with a subpoena which directed him to appear before officials of the Office of Price Administration and to produce "all duplicate sales invoices, sales books, ledgers, inventory records, contracts and records relating to the sale of all commodities"[64] for a designated period of time. The petitioner claimed that the records were private business records, and as such, were within the constitutional privilege against self-incrimination. The Court rejected this claim stating that: "the privilege which exists as to private papers cannot be maintained in relation to 'records required by law to be kept in order that there may be suitable information of transactions which are the appropriate subjects of government regulation and the enforcement of restrictions validly established.' "[65]

The implications of *Shapiro* can only be appreciated when one considers the pervasive nature of recordkeeping requirements. "If records merely because required to be kept by law *ipso facto* become public

59. Id. at 589–90, 66 S.Ct. at 1259–60 (this distinction was first announced in Wilson v. United States, 221 U.S. 361, 380, 31 S.Ct. 538, 55 L.Ed. 771 (1911)).

60. Id. at 591, 66 S.Ct. at 1260.

61. Id.

62. 335 U.S. 1, 68 S.Ct. 1375, 92 L.Ed. 1787 (1948), reh'g denied, 335 U.S. 836, 69 S.Ct. 9, 93 L.Ed. 388 (1948).

63. Emergency Price Control Act, ch. 26, 56 Stat. 23 (1942) (originally codified as amended at 50 U.S.C.A. §§ 901–946 (omitted as terminated)).

64. 335 U.S. at 4, 68 S.Ct. at 1377.

65. Id. at 33, 68 S.Ct. at 1292 (quoting *Davis,* 328 U.S. at 589–90, 66 S.Ct. at 1259–60). The Court relied on its prior holding in *Wilson,* where it held that a corporation cannot resist production of records upon the ground of self-incrimination and further that a corporation's officers may not refuse, upon demand, to come forward with the corporate records on the ground that the records may incriminate the officer personally.

Justice Frankfurter, however, sharply criticized the majority for its reliance on *Wilson:* "The conclusion reached today that *all* records required to be kept by law are *public* records cannot lean on the *Wilson* opinion." Id. at 58, 68 S.Ct. at 1404 (Frankfurter, J., dissenting) (emphasis in the original).

records, we are indeed living in glass houses."[66] In a community in which regulation has become a basic fact of economic life, recordkeeping requirements cut across every aspect of the business spectrum. Indeed, recordkeeping requirements and hence, the *Shapiro* exception, do not pertain solely to business entities or to business records. For instance, personal bank and tax records are available to the government for inspection. Government access to this information could have disturbing implications for a right to privacy; these documents clearly express much about the beliefs, associations, and activities of the owners.

Control over one's ability to project a certain image to the world, as well as, and perhaps more importantly, limitations on the government's power to coerce the disclosure of information, become more difficult and more crucial as the government's capacity to gain and store information increases. Most troublesome to individual liberty interests is the permanent memory of computers. "Records are mechanical memories not subject to the erosions of forgetfulness and the promise of eventual obliteration. The threat of misuse becomes as permanent as the records themselves. The risks to autonomy multiply not simply because of the heightened possibilities of uncontested reproduction and distribution at any given time, but also because those possibilities, however reduced by regulation, now extend indefinitely through time. Such a chronic and enduring risk must count as itself an injury."[67]

Recognizing that exempting public and required records from fifth amendment protection, as propounded by Shapiro, could have potentially abusive results, the Court in *Marchetti v. United States*[68] has limited the *Shapiro* holding to some extent. The defendant in *Marchetti* was convicted of failing to register before engaging in the business of accepting wagers and for failing to pay an occupational tax. He challenged the conviction on the basis that the statutory obligations to register and to pay an occupational tax violated his fifth amendment privilege against self-incrimination. The Court agreed, deciding that the required report doctrine of *Shapiro* did not apply in this case.

In distinguishing *Marchetti* from *Shapiro,* the Court found that the three principal elements of the required records doctrine described in *Shapiro* were absent in *Marchetti.* First, *Marchetti* was being required to keep records of the kind not customarily kept. "This requirement is not significantly different from a demand that he provide oral testimony."[69] Second, the information demanded of *Marchetti* had none of the "public aspects" noted in *Shapiro.*[70] Third, "the requirements at issue in *Shapi-*

66. Id. at 51, 68 S.Ct. at 1401 (Frankfurter, J., dissenting).

67. Gerety, Redefining Privacy, 12 Harv. C.R.–C.L.L.Rev. 233, 288 (1977). See generally, Alfred C. Aman, Jr., Information, Privacy, and Technology: Citizens, Clients, or Consumers? in Freedom of Expression And Freedom of Information, 325–48 (Oxford Univ. Press, 2000) (Jack Beatson and Yvonne Cripps, eds).

68. 390 U.S. 39, 88 S.Ct. 697, 19 L.Ed.2d 889 (1968), superseded by statute as stated in State v. Hall, 196 Wis.2d 850, 540 N.W.2d 219 (1995).

69. Id. at 57, 88 S.Ct. at 707.

70. "The Government's anxiety to obtain information known to a private individual does not without more render that information public; if it did, no room would

ro were imposed in 'an essentially non-criminal and regulatory area of inquiry' while those [in *Marchetti* were] directed to a 'selective group inherently suspect of criminal activities.' "[71]Thus *Marchetti* not only clarified the *Shapiro* holding, but implicitly narrowed it as well.[72] The Court did not find the wage or tax requirement unconstitutional, but it did determine that those who asserted their privilege may not be criminally prosecuted for failure to comply with the registration requirement.

In sum, a required report which is not inherently criminal but contains certain answers which could incriminate the individual, for example a tax return form, is generally not protected by the fifth amendment in its entirety, so the report must be filed; however, the party may claim the privilege as to particular answers.[73]

remain for the application of the constitutional privilege. Nor does it stamp information with a public character that the Government has formalized its demands in the attire of a statute; if this alone were sufficient, the constitutional privilege could be entirely abrogated by any Act of Congress." Id.

71. Id.

72. Id. The Court suggests in *Marchetti* that the *Shapiro* holding could be further narrowed; however, "[t]here is no need to explore further the elements and limitations of *Shapiro* and the cases involving public papers." Id. See also Grosso v. United States, 390 U.S. 62, 88 S.Ct. 709, 19 L.Ed.2d 906 (1968) (the Court describes the premises of the Shapiro doctrine as: "first, the purposes of the United States' inquiry must be essentially regulatory; second, information is to be obtained by requiring the preservation of records of a kind which the regulated party has customarily kept; and third, the records themselves must have assumed 'public aspects' which render them at least analogous to public documents" Id. at 67–68, 88 S.Ct. at 714); Haynes v. United States, 390 U.S. 85, 88 S.Ct. 722, 19 L.Ed.2d 923 (1968), superseded by statute as stated in U.S. v. Dorsey, 77 F.3d 490 (9th Cir.1996) (the Court found that a proper claim of the fifth amendment provides a full defense to prosecution for failure to register an illegal firearm or for possession of unregistered firearms under the National Firearm Act); Albertson v. Subversive Activities Control Board, 382 U.S. 70, 86 S.Ct. 194, 15 L.Ed.2d 165 (1965) (The Court held that a S.A.C.B. order requiring that all members of the communist party register was incriminating under the fifth amendment because the admission of party membership may be used as evidence in criminal prosecution. "Petitioners' claims are not asserted in an essentially non-criminal and regulatory area of inquiry, but against an inquiry in an area permeated with criminal statutes, where response to any of the form's questions in context might involve the petitioners in the admission of a crucial element of a crime." Id. at 79, 88 S.Ct. at 199); Leary v. United States, 395 U.S. 6, 89 S.Ct. 1532, 23 L.Ed.2d 57 (1969), appeal after remand, 431 F.2d 85 (5th Cir.1970). (Defendant successfully claimed the fifth to a reporting requirement that all marijuana deals be reported to the I.R.S. "[s]ince compliance with the transfer tax provisions would have required petitioner unmistakably to identify himself as a member of this 'selective' and 'suspect' group." Id. at 18, 89 S.Ct. at 1538); Cf. United States v. Ward, 448 U.S. 242, 100 S.Ct. 2636, 65 L.Ed.2d 742 (1980), reh'g denied, 448 U.S. 916, 101 S.Ct. 37, 65 L.Ed.2d 1179 (1980) (where the Court upheld a Federal Water Pollution Control Act provision which required the reporting of all prohibited discharges of oil into navigable waters because the penalty for such discharges was defined as "civil" in nature, therefore, the constitutional protections of the fifth did not apply).

73. See United States v. Sullivan, 274 U.S. 259, 47 S.Ct. 607, 71 L.Ed. 1037 (1927) (the Fifth Amendment does not protect the recipient of income derived from illicit traffic in liquor from prosecution for willful refusal to make any return under income tax law; defendant could have raised objections to particular answers in the return but he could not be excused from filing a return). See generally Meltzer, Required Records, the McCarran Act and the Privilege Against Self–Incrimination, 18 U.Chic.L.Rev. 687 (1951); J. Mansfield, The Albertson Case: Conflict Between the Privilege Against Self–Incrimination and the Government's Need for Information, 1966 Sup.Ct.Rev. 103; R. McKay, Self–Incrimina-

(c) Statutory Use Immunity

In addition to exempting corporations from protection under the fifth amendment, grants of immunity from prosecution are also used to gain information. Some agency enabling statutes, however, prevent the use of testimony compelled from a witness from being used against that witness.[74] The end effect is that a witness cannot refuse to testify or produce documents on the grounds that the evidence is incriminating because no danger of prosecution based on the information disclosed by that witness exists.[75]

The Court upheld the constitutionality of statutory use immunity in *Kastigar v. United States* but noted that the immunity is only as to use, not transactions, and outside materials not obtained from the witness are not covered by the immunity.[76] In *United States v. Doe,*[77] the Court was urged to adopt a doctrine of constructive use immunity: "Under this doctrine, the courts would impose a requirement on the Government not to use the incriminatory aspects of the act of production against the person claiming the privilege even though the statutory procedures have not been followed."[78] The Court failed to adopt the doctrine of constructive use immunity reasoning that "[t]he decision to seek use immunity necessarily involves a balancing of the Government's interest in obtaining information against the risk that immunity will frustrate the Government's attempts to prosecute the subject of the investigation. Congress expressly left this decision exclusively to the Justice Department."[79]

§ 20.4 OTHER LIMITATIONS ON AGENCY ACQUISITION OF INFORMATION

In addition to the fourth and fifth amendments, there are other limitations on an agency's power to compel disclosure of information. First, an agency's demand for information must be authorized by stat-

tion and the New Privacy, 1967 Sup.Ct.Rev. 193; Note, Business Records and the Fifth Amendment Right Against Self–Incrimination, 38 Ohio St.L.J. 351 (1977).

74. The Compulsory Testimony Act, ch. 83, § 1, 27 Stat. 443 (1893) repealed by Act of Oct. 15, 1970, Pub.L. No. 91–452, § 245, 84 Stat. 923, 931.

75. 18 U.S.C.A. § 6002. That statute provides that:

> Whenever a witness refuses, on the basis of his privilege against self-incrimination, to testify or provide other information in a proceeding before or ancillary to ... (2) an agency of the United States, ... and the person presiding over the proceeding communicates to the witness an order issued under this part, the witness may not refuse to comply with the order on the basis of his privilege ... ; but no testimony or other information compelled under the order ... may be used against the witness in any criminal case ...

76. 406 U.S. 441, 92 S.Ct. 1653, 32 L.Ed.2d 212 (1972), reh'g denied, 408 U.S. 931, 92 S.Ct. 2478, 33 L.Ed.2d 345 (1972).

77. 465 U.S. 605, 104 S.Ct. 1237, 79 L.Ed.2d 552 (1984).

78. Id. at 616, 104 S.Ct. at 1244.

79. Id. at 616–17, 104 S.Ct. at 1244–45 (citation omitted). Cf. Braswell v. United States, 487 U.S. 99, 118, 108 S.Ct. 2284, 2295, 101 L.Ed.2d 98 (1988). ("We reject the suggestion that the limitation on evidentiary use of the custodian's act of production is the equivalent of constructive use immunity barred ... in *Doe.*").

ute. Second, this authority may not be exercised improperly. Third, the request for information must be relevant to a lawful subject of inquiry and not too indefinite or unreasonably burdensome. Finally, subsection (c) discusses the limitations on an agency's use of a subpoena to acquire information. First, an agency must have jurisdiction over the subpoenaed party. Second, the subpoena must be issued by the proper person. Third, the use of a subpoena may be limited by privileges.

Another area in which claims often are made to limit the disclosure powers of agencies involves the transferability of information between agencies. This question was raised in *Shell Oil Co. v. DOE.*[1] The Department of Energy had broad authority to collect the information necessary for it to formulate energy policy. This information, however, was subject to sharing with the Federal Trade Commission and the Department of Justice's Antitrust Divisions. While such sharing arrangements can increase governmental investigative efficiency as well as hold down the private costs of compliance,[2] it raises difficulties as well. As Justice Powell noted in his dissent to the denial of certiorari in this case:

> The dissemination of this extraordinary volume of data to those prosecutorial Government agencies raises a serious question, as these agencies may thereby obtain information that statutory and constitutional safeguards would bar them from obtaining directly in antitrust unenforcement actions. The likelihood that rights of potential antitrust defendants will be violated increases as DOE demands increasingly more data from companies subject to its regulation and then disseminates the information to prosecutorial agencies. Congress has given DOE an investigative power that appears to be intrusive as well as excessively burdensome in its own right. But that power should not become a blanket discovery authority for the use of the Department of Justice and the Federal Trade Commission without the safeguards provided by law against abuse of legal rights.[3]

§ 20.4.1 Agency Request for Information Must Be Authorized by Statute

Section 555 of the Administrative Procedure Act states: "Process, requirement of a report, in section or other investigative act or demand may not be issued, made or enforced except *as authorized by law.*"[4] The

§ 20.4

1. 477 F.Supp. 413 (D.Del.1979), aff'd 631 F.2d 231 (3d Cir.1980), cert. denied, 450 U.S. 1024, 101 S.Ct. 1730, 68 L.Ed.2d 219 (1981).

2. See Gelhorn et al., Administrative Law 876 (9th ed. 1995).

3. Shell Oil Co. v. Department of Energy, 450 U.S. 1024, 101 S.Ct. 1730, 68 L.Ed.2d 219 (1981). See generally Stevenson, Panel Discussion: Agency Release and Sharing of Information, 34 Admin.L.Rev. 159, 160 (1982); Emerson Electric Co. v. Schlesinger, 609 F.2d 898 (8th Cir.1979). For statutes that explicitly restrict the transfer of information, see, e.g., The Right to Financial Privacy Act of 1978, codified as amended at 12 U.S.C.A. §§ 3401, 3421. See also Carey v. Klutznick, 653 F.2d 732 (2d Cir.1981), cert. denied 455 U.S. 999, 102 S.Ct. 1630, 71 L.Ed.2d 866 (1982) (where district court's order that the Census Bureau produce the master address registers for every municipality in New York was found to have been improvidently granted).

4. 5 U.S.C.A. § 555(c) (emphasis added).

statutory provisions that authorize agency investigations are almost uniformly broad and extensive.[5] In addition to the power to investigate, the agencies must also have specific authorization from Congress to issue subpoenas and require reports.[6] These authorizing statutes are common and may be found in the general enabling statutes or may be enacted for a specific investigation.[7]

§ 20.4.2 Improper Use of Investigative Powers Is Prohibited

An agency must at all times exercise its extensive investigatory powers in good faith. The burden of proving that an agency is acting with illegitimate motives, however, is difficult to meet.[8] But if illegitimate motives are proved, the court will interfere in the administrative process and refuse to invoke judicial process to enforce agency authority that is being used abusively and in bad faith.[9] The Court in *United States*

5. See infra note 7.

6. See, e.g., Serr v. Sullivan, 390 F.2d 619, 620 (3d Cir.1968) ("Federal Alcohol Administration Act did not.... expressly or impliedly empower the Director of the Alcohol and Tobacco Division ... to issue subpoenas *duces tecum* pursuant thereto"); United States v. Exxon Corp., 628 F.2d 70 (D.C.Cir.1980), cert. denied 446 U.S. 964, 100 S.Ct. 2940, 64 L.Ed.2d 823 (1980) (A special grant of subpoena power was not necessary for this particular investigation because the Department of Energy could have conducted the investigation under its general investigatory powers. Thus, the D.O.E. may rely on its general subpoena power grant.). But see United States v. Minker, 350 U.S. 179, 76 S.Ct. 281, 100 L.Ed. 185 (1956) (Court concludes that statutory term "witness" does not include persons under investigation).

7. See, e.g., 15 U.S.C.A. §§ 46(b), 49. These statutory provisions are typical of statutes authorizing the use of reports and subpoenas in investigations. 15 U.S.C.A. § 46(b) provides that the Commission shall have the power to "require, by general or special orders, persons, partnerships, and corporations engaged in.... commerce ... to file with the Commission in such form as the Commission may prescribe annual or special ... reports or answers in writing to specific questions, furnishing to the Commission such information as it may require." 15 U.S.C.A. § 49 provides that "the Commission ... shall at all reasonable times have access to, for the purpose of examination, and the right to copy any documentary evidence of any person, partnership, or corporation being investigated or proceeded against; and the Commission shall have power to require by subpoena ... the production of all such documentary evidence relating to any matter under investigation."

8. The Court in United States v. LaSalle Nat. Bank, 437 U.S. 298, 316, 98 S.Ct. 2357, 2367, 57 L.Ed.2d 221 (1978), on remand, 79-2 USTC P 9643, 1979 WL 1472 (N.D.Ill.), for example, said that a party challenging an I.R.S. subpoena on the grounds that the investigation's sole purpose is to gather evidence for criminal prosecution had the burden of disproving the actual existence of any valid civil tax determination or collection purpose by the Service. Given the often intertwined elements of civil and criminal liabilities, the court acknowledged that "[w]ithout doubt, this burden is a heavy one." See also United States v. Powell, 379 U.S. 48, 85 S.Ct. 248, 13 L.Ed.2d 112 (1964); United States v. Litton Industries, Inc., 462 F.2d 14 (9th Cir.1972).

9. See, e.g., Donaldson v. United States, 400 U.S. 517, 536, 91 S.Ct. 534, 545, 27 L.Ed.2d 580 (1971), superseded by statute as stated in Ip v. U.S., 205 F.3d 1168 (9th Cir.2000) ("We hold that ... an internal revenue summons may be issued in aid of an investigation if it is issued in good faith and prior to a recommendation for criminal prosecution."); United States v. LaSalle Nat. Bank, 437 U.S. 298, 307–11, 98 S.Ct. 2357, 2362–65, 57 L.Ed.2d 221 (1978); SEC v. Wheeling–Pittsburgh Steel Corp., 648 F.2d 118 (3d Cir.1981); Shasta Minerals & Chem. Co. v. SEC, 328 F.2d 285 (10th Cir.1964). See also Comment, Bad Faith and the Abuse-of-Process Defense to Administrative Subpoenas, 82 Colum.L.Rev. 811 (1981).

v. Powell[10] deferred to the Commissioner's determination of the scope of his investigatory powers and upheld the enforcement of a subpoena issued by the Internal Revenue Service, under the authority of the Internal Revenue Code.[11] The Court, however, warned that it would inquire into the legitimacy of an investigation when given cause in order to prevent abuse of judicial process.[12] Good faith, as defined by the *Powell* Court, involved a showing by the agency that the investigation was conducted pursuant to a legitimate purpose, that the inquiry was relevant to that purpose, that the information sought had not already been within the agency's possession and that the administrative steps required by the Code were followed.[13]

Another area of dispute regarding good faith behavior of agencies is where agency investigations may lead to criminal as well as civil sanctions. Because the regulations involving criminal and civil sanctions are often intertwined, most courts agree that an agency investigation that may lead to civil liability as well as criminal prosecution is legitimate.[14] Only when the agency's "sole purpose" is to investigate for criminal violations will the court interfere.[15] Even then, summonses are likely to be enforced unless issued after a criminal proceeding has been initiated.[16]

10. 379 U.S. 48, 85 S.Ct. 248, 13 L.Ed.2d 112 (1964).

11. The Internal Revenue Code of 1954, ch. 78, § 7602(a), 68A Stat. 901 (codified as amended at 26 U.S.C.A. § 7602(a)) provides that the Secretary of the IRS or his delegates may examine relevant material "[f]or the purpose of ascertaining the correctness of any return, making a return where none has been made, determining the liability of any person for any internal revenue tax or the liability at law or in equity of any transferee or fiduciary of any person in respect of any internal revenue tax, or collecting any such liability."

Section 7601 of the Internal Revenue Code, directs the Secretary or his delegate "to the extent he deems it practicable" to cause Treasury Department officers or employees "to proceed ... and inquire after" all persons "who may be liable to pay any internal revenue tax."

12. "Nor does our reading of the statutes mean that under no circumstances may the court inquire into the underlying reasons for the examination. It is the court's process which is invoked to enforce the administrative summons and a court may not permit its process to be abused. Such an abuse would take place if the summons had been issued for an improper purpose, such as to harass the taxpayer or to put pressure on him to settle a collateral dispute, or for any other purpose reflecting on the good faith of the particular investigation. The burden of showing an abuse of the court's process is on the [challenger]...." 379 U.S. at 58, 85 S.Ct. at 255 (footnotes omitted).

13. Id. at 57–58, 85 S.Ct. at 255. See also SEC v. Wheeling–Pittsburgh Steel Corp., 648 F.2d 118, 126 (3d Cir.1981) ("An administrative agency that undertakes an extensive investigation at the insistence of a powerful United States Senator 'with no reasonable expectation' of proving a violation and then seeks federal court enforcement of its subpoena could be found to be using the judiciary for illicit purposes."); Comment, supra note 118.

14. Donaldson v. United States, 400 U.S. 517, 531–36, 91 S.Ct. 534, 542–45, 27 L.Ed.2d 580 (1971), superseded by statute as stated in Ip v. U.S., 205 F.3d 1168 (9th Cir.2000); United States v. LaSalle Nat. Bank, 437 U.S. 298, 307–11, 98 S.Ct. 2357, 2362–65, 57 L.Ed.2d 221 (1978), on remand 79-2 USTC P 9643, 1979 WL 1472 (N.D.Ill.).

15. The Court in United States v. LaSalle Nat. Bank, 437 U.S. 298, 316, 98 S.Ct. 2357, 2367, 57 L.Ed.2d 221 (1978), on remand 79-2 USTC P 9643, 1979 WL 1472 (N.D.Ill.) stated that "the question of whether an investigation has solely criminal purposes must be answered only by an examination of the institutional posture of the [agency,]" not the personal motive held by the individual agent.

16. The *LaSalle* Court recognized that delays in submitting recommendations for criminal prosecution when the agency had already decided to do so for the purposes of

Generally, the investigatory powers of agencies are so broad and the burden of proving illegitimate motives is so difficult that challenges to an agency request on the grounds that the investigatory powers are being used in bad faith are almost always unsuccessful.

§ 20.4.3 Request for Information Must Be Relevant and Not Too Indefinite or Unreasonably Burdensome

Closely related to the authority of an agency to compel the production of information is the question of whether the information sought is relevant to the inquiry. Consistent with the loose application of the fourth amendment in the administrative context, a claim of irrelevancy will invalidate an agency request only when it is "plainly incompetent or irrelevant."[17] Relevancy is measured in relation to the general purpose of the investigation defined by the agency.[18] It is imperative, therefore, that the agency state its purpose in conducting the investigation so courts have a means of determining the information's relevance. If no purpose is stated, or the purpose stated is so broad as to be virtually all inclusive, courts will generally not enforce the subpoena on the grounds that they cannot determine the materiality of the requested information.[19] Courts have recognized, however, that in the precomplaint stage, propounding a narrowly focused purpose may be difficult because the issues have yet to be investigated. In such cases general statements of purpose by the agency will suffice, so long as they provide some objective against which the relevancy of the request may be measured.[20] If a purpose is stated, the measure of relevance is that the materials requested must possibly be useful or are at least reasonably relevant to the investigative purpose cited by the agency.[21]

gathering more information for prosecution or using agencies as information gathering bodies for other departments would violate good faith standards of investigation, 437 U.S. at 316–17, 98 S.Ct. at 2367–68.

17. Endicott Johnson v. Perkins, 317 U.S. 501, 509, 63 S.Ct. 339, 343, 87 L.Ed. 424 (1943).

18. FTC v. Texaco, Inc., 555 F.2d 862 (D.C.Cir.1977), cert. denied 431 U.S. 974, 97 S.Ct. 2940, 53 L.Ed.2d 1072 (1977).

19. See, e.g., CAB v. United Airlines, Inc., 542 F.2d 394 (7th Cir.1976) (where the court found that an agency's investigation powers, although broad, are not limitless). See also Montship Lines, Ltd. v. Federal Maritime Bd., 295 F.2d 147, 155 (D.C.Cir. 1961) (the agency may investigate just to satisfy its curiosity that a violation is not taking place, but this does not allow the absence altogether of any indication of the investigation's purpose); Hellenic Lines Ltd. v. Federal Maritime Bd., 295 F.2d 138 (D.C.Cir.1961) (statement of purpose being to effectuate the Board's regulatory duties under the Act provides no standard for determining relevance).

20. In FTC v. Texaco, Inc., 555 F.2d 862, 874 (D.C.Cir.1977), cert. denied 431 U.S. 974, 97 S.Ct. 2940, 53 L.Ed.2d 1072 (1977), reh'g denied, 434 U.S. 883, 98 S.Ct. 251, 54 L.Ed.2d 168 (1977) the court stated, "the better approach is simply to recognize that in the pre-complaint stage, an investigating agency is under no obligation to propound a narrowly focused theory of a possible future case. Accordingly, the relevance of the agency's subpoena requests may be measured only against the general purposes of its investigation. The district court is not free to speculate about the possible charges that might be included in a future complaint, and then to determine the relevance of the subpoena requests by reference to those hypothetical charges."

21. See generally Note, Reasonable Relation Reassessed, 56 N.Y.U.L.R. 742 (1981). See also FTC v. Texaco, Inc., 555 F.2d 862 (D.C.Cir.1977), cert. denied, 431

As first noted in *Oklahoma Press,* some agency requests for information may be defeated if the requirement is unduly burdensome. In reality, this seldom amounts to much of a limitation. Generally, the cases reveal that courts are willing to enforce all but the most impossible vague and oppressive subpoena requests. One of the leading cases, *CAB v. Hermann,*[22] indicates that the Court will tolerate voluminous and burdensome requests so long as they are reasonably relevant to the investigation. The subpoena upheld in that case requested broad categories of documents covering substantial periods of time. The Court found that because the information requested was not irrelevant and because the district court had made appropriate provisions for assuring minimum interference with the daily business of respondents, the subpoena request was not unreasonable.[23]

In *Appeal of FTC Line of Business Report Litigation,*[24] the D.C. Circuit examined a reporting scheme in which the Commission ordered 450 of the nation's largest manufacturers to file reports disclosing certain financial data for 1974. The data was to be reported in terms of the different lines of business in which the manufacturers were engaged. The manufacturers objected on the grounds that creating the information in the requested manner was overly burdensome as it was not the practice of the companies to maintain their records along the categories set out by the Commission. The court rejected the companies' assertion, finding that even "assuming the accuracy of the most extravagant cost estimates, the costs of compliance were *de minimis* relative to the overall corporate operating budgets."[25]

U.S. 974, 97 S.Ct. 2940, 53 L.Ed.2d 1072 (1977), rehearing denied, 434 U.S. 883, 98 S.Ct. 251, 54 L.Ed.2d 168 (1977); Lee v. Federal Maritime Bd., 284 F.2d 577 (9th Cir.1960) (that the Board may later find the information not helpful does not render it irrelevant because relevance must be considered in broad terms); Appeal of FTC Line of Business Report Litigation, 595 F.2d 685, 703 (D.C.Cir.1978), cert. denied 439 U.S. 958, 99 S.Ct. 362, 58 L.Ed.2d 351 (1978) (district court finding that "the data sought in the [line of business] program is not totally useless" was upheld) (footnote omitted); Kerr Steamship Co. v. United States, 284 F.2d 61 (2d Cir.1960), petition for review dismissed as moot 369 U.S. 422, 82 S.Ct. 874, 7 L.Ed.2d 847 (1962); United States v. Theodore, 479 F.2d 749 (4th Cir. 1973) (holding an I.R.S. demand on a preparer of tax return too "vague" and "burdensome").

22. 353 U.S. 322, 77 S.Ct. 804, 1 L.Ed.2d 852 (1957), reh'g denied, 354 U.S. 927, 77 S.Ct. 1376, 1 L.Ed.2d 1441 (1957).

23. For a general description of what a court may consider too vague to be considered reasonable, see Adams v. FTC, 296 F.2d 861 (8th Cir.1961), cert. denied, 369 U.S. 864, 82 S.Ct. 1029, 8 L.Ed.2d 83 (1962) where broadness alone was an insufficient justification to refuse enforcement so long as the material was relevant. Where the request is too broad, however, a court may impose restrictions on the request without invalidating the entire subpoena. See also Kerr Steamship Co. v. United States, 284 F.2d 61 (2d Cir.1960) (where the court acknowledged that the terms of the request were very broad and not precisely defined but upheld the subpoena because, given the type of investigation, limited demands were not practical); United States v. Theodore, 479 F.2d 749 (4th Cir.1973) (refusing to enforce I.R.S. summons because request was too vague).

24. 595 F.2d 685 (D.C.Cir.1978).

25. Id. at 704 (footnote omitted). See generally Business Disclosure: Government's Need to Know (Harvey J. Goldschmid, ed. 1979); Note, The F.T.C.'s Annual Line of Business Reporting Program, 1975 Duke L.J. 389 (1975); Benston, An Appraisal of the Costs and Benefits of Government Required Disclosure: S.E.C. and F.T.C. Requirements, 41 L. & Contemp.Probs. 30 (1977); W. Breit & K. Elzinger, Information for Antitrust and Business Activity: Line of

For a party to gain judicial review of a claim that an agency request for information is unreasonably burdensome, usually the agency itself must first review the claim. Courts will then get involved if an enforcement proceeding is initiated. Courts will on occasion modify the request so as to keep it within the bounds of reasonableness. For a court to do this, however, requires that claims of financial burden caused by the document production and lost person-hours or detriment to the everyday running of the business are set forth very clearly. Such claims are rarely successful in invalidating a request.[26] Courts may, however, grant a protective order where a party claims that a subpoena request is burdensome because it forces them to disclose trade secrets that may be harmful if revealed to competitors.[27]

§ 20.4.4 Limitations Specific to Agency Reporting Powers—Request for Information Must Comply With the Paperwork Reduction Act

Not only must an agency's request for information be authorized by statute and be consistent with the general constitutional principles described in the preceding subsections, but the request must comply with the specific procedural requirements of the Paperwork Reduction Act, enacted in 1980 and amended in 1995.[28] Although the Act has multiple purposes, a primary goal is to minimize the federally imposed paperwork burden on the private sector.[29] To this end, the Act established within the OMB the Office of Information and Regulatory Affairs (OIRA).[30] The director of OMB was required to delegate the authority to administer all functions under the Act to OIRA's administrator.[31] Before imposing a new demand for information on the private sector, an agency must show that the information requested "is necessary for the proper performance of the functions of the agency, . . . and will have practical

Business Reporting, in The Federal Trade Commission Since 1970, Economic Regulation and Bureaucratic Behavior (K. Clarkson & T. Muris eds. 1980).

26. See FTC v. Standard Am., Inc., 306 F.2d 231 (3d Cir.1962); Genuine Parts Co. v. FTC, 445 F.2d 1382, 1391 (5th Cir.1971); Hunt Foods and Industries, Inc. v. FTC, 286 F.2d 803, 811–812 (9th Cir.1960), cert. denied, 365 U.S. 877, 81 S.Ct. 1027, 6 L.Ed.2d 190 (1961); SEC v. Blackfoot Bituminous, Inc., 622 F.2d 512 (10th Cir.1980), cert. denied, 449 U.S. 955, 101 S.Ct. 362, 66 L.Ed.2d 220 (1980).

27. See, e.g., 595 F.2d at 705–07; FTC v. Lonning, 539 F.2d 202, 210–11 (D.C.Cir. 1976); FTC v. Owens–Corning Fiberglas Corp., 626 F.2d 966 (D.C.Cir.1980).

28. The Paperwork Reduction Act of 1995, 44 U.S.C.A. §§ 3501–3520, slightly amended the 1980 Act. For a discussion of the 1980 Act and its basic purposes, which remain relevant today, see generally Funk, The Paperwork Reduction Act: Paperwork Reduction Meets Administrative Law, 24 Harv.J. on Legis. 1 (1987). [hereinafter Funk, Paperwork Reduction Meets Administrative Law].

29. 44 U.S.C.A. §§ 3501(1) and 3592(15) (broadly defining person).

30. Id. § 3503. Originally the administrator of OIRA was appointed by the director of OMB; however, in an effort to gain more control over OIRA, Congress amended the Act so that the administrator is "appointed by the President, by and with the consent of the Senate." Funk, Paperwork Reduction Act Amendment, 12 Admin.L.News 3 (Spring 1987) (analyzing the Paperwork Reduction Act of 1986, Pub.L. No. 99–591, 100 Stat. 3341).

31. 44 U.S.C.A. § 3503(b).

utility."[32] OIRA makes the final determination of whether a new demand for information meets the ten statutory criteria necessary before these costs may be imposed.[33] OIRA cannot veto an information request that is required by an agency's own enabling statute, but the Paperwork Reduction Act does authorize OIRA to review such proposals[34] before they go into effect. OIRA can veto requests for additional information not so authorized; however, such vetoes can be overridden if a majority of the members of an independent agency vote to do so.[35]

The 1980 Act generally protected OIRA decisions from judicial review of any kind,[36] but the 1995 amendments speak to this issue only in one place. Section 3507(6) states: "The decision by the Director to approve or not act upon a collection of information contained in an agency rule shall not be subject to judicial review."[37]

The 1995 amendments to the Act explicitly make one other change. The Paperwork Reduction Act of 1980 came into play any time an agency sought to impose a reporting or recordkeeping requirement on ten or more persons.[38] In *Dole v United Steelworkers*,[39] the Supreme Court held that this requirement applied only to disclosures to the government, not to third parties. The 1995 amendments, however, overrule this interpretation of the Act, making it clear that the Act now applied if agencies require disclosure either to the government or to members of the public.[40]

32. 44 U.S.C. § 3506 (c)(3).

33. Id. at § 3506 (c)(3)(A)-(J). These criteria are: (A) is necessary for the proper performance of the functions of the agency, including that the information has practical utility; (B) is not unnecessarily duplicative of information otherwise reasonably accessible to the agency; (C) reduces to the extent practicable and appropriate the burden on persons who shall provide information to or for the agency, including with respect to small entities, as defined under section 601(6) of title 5, the use of such techniques as (i) establishing differing compliance or reporting requirements or timetables that take into account the resources available to those who are to respond; (ii) the clarification, consolidation, or simplification of compliance and reporting requirements; or (iii) an exemption from coverage of the collection of information, or any part thereof; (D) is written using plain, coherent, and unambiguous terminology and is understandable to those who are to respond; (E) is to be implemented in ways consistent and compatible, to the maximum extent practicable, with the existing reporting and recordkeeping practices of those who are to respond; (F) indicates for each recordkeeping requirement the length of time persons are required to maintain the records specified; (G) contains the statement required under paragraph (1)(B)(iii); (H) has been developed by an office that has planned and allocated resources for the efficient and effective management and use of the information to be collected, including the processing of the information in a manner which shall enhance, where appropriate, the utility of the information to agencies and the public; (I) uses effective and efficient statistical survey methodology appropriate to the purpose for which the information is to be collected; and (J) to the maximum extent practicable, uses information technology to reduce burden and improve data quality, agency efficiency and responsiveness to the public.

34. Id. at § 3507 (d)(4).

35. Id. at § 3507 (f)(1)(A).

36. § 3504(h) (1980 Act).

37. § 3507 (6) (1996 Amendment).

38. § 3502 (3)(A)(i).

39. 494 U.S. 26, 110 S.Ct. 929, 108 L.Ed.2d 23 (1990), superseded by statute as stated in In re Lazarus, Inc., 7 E.A.D. 318, 1997 WL 603524 (E.P.A.1997).

40. § 3502(3) redefines "collection of information" to mean "the obtaining, causing to be obtained, soliciting, or requiring the disclosure to third parties or the public, of facts or opinions for an agency, regardless of form or format...."

In addition to monitoring and controlling the information costs imposed on the private sector, another important reason Congress enacted the Paperwork Reduction Act was to eliminate the numerous exemptions which its predecessor, the Federal Reports Act, gave to different agencies.[41] Nonetheless, courts have begun to chip away at the Act's intended inclusiveness as illustrated by *Shane v. Buck.*[42] In *Shane,* the United States Postal Service (USPS) notified the operator of a private mail-forwarding agency that he and his clients were required to file Form 1583, "Application for Delivery of the Mail Through Agent." The form solicits such information as the names and addresses of the applicant and its agent and if applicable, the business address of the firm or corporation, the type of business involved, and the members or officers of the firm or corporation whose mail is authorized to be delivered to the agent. Shane refused to comply and challenged the validity of the form. Shane argued that the USPS is subject to the Act, therefore, a collection of information sponsored by the USPS, such as Form 1583, must be approved by OMB and contain a control number.[43] The court found that Form 1583 was a "collection of information" as defined by § 3502; therefore, notwithstanding the language of the Act, the determinative issue was whether the USPS was an "agency" or an "independent regulatory agency."

The court noted that § 3502(1) defined agency as "any executive department, ... Government controlled corporation or other establishment in the executive branch of the Government ..., or any independent regulatory agency...." Although the USPS is statutorily defined as an "independent establishment within the executive branch,"[44] the court found that it was not clearly encompassed by the "any executive department" or "other establishment in the executive branch" clauses in the definition of agency.

After the court found that the USPS was not included within the definitions of agency or independent regulatory agency, the court held that the USPS is not subject to the Act. Therefore, Postal Service Form 1583 need not be reviewed by OMB nor have a control number.

This conclusion is relevant for several reasons. First, *Shane* is one of the few cases interpreting the Act and, even though the court's analysis is suspect,[45] its reasoning was adopted by the second circuit in *Kuzma v. United States Postal Service.*[46] Second, the holding of *Shane* is contrary to the general congressional goal of making all government actions of this type subject to the Act. Not only does this undermine the effective-

41. Funk, Paperwork Reduction Meets Administrative Law, supra note 139, at 73 n. 398.

42. 658 F.Supp. 908 (D.Utah 1985), affirmed 817 F.2d 87 (10th Cir.1987).

43. 44 U.S.C.A. § 3507(f) ("An agency shall not engage in a collection of information without obtaining from the Director a control number to be displayed upon the information collection request.").

44. 39 U.S.C.A. § 201.

45. See, e.g., Funk, Paperwork Reduction Meets Administrative Law, supra note 139, at 73 n. 398.

46. 798 F.2d 29 (2d Cir.1986), cert. denied, 479 U.S. 1043, 107 S.Ct. 906, 93 L.Ed.2d 856 (1987).

ness of the Act generally, but more importantly, it defeats the purpose of the public protection provision. If individuals are uncertain as to which forms or agencies the provision applies, then they are likely to comply with the information request even though it lacks a control number.[47] The public protection provision loses its effectiveness as a check against agency abuse if individuals are subject to penalization when they refuse to comply with information requests lacking OMB control numbers. On the other hand, the *Shane* court may have had other considerations in mind. Some members of Congress, at least, have expressed concern about the potential for OMB to misuse its legal authority under the Act to affect the substance of agency programs.[48] By curtailing OMB's jurisdiction under the Act, *Shane* evidences a judicial response to that trend.

Nevertheless, since the Act came into existence, agencies have made substantial progress in reducing paperwork funding. In part, this may be due to the fact that a great deal of information can now be collected electronically. For example, President Clinton directed federal agencies to avoid traditional paper approaches, where electronic means were available. In 1997, for example, "the Internal Revenue Service (IRS) offered Telefile to most single filers who did not claim dependents, allowing over 4 million tax payers who had previously filed the 1040 EZ paper form to file their tax returns using a touch-tone phone."[49]

§ 20.5 LIMITATIONS SPECIFIC TO AGENCY SUBPOENA POWERS

This section discusses the limitations on an agency's use of a subpoena to acquire information. These limitations are, first, that an agency have jurisdiction over the subpoenaed party and second, that the subpoena be issued by the proper person. The use of a subpoena may also be limited by certain privileges.

When the transferability of information between agencies is involved, claims often are made to limit the disclosure powers of agencies. In *Shell Oil Co. v. DOE*,[1] for example, the Department of Energy used its broad authority to collect the information necessary for it to formulate an appropriate energy policy. This information, however, had to be

47. Failure to obtain control numbers can have serious consequences. See Saco River Cellular, Inc. v. FCC, 133 F.3d 25 (D.C.Cir.1998), cert. denied, 525 U.S. 813, 119 S.Ct. 47, 142 L.Ed.2d 37 (1998).

48. For example, in introducing his bill to reauthorize the Act, Senator Bingaman stated: "[T]he record of the past 8 years shows that there is a need to increase public participation in, and improve the accountability of [OMB] and Federal agency decision making." His introduction outlined several of his bills proposals designed to check OMB power. See 135 Cong.Rec. S12926 (daily ed. Oct. 6, 1989).

See also, Funk, Paperwork Reduction Meets Administrative Law, supra note 139, at 103–110.

49. OMB, Reports to Congress Under the Paperwork Reduction Act of 1995 (1997), *cited* by Jerry Masher, Richard Merrill, Peter Chance, Administrative Law, The American Public Law System, 647 (West Group, 1998).

§ 20.5

1. 477 F.Supp. 413 (D.Del.1979), aff'd, 631 F.2d 231 (3d Cir.1980), cert. denied 450 U.S. 1024, 101 S.Ct. 1730, 68 L.Ed.2d 219 (1981).

shared with the Federal Trade Commission and the Department of Justice's Antitrust Divisions. While such sharing arrangements can increase governmental investigative efficiency as well as hold down the private costs of compliance,[2] it raises difficulties as well. As Justice Powell noted in his dissent to the denial of certiorari in this case:

> The dissemination of this extraordinary volume of data to those prosecutorial Government agencies raises a serious question, as these agencies thereby may obtain information that statutory and constitutional safeguards would bar them from obtaining directly in antitrust enforcement actions. The likelihood that rights of potential antitrust defendants will be violated increases as DOE demands increasingly more data from companies subject to its regulation and then disseminates the information to prosecutorial agencies. Congress has given DOE an investigative power that appears to be intrusive as well as excessively burdensome in its own right. But that power should not become a blanket discovery authority for the use of the Department of Justice and the Federal Trade Commission without the safeguards provided by law against abuse of legal rights.[3]

(a) Jurisdiction Over the Subpoenaed Party Must Exist

For a subpoena issued under an agency investigation to be legal, the agency must have jurisdiction to conduct the investigation. What the agency is authorized to investigate is generally set out in the various empowering statutes discussed in earlier sections. Who falls within these guidelines and over whom the agency may assert its authority, however, is often the subject of litigation. The unanimous practice in the courts today is that the initial determination of the coverage of an administrative act or investigation is in the control of the head of the agency and should not be reviewed by the district courts in an enforcement proceeding.[4] This principle was first established in *Endicott Johnson Corp. v.*

2. See Walter Gellhorn et al., Administrative Law 666 (8th ed. 1986).

3. Shell Oil Co. v. Department of Energy, 450 U.S. 1024, 101 S.Ct. 1730, 68 L.Ed.2d 219 (1981). Se generally Stevenson, Panel Discussion: Agency Release and Sharing of Information, 34 Admin.L.Rev. 159, 160 (1982); Emerson Electric Co. v. Schlesinger, 609 F.2d 898 (8th Cir.1979). For statutes that explicitly restrict the transfer of information, see, e.g., The Right to Financial Privacy Act of 1978, codified as amended at 12 U.S.C.A. §§ 3401, 3421 (1988). See also Carey v. Klutznick, 653 F.2d 732 (2d Cir.1981) (where district court's order that the Census Bureau produce the master address registers for every municipality in New York was found to have been improvidently granted, cert. denied 455 U.S. 999, 102 S.Ct. 1630, 71 L.Ed.2d 866 (1982)).

4. See, e.g., SEC v. Wall St. Transcript Corp., 422 F.2d 1371, 1375 (2d Cir.1970), cert. denied 398 U.S. 958, 90 S.Ct. 2170, 26 L.Ed.2d 542 (1970) ("it has long been established that the question of the inclusion of a particular person or entity within the coverage of a regulatory statute is generally for initial determination by an agency, subject to review on direct appeal, rather than for a district court whose jurisdiction is invoked to enforce an administrative subpoena"); SEC v. Brigadoon Scotch Distributing Co., 480 F.2d 1047, 1052–53 (2d Cir.1973), cert. denied, 415 U.S. 915, 94 S.Ct. 1410, 39 L.Ed.2d 469 (1974) ("The Commission must be free without undue interference or delay to conduct an investigation which will adequately develop a factual basis for a determination as to whether particular activities come within the Commission's regulatory authority."); FTC v. Texaco, Inc., 555 F.2d

Perkins[5] when the Court was asked who should determine the applicability of the Walsh–Healy Public Contracts Act. The Court held that the Secretary of Labor must have exclusive authority to determine who and what the Act covered before investigating. Authority to investigate the existence of possible violations necessarily must include the authority to investigate possible coverage of the Act otherwise the Secretary would be forced to determine issues before investigating what the investigation was designed to illuminate. Such a practice, the Court acknowledged, would be of "dubious propriety" and "doubtful practicality" given the agency's broad purpose of regulating and raising labor standards.[6] Three years later in *Oklahoma Press Publishing Co. v. Walling,*[7] the Court confirmed that it is the role of the administrator, not the district courts, to determine the question of coverage in the preliminary investigation of possible violations.[8]

Given this general rule against reviewing jurisdiction of an administrative act in an enforcement proceeding, there are nevertheless limited exceptions to this prohibition. In *FTC v. Miller,*[9] the respondent successfully defeated the enforcement of an agency subpoena on the grounds that he fell squarely within the common carrier exemption from investigations by the Federal Trade Commission in 15 U.S.C.A. § 46:[10] "[T]he agency's power to investigate is specifically limited by statute . . ., and thus the policy against interfering with administrative investigations must give way."[11] Citing *FTC v. Feldman,*[12] the court laid out "three situations in which . . . coverage issues may be litigated in subpoena-enforcement proceedings . . . : (1) when the agency has clearly violated a right secured by statute or agency regulation; (2) the issue involved is a strictly legal one not involving the agency's expertise or any factual

862, 879 (D.C.Cir.1977), cert. denied, 431 U.S. 974, 97 S.Ct. 2940, 53 L.Ed.2d 1072 (1977) ("As a general rule, substantive issues which may be raised in defense against an administrative complaint are premature in an enforcement proceeding.... The reasons for this rule are obvious. If parties under investigation could contest substantive issues in an enforcement proceeding, when the agency lacks the information to establish its case, administrative investigation would be foreclosed or at least substantially delayed."); Donovan v. Shaw 668 F.2d 985, 989 (8th Cir.1982) ("It is well-settled that a subpoena enforcement proceeding is not the proper forum in which to litigate the question of coverage under a particular federal statute. This question, reserved for initial determination by the administrative agency seeking judicial enforcement of its subpoena, cannot be resolved before the agency has had an opportunity to examine the relevant records." (citations omitted)).

5. 317 U.S. 501, 63 S.Ct. 339, 87 L.Ed. 424 (1943).

6. Id. at 508, 63 S.Ct. at 343.

7. 327 U.S. 186, 66 S.Ct. 494, 90 L.Ed. 614 (1946)

8. Id. at 213–14, 66 S.Ct. at 508, 90 L.Ed. 614 (1946). The Court acknowledged that giving the Administrator such power may in some instances infringe on privacy interests which the investigation may later reveal were not within the authority of the administration to investigate. But if the issue of coverage had to be determined prior to investigation and was reviewable by the courts in a subpoena enforcement action, the effect would be to "stop much if not all of investigation in the public interest at the threshold of inquiry.... [T]his would render substantially impossible [the Administrator's] effective discharge of the duties of investigation and enforcement which Congress had placed upon him." Id. at 213, 66 S.Ct. at 508.

9. 549 F.2d 452 (7th Cir.1977).

10. 549 F.2d at 462.

11. Id.

12. 532 F.2d 1092 (7th Cir.1976).

determinations; or (3) when the issue cannot be raised upon judicial review [of a later order] of the agency."[13]

Jurisdiction to investigate a party is not necessary to gain access to that party's records. If the documents of a third party, admittedly not subject to the investigatory powers of an agency, are relevant to an authorized investigation, then the agency may subpoena that party for those documents. The defense that the person subpoenaed is not subject to the administrative regulation has not been recognized, provided the agency considers the information subpoenaed within the regulation's coverage.[14]

(b) Subpoena Must Be Issued by the Proper Person

Generally, only the administrator is authorized to issue subpoenas. This restriction, however, only minimally limits an agency's subpoena powers. The subpoenas usually are signed in blank and provided to the administrator's subordinates. Courts uphold this practice[15] as well as an administrator's decision to delegate his or her authority to sign subpoenas.[16]

(c) Effect of Privilege on Agency Subpoena Power

Generally, privileges are vague, developed through the common law,[17] and have but limited force in administrative proceedings.[18]

13. 549 F.2d at 460 (citations omitted). See also United States v. Frontier Airlines, Inc., 563 F.2d 1008 (10th Cir.1977) (use of the flight recorder data for investigations of airline behavior other than accidents was not contemplated and subpoena requesting the information will not be enforced as outside its statutory authority).

14. See, e.g., Freeman v. Brown Bros. Harriman & Co., 250 F.Supp. 32 (S.D.N.Y. 1966), aff'd, 357 F.2d 741 (2d Cir.1966), cert. denied 384 U.S. 933, 86 S.Ct. 1446, 16 L.Ed.2d 532 (1966) (subpoena issued under authority of the Agricultural Marketing Agreement Act, 7 U.S.C.A. § 610(h), was enforced for the records of a customer's account even though the holder of the records was not subject to the Act). See also United States v. Marshall Durbin & Co. of Haleyville, Inc., 363 F.2d 1 (5th Cir.1966) (although the party subpoenaed is arguably not subject to regulation, the subpoena will be enforced because the records requested are relevant to an investigation).

15. See, e.g., NLRB v. Lewis, 249 F.2d 832, 835 (9th Cir.1957) ("subpoenas may validly be issued by a Regional Director under the facsimile signature of a Board member"), aff'd, 357 U.S. 10, 78 S.Ct. 1029, 2 L.Ed.2d 1103 (1958); NLRB v. John S. Barnes Corp., 178 F.2d 156, 159 (7th Cir. 1949) ("expressed power to delegate the authority to prosecute" includes "the incidental power to issue subpoenas").

16. Fleming v. Mohawk Wrecking & Lumber Co., 331 U.S. 111, 67 S.Ct. 1129, 91 L.Ed. 1375 (1947). Cf. NLRB v. Duval Jewelry Co., 357 U.S. 1, 78 S.Ct. 1024, 2 L.Ed.2d 1097 (1958) (regards the delegability of the power to revoke a subpoena).

See also SEC v. Arthur Young & Co., 584 F.2d 1018, 1026 (D.C.Cir.1978) ("To require Commission members to exercise the substantial amount of supervision that subpoena-detailing would require is to grind its operations to a halt."), cert. denied, 439 U.S. 1071, 99 S.Ct. 841, 59 L.Ed.2d 37 (1979); and Donovan v. National Bank of Alaska, 696 F.2d 678, 682 (9th Cir.1983) ("with regard to issuing subpoenas, ERISA expressly makes available to the Secretary [of Labor] 'or any officers designated by him' these provisions of the Federal Trade Commission Act relating to the attendance of witnesses and the production of documents" (citation omitted)).

17. "Except as otherwise required by the Constitution of the United States or provided by Act of Congress or in rules prescribed by the Supreme Court pursuant to statutory authority, the privilege of a witness, ... shall be governed by the principles of the common law as they may be

This subsection addresses the applicability of the more frequently invoked privileges, including: the executive privilege, the lawyer-client privilege, the accountant-client privilege, and the spousal privilege.

There is no mention of an executive privilege in the Constitution nor the constitutional debates; however, presidents have invoked the privilege whenever it appeared necessary "to don the shroud of secrecy."[19] When considering the applicability of the privilege, courts employ a balancing test, "weighing 'the detrimental effects of disclosure against the necessity for production shown.' "[20] One addresses the first half of the balance by asking whether the requested information is within the privilege's scope. One determines the "weight" of the second half of the balance by asking whether the privilege should be recognized in the specific proceeding at hand.[21] *United States v. Nixon*[22] is one of the most significant cases for this inquiry.

United States v. Nixon arose out of *United States v. Mitchell,*[23] a case prosecuting former government and presidential campaign officials for numerous offenses including conspiracy to defraud the United States and to obstruct justice. The President was not among the defendants in *Mitchell;* however, the Special Prosecutor in *Mitchell* moved for a subpoena *duces tecum* requiring the President to produce certain tapes and papers. The district court issued the subpoena; the President's refusal to comply led to *United States v. Nixon.*

After holding that it had jurisdiction, that a justiciable controversy existed, that it was not a political question, and that the subpoena had been issued properly, the Court determined the extent to which the President was immune to such subpoenas. The President first argued "that the separation of powers doctrine precluded review of a President's claim of privilege."[24] Relying on *Marbury v. Madison,*[25] the Court reaffirmed its "province and duty ... 'to say what the law is' " with respect to the claim of privilege.[26] The Court then acknowledged the existence and importance of the executive's privilege, but concluded that it was not absolute because such an unqualified privilege would impede the judicia-

interpreted by the courts ... in the light of reason and experience." Fed.R.Evid. 501.

18. See, e.g., Ryan v. Commissioner, 568 F.2d 531 (7th Cir.1977), cert. denied 439 U.S. 820, 99 S.Ct. 84, 58 L.Ed.2d 111 (1978) (claim of marital privilege was denied on the facts of the case). See generally Note, Formalism, Legal Realism and Constitutionally Protected Privacy Under the Fourth and Fifth Amendments, 90 Harv. L.Rev. 945 (1977); Note, Privileged Communications Before Federal Administrative Agencies, 31 Chi.L.R. 395 (1964); Gerety, Redefining Privacy, 12 Harv. C.R.C.L.L.Rev. 233 (1977); McKenna, The Constitutional Protection of Private Papers: The Role of a Hierarchical Fourth Amendment, 53 Ind.L.J. 55 (1977).

19. L. Tribe, American Constitutional Law 275 (2d ed. 1988) (citing Berger, The Incarnation of Executive Privilege, 22 U.C.L.A. L.Rev. 4 (1974)).

20. Dellums v. Powell, 561 F.2d 242, 246 (D.C.Cir.1977), cert. denied, 434 U.S. 880, 98 S.Ct. 234, 54 L.Ed.2d 160 (1977) (citations omitted).

21. See generally Tribe, supra note 19, at 275–285.

22. 418 U.S. 683, 94 S.Ct. 3090, 41 L.Ed.2d 1039 (1974).

23. 377 F.Supp. 1326 (D.D.C.1974).

24. 418 U.S. at 703, 94 S.Ct. at 3105.

25. 5 U.S. (1 Cranch) 137, 2 L.Ed. 60 (1803).

26. 418 U.S. at 703, 94 S.Ct. at 3105.

ry's constitutional duty to do justice in criminal prosecutions. Citing *Nixon v. Sirica,*[27] the Court accepted presidential communications as "presumptively privileged;" however, the Court said that "this presumptive privilege must be considered in light of our historic commitment to the rule of law."[28]

In addressing these considerations, the Court emphasized that the information was being subpoenaed for a criminal prosecution and that "[t]he ends of criminal justice would be defeated if judgments were to be founded on a partial or speculative presentation of the facts."[29] Furthermore, "[t]he right to the production of all evidence at a criminal trial similarly has constitutional dimensions" implicating both the fifth and the sixth amendments.[30] In light of this fundamental need for a "fair administration of criminal justice," the Court analyzed the importance of a "general privilege of confidentiality for Presidential communications."[31] The Court found it significant that the President's challenge to the subpoena was based "on the claim that he [had] a privilege against disclosure of confidential communications. He [did] not place his claim of privilege on the ground they [were] military or diplomatic secrets."[32] The Court makes clear that had the documents subject to the subpoena contained military or diplomatic secrets the analysis would have been different.[33]

The Court concluded "that when the ground for asserting privilege as to subpoenaed materials sought for use in a criminal trial is based only on the generalized interest in confidentiality, it cannot prevail over the fundamental demands of due process of law in the fair administration of criminal justice."[34]

Consequently, the Court in *United States v. Nixon* reveals much about the two questions asked at the beginning of this subsection. Regarding the scope of the privilege, the Court states that a "generalized interest in confidentiality" is insufficient to be included. The Court strongly suggests that military or diplomatic secrets, or "state secrets," could be covered by the privilege. Regarding the type of proceeding in which the privilege should be recognized, the Court emphasizes the serious constitutional implications which denying evidence in a criminal trial would have on the fundamental demands of due process. Beyond the concern of denying the accused information necessary for a defense is the reality that in a criminal prosecution the government can always preserve the confidentiality of information sought by dropping the charge against the accused.[35]

27. 487 F.2d 700 (D.C.Cir.1973).

28. 418 U.S. at 708, 94 S.Ct. at 3107.

29. Id. at 709, 94 S.Ct. at 3108.

30. Id. at 711, 94 S.Ct. at 3109.

31. Id.

32. Id. at 710, 94 S.Ct. at 3108.

33. "[T]he courts have traditionally shown the utmost deference to Presidential responsibilities" in these areas of Article II duties. Id.

34. Id. at 713, 94 S.Ct. at 3110.

35. "The rationale of the criminal cases is that, since the Government which prosecutes an accused also has the duty to see that justice is done, it is unconscionable to allow it to undertake prosecution and then invoke its governmental privileges to

Two cases arose during the Clinton Administration, that help refine to some extent the scope of executive privilege.[36] In Re Sealed Case involved an investigation of Secretary of Agriculture, Mike Espy, by the Office of Independent Counsel (OIC). The Independent Counsel (IC) sought documents prepared by White House Counsel. That Counsel had been asked by President Clinton to investigate allegations of impropriety by Secretary Espy and to advise him of what action should be taken. The Independent Counsel sought these documents, which had been prepared as part of the White House Counsel's investigation. On appeal from a district court order upholding the White House's claims of privilege, the appellate court agreed that executive privilege was not limited to communications directly involving the President, but also covered communications made by presidential advisors in the course of preparing advice for the President.[37] *In re Grand Jury Proceedings*[38] arose when the Independent Counsel sought to compel the testimony of senior advisors to the President. The District Court noted that this testimony was presumptively privileged, even though the matters discussed involved private conduct; however, the court noted that "the President does need to address personal matters in the context of his official decisions."[39] Since the issues in this case involved advice regarding whether or not to assert official privileges, impeachment proceedings, the President's State of the Union address and a visit by a foreign head of state, the court held that executive privilege applied and the Independent Counsel had to demonstrate a need sufficient to overcome the presumptive privilege.[40] The court found that this need was demonstrated.[41] The criminal nature of both cases ultimately required submission of most of the information sought by the Independent Counsel in these cases.

As these cases and the Court in *United States v. Nixon* makes clear, executive privilege is not absolute, especially in the criminal context.[42] Other cases are helpful for further defining the privilege in the context of a civil proceeding. In *United States v. Reynolds,*[43] the plaintiffs filed a

deprive the accused of anything which might be material to his defense." United States v. Reynolds, 345 U.S. 1, 12, 73 S.Ct. 528, 534, 97 L.Ed. 727 (1953). See also Tribe, supra note 19, at 282.

36. In re Sealed Case, 121 F.3d 729 (D.C.Cir.1997); In re Grand Jury Proceedings, 5 F.Supp. 2d 21 (D.D.C.1998), affirmed in part, reversed in part In re Lindsey, 158 F.3d 1263 (D.C.Cir.1998), cert. denied Office of President v. Office of Independent Counsel, 525 U.S. 996, 119 S.Ct. 466, 142 L.Ed.2d 418 (1998).

37. 121 F.3d at 750–52. This case also clarified some other aspects of the scope of the privilege, including the appropriate standards for determining whether the privilege was overcome. Id. at 753–56.

38. 5 F.Supp. 2d 21 (D.D.C.1998), affirmed in part, reversed in part In re Lindsey, 158 F.3d 1263 (D.C.Cir.1998), cert. denied Office of President v. Office of Independent Counsel, 525 U.S. 996, 119 S.Ct. 466, 142 L.Ed.2d 418 (1998).

39. Id. at 26.

40. Id. at 28.

41. Id.

42. See especially United States v. Smith, 750 F.2d 1215 (4th Cir.1984) where the court "conclude[d] that a district court . . . is not empowered . . . to exclude classified evidence that is relevant to the accused's defense on the ground that the prevention of harm to the national security outweighs defendant's need. . . . [T]he Executive [is left] the ultimate decision whether to expose the classified material. . . ." Id. at 1220.

43. 345 U.S. 1, 73 S.Ct. 528, 97 L.Ed. 727 (1953).

civil suit under the Federal Tort Claims Act[44] and requested information from the Air Force's official accident report concerning the fatal crash which gave rise to this suit. Taking judicial notice that the accident occurred at "a time of vigorous preparation for national defense" and that "air power is one of the most potent weapons in our scheme of defense," the Court found that the information was reasonably within the scope of the privilege. The Court then looked to the nature of the proceeding and found only "a dubious showing of necessity" for disclosure. The Court stated: "Where there is a strong showing of necessity, the claim of privilege should not be lightly accepted, but even the most compelling necessity cannot overcome the claim of privilege if the court is ultimately satisfied that military secrets are at stake."[45]

Reynolds should not be understood as suggesting that the executive privilege will be upheld merely because the underlying proceeding is civil rather than criminal, as in *U.S. v. Nixon.* For example, in *Dellums v. Powell*[46] the D.C. Circuit affirmed the district court's ruling that the civil "plaintiffs completely [had overcome] whatever presumptive executive privilege may attach to the former President's interest in the tapes."[47] The allegations were that Nixon's tapes would reveal a conversation between the President and the attorney general regarding an executive conspiracy to disrupt "May Day" celebrations by unconstitutionally harassing and arresting plaintiffs. The circuit court balanced the severity of the alleged constitutional violations, the materiality of the information sought to the case, and the likelihood that the tapes would reveal the evidence and concluded that the plaintiffs had overcome the rebuttable presumption of privilege of the executive.[48] The court made clear, however, that the plaintiffs would have access to the record only if such recorded conversations existed.[49] *Dellums* thus shows that it is possible for a civil plaintiff to overcome the executive privilege.[50]

Courts have also wrestled with the issue of being able to recognize the appropriate circumstances for the privilege without undermining its

44. 28 U.S.C.A. § 2674.

45. 345 U.S. at 11, 73 S.Ct. at 533 (citing Totten v. United States, 92 U.S. (2 Otto) 105, 23 L.Ed. 605 (1875) (viewed as one of the first judicial recognitions of a state secrets doctrine)).

46. 561 F.2d 242 (D.C.Cir.1977), cert. denied, 434 U.S. 880, 98 S.Ct. 234, 54 L.Ed.2d 160 (1977).

47. Id. at 248 (quoting from the district court opinion).

48. Id. at 249 ("Given the substantial violations of constitutional right sought to be vindicated, given the high-level meeting of the Justice Department to prepare for the May Day demonstration, the attendance of a White House aide and briefing of Mr. Mitchell as attorney general on these matters, plaintiffs have made a showing of substantial need, in their attempt to establish Mr. Mitchell's responsibility for the violations, for overcoming the presumption of the privilege assumed to exist for former presidents.").

49. Id.

50. Attorney General v. Irish People, Inc., 684 F.2d 928, 953 (D.C.Cir.1982), cert. denied 459 U.S. 1172, 103 S.Ct. 817, 74 L.Ed.2d 1015 (1983), reh'g denied, 460 U.S. 1056, 103 S.Ct. 1509, 75 L.Ed.2d 937 (1983). *Irish People, Inc.* is a civil enforcement action where the court found that the "likelihood of injustice to defendant [was] small indeed ... no constitutional rights [were] threatened, only registration [was] imminent, no jail sentence loom[ed].... On the other hand, the consequences of revealing the evidence [were] of the same magnitude as revealing the military secrets in Reynolds...." Id. at 953–54.

very purpose: "Too much judicial inquiry into the claim of privilege would force disclosure of the thing the privilege was meant to protect, while a complete abandonment of judicial control would lead to intolerable abuses."[51] Analogizing to the privilege against self-incrimination, the *Reynolds* Court found that when circumstantial evidence shows a reasonable danger that disclosure of the evidence would expose national security matters which should not be divulged, then "the occasion for the privilege is appropriate, and the court should not jeopardize the security which the privilege is meant to protect by insisting upon an examination of the evidence, even by the judge alone, in chambers."[52] The Classified Information Procedures Act[53] now provides for a process in criminal cases which permits "the trial judge to rule on questions of admissibility involving classified information before introduction of the evidence in open court."[54]

Another area of privilege that sometimes is recognized in information disclosure disputes is the lawyer/client relationship. In order to encourage clients to obtain legal assistance and to make full disclosure to their attorneys, the privilege "protects only those disclosures—necessary to obtain legal advice—which would not have been made absent the privilege."[55] Therefore, courts have "uniformly held that pre-existing documents which could have been obtained by court process from the client when [the client] was in possession may also be obtained from the attorney by similar process following transfer by the client in order to obtain more informed legal advice."[56]

Another Clinton Administration case involved attorney-client privilege. Independent Counsel Starr pursued the issues in two cases, one before the Eighth Circuit[57] and the other before the D.C. Circuit.[58] Both cases raised essentially the same issues. The IC sought to compel the testimony of the Deputy White House Counsel. The White House took the position that in seeking advice from counsel, the President could rely on an absolute attorney-client privilege. The D.C. Circuit, however,

51. United States v. Reynolds, 345 U.S. at 8, 73 S.Ct. at 532.

52. Id. at 10, 73 S.Ct. at 533.

53. 18 U.S.C.A. §§ 1–16.

54. S.Rep. No. 823, 96th Cong., 2d Sess. 1 (1980), reprinted in 1980 U.S.C.C.A.N. 4294.

55. Fisher v. United States, 425 U.S. 391, 403, 96 S.Ct. 1569, 1577, 48 L.Ed.2d 39 (1976) (citations omitted).

56. Id. at 403, 404, 96 S.Ct. at 1577, 1578 (citations omitted); see, e.g., In re Two Grand Jury Subpoenae Duces Tecum Dated August 21, 1985, 793 F.2d 69, 71 (2d Cir. 1986) ("purpose [of the privilege] is not served by protecting information about client awards and fee arrangements from disclosure" because such information is often disclosed in pleadings, discovery, trials and appeals); In re Grand Jury Proceedings, 791 F.2d 663, 665 (8th Cir.1986) ("matters existing in public eye, such as a person's appearance and handwriting, are generally not confidential communications"); In re Antitrust Grand Jury, 805 F.2d 155, 162 (6th Cir.1986) ("reasons for the attorney-client privilege are completely eviscerated when a client consults an attorney not for advice on past misconduct, but for legal assistance in carrying out a contemplated . . . crime").

57. In Re Grand Jury Subpoena Duces Tecum, 112 F.3d 910, cert. denied, 521 U.S. 1105, 117 S.Ct. 2482, 138 L.Ed.2d 991 (1997).

58. In Re Lindsey, 158 F.3d 1263 (D.C.Cir.1998), cert. denied Office of the President v. Office of the Independent Counsel, 525 U.S. 996, 119 S.Ct. 466, 142 L.Ed.2d 418 (1998).

found that no attorney-client privilege existed when information was sought from a government attorney by the Independent Counsel.[59] The court noted that such a privilege usually existed for a government lawyer and a client in the context of a civil litigation,[60] but whenever a government attorney is called to give evidence about alleged crimes, the lawyer's duty is to provide that evidence.[61] A government lawyer has a special role to play and must uphold the public trust.[62] For the President to be protected in such a case, he would have had to retain a private attorney.[63]

The Court in *Upjohn Co. v. United States*[64] addressed whether the lawyer-client privilege applies when the client is a corporation. With little discussion, the Court assumed that it did.[65] Due to the artificiality of corporations, however, application of the privilege in this context is more complicated than when the client is an individual. The problem arises when a court must determine which of the corporation's employees will have their communications protected by the privilege. The Court of Appeals for the Sixth Circuit decided that the privilege only extended to the "control group," finding that "only the senior management, guiding and integrating the several operations . . . can be said to possess an identity analogous to the corporation as a whole."[66] The Supreme Court reversed, noting that the "control group test . . . frustrates the very purpose of the privilege,"[67] and results in the unpredictable application of the test.[68]

The Court explicitly concluded that "the narrow 'control group test' . . . cannot, consistent with 'the principles of the common law as . . . interpreted . . . in the light of reason and experience,' govern the development of the law in this area."[69] The Court, however, failed to adopt a different test relying instead on a "case-by-case" determination.[70]

59. Id. at 1272–73.

60. Id.

61. Id.

62. Id.

63. Id. at 1276.

64. 449 U.S. 383, 101 S.Ct. 677, 66 L.Ed.2d 584 (1981).

65. Id. at 389–90, 101 S.Ct. at 682–83 (citing United States v. Louisville & Nashville R. Co., 236 U.S. 318, 336, 35 S.Ct. 363, 369, 59 L.Ed. 598 (1915)).

66. Id. at 390, 101 S.Ct. at 683 (quoting United States v. Upjohn Co., 600 F.2d 1223, 1226 (6th Cir.1979)).

67. "The narrow scope given the attorney-client privilege by the court below not only makes it difficult for corporate attorneys to formulate sound advice when their client is faced with a specific legal problem but also threatens to limit the valuable efforts of corporate counsel to ensure their client's compliance with the law." Id. at 392, 101 S.Ct. at 684.

68. Id. at 393, 101 S.Ct. at 684.

69. Id. at 397, 101 S.Ct. at 686 (quoting Fed.Rule Evid. 501).

70. Id. at 396, 101 S.Ct. at 686. The following passage describes the context in which the Court held the privilege applicable to communication between non-management employees and the corporation's lawyer:

> The communications at issue were made by Upjohn employees to counsel for Upjohn.... Information, not available from upper-echelon management, was needed to supply a basis for legal advice.... The communications concerned matters within the scope of the employees' corporate duties, and the employees themselves were sufficiently aware that they were being questioned in order that the corporation could obtain legal

The privilege, however, between accountant and client has uniformly been rejected.[71] In particular, the accountant-client privilege is frequently claimed in I.R.S. subpoena cases. The Court in *United States v. Arthur Young & Co.*[72] expressly held that this privilege did not exist in the tax context. The Court, however, refused to recognize the privilege because of the relevant language in the Code authorizing the I.R.S.'s summons power, not because of any inherent characteristics of the privilege itself.[73]

The privilege against adverse spousal testimony has been restricted in recent years. Based on the medieval concept that husband and wife were legally one, the spousal privilege prevented one's spouse from testifying when the individual could not testify on their own behalf. Generally, commentators have been critical of the privilege;[74] nonetheless, the Court in *Hawkins v. United States*[75] recognized the privilege as barring the testimony of one spouse against the other unless both consent. The rule from *Hawkins* was reconsidered in *Trammel v. United States*[76] where the Court concluded that the privilege was impermissibly broad in light of its history and purpose. Accordingly, the *Hawkins* rule was "modified so that the witness spouse alone has a privilege to refuse to testify adversely; the witness may be neither compelled to testify nor

> advice.... The questionnaire identified ... "the company's General Counsel" and referred in its opening sentence to the possible illegality of payments such as the ones on which information was being sought. A statement of policy accompanying the questionnaire clearly indicated the legal implications of the investigation.... This statement was issued to Upjohn employees worldwide, so that even those interviewees not receiving a questionnaire were aware of the legal implications of the interviews. Pursuant to explicit instructions from the Chairman of the Board, the communications were considered "highly confidential" when made and have been kept confidential by the company. Consistent with the underlying purposes of the attorney-client privilege, these communications must be protected against compelled disclosure.

Id. at 394–95, 101 S.Ct. at 685–86 (citations omitted). See also Liberty Lobby, Inc. v. Dow Jones & Co., 838 F.2d 1287, 1302 (D.C.Cir.1988), cert. denied, 488 U.S. 825, 109 S.Ct. 75, 102 L.Ed.2d 51 (1988) (applying the Upjohn decision, the circuit court states that "[p]re-publication discussions between libel counsel and editors or reporters would seem to come squarely within the scope of the privilege").

71. Couch v. United States, 409 U.S. 322, 93 S.Ct. 611, 34 L.Ed.2d 548 (1973). See also United States v. El Paso Co., 682 F.2d 530 (5th Cir.1982), reh'g denied, 688 F.2d 840 (1982); Sutton v. United States, 658 F.2d 782 (10th Cir.1981); Matter of International Horizons, Inc., 689 F.2d 996 (11th Cir.1982); In re Newton, 718 F.2d 1015 (11th Cir.1983), cert. denied, 466 U.S. 904, 104 S.Ct. 1678, 80 L.Ed.2d 153 (1984).

72. 465 U.S. 805, 104 S.Ct. 1495, 79 L.Ed.2d 826 (1984).

73. "In light of this explicit statement by the Legislative Branch, courts should be chary in recognizing exceptions to the broad summons authority of the IRS or in fashioning new privileges that would curtail disclosure under § 7602. If the broad latitude granted to the IRS by § 7602 is to be circumscribed, that is a choice for Congress, and not this Court, to make." Id. at 816–17, 104 S.Ct. at 1502 (citations omitted).

74. Professor Wigmore has called the privilege "the merest anachronism in legal theory and an indefensible obstruction to truth in practice." 8 John Henry Wigmore, Evidence in Trials at Common Law § 2228 (John T. McNaughton rev. 1961).

75. 358 U.S. 74, 79 S.Ct. 136, 3 L.Ed.2d 125 (1958). The Court reasoned "that the law should not force or encourage testimony which might alienate husband and wife, or further inflame existing domestic differences." Id. at 79, 79 S.Ct. at 139.

76. 445 U.S. 40, 100 S.Ct. 906, 63 L.Ed.2d 186 (1980).

foreclosed from testifying. This modification ... furthers the important public interest in marital harmony without unduly burdening legitimate law enforcement needs."[77]

The spousal privilege, where recognized, has several limitations. First, the privilege does not survive the marriage.[78] Second, the privilege does not extend beyond its purpose of protecting marital harmony. Consequently, where the marriage is considered a sham, the privilege is unavailable.[79]

The so-called "protective function" privilege was at issue after a federal district court refused to find that officers of the U.S. Secret Service (USSS) could not refuse to answer questions as part of a grand jury proceeding of the Office of Independent Counsel (OIC).[80] The U.S. Secretary of the Treasury argued that without a protective function privilege, the President would physically distance himself from the USSS rather than risk the chance of USSS agents overhearing comments or observing behavior of the President that might implicate him in a felony. If the President withdrew from USSS protection, argued the Secretary of the Treasury, it would place the President in danger. The court of appeals stated that it was not prohibited from recognizing a novel privilege,[81] but that the Secretary of the Treasury would have to "demonstrate with a high degree of clarity and certainty" that the proposed privilege would "effectively advance the public good."[82]

The court concluded that the Secretary of Treasury had failed to show the need for a protective function privilege. The court analyzed congressional policy, agency practice, whether there was a tight means-end fit between the proposed privilege and the goal it was purported to achieve, and the opinions of former Presidents. The court found that congressional policy placed a statutory duty on the President to accept USSS protection[83] and that the USSS was required by statute to report relevant information to the OIC.[84] Second, no agency rule prohibited former USSS agents from testifying in criminal proceedings, which weakened any argument to exempt current agents from giving such testimony.[85] Third, the privilege itself suffered from at least three weaknesses: it only protected agents from testifying about conduct that they knew was felonious *at the very moment* they witnessed it;[86] the privilege was vested in the Secretary of the Treasury and not in the President, which would leave former Presidents unable to invoke the privilege;[87] and the privilege was most useful in private whereas the

77. Id. at 53, 100 S.Ct. at 914.

78. See United States v. Bolzer, 556 F.2d 948 (9th Cir.1977) (even when the divorce judgment is being appealed).

79. See Lutwak v. United States, 344 U.S. 604, 73 S.Ct. 481, 97 L.Ed. 593 (1953), reh'g denied, 345 U.S. 919, 73 S.Ct. 726, 97 L.Ed. 1352 (1953).

80. In re Sealed Case, 148 F.3d 1073 (D.C.Cir.1998), per curiam.

81. Id. at 1075.

82. Id. at 1076.

83. Id. at 1077.

84. Id. at 1078.

85. Id. at 1077.

86. Id.

87. Id. at 1077–78.

President was at greatest risk in public.[88] Finally, the court noted that not all former Presidents agreed that the privilege should shield the USSS from testifying in criminal trials.[89]

§ 20.6 JUDICIAL ENFORCEMENT OF AGENCY ORDERS TO DISCLOSE INFORMATION

Upon issuance of a subpoena or reporting requirement, most parties voluntarily comply and turn over the requested information. If, however, the party refuses to cooperate, most agencies have no inherent power to enforce compliance. They must enlist the aid of the courts. To do so, an agency usually must also persuade the Department of Justice to seek enforcement on their behalf.[1]

ICC v. Brimson[2] established that enforcement of a legal duty, such as the duty to turn over documents lawfully subpoenaed by an agency, and the imposition of criminal sanctions when a compliance order is disobeyed, is a judicial function.[3] Authorization for an agency to turn to the judiciary for enforcement is usually incorporated in agency enabling statutes.[4]

A review of what happens when an agency faces a contumacious witness helps to clarify the enforcement process. Upon refusal of a party to comply with an agency order, either by submitting a refusal or by simply letting the date of compliance pass, the Department of Justice will usually file a petition on behalf of the agency for enforcement in the appropriate federal district court.[5] The court will then review the request of the agency and either uphold its validity and issue a compliance order or invalidate it. What the court may look to in determining whether to enforce the subpoena and how the non-complying party may challenge the subpoena are often the subject of the proceeding. The Administrative Procedure Act,[6] which provides that courts shall enforce the subpoena so long as it is "found to be in accordance with law," is not much guidance. Judicially created standards of validity, however, have been created and

88. Id. at 1078.

89. Id. at 1076–77.

§ 20.6

1. See generally S & E Contractors, Inc. v. United States, 406 U.S. 1, 92 S.Ct. 1411, 31 L.Ed.2d 658 (1972).

2. 154 U.S. 447, 14 S.Ct. 1125, 38 L.Ed. 1047 (1894).

3. Id. at 487–89, 14 S.Ct. at 1137–38. The Court also found that an enforcement proceeding was within its jurisdiction because it was a valid "case or controversy" and not just an ancillary or advisory proceeding. Id. at 487, 14 S.Ct. at 1137. See also Shasta Minerals & Chemical Co. v. SEC, 328 F.2d 285, 286 (10th Cir.1964) (power to punish for contempt "is not generally available to federal administrative agencies"); United States v. Feaster, 376 F.2d 147 (5th Cir.1967), cert. denied 389 U.S. 920, 88 S.Ct. 237, 19 L.Ed.2d 265 (1967).

4. The I.C.C. authorizing statute, 49 U.S.C.A. § 10321c(1), (3), is typical: "If a witness disobeys a subpoena, the Commission ... may petition a court of the United States to enforce that subpoena.... [t]he court may punish a refusal to obey a subpoena as a contempt of court."

5. Generally, the district courts of the United States are given jurisdiction to enforce an agency subpoena by statute. See, e.g., 49 U.S.C.A. § 10321c(3).

6. 5 U.S.C.A. § 555(d).

usually are relied upon to review agency orders.[7]

Upon a finding of validity, the court will order the party to comply. Usually imposition of fines or finding of contempt for non-compliance will take place only upon refusal to comply with the court order. In some cases, however, the legislature may provide that criminal sanctions may attach immediately upon finding the disclosure request valid, with no subsequent chance for compliance.[8] Likewise, provisions for imposing fines for refusal to obey an agency default decree will often automatically attach within a given time after the decree is issued. Because of the harsh results of these statutes, courts will often exercise their discretion in imposing the sanctions, especially if a timely challenge to the order is made in good faith.[9] Once legislatively created fines attach and the alleged violator has brought no challenge to the request before accrual of the fines begins, courts are usually powerless to deny these forfeitures retroactively.[10]

7. Courts apply the test created in *Endicott Johnson/Oklahoma Press,* see sec. 20.2, supra notes 11 and 14 and accompanying text.

8. See, e.g., 15 U.S.C.A. § 78u(c) ("Any person who shall, without just cause, fail or refuse to ... [obey] the subpoena of the [Securities and Exchange] Commission, shall be guilty of a misdemeanor and, upon conviction, shall be subject to a fine of not more than $1000 or to imprisonment for a term of not more than one year, or both."). But see, Guaranty Underwriters v. Johnson, 133 F.2d 54, 56 (5th Cir.1943) (applying 15 U.S.C.A. § 78u(c), the court held that the remedy for a party claiming that the S.E.C. was making unreasonable demands "lies in refusing compliance with unlawful demands for records or testimony, which can be enforced only by application to the District Court under [§ 78u(c)]. A bonafide contention of this sort will not result in punishment under the last sentence of [§ 78u(c)].").

9. Casey v. FTC, 578 F.2d 793, 797 (9th Cir.1978) ("there is no risk of criminal prosecution where one in good faith challenges an agency subpoena by noncompliance"); St. Regis Paper Co. v. United States, 368 U.S. 208, 226–27, 82 S.Ct. 289, 299–300, 7 L.Ed.2d 240 (1961) reh'g denied, 368 U.S. 972, 82 S.Ct. 437, 7 L.Ed.2d 401 (1962) (In dictum, the Court stated that petitioner had an opportunity to seek relief from penalties under § 10 of the F.T.C. Act before they began accruing. When a party makes a good faith challenge to the validity of Commission orders, a court may stay the accrual of such penalties.); Genuine Parts Co. v. FTC, 445 F.2d 1382, 1394 (5th Cir. 1971) ("The implication is that a stay of the accrual of Section 10 penalties would be appropriate whenever the challenged order 'appears suspect' and the review seeks a 'good faith test' of 'reasonable objections' to the order.").

Recognizing the restrictions on parties' ability to challenge subpoenas that these criminal sanctions imposed, Congress amended the Federal Trade Commission Act in 1980, stating: "An additional provision of the bill would eliminate the threat of criminal sanctions applied to those recipients of a Commission subpoena who in good faith resist unnecessary investigations by making such sanctions inapplicable until a court has acted in enforcement." S.Rep. No. 500, 96th Cong., 2d Sess. 4 (1980) reprinted in 1980 U.S.C.C.A.N. 1102, 1205 (referring to Federal Trade Commission Improvements Act of 1980, Pub.L. No. 96–252, § 6, 94 Stat. 374, 376 (1980) (codified at 15 U.S.C.A. § 50)).

10. See, e.g., United States v. W.H. Hodges & Co., 533 F.2d 276 (5th Cir.1976) (once statutory penalties legally attach, the court cannot forgive them; "a party could have instituted a suit prior to the forfeitures attaching and the courts could then have stayed the accrual based on the good faith challenge") (citing St. Regis Paper Co. v. United States, 368 U.S. 208, 82 S.Ct. 289, 7 L.Ed.2d 240 (1961), reh'g denied, 368 U.S. 972, 82 S.Ct. 437, 7 L.Ed.2d 401 (1962)).

§ 20.7 PHYSICAL INSPECTIONS

The ability to conduct physical on-site inspections or visitations of private and business premises is one of the most powerful tools agencies have for ensuring compliance with regulatory acts. For example, allowing agents to enter and inspect manufacturing plants, meat packing plants and storage warehouses is critical to maintaining health and safety standards. Similarly, federal agencies such as OSHA rely heavily on inspections to determine whether its workplace safety rules are being obeyed.[1] Agencies must exercise this power with restraint to avoid violating equally important rights of the citizens protected by the Constitution, the fourth amendment in particular. Because significant public concerns are also at stake, courts have tended to apply the fourth amendment to administrative searches more loosely than in criminal contexts.[2] In addition, this area of the law seems always to be in a state of flux.

§ 20.7.1 Extent of Fourth Amendment Protection

It was not until 1959 that the Supreme Court dealt specifically with the extent to which the fourth amendment applies to administrative searches. In *Frank v. Maryland,*[3] the Court held that the Baltimore City Health Department could conduct a warrantless search of private premises as part of an inspection to ensure compliance with the Baltimore City Code. Acting on a complaint of rat infestation, a Baltimore City Health Department inspector conducted an inspection of the houses in the vicinity of the infestation. An exploration of the outside of the defendant's home revealed that the House was in extreme decay and that there was a pile of rodent feces and debris in the rear of the House. The inspector demanded entry to inspect the defendant's basement. The defendant refused to permit the warrantless inspection, and was arrested and was found guilty of the offense.[4]

§ 20.7

1. See generally Eugene Bardach and Robert A. Kagan, Going By The Book: The Problems of Regulatory Unreasonableness (1982).

2. See, e.g., Vernonia School District 47J v. Acton, 515 U.S. 646, 115 S.Ct. 2386, 132 L.Ed.2d 564 (1995) (upholding a school rule requiring as a condition of participation in school athletics that team members participate in periodic, random testing of urine samples for certain drugs). As with administrative subpoenas and required reporting, the agencies must have statutory authority to conduct physical inspections. An example is found in the Food and Drug Act, 21 U.S.C.A. § 374(a)(1), which authorizes the administrator "(A) to enter, at reasonable times, any factory, warehouse, or establishment in which food, drugs, devices or cosmetics are manufactured, processed, packed, or held, for introduction into interstate commerce.... and (B) to inspect, at reasonable times and within reasonable limits and in a reasonable manner, such factory, warehouse, establishment, or vehicle and all pertinent equipment, finished and unfinished materials; containers, and labeling therein." (footnote omitted).

3. 359 U.S. 360, 79 S.Ct. 804, 3 L.Ed.2d 877 (1959), reh'g denied, 360 U.S. 914, 79 S.Ct. 1292, 3 L.Ed.2d 1263; 360 U.S. 914, 79 S.Ct. 1292, 3 L.Ed.2d 1263 (1959).

4. Sec. 120 of Art. 12 of the Baltimore City Code provides:

> Whenever the Commissioner of Health shall have cause to suspect that a nuisance exists in any House, cellar or enclosure, he may demand entry therein in the day time, and if the owner or occupier shall refuse or delay to open the same

On appeal, the Court reviewed its prior decisions concerning the "security of one's privacy against arbitrary intrusion by the police."[5] It concluded that two protections emerge from the general proscription against such intrusion: 1) "the right to be secure from intrusion into personal privacy, the right to shut the door on officials of the state unless their entry is under proper authority of law"[6] and 2) "the right to resist unauthorized entry which has as its design the securing of information to fortify the coercive power of the state against the individual, information which may be used to effect a further deprivation of life or liberty or property."[7] The Court noted that this second aspect of the constitutional protection against invasion of privacy served as the historic basis of the fourth amendment. While the Court also noted that the fourth amendment is not restricted to these "historic bounds," its protection could not be invoked in this case because "[n]o evidence for a criminal prosecution [was] sought."[8] In addition, the power of inspection granted by the Baltimore City Code was limited: "[v]alid grounds for suspicion of the existence of a nuisance must exist," the "inspection must be made in the day time," and forced entry was prohibited.[9] According to the Court, not only did the inspection touch, at most, upon the "periphery" of privacy interests, but it was also designed to cause only the slightest intrusion on privacy.

Seven years later, however, in *Camara v. Municipal Court*[10] and the companion case of *See v. City of Seattle,*[11] the Supreme Court significantly changed the law in this area. In *Camara,* appellant was awaiting trial on a criminal charge of violating the San Francisco Housing Code for refusing to permit a warrantless inspection of his personal residence. Appellant lived in an apartment building that was subject to a routine annual inspection for possible violations of the city's Housing Code. The building's manager informed the inspector that appellant was leasing the ground floor for a personal residence. Alleging that the building's occupancy permit did not allow residential use of the ground floor, the inspector demanded entry to and inspection of appellant's dwelling. Appellant refused to allow the inspection because the inspector lacked a warrant.

The Court's analysis in *Camara* was based on the premise that, "except in certain carefully defined classes of cases, a search of private property without proper consent is 'unreasonable' unless it has been authorized by a valid search warrant."[12] According to the Court, the *Frank* decision had been generally interpreted as carving out an exception to this rule. While the *Camara* Court continued to agree with its

and admit a free examination, he shall forfeit and pay for each such refusal the sum of Twenty Dollars. (as reprinted in 359 U.S. at 361, 79 S.Ct. at 806).

5. 359 U.S. at 362, 79 S.Ct. at 806 (quoting Wolf v. Colorado, 338 U.S. 25, 27, 69 S.Ct. 1359, 93 L.Ed. 1782 (1949)).

6. Id. at 365, 79 S.Ct. at 808.

7. Id.

8. Id. at 366, 79 S.Ct. at 808.

9. Id. at 366, 367, 79 S.Ct. at 808, 809.

10. 387 U.S. 523, 87 S.Ct. 1727, 18 L.Ed.2d 930 (1967).

11. 387 U.S. 541, 87 S.Ct. 1737, 18 L.Ed.2d 943 (1967).

12. 387 U.S. at 528–29, 87 S.Ct. at 1730–31.

statement in *Frank* "that a routine inspection of the physical condition of private property is a less hostile intrusion than the typical policeman's search for the fruits and instrumentalities of crime," the *Camara* Court nonetheless rejected the *Frank* view "that the fourth amendment interests at stake in these inspection cases [were] merely 'peripheral.' It is surely anomalous to say that the individual and his private property are fully protected by the fourth amendment only when the individual is suspected of criminal behavior."[13] Thus, "law abiding citizens" have an interest in limiting the circumstances under which the sanctity of their home is broken. Even accepting *Frank*'s rather "remarkable premise," inspections of this kind do jeopardize "self-protection" interests of the property owners.[14] The Court pointed out that in some cities discovery of a violation by the inspector leads to a criminal complaint; in cities where such a discovery results in only an administrative compliance order, refusal to comply is a criminal offense, punishable by a fine or jail sentence.

The Court also rejected the other justifications utilized in *Frank* to permit warrantless inspections. In *Frank,* the Court had relied on its finding that the "inspections [were] designed to make the least possible demand on the individual occupant" and that the inspector's entry "must comply with the constitutional standard of reasonableness even if he may enter without a warrant." Second, the *Frank* Court argued that the warrant process would be misplaced because the "decision to inspect an entire municipal area is based upon legislative or administrative assessment[s]."[15] Unless the magistrate reviewed these policy rationales he would simply be issuing a "rubber stamp" warrant which provides no protection at all to the property owner. The *Camara* Court dismissed this justification, noting that "[i]t has nowhere been urged that fire, health, and housing code inspection programs could not achieve their goals within the confines of a reasonable search warrant requirement."[16] Furthermore, the Court reasoned that:

> The practical effect of [the *Frank* approach] is to leave the occupant subject to the discretion of the official in the field. This is precisely the discretion to invade private property which we have consistently circumscribed by a requirement that a disinterested party warrant the need to search.... [B]road statutory safeguards are no substitute for individualized review, particularly when those safeguards may only be invoked at the risk of a criminal penalty.[17]

The *Camara* Court, however, did reject the more onerous requirement that warrants for code enforcement inspection programs could only be issued upon "probable cause" that a particular dwelling contained

13. Id. at 530, 87 S.Ct. at 1731 (footnote omitted).

14. This is the first of the two historic Fourth Amendment protections which the *Frank* Court found inapplicable in the administrative regulatory context.

15. 387 U.S. at 531–32, 87 S.Ct. at 1732 (footnote omitted).

16. Id. at 533, 87 S.Ct. at 1733.

17. Id. at 532–33, 87 S.Ct. at 1732–33.

code violations.[18] This constitutional mandate had been met, the Court concluded, because the area inspection was a "reasonable" search of private property. The probable cause and reasonableness determinations "may be based upon the passage of time, the nature of the building . . . , or the condition of the entire area, but they will not necessarily depend upon specific knowledge of the condition of the particular dwelling."[19] Thus, the Court held that reasonableness is the ultimate standard for judging the propriety of the warrant. If a valid public interest justified the intrusion contemplated and the search was thereby reasonable, the Court would find "probable cause to issue a suitably restricted search warrant."[20] Additionally, the Court noted that it did not intend to foreclose prompt warrantless inspections in emergency situations.

See v. City of Seattle[21] extended the *Camara* rationale to commercial premises. This case involved an action against a warehouse owner who refused to permit a representative of the city fire department to enter and inspect his commercial warehouse without a warrant and without probable cause to believe that a violation of the fire code existed. The Court held that *Camara* applied to inspections of commercial structures which are not used as private residences: "The businessman, like the occupant of a residence, has a constitutional right to go about his business free from unreasonable official entries upon his private com-

18. " '[P]robable' cause is the standard by which a particular decision to search is tested against the constitutional mandate of reasonableness." Id. at 534, 87 S.Ct. at 1734.

19. Id. at 538, 87 S.Ct. at 1735.

20. Id. at 539, 87 S.Ct. at 1736. The administrative standard of probable cause has been applied, with the approval of several courts, to hybrid administrative/criminal cases. For instance in Kotler Industries, Inc. v. INS, 586 F.Supp. 72, 75–76 (N.D.Ill. 1984), the court held that a warrant authorizing a noncriminal search of a business's illegal aliens, could be issued upon the *Camara* standard of probable cause. The *Kotler* court relied upon Blackie's House of Beef v. Castillo, 659 F.2d 1211 (D.C.Cir. 1981), cert. denied, 455 U.S. 940, 102 S.Ct. 1432, 71 L.Ed.2d 651 (1982) reaching a similar result.

Additionally, warrants issued ex parte for area wide inspections provide an occupant with no greater fourth amendment protection than that provided by a warrantless search. Of course, some statutes require notice of inspection and therefore afford the owner or occupant some protection. Most administrative inspection schemes, however, do not include a notice requirement. Thus, the crucial issue is really that of notice and not whether a warrant exists or not.

Nonetheless, the warrant requirement, arguably serves three purposes: First, it informs the owner or occupant that the search is in fact one conducted by government inspectors for an administrative purpose rather than a search performed by police officers for the purpose of detecting criminal activity. Second, the warrant may ensure against repeated inspections conducted for the purpose of harassment. If the inspectors have illegitimate motives, however, the warrant is probably no protection. In this situation the inspectors are just as likely to conduct improper searches without a warrant (i.e., without any judicial record). Third, the warrant delineates the permissible scope of the search. This protection, however, is probably negligible because most administrative inspectors are trained and therefore know the reasonable parameters of a search. Again, if an inspector's motive is disingenuous, he or she may perform an impermissibly broad search, but is unlikely to admit it.

In sum, a surprise visit may not be inappropriate in the administrative context, particularly where notice would allow for the temporary concealment of a violation. The Court, however, should be forthright and not justify its holding upon spurious protections.

21. 387 U.S. 541, 87 S.Ct. 1737, 18 L.Ed.2d 943 (1967).

mercial property."[22]

In so doing, the Court said that it was not questioning "such accepted regulatory techniques as licensing programs which require inspections prior to operating a business or marketing a product"[23] or whether warrants to inspect business premises may be issued only after access is refused. Recognizing that "surprise may often be a crucial aspect of routine inspections of business establishments," the Court held that "the reasonableness of warrants issued in advance of inspection will necessarily vary with the nature of the regulation involved and may differ from standards applicable to private homes."[24]

Exceptions to the *Camara* and *See* doctrine do exist, however, particularly with businesses having a history of regulation. For example, in *Colonnade Catering Corp. v. United States*[25] the Court states that Congress may establish the reasonableness standard for searches in the liquor industry because of that industry's long history of close supervision and inspection. In *Colonnade,* an agent of the Alcohol and Tobacco Tax Division noticed a possible violation of the federal excise tax law while a guest on petitioner's premises. When federal agents revisited the place, they noticed that liquor was being served again. Without the manager's consent, they inspected the cellar and asked the manager to open the locked liquor storeroom. After repeated refusals, an agent broke the lock and entered. The agents removed bottles of liquor which they apparently suspected of being refilled contrary to federal law. Under the applicable statute, the Secretary of the Treasury has broad authority to enter and inspect the premises of liquor dealers; refusal could result in a $500 fine.[26]

The Court recognized "that Congress has broad authority to fashion standards of reasonableness for searches and seizures. [However,] under the existing statutes, Congress selected a standard that does not include forcible entries without a warrant."[27] Therefore, the general rule laid down in *See*—that the warrant procedure must be complied with for an administrative entry made without consent—was inapplicable in *Colonnade* because of the regulatory history of the liquor industry. Nonetheless, "[w]here Congress has authorized inspection but made no rules governing the procedure that inspectors must follow, the fourth amendment and its various restrictive rules apply;"[28] therefore, the petitioner's conviction had to be overturned.

22. 387 U.S. at 543, 87 S.Ct. at 1739.

23. 387 U.S. at 546, 87 S.Ct. at 1741. See generally Note, Inspections by Administrative Agencies: Clarification of the Warrant Requirement, 49 Notre Dame L.Rev. 879 (1974); Note, Administrative Inspection and the Fourth Amendment—A Rationale, 65 Colum.L.Rev. 288 (1965); LaFave, Administrative Searches and the Fourth Amendment: The *Camara* and *See* Cases, 1967 Sup.Ct.Rev. 1.

24. 387 U.S. at 545 n. 6, 87 S.Ct. at 1740.

25. 397 U.S. 72, 90 S.Ct. 774, 25 L.Ed.2d 60 (1970).

26. I.R.C. §§ 5146(b) and 7342.

27. 397 U.S. at 77, 90 S.Ct. at 777.

28. Id.

In *United States v. Biswell*,[29] the Court continued to develop the industry based exception to the *Camara* and *See* rationale. The Court upheld the Gun Control Act of 1968[30] authorizing official entry during business hours to the premises of any firearms or ammunition dealer for the purpose of inspecting records and firearms or ammunitions. Respondent was a pawn shop operator licensed to deal in sporting weapons. He was visited by a Federal Treasury agent who requested entry into a locked gun storeroom. Though the agent had no warrant, he showed respondent a copy of the statute which authorized entry without a warrant. Respondent allowed him to enter and the agent found and seized two unlicenced sawed-off rifles. He was later convicted for dealing in firearms without having paid the required special occupational tax.

The Court noted that "[f]ederal regulation of . . . firearms is not as deeply rooted in history as is governmental control of the liquor industry,[31] but close scrutiny of [firearms] traffic is undeniably of central importance to the federal efforts to prevent violent crime and to assist the States in regulating the firearms traffic within their borders."[32] In addition, for inspection to be effective, warrants could not be required. The Court thus distinguished the present case from *See,* where "the inspection system was to discover . . . conditions that were relatively difficult to conceal or to correct in a short time. . . . [W]arrants could be required and privacy [protected] with little if any threat to the effectiveness of the inspection system"[33] at issue in that case. Here, however, if inspection was to serve as a credible deterrent, unannounced, even frequent inspections were essential. The Court believed that "[i]n this context, the prerequisite of a warrant could easily frustrate inspection, and if the necessary flexibility as to time, scope, and frequency was to be preserved, the protection afforded by a warrant would be negligible.[34] The Court went on to explain:"

> "It is also plain that inspections for compliance with the Gun Control Act pose only limited threats to the dealer's justifiable expectations of privacy. When a dealer chooses to engage in this pervasively regulated business and to accept a federal license, he does so with the knowledge that his business records, firearms, and ammunition will be subject to effective inspection."[35]

29. 406 U.S. 311, 92 S.Ct. 1593, 32 L.Ed.2d 87 (1972).

30. Pub.L. No. 90–618, 82 Stat. 1397 (codified as amended at 18 U.S.C.A. §§ 921–928).

31. The *Colonnade* exception is generally thought of as an exception for "closely regulated industry long subject to close supervision and inspection," whereas the *Biswell* exception is one that is applicable to "pervasively regulated businesses," irrespective of the presence or absence of a history of regulation.

32. 406 U.S. at 315, 92 S.Ct. at 1596.

33. Id. at 316, 92 S.Ct. at 1596.

34. Id.

35. Id. The Court's reliance on a notion of implied consent is problematic when one considers that regulations allowing for inspections may have been enacted subsequent to the time that a particular entrepreneur entered the market. The limitations on a person's privacy should not be dependent upon that person's awareness that the limitations exist. Rather, the infringement on privacy is either permissible or it is not.

In *Marshall v. Barlow's, Inc.*,[36] the Court retreated from its lenient approach in *Colonnade* and *Biswell* and was seemingly more solicitous of the "privacy" interests of entrepreneurs.[37] The Court held that the Occupational Safety and Health Act of 1970 (OSHA), which empowered agents of the Secretary of Labor to search employment facilities for safety hazards and violations, was unconstitutional insofar as it purported to authorize inspections without a warrant or its equivalent.

The Secretary of Labor had argued that two exceptions should apply in this case: 1) This was a pervasively regulated business (*Biswell*) and 2) it had long been subject to close supervision and inspection (*Colonnade*). The Court rejected these contentions because, it stated, these exceptions were responses to relatively unique circumstances that did not exist here: "Certain industries have such a history of government over-sight or involve such activities that no reasonable expectation of privacy could exist. . . ."[38] Indeed, the closely regulated industry is the exception, not the rule.[39]

The Secretary argued further that because "reasonableness" is still the ultimate standard under *Camara,* the Court should determine if a warrant is required by balancing the administrative necessity of inspections and the incremental protection provided by a warrant against a business owner's privacy. The Secretary argued that only by exempting OSHA inspections from the requirements of the Fourth Amendment could the competing public and private interests be fully recognized. According to the Secretary, proper enforcement of OSHA requires warrantless searches in order to preserve the advantages of surprise so that the plant owner would not have time to correct violations after initial permission to inspect had been refused and before the inspector could return with a warrant. Although warrants issued *ex parte* could preserve the element of surprise if issued without delay or prior notice, the Secretary argued that such a practice would place the courts and the inspection system under an administrative strain.[40]

The Court was unconvinced by the administrative burden argument and did not think that a warrantless inspection was essential to OSHA's effectiveness. The Court reasoned that most businessmen can be expect-

36. 436 U.S. 307, 98 S.Ct. 1816, 56 L.Ed.2d 305 (1978).

37. I use the term theoretically because the warrant required in *Barlow's* suffered from the same flaws as the warrant required in *Camara*. Infra note 168. Of course, the crucial issue is whether the regulatory scheme allows for surprise inspections. The warrant requirement does not speak to this issue.

38. 436 U.S. at 313, 98 S.Ct. at 1820 (citing Katz v. United States, 389 U.S. 347, 351–52, 88 S.Ct. 507, 511–12, 19 L.Ed.2d 576 (1967)).

39. "It is quite unconvincing to argue that the imposition of minimum wages and maximum hours on employees who contracted with the Government under the Walsh–Healey Act prepared the entirety of American interstate commerce for regulation of working conditions to the minutest detail. Nor can any but the most fictional sense of voluntary consent to later searches be found in the single fact that one conducts a business affecting interstate commerce; under current practice and law, few businesses can be conducted without having some effect on interstate commerce." 436 U.S. at 314, 98 S.Ct. at 1821.

40. Id. at 316, 98 S.Ct. at 1822.

ed to consent to inspection without notice. Furthermore, the Secretary had already promulgated a regulation providing compulsory process in situations where permission was refused.[41] Under this regulation, "the Act's effectiveness has not been crippled by providing those owners who wish to refuse an initial requested entry with a time lapse while the inspector obtains the necessary process."[42]

The Court in *Barlow's* also discussed the probable cause requirement for issuance of a warrant. The Court held that the probable cause standard would be satisfied by either showing "specific evidence of an existing violation"[43] or that the warrant was based on an enforcement plan derived by the agency from neutral sources.[44] Finally, the Court stated that requiring a warrant in the OSHA context does not imply that warrantless search provisions in other regulatory statutes will be constitutionally invalid because "[t]he reasonableness of a warrantless search . . . depend[s] upon the specific enforcement needs and privacy guarantees of each statute."[45]

Shortly after *Barlow's,* the Court somewhat limited the reach of this decision. In *Donovan v. Dewey,*[46] it held that warrantless inspections of mines and quarries to insure compliance with the Federal Mine Safety and Health Act of 1977[47] did not violate the Fourth Amendment. Not unlike the provision in the OSHA Act which the Court struck down in *Barlow's,* section 103(a) of the Mine Safety and Health Act also requires routine inspections of mines and grants inspectors the right of entry to any mine. Advance notice is not required. If a mine operator refuses to allow a warrantless inspection, the Secretary of Labor is authorized to bring a civil action for injunctive or other relief.

The Court nonetheless upheld this warrantless provision reasoning that, unlike searches of private homes, statutes authorizing warrantless administrative searches of commercial property do not necessarily violate the Fourth Amendment. This is because the expectation of privacy that a

41. 29 C.F.R. § 1903.4 (1992).

42. 436 U.S. at 318, 98 S.Ct. at 1823.

43. Id. at 320, 98 S.Ct. at 1824 (footnote omitted).

Courts have found that employee complaints could constitute "specific elements of a violation." These complaints do not have to be supported by detailed signed statements, nor does the agency have to establish employee credibility if the complaint yields a reasonable belief that a violation exists. When applying for the warrant, however, the agency is required to set forth specifics of the complaint sufficient to give the magistrate some evidence upon which to base his or her decision. A mere statement that an employee complaint had been received does not satisfy the standard. See In re Establishment Inspection of Gilbert & Bennett Mfg. Co., 589 F.2d 1335 (7th Cir. 1979), cert. denied, 444 U.S. 884, 100 S.Ct. 174, 62 L.Ed.2d 113 (1979); Weyerhaeuser Co. v. Marshall, 592 F.2d 373 (7th Cir. 1979).

44. 436 U.S. at 321, 98 S.Ct. at 1824.

Neutral regulatory schemes that have been upheld include preboarding screening of airline passengers and searches of those entering federal buildings. See United States v. Davis, 482 F.2d 893 (9th Cir. 1973). See generally Rader, OSHA Warrants and Administrative Probable Cause, 33 Baylor L.Rev. 97 (1981); Rothstein, OSHA Inspection After Marshall v. Barlow's, Inc., 1979 Duke L.J. 63 (1979); Note, Administrative Agency Searches Since *Marshall v. Barlow's, Inc.,* 70 Geo.L.J. 1183 (1982).

45. 436 U.S. at 321, 98 S.Ct. at 1824.

46. 452 U.S. 594, 101 S.Ct. 2534, 69 L.Ed.2d 262 (1981).

47. 30 U.S.C.A. §§ 801–962.

commercial property owner enjoys differs significantly from the expectation of privacy in one's home. The Fourth Amendment, however, does provide some protection for a property owner from unreasonable intrusions. Inspections of commercial property may be unreasonable if they are unauthorized by law, unnecessary for furthering federal interests, or so random, infrequent, or unpredictable that the owner has no real expectation that his property will from time to time be inspected by government officials.[48] Pursuant to the Mine Safety and Health Act, the Court found a substantial federal interest in improving the health and safety conditions in mines.[49] Thus, Congress could reasonably determine, as it did in *Biswell,* that a system of warrantless inspections was necessary if the law was to be enforced properly and the inspection made effective.[50]

Having concluded that a warrant requirement would impede the enforcement needs of the Act, the only real issue for the Court was whether the statute's inspection program—its certainty and the regularity of its application—provided a constitutionally adequate substitute for a warrant. By requiring the inspection of all mines and specifically defining the frequency of inspection, the Act is tailored to address these concerns.[51] Furthermore, mine owners are informed of the standards with which they must comply. Thus, the Court concluded, "rather than leaving the frequency and purpose of inspection to the unchecked discretion of Government officers, the Act establishes a predictable and guided federal regulatory presence."[52] Finally, the Act provides for accommodating special privacy concerns that a mine operator might have by prohibiting forcible entries and instead requiring the Secretary of Labor to file a civil action in federal court to obtain an injunction against future refusals.[53]

The Court distinguished inspections under the Mine Safety and Health Act from those under OSHA by noting that OSHA failed to tailor the scope and frequency of inspections to the particular health and safety concerns posed by the numerous and divergent business regulated by the statute.... Similarly, [OSHA did] not provide any standards to guide inspectors either in their selection of establishments to be searched or in the exercise of their authority to search. The statute instead simply provided that such searches must be performed "at ...

48. 452 U.S. at 598–599, 101 S.Ct. at 2537–38. Reaffirming its holdings in *Biswell* and *Colonnade,* the Court stated that "a warrant may not be constitutionally required when Congress has not reasonably determined that warrantless searches are necessary to further a regulatory scheme and the federal regulatory presence is sufficiently comprehensive and defined that the owner of commercial property cannot help but be aware that his property will be subject to periodic inspections undertaken for specific purposes." Id. at 600, 101 S.Ct.

49. Id. at 602, 101 S.Ct. at 2539.

50. In reaching this conclusion, the Court noted on the following legislative explanation of § 103(a): "[I]n [light] of the notorious ease with which many safety or health hazards may be concealed if advance warning of inspection is obtained, a warrant requirement would seriously undercut this Act's objectives." S.Rep. No. 181, 95th Cong., 1st Sess. 27 (1977).

51. 452 U.S. at 603–604, 101 S.Ct. at 2540–41.

52. Id. at 604, 101 S.Ct. at 2541.

53. Id. at 604, 101 S.Ct. at 2540–41.

reasonable times, and within reasonable limits and in a reasonable manner."[54]

Appellees contended that even if § 103(a) were constitutional as applied to most segments of the mining industry, it nonetheless violated the Fourth Amendment in its authorization of warrantless inspections of stone quarries. There was no long tradition of government regulation in that field. The Court responded, however, that "it is the pervasiveness and regularity of the federal regulation that ultimately determines whether a warrant is necessary."[55] Thus, the Court emphasized that in *Biswell,* it upheld the warrantless search provisions of the Gun Control Act even though government regulation of firearms was not as deeply rooted in history as was regulation of the liquor industry (*Colonnade*). The Court did remark, however, that "the duration of a particular regulatory scheme will often be an important factor in determining whether it is sufficiently pervasive to make the imposition of a warrant requirement unnecessary. But, if the length of regulation were the only criterion, absurd results would occur.... [N]ew or emerging industries, including ones such as the nuclear power industry that pose enormous potential safety and health problems, could never be subject to warrantless searches."[56]

§ 20.7.2 Further Definition of the Range of Exceptions to the Warrant Requirement and the Permissible Scope of Inspections

Colonnade and *Biswell* set out a narrow class of cases where constructive notice of inspection waived the warrant requirement. These situations are 1) where the business subject to inspection had a long history of regulation by the government, and 2) where the inspection scheme was sufficiently pervasive to give adequate notice to businesses of the possibility of inspections, their scope and frequency. In addition, courts have recognized and defined other situations in which warrantless searches also are acceptable.

(a) Emergency Situations

In *Michigan v. Tyler,*[57] the Court upheld the right of a fire inspector to search the remains of a fire to determine the cause, so long as the initial entry into the building was for the purpose of extinguishing the blaze. Citing the need to find the cause of a fire quickly to prevent reoccurrence or to preserve evidence, the Court stated, "in the regulatory field, our cases have recognized the importance of 'prompt inspections, even without a warrant ... in emergency situations.' "[58]The Court went on to hold that "officials need no warrant to remain in a building

54. Id. at 601, 101 S.Ct. at 2539.

55. Id. at 606, 101 S.Ct. at 2542.

56. Id. at 606, 101 S.Ct. at 2542.

57. 436 U.S. 499, 98 S.Ct. 1942, 56 L.Ed.2d 486 (1978).

58. Id. at 509, 98 S.Ct. at 1949 (citing Camara v. Municipal Court of San Francisco, 387 U.S. 523, 87 S.Ct. 1727, 18 L.Ed.2d 930 (1967)).

for a reasonable time to investigate the cause of a blaze after it has been extinguished."[59] Subsequent inspections that were clearly detached from the initial entry were held unlawful, however, because they were not conducted pursuant to a warrant or with consent.

(b) Entry and Inspection of Open or Public Spaces

The "open fields" exception to the warrant requirement has long been recognized in both criminal and administrative searches.[60] In *Dow Chemical Co. v. United States,*[61] the Court expanded the notion of "open fields" to include areas that are visible from above, even if the area is walled off intentionally at the ground level. Dow Chemical owned a 2000 acre chemical plant that had a security system barring public view from the ground. Agents from the E.P.A. requested an on-site inspection which was denied by the company. Instead of obtaining an inspection warrant, the E.P.A. employed a commercial aerial photographer who used standard precision aerial mapping cameras to inspect the area. Dow sued for an injunction on the grounds that the aerial surveillance violated their fourth amendment protection against warrantless searches.

The Court determined that, although Dow had a legitimate expectation of privacy for the buildings covered by roofs, the uncovered areas of the plant were more analogous to open fields than to "curtilage" and no warrant was necessary to inspect them from the air.[62] "The intimate activities associated with family privacy and the home and its curtilage do not reach the outdoor areas or spaces between structures and buildings of a manufacturing plant."[63] The Court acknowledged that had the inspectors physically entered the plant, Fourth Amendment concerns would have been raised. In this instance, however, it found that an aerial inspection taken from lawfully navigable airspace with equipment that is commercially available to the public was not a search under the fourth amendment and, consequently, no warrant was necessary.[64] Regarding

59. Id. at 510, 98 S.Ct. at 1950 (footnote omitted explaining what constitutes a "reasonable time to investigate"). In this case, remaining in the building "for a reasonable time" allowed the inspectors to leave the building for several hours because of poor visibility and conditions and return to continue their inspection.

60. The "open fields" exception is that any evidence that exists in an open or public area and that is effortlessly visible to anyone in that area may be used without obtaining a warrant. In Oliver v. United States, the Court said that "open fields do not provide the setting for those intimate activities that the [Fourth] Amendment is intended to shelter from government interference or surveillance." 466 U.S. 170, 179, 104 S.Ct. 1735, 1737, 1741, 80 L.Ed.2d 214 (1984). The Court concluded that "an individual has no legitimate expectation that open fields will remain free from warrantless intrusion by government officers." Id. at 181, 104 S.Ct. at 1742.

61. 476 U.S. 227, 106 S.Ct. 1819, 90 L.Ed.2d 226 (1986).

62. The "curtilage" of a dwelling is described as "the area to which extends the intimate activity associated with the 'sanctity of a man's home and the privacies of life.' "Id. at 236, 106 S.Ct. at 1825 (quoting Oliver v. United States, 466 U.S. 170, 180, 104 S.Ct. 1735, 1742, 80 L.Ed.2d 214 (1984)).

63. 476 U.S. at 236, 106 S.Ct. at 1825.

64. The Court did recognize the potential for abuse by making use of sophisticated technology which could more thoroughly penetrate the intimate details of the plant

regulatory inspections, the Court stated that "what is observable by the public is observable without a warrant by the Government inspector as well."[65]

(c) *Permissible Scope of Searches*

When a search is permissible without a warrant, or even once an inspector has obtained a warrant, the allowable scope of that inspection is often the subject of litigation. The conflicting goals of administrative convenience and individual privacy have left this area of the law in a state of flux. In *Donovan v. Sarasota Concrete Co.*,[66] the court restricted the scope of a permissible inspection based on an employee complaint to determine only whether the complaint was valid. A search of the entire work place was deemed unreasonable given the limited evidence of probable cause of a violation:

> [E]mployee complaints lack administrative guidelines that insure that the target of the search was not chosen for the purpose of harassment.... Because of this increased danger of abuse of discretion and intrusiveness, [we decide] ... that a complaint inspection must bear an appropriate relationship to the violation alleged in the complaint.... When nothing more is offered than a specific complaint relating to a localized condition, probable cause exists for a search to determine only whether the complaint is valid.... Under other circumstances it is conceivable that a specific violation plus a past pattern of violations may be probable cause for a full scope inspection. In addition, a specific complaint may allege a violation which permeates the workplace so that a full scope inspection is reasonably related to the complaint.[67]

from the air. If such a situation would ever arise, the Court suggested that violations of fourth amendment rights would be at issue. "Here, the EPA was not employing some unique sensory device that ... could penetrate the walls of buildings and record conversations in Dow's plants, offices or laboratories, but rather a conventional, albeit precise, commercial camera commonly used in map making...."

> "[I]t may well be ... that surveillance of private property by using highly sophisticated surveillance equipment not generally available to the public, such as satellite technology, might be constitutionally proscribed absent a warrant. But the photographs here are not so revealing of intimate details as to raise constitutional concerns.... The mere fact that human vision is enhanced somewhat, at least to the degree here, does not give rise to constitutional problems. An electronic device to penetrate walls or windows so as to hear and record confidential discussions ... would raise very different and far more serious questions ..." Id. at 238–239, 106 S.Ct. at 1826–27 (footnote omitted).

65. Id. at 238, 106 S.Ct. at 1826 (quoting *Barlow's*, 436 U.S. at 315, 98 S.Ct. at 1821). See also, Donovan v. Lone Steer, Inc., 464 U.S. 408, 104 S.Ct. 769, 78 L.Ed.2d 567 (1984) (entry into a public area of a hotel or restaurant for the purposes of serving a subpoena is not a search and does not require a warrant); and Air Pollution Variance Bd. v. Western Alfalfa Corp., 416 U.S. 861, 94 S.Ct. 2114, 40 L.Ed.2d 607 (1974) (a health inspector entering respondent's outdoor premises which were open to the public, without consent or knowledge of the owners, to test chimney smoke was not a search because the inspector had sighted what anyone who was near the plant could see).

66. 693 F.2d 1061 (11th Cir.1982).

67. Id. at 1068–69 (footnotes and citations omitted). Compare with Hern Iron Works, Inc. v. Donovan, 670 F.2d 838 (9th Cir.1982), cert. denied 459 U.S. 830, 103 S.Ct. 69, 74 L.Ed.2d 69 (1982) (the court upheld a full workplace inspection based on

§ 20.7.3 Consent to Inspections

Generally, when an agency official requests entrance to a premises for the purposes of inspection, the owner grants permission and waives any constitutional protections against warrantless searches. If consent is not given and the search does not fall into one of the above defined exceptions, no waiver occurs and the agent must go to a magistrate to obtain a warrant to conduct the inspection. In a criminal context, a person must knowingly and voluntarily waive his or her constitutional rights for the waiver to be effective.[68] In an administrative regulatory context, however, the standard is less rigid.[69] The issue of voluntary consent to an inspection can become difficult if some government benefit, such as granting a license, depends on that inspection being carried out. Courts have held that the government may not use its power to take away constitutionally protected rights in exchange for government favors.[70] This issue arose in *Wyman v. James,*[71] where the Court held that a beneficiary of the program for Aid to Families with Dependent Children (AFDC) may not refuse a warrantless "home visit" by her caseworker without risking the termination of benefits.

The periodic home visit in *Wyman* was required by New York statutes and regulations as a condition for the continuance of assistance under the program. The District Court held that a home visit constituted a search and, therefore, the fourth amendment required either the beneficiary's consent or a warrant based on probable cause before the visit could occur. The Supreme Court reversed this decision, failing to find that the visit in question was actually a search within the meaning

an employee complaint of safety violations in "metal pouring areas" and ventilation defects). See generally Note, Permissible Scope of OSHA Inspection Warrants, 66 Corn.L.Rev. 1254 (1981); Note, F.D.A., E.P.A. and O.S.H.A. Inspections—Practical Considerations in Light of *Marshall v. Barlow's, Inc.,* 39 Md.L.Rev. 715 (1980).

68. See Bumper v. North Carolina, 391 U.S. 543, 88 S.Ct. 1788, 20 L.Ed.2d 797 (1968) (where the Court held that there was no consent because entry was obtained coercively).

69. See, e.g., United States v. Thriftimart, Inc., 429 F.2d 1006 (9th Cir.1970), cert. denied 400 U.S. 926, 91 S.Ct. 188, 27 L.Ed.2d 185 (1970). That inspectors for F.D.A. did not warn defendant's warehouse managers of their rights to insist upon a warrant before conducting food inspection, and the possibility that the managers were not aware of the precise nature of their rights under the fourth amendment, did not render their consent to inspection unknowing or involuntary. See also United States v. J.B. Kramer Grocery Co., 418 F.2d 987 (8th Cir.1969) (issue of whether consent was actually given is for the trier of fact to determine); Stephenson Enter., Inc. v. Marshall, 578 F.2d 1021 (5th Cir.1978) (fourth amendment restrictions of *Barlow's* do not apply because plant manager consented to the inspections).

70. Frost & Frost Trucking Co. v. Railroad Comm'n of Calif., 271 U.S. 583, 593–594, 46 S.Ct. 605, 607, 70 L.Ed. 1101 (1926) ("the power of the state . . . is not unlimited; and one of the limitations is that it may not impose conditions which require the relinquishment of constitutional rights"). See also FCC v. League of Women Voters of Calif., 468 U.S. 364, 104 S.Ct. 3106, 82 L.Ed.2d 278 (1984) (Court rejected statute which severely restricted first amendment rights of broadcasting groups who received government funding); cf. Selective Service System v. Minn. Pub. Interest Research Group, 468 U.S. 841, 104 S.Ct. 3348, 82 L.Ed.2d 632 (1984) (Court upheld provision which denied eligibility for federal assistance to those who resisted registration for the draft).

71. 400 U.S. 309, 91 S.Ct. 381, 27 L.Ed.2d 408 (1971).

of the fourth amendment.[72] The Court concluded that even if the visit did possess some of the characteristics of a search in the traditional sense, it did not violate the Fourth Amendment because it was not unreasonable.[73] The rationale behind requiring a warrant is that the warrant requires probable cause. In the welfare context, probable cause requires more than the mere need of the caseworker to see the child in the home and to have the assurance that the child is receiving the benefit of the prescribed aid. Therefore, the intended purposes of the home visit would be precluded by requiring a warrant based on probable cause. To illustrate that a warrant is unnecessary and out of place in the welfare context, the Court compared a home visit, and the resulting loss of benefits if the visit is refused, to a civil audit of an income tax return and the resulting tax detriment if the taxpayer fails to produce proof of his or her return.[74]

72. "It is true that the governing statute and regulations appear to make mandatory the initial home visit and the subsequent periodic 'contacts' (which may include home visits) for the inspection and continuance of aid. It is also true that the caseworker's posture in the home visit is perhaps, in a sense, both rehabilitative and investigative. But this latter aspect, we think, is given too broad a character and far more emphasis than it deserves if it is equated with a search in the traditional criminal law context. We note, too, that the visitation in itself is not forced or compelled, and that the beneficiary's denial of permission is not a criminal act. If consent to the visitation is withheld, no visitation takes place. The aid then never begins or merely ceases, as the case may be. There is no entry of the home and there is no search." Id. at 317–318, 91 S.Ct. at 385–86.

73. The Court based its determination on the following factors: (1) The program focuses on the dependent child's needs and not the interests of the mother. (2) The agency, through tax funds, is fulfilling a public trust. The state has an interest in assuming that the intended and proper objects of that tax-produced assistance are the ones who benefit from the aid it dispenses. (3) The public as a dispenser of purely private charity has an interest if not an obligation to know how its charitable funds are utilized and put to work. (4) The emphasis of the statutes and regulation is rehabilitative. The visit is essential to this goal. (5) The means emphasize privacy: Advance written notice is provided; the applicant-recipient is the primary source of information; outside informational sources, other than public records, are consulted only with the beneficiary's consent; and forcible entry or entry under false pretenses or visitation outside working hours or snooping in the home are forbidden. (6) The record presents no specific complaint of any unreasonable intrusion into appellant's home. (7) Secondary sources of information would not be sufficient. For instance, the caseworker could not assure verification of actual residence or of physical presence in the home, which are requisites for AFDC benefits. (8) The visit is not one by uniformed authority, but by a caseworker whose primary objective is, or should be, the welfare not the prosecution of the recipient. (9) The home visit is not a criminal investigation or part of any criminal proceeding. (10) The warrant procedure is out of place in the welfare context. If the warrant could be obtained, it presumably could be applied for *ex parte*. On this basis, execution of the warrant would require no notice, would justify entry by force, would not be as limited as those prescribed for home visitation and would necessarily imply either civil or criminal misconduct. Id. at 318–324, 91 S.Ct. at 386–89.

74. Id. at 324, 91 S.Ct. at 389. "It seems to us that the situation is akin to that where an Internal Revenue Service agent, in making a routine civil audit of a taxpayer's income tax return, asks that the taxpayer produce for the agent's review some proof of a deduction the taxpayer has asserted to his benefit in the computation of his tax. If the taxpayer refuses, there is, absent fraud, only a disallowance of the claimed deduction and a consequent additional tax. The taxpayer is fully within his 'rights' in refusing to produce the proof, but in maintaining and asserting those rights a tax detriment results and it is a detriment of the taxpayer's own making. So here [the beneficiary] has the 'right' to refuse the home visit, but a consequence in the form of cessation of aid, similar to the taxpayer's

The Court noted that the holdings in *Camara* and *See* were not inconsistent with the result here because those cases concerned a "true search for violations." Each case arose in a criminal context where a genuine search was denied and prosecution followed. In contrast, the beneficiary in *Wyman* is not being prosecuted or about to be prosecuted for her refusal to permit the home visit. Her refusal results only in cessation of benefits. "If a statute made her refusal a criminal offense, and if this case were one concerning her prosecution under that statute, *Camara* and *See* would have conceivable pertinency."[75] Finally, the Court limited its holding by noting "that a termination of benefits upon refusal of a home visit would not be upheld against constitutional challenge under all conceivable circumstances."[76]

resultant additional tax, flows from that refusal. The choice is entirely hers, and nothing of constitutional magnitude is involved."

75. Id. at 325, 91 S.Ct. at 389–90.

76. Id. at 326, 91 S.Ct. at 390. Justice Douglas, in his dissenting opinion, pointed out that the central question in this case is really whether the government by force of its largess has the power to "buy up" rights guaranteed by the Constitution. "But for the assertion of her constitutional right, Barbara James [the appellant] in this case would have received the welfare benefit." 400 U.S. at 328, 91 S.Ct. at 391. After surveying a series of first amendment cases, Justice Douglas stated: "The rule is that the right to continue the exercise of a privilege granted by the state cannot be made to depend upon the grantee's submission to a condition prescribed by the state which is hostile to the provisions of the federal Constitution." Id. at 329, 91 S.Ct. at 391 (quoting United States v. Chicago, Milw., St. Paul and Pac. R.R. Co., 282 U.S. 311, 328–329, 51 S.Ct. 159, 163–64, 75 L.Ed. 359) (footnote omitted). This rule, according to Douglas, should be just as applicable in the Fourth Amendment context. Criticizing the majority for not applying *Camara* and *See* in the welfare context, Douglas states that: "It is a strange jurisprudence indeed which safeguards the businessman at his place of work from warrantless searches but will not do the same for a mother in her home." Id. at 331, 91 S.Ct. at 392.

In his dissenting opinion, Justice Marshall differed with the majority's conclusion that there was no search: "I should have thought that the Amendment governs all intrusions by agents of the public upon personal security." Id. at 338, 91 S.Ct. at 397 (citation omitted). Even if the fourth amendment does not apply to each governmental entry into the home, Marshall continued, the home visit is not a purely benevolent inspection. Social Services repeatedly emphasized the need to enter recipients' homes to prevent welfare fraud and child abuse, both of which are felonies. The New York statutes require all caseworkers to report any evidence of fraud that a home visit uncovers. According to Marshall, the home visit is an even more severe intrusion upon privacy and family dignity than the type of inspection proscribed by *Camara*. Both the home visit and the search in *Camara* may convey penalties. "The fact that one purpose of the visit is to provide evidence that may lead to an elimination of benefits is sufficient to grant appellee protection since *Camara* stated that the Fourth Amendment applies to inspections which can result in only civil violations. But here the case is stronger since the home visit, like many housing inspections, may lead to criminal convictions." Id. at 340, 91 S.Ct. at 398 (citation omitted).

Marshall also rejected the majority's claim that *See* and *Camara*, but not *Wyman*, involved "true" and "genuine searches." According to Marshall, the only basis for this distinction was that *See* and *Camara* concerned criminal prosecutions for refusal to permit a search; the magnitude of the penalty should not be a relevant criterion for determining whether an inspection/home visit is a search.

> "[T]here is neither logic in, nor precedent for, the view that the ambit of the Fourth Amendment depends not on the character of the governmental intrusion but on the size of the club that the State wields against a resisting citizen." 400 U.S. at 340–341, 91 S.Ct. at 398–99. For an argument that government largess, such as welfare aid, should be a vested property right and that forfeiture of that right based on refusal to meet certain government conditions must be justly compensated, see Reich, The New Property, 73 Yale L.J. 733, 768–774, 785 (1964).

§ 20.7.4 Remedies Available When Permissible Warrantless Entry Is Refused

In *Colonnade* and *Biswell,* the Court addressed the issue of what steps agents could take upon being refused admission to a premises. In both cases the Court found that the statutory scheme providing the authority to conduct warrantless physical inspections determined the permissible actions of the agents. In *Colonnade,* the Court noted that the statutory provision which provided that a fine would be imposed for not allowing a search, precluded forcible entry into the premises. The agents' seizure of the illicit liquor was thus a violation of their statutory authority: "[Congress] resolved the issue, not by authorizing forcible, warrantless entries, but by making it an offense for a licensee to refuse admission to the inspector."[77] On the other hand, in *Biswell,* the Gun Control Act specifically provided for official entry onto the premises of any firearms or ammunition dealer for inspection purposes during business hours. Under this particular statutory scheme, no consent was needed to inspect. The Court had "little difficulty in concluding that where ... regulatory inspections further urgent federal interests and the possibilities of abuse and the threat to privacy are not of impressive dimensions, the inspection may proceed without a warrant where specifically authorized by statute."[78]

Whether or not evidence obtained through an erroneous search should be excluded from use is determined by balancing the interest in protecting companies from unlawful searches with that of protecting the public from unlawful company behavior.[79] In *Donovan v. Sarasota Concrete Co.,*[80] for example, the court adopted a balancing test regarding the application of the exclusionary rule. It held that in civil cases exclusion of evidence gained through an impermissible search would depend on whether the deterrent factor to abuse in that particular situation would

For discussion on the impact of and a critique of *Wyman,* see Note, Administrative Investigations of Welfare Recipients, 22 Case West.L.Rev. 581, 588 (1971); Note, Welfare Home Visits and a Strict Construction of the Fourth Amendment, 66 Nw. U.L.Rev. 714, 734 (1971); Note, Wyman v. James: New Restrictions Placed Upon the Individual's Right to Privacy, 21 De Paul L.Rev. 1081 (1972); R.A. Burt, Forcing Protection on Children and Their Parents: The Impact of Wyman v. James, 69 Mich.L.Rev. 1259 (1971); Dembitz, The Good of the Child Versus the Rights of the Parent, 86 Pol.Sci.Q. 389, 395–396 (1971).

For discussion of consent and conditions on government benefits, see generally, W. Van Alstyne, The Demise of the Right–Privilege Distinction in Constitutional Law, 81 Harv.L.Rev. 1439, 1448 (1968); Note, Administrative Searches and the Implied Consent Doctrine: Beyond the Fourth Amendment, 42 Brooklyn L.Rev. 91 (1976); Comment, Entitlement, Enjoyment and Due Process of Law, 1974 Duke L.J. 89, 108–112; Robert M. O'Neil, The Price of Dependency, 39–57 (1970); Comment, Another Look at Unconstitutional Conditions, 117 U.Pa.L.Rev. 144 (1968); Note, Unconstitutional Conditions, 73 Harv.L.Rev. 1595 (1960); Hale, Unconstitutional Condition and Constitutional Rights, 35 Colum.L.Rev. 321 (1935).

77. Colonnade Catering Corp. v. United States, 397 U.S. 72, 77, 90 S.Ct. 774, 777, 25 L.Ed.2d 60 (1970).

78. United States v. Biswell, 406 U.S. 311, 317, 92 S.Ct. 1593, 1597, 32 L.Ed.2d 87 (1972).

79. See, e.g., Cerro Metal Prod. v. Marshall, 620 F.2d 964, 974 (3d Cir.1980).

80. 693 F.2d 1061 (11th Cir.1982).

be significant.[81] A good faith exception to the exclusionary rule also has been recognized. Courts have permitted the use of evidence obtained through a search or warrant which was obtained in good faith but later held invalid. The exclusionary rule exists to prevent abusive activity by agencies. It "can have no deterrent effect when ... law enforcement personnel have acted mistakenly, but in good faith and on reasonable grounds."[82]

81. The primary function of an exclusionary sanction is to deter unlawful conduct.... Whether exclusion of evidence is appropriate in a particular proceeding depends upon whether the deterrent effect of the sanction outweighs the cost to society of suppressing relevant evidence. 693 F.2d 1061, 1070 (citations omitted).

82. See Donovan v. Federal Clearing Die Casting Co., 695 F.2d 1020 (7th Cir. 1982) (citing United States v. Williams, 622 F.2d 830 (5th Cir.1980)). Cf., Donovan v. Sarasota Concrete Co., 693 F.2d 1061 (11th Cir.1982) (no good faith exception where OSHA officials decided to risk what was clearly a questionable search).

Appendix A

STATUTORY APPENDIX

Note: The Administrative Procedure Act was enacted in 1946, by Pub.L. No. 404. In 1966, the Act was incorporated into Title 5 of the United States Code. Pub.L. No. 89–554. Over the years, other enactments have been added to the Administrative Procedure Act and Title 5. These Acts are the Freedom of Information Act (Pub.L. No. 89–554), the Privacy Act (Pub.L. No. 93–579), the Government in the Sunshine Act (Pub.L. No. 94–409), and most recently the Administrative Dispute Resolution Act (Pub.L. No. 101–552) and the Negotiated Rulemaking Act (Pub.L. No. 101–648). Except for the Freedom of Information Act, which is at 5 U.S.C.A. § 552, we list these acts separately in this appendix, after the main body of the Administrative Procedure Act. However, these acts are part of the Administrative Procedure Act and codified within it, and we list them separately purely for simplicity.

Finally, Congress inadvertently gave the Administrative Dispute Resolution and the Negotiated Rulemaking Acts the same section numbers in the U.S. Code. As originally enacted, both Acts commenced at 5 U.S.C.A. § 581. As this Treatise goes to press, Congress has passed H.R. 2549, the Administrative Procedure Technical Amendments Act of 1991 (sent to the President on August 6, 1992) to correct this overlap. Once signed into law, this Act will redesignate the sections from both of the earlier Acts in sequence from § 561 through § 583.

ADMINISTRATIVE PROCEDURE ACT

United States Code, Chapter Five of Title 5
ADMINISTRATIVE PROCEDURE

§ 551. Definitions

For the purpose of this subchapter—

(1) "agency" means each authority of the Government of the United States, whether or not it is within or subject to review by another agency, but does not include—

(A) the Congress;

(B) the courts of the United States;

(C) the governments of the territories or possessions of the United States;

(D) the government of the District of Columbia;

or except as to the requirements of section 552 of this title—

(E) agencies composed of representatives of the parties or of representatives of organizations of the parties to the disputes determined by them;

(F) courts martial and military commissions;

(G) military authority exercised in the field in time of war or in occupied territory; or

(H) functions conferred by sections 1738, 1739, 1743, and 1744 of title 12; chapter 2 of title 41; subchapter II of chapter 471 of title 49; or sections, 1884, 1891–1902, and former section 1641(b)(2), of title 50, appendix;

(2) "person" includes an individual, partnership, corporation, association, or public or private organization other than an agency;

(3) "party" includes a person or agency named or admitted as a party, or properly seeking and entitled as of right to be admitted as a party, in an agency proceeding, and a person or agency admitted by an agency as a party for limited purposes;

(4) "rule" means the whole or a part of an agency statement of general or particular applicability and future effect designed to implement, interpret, or prescribe law or policy or describing the organization, procedure, or practice requirements of an agency and includes the approval or prescription for the future of rates, wages, corporate or financial structures or reorganizations thereof, prices, facilities, appliances, services or allowances therefor or of valuations, costs, or accounting, or practices bearing on any of the foregoing;

(5) "rule making" means agency process for formulating, amending, or repealing a rule;

(6) "order" means the whole or a part of a final disposition, whether affirmative, negative, injunctive, or declaratory in form, of

an agency in a matter other than rule making but including licensing;

(7) "adjudication" means agency process for the formulation of an order;

(8) "license" includes the whole or a part of an agency permit, certificate, approval, registration, charter, membership, statutory exemption or other form of permission;

(9) "licensing" includes agency process respecting the grant, renewal, denial, revocation, suspension, annulment, withdrawal, limitation, amendment, modification, or conditioning of a license;

(10) "sanction" includes the whole or a part of an agency—

(A) prohibition, requirement, limitation, or other condition affecting the freedom of a person;

(B) withholding of relief;

(C) imposition of penalty or fine;

(D) destruction, taking, seizure, or withholding of property;

(E) assessment of damages, reimbursement, restitution, compensation, costs, charges, or fees;

(F) requirement, revocation, or suspension of a license; or

(G) taking other compulsory or restrictive action;

(11) "relief" includes the whole or a part of an agency—

(A) grant of money, assistance, license, authority, exemption, exception, privilege, or remedy;

(B) recognition of a claim, right, immunity, privilege, exemption, or exception; or

(C) taking of other action on the application or petition of, and beneficial to, a person;

(12) "agency proceeding" means an agency process as defined by paragraphs (5), (7), and (9) of this section;

(13) "agency action" includes the whole or a part of an agency rule, order, license, sanction, relief, or the equivalent or denial thereof, or failure to act; and

(14) "ex parte communication" means an oral or written communication not on the public record with respect to which reasonable prior notice to all parties is not given, but it shall not include requests for status reports on any matter or proceeding covered by this subchapter.

§ 552. Public Information; Agency Rules, Opinions, Orders, Records, and Proceedings

(a) Each agency shall make available to the public information as follows:

(1) Each agency shall separately state and currently publish in the Federal Register for the guidance of the public—

(A) descriptions of its central and field organization and the established places at which, the employees (and in the case of a uniformed service, the members) from whom, and the methods whereby, the public may obtain information, make submittals or requests, or obtain decisions;

(B) statements of the general course and method by which its functions are channeled and determined, including the nature and requirements of all formal and informal procedures available;

(C) rules of procedure, descriptions of forms available or the places at which forms may be obtained, and instructions as to the scope and contents of all papers, reports, or examinations;

(D) substantive rules of general applicability adopted as authorized by law, and statements of general policy or interpretations of general applicability formulated and adopted by the agency; and

(E) each amendment, revision, or repeal of the foregoing. Except to the extent that a person has actual and timely notice of the terms thereof, a person may not in any manner be required to resort to, or be adversely affected by, a matter required to be published in the Federal Register and not so published. For the purpose of this paragraph, matter reasonably available to the class of persons affected thereby is deemed published in the Federal Register when incorporated by reference therein with the approval of the Director of the Federal Register.

(2) Each agency, in accordance with published rules, shall make available for public inspection and copying—

(A) final opinions, including concurring and dissenting opinions, as well as orders, made in the adjudication of cases;

(B) those statements of policy and interpretations which have been adopted by the agency and are not published in the Federal Register;

(C) administrative staff manuals and instructions to staff that affect a member of the public;

(D) copies of all records, regardless of form or format, which have been released to any person under paragraph (3) and which, because of the nature of their subject matter, the agency determines have become or are likely to become the subject of subsequent requests for substantially the same records; and

(E) a general index of the records referred to under subparagraph (D); unless the materials are promptly published and copies offered for sale. For records created on or after November 1, 1996, within one year after such date, each agency shall make such records available, including by computer telecommunications or, if computer telecommunications means have not been established by the agency, by other electronic means. To the extent required to prevent a clearly unwarranted invasion of personal privacy, an agency may delete identifying details when it makes available or publishes an opinion, statement of policy, interpretation, staff manual, instruction, or copies of records referred to in subparagraph (D). However, in each case the justification for the deletion shall be explained fully in writing, and the extent of such deletion shall be indicated on the portion of the record which is made available or published, unless including that indication would harm an interest protected by the exemption in subsection (b) under which the deletion is made. If technically feasible, the extent of the deletion shall be indicated at the place in the record where the deletion was made. Each agency shall also maintain and make available for public inspection and copying current indexes providing identifying information for the public as to any matter issued, adopted, or promulgated after July 4, 1967, and required by this paragraph to be made available or published. Each agency shall make the index referred to in subparagraph (E) available by computer telecommunications by December 31, 1999. Each agency shall promptly publish, quarterly or more frequently, and distribute (by sale or otherwise) copies of each index or supplements thereto unless it determines by order published in the Federal Register that the publication would be unnecessary and impracticable, in which case the agency shall nonetheless provide copies of such index on request at a cost not to exceed the direct cost of duplication. A final order, opinion, statement of policy, interpretation, or staff manual or instruction that affects a member of the public may be relied on, used, or cited as precedent by an agency against a party other than an agency only if—

(i) it has been indexed and either made available or published as provided by this paragraph; or

(ii) the party has actual and timely notice of the terms thereof.

(3) (A) Except with respect to the records made available under paragraphs (1) and (2) of this subsection, each agency, upon any request for records which (i) reasonably describes such records and (ii) is made in accordance with published rules stating the time, place, fees (if any), and procedures to be followed, shall make the records promptly available to any person.

(B) In making any record available to a person under this paragraph, an agency shall provide the record in any form or format requested by the person if the record is readily reproducible by the agency in that form or format. Each agency shall make reasonable efforts to maintain its records in forms or formats that are reproducible for purposes of this section.

(C) In responding under this paragraph to a request for records, an agency shall make reasonable efforts to search for the records in electronic form or format, except when such efforts would significantly interfere with the operation of the agency's automated information system.

(D) For purposes of this paragraph, the term "search" means to review, manually or by automated means, agency records for the purpose of locating those records which are responsive to a request.

(4) (A) (i) In order to carry out the provisions of this section, each agency shall promulgate regulations, pursuant to notice and receipt of public comment, specifying the schedule of fees applicable to the processing of requests under this section and establishing procedures and guidelines for determining when such fees should be waived or reduced. Such schedule shall conform to the guidelines which shall be promulgated, pursuant to notice and receipt of public comment, by the Director of the Office of Management and Budget and which shall provide for a uniform schedule of fees for all agencies.

(ii) Such agency regulations shall provide that—

(I) fees shall be limited to reasonable standard charges for document search, duplication, and review, when records are requested for commercial use;

(II) fees shall be limited to reasonable standard charges for document duplication when records are not sought for commercial use and the request is made by an educational or noncommercial scientific institution, whose purpose is scholarly or scientific research; or a representative of the news media; and

(III) for any request not described in (I) or (II), fees shall be limited to reasonable standard charges for document search and duplication.

(iii) Documents shall be furnished without any charge or at a charge reduced below the fees established under clause (ii) if disclosure of the information is in the public interest because it is likely to contribute significantly to public understanding of the operations or activities of the government and is not primarily in the commercial interest of the requester.

(iv) Fee schedules shall provide for the recovery of only the direct costs of search, duplication, or review. Review costs shall include only the direct costs incurred during the initial examination of a document for the purposes of determining whether the documents must be disclosed under this section and for the purposes of withholding any portions exempt from disclosure under this section. Review costs may not include any costs incurred in resolving issues of law or policy that may be raised in the course of processing a request under this section. No fee may be charged by any agency under this section—

(I) if the costs of routine collection and processing of the fee are likely to equal or exceed the amount of the fee; or

(II) for any request described in clause (ii)(II) or (III) of this subparagraph for the first two hours of search time or for the first one hundred pages of duplication.

(v) No agency may require advance payment of any fee unless the requester has previously failed to pay fees in a timely fashion, or the agency has determined that the fee will exceed $250.

(vi) Nothing in this subparagraph shall supersede fees chargeable under a statute specifically providing for setting the level of fees for particular types of records.

(vii) In any action by a requester regarding the waiver of fees under this section, the court shall determine the matter de novo: Provided, That the court's review of the matter shall be limited to the record before the agency.

(B) On complaint, the district court of the United States in the district in which the complainant resides, or has his principal place of business, or in which the agency records are situated, or in the District of Columbia, has jurisdiction to enjoin the agency from withholding agency records and to order the production of any agency records improperly withheld from the complainant. In such a case the court shall determine the matter de novo, and may examine the contents of such agency records in camera to determine whether such records or any part thereof shall be withheld under any of the exemptions set forth in subsection (b) of this section, and the burden is on the agency to sustain its action. In addition to any other matters to which a court accords substantial weight, a court shall accord substantial weight to an affidavit of an agency concerning the agency's determination as to technical feasibility under paragraph (2)(C) and subsection (b) and reproducibility under paragraph (3)(B).

(C) Notwithstanding any other provision of law, the defendant shall serve an answer or otherwise plead to any complaint made under this subsection within thirty days after service upon the defendant of the pleading in which such complaint is made, unless the court otherwise directs for good cause shown.

(D) [Repealed]

(E) The court may assess against the United States reasonable attorney fees and other litigation costs reasonably incurred in any case under this section in which the complainant has substantially prevailed.

(F) Whenever the court orders the production of any agency records improperly withheld from the complainant and assesses against the United States reasonable attorney fees and other litigation costs, and the court additionally issues a written finding that the circumstances surrounding the withholding raise questions whether agency personnel acted arbitrarily or capriciously with respect to the withholding, the Special Counsel shall promptly initiate a proceeding to determine whether disciplinary action is warranted against the officer or employee who was primarily responsible for the withholding. The Special Counsel, after investigation and consideration of the evidence submitted, shall submit his findings and recommendations to the administrative authority of the agency concerned and shall send copies of the findings and recommendations to the officer or employee or his representative. The administrative authority shall take the corrective action that the Special Counsel recommends.

(G) In the event of noncompliance with the order of the court, the district court may punish for contempt the responsible employee, and in the case of a uniformed service, the responsible member.

(5) Each agency having more than one member shall maintain and make available for public inspection a record of the final votes of each member in every agency proceeding.

(6) (A) Each agency, upon any request for records made under paragraph (1), (2), or (3) of this subsection, shall—

(i) determine within 20 days (excepting Saturdays, Sundays, and legal public holidays) after the receipt of any such request whether to comply with such request and shall immediately notify the person making such request of such determination and the reasons therefor, and of the right of such person to appeal to the head of the agency any adverse determination; and

(ii) make a determination with respect to any appeal within twenty days (excepting Saturdays, Sundays, and legal public holidays) after the receipt of such appeal. If on appeal the denial of the request for records is in whole or in part upheld, the agency shall notify the person making such request of the provisions for judicial review of that determination under paragraph (4) of this subsection.

(B) (i) In unusual circumstances as specified in this subparagraph, the time limits prescribed in either clause (i) or clause (ii) of subparagraph (A) may be extended by written notice to the person making such request setting forth the unusual circumstances for such extension and the date on which a determination is expected to be dispatched. No such notice shall specify a date that would result in an extension for more than ten working days, except as provided in clause (ii) of this subparagraph.

(ii) With respect to a request for which a written notice under clause (i) extends the time limits prescribed under clause (i) of subparagraph (A), the agency shall notify the person making the request if the request cannot be processed within the time limit specified in that clause and shall provide the person an opportunity to limit the scope of the request so that it may be processed within that time limit or an opportunity to arrange with the agency an alternative time frame for processing the request or a modified request. Refusal by the person to reasonably modify the request or arrange such an alternative time frame shall be considered as a factor in determining whether exceptional circumstances exist for purposes of subparagraph (C).

(iii) As used in this subparagraph, "unusual circumstances" means, but only to the extent reasonably necessary to the proper processing of the particular requests—

(I) the need to search for and collect the requested records from field facilities or other establishments that are separate from the office processing the request;

(II) the need to search for, collect, and appropriately examine a voluminous amount of separate and distinct records which are demanded in a single request; or

(III) the need for consultation, which shall be conducted with all practicable speed, with another agency having a substantial interest in the determination of the request or among two or more components of the agency having substantial subject-matter interest therein.

(iv) Each agency may promulgate regulations, pursuant to notice and receipt of public comment, providing for the aggregation of certain requests by the same requestor, or by a group of requestors acting in concert, if the agency reasonably believes that such requests actually constitute a single request, which would otherwise satisfy the unusual circumstances specified in this subparagraph, and the requests involve clearly related matters. Multiple requests involving unrelated matters shall not be aggregated.

(C) (i) Any person making a request to any agency for records under paragraph (1), (2), or (3) of this subsection shall be deemed to have exhausted his administrative remedies with respect to such request if the agency fails to comply with the applicable time limit provisions of this paragraph. If the Government can show exceptional circumstances exist and that the agency is exercising due diligence in responding to the request, the court may retain jurisdiction and allow the agency additional time to complete its review of the records. Upon any determination by an agency to comply with a request for records, the records shall be made promptly available to such person making such request. Any notification of denial of any request for records under this subsection shall set forth the names and titles or positions of each person responsible for the denial of such request.

(ii) For purposes of this subparagraph, the term "exceptional circumstances" does not include a delay that results from a predictable agency workload of requests under this section, unless the agency demonstrates reasonable progress in reducing its backlog of pending requests.

(iii) Refusal by a person to reasonably modify the scope of a request or arrange an alternative time frame for processing a request (or a modified request) under clause (ii) after being given an opportunity to do so by the agency to whom the person made the request shall be considered as a factor in determining whether exceptional circumstances exist for purposes of this subparagraph.

(D) (i) Each agency may promulgate regulations, pursuant to notice and receipt of public comment, providing for multitrack processing of requests for records based on the amount of work or time (or both) involved in processing requests.

(ii) Regulations under this subparagraph may provide a person making a request that does not qualify for the fastest multitrack processing an opportunity to limit the scope of the request in order to qualify for faster processing.

(iii) This subparagraph shall not be considered to affect the requirement under subparagraph (C) to exercise due diligence.

(E) (i) Each agency shall promulgate regulations, pursuant to notice and receipt of public comment, providing for expedited processing of requests for records—

(I) in cases in which the person requesting the records demonstrates a compelling need; and

(II) in other cases determined by the agency.

(ii) Notwithstanding clause (i), regulations under this subparagraph must ensure—

(I) that a determination of whether to provide expedited processing shall be made, and notice of the determination shall be provided to the person making the request, within 10 days after the date of the request; and

(II) expeditious consideration of administrative appeals of such determinations of whether to provide expedited processing.

(iii) An agency shall process as soon as practicable any request for records to which the agency has granted expedited processing under this subparagraph. Agency action to deny or affirm denial of a request for expedited processing pursuant to this subparagraph, and failure by an agency to respond in a timely manner to such a request shall be subject to judicial review under paragraph (4), except that the judicial review shall be based on the record before the agency at the time of the determination.

(iv) A district court of the United States shall not have jurisdiction to review an agency denial of expedited processing of a request for records after the agency has provided a complete response to the request.

(v) For purposes of this subparagraph, the term "compelling need" means—

(I) that a failure to obtain requested records on an expedited basis under this paragraph could reasonably be expected to pose an imminent threat to the life or physical safety of an individual; or

(II) with respect to a request made by a person primarily engaged in disseminating information, urgency to inform the public concerning actual or alleged Federal Government activity.

(vi) A demonstration of a compelling need by a person making a request for expedited processing shall be made by a statement certified by such person to be true and correct to the best of such person's knowledge and belief.

(F) In denying a request for records, in whole or in part, an agency shall make a reasonable effort to estimate the volume of any requested matter the provision of which is denied, and shall provide any such estimate to the person making the request, unless providing such estimate would harm an interest protected by the exemption in subsection (b) pursuant to which the denial is made.

(b) This section does not apply to matters that are—

(1) (A) specifically authorized under criteria established by an Executive order to be kept secret in the interest of national defense or foreign policy and (B) are in fact properly classified pursuant to such Executive order;

(2) related solely to the internal personnel rules and practices of an agency;

(3) specifically exempted from disclosure by statute (other than section 552b of this title) provided that such statute (A) requires that the matters be withheld from the public in such a manner as to leave no discretion on the issue, or (B) establishes particular criteria for withholding or refers to particular types of matters to be withheld;

(4) trade secrets and commercial or financial information obtained from a person and privileged or confidential;

(5) inter-agency or intra-agency memorandums or letters which would not be available by law to a party other than an agency in litigation with the agency;

(6) personnel and medical files and similar files the disclosure of which would constitute a clearly unwarranted invasion of personal privacy;

(7) records or information compiled for law enforcement purposes, but only to the extent that the production of such law enforcement records or information (A) could reasonably be expected to interfere with enforcement proceedings, (B) would deprive a person of a right to a fair trial or an impartial adjudication, (C) could reasonably be expected to constitute an unwarranted invasion of personal privacy, (D) could reasonably be expected to disclose the identity of a confidential source, including a State, local, or foreign agency or authority or any private institution which furnished information on a confidential basis, and, in the case of a record or information compiled by criminal law enforcement authority in the course of a criminal investigation or by an agency conducting a lawful national security intelligence investigation, information furnished by a confidential source, (E) would disclose techniques and procedures for law enforcement investigations or prosecutions, or would disclose guidelines for law enforcement investigations or prosecutions if such disclosure could reasonably be expected to risk circumvention of the law, or (F) could reasonably be expected to endanger the life or physical safety of any individual;

(8) contained in or related to examination, operating, or condition reports prepared by, on behalf of, or for the use of an agency responsible for the regulation or supervision of financial institutions; or

(9) geological or geophysical information and data, including maps, concerning wells. Any reasonably segregable portion of a record shall be provided to any person requesting such record after deletion of the portions which are exempt under this subsection. The amount of information deleted shall be indicated on the released portion of the record, unless including that indication would harm an interest protected by the exemption in this subsection under which the deletion is made. If technically feasible, the amount of the information deleted shall be indicated at the place in the record where such deletion is made.

(c) (1) Whenever a request is made which involves access to records described in subsection (b)(7)(A) and—

(A) the investigation or proceeding involves a possible violation of criminal law; and

(B) there is reason to believe that (i) the subject of the investigation or proceeding is not aware of its pendency, and (ii) disclosure of the existence of the records could reasonably be expected to interfere with enforcement proceedings, the agency may, during only such time as that circumstance continues, treat the records as not subject to the requirements of this section.

(2) Whenever informant records maintained by a criminal law enforcement agency under an informant's name or personal identifier are requested by a third party according to the informant's name or personal identifier, the agency may treat the records as not subject to the requirements of this section unless the informant's status as an informant has been officially confirmed.

(3) Whenever a request is made which involves access to records maintained by the Federal Bureau of Investigation pertaining to foreign intelligence or counterintelligence, or international terrorism, and the existence of the records is classified information as provided in subsection (b)(1), the Bureau may, as long as the existence of the records remains classified information, treat the records as not subject to the requirements of this section.

(d) This section does not authorize withholding of information or limit the availability of records to the public, except as specifically stated in this section. This section is not authority to withhold information from Congress.

(e) (1) On or before February 1 of each year, each agency shall submit to the Attorney General of the United States a report which shall cover the preceding fiscal year and which shall include—

(A) the number of determinations made by the agency not to comply with requests for records made to such agency under subsection (a) and the reasons for each such determination;

(B) (i) the number of appeals made by persons under subsection (a)(6), the result of such appeals, and the reason for the action upon each appeal that results in a denial of information; and

(ii) a complete list of all statutes that the agency relies upon to authorize the agency to withhold information under subsection (b)(3), a description of whether a court has upheld the decision of the agency to withhold information under each such statute, and a concise description of the scope of any information withheld;

(C) the number of requests for records pending before the agency as of September 30 of the preceding year, and the median number of days that such requests had been pending before the agency as of that date;

(D) the number of requests for records received by the agency and the number of requests which the agency processed;

(E) the median number of days taken by the agency to process different types of requests;

(F) the total amount of fees collected by the agency for processing requests; and

(G) the number of full-time staff of the agency devoted to processing requests for records under this section, and the total amount expended by the agency for processing such requests.

(2) Each agency shall make each such report available to the public including by computer telecommunications, or if computer telecommunications means have not been established by the agency, by other electronic means.

(3) The Attorney General of the United States shall make each report which has been made available by electronic means available at a single electronic access point. The Attorney General of the United States shall notify the Chairman and ranking minority member of the Committee on Government Reform and Oversight of the House of Representatives and the Chairman and ranking minority member of the Committees on Governmental Affairs and the Judiciary of the Senate, no later than April 1 of the year in which each such report is issued, that such reports are available by electronic means.

(4) The Attorney General of the United States, in consultation with the Director of the Office of Management and Budget, shall develop reporting and performance guidelines in connection with reports required by this subsection by October 1, 1997, and may establish additional requirements for such reports as the Attorney General determines may be useful.

(5) The Attorney General of the United States shall submit an annual report on or before April 1 of each calendar year which shall include for the prior calendar year a listing of the number of cases arising under this section, the exemption involved in each case, the disposition of such case, and the cost, fees, and penalties assessed under subparagraphs (E), (F), and (G) of subsection (a)(4). Such report shall also include a description of the efforts undertaken by the Department of Justice to encourage agency compliance with this section.

(f) For purposes of this section, the term—

(1) "agency" as defined in section 551(1) of this title includes any executive department, military department, Government corpo-

ration, Government controlled corporation, or other establishment in the executive branch of the Government (including the Executive Office of the President), or any independent regulatory agency; and

(2) "record" and any other term used in this section in reference to information includes any information that would be an agency record subject to the requirements of this section when maintained by an agency in any format, including an electronic format.

(g) The head of each agency shall prepare and make publicly available upon request, reference material or a guide for requesting records or information from the agency, subject to the exemptions in subsection (b), including—

(1) an index of all major information systems of the agency;

(2) a description of major information and record locator systems maintained by the agency; and

(3) a handbook for obtaining various types and categories of public information from the agency pursuant to chapter 35 of title 44 [44 USCS §§ 3501 et seq.], and under this section.

§ 553. Rule Making

(a) This section applies, according to the provisions thereof, except to the extent that there is involved—

(1) a military or foreign affairs function of the United States; or

(2) a matter relating to agency management or personnel or to public property, loans, grants, benefits, or contracts.

(b) General notice of proposed rule making shall be published in the Federal Register unless persons subject thereto are named and either personally served or otherwise have actual notice thereof in accordance with law. The notice shall include—

(1) a statement of the time, place, and nature of public rule making proceedings;

(2) reference to the legal authority under which the rule is proposed; and

(3) either the terms or substance of the proposed rule or a description of the subjects and issues involved.

Except when notice or hearing is required by statute, this subsection does not apply—

(A) to interpretative rules, general statements of policy, or rules of agency organization, procedure, or practice; or

(B) when the agency for good cause finds (and incorporates the finding and a brief statement of reasons therefor in the rules issued) that notice and public procedure thereon are impracticable, unnecessary, or contrary to the public interest.

(c) After notice required by this section, the agency shall give interested persons an opportunity to participate in the rule making through submission of written data, views, or arguments with or without opportunity for oral presentation. After consideration of the relevant matter presented, the agency shall incorporate in the rules adopted a concise general statement of their basis and purpose. When rules are required by statute to be made on the record after opportunity for an agency hearing sections 556 and 557 of this title apply instead of this subsection.

(d) The required publication or service of substantive rule shall be made not less than 3 days before its effective date, except—

(1) a substantive rule which grants or recognizes an exemption or relieves a restriction;

(2) interpretative rules and statements on policy; or

(3) as otherwise provided by the agency for good cause found and published with the rule.

(e) Each agency shall give an interested person the right to petition for the issuance, amendment, or repeal of a rule.

§ 554. Adjudications

(a) This section applies, according to the provisions thereof, in every case of adjudication required by statute to be determined on the record after opportunity for an agency hearing, except to the extent that there is involved—

(1) a matter subject to a subsequent trial of the law and the facts de novo in a court;

(2) the selection or tenure of an employee, except an administrative law judge appointed under section 3105 of this title;

(3) proceedings in which decisions rest solely on inspections, tests, or elections;

(4) the conduct of military or foreign affairs functions;

(5) cases in which an agency is acting as an agent for a court; or

(6) the certification of worker representatives.

(b) Persons entitled to notice of an agency hearing shall be timely informed of—

(1) the time, place, and nature of the hearing;

(2) the legal authority and jurisdiction under which the hearing is to be held; and

(3) the matters of fact and law asserted.

When private persons are the moving parties, other parties to the proceeding shall give prompt notice of issues controverted in fact or law; and in other instances agencies may by rule require responsive pleading.

In fixing the time and place for hearings, due regard shall be had for the convenience and necessity of the parties or their representatives.

(c) The agency shall give all interested parties opportunity for—

(1) the submission and consideration of facts, arguments, offers of settlement, or proposals of adjustment when time, the nature of the proceeding, and the public interest permit; and

(2) to the extent that the parties are unable so to determine a controversy by consent, hearing and decision on notice and in accordance with sections 556 and 557 of this title.

(d) The employee who presides at the reception of evidence pursuant to section 556 of this title shall make the recommended decision or initial decision required by section 557 of this title, unless he becomes unavailable to the agency. Except to the extent required for the disposition of ex parte matters as authorized by law, such an employee may not—

(1) consult a person or party on a fact in issue, unless on notice and opportunity for all parties to participate; or

(2) be responsible to or subject to the supervision or direction of an employee or agent engaged in the performance of investigative or prosecuting functions for an agency.

An employee or agent engaged in the performance of investigative or prosecuting functions for an agency in a case may not, in that or a factually related case, participate or advise in the decision, recommended decision, or agency review pursuant to section 557 of this title, except as witness or counsel in public proceedings. This subsection does not apply—

(A) in determining applications for initial licenses;

(B) to proceedings involving the validity or application of rates, facilities, or practices of public utilities or carriers; or

(C) to the agency or a member or members of the body comprising the agency.

(e) The agency, with like effect as in the case of other orders, and in its sound discretion, may issue a declaratory order to terminate a controversy or remove uncertainty.

§ 555. Ancillary Matters

(a) This section applies, according to the provisions thereof, except as otherwise provided in this subchapter.

(b) A person compelled to appear in person before an agency or representative thereof is entitled to be accompanied, represented, and advised by counsel or, if permitted by the agency, by other qualified representative. A party is entitled to appear in person or by or with counsel or other duly qualified representative in an agency proceeding. So far as the orderly conduct of public business permits, an interested person may appear before an agency or its responsible employees for the presentation, adjustment, or determination of an issue, request, or controversy in a proceeding, whether interlocutory, summary, or otherwise, or in connection with an agency function. With due regard for the convenience and necessity of the parties or their representatives and within reasonable time, each agency shall proceed to conclude a matter presented to it. This subsection does not grant or deny a person who is not a lawyer the right to appear for or represent others before an agency or in an agency proceeding.

(c) Process, requirement of a report, institution, or other investigative act or demand may not be issued, made, or enforced except as authorized by law. A person compelled to submit data or evidence is entitled to retain or, on payment of lawfully prescribed costs, procure a copy or transcript thereof, except that in a nonpublic investigatory proceeding the witness may for good cause be limited to inspection of the official transcript of his testimony.

(d) Agency subpenas authorized by law shall be issued to a party on request and, when required by rules of procedure, on a statement or showing of general relevance and reasonable scope of the evidence sought. On contest, the court shall sustain the subpena or similar process or demand to the extent that it is found to be in accordance with law. In a proceeding enforcement, the court shall issue an order requiring the appearance of the witness or the production of the evidence or data within a reasonable time under penalty of punishment for contempt in case of contumacious failure to comply.

(e) Prompt notice shall be given of the denial in whole or in part of a written application, petition, or other request of an interested person made in connection with any agency proceeding. Except in affirming a prior denial or when the denial is self-explanatory, the notice shall be accompanied by a brief statement of the grounds for denial.

§ 556. Hearings; Presiding Employees; Powers and Duties; Burden of Proof; Evidence; Record as Basis of Decision

(a) This section applies, according to the provisions thereof, to hearings required by section 553 or 554 of this title to be conducted in accordance with this section.

(b) There shall preside at the taking of evidence—

(1) the agency;

(2) one or more members of the body which comprises the agency; or

(3) one or more administrative law judges appointed under section 3105 of this title.

This subchapter does not supersede the conduct of specified classes of proceedings, in whole or in part, by or before boards or other employees specially provided for by or designated under statute. The functions of presiding employees and of employees participating in decisions in accordance with section 557 of this title shall be conducted in an impartial manner. A presiding or participating employee may at any time disqualify himself. On the filing in good faith of a timely and sufficient affidavit of personal bias or other disqualification of a presiding or participating employee, the agency shall determine the matter as a part of the record and decision in the case.

(c) Subject to published rules of the agency and within its powers, employees presiding at hearings may—

(1) administer oaths and affirmations;

(2) issue subpenas authorized by law;

(3) rule on offers of proof and receive relevant evidence;

(4) take depositions or have depositions taken when the ends of justice would be served;

(5) regulate the course of the hearing;

(6) hold conferences for the settlement or simplification of the issues by consent of the parties or by the use of alternative means of dispute resolution as provided in subchapter IV of this chapter [5 USCS § 571–583];

(7) inform the parties as to the availability of one or more alternative means of dispute resolution, and encourage use of such methods;

(8) require the attendance at any conference held pursuant to paragraph (6) of at least one representative of each party who has authority to negotiate concerning resolution of issues in controversy;

(9) dispose of procedural requests or similar matters;

(10) make or recommend decisions in accordance with section 557 of this title; and

(11) take other action authorized by agency rule consistent with this subchapter [5 U.S.C.A. §§ 551–559].

(d) Except as otherwise provided by statute, the proponent of a rule or order has the burden of proof. Any oral or documentary evidence may be received, but the agency as a matter of policy shall provide for the exclusion of irrelevant, immaterial, or unduly repetitious evidence. A sanction may not be imposed or rule or order issued except on consideration of the whole record or those parts thereof cited by a party and supported by and in accordance with the reliable, probative, and substantial evidence. The agency may, to the extent consistent with the interests of justice and the policy of the underlying statutes administered by the agency, consider a violation of section 557(d) of this title sufficient grounds for a decision adverse to a party who has knowingly committed such violation or knowingly caused such violation to occur. A party is entitled to present his case or defense by oral or documentary evidence, to submit rebuttal evidence, and to conduct such cross-examination as may be required for a full and true disclosure of the facts. In rule making or determining claims for money or benefits or applications for initial licenses an agency may, when a party will not be prejudiced thereby, adopt procedures for the submission of all or part of the evidence in written form.

(e) The transcript of testimony and exhibits, together with all papers and requests filed in the proceeding, constitutes the exclusive record for decision in accordance with section 557 of this title and, on payment of lawfully prescribed costs, shall be made available to the parties. When an agency decision rests on official notice of a material fact not appearing in the evidence in the record, a party is entitled, on timely request, to an opportunity to show the contrary.

§ 557. Initial Decisions; Conclusiveness; Review by Agency; Submissions by Parties; Contents of Decisions; Record

(a) This section applies, according to the provisions thereof, when a hearing is required to be conducted in accordance with section 556 of this title.

(b) When the agency did not preside at the reception of the evidence, the presiding employee or, in cases not subject to section 554(d) of this title, an employee qualified to preside at hearings pursuant to section 556 of this title, shall initially decide the case unless the agency requires, either in specific cases or by general rule, the entire record to be certified to it for decision. When the presiding employee makes an initial decision, that decision then becomes the decision of the agency without further proceedings unless there is an appeal to, or review on motion of, the agency within time provided by rule. On appeal from or review of the initial decision, the agency has all the powers which it would have in making the initial decision except as it may limit the issues on notice or by rule. When the agency makes the decision without having presided at the reception of the evidence, the presiding employee or an employee qualified to preside at hearings pursuant to section 556 of this title shall first recommend a decision, except that in rule making or determining applications for initial licenses—

(1) instead thereof the agency may issue a tentative decision or one of its responsible employees may recommend a decision; or

(2) this procedure may be omitted in a case in which the agency finds on the record that due and timely execution of its functions imperatively and unavoidably so requires.

(c) Before a recommended, initial, or tentative decision, or a decision on agency review of the decision of subordinate employees, the parties are entitled to a reasonable opportunity to submit for the consideration of the employees participating in the decisions—

(1) proposed findings and conclusions; or

(2) exceptions to the decisions or recommended decisions of subordinate employees or to tentative agency decisions; and

(3) supporting reasons for the exceptions or proposed findings or conclusions.

The record shall show the ruling on each finding, conclusion, or exception presented. All decisions, including initial, recommended, and tentative decisions, are a part of the record and shall include a statement of—

(A) findings and conclusions, and the reasons or basis therefor, on all the material issues of fact, law, or discretion presented on the record; and

(B) the appropriate rule, order, sanction, relief, or denial thereof.

(d)(1) In any agency proceeding which is subject to subsection (a) of this section, except to the extent required for the disposition of ex parte matters as authorized by law—

(A) no interested person outside the agency shall make or knowingly cause to be made to any member of the body comprising the agency, administrative law judge, or other employee who is or may reasonably be expected to be involved in the decisional process of the proceeding, an ex parte communication relevant to the merits of the proceeding;

(B) no member of the body comprising the agency, administrative law judge, or other employee who is or may reasonably expected to be involved in the decisional process of the proceeding, shall make or knowingly cause to be made to any interested person outside the agency an ex parte communication relevant to the merits of the proceeding;

(C) a member of the body comprising the agency, administrative law judge, or other employee who is or may reasonably be expected to be involved in the who receives, or who makes or knowingly causes to be made, a communication prohibited by this subsection shall place on the public record of the proceeding:

(i) all such written communications;

(ii) memoranda stating the substance of all such oral communications; and

(iii) all written responses, and memoranda stating the substances of all oral responses, to the materials described in clauses (i) and (ii) of this subparagraph;

(D) upon receipt of a communication knowingly made or knowingly caused to be made by a party in violation of this subsection, the agency, administrative law judge, or other employee presiding at the hearing may, to the extent consistent with the interests of justice and the policy of the underlying statutes, require the party to show cause why his claim or interest in the proceeding should not be dismissed, denied, disregarded, or otherwise adversely affected on account of such violation; and

(E) the prohibitions of this subsection shall apply beginning at such time as the agency may designate, but in no case shall they begin to apply later than the time at which a proceeding is noticed for hearing unless the person responsible for the communication has knowledge that it will be noticed, in which case the prohibitions shall apply beginning at the time of his acquisition of such knowledge.

(2) This subsection does not constitute authority to withhold information from Congress.

§ 558. Imposition of Sanctions; Determination of Applications for Licenses; Suspension, Revocation, and Expiration of Licenses

(a) This section applies, according to the provisions thereof, to the exercise of a power or authority.

(b) A sanction may not be imposed or a substantive rule or order issued except within jurisdiction delegated to the agency and as authorized by law.

(c) When application is made for a license required by law, the agency, with due regard for the rights and privileges of all the interested parties or adversely affected persons and within a reasonable time, shall set and complete proceedings required to be conducted in accordance with sections 556 and 557 of this title or other proceedings required by law and shall make its decision. Except in cases of willfulness or those in which public health, interest, or safety requires otherwise, the withdrawal, suspension, revocation, or annulment of a license is lawful only if, before the institution of agency proceedings therefor, the licensee has been given—

(1) notice by the agency in writing of the facts or conduct which may warrant the action; and

(2) opportunity to demonstrate or achieve compliance with all lawful requirements.

When the licensee has made timely and sufficient application for a renewal or a new license in accordance with agency rules, a license with reference to an activity of a continuing nature does not expire until the application has been finally determined by the agency.

§ 559. Effect on Other Law; Effect of Subsequent Statute

This subchapter, chapter 7, and sections 1305, 3105, 3344, 4301(2)(E), 5372, and 7521 of this title, and the provisions of section 5335(a)(B) of this title that relate to administrative law judges, do not limit or repeal additional requirements imposed by statute or otherwise recognized by law. Except as otherwise required by law, requirements or privileges relating to evidence or procedure apply equally to agencies and persons. Each agency is granted the authority necessary to comply with the requirements of this subchapter through the issuance of rules or otherwise. Subsequent statute may not be held to supersede or modify this subchapter, chapter 7, sections 1305, 3105, 3344, 4301(2)(E), 5372, or 7521 of this title, or the provisions of section 5335(a)(B) of this title that relate to administrative law judges, except to the extent that it does so expressly.

JUDICIAL REVIEW

---

§ 701. Application; Definitions

(a) This chapter applies, according to the provisions thereof, except to the extent that—

(1) statutes preclude judicial review; or

(2) agency action is committed to agency discretion by law.

(b) For the purpose of this chapter—

(1) "agency" means each authority of the Government of the United States, whether or not it is within or subject to review by another agency, but does not include—

(A) the Congress;

(B) the courts of the United States;

(C) the governments of the territories or possessions of the United States;

(D) the government of the District of Columbia;

(E) agencies composed of representatives of the parties or of representatives of organizations of the parties to the disputes determined by them;

(F) courts martial and military commissions;

(G) military authority exercised in the field in time of war or in occupied territory; or

(H) functions conferred by sections 1738, 1739, 1743, and 1744 of title 12; chapter 2 of title 41; subchapter II of chapter 471 of title 49; or sections, 1884, 1891–1902, and former section 1641(b)(2), of title 50, appendix; and

(2) "person", "rule", "order", "license", "sanction", "relief" and "agency action" have the meanings given them by section 551 of this title.

§ 702. Right of Review

A person suffering legal wrong because of agency action, or adversely affected or aggrieved by agency action within the meaning of a relevant statute, is entitled to judicial review thereof. An action in a court of the United States seeking relief other than money damages and stating a claim that an agency or an officer or employee thereof acted or failed to act in an official capacity or under color of legal authority shall not be dismissed nor relief therein be denied on the ground that it is against the United States or that the United States is an indispensable party. The United States may be named as a defendant in any such action, and a judgment or decree may be entered against the United States: Provided, That any mandatory or injunctive decree shall specify the Federal officer or officers (by name or by title), and their successors in office, personally responsible for compliance. Nothing herein (1) affects other limitations on judicial review or the power or duty of the court to dismiss any action or deny relief on any other appropriate legal or equitable ground; or (2) confers authority to grant relief if any other statute that grants consent to suit expressly or impliedly forbids the relief which is sought.

§ 703. Form and Venue of Proceeding

The form of proceeding for judicial review is the special statutory review proceeding relevant to the subject matter in a court specified by statute or, in the absence or inadequacy thereof, any applicable form of legal action, including actions for declaratory judgments or writs of prohibitory or mandatory injunction or habeas corpus, in a court of competent jurisdiction. If no special statutory review proceeding is applicable, the action for judicial review may be brought against the United States, the agency by its official title, or the appropriate officer. Except to the extent that prior, adequate, and exclusive opportunity for judicial review is provided by law, agency action is subject to judicial review in civil or criminal proceedings for judicial enforcement.

§ 704. Actions Reviewable

Agency action made reviewable by statute and final agency action for which there is no other adequate remedy in a court are subject to judicial review. A preliminary, procedural, or intermediate agency action or ruling not directly reviewable is subject to review on the review of the final agency action. Except as otherwise expressly required by statute, agency action otherwise final is final for the purposes of this section whether or not there has been presented or determined an application for a declaratory order, for any form of reconsiderations, or, unless the agency otherwise requires by rule and provides that the action meanwhile is inoperative, for an appeal to superior agency authority.

§ 705. Relief Pending Review

When an agency finds that justice so requires, it may postpone the effective date of action taken by it, pending judicial review. On such conditions as may be required and to the extent necessary to prevent irreparable injury, the reviewing court, including the court to which a case may be taken on appeal from or on application for certiorari or other writ to a reviewing court, may issue all necessary and appropriate process to postpone the effective date of an agency action or to preserve status or rights pending conclusion of the review proceedings.

§ 706. Scope of Review

To the extent necessary to decision and when presented, the reviewing court shall decide all relevant questions of law, interpret constitutional and statutory provisions, and determine the meaning or applicability of the terms of an agency action. The reviewing court shall—

(1) compel agency action unlawfully withheld or unreasonably delayed; and

(2) hold unlawful and set aside agency action, findings, and conclusions found to be—

(A) arbitrary, capricious, an abuse of discretion, or otherwise not in accordance with law;

(B) contrary to constitutional right, power, privilege, or immunity;

(C) in excess of statutory jurisdiction, authority, or limitations, or short of statutory right;

(D) without observance of procedure required by law;

(E) unsupported by substantial evidence in a case subject to sections 556 and 557 of this title or otherwise reviewed on the record of an agency hearing provided by statute; or

(F) unwarranted by the facts to the extent that the facts are subject to trial de novo by the reviewing court.

In making the foregoing determinations, the court shall review the whole record or those parts of it cited by a party, and due account shall be taken of the rule of prejudicial error.

THE PRIVACY ACT*

§ 552a. Records Maintained on Individuals

(a) Definitions. For purposes of this section—

(1) the term "agency" means agency as defined in section 552[(f)](e) of this title;

* Pub.L. 93–579 (1974).

(2) the term "individual" means a citizen of the United States or an alien lawfully admitted for permanent residence;

(3) the term "maintain" includes maintain, collect, use, or disseminate;

(4) the term "record" means any item, collection, or grouping of information about an individual that is maintained by an agency, including, but not limited to, his education, financial transactions, medical history, and criminal or employment history and that contains his name, or the identifying number, symbol, or other identifying particular assigned to the individual, such as a finger or voice print or a photograph;

(5) the term "system of records" means a group of any records under the control of any agency from which information is retrieved by the name of the individual or by some identifying number, symbol, or other identifying particular assigned to the individual;

(6) the term "statistical record" means a record in a system of records maintained for statistical research or reporting purposes only and not used in whole or in part in making any determination about an identifiable individual, except as provided by section 8 of title 13;

(7) the term "routine use" means, with respect to the disclosure of a record, the use of such record for a purpose which is compatible with the purpose for which it was collected; and

(8) the term "matching program"—

(A) means any computerized comparison of—

(i) two or more automated systems of records or a system of records with non-Federal records for the purpose of—

(I) establishing or verifying the eligibility of, or continuing compliance with statutory and regulatory requirements by, applicants for, recipients or beneficiaries of, participants in, or providers of services with respect to, cash or in-kind assistance or payments under Federal benefit programs, or

(II) recouping payments or delinquent debts under such Federal benefit programs, or

(ii) two or more automated Federal personnel or payroll systems of records or a system of Federal personnel or payroll records with non-Federal records,

(B) but does not include—

(i) matches performed to produce aggregate statistical data without any personal identifiers;

(ii) matches performed to support any research or statistical project, the specific data of which may not be used to make decisions concerning the rights, benefits, or privileges of specific individuals;

(iii) matches performed, by an agency (or component thereof) which performs as its principal function any activity pertaining to the enforcement of criminal laws, subsequent to the initiation of a specific criminal or civil law enforcement investigation of a named person or persons for the purpose of gathering evidence against such person or persons;

(iv) matches of tax information (I) pursuant to section 6103(d) of the Internal Revenue Code of 1986 [26 USCS § 6103(d)], (II) for purposes of tax administration as defined in section 6103(b)(4) of such Code [26 USCS § 6103(b)(4)], (III) for the purpose of intercepting a tax refund due an individual under authority granted by section 404(e), 464, or 1137 of the Social Security Act [42 USCS § 604(e), 664, or 1337]; or (IV) for the purpose of intercepting a tax refund due an individual under any other tax refund intercept program authorized by statute which has been determined by the Director of the Office of Management and Budget to contain verification, notice, and hearing requirements that are substantially similar to the procedures in section 1137 of the Social Security Act [42 USCS § 1320b–7];

(v) matches—

(I) using records predominantly relating to Federal personnel, that are performed for routine administrative purposes (subject to guidance provided by the Director of the Office of Management and Budget pursuant to subsection (v)); or

(II) conducted by an agency using only records from systems of records maintained by that agency; if the purpose of the match is not to take any adverse financial, personnel, disciplinary, or other adverse action against Federal personnel;

(vi) matches performed for foreign counterintelligence purposes or to produce background checks for security clearances of Federal personnel or Federal contractor personnel;

(vii) matches performed incident to a levy described in section 6103(k)(8) of the Internal Revenue Code of 1986 [26 USCS § 6103(k)(8)]; or

(viii) matches performed pursuant to section 202(x)(3) or 1611(e)(1) of the Social Security Act (42 U.S.C. 402(x)(3), 1382(e)(1));

(9) the term "recipient agency" means any agency, or contractor thereof, receiving records contained in a system of records from a source agency for use in a matching program;

(10) the term "non-Federal agency" means any State or local government, or agency thereof, which receives records contained in a system of records from a source agency for use in a matching program;

(11) the term "source agency" means any agency which discloses records contained in a system of records to be used in a matching program, or any State or local government, or agency thereof, which discloses records to be used in a matching program;

(12) the term "Federal benefit program" means any program administered or funded by the Federal Government, or by any agent or State on behalf of the Federal Government, providing cash or in-kind assistance in the form of payments, grants, loans, or loan guarantees to individuals; and

(13) the term "Federal personnel" means officers and employees of the Government of the United States, members of the uniformed services (including members of the Reserve Components), individuals entitled to receive immediate or deferred retirement benefits under any retirement program of the Government of the United States (including survivor benefits).

(b) Conditions of disclosure. No agency shall disclose any record which is contained in a system of records by any means of communication to any person, or to another agency, except pursuant to a written request by, or with the prior written consent of, the individual to whom the record pertains, unless disclosure of the record would be—

(1) to those officers and employees of the agency which maintains the record who have a need for the record in the performance of their duties;

(2) required under section 552 of this title;

(3) for a routine use as defined in subsection (a)(7) of this section and described under subsection (e)(4)(D) of this section;

(4) to the Bureau of the Census for purposes of planning or carrying out a census or survey or related activity pursuant to the provisions of title 13;

(5) to a recipient who has provided the agency with advance adequate written assurance that the record will be used solely as a statistical research or reporting record, and the record is to be transferred in a form that is not individually identifiable;

(6) to the National Archives and Records Administration as a record which has sufficient historical or other value to warrant its continued preservation by the United States Government, or for evaluation by the Archivist of the United States or the designee of the Archivist to determine whether the record has such value;

(7) to another agency or to an instrumentality of any governmental jurisdiction within or under the control of the United States for a civil or criminal law enforcement activity if the activity is authorized by law, and if the head of the agency or instrumentality has made a written request to the agency which maintains the record specifying the particular portion desired and the law enforcement activity for which the record is sought;

(8) to a person pursuant to a showing of compelling circumstances affecting the health or safety of an individual if upon such disclosure notification is transmitted to the last known address of such individual;

(9) to either House of Congress, or, to the extent of matter within its jurisdiction, any committee or subcommittee thereof, any joint committee of Congress or subcommittee of any such joint committee;

(10) to the Comptroller General, or any of his authorized representatives, in the course of the performance of the duties of the General Accounting Office;

(11) pursuant to the order of a court of competent jurisdiction; or

(12) to a consumer reporting agency in accordance with section 3711(e) of title 31.

(c) Accounting of certain disclosures. Each agency, with respect to each system of records under its control, shall—

(1) except for disclosures made under subsections (b)(1) or (b)(2) of this section, keep an accurate accounting of—

(A) the date, nature, and purpose of each disclosure of a record to any person or to another agency made under subsection (b) of this section; and

(B) the name and address of the person or agency to whom the disclosure is made;

(2) retain the accounting made under paragraph (1) of this subsection for at least five years or the life of the record, whichever is longer, after the disclosure for which the accounting is made;

(3) except for disclosures made under subsection (b)(7) of this section, make the accounting made under paragraph (1) of this subsection available to the individual named in the record at his request; and

(4) inform any person or other agency about any correction or notation of dispute made by the agency in accordance with subsection (d) of this section of any record that has been disclosed to the person or agency if an accounting of the disclosure was made.

(d) Access to records. Each agency that maintains a system of records shall—

(1) upon request by any individual to gain access to his record or to any information pertaining to him which is contained in the system, permit him and upon his request, a person of his own choosing to accompany him, to review the record and have a copy made of all or any portion thereof in a form comprehensible to him, except that the agency may require the individual to furnish a written statement authorizing discussion of that individual's record in the accompanying person's presence;

(2) permit the individual to request amendment of a record pertaining to him and—

(A) not later than 10 days (excluding Saturdays, Sundays, and legal public holidays) after the date of receipt of such request, acknowledge in writing such receipt; and

(B) promptly, either—

(i) make any correction of any portion thereof which the individual believes is not accurate, relevant, timely, or complete; or

(ii) inform the individual of its refusal to amend the record in accordance with his request, the reason for the refusal, the procedures established by the agency for the individual to request a review of that refusal by the head of the agency or an officer designated by the head of the agency, and the name and business address of that official;

(3) permit the individual who disagrees with the refusal of the agency to amend his record to request a review of such refusal, and not later than 30 days (excluding Saturdays, Sundays, and legal public holidays) from the date on which the individual requests such review, complete such review and make a final determination unless, for good cause shown, the head of the agency extends such 30–day period; and if, after his review, the reviewing official also refuses to amend the record in accordance with the request, permit the individual to file with the agency a concise statement setting forth the reasons for his disagreement with the refusal of the agency, and notify the individual of the provisions for judicial review of the reviewing official's determination under subsection (g)(1)(A) of this section;

(4) in any disclosure, containing information about which the individual has filed a statement of disagreement, occurring after the filing of the statement under paragraph (3) of this subsection, clearly note any portion of the record which is disputed and provide copies of the statement and, if the agency deems it appropriate, copies of a concise statement of the reasons of the agency for not making the amendments requested, to persons or other agencies to whom the disputed record has been disclosed; and

(5) nothing in this section shall allow an individual access to any information compiled in reasonable anticipation of a civil action or proceeding.

(e) Agency requirements. Each agency that maintains a system of records shall—

(1) maintain in its records only such information about an individual as is relevant and necessary to accomplish a purpose of the agency required to be accomplished by statute or by executive order of the President;

(2) collect information to the greatest extent practicable directly from the subject individual when the information may result in adverse determinations about an individual's rights, benefits, and privileges under Federal programs;

(3) inform each individual whom it asks to supply information, on the form which it uses to collect the information or on a separate form that can be retained by the individual—

(A) the authority (whether granted by statute, or by executive order of the President) which authorizes the solicitation of the information and whether disclosure of such information is mandatory or voluntary;

(B) the principal purpose or purposes for which the information is intended to be used;

(C) the routine uses which may be made of the information, as published pursuant to paragraph (4)(D) of this subsection; and

(D) the effects on him, if any, of not providing all or any party of the requested information;

(4) subject to the provisions of paragraph (11) of this subsection, publish in the Federal Register upon establishment or revision a notice of the existence and character of the system of records, which notice shall include—

(A) the name and location of the system;

(B) the categories of individuals on whom records are maintained in the system;

(C) the categories of records maintained in the system;

(D) each routine use of the records contained in the system, including the categories of users and the purpose of such use;

(E) the policies and practices of the agency regarding storage, retrievability, access controls, retention, and disposal of the records;

(F) the title and business address of the agency official who is responsible for the system of records;

(G) the agency procedures whereby an individual can be notified at his request if the system of records contains a record pertaining to him;

(H) the agency procedures whereby an individual can be notified at his request how he can gain access to any record pertaining to him contained in the system of records, and how he can contest its content; and

(I) the categories of sources or records in the system;

(5) maintain all records which are used by the agency in making any determination about any individual with such accuracy, relevance, timeliness, and completeness as is reasonably necessary to assure fairness to the individual in the determination;

(6) prior to disseminating any record about an individual to any person other than an agency, unless the dissemination is made pursuant to subsection (b)(2) of this section, make reasonable efforts to assure that such records are accurate, complete, timely, and relevant for agency purposes;

(7) maintain no record describing how any individual exercises rights guaranteed by the First Amendment unless expressly authorized by statute or by the individual about whom the record is maintained or unless pertinent to and within the scope of an authorized law enforcement activity;

(8) make reasonable efforts to serve notice on an individual when any record on such individual is made available to any person under compulsory legal process when such process becomes a matter of public record;

(9) establish rules of conduct for persons involved in the design, development, operation, or maintenance of any system of records, or in maintaining any record, and instruct each such person with respect to such rules and the requirements of this section, including any other rules and procedures adopted pursuant to this section and the penalties for noncompliance;

(10) establish appropriate administrative, technical, and physical safeguards to insure the security and confidentiality of records and to protect against any anticipated threats or hazards to their security or integrity which could result in substantial harm, embarrassment, inconvenience, or unfairness to any individual on whom information is maintained;

(11) at least 30 days prior to publication of information under paragraph (4)(D) of this subsection, publish in the Federal Register notice of any new use or intended use of the information in the system, and provide an opportunity for interested persons to submit written data, views, or arguments to the agency; and

(12) [Caution: For effective date, see 1988 Amendment note] if such agency is a recipient agency or a source agency in a matching

program with a non-Federal agency, with respect to any establishment or revision of a matching program, at least 30 days prior to conducting such program, publish in the Federal Register notice of such establishment or revision.

(f) Agency Rules. In order to carry out the provisions of this section, each agency that maintains a system of records shall promulgate rules, in accordance with the requirements (including general notice) of section 553 of this title, which shall—

(1) establish procedures whereby an individual can be notified in response to his request if any system of records named by the individual contains a record pertaining to him;

(2) define reasonable times, places, and requirements for identifying an individual who requests his record or information pertaining to him before the agency shall make the record or information available to the individual;

(3) establish procedures for the disclosure to an individual upon his request of his record or information pertaining to him, including special procedure, if deemed necessary, for the disclosure to an individual of medical records, including psychological records, pertaining to him;

(4) establish procedures for reviewing a request from an individual concerning the amendment of any record or information pertaining to the individual, for making a determination on the request, for an appeal within the agency of an initial adverse agency determination, and for whatever additional means may be necessary for each individual to be able to exercise fully his rights under this section; and

(5) establish fees to be charged, if any, to any individual for making copies of his record, excluding the cost of any search for and review of the record. The Office of the Federal Register shall biennially compile and publish the rules promulgated under this subsection and agency notices published under subsection (e)(4) of this section in a form available to the public at low cost.

(g) Civil remedies.

(1) Whenever any agency—

(A) makes a determination under subsection (d)(3) of this section not to amend an individual's record in accordance with his request, or fails to make such review in conformity with that subsection;

(B) refuses to comply with an individual request under subsection (d)(1) of this section;

(C) fails to maintain any record concerning any individual with such accuracy, relevance, timeliness, and completeness as is necessary to assure fairness in any determination relating to the qualifications, character, rights, or opportunities of, or benefits to the individual that may be made on the basis of such record, and consequently a determination is made which is adverse to the individual; or

(D) fails to comply with any other provision of this section, or any rule promulgated thereunder, in such a way as to have an adverse effect on an individual, the individual may bring a civil action against the agency, and the district courts of the United States shall have jurisdiction in the matters under the provisions of this subsection.

(2) (A) In any suit brought under the provisions of subsection (g)(1)(A) of this section, the court may order the agency to amend the individual's record in accordance with his request or in such other way as the court may direct. In such a case the court shall determine the matter de novo.

(B) The court may assess against the United States reasonable attorney fees and other litigation costs reasonably incurred in any case under this paragraph in which the complainant has substantially prevailed.

(3) (A) In any suit brought under the provisions of subsection (g)(1)(B) of this section, the court may enjoin the agency from withholding the records and order the production to the complainant of any agency records improperly withheld from him. In such a case the court shall determine the matter de novo, and may examine the contents of any agency records in camera to determine whether the records or any portion thereof may be withheld under any of the exemptions set forth in subsection (k) of this section, and the burden is on the agency to sustain its action.

(B) The court may assess against the United States reasonable attorney fees and other litigation costs reasonably incurred in any case under this paragraph in which the complainant has substantially prevailed.

(4) In any suit brought under the provisions of subsection (g)(1)(C) or (D) of this section in which the court determines that the agency acted in a manner which was intentional or willful, the United States shall be liable to the individual in an amount equal to the sum of—

(A) actual damages sustained by the individual as a result of the refusal or failure, but in no case shall a person entitled to recovery receive less than the sum of $1,000; and

(B) the costs of the action together with reasonable attorney fees as determined by the court.

(5) An action to enforce any liability created under this section may be brought in the district court of the United States in the district in which the complainant resides, or has his principal place of business, or in which the agency records are situated, or in the District of Columbia, without regard to the amount in controversy,

within two years from the date on which the cause of action arises, except that where an agency has materially and willfully misrepresented any information required under this section to be disclosed to an individual and the information so misrepresented is material to establishment of the liability of the agency to the individual under this section, the action may be brought at any time within two years after discovery by the individual of the misrepresentation. Nothing in this section shall be construed to authorize any civil action by reason of any injury sustained as the result of a disclosure of a record prior to September 27, 1975.

(h) Rights of legal guardians. For the purposes of this section, the parent of any minor, or the legal guardian of any individual who has been declared to be incompetent due to physical or mental incapacity or age by a court of competent jurisdiction, may act on behalf of the individual.

(i) Criminal penalties.

(1) Any officer or employee of an agency, who by virtue of his employment or official position, has possession of, or access to, agency records which contain individually identifiable information the disclosure of which is prohibited by this section or by rules or regulations established thereunder, and who knowing that disclosure of the specific material is so prohibited, willfully discloses the material in any manner to any person or agency not entitled to receive it, shall be guilty of a misdemeanor and fined not more than $5,000.

(2) Any officer or employee of any agency who willfully maintains a system of records without meeting the notice requirements of subsection (e)(4) of this section shall be guilty of a misdemeanor and fined not more than $5,000.

(3) Any person who knowingly and willfully requests or obtains any record concerning an individual from an agency under false pretenses shall be guilty of a misdemeanor and fined not more than $5,000.

(j) General exemptions. The head of any agency may promulgate rules, in accordance with the requirements (including general notice) of sections 553(b)(1), (2), and (3), (c), and (e) of this title, to exempt any system of records within the agency from any part of this section except subsections (b), (c)(1) and (2), (e)(4)(A) through (F), (e)(6), (7), (9), (10), and (11), and (i) if the system of records is—

(1) maintained by the Central Intelligence Agency; or

(2) maintained by an agency or component thereof which performs as its principal function any activity pertaining to the enforcement of criminal laws, including police efforts to prevent, control, or reduce crime or to apprehend criminals, and the activities of prosecutors, courts, correctional, probation, pardon, or parole authorities, and which consists of (A) information compiled for the purpose of

identifying individual criminal offenders and alleged offenders and consisting only of identifying data and notations of arrests, the nature and disposition of criminal charges, sentencing, confinement, release, and parole and probation status; (B) information compiled for the purpose of a criminal investigation, including reports of informants and investigators, and associated with an identifiable individual; or (C) reports identifiable to an individual compiled at any stage of the process of enforcement of the criminal laws from arrest or indictment through release from supervision. At the time rules are adopted under this subsection, the agency shall include in the statement required under section 553(c) of this title, the reasons why the system of records is to be exempted from a provision of this section.

(k) Specific exemptions. The head of any agency may promulgate rules, in accordance with the requirements (including general notice) of sections 553(b)(1), (2), and (3), (c), and (e) of this title, to exempt any system of records within the agency from subsections (c)(3), (d), (e)(1), (e)(4)(G), (H), and (I) and (f) of this section if the system of records is—

(1) subject to provisions of section 552(b)(1) of this title;

(2) investigatory material compiled for law enforcement purposes, other than material within the scope of subsection (j)(2) of this section: Provided, however, That if any individual is denied any right, privilege, or benefit that he would otherwise be entitled by Federal law, or for which he would otherwise be eligible, as a result of the maintenance of such material, such material shall be provided to such individual, except to the extent that the disclosure of such material would reveal the identity of a source who furnished information to the Government under an express promise that the identity of the source would be held in confidence, or, prior to the effective date of this section, under an implied promise that the identity of the source would be held in confidence;

(3) maintained in connection with providing protective services to the President of the United States or other individuals pursuant to section 3056 of title 18;

(4) required by statute to be maintained and used solely as statistical records;

(5) investigatory material compiled solely for the purpose of determining suitability, eligibility, or qualifications for Federal civilian employment, military service, Federal contracts, or access to classified information, but only to the extent that the disclosure of such material would reveal the identity of a source who furnished information to the Government under an express promise that the identity of the source would be held in confidence, or, prior to the effective date of this section, under an implied promise that the identity of the source would be held in confidence;

(6) testing or examination material used solely to determine individual qualifications for appointment or promotion in the Federal service the disclosure of which would compromise the objectivity or fairness of the testing or examination process; or

(7) evaluation material used to determine potential for promotion in the armed services, but only to the extent that the disclosure of such material would reveal the identity of a source who furnished information to the Government under an express promise that the identity of the source would be held in confidence, or, prior to the effective date of this section, under an implied promise that the identity of the source would be held in confidence. At the time rules are adopted under this subsection, the agency shall include in the statement required under section 553(c) of this title, the reasons why the system of records is to be exempted from a provision of this section.

(*l*) Archival records.

(1) Each agency record which is accepted by the Archivist of the United States for storage, processing, and servicing in accordance with section 3103 of title 44 shall, for the purposes of this section, be considered to be maintained by the agency which deposited the record and shall be subject to the provisions of this section. The Archivist of the United States shall not disclose the record except to the agency which maintains the record, or under rules established by that agency which are not inconsistent with the provisions of this section.

(2) Each agency record pertaining to an identifiable individual which was transferred to the National Archives of the United States as a record which has sufficient historical or other value to warrant its continued preservation by the United States Government, prior to the effective date of this section, shall, for the purposes of this section, be considered to be maintained by the National Archives and shall not be subject to the provisions of this section, except that a statement generally describing such records (modeled after the requirements relating to records subject to subsections (e)(4)(A) through (G) of this section) shall be published in the Federal Register.

(3) Each agency record pertaining to an identifiable individual which is transferred to the National Archives of the United States as a record which has sufficient historical or other value to warrant its continued preservation by the United States Government, on or after the effective date of this section [effective 270 days following Dec. 31, 1974], shall, for the purposes of this section, be considered to be maintained by the National Archives and shall be exempt from the requirements of this section except subsections (e)(4)(A) through (G) and (e)(9) of this section.

(m) Government contractors.

(1) When an agency provides by a contract for the operation by or on behalf of the agency of a system of records to accomplish an agency function, the agency shall, consistent with its authority, cause the requirements of this section to be applied to such system. For purposes of subsection (i) of this section any such contractor and any employee of such contractor, if such contract is agreed to on or after the effective date of this section, shall be considered to be an employee of an agency.

(2) A consumer reporting agency to which a record is disclosed under section 3711(e) of title 31 shall not be considered a contractor for the purposes of this section.

(n) Mailing lists. An individual's name and address may not be sold or rented by an agency unless such action is specifically authorized by law. This provision shall not be construed to require the withholding of names and addresses otherwise permitted to be made public.

(*o*) Matching agreements.

(1) No record which is contained in a system of records may be disclosed to a recipient agency or non-Federal agency for use in a computer matching program except pursuant to a written agreement between the source agency and the recipient agency or non-Federal agency specifying—

(A) the purpose and legal authority for conducting the program;

(B) the justification for the program and the anticipated results, including a specific estimate of any savings;

(C) a description of the records that will be matched, including each data element that will be used, the approximate number of records that will be matched, and the projected starting and completion dates of the matching program;

(D) procedures for providing individualized notice at the time of application, and notice periodically thereafter as directed by the Data Integrity Board of such agency (subject to guidance provided by the Director of the Office of Management and Budget pursuant to subsection (v)), to—

(i) applicants for and recipients of financial assistance or payments under Federal benefit programs, and

(ii) applicants for and holders of positions as Federal personnel, that any information provided by such applicants, recipients, holders and individuals may be subject to verification through matching programs;

(E) procedures for verifying information produced in such matching program as required by subsection (p);

(F) procedures for the retention and timely destruction of identifiable records created by a recipient agency or non-Federal agency in such matching program;

(G) procedures for ensuring the administrative, technical, and physical security of the records matched and the results of such programs;

(H) prohibitions on duplication and redisclosure of records provided by the source agency within or outside the recipient agency or the non-Federal agency, except where required by law or essential to the conduct of the matching program;

(I) procedures governing the use by a recipient agency or non-Federal agency of records provided in a matching program by a source agency, including procedures governing return of the records to the source agency or destruction of records used in such program;

(J) information on assessments that have been made on the accuracy of the records that will be used in such matching program; and

(K) that the Comptroller General may have access to all records of a recipient agency or a non-Federal agency that the Comptroller General deems necessary in order to monitor or verify compliance with the agreement.

(2) (A) A copy of each agreement entered into pursuant to paragraph (1) shall—

(i) be transmitted to the Committee on Governmental Affairs of the Senate and the Committee on Government Operations of the House of Representatives; and

(ii) be available upon request to the public.

(B) No such agreement shall be effective until 30 days after the date on which such a copy is transmitted pursuant to subparagraph (A)(i).

(C) Such an agreement shall remain in effect only for such period, not to exceed 18 months, as the Data Integrity Board of the agency determines is appropriate in light of the purposes, and length of time necessary for the conduct, of the matching program.

(D) Within 3 months prior to the expiration of such an agreement pursuant to subparagraph (C), the Data Integrity Board of the agency may, without additional review, renew the matching agreement for a current, ongoing matching program for not more than one additional year if—

(i) such program will be conducted without any change; and

(ii) each party to the agreement certifies to the Board in writing that the program has been conducted in compliance with the agreement.

(p) Verification and opportunity to contest findings.

(1) In order to protect any individual whose records are used in a matching program, no recipient agency, non-Federal agency, or source agency may suspend, terminate, reduce, or make a final denial of any financial assistance or payment under a Federal benefit program to such individual, or take other adverse action against such individual, as a result of information produced by such matching program, until—

(A) (i) the agency has independently verified the information; or

(ii) the Date Integrity Board of the agency, or in the case of a non-Federal agency the Data Integrity Board of the source agency, determines in accordance with guidance issued by the Director of the Office of Management and Budget that—

(I) the information is limited to identification and amount of benefits paid by the source agency under a Federal benefit program; and

(II) there is a high degree of confidence that the information provided to the recipient agency is accurate;

(B) the individual receives a notice from the agency containing a statement of its findings and informing the individual of the opportunity to contest such findings; and

(C) (i) the expiration of any time period established for the program by statute or regulation for the individual to respond to that notice; or

(ii) in the case of a program for which no such period is established, the end of the 30-day period beginning on the date on which notice under subparagraph (B) is mailed or otherwise provided to the individual.

(2) Independent verification referred to in paragraph (1) requires investigation and confirmation of specific information relating to an individual that is used as a basis for an adverse action against the individual, including where applicable investigation and confirmation of—

(A) the amount of any asset or income involved;

(B) whether such individual actually has or had access to such asset or income for such individual's own use; and

(C) the period or periods when the individual actually had such asset or income.

(3) Notwithstanding paragraph (1), an agency may take any appropriate action otherwise prohibited by such paragraph if the agency determines that the public health or public safety may be adversely affected or significantly threatened during any notice period required by such paragraph.

(q) Sanctions.

(1) Notwithstanding any other provision of law, no source agency may disclose any record which is contained in a system of records to a recipient agency or non-Federal agency for a matching program if such source agency has reason to believe that the requirements of subsection (p), or any matching agreement entered into pursuant to subsection (*o*), or both, are not being met by such recipient agency.

(2) No source agency may renew a matching agreement unless—

(A) the recipient agency or non-Federal agency has certified that it has complied with the provisions of that agreement; and

(B) the source agency has no reason to believe that the certification is inaccurate.

(r) Report on new systems and matching programs. Each agency that proposes to establish or make a significant change in a system of records or a matching program shall provide adequate advance notice of any such proposal (in duplicate) to the Committee on Government Operations of the House of Representatives, the Committee on Governmental Affairs of the Senate, and the Office of Management and Budget in order to permit an evaluation of the probable or potential effect of such proposal on the privacy or other rights of individuals.

(s) Biennial report. The President shall biennially submit to the Speaker of the House of Representatives and the President pro tempore of the Senate a report—

(1) describing the actions of the Director of the Office of Management and Budget pursuant to section 6 of the Privacy Act of 1974 during the preceding 2 years;

(2) describing the exercise of individual rights of access and amendment under this section during such years;

(3) identifying changes in or additions to systems of records;

(4) containing such other information concerning administration of this section as may be necessary or useful to the Congress in reviewing the effectiveness of this section in carrying out the purposes of the Privacy Act of 1974 [note to this section].

(t) Effect of other laws.

(1) No agency shall rely on any exemption contained in section 552 of this title to withhold from an individual any record which is otherwise accessible to such individual under the provisions of this section.

(2) No agency shall rely on any exemption in this section to withhold from an individual any record which is otherwise accessible to such individual under the provisions of section 552 of this title.

(u) Data Integrity Boards.

(1) Every agency conducting or participating in a matching program shall establish a Data Integrity Board to oversee and coordinate among the various components of such agency the agency's implementation of this section.

(2) Each Data Integrity Board shall consist of senior officials designated by the head of the agency, and shall include any senior official designated by the head of the agency as responsible for implementation of this section, and the inspector general of the agency, if any. The inspector general shall not serve as chairman of the Data Integrity Board.

(3) Each Data Integrity Board—

(A) shall review, approve, and maintain all written agreements for receipt or disclosure of agency records for matching programs to ensure compliance with subsection (*o*), and all relevant statutes, regulations, and guidelines;

(B) shall review all matching programs in which the agency has participated during the year, either as a source agency or recipient agency, determine compliance with applicable laws, regulations, guidelines, and agency agreements, and assess the costs and benefits of such programs;

(C) shall review all recurring matching programs in which the agency has participated during the year, either as a source agency or recipient agency, for continued justification for such disclosures;

(D) shall compile an annual report, which shall be submitted to the head of the agency and the Office of Management and Budget and made available to the public on request, describing the matching activities of the agency, including—

(i) matching programs in which the agency has participated as a source agency or recipient agency;

(ii) matching agreements proposed under subsection (*o*) that were disapproved by the Board;

(iii) any changes in membership or structure of the Board in the preceding year;

(iv) the reasons for any waiver of the requirement in paragraph (4) of this section for completion and submission of a cost-benefit analysis prior to the approval of a matching program;

(v) any violations of matching agreements that have been alleged or identified and any corrective action taken; and

(vi) any other information required by the Director of the Office of Management and Budget to be included in such report;

(E) shall serve as a clearinghouse for receiving and providing information on the accuracy, completeness, and reliability of records used in matching programs;

(F) shall provide interpretation and guidance to agency components and personnel on the requirements of this section for matching programs;

(G) shall review agency recordkeeping and disposal policies and practices for matching programs to assure compliance with this section; and

(H) may review and report on any agency matching activities that are not matching programs.

(4) (A) Except as provided in subparagraphs (B) and (C), a Data Integrity Board shall not approve any written agreement for a matching program unless the agency has completed and submitted to such Board a cost-benefit analysis of the proposed program and such analysis demonstrates that the program is likely to be cost effective.

(B) The Board may waive the requirements of subparagraph (A) of this paragraph if it determines in writing, in accordance with guidelines prescribed by the Director of the Office of Management and Budget, that a cost-benefit analysis is not required.

(C) A cost-benefit analysis shall not be required under subparagraph (A) prior to the initial approval of a written agreement for a matching program that is specifically required by statute. Any subsequent written agreement for such a program shall not be approved by the Data Integrity Board unless the agency has submitted a cost-benefit analysis of the program as conducted under the preceding approval of such agreement.

(5) (A) If a matching agreement is disapproved by a Data Integrity Board, any party to such agreement may appeal the disapproval to the Director of the Office of Management and Budget. Timely notice of the filing of such an appeal shall be provided by the Director of the Office of Management and Budget to the Committee on Governmental Affairs of the Senate and the Committee on Government Operations of the House of Representatives.

(B) The Director of the Office of Management and Budget may approve a matching agreement notwithstanding the disapproval of a Data Integrity Board if the Director determines that—

(i) the matching program will be consistent with all applicable legal, regulatory, and policy requirements;

(ii) there is adequate evidence that the matching agreement will be cost-effective; and

(iii) the matching program is in the public interest.

(C) The decision of the Director to approve a matching agreement shall not take effect until 30 days after it is reported to committees described in subparagraph (A).

(D) If the Data Integrity Board and the Director of the Office of Management and Budget disapprove a matching program proposed by the inspector general of an agency, the inspector general may report the disapproval to the head of the agency and to the Congress.

(6) In the reports required by paragraph (3)(D), agency matching activities that are not matching programs may be reported on an aggregate basis, if and to the extent necessary to protect ongoing law enforcement or counterintelligence investigations.

(7) [Redesignated]

(v) Office of Management and Budget responsibilities. The Director of the Office of Management and Budget shall—

(1) develop and, after notice and opportunity for public comment, prescribe guidelines and regulations for the use of agencies in implementing the provisions of this section; and

(2) provide continuing assistance to and oversight of the implementation of this section by agencies.

THE GOVERNMENT IN THE SUNSHINE ACT*

§ 552b. Open Meetings

(a) For purposes of this section—

(1) the term "agency" means any agency, as defined in section 552(e) of this title, headed by a collegial body composed of two or more individual members, a majority of whom are appointed to such position by the President with the advice and consent of the Senate, and any subdivision thereof authorized to act on behalf of the agency;

(2) the term "meeting" means the deliberations of at least the number of individual agency members required to take action on behalf of the agency where such deliberations determine or result in the joint conduct or disposition of official agency business, but does not include deliberations required or permitted by subsection (d) or (e); and

(3) the term "member" means an individual who belongs to a collegial body heading an agency.

(b) Members shall not jointly conduct or dispose of agency business other than in accordance with this section. Except as provided in subsection (c), every portion of every meeting of an agency shall be open to public observation.

* Pub.L. 94–409 (1976).

(c) Except in a case where the agency finds that the public interest requires otherwise, the second sentence of subsection (b) shall not apply to any portion of an agency meeting, and the requirements of subsections (d) and (e) shall not apply to any information pertaining to such meeting otherwise required by this section to be disclosed to the public, where the agency properly determines that such portion or portions of its meeting or the disclosure of such information is likely to—

(1) disclose matters that are (A) specifically authorized under criteria established by an Executive order to be kept secret in the interests of national defense or foreign policy and (B) in fact properly classified pursuant to such Executive order;

(2) relate solely to the internal personnel rules and practices of an agency;

(3) disclose matters specifically exempted from disclosure by statute (other than section 552 of this title), provided that such statute (A) requires that the matters be withheld from the public in such a manner as to leave no discretion on the issue, or (B) establishes particular criteria for withholding or refers to particular types of matters to be withheld;

(4) disclose trade secrets and commercial or financial information obtained from a person and privileged or confidential;

(5) involve accusing any person of a crime, or formally censuring any person;

(6) disclose information of a personal nature where disclosure would constitute a clearly unwarranted invasion of personal privacy;

(7) disclose investigatory records compiled for law enforcement purposes, or information which if written would be contained in such records, but only to the extent that the production of such records or information would (A) interfere with enforcement proceedings, (B) deprive a person of a right to a fair trial or an impartial adjudication, (C) constitute an unwarranted invasion of personal privacy, (D) disclose the identity of a confidential source and, in the case of a record compiled by a criminal law enforcement authority in the course of a criminal investigation, or by an agency conducting a lawful national security intelligence investigation, confidential information furnished only by the confidential source, (E) disclose investigative techniques and procedures, or (F) endanger the life or physical safety of law enforcement personnel;

(8) disclose information contained in or related to examination, operating, or condition reports prepared by, on behalf of, or for the use of an agency responsible for the regulation or supervision of financial institutions;

(9) disclose information the premature disclosure of which would—

(A) in the case of an agency which regulates currencies, securities, commodities, or financial institutions, be likely to (i) lead to significant financial speculation in currencies, securities, or commodities, or (ii) significantly endanger the stability of any financial institution; or

(B) in the case of any agency, be likely to significantly frustrate implementation of a proposed agency action.

except that subparagraph (B) shall not apply in any instance where the agency has already disclosed to the public the content or nature of its proposed action, or where the agency is required by law to make such disclosure on its own initiative prior to taking final agency action on such proposal; or

(10) specifically concern the agency's issuance of a subpena, or the agency's participation in a civil action or proceeding, an action in a foreign court or international tribunal, or an arbitration, or the initiation, conduct, or disposition by the agency of a particular case of formal agency adjudication pursuant to the procedures in section 554 of this title or otherwise involving a determination on the record after opportunity for a hearing.

(d)(1) Action under subsection (c) shall be taken only when a majority of the entire membership of the agency (as defined in subsection (a)(*l*)) votes to take such action. A separate vote of the agency members shall be taken with respect to each agency meeting a portion or portions of which are proposed to be closed to the public pursuant to subsection (c), or with respect to any information which is proposed to be withheld under subsection (c). A single vote may be taken with respect to a series of meetings, a portion or portions of which are proposed to be closed to the public, or with respect to any information concerning such series of meetings, so long as each meeting in such series involves the same particular matters and is scheduled to be held no more than thirty days after the initial meeting in such series. The vote of each agency member participating in such vote shall be recorded and no proxies shall be allowed.

(2) Whenever any person whose interests may be directly affected by a portion of a meeting requests that the agency close such portion to the public for any of the reasons referred to in paragraph (5), (6), or (7) of subsection (c), the agency, upon request of any one of its members, shall vote by recorded vote whether to close such meeting.

(3) Within one day of any vote taken pursuant to paragraph (1) or (2), the agency shall make publicly available a written copy of such vote reflecting the vote of each member on the question. If a portion of a meeting is to be closed to the public, the agency shall, within one day of the vote taken pursuant to paragraph (1) or (2) of this subsection, make publicly available a full written explanation of its action closing the portion together with a list of all persons expected to attend the meeting and their affiliation.

(4) Any agency, a majority of whose meetings may properly be closed to the public pursuant to paragraph (4), (8), (9)(A), or (10) of subsection (c), or any combination thereof, may provide by regulation for the closing of such meetings or portions thereof in the event that a majority of the members of the agency votes by recorded vote at the beginning of such meeting, or portion thereof, to close the exempt portion or portions of the meeting, and a copy of such vote, reflecting the vote of each member on the question, is made available to the public. The provisions of paragraphs (1), (2), and (3) of this subsection and subsection (e) shall not apply to any portion of a meeting to which such regulations apply: Provided, That the agency shall, except to the extent that such information is exempt from disclosure under the provisions of subsection (c), provide the public with public announcement of the time, place, and subject matter of the meeting and of each portion thereof at the earliest practicable time.

(e)(*l*) In the case of each meeting, the agency shall make public announcement, at least one week before the meeting, of the time, place, and subject matter of the meeting, whether it is to be open or closed to the public, and the name and phone number of the official designated by the agency to respond to requests for information about the meeting. Such announcement shall be made unless a majority of the members of the agency determines by a recorded vote that agency business requires that such meeting be called at an earlier date, in which case the agency shall make public announcement of the time, place, and subject matter of such meeting, and whether open or closed to the public, at the earliest practicable time.

(2) The time or place of a meeting may be changed following the public announcement required by paragraph (1) only if the agency publicly announces such change at the earliest practicable time. The subject matter of a meeting, or the determination of the agency to open or close a meeting, or portion of a meeting, to the public, may be changed following the public announcement required by this subsection only if (A) a majority of the entire membership of the agency determines by a recorded vote that agency business so requires and that no earlier announcement of the change was possible, and (B) the agency publicly announces such change and the vote of each member upon such change at the earliest practicable time.

(3) Immediately following each public announcement required by this subsection, notice of the time, place, and subject matter of a meeting, whether the meeting is open or closed, any change in one of the preceding, and the name and phone number of the official designated by the agency to respond to requests for information about the meeting, shall also be submitted for publication in the Federal Register.

(f)(1) For every meeting closed pursuant to paragraphs (1) through (10) of subsection (c), the General Counsel or chief legal officer of the agency shall publicly certify that, in his or her opinion, the meeting may be closed to the public and shall state each relevant exemptive provision. A copy of such certification, together with a statement from the presiding officer of the meeting setting forth the time and place of the meeting, and the persons present, shall be retained by the agency. The agency shall maintain a complete transcript or electronic recording adequate to record fully the proceedings of each meeting, or portion of a meeting, closed to the public, except that in the case of a meeting, or portion of a meeting, closed to the public pursuant to paragraph (8), (9)(A), or (10) of subsection (c), the agency shall maintain either such a transcript or recording, or a set of minutes. Such minutes shall fully and clearly describe all matters discussed and shall provide a full and accurate summary of any actions taken, and the reasons therefor, including a description of each of the views expressed on any item and the record of any rollcall vote (reflecting the vote of each member on the question). All documents considered in connection with any action shall be identified in such minutes.

(2) The agency shall make promptly available to the public, in a place easily accessible to the public, the transcript, electronic recording, or minutes (as required by paragraph (1)) of the discussion of any item on the agenda, or of any item of the testimony of any witness received at the meeting, except for such item or items of such discussion or testimony as the agency determines to contain information which may be withheld under subsection (c). Copies of such transcript, or minutes, or a transcription of such recording disclosing the identity of each speaker, shall be furnished to any person at the actual cost of duplication or transcription. The agency shall maintain a complete verbatim copy of the transcript, a complete copy of the minutes, or a complete electronic recording of each meeting, or portion of a meeting, closed to the public, for a period of at least two years after such meeting, or until one year after the conclusion of any agency proceeding with respect to which the meeting or portion was held, whichever occurs later.

(g) Each agency subject to the requirements of this section shall. within 180 days after the date of enactment of this section, following consultation with the Office of the Chairman of the Administrative Conference of the United States and published notice in the Federal Register of at least thirty days and opportunity for written comment by any person, promulgate regulations to implement the requirements of subsections (b) through (f) of this section. Any person may bring a proceeding in the United States District Court for the District of Columbia to require an agency to promulgate such regulations if such agency has not promulgated such regulations within the time period specified herein. Subject to any limitations of time provided by law, any person may bring a proceeding in the United States Court of Appeals for the

District of Columbia to set aside agency regulations issued pursuant to this subsection that are not in accord with the requirements of subsections (b) through (f) of this section and to require the promulgation of regulations that are in accord with such subsections.

(h)(*l*) The district courts of the United States shall have jurisdiction to enforce the requirements of subsections (b) through (f) of this section by declaratory judgment, injunctive relief, or other relief as may be appropriate. Such actions may be brought by any person against an agency prior to, or within sixty days after, the meeting out of which the violation of this section arises, except that if public announcement of such meeting is not initially provided by the agency in accordance with the requirements of this section, such action may be instituted pursuant to this section at any time prior to sixty days after any public announcement of such meeting. Such actions may be brought in the district court of the United States for the district in which the agency meeting is held or in which the agency in question has its headquarters, or in the District Court for the District of Columbia. In such actions a defendant shall serve his answer within thirty days after the service of the complaint. The burden is on the defendant to sustain his action. In deciding such cases the court may examine in camera any portion of the transcript, electronic recording, or minutes of a meeting closed to the public, and may take such additional evidence as it deems necessary. The court, having due regard for orderly administration and the public interest, as well as the interests of the parties, may grant such equitable relief as it deems appropriate, including granting an injunction against future violations of this section or ordering the agency to make available to the public such portion of the transcript, recording, or minutes of a meeting as is not authorized to be withheld under subsection (c) of this section.

(2) Any Federal court otherwise authorized by law to review agency action may, at the application of any person properly participating in the proceeding pursuant to other applicable law, inquire into violations by the agency of the requirements of this section and afford such relief as it deems appropriate. Nothing in this section authorizes any Federal court having jurisdiction solely on the basis of paragraph (1) to set aside, enjoin, or invalidate any agency action (other than an action to close a meeting or to withhold information under this section) taken or discussed at any agency meeting out of which the violation of this section arose.

(i) The court may assess against any party reasonable attorney fees and other litigation costs reasonably incurred by any other party who substantially prevails in any action brought in accordance with the provisions of subsection (g) or (h) of this section, except that costs may be assessed against the plaintiff only where the court finds that the suit was initiated by the plaintiff primarily for frivolous or dilatory purposes. In the case of assessment of costs against an agency, the costs may be assessed by the court against the United States.

(j) Each agency subject to the requirements of this section shall annually report to the Congress regarding the following:

(1) The changes in the policies and procedures of the agency under this section that have occurred during the preceding 1–year period.

(2) A tabulation of the number of meetings held, the exemptions applied to close meetings, and the days of public notice provided to close meetings.

(3) A brief description of litigation or formal complaints concerning the implementation of this section by the agency.

(4) A brief explanation of any changes in law that have affected the responsibilities of the agency under this section.

(k) Nothing herein expands or limits the present rights of any person under section 552 of this title, except that the exemptions set forth in subsection (c) of this section shall govern in the case of any request made pursuant to section 552 to copy or inspect the transcripts. recordings, or minutes described in subsection (f) of this section. The requirements of Chapter 33 of title 44, United States Code, shall not apply to the transcripts, recordings, and minutes described in subsection (f) of this section.

(*l*) This section does not constitute authority to withhold any information from Congress, and does not authorize the closing of any agency meeting or portion thereof required by any other provision of law to be open.

(m) Nothing in this section authorizes any agency to withhold from any individual any record, including transcripts, recordings, or minutes required by this section, which is otherwise accessible to such individual under section 552a of this title.

ALTERNATIVE MEANS OF DISPUTE RESOLUTION IN THE ADMINISTRATIVE PROCESS*

* Pub.L. 101–552 (1990). As originally enacted, both this Act and the Negotiated Rulemaking Act commenced at 5 U.S.C.A. § 581.

The Administrative Dispute Resolution Act contains a "sunset provision" which provides that "The authority of agencies to use dispute resolution proceedings under this Act and the amendments made by this Act shall terminate on October 1, 1995, except that such authority shall continue in effect with respect to then pending proceedings which, in the judgment of the agencies that are parties to the dispute resolution proceedings, require such continuation, until such proceedings terminate."

§ 571. Definitions

For the purposes of this subchapter [5 USCS §§ 571 et seq.], the term—

(1) "agency" has the same meaning as in section 551(1) of this title;

(2) "administrative program" includes a Federal function which involves protection of the public interest and the determination of rights, privileges, and obligations of private persons through rule making, adjudication, licensing, or investigation, as those terms are used in subchapter II of this chapter [5 USCS §§ 551 et seq.];

(3) "alternative means of dispute resolution" means any procedure that is used to resolve issues in controversy, including, but not limited to, conciliation, facilitation, mediation, factfinding, minitrials, arbitration, and use of ombuds, or any combination thereof;

(4) "award" means any decision by an arbitrator resolving the issues in controversy;

(5) "dispute resolution communication" means any oral or written communication prepared for the purposes of a dispute resolution proceeding, including any memoranda, notes or work product of the neutral, parties or nonparty participant; except that a written agreement to enter into a dispute resolution proceeding, or final written agreement or arbitral award reached as a result of a dispute resolution proceeding, is not a dispute resolution communication;

(6) "dispute resolution proceeding" means any process in which an alternative means of dispute resolution is used to resolve an issue in controversy in which a neutral is appointed and specified parties participate;

(7) "in confidence" means, with respect to information, that the information is provided—

(A) with the expressed intent of the source that it not be disclosed; or

(B) under circumstances that would create the reasonable expectation on behalf of the source that the information will not be disclosed;

(8) "issue in controversy" means an issue which is material to a decision concerning an administrative program of an agency, and with which there is disagreement—

(A) between an agency and persons who would be substantially affected by the decision; or

(B) between persons who would be substantially affected by the decision;

(9) "neutral" means an individual who, with respect to an issue in controversy, functions specifically to aid the parties in resolving the controversy;

(10) "party" means—

(A) for a proceeding with named parties, the same as in section 551(3) of this title; and

(B) for a proceeding without named parties, a person who will be significantly affected by the decision in the proceeding and who participates in the proceeding;

(11) "person" has the same meaning as in section 551(2) of this title; and

(12) "roster" means a list of persons qualified to provide services as neutrals.

§ 572. General Authority

(a) An agency may use a dispute resolution proceeding for the resolution of an issue in controversy that relates to an administrative program, if the parties agree to such proceeding.

(b) An agency shall consider not using a dispute resolution proceeding if—

(1) a definitive or authoritative resolution of the matter is required for precedential value, and such a proceeding is not likely to be accepted generally as an authoritative precedent;

(2) the matter involves or may bear upon significant questions of Government policy that require additional procedures before a final resolution may be made, and such a proceeding would not likely serve to develop a recommended policy for the agency;

(3) maintaining established policies is of special importance, so that variations among individual decisions are not increased and such a proceeding would not likely reach consistent results among individual decisions;

(4) the matter significantly affects persons or organizations who are not parties to the proceeding;

(5) a full public record of the proceeding is important, and a dispute resolution proceeding cannot provide such a record; and

(6) the agency must maintain continuing jurisdiction over the matter with authority to alter the disposition of the matter in the light of changed circumstances, and a dispute resolution proceeding would interfere with the agency's fulfilling that requirement.

(c) Alternative means of dispute resolution authorized under this subchapter are voluntary procedures which supplement rather than limit other available agency dispute resolution techniques.

§ 573. Neutrals

(a) A neutral may be a permanent or temporary officer or employee of the Federal Government or any other individual who is acceptable to the parties to a dispute resolution proceeding. A neutral shall have no official, financial, or personal conflict of interest with respect to the issues in controversy, unless such interest is fully disclosed in writing to all parties and all parties agree that the neutral may serve.

(b) A neutral who serves as a conciliator, facilitator, or mediator serves at the will of the parties.

(c) The President shall designate an agency or designate or establish an interagency committee to facilitate and encourage agency use of dispute resolution under this subchapter [5 USCS §§ 571 et seq.]. Such agency or interagency committee, in consultation with other appropriate Federal agencies and professional organizations experienced in matters concerning dispute resolution, shall—

(1) encourage and facilitate agency use of alternative means of dispute resolution; and

(2) develop procedures that permit agencies to obtain the services of neutrals on an expedited basis.

(d) An agency may use the services of one or more employees of other agencies to serve as neutrals in dispute resolution proceedings. The agencies may enter into an interagency agreement that provides for the reimbursement by the user agency or the parties of the full or partial cost of the services of such an employee.

(e) Any agency may enter into a contract with any person for services as a neutral, or for training in connection with alternative means of dispute resolution. The parties in a dispute resolution proceeding shall agree on compensation for the neutral that is fair and reasonable to the Government.

§ 574. Confidentiality

(a) Except as provided in subsections (d) and (e), a neutral in a dispute resolution proceeding shall not voluntarily disclose or through discovery or compulsory process be required to disclose any dispute resolution communication or any communication provided in confidence to the neutral, unless—

(1) all parties to the dispute resolution proceeding and the neutral consent in writing, and, if the dispute resolution communi-

cation was provided by a nonparty participant, that participant also consents in writing;

(2) the dispute resolution communication has already been made public;

(3) the dispute resolution communication is required by statute to be made public, but a neutral should make such communication public only if no other person is reasonably available to disclose the communication; or

(4) a court determines that such testimony or disclosure is necessary to—

(A) prevent a manifest injustice;

(B) help establish a violation of law; or

(C) prevent harm to the public health or safety, of sufficient magnitude in the particular case to outweigh the integrity of dispute resolution proceedings in general by reducing the confidence of parties in future cases that their communications will remain confidential.

(b) A party to a dispute resolution proceeding shall not voluntarily disclose or through discovery or compulsory process be required to disclose any dispute resolution communication, unless—

(1) the communication was prepared by the party seeking disclosure;

(2) all parties to the dispute resolution proceeding consent in writing;

(3) the dispute resolution communication has already been made public;

(4) the dispute resolution communication is required by statute to be made public;

(5) a court determines that such testimony or disclosure is necessary to—

(A) prevent a manifest injustice;

(B) help establish a violation of law; or

(C) prevent harm to the public health and safety, of sufficient magnitude in the particular case to outweigh the integrity of dispute resolution proceedings in general by reducing the confidence of parties in future cases that their communications will remain confidential;

(6) the dispute resolution communication is relevant to determining the existence or meaning of an agreement or award that resulted from the dispute resolution proceeding or to the enforcement of such an agreement or award; or

(7) except for dispute resolution communications generated by the neutral, the dispute resolution communication was provided to or was available to all parties to the dispute resolution proceeding.

(c) Any dispute resolution communication that is disclosed in violation of subsection (a) or (b), shall not be admissible in any proceeding relating to the issues in controversy with respect to which the communication was made.

(d) (1) The parties may agree to alternative confidential procedures for disclosures by a neutral. Upon such agreement the parties shall inform the neutral before the commencement of the dispute resolution proceeding of any modifications to the provisions of subsection (a) that will govern the confidentiality of the dispute resolution proceeding. If the parties do not so inform the neutral, subsection (a) shall apply.

(2) To qualify for the exemption established under subsection (j), an alternative confidential procedure under this subsection may not provide for less disclosure than the confidential procedures otherwise provided under this section.

(e) If a demand for disclosure, by way of discovery request or other legal process, is made upon a neutral regarding a dispute resolution communication, the neutral shall make reasonable efforts to notify the parties and any affected nonparty participants of the demand. Any party or affected nonparty participant who receives such notice and within 15 calendar days does not offer to defend a refusal of the neutral to disclose the requested information shall have waived any objection to such disclosure.

(f) Nothing in this section shall prevent the discovery or admissibility of any evidence that is otherwise discoverable, merely because the evidence was presented in the course of a dispute resolution proceeding.

(g) Subsections (a) and (b) shall have no effect on the information and data that are necessary to document an agreement reached or order issued pursuant to a dispute resolution proceeding.

(h) Subsections (a) and (b) shall not prevent the gathering of information for research or educational purposes, in cooperation with other agencies, governmental entities, or dispute resolution programs, so long as the parties and the specific issues in controversy are not identifiable.

(i) Subsections (a) and (b) shall not prevent use of a dispute resolution communication to resolve a dispute between the neutral in a dispute resolution proceeding and a party to or participant in such proceeding, so long as such dispute resolution communication is disclosed only to the extent necessary to resolve such dispute.

(j) A dispute resolution communication which is between a neutral and a party and which may not be disclosed under this section shall also be exempt from disclosure under section 552(b)(3).

§ 575. Authorization of Arbitration

(a) (1) Arbitration may be used as an alternative means of dispute resolution whenever all parties consent. Consent may be obtained either before or after an issue in controversy has arisen. A party may agree to—

(A) submit only certain issues in controversy to arbitration; or

(B) arbitration on the condition that the award must be within a range of possible outcomes.

(2) The arbitration agreement that sets forth the subject matter submitted to the arbitrator shall be in writing. Each such arbitration agreement shall specify a maximum award that may be issued by the arbitrator and may specify other conditions limiting the range of possible outcomes.

(3) An agency may not require any person to consent to arbitration as a condition of entering into a contract or obtaining a benefit.

(b) An officer or employee of an agency shall not offer to use arbitration for the resolution of issues in controversy unless such officer or employee—

(1) would otherwise have authority to enter into a settlement concerning the matter; or

(2) is otherwise specifically authorized by the agency to consent to the use of arbitration.

(c) Prior to using binding arbitration under this subchapter [5 USCS §§ 571 et seq.], the head of an agency, in consultation with the Attorney General and after taking into account the factors in section 572(b), shall issue guidance on the appropriate use of binding arbitration and when an officer or employee of the agency has authority to settle an issue in controversy through binding arbitration.

§ 576. Enforcement of Arbitration Agreements

An agreement to arbitrate a matter to which this subchapter applies is enforceable pursuant to section 4 of title 9, and no action brought to enforce such an agreement shall be dismissed nor shall relief therein be denied on the grounds that it is against the United States or that the United States is an indispensable party.

§ 577. Arbitrators

(a) The parties to an arbitration proceeding shall be entitled to participate in the selection of the arbitrator.

(b) The arbitrator shall be a neutral who meets the criteria of section 573 of this title.

§ 578. Authority of the Arbitrator

An arbitrator to whom a dispute is referred under this subchapter may—

(1) regulate the course of and conduct arbitral hearings;

(2) administer oaths and affirmations;

(3) compel the attendance of witnesses and production of evidence at the hearing under the provisions of section 7 of title 9 only to the extent the agency involved is otherwise authorized by law to do so; and

(4) make awards.

§ 579. Arbitration Proceedings

(a) The arbitrator shall set a time and place for the hearing on the dispute and shall notify the parties not less than 5 days before the hearing.

(b) Any party wishing a record of the hearing shall—

(1) be responsible for the preparation of such record;

(2) notify the other parties and the arbitrator of the preparation of such record;

(3) furnish copies to all identified parties and the arbitrator; and

(4) pay all costs for such record, unless the parties agree otherwise or the arbitrator determines that the costs should be apportioned.

(c)(*l*) The parties to the arbitration are entitled to be heard, to present evidence material to the controversy, and to cross-examine witnesses appearing at the hearing.

(2) The arbitrator may, with the consent of the parties, conduct all or part of the hearing by telephone, television, computer, or other electronic means, if each party has an opportunity to participate.

(3) The hearing shall be conducted expeditiously and in an informal manner.

(4) The arbitrator may receive any oral or documentary evidence, except that irrelevant, immaterial, unduly repetitious, or privileged evidence may be excluded by the arbitrator.

(5) The arbitrator shall interpret and apply relevant statutory and regulatory requirements, legal precedents, and policy directives.

(d) No interested person shall make or knowingly cause to be made to the arbitrator an unauthorized ex parte communication relevant to the merits of the proceeding, unless the parties agree otherwise. If a communication is made in violation of this subsection, the arbitrator shall ensure that a memorandum of the communication is prepared and made a part of the record, and that an opportunity for rebuttal is allowed. Upon receipt of a communication made in violation of this subsection, the arbitrator may, to the extent consistent with the interests of justice and the policies underlying this subchapter, require the offending party to show cause why the claim of such party should not be resolved against such party as a result of the improper conduct.

(e) The arbitrator shall make the award within 30 days after the close of the hearing, or the date of the filing of any briefs authorized by the arbitrator, whichever date is later, unless—

(1) the parties agree to some other time limit; or

(2) the agency provides by rule for some other time limit.

§ 580. Arbitration Awards

(a)(1) Unless the agency provides otherwise by rule, the award in an arbitration proceeding under this subchapter [5 USCS §§ 571 et seq.] shall include a brief, informal discussion of the factual and legal basis for the award, but formal findings of fact or conclusions of law shall not be required.

(2) The prevailing parties shall file the award with all relevant agencies, along with proof of service on all parties.

(b) The award in an arbitration proceeding shall become final 30 days after it is served on all parties. Any agency that is a party to the proceeding may extend this 30–day period for an additional 30–day period by serving a notice of such extension on all other parties before the end of the first 30–day period.

(c) A final award is binding on the parties to the arbitration proceeding, and may be enforced pursuant to sections 9 through 13 of title 9. No action brought to enforce such an award shall be dismissed nor shall relief therein be denied on the grounds that it is against the United States or that the United States is an indispensable party.

(d) An award entered under this subchapter [5 USCS §§ 571 et seq.] in an arbitration proceeding may not serve as an estoppel in any other proceeding for any issue that was resolved in the proceeding. Such an award also may not be used as precedent or otherwise be considered in any factually unrelated proceeding, whether conducted under this subchapter [5 USCS §§ 571 et seq.], by an agency, or in a court, or in any other arbitration proceeding.

§ 581. Judicial Review

(a) Notwithstanding any other provision of law, any person adversely affected or aggrieved by an award made in an arbitration proceeding conducted under this subchapter [5 USCS §§ 571 et seq.] may bring an action for review of such award only pursuant to the provisions of sections 9 through 13 of title 9.

(b) A decision by an agency to use or not to use a dispute resolution proceeding under this subchapter [5 USCS §§ 571 et seq.] shall be committed to the discretion of the agency and shall not be subject to judicial review, except that arbitration shall be subject to judicial review under section 10(b) of title 9.

§ 582. Repealed. Pub. L. 104–320, Sec. 4(b)(1), Oct. 19, 1996, 110 Stat. 3871.

§ 583. Support Services

For the purposes of this subchapter, an agency may use (with or without reimbursement) the services and facilities of other Federal agencies, State, local, and tribal governments, public and private organizations and agencies, and individuals, with the consent of such agencies, organizations, and individuals. An agency may accept voluntary and uncompensated services for the purposes of this subchapter without regard to the provisions of section 1342 of title 31.

NEGOTIATED RULEMAKING PROCEDURE*

Sec.

§ 561. Purpose

The purpose of this subchapter is to establish a framework for the conduct of negotiated rulemaking, consistent with section 553 of this title, to encourage agencies to use the process when it enhances the informal rulemaking process. Nothing in this subchapter should be construed as an attempt to limit innovation and experimentation with the negotiated rulemaking process or with other innovative rulemaking procedures otherwise authorized by law.

§ 562. Definitions

For the purposes of this subchapter, the term—

* Pub.L. 101–648 (1990). As originally enacted, both this Act and the Administrative Dispute Resolution Act commenced at 5 U.S.C.A. § 581 (with both designated as subchapter IV).

Subchapter III of chapter 6 of title 5, United States Code (enacted as subchapter IV of chapter 6 of title 5, United States Code, by section 3 of this Act and redesignated as subchapter III of such chapter 5 by section (3)(a) of the Administrative Procedure Technical Amendments Act of 1991) and that portion of the table of sections at the beginning of chapter 5 of title 5, United States Code, relating to subchapter in, are repealed, effective 6 years after the date of the enactment of this Act [Nov. 29, 1990], except that the provisions of such subchapter shall continue to apply after the date of the repeal with respect to then pending negotiated rulemaking proceedings initiated before the date of repeal which, in the judgment of the agencies which are convening or have convened such proceedings, require such continuation, until such negotiated rulemaking proceedings terminate pursuant to such subchapter.

(1) "agency" has the same meaning as in section 551(1) of this title;

(2) "consensus" means unanimous concurrence among the interests represented on a negotiated rulemaking committee established under this subchapter, unless such committee—

(A) agrees to define such term to mean a general but not unanimous concurrence; or

(B) agrees upon another specified definition;

(3) "convener" means a person who impartially assists an agency in determining whether establishment of a negotiated rulemaking committee is feasible and appropriate in a particular rulemaking;

(4) "facilitator" means a person who impartially aids in the discussions and negotiations among the members of a negotiated rulemaking committee to develop a proposed rule;

(5) "interest" means, with respect to an issue or matter, multiple parties which have a similar point of view or which are likely to be affected in a similar manner;

(6) "negotiated rulemaking" means rulemaking through the use of a negotiated rulemaking committee;

(7) "negotiated rulemaking committee" or "committee" means an advisory committee established by an agency in accordance with this subchapter and the Federal Advisory Committee Act to consider and discuss issues for the purpose of reaching a consensus in the development of a proposed rule;

(8) "party" has the same meaning as in section 551(3) of this title;

(9) "person" has the same meaning as in section 551(2) of this title;

(10) "rule" has the same meaning as in section 551(4) of this title; and

(11) "rulemaking" means "rule making" as that term is defined in section 551(5) of this title.

§ 563. Determination of Need for Negotiated Rulemaking Committee

(a) Determination of Need by the Agency. An agency may establish a negotiated rulemaking committee to negotiate and develop a proposed rule, if the head of the agency determines that the use of the negotiated rulemaking procedure is in the public interest. In making such a determination, the head of the agency shall consider whether—

(1) there is a need for a rule;

(2) there are a limited number of identifiable interests that will be significantly affected by the rule;

(3) there is a reasonable likelihood that a committee can be convened with a balanced representation of persons who—

(A) can adequately represent the interests identified under paragraph (2); and

(B) are willing to negotiate in good faith to reach a consensus on the proposed rule;

(4) there is a reasonable likelihood that a committee will reach a consensus on the proposed rule within a fixed period of time;

(5) the negotiated rulemaking procedure will not unreasonably delay the notice of proposed rulemaking and the issuance of the final rule;

(6) the agency has adequate resources and is willing to commit such resources, including technical assistance, to the committee; and

(7) the agency, to the maximum extent possible consistent with the legal obligations of the agency, will use the consensus of the committee with respect to the proposed rule as the basis for the rule proposed by the agency for notice and comment.

(b) Use of Conveners.

(1) Purposes of conveners. An agency may use the services of a convener to assist the agency in—

(A) identifying persons who will be significantly affected by a proposed rule, including residents of rural areas; and

(B) conducting discussions with such persons to identify the issues of concern to such persons, and to ascertain whether the establishment of a negotiated rulemaking committee is feasible and appropriate in the particular rulemaking.

(2) Duties of conveners. The convener shall report findings and may make recommendations to the agency. Upon request of the agency, the convener shall ascertain the names of persons who are willing and qualified to represent interests that will be significantly affected by the proposed rule, including residents of rural areas. The report and any recommendations of the convener shall be made available to the public upon request.

§ 564. Publication of notice; applications for membership on committees

(a) Publication of Notice. If, after considering the report of a convener or conducting its own assessment, an agency decides to establish a negotiated rulemaking committee, the agency shall publish in the Federal Register and, as appropriate, in trade or other specialized publications, a notice which shall include—

(1) an announcement that the agency intends to establish a negotiated rulemaking committee to negotiate and develop a proposed rule;

(2) a description of the subject and scope of the rule to be developed, and the issues to be considered;

(3) a list of the interests which are likely to be significantly affected by the rule;

(4) a list of the persons proposed to represent such interests and the person or persons proposed to represent the agency;

(5) a proposed agenda and schedule for completing the work of the committee, including a target date for publication by the agency of a proposed rule for notice and comment;

(6) a description of administrative support for the committee to be provided by the agency, including technical assistance;

(7) a solicitation for comments on the proposal to establish the committee, and the proposed membership of the negotiated rulemaking committee; and

(8) an explanation of how a person may apply or nominate another person for membership on the committee, as provided under subsection (b).

(b) Applications for Membership or [sic] Committee. Persons who will be significantly affected by a proposed rule and who believe that their interests will not be adequately represented by any person specified in a notice under subsection (a)(4) may apply for, or nominate another person for, membership on the negotiated rulemaking committee to represent such interests with respect to the proposed rule. Each application or nomination shall include—

(1) the name of the applicant or nominee and a description of the interests such person shall represent;

(2) evidence that the applicant or nominee is authorized to represent parties related to the interests the person proposes to represent;

(3) a written commitment that the applicant or nominee shall actively participate in good faith in the development of the rule under consideration; and

(4) the reasons that the persons specified in the notice under subsection (a)(4) do not adequately represent the interests of the person submitting the application or nomination.

(c) Period for Submission of Comments and Applications. The agency shall provide for a period of at least 30 calendar days for the submission of comments and applications under this section.

§ 565. Establishment of Committee

(a) Establishment.

(1) Determination to establish committee. If after considering comments and applications submitted under section 564, the agency determines that a negotiated rulemaking committee can adequately

represent the interests that will be significantly affected by a proposed rule and that it is feasible and appropriate in the particular rulemaking, the agency may establish a negotiated rule-making committee. In establishing and administering such a committee, the agency shall comply with the Federal Advisory Committee Act with respect to such committee, except as otherwise provided in this subchapter.

(2) Determination not to establish committee. If after considering such comments and applications, the agency decides not to establish a negotiated rulemaking committee, the agency shall promptly publish notice of such decision and the reasons therefor in the Federal Register and, as appropriate, in trade or other specialized publications, a copy of which shall be sent to any person who applied for, or nominated another person for membership on the negotiating rulemaking committee to represent such interests with respect to the proposed rule.

(b) Membership, The agency shall limit membership on a negotiated rulemaking committee to 25 members, unless the agency head determines that a greater number of members is necessary for the functioning of the committee or to achieve balanced membership. Each committee shall include at least one person representing the agency.

(c) Administrative Support. The agency shall provide appropriate administrative support to the negotiated rulemaking committee, including technical assistance.

§ 566. Conduct of Committee Activity

(a) Duties of Committee. Each negotiated rulemaking committee established under this subchapter shall consider the matter proposed by the agency for consideration and shall attempt to reach a consensus concerning a proposed rule with respect to such matter and any other matter the committee determines is relevant to the proposed rule.

(b) Representatives of Agency on Committee. The person or persons representing the agency on a negotiated rulemaking committee shall participate in the deliberations and activities of the committee with the same rights and responsibilities as other members of the committee, and shall be authorized to fully represent the agency in the discussions and negotiations of the committee.

(c) Selecting Facilitator. Notwithstanding section 10(e) of the Federal Advisory Committee Act, an agency may nominate either a person from the Federal Government or a person from outside the Federal Government to serve as a facilitator for the negotiations of the committee, subject to the approval of the committee by consensus. If the committee does not approve the nominee of the agency for facilitator, the agency shall submit a substitute nomination. If a committee does not approve any nominee of the agency for facilitator, the committee shall select by consensus a person to serve as facilitator. A person designated to represent the agency in substantive issues may not serve as facilitator or otherwise chair the committee.

(d) Duties of Facilitator. A facilitator approved or selected by a negotiated rulemaking committee shall—

(1) chair the meetings of the committee in an impartial manner;

(2) impartially assist the members of the committee in conducting discussions and negotiations; and

(3) manage the keeping of minutes and records as required under section ICK(b) and (c) of the Federal Advisory Committee Act, except that any personal notes and materials of the facilitator or of the members of a committee shall not be subject to section 552 of this title.

(e) Committee Procedures. A negotiated rulemaking committee established under this subchapter may adopt procedures for the operation of the committee. No provision of section 553 of this title shall apply to the procedures of a negotiated rulemaking committee.

(f) Report of Committee. If a committee reaches a consensus on a proposed rule, at the conclusion of negotiations the committee shall transmit to the agency that established the committee a report containing the proposed rule. If the committee does not reach a consensus on a proposed rule, the committee may transmit to the agency a report specifying any areas in which the committee reached a consensus. The committee may include in a report any other information, recommendations, or materials that the committee considers appropriate. Any committee member may include as an addendum to the report additional information, recommendations, or materials.

(g) Records of Committee. In addition to the report required by subsection (f), a committee shall submit to the agency the records required under section i0(b) and (c) of the Federal Advisory Committee Act.

§ 567. Termination of Committee

A negotiated rulemaking committee shall terminate upon promulgation of the final rule under consideration, unless the committee's charter contains an earlier termination date or the agency, after consulting the committee, or the committee itself specifies an earlier termination date.

§ 568 [§ 588]. Services, Facilities, and Payment of Committee Member Expenses

(a) Services of Conveners and Facilitators.

(1) In general. An agency may employ or enter into contracts for the services of an individual or organization to serve as a convener or facilitator for a negotiated rulemaking committee under

this subchapter, or may use the services of a Government employee to act as a convener or a facilitator for such a committee.

(2) Determination of conflicting interests. An agency shall determine whether a person under consideration to serve as convener or facilitator of a committee under paragraph (1) has any financial or other interest that would preclude such person from serving in an impartial and independent manner.

(b) Services and Facilities of Other Entities. For purposes of this subchapter, an agency may use the services and facilities of other Federal agencies and public and private agencies and instrumentalities with the consent of such agencies and instrumentalities, and with or without reimbursement to such agencies and instrumentalities, and may accept voluntary and uncompensated services without regard to the provisions of section 1342 of title 31. The Federal Mediation and Conciliation Service may provide services and facilities, with or without reimbursement, to assist agencies under this subchapter, including furnishing conveners, facilitators, and training in negotiated rulemaking.

(c) Expenses of Committee Members. Members of a negotiated rulemaking committee shall be responsible for their own expenses of participation in such committee, except that an agency may, in accordance with section 7(d) of the Federal Advisory Committee Act, pay for a member's reasonable travel and per diem expenses, expenses to obtain technical assistance, and a reasonable rate of compensation, if—

(1) such member certifies a lack of adequate financial resources to participate in the committee; and

(2) the agency determines that such member's participation in the committee is necessary to assure an adequate representation of the member's interest.

(d) Status of Member as Federal Employee. A member's receipt of funds under this section or section 569 shall not conclusively determine for purposes of sections 202 through 209 of title 18 whether that member is an employee of the United States Government.

§ 569. Encouraging negotiated rulemaking

(a) The President shall designate an agency or designate or establish an interagency committee to facilitate and encourage agency use of negotiated rulemaking. An agency that is considering, planning, or conducting a negotiated rulemaking may consult with such agency or committee for information and assistance.

(b) To carry out the purposes of this subchapter [5 USCS §§ 561 et seq.], an agency planning or conducting a negotiated rulemaking may accept, hold, administer, and utilize gifts, devises, and bequests of property, both real and personal if that agency's acceptance and use of such gifts, devises, or bequests do not create a conflict of interest. Gifts and bequests of money and proceeds from sales of other property received as gifts, devises, or bequests shall be deposited in the Treasury and shall be disbursed upon the order of the head of such agency. Property accepted pursuant to this section, and the proceeds thereof, shall be used as nearly as possible in accordance with the terms of the gifts, devises, or bequests.

§ 570. Judicial Review

Any agency action relating to establishing, assisting, or terminating a negotiated rulemaking committee under this subchapter shall not be subject to judicial review. Nothing in this section shall bar judicial review of a rule if such judicial review is otherwise provided by law. A rule which is the product of negotiated rulemaking and is subject to judicial review shall not be accorded any greater deference by a court than a rule which is the product of other rulemaking procedures.

§ 570a. Authorization of appropriations

There are authorized to be appropriated such sums as may be necessary to carry out the purposes of this subchapter.

§ 801. Congressional review

(a) (1) (A) Before a rule can take effect, the Federal agency promulgating such rule shall submit to each House of the Congress and to the Comptroller General a report containing—

(i) a copy of the rule;

(ii) a concise general statement relating to the rule, including whether it is a major rule; and

(iii) the proposed effective date of the rule.

(B) On the date of the submission of the report under subparagraph (A), the Federal agency promulgating the rule shall submit to the Comptroller General and make available to each House of Congress—

(i) a complete copy of the cost-benefit analysis of the rule, if any;

(ii) the agency's actions relevant to sections 603, 604, 605, 607, and 609;

(iii) the agency's actions relevant to sections 202, 203, 204, and 205 of the Unfunded Mandates Reform Act of 1995 [2 USCS §§ 1532–1535]; and

(iv) any other relevant information or requirements under any other Act and any relevant Executive orders.

(C) Upon receipt of a report submitted under subparagraph (A), each House shall provide copies of the report to the chairman and ranking member of each standing committee with jurisdiction under the rules of the House of Representatives or the Senate to report a bill to amend the provision of law under which the rule is issued.

(2) (A) The Comptroller General shall provide a report on each major rule to the committees of jurisdiction in each House of the Congress by the end of 15 calendar days after the submission or publication date as provided in section 802(b)(2). The report of the Comptroller General shall include an assessment of the agency's compliance with procedural steps required by paragraph (1)(B).

(B) Federal agencies shall cooperate with the Comptroller General by providing information relevant to the Comptroller General's report under subparagraph (A).

(3) A major rule relating to a report submitted under paragraph (1) shall take effect on the latest of—

(A) the later of the date occurring 60 days after the date on which—

(i) the Congress receives the report submitted under paragraph (1); or

(ii) the rule is published in the Federal Register, if so published;

(B) if the Congress passes a joint resolution of disapproval described in section 802 relating to the rule, and the President signs a veto of such resolution, the earlier date—

(i) on which either House of Congress votes and fails to override the veto of the President; or

(ii) occurring 30 session days after the date on which the Congress received the veto and objections of the President; or

(C) the date the rule would have otherwise taken effect, if not for this section (unless a joint resolution of disapproval under section 802 is enacted).

(4) Except for a major rule, a rule shall take effect as otherwise provided by law after submission to Congress under paragraph (1).

(5) Notwithstanding paragraph (3), the effective date of a rule shall not be delayed by operation of this chapter beyond the date on which either House of Congress votes to reject a joint resolution of disapproval under section 802.

(b) (1) A rule shall not take effect (or continue), if the Congress enacts a joint resolution of disapproval, described under section 802, of the rule.

(2) A rule that does not take effect (or does not continue) under paragraph (1) may not be reissued in substantially the same form, and a new rule that is substantially the same as such a rule may not be issued, unless the reissued or new rule is specifically authorized by a law enacted after the date of the joint resolution disapproving the original rule.

(c) (1) Notwithstanding any other provision of this section (except subject to paragraph (3)), a rule that would not take effect by reason of subsection (a)(3) may take effect, if the President makes a determination under paragraph (2) and submits written notice of such determination to the Congress.

(2) Paragraph (1) applies to a determination made by the President by Executive order that the rule should take effect because such rule is—

(A) necessary because of an imminent threat to health or safety or other emergency;

(B) necessary for the enforcement of criminal laws;

(C) necessary for national security; or

(D) issued pursuant to any statute implementing an international trade agreement.

(3) An exercise by the President of the authority under this subsection shall have no effect on the procedures under section 802 or the effect of a joint resolution of disapproval under this section.

(d) (1) In addition to the opportunity for review otherwise provided under this chapter, in the case of any rule for which a report was submitted in accordance with subsection (a)(1)(A) during the period beginning on the date occurring—

(A) in the case of the Senate, 60 session days, or

(B) in the case of the House of Representatives, 60 legislative days, before the date the Congress adjourns a session of Congress through the date on which the same or succeeding Congress first convenes its next session, section 802 shall apply to such rule in the succeeding session of Congress.

(2) (A) In applying section 802 for purposes of such additional review, a rule described under paragraph (1) shall be treated as though—

(i) such rule were published in the Federal Register (as a rule that shall take effect) on—

(I) in the case of the Senate, the 15th session day, or

(II) in the case of the House of Representatives, the 15th legislative day, after the succeeding session of Congress first convenes; and

(ii) a report on such rule were submitted to Congress under subsection (a)(1) on such date.

(B) Nothing in this paragraph shall be construed to affect the requirement under subsection (a)(1) that a report shall be submitted to Congress before a rule can take effect.

(3) A rule described under paragraph (1) shall take effect as otherwise provided by law (including other subsections of this section).

(e) (1) For purposes of this subsection, section 802 shall also apply to any major rule promulgated between March 1, 1996, and the date of the enactment of this chapter.

(2) In applying section 802 for purposes of Congressional review, a rule described under paragraph (1) shall be treated as though—

(A) such rule were published in the Federal Register on the date of enactment of this chapter; and

(B) a report on such rule were submitted to Congress under subsection (a)(1) on such date.

(3) The effectiveness of a rule described under paragraph (1) shall be as otherwise provided by law, unless the rule is made of no force or effect under section 802.

(f) Any rule that takes effect and later is made of no force or effect by enactment of a joint resolution under section 802 shall be treated as though such rule had never taken effect.

(g) If the Congress does not enact a joint resolution of disapproval under section 802 respecting a rule, no court or agency may infer any intent of the Congress from any action or inaction of the Congress with regard to such rule, related statute, or joint resolution of disapproval.

§ 802. Congressional disapproval procedure

(a) For purposes of this section, the term "joint resolution" means only a joint resolution introduced in the period beginning on the date on which the report referred to in section 801(a)(1)(A) is received by Congress and ending 60 days thereafter (excluding days either House of Congress is adjourned for more than 3 days during a session of Congress), the matter after the resolving clause of which is as follows: "That Congress disapproves the rule submitted by the ___ relating to ___, and such rule shall have no force or effect." (The blank spaces being appropriately filled in).

(b)(1) A joint resolution described in subsection (a) shall be referred to the committees in each House of Congress with jurisdiction.

(2) For purposes of this section, the term "submission or publication date" means the later of the date on which—

(A) the Congress receives the report submitted under section 801(a)(1); or

(B) the rule is published in the Federal Register, if so published.

(c) In the Senate, if the committee to which is referred a joint resolution described in subsection (a) has not reported such joint resolution (or an identical joint resolution) at the end of 20 calendar days after the submission or publication date defined under subsection (b)(2), such committee may be discharged from further consideration of such joint resolution upon a petition supported in writing by 30 Members of the Senate, and such joint resolution shall be placed on the calendar.

(d)(1) In the Senate, when the committee to which a joint resolution is referred has reported, or when a committee is discharged (under subsection (c)) from further consideration of a joint resolution described in subsection (a), it is at any time thereafter in order (even though a previous motion to the same effect has been disagreed to) for a motion to proceed to the consideration of the joint resolution, and all points of order against the joint resolution (and against consideration of the joint resolution) are waived. The motion is not subject to amendment, or to a motion to postpone, or to a motion to proceed to the consideration of other business. A motion to reconsider the vote by which the motion is agreed to or disagreed to shall not be in order. If a motion to proceed to the consideration of the joint resolution is agreed to, the joint resolution shall remain the unfinished business of the Senate until disposed of.

(2) In the Senate, debate on the joint resolution, and on all debatable motions and appeals in connection therewith, shall be limited to not more than 10 hours, which shall be divided equally between those favoring and those opposing the joint resolution. A motion further to limit debate is in order and not debatable. An amendment to, or a motion to postpone, or a motion to proceed to the consideration of other business, or a motion to recommit the joint resolution is not in order.

(3) In the Senate, immediately following the conclusion of the debate on a joint resolution described in subsection (a), and a single quorum call at the conclusion of the debate if requested in accordance with the rules of the Senate, the vote on final passage of the joint resolution shall occur.

(4) Appeals from the decisions of the Chair relating to the application of the rules of the Senate to the procedure relating to a joint resolution described in subsection (a) shall be decided without debate.

(e) In the Senate the procedure specified in subsection (c) or (d) shall not apply to the consideration of a joint resolution respecting a rule—

(1) after the expiration of the 60 session days beginning with the applicable submission or publication date, or

(2) if the report under section 801(a)(1)(A) was submitted during the period referred to in section 801(d)(1), after the expiration of the 60 session days beginning on the 15th session day after the succeeding session of Congress first convenes.

(f) If, before the passage by one House of a joint resolution of that House described in subsection (a), that House receives from the other House a joint resolution described in subsection (a), then the following procedures shall apply:

(1) The joint resolution of the other House shall not be referred to a committee.

(2) With respect to a joint resolution described in subsection (a) of the House receiving the joint resolution—

(A) the procedure in that House shall be the same as if no joint resolution had been received from the other House; but

(B) the vote on final passage shall be on the joint resolution of the other House.

(g) This section is enacted by Congress—

(1) as an exercise of the rulemaking power of the Senate and House of Representatives, respectively, and as such it is deemed a part of the rules of each House, respectively, but applicable only with respect to the procedure to be followed in that House in the case of a joint resolution described in subsection (a), and it supersedes other rules only to the extent that it is inconsistent with such rules; and

(2) with full recognition of the constitutional right of either House to change the rules (so far as relating to the procedure of that House) at any time, in the same manner, and to the same extent as in the case of any other rule of that House.

§ 803. Special rule on statutory, regulatory, and judicial deadlines

(a) In the case of any deadline for, relating to, or involving any rule which does not take effect (or the effectiveness of which is terminated) because of enactment of a joint resolution under section 802, that deadline is extended until the date 1 year after the date of enactment of the joint resolution. Nothing in this subsection shall be construed to affect a deadline merely by reason of the postponement of a rule's effective date under section 801(a).

(b) The term "deadline" means any date certain for fulfilling any obligation or exercising any authority established by or under any Federal statute or regulation, or by or under any court order implementing any Federal statute or regulation.

§ 804. Definitions

For purposes of this chapter [5 USCS §§ 801 et seq.]—

(1) The term "Federal agency" means any agency as that term is defined in section 551(1).

(2) The term "major rule" means any rule that the Administrator of the Office of Information and Regulatory Affairs of the Office of Management and Budget finds has resulted in or is likely to result in—

(A) an annual effect on the economy of $100,000,000 or more;

(B) a major increase in costs or prices for consumers, individual industries, Federal, State, or local government agencies, or geographic regions; or

(C) significant adverse effects on competition, employment, investment, productivity, innovation, or on the ability of United States-based enterprises to compete with foreign-based enterprises in domestic and export markets. The term does not include any rule promulgated under the Telecommunications Act of 1996 and the amendments made by that Act.

(3) The term "rule" has the meaning given such term in section 551, except that such term does not include—

(A) any rule of particular applicability, including a rule that approves or prescribes for the future rates, wages, prices, services, or allowances therefor, corporate or financial structures, reorganizations, mergers, or acquisitions thereof, or accounting practices or disclosures bearing on any of the foregoing;

(B) any rule relating to agency management or personnel; or

(C) any rule of agency organization, procedure, or practice that does not substantially affect the rights or obligations of non-agency parties.

§ 805. Judicial review

No determination, finding, action, or omission under this chapter [5 USCS §§ 801 et seq.] shall be subject to judicial review.

§ 806. Applicability; severability

(a) This chapter [5 USCS §§ 801 et seq.] shall apply notwithstanding any other provision of law.

(b) If any provision of this chapter [5 USCS §§ 801 et seq.] or the application of any provision of this chapter [5 USCS §§ 801 et seq.] to any person or circumstance, is held invalid, the application of such provision to other persons or circumstances, and the remainder of this chapter [5 USCS §§ 801 et seq.], shall not be affected thereby.

§ 807. Exemption for monetary policy

Nothing in this chapter [5 USCS §§ 801 et seq.] shall apply to rules that concern monetary policy proposed or implemented by the Board of Governors of the Federal Reserve System or the Federal Open Market Committee.

§ 808. Effective date of certain rules

Notwithstanding section 801—

(1) any rule that establishes, modifies, opens, closes, or conducts a regulatory program for a commercial, recreational, or subsistence activity related to hunting, fishing, or camping, or

(2) any rule which an agency for good cause finds (and incorporates the finding and a brief statement of reasons therefor in the rule issued) that notice and public procedure thereon are impracticable, unnecessary, or contrary to the public interest, shall take effect at such time as the Federal agency promulgating the rule determines.

*

Appendix B

ADMINISTRATIVE LAW, SECOND EDITION, RESEARCH ON WESTLAW

Analysis

Section 1. Introduction

Administrative Law, Second Edition, provides a strong base for analyzing even the most complex problem involving administrative law. Whether your research requires examination of case law, statutes, expert commentary, or other materials, West books and Westlaw are excellent sources of information.

To keep you abreast of current developments, Westlaw provides frequently updated databases. With Westlaw, you have unparalleled legal research resources at your fingertips.

Additional Resources

If you have not previously used Westlaw or have questions not covered in this appendix, call the West Group Reference Attorneys at 1–800–REF–ATTY (1–800–733–2889). The West Group Reference Attorneys are trained, licensed attorneys, available 24 hours a day to assist you with your Westlaw search questions. To subscribe to Westlaw, call 1–800–344–5008 or visit the West Group Web site at **www.westgroup.com**.

Section 2. Westlaw Databases

Each database on Westlaw is assigned an abbreviation called an *identifier*, which you use to access the database. You can find identifiers for all databases in the online Westlaw Directory and in the printed *Westlaw Database Directory*. When you need to know more detailed information about a database, use Scope. Scope contains coverage information, lists of related databases, and valuable search tips. To access Scope, click **Scope** after you access the database.

The following chart lists selected Westlaw databases that contain information pertaining to administrative law. For a complete list of administrative law databases, see the online Westlaw Directory or the printed *Westlaw Database Directory*. Because new information is continually being added to Westlaw, you should also check Welcome to Westlaw and the Westlaw Directory for new database information.

Selected Administrative Law Databases on Westlaw

Database	Identifier	Coverage
Federal Statutes and Regulations		
United States Code Annotated®	USCA	Current data
United States Code Annotated (historical) 1990–2000	USCAYY (where YY is the last two digits of a year)	Varies by database
Code of Federal Regulations	CFR	Current data
Code of Federal regulations (historical) 1984–1999	CFRYY (where YY is the last two digits of a year)	Varies by database
Federal Register	FR	July 1980
State Statutes and Regulations		
State Statutes–Annotated	ST–ANN–ALL	Varies by state

Database	Identifier	Coverage
Individual State Statutes–Annotated	XX–ST–ANN (where XX is a state's two-letter postal abbreviation)	Varies by states
State Administrative Code Multibase	ADC–ALL	Varies by state
Individual State Administrative Code	XX–ADC (where XX is a state's two-letter postal abbreviation)	Varies by state
Multistate Insurance Administrative Code	MIN–ADC	Varies by state
Individual State Insurance Administrative Code	XXIN–ADC (where XX is a state's two-letter postal abbreviation)	Varies by state
ENFLEX State Environmental, Health and Safety Regulations	ENFLEX–STATE	Current data
Individual State Environmental, Health and Safety Regulations	ENFLEX–XX (where XX is a state's two-letter postal abbreviation)	Current data
Federal Case Law		
All Federal Cases	ALLFEDS	Begins with 1945
U.S. Supreme Court Cases	SCT	Begins with 1945
U.S. Courts of Appeals Cases	CTA	Begins with 1945
U.S. Court of Appeals Individual Circuit Cases	CTAX (where XX is DC, F, or a number)	Begins with 1945
U.S. District Courts Cases	DCT	Begins with 1945
State Case Law		
All State Cases	ALLSTATES	Begins with 1945
Individual State Cases	XX–CS (where XX is a state's two-letter postal abbreviation)	Varies by state
Federal Administrative Decisions		
Comptroller General Decisions	CG	Begins with 1921
Customs Bulletin and Decisions	FINT–CUSTB	Begins with 1962
Department of the Interior Decisions	INTDEC	Begins with 1881

Database	Identifier	Coverage
Directorate for Industrial Security Clearance Review Decisions	FMIL–DISCR	Begins with 1992
Fair Housing Administrative Decisions	FAIRHOUS	Begins with 1989
Federal Antitrust & Trade Regulation–Federal Trade Commission Decisions	FATR–FTC	Begins with 1959
Federal Aviation Administration Decisions	FTRAN–FAA	Begins with November 1989
Federal Communications–Federal Communications Commission Decisions and Daily Digest	FCOM–ADMIN	Varies by source
Federal Energy–Federal Energy Regulatory Commission Decisions	FEN–FERC	
Federal Energy Guidelines		Begins with 1977
Federal Power Commission Reports:		1931–1977
Federal Environmental Law–E.P.A. Decisions	FENV–EPA	Begins with 1974
Federal Environmental Law–E.P.A. Federal Insecticide, Fungicide and Rodenticide Act Decisions	FENV–FIFRA	Begins with 1978
Federal Environmental Law–E.P.A. Resource Conservation and Recovery Act Decisions	FENV–RCRA	Begins with 1981
Federal Environmental Law–E.P.A. Toxic Substances Control Act Decisions	FENV–TSCA	Begins with 1980
Federal Finance & Banking–Federal Deposit Insurance Corporation (FDIC) Decisions and Interpretive Letters	FFIN–FDIC	
Decisions		Begins with February 1981
Letters		Begins with January 1979
Federal Government Contracts–All Board of Contract Appeals Decisions	FGC–BCA	Varies by source

Database	Identifier	Coverage
Federal Government Contracts–Contract Adjustment Board Decisions	FGC–CAB	Begins with 1951
Federal Government Contracts–Housing and Urban Development Debarment Decisions	FGC–HUDDEBAR	Begins with 1980
Federal Government Contracts–Small Business Administration Office of Hearings and Appeals Decisions	FGC–SBA	Begins with December 1983
Federal Health Law–Health and Human Services Decisions	FHTH–HHS	Begins with March 1974
Federal Health Law–Provider	FHTH–PRRB	
Reimbursement Review Board Hearing and Appeals Decisions		
Provider Reimbursement Review Board		Begins with 1994
Health Care Financing Administration		Begins with 1996
Federal Immigration Administrative Decisions Combined	FIM–ADMIN	Varies by source
Federal Intellectual Property–Patent & Trademark Office Decisions	FIP–PTO	Begins with January 1987
Federal International Law–Treasury Decisions	FINT–TD	Begins with August 1980
Federal Labor & Employment–Employees' Compensation Appeals Board Decisions	FLB–ECAB	Begins with October 1976
Federal Labor & Employment–Equal Employment Opportunity Commission Decisions	FLB–EEOC	
Private sector		Begins with July 1969
Public sector		Begins with April 1994
Federal Labor & Employment–National Mediation Board Decisions	FLB–NMB	Begins with 1935
Federal Native Americans Law–Interior Board of Indian Appeals Decisions	FNAM–IBIA	Begins with 1970

Database	Identifier	Coverage
Federal Securities and Blue Sky Law–Commodity Futures Trading Commission Decisions	FSEC–CFTC	
CFTC decisions		Begins with 1976
Administrative law judge decisions		Begins with 1983
Federal Taxation–IRS Actions on Decisions	FTX–AOD	Begins with 1967
Federal Taxation–IRS Combined Releases	FTX–RELS	Varies by source
Federal Taxation–Treasury Decisions	FTX–TD	Begins with August 1980
Federal Transportation–Department of Transportation, Aviation Decisions	FTRAN–DOT	Begins with 1979
Federal Transportation–Interstate Commerce Commission Decisions	FTRAN–ICC	Begins with July 1977
Federal Transportation–National Transportation Safety Board Decisions	FTRAN–NTSB	Begins with 1967
Office of Federal Contract Compliance Programs Decisions	OFCCP	Begins with 1968
Office of Personnel Management–Digest of Significant Classification Decisions	FHR–DSCDO	Begins with 1981
United States Department of Agriculture Decisions	USDA	Begins with 1977
United States Department of Education Decisions	FED–ADMIN	Begins with 1987
State Administrative Decisions		
Multistate Environmental Law–Administrative Decisions	MENV–ADMIN	Varies by state
Individual State Environmental Law Administrative Decisions	XXENV–ADMIN (where XX is a state's two-letter postal abbreviation)	Varies by state
Multistate Securities and Blue Sky Law–Administrative Decisions	MSEC–ADMIN	Varies by state
Individual State Securities and Blue Sky Law Administrative	XXSEC–ADMIN (where XX is a state's	Varies by state

Database	Identifier	Coverage
Decisions	two-letter postal abbreviation)	
Multistate Taxation–Administrative Decisions	MTX–ADMIN	Varies by jurisdiction
Individual State Taxation Administrative Decisions	XXTX–ADMIN (where XX is a state's two-letter postal abbreviation)	Varies by jurisdiction
Multistate Workers' Compensation–Administrative Decisions	MWC–ADMIN	Varies by state
Individual State Workers' Compensation Administrative Decisions	XXWC–ADMIN (where XX is a state's two-letter postal abbreviation)	Varies by state
Legal Texts and Periodicals		
Administrative Law–Law Reviews, Texts & Bar Journals	AD–TP	Varies by publication
Administrative and Regulatory Law News	ADMRLN	Selected coverage begins with 1994 (vol. 19)
Administrative Law Journal of the American University	ADMLJAMU	Selected coverage begins with 1987 (vol. 1); full coverage begins with 1993 (vol. 7)
Administrative Law Review	ADMLR	Selected coverage begins with 1987 (vol. 39); full coverage begins with 1993 (vol. 46)
California Regulatory Law Reporter	CARLR	Full coverage begins with 1994 (vol. 14)
Journal of the National Association of Administrative Law Judges	JNAALJ	Full coverage begins with 2000 (vol. 20)
Yale Journal on Regulation	YJR	Selected coverage begins with 1983 (vol. 1); full coverage begins with 1984 (vol. 2)

Section 3. Retrieving a Document with a Citation: Find and Hypertext Links

3.1 Find

Find is a Westlaw service that allows you to retrieve a document by entering its citation. Find allows you to retrieve documents from anywhere in Westlaw without accessing or changing databases. Find is available for many documents, including administrative materials, case law (state and federal), the *United States Code Annotated*, state statutes, and texts and periodicals.

To use Find, simply access the Find service and type the citation. The following list provides some examples:

To Find This Document	Access Find and Type
43 C.F.R. § 29.7	**43 cfr s 29.7**
57 F.R. 514	**57 fr 514**
14 F.C.C.R. 1700	**14 fccr 1700**
Goldberg v. Kelly, 90 S. Ct. 1011 (1969)	**90 sct 1011**
43 U.S.C.A. § 1651	**43 usca s 1651**

For a complete list of publications that can be retrieved with Find and their abbreviations, consult the Publications List after accessing Find.

3.2 Hypertext Links

Use hypertext links to move from one location to another on Westlaw. For example, use hypertext links to go directly from the statute, case, or law review article you are viewing to a cited statute, case, or article; from a headnote to the corresponding text in the opinion; or from an entry in a statutes index database to the full text of the statute.

Section 4. Searching with Natural Language

Overview: With Natural Language, you can retrieve documents by simply describing your issue in plain English. If you are a relatively new Westlaw user, Natural Language searching can make it easier for you to retrieve cases that are on point. If you are an experienced Westlaw user, Natural Language gives you a valuable alternative search method.

When you enter a Natural Language description, Westlaw automatically identifies legal phrases, removes common words and generates variations of terms in your description. Westlaw then searches for the concepts in your description. Concepts may include significant terms, phrases, legal citations, or topic and key numbers. Westlaw retrieves the 20 documents that most closely match your description, beginning with the document most likely to match.

4.1 Natural Language Search

Access a database, such as the Administrative Law–Law Reviews, Texts & Bar Journals database (AD–TP). In the text box, type a Natural Language description such as the following:

distinction between rule-making and adjudication

4.2 Next Command

Westlaw displays the 20 documents that most closely match your description, beginning with the document most likely to match. If you want to view additional documents, use the Next command, click the **Document** or **Doc** arrow at the bottom of the page, or click the right arrow in the left frame.

4.3 Natural Language Browse Commands

Best Mode: To display the best portion (the portion that most closely matches your description) of each document in your search result, click the **Best Section** or **Best** arrow at the bottom of the window or page.

Standard Browsing Commands: You can also browse your Natural Language search result using standard Westlaw browsing commands, such as citations list, Locate, and term mode.

Section 5. Searching with Terms and Connectors

Overview: With Terms and Connectors searching, you enter a query, which consists of key terms from your issue and connectors specifying the relationship between these terms.

Terms and Connectors searching is useful when you want to retrieve a document for which you know specific details, such as the title or the fact situation. Terms and Connectors searching is also useful when you want to retrieve documents relating to a specific issue.

5.1 Terms

Plurals and Possessives: Plurals are automatically retrieved when you enter the singular form of a term. This is true for both regular and irregular plurals (e.g., **child** retrieves *children*). If you enter the plural form of a term, you will not retrieve the singular form.

If you enter the nonpossessive form of a term, Westlaw automatically retrieves the possessive form as well. However, if you enter the possessive form, only the possessive form is retrieved.

Automatic Equivalencies: Some terms have alternative forms or equivalencies; for example, *5* and *five* are equivalent terms. Westlaw automatically retrieves equivalent terms. The *Westlaw Reference Manual* contains a list of equivalent terms.

Compound Words, Abbreviations, and Acronyms: When a compound word is one of your search terms, use a hyphen to retrieve all forms of the word. For example, the term **along-side** retrieves *along-side, alongside,* and *along side.*

When using an abbreviation or acronym as a search term, place a period after each of the letters to retrieve any of its forms. For example, the term **n.l.r.b.** retrieves *nlrb, n.l.r.b., n l r b,* and *n. l. r. b.* Note: The abbreviation does *not* retrieve *national labor relations board*, so remember to add alternative terms to your query such as **"national labor relations board"**.

The Root Expander and the Universal Character: When you use the Terms and Connectors search method, placing the root expander (!) at the end of a root term generates all other terms with that root. For example, adding the ! to the root *participat!* in the query

public /s participat!

instructs Westlaw to retrieve such terms as *participate, participation, participating,* and *participated.*

The universal character (*) stands for one character and can be inserted in the middle or at the end of a term. For example, the term

withdr*w

will retrieve *withdraw* and *withdrew*. Adding three asterisks to the root *elect*

elect* * *

instructs Westlaw to retrieve all forms of the root with up to three additional characters. Terms such as *elected* or *election* are retrieved by this query. However, terms with more than three letters following the root, such as *electronic,* are not retrieved. Plurals are always retrieved, even if more than three letters follow the root.

Phrase Searching: To search for an exact phrase, place it within quotation marks. For example, to search for references to *tender offer*, type "**tender offer**". When you are using the Terms and Connectors search method, you should use phrase searching only if you are certain that the terms in the phrase will not appear in any other order.

5.2 Alternative Terms

After selecting the terms for your query, consider which alternative terms are necessary. For example, if you are searching for the term *admissible*, you might also want to search for the term *inadmissible.* You should consider both synonyms and antonyms as alternative terms. You can also use the Westlaw thesaurus to add alternative terms to your query.

5.3 Connectors

After selecting terms and alternative terms for your query, use connectors to specify the relationship that should exist between search terms in your retrieved documents. The connectors are described below:

Use:	To retrieve documents with:	Example:
& (and)	both terms	**registration & filing**
or (space)	either term or both terms	**sale sell**
/p	search terms in the same paragraph	**churning! /p liab!**
/s	search terms in the same sentence	**registration /s requir!**
+s	the first search term preceding the second within the same sentence	**agency +s discretion**
/n	search terms within "n" terms of each other (where "n" is a number)	**action period statut! /3 limit!**
+n	the first search term preceding the second by "n" terms (where "n" is a number)	**final +3 rulemaking**
" "	search terms appearing in the same order as in the quotation marks	**"hard look doctrine"**

Use:	To retrieve documents with:	Example:
% (but not)	search terms following the %	**registration % filing**

5.4 Field Restrictions

Overview: Documents in each Westlaw database consist of several segments, or fields. One field may contain the citation, another the title, another the synopsis and so forth. Not all databases contain the same fields. Also depending on the database, fields with the same name may contain different types of information.

To view a list of fields for a specific database and their contents, see Scope for that database. Note that in some databases not every field is available for every document.

To retrieve only those documents containing your search terms in a specific field, restrict your search to that field. To restrict your search to a specific field, type the field name or abbreviation followed by your search terms enclosed in parentheses. For example, to retrieve an Eighth Circuit Court of Appeals case titled *Newton County Wildlife Association v. Rogers,* access the U.S. Court of Appeals for the Eighth Circuit Cases database (CTA8) and search for your terms in the title field (ti):

ti("newton county" & rogers)

The fields discussed below are available in Westlaw databases you might use for researching administrative law issues.

Digest and Synopsis Fields: The digest (di) and synopsis (sy) fields, added to case law databases by West's attorney-editors, summarize the main points of a case. The synopsis field contains a brief description of a case. The digest field contains the topic and headnote fields and includes the complete hierarchy of concepts used by West's editors to classify the headnotes to specific West digest topic and key numbers. Restricting your search to the synopsis and digest fields limits your result to cases in which your terms are related to a major issue in the case.

Consider restricting your search to one or both of these fields if

- you are searching for common terms or terms with more than one meaning, and you need to narrow your search; or
- you cannot narrow your search by using a smaller database.

For example, to retrieve cases from the U.S. Court of Appeals for the Tenth Circuit that discuss what constitutes final agency action, access the U.S. Court of Appeals for the Tenth Circuit Cases database (CTA10) and type the following query:

sy,di(final /s agency /s action)

Headnote Field: The headnote field (he) is part of the digest field but does not contain topic numbers, hierarchical classification information, or key numbers. The headnote field contains a one-sentence summary for each point of law in a case and any supporting citations given by the author of the opinion. A headnote field restriction is useful when you are searching for specific statutory sections or rule numbers. For example, to retrieve headnotes from cases from the U.S. Court of Appeals for the First Circuit that cite 15 U.S.C.A. § 78n(a), access the U.S. Court of Appeals for the First Circuit Cases database (CTA1) and type the following query:

he(15 +5 78n(a))

Topic Field: The topic field (to) is also part of the digest field. It contains hierarchical classification information, including the West digest topic names and numbers and the key numbers. You should restrict search terms to the topic field in a case law database if

- a digest field search retrieves too many documents; or
- you want to retrieve cases with digest paragraphs classified under more than one topic.

For example, the topic Administrative Law and Procedure has the topic number 15a. To retrieve federal district court cases that discuss the standard of review a court uses in reviewing administrative agency action, access the U.S. District Courts Cases database (DCT) and type a query like the following:

to(15a) /p "standard of review" /p agency /5 action

To retrieve cases classified under more than one topic and key number, search for your terms in the topic field. For example, to retrieve U.S. Supreme Court cases discussing exhaustion of administrative remedies, which may be classified to Administrative Law and Procedure (15a), Civil Rights (78), or Social Security and Public Welfare (356a), among other topics, access the U.S. Supreme Court Cases database (SCT) and type a query like the following:

to(exhaust! /s administrative /s remedy)

For a complete list of West digest topics and their corresponding topic numbers, access the Key Number Service.

> *Note*: Slip opinions, cases not reported by West, and cases from topical services, do not contain the digest, headnote, and topic fields.

Prelim and Caption Fields: When searching in a database containing statutes, rules, Prelim and Captor regulations, restrict your search to the prelim (pr) and caption (ca) fields to retrieve documents in which your terms are important enough to appear in a section name or heading. For example, to retrieve federal regulations about accessing records under the Freedom of Information Act (FOIA), access the Code of Federal Regulations database (CFR) and type the following:

pr,ca("freedom of information" f.o.i.a. & access! /s record)

5.5 Date Restrictions

You can use Westlaw to retrieve documents *decided* or *issued* before, after, or on a specified date, as well as within a range of dates. The following sample queries contain date restrictions:

da(1999) & "informal adjudication"

da(aft 1995) & promulgat! /3 rule

da(12/27/2000) & "judicial review"

You can also search for documents *added to a database* on or after a specified date, as well as within a range of dates. The following sample queries contain added-date restrictions:

ad(aft 1995) & delegat! /5 authority /5 agency

ad(aft 2/1/1998 & bef 5/15/1998) & "nondelegation doctrine"

Section 6. Searching with Topic and Key Numbers

To retrieve cases that address a specific point of law, use topic and key numbers as your search terms. If you have an on-point case, run a search using the topic and key number from the relevant headnote in an appropriate database to find other cases containing headnotes classified to that topic and key number. For example, to search for federal cases containing headnotes classified under topic 15a (Administrative Law and Procedure) and key number 442 (What Constitutes an Adjudication), access the Federal Case Law database (ALLFEDS) and enter the following query:

15ak442

For a complete list of West digest topic and key numbers, access the Key Number Service.

> *Note*: Slip opinions, cases not reported by West, and cases from topical services do not contain West topic and key numbers.

Section 7. Verifying Your Research with Citation Research Services

Overview: A citation research service is a tool that helps you ensure that your cases are good law; helps you retrieve cases, legislation, or articles that cite a case, rule, or statute; and helps you verify that the spelling and format of your citations are correct.

7.1 KeyCite

KeyCite is the citation research service from West Group.

KeyCite for cases covers case law on Westlaw, including unpublished opinions.

KeyCite for statutes covers the *United States Code Annotated* (USCA®), the *Code of Federal Regulations* (CFR), and statutes from all 50 states.

KeyCite Alert monitors the status of your cases or statutes and automatically sends you updates at the frequency you specify when their KeyCite information changes.

KeyCite provides the following:

- Direct appellate history of a case, including related references, which are opinions involving the same parties and facts but resolving different issues
- Negative indirect history of a case, which consists of cases outside the direct appellate line that may have a negative impact on its precedential value
- The title, parallel citations, court of decision, docket number, and filing date of a case
- Citations to cases, administrative decisions, and secondary sources on Westlaw that have cited a case
- Complete integration with the West Key Number System® so you can track legal issues discussed in a case
- Links to session laws amending or repealing a statute
- Statutory credits and historical notes
- Citations to pending legislation affecting a federal statute or a statute from California or New York
- Citations to cases, administrative decisions, and secondary sources that have cited a statute or federal regulation

7.2 Westlaw As a Citator

For citations not covered by KeyCite, including persuasive secondary authority such as restatements and treatises, use Westlaw as a citator to retrieve cases that cite your authority.

For example, to retrieve federal cases citing the law review article "Setting No Records: The Failed Attempts to Limit the Record in Review of Administrative Action," 36 Admin. L. Rev. 333 (1984), access the Federal Case Law database (ALLFEDS) and type a query like the following:

record /s review /s 36 /s 333

Section 8. Researching with Westlaw—Examples

8.1 Retrieving Law Review Articles

Recent law review articles are often a good place to begin researching a legal issue because law review articles serve 1) as an excellent introduction to a new topic or review for a stale one, providing terminology to help you formulate a query; 2) as a finding tool for pertinent primary authority, such as rules, statutes, and cases; and 3) in some instances, as persuasive secondary authority.

Suppose you need to gather background information on how courts distinguish legislative rules from interpretative rules.

Solution

- To retrieve recent law review articles relevant to your issue, access the Administrative Law–Law Reviews, Texts & Bar Journals database (AD–TP). Using the Natural Language search method, enter a description like the following:

  distinguishing interpretative rules from legislative rules

- If you have a citation to an article in a specific publication, use Find to retrieve it. For more information on Find, see Section 3.1 of this appendix. For example, to retrieve the article found at 31 Wake Forest L. Rev. 667, access Find and type

  31 wake forest l rev 667

- If you know the title of an article but not which journal it appeared in, access the Administrative Law–Law Reviews, Texts & Bar Journals database (AD–TP) and search for key terms using the title field. For example, to retrieve the article "Legislative Reform of Judicial Review of Agency Actions," type the following Terms and Connectors query:

  ti("legislative reform" & judicial & review & agency)

8.2 Retrieving Case Law

Suppose you need to retrieve federal district court case law dealing with abuse of agency discretion.

Solution

- Access the U.S. District Courts Cases database (DCT). Type a Natural Language description such as the following:

abuse of agency discretion

- When you know the citation for a specific case, use Find to retrieve it. For more information on Find, see Section 3.1 of this appendix. For example, to retrieve *Shanti, Inc. v. Reno,* 36 F. Supp. 2d 1151 (D. Minn. 1999), access Find and type

36 fsupp2d 1151

- If you find a topic and key number that is on point, run a search using that topic and key number to retrieve additional cases discussing that point of law. For example, to retrieve cases containing headnotes classified under topic 15a (Administrative Law and Procedure) and key number 754 (Discretion of Administrative Agency), type the following query:

15ak754

- To retrieve cases written by a particular judge, add a judge field (ju) restriction to your query. For example, to retrieve cases written by Justice Anthony Kennedy of the U.S. Supreme Court that contain headnotes classified under topic 15a (Administrative Law and Procedure), access the U.S. Supreme Court Cases database (SCT) and type the following query:

ju(kennedy) & to(15a)

8.3 Retrieving Statutes and Regulations

Suppose you need to retrieve sections of the Administrative Procedure Act found in various sections of Title 5, Subchapter II of the *United States Code Annotated.*

Solution

- Access the U.S. Code Annotated database (USCA). Search for your terms in the prelim and caption fields using the Terms and Connectors search method:

pr,ca("administrative procedure" & "title 5" & "subchapter ii")

- When you know the citation for a specific statute, use Find to retrieve it. For example, to retrieve 5 U.S.C.A. § 553, access Find and type

5 usca s 553

- To look at surrounding sections, use the Table of Contents service. Click a hypertext link in the prelim or caption field, or click the **TOC** tab in the left frame. You can also use Documents in Sequence to retrieve the section following § 553, even if that subsequent section was not retrieved with your search or Find request.

- When you retrieve a statute on Westlaw, it will contain a message if legislation amending or repealing it is available online. To display this legislation, click the hypertext link in the message.

> Because slip copy versions of laws are added to Westlaw before they contain full editorial enhancements, they are not retrieved with the update feature. To retrieve slip copy versions of laws, access the United States Public Laws database (US–PL) or a states's legislative service databases (XX–LEGIS, where XX is the state's two–letter postal abbreviation). Then type **ci(slip)** and descriptive terms, e.g., **ci(slip) & fiduciary**. Slip copy documents are replaced by the editorially enhanced versions within a few working days. The update feature also does not retrieve legislation that enacts a new statute or covers a topic that will not be incorporated into the statutes. To retrieve this legislation, access US–PL or a legislative service database and enter a query containing terms that describe the new legislation.

Suppose you need to retrieve federal regulations regarding the use of settlement judges.

Solution

- Access the Code of Federal Regulations database (CFR). Search for your terms in the prelim and caption fields using the Terms and Connectors search method:

  pr,ca(settlement /s judge)

- When you retrieve a CFR section on Westlaw, it will contain a message if documents amending it are available in the Federal Register database (FR). To display the *Federal Register* documents, click the hypertext link in the message.

8.4 Using KeyCite

Suppose one of the cases you retrieve in your case law research is *AT & T Corp. v. F.C.C.*, 236 F.3d 729 (D.C. Cir. 2000). You want to determine whether this case is good law and to find other cases that have cited this case.

Solution

- Use KeyCite to retrieve direct history and negative indirect history for *AT & T Corp. v. F.C.C.*
- Use KeyCite to display citing references for *AT & T Corp. v. F.C.C.*

*

Table of Cases

A

Abbott Laboratories v. Gardner, 387 U.S. 136, 87 S.Ct. 1507, 18 L.Ed.2d 681 (1967)—**§ 5.3, n. 4; § 12.4; § 12.4, n. 8, 14; § 12.5, n. 16; § 12.7, n. 22, 74; § 12.8; § 12.8, n. 6; § 12.9; § 12.9, n. 2.**

Abbotts Dairies Division of Fairmont Foods, Inc. v. Butz, 389 F.Supp. 1 (E.D.Pa. 1975)—**§ 13.4, n. 31.**

Abernethy v. I.R.S., 909 F.Supp. 1562 (N.D.Ga.1995)—**§ 18.1, n. 85; § 18.6, n. 1.**

ABF Freight System, Inc. v. N.L.R.B., 510 U.S. 317, 114 S.Ct. 835, 127 L.Ed.2d 152 (1994)—**§ 13.4, n. 7.**

Abilene & S. Ry. Co., United States v., 265 U.S. 274, 44 S.Ct. 565, 68 L.Ed. 1016 (1924)—**§ 8.4; § 8.4, n. 129.**

Abraham & Rose, P.L.C. v. United States, 138 F.3d 1075 (6th Cir.1998)—**§ 17.4, n. 40, 50.**

Accardi, United States ex rel. v. Shaughnessy, 347 U.S. 260, 74 S.Ct. 499, 98 L.Ed. 681 (1954)—**§ 7.2, n. 5; Ch. 10, n. 1.**

Action Alliance of Senior Citizens of Greater Philadelphia v. Heckler, 789 F.2d 931, 252 U.S.App.D.C. 249 (D.C.Cir.1986)—**§ 12.9, n. 5.**

Action for Children's Television v. F.C.C., 821 F.2d 741, 261 U.S.App.D.C. 253 (D.C.Cir.1987)—**§ 13.10, n. 92.**

Action for Children's Television v. F. C. C., 564 F.2d 458, 183 U.S.App.D.C. 437 (D.C.Cir.1977)—**§ 9.5, n. 270; § 13.10, n. 90; § 15.2, n. 3.**

Action on Smoking and Health v. C.A.B., 699 F.2d 1209, 226 U.S.App.D.C. 57 (D.C.Cir.1983)—**§ 2.1, n. 72; § 13.10, n. 64, 90, 92.**

Acton Corp., United States v., 733 F.Supp. 869 (D.N.J.1990)—**§ 9.5, n. 144.**

Adams v. F. T. C., 296 F.2d 861 (8th Cir. 1961)—**§ 20.4, n. 23.**

Adams v. Richardson, 480 F.2d 1159, 156 U.S.App.D.C. 267 (D.C.Cir.1973)—**§ 12.6; § 12.6, n. 40.**

Adams v. Richardson, 356 F.Supp. 92 (D.D.C.1973)—**§ 12.6, n. 41.**

Addison v. Holly Hill Fruit Products, 322 U.S. 607, 64 S.Ct. 1215, 88 L.Ed. 1488 (1944)—**§ 13.8; § 13.8, n. 16.**

Administrator, Federal Aviation Administration v. Robertson, 422 U.S. 255, 95 S.Ct. 2140, 45 L.Ed.2d 164 (1975)—**§ 17.2; § 17.2, n. 43.**

Advance Bronze, Inc. v. Dole, 917 F.2d 944 (6th Cir.1990)—**§ 8.4, n. 46.**

Advanced Electronics, 21 F.C.C.2d 239 (F.C.C.1970)—**§ 4.5, n. 16.**

Advanced Micro Devices v. C.A.B., 742 F.2d 1520, 239 U.S.App.D.C. 367 (D.C.Cir. 1984)—**§ 13.10, n. 92.**

Advocates for Highway and Auto Safety v. Federal Highway Admin., 28 F.3d 1288, 307 U.S.App.D.C. 421 (D.C.Cir.1994)—**§ 2.1, n. 36.**

A. G. Becker Inc. v. Board of Governors of Federal Reserve System, 502 F.Supp. 378 (D.D.C.1980)—**§ 19.1, n. 55, 60.**

Agee v. Central Intelligence Agency, 517 F.Supp. 1335 (D.D.C.1981)—**§ 17.4, n. 22.**

Agosto v. Immigration and Naturalization Service, 436 U.S. 748, 98 S.Ct. 2081, 56 L.Ed.2d 677 (1978)—**§ 13.6, n. 10, 18.**

Air Courier Conference of America v. American Postal Workers Union AFL–CIO, 498 U.S. 517, 111 S.Ct. 913, 112 L.Ed.2d 1125 (1991)—**§ 12.7; § 12.7, n. 84.**

Aircraft & Diesel Equipment Corp. v. Hirsch, 331 U.S. 752, 67 S.Ct. 1493, 91 L.Ed. 1796 (1947)—**§ 12.11, n. 16.**

Air Line Pilots Ass'n, Intern. v. Department of Transp., 791 F.2d 172, 253 U.S.App. D.C. 1 (D.C.Cir.1986)—**§ 13.10, n. 29.**

Air Line Pilots Ass'n, Intern. v. Quesada, 276 F.2d 892 (2nd Cir.1960)—**§ 7.1, n. 10; § 9.4, n. 21.**

Airmark Corp. v. F.A.A., 758 F.2d 685, 244 U.S.App.D.C. 365 (D.C.Cir.1985)—**§ 13.10, n. 92.**

Air Pollution Variance Bd. of Colorado v. Western Alfalfa Corp., 416 U.S. 861, 94 S.Ct. 2114, 40 L.Ed.2d 607 (1974)—**§ 20.7, n. 65.**

Air Products & Chemicals, Inc. v. Federal Energy Regulatory Commission, 650 F.2d 687 (5th Cir.1981)—**§ 8.4; § 8.4, n. 135; § 8.5, n. 87; § 13.4, n. 29.**

Air Transport Ass'n of America v. C.A.B., 732 F.2d 219, 235 U.S.App.D.C. 333 (D.C.Cir.1984)—**§ 2.1, n. 56.**

Alabama Ass'n of Ins. Agents v. Board of Governors of Federal Reserve System,

B

Bowen v. United States Food and Drug Admin., 925 F.2d 1225 (9th Cir.1991)—**§ 17.4, n. 104.**
Bowles v. Willingham, 321 U.S. 503, 64 S.Ct. 641, 88 L.Ed. 892 (1944)—**§ 7.7, n. 4; § 9.4; § 9.4, n. 49.**
Bowman v. United States Bd. of Parole, 411 F.Supp. 329 (W.D.Wis.1976)—**§ 9.3, n. 18.**
Bowman Transp., Inc. v. Arkansas–Best Freight System, Inc., 419 U.S. 281, 95 S.Ct. 438, 42 L.Ed.2d 447 (1974)—**§ 13.4, n. 26; § 13.10, n. 14, 15, 81.**
Boyd v. Secretary of the Navy, 709 F.2d 684 (11th Cir.1983)—**§ 18.1, n. 73; § 18.3, n. 7.**
Boyd v. United States, 116 U.S. 616, 6 S.Ct. 524, 29 L.Ed. 746 (1886)—**§ 20.3, n. 39.**
Bradley v. Fisher, 80 U.S. 335, 20 L.Ed. 646 (1871)—**§ 14.3, n. 7.**
Brae Corp. v. United States, 740 F.2d 1023, 238 U.S.App.D.C. 352 (D.C.Cir.1984)—**§ 13.10, n. 69, 90, 92.**
Brandt v. Hickel, 427 F.2d 53 (9th Cir. 1970)—**§ 11.2, n. 1, 21, 29.**
Braniff Airways, Inc. v. C. A. B., 379 F.2d 453, 126 U.S.App.D.C. 399 (D.C.Cir. 1967)—**§ 8.5, n. 19.**
Braniff Master Executive Council of Air Line Pilots Ass'n Intern. v. C.A.B., 693 F.2d 220, 224 U.S.App.D.C. 105 (D.C.Cir.1982)—**§ 19.1, n. 70.**
Brant Const. Co., Inc. v. United States E.P.A., 778 F.2d 1258 (7th Cir.1985)—**§ 17.4, n. 220.**
Braswell v. United States, 487 U.S. 99, 108 S.Ct. 2284, 101 L.Ed.2d 98 (1988)—**§ 20.3; § 20.3, n. 46, 79.**
Brennan v. Gilles & Cotting, Inc., 504 F.2d 1255 (4th Cir.1974)—**§ 16.1, n. 13.**
Briggs v. Dalton, 939 F.Supp. 753 (D.Hawai'i 1996)—**§ 13.6, n. 6.**
Brinkley v. Hassig, 83 F.2d 351 (10th Cir. 1936)—**§ 8.5, n. 114.**
Brinton v. Department of State, 636 F.2d 600, 204 U.S.App.D.C. 328 (D.C.Cir. 1980)—**§ 17.3, n. 100; § 17.4, n. 145.**
Briscoe v. Bell, 432 U.S. 404, 97 S.Ct. 2428, 53 L.Ed.2d 439 (1977)—**§ 12.5, n. 23.**
British Caledonian Airways, Ltd. v. C. A. B., 584 F.2d 982, 190 U.S.App.D.C. 1 (D.C.Cir.1978)—**§ 4.2, n. 16; § 4.5, n. 46.**
Britt v. Naval Investigative Service, 886 F.2d 544 (3rd Cir.1989)—**§ 18.2, n. 20.**
B.R. MacKay & Sons, Inc. v. United States, 633 F.Supp. 1290 (D.Utah 1986)—**§ 9.5, n. 113.**
Brock v. Roadway Exp., Inc., 481 U.S. 252, 107 S.Ct. 1740, 95 L.Ed.2d 239 (1987)—**§ 7.6, n. 1, 18, 20, 29.**
Brown v. Federal Bureau of Investigation, 658 F.2d 71 (2nd Cir.1981)—**§ 18.2, n. 14; § 18.5, n. 4.**
Brumley v. United States Dept. of Labor, 767 F.2d 444 (8th Cir.1985)—**§ 17.3, n. 4, 50, 63.**
Bryant v. Bowen, 683 F.Supp. 95 (D.N.J. 1988)—**§ 8.4, n. 62.**
Buchman v. S. E. C., 553 F.2d 816 (2nd Cir.1977)—**§ 13.4, n. 47.**
Buckley v. Valeo, 424 U.S. 1, 96 S.Ct. 612, 46 L.Ed.2d 659 (1976)—**§ 9.5, n. 178; § 15.3; § 15.3, n. 3; § 15.4; § 15.4, n. 58, 63.**
Buckner v. I.R.S., 25 F.Supp.2d 893 (N.D.Ind.1998)—**§ 17.4, n. 58.**
Buckner Trucking, Inc. v. United States, 354 F.Supp. 1210 (S.D.Tex.1973)—**§ 8.4, n. 39.**
Bumper v. North Carolina, 391 U.S. 543, 88 S.Ct. 1788, 20 L.Ed.2d 797 (1968)—**§ 20.7, n. 68.**
Bunker Hill Co. v. E.P.A., 572 F.2d 1286 (9th Cir.1977)—**§ 8.4, n. 64.**
Bureau of Nat. Affairs, Inc. v. United States Dept. of Justice, 742 F.2d 1484, 239 U.S.App.D.C. 331 (D.C.Cir.1984)—**§ 17.3, n. 28, 32.**
Burka v. United States Dept. of Health and Human Services, 87 F.3d 508, 318 U.S.App.D.C. 274 (D.C.Cir.1996)—**§ 17.4, n. 113, 156.**
Burkins v. United States, 865 F.Supp. 1480 (D.Colo.1994)—**§ 17.4, n. 123; § 18.5, n. 5.**
Burley v. United States Drug Enforcement Administration, 443 F.Supp. 619 (M.D.Tenn.1977)—**§ 18.1, n. 36; § 18.2, n. 22, 26.**
Burlington, City of v. Dague, 505 U.S. 557, 112 S.Ct. 2638, 120 L.Ed.2d 449 (1992)—**§ 18.6, n. 4.**
Burlington Truck Lines, Inc. v. United States, 371 U.S. 156, 83 S.Ct. 239, 9 L.Ed.2d 207 (1962)—**§ 13.8, n. 69.**
Burnap v. United States, 252 U.S. 512, 40 S.Ct. 374, 64 L.Ed. 692 (1920)—**§ 15.3, n. 11.**
Bush v. Lucas, 462 U.S. 367, 103 S.Ct. 2404, 76 L.Ed.2d 648 (1983)—**§ 14.2, n. 6.**
Butler v. Department of Air Force, 888 F.Supp. 174 (D.D.C.1995)—**§ 17.4, n. 196, 203; § 18.4, n. 7.**
Butta–Brinkman v. FCA Intern., Ltd., 164 F.R.D. 475 (N.D.Ill.1995)—**§ 17.4, n. 117.**
Buttfield v. Stranahan, 192 U.S. 470, 24 S.Ct. 349, 48 L.Ed. 525 (1904)—**§ 1.1, n. 22.**
Buttrey v. United States, 690 F.2d 1170 (5th Cir.1982)—**§ 8.2, n. 36.**
Butz v. Economou, 438 U.S. 478, 98 S.Ct. 2894, 57 L.Ed.2d 895 (1978)—**§ 8.5, n. 29; § 14.3; § 14.3, n. 2, 7, 9, 22, 25.**
Butz v. Glover Livestock Commission Co., Inc., 411 U.S. 182, 93 S.Ct. 1455, 36 L.Ed.2d 142 (1973)—**§ 9.2, n. 21.**

C

D

E

F

G

H

J

K

L

M

Montgomery Imp. Ass'n, Inc. v. United States Dept. of Housing and Urban Development, 543 F.Supp. 603 (M.D.Ala. 1982)—**§ 13.6, n. 6.**
Montgomery Ward & Co., Inc. v. F.T.C., 691 F.2d 1322 (9th Cir.1982)—**§ 4.5; § 4.5, n. 57.**
Montilla v. United States, 198 Ct.Cl. 48, 457 F.2d 978 (Ct.Cl.1972)—**§ 11.2, n. 19.**
Montrose Chemical Corp. of California v. Train, 491 F.2d 63, 160 U.S.App.D.C. 270 (D.C.Cir.1974)—**§ 17.4, n. 127.**
Montship Lines, Limited v. Federal Maritime Bd., 295 F.2d 147, 111 U.S.App. D.C. 160 (D.C.Cir.1961)—**§ 20.4, n. 19.**
Moore, United States v., 95 U.S. 760, 5 Otto 760, 24 L.Ed. 588 (1877)—**§ 15.3, n. 11.**
Morgan v. United States, 304 U.S. 1, 58 S.Ct. 773, 82 L.Ed. 1129 (1938)—**§ 8.5, n. 1, 8.**
Morgan v. United States, 298 U.S. 468, 56 S.Ct. 906, 80 L.Ed. 1288 (1936)—**§ 8.5, n. 1, 3.**
Morgan v. United States Postal Service, 798 F.2d 1162 (8th Cir.1986)—**§ 8.4, n. 32.**
Morgan, United States v., 313 U.S. 409, 61 S.Ct. 999, 85 L.Ed. 1429 (1941)—**§ 8.5, n. 1, 14; § 13.9, n. 3; § 13.10, n. 67.**
Morgan, United States v., 307 U.S. 183, 59 S.Ct. 795, 83 L.Ed. 1211 (1939)—**§ 8.5, n. 1, 14.**
Morrison v. Olson, 487 U.S. 654, 108 S.Ct. 2597, 101 L.Ed.2d 569 (1988)—**§ 9.5; § 9.5, n. 172, 174; § 15.3; § 15.3, n. 2, 14; § 15.4, n. 19, 82.**
Morrissey v. Brewer, 408 U.S. 471, 92 S.Ct. 2593, 33 L.Ed.2d 484 (1972)—**§ 7.5; § 7.5, n. 15; § 7.6; § 7.6, n. 1, 6, 7, 10, 15, 26, 41.**
Morton v. Ruiz, 415 U.S. 199, 94 S.Ct. 1055, 39 L.Ed.2d 270 (1974)—**Ch. 2, n. 1; § 3.2; § 3.2, n. 4; § 4.3, n. 8, 25; § 4.5; § 4.5, n. 40, 44, 54; Ch. 10, n. 3; § 11.2, n. 18; § 13.8; § 13.8, n. 65, 82; § 13.9, n. 6.**
Morton Salt Co., United States v., 338 U.S. 632, 70 S.Ct. 357, 94 L.Ed. 401 (1950)—**§ 20.2; § 20.2, n. 23, 26; § 20.3, n. 3, 41.**
Moser v. United States, 341 U.S. 41, 71 S.Ct. 553, 95 L.Ed. 729 (1951)—**§ 9.4, n. 24.**
Motor Vehicle Mfrs. Ass'n of United States, Inc. v. E.P.A., 768 F.2d 385, 247 U.S.App.D.C. 268 (D.C.Cir.1985)—**§ 13.10, n. 26.**
Motor Vehicle Mfrs. Ass'n of United States, Inc. v. State Farm Mut. Auto. Ins. Co., 463 U.S. 29, 103 S.Ct. 2856, 77 L.Ed.2d 443 (1983)—**§ 13.10; § 13.10, n. 18, 72, 91, 92.**
Mouat, United States v., 124 U.S. 303, 23 Ct.Cl. 490, 8 S.Ct. 505, 31 L.Ed. 463 (1888)—**§ 15.3, n. 11.**
Mount v. United States Postal Service, 79 F.3d 531 (6th Cir.1996)—**§ 18.2, n. 20, 25.**
Mourning v. Family Publications Service, Inc., 411 U.S. 356, 93 S.Ct. 1652, 36 L.Ed.2d 318 (1973)—**§ 13.8, n. 14.**
Mower v. Britton, 504 F.2d 396 (10th Cir. 1974)—**§ 9.3, n. 1.**
Mt. Diablo Hosp. Dist. v. Bowen, 860 F.2d 951 (9th Cir.1988)—**§ 4.3, n. 21, 33.**
Mudge Rose Guthrie Alexander & Ferdon v. United States Intern. Trade Com'n, 846 F.2d 1527, 270 U.S.App.D.C. 68 (D.C.Cir.1988)—**§ 17.4, n. 75.**
Mullane v. Central Hanover Bank & Trust Co., 339 U.S. 306, 70 S.Ct. 652, 94 L.Ed. 865 (1950)—**§ 7.6, n. 19; § 8.4, n. 36, 37.**
Mullins, In re, 84 F.3d 1439, 318 U.S.App. D.C. 65 (D.C.Cir.1996)—**§ 18.1, n. 49; § 18.5, n. 2.**
Multi-State Communications, Inc. v. F.C.C., 728 F.2d 1519, 234 U.S.App.D.C. 285 (D.C.Cir.1984)—**§ 8.3, n. 4.**
Muniz, United States v., 374 U.S. 150, 83 S.Ct. 1850, 10 L.Ed.2d 805 (1963)—**§ 14.1, n. 12.**
Murff, United States ex rel. Exarchou v., 265 F.2d 504 (2nd Cir.1959)—**§ 13.4, n. 43.**
Murray v. Hoboken Land & Imp. Co., 59 U.S. 272, 18 How. 272, 15 L.Ed. 372 (1855)—**§ 5.1, n. 6, 12; § 7.2; § 7.2, n. 2, 7; § 7.6, n. 14; § 7.8; § 7.8, n. 18.**
Murty v. Office of Personnel Management, 707 F.2d 815 (4th Cir.1983)—**§ 17.3, n. 111.**
Myers v. Bethlehem Shipbuilding Corp., 303 U.S. 41, 58 S.Ct. 459, 82 L.Ed. 638 (1938)—**§ 12.10; § 12.10, n. 4.**
Myers v. United States, 272 U.S. 52, 47 S.Ct. 21, 71 L.Ed. 160 (1926)—**§ 15.3, n. 11; § 15.4; § 15.4, n. 4.**
Myers, Estate of v. United States, 842 F.Supp. 1297 (E.D.Wash.1993)—**§ 18.5, n. 4.**
Myron v. Hauser, 673 F.2d 994 (8th Cir. 1982)—**Ch. 5, n. 3; § 5.1, n. 5, 11; § 6.2; § 6.2, n. 7.**

N

N. A. A. C. P. v. F. C. C., 682 F.2d 993, 221 U.S.App.D.C. 44 (D.C.Cir.1982)—**§ 13.10, n. 46.**
NAACP Legal Defense Fund and Educational Fund, Inc. v. United States Dept. of Justice, 612 F.Supp. 1143 (D.D.C.1985)—**§ 17.4, n. 148.**
Nader v. Allegheny Airlines, Inc., 426 U.S. 290, 96 S.Ct. 1978, 48 L.Ed.2d 643 (1976)—**§ 12.11; § 12.11, n. 10, 11, 20.**
Nader v. Bork, 366 F.Supp. 104 (D.D.C. 1973)—**§ 3.1, n. 3; Ch. 10, n. 1.**

Nader v. Nuclear Regulatory Commission, 513 F.2d 1045, 168 U.S.App.D.C. 255 (D.C.Cir.1975)—**§ 13.9, n. 6.**

Nader v. Sawhill, 514 F.2d 1064 (Temp.Emer.1975)—**§ 4.4; § 4.4, n. 8.**

Nader v. Volpe, 466 F.2d 261, 151 U.S.App. D.C. 90 (D.C.Cir.1972)—**§ 12.4, n. 11.**

Nadler v. F.D.I.C., 92 F.3d 93 (2nd Cir. 1996)—**§ 17.4, n. 99.**

Nagel v. United States Dept. of Health, Educ. and Welfare, 725 F.2d 1438, 233 U.S.App.D.C. 332 (D.C.Cir.1984)—**§ 18.2, n. 34; § 18.3, n. 7.**

Na Iwi O Na Kupuna O Mokapu v. Dalton, 894 F.Supp. 1397 (D.Hawai'i 1995)—**§ 17.4, n. 162; § 17.5, n. 8.**

Nasem v. Brown, 595 F.2d 801, 193 U.S.App.D.C. 416 (D.C.Cir.1979)—**§ 11.1, n. 18.**

Nash v. Califano, 613 F.2d 10 (2nd Cir. 1980)—**§ 8.5, n. 21, 30.**

National Ass'n for Advancement of Colored People v. Wilmington Medical Center, Inc., 453 F.Supp. 280 (D.Del.1978)—**§ 13.6, n. 6.**

National Ass'n of Broadcasters v. Copyright Royalty Tribunal, 675 F.2d 367, 218 U.S.App.D.C. 348 (D.C.Cir.1982)—**§ 13.4, n. 29.**

National Ass'n of Broadcasters v. Librarian of Congress, 146 F.3d 907, 330 U.S.App. D.C. 394 (D.C.Cir.1998)—**§ 9.5, n. 151.**

National Ass'n of Home Health Agencies v. Schweiker, 690 F.2d 932, 223 U.S.App. D.C. 209 (D.C.Cir.1982)—**§ 4.2; § 4.2, n. 9.**

National Ass'n of Independent Television Producers and Distributors v. F. C. C., 516 F.2d 526 (2nd Cir.1975)—**§ 13.10, n. 17, 18, 20, 24, 26.**

National Ass'n of Radiation Survivors v. Derwinski, 994 F.2d 583 (9th Cir. 1992)—**§ 8.2, n. 15.**

National Ass'n of Recycling Industries, Inc. v. Federal Maritime Commission, 658 F.2d 816, 212 U.S.App.D.C. 68 (D.C.Cir. 1980)—**§ 8.4, n. 75, 89.**

National Ass'n of Regulatory Utility Com'rs v. United States Dept. of Energy, 851 F.2d 1424, 271 U.S.App.D.C. 197 (D.C.Cir.1988)—**§ 2.1, n. 21.**

National Ass'n of Securities Dealers, Inc., United States v., 422 U.S. 694, 95 S.Ct. 2427, 45 L.Ed.2d 486 (1975)—**§ 12.11; § 12.11, n. 24.**

National Ass'n of Women's & Children's Apparel Salesmen, Inc. v. F.T.C., 479 F.2d 139 (5th Cir.1973)—**§ 11.1, n. 21.**

National Automatic Laundry and Cleaning Council v. Shultz, 443 F.2d 689, 143 U.S.App.D.C. 274 (D.C.Cir.1971)—**§ 12.9; § 12.9, n. 16, 17.**

National Black Media Coalition v. F.C.C., 775 F.2d 342, 249 U.S.App.D.C. 292 (D.C.Cir.1985)—**§ 13.10, n. 92.**

National Broadcasting Co. v. F.C.C., 132 F.2d 545, 76 U.S.App.D.C. 238 (D.C.Cir. 1942)—**§ 8.4, n. 14.**

National Broadcasting Co. v. United States, 319 U.S. 190, 63 S.Ct. 997, 87 L.Ed. 1344 (1943)—**§ 1.1, n. 15.**

National Broadcasting Co. v. United States Small Business Admin., 836 F.Supp. 121 (S.D.N.Y.1993)—**§ 17.4, n. 145, 255.**

National Cable Television Ass'n, Inc. v. F. C. C., 479 F.2d 183, 156 U.S.App.D.C. 91 (D.C.Cir.1973)—**§ 17.3, n. 72.**

National Cable Television Ass'n, Inc. v. United States, 415 U.S. 336, 94 S.Ct. 1146, 39 L.Ed.2d 370 (1974)—**Pt. 1, n. 2; 1.1; § 1.1, n. 28; § 1.2, n. 5.**

National Citizens Committee For Broadcasting v. F. C. C., 567 F.2d 1095, 186 U.S.App.D.C. 102 (D.C.Cir.1977)—**§ 13.10, n. 91.**

National Classification Committee v. I.C.C., 765 F.2d 1146, 246 U.S.App.D.C. 393 (D.C.Cir.1985)—**§ 13.9, n. 7.**

National Conservative Political Action Committee v. Federal Election Commission, 626 F.2d 953, 200 U.S.App.D.C. 89 (D.C.Cir.1980)—**Ch. 10, n. 5.**

National Credit Union Admin. v. First Nat. Bank & Trust Co., 522 U.S. 479, 118 S.Ct. 927, 140 L.Ed.2d 1 (1998)—**§ 12.7; § 12.7, n. 85; § 13.7, n. 42, 69, 78.**

National Federation of Federal Emp. v. Devine, 671 F.2d 607, 217 U.S.App.D.C. 101 (D.C.Cir.1982)—**§ 4.4, n. 4, 6.**

National Fuel Gas Supply Corp. v. F.E.R.C., 811 F.2d 1563, 258 U.S.App.D.C. 374 (D.C.Cir.1987)—**§ 13.7, n. 42.**

National Helium Corp. v. Federal Energy Admin., 569 F.2d 1137 (Temp.Emer.1977)—**§ 4.3, n. 1.**

National Lime Ass'n v. Environmental Protection Agency, 627 F.2d 416, 200 U.S.App.D.C. 363 (D.C.Cir.1980)—**§ 13.9, n. 29; § 13.10, n. 24, 71.**

National Medical Enterprises, Inc. v. Sullivan, 916 F.2d 542 (9th Cir.1990)—**§ 13.8, n. 7.**

National Mut. Ins. Co. of Dist. of Col. v. Tidewater Transfer Co., 337 U.S. 582, 69 S.Ct. 1173, 93 L.Ed. 1556 (1949)—**Ch. 5, n. 7.**

National Nutritional Foods Ass'n v. Food and Drug Administration, United States Dept. of Health, Ed. and Welfare, 491 F.2d 1141 (2nd Cir.1974)—**§ 8.5, n. 19.**

National Nutritional Foods Ass'n v. Weinberger, 512 F.2d 688 (2nd Cir.1975)—**§ 13.5, n. 14; § 13.8, n. 14.**

National Organization for Women, Washington, D.C. Chapter v. Social Sec. Admin. of Dept. of Health and Human Services, 736 F.2d 727, 237 U.S.App.D.C. 118 (D.C.Cir.1984)—**§ 13.6, n. 7.**

O

P

Philco Corp. v. F.C.C., 257 F.2d 656, 103 U.S.App.D.C. 278 (D.C.Cir.1958)—**§ 8.4, n. 15.**

Phillippi v. Central Intelligence Agency, 546 F.2d 1009, 178 U.S.App.D.C. 243 (D.C.Cir.1976)—**§ 17.3; § 17.3, n. 117; § 17.4; § 17.4, n. 18.**

Phillips v. Commissioner, 283 U.S. 589, 51 S.Ct. 608, 75 L.Ed. 1289 (1931)—**§ 9.4, n. 50.**

Phillips Petroleum Co. v. State of Wisconsin, 347 U.S. 672, 74 S.Ct. 794, 98 L.Ed. 1035 (1954)—**§ 13.7, n. 7.**

Pickus v. United States Bd. of Parole, 507 F.2d 1107, 165 U.S.App.D.C. 284 (D.C.Cir.1974)—**§ 4.2; § 4.2, n. 12, 14; § 4.3; § 4.3, n. 3, 38.**

Pierce Auto Freight Lines, United States v., 327 U.S. 515, 66 S.Ct. 687, 90 L.Ed. 821 (1946)—**§ 8.4, n. 139.**

Pierson v. Ray, 386 U.S. 547, 87 S.Ct. 1213, 18 L.Ed.2d 288 (1967)—**§ 14.3, n. 18.**

Pillai v. C. A. B., 485 F.2d 1018, 158 U.S.App.D.C. 239 (D.C.Cir.1973)—**§ 13.10, n. 91.**

Pillsbury Co. v. F. T. C., 354 F.2d 952 (5th Cir.1966)—**§ 8.5, n. 115; § 16.2; § 16.2, n. 9.**

Pilon v. United States Dept. of Justice, 73 F.3d 1111, 315 U.S.App.D.C. 329 (D.C.Cir.1996)—**§ 18.2, n. 28.**

Pippinger v. Rubin, 129 F.3d 519 (10th Cir.1997)—**§ 18.2, n. 20, 40.**

Pittsburgh Plate Glass Co. v. N.L.R.B., 313 U.S. 146, 61 S.Ct. 908, 85 L.Ed. 1251 (1941)—**§ 8.4, n. 66, 82.**

Pittsburgh S. S. Co. v. Brown, 171 F.2d 175 (7th Cir.1948)—**§ 13.6, n. 17.**

Plato v. Roudebush, 397 F.Supp. 1295 (D.Md.1975)—**§ 12.5, n. 20.**

Playboy Enterprises, Inc. v. Department of Justice, 677 F.2d 931, 219 U.S.App.D.C. 343 (D.C.Cir.1982)—**§ 17.4, n. 119, 127, 135.**

Plumbers Local Union No. 519 of United Ass'n of Journeymen and Apprentices of Plumbing and Pipe Fitting Industry of United States and Canada, AFL–CIO v. Construction Industry Stabilization Committee, 479 F.2d 1052 (Temp.Emer.1973)—**§ 9.3, n. 10.**

Policy Statement on Comparative Broadcast Hearings, 1 F.C.C.2d 393 (F.C.C.1965)—**§ 8.3, n. 5.**

Pollard v. F.B.I., 705 F.2d 1151 (9th Cir. 1983)—**§ 17.4, n. 224.**

Porter v. Califano, 592 F.2d 770 (5th Cir. 1979)—**§ 13.2, n. 17; § 13.6; § 13.6, n. 7, 10, 19; § 13.7, n. 9.**

Porter v. United States Dept. of Justice, 717 F.2d 787 (3rd Cir.1983)—**§ 17.4, n. 83; § 18.1, n. 60.**

Porter & Dietsch, Inc. v. F. T. C., 605 F.2d 294 (7th Cir.1979)—**§ 11.1, n. 8.**

Portland Audubon Soc. v. Oregon Lands Coalition, 984 F.2d 1534 (9th Cir. 1993)—**§ 15.2, n. 3.**

Portland Cement Ass'n v. Ruckelshaus, 486 F.2d 375, 158 U.S.App.D.C. 308 (D.C.Cir.1973)—**§ 2.1; § 2.1, n. 48, 49, 56, 59, 61; § 13.9; § 13.9, n. 24; § 13.10, n. 48, 90.**

Portland Cement Ass'n v. Train, 513 F.2d 506, 168 U.S.App.D.C. 248 (D.C.Cir. 1975)—**§ 13.9, n. 26.**

Portmann v. United States, 674 F.2d 1155 (7th Cir.1982)—**§ 11.2; § 11.2, n. 7, 19, 21, 37; § 11.3; § 11.3, n. 1, 4.**

Port Norris Exp. Co., Inc. v. I. C. C., 687 F.2d 803 (3rd Cir.1982)—**§ 13.4, n. 31.**

Port of Boston Marine Terminal Ass'n v. Rederiaktiebolaget Transatlantic, 400 U.S. 62, 91 S.Ct. 203, 27 L.Ed.2d 203 (1970)—**§ 12.11, n. 16.**

Posadas de Puerto Rico Associates v. Tourism Co. of Puerto Rico, 478 U.S. 328, 106 S.Ct. 2968, 92 L.Ed.2d 266 (1986)—**§ 18.8, n. 18.**

Powell, United States v., 379 U.S. 48, 85 S.Ct. 248, 13 L.Ed.2d 112 (1964)—**§ 20.4; § 20.4, n. 8, 10.**

PPG Industries, Inc. v. Costle, 659 F.2d 1239, 212 U.S.App.D.C. 355 (D.C.Cir. 1981)—**§ 2.1, n. 49, 50; § 13.9, n. 4.**

PPG Industries, Inc. v. Stauffer Chemical Co., 637 F.Supp. 85 (D.D.C.1986)—**§ 9.5, n. 222.**

Pratt v. Webster, 673 F.2d 408, 218 U.S.App.D.C. 17 (D.C.Cir.1982)—**§ 17.4, n. 202.**

Pray v. Department of Justice, 902 F.Supp. 1 (D.D.C.1995)—**§ 17.4, n. 244.**

Prentis v. Atlantic Coast Line Co., 211 U.S. 210, 29 S.Ct. 67, 53 L.Ed. 150 (1908)—**§ 4.5, n. 1.**

Printz v. United States, 521 U.S. 898, 117 S.Ct. 2365, 138 L.Ed.2d 914 (1997)—**§ 9.5; § 9.5, n. 176.**

Process Gas Consumers Group v. Consumer Energy Council of America, 463 U.S. 1216, 103 S.Ct. 3556, 77 L.Ed.2d 1402, 77 L.Ed.2d 1403, 77 L.Ed.2d 1413 (1983)—**§ 16.3, n. 3.**

Process Gas Consumers Group v. United States Dept. of Agriculture, 694 F.2d 728, 224 U.S.App.D.C. 162 (D.C.Cir. 1981)—**§ 13.10, n. 20, 26.**

Professional Air Traffic Controllers Organization v. Federal Labor Relations Authority, 685 F.2d 547, 222 U.S.App.D.C. 97 (D.C.Cir.1982)—**§ 8.5; § 8.5, n. 50.**

Professional Drivers Council v. Bureau of Motor Carrier Safety, 706 F.2d 1216, 227 U.S.App.D.C. 312 (D.C.Cir.1983)—**§ 2.1, n. 20.**

Professional Pilots Federation v. F.A.A., 118 F.3d 758, 326 U.S.App.D.C. 157 (D.C.Cir.1997)—**§ 13.10, n. 87.**

Q

R

Rugiero v. United States Dept. of Justice, 35 F.Supp.2d 977 (E.D.Mich.1998)—**§ 17.4, n. 143.**

Rural Housing Alliance v. United States Dept. of Agriculture, 498 F.2d 73, 162 U.S.App.D.C. 122 (D.C.Cir.1974)—**§ 17.4, n. 160, 172, 195.**

Rushforth v. Council of Economic Advisers, 762 F.2d 1038, 246 U.S.App.D.C. 59 (D.C.Cir.1985)—**§ 17.3, n. 20.**

Russell v. Department of the Air Force, 682 F.2d 1045, 221 U.S.App.D.C. 96 (D.C.Cir.1982)—**§ 17.4, n. 122.**

Russell v. United States General Services Admin., 935 F.Supp. 1142 (D.Colo. 1996)—**§ 18.2, n. 20.**

Russell–Newman Mfg. Co. v. N. L. R. B., 370 F.2d 980 (5th Cir.1966)—**§ 8.4, n. 66.**

Rust v. Sullivan, 500 U.S. 173, 111 S.Ct. 1759, 114 L.Ed.2d 233 (1991)—**§ 13.7, n. 69; § 13.8, n. 3.**

Rutherford, United States v., 442 U.S. 544, 99 S.Ct. 2470, 61 L.Ed.2d 68 (1979)—**§ 13.8; § 13.8, n. 72.**

Ryan v. Commissioner, 568 F.2d 531 (7th Cir.1977)—**§ 20.5, n. 18.**

Ryan v. Department of Justice, 617 F.2d 781, 199 U.S.App.D.C. 199 (D.C.Cir. 1980)—**§ 17.4, n. 120.**

Ryan v. Department of Justice, 595 F.2d 954 (4th Cir.1979)—**§ 18.4, n. 3; § 18.5, n. 7.**

S

Saco River Cellular, Inc. v. F.C.C., 133 F.3d 25, 328 U.S.App.D.C. 162 (D.C.Cir. 1998)—**§ 20.4, n. 47.**

S.A. Empresa de Viacao Aerea Rio Grandense (Varig Airlines), United States v., 467 U.S. 797, 104 S.Ct. 2755, 81 L.Ed.2d 660 (1984)—**§ 14.1, n. 17.**

Saginaw Broadcasting Co. v. F.C.C., 96 F.2d 554 (D.C.Cir.1938)—**§ 13.3; § 13.3, n. 14.**

Salt Lake City v. International Ass'n of Firefighters, Locals 1645, 593, 1654 and 2064, 563 P.2d 786 (Utah 1977)—**§ 1.3, n. 4.**

Samuels v. Mackell, 401 U.S. 66, 91 S.Ct. 764, 27 L.Ed.2d 688 (1971)—**§ 9.4, n. 27.**

Sangamon Val. Television Corp. v. United States, 269 F.2d 221, 106 U.S.App.D.C. 30 (D.C.Cir.1959)—**§ 15.2, n. 3.**

Santa Clara, Cal., City of v. Andrus, 572 F.2d 660 (9th Cir.1978)—**§ 12.6, n. 10; § 13.9, n. 5.**

Santa Fe Natural Tobacco Co., Inc. v. Judge, 963 F.Supp. 437 (M.D.Pa.1997)—**§ 1.3, n. 4.**

Santoni v. Federal Deposit Ins. Corp., 677 F.2d 174 (1st Cir.1982)—**§ 11.2, n. 9.**

Savada v. United States Dept. of Defense, 755 F.Supp. 6 (D.D.C.1991)—**§ 18.4, n. 20.**

Savarese v. United States Dept. of Health, Ed. and Welfare, 479 F.Supp. 304 (N.D.Ga.1979)—**§ 18.1, n. 80.**

Save Our Cumberland Mountains, Inc. v. Clark, 725 F.2d 1422, 233 U.S.App.D.C. 316 (D.C.Cir.1984)—**§ 12.4, n. 28.**

Saxbe v. Bustos, 419 U.S. 65, 95 S.Ct. 272, 42 L.Ed.2d 231 (1974)—**§ 13.8; § 13.8, n. 49.**

Scenic Hudson Preservation Conference v. Federal Power Commission, 453 F.2d 463 (2nd Cir.1971)—**§ 13.10, n. 16.**

Scenic Hudson Preservation Conference v. Federal Power Commission, 354 F.2d 608 (2nd Cir.1965)—**§ 8.4; § 8.4, n. 19; § 12.7, n. 18; § 13.10, n. 69, 90.**

Scheer v. United States Dept. of Justice, 35 F.Supp.2d 9 (D.D.C.1999)—**§ 17.4, n. 203.**

Schering Corp. v. Heckler, 779 F.2d 683, 250 U.S.App.D.C. 293 (D.C.Cir.1985)—**§ 13.11, n. 22.**

Scheuer v. Rhodes, 416 U.S. 232, 94 S.Ct. 1683, 40 L.Ed.2d 90 (1974)—**§ 14.2, n. 5; § 14.3; § 14.3, n. 1, 19.**

Schiffer v. F.B.I., 78 F.3d 1405 (9th Cir. 1996)—**§ 17.4, n. 217.**

Schlefer v. United States, 702 F.2d 233, 226 U.S.App.D.C. 254 (D.C.Cir.1983)—**§ 17.4, n. 145.**

Schmerler v. F.B.I., 900 F.2d 333, 283 U.S.App.D.C. 349 (D.C.Cir.1990)—**§ 17.4, n. 234.**

School Bd. of Broward County, Florida v. Department of Health, Ed. and Welfare, United States Office of Ed., 525 F.2d 900 (5th Cir.1976)—**§ 8.4, n. 89.**

Schor v. Commodity Futures Trading Com'n, 740 F.2d 1262, 239 U.S.App.D.C. 159 (D.C.Cir.1984)—**§ 9.5; § 9.5, n. 162.**

Schrecker v. United States Dept. of Justice, 74 F.Supp.2d 26 (D.D.C.1999)—**§ 17.4, n. 57.**

Schuhl v. United States, 3 Cl.Ct. 207 (Cl.Ct. 1983)—**§ 11.2, n. 26.**

Schwaner v. Department of Air Force, 898 F.2d 793, 283 U.S.App.D.C. 196 (D.C.Cir.1990)—**§ 17.4, n. 51.**

Schwaner v. Department of Air Force, 698 F.Supp. 4 (D.D.C.1988)—**§ 17.3, n. 1.**

Schware v. Board of Bar Exam. of State of N.M., 353 U.S. 232, 77 S.Ct. 752, 1 L.Ed.2d 796 (1957)—**§ 7.5, n. 9.**

Schweiker v. Hansen, 450 U.S. 785, 101 S.Ct. 1468, 67 L.Ed.2d 685 (1981)—**§ 11.2; § 11.2, n. 21, 28.**

Schweiker v. McClure, 456 U.S. 188, 102 S.Ct. 1665, 72 L.Ed.2d 1 (1982)—**§ 9.5; § 9.5, n. 223; § 13.9, n. 3.**

SDC Development Corp. v. Mathews, 542 F.2d 1116 (9th Cir.1976)—**§ 17.2;**

T

U

V

W

Y

Z

Table of Statutes

UNITED STATES

UNITED STATES CONSTITUTION

UNITED STATES CONSTITUTION

UNITED STATES CONSTITUTION

UNITED STATES CONSTITUTION

UNITED STATES CODE ANNOTATED

2 U.S.C.A.—The Congress

5 U.S.C.A.—Government Organization and Employees

UNITED STATES CODE ANNOTATED

5 U.S.C.A.—Government Organization and Employees

UNITED STATES CODE ANNOTATED

5 U.S.C.A.—Government Organization and Employees

UNITED STATES CODE ANNOTATED

5 U.S.C.A.—Government Organization and Employees

UNITED STATES CODE ANNOTATED

5 U.S.C.A.—Government Organization and Employees

Sec.	This Work Sec.	Note
601—612	16.2	17
601(6)	20.4	33
611	16.2	19
701	12.6	8
701—706	Intro., p. 4	11
701—706	13.2	1
701 et seq.	17.4	67
701(a)(1)	2.1	20
701(a)(1)	12.5	15
701(a)(2)	12.6	3
701(a)(2)	13.2	16
701(a)(2)	13.11	4
702	12.1	7
702	12.4	3
702	12.4	10
702	12.7	21
702	12.7	73
703	12.3	8
703	12.4	7
704	12.10	6
704	12.10	32
706	12.6	7
706	13.2	15
706	13.4	11
706	13.7	1
706	13.11	3
706(1)	13.2	3
706(2)	12.6	27
706(2)	13.7	2
706(2)(A)	10.2	4
706(2)(A)	13.2	9
706(2)(A)	13.4	6
706(2)(A)	13.7	6
706(2)(A)	13.8	15
706(2)(A)	13.10	71
706(2)(A)	13.11	59
706(2)(A)	17.5	7
706(2)(B)	13.2	4
706(2)(B)	13.7	3
706(2)(C)	13.2	2
706(2)(C)	13.7	4
706(2)(D)	13.2	8
706(2)(D)	13.7	5
706(2)(D)	13.9	1
706(2)(E)	13.2	10
706(2)(E)	13.2	13
706(2)(E)	13.2	15
706(2)(E)	13.4	5
706(2)(E)	13.5	18
706(2)(F)	13.2	11
706(2)(F)	13.2	17
706(2)(F)	13.4	4
706(2)(F)	13.6	1
801—808	16.3	5
801(a)(1)(B)	16.3	7
801(a)(3)(B)	16.3	10
801(a)(4)	16.3	8
802	16.3	9

UNITED STATES CODE ANNOTATED

5 U.S.C.A.—Government Organization and Employees

Sec.	This Work Sec.	Note
807	16.3	6
824	15.1	31
1201	8.1	15
1305	Intro., p. 4	11
3105	Intro., p. 4	11
3105	5.2	18
3344	Intro., p. 4	11
4301	8.5	26
5362	8.5	24
5372	Intro., p. 4	11
5372	5.2	18
7521	Intro., p. 4	11
7521	5.2	18

5 U.S.C.A.App.—Government Organization and Employees

Sec.	This Work Sec.	Note
1—15	9.5	246
3(2)	19.1	85
5(b)(2)	19.1	80
5(c)	19.1	80
10	9.5	260

7 U.S.C.A.—Agriculture

Sec.	This Work Sec.	Note
8	13.4	24
18(g)	5.1	11
136 et seq.	5.2	1
136a(c)(1)(F)(iii)	9.5	138
136k(a)—(c)	9.4	48
211(a)	8.5	2
608(c)(15)	12.4	29
610(h)	20.5	14
671	9.5	138
671(a)	9.5	140
950(a)	16.1	20
950(a)	16.1	22
1021	8.5	2

8 U.S.C.A.—Aliens and Nationality

Sec.	This Work Sec.	Note
1101(a)(27)(B)	13.8	50
1105(a)(2)	12.4	29
1181(b)	13.8	52
1254(a)(1)	15.4	31
1254(c)(1)	15.4	32
1254(c)(2)	15.4	30

UNITED STATES CODE ANNOTATED

9 U.S.C.A.—Arbitration

Sec.	This Work Sec.	Note
9—13	9.5	
10(a)	9.5	153

10 U.S.C.A.—Armed Forces

Sec.	This Work Sec.	Note
2305(g)	17.4	76

12 U.S.C.A.—Banks and Banking

Sec.	This Work Sec.	Note
36	12.7	82
81	12.7	82
241	16.1	4
1842	9.4	32
1848	13.5	26
1904	1.4	5
3401	20.4	3
3401	20.5	3
3421	20.4	3
3421	20.5	3

15 U.S.C.A.—Commerce and Trade

Sec.	This Work Sec.	Note
41	15.4	13
41	16.1	5
41—58	15.4	2
45	Ch. 5, p. 121	12
45(a)	1.1	22
45(a)(2)	20.1	3
45(b)	8.4	10
45(b)	12.10	30
45(c)	12.4	2
45(c)	12.4	27
45(c)	12.4	29
46	20.2	6
46	20.5	
46(a)	20.1	4
46(b)	20.2	25
46(b)	20.4	7
49	20.2	15
49	20.4	7
50	20.6	9
57(a)	2.1	15
57a	2.2	2
57a(e)	12.4	13
57a(e)(3)(A)	13.5	3
77	Ch. 1, p. 11	11
78u(c)	20.6	8
78y(b)(4)	13.5	3
402(b)	12.4	30
717	13.8	41
717r(b)	13.5	12
766(c)	12.4	30
1410	9.4	17

UNITED STATES CODE ANNOTATED

15 U.S.C.A.—Commerce and Trade

Sec.	This Work Sec.	Note
1417	9.4	17
1608	15.1	72
1710(a)	13.5	3
2001 et seq.	12.6	36
2052—2083	13.5	12
2058(d)	2.1	15
2060(c)	13.5	3
2061	9.4	48
2601 et seq.	2.1	24
2618(c)(1)(B)(i)	13.5	3
3412(c)	9.4	16
6801—6827	18.8	21

16 U.S.C.A.—Conservation

Sec.	This Work Sec.	Note
973n	9.5	138
8251(b)	8.4	20

17 U.S.C.A.—Copyrights

Sec.	This Work Sec.	Note
801	9.5	138

18 U.S.C.A.—Crimes and Criminal Procedure

Sec.	This Work Sec.	Note
1—16	20.5	53
921—928	20.7	30
1905	17.4	70
1905	17.4	90
1905	17.5	4
6002	20.3	75

19 U.S.C.A.—Customs and Duties

Sec.	This Work Sec.	Note
1526	13.7	66

21 U.S.C.A.—Food and Drugs

Sec.	This Work Sec.	Note
301—395	13.7	83
334	9.4	48
355	13.8	73
355	13.8	74
374(a)(1)	20.7	2
455(c)	9.4	48
606(b)(2)	9.4	48
1034(c)	9.4	48

22 U.S.C.A.—Foreign Relations and Intercourse

Sec.	This Work Sec.	Note
1978	12.6	26

UNITED STATES CODE ANNOTATED

26 U.S.C.A.—Internal Revenue Code

Sec.	This Work Sec.	This Work Note
501(c)(3)	12.7	44
5146(b)	20.7	26
6103	17.4	65
6223 et seq.	8.4	
7342	20.7	26
7601	20.4	11
7602(a)	20.4	11

28 U.S.C.A.—Judiciary and Judicial Procedure

Sec.	This Work Sec.	This Work Note
49	15.3	15
49	15.3	16
49	15.4	84
455	8.5	118
546	15.3	34
591 et seq.	15.3	15
596(a)(1)	15.4	84
636(b)(1)	5.3	3
651—658	9.5	4
651 et seq.	9.5	17
1137	12.4	9
1331	12.3	
1331	12.4	
1331	12.4	8
1331	12.4	9
1331	12.10	8
1343(3)	12.4	
1346	12.4	9
1346(b)	14.1	2
1346(b)	14.1	9
1346(b)	14.1	10
1346(f)	12.1	9
1361	12.3	1
1361	12.4	9
1391	12.4	
1391(e)	12.4	
1391(e)	12.4	26
1402(d)	12.1	9
1404(a)	12.4	35
1491	14.1	24
1582	Ch. 5, p. 121	12
1651(a)	12.3	1
1651(a)	12.4	19
2112(3)	12.4	31
2112(3)	12.4	34
2112(5)	12.4	
2112(5)	12.4	35
2112(a)	12.4	35
2342(1)	12.4	16
2409(a)	12.1	9
2671 et seq.	14.1	2
2674	14.1	2
2674	14.1	9
2674	20.5	44
2679(b)(1)	14.1	4
2679(b)(1)	14.1	11

UNITED STATES CODE ANNOTATED

28 U.S.C.A.—Judiciary and Judicial Procedure

Sec.	This Work Sec.	This Work Note
2679(d)(4)	14.1	6
2680(a)	14.1	16
2680(h)	14.1	14
2680(h)	14.2	13
2680(k)	14.1	8

29 U.S.C.A.—Labor

Sec.	This Work Sec.	This Work Note
160(b)	8.4	76
160(e)	12.10	24
160(e)	13.4	12
209	20.2	15
211(a)	20.1	3
211(a)	20.2	15
433	13.11	36
440	13.11	36
481 et seq.	13.11	
482	13.11	
482	13.11	34
651—678	15.1	8
651—678	16.1	10
651 et seq.	2.1	15
651 et seq.	6.2	1
655(b)(5)	1.1	32
655(c)	2.1	25
655(f)	13.5	3
655(f)	13.5	12
655(f)	13.5	16
661	8.1	12
665	9.4	11
665	9.4	20
665(f)	13.5	6

30 U.S.C.A.—Mineral Lands and Mining

Sec.	This Work Sec.	This Work Note
801—962	20.7	47
811(c)	9.4	17
811(e)	9.4	17
814(g)	9.4	17
816(a)	13.5	3
823	8.1	13

31 U.S.C.A.—Money and Finance

Sec.	This Work Sec.	This Work Note
16	15.1	31
16	15.1	34
483a	1.1	29
1400—1407	15.1	37
1400—1407	15.1	38
9101(3)	16.1	22

UNITED STATES CODE ANNOTATED

33 U.S.C.A.—Navigation and Navigable Waters

Sec.	This Work Sec.	Note
901 et seq.	8.4	87
1251 et seq.	8.2	19
1317(a)	12.6	36
1342	9.4	17

38 U.S.C.A.—Veterans' Benefits

Sec.	This Work Sec.	Note
211(a)	12.5	9
211(a)	12.5	13

39 U.S.C.A.—Postal Service

Sec.	This Work Sec.	Note
201	20.4	44
1207	9.5	138

41 U.S.C.A.—Public Contracts

Sec.	This Work Sec.	Note
35—45	20.2	9
253b(m)	17.4	76

42 U.S.C.A.—The Public Health and Welfare

Sec.	This Work Sec.	Note
300g-4	9.4	17
405	18.1	24
405(b)	8.4	70
405(g)	12.4	4
405(g)	12.4	6
405(g)	12.4	29
405(g)	12.5	2
405(g)	12.5	8
405(h)	12.4	9
421(d)	12.4	6
601—612	2.1	12
901—927	18.1	4
1383(c)(1)	8.4	120
1395(ii)	12.5	23
1888	12.4	21
1973(b)	12.5	23
1983	11.1	
1983	12.4	21
2155a	9.4	17
3501—3520	Ch. 16, p. 613	3
3604(d)	12.7	29
3612	6.1	4
4083	9.5	138
4321	16.2	13
4321—4361	Ch. 16, p. 613	2
4321 et seq.	Ch. 1, p. 13	15

UNITED STATES CODE ANNOTATED

42 U.S.C.A.—The Public Health and Welfare

Sec.	This Work Sec.	Note
4331 et seq.	2.1	11
6901—6987	9.5	102
6924(d)(1)	Ch. 16, p. 614	6
7174(a)	9.4	7
7194(a)	9.4	19
7409	13.7	33
7410	9.4	17
7502(b)(6)	13.7	34
7607(3)	2.1	49
7607(b)—(d)	13.5	12
7607(d)	2.1	14
7607(d)	2.1	15
7607(d)(7)(A)	2.1	79
9601—9675	9.5	88
9613(h)	9.5	90
9613(j)(1)	9.5	90
9613(j)(2)	9.5	90
9622	9.5	48
9622	9.5	51
9622	9.5	86
9622(a)	9.5	49
9622(a)	9.5	87
9622(a)	9.5	88
9622(b)	9.5	91
9622(b)	9.5	96
9622(d)	9.5	95
9622(e)	9.5	97
9622(e)(3)(B)	9.5	89
9622(f)	9.5	93
9622(g)	9.5	92
9622(g)	9.5	99
9622(h)	9.5	94
9622(h)(2)	9.5	138
9622(h)(2)	9.5	144
9622(i)(3)	9.5	100
9651(h)(3)	16.2	3
11046(a)1	12.7	54

44 U.S.C.A.—Public Printing and Documents

Sec.	This Work Sec.	Note
301	3.2	1
3501	15.1	64
3501—3520	15.1	63
3501—3520	20.4	28
3501 et seq.	2.1	12
3501(1)	20.4	29
3502(10)	16.1	6
3503(b)	20.4	31
3506(c)(3)	20.4	32
3506(c)(3)(A)—(c)(3)(J)	20.4	33
3507(d)(4)	20.4	34
3507(f)	20.4	43
3507(f)(1)(A)	20.4	35
3592(15)	20.4	29

UNITED STATES CODE ANNOTATED

46 U.S.C.A.—Shipping

Sec.	This Work Sec.	Note
814	9.4	17
833a	9.4	17

47 U.S.C.A.—Telegraphs, Telephones, and Radiotelegraphs

Sec.	This Work Sec.	Note
151 et seq.	8.3	2
154(c)	16.1	4
203(b)(2)	9.4	8
203(b)(2)	9.4	17
214(a)	9.4	17
303	1.1	17
305	18.1	4
316	9.4	17
316(a)	9.4	8
359	9.4	17

49 U.S.C.A.—Transportation

Sec.	This Work Sec.	Note
1(14)(a)	8.2	39
5b	12.11	22
12	20.2	4
13	20.2	4
21	20.2	4
1384	12.11	22
1386(b)(1)	9.4	17
1429	8.1	14
1432(c)	9.4	17
1442	8.1	14
1653(f)	9.2	6
10101 et seq.	8.2	33
10311	20.2	4
10321	20.2	4
10321c(1)	20.6	4
10321c(3)	20.6	4
10321c(3)	20.6	5
10326	20.2	4
10505	20.2	4
11501	20.2	4
11502	20.2	4
11701	20.2	4
11703	20.2	4

49 U.S.C.A.App.—Transportation

Sec.	This Work Sec.	Note
2520	16.2	3

50 U.S.C.A.—War and National Defense

Sec.	This Work Sec.	Note
403–3(c)(6)	17.4	59
431	17.2	25
435	17.4	35
435	17.4	261

UNITED STATES CODE ANNOTATED

50 U.S.C.A.—War and National Defense

Sec.	This Work Sec.	Note
633	20.3	57
645	20.3	57
901—946	20.3	63

STATUTES AT LARGE

Year	This Work Sec.	Note
1887, Ch. 104	12.11	4
1887, Ch. 104	20.2	4
1887, Ch. 359	14.1	24
1893, Ch. 83	20.3	74
1914, Ch. 311	15.4	13
1914, Ch. 311	20.2	6
1921, Ch. 18	15.1	29
1933, Ch. 25	9.5	139
1934, Ch. 652	1.1	17
1937, Ch. 296	9.5	139
1938, Ch. 556	13.8	41
1942, Ch. 26	20.3	63
1946, Ch. 324	17.2	6
1947, Ch. 114	5.2	17
1950, Ch. 1052	8.2	9
1952, Ch. 477	13.8	50
1954, Ch. 736	20.4	11
1958, P.L. 85–619	17.2	5
1965, P.L. 89–236	13.8	50
1966, P.L. 89–487	17.1	1
1966, P.L. 89–487	17.2	8
1967, P.L. 90–23	17.2	7
1967, P.L. 90–23	17.4	185
1968, P.L. 90–618	20.7	30
1970, P.L. 91–190	16.2	13
1970, P.L. 91–452	20.3	74
1971, P.L. 91–696	15.1	31
1972, P.L. 92–463	9.5	246
1972, P.L. 92–463	17.1	6
1972, P.L. 92–463	19.1	77
1974, P.L. 93–250	15.1	34
1974, P.L. 93–253	14.1	15
1974, P.L. 93–344	15.1	37
1974, P.L. 93–344	15.1	38
1974, P.L. 93–443	15.3	4
1974, P.L. 93–502	17.1	2
1974, P.L. 93–502	17.2	24
1974, P.L. 93–502	17.4	187
1974, P.L. 93–579	17.1	9
1974, P.L. 93–579	18.1	9
1974, P.L. 93–579	18.1	14
1974, P.L. 93–579	18.1	17
1976, P.L. 94–409	17.1	2
1976, P.L. 94–409	17.1	7
1976, P.L. 94–409	19.1	1
1976, P.L. 94–409	19.1	2
1976, P.L. 94–409	19.1	78
1976, P.L. 94–574	12.1	7
1980, P.L. 96–252	20.6	9
1980, P.L. 96–354	16.2	18
1980, P.L. 96–510	9.5	143
1980, P.L. 96–511	17.2	69

STATUTES AT LARGE

Year	This Work Sec.	Note
1982, P.L. 97–375	18.1	25
1984, P.L. 98–447	17.2	56
1984, P.L. 98–477	17.3	10
1984, P.L. 98–477	17.4	24
1984, P.L. 98–477	17.4	84
1984, P.L. 98–477	18.1	61
1984, P.L. 98–477	18.2	9
1984, P.L. 98–477	18.2	11
1984, P.L. 98–477	18.2	12
1984, P.L. 98–620	17.2	57
1985, P.L. 99–177	15.4	48
1986, P.L. 99–499	9.5	48
1986, P.L. 99–499	9.5	86
1986, P.L. 99–570	17.1	2
1986, P.L. 99–570	17.2	53
1986, P.L. 99–570	17.4	189
1986, P.L. 99–591	20.4	30
1988, P.L. 100–236	12.4	32
1988, P.L. 100–236	12.4	34
1988, P.L. 100–330	9.5	141
1988, P.L. 100–503	18.7	2
1988, P.L. 100–687	12.5	9
1988, P.L. 100–687	12.5	13
1988, P.L. 100–694	14.1	4
1990, P.L. 101–549	16.2	27
1990, P.L. 101–552	9.5	28
1990, P.L. 101–552	9.5	152
1990, P.L. 101–648	9.5	227
1990, P.L. 101–648	9.5	263
1992, P.L. 102–538	18.1	4
1993, P.L. 103–62	16.2	26
1994, P.L. 103–238	17.4	27
1995, P.L. 104–4	16.2	20
1995, P.L. 104–13	15.1	63
1996, P.L. 104–121	16.2	17
1996, P.L. 104–121	16.2	19
1996, P.L. 104–130	15.4	110
1996, P.L. 104–130	15.4	111
1996, P.L. 104–201	17.4	76
1996, P.L. 104–231	17.1	2
1996, P.L. 104–231	17.2	60
1996, P.L. 104–320	2.1	27
1996, P.L. 104–320	9.5	28
1996, P.L. 104–320	9.5	152
1996, P.L. 104–320	9.5	227
1997, P.L. 105–33	15.4	107
1997, P.L. 105–34	15.4	108
1998, P.L. 105–315	9.5	4
1998, P.L. 105–315	9.5	17
1999, P.L. 106–102	18.8	21
2000, P.L. 106–120	17.2	49

POPULAR NAME ACTS

ADMINISTRATIVE DISPUTE RESOLUTION ACT

Sec.	This Work Sec.	Note
5—8	9.5	

ADMINISTRATIVE DISPUTE RESOLUTION ACT

Sec.	This Work Sec.	Note
9	9.5	

ADMINISTRATIVE PROCEDURE ACT

Sec.	This Work Sec.	Note
3	17.2	
3	17.2	6
7(c)	8.4	
7(c)	8.4	65
7(d)	8.4	107
551(4)	16.3	
552	3.2	
552(a)(1)	3.2	
553	2.1	
553	2.1	16
553	2.1	39
553	2.1	60
553	2.1	65
553	2.1	69
553	2.1	72
553	2.2	
553	2.2	6
553	3.2	
553	3.3	9
553	Ch. 4, p. 75	
553	4.1	
553	4.2	
553	4.2	1
553	4.2	10
553	4.3	
553	4.3	4
553	4.3	20
553	4.3	25
553	4.4	
553	4.5	
553	4.5	38
553	4.6	
553	8.2	
553	13.2	
553	13.2	13
553	13.4	
553	13.7	
553	13.9	
553	13.10	
553	15.2	
553	18.1	
553(a)(2)	9.4	
553(b)	2.1	
553(b)	4.2	
553(c)	2.1	
553(c)	2.1	65
553(c)	2.1	69
553(c)	2.1	73
553(c)	2.2	6
553(c)	8.2	
553(c)	13.9	
553(e)	2.1	
553(e)	2.1	18

CLEAN WATER ACT

Sec.	This Work Sec.	Note
301(1)	13.7	

COMMUNICATIONS ACT OF 1934

Sec.	This Work Sec.	Note
203(b)(2)	13.7	77
303	1.1	
303	1.1	17

COMPREHENSIVE ENVIRONMENTAL RESPONSE, COMPENSATION AND LIABILITY ACT

Sec.	This Work Sec.	Note
104	9.5	90
106	9.5	90
106(a)	9.5	90
107	9.5	90
107	9.5	109
310	9.5	90

CONSUMER PRODUCT SAFETY ACT

Sec.	This Work Sec.	Note
11(c)	13.5	3

DEPARTMENT OF TRANSPORTATION ACT

Sec.	This Work Sec.	Note
4(f)	9.2	

FAIR HOUSING ACT

Sec.	This Work Sec.	Note
804(d)	12.7	

FAIR LABOR STANDARDS ACT

Sec.	This Work Sec.	Note
9	20.2	15
11(a)	20.2	15
211(a)	20.1	3

FEDERAL ADVISORY COMMITTEE ACT

Sec.	This Work Sec.	Note
7(d)	9.5	265
10(b)	9.5	264
10(c)	9.5	264

FEDERAL AVIATION ACT

Sec.	This Work Sec.	Note
1104	17.2	

FEDERAL COAL MINE HEALTH AND SAFETY ACT

Sec.	This Work Sec.	Note
106(a)	13.5	3

FEDERAL COMMUNICATIONS ACT

Sec.	This Work Sec.	Note
309(a)	8.3	

FEDERAL FOOD, DRUG AND COSMETICS ACT

Sec.	This Work Sec.	Note
201	13.8	73
346	13.7	
505	13.8	74

FEDERAL POWER ACT

Sec.	This Work Sec.	Note
313(b)	8.4	20

FEDERAL TRADE COMMISSION ACT

Sec.	This Work Sec.	Note
5	20.1	3
6	20.1	4
6	20.2	25
6(a)	20.2	6
6(c)	20.2	6
9	20.2	15
10	20.6	9

FEDERAL TRADE COMMISSION IMPROVEMENT ACT OF 1975

Sec.	This Work Sec.	Note
202(e)(3)(A)	13.5	3

FREEDOM OF INFORMATION ACT

Sec.	This Work Sec.	Note
552	17.2	
552(a)(1)	17.3	
552(a)(2)	17.3	
552(a)(3)	17.3	
552(a)(3)	17.3	13

FREEDOM OF INFORMATION ACT

Sec.	This Work Sec.	Note
552(a)(4)	17.3	
552(a)(4)(B)	17.3	
552(a)(4)(E)	17.3	55
552(a)(6)	17.3	6
552(b)	17.3	
552(b)	17.4	
552(b)	17.5	
552(b)(1)	17.2	
552(b)(1)	17.4	
552(b)(1)	18.2	9
552(b)(1)	18.2	25
552(b)(2)	17.4	
552(b)(3)	17.2	
552(b)(3)	17.4	
552(b)(3)	18.2	
552(b)(4)	17.4	
552(b)(5)	17.4	
552(b)(5)	17.4	120
552(b)(5)	19.1	
552(b)(6)	17.4	
552(b)(6)	18.2	
552(b)(7)	17.2	
552(b)(7)	17.2	28
552(b)(7)	17.4	
552(b)(7)(A)	17.4	
552(b)(7)(B)	17.4	
552(b)(7)(C)	17.4	
552(b)(7)(D)	17.4	
552(b)(7)(E)	17.4	
552(b)(7)(F)	17.4	
552(b)(8)	17.4	
552(b)(9)	17.4	
552(c)	17.3	
552(c)	17.4	
552(c)(1)	17.4	
552(c)(2)	17.3	
552(c)(2)	17.3	118
552(c)(2)	17.4	
552(c)(3)	17.3	
552(c)(3)	17.4	
552(d)	17.3	
552(e)	17.3	
552(f)	17.3	
552(g)	17.3	

GOVERNMENT IN SUNSHINE ACT

Sec.	This Work Sec.	Note
551b(a)(1)	19.1	
552b(a)	19.1	
552b(a)(1)	19.1	
552b(a)(2)	19.1	
552b(b)	19.1	
552b(c)	19.1	
552b(c)(4)	19.1	
552b(c)(9)	19.1	
552b(c)(9)(B)	19.1	51
552b(c)(10)	19.1	
552b(h)(2)	19.1	

GOVERNMENT PERFORMANCE AND RESULTS ACT

Sec.	This Work Sec.	Note
2(b)(3)	16.2	26

IMMIGRATION AND NATIONALITY ACT

Sec.	This Work Sec.	Note
241(a)(11)	8.2	11
244(a)(1)	15.4	
244(c)(1)	15.4	
244(c)(2)	15.4	

IMMIGRATION AND NATURALIZATION ACT

Sec.	This Work Sec.	Note
101(a)(27)(B)	13.8	50
208(a)	13.7	
243(h)	13.7	

INDIAN REORGANIZATION ACT

Sec.	This Work Sec.	Note
465	1.1	

INTERSTATE COMMERCE ACT

Sec.	This Work Sec.	Note
1(14)(a)	8.2	
1(14)(a)	8.2	39
1(14)(a)	8.2	45

INTERSTATE LAND SALES FULL DISCLOSURE ACT

Sec.	This Work Sec.	Note
1411(a)	13.5	3

LABOR MANAGEMENT REPORTING AND DISCLOSURE ACT OF 1959

Sec.	This Work Sec.	Note
203	13.11	36
402	13.11	

MINE SAFETY AND HEALTH ACT

Sec.	This Work Sec.	Note
103(a)	20.7	
103(a)	20.7	50

NATIONAL INDUSTRIAL RECOVERY ACT

Sec.	This Work Sec.	Note
9(c)	1.1	

NATIONAL LABOR RELATIONS ACT

Sec.	This Work Sec.	Note
7	13.7	9
8(b)(4)(ii)(B)	13.7	9

OCCUPATIONAL SAFETY AND HEALTH ACT

Sec.	This Work Sec.	Note
6(f)	13.5	3

PAPERWORK REDUCTION ACT

Sec.	This Work Sec.	Note
3502	20.4	
3502(1)	20.4	
3502(3)	20.4	40
3502(3)(A)(i)	20.4	38
3504(h)	20.4	36
3507(6)	20.4	
3507(6)	20.4	37

PRIVACY ACT OF 1974

Sec.	This Work Sec.	Note
3	18.1	17
5	18.1	
6	18.1	
7	18.1	
552a	18.1	
552a(a)	18.1	
552a(b)	18.2	
552a(d)(5)	18.4	20
552a(e)	18.2	
552a(e)	18.3	
552a(e)(1)—(e)(12)	18.2	
552a(e)(7)	18.3	
552a(g)(1)(A)	18.1	
552a(g)(1)(B)	18.1	
552a(g)(1)(C)	18.1	
552a(g)(1)(D)	18.1	
552a(j)	18.4	
552a(j)(1)	18.4	
552a(j)(2)	18.1	
552a(j)(2)	18.4	
552a(j)(2)	18.4	8
552a(j)(2)	18.4	20
552a(k)	18.4	
552a(k)(2)	18.4	
552a(k)(2)	18.4	8
552a(k)(2)	18.4	11

RURAL ELECTRIFICATION ACT

Sec.	This Work Sec.	Note
410(a)	16.1	20
410(a)	16.1	22

SECURITIES EXCHANGE ACT OF 1934

Sec.	This Work Sec.	Note
3(a)(10)	13.8	61
3(a)(14)	13.8	62
14(b)	4.3	
25(b)(4)	13.5	3

SECURITIES ACT OF 1933

Sec.	This Work Sec.	Note
2(1)	13.8	61
2(3)	13.8	62

SOCIAL SECURITY ACT

Sec.	This Work Sec.	Note
405(h)	12.5	
405(h)	12.5	23

TARIFF ACT

Sec.	This Work Sec.	Note
525	13.7	
526	13.7	
777	17.4	75

TAXPAYER RELIEF ACT

Sec.	This Work Sec.	Note
968	15.4	

TOXIC SUBSTANCE CONTROL ACT

Sec.	This Work Sec.	Note
9	15.1	
19(c)(1)(B)(i)	13.5	3

TRADE ACT OF 1974

Sec.	This Work Sec.	Note
231	13.7	64

UNITED STATES HOUSING ACT OF 1937

Sec.	This Work Sec.	Note
8	7.4	20

CODE OF FEDERAL REGULATIONS

Tit.	This Work Sec.	Note
18, § 385.603(c)(2)	9.5	56
18, § 385.603(g)	9.5	41
18, § 385.603(g)	9.5	59
20, § 416.1457(a)	8.4	121
26, § 601.201(d)	9.4	25
26, § 602.201(a)	9.4	25
28, § 16.7	17.5	2
28, § 16.11	17.3	5
28, § 16.11	17.3	104
28, § 50.2	9.4	60
29, § 18.44	8.4	76
29, § 102.30(a)	8.4	54
29, § 102.117	8.4	54
29, § 220.101	9.5	58
29, § 1903.4	20.7	41
29, § 2570.65	9.5	24
36, Pt. 600	15.1	24
47, § 1.3	9.4	9

FEDERAL REGISTER

Vol.	This Work Sec.	Note
18, p. 4899	15.1	28
27, p. 11527	15.1	28
32, p. 14303	15.1	28
37, p. 16504	13.11	10
42, p. 61445	19.1	79
43, p. 511375	15.1	24
44, p. 34936	9.5	52
46, p. 53423	13.10	83
50, p. 5036	9.5	91
50, p. 5036	9.5	99
50, p. 47212	9.5	104
51, p. 3738	15.1	73
52, p. 10012	17.3	104
52, p. 10017	17.3	104
52, p. 23781	17.4	106
52, p. 23781	17.5	9
52, p. 41685	15.1	27
53, p. 11414	15.1	76
53, p. 51003	9.5	287
56, p. 55195	9.5	181
58, p. 48255	15.1	5
59, p. 47887	8.2	15
61, p. 4729	9.5	181
62, p. 66370	9.5	10

*

Index

References are to Pages

†